# THE COMPLETE JEFFERSON

# THE COMPLETE JEFFERSON

*Containing His Major Writings, Published and Unpublished, Except His Letters*

ASSEMBLED AND ARRANGED BY

SAUL K. PADOVER

*With Illustrations and analytic index*

*Select Bibliographies Reprint Series*

BOOKS FOR LIBRARIES PRESS
FREEPORT, NEW YORK

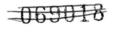

Reprinted 1969 by arrangement

STANDARD BOOK NUMBER:
8369-5027-5

LIBRARY OF CONGRESS CATALOG CARD NUMBER:
78-80623

PRINTED IN THE UNITED STATES OF AMERICA

# PREFACE

## BY THOMAS JEFFERSON

(From a letter to John W. Campbell, September 3, 1809)

*In answer to your proposition for publishing a complete edition of my different writings, I must observe that no writings of mine, other than those merely official, have been published,*[1] *except the Notes on Virginia*[2] *and a small pamphlet under the title of a Summary View of the rights of British America.*[3] *The Notes on Virginia, I have always intended to enlarge, and have, from time to time, laid by materials for that purpose.*

*The Summary View was not written for publication. It was a draught I had prepared for a petition to the king . . . , as a member of the convention of 1774. . . . If it had any merit, it was that of first taking our true ground. . . .*

*I do not mention the Parliamentary Manual, published for the use of the Senate of the United States, because it was a mere compilation, into which nothing entered of my own but the arrangement, and a few observations necessary to explain that and some of the cases.*

*I do not know whether your view extends to official papers of mine which have been published. Many of these would be like old newspapers, materials for future historians, but no longer interesting to the readers of the day. They would consist of reports, correspondences, messages, answers to addresses;*[4] *a few of my reports while Secretary of State, might perhaps be read by some as essays on abstract subjects. Such as the report on measures, weights and coins, on the mint, on the fisheries, on commerce, on the use of distilled sea-water, &c. The correspondence with the British and French ministers, Hammond and Genet, were published by Congress. The messages to Congress, which might have been interesting at the moment, would*

[1] See the Selected Bibliography of Jefferson's writings, p. 1301.

[2] The *Notes on Virginia* went through several editions even during Jefferson's lifetime. An eighth American edition was published in New York in 1801, the year he was inaugurated President.

[3] The year of its publication, 1774, saw three editions, one in Philadelphia and two in London.

[4] For a list of his reports, drafts, resolutions, and other official papers, see P. L. Ford, *The Writings of Thomas Jefferson*, vol. X, pp. 427-431.

*scarcely be read a second time, and answers to addresses are hardly read a first time.*

*So that on a review of these various materials, I see nothing encouraging a printer to a re-publication of them. They would probably be bought by those only who are in the habit of preserving State papers, and who are not many.*

*I say nothing of numerous draughts of reports, resolutions, declarations, &c., drawn as a Member of Congress or of the Legislature of Virginia, such as the Declaration of Independence, Report on the Money Mint of the United States, the act of religious freedom, &c., &c.;*[5] *these having become the acts of public bodies, there can be no personal claim to them, and they would no more find readers now, than the journals and statute books in which they are deposited. . . .*

*They belong mostly to a class of papers not calculated for popular reading, and not likely to offer profit, or even indemnification to the re-publisher.*

[5] All of these are included in this volume.

# INTRODUCTION

This is a one-volume Jefferson library, here brought together between two covers for the first time. It contains all of Jefferson's major writings, except his letters, and it is arranged by subject matter in such a way that it may be read for pleasure or consulted for reference.

The earliest piece was written about 1765, when Jefferson was twenty-two, and the last one in 1826, the year he died. The book is, therefore, the product of sixty remarkable years.

This is neither an anthology nor an assortment of excerpts. It is, excepting the letters, complete. Every important paper is included, and in each instance the full text is given. Likewise, Jefferson's two books—*Notes on Virginia* and *Manual of Parliamentary Practice,* both published in his lifetime—are reproduced in full, in smaller type to save space. Minor pieces, such as routine messages or unimportant papers, have been omitted. Nor will the reader find here narrowly technical papers or collections made by Jefferson. Thus, for example, the "Batture of New Orleans," which is a legal brief, is not included, nor is the so-called "Jefferson Bible," which is a collection culled from the New Testament.

The volume contains about eighty letters. These are included either because they supply the necessary background for some text or because they are the only source of certain basic ideas. For instance, while Jefferson deeply concerned himself with such questions as the Bill of Rights and the Supreme Court, he did not embody his thoughts on them in any official or public papers, but expressed them fully in letters only. Such letters are, therefore, included in order to fill challenging gaps.

Most of the documents in this book have been garnered from the published many-volumed Jefferson collections.[1] About fifteen pages, however, or one and one-fourth per cent of the total, are from archives and are here published for the first time. Another thirty-five pages, or approximately three per cent of the whole, are from scattered and little-known publications. In the unpublished materials the orthography has been reproduced as in the original. In the previously published ones, textual alterations have been confined to occasional modernization of the spelling and slight changes for

[1] See the Bibliography, p. 1301.

the sake of consistency, such as the "and" in place of Jefferson's favorite "&."

In one sense, this is not a book; it is an arsenal. Here are all the great ideas of democracy's most articulate champion. Here are the fundamental State papers of the architect of American liberty. Here are the basic arguments of the philosopher who had "sworn upon the altar of God, eternal hostility against every form of tyranny over the mind of man." Here are the thoughts of the statesman who told his friend John Adams: "I cannot live without books."

This condensation of Jefferson's writings in one volume brings out sharply the immensity of his interests. His mind is here displayed in panoramic view, and the effect is breath-taking. There has probably never been anything like it since the Italian Renaissance. In these pages the multi-minded Sage of Monticello speaks on liberty, discourses on philosophy, discusses religion, writes on agriculture, proposes educational systems, analyzes linguistics, suggests labor-saving devices, sketches inventions, comments on scientific classifications, tells how to construct a pedometer, explains how to survey a plat, introduces a new system of coinage, and—pens a poem to his love. The Jefferson who emerges from these pages is nearly incredible.

The book also reveals Jefferson the literary artist. Contemporaries considered him a master draftsman of bills and declarations; modern readers will find him a writer of matchless skill and beguiling felicity. In this collection of some 600,000 words—written, be it remembered, by a busy statesman and not by a professional writer—the literary standard is remarkably high. He was, despite the seeming effortlessness of his style, a conscious literary craftsman, although on occasion he was capable of sinking into that queer verbosity that is the favorite of lawyers the world over. Such occasions, however, were rare, as the careful reader will discover. As a young man he remarked that "the most valuable of all talents is that of never using two words where one will do." He chose his words meticulously and poured them out in a rhythm that was definitely his own. A deeply learned scholar and a disciplined scientist, he was yet so sensitive to beauty in all its forms that he rarely allowed the discussion of even a complex subject to mar the limpidity of his style.

Here, then, is Jefferson in his fullness. It is his book, and what he says in it is timeless.

SAUL K. PADOVER

*Washington, D. C.*

# CONTENTS



## PART I. POLITICS AND GOVERNMENT

### CHAPTER I. THE AMERICAN REVOLUTION: I, DECLARATIONS

CHAPTER II. THE AMERICAN REVOLUTION: II, HISTORY



CHAPTER III. LAWS AND CONSTITUTIONS

## Chapter IV. Foreign Policy: I, Relations



## Chapter V. Foreign Policy: II, Commerce

CHAPTER VI. THE NATIONAL CAPITAL



CHAPTER VII. THE WESTERN TERRITORIES



CHAPTER VIII. POLITICS AND POLITICAL THEORY

## Chapter IX. Government and Administration

CHAPTER X. THE NATIONAL ECONOMY



PART II. SPEECHES

CHAPTER XI. ADDRESSES AND MESSAGES

Chapter XIII. Replies to Addresses

## PART III. BOOKS, JOURNALS, AND ESSAYS

### Chapter XIV. Notes on the State of Virginia



### Chapter XV. A Manual of Parliamentary Practice



### Chapter XVI. Memoranda of Travels in Europe

## Chapter XVII. Literature and Language



## Chapter XVIII. Biographic Sketches

## PART IV. RELIGION, SCIENCE, AND PHILOSOPHY

### Chapter XIX. Religion



### Chapter XX. Science and Invention

### Chapter XXI. Philosophy and Conduct



## PART V. EDUCATION

### Chapter XXII. Ideas and Projects

### Chapter XXIII. The University of Virginia



## PART VI. PERSONAL PAPERS

### Chapter XXIV. Autobiography



### Chapter XXV. Diaries and Notes

# ILLUSTRATIONS

*Part I*

# POLITICS AND GOVERNMENT

*Chapter I*

# THE AMERICAN REVOLUTION: I, DECLARATIONS

## RESOLUTIONS OF THE VIRGINIA HOUSE OF BURGESSES [1]

May 8, 1769

*Resolved, Nemine contradicente,* That a most humble and dutiful Address be presented to his Excellency the Governor [Botetourt], returning Thanks for his very affectionate Speech at the Opening of the Session;

Expressing our firm Attachment to his Majesty's sacred Person and Government, and a lively Sense of his Royal Favour, manifested by frequent Approbations of our former Conduct; by extending his Paternal Regard to all his Subjects, however remote; and, by his gracious Purpose, that our Chief Governor shall, in future, reside among us;

Declaring, that we esteem, as a peculiar Mark of his Attention to our Happiness, the Appointment of his Lordship to preside over this Colony; and, that his Virtues and Abilities, manifested ever since his Arrival here, are to us the firmest Assurance, that Wisdom and Benevolence will distinguish his Administration;

Joining, in Congratulations on the Birth of another Princess, and the happy Restoration of her Majesty's Health;

Assuring his Excellency, that we shall, with Candour, proceed to the important Business on which we are met in General Assembly; and that, if in the Course of our Deliberations, any Matters shall arise, which may in any wise affect the Interests of *Great-Britain,* these shall ever be discussed on this ruling Principle, that her Interests, and ours, are inseparably the same; And finally, offering our Prayers, that Providence, and the Royal Pleasure, may long continue his Lordship the happy Ruler of a free and happy People.

[1] This draft is interesting mainly because it is Jefferson's first public paper. Twenty-six years old, he had just been elected to the Burgesses, where he was beginning to learn parliamentary rules and, particularly, the drafting of public papers and bills, an art in which he was to become a master.

A

SUMMARY VIEW

OF THE

RIGHTS

OF

BRITISH AMERICA.

SET FORTH IN SOME

RESOLUTIONS

INTENDED FOR THE

INSPECTION

OF THE PRESENT

DELEGATES

OF THE

PEOPLE OF VIRGINIA.

NOW IN

CONVENTION.

---

BY A NATIVE, AND MEMBER OF THE HOUSE OF BURGESSES.

by Thomas Jefferson

---

WILLIAMSBURG:

PRINTED BY CLEMENTINA RIND.

# A SUMMARY VIEW OF THE RIGHTS OF BRITISH AMERICA[1]

## August, 1774

The Legislature of Virginia happened to be in session, in Williamsburg, when news was received of the passage, by the British Parliament, of the Boston Port Bill, which was to take effect on the first day of June then ensuing. The House of Burgesses, thereupon, passed a resolution, recommending to their fellow-citizens, that that day should be set apart for fasting and prayer to the Supreme Being, imploring him to avert the calamities then threatening us, and to give us one heart and one mind to oppose every invasion of our liberties. The next day, May the 20th, 1774, the Governor dissolved us. We immediately repaired to a room in the Raleigh tavern, about one hundred paces distant from the Capitol, formed ourselves into a meeting, Peyton Randolph in the chair, and came to resolutions, declaring, that an attack on one colony, to enforce arbitrary acts, ought to be considered as an attack on all, and to be opposed by the united wisdom of all. We, therefore, appointed a Committee of correspondence, to address letters to the Speakers of the several Houses of Representatives of the colonies, proposing the appointment of deputies from each, to meet annually in a General Congress, to deliberate on their common interests, and on the measures to be pursued in common. The members then separated to their several homes, except those of the Committee, who met the next day, prepared letters according to instructions, and despatched them by messengers express, to their several destinations. It had been agreed, also, by the meeting, that the Burgesses, who should be elected under the writs then issuing, should be requested to meet in Convention, on a certain day in August, to learn the results of these letters, and to appoint delegates to a Congress, should that measure be approved by the other colonies. At the election, the people re-elected every man of the former Assembly, as a proof of their approbation of what they had done.

Before I left home, to attend the Convention, I prepared what I thought might be given, in instruction, to the Delegates who should be appointed to attend the General Congress proposed. They were drawn in haste, with a number of blanks, with some uncertainties and inaccuracies of historical facts, which I neglected at the moment, knowing they could be readily corrected at the meeting. I set out on my journey, but was taken sick on the road, and was unable to proceed. I therefore sent on, by express, two copies, one under cover to Patrick Henry, the other to Peyton Randolph, who I knew would be in the chair of the Convention. Of the former, no more was ever heard or known. Mr. Henry probably thought it too bold, as a first measure, as the majority of the members did. On the other copy being laid on the table of the Convention, by Peyton Randolph, as the proposition of a member, who was prevented from attendance by sickness on the road, tamer sentiments were preferred, and, I believe, wisely preferred; the

[1] Jefferson originally called this paper "Instructions." It was printed in pamphlet form under the title, *A Summary View of the Rights of British America,* and it went through several editions, especially in England, where it caused a sensation. The title page of one American edition, printed at Williamsburg, is shown facing this page. The text in this book is based upon that in the Congress Edition of Jefferson's *Writings.*

leap I proposed being too long, as yet, for the mass of our citizens. The distance between these, and the instructions actually adopted, is of some curiosity, however, as it shews the inequality of pace with which we moved, and the prudence required to keep front and rear together. My creed had been formed on unsheathing the sword at Lexington. They printed the paper, however, and gave it the title of "A Summary view of the rights of British America." In this form it got to London, where the opposition took it up, shaped it to opposition views, and, in that form, it ran rapidly through several editions: [2]

Resolved, That it be an instruction to the said deputies, when assembled in General Congress, with the deputies from the other states of British America, to propose to the said Congress, that an humble and dutiful address be presented to his Majesty, begging leave to lay before him, as Chief Magistrate of the British empire, the united complaints of his Majesty's subjects in America; complaints which are excited by many unwarrantable encroachments and usurpations, attempted to be made by the legislature of one part of the empire, upon the rights which God, and the laws, have given equally and independently to all. To represent to his Majesty that these, his States, have often individually made humble application to his imperial Throne, to obtain, through its intervention, some redress of their injured rights; to none of which, was ever even an answer condescended. Humbly to hope that this, their joint address, penned in the language of truth, and divested of those expressions of servility, which would persuade his Majesty that we are asking favors, and not rights, shall obtain from his Majesty a more respectful acceptance; and this his Majesty will think we have reason to expect, when he reflects that he is no more than the chief officer of the people, appointed by the laws, and circumscribed with definite powers, to assist in working the great machine of government, erected for their use, and, consequently, subject to their superintendence; and, in order that these, our rights, as well as the invasions of them, may be laid more fully before his Majesty, to take a view of them, from the origin and first settlement of these countries.

To remind him that our ancestors, before their emigration to America, were the free inhabitants of the British dominions in Europe, and possessed a right, which nature has given to all men, of departing from the country in which chance, not choice, has placed them, of going in quest of new habitations, and of there establishing new societies, under such laws and regulations as, to them, shall seem most likely to promote public happiness. That their Saxon ancestors had, under this universal law, in like manner, left their native wilds and woods in the North of Europe, had possessed themselves of the Island of Britain, then less charged with inhabitants, and had established there that system of laws which has so long been the glory

[2] From Jefferson's *Autobiography*, Appendix.

and protection of that country. Nor was ever any claim of superiority or dependence asserted over them, by that mother country from which they had migrated: and were such a claim made, it is believed his Majesty's subjects in Great Britain have too firm a feeling of the rights derived to them from their ancestors, to bow down the sovereignty of their state before such visionary pretensions. And it is thought that no circumstance has occurred to distinguish, materially, the British from the Saxon emigration. America was conquered, and her settlements made and firmly established, at the expense of individuals, and not of the British public. Their own blood was spilt in acquiring lands for their settlement, their own fortunes expended in making that settlement effectual. For themselves they fought, for themselves they conquered, and for themselves alone they have right to hold. No shilling was ever issued from the public treasures of his Majesty, or his ancestors, for their assistance, till of very late times, after the colonies had become established on a firm and permanent footing. That then, indeed, having become valuable to Great Britain for her commercial purposes, his Parliament was pleased to lend them assistance against an enemy who would fain have drawn to herself the benefits of their commerce, to the great aggrandisement of herself, and danger of Great Britain. Such assistance, and in such circumstances, they had often before given to Portugal and other allied states, with whom they carry on a commercial intercourse. Yet these states never supposed, that by calling in her aid, they thereby submitted themselves to her sovereignty. Had such terms been proposed, they would have rejected them with disdain, and trusted for better, to the moderation of their enemies, or to a vigorous exertion of their own force. We do not, however, mean to underrate those aids, which, to us, were doubtless valuable, on whatever principles granted: but we would shew that they cannot give a title to that authority which the British Parliament would arrogate over us; and that may amply be repaid by our giving to the inhabitants of Great Britain such exclusive privileges in trade as may be advantageous to them, and, at the same time, not too restrictive to ourselves. That settlement having been thus effected in the wilds of America, the emigrants thought proper to adopt that system of laws, under which they had hitherto lived in the mother country, and to continue their union with her, by submitting themselves to the same common sovereign, who was thereby made the central link, connecting the several parts of the empire thus newly multiplied.

But that not long were they permitted, however far they thought themselves removed from the hand of oppression, to hold undisturbed the rights thus acquired at the hazard of their lives and loss of their fortunes. A family of Princes was then on the British throne, whose treasonable crimes against their people, brought on them, afterwards, the exertion of those sacred and sovereign rights of punishment, reserved in the hands of the people for cases of extreme necessity, and judged by the constitution unsafe to be delegated to any other judicature. While every day brought forth some new and unjustifiable exertion of power over their subjects on that side of the water, it was not to be expected that those here, much less able at that time to oppose the designs of despotism, should be exempted from injury. Accordingly, this country which had been acquired by the lives, the labors, and fortunes of individual adventurers, was by these Princes, several times, parted out and distributed among the favorites and followers of their fortunes; and, by an assumed right of the Crown alone, were erected into distinct and independent governments; a measure, which it is believed, his Majesty's prudence and understanding would prevent him from imitating at this day; as no exercise of such power, of dividing and dismembering a country, has ever occurred in his Majesty's realm of England, though now of very ancient standing; nor could it be justified or acquiesced under there, or in any part of his Majesty's empire.

That the exercise of a free trade with all parts of the world, possessed by the American colonists, as of natural right, and which no law of their own had taken away or abridged, was next the object of unjust encroachment. Some of the colonies having thought proper to continue the administration of their government in the name and under the authority of his Majesty, King Charles the first, whom, notwithstanding his late deposition by the Commonwealth of England, they continued in the sovereignty of their State, the Parliament, for the Commonwealth, took the same in high offence, and assumed upon themselves the power of prohibiting their trade with all other parts of the world, except the Island of Great Britain. This arbitrary act, however, they soon recalled, and by solemn treaty entered into on the 12th day of March, 1651, between the said Commonwealth, by their Commissioners, and the colony of Virginia by their House of Burgesses, it was expressly stipulated by the eighth article of the said treaty, that they should have "free trade as the people of England do enjoy to all places and with all nations, according to the laws of that Commonwealth." But that, upon the restoration of his Majesty, King Charles the second, their rights of free commerce fell once more a victim to arbitrary power; and by several acts of his reign, as well as of some of his successors, the trade of the colonies was laid under such restrictions, as show what hopes they might form from the justice of a British Parliament, were its uncontrolled power admitted over these States. History has informed us, that bodies of men as well as of individuals, are susceptible of the spirit of tyranny. A view of these acts of Parliament for regulation, as it has been affectedly called, of the American trade, if all other evidences were removed out of the case, would undeniably evince the truth of this observation. Besides the duties they impose on our articles of export and import, they prohibit our going to any markets Northward of Cape Finisterra, in the kingdom of Spain, for the sale of commodities which Great Britain will not take from us, and for the purchase of others, with which she cannot supply us; and that, for no other than the arbitrary purpose of purchasing for themselves, by a sacrifice of our rights and interests, certain privileges in their commerce with an allied state, who, in confidence, that their exclusive trade with America will be continued, while the principles and power of the British Parliament be the same, have indulged themselves in every exorbitance which their avarice could dictate or our necessity extort: have raised their commodities called for in America, to the double and treble of what they sold for, before such exclusive privileges were given them, and of what better commodities of the same kind would cost us elsewhere; and, at the same time, give us much less for what we carry thither, than might be had at more convenient ports. That these acts prohibit us from carrying, in quest of other purchasers, the surplus of our tobaccos, remaining after the consumption of Great Britain is supplied: so that we must leave them with the British merchant, for whatever he will please to allow us, to be by him re-shipped to foreign markets, where he will reap the benefits of making sale of them for full value. That, to heighten still the idea of Parliamentary justice, and to show with what moderation they are like to exercise power, where themselves are to feel no part of its weight, we take leave to mention to his Majesty, certain other acts of the British Parliament, by which they would prohibit us from manufacturing, for our own use, the articles we raise on our own lands, with our own labor. By an act passed in the fifth year of the reign of his late Majesty, King George the second, an American subject is forbidden to make a hat for himself, of the fur which he has taken, perhaps, on his own soil; an instance of despotism, to which no parallel can be produced in the most arbitrary ages of British history. By one other act, passed in the twenty-third year of the same reign, the iron which we make, we are forbidden to manufacture; and, heavy as that article is, and necessary in every branch of husbandry, besides commission and insurance, we are to pay freight for it to Great Britain, and freight for it back again, for the purpose of supporting, not men, but machines, in the island of Great Britain. In the same spirit of equal and impartial legislation, is to be viewed the act of Parliament, passed in the fifth year of the same reign, by which American lands are made subject to the demands of British creditors, while their own lands were still continued unanswerable for their debts; from which, one of these conclusions must necessarily follow, either that justice is not the same thing in America as in Britain, or else, that the British Parliament pay less regard to it here than there. But, that we do not point out to his Majesty the injustice of these acts, with intent to rest on that principle the cause of their nullity; but to show that experience confirms the propriety of those political principles, which exempt us from the jurisdiction of the British Parliament. The true ground on which we declare these acts void, is, that the British Parliament has no right to exercise authority over us.

That these exercises of usurped power have not been confined to instances alone, in which themselves were interested; but they have also intermeddled with the regulation of the internal affairs of the colonies. The act of the 9th

JEFFERSON'S CHAIR AND WRITING TABLE

of Anne for establishing a post office in America, seems to have had little connection with British convenience, except that of accommodating his Majesty's ministers and favorites with the sale of a lucrative and easy office.

That thus have we hastened through the reigns which preceded his Majesty's, during which the violation of our rights were less alarming, because repeated at more distant intervals, than that rapid and bold succession of injuries, which is likely to distinguish the present from all other periods of American story. Scarcely have our minds been able to emerge from the astonishment into which one stroke of Parliamentary thunder has involved us, before another more heavy and more alarming is fallen on us. Single acts of tyranny may be ascribed to the accidental opinion of a day; but a series of oppressions, begun at a distinguished period, and pursued unalterably through every change of ministers, too plainly prove a deliberate, systematical plan of reducing us to slavery.

That the act passed in the fourth year of his Majesty's reign, entitled "an act

Act for granting certain duties.

One other act passed in the fifth year of his reign, entitled "an act

Stamp act.

One other act passed in the sixth year of his reign, entitled "an act

Act declaring the right of Parliament over the colonies.

And one other act passed in the seventh year of his reign, entitled "an act

Act for granting duties on paper, tea, &c.

Form that connected chain of Parliamentary usurpation, which has already been the subject of frequent applications to his Majesty, and the Houses of Lords and Commons of Great Britain; and, no answers having yet been condescended to any of these, we shall not trouble his Majesty with a repetition of the matters they contained.

But that one other act passed in the same seventh year of his reign, having been a peculiar attempt, must ever require peculiar mention. It is entitled "an act

Act suspending legislature of New York.

One free and independent legislature, hereby takes upon itself to suspend the powers of another, free and independent as itself. Thus exhibiting a phenomenon unknown in nature, the creator, and creature of its own power. Not only the principles of common sense, but the common feelings of human nature must be surrendered up, before his Majesty's subjects here, can be persuaded to believe, that they hold their political existence at the will of a British Parliament. Shall these governments be dissolved, their property annihilated, and their people reduced to a state of nature, at the imperious breath of a body of men whom they never saw, in whom they never confided, and over whom they have no powers of punishment or removal, let their crimes against the American public be ever so great? Can any one reason be assigned, why one hundred and sixty thousand electors in the island of Great Britain, should give law to four millions in the States of America, every individual of whom is equal to every individual of them in virtue, in understanding, and in bodily strength? Were this to be admitted, instead of being a free people, as we have hitherto supposed, and mean to continue ourselves, we should suddenly be found the slaves, not of one, but of one hundred and sixty thousand tyrants; distinguished, too, from all others, by this singular circumstance, that they are removed from the reach of fear, the only restraining motive which may hold the hand of a tyrant.

That, by "an act to discontinue in such manner, and for such time as are therein mentioned, the landing and discharging, lading or shipping of goods, wares and merchandize, at the town and within the harbor of Boston, in the province of Massachusetts bay, in North America," which was past at the last session of the British Parliament, a large and populous town, whose trade was their sole subsistence, was deprived of that trade, and involved in utter ruin. Let us for a while, suppose the question of right suspended, in order to examine this act on principles of justice. An act of Parliament had been passed, imposing duties on teas, to be paid in America, against which act the Americans had protested, as inauthoritative. The East India Company, who till that time, had never sent a pound of tea to America on their own account, step forth on that occasion, the asserters of Parliamentary right, and send hither many ship loads of that obnoxious commodity. The masters of their several vessels, however, on their arrival in America, wisely attended to admonition, and returned with their cargoes. In the province of New-England alone, the remonstrances of the people were disregarded, and a compliance, after being many days waited for, was flatly refused. Whether in this, the master of the vessel was governed by his obstinacy, or his instructions, let those who know, say. There are extraordinary situations which require extraordinary interposition. An exasperated people, who feel that they possess power, are not easly restrained within limits strictly regular. A number of them assembled in the town of Boston, threw the tea into the ocean, and dispersed without doing any other act of violence. If in this they did wrong, they were known, and were amenable to the laws of the land; against which, it could not be objected, that they had ever, in any instance, been obstructed or diverted from the regular course, in favor of popular offenders. They should, therefore, not have been distrusted on this occasion. But that ill-fated colony had formerly been bold in their enmities against the House of Stuart, and were now devoted to ruin, by that unseen hand which governs the momentous affairs of this great empire. On the partial representations of a few worthless ministerial dependants, whose constant office it has been to keep that government embroiled, and who, by their treacheries, hope to obtain the dignity of British knighthood, without calling for a party accused, without asking a proof, without attempting a distinction between the guilty and the innocent, the whole of that ancient and wealthy town, is in a moment reduced from opulence to beggary. Men who had spent their lives in extending the British commerce, who had invested, in that place, the wealth their honest endeavors had merited, found themselves and their families, thrown at once on the world, for subsistence by its charities. Not the hundredth part of the inhabitants of that town, had been concerned in the act complained of; many of them were in Great Britain, and in other parts beyond sea; yet all were involved in one indiscriminate ruin, by a new executive power, unheard of till then, that of a British Parliament. A property of the value of many millions of money, was sacrificed to revenge, not repay, the loss of a few thousands. This is administering justice with a heavy hand indeed! And when is this tempest to be arrested in its course? Two wharves are to be opened again when his Majesty shall think proper: the residue, which lined the extensive shores of the bay of Boston, are forever interdicted the exercise of commerce. This little exception seems to have been thrown in for no other purpose, than that of setting a precedent for investing his Majesty with legislative powers. If the pulse of his people shall beat calmly under this experiment, another and another will be tried, till the measure of despotism be filled up. It would be an insult on common sense, to pretend that this exception was made, in order to restore its commerce to that great town. The trade, which cannot be received at two wharves alone, must of necessity be transferred to some other place; to which it will soon be followed by that of the two wharves. Considered in this light, it would be an insolent and cruel mockery at the annihilation of the town of Boston. By the act for the suppression of riots and tumults in the town of Boston, passed also in the last session of Parliament, a murder committed there, is, if the Governor pleases, to be tried in the court of King's bench, in the island of Great Britain, by a jury of Middlesex. The witnesses, too, on receipt of such a sum as the Governor shall think it reasonable for them to expend, are to enter into recognizance to appear at the trial. This is, in other words, taxing them to the amount of their recognizance; and that amount may be whatever a Governor pleases. For who does his Majesty think can be prevailed on to cross the Atlantic for the sole purpose of bearing evidence to a fact? His expenses are to be borne, indeed, as they shall be estimated by a Governor; but who are to feed the wife and children whom he leaves behind, and who have had no other subsistence but his daily labor? Those epidemical disorders, too, so terrible in a foreign climate, is the cure of them to be estimated among the articles of expense, and their danger to be warded off by the Almighty power of a Parliament? And the wretched criminal, if he happen to have offended on the American side, stripped of his privilege of trial by peers of his vicinage, removed from the place where alone full evidence could be obtained, without money, without counsel, without friends, without exculpatory proof, is tried before Judges predetermined to condemn. The cowards who would suffer a countryman to be torn from the bowels of their society, in order to be thus offered a sacrifice to Parliamentary tyranny, would merit that everlasting infamy now fixed on the authors of the act! A clause, for a similar purpose, had been introduced into an act passed in the twelfth year of his Majesty's reign, entitled, "an act for the better securing and preserving his Majesty's Dock-yards, Magazines, Ships, Ammunition and Stores"; against which, as meriting the same censures, the several colonies have already protested.

That these are the acts of power, assumed by a body of men foreign to our constitutions, and unacknowledged by our laws; against which we do, on behalf of the inhabitants of British America, enter this, our solemn and determined protest. And we do earnestly intreat his Majesty, as yet the only mediatory power between the several States of the British empire, to recommend to his Parliament of Great Britain, the total revocation of these acts, which, however nugatory they may be, may yet prove the cause of further discontents and jealousies among us.

That we next proceed to consider the conduct of his Majesty, as holding the Executive powers of the laws of these States, and mark out his deviations from the line of duty. By the Constitution of Great Britain, as well as of the several American States, his Majesty possesses the power of refusing to pass into a law, any bill which has already passed the other two branches of the legislature. His Majesty, however, and his ancestors, conscious of the impropriety of opposing their single opinion to the united wisdom of two Houses of Parliament, while their proceedings were unbiassed by interested principles, for several ages past, have modestly declined the exercise of this power, in that part of his empire called Great Britain. But, by change of circumstances, other principles than those of justice simply, have obtained an influence on their determinations. The addition of new States to the British empire has produced an addition of new, and, sometimes, opposite interests. It is now, therefore, the great office of his Majesty to resume the exercise of his negative power, and to prevent the passage of laws by any one legislature of the empire, which might bear injuriously on the rights and interests of another. Yet this will not excuse the wanton exercise of this power, which we have seen his Majesty practice on the laws of the American legislature. For the most trifling reasons, and, sometimes for no conceivable reason at all, his Majesty has rejected laws of the most salutary tendency. The abolition of domestic slavery is the great object of desire in those colonies, where it was, unhappily, introduced in their infant state. But previous to the enfranchisement of the slaves we have, it is necessary to exclude all further importations from Africa. Yet our repeated attempts to effect this, by prohibitions, and by imposing duties which might amount to a prohibition, having been hitherto defeated by his Majesty's negative: thus preferring the immediate advantages of a few British corsairs, to the lasting interests of the American States, and to the rights of human nature, deeply wounded by this infamous practice. Nay, the single interposition of an interested individual against a law was scarcely ever known to fail of success, though, in the opposite scale, were placed the interests of a whole country. That this is so shameful an abuse of a power, trusted with his Majesty for other purposes, as if, not reformed, would call for some legal restrictions.

With equal inattention to the necessities of his people here has his Majesty permitted our laws to lie neglected, in England, for years, neither confirming them by his assent, nor annulling them by his negative: so, that such of them as have no suspending clause, we hold on the most precarious of all tenures, his Majesty's will; and such of them as suspend themselves till his Majesty's assent be obtained, we have feared might be called into existence at some future and distant period, when time and change of circumstances shall have rendered them destructive to his people here. And, to render this grievance still more oppressive, his Majesty, by his instructions, has laid his Governors under such restrictions, that they can pass no law, of any moment, unless it have such suspending clause: so that, however immediate may be the call for legislative interposition, the law cannot be executed, till it has twice crossed the Atlantic, by which time the evil may have spent its whole force.

But in what terms reconcilable to Majesty, and at the same time to truth, shall we speak of a late instruction to his Majesty's Governor of the colony of Virginia, by which he is forbidden to assent to any law for the division of a county, unless the new county will consent to have no representative in Assembly? That colony has as yet affixed no boundary to the Westward. Their Western counties, therefore, are of an indefinite extent. Some of them are actually seated many hundred miles from their Eastern limits. Is it possible, then, that his Majesty can have bestowed a single thought on the situation of those people, who in order to obtain justice for injuries, however great or small, must, by the laws of that colony, attend their county court at such a distance, with all their witnesses, monthly, till their litigation be determined? Or does his Majesty seriously wish, and publish it to the world, that his subjects should give up the glorious right of representation, with all the benefits derived from that, and submit themselves the absolute slaves of his sovereign will? Or is it rather meant to confine the legislative body to their present numbers, that they may be the cheaper bargain, whenever they shall become worth a purchase?

One of the articles of impeachment against Tresilian, and the other Judges of Westminster Hall, in the reign of Richard the Second, for which they suffered death, as traitors to their country, was, that they had advised the King, that he might dissolve his Parliament at any time; and succeeding kings have adopted the opinion of these unjust Judges. Since the establishment, however, of the British constitution, at the glorious Revolution, on its free and ancient principles, neither his Majesty, nor his ancestors, have exercised such a power of dissolution in the island of Great Britain;[3] and when his Majesty was petitioned, by the united voice of his people there, to

[3] On further inquiry, I find two instances of dissolution before the Parliament would, of itself, have been at an end: *viz.*, the Parliament called to meet August 24, 1698, was dissolved by King William, December 19, 1700, and a new one called, to meet February 6, 1701, which was also dissolved, November 11, 1701, and a new one met December 30, 1701.—T. J.

dissolve the present Parliament, who had become obnoxious to them, his Ministers were heard to declare, in open Parliament, that his Majesty possessed no such power by the constitution. But how different their language, and his practice, here! To declare, as their duty required, the known rights of their country, to oppose the usurpation of every foreign judicature, to disregard the imperious mandates of a Minister or Governor, have been the avowed causes of dissolving Houses of Representatives in America. But if such powers be really vested in his Majesty, can he suppose they are there placed to awe the members from such purposes as these? When the representative body have lost the confidence of their constituents, when they have notoriously made sale of their most valuable rights, when they have assumed to themselves powers which the people never put into their hands, then, indeed, their continuing in office becomes dangerous to the State, and calls for an exercise of the power of dissolution. Such being the cause for which the representative body should, and should not, be dissolved, will it not appear strange, to an unbiassed observer, that that of Great Britain was not dissolved, while those of the colonies have repeatedly incurred that sentence?

But your Majesty, or your Governors, have carried this power beyond every limit known or provided for by the laws. After dissolving one House of Representatives, they have refused to call another, so that, for a great length of time, the legislature provided by the laws, has been out of existence. From the nature of things, every society must, at all times, possess within itself the sovereign powers of legislation. The feelings of human nature revolt against the supposition of a State so situated, as that it may not, in any emergency, provide against dangers which, perhaps, threaten immediate ruin. While those bodies are in existence to whom the people have delegated the powers of legislation, they alone possess, and may exercise, those powers. But when they are dissolved, by the lopping off one or more of their branches, the power reverts to the people, who may use it to unlimited extent, either assembling together in person, sending deputies, or in any other way they may think proper. We forbear to trace consequences further; the dangers are conspicuous with which this practice is replete.

That we shall, at this time also, take notice of an error in the nature of our land holdings, which crept in at a very early period of our settlement. The introduction of the feudal tenures into the kingdom of England, though ancient, is well enough understood to set this matter in a proper light. In the earlier ages of the Saxon settlement, feudal holdings were certainly altogether unknown, and very few, if any, had been introduced at the time of the Norman conquest. Our Saxon ancestors held their lands, as they did their personal property, in absolute dominion, disincumbered with any superior, answering nearly to the nature of those possessions which the feudalist term Allodial. William the Norman, first introduced that system generally. The lands which had belonged to those who fell in the battle of Hastings, and in the subsequent insurrections of his reign, formed a considerable proportion of the lands of the whole kingdom. These he granted out, subject to feudal duties, as did he also those of a great number of his new subjects, who, by persuasions or threats, were induced to surrender them for that purpose. But still, much was left in the hands of his Saxon subjects, held of no superior, and not subject to feudal conditions. These, therefore, by express laws, enacted to render uniform the system of military defence, were made liable to the same military duties as if they had been feuds; and the Norman lawyers soon found means to saddle them, also, with the other feudal burthens. But still they had not been surrendered to the King, they were not derived from his grant, and therefore they were not holden of him. A general principle was introduced, that "all lands in England were held either mediately or immediately of the Crown"; but this was borrowed from those holdings which were truly feudal, and only applied to others for the purposes of illustration. Feudal holdings were, therefore, but exceptions out of the Saxon laws of possession, under which all lands were held in absolute right. These, therefore, still form the basis or groundwork of the Common law, to prevail wheresoever the exceptions have not taken place. America was not conquered by William the Norman, nor its lands surrendered to him or any of his successors. Possessions there are, undoubtedly, of the Allodial nature. Our ancestors, however, who migrated hither, were laborers, not lawyers. The fictitious principle, that all lands belong originally to the King, they were early persuaded to believe real, and accordingly took grants of their own lands from the Crown. And while the Crown continued to grant for small sums and on reasonable rents, there was no inducement to arrest the error, and lay it open to public view. But his Majesty has lately taken on him to advance the terms of purchase and of holding, to the double of what they were; by which means, the acquisition of lands being rendered difficult, the population of our country is likely to be checked. It is time, therefore, for us to lay this matter before his Majesty, and to declare, that he has no right to grant lands of himself. From the nature and purpose of civil institutions, all the lands within the limits, which any particular party has circumscribed around itself, are assumed by that society, and subject to their allotment; this may be done by themselves assembled collectively, or by their legislature, to whom they may have delegated sovereign authority; and, if they are allotted in neither of these ways, each individual of the society, may appropriate to himself such lands as he finds vacant, and occupancy will give him title.

That, in order to enforce the arbitrary measures before complained of, his Majesty has, from time to time, sent among us large bodies of armed forces, not made up of the people here, nor raised by the authority of our laws. Did his Majesty possess such a right as this, it might swallow up all our other rights, whenever he should think proper. But his Majesty has no right to land a single armed man on our shores; and those whom he sends here are liable to our laws, for the suppression and punishment of riots, routs, and unlawful assemblies, or are hostile bodies invading us in defiance of law. When, in the course of the late war, it became expedient that a body of Hanoverian troops should be brought over for the defence of Great Britain, his Majesty's grandfather, our late sovereign, did not pretend to introduce them under any authority he possessed. Such a measure would have given just alarm to his subjects of Great Britain, whose liberties would not be safe if armed men of another country, and of another spirit, might be brought into the realm at any time, without the consent of their legislature. He, therefore, applied to Parliament, who passed an act for that purpose, limiting the number to be brought in, and the time they were to continue. In like manner is his Majesty restrained in every part of the empire. He possesses indeed the executive power of the laws in every State; but they are the laws of the particular State, which he is to administer within that State, and not those of any one within the limits of another. Every State must judge for itself, the number of armed men which they may safely trust among them, of whom they are to consist, and under what restrictions they are to be laid. To render these proceedings still more criminal against our laws, instead of subjecting the military to the civil power, his majesty has expressly made the civil subordinate to the military. But can his Majesty thus put down all law under his feet? Can he erect a power superior to that which erected himself? He has done it indeed by force; but let him remember that force cannot give right.

That these are our grievances, which we have thus laid before his Majesty, with that freedom of language and sentiment which becomes a free people, claiming their rights as derived from the laws of nature, and not as the gift of their Chief Magistrate. Let those flatter, who fear: it is not an American art. To give praise where it is not due might be well from the venal, but would ill beseem those who are asserting the rights of human nature. They know, and will, therefore, say, that Kings are the servants, not the proprietors of the people. Open your breast, Sire, to liberal and expanded thought. Let not the name of George the third, be a blot on the page of history. You are surrounded by British counsellors, but remember that they are parties. You have no ministers for American affairs, because you have none taken from among us, nor amenable to the laws on which they are to give you advice. It behooves you, therefore, to think and to act for yourself and your people. The great principles of right and wrong are legible to every reader; to pursue them, requires not the aid of many counsellors. The whole art of government consists in the art of being honest. Only aim to do your duty, and mankind will give you credit where you fail. No longer persevere in sacrificing the rights of one part of the empire to the inordinate desires of another; but deal out to all, equal and impartial right. Let no act be passed by any one legislature, which may infringe on the rights and liberties of another. This is the important post in which fortune has placed you, holding the balance of a great, if a well-poised empire. This, Sire, is the advice of your great American council, on the observance of which may perhaps depend your felicity and future fame, and the preservation of that harmony which alone can continue, both to Great Britain and America, the reciprocal advantages of their connection. It is neither our wish nor our interest to separate from her. We are willing, on our part, to sacrifice everything which reason can ask, to the restoration of that tranquillity for which all must wish. On their part, let them be ready to establish union on a generous plan. Let them name their terms, but let them be just. Accept of every commercial preference it is in our power to give, for such things as we can raise for their use, or they make for ours. But let them not think to exclude us from going to other markets to dispose of those commodities which they cannot use, nor to supply those wants which they cannot supply. Still less, let it be proposed, that our properties, within our own territories, shall be taxed or regulated by any power on earth, but our own. The God who gave us life, gave us liberty at the same time: the hand of force may destroy, but cannot disjoin them. This, Sire, is our last, our determined resolution. And that you will be pleased to interpose, with that efficacy which your earnest endeavors may insure, to procure redress of these our great grievances, to quiet the minds of your subjects in British America against any apprehensions of future encroachment, to establish fraternal love and harmony through the whole empire, and that that may continue to the latest ages of time, is the fervent prayer of all British America.

## ADDRESS TO GOVERNOR DUNMORE[1]

June 12, 1775

MY LORD: We, His majesty's dutiful and loyal subjects, the Burgesses of Virginia, now met in General Assembly, have taken into our consideration the joint Address of the two Houses of Parliament, His Majesty's Answer, and the Resolution of the Commons, which your Lordship has been pleased to lay before us. Wishing nothing so sincerely as the perpetual continuance

[1] Jefferson drew up this address as a member of a committee of eight which the Virginia House of Burgesses appointed to make a reply to Lord North's "conciliatory propositions" of February, 1775. The address was submitted on June 12, and after a few changes it was passed "with unanimity or a vote approaching it." The address is a forerunner of the Declaration of Independence.

of that brotherly love which we bear to our fellow-subjects of Great Britain, and still continuing to hope and believe that they do not approve the measures which have so long oppressed their brethren in America, we were pleased to receive your Lordship's notification, that a benevolent tender had at length been made by the British House of Commons towards bringing to a good end our unhappy disputes with the Mother Country. Next to the possession of liberty, my Lord, we should consider such a reconciliation as the greatest of all human blessings. With these dispositions we entered into the consideration of that Resolution; we examined it minutely; we viewed it in every point of light in which we were able to place it; and, with pain and disappointment, we must ultimately declare it only changes the form of oppression, without lightening its burden. We cannot, my Lord, close with the terms of that Resolution, for these reasons:

Because the British Parliament has no right to intermeddle with the support of civil Government in the Colonies. For us, not for them, has Government been instituted here. Agreeable to our ideas, provision has been made for such officers as we think necessary for the administration of publick affairs; and we cannot conceive that any other legislature has a right to prescribe either the number or pecuniary appointments of our offices. As a proof that the claim of Parliament to interfere in the necessary provisions for the support of civil Government is novel, and of a late date, we take leave to refer to an Act of our Assembly, passed so long since as the thirty-second year of the reign of King Charles the Second, intituled, "An Act for raising a publick revenue, and for the better support of the Government of His Majesty's Colony of Virginia." This act was brought over by Lord Culpeper, then Governour, under the great seal of England, and was enacted in the name of the "King's most Excellent Majesty, by and with the consent of the General Assembly."

Because to render perpetual our exemption from an unjust taxation, we must saddle ourselves with a perpetual tax, adequate to the expectations, and subject to the disposal of Parliament alone; Whereas, we have a right to give our money, as the Parliament do theirs, without coercion, from time to time, as public exigencies may require. We conceive that we alone are the judges of the condition, circumstances, and situation of our people, as the Parliament are of theirs. It is not merely the mode of raising, but the freedom of granting our money, for which we have contended. Without this, we possess no check on the royal prerogative; and what must be lamented by dutiful and loyal subjects, we should be stripped of the only means, as well of recommending this Country to the favours of our most gracious Sovereign, as of strengthening those bands of amity with our fellow-subjects, which we would wish to remain indissoluble.

Because on our undertaking to grant money, as is proposed, the Commons only resolve to forbear levying pecuniary taxes on us, still leaving unrepealed their several Acts passed for the purposes of restraining the Trade, and altering the form of Government of the Eastern Colonies; extending the boundaries, and changing the Government and Religion of Quebeck; enlarging the jurisdiction of the Courts of Admiralty; taking from us the right of Trial by Jury, and transporting us into other countries to be tried for criminal offences. Standing Armies, too, are still to be kept among us, and the other numerous grievances, of which ourselves and sister Colonies, separately and by our Representatives in General Congress, have so often complained, are still to continue without redress.

Because, at the very time of requiring from us grants of money, they are making disposition to invade us with large armaments by sea and land, which is a style of asking gifts not reconcilable to our freedom. They are also proceeding to a repetition of injury, by passing Acts for restraining the Commerce and Fisheries of the Provinces of New England, and for prohibiting the Trade of the other Colonies with all parts of the world, except the Island of Great Britain, Ireland, and the West Indies. This seems to bespeak no intention to discontinue the exercise of this usurped power over us in future.

Because on our agreeing to contribute our proportion towards the common defence, they do not propose to lay open to us a free trade with all the world: whereas, to us it appears just that those who bear equally the burdens of Government should equally participate of its benefits; either be contented with the monopoly of our trade, which brings greater loss to us and benefit to them than the amount of our proportional contributions to the common defence; or, if the latter be preferred, relinquish the former, and do not propose, by holding both, to exact from us double contributions. Yet we would remind Government, that on former emergencies, when called upon as a free people, however cramped by this monopoly in our resources of wealth, we have liberally contributed to the common defence. Be assured, then, that we shall be as generous in future as in past times, disclaiming the shackles of proportion when called to our free station in the general system of the Empire.

Because the proposition now made to us involves the interests of all the other Colonies. We are now represented in General Congress by members approved by this House, where the former union, it is hoped, will be so strongly cemented, that no partial applications can produce the slightest departure from the common cause. We consider ourselves as bound in honour, as well as interest, to share one general fate with our sister Colonies; and should hold ourselves base deserters of that union to which we have acceded, were we to agree on any measures distinct and apart from them.

There was, indeed, a plan of accommodation offered in Parliament, which, though not entirely equal to the terms we had a right to ask, yet differed but in few points from what the General Congress had held out. Had Parliament been disposed sincerely, as we are, to bring about a reconciliation, reasonable men had hoped, that by meeting us on this ground, something might have been done. Lord Chatham's Bill, on the one part, and the terms of Congress on the other, would have formed a basis for negotiations, which a spirit of accommodation on both sides might, perhaps, have reconciled. It came recommended, too, from one whose successful experience in the art of Government should have insured it some attention from those to whom it was intended. He had shown to the world, that Great Britain, with her Colonies united firmly under a just and honest Government, formed a power which might bid defiance to the most potent enemies. With a change of Ministers, however, a total change of measures took place. The component parts of the Empire have, from that moment, been falling asunder, and a total annihilation of its weight in the political scale of the world, seems justly to be apprehended.

These, my Lord, are our sentiments on this important subject, which we offer only as an individual part of the whole Empire. Final determination we leave to the General Congress, now sitting,[2] before whom we shall lay the papers your Lordship has communicated to us. To their wisdom we commit the improvement of this important advance; if it can be wrought into any good, we were assured they will do it. To them, also we refer the discovery of that proper method of representing our well-founded grievances, which your Lordship assures us will meet with the attention and regard so justly due to them. For ourselves, we have exhausted every mode of application which our invention could suggest as proper and promising. We have decently remonstrated with Parliament: they have added new injuries to the old. We have wearied our King with applications: he has not deigned to answer us. We have appealed to the native honour and justice of the British Nation. Their efforts in our favour have been hitherto ineffectual. What, then, remains to be done? That we commit our injuries to the evenhanded justice of the Being who doth no wrong, earnestly beseeching him to illuminate the counsels, and prosper the endeavours of those to whom America hath confided her hopes, that through their wise direction we may again see reunited the blessings of liberty, property, and harmony with Great Britain.

[2] The Second Continental Congress, in Philadelphia, of which Jefferson was a member.

## DECLARATION ON TAKING UP ARMS [1]

July 6, 1775

A Declaration ~~of~~ by

~~We~~ the representatives of the United colonies of America now sitting in General Congress, ~~to all nations send greeting of~~ setting forth the causes and necessity of their taking up arms.

The large strides of late taken by the *legislature of Great Britain* towards establishing over these colonies their absolute rule, and the hardiness of the present attempt to effect by force of arms what by law or right they could never effect, *render* it necessary for us also to change the ground of opposition, and to close with their last appeal from reason to arms. And it behooves those, who *are called to this great decision,* to be assured that their cause is approved before supreme reason; so is it of great avail that its justice be made known to the world, whose affections will ever take part with those encountering oppression. Our forefathers, inhabitants of the island of Great Britain, ~~having long endeavored to bear up against the evils of misrule,~~ left their native lands to seek on these shores a residence for civil and religious freedom. At the expence of their blood, ~~with~~ to the ruin of their fortunes, with the relinquishment of everything quiet and comfortable in life, they effected settlements in the hospitable wilds of America; ~~they~~ and there established civil societies with various forms of constitution. ~~But possessing all, what is inherent in all, the full and perfect powers of legislation.~~ To continue their connection with the friends whom they had left, they arranged themselves by charters of compact under ~~one~~ the same common king, who thus completed their powers of full and perfect legislation and became the link of union between the several parts of the empire. Some occasional assumptions of power by the parliament of Great Britain, however unacknowledged by the constitution of our governments, were finally acquiesced in through warmth of affection. Proceeding thus in the fullness of mutual harmony and confidence, both parts of the empire increased in population and wealth with a rapidity unknown in the history of man. The political institutions of America, its various soils and climates opened a certain resource to the unfortunate and to the enterprising of every country, and ensured to them the acquisition and free possession of property. Great Britain too acquired a lustre and a weight among the powers of the earth which

[1] On June 26, the Second Continental Congress, at Philadelphia, appointed Jefferson and John Dickinson to a committee to "prepare a declaration of the causes of taking up arms" against Britain. Jefferson drew up the above draft. It was "too strong" for the Congress, which adopted a milder version by Dickinson. The latter, however, retained a number of Jeffersonian phrases. Jefferson's draft is a comparatively pale, but important, predecessor of the Declaration of Independence.

The words crossed out were corrections made by Jefferson himself.

her internal resources could never have given her. To a communication of the wealth and power of ~~the whole~~ every part of the empire we may surely ascribe in some measure the illustrious character she sustained through her last European war, and its successful event. At the close of that war ~~however having subdued all her foes~~[2] it pleased our sovereign to make a change in his counsels. The new ministry finding all the foes of Britain subdued she took up the unfortunate idea of subduing her friends also. By them [3] and her parliament then for the first time ~~asserted a right~~ [4] assumed a power of unbounded legislation over the colonies of America; and in the ~~space~~ course of ten years ~~during which they have proceeded to exercise this right,~~ have given such decisive specimens of the spirit of this new legislation, as leaves no room to doubt the consequence of acquiescence under it. By several acts of parliament passed within that ~~space of~~ time they have ~~attempted to take from us~~ undertaken to give and grant our money without our consent: a right of which we have ever had the exclusive exercise: they have interdicted all commerce to one of our principal towns, thereby annihilating its property in the hands of the holders; they have cut off the commercial intercourse of whole colonies with foreign countries; they have extended the jurisdiction of courts of admiralty beyond their ancient limits; ~~thereby~~ they have ~~depriving~~ deprived us of the inestimable ~~right~~ privilege of trial by a jury of the vicinage, in cases affecting both life and property; they have declared that American Subjects charged with certain offenses shall be transported beyond sea to be tried before the very persons against whose pretended sovereignty the offense is supposed to be committed; they have attempted fundamentally to alter the form of government in one of these colonies, a form ~~established~~ secured by charters on the part of the crown and confirmed by acts of its own legislature; ~~and further secured by charters on the part of the crown;~~ they have erected in a neighboring province acquired by the joint arms of Great Britain and America, a tyranny dangerous to the very existence of all these colonies. But why should we enumerate their injuries in the detail? By one act they have suspended the powers of one American legislature, and by another have declared they may legislate for us themselves in all cases whatsoever. These two acts alone form a basis broad enough whereon to erect a despotism of unlimited extent. And what is to secure us against this dreaded evil? The persons assuming these powers are not chosen by us, are not subject to our controul or influence, are exempted by their situation from the operation of these laws, and lighten their own burthens in proportion as they increase ours. These temptations might put to trial the severest characters of ancient virtue: with what new

[2] Insertion by John Dickinson: "her successful and glorious ministry."

[3] Alteration by Dickinson: "by their influence."

[4] Alteration by Dickinson: "were persuaded to assume and assert."

armour then shall a British parliament encounter the rude assault? towards these deadly injuries from the tender plant of liberty which we have brought over, and with so much affection fostered on these our own shores, we have pursued every temperate, every respectful measure. We have supplicated our king at various times, in terms almost disgraceful to freedom; we have reasoned, we have remonstrated with parliament in the most mild and decent language; we have even proceeded to break off our commercial intercourse with our fellow subjects, as the last peaceful admonition that our attachment to no nation on earth should supplant our attachment to liberty. And here we had well hoped was the ultimate step of the controversy. But subsequent events have shewn how vain was even this last remain of confidence in the moderation of the British ministry.[5] During the course of the last year their troops in a hostile manner invested the town of Boston in the province of Massachusets bay, and from that time have held the same beleaguered by sea and land. On the 19th day of April in the present year they made an unprovoked ~~attack~~ assault on the inhabitants of the said province at the town of Lexington, murdered eight of them on the spot and wounded many others. From thence they proceeded in ~~the~~ all the array of war to the town of Concord, where they set upon another party of the inhabitants of the same province, killing many of them also, burning houses, and laying waste property, until repressed by ~~the arms~~[6] the people[7] suddenly assembled to oppose this cruel aggression. Hostilities thus commenced on the part of the ministerial army have been since by them pursued without regard to faith or to fame. The inhabitants of the town of Boston in order to procure their enlargement having entered into treaty with ~~a certain Thomas Gage~~ General Gage their Governor ~~principal instigator of these enormities~~[8] it was stipulated that the said inhabitants,[9] having first deposited their arms with their own magistrates ~~their arms and military stores~~ should have liberty to depart from out of the said town taking with them their other ~~goods and~~ effects. Their arms ~~and military stores~~ they accordingly delivered in, and claimed the stipulated license of departing with their effects. But in open violation of plighted faith and honour, in defiance of the sacred obligations of treaty which even savage nations observe, their arms and warlike stores deposited with their own magistrates to be preserved as their property, were immediately seized by a body of armed men under orders from the said ~~Thomas Gage~~ General, the greater part of the inhabitants were detained in the town, and the few permitted to depart were compelled to

[5] Marginal notation by Dickinson: "Here insert substance of the Address declaring a Rebellion to exist in Massachusetts Bay, &c."

[6] Insertion by Dickinson: "Country."

[7] Insertion by Dickinson: "Only."

[8] Insertion by Dickinson: "To procure their Enlargement."

[9] Insertion by Dickinson: "after."

leave their most valuable effects behind. We leave the world to ~~their own~~ its own reflections on this atrocious perfidy. That we might no longer doubt the ultimate aim of these ministerial maneuvers ~~the same Thomas~~ General Gage, by proclamation bearing date the 12th day of June, after reciting the grossest falsehoods and calumnies against the good people of these colonies, proceeds to declare them all, either by name or description, to be rebels and traitors, to supersede ~~by his own authority~~ the exercise of the common law of the said province, and to proclaim and order instead thereof the use and exercise of the law martial. This bloody edict issued, he has proceeded to commit further ravages and murders in the same province, burning the town of Charlestown, attacking and killing great numbers of the people residing or assembled therein; and is now going on in an avowed course of murder and devastation, taking every occasion to destroy the lives and properties of the inhabitants ~~of the said province.~~ To oppose his arms we also have taken up arms. We should be wanting to ourselves, we should be perfidious to posterity, we should be unworthy that free ancestry from ~~whom~~ which we derive our descent, should we submit with folded arms to military butchery and depredation, to gratify the lordly ambition, or sate the avarice of a British ministry. We do then most solemnly, before God and the world declare that, regardless of every consequence, at the risk of every distress, the arms we have been compelled to assume we will ~~wage~~ use with the perseverance, exerting to their utmost energies all those powers which our creator hath given us, to ~~guard~~ preserve that liberty which he committed to us in sacred deposit and to protect from every hostile hand our lives and our properties. But that this our declaration may not disquiet the minds of our good fellow subjects[10] in any parts of the empire, we do further assure them that we mean not in any wise to affect that union with them in which we have so long and so happily lived and which we wish so much to see again restored. That necessity must be hard indeed which may force upon us that desperate measure, or induce us to avail ourselves of any aid which their enemies might proffer. We did not embody a soldiery to commit aggression on them; we did not raise armies for glory or for conquest; we did not invade their island carrying death or slavery to its inhabitants. ~~We took up arms~~ in defence of our persons and properties under actual violation, we took up arms. ~~we have taken up arms~~ When that violence shall be removed, when hostilities shall cease on the part of the aggressors, hostilities shall cease on our part also. ~~The moment they withdraw their armies, we will disband ours.~~ For the achievement of this happy event, we call for and confide in the good offices of our fellow subjects beyond the Atlantic. Of their friendly dispositions we do not cease to hope; aware, as they must be, that they have nothing more to expect from the same common enemy, than

[10] Insertion by Dickinson: "In Britain or other."

the humble favour of being last devoured. And we devoutly implore assistance of Almighty God to conduct us happily through this great conflict, to dispose ~~the minds of~~ his majesty, his ministers, and parliament to ~~reasonable terms~~ reconciliation with us on reasonable terms, and to deliver us from the evils of a civil war.

## DECLARATION CONCERNING ETHAN ALLEN[1]

December 2, 1775 (?)

A DECLARATION (OR A LETTER TO HOWE) ON ALLEN'S CASE

When necessity compelled us to take up arms against Great Britain in defence of our just rights, we thought it a circumstance of comfort that our enemy was brave and civilized. It is the happiness of modern times that the evils of necessary war are softened by the refinement of manners and sentiment and that an enemy is an object of vengeance, in arms, and in the field only. It is with pain we hear that Mr. Allen and others taken with him while fighting bravely in their country's cause, are sent to Britain in irons, to be punished for pretended treason; treason too created by one of those very laws whose obligation we deny, and mean to contest by the sword. This question will not be decided by reeking vengeance on a few helpless captives but by achieving success in the fields of war, and gathering there those laurels which grow for the warrior brave. In this light we view the object between us, in this line we have hitherto conducted ourselves for its attainment. To those who bearing your arms have fallen into our hands we afforded every comfort for which captivity and misfortune call for. Enlargement and comfortable subsistence have been extended to both officers and men, and their restraint is a restraint of honor only. Should you think proper in these days to revive ancient barbarism and again disgrace our nature with the sacrifice the fortune of war has put it into our power subjects for multiplied retaliation. To them, to you, and to the world we declare they shall not be wretched unless their imprudence or your example shall oblige us to make them so; but we declare that their lives shall teach our enemies to respect the rights of nations. We have ordered Brigadier General Prescot to be bound in irons and to be confined in close jail, there to experience corresponding miseries to those which shall be inflicted on Mr. Allen. His life shall answer for that of Mr. Allen, and the lives of as many others of the brave men captivated with him. We deplore the event which shall oblige us to shed blood for blood, and shall resort to retaliation but as the means of stopping the progress of butchery. This it is a duty we owe to those

[1] This proposal, written on the arrival of the news of Allen's imprisonment, was not accepted by Congress.

engaged in the cause of their country, to assure them that if any unlucky circumstance baffling the efforts of their bravery shall put them in the power of their enemies, we will use the pledges in our hands to warrant their lives from sacrifice.

## A DECLARATION BY THE REPRESENTATIVES OF THE UNITED STATES OF AMERICA, IN GENERAL CONGRESS ASSEMBLED[1]

July 4, 1776

When, in the course of human events, it becomes necessary for one people to dissolve the political bands which have connected them with another, and to assume among the powers of the earth the separate and equal station to which the laws of nature and of nature's God entitle them, a decent respect to the opinions of mankind requires that they should declare the causes which impel them to the separation.

We hold these truths to be self-evident; that all men are created equal; that they are endowed by their creator
certain — with [*inherent and*] inalienable rights; that among these are life, liberty, and the pursuit of happiness; that to secure these rights, governments are instituted among men, deriving their just powers from the consent of the governed; that whenever any form of government becomes destructive of these ends, it is the right of the people to alter or to abolish it, and to institute new government, laying its foundation on such principles, and organizing its powers in such form, as to them shall seem most likely to effect their safety and happiness. Prudence, indeed, will dictate that governments long established should not be changed for light and transient causes; and accordingly all experience hath shown that mankind are more disposed to suffer while evils are sufferable, than to right themselves by abolishing the forms to which they are accustomed. But when a long train of abuses and usurpations [*begun at a distinguished*

[1] This was Jefferson's original title. Congress changed it, on July 19, 1776, to "The Unanimous Declaration of the thirteen united States of America."

Since this is Jefferson's most famous paper, the text is given here as he first wrote it and as it was finally corrected. The parts stricken out by Congress are shown in brackets and in italics, and insertions are given in the margin or in a parallel column.

A Declaration by the Representatives of the UNITED STATES OF AMERICA, in General Congress assembled.

When in the course of human events it becomes necessary for one ~~a~~ people to dissolve the political bands which have connected them with another, and to [~~advance from that subordination in which they have hitherto remained, & to~~] assume among the powers of the earth the separate and equal ~~equal & independant~~ station to which the laws of nature & of nature's god entitle them, a decent respect to the opinions of mankind requires that they should declare the causes which impel them to ~~the change~~ the separation.

We hold these truths to be self-evident ~~sacred & undeniable~~; that all men are created equal ~~& independant~~; that they are endowed by their creator with ~~equal~~ [~~from that equal creation they derive~~] ~~rights~~ certain [inherent &] inalienable rights, that among ~~which~~ these are ~~the preservation of~~ life, & liberty, & the pursuit of happiness; that to secure these rights ~~ends~~, governments are instituted among men, deriving their just powers from the consent of the governed; that whenever any form of government ~~shall~~ becomes destructive of these ends, it is the right of the people to alter or to abolish it, & to institute new government, laying it's foundation on such principles & organising it's powers in such form, as to them shall seem most likely to effect their safety & happiness. prudence indeed will dictate that governments long established should not be changed for light & transient causes: and accordingly all experience hath shewn that mankind are more disposed to suffer while evils are sufferable, than to right themselves by abolishing the forms to which they are accustomed. but when a long train of abuses & usurpations [begun at a distinguished period, &] pursuing invariably the same object, evinces a design to ~~subject~~ reduce them under absolute Despotism ~~to arbitrary power~~, it is their right, it is their duty, to throw off such government & to provide new guards for their future security. such has been the patient sufferance of these colonies; & such is now the necessity which constrains them to [expunge] alter their former systems of government. the history of ~~his~~ the present King of Great Britain ~~majesty~~ is a history of [unremitting] repeated injuries and usurpations, [among which appears no solitary fact ~~one of which ...~~ to contradict the uniform tenor of the rest, ~~all of which~~ but all have] having] in direct object the establishment of an absolute tyranny over these states. to prove this let facts be submitted to a candid world. [for the truth of which we pledge a faith yet unsullied by falsehood]

Dr. Franklin handwriting

Mr. Adams handwriting

THE DECLARATION OF INDEPENDENCE. JEFFERSON'S ROUGH DRAFT AS IT WAS REPORTED BY THE COMMITTEE TO CONGRESS.

*period and*] pursuing invariably the same object, evinces a design to reduce them under absolute despotism, it is their right, it is their duty to throw off such government, and to provide new guards for their future security. Such has been the patient sufferance of these Colonies; and such is now the necessity which constrains
alter them to [*expunge*] their former systems of government. The history of the present King of Great Britain is a his-
repeated tory of [*unremitting*] injuries and usurpations, [*among which appears no solitary fact to contradict the uniform*
all having *tenor of the rest, but all have*] in direct object the establishment of an absolute tyranny over these States. To prove this, let facts be submitted to a candid world [*for the truth of which we pledge a faith yet unsullied by falsehood*].

He has refused his assent to laws the most wholesome and necessary for the public good.

He has forbidden his governors to pass laws of immediate and pressing importance, unless suspended in their operation till his assent should be obtained; and, when so suspended, he has utterly neglected to attend to them.

He has refused to pass other laws for the accommodation of large districts of people, unless those people would relinquish the right of representation in the Legislature, a right inestimable to them, and formidable to tyrants only.

He has called together legislative bodies at places unusual, uncomfortable, and distant from the depository of their public records, for the sole purpose of fatiguing them into compliance with his measures.

He has dissolved representative houses repeatedly [*and continually*] for opposing with manly firmness his invasions on the rights of the people.

He has refused for a long time after such dissolutions to cause others to be elected, whereby the legislative powers, incapable of annihilation, have returned to the people at large for their exercise, the State remaining, in the meantime, exposed to all the dangers of invasion from without and convulsions within.

He has endeavored to prevent the population of these States; for that purpose obstructing the laws for naturalization of foreigners, refusing to pass others to encourage their migrations hither, and raising the conditions of new appropriations of lands.

He has [*suffered*] the administration of justice [*totally to cease in some of these States*] refusing his assent to laws for establishing judiciary powers.

obstructed
by

He has made [*our*] judges dependent on his will alone for the tenure of their offices, and the amount and payment of their salaries.

He has erected a multitude of new offices, [*by a self-assumed power*] and sent hither swarms of new officers to harass our people and eat out their substance.

He has kept among us in times of peace standing armies [*and ships of war*] without the consent of our Legislatures.

He has affected to render the military independent of, and superior to, the civil power.

He has combined with others to subject us to a jurisdiction foreign to our constitutions and unacknowledged by our laws, giving his assent to their acts of pretended legislation for quartering large bodies of armed troops among us; for protecting them by a mock trial from punishment for any murders which they should commit on the inhabitants of these States; for cutting off our trade with all parts of the world; for imposing taxes on us without our consent; for depriving us [ ] of the benefits of trial by jury; for transporting us beyond seas to be tried for pretended offences; for abolishing the free system of Engish laws in a neighboring province, establishing therein an arbitrary government, and enlarging its boundaries, so as to render it at once an example and fit instrument for introducing the same absolute rule into these [*States*]; for taking away our charters, abolishing our most valuable laws, and altering fundamentally the forms of our governments; for suspending our own Legislatures, and declaring themselves invested with power to legislate for us in all cases whatsoever.

in many cases

Colonies

He has abdicated government here [*withdrawing his governors, and declaring us out of his allegiance and protection*].

by declaring us out of his protection, and waging war against us.

He has plundered our seas, ravaged our coasts, burnt our towns, and destroyed the lives of our people.

He is at this time transporting large armies of foreign mercenaries to complete the works of death, desolation, and tyranny already begun with circumstances of cruelty and perfidy [ ] unworthy the head of a civilized nation.

scarcely paralleled in the most barbarous ages, and totally

He has constrained our fellow-citizens taken captive on the high seas to bear arms against their country, to become the executioners of their friends and brethren, or to fall themselves by their hands.

excited domestic insurrection among us, and has

He has [ ] endeavored to bring on the inhabitants of our frontiers the merciless Indian savages, whose known rule of warfare is an undistinguished destruction of all ages, sexes, and conditions [*of existence*].

[*He has incited treasonable insurrections of our fellow-citizens, with the allurements of forfeiture and confiscation of our property.*

*He has waged cruel war against human nature itself, violating its most sacred rights of life and liberty in the persons of a distant people who never offended him, captivating and carrying them into slavery in another hemisphere, or to incur miserable death in their transportation thither. This piratical warfare, the opprobrium of* INFIDEL *powers, is the warfare of the* CHRISTIAN *King of Great Britain. Determined to keep open a market where* MEN *should be bought and sold, he has prostituted his negative for suppressing every legislative attempt to prohibit or to restrain this execrable commerce. And that this assemblage of horrors might want no fact of distinguished die, he is now exciting those very people to rise in arms among us, and to purchase that liberty of which he has deprived them, by murdering the people on whom he also obtruded them: thus paying off former crimes committed against the* LIBERTIES *of one people with crimes which he urges them to commit against the* LIVES *of another.*]

In every stage of these oppressions we have petitioned for redress in the most humble terms: our repeated petitions have been answered only by repeated injuries.

free

A Prince whose character is thus marked by every act which may define a tyrant is unfit to be the ruler of a [ ] people [*who mean to be free. Future ages will scarcely believe that the hardiness of one man adventured, within the short compass of twelve years only, to lay a foundation so broad and so undisguised for tyranny over a people fostered and fixed in principles of freedom.*]

Nor have we been wanting in attentions to our British brethren. We have warned them from time to time of attempts by their legislature to extend [*a*] jurisdiction over [*these our States*]. We have reminded them of the circumstances of our emigration and settlement here, [*no one of which could warrant so strange a pretension: that these were effected at the expense of our own blood and treasure, unassisted by the wealth or the strength of Great Britain: that in constituting indeed our several forms of government, we had adopted one common king, thereby laying a foundation for perpetual league and amity with them: but that submission to their parliament was no part of our Constitution, nor ever in idea, if history may be credited: and,*] we [ ] appealed to their native justice and magnanimity [*as well as to*] the ties of our common kindred to disavow these usurpations which [*were likely to*] interrupt our connection and correspondence. They too have been deaf to the voice of justice and of consanguinity, [*and when occasions have been given them, by the regular course of their laws, of removing from their councils the disturbers of our harmony, they have, by their free election, re-established them in power. At this very time too, they are permitting their chief magistrate to send over not only soldiers of our common blood, but Scotch and foreign mercenaries to invade and destroy us. These facts have given the last stab to agonizing affection, and manly spirit bids us to renounce forever these unfeeling brethren. We must endeavor to forget our former love for them, and hold them as we hold the rest of mankind, enemies in war, in peace friends. We might have been a free and a great people together; but a communication of grandeur and of freedom, it seems, is below their dignity. Be it so, since they will have it. The road to happiness and to glory is open to us too. We will tread it apart from them, and*] acquiesce in the necessity which denounces our [*eternal*] separation [ ]!

an unwarrantable

us

have

and we have conjured them by

would inevitably

We must therefore

and hold them as we hold the rest of mankind, enemies in war, in peace friends.

We therefore the representatives of the United States of America in General Congress assembled, appealing to the supreme judge of the world for the rectitude of our intentions, do in the name, and by the authority of the good people of these Colonies, solemnly publish and declare, that these united Colonies are, and of right ought to be, free and independent States; that they are absolved from all allegiance to the British crown, and that all political connection between them and the state of Great Britain is, and ought to be, totally dissolved; and that as free and independent States, they have full power to levy war, conclude peace, contract alliances, establish commerce, and to do all other acts and things which independent States may of right do.

And for the support of this declaration, with a firm reliance on the protection of divine providence, we mutually pledge to each other our lives, our fortunes, and our sacred honor.

We therefore the representatives of the United States of America in General Congress assembled, do in the name, and by the authority of the good people of these [*States reject and renounce all allegiance and subjection to the kings of Great Britain and all others who may hereafter claim by, through, or under them; we utterly dissolve all political connection which may heretofore have subsisted between us and the people or parliament of Great Britain: and finally we do assert and declare these Colonies to be free and independent States,*] and that as free and independent States, they have full power to levy war, conclude peace, contract alliances, establish commerce, and to do all other acts and things which independent States may of right do.

And for the support of this declaration, we mutually pledge to each other our lives, our fortunes, and our sacred honor.

## EXTRACT FROM THE POCKET EXPENSE ACCOUNT BOOK[1]

June 2-July 4, 1776

| | | | |
|---|---|---|---|
| June | 2 | pd for a comb | 5/ |
| | | pd Graaf one week's lodging | 35/ |
| | | pd for tea & canister | 20/ |
| | | pd for [illegible] | |
| | | pd at Duff's for punch | 2/ |
| | 5 | pd at Greentree's dinner & club | 7/ |
| | 6 | pd for window shutter rings | 25/2 |
| | 7 | pd at Smith's dinner | 5/6 |
| | | pd for Shoes for Bob | 8/ |
| | 8 | pd forage for horses | $6^{d}$ |
| | 9 | pd for 7 wash bnls | 10/6 |
| | | pd for stockings for Bob | 7/ |

[1] MS. in the Massachusetts Historical Society. This extract covers the period of writing the Declaration of Independence; hence its intrinsic interest.

| | | | |
|---|---|---|---|
| June | 9 | pd Mrs. Graaf one week's lodging | 35/ |
| | 10 | pd dinner at Smith's | 6/ |
| | 11 | pd for window shutter rings | £1-18-2 |
| | 12 | rec[d] from Mr. Eppes by Myles Taylor | 16 Doll[rs] |
| | 13 | pd dinner at Smith's | 6/ |
| | 17 | pd dinner at Smith's | 7/6 |
| | 18 | pd for a nest of trunks | 7/6 |
| | | pd forage of horses | 6[d] |
| | | pd dinner at Smith's | 6/6 |
| | 19 | pd King for handling six Spring bulbs | 30/ |
| | | pd Greentree for wine | 6/ |
| | | pd Come [?] in full | 30/6 |
| | | pd Fox for 2 knives for myself | 18/9 |
| | | pd for 1 d[o] for R. Harvie | 12/6 |
| | 20 | pd dinner at Smith's | 7/ |
| | | pd Hugh Walker for waggonage of sundries | 27/6 |
| | | pd Walker for lining a map | 5 |
| | 22 | pd dinner at Smith's | 7/6 |
| | | pd Sparhawk for p[r] spurs | 25/ |
| | | pd feriage over Schuylkill | 10[d] |
| | 23 | pd Graaf 2 weeks lodging | £3-10 |
| | 24 | pd dinner at Smith's | 5/6 |
| | 25 | pd for 2 p[r] stockings for Bob | 15/ |
| | | pd dinner at Smith's | 5/ |
| | | pd for a straw hat | 10/ |
| | 27 | pd Byrne for weeks shaving & dressing | 30/ |
| | 28 | pd Mrs. Lovemore washing in full | 39/9 |
| | 30 | pd Sparhawk for a pencil | 1/6 |
| | | a map | 7/6 |
| | | pd dinner at Smith's | 8/6 |
| | 31 | pd expences riding | 2/4 |
| July | 1 | pd forage of horses | 6[d] |
| | 3 | pd Towne for Doctor Gilmer | 7/6 |
| | | pd for myself | 7/6 |
| | | pd Smith in full | 15/6 |
| | 4 | pd Sparhawk for a thermometer | £3-15 |
| | | pd for 7 p[r] women's gloves | 27/ |
| | | pd for charity | 1/6 |

## OBSERVATION ON THE WEATHER[1]

### July 1-4, 1776

| JULY | HOUR | | THERMOMETER |
|---|---|---|---|
| 1 | 9 | A.M. | 81½ |
| | 7 | P.M. | [illegible] |
| 2 | 6 | A.M. | 70 |
| | 9:40 | A.M. | 78 |
| | 9 | P.M. | [illegible] |
| 3 | 5:30 | A.M. | 74 |
| | 1:30 | P.M. | 76 |
| | 8:10 | | 74 |
| 4 | 6 | A.M. | 68 |
| | 9 | | 72¼ |
| | 1 | P.M. | 76 |
| | 9 | | 73½ |

## RESOLUTION TO ENCOURAGE DESERTIONS OF HESSIAN OFFICERS[2]

### August, 1776

The Congress proceeding to take into further consideration the expediency of inviting from the service of his Britannic majesty such foreigners as by the compulsive authority of their prince may have been engaged therein and sent hither for the purpose of waging war against these states, and expecting that the enlightened minds of the officers having command in those foreign corps will feel more sensibly the agency of the principles urged in our resolution of the 14th instant, principles which be derived from the unalterable laws of God and nature cannot be superseded by any human authority or engagement, and willing to tender to them also, as they had before done to the soldiery of their corps a participation of the blessings of peace, liberty, property and mild government, on their relinquishing the disgraceful office on which they have been sent hither: Resolved that they will give all such of the said foreign officers as shall leave the armies of his Britannic majesty in America and chuse to become citizens of these states, unappropriated lands in the following quantities and proportions to them and their heirs in absolute dominion: To a colonel 1,000 acres, to a Lt. Col. 800 acres, to a Major 600 acres, to a Captain 400 acres, to an Ensign 200 acres, to every non commissioned officer 100 acres and to every other officer

[1] MS. in the Massachusetts Historical Society.

[2] Drawn by Jefferson as member of a committee (together with Franklin and John Adams); it was adopted on August 27, 1776.

or person employed in the said foreign corps and whose office or employment is not here specifically named, lands in the like proportion to their rank or pay in the said corps: and moreover that where any officers shall bring with them a number of the said foreign soldiers, this Congress, besides the lands before promised to the said officers and soldiers will give to such officers further rewards proportionate to the numbers they shall bring over and suited to the nature of their wants. Provided that such foreign officers or soldiers shall come within over from the said service before these offers be recalled, or within after a reasonable time.

## PROCLAMATION CONCERNING FOREIGNERS

February 5, 1781

BY HIS EXCELLENCY THOMAS JEFFERSON, ESQR., GOVN. OF THE COMMONWEALTH OF VIRGINIA

*A Proclamation*

Whereas Congress considering that it had been the wise policy of these States to extend the protection of their Laws to all those who should settle among them of whatsoever nation or religion they might be, and to admit them to a participation of the Benefits of Civil and religious freedom, and that the Benevolence of this practice, as well as its salutary effects had rendered it worthy of being continued in future times: That his Britannic Majesty in order to destroy our Freedom and Happiness, had commenced against us, a cruel and unprovoked War, and unable to engage Britons sufficient to execute his sanguinary measures, had applied for aid to Foreign Princes, who were in the habit of selling the blood of their people for money, and from them had procured and transported hither, considerable number of Foreigners, if apprised of the practice of these States would chuse to accept of Lands, Liberty and Safety and a Communion of good Laws and mild Government, in a Country where many of their Friends and relations were already happily settled, rather than continue exposed to the toils and Dangers of a long and bloody War, waged against a people guilty of no other Crime, than that of refusing to exchange freedom for Slavery: And that they would do this the more especially, when they should reflect they had violated every Christian and moral precept by invading and attempting to destroy those who had never injured them or their Country, their only reward, if they escaped Death and Captivity, would be, a return to the Despotism of their Prince, to be by him again sold to do the drudgery of some other Enemy to the rights of Mankind: and that our enemies had thought fit, not only to invite our Troops to desert our service, but to compel our citizens falling into their hands to serve against their Country, Did resolve, that these States would receive all such foreigners who should leave the armies of his Britannic Majesty, in America and should chuse to become members of any of these States, and that they should be protected in the free Exercise of their respective religions, and be invested with the rights, privileges, and immunities of natives as Established by the Laws of these States, and moreover that they would provide for every such Person 50 Acres of un-appropriated Lands in some of these States to be held by him and his Heirs in Absolute property.

I therefore have thought fit, by and with the advice of the Council of State, to issue this my Proclamation, hereby notifying more generally the said Engagement of Congress, and further promising to all such Foreigners, who shall leave the armies of his Britannic Majesty while in this State, and repair forthwith to me at this place, that they shall receive from this Commonwealth a further donation of two Cows and an exemption during the present War, and their continuance in this State, from all taxes, for the support thereof, and from all Militia and Military Service. And moreover that they shall receive a full compensation for any arms or accoutrements which they shall bring with them, and deliver to the Commanding officer at any of the Posts holden by our Forces, taking his receipt for the same.

Given under my hand and the Seal of the Commonwealth at Richmond, this Second day of February in the year of our Lord 1781 and of the Commonwealth the fifth.

# *Chapter II*

# THE AMERICAN REVOLUTION: II, HISTORY

## ANSWERS TO QUESTIONS PROPOUNDED BY M. DE MEUSNIER[1]

January 24, 1786

1. On the original establishment of the several States, the civil code of England, from whence they had emigrated, was adopted. This of course could extend only to general laws, and not to those which were particular to certain places in England only. The circumstances of the new States obliged them to add some new laws, which their special situation required, and even to change some of the general laws of England in cases which did not suit their circumstances or ways of thinking. The law of descents, for instance, was changed in several States. On the late revolution, the changes which under their new form of government rendered necessary were easily made. It was only necessary to say that the powers of legislation, the judiciary, and the executive powers, heretofore exercised by persons of such and such description, shall henceforth be exercised by persons to be appointed in such and such manners. This was what their constitution did. Virginia thought it might be necessary to examine the whole code of law, to reform such parts of it as had been calculated to produce a devotion to monarchy, and to

[1] Meusnier, author of the economic, political, and diplomatic section of the *Encyclopédie Politique,* asked Jefferson to supply him with informatoin on the United States. Meusnier based his article on Jefferson's replies. On August 27, 1786, Jefferson wrote to John Adams: "I enclose you the article 'Etats Unis' of one of the volumes of the Encyclopedie, lately published. The author, M. de Meusnier, . . . asked of me information on the subject of our states, and left with me a number of queries to answer. Knowing the importance of setting to rights a book so universally diffused and which will go down to late ages, I answered his queries as fully as I was able, went into a great many calculations for him, and offered to give him further explanations when necessary. He then put his work into my hands. I read it, and was led by that into a still greater number of details by way of correcting what he had written, which was indeed a mass of errors and misconceptions from beginning to end. I returned him his work and dry details, but he did not communicate it to me after he had corrected it. It has therefore come out with many errors which I would have advised him to correct."

reduce into smaller volume such useful parts as had become too diffuse. A committee was appointed to execute this work; they did it; and the Assembly began in October, 1785, the examination of it, in order to change such parts of the report as might not meet their approbation, and to establish what they should approve. We may expect to hear the result of their deliberations about the last of February next.

I have heard that Connecticut undertook a like work; but I am not sure of this, nor do I know whether any other of the States have or have not done the same.

2. The constitution of New Hampshire, established in 1776, having been expressly made to continue only during the contest with Great Britain, they proceeded, after the close of that, to form and establish a permanent one, which they did. The Convention of Virginia which organized their new government, had been chosen before a separation from Great Britain had been thought of in their State. They had, therefore, none but the ordinary powers of legislation. This leaves their act for organizing the government subject to be altered by every legislative assembly; and though no general change in it has been made, yet its effect has been controlled in several special cases. It is therefore thought that that State will appoint a convention for the special purpose of forming a stable constitution. I think no change has been made in any other of the States.

3. The following is a rough estimate of the particular debts of some of the States as they existed in the year 1784:

| | | | |
|---|---|---|---|
| New Hampshire | $ 500,000 | United States' principal of foreign debt nearly | $ 7,000,000 |
| Rhode Island | 5,000,000 | | |
| Massachusetts | 430,000 | The principal of the domestic debt is somewhere between 27½ millions and 35½ millions, call it therefore | 31,300,000 |
| Connecticut | 3,439,086⅔ | | |
| Virginia | 2,300,000 | | |
| | | | $38,300,000 |

The other States not named here, are probably indebted in the same proportion to their abilities. If so, and we estimate their abilities by the rule of quotaing them, those eight States will owe about fourteen millions, and consequently the particular debts of all the States will amount to twenty-five or twenty-six millions of dollars.

5. A particular answer to this question would lead to very minute details: one general idea, however, may be applied to all the States. Each having their separate debt, and a determinate proportion of the Federal debt, they endeavor to lay taxes sufficient to pay the interest of both of these, and to support their own and the Federal Government. These taxes are gen-

erally about one or one and a-half per cent on the value of property; and from two and a-half to five per cent on foreign merchandise imported. But the payment of this interest regularly, is not accomplished in many of the States. The people are as yet not recovered from the depredations of the war. When that ended their houses were in ruin, their farms waste, themselves distressed for clothing and necessaries for their households. They cannot as yet, therefore, bear heavy taxes. For the payment of the principal no final measures are yet taken. Some States will have land for sale, the produce of which may pay the principal debt. Some will endeavor to have an exceeding of their taxes to be applied as a sinking fund; and all of them look forward to the increase of population, and of course an increase of productions in their present taxes, to enable them to be sinking their debt. This is a general view. Some of the States have not yet made even just efforts for satisfying either the principal or interest of their public debt.

6. By the close of the year 1785 there had probably passed over about 50,000 emigrants. Most of these were Irish. The greatest number of the residue were Germans. Philadelphia receives most of them, and next to that, Baltimore and New York.

7. Nothing is decided as to Vermont. The four northernmost States wish it to be received into the Union. The Middle and Southern States are rather opposed to it. But the great difficulty arises with New York, which claims that territory. In the beginning every individual revolted at the idea of giving them up. Congress therefore only interfered from time to time, to prevent the two parties from coming to an open rupture. In the meanwhile the minds of the New Yorkers have been familiarizing to the idea of a separation, and I think it will not be long before they will consent to it. In that case, the Southern and Middle States will doubtless acquiesce, and Vermont will be received into the Union.

8. LeMaine, a part of the government of Massachusetts, but detached from it (the State of New Hampshire lying between), begins to desire to be separated. They are very weak in numbers as yet: but whenever they shall attain a certain degree of population, there are circumstances which render it highly probable they will be allowed to become a separate member of the Union.

9. It is believed that the State of Virginia has by this time made a second cession of lands to Congress, comprehending all those between the meridian of the mouth of the Great Kanhaway, the Ohio, Mississippi, and Carolina boundary. Within this lies Kentucky. I believe that their numbers are sufficient already to entitle them to come into Congress. And their reception there will only increase the delay necessary for taking the consent of the several Assemblies. There is no other new State as yet approaching the time of its reception.

10. The number of Royalists which left New York, South Carolina and Georgia, when they were evacuated by the British army was considerable, but I am absolutely unable to conjecture their numbers. From all the other States, I suppose perhaps two thousand may have gone.

11. The Confederation is a wonderfully perfect instrument, considering the circumstances under which it was formed. There are, however, some alterations which experience proves to be wanting. These are principally three. 1. To establish a general rule for the admission of new States into the Union. By the confederation no new States, except Canada, can be permitted to have a vote in Congress without first obtaining the consent of all the thirteen legislatures. It becomes necessary to agree what districts may be established into separate States, and at what period of their population they may come into Congress. The act of Congress of April 23, 1784, has pointed out what ought to be agreed on, to say also what number of votes must concur when the number of voters shall be thus enlarged. 2. The Confederation, in its eighth article, decides that the quota of money to be contributed by the several States shall be proportioned to the value of the landed property in the State. Experience has shown it impracticable to come at this value. Congress have therefore recommended to the States to agree that their quotas shall be in proportion to the number of their inhabitants, counting five slaves, however, but as equal to three free inhabitants. I believe all the States have agreed to this alteration except Rhode Island. 3. The Confederation forbids the States individually to enter into treaties of commerce, or of any other nature, with foreign nations: and it authorizes Congress to establish such treaties, with two reservations however, *viz.,* that they shall agree to no treaty which would, 1. restrain the legislatures from imposing such duties on foreigners as natives are subject to; or 2., from prohibiting the exportation or importation of any species of commodities. Congress may therefore be said to have a power to regulate commerce so far as it can be effected by conventions with other nations, and by conventions which do not infringe the two fundamental reservations before mentioned. But this is too imperfect. Because, till a convention be made with any particular nation, the commerce of any one of our States with that nation may be regulated by the State itself, and even when a convention is made, the regulation of the commerce is taken out of the hands of the several States only so far as it is covered or provided for by that convention or treaty. But treaties are made in such general terms, that the greater part of the regulations would still result to the legislatures. Let us illustrate these observations by observing how far the commerce of France and England can be affected by the State Legislatures. As to England, any one of the legislatures may impose on her goods double the duties which are paid other nations; may prohibit their goods altogether; may refuse them the usual facilities for recovering their

debts or withdrawing their property; may refuse to receive their Consuls or to give those Consuls any jurisdiction. But with France, whose commerce is protected by a treaty, no State can give any molestation to that commerce which is defended by the treaty. Thus, though a State may exclude the importation of all wines (because one of the reservations aforesaid is that they may prohibit the importation of any species of commodities), yet they cannot prohibit the importation of French wines, particularly while they allow wines to be brought in from other countries. They cannot impose heavier duties on French commodities than on those of other nations. They cannot throw peculiar obstacles in the way of their recovery of debts due to them, &c., &c., because those things are provided for by treaty. Treaties, however, are very imperfect machines for regulating commerce in the detail. The principal objects in the regulation of our commerce would be: 1. to lay such duties, restrictions, or prohibitions on the goods of any particular nation, as might oblige that nation to concur in just and equal arrangements of commerce. 2. To lay such unifom duties on the articles of commerce throughout all the States, as may avail them of that fund for assisting to bear the burthen of public expenses. Now, this cannot be done by the States separately, because they will not separately pursue the same plan. New Hampshire cannot lay a given duty on a particular article unless Massachusetts will do the same, because it will turn the importation of that article from her ports into those of Massachusetts, from whence they will be smuggled into New Hampshire by land. But though Massachusetts were willing to concur with New Hampshire in laying the same duty, yet she cannot do it for the same reason, unless Rhode Island will also, nor can Rhode Island without Connecticut, nor Connecticut without New York, nor New York without New Jersey, and so on quite to Georgia. It is visible, therefore, that the commerce of the States cannot be regulated to the best advantage but by a single body, and no body so proper as Congress. Many of the States have agreed to add an article to the Confederation for allowing to Congress the regulation of their commerce, only providing that the revenues to be raised on it shall belong to the States in which they are levied. Yet it is believed that Rhode Island will prevent this also. An everlasting recurrence to this same obstacle will occasion a question to be asked. How happens it that Rhode Island is opposed to every useful proposition? Her geography accounts for it, with the aid of one or two observations. The cultivators of the earth are the most virtuous citizens, and possess most of the amor patriæ. Merchants are the least virtuous, and possess the least of the amor patriæ. The latter reside principally in the seaport towns, the former in the interior country. Now, it happened that of the territory constituting Rhode Island and Connecticut, the part containing the seaports was erected into a State by itself, called Rhode Island, and that containing the interior country was erected into another State called Connecticut. For though it has a little sea-coast, there are no good ports in it. Hence it happens that there is scarcely one merchant in the whole State of Connecticut, while there is not a single man in Rhode Island who is not a merchant of some sort. Their whole territory is but a thousand square miles, and what of that is in use is laid out in grass farms almost entirely. Hence they have scarcely any body employed in agriculture. All exercise some species of commerce. This circumstance has decided the characters of these two States. The remedies to this evil are hazardous. One would be to consolidate the two States into one. Another would be to banish Rhode Island from the Union. A third, to compel her submission to the will of the other twelve. A fourth, for the other twelve to govern themselves according to the new propositions, and to let Rhode Island go on by herself according to the ancient articles. But the dangers and difficulties attending all these remedies are obvious.

These are the only alterations proposed to the Confederation, and the last of them is the only additional power which Congress is thought to need.

12. Congress have not yet ultimately decided at what rates they will redeem the paper money in the hands of the holders. But a resolution of 1784 has established the principle, so that there can be little doubt but that the holders of paper money will receive as much real money as the paper was actually worth at the time they received it, and an interest of six per cent from the time they received it. Its worth will be found in the depreciation table of the State wherein it was received; these depreciation tables having been formed according to the market price of the paper money at different epochs.

13. Those who talk of the bankruptcy of the United States, are of two descriptions: 1. Strangers who do not understand the nature and history of our paper money. 2. Holders of that paper money who do not wish that the world should understand it. Thus, when in March, 1780, the paper money being so far depreciated that forty dollars of it would purchase only one silver dollar, Congress endeavored to correct the progress of that depreciation by declaring they would emit no more, and would redeem what was in circulation at the rate of one dollar of silver for forty of paper; this was called by the brokers in paper money, a bankruptcy. Yet these very people who had only given one dollar's worth of provisions, of manufactures, or perhaps of silver, for their forty dollars, were displeased that they could not in a moment multiply their silver into forty. If it were decided that the United States should pay a silver dollar for every paper dollar they emitted, I am of opinion (conjecturing from loose data of my memory only as to the amount and true worth of the sums emitted by Congress and by the several States) that a debt, which in its just amount is not more, perhaps, than six millions of dollars, would amount up to four hundred millions, and instead

of assessing every inhabitant with a debt of about two dollars, would fix on him thirty guineas, which is considerably more than the national debt of England affixes on each of its inhabitants, and would make a bankruptcy where there is none. The real just debts of the United States, which were stated under the third query, will be easily paid by the sale of their lands, which were ceded on the fundamental condition of being applied as a sinking fund for this purpose.

14. The whole army of the United States was disbanded at the close of the war. A few guards only were engaged for their magazines. Lately they have enlisted some two or three regiments to garrison the posts along the Northern boundary of the United States.

16. The United States do not own, at present, a single vessel of war; nor has Congress entered into any resolution on that subject.

17. I conjecture there are six hundred and fifty thousand Negroes in the five southernmost States, and not fifty thousand in the rest. In most of these latter, effectual measures have been taken for their future emancipation. In the former, nothing is done towards that. The disposition to emancipate them is strongest in Virginia. Those who desire it, form, as yet, the minority of the whole State, but it bears a respectable portion to the whole in numbers and weight of character, and it is continually recruiting by the addition of nearly the whole of the young men as fast as they come into public life. I flatter myself it will take place there at some period of time not very distant. In Maryland and North Carolina a very few are disposed to emancipate. In South Carolina and Georgia, not the smallest symptom of it, but, on the contrary, these two States, and North Carolina, continue importations of Negroes. These have been long prohibited in all the other States.

18. In Virginia, where a great proportion of the legislature consider the constitution but as other acts of legislation, laws have been frequently passed which controlled its effects. I have not heard that in the other States they have ever infringed their constitution, and I suppose they have not done it, as the Judges would consider any law as void which was contrary to the constitution. Pennsylvania is divided into two parties very nearly equal, the one desiring to change the constitution, the other opposing a change. In Virginia there is a part of the State which considers the act for organizing their government as a constitution, and are content to let it remain; there is another part which considers it only as an ordinary act of the legislature, who, therefore, wish to form a real constitution, correcting some defects which have been observed in the act now in force. Most of the young people as they come into office arrange themselves on this side, and I think they will prevail ere long. But there are no heats on this account. I do not know that any of the other States propose to change their constitution.

19. I have heard of no malversations in office which have been of any consequence, unless we consider as such some factious transactions in the Pennsylvania Assembly; or some acts of the Virginia Assembly which have been contrary to their constitution. The causes of these were explained in the preceding article.

20. Broils among the States may happen in the following ways: 1. A State may be embroiled with the other twelve by not complying with the lawful requisitions of Congress. 2. Two States may differ about their boundaries. But the method of settling these is fixed by the Confederation, and most of the States which have any differences of this kind, are submitting them to this mode of determination, and there is no danger of opposition to the decree by any State. The individuals interested may complain, but this can produce no difficulty. 3. Other contestations may arise between two States, such as pecuniary demands, affrays among their citizens, and whatever else may arise between any two nations, with respect to these, there are two opinions. One that they are to be decided according to the ninth article of the Confederation, which says that Congress shall be the last resort in all differences between two or more States, concerning boundary jurisdiction, *or any other cause whatever;* and prescribes the mode of decision, and the weight of reason is undoubtedly in favor of this opinion, yet there are some who question it.

It has been often said that the decisions of Congress are impotent because the Confederation provides no compulsory power. But when two or more nations enter into compact, it is not usual for them to say what shall be done to the party who infringes it. Decency forbids this, and it is as unnecessary as indecent, because the right of compulsion naturally results to the party injured by the breach. When any one State in the American Union refuses obedience to the Confederation by which they have bound themselves, the rest have a natural right to compel them to obedience. Congress would probably exercise long patience before they would recur to force; but if the case ultimately required it, they would use that recurrence. Should this case ever arise, they will probably coerce by a naval force, as being more easy, less dangerous to liberty, and less likely to produce much bloodshed.

It has been said, too, that our governments, both federal and particular, want energy; that it is difficult to restrain both individuals and States from committing wrong. This is true, and it is an inconvenience. On the other hand, that energy which absolute governments derive from an armed force, which is the effect of the bayonet constantly held at the breast of every citizen, and which resembles very much the stillness of the grave, must be admitted also to have its inconveniences. We weigh the two together, and like best to submit to the former. Compare the number of wrongs committed with impunity by citizens among us with those committed by the sovereign in other countries, and the last will be found most numerous, most oppressive on the mind, and most degrading of the dignity of man.

22. The States differed very much in their proceedings as to British property, and I am unable to give the details. In Virginia, the sums sequestered in the treasury remain precisely as they did at the conclusion of the peace. The British having refused to make satisfaction for the slaves they carried away, contrary to the treaty of peace, and to deliver up the ports within our limits, the execution of that treaty is in some degree suspended. Individuals, however, are paying off their debts to British subjects, and the laws even permit the latter to recover them judicially. But as the amount of these debts are twenty or thirty times the amount of all the money in circulation in that State, the same laws permit the debtor to pay his debts in seven equal and annual payments.

## ADDITIONAL QUESTIONS OF M. DE MEUSNIER, AND ANSWERS

1. What has led Congress to determine, that the concurrence of seven votes is requisite in questions which, by the Confederation, are submitted to the decision of a majority of the United States in Congress assembled?

The ninth article of Confederation, section six, evidently establishes three orders of questions in Congress. 1. The greater ones, which relate to making peace or war, alliances, coinage, requisitions for money, raising military force, or appointing its commander-in-chief. 2. The lesser ones, which comprehend all other matters submitted by the Confederation to the federal head. 3. The single question of adjourning from day to day. This gradation of questions is distinctly characterized by the article.

In proportion to the magnitude of these questions, a greater concurrence of the voices composing the Union was thought necessary. Three degrees of concurrence, well distinguished by substantial circumstances, offered themselves to notice. 1. A concurrence of a *majority of the people* of the Union. It was thought that this would be insured, by requiring the voices of nine States; because, according to the loose estimates which had been made of the inhabitants, and the proportion of them which were free, it was believed that even the nine smallest would include a majority of the free citizens of the Union. The voices, therefore, of nine States were required in the greater questions. 2. A concurrence of the *majority of the States.* Seven constitute that majority. This number, therefore, was required in the lesser questions. 3. A concurrence of the *majority of Congress,* that is to say, of the States actually present in it. As there is no Congress, when there are not seven States present, this concurrence could never be of less than four States. But these might happen to be the four smallest, which would not include one-ninth part of the free citizens of the Union. This kind of majority, therefore, was entrusted with nothing but the power of adjourning themselves from day to day.

Here then are three kind of majorities. 1. Of the people. 2. Of the States. 3. Of the Congress: each of which is entrusted to a certain length.

Though the paragraph in question be clumsily expressed, yet it strictly announces its own intentions. It defines with precision, the *greater* questions, for which nine votes shall be requisite. In the *lesser* questions, it then requires a *majority of the United States in Congress assembled:* a term which will apply either to the number seven, as being a *majority of the States,* or to the number four as being a *majority of Congress.* Which of the two kinds of majority, was meant? Clearly, that which would leave a still smaller kind, for the decision of the question of adjournment. The contrary construction would be absurd.

This paragraph, therefore, should be understood, as if it had been expressed in the following terms: "The United States, in Congress assembled, shall never engage in war, &c., but with the consent of nine States: nor determine any other question, but with the consent of a majority of the whole States, except the question of adjournment from day to day, which may be determined by a majority of the States actually present in Congress."

2. How far is it permitted, to bring on the reconsideration of a question which Congress has once determined?

The first Congress which met, being composed mostly of persons who had been members of the legislatures of their respective States, it was natural for them to adopt those rules in their proceedings, to which they had been accustomed in their legislative houses; and the more so, as these happened to be nearly the same, as having been copied from the same original, those of the British parliament. One of those rules of proceeding was, that "a question once determined, cannot be proposed, a second time, in the same session." Congress, during their first session, in the autumn of 1774, observed this rule strictly. But before their meeting in the spring of the following year, the war had broken out. They found themselves at the head of that war, in an executive as well as legislative capacity. They found that a rule, wise and necessary for a legislative body, did not suit an executive one, which, being governed by events, must change their purposes as those change. Besides, their session was then to become of equal duration with the war; and a rule, which should render their legislation immutable, during all that period, could not be submitted to. They, therefore, renounced it in practice, and have ever since continued to reconsider their questions freely. The only restraint as yet provided against the abuse of this permission to reconsider, is, that when a question has been decided, it cannot be proposed for reconsideration, but by someone who voted in favor of the former decision, and declares that he has since changed his opinion. I do not recollect accurately enough, whether it be necessary that his vote should have decided that of his State, and the vote of his State have decided that of Congress.

Perhaps it might have been better, when they were forming the federal constitution, to have assimilated it, as much as possible, to the particular constitutions of the States. All of these have distributed the legislative, executive and judiciary powers, into different departments. In the federal constitution, the judiciary powers are separated from the others; but the legislative and executive are both exercised by Congress. A means of amending this defect has been thought of. Congress having a power to establish what committees of their own body they please, and to arrange among them the distribution of their business, they might, on the first day of their annual meeting, appoint an executive committee, consisting of a member from each State, and refer to them all executive business which should occur during their session; confining themselves to what is of a legislative nature, that is to say, to the heads described in the ninth article, as of the competence of nine States only, and to such other questions as should lead to the establishment of general rules. The journal of this committee, of the preceding day, might be read the next morning in Congress, and considered as approved, unless a vote was demanded on a particular article, and that article changed. The sessions of Congress would then be short, and when they separated, the Confederation authorizes the appointment of a committee of the States, which would naturally succeed to the business of the executive committee. The legislative business would be better done, because the attention of the members would not be interrupted by the details of execution; and the executive business would be better done, because, business of this nature is better adapted to small, than great bodies. A monarchical head should confide the execution of its will to departments, consisting, each, of a plurality of hands, who would warp that will, as much as possible, towards wisdom and moderation, the two qualities it generally wants. But, a republican head, founding its decrees, originally, in these two qualities, should commit them to a single hand for execution, giving them, thereby, a promptitude which republican proceedings generally want. Congress could not, indeed, confide their executive business to a smaller number than a committee consisting of a member from each State. This is necessary to insure the confidence of the Union. But it would be gaining a great deal, to reduce the executive head to thirteen, and to relieve themselves of those details. This, however, has as yet been the subject of private conversations only.

3. A succinct account of paper money in America?

Previous to the Revolution, most of the States were in the habit, whenever they had occasion for more money than could be raised immediately by taxes, to issue paper notes or bills, in the name of the State, wherein they promised to pay to the bearer the sum named in the note or bill. In some of the States no time of payment was fixed, nor tax laid to enable payment. In these, the bills depreciated. But others of the States named in the bill the day when it should be paid, laid taxes to bring in money enough for that purpose, and paid the bills punctually, on or before the day named. In these States, paper money was in as high estimation as gold and silver. On the commencement of the late Revolution, Congress had no money. The external commerce of the States being suppressed, the farmer could not sell his produce, and, of course, could not pay a tax. Congress had no resource then but in paper money. Not being able to lay a tax for its redemption, they could only promise that taxes should be laid for that purpose, so as to redeem the bills by a certain day. They did not foresee the long continuance of the war, the almost total suppression of their exports, and other events, which rendered the performance of their engagement impossible. The paper money continued for a twelvemonth equal to gold and silver. But the quantities which they were obliged to emit for the purpose of the war, exceeded what had been the usual quantity of the circulating medium. It began, therefore, to become cheaper, or, as we expressed it, it depreciated, as gold and silver would have done, had they been thrown into circulation in equal quantities. But not having, like them, an intrinsic value, its depreciation was more rapid and greater than could ever have happened with them. In two years, it had fallen to two dollars of paper money for one of silver; in three years, to four for one; in nine months more, it fell to ten for one; and in the six months following, that is to say, by September, 1779, it had fallen to twenty for one.

Congress, alarmed at the consequences which were to be apprehended, should they lose this resource altogether, thought it necessary to make a vigorous effort to stop its further depreciation. They therefore determined, in the first place, that their emissions should not exceed two hundred millions of dollars, to which term they were then nearly arrived; and though they knew that twenty dollars of what they were then issuing, would buy no more for their army than one silver dollar would buy, yet they thought it would be worth while to submit to the sacrifice of nineteen out of twenty dollars, if they could thereby stop further depreciation. They, therefore, published an address to their constituents, in which they renewed their original declarations, that this paper money should be redeemed at dollar for dollar. They proved the ability of the States to do this, and that their liberty would be cheaply bought at that price. The declaration was ineffectual. No man received the money at a better rate; on the contrary, in six months more, that is, by March, 1780, it had fallen to forty for one. Congress then tried an experiment of a different kind. Considering their former offers to redeem this money at par, as relinquished by the general refusal to take it, but in progressive depreciation, they required the whole to be brought in, declared it should be redeemed at its present value, of forty for one, and that they would give to the holders new bills, reduced in their denomination to the sum of gold or silver, which was actually to be paid for them. This would reduce the nominal sum of the mass in circulation to the present worth of that mass, which was five millions; a sum not too great for the circulation of the States, and which, they therefore hoped, would not depreciate further, as they continued firm in their purpose of emitting no more. This effort was as unavailing as the former. Very little of the money was brought in. It continued to circulate and to depreciate, till the end of 1780, when it had fallen to seventy-five for one, and the money circulated from the French army, being, by that time, sensible in all the States north of the Potomac, the paper ceased its circulation altogether in those States. In Virginia and North Carolina it continued a year longer, within which time it fell to one thousand for one, and then expired, as it had done in the other States, without a single groan. Not a murmur was heard on this occasion, among the people. On the contrary, universal congratulations took place on their seeing this gigantic mass, whose dissolution had threatened convulsions which should shake their infant confederacy to its centre, quietly interred in its grave. Foreigners, indeed, who do not, like the natives, feel indulgence for its memory, as of a being which has vindicated their liberties, and fallen in the moment of victory, have been loud, and still are loud in their complaints. A few of them have reason; but the most noisy are not the best of them. They are persons who have become bankrupt by unskilful attempts at commerce with America. That they may have some pretext to offer to their creditors, they have bought up great masses of this dead money in America, where it is to be had at five thousand for one, and they show the certificates of their paper possessions, as if they had all died in their hands, and had been the cause of their bankruptcy. Justice will be done to all, by paying to all persons what this money actually cost them, with an interest of six per cent from the time they received it. If difficulties present themselves in the ascertaining the epoch of the receipt, it has been thought better that the State should lose, by admitting easy proofs, than that individuals, and especially foreigners, should, by being held to such as would be difficult, perhaps impossible.

4. Virginia certainly owed two millions sterling to Great Britain at the conclusion of the war. Some have conjectured the debt as high as three millions. I think that State owed near as much as all the rest put together. This is to be ascribed to peculiarities in the tobacco trade. The advantages made by the British merchants, on the tobaccos consigned to them, were so enormous, that they spared no means of increasing those consignments. A powerful engine for this purpose, was the giving good prices and credit to the

planter, till they got him more immersed in debt than he could pay, without selling his lands or slaves. They then reduced the prices given for his tobacco, so that let his shipments be ever so great, and his demand of necessaries ever so economical, they never permitted him to clear off his debt. These debts had become hereditary from father to son, for many generations, so that the planters were a species of property, annexed to certain mercantile houses in London.

5. The members of Congress are differently paid by different States. Some are on fixed allowances, from four to eight dollars a day. Others have their expenses paid, and a surplus for their time. This surplus is of two, three, or four dollars a day.

6. I do not believe there has ever been a moment, when a single Whig, in any one State, would not have shuddered at the very idea of a separation of their State from the confederacy. The Tories would, at all times, have been glad to see the confederacy dissolved, even by particles at a time, in hopes of their attaching themselves again to Great Britain.

7. The 11th article of Confederation admits Canada to accede to the Confederation at its own will, but adds, "no other colony shall be admitted to the same, unless such admission be agreed to by nine States." When the plan of April, 1784, for establishing new States was on the carpet, the committee who framed the report of that plan, had inserted this clause, "provided nine States agree to such admission, according to the reservation of the 11th of the articles of Confederation." It was objected, 1. That the words of the confederation, "no other colony," could refer only to the residuary possessions of Great Britain, as the two Floridas, Nova Scotia, &c., not being already parts of the Union; that the law for "admitting" a new member into the Union, could not be applied to a territory which was already in the Union, as making part of a State which was a member of it. 2. That it would be improper to allow "nine" States to receive a new member, because the same reasons which rendered that number proper now, would render a greater one proper, when the number composing the Union should be increased. They therefore struck out this paragraph and inserted a proviso, that "the consent of so many States, in Congress, shall be first obtained, as may, at the time, be competent"; thus leaving the question, whether the 11th article applies to the admission of new States, to be decided when that admission shall be asked. See the Journal of Congress of April 20, 1784. Another doubt was started in this debate, *viz.:* whether the agreement of the nine States, required by the Confederation, was to be made by their legislatures, or by their delegates in Congress? The expression adopted, *viz.:* "so many States, in Congress, is first obtained," show what was their sense of this matter. If it be agreed that the 11th article of the Confederation is not to be applied to the admission of these new States, then it is contended that their admis-

sion comes within the 13th article, which forbids "any alteration, unless agreed to in a Congress of the United States, and afterwards confirmed by the legislatures of every State." The independence of the new States of Kentucky and Franklin, will soon bring on the ultimate decision of all these questions.

8. Particular instances whereby the General Assembly of Virginia have shown that they considered the ordinance called their constitution, as every other ordinance, or act of the legislature, subject to be altered by the legislature for the time being.

1. The convention which formed that constitution, declared themselves to be the House of Delegates, during the term for which they were originally elected, and in the autumn of the year met the Senate, elected under the new constitution, and did legislative business with them. At this time, there were malefactors in the public jail, and there was as yet no court established for their trial. They passed a law, appointing certain members by name, who were then members of the Executive Council, to be a court for the trial of these malefactors, though the constitution had said, in express words, that no person should exercise the powers of more than one of the three departments, legislative, executive and judiciary at the same time. This proves that the very men who had made that constitution understood that it would be alterable by the General Assembly. This court was only for that occasion. When the next General Assembly met, after the election of the ensuing year, there was a new set of malefactors in the jail, and no court to try them. This Assembly passed a similar law to the former, appointing certain members of the Executive Council to be an occasional court for this particular case. Not having the journals of Assembly by me, I am unable to say whether this measure was repealed afterwards. However, they are instances of *executive* and *judiciary* powers exercised by the same persons, under the authority of a law, made in contradiction to the constitution.

2. There was a process depending in the ordinary courts of justice, between two individuals of the names of Robinson and Fauntleroy, who were relations, of different descriptions, to one Robinson, a British subject, lately dead. Each party claimed a right to inherit the lands of the decedent according to the laws. Their right should by the constitution have been decided by the judiciary courts; and it was actually depending before them. One of the parties petitioned the Assembly (I think it was in the year 1782), who passed a law deciding the right in his favor. In the following year, a Frenchman, master of a vessel, entered into port without complying with the laws established in such cases, whereby he incurred the forfeitures of the law to any person who would sue for them. An individual instituted a legal process to recover these forfeitures according to the law of the land. The Frenchman petitioned the Assembly, who passed a law deciding the question of for-

feiture in his favor. These acts are occasional repeals of that part of the constitution which forbids the same persons to exercise *legislative* and *judiciary* powers at the same time.

The Assembly is in the habitual exercise, during their sessions, of directing the Executive what to do. There are few pages of their journals which do not show proofs of this, and consequently instances of the *legislative* and *executive* powers exercised by the same persons at the same time. These things prove that it has been the uninterrupted opinion of every Assembly, from that which passed the ordinance called the constitution down to the present day, that their acts may control that ordinance, and, of course, that the State of Virginia has no fixed constitution at all.

[THE following observations were made by Jefferson on an article entitled "États Unis," prepared for the Encyclopédie Méthodique, June 22, 1786.]

Page 8. The malefactors sent to America were not sufficient in number to merit enumeration, as one class out of three which peopled America. It was at a late period of their history that this practice began. I have no book by me which enables me to point out the date of its commencement. But I do not think the whole number sent would amount to two thousand, and being principally men, eaten up with disease, they married seldom and propagated little. I do not suppose that themselves and their descendants are at present four thousand, which is little more than one thousandth part of the whole inhabitants.

Indented servants formed a considerable supply. These were poor Europeans, who went to America to settle themselves. If they could pay their passage, it was well. If not, they must find means of paying it. They were at liberty, therefore, to make an agreement with any person they chose, to serve him such a length of time as they agreed on, upon condition that he would repay to the master of the vessel the expenses of their passage. If, being foreigners, unable to speak the language, they did not know how to make a bargain for themselves, the captain of the vessel contracted for them with such persons as he could. This contract was by deed indented, which occasioned them to be called indented servants. Sometimes they were called redemptioners, because by their agreement with the master of the vessel, they could *redeem* themselves from his power by paying their passage, which they frequently effected by hiring themselves on their arrival, as is before mentioned. In some States I know that these people had a right of marrying themselves without their master's leave, and I did suppose they had that right everywhere. I did not know that in any of the States they demanded so much as a week for every day's absence without leave. I suspect this must have been at a very early period, while the governments were in the hands of the first emigrants, who, being mostly laborers, were narrow-minded and severe. I know that in Virginia the laws allowed their servitude to be protracted only two days for every one they were absent without leave. So mild was this kind of servitude, that it was very frequent for foreigners, who carried to America money enough not only to pay their passage, but to buy themselves a farm, to indent themselves to a master for three years for a certain sum of money, with a view to learn the husbandry of the country. I will here make a general observation. So desirous are the poor of Europe to get to America, where they may better their condition, that being unable to pay their passage, they will agree to serve two or three years on their arrival here, rather than not go. During the time of that service, they are better fed, better clothed, and have lighter labor, than while in Europe. Continuing to work for hire a few years longer, they buy a farm, marry, and enjoy all the sweets of a domestic society of their own. The American governments are censured for permitting this species of servitude, which lays the foundation of the happiness of these people. But what should these governments do? Pay the passage of all those who choose to go into their country? They are not able; nor were they able, do they think the purchase worth the price? Should they exclude these people from their shores? Those who know their situations in Europe and America, would not say that this is the alternative which humanity dictates. It is said that these people are deceived by those who carry them over. But this is done in Europe. How can the American governments prevent it? Should they punish the deceiver? It seems more incumbent on the European government, where the act is done, and where a public injury is sustained from it. However, it is only in Europe that this deception is heard of. The individuals are generally satisfied in America with their adventure, and very few of them wish not to have made it. I must add that the Congress have nothing to do with this matter. It belongs to the legislatures of the several States.

Page 26. *"Une puissance, en effet,"* &c. The account of the settlement of the colonies, which precedes this paragraph, shows that that settlement was not made by public authority, or at the public expense of England; but by the exertions, and at the expense of individuals. Hence it happened, that their constitutions were not formed systematically, but according to the circumstances which happened to exist in each. Hence, too, the principles of the political connection between the old and new countries, were never settled. That it would have been advantageous to have settled them, is certain; and, particularly, to have provided a body which should decide, in the last resort, all cases wherein both parties were interested. But it is not certain that that right would have been given, or ought to have been given to the Parliament; much less, that it resulted to the Parliament, without having been given to it expressly. Why was it necessary that there should have been a body to decide in the last resort? Because, it would have been for the good of both parties.

But this reason shows it ought not to have been the Parliament, since that would have exercised it for the good of one party only.

Page 105. As to the change of the 8th article of Confederation, for quoting requisitions of money on the States.

By a report of the Secretary of Congress, dated January the 4th, 1786, eight States had then acceded to the proposition; to wit, Massachusetts, Connecticut, New York, New Jersey, Pennsylvania, Maryland, Virginia, and North Carolina.

Congress, on the 18th of April, 1783, recommended to the States to invest them with a power, for twenty-five years, to levy an impost of five per cent on all articles imported from abroad. New Hampshire, Massachusetts, Connecticut, New Jersey, Pennsylvania, Delaware, Virginia, North Carolina, and South Carolina, had complied with this, before the 4th of January, 1786. Maryland had passed an act for the same purpose; but, by a mistake in referring to the date of the recommendation of Congress, the act failed of its effect. This was therefore to be rectified. Since the 4th of January, the public papers tell us that Rhode Island has complied fully with this recommendation. It remains still for New York and Georgia to do it. The exportations of America, which are tolerably well known, are the best measure for estimating the importations. These are probably worth about twenty millions of dollars, annually. Of course, this impost will pay the interest of a debt to that amount. If confined to the foreign debt, it will pay the whole interest of that, and sink half a million of the capital, annually. The expenses of collecting this impost, will probably be six per cent on its amount, this being the usual expense of collection in the United States. This will be sixty thousand dollars.

On the 30th of April, 1784, Congress recommended to the States, to invest them with a power, for fifteen years, to exclude from their ports the vessels of all nations, not having a treaty of commerce with them; and to pass, as to all nations, an act on the principles of the British navigation act. Not that they were disposed to carry these powers into execution, with such as would meet them in fair and equal arrangements of commerce; but that they might be able to do it against those who should not. On the 4th of January, 1786, New Hampshire, Massachusetts, Rhode Island, Connecticut, New York, Pennsylvania, Maryland, Virginia, and North Carolina, had done it. It remained for New Jersey, Delaware, South Carolina, and Georgia, to do the same.

In the meantime, the general idea has advanced before the demands of Congress, and several States have passed acts, for vesting Congress with the whole regulation of their commerce, reserving the revenue arising from these regulations, to the disposal of the State in which it is levied. The States which, according to the public papers, have passed such acts, are New Hampshire, Massachusetts, Rhode Island, New Jersey, Delaware, and Virginia; but the Assembly of Virginia, apprehensive that this disjointed method of proceeding may fail in its effect, or be much retarded, passed a resolution on the 21st of January, 1786, appointing commissioners to meet others from the other States, whom they invite into the same measure, to digest the form of an act, for investing Congress with such powers over their commerce, as shall be thought expedient, which act is to be reported to their several Assemblies, for their adoption. This was the state of the several propositions relative to the impost, and regulation of commerce, at the date of our latest advices from America.

Page 125. The General Assembly of Virginia, at their session in 1785, passed an act, declaring that the district, called Kentucky, shall be a separate and independent State, on these conditions. 1. That the people of that district shall consent to it. 2. That Congress shall consent to it, and shall receive them into the federal Union. 3. That they shall take on themselves a proportionable part of the public debt of Virginia. 4. That they shall confirm all titles to lands within their district, made by the State of Virginia, before their separation.

Page 139. It was in 1783, and not in 1781, that Congress quitted Philadelphia.

Page 140. *"Le Congrès qui se trouvoit à la portée des rebelles fut effrayé."* I was not present on this occasion, but I have had relations of the transaction from several who were. The conduct of Congress was marked with indignation and firmness. They received no propositions from the mutineers. They came to the resolutions, which may be seen in the journals of June the 21st, 1783, then adjourned regularly, and went through the body of the mutineers to their respective lodgings. The measures taken by Dickinson, the President of Pennsylvania, for punishing this insult, not being satisfactory to Congress, they assembled, nine days after, at Princeton, in Jersey. The people of Pennsylvania sent petitions declaring their indignation at what had passed, their devotion to the federal head, and their dispositions to protect it, and praying them to return; the legislature, as soon as assembled, did the same thing; the Executive, whose irresolution had been so exceptionable, made apologies. But Congress were now removed; and, to the opinion that this example was proper, other causes were now added, sufficient to *prevent* their return to Philadelphia.

Page 155. 1. 2. Omit *"La dette actuelle,"* &c.

And also, *"Les détails,"* &c., &c., to the end of the paragraph, *"celles des États Unis"*; page 156. The reason is, that these passages seem to suppose, that the several sums emitted by Congress, at different times, amounting nominally to two hundred millions of dollars, had been actually worth that at the time of emission, and, of course, that the soldiers and others had received that sum from Congress. But nothing is further from the truth. The soldier, victualler, or other persons who received forty dollars for a service, at the close of the year 1779, received, in fact, no more than he who received one dollar for the same service, in the year 1775, or 1776; because, in those years, the paper money was at par with silver; whereas, by the close of 1779, forty paper dollars were worth but one of silver, and would buy no more of the necessaries of life. To know what the monies emitted by Congress were worth to the people, at the time they received them, we will state the date and amount of every several emission, the depreciation of paper money at the time, and the real worth of the emission in silver or gold.

| EMISSION | | SUM EMITTED | DEPRECIATION | WORTH OF THE SUM EMITTED, IN SILVER DOLLARS |
|---|---|---|---|---|
| 1775. | June 23 | 2,000,000 | .... | 2,000,000 |
| " | November 29 | 3,000,000 | .... | 3,000,000 |
| 1776. | Feb. 17 | 4,000,000 | .... | 4,000,000 |
| " | August 13 | 5,000,000 | .... | 5,000,000 |
| 1777. | May 20 | 5,000,000 | 2⅔ | 1,877,273 |
| " | August 15 | 1,000,000 | 3 | 333,333⅓ |
| " | Nov. 7 | 1,000,000 | 4 | 250,000 |
| " | Dec. 3 | 1,000,000 | 4 | 250,000 |
| 1778. | January 8 | 1,000,000 | 4 | 250,000 |
| " | January 22 | 2,000,000 | 4 | 500,000 |
| " | February 16 | 2,000,000 | 5 | 400,000 |
| " | March 5 | 2,000,000 | 5 | 400,000 |
| " | April 4 | 1,000,000 | 6 | 166,666⅔ |
| " | April 11 | 5,000,000 | 6 | 833,333⅓ |
| " | April 18 | 500,000 | 6 | 83,333⅓ |
| " | May 22 | 5,000,000 | 5 | 1,000,000 |
| " | June 20 | 5,000,000 | 4 | 1,250,000 |
| " | July 30 | 5,000,000 | 4½ | 1,111,111 |
| " | September 5 | 5,000,000 | 5 | 1,000,000 |
| " | September 26 | 10,000,100 | 5 | 2,000,020 |
| " | November 4 | 10,000,100 | 6 | 1,666,683⅓ |
| " | December 14 | 10,000,100 | 6 | 1,666,683⅓ |
| 1779. | January 14 | 24,447,620 | 8 | 3,055,952½ |
| " | February 3 | 5,000,160 | 10 | 500,016 |
| " | February 12 | 5,000,160 | 10 | 500,016 |
| " | April 2 | 5,000,160 | 17 | 294,127 |
| " | May 5 | 10,000,100 | 24 | 416,670⅚ |
| " | June 4 | 10,000,100 | 20 | 500,005 |
| " | July 17 | 15,000,280 | 20 | 750,014 |
| " | September 17 | 15,000,260 | 24 | 625,010⅚ |
| " | October 14 | 5,000,180 | 30 | 166,672⅔ |
| " | November 17 | 10,050,540 | 38½ | 261,053 |
| " | November 29 | 10,000,140 | 38½ | 259,743 |
| | | 200,000,000 | | 36,367,719⅚ |

Thus, it appears, that the two hundred millions of dollars, emitted by Congress, were worth, to those who received them, but about thirty-six millions of silver dollars. If we estimate at the same value, the like sum of two hundred millions, supposed to have been emitted by the States, and reckon the Federal debt, foreign and domestic, at about forty-three millions, and the State debts, at about twenty-five millions, it will form an amount of one hundred and forty millions of dollars, or seven hundred and thirty-five millions of livres, Tournois, the total sum which the war has cost the inhabitants of the United States. It continued eight years, from the battle of Lexington to the cessation of hostilities in America. The annual expense, then, was about seventeen millions and five hundred thousand dollars, while that of our enemies was a greater number of guineas.

It will be asked, how will the two masses of Continental and of State money have cost the people of the United States seventy-two millions of dollars, when they are to be redeemed, now, with about six millions? I answer, that the difference, being sixty-six millions, has been lost on the paper bills, separately, by the successive holders of them. Everyone, through whose hands a bill passed, lost on that bill what it lost in value, during the time it was in his hands. This was a real tax on him; and, in this way, the people of the United States actually contributed those sixty-six millions of dollars, during the war, and by a mode of taxation the most oppressive of all, because the most unequal of all.

Page 166; bottom line. Leave out *"Et c'est une autre économie,"* &c. The reason of this, is, that in 1784, purchases of lands were to be made of the Indians, which were accordingly made. But in 1785, they did not propose to make any purchase. The money desired in 1785, five thousand dollars, was probably to pay agents residing among the Indians, or balances of the purchases of 1784. These purchases will not be made every year; but only at distant intervals, as our settlements are extended; and it may be regarded as certain, that not a foot of land will ever be taken from the Indians, without their own consent. The sacredness of their rights, is felt by all thinking persons in America, as much as in Europe.

Page 170. Virginia was quotaed the highest of any State in the Union. But during the war, several States appear to have paid more, because they were free from the enemy, whilst Virginia was cruelly ravaged. The requisition of 1784, was so quotaed on the several States, as to bring up their arrearages; so that when they should have paid the sums then demanded, all would be on an equal footing. It is necessary to give a further explanation of this requisition. The requisitions of one million and two hundred thousand dollars, of eight millions, and two millions, had been made during the war, as an experiment, to see whether, in that situation, the States could furnish the necessary supplies. It was found they could not. The money was thereupon obtained by loans in Europe; and Congress meant, by their requisition of 1784, to abandon the requisitions of one million and two hundred thousand dollars, and of two millions, and also one-half of the eight millions. But as all the States, almost, had made some payments in part of that requisition, they were obliged to retain such a proportion of it, as would enable them to call for equal contributions from all the others.

Page 170. I cannot say how it has happened, that the debt of Connecticut is greater than that of Virginia. The latter is the richest in productions, and, perhaps, made greater exertions to pay for her supplies in the course of the war.

Page 172. *"Les Américains serant après une banqueroute,"* &c. The objections made to the United States, being here condensed together in a short compass, perhaps, it would not be improper to condense the answers in as small a compass, in some such form as follows. That is, after the words *"aucun espoir,"* add, "But to these charges it may be justly answered, that those are no bankrupts who acknowledge the sacredness of their debts, in their just and real amount, who are able, within a reasonable time, to pay them, and who are actually proceeding in that payment; that they furnish, in fact, the supplies necessary for the support of their government; that their officers and soldiers are satisfied, as the interest of their debt is paid regularly, and the principal is in a course of payment; that the question, whether they fought ill, should be asked of those who met them at Bunker's hill, Bennington, Stillwater, King's mountain, the Cowpens, Guilford, and the Eutaw. And that the charges of ingratitude, madness, infidelity and corruption, are easily made by those to whom falsehoods cost nothing; but that no instances, in support of them, have been produced, or can be produced."

Page 187. *"Les officiers et les soldats ont eté payés,"* &c. The balances due to the officers and soldiers have been ascertained, and a certificate of the sum given to each; on these, the interest is regularly paid; and every occasion is seized of paying the principal, by receiving these certificates as money, whenever public property is sold, till a more regular and effectual method can be taken, for paying the whole.

Page 191. *"Quoique la loi dont nous parlons, ne s'observe plus en Angleterre."* "An alien born may purchase lands or other estates, but not for his own use; for the King is thereupon entitled to them." "Yet an alien may acquire a property in goods, money and other personal estate, or may hire a house for his habitation. For this is necessary for the advancement of trade." "Also, an alien may bring an action concerning personal property, and may make a will, and dispose of his personal estate." "When I mention these rights of an alien, I must be understood of alien *friends* only, or such whose countries are in peace with ours; for alien *enemies* have no rights, no privileges, unless by the King's special favor, during the time of war."

Blackstone, B. 1. c. 10, page 372. "An alien *friend* may have personal actions, but not real; an alien *enemy* shall have neither real, personal, or mixed actions. The reason why an alien *friend* is allowed to maintain a personal action, is, because he would otherwise be incapacitated to merchandise, which may be as much to our prejudice as his." Cunningham's law dict. title, Aliens. The above is the clear law of England, practiced from the earliest ages to this day, and never denied. The passage quoted by M. de Meusnier from 2 Blackstone, c. 26, is from his chapter, "Of title to things *personal by occupancy.*" The word "personal," shows, that nothing in this chapter relates to lands, which are *real* estate; and, therefore, this passage does not contract the one before quoted from the same author, (1 Bl. c. 10.) which says, that the lands of an alien belong to the King. The words, "of title by *occupancy,*" show, that it does not relate to *debts,* which, being a moral existence only, cannot be the subject of *occupancy.* Blackstone, in this passage, (B. 2. c. 26.) speaks only of personal goods of an alien, which another may find, and seize as prime occupant.

Page 193. *"Le remboursement présentera des difficultés des sommes considérables,"* &c. There is no difficulty nor doubts on this subject. Everyone is sensible how this is to be ultimately settled. Neither the British creditor, nor the State, will be permitted to lose by these payments. The debtor will be credited for what he paid, according to what it was really worth at the time he paid it, and he must pay the balance. Nor does he lose by this; for if a man who owed one thousand dollars to a British merchant, paid eight hundred paper dollars into the treasury, when the depreciation was at eight for one, it is clear he paid but one hundred real dollars, and must now pay nine hundred. It is probable, he received those eight hundred dollars for one hundred bushels of wheat, which were never worth more than one hundred silver dollars. He is credited, therefore, the full worth of his wheat. The equivoque is in the use of the word "dollar."

Page 226. *"Qu' on abolisse les privilèges du clergé."* This privilege, originally allowed to the clergy, is now extended to every man, and even to women. It is a right of exemption from capital punishment, for the first offence, in most cases. It is, then, a pardon by the law. In other cases, the Executive gives the pardon. But when laws are made as mild as they should be, both those pardons are absurd. The principle of Beccaria is sound. Let the legislators be merciful, but the executors of the law inexorable. As the term *"privilèges du clergé"* may be understood by foreigners, perhaps, it will be better to strike it out here, and substitute the word "pardon."

Page 239. *"Les commissaires veulent,"* &c. Manslaughter is the killing a man with design, but in a sudden gust of passion, and where the killer has not had time to cool. The first offence is not punished capitally, but the second is. This is the law of England and of all the American States; and is not now a new proposition. Those laws have supposed that a man, whose passions have so much dominion over him, as to lead him to repeated acts of murder, is unsafe to society: that it is better he should be put to death by the law, than others, more innocent than himself, on the movements of his impetuous passions.

Ibid. *"Mal-aisé d' indiquer la nuance précise,"* &c. In forming a scale of crimes and punishments, two considerations have principal weight. 1. The atrocity of the crime. 2. The peculiar circumstances of a country, which furnish greater temptations to commit it, or greater facilities for escaping detection. The punishment must be heavier to counterbalance this. Were the first the only consideration, all nations would form the same scale. But, as the circumstances of a country have influence on the punishment, and no two countries exist precisely under the same circumstances, no two countries will form the same scale of crimes and punishments. For example; in America, the inhabitants let their horses go at large, in the uninclosed lands, which are so extensive, as to maintain them altogether. It is easy, therefore, to steal them, and easy to escape. Therefore, the laws are obliged to oppose these temptations with a heavier degree of punishment. For this reason, the stealing of a horse in America, is punished more severely, than stealing the same value in any other form. In Europe, where horses are confined so securely, that it is impossible to steal them, that species of theft need not be punished more severely than any other. In some countries of Europe, stealing fruit from trees is punished capitally. The reason is, that it being impossible to lock fruit trees up in coffers, as we do our money, it is impossible to oppose physical bars to this species of theft. Moral ones are, therefore, opposed by the laws. This, to an unreflecting American, appears the most enormous of all the abuses of power; because, he has been used to see fruits hanging in such quantities, that, if not taken by men, they would rot: he has been used to consider them, therefore, as of no value, and as not furnishing materials for the commission of a crime. This must serve as an apology for the arrangements of crimes and punishments, in the scale under our consideration. A different one would be formed here; and still different ones in Italy, Turkey, China, &c.

Page 240. *"Les officiers Américains,"* &c., to page 264, *"qui le méritoient."* I would propose to new model this section, in the following manner. 1. Give a succinct history of the origin and establishment of the Cincinnati. 2. Examine whether, in its present form, it threatens any dangers to the State. 3. Propose the most practicable method of preventing them.

Having been in America, during the period in which this institution was formed, and being then in a situation which gave me opportunities of seeing it, in all its stages, I may venture to give M. de Meusnier materials for the first branch of the preceding distribution of the subject. The second and third, he will best execute himself. I should write its history in the following form:

When, on the close of that war, which established the independence of America, its army was about to be disbanded, the officers, who, during the course of it, had gone through the most trying scenes together, who, by mutual aids and good offices, had become dear to one another, felt with great oppression of mind, the approach of that moment which was to separate them, never, perhaps, to meet again. They were from different States, and from distant parts of the same State. Hazard alone could, therefore, give them but rare and partial occasions of seeing each other. They were, of course, to abandon altogether the hope of ever meeting again, or to devise some occasion which might bring them together. And why not come together on purpose, at stated times? Would not the trouble of such a journey be greatly overpaid, by the pleasure of seeing each other again, by the sweetest of all consolations, the talking over the scenes of difficulty and of endearment they had gone through? This, too, would enable them to know who of them should succeed in the world, who should be unsuccessful, and to open the purses of all to every laboring brother. This idea was too soothing, not to be cherished in conversation. It was improved into that of a regular association, with an organized administration, with periodical meetings, general and particular, fixed contributions for those who should be in distress, and a badge, by which, not only those who had not had occasion to become personally known, should be able to recognize one another, but which should be worn by their descendants, to perpetuate among them the friendships which had bound their ancestors together.

General Washington was, at that moment, oppressed with the operation of disbanding an army which was not paid, and the difficulty of this operation was increased, by some two or three States having expressed sentiments, which did not indicate a sufficient attention to their payment. He was sometimes present, when his officers were fashioning in their conversations, their newly proposed society. He saw, the innocence of its origin, and foresaw no effects less innocent. He was, at that time, writing his valedictory letter to the States, which has been so deservedly applauded by the world. Far from thinking it a moment to multiply the causes of irritation, by thwarting a proposition which had absolutely no other basis but that of benevolence and friendship, he was rather satisfied to find himself aided in his difficulties by this new incident, which occupied, and, at the same time, soothed the minds of the officers. He thought, too, that this institution would be one instrument the more for strengthening the federal bond, and for promoting federal ideas. The institution was formed. They incorporated into it the officers of the French army and navy, by whose sides they had fought, and with whose aid they had finally prevailed, extending it to such grades as they were told might be permitted to enter into it. They sent an officer to France, to make the proposition to them, and to procure the badges which they had devised for their order. The moment of disbanding the army having come, before they could have a full meeting to appoint their President, the General was prayed to act in that office till their first general meeting, which was to be held at Philadelphia, in the month of May following.

The laws of the society were published. Men who read them in their closets, unwarmed by those sentiments of friendship which had produced them, inattentive to those pains which an approaching separation had excited in the minds of the institutors, politicians, who see in everything only the dangers with which it threatens civil society, in fine, the laboring people, who, shielded by equal laws, had never seen any difference between man and man, but had read of terrible oppressions, which people of their description experience in other countries, from those who are distinguished by titles and badges, began to be alarmed at this new institution. A remarkable silence, however, was observed. Their solicitudes were long confined within the circles of private conversation. At length, however, a Mr. Burke, Chief Justice of South Carolina, broke that silence. He wrote against the new institution, foreboding its dangers, very imperfectly indeed, because he had nothing but his imagination to aid him. An American could do no more; for to detail the real evils of aristocracy, they must be seen in Europe. Burke's fears were thought exaggerations in America; while in Europe, it is known that even Mirabeau has but faintly sketched the curses of hereditary aristocracy as they are experienced here, and as they would have followed in America, had this institution remained. The epigraph of Burke's pamphlet, was, "Blow ye the trumpet in Zion." Its effect corresponded with its epigraph. This institution became, first, the subject of general conversation. Next, it was made the subject of deliberation in the legislative Assemblies of some of the States. The Governor of South Carolina censured it, in an address to the Assembly of that State. The Assemblies of Massachusetts, Rhode Island, and Pennsylvania, condemned its principles. No circumstance, indeed, brought the consideration of it expressly before Congress; yet it had sunk deep into their minds. An offer having been made to them, on the part of the Polish order of Divine Providence, to receive some of their distinguished citizens into that order, they made that an occasion to declare, that these distinctions were contrary to the principles of their Confederation.

The uneasiness excited by this institution, had very early caught the notice of General Washington. Still recollecting all the purity of the motives which gave it birth, he became sensible that it might produce political evils, which the warmth of those motives had masked. Add to this, that it was disapproved by the mass of citizens of the Union. This, alone, was reason strong enough, in a country where the will of the majority is the law, and ought to be the law. He saw that the objects of the institution were too light, to be opposed to considerations as serious as these; and that it was become necessary to annihilate it absolutely. On this, therefore, he was decided. The first annual meeting at Philadelphia was now at hand; he went to that, determined to exert all his influence for its suppression. He proposed it to his fellow officers, and urged it with all his powers. It met an opposition which was observed to cloud his face with an anxiety, that the most distressful scenes of the war had scarcely ever produced. It was canvassed for several days, and, at length, it was no more a doubt what would be its ultimate fate. The order was on the point of receiving its annihilation, by the vote of a great majority of its members. In this moment, their envoy arrived from France, charged with letters from the French officers, accepting with cordiality the proposed badges of union, with solicitations from others to be received into the order, and with notice that their respectable Sovereign had been pleased to recognize it, and permit his officers to wear its badges. The prospect now changed. The question assumed a new form. After the offer made by them, and accepted by their friends, in what words could they clothe a proposition to retract it, which would not cover themselves with the reproaches of levity and ingratitude? which would not appear an insult to those whom they loved? Federal principles, popular discontent, were considerations whose weight was known and felt by themselves. But would foreigners know and feel them equally? Would they so far acknowledge their cogency, as to permit without any indignation, the eagle and ribbon to be torn from their breasts, by the very hands which had placed them there? The idea revolted the whole society. They found it necessary, then, to preserve so much of their institution as might continue to support this foreign branch, while they should prune off every other, which would give offence to their fellow citizens: thus sacrificing, on each hand, to their friends and to their country.

The society was to retain its existence, its name, its meetings, and its charitable funds: but these last were to be deposited with their respective legislatures. The order was to be no longer hereditary, a reformation, which had been pressed even from this side the Atlantic; it was to be communicated to no new members; the general meetings, instead of annual, were to be triennial only. The eagle and ribbon, indeed, were retained; because they were worn, and they wished them to be worn by their friends who were in a country where they would not be objects of offence; but themselves never wore them. They laid them up in their bureaus with the medals of American Independence, with those of the trophies they had taken, and the battles they had won. But through all the United States, no officer is seen to offend the public eye, with the display of this badge. These changes have tranquillized the American States. Their citizens feel too much interest in the reputation of their officers, and value too much, whatever may serve to recall to the memory of their allies, the moments wherein they formed but one people, not to do justice to the circumstance which prevented a total annihilation of the order. Though they are obliged by a prudent foresight, to keep out everything from among themselves, which might pretend to divide them into orders, and to degrade one description of men below another, yet they hear with pleasure, that their allies, whom circumstances have already placed under these distinctions, are willing to consider it as one, to have aided them in the establishment of their liberties, and to wear a badge which may recall them to their remembrance; and it would be an extreme affliction to them, if the domestic reformation which has been found necessary, if the censures of individual writers, or if any other circumstance should discourage the wearing their badge or lessen its reputation.

This short but true history of the order of the Cincinnati, taken from the mouths of persons on the spot, who were privy to its origin and progress, and who knew its present state, is the best apology which can be made for an insinuation, which appeared to be, and was really, so heterogeneous to the governments in which it was erected.

It should be further considered, that in America no other distinction between man and man had ever been known, but that of persons in office, exercising powers by authority of the laws, and private individuals. Among these last, the poorest laborer stood on equal ground with the wealthiest millionnaire, and generally on a more favored one, whenever their rights seemed to jar. It has been seen that a shoemaker or other artisan, removed by the voice of his country from his work bench into a chair of office, has instantly commanded all the respect and obedience which the laws ascribe to his office. But of distinction by birth or badge, they had no more idea than they had of the mode of existence in the moon or planets. They had heard only that there were such, and knew that they must be wrong. A due horror of the evils which flow from these distinctions, could be excited in Europe only, where the dignity of man is lost in arbitrary distinctions, where the human species is classed into several stages of degradation, where the many are crushed under the weight of the few, and where the order established, can present to the contemplation of a thinking being, no other picture than that of God Almighty and his angels, trampling under foot the host of the damned. No wonder, then, that the institution of the Cincinnati should be innocently conceived by one order of American citizens, should raise in the other orders, only a slow, temperate, and rational opposition, and should be viewed in Europe as a detestable parricide.

The second and third branches of this subject, no body can better execute than M. de Meusnier. Perhaps it may be curious to him to see how they strike an American mind at present. He shall, therefore, have the ideas of one who was an enemy to the institution from the first moment of its conception, but who was always sensible that the officers neither foresaw nor intended the injury they were doing to their country.

As to the question, then, whether any evil can proceed from the institution as it stands at present, I am of opinion there may. 1. From the meetings. These will keep the officers formed into a body; will continue a distinction between the civil and military, which it would be for the good of the whole to obliterate, as soon as possible; and the military assemblies will not only keep alive the jealousies and fears of the civil government, but give ground for these fears and jealousies. For when men meet together, they will make business if they have none; they will collate their grievances, some real, some imaginary, all highly painted; they will communicate to each other the sparks of discontent; and these may engender a flame which will consume their particular, as well as the general happiness. 2. The charitable part of the institution is still more likely to do mischief, as it perpetuates the dangers apprehended in the preceding clause. For here is a fund provided of permanent existence. To whom will it belong? To the descendants of American officers of a certain description. These descendants, then, will form a body, having sufficient interest to keep up an attention to their description, to continue meetings, and perhaps, in some moment, when the political eye shall be slumbering, or the firmness of their fellow citizens relaxed, to replace the insignia of the order and revive all its pretensions. What good can the officers propose which may weigh against these possible evils? The securing their descendants against want? Why afraid to trust them to the same fertile soil, and the same genial climate, which will secure from want the descendants of their other fellow citizens? Are they afraid they will be reduced to labor the earth for their sustenance? They will be rendered thereby both more honest and happy. An industrious farmer occupies a more dignified place in the scale of beings, whether moral or political, than a lazy lounger, valuing himself on his family, too proud to work, and drawing out a miserable existence, by eating on that surplus of other men's labor, which is the sacred fund of the helpless poor. A pitiful annuity will only prevent them from exerting that industry and those talents which would soon lead them to better fortune.

How are these evils to be prevented? 1. At their first general meeting, let them distribute the funds on hand to the existing objects of their destination, and discontinue all further contributions. 2. Let them declare, at the same time, that their meetings, general and particular, shall thenceforth cease. 3. Let them melt up their eagles and add the mass to the distributable fund, that their descendants may have no temptation to hang them in their button holes.

These reflections are not proposed as worthy the notice of M. de Meusnier.

He will be so good as to treat the subject in his own way, and no body has a better. I will only pray him to avail us of his forcible manner, to evince that there is evil to be apprehended, even from the ashes of this institution, and to exhort the society in America to make their reformation complete; bearing in mind, that we must keep the passions of men on our side, even when we are persuading them to do what they ought to do.

Page 268. *"Et en effet la population,"* &c. Page 270. *"Plus de confiance."*

To this we answer that no such census of the numbers was ever given out by Congress, nor ever presented to them: and further, that Congress never have, at any time, declared by their vote, the number of inhabitants in their respective States. On the 22d of June, 1775, they first resolved to emit paper money. The sum resolved on was two millions of dollars. They declared, then, that the twelve confederate colonies (for Georgia had not yet joined them) should be pledged for the redemption of these bills. To ascertain in what proportion each State should be bound, the members from each were desired to say, as nearly as they could, what was the number of the inhabitants of their respective States. They were very much unprepared for such a declaration. They guessed, however, as well as they could. The following are the numbers, as they conjectured them, and the consequent apportionment of the two millions of dollars.

| | INHABITANTS | DOLLARS |
|---|---|---|
| New Hampshire | 100,000 | 82,713 |
| Massachusetts | 350,000 | 289,496 |
| Rhode Island | 58,000 | 47.973 |
| Connecticut | 200,000 | 165,426 |
| New York | 200,000 | 165,426 |
| New Jersey | 130,000 | 107,527 |
| Pennsylvania | 300,000 | 248,139 |
| Delaware | 30,000 | 24,813 |
| Maryland | 250,000 | 206,783 |
| Virginia | 400,000 | 330,852 |
| North Carolina | 200,000 | 165,426 |
| South Carolina | 200,000 | 165,426 |
| | 2,418,000 | 2,000,000 |

Georgia having not yet acceded to the measures of the other States, was not quotaed; but her numbers were generally estimated at about thirty thousand, and so would have made the whole two million four hundred and forty-eight thousand persons, of every condition. But it is to be observed, that though Congress made this census the basis of their apportionment, yet they did not even give it a place on their journals; much less publish it to the world with their sanction. The way it got abroad was this: As the members declared from their seats the number of inhabitants which they conjectured to be in their State, the secretary of Congress wrote them on a piece of paper, calculated the portion of two millions of dollars to be paid by each, and entered the sum only in the journals. The members, however, for their own satisfaction, and the information of their States, took copies of this enumeration and sent them to their States. From thence they got into the public papers: and when the English news writers found it answer their purpose to compare this with the enumeration of 1783, as their principle is "to lie boldly that they may not be suspected of lying," they made it amount to three millions one hundred and thirty-seven thousand eight hundred and nine, and ascribed its publication to Congress itself.

In April, 1785, Congress being to call on the States to raise a million and a half of dollars annually for twenty-five years, it was necessary to apportion this among them. The States had never furnished them with their exact numbers. It was agreed, too, that in this apportionment five slaves should be counted as three freemen only. The preparation of this business was in the hands of a committee; they applied to the members for the best information they could give them of the number of their States. Some of the States had taken pains to discover their numbers. Others had done nothing in that way, and, of course, were now where they were in 1775, when their numbers were first called on to declare their numbers. Under these circumstances, and on the principle of counting three-fifths only of the slaves, the committee apportioned the money among the States, and reported their work to Congress. In this they had assessed South Carolina as having one hundred and seventy thousand inhabitants. The delegate for that State, however, prevailed on Congress to assess them on the footing of one hundred and fifty thousand only, in consideration of the state of total devastation in which the enemy had left their country. The difference was then laid on the other States, and the following was the result:

| | INHABITANTS | DOLLARS |
|---|---|---|
| New Hampshire | 82,200 | 52,708 |
| Massachusetts | 350,000 | 224,427 |
| Rhode Island | 50,400 | 32,318 |
| Connecticut | 206,000 | 132,091 |
| New York | 200,000 | 128,243 |
| New Jersey | 130,000 | 83,358 |
| Pennsylvania | 320,000 | 205,189 |
| Delaware | 35,000 | 22,443 |
| Maryland | 220,700 | 141,517 |
| Virginia | 400,000 | 256,487 |
| North Carolina | 170,000 | 109,006 |
| South Carolina | 150,000 | 96,183 |
| Georgia | 25,000 | 16,030 |
| | 2,339,300 | 1,500,000 |

Still, however, Congress refused to give the enumeration the sanction of a place on their journals, because it was not formed on such evidence as a strict attention to accuracy and truth required. They used it from necessity, because they could get no better rule, and they entered on their journals only the apportionment of money. The members, however, as before, took copies of the enumeration, which was the groundwork of the apportionment, sent them to their States, and thus this second enumeration got into the public papers, and was by the English ascribed to Congress as their declaration of their present numbers. To get at the real numbers which this enumeration supposes, we must add twenty thousand to the number on which South Carolina was quoted; we must consider that seven hundred thousand slaves are counted but as four hundred and twenty thousand persons, and add, on that account, two hundred and eighty thousand. This will give us a total of two millions six hundred and thirty-nine thousand three hundred inhabitants of every condition in the thirteen States, being two hundred and twenty-one thousand three hundred more than the enumeration of 1775, instead of seven hundred and ninety-eight thousand five hundred and nine less, which the English papers asserted to be the diminution of numbers in the United States, according to the confession of Congress themselves.

Page 272. "*Comportera peut-être une population de trente millions.*"

The territory of the United States contains about a million of square miles, English. There is, in them, a greater proportion of fertile lands than in the British dominions in Europe. Suppose the territory of the United States, then, to attain an equal degree of population with the British European dominions, they will have an hundred millions of inhabitants. Let us extend our views to what may be the population of the two continents of North and South America, supposing them divided at the narrowest part of the isthmus of Panama. Between this line and that of 50° of north latitude, the northern continent contains about five millions of square miles, and south of this line of division the southern continent contains about seven millions of square miles. I do not pass the 50th degree of northern latitude in my reckoning, because we must draw a line somewhere, and considering the soil and climate beyond that, I would only avail my calculation of it, as a make weight, to make good what the colder regions within that line may be supposed to fall short in their future population. Here are twelve millions of square miles, then, which, at the rate of population before assumed, will nourish twelve hundred millions of inhabitants, a number greater than the present population of the whole globe is supposed to amount to. If those who propose medals for the resolution of questions, about which nobody makes any question, those who have invited discussion on the pretended problem, Whether the discovery of America was for the good of mankind? if they, I say, would have viewed it only as doubling the numbers of mankind, and, of course, the quantum of existence and happiness, they might have saved the money and the reputation which their proposition has cost them. The present population of the inhabited parts of the United States is of about ten to the square mile; and experience has shown us, that wherever we reach that, the inhabitants become uneasy, as too much compressed, and go off in great numbers to search for vacant country. Within forty years their whole territory will be peopled at that rate. We may fix that, then, as the term beyond which the people of those States will not be restrained within their present limits; we may fix that population, too, as the limit which they will not exceed till the whole of those two continents are filled up to that mark, that is to say, till they shall contain one hundred and twenty millions of inhabitants. The soil of the country on the western side of the Mississippi, its climate, and its vicinity to the United States, point it out as the first which will receive population from that nest. The present occupiers will just have force enough to repress and restrain the emigrations to a certain degree of consistence. We have seen lately a single person go and decide on a settlement in Kentucky, many hundred miles from any white inhabitant, remove thither with his family and a few neighbors; and though perpetually harassed by the Indians, that settlement in the course of ten years has acquired thirty thousand inhabitants. Its numbers are increasing while we are writing, and the State, of which it formerly made a part, has offered it independence.

Page 280, line five. *"Huit des onze États,"* &c. Say, "There were ten States present; six voted unanimously for it, three against it, and one was divided; and seven votes being requisite to decide the proposition affirmatively, it was lost. The voice of a single individual of the State which was divided, or of one of those which were of the negative, would have prevented this abominable crime from spreading itself over the new country. Thus we see the fate of millions unborn hanging on the tongue of one man, and heaven was silent in that awful moment! But it is to be hoped it will not always be silent, and that the friends to the rights of human nature will in the end prevail.

"On the 16th of March, 1785, it was moved in Congress that the same proposition should be referred to a committee, and it was referred by the votes of eight States against three. We do not hear that anything further is yet done on it."

Page 286. *"L'autorité du Congrès étoit nécessaire."* The substance of the passage alluded to in the journal of Congress, May the 26th, 1784, is, "That the authority of Congress to make *requisitions* of troops during peace is questioned; that such an authority would be dangerous, combined with the acknowledged one of emitting or borrowing money; and that a few troops only being wanted to guard magazines and garrison the frontier posts, it would be more proper at present to *recommend* than to require."

---

Mr Jefferson presents his compliments to M. de Meusnier, and sends him copies of the thirteenth, twenty-third, and twenty-fourth articles of treaty between the King of Prussia and the United States.

If M. de Meusnier proposes to mention the facts of cruelty of which he and Mr. Jefferson spoke yesterday, the twenty-fourth article will introduce them properly, because they produced a sense of the necessity of that article. These facts are, 1. The death of upwards of eleven thousand American prisoners in one prison ship (the Jersey), and in the space of three years. 2. General Howe's permitting our prisoners, taken at the battle of Germantown, and placed under a guard in the yard of the State-house of Philadelphia, to be so long without any food furnished them that many perished with hunger. Where the bodies laid, it was seen that they had eaten all the grass around them within their reach, after they had lost the power of rising, or moving from their place. 3. The second fact was the act of a commanding officer; the first, of several commanding officers, and for so long a time as must suppose the approbation of government. But the following was the act of government itself. During the periods that our affairs seemed unfavorable, and theirs successful, that is to say, after the evacuation of New York, and again, after the taking of Charleston, in South Carolina, they regularly sent our prisoners, taken on the seas and carried to England, to the East Indies. This is so certain, that in the month of November or December, 1785, Mr. Adams having officially demanded a delivery of the American prisoners sent to the East Indies, Lord Cærmarthen answered, officially, "That orders were immediately issued for their discharge." M. de Meusnier is at liberty to quote this fact. 4. A fact to be ascribed not only to the government, but to the parliament, who passed an act for that purpose in the beginning of the war, was the obliging our prisoners taken at sea, to join them, and fight against their countrymen. This they effected by starving and whipping them. The insult on Captain Stanhope, which happened at Boston last year, was a consequence of this. Two persons, Dunbar and Lowthorp, whom Stanhope had treated in this manner (having particularly inflicted twenty-four lashes on Dunbar), meeting him at Boston, attempted to beat him. But the people interposed and saved him. The fact is referred to in that paragraph of the Declaration of Independence, which says, "He has constrained our fellow-citizens, taken captive on the high seas, to bear arms against their country, to become the executioners of their friends and brethren, or to fall themselves by their hands." This was the most afflicting to our prisoners of all the cruelties exercised on them. The others affected the body only, but this the mind; they were haunted by the horror of having, perhaps, themselves shot the ball by which a father or a brother fell. Some of them had constancy enough to hold out against half allowance of food and repeated whippings. These were generally sent to England, and from thence to the East Indies. One of them escaped from the East Indies, and got back to Paris, where he gave an account of his sufferings to Mr. Adams, who happened to be then at Paris.

M. de Meusnier, where he mentions that the slave law has been passed in Virginia, without the clause of emancipation, is pleased to mention, that neither Mr. Wythe, nor Mr. Jefferson was present, to make the proposition they had meditated; from which, people, who do not give themselves the trouble to reflect or inquire, might conclude hastily, that their absence was the cause why the proposition was not made; and, of course, that there were not in the Assembly, persons of virtue and firmness enough to propose the clause for emancipation. This supposition would not be true. There were persons there, who wanted neither the virtue to propose, nor talents to enforce the proposition, had they seen that the disposition of the legislature was ripe for it. These worthy characters would feel themselves wounded, degraded, and discouraged by this idea. Mr. Jefferson would therefore be obliged to M. de Meusnier, to mention it in some such manner as this. "Of the two commissioners, who had concerted the amendatory clause for the gradual emancipation of slaves, Mr. Wythe could not be present, he being a member of the judiciary department, and Mr. Jefferson was absent on the legation to France. But there were not wanting in that Assembly, men of virtue enough to propose, and talents to vindicate this clause. But they saw, that the moment of doing it with success was not yet arrived, and that an unsuccessful effort, as too often happens, would only rivet still closer the chains of bondage, and retard the moment of delivery to this oppressed description of men. What a stupendous, what an incomprehensible machine is man! who can endure toil, famine, stripes, imprisonment, and death itself, in vindication of his own liberty, and, the next moment be deaf to all those motives whose power supported him through his trial, and inflict on his fellow men a bondage, one hour of which is fraught with more misery, than ages of that which he rose in rebellion to oppose. But we must await, with patience, the workings of an overruling Providence, and hope that that is preparing the deliverance of these, our suffering brethren. When the measure of their tears shall be full, when their groans shall have involved heaven itself in darkness, doubtless, a God of justice will awaken to their distress, and by diffusing light and liberality among their oppressors, or, at length, by his exterminating thunder, manifest his attention to the things of this world, and that they are not left to the guidance of a blind fatality."

## TO THE EDITOR OF THE *JOURNAL DE PARIS*

August 29, 1787

SIR: I am a citizen of the United States of America, and have passed in those States almost the whole of my life. When young, I was passionately fond of reading books of history and travels. Since the commencement of the late revolution which separated us from Great Britain, our country too, has been thought worthy to employ the pens of historians and travellers. I cannot paint to you, Sir, the agonies which these have cost me, in obliging me to renounce these favorite branches of reading, and in discovering to me at length, that my whole life has been employed in nourishing my mind with fables and falsehoods. For thus I reason. If the histories of d' Auberteuil and of Longchamps, and the travels of the Abbé Robin can be published in the face of the world, and can be read and believed by those who are contemporary with the events they pretend to relate, how may we expect that future ages shall be better informed? Will those rise from their graves to bear witness to the truth, who would not, while living, lift their voices against falsehood? If contemporary histories are thus false, what will future compilations be? And what are all those of preceding times? In your journal of this day, you announce and criticise a book under the title of *"Les ligues Achéenne, Suisse, & Hollandoise, et révolution des états unis de l'Amérique par M. de Mayer."* I was no part of the Achaean, Swiss or Dutch confederacies, and have therefore nothing to say against the facts related of them. And you cite only one fact from his account of the American revolution. It is in these words: *"Monsieur Mayer assure qu'une seule voix, un seul homme, prononça l'indépendance des États unis. Ce fut, dit il, John Dickinson, un des Députés de la Pensilvanie au Congrès. La veille, il avoit voté pour la soumission, l'égalité des suffrages avoit suspendu la résolution; s'il eut persisté, le Congrès ne déliberoit point, il fut foible: il céda aux instances de ceux qui avoient plus d'énergie, plus d' éloquence, et plus de lumières; il donna sa voix: l'Amérique lui doit une reconnaissance éternelle; c'est Dickinson qui l'a affranchie."* The modesty and candor of Mr. Dickinson himself, Sir, would disavow every word of this paragraph, except these—*"il avoit voté pour la soumission."* These are true, every other tittle false. I was on the spot, and can relate to you this transaction with precision. On the 7th of June, 1776, the delegates from Virginia moved, in obedience to instructions from their constituents, that Congress should declare the thirteen united colonies to be independent of Great Britain, that a confederation should be formed to bind them together, and measures be taken for procuring the assistance of foreign powers. The House ordered a punctual attendance of all their members the next day at ten o'clock, and then resolved themselves into a committee of the whole and entered on the discussion. It appeared in the course of the debates that seven States: *viz.,* New Hampshire, Massachusetts, Rhode Island, Connecticut, Virginia, North Carolina and Georgia, were decided for a separation; but that six others still hesitated, to wit: New York, New Jersey, Pennsylvania, Delaware, Maryland, and South Carolina. Congress, desirous of unanimity, and seeing that the public mind was advancing rapidly to it, referred the further discussion to the first of July, appointing, in the mean time, a committee to prepare a declaration of independence, a second to form articles for the confederation of the States, and a third to propose measures for obtaining foreign aid. On the 28th of June, the Declaration of Independence was reported to the House, and was laid on the table for the consideration of the members. On the first day of July, they resolved themselves into a committee of the whole, and resumed the consideration of the motion of June 7th. It was debated through the day, and at length was decided in the affirmative by the vote of nine States: *viz.,* New Hampshire, Massachusetts, Rhode Island, Connecticut, New Jersey, Maryland, Virginia, North Carolina, and Georgia. Pennsylvania and South Carolina voted against it. Delaware, having but two members present, was divided. The delegates from New York declared they were for it, and their constituents also; but that the instructions against it which had been given them a twelvemonth before, were still unrepealed; that their convention was to meet in a few days, and they asked leave to suspend their vote till they could obtain a repeal of their instructions. Observe that all this was in a committee of the whole Congress, and that according to the mode of their proceedings, the resolution of that committee to declare themselves independent, was to be put to the same persons re-assuming their form as a Congress. It was now evening, the members exhausted by a debate of nine hours, during which all the powers of the soul had been distended with the magnitude of the object—without refreshment, without a pause—and the delegates of South Carolina desired that the final decision might be put off to the next morning, that they might still weigh in their own minds their ultimate vote. It was put off, and in the morning of the second of July they joined the other nine States in voting for it. The members of the Pennsylvania delegation too, who had been absent the day before, came in and turned the vote of their State in favor of independence; and a third member of the State of Delaware, who, hearing of the division in the sentiments of his two colleagues, had travelled post to arrive in time, now came in and decided the vote of that State also for the resolution. Thus twelve States voted for it at the time of its passage, and the delegates of New York, the thirteenth State, received instructions within a few days to add theirs to the general vote: so that, instead of the *"égalité des suffrages"* spoken of by M. Mayer, there was not a dissenting voice. Congress proceeded immediately to consider the Declaration of Independence which had been reported by their committee on the 28th of June. The several paragraphs of that were debated for three days: *viz.,* the second, third, and fourth of July. In the evening of the fourth they were finally closed, and the instrument approved by an unanimous vote and signed by every member, *except Mr. Dickinson.* Look into the Journal of Congress of that day, Sir, and you will see the instrument and the names of the signers, and that Mr. Dickinson's name is not among them. Then read again those words of your paper: *"il (M. Mayer) assure qu'une seule voix, un seul homme, prononça l'indépendance des états unis, ce fut John Dickinson.—l'Amérique lui doit une reconnaissance éternelle; c'est Dickinson qui l'a affranchie."* With my regrets, and my adieus to history, to travels, to Mayer, and to you, Sir, permit me to mingle assurances of the great respect with which I have the honor to be, Sir, your most obedient and most humble servant.

## NOTES ON PROFESSOR EBELING'S LETTER OF JULY 30, 1795 [1]

1795

Professor Ebeling mentioning the persons in America from whom he derives information for his work, it may be useful for him to know how far he may rely on their authority.

President Stiles, an excellent man, of very great learning, but remarkable for his credulity.

| | |
|---|---|
| Dr. Willard.<br>Dr. Barton.<br>Dr. Ramsey.<br>Mr. Barlow. | All these are men of respectable characters worthy of confidence as to any facts they may state, and rendered, by their good sense, good judges of them. |
| Mr. Morse.<br>Mr. Webster. | Good authorities for whatever relates to the Eastern states, and perhaps as far South as the Delaware. |

But South of that their information is worse than none at all, except as far as they quote good authorities. They both I believe took a single journey through the Southern parts, merely to acquire the right of being considered as eye-witnesses. But to pass once along a public road through a country, and in one direction only, to put up at its taverns, and get into conversation with the idle, drunken individuals who pass their time lounging in these taverns, is not the way to know a country, its inhabitants, or manners. To generalize a whole nation from these specimens is not the sort of information which Professor Ebeling would wish to compose *his work* from.

[1] Christoph Daniel Ebeling was preparing his *Geography and History of North America* (5 vols., 1796-1816), for which he asked Jefferson for information.

Fenno's *Gazette of the U.S.*
Webster's *Minerva.*
*Columbian Centinel.*

To form a just judgment of a country from its newspapers the character of these papers should be known, in order that proper allowances and corrections may be used. This will require a long explanation, without which, these particular papers would give a foreigner a very false view of American affairs.

The people of America, before the revolution-war, being attached to England, had taken up, without examination, the English ideas of the superiority of their constitution over every thing of the kind which ever had been or ever would be tried. The revolution forced them to consider the subject for themselves, and the result was an universal conversion to republicanism. Those who did not come over to this opinion, either left us, and were called Refugees, or staid with us under the name of tories; and some, preferring profit to principle took side with us and floated with the general tide. Our first federal constitution, or Confederation as it was called, was framed in the first moments of our separation from England, in the highest point of our jealousies of independence as to her and as to each other. It formed therefore too weak a bond to produce an union of action as to foreign nations. This appeared at once on the establishment of peace, when the pressure of a common enemy which had hooped us together during the war, was taken away. Congress was found to be quite unable to point the action of the several states to a common object. A general desire therefore took place of amending the federal constitution. This was opposed by some of those who wished for monarchy, to wit, the Refugees now returned, the old tories, and the timid whigs who prefer tranquility to freedom, hoping monarchy might be the remedy if a state of complete anarchy could be brought on. A Convention however being decided on, some of the monocrats got elected, with a hope of introducing an English constitution as nearly as was attainable. In this they were not altogether without success; insomuch that the monarchical features of the new constitution produced a violent opposition to it from the most zealous republicans in the several states. For this reason, and because they also thought it carried the principle of a consolidation of the states farther than was requisite for the purpose of producing an union of action as to foreign powers, it is still doubted by some whether a majority of the people of the U.S. were not against adopting it. However it was carried through all the assemblies of the states, though by very small majorities in the largest states. The inconveniences of an inefficient government, driving the people as is usual, into the opposite extreme, the elections to the first Congress ran very much in favor of those who were known to favor a very strong government. Hence the anti-republicans appeared a considerable majority in both houses of Congress. They pressed forward the plan therefore of strengthening all the features of the government which gave it resemblance to an English constitution, of adopting the English forms and principles of administration, and of forming like them a monied interest, by means of a funding system, not calculated to pay the public debt, but to render it perpetual, and to make it an engine in the hands of the executive branch of government which, added to the great patronage it possessed in the disposal of public offices, might enable it to assume by degrees a kingly authority. The biennial period of Congress being too short to betray to the people, spread over this great continent, this train of things during the first Congress, little change was made in the members to the second. But in the mean time two very distinct parties had formed in Congress; and before the third election, the people in general became apprised of the game which was playing for drawing over them a kind of government which they never had in contemplation. At the 3d election therefore a decided majority of Republicans were sent to the lower house of Congress; and as information spread still farther among the people after the 4th election the anti-republicans have become a weak minority. But the members of the Senate being changed but once in 6 years, the completion of that body will be much slower in its assimilation to that of the people. This will account for the differences which may appear in the proceedings and spirit of the two houses. Still however it is inevitable that the Senate will at length be formed to the republican model of the people, and the two houses of the legislature, once brought to act on the true principles of the Constitution, backed by the people, will be able to defeat the plan of sliding us into monarchy, and to keep the Executive within republican bounds, notwithstanding the immense patronage it possesses in the disposal of public offices, notwithstanding it has been able to draw into this vortex the judiciary branch of the government and by their expectancy of sharing the other offices in the Executive gift to make them auxiliary to the Executive in all its views instead of forming a balance between that and the legislature as it was originally intended and notwithstanding the funding phalanx which a respect for public faith must protect, though it was engaged by false brethren. Two parties then do exist within the U.S. they embrace respectively the following descriptions of persons.

The Anti-republicans consist of

1. The old refugees and tories.

2. British merchants residing among us, and composing the main body of our merchants.

3. American merchants trading on British capital. Another great portion.

4. Speculators and holders in the banks and public funds.

5. Officers of the federal government with some exceptions.

6. Office-hunters, willing to give up principles for places. A numerous and noisy tribe.

7. Nervous persons, whose languid fibres have more analogy with a passive than active state of things.

The Republican part of our Union comprehends

1. The entire body of landholders throughout the United States.

2. The body of labourers, not being landholders, whether in husbanding or the arts.

The latter is to the aggregate of the former party probably as 500 to one; but their wealth is not as disproportionate, though it is also greatly superior, and is in truth the foundation of that of their antagonists. Trifling as are the numbers of the Anti-republican party, there are circumstances which give them an appearance of strength and numbers. They all live in cities, together, and can act in a body readily and at all times; they give chief employment to the newspapers, and therefore have most of them under their command. The Agricultural interest is dispersed over a great extent of country, have little means of intercommunication with each other, and feeling their own strength and will, are conscious that a single exertion of these will at any time crush the machinations against their government. As in the commerce of human life, there are commodities adapted to every demand, so there are newspapers adapted to the Anti-republican palate, and others to the republican. Of the former class are the *Columbian Centinel,* the Hartford newspaper, Webster's *Minerva,* Fenno's *Gazette of the U.S.,* Davies's Richmond paper &c. Of the latter are Adams's Boston paper, Greenleaf's of New York, Freneau's of New Jersey, Bache's of Philadelphia, Pleasant's of Virginia &c. Pleasant's paper comes out twice a week, Greenleaf's and Freneau's once a week, Bache's daily. I do not know how often Adams's. I shall according to your desire endeavor to get Pleasant's for you for 1794, and 95 and will have it forwarded through 96 from time to time to your correspondent at Baltimore.

While on the subject of authorities and information, the following works are recommended to Professor Ebeling.

Minot's history of the insurrection in Massachusetts in 1786. 8^vo^.

Mazzei. *Recherches historiques et politiques sur les E.U de l'Amérique.* 4 vol. 8^vo^. This is to be had from Paris. The author is an exact man.

The article *États Unis de l'Amérique* in the *Dictionnarie d'Économie politique et diplomatique, de l'Encyclopédie méthodique.* This article occupies about 90 pages, is by De Meusnier,[2] and his materials were worthy of confidence, except so far as they were taken from the Abbé Raynal. Against these effusions of an imagination in delirio it is presumed Professor Ebeling needs not be put on his guard. The earlier editions of the Abbé Raynal's work were equally bad as to both South and North America. A gentleman

[2] See pages 39-73, for Jefferson's comments.

however of perfect information as to South America, undertook to reform that part of the work, and his changes and additions were for the most part adopted by the Abbé in his latter editions. But the North American part remains in its original state of worthlessness.

## NOTES ON THE FIFTH VOLUME OF MARSHALL'S *LIFE OF WASHINGTON*

1809

Page 2. *"The practicability of perpetuating his authority,"* &c. I am satisfied that General Washington had not a wish to perpetuate his authority; but he who supposes it was practicable, had he wished it, knows nothing of the spirit of America, either of the people or of those who possessed their confidence. There was indeed a cabal of the officers of the army who proposed to establish a monarchy and to propose it to General Washington. He frowned indignantly at the proposition [according to the information which got abroad], and Rufus King and some few civil characters, chiefly [indeed, I believe, to a man] north of Maryland, who joined in this intrigue. But they never dared openly to avow it, knowing that the spirit which had produced a change in the form of government was alive to the preservation of it.

Page 28. The member of Congress here alluded to was myself, and the extracts quoted, was part of a letter from myself in answer to one General Washington wrote. General Washington called on me at Annapolis (where I then was as a member of Congress), on his way to the meeting of the Cincinnati in Philadelphia. We had much conversation on the institution, which was chiefly an amplification of the sentiments in our letters, and, in conclusion, after I had stated to him the modifications which I thought might remove all jealousies, as well as dangers, and the parts which might still be retained, he appeared to make up his mind, and said: "No! not a fibre of it must be retained—no half-way reformation will suffice. If the thing be bad, it must be totally abolished." And he declared his determination to use his utmost endeavors to have it entirely abolished. On his return from Philadelphia he called on me again at Annapolis, and sat with me until a very late hour in the night, giving me an account of what passed in their convention. The sum of it was that he had exerted his whole influence in every way in his power to procure an abolition; that the opposition to it was extreme, and especially from some of the younger members; but that after several days of struggle within doors and without, a general sentiment was obtained for its entire abolition. Whether any vote had been taken on it or not, I do not remember; but his affirmation to me was, that within a few days (I think he said two or three) it would have been formally abolished. Just in that moment arrived Major L'Enfant, who had been sent to France to procure the Eagles, and to offer the order to the French officers who had served in America. He brought the King's permission to his officers to accept it, the letters of thanks of these officers accepting it, letters of solicitation from other officers to obtain it, and the Eagles themselves. The effect of all this on the minds of the members was to undo much of what had been done; to rekindle all the passions which had produced the institution, and silence all the dictates of prudence, which had been operating for its abolition. After this, the General said, the utmost that could be effected was the modification which took place, and which provided for its extinction with the death of the existing members. He declined the Presidency, and, I think, Baron Steuben was appointed. I went soon after to France. While there, M. de Meusnier, charged with that part of the *Encyclopédie Méthodique* which relates to economy politique and diplomatique, called on me with the article of that dictionary, *"États Unis,"* which he had prepared ready for the press, and begged I would revise it and make any notes on it which I should think necessary towards rendering it correct. I furnished him most of the matter of his fifth, sixth, eighth, ninth, and tenth sections of the article *"États Unis,"* with which, however, he intermixed some of his own. The ninth is that which relates to the Cincinnati. On this subject, the section, as prepared by him, was an unjust and incorrect Philippic against General Washington and the American officers in general. I wrote a substitute for it, which he adopted, but still retaining considerable of his own matter, and interspersing it in various parts.

Page 33. *"In a government constituted," &c.* Here begins the artful complexion he has given to the two parties, federal and republican. In describing the first by their views and motives, he implies an opposition to those motives in their opponents which is totally untrue. The real difference consisted in their different degrees of inclination to monarchy or republicanism. The federalists wished for everything which would approach our new government to a monarchy. The republicans to preserve it essentially republican. This was the true origin of the division, and remains still the essential principle of difference between the two parties.

---

## BACKGROUND OF THE DECLARATION OF INDEPENDENCE[1]

May 12, 1819

An absence of some time at an occasional and distant residence, must apologize for the delay in acknowledging the receipt of your favor of April

[1] Letter to Samuel A. Wells, grandson of Samuel Adams.

12; and, candor obliges me to add, that it has been somewhat extended by an aversion to writing, as well as to calls on my memory for facts so much obliterated from it by time, as to lessen my own confidence in the traces which seem to remain. One of the inquiries in your letter, however, may be answered without an appeal to the memory. It is that respecting the question, whether committees of correspondence originated in Virginia, or Massachusetts? on which you suppose me to have claimed it for Virginia; but certainly I have never made such a claim. The idea, I suppose, has been taken up from what is said in Wirt's history of Mr. Henry, page 87, and from an inexact attention to its precise terms. It is there said, "this House (of Burgesses, of Virginia) had the merit of originating that powerful engine of resistance, corresponding committees *between the legislatures of the different colonies.*" That the fact, as here expressed, is true, your letter bears witness, when it says, that the resolutions of Virginia, for this purpose, were transmitted to the speakers of the different assemblies, and by that of Massachusetts, was laid, at the next session, before that body, who appointed a committee for the specified object: adding, "thus, in Massachusetts, there were two committees of correspondence, one chosen by the people, the other appointed by the House of Assembly; in the former, Massachusetts preceded Virginia; in the latter, Virginia preceded Massachusetts." To the origination of committees for the interior correspondence between the counties and towns of a State, I know of no claim on the part of Virginia; and certainly none was ever made by myself. I perceive, however, one error, into which memory had led me. Our committee for national correspondence, was appointed in March, '73, and I well remember, that going to Williamsburg, in the month of June following, Peyton Randolph, our Chairman, told me that messengers bearing despatches between the two States, had crossed each other by the way, that of Virginia carrying our propositions for a committee of national correspondence, and that of Massachusetts, bringing, as my memory suggested, a similar proposition. But here I must have misremembered; and the resolutions brought us from Massachusetts, were probably those you mention of the town-meeting of Boston, on the motion of Mr. Samuel Adams, appointing a committee "to state the rights of the colonists, and of that province in particular, and the infringements of them; to communicate them to the several towns, as the sense of the town of Boston, and to request, of each town, a free communication of its sentiments on the subject." I suppose, therefore, that these resolutions were not received, as you think, while the House of Burgesses was in session in March, 1773, but a few days after we rose, and were probably what was sent by the messenger, who crossed ours by the way. They may, however, have been still different. I must, therefore, have been mistaken in supposing, and stating to Mr. Wirt, that the proposition of a committee for national correspondence, was nearly simultaneous in Virginia and Massachusetts.

A similar misapprehension of another passage in Mr. Wirt's book, for which I am also quoted, has produced a similar reclamation on the part of Massachusetts, by some of her most distinguished and estimable citizens. I had been applied to by Mr. Wirt, for such facts respecting Mr. Henry, as my intimacy with him, and participation in the transactions of the day, might have placed within my knowledge. I accordingly committed them to paper; and Virginia being the theatre of his action, was the only subject within my contemplation. While speaking of him, of the resolutions and measures here, in which he had the acknowledged lead, I used the expression, that "Mr. Henry certainly gave the first impulse to the ball of revolution." [Wirt, page 41.] The expression is indeed general, and in all its extension, would comprehend all the sister States; but indulgent construction would restrain it, as was really meant, to the subject matter under contemplation, which was Virginia alone; according to the rule of the lawyers, and a fair canon of general criticism, that every expression should be construed *secundum subjectam materiam*. Where the first attack was made, there must have been of course, the first act of resistance, and that was in Massachusetts. Our first overt act of war, was Mr. Henry's embodying a force of militia from several counties, regularly armed and organized, marching them in military array, and making reprisal on the King's treasury at the seat of government, for the public powder taken away by his Governor. This was on the last days of April, 1775. Your formal battle of Lexington, was ten or twelve days before that, and greatly overshadowed in importance, as it preceded in time, our little affray, which merely amounted to a levying of arms against the King; and very possibly, you had had military affrays before the regular battle of Lexington.

These explanations will, I hope, assure you, Sir, that so far as either facts or opinions have been truly quoted from me, they have never been meant to intercept the just fame of Massachusetts, for the promptitude and perseverance of her early resistance. We willingly cede to her the laud of having been (although not exclusively) "the cradle of sound principles," and, if some of us believe she has deflected from them in her course, we retain full confidence in her ultimate return to them.

I will now proceed to your quotation from Mr. Galloway's statement of what passed in Congress, on their Declaration of Independence; in which statement there is not one word of truth, and where bearing some resemblance to truth, it is an entire perversion of it. I do not charge this on Mr. Galloway himself; his desertion having taken place long before these measures, he doubtless received his information from some of the loyal friends whom he left behind him. But as yourself, as well as others, appear embarrassed by inconsistent accounts of the proceedings on that memorable occasion, and as those who have endeavored to restore the truth, have themselves committed some errors, I will give you some extracts from a written document on that subject; for the truth of which I pledge myself to heaven and earth; having, while the question of Independence was under consideration before Congress, taken written notes, in my seat, of what was passing, and reduced them to form on the final conclusion. I have now before me that paper, from which the following are extracts. "Friday, June 7th, 1776. The delegates from Virginia moved, in obedience to instructions from their constituents, that the Congress should declare that these United Colonies are, and of right ought to be, free and independent States; that they are absolved from all allegiance to the British crown, and that all political connection between them and the State of Great Britain is, and ought to be totally dissolved; that measures should be immediately taken for procuring the assistance of foreign powers, and a Confederation be formed to bind the colonies more closely together. The House, being obliged to attend at that time to some other business, the proposition was referred to the next day, when the members were ordered to attend punctually at ten o'clock, Saturday, June 8th. They proceeded to take it into consideration, and referred it to a committee of the whole, into which they immediately resolved themselves, and passed that day in debating on the subject.

"It appearing in the course of these debates, that the colonies of New York, New Jersey, Pennsylvania, Delaware, Maryland and South Carolina, were not yet matured for falling from the parent stem, but that they were fast advancing to that state, it was thought most prudent to wait a while for them, and to postpone the final decision to July 1st. But that this might occasion as little delay as possible, a Committee was appointed to prepare a Declaration of Independence. The Committee were John Adams, Dr. Franklin, Roger Sherman, Robert R. Livingston and myself. This was reported to the House on Friday, the 28th of June, when it was read and ordered to lie on the table. On Monday, the 1st of July, the House resolved itself into a Committee of the whole, and resumed the consideration of the original motion made by the delegates of Virginia, which, being again debated through the day, was carried in the affirmative by the votes of New Hampshire, Connecticut, Massachusetts, Rhode Island, New Jersey, Maryland, Virginia, North Carolina and Georgia. South Carolina and Pennsylvania voted against it. Delaware had but two members present, and they were divided. The delegates from New York declared they were for it themselves, and were assured their constituents were for it; but that their instructions having been drawn near a twelvemonth before, when reconciliation was still the general object, they were enjoined by them, to do nothing which should impede that object. They, therefore, thought themselves not justifiable in voting on either side, and asked leave to withdraw from the question, which was given them. The Committee rose, and reported their resolutions to the House. Mr. Rutledge, of South Carolina, then requested the determination might be put off to the next day, as he believed his colleagues, though they disapproved of the resolution, would then join in it for the sake of unanimity. The ultimate question, whether the House would agree to the resolution of the Committee, was accordingly postponed to the next day, when it was again moved, and South Carolina concurred in voting for it. In the meantime, a third member had come post from the Delaware counties, and turned the vote of that colony in favor of the resolution. Members of a different sentiment attending that morning from Pennsylvania also, her vote was changed; so that the whole twelve colonies, who were authorized to vote at all, gave their votes for it; and within a few days [July 9th] the convention of New York approved of it, and this supplied the void occasioned by the withdrawing of their delegates from the vote." [Be careful to observe, that this vacillation and vote were on the original motion of the 7th of June, by the Virginia delegates, that Congress should declare the colonies independent.] "Congress proceeded, the same day, to consider the Declaration of Independence, which had been reported and laid on the table the Friday preceding, and on Monday, referred to a Committee of the whole. The pusillanimous idea, that we had friends in England worth keeping terms with, still haunted the minds of many. For this reason, those passages which conveyed censures on the people of England were struck out, lest they should give them offence. The debates having taken up the greater parts of the second, third and fourth days of July, were, in the evening of the last, closed; the Declaration was reported by the Committee, agreed to by the House, and signed by every member present except Mr. Dickinson." So far my notes.

Governor M'Kean, in his letter to McCorkle of July 16th, 1817, has thrown some lights on the transactions of that day; but, trusting to his memory chiefly, at an age when our memories are not to be trusted, he has confounded two questions, and ascribed proceedings to one which belonged to the other. These two questions were, 1st, the Virginia motion of June the 7th, to declare Independence; and 2d, the actual Declaration, its matter and form. Thus he states the question on the Declaration itself, as decided on the 1st of July; but it was the Virginia motion which was voted on that day in committee of the whole; South Carolina, as well as Pennsylvania, then voting against it. But the ultimate decision in *the House,* on the report of the Committee, being, by request, postponed to the next morning, all the States voted for it, except New York, whose vote was delayed for the reason before stated. It was not till the 2d of July, that the Declaration itself was taken up; nor till the 4th, that it was decided, and it was signed by every member present, except Mr. Dickinson.

The subsequent signatures of members who were not then present, and some of them not yet in office, is easily explained, if we observe who they were; to wit, that they were of New York and Pennsylvania. New York did not sign till the 15th, because it was not till the 9th (five days after the general signature), that their Convention authorized them to do so. The Convention of Pennsylvania, learning that it had been signed by a minority only of their delegates, named a new delegation on the 20th, leaving out Mr. Dickinson, who had refused to sign, Willing and Humphreys who had withdrawn, reappointing the three members who had signed, Morris, who had not been present, and five new ones, to wit, Rush, Clymer, Smith, Taylor and Ross: and Morris, and the five new members were permitted to sign, because it manifested the assent of their full delegation, and the express will of their Convention, which might have been doubted on the former signature of a minority only. Why the signature of Thornton, of New Hampshire, was permitted so late as the 4th of November, I cannot now say; but undoubtedly for some particular reason, which we should find to have been good, had it been expressed. These were the only post-signers, and you see, Sir, that there were solid reasons for receiving those of New York and Pennsylvania, and that this circumstance in no wise affects the faith of this Declaratory Charter of our rights, and of the rights of man.

With a view to correct errors of fact before they become inveterate by repetition, I have stated what I find essentially material in my papers, but with that brevity, which the labor of writing constrains me to use.

On the four particular articles of enquiry in your letter, respecting your grandfather, the venerable Samuel Adams, neither memory nor memorandums enable me to give any information. I can say that he was truly a great man, wise in council, fertile in resources, immoveable in his purposes, and had, I think, a greater share than any other member, in advising and directing our measures, in the Northern war. As a speaker, he could not be compared with his living colleague and namesake, whose deep conceptions, nervous style, and undaunted firmness, made him truly our bulwark in debate. But Mr. Samuel Adams, although not of fluent elocution, was so rigorously logical, so clear in his views, abundant in good sense, and master always of his subject, that he commanded the most profound attention, whenever he rose in an assembly, by which the froth of declamation was heard with the most sovereign contempt. I sincerely rejoice, that the record of his worth is to be undertaken by one so much disposed as you will be, to hand him down fairly to that posterity for whose liberty and happiness he was so zealous a laborer.

With sentiments of sincere veneration for his memory, accept yourself this tribute to it, with the assurance of my great respect.

P.S. August 6th, 1822. Since the date of this letter, to-wit, this day, August 6, '22, I have received the new publication of the Secret Journals of Congress, wherein is stated a resolution of July 19th, 1776, that the Declaration passed on the 4th, be fairly engrossed on parchment, and when engrossed, be signed by every member; and another of August 2nd, that being engrossed and compared at the table, it was signed by the members; that is to say, the copy engrossed on parchment (for durability) was signed by the members, after being compared at the table, with the original one signed on paper as before stated. I add this P.S. to the copy of my letter to Mr. Wells, to prevent confounding the signature of the original with that of the copy engrossed on parchment.

---

*Chapter III*

# LAWS AND CONSTITUTIONS

## BILL TO ABOLISH ENTAILS[1]

1776

A BILL TO ENABLE TENANTS IN TAIL TO CONVEY THEIR LANDS IN FEE-SIMPLE

Whereas the perpetuation of property in certain families by means of gifts made to them in fee-simple is contrary to good policy, tends to deceive fair traders who give credit on the visible possession of such estates, discourages the holder thereof from taking care and improving the same, and sometimes does injury to the morals of youth by rendering them independent of, and disobedient to, their parents; and whereas the former method of docking such estates tail by special act of assembly formed for every particular case employed very much time of the legislature, was burthensome to the public, and also to the individual who made application for such acts:

Be it therefore enacted by—[2]

and it is hereby enacted by authority of the same that any person who now hath, or hereafter may have any estate in fee tail general or special in any lands or slaves in possession, or who now is or hereafter may be entitled to any such estate tail in reversion or remainder after the determination of any estate for life or lives or of any lesser estate, whether such estate hath been or shall be created by deed, will, act of assembly, or any other ways or means shall have full power to pass, convey, or assure in fee-simple or for any lesser

[1] Jefferson introduced this bill into the Virginia legislature on October 14, 1776; it was amended and passed on October 23 by the lower house and on November 1 by the Senate. He considered this bill the first important attack on the Virginia aristocracy, as he tells in his *Autobiography*: "The transmission of this property from generation to generation in the same name raised up a distinct set of families who, being privileged by law in the perpetuation of their wealth, were thus formed into a Patrician order. . . . To annual this privilege, and instead of an aristocracy of wealth, of more harm and danger, than benefit, to society, to make an opening for the aristocracy of virtue and talent . . . , was deemed essential to a well-ordered republic."

[2] The State Constitution had just been adopted and the enacting clause was not yet defined; hence the blank in Jefferson's draft.

estate the said lands or slaves, or use in lands or slaves or such reversion or remainder therein, or any part or parcel thereof, to any person or persons whatsoever by deed or deeds of feoffment, gift, grant, exchange, partition, lease, release, bargain, and sale, covenant to stand seized to uses, deed to lead uses, or by his last will and testament, or by any other mode or form of conveyance or assurance by which such lands or slaves, or use in lands or slaves, or such reversion or remainder therein might have been passed, conveyed or assured had the same been held in fee-simple by the person so passing, conveying or assuring the same: and such deed, will or other conveyance shall be good and effectual to bar the issue in tail and those in remainder and revert as to such estate or estates so passed, conveyed, or assured by such deed, will, or other conveyance.

Provided nevertheless that such deed, will, or other conveyance shall be executed, acknowledged, or proved, and recorded in like manner as, and in all cases where, the same should have been done, had the person or persons so conveying or assuring held the said lands or slaves, or use of lands and slaves or such reversion or remainder in fee-simple.

## A BILL CONCERNING SLAVES[1]

### 1779

SECTION I. Be it enacted by the General Assembly, that no persons shall, henceforth, be slaves within this commonwealth, except such as were so on the first day of this present session of Assembly, and the descendants of the females of them.

SECTION II. Negroes and mulattoes which shall hereafter be brought into this commonwealth and kept therein one whole year, together, or so long at different times as shall amount to one year, shall be free. But if they shall not depart the commonwealth within one year thereafter they shall be out of the protection of the laws.

SECTION III. Those which shall come into this commonwealth of their own accord shall be out of the protection of the laws; save only such as being seafaring persons and navigating vessels hither, shall not leave the same while here more than twenty four hours together.

SECTION IV. It shall not be lawful for any person to emancipate a slave but by deed executed, proved and recorded as is required by law in the case of a conveyance of goods and chattels, on consideration not deemed valuable in law, or by last will and testament, and with the free consent of such slave, expressed in presence of the court of the county wherein he resides. And if such slave, so emancipated, shall not within one year thereafter,

[1] Ch. LI of the *Report of the Revisors.*

depart the commonwealth, he shall be out of the protection of the laws. All conditions, restrictions and limitations annexed to any act of emancipation shall be void from the time such emancipation is to take place.

SECTION V. If any white woman shall have a child by a Negro or mulatto, she and her child shall depart the commonwealth within one year thereafter. If they shall fail so to do, the woman shall be out of the protection of the laws, and the child shall be bound out by the Aldermen of the county, in like manner as poor orphans are by law directed to be, and within one year after its term of service expired shall depart the commonwealth, or on failure so to do, shall be out of the protection of the laws.

SECTION VI. Where any of the persons before described shall be disabled from departing the commonwealth by grievous sickness, the protection of the law shall be continued to him until such disability be removed: And if the county shall in the meantime, incur any expense in taking care of him, as of other county poor, the Aldermen shall be entitled to recover the same from his master, if he had one, his heirs, executors and administrators.

SECTION VII. No Negro or mulatto shall be a witness except in pleas of the commonwealth against Negroes or mulattoes, or in civil pleas wherein Negroes or mulattoes alone shall be parties.

SECTION VIII. No slave shall go from the tenements of his master, or other person with whom he lives, without a pass, or some letter or token whereby it may appear that he is proceeding by authority from his master, employer, or overseer: If he does, it shall be lawful for any person to apprehend and carry him before a Justice of the Peace, to be by his order punished with stripes, or not in his direction.

SECTION IX. No slaves shall keep any arms whatever, nor pass, unless with written orders from his master or employer, or in his company, with arms from one place to another. Arms in possession of a slave contrary to this prohibition shall be forfeited to him who will seize them.

SECTION X. Riots, routs, unlawful assemblies, trespasses and seditious speeches by a Negro or mulatto shall be punished with stripes at the discretion of a Justice of the Peace; and he who will may apprehend and carry him before such a Justice.

## A BILL FOR PROPORTIONING CRIMES AND PUNISHMENTS[1]

1779

Whereas, it frequently happens that wicked and dissolute men, resigning themselves to the dominion of inordinate passions, commit violations on the

[1] This forms Ch. LXIV of the *Report of the Revisors*. The text is taken from the Congress Edition of the *Writings*.

On November 1, 1778, Jefferson wrote to George Wythe: "I have got through the bill for lives, liberties, and property of others, and, the secure enjoyment of these having principally induced men to enter into society, government would be defective in its principal purpose, were it not to restrain such criminal acts, by inflicting due punishments on those who perpetrate them; but it appears, at the same time, equally deducible from the purposes of society, that a member thereof, committing an inferior injury, does not wholly forfeit the protection of his fellow citizens, but, after suffering a punishment in proportion to his offence, is entitled to their protection from all greater pain, so that it becomes a duty in the legislature to arrange, in a proper scale, the crimes which it may be necessary for them to repress, and to adjust thereto a corresponding gradation of punishments.

And whereas, the reformation of offenders, though an object worthy the attention of the laws, is not effected at all by capital punishments, which exterminate instead of reforming, and should be the last melancholy resource against those whose existence is become inconsistent with the safety of their fellow citizens, which also weaken the State, by cutting off so many who, if reformed, might be restored sound members to society, who, even under a course of correction, might be rendered useful in various labors for the public, and would be living and long-continued spectacles to deter others from committing the like offences.

And forasmuch as the experience of all ages and countries hath shown, that cruel and sanguinary laws defeat their own purpose, by engaging the

'proportioning crimes and punishments in cases heretofore capital,' and now enclose it to you with a request that you will be so good, as scrupulously to examine and correct it, that it may be presented to our committee with as few defects as possible. In its style, I have aimed at accuracy, brevity, and simplicity, preserving, however, the very words of the established law, wherever their meaning had been sanctioned by judicial decisions, or rendered technical by usage. The same matter, if couched in the modern statutory language, with all its tautologies, redundancies, and circumlocutions, would have spread itself over many pages, and been unintelligible to those whom it most concerns. Indeed, I wished to exhibit a sample of reformation in the barbarous style into which modern statutes have degenerated from their ancient simplicity. And I must pray you to be as watchful over what I have not said, as what is said; for the omissions of this bill have all their positive meaning. I have thought it better to drop, in silence, the laws we mean to discontinue, and let them be swept away by the general negative words of this, than to detail them in clauses of express repeal. By the side of the text I have written the notes I made, as I went along, for the benefit of my own memory. They may serve to draw your attention to questions, to which the expressions or the omissions of the text may give rise. The extracts from the Anglo-Saxon laws, the sources of the Common law, I wrote in their original, for my own satisfaction; but I have added Latin, or liberal English translations. From the time of Canute to that of the Magna Charta, you know, the text of our statutes is preserved to us in Latin only, and some old French.

"I have strictly observed the scale of punishments settled by the Committee, without being entirely satisfied with it. The *Lex talionis,* although a restitution of the Common law, to the simplicity of which we have generally found it so advantageous to return, will be revolting to the humanized feelings of modern times. An eye for an eye, and a hand for a hand, will exhibit spectacles in execution whose moral effect would be questionable; and even the *membrum pro membro* of Bracton, or the punishment of the offending member, although long authorized by our law, for the same offence in a slave has, you know, been not long since repealed in conformity with public sentiment. This needs reconsideration."

benevolence of mankind to withhold prosecutions, to smother testimony, or to listen to it with bias, when, if the punishment were only proportioned to the injury, men would feel it their inclination, as well as their duty, to see the laws observed.

For rendering crimes and punishments, therefore, more proportionate to each other:

Be it enacted by the General Assembly, that no crime shall be henceforth punished by the deprivation of life or limb,[2] except those hereinafter ordained to be so punished.

[3] If a man do levy war [4] against the Commonwealth [*in the same*], or be adherent to the enemies of the Commonwealth [*within the same*],[5] giving to them aid or comfort in the Commonwealth, or elsewhere, and thereof be convicted of open deed, by the evidence of two sufficient witnesses, or his own voluntary confession, the said cases, and no [6] others, shall be adjudged treasons which extend to the Commonwealth, and the person so convicted shall suffer death, by hanging,[7] and shall forfeit his lands and goods to the Commonwealth.

If any person commit petty treason, or a husband murder his wife, a parent [8] his child, or a child his parent, he shall suffer death by hanging, and his body be delivered to anatomists to be dissected.

[2] This takes away the punishment of cutting off the hand of a person striking another, or drawing his sword in one of the superior courts of justice. Stamf. P. C. 38. 33. H. 8. c. 12. In an earlier stage of the Common law, it was death. Gif hwa gefeohte on Cyninges huse sy he scyldig ealles his yrfes, and sy on Cyninges dome hwæther he lif age de nage: *si quis in regis domo pugnet, perdat omnem suam haereditatem, et in regis sit arbitrio, possideat vitam an non possideat.* Ll. Inae. 6. Gif hwa on Cyninges healle gefeohte, oththe his wæpne gebrede, and hine mon gefo, sy thæt on Cyninges dome swa death, swa lif, swa he him forgyfan wille: *si quis in aula regia pugnet, vel arma sua extrahat et capiatur, sit in regis arbitrio tam mors quam vita, sicut ei condonare voluerit.* Ll. Alfr. 7. Gif hwa on Cyninges hirede gefeohte tholige thæt lifes, buton se Cyning him gearian wille: *si quis in regia dimicat, perdat vitam, nisi rex hoc illi condonare velit.* Ll. Cnuti. 56. 4. Bl. 125.—T. J.

[3] 25. E. 3. st. 5. c. 2. 7. W. 3. c. 3. § 2.—T. J.

[4] Though the crime of an accomplice in treason is not here described, yet, Lord Coke says, the partaking and maintaining a treason herein described, makes him a principal in that treason: it being a rule that in treason all are principals. 3 Inst. 138. 2 Inst. 590. 1 H. 6. 5.—T. J.

[5] These words in the English statute narrow its operation. A man adhering to the enemies of the Commonwealth, in a foreign country, would certainly not be guilty of treason with us, if these words be retained. The convictions of treason of that kind in England have been under that branch of the statute which makes the compassing the king's death treason. Foster 196. 197. But as we omit that branch, we must by other means reach this flagrant case.—T. J.

[6] The stat. 25. E. 3. directs all other cases of treasons to await the opinion of Parliament. This has the effect of negative words, excluding all other treasons. As we drop that part of the statute, we must, by negative words, prevent an inundation of common law treasons. I strike out the word "it," therefore, and insert "the said cases, and no others." Quære, how far those negative words may affect the case of accomplices above mentioned? Though if their case was within the statute, so as that it needed not await the opinion of Parliament, it should seem to be also within our act, so as not to be ousted by the negative words.—T. J.

[7] This implies "by the neck." See 2 Hawk. 544. notes n. o.—T. J.

[8] By the stat. 21. Jac. 1. c. 27. and Act Ass. 1170. c. 12. concealment by the mother of the death of a bastard child is made murder. In justification of this, it is said, that shame is a feeling which operates so strongly on the mind, as frequently to induce the mother of such a child to murder it, in order to conceal her disgrace. The act of concealment, therefore,

Whosoever committeth murder by poisoning shall suffer death by poison.

Whosoever committeth murder by way of duel shall suffer death by hanging; and if he were the challenger, his body, after death, shall be gibbetted.[9] He who removeth it from the gibbet shall be guilty of a misdemeanor; and the officer shall see that it be replaced.

Whosoever shall commit murder in any other way shall suffer death by hanging.

And in all cases of petty treason and murder, one half of the lands and goods of the offender, shall be forfeited to the next of kin to the person killed, and the other half descend and go to his own representatives. Save only, where one shall slay the challenger in a duel,[10] in which case, no part of his lands or goods shall be forfeited to the kindred of the party slain, but, instead thereof, a moiety shall go to the Commonwealth.

The same evidence[11] shall suffice, and order and course[12] of trial

proves she was influenced by shame, and that influence produces a presumption that she murdered the child. The effect of this law then is, to make what, in its nature, is only presumptive evidence of a murder conclusive of that fact. To this I answer, 1. So many children die before or soon after birth, that to presume all those murdered who are found dead, is a presumption which will lead us oftener wrong than right, and consequently would shed more blood than it would save. 2. If the child were born dead, the mother would naturally choose rather to conceal it, in hopes of still keeping a good character in the neighborhood. So that the act of concealment is far from proving the guilt of murder on the mother. 3. If shame be a powerful affection of the mind, is not parental love also? Is it not the strongest affection known? Is it not greater than even that of self-preservation? While we draw presumptions from shame, one affection of the mind, against the life of the prisoner, should we not give some weight to presumptions from parental love, an affection at least as strong, in favor of life? If concealment of the fact is a presumptive evidence of murder, so strong as to overbalance all other evidence that may possibly be produced to take away the presumption, why not trust the force of this incontestable presumption to the jury, who are, in a regular course, to hear presumptive, as well as positive testimony? If the presumption arising from the act of concealment, may be destroyed by proof positive or circumstantial to the contrary, why should the legislature preclude that contrary proof? Objection. The crime is difficult to prove, being usually committed in secret. Answer. But circumstantial proof will do; for example, marks of violence, the behavior, countenance, &c. of the prisoner, &c. And if conclusive proof be difficult to be obtained, shall we therefore fasten irremovably upon equivocal proof? Can we change the nature of what is contestable, and make it incontestable? Can we make that conclusive which God and nature have made inconclusive? Solon made no law against parricide, supposing it impossible that anyone could be guilty of it; and the Persians, from the same opinion, adjudged all who killed their reputed parents to be bastards; and although parental be yet stronger than filial affection, we admit saticide proved on the most equivocal testimony, whilst they rejected all proof of an act certainly not more repugnant to nature, as of a thing impossible, unprovable. See Beccaria, § 31.—T. J.

[9] 25. G. 2. c. 37.—T. J.

[10] Quære, if the estates of both parties in a duel, should not be forfeited? The deceased is equally guilty with a suicide.—T. J.

[11] Quære, if these words may not be omitted? By the Common law, one witness in treason was sufficient. Foster 233. Plowd. 8. a. Mirror c. 3. § 34. Waterhouse on Fortesc. de laud. 252. Carth. 144. per. Holt. But Lord Coke, contra 3 inst. 26. The stat. 1. E. 6. c. 12. & 5. E. 6. c. 11. first required two witnesses in treason. The clause against high treason supra, does the same as to high treason; but it seems if 1st and 5th E. 6. are dropped, Petty treason will be tried and proved, as at Common law, by one witness. But quære, Lord Coke being contra, whose opinion it is ever dangerous to neglect.—T. J.

[12] These words are intended to take away the peremptory challenge of thirty-five jurors. The same words being used 1. 2. Ph. & M. c. 10. are deemed to have restored the peremptory challenge in high treason; and consequently are sufficient to take it away. Foster 237. —T. J.

be observed in cases of petty treason, as in those of other[13] murders.

Whosoever shall be guilty of manslaughter,[14] shall, for the first offence, be condemned to hard[15] labor for seven years in the public works, shall forfeit one half of his lands and goods to the next of kin to the person slain; the other half to be sequestered during such term, in the hands and to the use of the Commonwealth, allowing a reasonable part of the profits for the support of his family. The second offence shall be deemed murder.

And where persons, meaning to commit a trespass[16] only, or larceny, or other unlawful deed, and doing an act from which involuntary homicide hath ensued, have heretofore been adjudged guilty of manslaughter, or of murder, by transferring such their unlawful intention to an act, much more penal than they could have in probable contemplation; no such case shall hereafter be deemed manslaughter, unless manslaughter was intended, nor murder, unless murder was intended.

In other cases of homicide, the law will not add to the miseries of the party, by punishments and forfeitures.[17]

[13] Petty treason is considered in law only as an aggravated murder. Foster 107. 323. A pardon of all murders, pardons petty treason. 1 Hale P. C. 378. see 2 H. P. C. 340. 342. It is also included in the word "felony," so that a pardon of all felonies, pardons petty treason.—T. J.

[14] Manslaughter is punishable at law, by burning in the hands, and forfeiture of chattels. —T. J.

[15] It is best, in this act, to lay down principles only, in order that it may not forever be undergoing change; and, to carry into effect the minuter parts of it, frame a bill "for the employment and government of felons, or malefactors, condemned to labor for the Commonwealth," which may serve as an Appendix to this, and in which all the particulars requisite may be directed; and as experience will, from time to time, be pointing out amendments, these may be made without touching this fundamental act. See More's Utopia p. 50. for some good hints. Fugitives might, in such a bill, be obliged to work two days for every one they absent themselves.—T. J.

[16] The shooting at a wild fowl, and killing a man, is homicide by misadventure. Shooting at a pullet, without any design to take it away, is manslaughter; and with a design to take it away, is murder. 6 Sta. tr. 222. To shoot at the poultry of another, and thereby set fire to his house, is arson, in the opinion of some. Dalt. c. 116. 1. Hale's P. C. 569. c. contra. —T. J.

[17] Beccaria. § 32. Suicide. Homicides are, 1. Justifiable. 2. Excusable. 3. Felonious. For the last, punishments have been already provided. The first are held to be totally without guilt, or rather commendable. The second are in some cases not quite unblamable. These should subject the party to marks of contrition; *viz.*, the killing of a man in defence of property; so also in defence of one's person, which is a species of excusable homicide; because, although cases may happen where these also are commendable, yet most frequently they are done on too slight appearance of danger; as in return for a blow, kick, fillip, &c.; or on a person's getting into a house, not *animo furandi*, but perhaps *veneris causa*, &c. Bracton says, "*si quis furem nocturnum occident, ita demum impune foret, si parcere ei sine periculo suo non potuit, si autem potuit, aliter erit. Item erit si quis hamsokne quae dicitur invasio domus contra pacem domini regis in domo sua se defenderit, et invasor occisus fuerit; impersecutus et insultus remanebit, si ille quem invasit aliter se defendere non potuit; dicitur enim quod non est dignus habere pacem qui non vult observare eam.*" L. 3. c. 23. § 3. "*Qui latronem occiderit, non tenetur, nocturnum vel diurnum, si aliter periculum evadere non possit; tenetur tamen si possit. Item non tenetur si per infortunium, et non animo et voluntate occidendi, nec dolus, nec culpa ejus inveniatur.*" L. 3. c. 36. § 1. The stat. 24. H. 8. c. 5. is therefore merely declaratory of the Common law. See on the general subject Puffend. 2. 5. § 10. 11. 12. 16. 17. Excusable homicides are by misadventure, or in self-defence. It is the opinion of some lawyers, that the Common law punished these with death, and that the statute of Marl-

Whenever sentence of death shall have been pronounced against any person for treason or murder, execution shall be done on the next day but one after such sentence, unless it be Sunday, and then on the Monday following.[18]

Whosoever shall be guilty of rape,[19] polygamy,[20] or sodomy[21] with man

bridge, c. 26. and Gloucester, c. 9. first took away this by giving them title to a pardon, as matter of right, and a writ of restitution of their goods. See 2. Inst. 148. 315. 3. Inst. 55. Bracton L. 3. c. 4. § 2. Fleta L. 1. c. 23. § 14. 15. 21. E. 3. 23. But it is believed never to have been capital. 1. H. P. C. 425. 1 Hawk. 75. Foster, 282. 4. Bl. 188. It seems doubtful also, whether at Common law, the party forfeited all his chattels in this case, or only paid a weregild. Foster, *ubi supra,* doubts, and thinks it of no consequence, as the statute of Gloucester entitles the party to Royal grace, which goes as well to forfeiture as life. To me there seems no reason for calling these excusable homicides, and the killing a man in defence of property, a justifiable homicide. The latter is less guiltless than misadventure or self-defence.

Suicide is by law punishable by forfeiture of chattels. This bill exempts it from forfeiture. The suicide injures the State less than he who leaves it with his effects. If the latter then be not punished, the former should not. As to the example, we need not fear its influence. Men are too much attached to life, to exhibit frequent instances of depriving themselves of it. At any rate, the quasi-punishment of confiscation will not prevent it. For if one be found who can calmly determine to renounce life, who is so weary of his existence here, as rather to make experiment of what is beyond the grave, can we suppose him, in such a state of mind, susceptible of influence from the losses to his family from confiscation? That men in general, too, disapprove of this severity, is apparent from the constant practice of juries finding the suicide in a state of insanity; because they have no other way of saving the forfeiture. Let it then be done away.—T. J.

[18] Beccaria. § 19. 25. G. 2. c. 37.—T. J.

[19] 13. E. 1. c. 34. Forcible abduction of a woman having substance, is felony by 3. H. 7. c. 2. 3. Inst. 61. 4. Bl. 208. If goods be taken, it will be felony as to them, without this statute; and as to the abduction of the woman, quære if not better to leave that, and also kidnapping, 4. Bl. 219. to the Common law remedies, *viz.,* fine, imprisonment, and pillory, Raym. 474. 2 Show. 221. Skin. 47. Comb. 10. the writs of Homine replegiando, Capias in Withernam, Habeas corpus, and the action of trespass? Rape was felony at the Common law. 3. Inst. 60. but see 2. Inst. 181. further—for its definition see 2. Inst. 180. Bracton, L. 3. c. 28. § 1. says the punishment of rape is *"amissio membrorum, ut sit membrum pro membro, quia virgo, cum corrumpitur, membrum amittit, et ideo corruptor puniatur in eo in quo deliquit; oculos igitur amittat propter aspectum decoris quo virginem concupivit; amittat et testiculos qui calorem stupri induxerunt. Olim quidem corruptores virginitatis et castitatis suspendebantur et eorum fautores, &c. Modernis tamen temporibus aliter observatur,"* &c. And Fleta, *"solet justiciarius pro quolibet mahemio ad amissionem testiculorum vel oculorum convictum condemnare, sed non sine errore, eo quod id judicium nisi in corruptione virginum tantum competebat; nam pro virginitatis corruptione solebant abscidi et merito judicari, ut sic pro membro quod abstulit, membrum per quod deliquit amitteret, viz., testiculos, qui calorem stupri induxerunt,"* &c. Fleta, L. 1. c. 40. § 4. "Gif theow man theowne to nydhed genyde, gabte mid his eowende:" *"Si servus servam ad stuprum coegerit, compenset hoc virga sua virili. Si quis puellam,"* &c. Ll. Aelfridi. 25. *"Hi purgist femme per forze forfait ad les membres."* Ll. Gul. conq. 19. In Dyer, 305, a man was indicted, and found guilty of a rape on a girl of seven years old. The court "doubted of the rape of so tender a girl; but if she had been nine years old, it would have been otherwise." 14. Eliz. Therefore the statute 18. Eliz. c. 6. says, "For plain declaration of law, be it enacted, that if any person shall unlawfully and carnally know and abuse any woman child, under the age of ten years, &c., he shall suffer as a felon, without allowance of clergy." Lord Hale, however, 1. P. C. 630. thinks it rape independent of that statute, to know carnally, a girl under twelve, the age of consent. Yet 4. Bl. 212. seems to neglect this opinion; and as it was founded on the words of 3. E. 1. c. 13. and this is with us omitted, the offence of carnally knowing a girl under twelve, or ten years of age, will not be distinguished from that of any other.—T. J.

[20] 1. Jac. 1. c. 11. Polygamy was not penal till the statute 1. Jac. The law contented itself with the nullity of the act. 4. Bl. 163. 3. Inst. 88.—T. J.

[21] 25. H. 8. c. 6. Buggery is twofold. 1. With mankind, 2. with beasts. Buggery is the genus, of which sodomy and bestiality, are the species. 12. Co. 37. says, "note that sodomy

or woman, shall be punished, if a man, by castration,[22] if a woman, by cutting through the cartilage of her nose a hole of one half inch in diameter at the least.

But no one shall be punished for polygamy, who shall have married after probable information of the death of his or her husband or wife, or after his or her husband or wife, hath absented him or herself, so that no notice of his or her being alive hath reached such person for seven years together, or hath suffered the punishments before prescribed for rape, polygamy, or sodomy.

Whosoever on purpose, and of malice forethought, shall maim [23] another, or shall disfigure him, by cutting out or disabling the tongue, slitting or cutting off a nose, lip, or ear, branding, or otherwise, shall be maimed, or disfigured in like [24] sort: or if that cannot be, for want of the same part, then as nearly as may be, in some other part of at least equal value and estimation, in the opinion of a jury, and moreover, shall forfeit one half of his lands and goods to the sufferer.

Whosoever shall counterfeit [25] any coin, current by law within this Com-

is with mankind." But Finch's L. B. 3. c. 24. "Sodomiary is a carnal copulation against nature, to wit, of man or woman in the same sex, or of either of them with beasts." 12. Co. 36. says, "it appears by the ancient authorities of the law that this was felony." Yet the 25. H. 8. declares it felony, as if supposed not to be so. Britton, c. 9. says, that sodomites are to be burnt. F.N.B. 269. b. Fleta, L. 1. c. 37. says, *"pecorantes et Sodomitae in terra vivi confodiantur."* The Mirror makes it treason. Bestiality can never make any progress; it cannot therefore be injurious to society in any great degree, which is the true measure of criminality in *foro civili,* and will ever be properly and severely punished, by universal derision. It may, therefore, be omitted. It was anciently punished with death, as it has been latterly. Ll. Aelfrid. 31. and 25. H. 8. c. 6. see Beccaria. § 31. Montesq.—T. J.

[22] Bracton, Fleta, &c.—T. J.

[23] 22. 23. Car. 2. c. 1. Maiming was felony at the Common law. Britton, c. 25. *"Mahemium autem dici poteri, aubi aliquis in aliqua parte sui corparis laesionem acceperit, per quam affectus sit inutilis ad pugnandum: ut si manus amputetur, vel pes, oculus privetur, vel scerda de osse capitis laveter, vel si quis dentes praecisores amiserit, vel castratus fuerit, et talis pro mahemiato poterit adjudicari."* Fleta L. 1. c. 40. *"Et volons que nul maheme ne soit tenus forsque de membre tollet dount home est plus feble a combatre, sicome del oyl, ou de la mayn, ou del pie, ou de la tete debruse, ou de les dentz devant."* Britton, c. 25. For further definitions, see Bracton, L. 3. c. 24. § 3. 4. Finch L. B. 3. c. 12. Co. L. 126. a. b. 288. a. 3. Bl. 121. 4. Bl. 205. Stamf. P. C. L. 1. c. 41. I do not find any of these definitions confine the offence to wilful and malicious perpetrations of it. 22. 23. Car. 2. c. 1. called the Coventry act, has the words "on purpose and of malice forethought." Nor does the Common law prescribe the same punishment for disfiguring, as for maiming.—T. J.

[24] The punishment was by retaliation. *"Et come ascun appele serra de tele felonie atteint et attende jugement, si soit le jugement tiel que il perde autriel membre come il avera tollet al pleintyfe. Et sy la pleynte soi faite de femme que avera tollet a home ses membres, en tiel cas perdra la femme la une meyn par jugement, come le membre dount ele axera trespasse."* Britton, c. 25. Fleta, B. 1. c. 40. Ll. Aelfr. 19. 40.—T. J.

[25] 25. E. 3. st. 5. c. 2. 5. El. c. 11. 18. El. c. 1. 8. 9. W. 3. c. 26. 15. 16. G. 2. c. 28. 7. Ann. c. 25. By the laws of Aethelstan and Canute, this was punished by cutting off the hand. "Gif se mynetere ful wurthe slea man tha hand of, the he that ful mid worthe and sette uppon tha mynet smiththan." In English characters and words "if the minter foul [criminal] wert, slay the hand off, that he the foul [crime] with wrought, and set upon the mint-smithery." Ll. Aethelst. 14. *"Et si quis praeter hanc, falsam fecerit, perdat manum quacum falsam confecit."* Ll. Cnuti. 8. It had been death by the Ll. Aethelredi sub fine. By those of H. 1. *"siquis cum falso*

monwealth, or any paper bills issued in the nature of money, or of certificates of loan on the credit of this Commonwealth, or of all or any of the United States of America, or any Inspectors' notes for tobacco, or shall pass any such counterfeit coin, paper, bills, or notes, knowing them to be counterfeit; or, for the sake of lucre, shall diminish,[26] case, or wash any such coin, shall be condemned to hard labor six years in the public works, and shall forfeit all his lands and goods to the Commonwealth.

[27] Whosoever committeth arson, shall be condemned to hard labor five years in the public works, and shall make good the loss of the sufferers threefold.[28]

If any person shall, within this Commonwealth, or being a citizen thereof, shall without the same, wilfully destroy,[29] or run [30] away with any sea-vessel, or goods laden on board thereof, or plunder or pilfer any wreck, he shall be condemned to hard labor five years in the public works, and shall make good the loss of the sufferers threefold.

*denario inventus fuerit—fiat justitia mea, saltem de dextro pugno et de testiculis.*" Anno 1108. "*Operae pretium vero est audire quam severus rex fuerit in pravos. Monetarios enim fere omnes totius Angliae fecit ementulari, et manus dextras abscindi, quia monetam furtive corruperant.*" Wilkins ib. et anno 1125. When the Common law became settled, it appears to have been punishable by death. "*Est aluid genus criminis quod sub nomine falsi continetur, et tangit coronam domini regis, et ultimum inducit supplicium, sicut de illis qui falsam fabricant monetam, et qui de re non reproba, faciunt reprobam; sicut sunt retonsores denariorum.*" Bract. L. 3. c. § 2. Fleta, L. 1. c. 22. § 4. Lord Hale thinks it was deemed petty treason at common law. 1. H. P. C. 220. 224. The bringing in false money with *intent* to merchandize, and make payment of it, is treason, by 25. E. 3. But the best proof of the intention, is the act of passing it, and why not leave room for repentance here, as in other cases of felonies intended? 1. H. P. C. 229.—T. J.

[26] Clipping, filing, rounding, impairing, scaling, lightening, (the words in the statues) are included in "diminishing"; gilding, in the word "casing"; coloring in the word "washing"; and falsifying, or making, is "counterfeiting."—T. J.

[27] 43. L. c. 13. confined to four counties. 22. 23. Car. 2. c. 7. 9. G. 1. c. 22. 9. G. 3. c. 29.—T. J.

[28] Arson was a felony at Common law—3. Inst. 66; punished by a fine, Ll. Aethelst. 6. But Ll. Cnuti, 61. make it a "*scelus inexpiable.*" "Hus brec and bærnet and open thyfth æberemorth and hlaford swice æfter woruld laga is botleds." Word for word, "house break and burnt, and open theft, and manifest murther, and lord-treachery, afterworld's law is bootless." Bracton says it was punished by death. "*Si quis turbida seditione incendium fecerit nequiter et in felonia, vel ob inimicitias, vel praedandi causa, capitali puniatur poena vel sententia.*" Bract. L. 3. 27. He defines it as commissible by burning "*aedes alienas.*'" Ib. Britton, c. 9. "*Ausi soit enquis de ceux que felonisement en temps de pecs eient autre* blees *ou autre* mesons *ars, et ceux que serrount de ceo atteyntz, soient ars issint que eux soient punys par mesme cele chose dount ilz pecherent.*" Fleta, L. 1. c. 37. is a copy of Bracton. The Mirror c. 1. § 8. says, "*Ardours sont que ardent citie, ville, maison home, maison beast, ou auters chatelx, de lour felonie en temps de pace pour haine ou vengeance.*" Again, c. 2. § 11. pointing out the words of the appellor "*jeo dise que Sebright, &c., enticl meason ou* biens *mist de feu.*" Coke 3. Inst. 67. says, "the ancient authors extended this felony further than houses, *viz.*, to sacks of corn, waynes or carts of coal, wood or other goods." He denies it as commissible, not only on the inset houses, parcel of the mansion house, but the outset also, as barn, stable, cowhouse, sheep house, dairy house, mill house, and the like, parcel of the mansion house. But "burning of a barn, being no parcel of a mansion house, is no felony," unless there be corn or hay within it. Ib. The 22. 23. Car. 2. and 9. G. 1. are the principal statutes against arson. They extend the offence beyond the Common law.—T. J.

[29] 1. Ann. st. 2. c. 9. 12. Ann. c. 18. 4. G. 1. c. 12. 26. G. 2. c. 19.—T. J.

[30] 11. 12. W. 3. c. 7.—T. J.

Whosoever committeth Robbery,[31] shall be condemned to hard labor four years in the public works, and shall make double reparation to the persons injured.

Whatsoever act, if committed on any Mansion house, would be deemed Burglary,[32] shall be Burglary, if committed on any other house; and he, who is guilty of Burglary, shall be condemned to hard labor four years in the public works, and shall make double reparation to the persons injured.

Whatsoever act, if committed in the night time, shall constitute the crime of Burglary, shall, if committed in the day, be deemed House-breaking;[33] and whosoever is guilty thereof, shall be condemned to hard labor three years in the public works, and shall make reparation to the persons injured.

Whosoever shall be guilty of Horse-stealing,[34] shall be condemned to hard

[31] Robbery was a felony at Common law. 3 Inst. 68. "*Scelus inexpiable*," by the Ll. Cnuti. 61. [See before in Arson.] It was punished with death. Britt. c. 15, "*de robbours et de larouns et de semblables mesfesours, soit ausi ententivement enquis—et tauntost soient ceux robbours juges a la mort.*" Fleta says, "*si quis convictus fuerit de bonis viri robbatis vel asportatis ad sectam regis judicium capitale subibit.*" L. 1. c. 39. See also Bract. L. 3. c. 32. § 1.—T. J.

[32] Burglary was felony at the Common law. 3 Inst. 63. It was not distinguished by ancient authors, except the Mirror, from simple House-breaking, ib. 65. Burglary and House-breaking were called "*Hamsockne diximus etiam de pacis violatione et de immunitatibus domus, si quis hoc in posterum fecerit ut perdat omne quod habet, et sit in regis arbitrio utrum vitam habeat.* Eac we quædon be mundbryce and be ham socnum, sethe hit ofer this do thæt he dolie ealles thæs the age, and sy on Cyninges dome hwæther he life age; and we quoth of mound-breach, and of home-seeking he who it after this do, that he dole all that he owe [owns], and is in king's doom whether he life owes [owns.]" Ll. Eadmundi. c. 6. and see Ll. Cnuti. 61. "hus brec," in notes on Arson. ante. A Burglar was also called a Burgessor. "*Et soit enquis de Burgessours et sunt tenus Burgessours trestous ceux que* felonisement *en temps de pees debrusont esglises ou auter mesons, ou murs ou portes de nos cytes, ou de nos Burghes.*" Britt. c. 10. "*Burglaria est nocturna diruptio habitaculi alicujus, vel ecclesiae, etiam murorum, partarumve civitatis aut burgi, ad feloniam aliquam perpetrandam.* Noctanter *dico, recentiores secutus; veteres enim hoc non adjungunt. Spelm. gloss. verb. Burglaria.*" It was punished with death. Ib. citn. from the office of a Coroner. It may be committed in the outset houses, as well as inset. 3 Inst. 65. though not under the same roof or contiguous, provided they be within the Curtilage or Homestall. 4 Bl. 225. As by the Common law, all felonies were clergiable, the stat. 23 H. 8. c. 1. 5. E. 6. c. 9. and 18 El. c. 7. first distinguished them, by taking the clerical privilege of impunity from the principals, and 3. 4. W. M. c. 9. from accessories before the fact. No *statute* defines what Burglary is. The 12 Ann. c. 7. decides the doubt whether, where breaking is subsequent to entry, it is Burglary. Bacon's Elements had affirmed, and 1. H. P. C. 554. had denied it. Our bill must distinguish them by different degrees of punishment.—T. J.

[33] At the Common law, the offence of Housebreaking was not distinguished from Burglary, and neither of them from any other larceny. The statutes at first took away clergy from Burglary, which made a leading distinction between the two offences. Later statutes, however, have taken clergy from so many cases of Housebreaking, as nearly to bring the offences together again. These are 23 H. 8. c. 1. 1. E. 6. c. 12. 5 and 6 E. 6. c. 9. 3 and 4 W. M. c. 9. 39 El. c. 15. 10 and 11 W. 3 c. 23. 12 Ann. c. 7. See Barr. 428. 4 Bl. 240. The circumstances which in these statutes characterize the offence, seem to have been occasional and unsystematical. The houses on which Burglary may be committed, and the circumstances which constitute that crime being ascertained, it will be better to define Housebreaking by the same subjects and circumstances, and let the crimes be distinguished only by the hour at which they are committed, and the degree of punishment.—T. J.

[34] The offence of Horse-stealing seems properly distinguishable from other larcenies, here, where these animals generally run at large, the temptation being so great and frequent, and the facility of commission so remarkable. See 1 E. 6. c. 12. 23 E. 6. c. 33. 31 El. c. 12.—T. J.

labor three years in the public works, and shall make reparation to the person injured.

Grand Larceny [35] shall be where the goods stolen are of the value of five dollars; and whosoever shall be guilty thereof, shall be forthwith put in the pillory for one half hour, shall be condemned to hard labor [36] two years in the public works, and shall make reparation to the person injured.

Petty Larceny shall be, where the goods stolen are of less value than five dollars; and whosoever shall be guilty thereof, shall be forthwith put in the pillory for a quarter of an hour, shall be condemned to hard labor one year in the public works, and shall make reparation to the person injured.

Robbery [37] or larceny of bonds, bills obligatory, bills of exchange, or promissory notes for the payment of money or tobacco, lottery tickets, paper bills issued in the nature of money, or of certificates of loan on the credit of this Commonwealth, or of all or any of the United States of America, or Inspectors' notes for tobacco, shall be punished in the same manner as robbery or larceny of the money or tobacco due on, or represented by such papers.

Buyers [38] and receivers of goods taken by way of robbery or larceny, knowing them to have been so taken, shall be deemed accessaries to such robbery or larceny after the fact.

[35] The distinction between grand and petty larceny is very ancient. At first 8d. was the sum which constituted grand larceny. Ll. Aethelst. c. 1. "*Ne parcatur ulli furi, qui furtum manutenens captus sit, supra 12. annos nato, et supra 8. denarios.*" Afterwards, in the same king's reign it was raised to 12d. "*non parcatur alicui furi ultra 12 denarios, et ultra 12 annos nato—ut occidemus illum et capiamus omne quod possidet, et imprimis sumamus rei furto ablatae pretium ab haerede, ac dividatur postea reliquum in duas partes, una pars uxori, si munda, et facinoris conscia non sit; et residuum in duo, dimidium capiat rex, dimidium societas.*" Ll. Aethelst. Wilkins, p. 65.—T. J.

[36] Ll. Inae. c. 7. "*Si quis furetur ita ut uxor ejus et infans ipsius nesciant, solvat 60. solidos poenae loco. Si autem furetur testantibus omnibus haeredibus suis,* abeant omnes in servitutem." Ina was king of the West-Saxons, and began to reign A. C. 688. After the union of the Heptarchy, i. e. temp. Aethelst. inter 924 and 940, we find it punishable with death as above. So it was inter 1017 and 1035, i. e. temp. Cnuti. Ll. Cnuti 61. cited in notes on Arson. In the time of William the conqueror, it seems to have been made punishable by fine only. Ll. Gul. conq. apud Wilk. p. 218, 220. This commutation, however, was taken away by Ll. H. 1. anno 1108. "*Si quis in furto vel latrocinio deprehensus fuisset, suspenderetur; sublata wirgildorum, id est, pecuniarae redemptionis lege.*" Larceny is the felonious taking and carrying away of the personal goods of another. 1. As to the taking, the 3. 4. W. M. c. 9 § 5. is not additional to the Common law, but declaratory of it; because where only the care or use, and not the possession, of things is delivered, to take them was larceny at the Common law. The 33. H. 6. c. 1. and 21 H. 8. c. 7. indeed, have added to the Common law, by making it larceny in a servant to convert things of his master's. But quære, if they should be imitated more than as to other breaches of trust in general. 2. As to the subject of larceny, 4 G. 2. c. 32. 6 G. 3. c. 36. 48. 43. El. c. 7. 15. Car. 2. c. 2. 23. G. 2. c. 26. 31. G. 2. c. 35. 9. G. 3. c. 41. 25. G. 2. c. 10. have extended larceny to things of various sorts either real, or fixed to the reality. But the enumeration is unsystematical, and in this country, where the produce of the earth is so spontaneous, as to have rendered things of this kind scarcely a breach of civility or good manners, in the eyes of the people, quære, if it would not too much enlarge the field of Criminal law? The same may be questioned of 9 G. 1. c. 22. 13 Car. 2. c. 10. 10 G. 2. c. 32. 5 G. 3. c. 14. 22 and 23 Car. 2. c. 25. 37 E. 3. c. 19. making it felony to steal animals feræ naturæ.—T. J.

[37] 2 G. 2. c. 25 § 3. 7 G. 3. c. 50.—T. J.

[38] 3. 4. W. M. c. 9. § 4. 5 Ann. c. 31. § 5. 4 G. 1. c. 11. § 1.—T. J.

Prison-breakers,[39] also, shall be deemed accessaries after the fact, to traitors or felons whom they enlarge from prison.[40]

All attempts to delude the people, or to abuse their understanding by exercise of the pretended arts of witchcraft, conjuration, enchantment, or sorcery, or by pretended prophecies, shall be punished by ducking and whipping, at the discretion of a jury, not exceeding fifteen stripes.[41]

If the principal offenders be fled,[42] or secreted from justice, in any case not touching life or member, the accessaries may, notwithstanding, be prosecuted as if their principal were convicted.[43]

If any offender stand mute of obstinacy,[44] or challenge peremptorily more

39 1 E. 2.—T. J.

40 Breach of prison at the Common law was capital, without regard to the crime for which the party was committed. *"Cum pro criminis qualitate in carcerem recepti fuerint, conspiraverint (ut ruptis vinculis aut fracto carcere) evadant, amplius (quam causa pro qua recepti sunt exposeit) puniendi sunt, videlicet ultimo supplicio, quamvis ex eo crimine innocentes inveniantur, propter quod inducti sunt in carcerem et imparcati."* Bracton L. 3. c. 9. § 4. Britt. c. 11. Fleta, L. 1. c. 26. § 4. Yet in the Y. B. Hill. 1. H. 7. 2. Hussey says, that by the opinion of Billing and Choke, and all the justices, it was a felony in strangers only, but not in the prisoner himself. S. C. Fitz. Abr. Coron. 48. They are principal felons, not accessaries. *ib.* Whether it was felony in the prisoner at Common law, is doubted. Stam. P. C. 30. b. The Mirror c. 5. § 1, says, *"abusion est a tener escape de prisoner, ou de bruserie del gaole pur peche mortell, car cel usage nest garrant per nul ley, ne in nul part est use forsque in cest realme, et en France, eins* [*mais*] *est leu garrantie de ceo faire per la ley de nature."* 2 Inst. 589. The stat. 1. E. 2. *de fraugentibus prisonam,* restrained the judgment of life and limb for prison breaking, to cases where the offence of the prisoner required such judgment.

It is not only vain, but wicked, in a legislator to frame laws in opposition to the laws of nature, and to arm them with the terrors of death. This is truly creating crimes in order to punish them. The law of nature impels everyone to escape from confinement; it should not, therefore, be subjected to punishment. Let the legislator restrain his criminal by walls, not by parchment. As to strangers breaking prison to enlarge an offender, they should, and may be fairly considered as accessaries after the fact. This bill says nothing of the prisoner releasing himself by breach of jail, he will have the benefit of the first section of the bill, which repeals the judgment of life and death at the common law.—T. J.

41 Gif wiccan owwe wigleras nansworan, owwe morthwyrhtan owwe fule afylede æbere horewenan ahwhar on lande wurthan agytene, thonne fyrsie man of earde and clænsie tha theode, owwe on earde forfare hi mid ealle, buton hi geswican and the deoper gebetan: if witches, or weirds, man-swearers, or murther-wroughters, or foul, defiled, open whore-queens, aywhere in the land were gotten, then force them off earth, and cleanse the nation, or in earth forth-fare them withal, buton they beseech, and deeply better. Ll. Ed. et Guthr. c. 11. *"Sagae, mulieres barbara, factitantes sacrificia, aut pestiferi, si cui mortem intulerint, neque id inficiari poterint, capitis poena esto."* Ll. Aethelst. c. 6. apud Lambard. Ll. Aelfr. 30. Ll. Cnuti. c. 4. *"Mesme cel jugement (d'etrears) eyent sorcers, et sorceresses, &c. ut supra. Fleta ut et ubi supra."* 3. Inst. 44. Trial of witches before Hale in 1664. The statutes 33 H. 8. c. 8. 5. El. c. 16 and 1. Jac. 1. c. 12. seem to be only in confirmation of the Common law. 9 G. 2. c. 25. punishes them with pillory, and a year's imprisonment. 3 E. 6. c. 15. 5 El. c. 15. punish fond, fantastical and false prophecies, by fine and imprisonment.—T. J.

42 1 Ann. c. 9. § 2.—T. J.

43 As every treason includes within it a misprision of treason, so every felony includes a misprision, or misdemeanor. 1 Hale P. C. 652. 708. *"Licet fuerit felonia, tamen in eo continetur misprisio."* 2 R. 3 10. Both principal and accessary, therefore, may be proceeded against in any case, either for felony or misprision, at the Common law. Capital cases not being mentioned here, accessaries to them will of course be triable for misprisions, if the offender flies.—T. J.

44 E. 1. c. 12.—T. J.

of the jurors than by law he may, being first warned of the consequence thereof, the court shall proceed as if he had confessed the charge.[45]

Pardon and Privilege of clergy, shall henceforth be abolished, that none may be induced to injure through hope of impunity. But if the verdict be against the defendant, and the court before whom the offence is heard and determined, shall doubt that it may be untrue for defect of testimony, or other cause, they may direct a new trial to be had.[46]

No attainder shall work corruption of blood in any case.

In all cases of forfeiture, the widow's dower shall be saved to her, during her title thereto; after which it shall be disposed of as if no such saving had been.

The aid of Counsel,[47] and examination of their witnesses on oath, shall be allowed to defendants in criminal prosecutions.

Slaves guilty of any offence [48] punishable in others by labor in the public

[45] Whether the judgment of penance lay at Common law. See 2 Inst. 178. 2 H. P. C. 321. 4 Bl. 322. It was given on standing mute; but on challenging more than the legal number, whether that sentence, or sentence of death is to be given, seems doubtful. 2 H. P. C. 316. Quære, whether it would not be better to consider the supernumerary challenge as merely void, and to proceed in the trial? Quære too, in case of silence?—T. J.

[46] "*Cum Clericus sic de crimine convictus degradetur non sequitur alia poena pro uno delicto, vel pluribus ante degradationem perpetratis. Satis enim sufficit ei pro poena degradatio, quae est magna capitis diminutio, nisi forte convictus fuerit de apostatia, quia hinc primo degradetur, et postea per manum laicalem comburetur, secundum quod accidit in concilio Oxoni celebrato a bonae memoriae S. Cantuanen. Archiepiscopo de quodam diacono, qui se apostatavit pro quadam Judaea; qui cum esset per episcopum degradatus, statim fuit igni traditus per manum laicalem.*" Bract. L. 3. c. 9. § 2. "*Et mesme cel jugement* (i.e., *qui ils soient ars*) *eyent sorcers et sorceresses, et sodomites et mescreauntz apertement atteyntz.*" Britt. c. 9. "*Christiani autem Apostatae, sortilegii, et hujusmodi detractari debent et comburi.*" Fleta, L. 1. c. 37. § 2. see 3. Inst. 39. 12. Rep. 92. 1. H. P. C. 393. The extent of the clerical privilege at the Common law. 1. As to the crimes, seems very obscure and uncertain. It extended to no case where the judgment was not of life, or limb. Note in 2. H. P. C. 326. This therefore excluded it in trespass, petty larceny, or killing *se defendendo.* In high treason against the person of the King, it seems not to have been allowed. Note 1. H. P. C. 185. Treasons, therefore, not against the King's person immediately, petty treasons and felonies, seem to have been the cases where it was allowed; and even of those, not for *insidiatio varium, depopulatio agrorum,* or *combustio domorum.* The statute de Clero, 25. E. 3. st. 3. c. 4. settled the law on this head. 2. As to the persons, it extended to all clerks, always, and *toties quoties.* 2. H. P. C. 374. To nuns also. Fitz. Abr. Corone. 461. 22. E. 3. The clerical habit and tonsure were considered as evidence of the person being clerical. 26. Assiz. 19. 20. E. 2. Fitz. Corone. 233. By the 9. E. 4. 28. b. 34. H. 6. 49 a. b. simple reading became the evidence. This extended impunity to a great number of laymen, and *toties quoties.* The stat. 4. H. 7. c. 13. directed that real clerks should, upon a second arraignment, produce their orders, and all others to be burnt in the hand with M. or T. on the first allowance of clergy, and not to be admitted to it a second time. A heretic, Jew, or Turk (as being incapable of orders) could not have clergy. 11. Co. Rep. 29 b. But a Greek, or other alien, reading in a book of his own country, might. Bro. Clergie. 20. So a blind man, if he could speak Latin. Ib. 21. qu. 11. Rep. 29. b. The orders entitling the party, were bishops, priests, deacons and subdeacons, the inferior being reckoned *Clerici in minoribus.* 2. H. P. C. 373. Quære, however, if this distinction is not founded on the stat. 23. H. 8. c. 1. 25. H. 8. c. 32. By merely dropping all the statutes, it should seem that none but clerks would be entitled to this privilege, and that they would, *toties quoties.*—T. J.

[47] 1. Ann. c. 9.—T. J.

[48] Manslaughter, counterfeiting, arson, asportation of vessels, robbery, burglary, house-breaking, horse-stealing, larceny.—T. J.

works, shall be transported to such parts in the West Indies, South America, or Africa, as the Governor shall direct, there to be continued in slavery.

---

## AUTHENTICATING PRINTED EDITIONS OF THE LAWS[1]

1791

The Secretary of State, to whom was referred the memorial of Andrew Brown, printer of Philadelphia, has had the same under his consideration, and thereupon makes the following report:

The memorialist states that he has in contemplation to publish a correct edition of the laws, treaties, and resolutions of the United States, and prays that such measures may be adopted for giving a public authentication to his work, as may ensure its reception throughout the United States.

The Secretary of State observes, that there exists, at present, but a single edition of the laws of the United States, to wit, the one printed by Childs and Swaine; that this edition is authentic, the proof sheets thereof having been carefully collated by sworn clerks with the original rolls in his office, and rendered literally conformable therewith; that the first volume of this edition can now rarely be found, the copies originally printed being mostly disposed of.

That it is desirable that copies of the laws should be so multiplied throughout the States, and in such cheap forms, as that every citizen of the United States may be able to procure them; that it is important, also, that such publications be rendered authentic, by a collation of the proof sheets with the original rolls by sworn clerks, when they are printed at the seat of Government, or in its neighborhood, and by a collation of the whole work, when printed at a distance, and a certified correction of its typographical errors annexed to each volume.

That this, however, if done at the public expense, would occasion an inconvenient augmentation of the number of clerks, as the act of collation requires the presence of three clerks, one to hold the roll, a second a printed copy already authenticated, and a third the proof sheet.

That it would be more reasonable that persons of confidence should be employed at the expense of the editor, to be named and sworn as clerks for the special occasion.

That, in this way, he is of opinion it will be advantageous to the public to permit that the laws to be printed by the memorialist be collated with and corrected by the original rolls, and that a certificate thereof by the Secretary of State be annexed to the edition.

[1] Communicated to the House of Representatives, February 7, 1791.

# PROPOSED CONSTITUTION FOR VIRGINIA [1]

June, 1776

[*A Bill*] for new-modelling the form of Government and for establishing the Fundamental principles thereof in future.

Whereas George

Guelf [2] king of Great Britain and Ireland and Elector of Hanover, heretofore entrusted with the exercise of the kingly office in this government hath endeavored to pervert the same into a destestable and insupportable tyranny;

by putting his negative on laws the most wholesome and necessary for ye public good;

by denying to his governors permission to pass laws of immediate and pressing importance, unless suspended in their operations for his assent, and, when so suspended, neglecting to attend to them for many years;

by refusing to pass certain other laws, unless the person to be benefited by them would relinquish the inestimable right of representation in the legislature

by dissolving legislative assemblies repeatedly and continually for opposing with manly firmness his invasions on the rights of the people;

when dissolved, by refusing to call others for a long space of time, thereby leaving the political system without any legislative head;

by endeavoring to prevent the population of our country, and for that purpose obstructing the laws for the naturalization of foreigners and raising the condition [*lacking appro*] [3] priations of lands;

[*by keeping among u*]s, in times of peace, standing armies and ships of war;

[*lack*]ing to render the military independent of and superior to the civil power;

by combining with others to subject us to a foreign jurisdiction, giving his assent to their pretended acts of legislation.

for quartering large bodies of troops among us;

for cutting off our trade with all parts of the world;

[1] Jefferson wrote this draft while he was in Philadelphia as a member of the Continental Congress. At this time he was also at work on the Declaration of Independence. The preamble, in fact, has a startling similarity to the Declaration, and it was adopted by the Virginia Convention on June 29. Jefferson wrote in 1825: "The fact is, that that Preamble was prior in composition to the Declaration; and both having the same object, of justifying our separation from Great Britain, they used necessarily the same materials of justification, and hence their similitude."

[2] "Guelf" or "Welf" was the name of a party in medieval Italy that opposed the German emperors.

[3] The bracketed words in italic are the insertions of Paul Leicester Ford, who first published this document in his collection: *The Writings of Thomas Jefferson,* Vol. II (1893), pp. 7-30. The bracketed words in Roman were so written by Jefferson; the same is true of the words crossed out.

for imposing taxes on us without our consent;

for depriving us of the benefits of trial by jury;

for transporting us beyond seas to be tried for pretended offences; and

for suspending our own legislatures and declaring themselves invested with power to legislate for us in all cases whatsoever;

by plundering our seas, ravaging our coasts, burning our towns and destroying the lives of our people;

by inciting insurrections of our fellow subjects with the allurements of forfeiture and confiscation;

by prompting our negroes to rise in arms among us; those very negroes whom ~~he hath from time to time~~ by an inhuman use of his negative he hath refused permission to exclude by law;

by endeavoring to bring on the inhabitants of our frontiers the merciless Indian savages, whose known rule of warfare is an undistinguished destruction of all ages, sexes, and conditions of existence;

by transporting at this time a large army of foreign mercenaries [*to complete*] the works of death, desolation and tyranny already begun with circum[*stances*] of cruelty and perfidy so unworthy the head of a civilized nation;

by answering our repeated petitions for redress with a repetition of injuries;

and finally by abandoning the helm of government and declaring us out of his allegiance and protection;

by which several acts of misrule the said George Guelf has forfeited the kingly office and has rendered it necessary for the preservation of the people that he should be immediately deposed from the same, and divested of all its privileges, powers, and prerogatives:

And forasmuch as the public liberty may be more certainly secured by abolishing an office which all experience hath shewn to be inveterately inimical thereto ~~or which~~ and it will thereupon become further necessary to re-establish such ancient principles as are friendly to the rights of the people and to declare certain others which may cooperate with and fortify the same in future.

Be it therefore enacted by the authority of the people that the said, George —— Guelf be, and he hereby is deposed from the kingly office within this government and absolutely divested of all its rights, powers, and prerogatives: and that he and his descendants and all persons acting by or through him, and all other persons whatsoever shall be and forever remain incapable of the same: and that the said office shall henceforth cease and never more either in name or substance be re-established within this colony.

And be it further enacted by the authority aforesaid that the following fundamental laws and principles of government shall henceforth be established.

The Legislative, Executive and Judiciary offices shall be kept forever separate; no person exercising the one shall be capable of appointment to the others, or to either of them.

### I. LEGISLATIVE

Legislation shall be exercised by two separate houses, to wit a house of Representatives, and a house of Senators, which shall be called the General Assembly of Virginia.

The said house of Representatives shall be composed of persons chosen by the people annually on the [1st day of October] and shall meet in General assembly on the [1st day of November] following and so from time to time on their own adjournments, or at any time when summoned by the Administrator and shall continue sitting so long as they shall think the publick service requires.

Vacancies in the said house by death or disqualification shall be filled by the electors under a warrant from the Speaker of the said house.

All male persons of full age and sane mind having a freehold estate in [one fourth of an acre] of land in any town, or in [25] acres of land in the country, and all persons resident in the colony who shall have paid scot and lot to government the last [two years] shall have right to give their vote in the election of their respective representatives. And every person so qualified to elect shall be capable of being elected, provided he shall have given no bribe either directly or indirectly to any elector, and shall take an oath of fidelity to the state and of duty in his office, before he enters on the exercise thereof. During his continuance in the said office he shall hold no public pension nor post of profit, either himself, or by another for his use.

The number of Representatives for each county or borough shall be so proportioned to the numbers of its qualified electors that the whole number of representatives shall not exceed [300] nor be less than [125]; for the present there shall be one representative for every [ ] qualified electors in each county or borough: but whenever this or any future proportion shall be likely to exceed or fall short of the limits beforementioned, it shall be again adjusted by the house of representatives.

The house of Representatives when met shall be free to act according to their own judgment and conscience.

The Senate shall consist of not less than [15] nor more than [50] members who shall be appointed by the house of Representatives. One third of them shall be removed out of office by lot at the end of the first [three] years and their places be supplied by a new appointment; one other third shall be removed by lot in like manner at the end of the second [three] years and their places be supplied by a new appointment; after which one third shall be removed annually at the end of every [three] years according to seniority. When once removed, they shall be forever incapable of being re-appointed to that house. Their qualifications shall be an oath of fidelity to the state, and of duty in their office, the being [31] years of age at the least, and the having given no bribe directly or indirectly to obtain their appointment. While in the senatorial office they shall be incapable of holding any public pension or post of profit either themselves, or by others for their use.

The judges of the General court and of the High court of Chancery shall have session and deliberative voice, but not suffrage in the house of Senators.

The Senate and the house of representatives shall each of them have power to originate and amend bills; save only that bills for levying money ~~bills~~ shall be originated and amended by the representatives only: the assent of both houses shall be requisite to pass a law.

The General assembly shall have no power to pass any law inflicting death for any crime, excepting murder, and ~~such~~ those offences in the military service for which they shall think punishment by death absolutely necessary: and all capital punishments in other cases are hereby abolished. Nor shall they have power to prescribe torture in any case whatever: nor shall there be power anywhere to pardon crimes or to remit fines or punishments: nor shall any law for levying money be in force longer than [ten years] from the time of its commencement.

[Two thirds] of the members of either house shall be a Quorum to proceed to business.

### II. EXECUTIVE

The executive powers shall be exercised in manner following.

One person to be called the [Administrator] shall be annually appointed by the house of Representatives on the second day of their first session, who after having acted [one] year shall be incapable of being again appointed to that office until he shall have been out of the same [three] years.

Under him shall be appointed by the same house and at the same time, a Deputy-Administrator to assist his principal in the discharge of his office, and to succeed, in case of his death before the year shall have expired, to the whole powers thereof during the residue of the year.

The administrator shall possess the power formerly held by the king: save only that, he shall be bound by acts of legislature though not expressly named;

he shall have no negative on the bills of the Legislature;

he shall be liable to action, though not to personal restraint for private duties or wrongs;

he shall not possess the prerogatives:

of dissolving, proroguing or adjourning either house of Assembly;
of declaring war or concluding peace;
of issuing letters of marque or reprisal;
of raising or introducing armed forces, building armed vessels, forts or strongholds;
of coining monies or regulating their values;
of regulating weights and measures;
of erecting courts, offices, boroughs, corporations, fairs, markets, ports, beacons, lighthouses, sea-marks.
of laying embargoes, or prohibiting the exportation of any commodity for a longer space than [40] days.
of retaining or recalling a member of the state but by legal process *pro delicto vel contractu.*
of making denizens.
~~of pardoning crimes, or remitting fines or punishments.~~
of creating dignities or granting rights or precedence.

but these powers shall be exercised by the legislature alone, and excepting also those powers which by these fundamentals are given to others, or abolished.

A Privy council shall be annually appointed by the house of representatives whose duties it shall be to give advice to the Administrator when called on by him. With them the Deputy Administrator shall have session and suffrage.

Delegates to represent this colony in the American Congress shall be appointed when necessary by the house of Representatives. After serving [one] year in that office they shall not be capable of being re-appointed to the same during an interval of [one] year.

A Treasurer shall be appointed by the house of Representatives who shall issue no money but by authority of both houses.

An Attorney general shall be appointed by the house of Representatives.

High Sheriffs and Coroners of counties shall be annually elected by those qualified to vote for representatives: and no person who shall have served as high sheriff [one] year shall be capable of being re-elected to the said office in the same county till he shall have been out of office [five] years.

All other Officers civil and military shall be appointed by the Administrator; but such appointment shall be subject to the negative of the Privy council, saving however to the Legislature a power of transferring to any other persons the appointment of such officers or any of them.

### III. JUDICIARY

The Judiciary powers shall be exercised
First, by County courts and other inferior jurisdictions:

Secondly, by a General court and a High court of Chancery:

Thirdly, by a Court of Appeals.

The judges of the county courts and other inferior jurisdictions shall be appointed by the Administrator, subject to the negative of the privy council. They shall not be fewer than [five] in number. Their jurisdictions shall be defined from time to time by the legislature: and they shall be removable for misbehavior by the court of Appeals.

The Judges of the General court and of the High court of Chancery shall be appointed by the Administrator and Privy council. If kept united they shall be [5] in number, if separate, there shall be [5] for the General court and [3] for the High court of Chancery. The appointment shall be made from the faculty of the law, and of such persons of that faculty as shall have actually exercised the same at the bar of some court or courts of record within this colony for [seven] years. They shall hold their commissions during good behavior, for breach of which they shall be removable by the court of Appeals. Their jurisdiction shall be defined from time to time by the Legislature.

The Court of Appeals shall consist of not less than [7] nor more than [11] members, to be appointed by the house of Representatives: they shall hold their offices during good behavior, for breach of which they shall be removable by an act of the legislature only. Their jurisdiction shall be to determine finally all causes removed before them from the General Court or High Court of Chancery, or of the county courts or other inferior jurisdictions for misbehavior: [*to try impeachments against high offenders lodged before them by the house of representatives for such crimes as shall hereafter be precisely defined by the Legislature, and for the punishment of which, the said legislature shall have previously prescribed certain and determinate pains*]. In this court the judges of the General court and High court of Chancery shall have session and deliberative voice, but no suffrage.

All facts in causes whether of Chancery, Common, Ecclesiastical, or Marine law, shall be tried by a jury upon evidence given *viva voce*, in open court: but where witnesses are out of the colony or unable to attend through sickness or other invincible necessity, their deposition may be submitted to the credit of the jury.

All Fines or Amercements shall be assessed, and Terms of imprisonment for Contempts and Misdemeanors shall be fixed by the verdict of a Jury.

All Process Original and Judicial shall run in the name of the court from which it issues.

Two thirds of the members of the General court, High court of Chancery, or Court of Appeals shall be a Quorum to proceed to business.

Unappropriated or Forfeited lands shall be appropriated by the Administrator with the consent of the Privy council.

Every person of full age neither owning nor having owned [50] acres of land, shall be entitled to an appropriation of [50] acres or to so much as shall make up what he owns or has owned [50] acres in full and absolute dominion. And no other person shall be capable of taking an appropriation.

Lands heretofore holden of the crown in fee simple, and those hereafter to be appropriated shall be holden in full and absolute dominion, of no superior whatever.

No lands shall be appropriated until purchased of the Indian native proprietors; nor shall any purchases be made of them but on behalf of the public, by authority of acts of the General assembly to be passed for every purchase specially.

The territories contained within the charters erecting the colonies of Maryland, Pennsylvania, North and South Carolina, are hereby ceded, released, and forever confirmed to the people of those colonies respectively, with all the rights of property, jurisdiction and government and all other rights whatsoever which might at any time heretofore have been claimed by this colony. The Western and Northern extent of this country shall in all other respects stand as fixed by the charter of —— until by act of the Legislature one or more territories shall be laid off Westward of the Alleghany mountains for new colonies, which colonies shall be established on the same fundamental laws contained in this instrument, and shall be free and independent of this colony and of all the world.

Descents shall go according to the laws Gavelkind, save only that females shall have equal rights with males.

No person hereafter coming into this county shall be held within the same in slavery under any pretext whatever.

All persons who by their own oath or affirmation, or by other testimony shall give satisfactory proof to any court of record in this colony that they propose to reside in the same [7] years at the least and who shall subscribe the fundamental laws, shall be considered as residents and entitled to all the rights of persons natural born.

All persons shall have full and free liberty of religious opinion; nor shall any be compelled to frequent or maintain any religious institution.

No freeman shall be debarred the use of arms [within his own lands].

There shall be no standing army but in time of actual war.

Printing presses shall be free, except so far as by commission of private injury cause may be given of private action.

All Forfeitures heretofore going to the king, shall go to the state; save only such as the legislature may hereafter abolish.

The royal claim to Wrecks, waifs, strays, treasure-trove, royal mines, royal fish, royal birds, are declared to have been usurpations on common right.

No Salaries or Perquisites shall be given to any officer but by some future act of the legislature. No salaries shall be given to the Administrator, members of the legislative houses, judges of the court of Appeals, judges of the County courts, or other inferior jurisdictions, Privy counsellors, or Delegates to the American Congress: but the reasonable expenses of the Administrator, members of the house of representatives, judges of the court of Appeals, Privy counsellors, and Delegates for subsistence while acting in the duties of their office, may be borne by the public, if the legislature shall so direct.

No person shall be capable of acting in any office Civil, Military [or Ecclesiastical] ~~The Qualifications of all not otherwise directed, shall be an oath of fidelity to state and the having given no bribe to obtain their office~~ who shall have given any bribe to obtain such office, or who shall not previously take an oath of fidelity to the state.

None of these fundamental laws and principles of government shall be repealed or altered, but by the personal consent of the people on summons to meet in their respective counties on one and the same day by an act of Legislature to be passed for every special occasion: and if in such county meetings the people of two thirds of the counties shall give their suffrage for any particular alteration or repeal referred to them by the said act, the same shall be accordingly repealed or altered, and such repeal or alteration shall take its place among these fundamentals and stand on the same footing with them, in lieu of the article repealed or altered.

The laws heretofore in force in this colony shall remain in force, except so far as they are altered by the foregoing fundamental laws, or so far as they may be hereafter altered by acts of the Legislature.

## DRAFT OF A CONSTITUTION FOR VIRGINIA [1]

June, 1783

To the citizens of the commonwealth of Virginia, and all others whom it may concern, the delegates for the said commonwealth in Convention assembled, send greeting:

It is known to you and to the world, that the government of Great Britain, with which the American States were not long since connected, assumed

[1] In 1786, while in Paris, Jefferson published this draft in pamphlet form, under the title: *Draught of a Fundamental Constitution for the Commonwealth of Virginia* (8vo, 14 pp.). He bound it with his *Notes on Virginia* as an Appendix.

over them an authority unwarrantable and oppressive; that they endeavored to enforce this authority by arms, and that the States of New Hampshire, Massachusetts, Rhode Island, Connecticut, New York, New Jersey, Pennsylvania, Delaware, Maryland, Virginia, North Carolina, South Carolina, and Georgia, considering resistance, with all its train of horrors, as a lesser evil than abject submission, closed in the appeal to arms. It hath pleased the Sovereign Disposer of all human events to give to this appeal an issue favorable to the rights of the States; to enable them to reject forever all dependence on a government which had shown itself so capable of abusing the trusts reposed in it; and to obtain from that government a solemn and explicit acknowledgment that they are free, sovereign, and independent States. During the progress of that war, through which we had to labor for the establishment of our rights, the legislature of the commonwealth of Virginia found it necessary to make a temporary organization of government for preventing anarchy, and pointing our efforts to the two important objects of war against our invaders, and peace and happiness among ourselves. But this, like all other acts of legislation, being subject to change by subsequent legislatures, possessing equal powers with themselves; it has been thought expedient, that it should receive those amendments which time and trial have suggested, and be rendered permanent by a power superior to that of the ordinary legislature. The general assembly therefore of this State recommend it to the good people thereof, to choose delegates to meet in general convention, with powers to form a constitution of government for them, and to declare those fundamentals to which all our laws present and future shall be subordinate; and, in compliance with this recommendation, they have thought proper to make choice of us, and to vest us with powers for this purpose.

We, therefore, the delegates, chosen by the said good people of this State for the purpose aforesaid, and now assembled in general convention, do in execution of the authority with which we are invested, establish the following constitution and fundamentals of government for the said State of Virginia:

The said State shall forever hereafter be governed as a commonwealth.

The powers of government shall be divided into three distinct departments, each of them to be confided to a separate body of magistracy; to wit, those which are legislative to one, those which are judiciary to another, and those which are executive to another. No person, or collection of persons, being of one of these departments, shall exercise any power properly belonging to either of the others, except in the instances hereinafter expressly permitted.

The legislature shall consist of two branches, the one to be called the House of Delegates, the other the Senate, and both together the General

Assembly. The concurrence of both of these, expressed on three several readings, shall be necessary to the passage of a law.

Delegates for the general assembly shall be chosen on the last Monday of November in every year. But if an election cannot be concluded on that day, it may be adjourned from day to day till it can be concluded.

The number of delegates which each county may send shall be in proportion to the number of its qualified electors; and the whole number of delegates for the State shall be so proportioned to the whole number of qualified electors in it, that they shall never exceed three hundred, nor be fewer than one hundred. Whenever such excess or deficiency shall take place, the House of Delegates so deficient or excessive shall, notwithstanding this, continue in being during its legal term; but they shall, during that term, re-adjust the proportion, so as to bring their number within the limits before mentioned at the ensuing election. If any county be reduced in its qualified electors below the number authorized to send one delegate, let it be annexed to some adjoining county.

For the election of senators, let the several counties be allotted by the senate, from time to time, into such and so many districts as they shall find best; and let each county at the time of electing its delegates, choose senatorial electors, qualified as themselves are, and four in number for each delegate their county is entitled to send, who shall convene, and conduct themselves, in such manner as the legislature shall direct, with the senatorial electors from the other counties of their district, and then choose, by ballot, one senator for every six delegates which their district is entitled to choose. Let the senatorial districts be divided into two classes, and let the members elected for one of them be dissolved at the first ensuing general election of delegates, the other at the next, and so on alternately forever.

All free male citizens, of full age, and sane mind, who for one year before shall have been resident in the county, or shall through the whole of that time have possessed therein real property of the value of ——; or shall for the same time have been enrolled in the militia, and no others, shall have a right to vote for delegates for the said county, and for senatorial electors for the district. They shall give their votes personally, and *viva voce.*

The general assembly shall meet at the place to which the last adjournment was, on the forty-second day after the day of election of delegates, and thenceforward at any other time or place on their own adjournment, till their office expires, which shall be on the day preceding that appointed for the meeting of the next general assembly. But if they shall at any time adjourn for more than one year, it shall be as if they had adjourned for one year precisely. Neither house, without the concurrence of the other, shall adjourn for more than one week, nor to any other place than the one at which they are sitting. The governor shall also have power, with the advice of the council of State, to call them at any other time to the same place, or to a different one, if that shall have become, since the last adjournment, dangerous from an enemy, or from infection.

A majority of either house shall be a quorum, and shall be requisite for doing business; but any smaller proportion which from time to time shall be thought expedient by the respective houses, shall be sufficient to call for, and to punish, their non-attending members, and to adjourn themselves for any time not exceeding one week.

The members, during their attendance on the general assembly, and for so long a time before and after as shall be necessary for travelling to and from the same, shall be privileged from all personal restraint and assault, and shall have no other privilege whatsoever. They shall receive during the same time, daily wages in gold or silver, equal to the value of two bushels of wheat. This value shall be deemed one dollar by the bushel till the year 1790, in which, and in every tenth year thereafter, the general court, at their first sessions in the year, shall cause a special jury, of the most respectable merchants and farmers, to be summoned, to declare what shall have been the averaged value of wheat duing the last ten years; which averaged value shall be the measure of wages for the ten subsequent years.

Of this general assembly, the treasurer, attorney general, register, ministers of the gospel, officers of the regular armies of this State, or of the United States, persons receiving salaries or emoluments from any power foreign to our confederacy, those who are not resident in the county for which they are chosen delegates, or districts for which they are chosen senators, those who are not qualified as electors, persons who shall have committed treason, felony, or such other crime as would subject them to infamous punishment, or who shall have been convicted by due course of law of bribery or corruption, in endeavoring to procure an election to the said assembly, shall be incapable of being members. All others, not herein elsewhere excluded, who may elect, shall be capable of being elected thereto.

Any member of the said assembly accepting any office of profit under this State, or the United States, or any of them, shall thereby vacate his seat, but shall be capable of being re-elected.

Vacancies occasioned by such disqualifications, by death, or otherwise, shall be supplied by the electors, on a writ from the speaker of the respective house.

The general assembly shall not have power to infringe this constitution; to abridge the civil rights of any person on account of his religious belief; to restrain him from professing and supporting that belief, or to compel him to contributions, other than those he shall have personally stipulated for the support of that or any other; to ordain death for any crime but treason or murder, or military offences; to pardon, or give a power of pardoning persons duly convicted of treason or felony, but instead thereof they may substitute one or two new trials, and no more; to pass laws for punishing actions done before the existence of such laws; to pass any bill of attainder of treason or felony; to prescribe torture in any case whatever; nor to permit the introduction of any more slaves to reside in this State, or the continuance of slavery beyond the generation which shall be living on the thirty-first day of December, one thousand eight hundred; all persons born after that day being hereby declared free.

The general assembly shall have power to sever from this State all or any parts of its territory westward of the Ohio, or of the meridian of the mouth of the Great Kanhaway, and to cede to Congress one hundred square miles of territory in any other part of this State, exempted from the jurisdiction and government of this State so long as Congress shall hold their sessions therein, or in any territory adjacent thereto, which may be tendered to them by any other State.

They shall have power to appoint the speakers of their respective houses, treasurer, auditors, attorney general, register, all general officers of the military, their own clerks and serjeants, and no other officers, except where, in other parts of this constitution, such appointment is expressly given them.

The executive powers shall be exercised by a *Governor,* who shall be chosen by joint ballot of both houses of assembly, and when chosen shall remain in office five years, and be ineligible a second time. During his term he shall hold no other office or emolument under this State, or any other State or power whatsoever. By executive powers, we mean no reference to those powers exercised under our former government by the crown as of its prerogative, nor that these shall be the standard of what may or may not be deemed the rightful powers of the governor. We give him those powers only, which are necessary to execute the laws (and administer the government), and which are not in their nature either legislative or judiciary. The application of this idea must be left to reason. We do however expressly deny him the prerogative powers of erecting courts, offices, boroughs, corporations, fairs, markets, ports, beacons, light-houses, and sea-marks; of laying embargoes, of establishing precedence, of retaining within the State, or recalling to it any citizen thereof, and of making denizens, except so far as he may be authorized from time to time by the legislature to exercise any of those powers. The power of declaring war and concluding peace, of contracting alliances, of issuing letters of marque and reprisal, of raising and introducing armed forces, of building armed vessels, forts, or strongholds, of coining money or regulating its value, of regulating weights and measures, we leave to be exercised under the authority of the confederation; but in all cases respecting them which are out of the said confederation, they shall be exercised by the governor, under the regulation of such laws as the legislature may think it expedient to pass.

The whole military of the State, whether regular, or of militia, shall be subject to his directions; but he shall leave the execution of those directions to the general officers appointed by the legislature.

His salary shall be fixed by the legislature at the session of the assembly in which he shall be appointed, and before such appointment be made; or if it be not then fixed, it shall be the same which his next predecessor in office was entitled to. In either case he may demand it quarterly out of any money which shall be in the public treasury; and it shall not be in the power of the legislature to give him less or more, either during his continuance in office, or after he shall have gone out of it. The lands, houses, and other things appropriated to the use of the governor, shall remain to his use during his continuance in office.

A *Council of State* shall be chosen by joint ballot of both houses of assembly, who shall hold their offices seven years, and be ineligible a second time, and who, while they shall be of the said council, shall hold no other office or emolument under this State, or any other State or power whatsoever. Their duty shall be to attend and advise the governor when called on by him, and their advice in any case shall be a sanction to him. They shall also have power, and it shall be their duty, to meet at their own will, and to give their advice, though not required by the governor, in cases where they shall think the public good calls for it. Their advice and proceedings shall be entered in books to be kept for that purpose, and shall be signed as approved or disapproved by the members present. These books shall be laid before either house of assembly when called for by them. The said council shall consist of eight members for the present; but their numbers may be increased or reduced by the legislature, whenever they shall think it necessary; provided such reduction be made only as the appointments become vacant by death, resignation, disqualification, or regular deprivation. A majority of their actual number, and not fewer, shall be a quorum. They shall be allowed for the present —— each by the year, payable quarterly out of any money which shall be in the public treasury. Their salary, however, may be increased or abated from time to time, at the discretion of the legislature; provided such increase or abatement shall not, by any ways or means, be made to affect either then, or at any future time, any one of those then actually in office. At the end of each quarter their salary shall be divided into equal portions by the number of days on which, during that quarter, a council has been held, or required by the governor, or by their own adjournment, and one of those portions shall be withheld from each member for every of the said days which, without cause allowed good by the board, he failed to attend, or departed before adjournment without their leave. If no board should have been held during that quarter, there shall be no deduction.

They shall annually choose a *President,* who shall preside in council in the absence of the governor, and who, in case of his office becoming vacant by death or otherwise, shall have authority to exercise all his functions, till a new appointment be made, as he shall also in any interval during which the governor shall declare himself unable to attend to the duties of his office.

The *Judiciary* powers shall be exercised by county courts and such other inferior courts as the legislature shall think proper to continue or to erect, by three superior courts, to wit, a Court of Admiralty, a general Court of Common Law, and a High Court of Chancery; and by one Supreme Court, to be called the Court of Appeals.

The judges of the high court of chancery, general court, and court of admiralty, shall be four in number each, to be appointed by joint ballot of both houses of assembly, and to hold their offices during good behavior. While they continue judges, they shall hold no other office or emolument, under this State, or any other State or power whatsoever, except that they may be delegated to Congress, receiving no additional allowance.

These judges, assembled together, shall constitute the Court of Appeals, whose business shall be to receive and determine appeals from the three superior courts, but to receive no original causes, except in the cases expressly permitted herein.

A majority of the members of either of these courts, and not fewer, shall be a quorum. But in the Court of Appeals nine members shall be necessary to do business. Any smaller numbers however may be authorized by the legislature to adjourn their respective courts.

They shall be allowed for the present —— each by the year, payable quarterly out of any money which shall be in the public treasury. Their salaries, however, may be increased or abated, from time to time, at the discretion of the legislature, provided such increase or abatement shall not by any ways or means, be made to affect, either then, or at any future time, any one of those then actually in office. At the end of each quarter their salary shall be divided into equal portions by the number of days on which, during that quarter, their respective courts sat, or should have sat, and one of these portions shall be withheld from each member for every of the said days which, without cause allowed good by his court, he failed to attend, or departed before adjournment without their leave. If no court should have been held during the quarter, there shall be no deduction.

There shall, moreover, be a *Court of Impeachments,* to consist of three members of the Council of State, one of each of the superior courts of Chancery, Common Law, and Admiralty, two members of the house of delegates and one of the Senate, to be chosen by the body respectively of which they are. Before this court any member of the three branches of government, that is to say, the governor, any member of the council, of the two houses of legislature, or of the superior courts, may be impeached by the governor, the council, or either of the said houses or courts, and by no other, for such misbehavior in office as would be sufficient to remove him therefrom; and the only sentence they shall have authority to pass shall be that of deprivation and future incapacity of office. Seven members shall be requisite to make a court, and two-thirds of those present must concur in the sentence. The offences cognizable by this court shall be cognizable by no other, and they shall be triers of the fact as well as judges of the law.

The justices or judges of the inferior courts already erected, or hereafter to be erected, shall be appointed by the governor, on advice of the council of State, and shall hold their offices during good behavior, or the existence of their courts. For breach of the good behavior, they shall be tried according to the laws of the land, before the Court of Appeals, who shall be judges of the fact as well as of the law. The only sentence they shall have authority to pass shall be that of deprivation and future incapacity of office, and two-thirds of the members present must concur in this sentence.

All courts shall appoint their own clerks, who shall hold their offices during good behavior, or the existence of their court; they shall also appoint all other attending officers to continue during their pleasure. Clerks appointed by the supreme or superior courts shall be removable by their respective courts. Those to be appointed by other courts shall have been previously examined, and certified to be duly qualified, by some two members of the general court, and shall be removable for breach of the good behavior by the Court of Appeals only, who shall be judges of the fact as well as of the law. Two-thirds of the members present must concur in the sentence.

The justices or judges of the inferior courts may be members of the legislature.

The judgment of no inferior court shall be final, in any civil case, of greater value than fifty bushels of wheat, as last rated in the general court for setting the allowance to the members of the general assembly, nor in any case of treason, felony, or other crime which should subject the party to infamous punishment.

In all causes depending before any court, other than those of impeachments, of appeals, and military courts, facts put in issue shall be tried by jury, and in all courts whatever witnesses shall give testimony *viva voce* in open court, wherever their attendance can be procured; and all parties shall be allowed counsel and compulsory process for their witnesses.

Fines, amercements, and terms of imprisonment left indefinite by the law, other than for contempts, shall be fixed by the jury, triers of the offence.

The governor, two councillors of State, and a judge from each of the superior Courts of Chancery, Common Law, and Admiralty, shall be a council to revise all bills which shall have passed both houses of assembly, in which council the governor, when present, shall preside. Every bill, before it becomes a law, shall be represented to this council, who shall have a right to advise its rejection, returning the bill, with their advice and reasons in writing, to the house in which it originated, who shall proceed to reconsider the said bill. But if after such reconsideration, two-thirds of the house shall be of opinion that the bill should pass finally, they shall pass and send it, with the advice and written reasons of the said Council of Revision, to the other house, wherein if two-thirds also shall be of opinion it should pass finally, it shall thereupon become law; otherwise it shall not.

If any bill, presented to the said council, be not, within one week (exclusive of the day of presenting it) returned by them, with their advice of rejection and reasons, to the house wherein it originated, or to the clerk of the said house, in case of its adjournment over the expiration of the week, it shall be law from the expiration of the week, and shall then be demandable by the clerk of the House of Delegates, to be filed of record in his office.

The bills which they approve shall become law from the time of such approbation, and shall then be returned to, or demandable by, the clerk of the House of Delegates, to be filed of record in his office.

A bill rejected on advice of the Council of Revision may again be proposed, during the same session of assembly, with such alterations as will render it conformable to their advice.

The members of the said Council of Revision shall be appointed from time to time by the board or court of which they respectively are. Two of the executive and two of the judiciary members shall be requisite to do business; and to prevent the evils of non-attendance, the board and courts may at any time name all, or so many as they will, of their members, in the particular order in which they would choose the duty of attendance to devolve from preceding to subsequent members, the preceding failing to attend. They shall have additionally for their services in this council the same allowance as members of assembly have.

The confederation is made a part of this constitution, subject to such future alterations as shall be agreed to by the legislature of this State, and by all the other confederating States.

The delegates to Congress shall be five in number; any three of whom, and no fewer, may be a representation. They shall be appointed by joint ballot of both houses of assembly for any term not exceeding one year, subject to be recalled, within the term, by joint vote of both the said houses. They may at the same time be members of the legislative or judiciary departments, but not of the executive.

The benefits of the writ of Habeas Corpus shall be extended, by the legislature, to every person within this State, and without fee, and shall be so facilitated that no person may be detained in prison more than ten days after he shall have demanded and been refused such writ by the judge appointed by law, or if none be appointed, then by any judge of a superior court, nor more than ten days after such writ shall have been served on the person detaining him, and no order given, on due examination, for his remandment or discharge.

The military shall be subordinate to the civil power.

Printing presses shall be subject to no other restraint than liableness to legal prosecution for false facts printed and published.

Any two of the three branches of government concurring in opinion, each by the voice of two-thirds of their whole existing number, that a convention is necessary for altering this constitution, or correcting breaches of it, they shall be authorized to issue writs to every county for the election of so many delegates as they are authorized to send to the general assembly, which elections shall be held, and writs returned, as the laws shall have provided in the case of elections of delegates of assembly, *mutatis mutandis,* and the said delegates shall meet at the usual place of holding assemblies, three months after date of such writs, and shall be acknowledged to have equal powers with this present convention. The said writs shall be signed by all the members approving the same.

*To introduce this government,* the following special and temporary provision is made.

This convention being authorized only to amend those laws which constituted the form of government, no general dissolution of the whole system of laws can be supposed to have taken place; but all laws in force at the meeting of this convention, and not inconsistent with this constitution, remain in full force, subject to alterations by the ordinary legislature.

The present general assembly shall continue till the forty-second day after the last Monday of November in this present year. On the said last Monday of November in this present year, the several counties shall by their electors qualified as provided by this constitution, elect delegates, which for the present shall be, in number, one for every —— militia of the said county, according to the latest returns in possession of the governor, and shall also choose senatorial electors in proportion thereto, which senatorial electors shall meet on the fourteenth day after the day of their election, at the court house of that county of their present district which would stand first in an alphabetical arrangement of their counties, and shall choose senators in the proportion fixed by this constitution. The elections and returns shall be conducted, in all circumstances not hereby particularly prescribed, by the same persons and under the same forms as prescribed by the present laws in elections of senators and delegates of assembly. The said senators and delegates shall constitute the first general assembly of the new government, and shall specially apply themselves to the procuring an exact return from every county of the number of its qualified electors, and to the settlement of the number of delegates to be elected for the ensuing general assembly.

The present governor shall continue in office to the end of the term for which he was elected.

All other officers of every kind shall continue in office as they would have done had their appointment been under this constitution, and new ones, where new are hereby called for, shall be appointed by the authority to which such appointment is referred. One of the present judges of the general court, he consenting thereto, shall by joint ballot of both houses of assembly, at their first meeting, be transferred to the High Court of Chancery.

## COMMENTS ON THE FEDERAL CONSTITUTION[1]

December 20, 1787

I like much the general idea of framing a government, which should go on of itself, peaceably, without needing continual recurrence to the State legislatures. I like the organization of the government into legislative, judiciary and executive. I like the power given the legislature to lexy taxes, and for that reason solely, I approve of the greater House being chosen by the people directly. For though I think a House so chosen, will be very far inferior to the present Congress, will be very illy qualified to legislate for the Union, for foreign nations, &c., yet this evil does not weigh against the good, of preserving inviolate the fundamental principle, that the people are not to be taxed but by representatives chosen immediately by themselves. I am captivated by the compromise of the opposite claims of the great and little States, of the latter to equal, and the former to proportional influence. I am much pleased too, with the substitution of the method of voting by person, instead of that of voting by States; and I like the negative given to the Executive, conjointly with a third of either House; though I should have liked it better, had the judiciary been associated for that purpose, or invested separately with a similar power. There are other good things of less moment. I will now tell you what I do not like. First, the omission of a bill of rights, providing clearly, and without the aid of sophism, for freedom of religion, freedom of the press, protection against standing armies, restriction of monopolies, the eternal and unremitting force of the habeas corpus laws, and trials by jury in all matters of fact triable by the laws of the land, and not by the laws of nations. To say, as Mr. Wilson does, that a bill of rights was not necessary, because all is reserved in the case of the general govern-

[1] Letter to James Madison.

ment which is not given, while in the particular ones, all is given which is not reserved, might do for the audience to which it was addressed; but it is surely a *gratis dictum,* the reverse of which might just as well be said; and it is opposed by strong inferences from the body of the instrument, as well as from the omission of the cause of our present Confederation, which had made the reservation in express terms. It was hard to conclude, because there has been a want of uniformity among the States as to the cases triable by jury, because some have been so incautious as to dispense with this mode of trial in certain cases, therefore, the more prudent States shall be reduced to the same level of calamity. It would have been much more just and wise to have concluded the other way, that as most of the States had preserved with jealousy this sacred palladium of liberty, those who had wandered, should be brought back to it; and to have established general right rather than general wrong. For I consider all the ill as established, which may be established. I have a right to nothing, which another has a right to take away; and Congress will have a right to take away trials by jury in all civil cases. Let me add, that a bill of rights is what the people are entitled to against every government on earth, general or particular; and what no just government should refuse, or rest on inference.

The second feature I dislike, and strongly dislike, is the abandonment, in every instance, of the principle of rotation in office, and most particularly in the case of the President. Reason and experience tell us, that the first magistrate will always be re-elected if he may be re-elected. He is then an officer for life. This once observed, it becomes of so much consequence to certain nations, to have a friend or a foe at the head of our affairs, that they will interfere with money and with arms. A Galloman, or an Angloman, will be supported by the nation he befriends. If once elected, and at a second or third election outvoted by one or two votes, he will pretend false votes, foul play, hold possession of the reigns of government, be supported by the States voting for him, especially if they be the central ones, lying in a compact body themselves, and separating their opponents; and they will be aided by one nation in Europe, while the majority are aided by another. The election of a President of America, some years hence, will be much more interesting to certain nations of Europe, than ever the election of a King of Poland was. Reflect on all the instances in history, ancient and modern, of elective monarchies, and say if they do not give foundation for my fears; the Roman Emperors, the Popes while they were of any importance, the German Emperors till they became hereditary in practice, the Kings of Poland, the Deys of the Ottoman dependencies. It may be said, that if elections are to be attended with these disorders, the less frequently they are repeated the better. But experience says, that to free them from disorder, they must be rendered less interesting by a necessity of change. No foreign power, nor domestic party, will waste their blood and money to elect a person, who must go out at the end of a short period. The power of removing every fourth year by the vote of the people, is a power which they will not exercise, and if they were disposed to exercise it, they would not be permitted. The King of Poland is removable every day by the diet. But they never remove him. Nor would Russia, the Emperor, &c., permit them to do it. Smaller objections are, the appeals on matters of fact as well as laws; and the binding all persons, legislative, executive and judiciary by oath, to maintain that constitution. I do not pretend to decide, what would be the best method of procuring the establishment of the manifold good things in this constitution, and of getting rid of the bad. Whether by adopting it, in hopes of future amendment; or after it shall have been duly weighed and canvassed by the people, after seeing the parts they generally dislike, and those they generally approve, to say to them, "We see now what you wish. You are willing to give to your federal government such and such powers; but you wish, at the same time, to have such and such fundamental rights secured to you, and certain sources of convulsion taken away. Be it so. Send together deputies again. Let them establish your fundamental rights by a sacrosanct declaration, and let them pass the parts of the constitution you have approved. These will give powers to your federal government sufficient for your happiness."

This is what might be said, and would probably produce a speedy, more perfect and more permanent form of government. At all events, I hope you will not be discouraged from making other trials, if the present one should fail. We are never permitted to despair of the commonwealth. I have thus told you freely what I like, and what I dislike, merely as a matter of curiosity; for I know it is not in my power to offer matter of information to your judgment, which has been formed after hearing and weighing everything which the wisdom of man could offer on these subjects. I own, I am not a friend to a very energetic government. It is always oppressive. It places the governors indeed more at their ease, at the expense of the people. The late rebellion in Massachusetts has given more alarm, than I think it should have done. Calculate that one rebellion in thirteen States in the course of eleven years, is but one for each State in a century and a half. No country should be so long without one. Nor will any degree of power in the hands of government, prevent insurrections. In England, where the hand of power is heavier than with us, there are seldom half a dozen years without an insurrection. In France, where it is still heavier, but less despotic, as Montesquieu supposes, than in some other countries, and where there are always two or three hundred thousand men ready to crush insurrections, there have been three in the course of the three years I have been here, in every one of which greater numbers were engaged than in Massachusetts, and a great deal more blood was spilt. In Turkey, where the sole nod of the despot is death, insurrections are the events of every day. Compare again the ferocious depredations of their insurgents, with the order, the moderation and the almost self-extinguishment of ours. And say, finally, whether peace is best preserved by giving energy to the government, or information to the people. This last is the most certain, and the most legitimate engine of government. Educate and inform the whole mass of the people. Enable them to see that it is their interest to preserve peace and order, and they will preserve them. And it requires no very high degree of education to convince them of this. They are the only sure reliance for the preservation of our liberty. After all, it is my principle that the will of the majority should prevail. If they approve the proposed constitution in all its parts, I shall concur in it cheerfully, in hopes they will amend it, whenever they shall find it works wrong. This reliance cannot deceive us, as long as we remain virtuous; and I think we shall be so, as long as agriculture is our principal object, which will be the case, while there remains vacant lands in any part of America. When we get piled upon one another in large cities, as in Europe, we shall become corrupt as in Europe, and go to eating one another as they do there. I have tired you by this time with disquisitions which you have already heard repeated by others, a thousand and a thousand times; and therefore, shall only add assurances of the esteem and attachment with which I have the honor to be, dear Sir, your affectionate friend and servant.

## BILL OF RIGHTS[1]

March 15, 1789

In the arguments in favor of a declaration of rights, you omit one which has great weight with me; the legal check which it puts into the hands of the judiciary. This is a body, which, if rendered independent and kept strictly to their own department, merits great confidence for their learning and integrity. In fact, what degree of confidence would be too much, for a body composed of such men as Wythe, Blair and Pendleton? On characters like these, the "*civium ardor prava jubentium*" would make no impression. I am happy to find that, on the whole, you are a friend to this amendment.

The declaration of rights is, like all other human blessings, alloyed with some inconveniences, and not accomplishing fully its object. But the good in this instance, vastly overweighs the evil. I cannot refrain from making short answers to the objections which your letter states to have been raised. 1. That the rights in question are reserved, by the manner in which the federal powers are granted. Answer. A constitutive act may, certainly, be so formed, as to need no declaration of rights. The act itself has the force of a

[1] Letter to James Madison.

declaration, as far as it goes; and if it goes to all material points, nothing more is wanting. In the draught of a constitution which I had once a thought of proposing in Virginia, and printed afterwards,[2] I endeavored to reach all the great objects of public liberty, and did not mean to add a declaration of rights. Probably the object was imperfectly executed; but the deficiencies would have been supplied by others, in the course of discussion. But in a constitutive act which leaves some precious articles unnoticed, and raises implications against others, a declaration of rights becomes necessary, by way of supplement. This is the case of our new federal constitution. This instrument forms us into one State, as to certain objects, and gives us a legislative and executive body for these objects. It should, therefore, guard us against their abuses of power, within the field submitted to them. 2. A positive declaration of some essential rights could not be obtained in the requisite latitude. Answer. Half a loaf is better than no bread. If we cannot secure all our rights, let us secure what we can. 3. The limited powers of the federal government, and jealousy of the subordinate governments, afford a security which exists in no other instance. Answer. The first member of this seems resolvable into the first objection before stated. The jealousy of the subordinate governments is a precious reliance. But observe that those governments are only agents. They must have principles furnished them, whereon to found their opposition. The declaration of rights will be the text, whereby they will try all the acts of the federal government. In this view, it is necessary to the federal government also; as by the same text, they may try the opposition of the subordinate governments. 4. Experience proves the inefficacy of a bill of rights. True. But though it is not absolutely efficacious under all circumstances, it is of great potency always, and rarely inefficacious. A brace the more will often keep up the building which would have fallen, with that brace the less. There is a remarkable difference between the characters of the inconveniences which attend a declaration of rights, and those which attend the want of it. The inconveniences of the declaration are, that it may cramp government in its useful exertions. But the evil of this is short-lived, moderate and reparable. The inconveniences of the want of a declaration are permanent, afflicting and irreparable. They are in constant progression from bad to worse. The executive, in our governments, is not the sole, it is scarcely the principal object of my jealousy. The tyranny of the legislatures is the most formidable dread at present, and will be for many years. That of the executive will come in its turn; but it will be at a remote period. I know there are some among us, who would now establish a monarchy. But they are inconsiderable in number and weight of character. The rising race are all republicans. We were educated in royalism; no wonder, if some of

[2] For text, see pp. 103-120.

us retain that idolatry still. Our young people are educated in republicanism; an apostasy from that to royalism, is unprecedented and impossible. I am much pleased with the prospect that a declaration of rights will be added; and I hope it will be done in that way, which will not endanger the whole frame of government, or any essential part of it.

## A CHARTER OF RIGHTS, ESTABLISHED BY THE [FRENCH] KING AND NATION[1]

June, 1789

1. The States-General shall assemble, uncalled, on the first day of November, annually, and shall remain together so long as they shall see cause. They shall regulate their own elections and proceedings, and until they shall ordain otherwise, their elections shall be in the forms observed in the present year, and shall be triennial.

2. The States-General alone shall levy money on the nation, and shall appropriate it.

3. Laws shall be made by the States-General only, with the consent of the King.

4. No person shall be restrained of his liberty, but by regular process from a court of justice, authorized by a general law. (Except that a Noble may be imprisoned by order of a court of justice, on the prayer of twelve of his nearest relations.) On complaint of an unlawful imprisonment, to any judge whatever, he shall have the prisoner immediately brought before him, and shall discharge him, if his imprisonment be unlawful. The officer in whose custody the prisoner is, shall obey the orders of the judge; and both judge and officer shall be responsible civilly and criminally, for a failure of duty herein.

5. The military shall be subordinate to the civil authority.

6. Printers shall be liable to legal prosecution for printing and publishing false facts, injurious to the party prosecuting; but they shall be under no other restraint.

7. All pecuniary privileges and exemptions, enjoyed by any description of persons, are abolished.

8. All debts already contracted by the King, are hereby made the debts of the nation; and the faith thereof is pledged for their payment in due time.

9. Eighty millions of livres are now granted to the King, to be raised by loan, and reimbursed by the nation; and the taxes heretofore paid, shall continue to be paid to the end of the present year, and no longer.

[1] Jefferson sent this draft to St. Etienne and Lafayette, for them to submit it to Louis XVI or to use it as a "canvas" on which to draw up a democratic constitution for France.

10. The States-General shall now separate, and meet again on the 1st day of November next.

Done, on behalf of the whole nation, by the King and their representatives in the States-General, at Versailles, this — day of June, 1789.

Signed by the King, and by every member individually, and in his presence.

## PETITION ON THE ELECTION OF JURORS[1]

October, 1798

TO THE GENERAL ASSEMBLY OF THE COMMONWEALTH OF VIRGINIA: The Petition of Sundry persons inhabitants of the county of Albemarle and citizens of the said Commonwealth respectfully sheweth.

That though civil government duly framed and administered be one of the greatest blessings and most powerful instruments for procuring safety and happiness to men collected in large societies, yet such is the proneness of those to whom its powers are necessarily deputed to pervert them to the attainment of personal wealth and dominion and to the utter oppression of their fellowmen, that it has become questionable whether the condition of our aboriginal neighbors who live without laws or magistrates but in the weight of their burthens. That the citizens of these U.S. impressed with this mortifying truth when they deposed the abusive government under which they have lived, founded their new forms, as well particular as general in that fact and principle, that the people themselves are the safest deposit of power, and that none therefore should be trusted to others which they can competently exercise themselves, that their own experience having proved that the people are competent to the appointment or election of their agents, that of their chief executive magistrates was reserved to be made by themselves or by others chosen by themselves: as was also the choice of their legislatures whether composed of one or more branches: that in the judiciary department, sensible that they were inadequate to questions of law, these were in ordinary cases confided to permanent judges, reserving to juries only extraordinary cases where a bias in the permanent judge might be suspected,

[1] On October 26, 1798, Jefferson wrote to James Madison: "The day after you left us, I sat down and wrote the petition I mentioned to you. It is not yet correct enough, and I enclose you a copy to which I pray your corrections, and to return it by the next post, that it may be set in motion. On turning to the judiciary law of the U.S. I find they established the designation of jurors *by lot otherwise as* NOW *practised in the several states;* should this prevent, in the first moment the execution of so much of the proposed law, as respects the federal courts, the people will be in possession of the right of electing jurors as to the state courts."

To John Taylor, Jefferson sent a copy of the same petition, on November 26, 1798, and asked him to correct it: "It is a petition for a reformation in the manner of appointing our juries. . . . Make it as perfect as you can. . . . It is the only thing which can yield us a little present protection against the dominion of a faction."

and where honest ignorance would be safer than perverted science: and reserving to themselves also the whole department of fact which constitutes indeed the great mass of judiciary litigations: that the wisdom of these reservations will be apparent on a recurrence to the history of that country from which we chiefly emigrated, where the faint glimmerings of liberty and safety now remaining to the nation are kept in feeble life by the reserved powers of the people only. That in the establishment of the trial by jury, however, a great inconsistence has been overlooked in this and some others of the states, or rather has been copied from their original without due attention: for while the competence of the people to the appointment even of the highest executive and the legislative agents is admitted and established, and their competence to be themselves the triers of judiciary facts, the appointment of the special individuals from among themselves who shall be such triers of fact has not been left in their hands, but has been placed by law in officers dependent on the executive or judiciary bodies: that triers of fact are therefore habitually taken in this state from among accidental bystanders and too often composed of foreigners attending on matters of business and of idle persons collected for purposes of dissipation, and in cases interesting to the powers of the public functionaries may be specially selected from descriptions of persons to be found in every country, whose ignorance or dependence renders them pliable to the will and designs of powers. That in others of these states [~~and particularly in those to the eastward of the union~~], this germ of rottedness in the constitution of juries has been carefully excluded and their laws have provided with laudable foresight for the appointment of jurors by selectmen chosen by the people themselves: and to a like restitution of principle and salutary precaution against the abuse of power by the public functionaries, who never did yet in any country fail to betray and oppress those for the care of whose affairs they were appointed, by force if they possessed it, or by fraud and delusion if they did not, your petitioners pray the timely attention of their legislature, while that legislature (and with a heartfelt satisfaction the petitioners pronounce it) are still honest enough to wish the preservation of the rights of the people, and wise enough to circumscribe in time the spread of that gangrene which sooner than many are aware may reach the vitals of our political existence.

And lest it should be supposed that the popular appointment of jurors may scarcely be practicable in a state so exclusive and circumstanced as ours, your petitioners will undertake to suggest one mode, not presuming to propose it for the adoption of the legislature, but firmly relying that their wisdom will devise a better: they observe then that by a law already passed for the establishment of schools provision has been made for laying off every country into districts or precincts; that this division which offers so many valuable resources for the purposes of information, of justice, of order and police, may be recurred to for the object now in contemplation, and may be completed for this purpose where it has not been done for the other, and the inhabitants of every precinct may meet at a given time and place in their precinct and in the presence of the constable or other head officer of the precinct, elect from among themselves someone to be a juror, that from among those so chosen in every county someone may be designated by lot, who shall attend the ensuing session of the federal court within the state to act as grand and petty jurors, one of those from every senatorial district being designated by lot for a grand juror, and the residue attending to serve as petty jurors to be in like manner designated by lot in every particular case: that of the others so chosen in every county composing a district for the itinerant courts of this Commonwealth so many may be taken by lot as shall suffice for grand and petty juries for the district court next ensuing their election; and the residue so chosen in each county may attend their own county courts for the same purposes till another election, or if too numerous the supernumeraries may be discharged by lot: and that such compensation may be allowed for these services as without rendering the office an object worth canvassing may yet protect the juror from actual loss. That an institution on this outline, or such better as the wisdom of the General assembly will devise, so modified as to guard it against the intrigue of parties, the influence of power, or irregularities of conduct, and further matured from time to time as experience shall develop its imperfections, may long preserve the trial by jury, in its pure and original spirit, as the true tribunal of the people, for a mitigation in the execution of hard laws when the power of preventing their passage is lost, and may afford some protection to persecuted man, whether alien or citizen, which the aspect of the times warns we may want.

And juror petitioners, waiving the expression of many important considerations which will offer themselves readily to the reflection of the general assembly, pray them to take the premises into deep and serious consideration and to do therein for their country what their wisdom shall deem best, and they as in duty bound shall ever pray, &c.

## THE KENTUCKY RESOLUTIONS [1]

November, 1798

1. *Resolved,* That the several States composing the United States of America, are not united on the principle of unlimited submission to their general government; but that, by a compact under the style and title of a Constitution for the United States, and of amendments thereto, they consti-

[1] Jefferson kept his authorship of these resolutions—a protest against the Alien and Sedition Acts—a secret. The resolutions were adopted by the Kentucky legislature on November 10, 1798.

tuted a general government for special purposes—delegated to that government certain definite powers, reserving, each State to itself, the residuary mass of right to their own self-government; and that whensoever the general government assumes undelegated powers, its acts are unauthoritative, void, and of no force: that to this compact each State acceded as a State, and is an integral party, its co-States forming, as to itself, the other party: that the government created by this compact was not made the exclusive or final judge of the extent of the powers delegated to itself; since that would have made its discretion, and not the Constitution, the measure of its powers; but that, as in all other cases of compact among powers having no common judge, each party has an equal right to judge for itself, as well of infractions as of the mode and measure of redress.

2. *Resolved,* That the Constitution of the United States, having delegated to Congress a power to punish treason, counterfeiting the securities and current coin of the United States, piracies, and felonies committed on the high seas, and offences against the law of nations, and no other crimes whatsoever; and it being true as a general principle, and one of the amendments to the Constitution having also declared, that "the powers not delegated to the United States by the Constitution, nor prohibited by it to the States, are reserved to the States respectively, or to the people," therefore the act of Congress, passed on the 14th day of July, 1798, and intituled "An Act in addition to the act intituled An Act for the punishment of certain crimes against the United States," as also the act passed by them on the — day of June, 1798, intituled "An Act to punish frauds committed on the bank of the United States," (and all their other acts which assume to create, define, or punish crimes, other than those so enumerated in the Constitution,) are altogether void, and of no force; and that the power to create, define, and punish such other crimes is reserved, and, of right, appertains solely and exclusively to the respective States, each within its own territory.

3. *Resolved,* That it is true as a general principle, and is also expressly declared by one of the amendments to the Constitution, that "the powers not delegated to the United States by the Constitution, nor prohibited by it to the States, are reserved to the States respectively, or to the people"; and that no power over the freedom of religion, freedom of speech, or freedom of the press being delegated to the United States by the Constitution, nor prohibited by it to the States, all lawful powers respecting the same did of right remain, and were reserved to the States or the people: that thus was manifested their determination to retain to themselves the right of judging how far the licentiousness of speech and of the press may be abridged without lessening their useful freedom, and how far those abuses which cannot be separated from their use should be tolerated, rather than the use be destroyed. And thus also they guarded against all abridgment by the United

States of the freedom of religious opinions and exercises, and retained to themselves the right of protecting the same, as this State, by a law passed on the general demand of its citizens, had already protected them from all human restraint or interference. And that in addition to this general principle and express declaration, another and more special provision has been made by one of the amendments to the Constitution, which expressly declares, that "Congress shall make no law respecting an establishment of religion, or prohibiting the free exercise thereof, or abridging the freedom of speech or of the press": thereby guarding in the same sentence, and under the same words, the freedom of religion, of speech, and of the press: insomuch, that whatever violated either, throws down the sanctuary which covers the others, and that libels, falsehood, and defamation, equally with heresy and false religion, are withheld from the cognizance of federal tribunals. That, therefore, the act of Congress of the United States, passed on the 14th day of July, 1798, intituled "An Act in addition to the act intituled An Act for the punishment of certain crimes against the United States," which does abridge the freedom of the press, is not law, but is altogether void, and of no force.

4. *Resolved,* That alien friends are under the jurisdiction and protection of the laws of the State wherein they are: that no power over them has been delegated to the United States, nor prohibited to the individual States, distinct from their power over citizens. And it being true as a general principle, and one of the amendments to the Constitution having also declared, that "the powers not delegated to the United States by the Constitution, nor prohibited by it to the States, are reserved to the States respectively, or to the people," the act of the Congress of the United States, passed on the — day of July, 1798, intituled "An Act concerning aliens," which assumes powers over alien friends, not delegated by the Constitution, is not law, but is altogether void, and of no force.

5. *Resolved,* That in addition to the general principle, as well as the express declaration, that powers not delegated are reserved, another and more special provision, inserted in the Constitution from abundant caution, has declared that "the migration or importation of such persons as any of the States now existing shall think proper to admit, shall not be prohibited by the Congress prior to the year 1808": that this commonwealth does admit the migration of alien friends, described as the subject of the said act concerning aliens: that a provision against prohibiting their migration, is a provision against all acts equivalent thereto, or it would be nugatory: that to remove them when migrated, is equivalent to a prohibition of their migration, and is, therefore, contrary to the said provision of the Constitution, and void.

6. *Resolved,* That the imprisonment of a person under the protection of the laws of this commonwealth, on his failure to obey the simple *order* of

the President to depart out of the United States, as is undertaken by said act intituled "An Act concerning aliens," is contrary to the Constitution, one amendment to which has provided that "no person shall be deprived of liberty without due progress of law"; and that another having provided that "in all criminal prosecutions the accused shall enjoy the right to public trial by an impartial jury, to be informed of the nature and cause of the accusation, to be confronted with the witnesses against him, to have compulsory process for obtaining witnesses in his favor, and to have the assistance of counsel for his defence," the same act, undertaking to authorize the President to remove a person out of the United States, who is under the protection of the law, on his own suspicion, without accusation, without jury, without public trial, without confrontation of the witnesses against him, without hearing witnesses in his favor, without defence, without counsel, is contrary to the provision also of the Constitution, is therefore not law, but utterly void, and of no force: that transferring the power of judging any person, who is under the protection of the laws, from the courts to the President of the United States, as is undertaken by the same act concerning aliens, is against the article of the Constitution which provides that "the judicial power of the United States shall be vested in courts, the judges of which shall hold their offices during good behavior"; and that the said act is void for that reason also. And it is further to be noted, that this transfer of judiciary power is to that magistrate of the general government who already possesses all the Executive, and a negative on all Legislative powers.

7. *Resolved,* That the construction applied by the General Government (as is evidenced by sundry of their proceedings) to those parts of the Constitution of the United States which delegate to Congress a power "to lay and collect taxes, duties, imports, and excises, to pay the debts, and provide for the common defence and general welfare of the United States," and "to make all laws which shall be necessary and proper for carrying into execution the powers vested by the Constitution in the government of the United States, or in any department or officer thereof," goes to the destruction of all limits prescribed to their power by the Constitution: that words meant by the instrument to be subsidiary only to the execution of limited powers, ought not to be so construed as themselves to give unlimited powers, nor a part to be so taken as to destroy the whole residue of that instrument: that the proceedings of the General Government under color of these articles, will be a fit and necessary subject of revisal and correction, at a time of greater tranquillity, while those specified in the preceding resolutions call for immediate redress.

8th. *Resolved,* That a committee of conference and correspondence be appointed, who shall have in charge to communicate the preceding resolutions to the Legislatures of the several States; to assure them that this commonwealth continues in the same esteem of their friendship and union which it has manifested from that moment at which a common danger first suggested a common union: that it considers union, for specified national purposes, and particularly to those specified in their late federal compact, to be friendly to the peace, happiness and prosperity of all the States: that faithful to that compact, according to the plain intent and meaning in which it was understood and acceded to by the several parties, it is sincerely anxious for its preservation: that it does also believe, that to take from the States all the powers of self-government and transfer them to a general and consolidated government, without regard to the special delegations and reservations solemnly agreed to in that compact, is not for the peace, happiness or prosperity of these States; and that therefore this commonwealth is determined, as it doubts not its co-States are, to submit to undelegated, and consequently unlimited powers in no man, or body of men on earth: that in cases of an abuse of the delegated powers, the members of the general government, being chosen by the people, a change by the people would be the constitutional remedy; but, where powers are assumed which have not been delegated, a nullification of the act is the rightful remedy: that every State has a natural right in cases not within the compact, (*casus non fœderis,*) to nullify of their own authority all assumptions of power by others within their limits: that without this right, they would be under the dominion, absolute and unlimited, of whosoever might exercise this right of judgment for them: that nevertheless, this commonwealth, from motives of regard and respect for its co-States, has wished to communicate with them on the subject: that with them alone it is proper to communicate, they alone being parties to the compact, and solely authorized to judge in the last resort of the powers exercised under it, Congress being not a party, but merely the creature of the compact, and subject as to its assumptions of power to the final judgment of those by whom, and for whose use itself and its powers were all created and modified: that if the acts before specified should stand, these conclusions would flow from them; that the general government may place any act they think proper on the list of crimes, and punish it themselves whether enumerated or not enumerated by the constitution as cognizable by them: that they may transfer its cognizance to the President, or any other person, who may himself be the accuser, counsel, judge and jury, whose *suspicions* may be the evidence, his *order* the sentence, his *officer* the executioner, and his breast the sole record of the transaction: that a very numerous and valuable description of the inhabitants of these States being, by this precedent, reduced, as outlaws, to the absolute dominion of one man, and the barrier of the Constitution thus swept away from us all, no rampart now remains against the passions and the powers of a majority in Congress to protect from a like exportation, or other more grievous punishment, the minority of the same body, the legislatures, judges, governors and counsellors of the States, nor their other peaceable inhabitants, who may venture to reclaim the constitutional rights and liberties of the States and people, or who for other causes, good or bad, may be obnoxious to the views, or marked by the suspicions of the President, or be thought dangerous to his or their election, or other interests, public or personal: that the friendless alien has indeed been selected as the safest subject of a first experiment; but the citizen will soon follow, or rather, has already followed, for already has a sedition act marked him as its prey: that these and successive acts of the same character, unless arrested at the threshold, necessarily drive these States into revolution and blood, and will furnish new calumnies against republican government, and new pretexts for those who wish it to be believed that man cannot be governed but by a rod of iron: that it would be a dangerous delusion were a confidence in the men of our choice to silence our fears for the safety of our rights: that confidence is everywhere the parent of despotism—free government is founded in jealousy, and not in confidence; it is jealousy and not confidence which prescribes limited constitutions, to bind down those whom we are obliged to trust with power: that our Constitution has accordingly fixed the limits to which, and no further, our confidence may go; and let the honest advocate of confidence read the Alien and Sedition acts, and say if the Constitution has not been wise in fixing limits to the government it created, and whether we should be wise in destroying those limits. Let him say what the government is, if it be not a tyranny, which the men of our choice have conferred on our President, and the President of our choice has assented to, and accepted over the friendly strangers to whom the mild spirit of our country and its laws have pledged hospitality and protection: that the men of our choice have more respected the bare *suspicions* of the President, than the solid right of innocence, the claims of justification, the sacred force of truth, and the forms and substance of law and justice. In questions of power, then, let no more be heard of confidence in man, but bind him down from mischief by the chains of the Constitution. That this commonwealth does therefore call on its co-States for an expression of their sentiments on the acts concerning aliens, and for the punishment of certain crimes herein before specified, plainly declaring whether these acts are or are not authorized by the federal compact. And it doubts not that their sense will be so announced as to prove their attachment unaltered to limited government, whether general or particular. And that the rights and liberties of their co-States will be exposed to no dangers by remaining embarked in a common bottom with their own. That they will concur with this commonwealth in considering the said acts as so palpably against the Constitution as to amount to an undisguised declaration that that compact is not meant to be the measure of the powers of the General Government, but that it will proceed in the exercise over these States, of all powers whatsoever: that they will view this as seizing the rights of the States, and consolidating them in the hands of the General Government, with a power assumed to bind the States (not merely as the cases made federal, *casus fœderis* but), in all cases whatsoever, by laws made, not with their consent, but by others against their consent: that this would be to surrender the form of government we have chosen, and live under one deriving its powers from its own will, and not from our authority; and that the co-States, recurring to their natural right in cases not made federal, will concur in declaring these acts void, and of no force, and will each take measures of its own for providing that neither these acts, nor any others of the General Government not plainly and intentionally authorized by the Constitution, shall be exercised within their respective territories.

9th. *Resolved,* That the said committee be authorized to communicate by writing or personal conferences, at any times or places whatever, with any person or persons who may be appointed by any one or more co-States to correspond or confer with them; and that they lay their proceedings before the next session of Assembly.

## THE SOLEMN DECLARATION AND PROTEST OF THE COMMONWEALTH OF VIRGINIA, ON THE PRINCIPLES OF THE CONSTITUTION OF THE UNITED STATES OF AMERICA, AND ON THE VIOLATIONS OF THEM

December, 1825.

We, the General Assembly of Virginia, on behalf, and in the name of the people thereof, do declare as follows:

The States in North America which confederated to establish their independence of the government of Great Britain, of which Virginia was one, became, on that acquisition, free and independent States, and as such, authorized to constitute governments, each for itself, in such form as it thought best.

They entered into a compact (which is called the Constitution of the United States of America), by which they agreed to unite in a single government as to their relations with each other, and with foreign nations, and as to certain other articles particularly specified. They retained at the same time, each to itself, the other rights of independent government, comprehending mainly their domestic interests.

For the administration of their federal branch, they agreed to appoint, in conjunction, a distinct set of functionaries, legislative, executive, and judiciary, in the manner settled in that compact: while to each, severally, and of course, remained its original right of appointing, each for itself, a separate set of functionaries, legislative, executive, and judiciary, also, for administering the domestic branch of their respective governments.

These two sets of officers, each independent of the other, constitute thus a *whole* of government, for each State separately; the powers ascribed to the one, as specifically made federal, exercised over the whole, the residuary powers, retained to the other, exercisable exclusively over its particular State, foreign herein, each to the others, as they were before the original compact.

To this construction of government and distribution of its powers, the commonwealth of Virginia does religiously and affectionately adhere, opposing, with equal fidelity and firmness, the usurpation of either set of functionaries on the rightful powers of the other.

But the federal branch has assumed in some cases, and claimed in others, a right of enlarging its own powers by constructions, inferences, and indefinite deductions from those directly given, which this assembly does declare to be usurpations of the powers retained to the independent branches, mere interpolations into the compact, and direct infractions of it.

They claim, for example, and have commenced the exercise of a right to construct roads, open canals, and effect other internal improvements within the territories and jurisdictions exclusively belonging to the several States, which this assembly does declare has not been given to that branch by the constitutional compact, but remains to each State among its domestic and unalienated powers, exercisable within itself and by its domestic authorities alone.

This assembly does further disavow and declare to be most false and unfounded, the doctrine that the compact, in authorizing its federal branch to lay and collect taxes, duties, imposts and excises to pay the debts and provide for the common defence and general welfare of the United States, has given them thereby a power to do whatever *they* may think, or pretend, would promote the general welfare, which construction would make that, of itself, a complete government, without limitation of powers; but that the plain sense and obvious meaning were, that they might levy the taxes necessary to provide for the general welfare, by the various acts of power therein specified and delegated to them, and by no others.

Nor is it admitted, as has been said, that the people of these States, by not investing their federal branch with all the means of bettering their condition, have denied to themselves any which may effect that purpose; since, in the distribution of these means they have given to that branch those which belong to its department, and to the States have reserved separately the residue which belong to them separately. And thus by the organization of the two branches taken together, have completely secured the first object of human association, the full improvement of their condition, and reserved to themselves all the faculties of multiplying their own blessings.

Whilst the General Assembly thus declares the rights retained by the States, rights which they have never yielded, and which this State will never voluntarily yield, they do not mean to raise the banner of disaffection, or of separation from their sister States, co-parties with themselves to this compact. They know and value too highly the blessings of their Union as to foreign nations and questions arising among themselves, to consider every infraction as to be met by actual resistance. They respect too affectionately the opinions of those possessing the same rights under the same instrument, to make every difference of construction a ground of immediate rupture. They would, indeed, consider such a rupture as among the greatest calamities which could befall them; but not the greatest. There is yet one greater, submission to a government of unlimited powers. It is only when the hope of avoiding this shall become absolutely desperate, that further forbearance could not be indulged. Should a majority of the co-parties, therefore, contrary to the expectation and hope of this assembly, prefer, at this time, acquiescence in these assumptions of power by the federal member of the government, we will be patient and suffer much, under the confidence that time, ere it be too late, will prove to them also the bitter consequences in which that usurpation will involve us all. In the meanwhile, we will breast with them, rather than separate from them, every misfortune, save that only of living under a government of unlimited powers. We owe every other sacrifice to ourselves, to our federal brethren, and to the world at large, to pursue with temper and perseverance the great experiment which shall prove that man is capable of living in society, governing itself by laws self-imposed, and securing to its members the enjoyment of life, liberty, property, and peace; and further to show, that even when the government of its choice shall manifest a tendency to degeneracy, we are not at once to despair but that the will and the watchfulness of its sounder parts will reform its aberrations, recall it to original and legitimate principles, and restrain it within the rightful limits of self-government. And these are the objects of this Declaration and Protest.

Supposing then, that it might be for the good of the whole, as some of its co-States seem to think, that the power of making roads and canals should be added to those directly given to the federal branch, as more likely to be systematically and beneficially directed, than by the independent action of the several States, this commonwealth, from respect to these opinions, and a desire of conciliation with its co-States, will consent, in concurrence with them, to make this addition, provided it be done regularly by an amendment of the compact, in the way established by that instrument, and provided also, it be sufficiently guarded against abuses, compromises, and corrupt practices, not only of possible, but of probable occurrence.

And as a further pledge of the sincere and cordial attachment of this commonwealth to the union of the whole, so far as has been consented to by the compact called "The Constitution of the United States of America" (constructed according to the plain and ordinary meaning of its language, to the common intendment of the time, and of those who framed it); to give also to all parties and authorities, time for reflection and for consideration, whether, under a temperate view of the possible consequences, and especially of the constant obstructions which an equivocal majority must ever expect to meet, they will still prefer the assumption of this power rather than its acceptance from the free will of their constituents; and to preserve peace in the meanwhile, we proceed to make it the duty of our citizens, until the legislature shall otherwise and ultimately decide, to acquiesce under those acts of the federal branch of our government which we have declared to be usurpations, and against which, in point of right, we do protest as null and void, and never to be quoted as precedents of right.

We therefore do enact, and be it enacted by the General Assembly of Virginia, that all citizens of this commonwealth, and persons and authorities within the same, shall pay full obedience at all times to the acts which may be passed by the Congress of the United States, the object of which shall be the construction of post roads, making canals of navigation, and maintaining the same in any part of the United States, in like manner as if said acts were, *totidem verbis,* passed by the Legislature of this Commonwealth.

## *Chapter IV*

# FOREIGN POLICY: I, RELATIONS

## OPINION ON THE QUESTION WHETHER THE SENATE HAS THE RIGHT TO NEGATIVE THE GRADE OF PERSONS APPOINTED BY THE EXECUTIVE TO FILL FOREIGN MISSIONS

April 24, 1790

The constitution having declared that the President shall *nominate* and, by and with the advice and consent of the Senate, shall *appoint* ambassadors, other public ministers, and consuls, the President desired my opinion whether the Senate has a right to negative the *grade* he may think it expedient to use in a foreign mission as well as the *person* to be appointed.

I think the Senate has no right to negative the *grade*.

The constitution has divided the powers of government into three branches, Legislative, Executive and Judiciary, lodging each with a distinct magistracy. The Legislative it has given completely to the Senate and House of Representatives. It has declared that the Executive powers shall be vested in the President, submitting special articles of it to a negative by the Senate, and it has vested the Judiciary power in the courts of justice, with certain exceptions also in favor of the Senate.

The transaction of business with foreign nations is Executive altogether. It belongs, then, to the head of that department, except as to such portions of it as are specially submitted to the Senate. Exceptions are to be construed strictly.

The constitution itself indeed has taken care to circumscribe this one within very strict limits; for it gives the *nomination* of the foreign agents to the President, the *appointments* to him and the Senate jointly, and the *commissioning* to the President.

This analysis calls our attention to the strict import of each term. To *nominate* must be to *propose*. *Appointment* seems that act of the will which constitutes or makes the agent, and the *commission* is the public evidence of it.

But there are still other acts previous to these not specially enumerated in the constitution, to wit: 1st. The destination of a mission to the particular country where the public service calls for it, and second the character or grade to be employed in it. The natural order of all these is first, destination; second, grade; third, nomination; fourth, appointment; fifth, commission. If *appointment* does not comprehend the neighboring acts of *nomination* or *commission,* (and the constitution says it shall not, by giving them exclusively to the President,) still less can it pretend to comprehend those previous and more remote, of *destination* and *grade.*

The constitution, analysing the three last, shows they do not comprehend the two first. The fourth is the only one it submits to the Senate, shaping it into a right to say that "A or B is unfit to be appointed." Now, this cannot comprehend a right to say that "A or B is indeed fit to be appointed," but the grade fixed on is not the fit one to employ, or, "our connections with the country of his destination are not such as to call for any mission."

The Senate is not supposed by the constitution to be acquainted with the concerns of the Executive department. It was not intended that these should be communicated to them, nor can they therefore be qualified to judge of the necessity which calls for a mission to any particular place, or of the particular grade, more or less marked, which special and secret circumstances may call for. All this is left to the President. They are only to see that no unfit person be employed.

It may be objected that the Senate may by continual negatives on the *person,* do what amounts to a negative on the *grade,* and so, indirectly, defeat this right of the President. But this would be a breach of trust; an abuse of power confided to the Senate, of which that body cannot be supposed capable. So the President has a power to convoke the Legislature, and the Senate might defeat that power by refusing to come. This equally amounts to a negative on the power of convoking. Yet nobody will say they possess such a negative, or would be capable of usurping it by such oblique means. If the constitution had meant to give the Senate a negative on the grade or destination, as well as the person, it would have said so in direct terms, and not left it to be effected by a sidewing. It could never mean to give them the use of one power through the abuse of another.

## OPINION RESPECTING THE EXPENSES AND SALARIES OF FOREIGN MINISTERS

July 17, 1790

The bill on the intercourse with foreign nations restrains the President from allowing to Ministers Plenipotentiary, or to Congress, more than

$9,000, and $4,500 for their "personal services, and other expenses." This definition of the objects for which the allowance is provided appearing vague, the Secretary of State thought it his duty to confer with the gentlemen heretofore employed as ministers in Europe, to obtain from them, in aid of his own information, an enumeration of the expenses incident to these offices, and their opinion which of them would be included within the fixed salary, and which would be entitled to be charged separately. He, therefore, asked a conference with the Vice-President, who was acquainted with the residences of London and the Hague, and the Chief Justice, who was acquainted with that of Madrid, which took place yesterday.

The Vice-President, Chief Justice, and Secretary of State, concurred in the opinion that the salaries named by the act are much below those of the same grade at the courts of Europe, and less than the public good requires they should be. Consequently, that the expenses not included within the definition of the law, should be allowed as an additional charge.

1. *Couriers, Gazettes, Translating necessary papers, Printing necessary papers, Aids to poor Americans.*—All three agreed that these ought to be allowed as additional charges, not included within the meaning of the phrase, "his personal services, and other expenses."

2. *Postage, Stationery, Court-fees.*—One of the gentlemen being of opinion that the phrase "personal services, and other expenses," was meant to comprehend all the *ordinary expenses* of the office, considered this second class of expenses as *ordinary,* and therefore included in the fixed salary. The first class before mentioned, he had viewed as *extraordinary*. The other two gentlemen were of opinion this second class was also out of the definition, and might be allowed in addition to the salary. One of them, particularly, considered the phrase as meaning "personal services and personal expenses," that is, expenses for his personal accommodation, comforts, and maintenance. This second class of expenses is not within that description.

3. *Ceremonies;* such as diplomatic and public dinners, galas, and illuminations. One gentleman only was of opinion these might be allowed.

The expenses of the first class may probably amount to about fifty dollars a year. Those of the second, to about four or five hundred dollars. Those of the third are so different at different courts, and so indefinite in all of them, that no general estimate can be proposed.

The Secretary of State thought it his duty to lay this information before the President, supposing it might be satisfactory to himself, as well as to the diplomatic gentlemen, to leave nothing uncertain as to their allowances; and because, too, a previous determination is in some degree necessary to the forming an estimate which may not exceed the whole sum appropriated.

The Secretary of State has also consulted on the subject of the Morocco consulship, with Mr. Barclay, who furnished him with the note, of which a copy accompanies this. Considering all circumstances, Mr. Barclay is of opinion, we had better have only a consul there, and that he should be the one now residing at Morocco, because, as secretary to the Emperor, he sees him every day, and possesses his ear. He is of opinion six hundred dollars a year might suffice for him, and that it should be proposed to him not as a salary, but as a sum in gross intended to cover his expenses, and to save the trouble of keeping accounts. That this consul should be authorized to appoint agents in the seaports, who would be sufficiently paid by the consignments of vessels. He thinks the consul at Morocco would most conveniently receive his allowance through the channel of our Chargé at Madrid, on whom, also, this consulate had better be made dependent for instructions, information, and correspondence, because of the daily intercourse between Morocco and Cadiz.

The Secretary of State, on a view of Mr. Barclay's note, very much doubts the sufficiency of the sum of six hundred dollars; he supposes a little money there may save a great deal; but he is unable to propose any specific augmentation till a view of the whole diplomatic establishments and its expenses, may furnish better grounds for it.

*Estimate of the Expenses of a Minister Plenipotentiary*

July 19, 1790

| | |
|---|---|
| Minister Plenipotentiary, his salary | $9,000 |
| His outfit, suppose it to happen once in seven years, will average | 1,285 |
| His reurn at a quarter's salary will average | 321 |
| Extras, *viz.:* Gazettes, Translating, Printing, Aids to poor American sailors, Couriers, and Postage, about | 350 |
| His Secretary | 1,350 |
| | $12,396 |

*Estimate for a Chargé des Affaires*

| | |
|---|---|
| Chargé des Affaires, his salary | $4,500 |
| His outfit, once in seven years, equal to an annual sum of | 643 |
| His return at a quarter's salary, do. | 161 |
| Extras, as above | 350 |
| | $5,654 |

| | |
|---|---|
| The Agent at The Hague, his salary | $1,300 |
| Extras | 100 |
| | $1,400 |

*Estimate of the Annual Expenses of the Establishment proposed*

| | |
|---|---|
| France, a Minister Plenipotentiary | $12,306 |
| London, do. do. | 12,306 |
| Madrid, a Chargé des Affaires | 5,654 |
| Lisbon, do. do. do. | 5,654 |
| Hague, an agent | 1,400 |
| Morocco, a consul | 1,800 |
| Presents to foreign ministers on taking leave, at $1,000 each, more or less, according to their favor and time. There will be five of them. If exchanged once in seven years, it will be annually | 715 |
| | $39,835 |

*Estimate of the probable calls on our foreign fund from July 1, 1790, when the act for foreign intercourse passed, to July 1, 1791*

| | | |
|---|---|---|
| France, a Minister Plenipotentiary, his outfit | $9,000 | |
| His salary, suppose it to commence August 1st | 8,250 | |
| Extras | 320 | |
| Secretary | 1,237.5 | —$18,807.5 |
| Chargé, suppose him to remain till November 1st. Salary | 1,500 | |
| Extras | 117 | |
| His return, a quarter's salary | 1,125 | — 2,742 |
| Madrid, a Chargé, his salary | 4,500 | |
| Extras | 350 | — 4,850 |
| Lisbon, a Chargé, (or Resident,) his outfit | 4,500 | |
| His salary, suppose it to commence January 1, 1791 | 2,250 | |
| Extras | 175 | — 6,925 |
| London, an Agent, suppose him to commence October 1st, at $1,350 salary | 1,012.5 | |
| Extras, (at $100 a year) | 75 | — 1,087.5 |
| Hague, an Agent | 1,400 | |
| Morocco, Consul | 1,800 | — 3,200 |
| Presents to foreign Ministers. The dye about | 500 | |
| Two medals and chains | 2,000 | — 2,500 |
| | | $40,112 |

## CIRCULAR OF THE CONSULS AND VICE-CONSULS OF THE UNITED STATES

August 26, 1790

SIR: I expected ere this, to have been able to send you an act of Congress, prescribing some special duties and regulations for the exercise of the consular offices of the United States; but Congress not having been able to mature the act sufficiently, it lies over to their next session. In the meanwhile, I beg leave to draw your attention to some matters of information, which it is interesting to receive.

I must beg the favor of you to communicate to me every six months, a report of the vessels of the United States which enter at the ports of your district, specifying the name and burthen of each vessel, of what description she is, (to wit, ship, snow, brig, &c.,) the names of the master and owners, and number of seamen, the port of the United States from which she cleared, places touched at, her cargo outward and inward, and the owners thereof, the port to which she is bound, and times of arrival and departure; the whole arranged in a table under different columns, and the reports closing on the last days of June and December.

We wish you to use your endeavors that no vessel enter as an American in the ports of your district, which shall not be truly such, and that none be sold under that name, which are not really of the United States.

That you give to me, from time to time, information of all military preparations, and other indications of war which may take place in your ports; and when a war shall appear imminent, that you notify thereof the merchants and vessels of the United States within your district, that they may be duly on their guard; and in general, that you communicate to me such political and commercial intelligence, as you may think interesting to the United States.

The consuls and vice-consuls of the United States are free to wear the uniform of their navy, if they choose to do so. This is a deep blue coat with red facings, lining and cuffs, the cuffs slashed and a standing collar; a red waistcoat (laced or not at the election of the wearer) and blue breeches; yellow buttons with a foul anchor, and black cockades and small swords.

Be pleased to observe, that the vice-consul of one district is not at all subordinate to the consul of another. They are equally independent of each other.

The ground of distinction between these two officers is this. Our government thinks, that to whatever there may be either of honor or profit resulting from the consular office, native citizens are first entitled, where such, of proper character, will undertake the duties; but where none such offer, a vice-consul is appointed of any other nation. Should a proper native come forward at any future time, he will be named consul; but this nomination will not revoke the commission of vice-consul; it will only suspend his functions during the continuance of the consul within the limits of his jurisdiction, and on his departure therefrom, it is meant that the vice-consular authority shall revive of course, without the necessity of a re-appointment.

It is understood, that consuls and vice-consuls have authority of course, to appoint their own agents in the several ports of their district, and that it is with themselves alone those agents are to correspond.

It will be best not to fatigue the government in which you reside, or those in authority under it, with applications in unimportant cases. Husband their good dispositions for occasions of some moment, and let all representations to them be couched in the most temperate and friendly terms, never indulging in any case whatever, a single expression which may irritate.

I have the honor to be, Sir, your most obedient, and most humble servant.

## OPINION FAVORING NEUTRALITY

August 28, 1790

I am so deeply impressed with the magnitude of the dangers which will attend our government, if Louisiana and the Floridas be added to the British empire, that, in my opinion, we ought to make ourselves parties in the *general war* expected to take place, should this be the only means of preventing the calamity.

But I think we should defer this step as long as possible; because war is full of chances, which may relieve us from the necessity of interfering; and if necessary, still the later we interfere, the better we shall be prepared.

It is often indeed more easy to prevent the capture of a place, than to retake it. Should it be so in the case in question, the difference between the two operations of preventing and retaking, will not be so costly as two, three, or four years more of war.

So that I am for preserving neutrality as long, and entering into the war as late, as possible.

If this be the best course, it decides, in a good degree, what should be our conduct, if the British ask leave to march troops through our territory, or march them without leave.

It is well enough agreed, in the laws of nations, that for a neutral power to give or refuse permission to the troops of either belligerent party to pass through their territory, is no breach of neutrality, provided the same refusal or permission be extended to the other party.

If we give leave of passage then to the British troops, Spain will have no just cause of complaint against us, provided we extend the same leave to her when demanded.

If we refuse (as indeed we have a right to do), and the troops should pass notwithstanding, of which there can be little doubt, we shall stand committed. For either we must enter immediately into the war, or pocket an acknowledged insult in the face of the world; and one insult pocketed soon produces another.

There is indeed a middle course, which I should be inclined to prefer; that is, to avoid giving any answer. They will proceed notwithstanding, but to do this under our silence, will admit of palliation, and produce apologies, from military necessity; and will leave us free to pass it over without dishonor, or to make it a handle of quarrel hereafter, if we should have use for it as such. But, if we are obliged to give an answer, I think the occasion not such as should induce us to hazard that answer which might commit us to the war at so early a stage of it; and therefore that the passage should be permitted.

If they should pass without having asked leave, I should be for expressing our dissatisfaction to the British court, and keeping alive an altercation on the subject, till events should decide whether it is most expedient to accept their apologies, or profit of the aggression as a cause of war.

## OPINION ON THE QUESTION WHETHER THE UNITED STATES HAVE A RIGHT TO RENOUNCE THEIR TREATIES WITH FRANCE, OR TO HOLD THEM SUSPENDED TILL THE GOVERNMENT OF THAT COUNTRY SHALL BE ESTABLISHED

April 28, 1793

I proceed in compliance with the requisition of the President to give an opinion in writing on the general question, whether the United States have a right to renounce their treaties with France, or to hold them suspended till the government of that country shall be established?

In the consultation at the President's on the 19th inst., the Secretary of the Treasury took the following positions and consequences. France was a monarchy when we entered into treaties with it; but it has declared itself a republic, and is preparing a republican form of government. As it may issue in a republic or a military despotism, or something else which may possibly render our alliance with it dangerous to ourselves, we have a right of election to renounce the treaty altogether, or to declare it suspended till their government shall be settled in the form it is ultimately to take; and then we may judge whether we will call the treaties into operation again, or declare them forever null. Having that right of election, now, if we receive their minister without any qualifications, it will amount to an act of election to continue the treaties; and if the change they are undergoing should issue in a form which should bring danger on us, we shall not be then free to renounce them. To elect to continue them is equivalent to the making a new treaty, at this time, in the same form, that is to say, with a clause of guarantee; but to make a treaty with a clause of guarantee, during a war, is a departure from neutrality, and would make us associates in the war. To renounce or suspend the treaties, therefore, is a necessary act of neutrality.

If I do not subscribe to the soundness of this reasoning, I do most fully to its ingenuity. I shall now lay down the principles which, according to my understanding, govern the case.

I consider the people who constitute a society or nation as the source of all authority in that nation; as free to transact their common concerns by any agents they think proper; to change these agents individually, or the organization of them in form or function whenever they please; that all the acts done by these agents under the authority of the nation, are the acts of the nation, are obligatory to them and enure to their use, and can in no wise be annulled or affected by any change in the form of the government, or of the persons administering it, consequently the treaties between the United States and France, were not treaties between the United States and Louis Capet, but between the two nations of America and France; and the nations remaining in existence, though both of them have since changed their forms of government, the treaties are not annulled by these changes. The law of nations, by which this question is to be determined, is composed of three branches. 1. The moral law of our nature. 2. The usages of nations. 3. Their special conventions. The first of these only concerns this question, that is to say the moral law to which man has been subjected by his creator, and of which his feelings or conscience, as it is sometimes called, are the evidence with which his creator has furnished him. The moral duties which exist between individual and individual in a state of nature, accompany them into a state of society, and the aggregate of the duties of all the individuals composing the society constitutes the duties of that society towards any other; so that between society and society the same moral duties exist as did between the individuals composing them, while in an unassociated state, and their maker not having released them from those duties on their forming themselves into a nation. Compacts then, between nation and nation, are obligatory on them by the same moral law which obliges individuals to observe their compacts. There are circumstances, however, which sometimes excuse the non-performance of contracts between man and man; so are there also between nation and nation. When performance, for instance, becomes *impossible,* non-performance is not immoral; so if performance becomes *self-destructive* to the party, the law of self-preservation overrules the laws of obligation in others. For the reality of these principles I appeal to the true fountains of evidence, the head and heart of every rational and honest man. It is there nature has written her moral laws, and where every man may read them for himself. He will never read there the permission to annul his obligations for a time, or forever, whenever they become dangerous, useless, or disagreeable; certainly not when merely useless or disagreeable, as seems to be said in an authority which has been quoted, (Vattel, p. 2, 197) and though he may, under certain degrees of danger, yet the danger must be imminent, and the degree great. Of these, it is true, that nations are to be judges for themselves; since no one nation has a right to sit in judgment over another, but the tribunal of our consciences remains, and that also of the opinion of the world. These will revise the sentence we pass in our own case, and as we respect these, we must see that in judging ourselves we have honestly done the part of impartial and rigorous judges.

But reason which gives this right of self-liberation from a contract in certain cases, has subjected it to certain just limitations.

I. The danger which absolves us must be great, inevitable and imminent. Is such the character of that now apprehended from our treaties with France? What is that danger? 1st. Is it that if their government issues in a military despotism, an alliance with them may taint us with despotic principles? But their government when we allied ourselves to it, was perfect despotism, civil, and military, yet the treaties were made in that very state of things, and, therefore, that danger can furnish no just cause.

2d. Is it that their government may issue in a republic, and too much strengthen our republican principles? But this is the hope of the great mass of our constituents, and not their dread. They do not look with longing to the happy mean of a limited monarchy.

3d. But, says the doctrine I am combatting, the change the French are undergoing, may possibly end in something we know not what, and may bring on us danger we know not whence. In short, it may end in a Raw-head and bloody bones in the dark. Very well—let Raw-head and bloody bones come. We shall be justified in making our peace with him by renouncing our ancient friends and his enemies; for observe, it is not the *possibility of danger* which absolves a party from his contract, for that possibility always exists, and in every case. It existed in the present one, at the moment of making the contract. If *possibilities* would void contracts, there never could be a valid contract, for possibilities hang over everything. Obligation is not suspended till the danger is become real, and the moment of it so imminent, that we can no longer avoid decision without forever losing the opportunity to do it. But can a danger which has not yet taken its shape, which does not yet exist, and never may exist which cannot therefore be defined—can such a danger, I ask, be so imminent that if we fail to pronounce on it in this moment, we can never have another opportunity of doing it?

4. As to the danger apprehended, Is it that (the treaties remaining valid) the clause guaranteeing their West Indian lands will engage us in the war? But does the guarantee engage us to enter into the war on any event? Are we to enter into it before we are called on by our allies?

Have we been called on by them? Shall we ever be called on?

Is it their interest to call on us?

Can they call on us before their islands are invaded, or immediately threatened?

If they can save them themselves, have they a right to call on us?

Are we obliged to go to war at once, without trying peaceable negotiations with their enemy?

If all these questions are against us, there are still others left behind.

Are we in a condition to go to war?

Can we be expected to begin before we are in condition?

Will the islands be lost if we do not save them?

Have we the means of saving them?

If we cannot save them, are we bound to go to war for a desperate object?

Many, if not most of these questions offer grounds of doubt whether the clause of guarantee will draw us into the war. Consequently, if this be danger apprehended, it is not yet certain enough to authorize us in sound morality to declare, at this moment, the treaties null.

5. Is danger apprehended from the 17th article of the treaty of commerce, which admits French ships of war and privateers to come and go freely, with prizes made on their enemies, while their enemies are not to have the same privilege with prizes made on the French? But Holland and Prussia have approved of this article in our treaty with France, by subscribing to an express salvo of it in our treaties with them. (Dutch treaty 22, convention 6. Prussian treaty 19.) And England, in her last treaty with France (Art. 40), has entered into the same stipulation verbatim, and placed us in her ports on the same footing in which she is in ours, in case of a war of either of us with France. If we are engaged in such a war, England must receive prizes made on us by the French, and exclude those made on the French by us. Nay, further; in this very article of her treaty with France, is a salvo of any similar article in any anterior treaty of either party; and ours with France being anterior, this salvo confirms it expressly. Neither of these three powers, then, have a right to complain of this article in our treaty.

6. Is the danger apprehended from the 22d article of our treaty of commerce, which prohibits the enemies of France from fitting out privateers in our posts, or selling their prizes here; but we are free to refuse the same thing to France, there being no stipulation to the contrary; and we ought to refuse it on principles of fair neutrality.

7. But the reception of a minister from the republic of France, without qualifications, it is thought, will bring us into danger; because this, it is said, will determine the continuance of the treaty, and take from us the right of self-liberation, when at any time hereafter our safety would require us to use it. The reception of the minister at all (in favor of which Colonel Hamilton has given his opinion, though reluctantly, as he confessed), is an acknowl-

edgment of the legitimacy of their government; and if the qualifications meditated are to deny that legitimacy, it will be a curious compound which is to admit and to deny the same thing. But I deny that the reception of a minister has anything to do with the treaties. There is not a word in either of them about sending ministers. This has been done between us under the common usage of nations, and can have no effect either to continue or annul the treaties.

But how can any act of election have the effect to continue a treaty which is acknowledged to be going on still?—for it was not pretended the treaty was void, but only voidable if we choose to declare it so. To make it void, would require an act of election, but to let it go on, requires only that we should do nothing; and doing nothing can hardly be an infraction of peace or neutrality.

But I go further and deny that the most explicit declaration made at this moment that we acknowledge the obligation of the treaties, could take from us the right of non-compliance at any future time, when compliance would involve us in great and inevitable danger.

I conclude, then, that few of these sources threaten any danger at all; and from none of them is it inevitable; and consequently, none of them give us the right at this moment of releasing ourselves from our treaties.

II. A second limitation on our right of releasing ourselves, is that we are to do it from so much of the treaties only as is bringing great and inevitable danger on us, and not from the residue, allowing the other party a right at the same time, to determine whether on our non-compliance with that part, they will declare the whole void. This right they would have, but we should not. Vattel, 2. 202. The only part of the treaty which can really lead us into danger, is the clause of guarantee. That clause is all that we could suspend in any case, and the residue will remain or not at the will of the other party.

III. A third limitation is that when a party from necessity or danger withholds compliance with part of a treaty, it is bound to make compensation where the nature of the case admits and does not dispense with it. 2 Vattel, 324. Wolf, 270. 443. If actual circumstances excuse us from entering into the war under the clause of guarantee, it will be a question whether they excuse us from compensation. Our weight in the war admits of an estimate; and that estimate would form the measure of compensation.

If, in withholding a compliance with any part of the treaties, we do it without just cause or compensation, we give to France a cause of war, and so become associated in it on the other side. An injured friend is the bitterest of foes, and France has not discovered either timidity, or over-much forbearance on the late occasions. Is this the position we wish to take for our constituents? It is certainly not the one they would take for themselves.

I will proceed now to examine the principal authority which has been relied on for establishing the right of self-liberation; because though just in part, it would lead us far beyond justice, if taken in all the latitude of which his expressions would admit. Questions of natural right are triable by their conformity with the moral sense and reason of man. Those who write treatises of natural law, can only declare what their own moral sense and reason dictate in the several cases they state. Such of them as happen to have feelings and a reason coincident with those of the wise and honest part of mankind, are respected and quoted as witnesses of what is morally right or wrong in particular cases. Grotius, Puffendorf, Wolf, and Vattel are of this number. Where they agree their authority is strong; but where they differ (and they often differ), we must appeal to our own feelings and reason to decide between them. The passages in question shall be traced through all these writers; that we may see wherein they concur, and where that concurrence is wanting. It shall be quoted from them in the order in which they wrote, that is to say, from Grotius first, as being the earliest writer, Puffendorf next, then Wolf, and lastly Vattel, as latest in time.

| GROTIUS 2. 16. 16. | PUFFENDORF 8. 9. 6. | WOLF 1146. | VATTEL 2. 197. |
|---|---|---|---|
| Hither must be referred the common question concerning personal and real treaties. If indeed it be with a free people, there can be no doubt but that the engagement is in its nature real, because the subject is a permanent thing, and even though the government of the State be changed into a kingdom, the treaty remains; because the same body remains though the head is changed; and as it was before now, the government which is exercised by a king does not cease to be the government of the people. There is an exception when the object seems peculiar to the government, as if free cities contract a league for the defence of their freedom. | It is certain that every alliance made with a republic is real in its nature, and continues consequently to the term agreed on by the treaty, although the magistrates who concluded it be dead before, so that the form of government is changed even from a democracy to a monarchy; for in this case the people do not cease to be the same, and the king, in the case supposed, being established by the consent of the people who abolished the republican government, is understood to accept the crown with all the engagements which the people confessing it had contracted as being free and governing themselves. There must nevertheless be an exception of the alliances contracted with a view to preserve the present government; as if two republics league for mutual defence against | The alliance which is made with a free people, or with a popular government, is a real alliance; and as when the form of government changes, the people remain the same (for it is the association which forms the people, and not the manner of administering the government). This alliance subsists, though the form of government changes, *unless,* as is evident, the reason of the alliance was particular to the popular state. | The same question presents itself in real alliances, and in general on every alliance made with a State, and not in particular with a king for the defence of his person. We ought, without doubt, to defend our ally against all invasion, against all foreign violence, and even against rebel subjects. We ought, in like manner, to defend a republic against the enterprises of an oppressor of the public liberty. But we ought to recollect that we are the ally of the state or of the nation, and not its judge. If the nation has deposed its king in form; if the people of a republic have driven away its magistrates, and have established themselves free, or if they have acknowledged the authority of an usurper, whether expressly or tacitly, to oppose these domestic arrangements |

| | |
|---|---|
| those who would undertake to invade their liberty; for if one of these two people consent afterwards voluntarily to change the form of the government, the alliance end of itself, because th reason on which i was founded no longe subsists. | —to contest their justice or validity—would be to meddle with the government of the nation, and to do it an injury. The ally remains the ally of the state, notwithstanding the change which has taken place; *but if this change renders the alliance useless, dangerous, or disagreeable to it, it is free to renounce it; for it may say with truth, that it would not have allied itself with this nation, if it had been under the present form of its government.* |

The doctrine then of Grotius, Puffendorf, and Wolf is, that "treaties remain obligatory, notwithstanding any change in the form of government, except in the single case, where the preservation of that form was the object of the treaty"; there the treaty extinguishes, not by the election or declaration of the party remaining in *statu quo,* but independently of that, by the evanishment of the object. Vattel lays down in fact the same doctrine, that treaties continue obligatory, notwithstanding a change of government by the will of the other party;—that to oppose that will would be a wrong; and that the ally remains an ally, notwithstanding the change. So far he concurs with all the previous writers:—but he then adds what they had not said nor could say; but if this change renders the alliance *useless, dangerous* or *disagreeable* to it, it is free to renounce it. It was unnecessary for him to have specified the exception of *danger* in this particular case, because the exception exists in all cases, and its extent has been considered; but when he adds that, because a contract is become merely *useless* or *disagreeable* we are free to renounce it,—he is in opposition to Grotius, Puffendorf, and Wolf, who admit no such license against the obligation of treaties, and he is in opposition to the morality of every honest man to whom we may safely appeal to decide whether he feels himself free to renounce a contract the moment it becomes *merely useless* or *disagreeable* to him. We may appeal to Vattel himself in those parts of his book where he cannot be misunderstood, and to his known character, as one of the most zealous and constant advocates for the preservation of good faith in all our dealings. Let us hear him on other occasions; and first where he shows what degree of danger or injury will authorize self-liberation from a treaty: "If simple lesion," (lesion—the loss sustained by selling a thing for less than half value, which degree of loss renders the sale void by the Roman law,) "if simple lesion," says he, "or some degree of disadvantage in a treaty does not suffice to render it invalid, it is not so as to inconvenience which would go to the *ruin* of the nation. As every treaty ought to be made by sufficient power, a treaty pernicious to the State is null, and not at all obligatory. No governor of a nation having power to engage things capable of *destroying* the State, for the safety of which the empire entrusts to him, the nation itself, bound necessarily to whatever its preservation and safety require, cannot enter into engagements contrary to its indispensable obligations." Here then we find that the degree of injury or danger which he deems sufficient to liberate us from a treaty, is that which would go to the absolute ruin or destruction of the State;—not simply the lesion of the Roman law, not merely the being disadvantageous or dangerous; for as he himself says, Section 158, "lesion cannot render a treaty invalid. It is his duty who enters into engagements, to weigh well all things before he concludes. He may do with his property what he pleases. He may relinquish his rights or renounce his advantages, as he judges proper. The acceptant is not obliged to inform himself of his motives nor to weigh their just value. If we could free ourselves from a compact because we find ourselves injured by it, there would be nothing firm in the contracts of nations. Civil laws may set limits to lesion, and determine the degree capable of producing a nullity of the contract; but sovereigns acknowledge no judge. How establish lesion among them? Who will determine the degree sufficient to invalidate a treaty? The happiness and peace of nations require manifestly that their treaties should not depend on a means of nullity so vague and so dangerous."

Let us hear him again on the general subject of the observation of treaties, Section 163: "It is demonstrated in natural law that he who promises another, confers on him a perfect right to require the thing promised, and that consequently, not to observe a perfect promise is to violate the right of another; it is as manifest injustice as to plunder anyone of their right. All the tranquillity, the happiness and security of mankind, rest on justice or the obligation to respect the rights of others. The respect of others for our right of domain and property is the security of our actual possessions. The faith of promises is the security for the things which cannot be delivered or executed on the spot. No more security, no more commerce among men, if they think themselves not bound to preserve faith, to keep their word. This obligation, then, is as necessary as it is natural and indubitable among nations who live together in a state of nature, and who acknowledge no superior on earth. To maintain order and peace in their society, nations and their governors then ought to observe inviolably their promises and their treaties. This is a great truth, although too often neglected in practice, is generally acknowledged by all nations, the reproach of perfidy is a bitter affront among sovereigns. Now he who does not observe a treaty is assuredly perfidious, since he violates his faith. On the contrary, nothing is so glorious to a prince and his nation as the reputation of inviolable fidelity to his word." Again, Section 219, "Who will doubt that treaties are of the things sacred among nations? They decide matters the most important; they impose rules on the pretensions of sovereigns, they cause the rights of nations to be acknowledged; they assume their most precious interests. Among political bodies, sovereigns, who acknowledge no superior on earth, treaties are the only means of adjusting their different pretensions; of establishing a rule, to know on what to count, on what to depend. But treaties are but vain words, if nations do not consider them as respectable engagements, as rules inviolable for sovereigns, and sacred through the whole earth." Section 220: "The faith of treaties, that firm and sincere will, that invincible constancy in fulfilling engagements, of which a declaration is made in a treaty, is then holy and sacred among nations, whose safety and repose it ensures; and if nations will not be wanting to themselves, they will load with infamy whoever violates his faith."

After evidence so copious and explicit of the respect of this author for the sanctity of treaties, we should hardly have expected that his authority would have been resorted to for a wanton invalidation of them whenever they should become merely *useless or disagreeable.* We should hardly have expected that, rejecting all the rest of his book, this scrap would have been culled and made the hook whereon to hang such a chain of immoral consequences. Had the passage accidentally met our eye, we should have imagined it had fallen from the author's pen under some momentary view, not sufficiently developed to found a conjecture what he meant, and we may certainly affirm that a fragment like this cannot weigh against the authority of all other writers; against the uniform and systematic doctrine of the very work from which it is torn; against the moral feelings and the reason of all honest men. If the terms of the fragment are not misunderstood, they are in full contradiction to all the written and unwritten evidences of morality. If they are misunderstood, they are no longer a foundation for the doctrines which have been built on them.

But even had this doctrine been as true as it is manifestly false, it would have been asked, to whom is it that the treaties with France have become *disagreeable?* How will it be proved that they are *useless?*

The conclusion of the sentence suggests a reflection too strong to be suppressed, "for the party may say with truth that it would not have allied itself with this nation if it had been under the present form of its government." The republic of the United States allied itself with France when under a despotic government. She changes her government, and declares it shall be a republic; prepares a form of republic extremely free, and in the meantime is governing herself as such. And it is proposed that America shall declare the treaties void, because it may say with truth that it would not have allied itself with that nation if it had been under the present form of its government. Who is the American who can say with truth that he would not have allied himself to France if she had been a republic? Or that a republic of any form would be as *disagreeable* as her ancient despotism?

Upon the whole I conclude, that the treaties are still binding, notwithstanding the change of government in France; that no part of them but the clause of guarantee holds up *danger,* even at a distance, and consequently that a liberation from no other part would be prepared in any case; that if that clause may ever bring *danger,* it is neither extreme nor imminent, nor even probable that the authority for renouncing a treaty, when *useless or disagreeable,* is either misunderstood or in opposition to itself, to all other writers, and to every moral feeling; that were it not so, these treaties are in fact neither useless or disagreeable; that the receiving a minister from France at this time is an act of no significance with respect to the treaties, amounting neither to an admission nor denial of them, forasmuch as he comes not under any stipulation in them; that were it an explicit admission, or were it an express declaration of their obligation now to be made, it would not take from us that right which exists at all times, of liberating ourselves when an adherence to the treaties would be *ruinous* or *destructive* to the society; and that the not renouncing the treaties now is so far from being a breach of neutrality, that the doing it would be the breach, by giving just cause of war to France.

## OPINION RELATIVE TO CASE OF A BRITISH VESSEL CAPTURED BY A FRENCH VESSEL, PURCHASED BY FRENCH CITIZENS, AND FITTED OUT AS A PRIVATEER IN ONE OF OUR PORTS

May 16, 1793

The facts suggested, or to be taken for granted, because the contrary is not known, in the case now to be considered, are, that a vessel was purchased at Charleston, and fitted out as a privateer by French citizens, manned with foreigners chiefly, but partly with citizens of the United States. The command given to a French citizen by a regular commission from his government; that she has made prize of an English vessel in the open sea, and sent her into Philadelphia. The British minister demands restitution, and the question is, whether the Executive of the United States shall undertake to make it?

This transaction may be considered, 1st, as an offence against the United States; 2d, as an injury to Great Britain.

In the first view it is not now to be taken up. The opinion being, that it has been an act of disrespect to the jurisdiction of the United States, of which proper notice is to be taken at a proper time.

Under the second point of view, it appears to me wrong on the part of the United States (where not constrained by treaties) to permit one party in the present war to do what cannot be permitted to the other. We cannot permit the enemies of France to fit out privateers in our ports, by the 22d article of our treaty. We ought not, therefore, to permit France to do it; the treaty leaving us free to refuse, and the refusal being necessary to preserve a fair neutrality. Yet considering that the present is the first case which has arisen; that it has been in the first moment of the war, in one of the most distant ports of the United States, and before measures could be taken by the government to meet all the cases which may flow from the infant state of our government, and novelty of our position, it ought to be placed by Great Britain among the accidents of loss to which a nation is exposed in a state of war, and by no means as a premeditated wrong on the part of the government. In the last light it cannot be taken, because the act from which it results placed the United States with the offended, and not the offending party. Her minister has seen himself that there could have been on our part neither permission or connivance. A very moderate apology then from the United States ought to satisfy Great Britain.

The one we have made already is ample, to wit, a pointed disapprobation of the transaction, a promise to prosecute and punish according to law such of our citizens as have been concerned in it, and to take effectual measures against a repetition. To demand more would be a wrong in Great Britain; for to demand satisfaction *beyond* what is adequate, is wrong. But it is proposed further to take the prize from the captors and restore her to the English. This is a very serious proposition.

The dilemma proposed in our conferences, appears to me unanswerable. Either the commission to the commander of the privateer was good, or not good. If not good, then the tribunals of the country will take cognizance of the transaction, receive the demand of the former owner, and make restitution of the capture; and there being, on this supposition, regular remedy at law, it would be irregular for the government to interpose. If the commission be good, then the capture having been made on the high seas, under a valid commission from a power at war with Great Britain, the British owner has lost all his right, and the prize would be deemed good, even in his own courts, were the question to be brought before his own courts. He has now no more claim on the vessel than any stranger would have who never owned her, his whole right being transferred by the laws of war to the captor.

The legal right then being in the captors, on what ground can we take it from him? Not on that of *right,* for the right has been transferred to him. It can only be by an act of *force,* that is to say, of reprisal for the offence committed against us in the port of Charleston. But the making reprisal on a nation is a very serious thing. Remonstrance and refusal of satisfaction ought to precede; and when reprisal follows, it is considered as an act of war, and never yet failed to produce it in the case of a nation able to make war; besides, if the case were important enough to require reprisal, and ripe for that step, Congress must be called on to take it; the right of reprisal being expressly lodged with them by the Constitution, and not with the Executive.

I therefore think that the satisfaction already made to the *government* of Great Britain is quite equal to what ought to be desired in the present case; that the property of the British *owner* is transferred by the laws of war to the *captor;* that for us to take it from the captor would be an act of force or reprisal, which the circumstances of the case do not justify, and to which the powers of the Executive are not competent by the constitution.

## CONFLICT WITH GENET [1]

August 16, 1793

SIR: In my letter of January the 13th, I enclosed to you copies of several letters which had passed between Mr. Ternant, Mr. Genet and myself, on the occurrences to which the present war had given rise within our ports. The object of this communication was to enable you to explain the principle on which our government was conducting itself towards the belligerent parties; principles which might not in all cases be satisfactory to all, but were meant to be just and impartial to all. Mr. Genet had been then but a little time with us; and but a little more was necessary to develop in him a character and conduct so unexpected and so extraordinary, as to place us in the most distressing dilemma, between our regard for his nation, which is constant and sincere, and a regard for our laws, the authority of which must be maintained; for the peace of our country, which the executive magistrate is charged to preserve; for its honor, offended in the person of that magistrate; and for its character grossly traduced, in the conversations and letters of this gentleman. In the course of these transactions, it has been a great comfort to us to believe, that none of them were within the intentions or expectations of his employers. These had been too recently expressed in acts which nothing could discolor, in the letters of the Executive Council, in the letter and decrees of the National Assembly, and in the general demeanor of the nation towards us, to describe to them things of so contrary a character. Our first duty, therefore, was, to draw a strong line between their intentions and the proceedings of their minister; our second, to lay those proceedings faithfully before them.

[1] Letter to Gouverneur Morris, the American Minister to Paris. Jefferson sent a copy to Genet.

On the declaration of war between France and England, the United States being at peace with both, their situation was so new and unexperienced by themselves, that their citizens were not, in the first instant, sensible of the new duties resulting therefrom, and of the restraints it would impose even *on their dispositions* towards the belligerent powers. Some of them imagined (and chiefly their transient sea-faring citizens) that they were free to indulge those dispositions, to take side with either party, and enrich themselves by depredations on the commerce of the other, and were meditating enterprises of this nature, as there was reason to believe. In this state of the public mind, and before it should take an erroneous direction, difficult to be set right and dangerous to themselves and their country, the President thought it expedient, through the channel of a proclamation, to remind our fellow-citizens that we were in a state of peace with all the belligerent powers, that in that state it was our duty neither to aid nor injure any, to exhort and warn them against acts which might contravene this duty, and particularly those of positive hostility, for the punishment of which the laws would be appealed to; and to put them on their guard also, as to the risks they would run, if they should attempt to carry articles of contraband to any. This proclamation, ordered on the 19th and signed the 22d day of April, was sent to you in my letter of the 26th of the same month.

On the day of its publication, we received, through the channel of the newspapers, the first intimation that Mr. Genet had arrived on the 8th of the month at Charleston, in the character of Minister Plenipotentiary from his nation to the United States, and soon after, that he had sent on to Philadelphia the vessel in which he came, and would himself perform the journey by land. His landing at one of the most distant ports of the Union from his points both of departure and destination, was calculated to excite attention; and very soon afterwards, we learned that he was undertaking to authorize the fitting and arming vessels in that port, enlisting men, foreigners and citizens, and giving them commissions to cruise and commit hostilities on nations at peace with us; that these vessels were taking and bringing prizes into our ports; that the consuls of France were assuming to hold courts of admiralty on them, to try, condemn, and authorize their sale as legal prize, and all this before Mr. Genet had presented himself or his credentials to the President, before he was received by him, without his consent or consultation, and directly in contravention of the state of peace existing, and declared to exist in the President's proclamation, and incumbent on him to preserve till the constitutional authority should otherwise declare. These proceedings became immediately, as was naturally to be expected, the subject of complaint by the representative here of that power against whom they would chiefly operate. The British minister presented several memorials thereon, to which we gave the answer of May the 15th, heretofore enclosed to you, corresponding in substance with a letter of the same date written to Mr. Ternant, the minister of France then residing here, a copy of which I send herewith. On the next day Mr. Genet reached this place, about five or six weeks after he had arrived at Charleston, and might have been at Philadelphia, if he had steered for it directly. He was immediately presented to the President, and received by him as the minister of the republic; and as the conduct before stated seemed to bespeak a design of forcing us into the war without allowing us the exercise of any free will in the case, nothing could be more assuaging than his assurance to the President at his reception, which he repeated to me afterwards in conversation, and in public to the citizens of Philadelphia in answer to an address from them, that on account of our remote situation and other circumstances, France did not expect that we should become a party to the war, but wished to see us pursue our prosperity and happiness in peace. In a conversation a few days after, Mr. Genet told me that M. de Ternant had delivered him my letter of May the 15th. He spoke something of the case of the Grange, and then of the armament at Charleston, explained the circumstances which had led him to it before he had been received by the government and had consulted its will, expressed a hope that the President had not so absolutely decided against the measure but that he would hear what was to be said in support of it, that he would write me a letter on the subject, in which he thought he could justify it under our treaty; but that if the President should finally determine otherwise, he must submit; for that assuredly his instructions were to do what would be agreeable to us. He accordingly wrote the letter of May the 27th. The President took the case again into consideration, and found nothing in that letter which could shake the grounds of his former decision. My letter of June the 5th notifying this to him, his of June the 8th and 14th, mine of the 17th, and his again of the 22d, will show what further passed on this subject, and that he was far from retaining his disposition to acquiesce in the ultimate will of the President.

It would be tedious to pursue this and our subsequent correspondence through all their details. Referring, therefore, for these to the letters themselves, which shall accompany this, I will present a summary view only of all the points of difference which have arisen, and the grounds on which they rest.

1. Mr. Genet asserts his right of arming in our ports and of enlisting our citizens, and that we have no right to restrain him or punish them. Examining this question under the law of nations, founded on the general sense and usage of mankind, we have produced proofs, from the most enlightened and approved writers on the subject, that a neutral nation must, in all things relating to the war, observe an exact impartiality towards the parties, that favors to one to the prejudice of the other, would import a fraudulent neu-

trality, of which no nation would be the dupe; that no succor should be given to either, unless stipulated by treaty, in men, arms, or anything else directly serving for war; that the right of raising troops being one of the rights of sovereignty, and consequently appertaining exclusively to the nation itself, no foreign power or person can levy men within its territory without its consent; and he who does, may be rightfully and severely punished; that if the United States have a right to refuse the permission to arm vessels and raise men within their ports and territories, they are bound by the laws of neutrality to exercise that right, and to prohibit such armaments and enlistments. To these principles of the law of nations Mr. Genet answers, by calling them "diplomatic subtleties," and "aphorisms of Vattel and others." But something more than this is necessary to disprove them; and till they are disproved, we hold it certain that the law of nations and the rules of neutrality forbid our permitting either party to arm in our ports.

But Mr. Genet says, that the twenty-second article of our treaty allows him *expressly* to arm in our ports. Why has he not quoted the very words of that article *expressly* allowing it? For that would have put an end to all further question. The words of the article are, "it shall not be lawful for any foreign privateers not belonging to subjects of the M. C. King, nor citizens of the said United States, who have commissions from any foreign Prince or State in enmity with either nation, to fit their ships in the ports of either the one or the other of the aforesaid parties." Translate this from the general terms in which it here stands, into the special case produced by the present war. "Privateers not belonging to France or the United States, and having commissions from the enemies of one of them," are, in the present state of things, "British, Dutch and Spanish privateers." Substituting these, then, for the equivalent terms, it will stand thus, "it shall not be lawful for British, Dutch or Spanish privateers to fit their ships in the ports of the United States." Is this an *express* permission to France to do it? Does the negative to the enemies of France, and silence as to France herself, imply an affirmative to France? Certainly not; it leaves the question as to France open, and free to be decided according to circumstances. And if the parties had meant an affirmative stipulation, they would have provided for it expressly; they would never have left so important a point to be inferred from mere silence or implications. Suppose they had desired to stipulate a refusal to their enemies, but nothing to themselves; what form of expression would they have used? Certainly the one they have used; an express stipulation as to their enemies, and silence as to themselves. And such an intention corresponds not only with the words, but with the circumstances of the times. It was of value to each party to exclude its enemies from arming in the ports of the other, and could in no case embarrass them. They therefore stipulated so far mutually. But each might be embarrassed by permitting the other to arm in its ports.

They therefore would not stipulate to permit that. Let us go back to the state of things in France when this treaty was made, and we shall find several cases wherein France could not have permitted us to arm in her ports. Suppose a war between these States and Spain. We know, that by the treaties between France and Spain, the former could not permit the enemies of the latter to arm in her ports. It was honest in her, therefore, not to deceive us by such a stipulation. Suppose a war between these States and Great Britain. By the treaties between France and Great Britain, in force at the signature of ours, we could not have been permitted to arm in the ports of France. She could not then have meant in this article to give us such a right. She has manifested the same sense of it in her subsequent treaty with England, made eight years after the date of ours, stipulating in the sixteenth article of it, as in our twenty-second, that foreign privateers, *not being subjects of either crown,* should not arm against either in the ports of the other. If this had amounted to an affirmative stipulation that the subjects of the other crown might arm in her ports *against us,* it would have been in direct contradiction to her twenty-second article with us. So that to give to these negative stipulations an affirmative effect, is to render them inconsistent with each other, and with good faith; to give them only their negative and natural effect, is to reconcile them to one another and to good faith, and is clearly to adopt the sense in which France herself has expounded them. We may justly conclude, then, that the article only obliges us to refuse this right, in the present case, to Great Britain and the other enemies of France. It does not go on to give it to France, either expressly or by implication. We may then refuse it. And since we are bound by treaty to refuse it to the one party, and are free to refuse it to that other, we are bound by the laws of neutrality to refuse it to the other. The aiding either party then with vessels, arms or men, being unlawful by the law of nations, and not rendered lawful by the treaty, it is made a question whether our citizens, joining in these unlawful enterprises, may be punished?

The United States being in a state of peace with most of the belligerent powers by treaty, and with all of them by the laws of nature, murders and robberies committed by our citizens within our territory, or on the high seas, on those with whom we are so at peace, are punishable equally as if committed on our own inhabitants. If I might venture to reason a little formally, without being charged with running into "subtleties and aphorisms," I would say that if one citizen has a right to go to war of his own authority, every citizen has the same. If every citizen has that right, then the nation (which is composed of all its citizens) has a right to go to war, by the authority of its individual citizen. But this is not true either on the general principles of society, or by our Constitution, which gives that power to Congress alone, and not to the citizens individually. Then the first position was not true;

and no citizen has a right to go to war of his own authority; and for what he does without right, he ought to be punished. Indeed, nothing can be more obviously absurd than to say, that all the citizens may be at war, and yet the nation at peace.

It has been pretended, indeed, that the engagement of a citizen in an enterprise of this nature, was a divestment of the character of citizen, and a transfer of jurisdiction over him to another sovereign. Our citizens are certainly free to divest themselves of that character by emigration and other acts manifesting their intention, and may then become the subjects of another power, and free to do whatever the subjects of that power may do. But the laws do not admit that the bare commission of a crime amounts of itself to a divestment of the character of citizen, and withdraws the criminal from their coercion. They would never prescribe an illegal act among the legal modes by which a citizen might disfranchise himself; nor render treason, for instance, innocent by giving it the force of a dissolution of the obligation of the criminal to his country. Accordingly, in the case of Henfeild, a citizen of these States, charged with having engaged in the port of Charleston, in an enterprise against nations at peace with us, and with having joined in the actual commission of hostilities, the Attorney General of the United States, in an official opinion, declared that the act with which he was charged was punishable by law. The same thing has been unanimously declared by two of the circuit courts of the United States, as you will see in the charges of Chief Justice Jay, delivered at Richmond, and Judge Wilson, delivered at Philadelphia, both of which are herewith sent. Yet Mr. Genet, in the moment he lands at Charleston, is able to tell the Governor, and continues to affirm in his correspondence here, that no law of the United States authorizes their government to restrain either its own citizens or the foreigners inhabiting its territory, from warring against the enemies of France. It is true, indeed, that in the case of Henfeild, the jury which tried, absolved him. But it appeared on the trial, that the crime was not knowingly and wilfully committed; that Henfeild was ignorant of the unlawfulness of his undertaking; that in the moment he was apprised of it he showed real contrition; that he had rendered meritorious services during the late war, and declared he would live and die an American. The jury, therefore, in absolving him, did no more than the constitutional authority might have done, had they found him guilty: the Constitution having provided for the pardon of offences in certain cases, and there being no case where it would have been more proper than where no offence was contemplated. Henfeild, therefore, was still an American citizen, and Mr. Genet's reclamation of him was as unauthorized as the first enlistment of him.

2. Another doctrine advanced by Mr. Genet is, that our courts can take no cognizance of questions whether vessels, *held by theirs* as prizes, are law-

ful prizes or not; that this jurisdiction belongs exclusively to their consulates here, which have been lately erected by the National Assembly into complete courts of admiralty.

Let us consider, first, what is the extent of jurisdiction which the consulates of France may rightfully exercise here. Every nation has of natural right, entirely and exclusively, all the jurisdiction which may be rightfully exercised in the territory it occupies. If it cedes any portion of that jurisdiction to judges appointed by another nation, the limits of their power must depend on the instrument of cession. The United States and France have, by their consular convention, given mutually to their consuls jurisdiction in certain cases especially enumerated. But that convention gives to neither the power of establishing complete courts of admiralty within the territory of the other, nor even of deciding the particular question of prize or not prize. The consulates of France, then, cannot take judicial cognizance of those questions here. Of this opinion Mr. Genet was when he wrote his letter of May the 27th, wherein he promises to correct the error of the consul at Charleston, of whom, in my letters of the 15th instant, I had complained, as arrogating to himself that jurisdiction; though in his subsequent letters he has thought proper to embark in the errors of his consuls.

But the United States, at the same time, do not pretend any right to try the validity of captures made *on the high seas,* by France, or any other nation, over its enemies. These questions belong, of common usage, to the sovereign of the captor, and whenever it is necessary to determine them, resort must be had to his courts. This is the case provided for in the seventeenth article of the treaty, which says, that such prizes shall not be arrested, nor cognizance taken of the validity thereof; a stipulation much insisted on by Mr. Genet and the consuls, and which we never thought of infringing or questioning. As the validity of captures then, made *on the high seas* by France over its enemies, cannot be tried within the United States by their consuls, so neither can they by our own courts. Nor is this the question between us, though we have been misled into it.

The real question is, whether the United States have not a right to protect vessels within their waters and on their coasts? The Grange was taken within the Delaware, between the shores of Jersey and of the Delaware State, and several miles above its mouth. The seizing her was a flagrant violation of the jurisdiction of the United States. Mr. Genet, however, instead of apologizing, takes great merit in his letters for giving her up. The William is said to have been taken within two miles of the shores of the United States. When the admiralty declined cognizance of the case, she was delivered to the French consul according to my letter of June the 25th, to be kept till the executive of the United States should examine into the case; and Mr. Genet was desired by my letter of June the 29th, to have them furnished with the evidence on behalf of the captors, as to the place of capture. Yet to this day it has never been done. The brig Fanny was alleged to be taken within five miles from our shore; the Catharine within two miles and a half. It is an essential attribute of the jurisdiction of every country to preserve peace, to punish acts in breach of it, and to restore property taken by force within its limits. Were the armed vessel of any nation to cut away one of our own from the wharves of Philadelphia, and to choose to call it a prize, would this exclude us from the right of redressing the wrong? Were it the vessel of another nation, are we not equally bound to protect it, while within our limits? Were it seized in any other of our waters, or on the shores of the United States, the right of redressing is still the same; and humble indeed would be our condition, were we obliged to depend for that on the will of a foreign consul, or on negotiation with diplomatic agents. Accordingly, this right of protection within its waters and to a reasonable distance on its coasts, has been acknowledged by every nation, and denied to none; and if the property seized be yet within their power, it is their right and duty to redress the wrong themselves. France herself has asserted the right in herself and recognized it in us, in the sixth article of our treaty, where we mutually stipulate that we will, *by all the means in our power* (not by negotiation), protect and defend each other's vessels and effects in our ports or roads, or on the seas near our countries, and recover and restore the same to the right owners. The United Netherlands, Prussia and Sweden, have recognized it also in treaties with us; and, indeed, it is a standing formula, inserted in almost all the treaties of all nations, and proving the principle to be acknowledged by all nations.

How, and by what organ of the government, whether judiciary or executive, it shall be redressed, is not yet perfectly settled with us. One of the subordinate courts of admiralty has been of opinion, in the first instance, in the case of the ship William, that it does not belong to the judiciary. Another, perhaps, may be of a contrary opinion. The question is still *sub judice,* and an appeal to the court of last resort will decide it finally. If finally the judiciary shall declare that it does not belong to the *civil* authority, it then results to the executive, charged with the direction of the *military* force of the Union, and the conduct of its affairs with foreign nations. But this is a mere question of internal arrangement between the different departments of the government, depending on the particular diction of the laws and Constitution; and it can in nowise concern a foreign nation to which department these have delegated it.

3. Mr. Genet, in his letter of July the 9th, requires that the ship Jane, which he calls an English privateer, shall be immediately ordered to depart; and to justify this, he appeals to the 22d article of our treaty, which provides that it shall not be lawful for any foreign *privateer* to fit their ships in our

ports, to sell *what they have taken,* or purchase victuals, &c. The ship Jane is an English merchant vessel, which has been many years employed in the commerce between Jamaica and these States. She brought here a cargo of produce from that island, and was to take away a cargo of flour. Knowing of the war when she left Jamaica, and that our coast was lined with small French privateers, she armed for her defence, and took one of those commissions usually called *letters of marque.* She arrived here safely without having had any rencounter of any sort. Can it be necessary to say that a merchant vessel is not a privateer? That though she has arms to defend herself in time of war, in the course of her regular commerce, this no more makes her a privateer, than a husbandman following his plough in time of war, with a knife or pistol in his pocket, is thereby made a soldier? The occupation of a privateer is attack and plunder, that of a merchant vessel is commerce and self-preservation. The article excludes the former from our ports, and from selling *what she has taken,* that is, what she has acquired by war, to show it did not mean the merchant vessel, and what she had acquired by commerce. Were the merchant vessels coming for our produce forbidden to have any arms for their defence, every adventurer who had a boat, or money enough to buy one, would make her a privateer, our coasts would swarm with them, foreign vessels must cease to come, our commerce must be suppressed, our produce remain on our hands, or at least that great portion of it which we have not vessels to carry away, our ploughs must be laid aside and agriculture suspended. This is a sacrifice no treaty could ever contemplate, and which we are not disposed to make out of mere complaisance to a false definition of the term *privateer.* Finding that the Jane had purchased new carriages to mount two or three additional guns, which she had brought in her hold, and that she had opened additional port-holes for them, the carriages were ordered to be re-landed, the additional port-holes stopped, and her means of defence reduced, to be exactly the same at her departure as at her arrival. This was done on the general principle of allowing no party to arm within our ports.

4. The seventeenth article of our treaty leaves armed vessels free to *conduct,* whithersoever they please, the ships and goods taken from their enemies without paying any duty, and to depart and be conducted freely to the places expressed in their commissions, which the captain shall be obliged to show. It is evident, that this article does not contemplate a freedom *to sell their prizes* here; but on the contrary, a *departure* to some other place, always to be expressed in their commission, where their validity is to be finally adjudged. In such case, it would be as unreasonable to demand duties on the goods they had taken from an enemy, as it would be on the cargo of a merchant vessel touching in our ports for refreshment or advices; and against this the article provides. But the armed vessels of France have been also ad-

mitted to land and sell their prize goods here for consumption, in which case, it is as reasonable they should pay duties, as the goods of a merchant-man landed and sold for consumption. They have however demanded, and as a matter of right, to sell them free of duty, a right, they say, given by this article of the treaty, though the article does not give the right to sell at all. Where a treaty does not give the principal right of selling, the additional one of selling duty free cannot be given; and the laws in admitting the principal right of selling, may withhold the additional one of selling duty free. It must be observed, that our revenues are raised almost wholly on imported goods. Suppose prize goods enough should be brought in to supply our whole consumption. According to their construction we are to lose our whole revenue. I put the extreme case to evince, more extremely, the unreasonableness of the claim. Partial supplies would affect the revenue but partially. They would lessen the evil, but not the error, of the construction; and I believe we may say, with truth, that neither party had it in contemplation, when penning this article, to abandon any part of its revenue for the encouragement of the sea robbers of the other.

5. Another source of complaint with Mr. Genet has been, that the English take French goods out of American vessels, which he says is against the law of nations and ought to be prevented by us. On the contrary, we suppose it to have been long an established principle of the law of nations, that the goods of a friend are free in an enemy's vessel, and an enemy's goods lawful prize in the vessel of a friend. The inconvenience of this principle which subjects merchant vessels to be stopped at sea, searched, ransacked, led out of their course, has induced several nations latterly to stipulate against it by treaty, and to substitute another in its stead, that free bottoms shall make free goods, and enemy bottoms enemy goods; a rule equal to the other in point of loss and gain, but less oppressive to commerce. As far as it has been introduced, it depends on the treaties stipulating it, and forms exceptions, in special cases, to the general operation of the law of nations. We have introduced it into our treaties with France, Holland and Prussia; and French goods found by the two latter nations in American bottoms are not made prize of. It is our wish to establish it with other nations. But this requires their consent also, is a work of time, and in the meanwhile, they have a right to act on the general principle, without giving to us or to France cause of complaint. Nor do I see that France can lose by it on the whole. For though she loses *her* goods when found in our vessels by the nations with whom we have no treaties, yet she gains *our* goods, when found in the vessels of the same and all other nations; and we believe the latter mass to be greater than the former. It is to be lamented, indeed, that the general principle has operated so cruelly in the dreadful calamity which has lately happened in St. Domingo. The miserable fugitives, who, to save their lives, had taken asylum

in our vessels, with such valuable and portable things as could be gathered in the moment out of the ashes of their houses and wrecks of their fortunes, have been plundered of these remains by the licensed sea rovers of their enemies. This has swelled, on this occasion, the disadvantages of the general principle, that "an enemy's goods are free prize in the vessels of a friend." But it is one of those deplorable and unforeseen calamities to which they expose themselves who enter into a state of war, furnishing to us an awful lesson to avoid it by justice and moderation, and not a cause or encouragement to expose our own towns to the same burning and butcheries, nor of complaint because we do not.

6. In a case like the present, where the missionary of one government construes differently from that to which he is sent, the treaties and laws which are to form a common rule of action for both, it would be unjust in either to claim an exclusive right of construction. Each nation has an equal right to expound the meaning of their common rules; and reason and usage have established, in such cases, a convenient and well-understood train of proceeding. It is the right and duty of the foreign missionary to urge his own constructions, to support them with reasons which may convince, and in terms of decency and respect which may reconcile the government of the country to a concurrence. It is the duty of that government to listen to his reasonings with attention and candor, and to yield to them when just. But if it shall still appear to them that reason and right are on their side, it follows of necessity, that exercising the sovereign powers of the country, they have a right to proceed on their own constructions and conclusions as to whatever is to be done within their limits. The minister then refers the case to his own government, asks new instructions, and, in the meantime, acquiesces in the authority of the country. His government examines his constructions, abandons them if wrong, insists on them if right, and the case then becomes a matter of negotiation between the two nations. Mr. Genet, however, assumes a new and bolder line of conduct. After deciding for himself ultimately, and without respect to the authority of the country, he proceeds to do what even his sovereign could not authorize, to put himself within the country on a line with its government, to act as co-sovereign of the territory; he arms vessels, levies men, gives commissions of war, independently of them, and in direct opposition to their orders and efforts. When the government forbids their citizens to arm and engage in the war, he undertakes to arm and engage them. When they forbid vessels to be fitted in their ports for cruising on nations with whom they are at peace, he commissions them to fit and cruise. When they forbid an unceded jurisdiction to be exercised within their territory by foreign agents, he undertakes to uphold that exercise, and to avow it openly. The privateers Citoyen Genet and Sans Culottes having been fitted out at Charleston (though without the permission of the

government, yet before it was forbidden) the President only required they might leave our ports, and did not interfere with their prizes. Instead, however, of their quitting our ports, the Sans Culottes remains still, strengthening and equipping herself, and the Citoyen Genet went out only to cruise on our coast, and to brave the authority of the country by returning into port again with her prizes. Though in the letter of June the 5th, the final determination of the President was communicated, that no future armaments in our ports should be permitted, the Vainqueur de La Bastille was afterwards equipped and commissioned in Charleston, the Anti-George in Savannah, the Carmagnole in Delaware, a schooner and a sloop in Boston, and the Polly or Republican was attempted to be equipped in New York, and was the subject of reclamation by Mr. Genet, in a style which certainly did not look like relinquishing the practice. The Little Sarah or Little Democrat was armed, equipped and manned, in the port of Philadelphia, under the very eye of the government, as if meant to insult it. Having fallen down the river, and being evidently on the point of departure for a cruise, Mr. Genet was desired in my letter of July the 12th, on the part of the President, to detain her till some inquiry and determination on the case should be had. Yet within three or four days after, she was sent out by orders from Mr. Genet himself, and is, at this time, cruising on our coasts, as appears by the protest of the master of one of our vessels maltreated by her.

The government thus insulted and set at defiance by Mr. Genet, and committed in its duties and engagements to others, determined still to see in these proceedings but the character of the individual, and not to believe, and it does not believe, that they are by instructions from his employers. They had assured the British minister here, that the vessels already armed to our ports should be obliged to leave them, and that no more should be armed in them. Yet more had been armed, and those before armed had either not gone away, or gone only to return with new prizes. They now informed him that the order for departure should be enforced, and the prizes made contrary to it should be restored or compensated. The same thing was notified to Mr. Genet in my letter of August the 7th, and that he might not conclude the promise of compensation to be of no concern to him, and go on in his courses, he was reminded that it would be a fair article of account against his nation.

Mr. Genet, not content with using our force, whether we will or not, in the military line against nations with whom we are at peace, undertakes also to direct the civil government; and particularly for the executive and legislative bodies, to pronounce what powers may or may not be exercised by the one or the other. Thus, in his letter of June the 8th, he promises to respect the political opinions of the President, *till the Representatives shall have confirmed or rejected them;* as if the President had undertaken to decide what belonged to the decision of Congress. In his letter of June the 4th, he says more openly, that the President ought not to have taken on himself to decide on the subject of the letter, but that it was of importance enough to have consulted Congress thereon; and in that of June the 22d, he tells the President in direct terms, that Congress ought already to have been occupied on certain questions which he had been too hasty in deciding; thus making himself, and not the President, the judge of the powers ascribed by the Constitution to the executive, and dictating to him the occasion when he should exercise the power of convening Congress at an earlier day than their own act had prescribed.

On the following expressions, no commentary shall be made:

July 9. "*Les principes philosophiques proclamées par le Président.*"

June 22. "*Les opinions privées ou publiques de M. le Président, et cette égide ne paroissant, pas suffisante.*"

June 22. "*Le gouvernement fédéral s'est empressé, poussé par je ne scais quelle influence.*"

June 22. "*Je ne puis attribuer, des démarches de cette nature qu'à des impressions étrangères dont le tems et la vérité triompheront.*"

June 25. "*On poursuit avec acharnement, en vertu des instructions de M. le Président, les armateurs Français.*"

June 14. "*Ce réfus tend à accomplir le système infernal du roi d'Angleterre, et des autres rois ses accomplices, pour faire périr par la famine les Républicains Français avec la liberté.*"

June 8. "*La lache abandon de ses amis.*"

July 25. "*En vain le désir de conserver la paix fait-il sacrifier les intérêts de la France à cet intérêt du moment; en vain le soif des richesses l'emporte-t-elle sur l'honneur dans la balance politique de l'Amérique. Tous ces ménagemens, toute cette condescendance, toute cette humilité n'aboutissent à rien; nos ennemis on rient, et les Français trop confiants sont punis pour avoir cru que la nation Américaine, avoit un pavillon, qu'elle avoit quelque égard pour ses loix, quelque conviction de ses forces, et qu'elle tenoit au sentiment de sa dignité. Il ne m'est pas possible de peindre toute ma sensibilité sur ce scandale qui tend à la diminution de votre commerce, à l'oppression du notre, et à l'abaissement, à l'avilissement des républiques. Si nos concitoyens ont été trompés, si vous n'êtes point en état de soutenir la souveraineté de votre peuple, parlez; nous l'avons garantié quand nous étions esclaves, nous saurons la rendre redoutable étant devenus libres.*"

We draw a veil over the sensations which these expressions excite. No words can render them; but they will not escape the sensibility of a friendly and magnanimous nation, who will do us justice. We see in them neither the portrait of ourselves, nor the pencil of our friends; but an attempt to embroil both; to add still another nation to the enemies of his country, and to draw on both a reproach, which it is hoped will never stain the history of either. The written proofs, of which Mr. Genet himself was the bearer, were too unequivocal to leave a doubt that the French nation are constant in their friendship to us. The resolves of their National Convention, the letters of their Executive Council, attest this truth, in terms which render it necessary to seek in some other hypothesis the solution of Mr. Genet's machinations against our peace and friendship.

Conscious, on our part, of the same friendly and sincere dispositions, we can with truth affirm, both for our nation and government, that we have never omitted a reasonable occasion of manifesting them. For I will not consider as of that character, opportunities of sallying forth from our ports to waylay, rob and murder defenceless merchants and others, who have done us no injury, and who were coming to trade with us in the confidence of our peace and amity. The violation of all the laws of order and morality which bind mankind together, would be an unacceptable offering to a just nation. Recurring then only to recent things, after so afflicting a libel, we recollect with satisfaction, that in the course of two years, by unceasing exertions, we paid up seven years' arrearages and instalments of our debt to France, which the inefficiency of our first form of government had suffered to be accumulating; that pressing on still to the entire fulfilment of our engagements, we have facilitated to Mr. Genet the effect of the instalments of the present year, to enable him to send relief to his fellow citizens in France, threatened with famine; that in the first moment of the insurrection which threatened the colony of St. Domingo, we stepped forward to their relief with arms and money, taking freely on ourselves the risk of an unauthorized aid, when delay would have been denial; that we have received according to our best abilities the wretched fugitives from the catastrophe of the principal town of that colony, who, escaping from the swords and flames of civil war, threw themselves on us naked and houseless, without food or friends, money or other means, their faculties lost and absorbed in the depth of their distresses; that the exclusive admission to sell here the prizes made by France on her enemies, in the present war, though unstipulated in our treaties, and unfounded in her own practice, or in that of other nations, as we believe; the spirit manifested by the late grand jury in their proceedings against those who had aided the enemies of France with arms and implements of war, the expressions of attachment to his nation, with which Mr. Genet was welcomed on his arrival and journey from south to north, and our long forbearance under his gross usurpations and outrages of the laws and authority of our country, do not bespeak the partialities intimated in his letters. And for these things he rewards us by endeavors to excite discord and distrust between our citizens and those whom they have entrusted with their government, between the different branches of our government, between our nation and his. But none of these things, we hope, will be found in his power. That friendship which dictates to us to bear with his conduct yet a while, lest the interests of his nation here should suffer injury, will hasten them to replace an agent whose dispositions are such a misrepresentation of theirs, and whose continuance here is inconsistent with order, peace, respect, and that friendly correspondence which we hope will ever subsist between the two nations. His government will see too that the case is pressing. That it is impossible for two sovereign and independent authorities to be going on within our territory at the same time without collision. They will foresee that if Mr. Genet perseveres in his proceedings, the consequences would be so hazardous to us, the example so humiliating and pernicious, that we may be forced even to suspend his functions before a successor can arrive to continue them. If our citizens have not already been shedding each other's blood, it is not owing to the moderation of Mr. Genet, but to the forbearance of the government. It is well known that if the authority of the laws had been resorted to, to stop the Little Democrat, its officers and agents were to have been resisted by the crew of the vessel, consisting partly of American citizens. Such events are too serious, too possible, to be left to hazard, or to what is more than hazard, the will of an agent whose designs are so mysterious.

Lay the case then immediately before his government. Accompany it with assurances, which cannot be stronger than true, that our friendship for the nation is constant and unabating; that, faithful to our treaties, we have fulfilled them in every point to the best of our understanding; that if in anything, however, we have construed them amiss, we are ready to enter into candid explanations, and to do whatever we can be convinced is right; that in opposing the extravagances of an agent, whose character they seem not sufficiently to have known, we have been urged by motives of duty to ourselves and justice to others, which cannot but be approved by those who are just themselves; and finally, that after independence and self-government, there is nothing we more sincerely wish than perpetual friendship with them.

I have the honor to be, with great respect and esteem, Dear Sir, your most obedient, and most humble servant.

## *CHESAPEAKE* PROCLAMATION[1]

July 2, 1807

During the wars which for some time have unhappily prevailed among the powers of Europe, the U.S. of America, firm in their principles of peace,

[1] The American frigate *Chesapeake* was attacked by the British warship *Leopard* outside Chesapeake Bay. Jefferson promptly ordered British warships out of American waters, by this Proclamation. He hoped that it would be a blow to Britain and that it would "save a war."

have endeavored by justice, by a regular discharge of all their national and social duties, and by every friendly office their situation admitted, to maintain, with all the belligerents, their accustomed relations of friendship, hospitality and commercial intercourse. Taking no part in the questions which animated these powers against each other, nor permitting themselves to entertain a wish, but for the restoration of general peace, they have observed with good faith the neutrality they assumed, and they believe that no instance of departure from its duties can be justly imputed to them by any nation. A free use of their harbours and waters, the means of refitting and of refreshment, of succour to their sick and suffering, have, at all times, and on equal principles been extended to all: and this too while the officers of one of the belligerents received among us have been in a continued course of insubordination to the laws, of violence to the persons, and of trespasses on the property of our citizens. These abuses of the laws of hospitality have become habitual to the Commanders of the British armed vessels hovering on our coasts and frequenting our harbours; they have been the subject of repeated representations to their government; assurances have been given that proper orders should restrain them within the limit of the rights, and of the respect belonging to a friendly nation: but those orders and assurances have been without effect; nor has a single instance of punishment for past wrongs taken place. And at length a deed, transcending all we have suffered, brings the public sensibility to a serious crisis, and forbearance to a necessary pause. A frigate of the U.S. trusting to. a state of peace and leaving her harbor on a distant service, has been surprised and attacked by a British vessel of superior force,[2] one of a squadron then lying in our waters to cover the transaction, and has been disabled from service with the loss of a number of men killed and wounded.[3] This enormity was not only without provocation or justifiable cause;[4] but was committed with the avowed purpose of taking by force from a ship of war of the U.S. a part of her crew: and that no circumstance might be wanting to make its character, the commander was apprised that the seamen thus forcibly [blank] were native citizens of the U.S. His purpose effected he returned to anchor with his squadron within our jurisdiction. Hospitality under such circumstances ceases to be a duty: and a continuance of it with such uncontrolled abuses would tend only, by multiplying injuries, and irritations, to bring on a rupture equally opposed to the interests of both nations, as to assurances of the most friendly dispositions on the part of the British government in the midst of which this outrage has been committed. The subject

[2] The American frigate *Chesapeake* had 38 guns, the British warship *Leopard* 50 guns.

[3] The *Leopard* killed three men and wounded eighteen on the *Chesapeake*.

[4] The cause for the attack was that the *Leopard* hailed the *Chesapeake* and demanded to "search for deserters." Naturally the American frigate refused, and was fired on.

cannot but present itself to that government, and strengthen the motives to an honorable reparation of the wrong which has been done, and that effectual control, of its naval commanders which alone can justify the government of the U.S. in the exercise of those hospitalities it is now constrained to discontinue.

IN CONSIDERATION of these circumstances, and of the right of every nation to regulate its own police, to provide for its peace and for the safety of its citizens, and consequently to refuse the admission of armed vessels into its harbors or waters, either in such numbers, or of such descriptions, as are inconsistent with these, or with the maintenance of the authority of the laws, I have thought proper in pursuance of the authority specially given by law to issue this my PROCLAMATION, hereby requiring all armed vessels bearing commissions under the government of Great Britain now within the harbors or waters of the U.S. immediately and without any delay to depart from the same: and interdicting the entrance of all the said harbors and waters to the said armed vessels, and to all others bearing commissions under the authority of the British government.

And if the said vessels or any of them, shall fail to depart as aforesaid, or if they or any others, so interdicted, shall hereafter enter the harbors or waters aforesaid, I do in that case forbid all intercourse with either or any of them, their officers or crews, and do prohibit all supplies and aid from being furnished to them or any of them.

And I do declare and make known that if any person from, or within, the jurisdictional limits of the U.S. shall afford any aid to any such vessel contrary to the prohibition contained in this proclamation, either in repairing any such vessel, or in furnishing her, her officers or crew, with supplies of any kind, or in any manner whatever, or if any pilot shall assist in navigating any of the said armed vessels, unless it be for the purpose of carrying them in the first instance, beyond the limits and jurisdiction of the U.S. or unless it be in the case of a vessel forced by distress, or charged with public dispatches as hereinafter provided for, such person or persons shall, on conviction, suffer all the pains and penalties by the laws provided for such offences.

And I do hereby enjoin and require all persons bearing office civil or military within or under the authority of the U.S., and all others, citizens or inhabitants thereof, or being within the same, with vigilance and promptitude to exert their respective authorities and to be aiding and assisting to the carrying this Proclamation and every part thereof into full effect.

Provided nevertheless that if any such vessel shall be forced into the harbors or waters of the U.S. by distress, by the dangers of the sea, or by the pursuit of an enemy, or shall enter them charged with dispatches or business from their government, or shall be a public packet for the conveyance of letters and dispatches, the commanding officer, immediately reporting his vessel to the collector of the district, stating the object or causes of entering the said harbors or waters, and conforming himself to the regulations in that case prescribed under the authority of the laws, shall be allowed the benefit of such regulations respecting repairs, supplies, stay, intercourse, and departure as shall be permitted under the same authority.

In testimony whereof I have caused the seal of the U.S. to be affixed to these presents and sign the same.

Given at the city of Washington the 2d day of July in the year of our Lord 1807 and of the sovereignty and independence of the U.S. the 31st.

## SUPPLEMENTARY EMBARGO BILL[1]

March 30, 1808

A BILL SUPPLEMENTARY TO THE SEVERAL ACTS FOR LAYING AN EMBARGO ON VESSELS, &C.

For vessels coming down rivers, &c.—Be it enacted, &c. that it shall not be lawful for any vessel laden with provisions or lumber to pass by or depart from any port of entry of the United States without examination and a special license from the collector of the customs of such port; nor shall any vessel be so laden on part of the coasts or shores of the United States without the limits of any port of entry until previously examined by some person authorized by the nearest collector of the customs, and a special license from the said collector to be so laden, and to depart according to her lawful destination, on pain of incurring the same penalties and forfeitures as if the said lading had been exported contrary to the tenor of the Acts for laying on embargo, &c. And it shall be lawful for all officers of the revenue and of the armed vessels of the United States to bring to and examine all vessels suspected to be laden with provisions or lumber, and to have departed, or to be

[1] On December 18, 1807, Jefferson sent the following message to Congress: "The communications now made, showing the great and increasing dangers with which our vessels, our seamen, and merchandise, are threatened on the high seas and elsewhere, from the belligerent powers of Europe, and it being of great importance to keep in safety these essential resources, I deem it my duty to recommend the subject to the consideration of Congress, who will doubtless perceive all the advantages which may be expected from an inhibition of the departure of our vessels from the ports of the United States.

"Their wisdom will also see the necessity of making every preparation for whatever events may grow out of the present crisis."

As a result of the message, Congress passed the Embargo Act, on December 22, tying up all American ships in American ports. The Embargo Act was openly flouted by the shipping interests and smugglers, and Jefferson admitted to Secretary of the Treasury Gallatin: "This embargo law is certainly the most embarrassing one we have ever had to execute. I did not expect a crop of so sudden & rank growth of fraud & open opposition by force could have grown up in the U.S." To tighten the law, Jefferson proposed a supplementary embargo act, which is given above. He called it a "very imperfect sketch." On April 16, Congress passed the supplementary Non-Importation Act.

about to depart, without having obtained such license, and on examination and probable grounds to seize and place the same under a due course of legal inquiry.

For Passamaquoddy and St. Mary's, and the secret coves and inlets of the coast.—And it be further enacted, &c., that wheresoever, in any port or on the coasts or shores of the United States elsewhere, a collection of provisions or of lumber shall be made or making which is suspected to be intended for exportation contrary to the provisions of the said laws for laying an embargo, it shall be lawful for the collector of the same port, or of the nearest port, by any agent to be appointed by him, to have the same deposited, if provisions, in warehouses to be approved by him, and to be duly secured by lock, the key of which shall remain with such agent; or if lumber, then to be placed under a sufficient guard by day and night, the expense of which shall be paid by the owner of such lumber, or be levied by sale of a sufficient part thereof; and not to permit the said provisions or lumber to be removed but to such other places, and on such conditions, as shall in his judgment sufficiently guard their being exported contrary to the provisions of the said Acts. And the said collectors and agents shall in all cases within the purview of this Act be governed by such regulations as shall be prescribed by the Secretary of the Treasury, with the approbation of the President of the United States, in all matters of detail necessary for preventing the evasion of this law and for carrying the same into effectual execution.

## ALLIANCE WITH GREAT BRITAIN[1]

October 24, 1823

DEAR SIR: The question presented by the letters you have sent me, is the most momentous which has ever been offered to my contemplation since that of Independence. That made us a nation, this sets our compass and points the course which we are to steer through the ocean of time opening on us. And never could we embark on it under circumstances more auspicious. Our first and fundamental maxim should be, never to entangle ourselves in the broils of Europe. Our second, never to suffer Europe to intermeddle with cis-Atlantic affairs. America, North and South, has a set of interests distinct from those of Europe, and peculiarly her own. She should therefore have a system of her own, separate and apart from that of Europe. While the last is laboring to become the domicil of despotism, our endeavor should surely be, to make our hemisphere that of freedom. One nation, most

[1] Letter to President Monroe. This letter led to the adoption, by President Monroe, of what has since been known as the "Monroe Doctrine." In this communication Jefferson reversed a lifelong policy when he advocated an alliance with Great Britain.

of all, could disturb us in this pursuit; she now offers to lead, aid, and accompany us in it. By acceding to her proposition, we detach her from the bands, bring her mighty weight into the scale of free government, and emancipate a continent at one stroke, which might otherwise linger long in doubt and difficulty. Great Britain is the nation which can do us the most harm of anyone, or all on earth; and with her on our side we need not fear the whole world. With her then, we should most sedulously cherish a cordial friendship; and nothing would tend more to knit our affections than to be fighting once more, side by side, in the same cause. Not that I would purchase even her amity at the price of taking part in her wars. But the war in which the present proposition might engage us, should that be its consequence, is not her war, but ours. Its object is to introduce and establish the American system, of keeping out of our land all foreign powers, of never permitting those of Europe to intermeddle with the affairs of our nations. It is to maintain our own principle, not to depart from it. And if, to facilitate this, we can effect a division in the body of the European powers, and draw over to our side its most powerful member, surely we should do it. But I am clearly of Mr. Canning's opinion, that it will prevent instead of provoking war. With Great Britain withdrawn from their scale and shifted into that of our two continents, all Europe combined would not undertake such a war. For how would they propose to get at either enemy without superior fleets? Nor is the occasion to be slighted which this proposition offers, of declaring our protest against the atrocious violations of the rights of nations, by the interference of anyone in the internal affairs of another, so flagitiously begun by Bonaparte, and now continued by the equally lawless Alliance, calling itself Holy.

But we have first to ask ourselves a question. Do we wish to acquire to our own confederacy any one or more of the Spanish provinces? I candidly confess, that I have ever looked on Cuba as the most interesting addition which could ever be made to our system of States. The control which, with Florida Point, this island would give us over the Gulf of Mexico, and the countries and isthmus bordering on it, as well as all those whose waters flow into it, would fill up the measure of our political well-being. Yet, as I am sensible that this can never be obtained, even with her own consent, but by war; and its independence, which is our second interest (and especially its independence of England), can be secured without it, I have no hesitation in abandoning my first wish to future chances, and accepting its independence, with peace and the friendship of England, rather than its association, at the expense of war and her enmity.

I could honestly, therefore, join in the declaration proposed, that we aim not at the acquisition of any of those possessions, that we will not stand in the way of any amicable arrangement between them and the mother country; but that we will oppose, with all our means, the forcible interposition of any other power, as auxiliary, stipendiary, or under any other form or pretext, and most especially, their transfer to any power by conquest, cession, or acquisition in any other way. I should think it, therefore, advisable, that the Executive should encourage the British government to a continuance in the dispositions expressed in these letters, by an assurance of his concurrence with them as far as his authority goes; and that as it may lead to war, the declaration of which requires an act of Congress, the case shall be laid before them for consideration at their first meeting, and under the reasonable aspect in which it is seen by himself.

I have been so long weaned from political subjects, and have so long ceased to take any interest in them, that I am sensible I am not qualified to offer opinions on them worthy of any attention. But the question now proposed involves consequences so lasting, and effects so decisive of our future destinies, as to rekindle all the interest I have heretofore felt on such occasions, and to induce me to the hazard of opinions, which will prove only my wish to contribute still my mite towards anything which may be useful to our country. And praying you to accept it at only what it is worth, I add the assurance of my constant and affectionate friendship and respect.

## *Chapter V*

# FOREIGN POLICY: II, COMMERCE

## INSTRUCTIONS TO THE MINISTERS PLENIPOTENTIARY APPOINTED TO NEGOTIATE TREATIES OF COMMERCE WITH THE EUROPEAN NATIONS

May 7, 1784

Whereas, instructions bearing date the 29th day of October, 1783, were sent to the Ministers Plenipotentiary of the United States of America at the Court of Versailles, empowered to negotiate a peace, or to any one or more of them, for concerting drafts or propositions for treaties of amity and commerce with the commercial powers of Europe:

*Resolved,* That it will be advantageous to these United States to conclude such treaties with Russia, the Court of Vienna, Prussia, Denmark, Saxony, Hamburg, Great Britain, Spain, Portugal, Genoa, Tuscany, Rome, Naples, Venice, Sardinia, and the Ottoman Porte.

*Resolved,* That in the formation of these treaties the following points be carefully stipulated:

1. That each party shall have a right to carry their own produce, manufactures, and merchandise, in their own bottoms to the ports of the other, and thence the produce and merchandise of the other, paying, in both cases, such duties only as are paid by the most favored nation, freely, where it is freely granted to such nation, or paying the compensation where such nation does the same.

2. That with the nations holding territorial possessions in America, a direct and similar intercourse be admitted between the United States and such possessions; or if this cannot be obtained, then a direct and similar intercourse between the United States and certain free ports within such possessions; and that if this neither can be obtained, permission be stipulated to bring from such possessions, in their own bottoms, the produce and merchandise

thereof to their States directly; and for these States to carry in their own bottoms their produce and merchandise to such possessions directly.

3. That these United States be considered in all such treaties, and in every case arising under them, as one nation, upon the principles of the federal constitution.

4. That it be proposed, though not indispensably required, that if war should hereafter arise between the two contracting parties, the merchants of either country, then residing in the other, shall be allowed to remain nine months to collect their debts and settle their affairs, and may depart freely, carrying off all their effects, without molestation or hinderance; and all fishermen, all cultivators of the earth, and all artisans or manufacturers, unarmed and inhabiting unfortified towns, villages or places, who labor for the common subsistence and benefit of mankind, and peaceably following their respective employments, shall be allowed to continue the same, and shall not be molested by the armed force of the enemy, in whose power, by the events of war, they may happen to fall; but if anything is necessary to be taken from them, for the use of such armed force, the same shall be paid for at a reasonable price; and all merchants and traders, exchanging the products of different places, and thereby rendering the necessaries, conveniences, and comforts of human life more easy to obtain and more general, shall be allowed to pass free and unmolested; and neither of the contracting powers shall grant or issue any commission to any private armed vessels empowering them to take or destroy such trading ships, or interrupt such commerce.

5. And in case either of the contracting parties shall happen to be engaged in war with any other nation, it be further agreed, in order to prevent all the difficulties and misunderstandings that usually arise respecting the merchandise heretofore called contraband, such as arms, ammunition and military stores of all kinds, that no such articles, carrying by the ships or subjects of one of the parties to the enemies of the other, shall, on any account, be deemed contraband, so as to induce confiscation, and a loss of property to individuals. Nevertheless, it shall be lawful to stop such ships and detain them for such length of time as the captors may think necessary, to prevent the inconvenience or damage that might ensue, from their proceeding on their voyage, paying, however, a reasonable compensation for the loss such arrest shall occasion to the proprietors; and it shall be further allowed to use in the service of the captors, the whole or any part of the military stores so detained, paying the owners the full value of the same, to be ascertained by the current price at the place of its destination. But if the other contracting party will not consent to discontinue the confiscation of contraband goods, then that it be stipulated, that if the master of the vessel stopped, will deliver out the goods charged to be contraband, he shall be admitted to do

it, and the vessel shall not in that case be carried into any port; but shall be allowed to proceed on her voyage.

6. That in the same case, when either of the contracting parties shall happen to be engaged in war with any other power, all goods, not contraband, belonging to the subjects of that other power, and shipped in the bottoms of the party hereto, who is not engaged in the war, shall be entirely free. And that to ascertain what shall constitute the blockade of any place or port, it shall be understood to be in such predicament, when the assailing power shall have taken such a station as to expose to imminent danger any ship or ships, that would attempt to sail in or out of the said port; and that no vessel of the party, who is not engaged in the said war, shall be stopped without a material and well-grounded cause; and in such cases justice shall be done, and an indemnification given, without loss of time to the persons aggrieved, and thus stopped without sufficient cause.

7. That no right be stipulated for aliens to hold real property within these States, this being utterly inadmissible by their several laws and policy; but when on the death of any person holding real estate within the territories of one of the contracting parties, such real estate would by their laws descend on a subject or citizen of the other, were he not disqualified by alienage, then he shall be allowed a reasonable time to dispose of the same, and withdraw the proceeds without molestation.

8. That such treaties be made for a term not exceeding ten years from the exchange of ratification.

9. That these instructions be considered as supplementary to those of October 29th, 1783; and not as revoking, except when they contradict them. That where in treaty with a particular nation they can procure particular advantages, to the specification of which we have been unable to descend, our object in these instructions having been to form outlines only and general principles of treaty with many nations, it is our expectation they will procure them, though not pointed out in these instructions; and where they may be able to form treaties on principles which, in their judgment, will be more beneficial to the United States than those herein directed to be made their basis, they are permitted to adopt such principles. That as to the duration of treaties, though we have proposed to restrain them to the term of ten years, yet they are at liberty to extend the same as far as fifteen years with any nation which may pertinaciously insist thereon. And that it will be agreeable to us to have supplementary treaties with France, the United Netherlands and Sweden, which may bring the treaties we have entered into with them as nearly as may be to the principles of those now directed; but that this be not pressed, if the proposal should be found disagreeable.

*Resolved,* That treaties of amity, or of amity and commerce, be entered into with Morocco, and the Regencies of Algiers, Tunis and Tripoli, to continue for the same term of ten years, or for a term as much longer as can be procured.

That our Ministers, to be commissioned for treating with foreign nations, make known to the Emperor of Morocco the great satisfaction which Congress feel from the amicable disposition he has shown towards these States, and his readiness to enter into alliance with them. That the occupations of the war, and distance of our situation have prevented our meeting his friendship so early as we wished. But the powers are now delegated to them for entering into treaty with him, in the execution of which they are ready to proceed, and that as to the expenses of his Minister, they do therein what is for the honor and interest of the United States.

*Resolved,* That a commission be issued to Mr. J. Adams, Mr. B. Franklin, and Mr. T. Jefferson, giving powers to them, or the greater part of them, to make and receive propositions for such treaties of amity and commerce, and to negotiate and sign the same, transmitting them to Congress for their final ratification; and that such commission be in force for a term not exceeding two years.

## REPORT OF A CONFERENCE WITH THE COUNT DE VERGENNES ON THE SUBJECT OF THE COMMERCE OF THE UNITED STATES WITH FRANCE[1]

1785

The next levee day at Versailles, I meant to bring again under the view of the Count de Vergennes, the whole subject of our commerce with France; but the number of audiences of ambassadors and other ministers, which take place, of course, before mine, and which seldom, indeed, leave me an opportunity of audience at all, prevented me that day. I was only able to ask the Count de Vergennes, as a particular favor, that he would permit me to wait on him some day that week. He did so, and I went to Versailles the Friday following (the 9th of December). M. de Reyneval was with the Count. Our conversation began with the usual topic; that the trade of the United States had not yet learned the way to France, but continued to centre in England, though no longer obliged by law to go there. I observed, that the real cause

[1] On January 2, 1786, Ambassador Jefferson wrote from Paris to John Jay:

"SIR: Several conferences and letters having passed between the Count de Vergennes and myself, on the subject of the commerce of this country with the United States, I think them sufficiently interesting to be communicated to Congress. They are stated in the form of a report, and are herein enclosed. The length of this despatch, perhaps, needs apology. Yet I have not been able to abridge it, without omitting circumstances which I thought Congress would rather choose to know. Some of the objects of these conferences present but small hopes for the present, but they seem to admit a possibility of success at some future moment."

Vergennes was Louis XVI's Minister of Foreign Affairs.

of this, was to be found in the difference of the commercial arrangements in the two countries; that merchants would not, and could not trade but where there was to be some gain; that the commerce between two countries could not be kept up, but by an exchange of commodities; that, if an American merchant was forced to carry his produce to London, it could not be expected he would make a voyage from thence to France, with the money, to lay it out here; and, in like manner, that if he could bring his commodities, with advantage, to this country, he would not make another voyage to England, with the money, to lay it out there, but would take in exchange the merchandise of this country. The Count de Vergennes agreed to this, and particularly that where there was no exchange of merchandise, there could be no durable commerce; and that it was natural for merchants to take their returns in the port where they sold their cargo. I desired his permission then, to take a summary view of the productions of the United States, that we might see which of them could be brought here to advantage.

1. Rice. France gets from the Mediterranean a rice not so good indeed, but cheaper than ours. He said that they bought of our rice, but that they got from Egypt also, rice of a very fine quality. I observed that such was the actual state of their commerce, in that article, that they take little from us. 2. Indigo. They make a plenty in their own colonies. He observed that they did, and that they thought it better than ours. 3. Flour, fish, and provisions of all sorts, they produce for themselves. That these articles might, therefore, be considered as not existing, for commerce, between the United States and the kingdom of France.

I proceeded to those capable of becoming objects of exchange between the two nations. 1. Peltry and furs. Our posts being in the hands of the English, we are cut off from that article. I am not sure even, whether we are not obliged to buy of them, for our own use. When these posts are given up, if ever they are, we shall be able to furnish France with skins and furs, to the amount of two millions of livres, in exchange for her merchandise; but at present, these articles are to be counted as nothing. 2. Potash. An experiment is making whether this can be brought here. We hope it may, but at present it stands for nothing. He observed that it was much wanted in France, and he thought it would succeed. 3. Naval stores. Trials are also making on these, as subjects of commerce with France. They are heavy, and the voyage long. The result, therefore, is doubtful. At present, they are as nothing in our commerce with this country. 4. Whale oil. I told him I had great hopes that the late diminution of duty would enable us to bring this article, with advantage, to France; that a merchant was just arrived (Mr. Barrett) who proposed to settle at L'Orient, for the purpose of selling the cargoes of this article, and choosing the returns. That he had informed me, that in the first year, it would be necessary to take one-third in money, and the remainder only in merchandise; because the fishermen require, indispensably, some money. But he thought that after the first year, the merchandise of the preceding year, would always produce money for the ensuing one, and that the whole amount would continue to be taken annually afterwards, in merchandise. I added, that though the diminution of duty was expressed to be but for one year, yet I hoped they would find their advantage in renewing and continuing it; for that if they intended really to admit it for one year only, the fishermen would not find it worth while to rebuild their vessels, and to prepare themselves for the business. The Count expressed satisfaction on the view of commercial exchange held up by this article. He made no answer as to the continuance of it; and I did not choose to tell him, at that time, that we should claim its continuance under their treaty with the Hanseatic towns, which fixes this duty for them, and our own treaty, which gives us the rights of the most favored nation. 5. Tobacco. I recalled to the memory of the Count de Vergennes, the letter I had written to him on this article; and the object of the present conversation being, how to facilitate the exchange of commerciable articles between the two countries, I pressed that of tobacco, in this point of view; observed that France, at present, paid us two millions of livres for this article; that for such portions of it as were bought in London, they sent the money directly there, and for what they bought in the United States, the money was still remitted to London, by bills of exchange; whereas, if they would permit our merchants to sell this article freely, they would bring it here, and take the returns on the spot, in merchandise, not money. The Count observed, that my proposition contained what was doubtless useful, but that the King received on this article, at present, a revenue of twenty-eight millions, which was so considerable, as to render them fearful of tampering with it; that the collection of this revenue by way of Farm, was of very ancient date, and that it was always hazardous to alter arrangements of long standing, and of such infinite combinations with the fiscal system. I answered, that the simplicity of the mode of collection proposed for this article, withdrew it from all fear of deranging other parts of their system; that I supposed they would confine the importation to some of their principal ports, probably not more than five or six; that a single collector in each of these, was the only new officer requisite; that he could get rich himself on six livres a hogshead, and would receive the whole revenue, and pay it into the treasury, at short hand. M. de Reyneval entered particularly into this part of the conversation, and explained to the Count, more in detail, the advantages and simplicity of it, and concluded by observing to me, that it sometimes happened that useful propositions, though not practicable at one time, might become so at another. I told him that that consideration had induced me to press the matter when I did, because I had understood the renewal of the Farm was then on the carpet, and that it was the precise moment when I supposed that this portion might be detached from the mass of the Farms. I asked Count de Vergennes whether, if the renewal of the Farm was pressing, this article might not be separated, merely in suspense, till government should have time to satisfy themselves on the expediency of renewing it. He said no promises could be made.

In the course of this conversation, he had mentioned the liberty we enjoyed of carrying our fish to the French islands. I repeated to him what I had hinted in my letter, of November the 20th, 1785, that I considered as a prohibition the laying such duties on our fish, and giving such premiums on theirs, as made a difference between their and our fishermen of fifteen livres the quintal, in an article which sold for but fifteen livres. He said it would not have that effect, for two reasons: 1. That their fishermen could not furnish supplies sufficient for their islands, and, of course, the inhabitants must, of necessity, buy our fish. 2. That from the constancy of our fishery, and the short season during which theirs continued, and also from the economy and management of ours, compared with the expense of theirs, we had always been able to sell our fish, in their islands, at twenty-five livres the quintal, while they were obliged to ask thirty-six livres. (I suppose he meant the livre of the French islands.) That thus, the duty and premium had been a necessary operation on their side, to place the sale of their fish on a level with ours, and that without this, theirs could not bear the competition.

I have here brought together the substance of what was said on the preceding subjects, not pretending to give it verbatim, which my memory does not enable me to do. I have, probably, omitted many things which were spoken, but have mentioned nothing which was not. It was interrupted, at times, with collateral matters. One of these was important. The Count de Vergennes complained, and with a good deal of stress, that they did not find a sufficient dependence on arrangements taken with us. This was the third time too, he had done it; first, in a conversation at Fontainebleau, when he first complained to me of the navigation acts of Massachusetts and New Hampshire; secondly, in his letter of October the 30th, 1785, on the same subject; and now, in the present conversation, wherein he added, as another instance, the case of the Chevalier de Mezières, heir of General Oglethorpe, who, notwithstanding that the 11th article of the treaty provides, that the subjects or citizens of either party shall succeed, *ab intestato,* to the lands of their ancestors, within the dominions of the other, had been informed from Mr. Adams, and by me also, that his right of succession to the General's estate in Georgia was doubtful. He observed too, that the administration of justice with us was tardy, insomuch that their merchants, when they had money due to them within our States, considered it as desperate; and that our commercial regulations, in general, were disgusting to them. These ideas were new, serious and delicate. I decided, therefore, not to enter into them at that moment, and the rather, as we were speaking in French, in which language I did not choose to hazard myself. I withdrew from the objections of the tardiness of justice with us, and the disagreeableness of our commercial regulations, by a general observation, that I was not sensible they were well founded. With respect to the case of the Chevalier de Mezières, I was obliged to enter into some explanations. They related chiefly to the legal operation of our Declaration of Independence, to the undecided question whether our citizens and British subjects were thereby made aliens to one another, to the general laws as to conveyances of land to aliens, and the doubt whether an act of the Assembly of Georgia might not have been passed, to confiscate General Oglethorpe's property, which would of course prevent its devolution on any heir. Mr. Reyneval observed, that in this case, it became a mere question of fact, whether a confiscation of these lands had taken place before the death of General Oglethorpe, which fact might be easily known by inquiries in Georgia, where the possessions lay. I thought it very material, that the opinion of this court should be set to rights on these points. On my return, therefore, I wrote the following observations on them, which, the next time I went to Versailles (not having an opportunity of speaking to the Count de Vergennes), I put into the hands of M. Reyneval, praying him to read them, and to ask the favor of the Count to do the same.

EXPLANATIONS ON SOME OF THE SUBJECTS OF CONVERSATION WHICH I HAD THE HONOR OF HAVING WITH HIS EXCELLENCY, THE COUNT DE VERGENNES, WHEN I WAS LAST AT VERSAILLES

The principal design of that conversation was, to discuss those articles of commerce which the United States could spare, which are wanted in France, and if received there on a convenient footing, would be exchanged for the productions of France. But in the course of the conversation, some circumstances were incidentally mentioned by the Count de Vergennes, which induced me to suppose he had received impressions, neither favorable to us, nor derived from perfect information.

The case of the Chevalier de Mezières was supposed to furnish an instance of our disregard to treaties; and the event of that case was inferred from opinions supposed to have been given by Mr. Adams and myself. This is ascribing a weight to our opinions, to which they are not entitled. They will have no influence on the decision of the case. The judges in our courts, would not suffer them to be read. Their guide is the law of the land, of which law its treaties make a part. Indeed, I know not what opinion Mr. Adams may have given on the case. And, if any be imputed to him derogatory of our regard to the treaty with France, I think his opinion has been misunderstood.

With respect to myself, the doubts which I expressed to the Chevalier de Mezières, as to the success of his claims, were not founded on any question whether the treaty between France and the United States would be observed. On the contrary, I venture to pronounce that it will be religiously observed, if his case comes under it. But I doubted whether it would come under the treaty. The case, as I understand it, is this: General Oglethorpe, a British subject, had lands in Georgia. He died since the peace, having devised these lands to his wife. His heirs are the Chevalier de Mezières, son of his elder sister, and the Marquis de Bellegarde, son of his younger sister. This case gives rise to legal questions, some of which have not yet been decided, either in England or America, the laws of which countries are nearly the same.

1. It is a question under the laws of those countries, whether persons *born before their separation,* and once completely invested, in both, with the character of natural subjects, can ever become aliens in either? There are respectable opinions on both sides. If the negative be right, then General Oglethorpe having never become an alien, and having devised his lands to his wife, who, on this supposition, also, was not an alien, the devise has transferred the lands to her, and there is nothing left for the treaty to operate on.

2. If the affirmative opinion be right, and the inhabitants of Great Britain and America, *born before the Revolution,* are become aliens to each other, it follows by the laws of both, that the lands which either possessed, within the jurisdiction of the other, became the property of the State in which they are. But a question arises, whether the transfer of the property took place on the Declaration of Independence, or not till an office, or an act of Assembly, had declared the transfer. If the property passed to the State on the Declaration of Independence, then it did not remain in General Oglethorpe, and, of course, at the time of his death, he having nothing, there was nothing to pass to his heirs, and so, nothing for the treaty to operate on.

3. If the property does not pass till declared by an office found by jury, or an act passed by the Assembly, the question then is, whether an office had been found, or an act of Assembly been passed for that purpose, before the peace? If there was, the lands had passed to the State during his life, and nothing being left in him, there is nothing for his heirs to claim under the treaty.

4. If the property had not been transferred to the State before the peace, either by the Declaration of Independence, or an office, or an act of Assembly, then it remained in General Oglethorpe at the epoch of the peace; and it will be insisted, no doubt, that, by the sixth article of the treaty of peace, between the United States and Great Britain, which forbids future confiscations, General Oglethorpe acquired a capacity of holding and of conveying his lands. He has conveyed them to his wife. But she being an alien, it will

be decided by the laws of the land, whether she took them for her own use, or for the use of the State. For it is a general principle of our law, that conveyances to aliens pass the lands to the State; and it may be urged, that though, by the treaty of peace, General Oglethorpe could convey, yet that treaty did not mean to give him a greater privilege of conveyance than natives hold, to wit: a privilege of transferring the property to persons incapable, by law, of taking it. However, this would be a question between the State of Georgia and the widow of General Oglethorpe, in the decision of which the Chevalier de Mezières is not interested, because, whether she takes the land by the will, for her own use, or for that of the State, it is equally prevented from descending to him: there is neither a conveyance to him, nor a succession *ab intestato* devolving on him, which are the cases provided for by our treaty with France. To sum up the matter in a few words; if the lands had passed to the State before the epoch of peace, the heirs of General Oglethorpe cannot say they have descended on them, and if they remained in the General at that epoch, the treaty saving them to him, he could convey them away from his heirs, and he has conveyed them to his widow, either for her own use, or for that of the State.

Seeing no event in which, according to the facts stated to me, the treaty could be applied to this case, or could give any right whatever, to the heirs of General Oglethorpe, I advised the Chevalier de Mezières not to urge his pretensions on the footing of right, nor under the treaty, but to petition the Assembly of Georgia for a grant of these lands. If, in the question between the State and the widow of General Oglethorpe, it should be decided that they were the property of the State, I expected from their generosity, and the friendly disposition in America towards the subjects of France, that they would be favorable to the Chevalier de Mezières. There is nothing in the preceding observations which would not have applied against the heir of General Oglethorpe, had he been a native citizen of Georgia, as it now applies against him, being a subject of France. The treaty has placed the subjects of France on a footing with natives, as to conveyances and descent of property. There was no occasion for the Assemblies to pass laws on this subject; the treaty being a law, as I conceive, superior to those of particular Assemblies, and repealing them, when they stand in the way of its operations.

The supposition that the treaty was disregarded on our part, in the instance of the acts of Assembly of Massachusetts and New Hampshire, which made a distinction between natives and foreigners, as to the duties to be paid on commerce, was taken notice of in the letter of November the 20th, which I had the honor of addressing to the Count de Vergennes. And while I express my hopes that, on a revision of these subjects, nothing will be found in them derogatory from either the letter or spirit of our treaty, I will add assurances that the United States will not be behind hand in going beyond both, whenever occasions shall offer of manifesting their sincere attachment to this country.

I will pass on to the observation, that our commercial regulations are difficult, and repugnant to the French merchants. To detail these regulations minutely, as they exist in every State, would be beyond my information. A general view of them, however, will suffice, because the States differ little in their several regulations. On the arrival of a ship in America, her cargo must be reported at the proper office. The duties on it are to be paid. These are commonly from two and a half to five per cent on its value. On many articles, the value of which is tolerably uniform, the precise sum is fixed by law. A tariff of these is presented to the importer, and he can see what he has to pay, as well as the officer. For other articles, the duty is such a per cent on their value. That value is either shown by the invoice, or by the oath of the importer. This operation being once over, and it is a very short one, the goods are considered as entered, and may then pass through the whole thirteen States without their being ever more subject to a question, unless they be reshipped. Exportation is still more simple; because, as we prohibit the exportation of nothing, and very rarely lay a duty on any article of export, the State is little interested in examining outward-bound vessels. The captain asks a clearance for his own purposes. As to the operations of internal commerce, such as matters of exchange, of buying, selling, bartering, &c., our laws are the same as the English. If they have been altered in any instance, it has been to render them more simple.

Lastly, as to the tardiness of the administration of justice with us, it would be equally tedious and impracticable for me to give a precise account of it in every State. But I think it probable that it is much on the same footing through all the States, and that an account of it in any one of them may found a general presumption of it in the others. Being best acquainted with its administration in Virginia, I shall confine myself to that. Before the Revolution, a judgment could not be obtained under eight years in the supreme court, where the suit was in the department of the common law, which department embraces about nine-tenths of the subject of legal contestation. In that of the chancery, from twelve to twenty years were requisite. This did not proceed from any vice in the laws, but from the indolence of the judges appointed by the King; and these judges holding their office during his will only, he could have reformed the evil at any time. This reformation was among the first works of the legislature after our independence. A judgment can now be obtained in the supreme court in one year at the common law, and in about three years in the chancery. But more particularly to protect the commerce of France, which, at that moment, was considerable with us, a law was passed, giving all suits wherein a foreigner was a party, a privilege to be tried immediately, on the return of his process, without waiting till those of natives, which stand before them, shall have been decided on. Out of this act, however, the British stand excluded by a subsequent one. This, with its causes, must be explained. The British army, after ravaging the State of Virginia, had sent off a very great number of slaves to New York. By the seventh article of the treaty of peace, they stipulated not to carry away any of these. Notwithstanding this, it was known, when they were evacuating New York, that they were carrying away the slaves. General Washington made an official demand of Sir Guy Carleton, that he should cease to send them away. He answered, that these people had come to them under promise of the King's protection, and that that promise should be fulfilled in preference to the stipulation in the treaty. The State of Virginia, to which nearly the whole of these slaves belonged, passed a law to forbid the recovery of debts due to British subjects. They declared, at the same time, they would repeal the law, if Congress were of opinion they ought to do it. But, desirous that their citizens should be discharging their debts, they afterwards permitted British creditors to prosecute their suits, and to receive their debts in seven equal and annual payments; relying that the demand for the slaves would be either admitted or denied in time to lay their hands on some of the latter payments for reimbursement. The immensity of this debt was another reason for forbidding such a mass of property to be offered for sale under execution at once, as, from the small quantity of circulating money, it must have sold for little or nothing, whereby the creditor would have failed to receive his money, and the debtor would have lost his whole estate without being discharged of his debt. This is the history of the delay of justice in that country in the case of British creditors. As to all others, its administration is as speedy as justice itself will admit. I presume it is equally so in all the other States, and can add, that it is administered in them all, with a purity and integrity of which few countries afford an example.

I cannot take leave altogether of the subjects of this conversation without recalling the attention of the Count de Vergennes to what had been its principal drift. This was to endeavor to bring about a direct exchange between France and the United States (without the intervention of a third nation), of those productions with which each could furnish the other. We can furnish to France (because we have heretofore furnished to England), of whale oil and spermaceti, of furs and peltry, of ships and naval stores, and of potash, to the amount of fifteen millions of livres; and the quantities will admit of increase. Of our tobacco, France consumes the value of ten millions more. Twenty-five millions of livres, then, mark the extent of that commerce of exchange, which is, at present, practicable between us. We want, in return, productions and manufactures, not money. If the duties on our produce are light, and the sale free, we shall undoubtedly bring it here, and lay out the proceeds on the spot in the productions and manufactures which we want. The merchants of France will, on their part, become active in the same business. We shall no more think, when we shall have sold our produce here, of making an useless voyage to another country to lay out the money, than we think at present, when we have sold it elsewhere, of coming here to lay out the money. The conclusion is, that there are commodities which form a basis of exchange to the extent of a million of guineas annually; it is for the wisdom of those in power to contrive that the exchange shall be made.

Having put this paper into the hands of Monsieur Reyneval, we entered into conversation again, on the subject of the Farms, which were now understood to be approaching to a conclusion. He told me, that he was decidedly of opinion, that the interest of the State required the Farm of tobacco to be discontinued, and that he had, accordingly, given every aid to my proposition, which laid within his sphere; that the Count de Vergennes was very clearly of the same opinion, and had supported it strongly with reasons of his own, when he transmitted it to the Comptroller General; but that the Comptroller, in the discussions of this subject which had taken place, besides the objections which the Count de Vergennes had repeated to me, and which are before mentioned, had added, that the contract with the Farmers General was now so far advanced, that the article of tobacco could not be withdrawn from it, without unravelling the whole transaction. Having understood that, in this contract, there was always reserved to the crown a right to discontinue it at any moment, making just reimbursements to the Farmers, I asked M. Reyneval, if the contract should be concluded in its present form, whether it might still be practicable to have it discontinued, as to the article of tobacco, at some future moment. He said it might be possible.

Upon the whole, the true obstacle to this proposition has penetrated, in various ways, through the veil which covers it. The influence of the Farmers General has been heretofore found sufficient to shake a minister in his office. Monsieur de Calonnes' continuance or dismission, has been thought, for some time, to be on a poise. Were he to shift this great weight, therefore, out of his own scale into that of his adversaries, it would decide their preponderance. The joint interests of France and America would be insufficient counterpoise in his favor.

It will be observed that these efforts to improve the commerce of the United States, have been confined to that branch only which respects France itself, and that nothing passed on the subject of our commerce with the

West Indies, except an incidental conversation as to our fish. The reason of this, was no want of a due sense of its importance. Of that, I am thoroughly sensible. But efforts in favor of this branch would, at present, be desperate. To nations with which we have not yet treated, and who have possessions in America, we may offer a free vent of their manufactures in the United States, for a full or modified admittance into those possessions. But to France, we are obliged to give that freedom for a different compensation; to wit, for her aid in effecting our independence. It is difficult, therefore, to say what we have now to offer her, for an admission into her West Indies. Doubtless, it has its price. But the question is, what this would be, and whether worth our while to give it. Were we to propose to give to each other's citizens all the rights of natives, they would, of course, count what they should gain by this enlargement of right, and examine whether it would be worth to them as much as their monopoly of their West India commerce. If not, that commercial freedom which we wish to preserve, and which, indeed, is so valuable, leaves us little to offer. An expression in my letter to the Count de Vergennes, of November the 20th, wherein I hinted that both nations might, perhaps, come into the opinion, that the condition of *natives* might be a better ground of intercourse for their citizens, than that of the *most favored* nation, was intended to furnish an opportunity to the minister of parleying on that subject, if he was so disposed, and to myself, of seeing whereabouts they would begin, that I might communicate it to Congress, and leave them to judge of the expediency of pursuing the subject. But no overtures have followed; for I have no right to consider as coming from the minister, certain questions which were, very soon after, proposed to me by an individual. It sufficiently accounts for these questions, that that individual had written a memorial on the subject, for the consideration of the minister, and might wish to know what we would be willing to do. The idea that I should answer such questions to him, is equally unaccountable, whether we suppose them originating with himself, or coming from the minister. In fact, I must suppose them to be his own; and I transmit them, only that Congress may see what one Frenchman, at least, thinks on the subject. If we can obtain from Great Britain reasonable conditions of commerce (which, in my idea, must forever include an admission into her islands), the freest ground between these two nations would seem to be the best. But if we can obtain no equal terms from her, perhaps Congress might think it prudent, as Holland has done, to connect us unequivocally with France. Holland has purchased the protection of France. The price she pays, is *aid in time of war*. It is interesting for us to purchase a free commerce with the French islands. But whether it is best to pay for it, by *aids in war, or by privileges in commerce, or not to purchase it at all,* is the question.

# OBSERVATIONS ON THE SUBJECT OF ADMITTING OUR WHALE OIL IN THE MARKETS OF FRANCE[1]

November 19, 1788

Whale oil enters, as a raw material, into several branches of manufacture, as of wool, leather, soap: it is used also, in painting, architecture and navigation. But its great consumption is in lighting houses and cities. For this last purpose, however, it has a powerful competitor in the vegetable oils. These do well in warm, still weather, but they fix with cold, they extinguish easily with the wind, their crop is precarious, depending on the seasons, and to yield the same light, a larger wick must be used, and greater quantity of oil consumed. Estimating all these articles of difference together, those employed in lighting cities find their account in giving about twenty-five per cent more for whale, than for vegetable oils. But higher than this, the whale oil, in its present form, cannot rise; because it then becomes more advantageous to the city lighters to use others. This competition, then, limits its price, higher than which no encouragement can raise it; and it becomes, as it were, a law of its nature. But, at this low price, the whale fishery is the poorest business into which a merchant or sailor can enter. If the sailor, instead of wages, has a part of what is taken, he finds that this, one year with another, yields him less than he could have got as wages in any other business. It is attended, too, with great risk, singular hardships, and long absence from his family. If the voyage is made solely at the expense of the merchant, he finds that, one year with another, it does not reimburse him his expense. As for example, an English ship of three hundred tons and forty-two hands, brings home, *communibus annis,* after four months' voyage, twenty-five tons of oil, worth four hundred and thirty-seven pounds ten shilling sterling. But the wages of the officers and seamen, will be four hundred pounds; the outfit, then, and the merchant's profit, must be paid by the government; and it is accordingly on this idea that the British bounty is calculated. From the poverty of this business, then, it has happened that the nations who have taken it up, have successively abandoned it. The Basques began it; but though the most economical and enterprising of the inhabitants of France, they could not continue it; and it is said they never employed more than thirty ships a year. The Dutch and Hanse towns succeeded them. The latter gave it up long ago. The English carried it on in competition with the Dutch, during the last and beginning of the present century; but it was too little profitable for them, in comparison with other branches of commerce open to them.

In the meantime, the inhabitants of the barren island of Nantucket had taken up this fishery, invited to it, by the whales presenting themselves on

[1] Enclosed in a letter to John Jay.

their own shore. To them, therefore, the English relinquished it, continuing to them, as British subjects, the importation of their oils into England, duty free, while foreigners were subject to a duty of eighteen pounds five shillings sterling, a ton. The Dutch were enabled to continue it long, because, 1st. They are so near the northern fishing grounds, that a vessel begins her fishing very soon after she is out of port. 2d. They navigate with more economy than the other nations of Europe. 3d. Their seamen are content with lower wages: and 4th, their merchants, with a lower profit on their capital. Under all these favorable circumstances, however, this branch of business, after long languishing, is, at length, nearly extinct with them. It is said, they did not send above half a dozen ships in pursuit of the whale, this present year. The Nantuckois, then, were the only people who exercised this fishery to any extent, at the commencement of the late war. Their country, from its barrenness yielding no subsistence, they were obliged to seek it in the sea which surrounded them. Their economy was more rigorous than that of the Dutch. Their seamen, instead of wages, had a share in what was taken: this induced them to fish with fewer hands, so that each had a greater dividend in the profit; it made them more vigilant in seeking game, bolder in pursuing it, and parsimonious in all their expenses. London was their only market. When, therefore, by the late Revolution, they became aliens in Great Britain, they became subject to the alien duty of eighteen pounds five shillings, the ton of oil, which being more than equal to the price of the common whale oil, they are obliged to abandon that fishery. So that this people, who, before the war, had employed upwards of three hundred vessels a year, in the whale fishery (while Great Britain had herself never employed one hundred), have now almost ceased to exercise it. But they still had the seamen, the most important material for this fishery; and they still retained the spirit for fishing: so that, at the re-establishment of peace, they were capable, in a very short time, of reviving their fishery, in all its splendor. The British government saw that the moment was critical. They knew that their own share in that fishery, was as nothing; that the great mass of fishermen was left with a nation now separated from them; that these fishermen, however, had lost their ancient market; had no other resource within their country, to which they could turn; and they hoped, therefore, they might, in the present moment of distress, be decoyed over to their establishments, and be added to the mass of their seamen. To effect this, they offered extravagant advantages to all persons who should exercise the whale fishery from British establishments. But not counting with much confidence, on a long connection with their remaining possessions on the continent of America, foreseeing that the Nantuckois would settle in them, preferably, if put on an equal footing with those of Great Britain, and that thus they might have to purchase them the second time, they confined their high offers to settlers in

Great Britain. The Nantuckois, left without resource by the loss of their market, began to think of removing to the British dominions; some to Nova Scotia, preferring smaller advantages, in the neighborhood of their ancient country and friends; others to Great Britain, postponing country and friends to high premiums. A vessel was already arrived from Halifax to Nantucket, to take off some of those who proposed to remove; two families had gone on board, and others were going, when a letter was received there, which had been written by Monsieur le Marquis de La Fayette, to a gentleman in Boston, and transmitted by him to Nantucket. The purport of the letter was, to dissuade their accepting the British proposals, and to assure them, that their friends in France would endeavor to do something for them. This instantly suspended their design: not another went on board, and the vessel returned to Halifax, with only the two families.

In fact, the French government had not been inattentive to the views of the British, nor insensible to the crisis. They saw the danger of permitting five or six thousand of the best seamen existing, to be transferred by a single stroke to the marine strength of their enemy, and to carry over with them an art, which they possessed almost exclusively. The counterplan which they set on foot, was, to tempt the Nantuckois, by high offers, to come and settle in France. This was in the year 1785. The British, however, had in their favor a sameness of language, religion, laws, habits, and kindred. Nine families only, of thirty-three persons in the whole, came to Dunkirk; so that this project was not likely to prevent their emigration to the English establishments, if nothing else had happened.

France had effectually aided in detaching the United States of America from the *force* of Great Britain; but, as yet, they seemed to have indulged only a silent wish, to detach them from her *commerce*. They had done nothing to induce that event. In the same year, 1785, while M. de Calonne was in treaty with the Nantuckois, an estimate of the commerce of the United States was submitted to the Count de Vergennes, and it was shown, that of three millions of pounds sterling, to which their exports amounted, one third might be brought to France, and exchanged against her productions and manufactures, advantageously for both nations; provided the obstacles of prohibition, monopoly and duty, were either done away or moderated, as far as circumstances would admit. A committee, which had been appointed to investigate a particular one of these objects, was thereupon instructed to extend its researches to the whole, and see what advantages and facilities the government could offer, for the encouragement of a general commerce with the United States. The committee was composed of persons well skilled in commerce; and after laboring assiduously for several months, they made their report: the result of which was given in the letter of his Majesty's Comptroller General, of the 22d of October, 1786, wherein he stated the principles which should be established, for the future regulation of the commerce between France and the United States. It was become tolerably evident, at the date of this letter, that the terms offered to the Nantuckois, would not produce their emigration to Dunkirk; and that it would be safest, in every event, to offer some other alternative, which might prevent their acceptance of the British offers. The obvious one was, to open the ports of France to their oils, so that they might still exercise their fishery, remaining in their native country, and find a new market for its produce, instead of that which they had lost. The article of whale oil was, accordingly, distinguished in the letter of M. de Calonne, by an immediate abatement of duty, and promise of further abatement, after the year 1790. This letter was instantly sent to America, and bid fair to produce there the effect intended, by determining the fishermen to carry on their trade from their own homes, with the advantage only of a free market in France, rather than remove to Great Britain, where a free market and great bounty were offered them. An *Arrêt* was still to be prepared, to give legal sanction to the letter of M. de Calonne. Monsieur Lambert, with a patience and assiduity almost unexampled, went through all the investigations necessary to assure himself, that the conclusion of the committee had been just. Frequent conferences on this subject were held in his presence; the deputies of the chambers of commerce were heard, and the result was, the *Arrêt* of December the 29th, 1787, confirming the abatements of duty, present and future, which the letter of October, 1786, had promised, and reserving to his Majesty, to grant still further favors to that production, if, on further information, he should find it for the interest of the two nations.

The English had now begun to deluge the markets of France, with their whale oils; and they were enabled by the great premiums given by their government, to undersell the French fisherman, aided by feebler premiums, and the American, aided by his poverty alone. Nor is it certain, that these speculations were not made at the risk of the British government, to suppress the French and American fishermen in their only market. Some remedy seemed necessary. Perhaps it would not have been a bad one, to subject, by a general law, the merchandise of every nation, and of every nature, to pay additional duties in the ports of France, exactly equal to the premiums and drawbacks given on the same merchandise, by their own government. This might not only counteract the effect of premiums in the instance of whale oils, but attack the whole British system of bounties and drawbacks, by the aid of which, they make London the centre of commerce for the whole earth. A less general remedy, but an effectual one, was, to prohibit the oils of all *European* nations; the treaty with England requiring only, that she should be treated as well as the most favored *European* nation. But the remedy adopted was, to prohibit all oils, without exception.

To know how this remedy will operate, we must consider the quantity of whale oil which France consumes annually, the quantity which she obtains from her own fishery; and, if she obtains less than she consumes, we are to consider what will follow the prohibition.

The annual consumption of France, as stated by a person who has good opportunities of knowing it, is as follows:

| | LBS. PESANT. | QUINTEAUX. | TONS. |
|---|---|---|---|
| Paris, according to the registers of 1786 | 2,800,000 | 28,000 | 1,750 |
| Twenty-seven other cities, lighted by M. Sangrain | 800,000 | 8,000 | 500 |
| Rouen | 500,000 | 5,000 | 312½ |
| Bordeaux | 600,000 | 6,000 | 375 |
| Lyons | 300,000 | 3,000 | 187½ |
| Other cities, leather and light | 3,000,000 | 30,000 | 1,875 |
| | 8,000,000 | 80,000 | 5,000 |

Other calcuations, or say rather, conjectures, reduce the consumption to about half this. It is treating these conjectures with great respect, to place them on an equal footing with the estimate of the person before alluded to, and to suppose the truth half way between them. But we will do it, and call the present consumption of France only sixty thousand quintals, or three thousand seven hundred and fifty tons a year. This consumption is increasing fast, as the practice of lighting cities is becoming more general, and the superior advantages of lighting them with whale oil, are but now beginning to be known.

What do the fisheries of France furnish? She has employed, this year, fifteen vessels in the southern, and two in the northern fishery, carrying forty-five hundred tons in the whole, or two hundred and sixty-five each, on an average. The English ships, led by Nantuckois as well as the French, have never averaged in the southern fishery, more than one-fifth of their burthen, in the best year. The fifteen ships of France, according to this ground of calculation, and supposing the present to have been one of the best years, should have brought, one with another, one-fifth of two hundred and sixty-five tons, or fifty-three tons each. But we are told, they have brought near the double of that, to wit, one hundred tons each, and fifteen hundred tons in the whole. Supposing the two northern vessels to have brought home the cargo which is common from the northern fishery, to wit, twenty-five tons each, the whole produce this year, will then be fifteen hundred and fifty tons. This is five and a half months' provision, or two-fifths of the annual consumption. To furnish for the whole year, would require forty ships of the same size, in years as fortunate as the present, and eighty-five *communibus annis;* forty-four tons, or one-sixth of the burthen, being as high an average as should be counted on, one year with another; and the number must be increased, with the increasing consumption. France, then, is evidently not yet in a condition to supply her own wants. It is said, indeed, she has a large stock on hand unsold, occasioned by the English competition. Thirty-three thousand quintals, including this year's produce, are spoken of: this is between six and seven months' provision; and supposing by the time this is exhausted that the next year's supply comes in, that will enable her to go on five or six months longer; say a twelvemonth in the whole. But at the end of the twelve month, what is to be done? The manufactures depending on this article, cannot maintain their competition against those of other countries, if deprived of their equal means. When the alternative, then, shall be presented, of letting them drop, or opening the ports to foreign whale oil, it is presumable the latter will be adopted as the lesser evil. But it will be too late for America. Her fishery, annihilated during the late war, only began to raise its head on the prospect of a market held out by this country. Crushed by the *Arrêt* of September the 28th, in its first feeble effort to revive, it will rise no more. Expeditions, which require the expense of the outfit of vessels, and from nine to twelve months' navigation, as the southern fishery does, most frequented by the Americans, cannot be undertaken in sole reliance on a market, which is opened and shut from one day to another, with little or no warning. The English alone, then, will remain to furnish these supplies, and they must be received even from them. We must accept bread from our enemies, if our friends cannot furnish it. This comes exactly to the point, to which that government has been looking. She fears no rivals in the whale fishery but America: or rather, it is the whale fishery of America, of which she is endeavoring to possess herself. It is for this object, she is making the present extraordinary efforts, by bounties and other encouragements; and her success, so far, is very flattering. Before the war, she had not one hundred vessels in the whale trade, while America employed three hundred and nine. In 1786, Great Britain employed one hundred and fifty-one vessels; in 1787, two hundred and eighty-six; in 1788, three hundred and fourteen, nearly the ancient American number; while the latter has fallen to about eighty. They have just changed places then; England having gained exactly what America has lost. France, by her ports and markets, holds the balance between the two contending parties, and gives the victory, by opening and shutting them, to which she pleases. We have still precious remains of seamen educated in this fishery, and capable, by their poverty, their boldness and address, of recovering it from the English in spite of their bounties. But this *Arrêt* endangers the transferring to Great Britain every man of them, who is not invincibly attached to his native soil. There is no other nation, in present condition, to maintain a competition with Great Britain in the whale fishery. The expense at which it is supported on her part, seems enormous. Two hundred and fifty-five vessels, of seventy-five thousand four hundred and thirty-six tons, employed by her this year, in the northern fishery, at forty-two men each; and fifty-nine in the southern, at eighteen men each, make eleven thousand seven hundred and seventy-two men. These are known to have cost the government fifteen pounds each, or one hundred and seventy-six thousand five hundred and eighty pounds, in the whole, and that, to employ the principal part of them, from three to four months only. The northern ships have brought home twenty, and the southern sixty tons of oil, on an average; making eighty-six hundred and forty tons. Every ton of oil, then, has cost the government twenty pounds in bounty. Still, if they can beat us out of the field and have it to themselves, they will think their money well employed. If France undertakes, solely, the competition against them, she must do it at equal expense. The trade is too poor to support itself. The eighty-five ships, necessary to supply even her present consumption, bountied, as the English are, will require a sacrifice of twelve hundred and eighty-five thousand two hundred livres a year, to maintain three thousand five hundred and seventy seamen, and that a part of the year only; and if she will put it to twelve thousand men, in competition with England, she must sacrifice, as they do, four or five millions a year. The same number of men might, with the same bounty, be kept in as constant employ, carrying stone from Bayonne to Cherbourg, or coal from Newcastle to Havre, in which navigations they would be always at hand, and become good seamen. The English consider among their best sailors, those employed in carrying coal from Newcastle to London. France cannot expect to raise her fishery, even to the supply of her own consumption in one year, or in several years. Is it not better, then, by keeping her ports open to the United States, to enable them to aid in maintaining the field against the common adversary, till she shall be in condition to take it herself, and to supply her own wants? Otherwise, her supplies must aliment that very force which is keeping her under. On our part, we can never be dangerous competitors to France. The extent to which we can exercise this fishery, is limited to that of the barren island of Nantucket, and a few similar barren spots; its duration, to the pleasure of this government, as we have no other market. A material observation must be added here: sudden vicissitudes of opening and shutting ports, do little injury to merchants settled on the opposite coast, watching for the opening, like the return of a tide, and ready to enter with it. But they ruin the adventurer, whose distance requires six months' notice. Those who are now arriving from America, in consequence of the *Arrêt* of December the 29th, will consider it as the false light which has led them to their ruin. They will be apt to say, that they come to the ports of France by invitation of that *Arrêt,* that the subsequent one of September the 28th, which drives them from those ports, founds itself on a single principle, *viz.* "that the prohibition of foreign oils, is the most useful encouragement which can be given to that branch of industry." They will say, that, if this be a true principle, it was as true on the 29th of December, 1787, as on the 20th of September, 1788; it was then weighed against other motives, judged weaker and overruled, and it is hard it should be now revived, to ruin them.

The refinery for whale oil, lately established at Rouen, seems to be an object worthy of national attention. In order to judge of its importance, the different qualities of whale oil must be noted. Three qualities are known in the American and English markets. 1st. That of the spermaceti whale. 2d. Of the Greenland whale. 3d. Of the Brazil whale. 1. The spermaceti whale found by the Nantuckois in the neighborhood of the western islands, to which they had gone in pursuit of other whales, retired thence to the coast of Guinea, afterwards to that of Brazil, and begins now to be best found in the latitude of the Cape of Good Hope, and even of Cape Horn. He is an active, fierce animal, and requires vast address and boldness in the fisherman. The inhabitants of Brazil make little expeditions from their coast, and take some of these fish. But the Americans are the only distant people who have been in the habit of seeking and attacking him, in numbers. The British, however, led by the Nantuckois, whom they have decoyed into their service, have begun this fishery. In 1785, they had eighteen ships in it; in 1787, thirty-eight; in 1788, fifty-four, or, as some say, sixty-four. I have calculated on the middle number, fifty-nine. Still they take but a very small proportion of their own demand; we furnish the rest. Theirs is the only market to which we carry that oil, because it is the only one where its properties are known. It is luminous, resists coagulation by cold, to the forty-first degree of Fahrenheit's thermometer, and fourth of Reaumur's, and yields no smell at all; it is used, therefore, within doors, to lighten shops, and even in the richest houses, for anti-chambers, stairs, galleries, &c. It sells at the London market for treble the price of common whale oil. This enables the adventurer to pay the duty of eighteen pounds five shillings sterling the ton, and still to have a living profit. Besides the mass of oil produced from the whole body of the whale, his head yields three or four barrels of what is called head matter, from which is made the solid spermaceti, used for medicine and candles. This sells by the pound, at double the price of the oil. The disadvantage of this fishery is, that the sailors are from nine to twelve months absent on the voyage; of course, they are not at hand on any sudden emergency, and are even liable to be taken before they know that war is begun. It must be added, on the subject of this whale, that he is rare and shy, soon abandoning the grounds where he is hunted. This fishery, less losing than the other, and often profitable, will occasion it to be so thronged, soon, as to bring it on a level with the other. It will then require the same extensive support, or to be abandoned.

The Greenland whale oil is next in quality. It resists coagulation by cold, to thirty-six degrees of Fahrenheit, and two of Reaumur; but it has a smell insupportable within doors, and is not luminous. It sells, therefore, in London, at about sixteen pounds the ton. This whale is clumsy and timid; he dives when struck, and comes up to breathe by the first cake of ice, where the fisherman needs little address or courage to find and take him. This is the fishery mostly frequented by European nations; it is this fish which yields the fin in quantity, and the voyages last about three or four months.

The third quality is that of the small Brazil whale. He was originally found on the coast of Nantucket, and first led that people to this pursuit; he retired, first to the Banks of Newfoundland, then to the western islands, and is now found within soundings on the coast of Brazil, during the months of December, January, February and March. His oil chills at fifty degrees of Fahrenheit, and eight of Reaumur, is black and offensive; worth, therefore, but thirteen pounds the ton, in London. In warm summer nights, however, it burns better than the Greenland oil.

To the qualities of the oils thus described, it is to be added, that an individual has discovered methods, 1, of converting a great part of the oils of the spermaceti whale into the solid substance called spermaceti, heretofore produced from his head alone; 2, of refining the Greenland whale oil, so as to take from it all smell, and render it limpid and luminous as that of the spermaceti whale; 3, of curdling the oil of the Brazil whale into tallow, resembling that of beef, and answering all its purposes. This person is engaged by the company, which has established the refinery at Rouen; their works will cost them half a million of livres; will be able to refine all the oil which can be used in the kingdom, and even to supply foreign markets. The effect of this refinery, then, would be, 1, to supplant the solid spermaceti of all other nations, by theirs, of equal quality, and lower price; 2, to substitute instead of spermaceti oil, their black whale oil refined, of equal quality, and lower price; 3, to render the worthless oil of the Brazil, equal in value to tallow; and 4, by accommodating these oils to uses, to which they could never otherwise have been applied, they will extend the demand beyond its present narrow limits, to any supply which can be furnished, and thus give the most effectual encouragement and extension to the whale fishery. But these works were calculated on the *Arrêt* of December the 29th, which admitted here, freely and fully, the produce of the American fishery. If confined to that of the French fishery alone, the enterprise may fail, for want of matter to work on.

After this review of the whale fishery as a political institution, a few considerations shall be added on its produce, as a basis of commercial exchange between France and the United States. The discussion it has undergone, on former occasions, in this point of view, leaves little new to be now urged.

The United States, not possessing mines of the precious metals, can purchase necessaries from other nations, so far only as their produce is received in exchange. Without enumerating our smaller articles, we have three of principal importance, proper for the French market; to wit, tobacco, whale oil and rice. The first and most important, is tobacco. This might furnish an exchange for eight millions of the productions of this country; but it is under a monopoly, and that not of a mercantile, but of a financiering company, whose interest is, to pay in money, and not in merchandise, and who are so much governed by the spirit of simplifying their purchases and proceedings, that they find means to elude every endeavor on the part of government, to make them diffuse their purchases among the merchants in general. Little profit is derived from this, then, as an article of exchange for the produce and manufactures of France. Whale oil might be next in importance; but that is now prohibited. American rice is not yet of great, but it is of growing consumption in France, and being the only article of the three which is free, it may become a principal basis of exchange. Time and trial may add a fourth, that is, timber. But some essays, rendered unsuccessful by unfortunate circumstances, place that, at present, under a discredit, which it will be found hereafter not to have merited. The English know its value, and were supplied with it before the war. A spirit of hostility, since that event, led them to seek Russian rather than American supplies; a new spirit of hostility has driven them back from Russia, and they are now making contracts for American timber. But of the three articles before mentioned, proved by experience to be suitable for the French market, one is prohibited, one under monopoly, and one alone free, and that the smallest and of very limited consumption. The way to encourage purchasers, is, to multiply their means of payment. Whale oil might be an important one. In one scale, are the interests of the millions who are lighted, shod, or clothed with the help of it, and the thousands of laborers and manufacturers, who would be employed in producing the articles which might be given in exchange for it, if received from America; in the other scale, are the interests of the adventurers in the whale fishery; each of whom, indeed, politically considered, may be of more importance to the State, than a simple laborer or manufacturer; but to make the estimate with the accuracy it merits, we should multiply the numbers in each scale into their individual importance, and see which preponderates.

Both governments have seen with concern that their commercial intercourse does not grow as rapidly as they would wish. The system of the

United States is, to use neither prohibitions nor premiums. Commerce there, regulates itself freely, and asks nothing better. Where a government finds itself under the necessity of undertaking that regulation, it would seem, that it should conduct it as an intelligent merchant would; that is to say, invite customers to purchase, by facilitating their means of payment, and by adapting goods to their taste. If this idea be just, government here has two operations to attend to, with respect to the commerce of the United States; 1, to do away, or to moderate, as much as possible, the prohibitions and monopolies of their materials for payment; 2, to encourage the institution of the principal manufactures, which the necessities or the habits of their new customers call for. Under this latter head, a hint shall be suggested, which must find its apology in the motive for which it flows; that is, a desire of promoting mutual interests and close friendship. Six hundred thousand of the laboring poor of America, comprehending slaves under that denomination, are clothed in three of the simplest manufactures possible; to wit, osnaburgs, plains and duffel blankets. The first is a linen; the two last, woollens. It happens, too, that they are used exactly by those who cultivate the tobacco and rice, and in a good degree by those employed in the whale fishery. To these manufactures they are so habituated, that no substitute will be received. If the vessels which bring tobacco, rice and whale oil, do not find them in the ports of delivery, they must be sought where they can be found; that is, in England, at present. If they were made in France, they would be gladly taken in exchange there. The quantities annually used by this description of people, and their value, are as follows:

| | | LIVRES |
|---|---|---|
| Osnaburgs | 2,700,000 aunes, at sixteen sous the aune, worth | 2,160,000 |
| Plains | 1,350,000 aunes, at two livres the aune, | 2,700,000 |
| Duffel blankets | 300,000 aunes, at seven and four-fifths livres each, | 2,160,000 |
| | | 7,020,000 |

It would be difficult to say how much should be added, for the consumption of inhabitants of other descriptions; a great deal surely. But the present view shall be confined to the one description named. Seven millions of livres, are nine millions of days work, of those who raise, spin and weave the wool and flax; and, at three hundred working days to the year, would maintain thirty thousand people. To introduce these simple manufactures, suppose government to give five per cent on the value of what should be exported of them, for ten years to come; if none should be exported, nothing would be to be paid; but on the other hand, if the manufactures, with this encouragement, should raise to the full demand, it will be a sacrifice of three hundred and fifty-one thousand livres a year, for ten years only, to produce a perpetual subsistence for more than thirty thousand people (for the demand will grow with our population), while she must expend perpetually one million two hundred and eighty-five thousand livres a year, to maintain the three thousand five hundred and seventy seamen, who would supply her with whale oil. That is to say, for each seaman, as much as for thirty laborers and manufacturers.

## OPINION RESPECTING OUR FOREIGN DEBT

August 26, 1790

On consideration of the letter of our banker, of January 25th, 1790, the Secretary of the Treasury's answer to it, and the draught of powers and instructions to him, I am of opinion, as I always have been, that the purchase of our debt to France by private speculators, would have been an operation extremely injurious to our credit; and that the consequence foreseen by our banker, that the purchasers would have been obliged, in order to make good their payments, to deluge the markets of Amsterdam with American paper of all sorts, and to sell it at any price, was a probable one. And the more so, as we know that the particular individuals who were engaged in that speculation, possess no means of their own adequate to the payments they would have had to make. While we must not doubt that these motives, together with a proper regard for the credit of the United States, had real and full weight with our bankers, towards inducing them to counterwork these private speculations; yet, to ascribe their industry in this business wholly to these motives, might lead to a too great and dangerous confidence in them. It was obviously their interest to defeat all such speculations, because they tended to take out of their hands, or at least to divide with them, the profits of the great operation of transferring the French debt to Amsterdam, an object of first rate magnitude to them, and on the undivided enjoyments of which they might count, if private speculators could be baffled. It has been a contest of dexterity and cunning, in which our champions have obtained the victory. The manœuvre of opening a loan of three millions of florins, has, on the whole, been useful to the United States, and though unauthorized, I think should be confirmed. The measure proposed by the Secretary of the Treasury, of sending a superintendent of their future operations, will effectually prevent their doing the like again, and the funding laws leave no danger that such an expedient might at any future time be useful to us.

The report of the Secretary of the Treasury, and the draught of instructions, present this plan to view: First, to borrow on the best terms we can, not exceeding those limited by the law, such a sum as may answer all demands of principal or interest of the foreign debts, due, or to become due before the end of 1791. [This I think he supposes will be about three and a half millions of dollars.] Second, to consider two of the three millions of florins already borrowed by our bankers as, so far, an execution of this operation; consequently, that there will remain but about two and a half millions of dollars to be borrowed on the old terms. Third, to borrow no more as yet, towards completing the transfer of the French debt to Amsterdam, unless we can do it on more advantageous terms. Fourth, to consider the third millions of florins already borrowed by our bankers, as, so far, an execution of the powers given the President to borrow two millions of dollars, by the act of the 12th of August. The whole of this appears to me to be wise. If the third million be employed in buying up our *foreign paper,* on the exchange of Amsterdam, by creating a demand for that species of paper, it will excite a cupidity in the monied men to obtain more of it by new loans, and consequently enable us to borrow more and on lower terms. The saving of interest, too, on the sum so to be bought, may be applied in buying up more principal, and thereby keep this salutary operation going.

I would only take the liberty of suggesting the insertion of some such clause as the following, into the instructions: "The agents to be employed shall never open a loan for more than one million of dollars at a time, nor open a new loan till the preceding one has been filled, and expressly approved by the President of the United States." A new man, alighting on the exchange of Amsterdam, with powers to borrow twelve millions of dollars, will be immediately beset with bankers and brokers, who will pour into his ear, from the most unsuspected quarters, such informations and suspicions as may lead him exactly into their snares. So wonderfully dexterous are they in wrapping up and complicating their propositions, they will make it evident, even to a clear-headed man (not in the habit of this business), that two and two make five. The agent, therefore, should be guarded, even against himself, by putting it out of his power to extend the effect of any erroneous calculation beyond one million of dollars. Were he able, under a delusive calculation, to commit such a sum as twelve millions of dollars, what would be said of the government? Our bankers told me themselves that they would not choose, in the conduct of this great loan, to open for more than two or three millions of florins at a time, and certainly never for more than five. By contracting for only one million of dollars at a time, the agent will have frequent occasions of trying to better the terms. I dare say that this caution, though not expressed in the instructions, is intended by the Secretary of the Treasury to be carried into their execution. But, perhaps, it will be desirable for the President, that his sense of it also should be expressed in writing.

## REPORT RELATIVE TO THE MEDITERRANEAN TRADE

December 28, 1790

The Secretary of State, to whom was referred by the House of Representatives so much of the speech of the President of the United States to both Houses of Congress, as relates to the trade of the United States in the Mediterranean, with instructions to report thereupon to the House, has had the same under consideration, and thereupon makes the following report:

The loss of the records of the custom houses in several of the States, which took place about the commencement and during the course of the late war, has deprived us of official information, as to the extent of our commerce and navigation in the Mediterranean sea. According to the best which may be obtained from other sources meriting respect, it may be concluded that about one-sixth of the wheat and flour exported from the United States, and about one-fourth in value of their dried and pickled fish, and some rice, found their best markets in the Mediterranean ports; that these articles constituted the principal part of what we sent into that sea; that that commerce loaded outwards from eighty to one hundred ships, annually, of twenty thousand tons, navigated by about twelve hundred seamen. It was abandoned early in the war. And after the peace which ensued, it was obvious to our merchants, that their adventures into that sea would be exposed to the depredations of the piratical States on the coast of Barbary. Congress, too, was very early attentive to this danger, and by a commission of the 12th of May, 1784, authorized certain persons, named ministers plenipotentiary for that purpose, to conclude treaties of peace and amity with the Barbary powers. And it being afterwards found more expedient that the negotiations should be carried on at the residences of those powers, Congress, by a farther commission, bearing date the 11th of March, 1785, empowered the same ministers plenipotentiary to appoint agents to repair to the said powers at their proper residences, and there to negotiate such treaties. The whole expenses were limited to eighty thousand dollars. Agents were accordingly sent to Morocco and Algiers.

Before the appointment of the one to Morocco, it was known that a cruiser of that State had taken a vessel of the United States; and that the emperor, on the friendly interposition of the court of Madrid had liberated the crew, and made restitution of the vessel and cargo, as far as their condition admitted. This was a happy presage of the liberal treaty he afterwards concluded with our agent, still under the friendly mediation of Spain, and at an expense of between nine and ten thousand dollars only. On his death, which has taken place not long since, it becomes necessary, according to their usage, to obtain immediately a recognition of the treaty by his successor, and consequently, to make provision for the expenses which may attend it. The amount of the former furnishes one ground of estimate; but the character and dispositions of the successor, which are unknown here, may influence it materially. The friendship of this power is important, because our Atlantic as well as Mediterranean trade is open to his annoyance, and because we carry on a useful commerce with his nation.

The Algerines had also taken two vessels of the United States, with twenty-one persons on board, whom they retained as slaves. On the arrival of the agent sent to that regency, the dey refused utterly to treat of peace on any terms, and demanded 59,496 dollars for the ransom of our captives. This mission therefore proved ineffectual.

While these negotiations were on foot at Morocco and Algiers, an ambassador from Tripoli arrived in London. The ministers plenipotentiary of the United States met him in person. He demanded for the peace of that State, thirty thousand guineas; and undertook to engage that of Tunis for a like sum. These demands were beyond the limits of Congress, and of reason, and nothing was done. Nor was it of importance, as, Algiers remaining hostile, the peace of Tunis and Tripoli was of no value, and when that of the former should be obtained, theirs would soon follow.

Our navigation, then, into the Mediterranean, has not been resumed at all since the peace. The sole obstacle has been the unprovoked war of Algiers; and the sole remedy must be to bring that war to an end, or to palliate its effects. Its effects may, perhaps, be palliated by insuring our ships and cargoes destined for that sea, and by forming a convention with the regency, for the ransom of our seamen, according to a fixed tariff. That tariff will, probably, be high, and the rate of insurance so settled, in the long run, as to pay for the vessels and cargoes captured, and something more. What proportion will be captured nothing but experience can determine. Our commerce differs from that of most of the nations with whom the predatory States are in habits of war. Theirs is spread all over the face of the Mediterranean, and therefore must be sought for all over its face. Ours must all enter at a strait only five leagues wide; so that their cruisers, taking a safe and commanding position near the strait's mouth, may very effectually inspect whatever enters it. So safe a station, with a certainty of receiving for their prisoners a good and stated price, may tempt their cupidity to seek our vessels particularly. Nor is it certain that our seamen could be induced to engage in that navigation, though with the security of Algerine faith that they would be liberated on the payment of a fixed sum. The temporary deprivation of liberty, perhaps chains, the danger of the pest, the perils of the engagement preceding their surrender, and possible delays of the ransom, might turn elsewhere the choice of men, to whom all the rest of the world is open. In every case, these would be embarrassments which would enter into the merchants' estimate, and endanger the preference of foreign bottoms not exposed to them. And upon the whole, this expedient does not fulfil our wish of a complete re-establishment of our commerce in that sea.

A second plan might be to obtain peace by purchasing it. For this we have the example of rich and powerful nations, in this instance counting their interest more than their honor. If, conforming to their example, we determine to purchase a peace, it is proper to inquire what a peace may cost. This being merely a matter of conjecture, we can only compare together such opinions as have been obtained, and from them form one for ourselves.

Mr. Wolf, a respectable Irishman, who had resided very long at Algiers, thought a peace might be obtained from that regency, and the redemption of our captives included, for sixty or seventy thousand pounds sterling. His character and opinion both merited respect. Yet his estimate being the lowest of all who have hazarded an opinion on this subject, one is apt to fear his judgment might have been biassed by the hope he entertained that the United States would charge him with this negotiation.

Captain O'Brien, one of our captives, who had been in Algiers four years and a half at the date of his last letter, a very sensible man, and to whom we are indebted for very minute information, supposes that peace alone, might be bought for that sum, that is to say, for three hundred and twenty-two thousand dollars.

The Tripoline ambassador, before mentioned, thought that peace could be made with the three smaller powers for ninety thousand pounds sterling, to which were to be added the expenses of the mission and other incidental expenses. But he could not answer for Algiers; they would demand more. The ministers plenipotentiary, who conferred with him, had judged that as much must be paid to Algiers as to the other three powers together; and consequently, that according to this measure, the peace of Algiers would cost from an hundred to an hundred and twenty-five thousand pounds sterling; or from four hundred and sixty to five hundred and seventy-five thousand dollars.

The latter sum seemed to meet the ideas of the Count de Vergennes, who, from a very long residence at Constantinople, was a good judge of what related to the Porte, or its dependencies.

A person whose name is not free to be mentioned here, a native of the continent of Europe, who had long lived, and still lives at Algiers, with whom the minister plenipotentiary of the United States, at Paris, had many and long conversations, and found his information full, clear, and consistent, was of opinion the peace of Algiers could not be bought by the United

States for less than one million of dollars. And when that is paid, all is not done. On the death of a dey (and the present one is between seventy and eighty years of age), respectable presents must be made to the successor, that he may recognize the treaty; and very often he takes the liberty of altering it. When a consul is sent or changed, new presents must be made. If these events leave a considerable interval, occasion must be made of renewing presents. And with all this they must see that we are in condition to chastise an infraction of the treaty; consequently some marine force must be exhibited in their harbor from time to time.

The late peace of Spain with Algiers is said to have cost from three to five millions of dollars. Having received the money, they take the vessels of that nation on the most groundless pretexts; counting, that the same force which bound Spain to so hard a treaty, may break it with impunity.

Their treaty with France, which had expired, was about two years ago renewed for fifty years. The sum given at the time of renewal is not known. But presents are to be repeated every ten years, and a tribute of one hundred thousand dollars to be annually paid. Yet perceiving that France, embarrassed at home with her domestic affairs, was less capable of acting abroad, they took six vessels of that nation in the course of the last year, and retain the captives, forty-four in number, in slavery.

It is the opinion of Captain O'Brien, that those nations are best treated who pay a smaller sum in the beginning, and an annual tribute afterwards. In this way he informs us that the Dutch, Danes, Swedes, and Venetians pay to Algiers, from twenty-four to thirty thousand dollars a year, each; the two first in naval stores, the two last chiefly in money. It is supposed, that the peace of the Barbary States costs Great Britain about sixty thousand guineas, or two hundred and eighty thousand dollars a year. But it must be noted that these facts cannot be authentically advanced; as from a principle of self-condemnation, the governments keep them from the public eye as much as possible.

Nor must we omit finally to recollect, that the Algerines, attentive to reserve always a sufficient aliment for their piracies, will never extend their peace beyond certain limits, and consequently, that we may find ourselves in the case of those nations to whom they refuse peace at any price.

The third expedient is to repel force by force. Several statements are hereto annexed of the naval force of Algiers, taken in 1785, 1786, 1787, 1788, and 1789, differing in small degrees, but concurring in the main. From these it results that they have usually had about nine chebecs, from ten to thirty-six guns, and four galleys, which have been reduced by losses to six chebecs and four galleys. They have a forty-gun frigate on the stocks, and expect two cruisers from the grand seignior. The character of their vessels is, that they are sharp built and swift, but so light as not to stand the broadside of a good frigate. Their guns are of different calibres, unskilfully pointed and worked. The vessels illy manœuvred, but crowded with men, one third Turks, the rest Moors, of determined bravery, and resting their sole hopes on boarding. But two of these vessels belong to the government, the rest being private property. If they come out of the harbor together, they separate immediately in quest of prey; and it is said they were never known to act together in any instance. Nor do they come out at all, when they know there are vessels cruising for them. They perform three cruises a year, between the middle of April and November, when they unrig and lay up for the winter. When not confined within the straits, they rove northwardly to the channel, and westwardly to the westward islands.

They are at peace at present, with France, Spain, England, Venice, the United Netherlands, Sweden, and Denmark; and at war with Russia, Austria, Portugal, Naples, Sardinia, Genoa, and Malta.

Should the United States propose to vindicate their commerce by arms, they would, perhaps, think it prudent to possess a force equal to the whole of that which may be opposed to them. What that equal force would be, will belong to another department to say.

At the same time it might never be necessary to draw out the whole at once, nor perhaps any proportion of it, but for a small part of the year; as it is reasonable to presume that a concert of operation might be arranged among the powers at war with the Barbary States, so as that, each performing a tour of given duration, and in given order, a constant cruise during the eight temperate months of every year, may be kept up before the harbor of Algiers, till the object of such operations be completely obtained. Portugal has singly, for several years past, kept up such a cruise before the straits of Gibraltar, and by that means has confined the Algerines closely within. But two of their vessels have been out of the straits in the last five years. Should Portugal effect a peace with them, as has been apprehended for some time, the Atlantic will immediately become the principal scene of their piracies; their peace with Spain having reduced the profits of their Mediterranean cruises below the expenses of equipment.

Upon the whole, it rests with Congress to decide between war, tribute, and ransom, as the means of re-establishing our Mediterranean commerce. If war, they will consider how far our own resources shall be called forth, and how far they will enable the Executive to engage, in the forms of the constitution, the co-operation of other powers. If tribute or ransom, it will rest with them to limit and provide the amount; and with the Executive, observing the same constitutional forms, to take arrangements for employing it to the best advantage.

# REPORT ON THE PRIVILEGES AND RESTRICTIONS ON THE COMMERCE OF THE UNITED STATES IN FOREIGN COUNTRIES[1]

December 16, 1793

SIR: According to the pleasure of the House of Representatives, expressed in their resolution of February 23, 1791, I now lay before them a report on the privileges and restrictions on the commerce of the United States in foreign countries. In order to keep the subject within those bounds which I supposed to be under the contemplation of the House, I have restrained my statements to those countries only with which we carry on a commerce of some importance, and to those articles also of our produce which are of sensible weight in the scale of our exports; and even these articles are sometimes grouped together, according to the degree of favor or restriction with which they are received in each country, and that degree expressed in general terms without detailing the exact duty levied on each article. To have gone fully into these minutiæ, would have been to copy the tariffs and books of rates of the different countries, and to have hidden, under a mass of details, those general and important truths, the extraction of which, in a simple form, I conceived would best answer the inquiries of the House, by condensing material information within those limits of time and attention, which this portion of their duties may justly claim. The plan, indeed, of minute details which have been impracticable with some countries, for want of information.

Since preparing this report, which was put into its present form in time to have been given in to the last session of Congress, alterations of the conditions of our commerce with some foreign nations have taken place—some of them independent of war; some arising out of it.

France has proposed to enter into a new treaty of commerce with us, on liberal principles; and has, in the meantime, relaxed some of the restraints mentioned in the report. Spain has, by an ordinance of June last, established New Orleans, Pensacola, and St. Augustine into free ports, for the vessels of friendly nations *having treaties of commerce* with her, provided they touch for a permit at Corcubion in Gallicia, or at Alicant; and our rice is, by the same ordinance, excluded from that country. The circumstances of war have necessarily given us freer access to the West Indian islands, whilst they have also drawn on our navigation vexations and depredations of the most serious nature.

To have endeavored to describe all these, would have been as impracticable as useless, since the scenes would have been shifting while under description. I therefore think it best to leave the report as it was formed, being adapted to a particular point of time, when things were in their settled order, that is to say, to the summer of 1792. I have the honor to be, &c.

*To the Speaker of the House of Representatives of the United States of America.*

[1] Transmitted to the Congress.

The Secretary of State, to whom was referred, by the House of Representatives, the report of a committee on the written message of the President of the United States, of the 14th of February, 1791, with instruction to report to Congress the nature and extent of the privileges and restrictions of the commercial intercourse of the United States with foreign nations, and the measures which he should think proper to be adopted for the improvement of the commerce and navigation of the same, has had the same under consideration, and thereupon makes the following Report:

The countries with which the United States have their chief commercial intercourse are Spain, Portugal, France, Great Britain, the United Netherlands, Denmark, and Sweden, and their American possessions; and the articles of export, which constitute the basis of that commerce, with their respective amounts, are,

| | |
|---|---|
| Bread-stuff, that is to say, bread grains, meals, and bread, to the annual amount of | $7,649,887 |
| Tobacco | 4,349,567 |
| Rice | 1,753,796 |
| Wood | 1,263,534 |
| Salted fish | 941,696 |
| Pot and pearl ash | 839,093 |
| Salted meats | 599,130 |
| Indigo | 537,379 |
| Horses and mules | 339,753 |
| Whale oil | 252,591 |
| Flax seed | 236,072 |
| Tar, pitch and turpentine | 217,177 |
| Live provisions | 137,743 |
| Ships | |
| Foreign goods | 620,274 |

To descend to articles of smaller value than these, would lead into a minuteness of detail neither necessary nor useful to the present object.

The proportions of our exports, which go to the nations before mentioned, and to their dominions, respectively, are as follows:

| | |
|---|---|
| To Spain and its dominions | $2,005,907 |
| Portugal and its dominions | 1,283,462 |
| France and its dominions | 4,698,735 |
| Great Britain and its dominions | 9,363,416 |
| The United Netherlands and their dominions | 1,963,880 |
| Denmark and its dominions | 224,415 |
| Sweden and its dominions | 47,240 |

Our imports from the same countries are:

| | |
|---|---|
| Spain and its dominions | 335,110 |
| Portugal and its dominions | 595,763 |
| France and its dominions | 2,068,348 |
| Great Britain and its dominions | 15,285,428 |
| United Netherlands and their dominions | 1,172,692 |
| Denmark and its dominions | 351,364 |
| Sweden and its dominions | 14,325 |

These imports consist mostly of articles on which industry has been exhausted.

Our *navigation,* depending on the same commerce, will appear by the following statement of the tonnage of our own vessels, entering in our ports, from those several nations and their possessions, in one year; that is to say, from October, 1789, to September, 1790, inclusive, as follows:

| | TONS |
|---|---|
| Spain | 19,695 |
| Portugal | 23,576 |
| France | 116,410 |
| Great Britain | 43,580 |
| United Netherlands | 58,858 |
| Denmark | 14,655 |
| Sweden | 750 |

Of our commercial objects, Spain receives favorably our bread-stuff, salted fish, wood, ships, tar, pitch, and turpentine. On our meals, however, as well as on those of other foreign countries, when re-exported to their colonies, they have lately imposed duties of from half-a-dollar to two dollars the barrel, the duties being so proportioned to the current price of their own flour, as that both together are to make the constant sum of nine dollars per barrel.

They do not discourage our rice, pot and pearl ash, salted provisions, or whale oil; but these articles, being in small demand at their markets, are carried thither but in a small degree. Their demand for rice, however, is increasing. Neither tobacco nor indigo are received there. Our commerce is permitted with their Canary islands under the same conditions.

Themselves, and their colonies, are the actual consumers of what they receive from us.

Our navigation is free with the kingdom of Spain; foreign goods being received there in our ships on the same conditions as if carried in their own, or in the vessels of the country of which such goods are the manufacture or produce.

*Portugal* receives favorably our grain and bread, salted fish, and other salted provisions, wood, tar, pitch, and turpentine.

For flax-seed, pot and pearl ash, though not discouraged, there is little demand.

Our ships pay 20 per cent on being sold to their subjects, and are then free-bottoms.

Foreign goods (except those of the East Indies) are received on the same footing in our vessels as in their own, or any others; that is to say, on general duties of from 20 to 28 per cent, and, consequently, our navigation is unobstructed by them. Tobacco, rice, and meals, are prohibited.

Themselves and their colonies consume what they receive from us.

These regulations extend to the Azores, Madeira, and the Cape de Verd islands, except that in these, meals and rice are received freely.

*France* receives favorably our bread-stuffs, rice, wood, pot and pearl ashes.

A duty of 5 sous the quintal, or nearly 4½ cents, is paid on our tar, pitch, and turpentine. Our whale oils pay 6 livres the quintal, and are the only foreign whale oils admitted. Our indigo pays 5 livres the quintal, their own 2½; but a difference of quality, still more than a difference of duty, prevents its seeking that market.

Salted beef is received freely for re-exportation; but if for home consumption, it pays five livres the quintal. Other salted provisions pay that duty in all cases, and salted fish is made lately to pay the prohibitory one of twenty livres the quintal.

Our ships are free to carry thither all foreign goods which may be carried in their own or any other vessels, except tobaccos not of our own growth; and they participate with theirs, the exclusive carriage of our whale oils and tobaccos.

During their former government, our tobacco was under a monopoly, but paid no duties; and our ships were freely sold in their ports, and converted into national bottoms. The first national assembly took from our ships this privilege. They emancipated tobacco from its monopoly, but subjected it to duties of eighteen livres, fifteen sous the quintal, carried in their own vessels, and five livres carried in ours—a difference more than equal to the freight of the article.

They and their colonies consume what they receive from us.

*Great Britain* receives our pot and pearl ashes free, whilst those of other nations pay a duty of two shillings and three pence the quintal. There is an equal distinction in favor of our bar iron; of which article, however, we do not produce enough for our own use. Woods are free from us, whilst they pay some small duty from other countries. Indigo and flax seed are free from all countries. Our tar and pitch pay eleven pence, sterling, the barrel. From other alien countries they pay about a penny and a third more.

Our tobacco, for their own consumption, pays one shilling and three pence, sterling, the pound, custom and excise, besides heavy expenses of collection; and rice, in the same case, pays seven shillings and fourpence, sterling, the hundred weight; which, rendering it too dear, as an article of common food, it is consequently used in very small quantity.

Our salted fish and other salted provisions, except bacon, are prohibited. Bacon and whale oils are under prohibitory duties; so are our grains, meals, and bread, as to internal consumption, unless in times of such scarcity as may raise the price of wheat to fifty shillings, sterling, the quarter, and other grains and meals in proportion.

Our ships, though purchased and navigated by their own subjects, are not permitted to be used, even in their trade with us.

While the vessels of other nations are secured by standing laws, which cannot be altered but by the concurrent will of the three branches of the British legislature, in carrying thither any produce or manufacture of the country to which they belong, which may be lawfully carried in any vessels, ours, with the same prohibition of what is foreign, are further prohibited by a standing law, (12 Car. 2, 18, sect. 3,) from carrying thither all and any of our own domestic productions and manufactures. A subsequent act, indeed, has authorized their executive to permit the carriage of our own productions in our own bottoms, at its sole discretion; and the permission has been given from year to year by proclamation, but subject every moment to be withdrawn on that single will; in which event, our vessels having anything on board, stand interdicted from the entry of all British ports. The disadvantage of a tenure which may be so suddenly discontinued, was experienced by our merchants on a late occasion,[2] when an official notification that this law would be strictly enforced, gave them just apprehensions for the fate of their vessels and cargoes despatched or destined for the ports of Great Britain. The minister of that court, indeed, frankly expressed his personal conviction, that the words of the order went farther than was intended, and so he afterwards officially informed us; but the embarrassments of the moment were real and great, and the possibility of their renewal lays our commerce to that country under the same species of discouragement as to other countries, where it is regulated by a single legislator; and the distinction is too remarkable not to be noticed, that our navigation is excluded from the security of fixed laws, while that security is given to the navigation of others.

Our vessels pay in their ports one shilling and nine pence, sterling, per ton, light and trinity dues, more than is paid by British ships, except in the port of London, where they pay the same as British.

The greater part of what they receive from us, is re-exported to other coun-

[2] April 12, 1792.

tries, under the useless charges of an intermediate deposit, and double voyage. From tables published in England, and composed, as is said, from the books of their customhouses, it appears, that of the indigo imported there in the years 1773, '4, '5, one-third was re-exported; and from a document of authority, we learn, that of the rice and tobacco imported there before the war, four-fifths were re-exported. We are assured, indeed, that the quantities sent thither for re-exportation since the war, are considerably diminished, yet less so than reason and national interest would dictate. The whole of our grain is re-exported when wheat is below fifty shillings the quarter, and other grains in proportion.

The *United Netherlands* prohibit our pickled beef and pork, meals and bread of all sorts, and lay a prohibitory duty on spirits distilled from grain.

All other of our productions are received on varied duties, which may be reckoned, on a medium, at about three per cent.

They consume but a small proportion of what they receive. The residue is partly forwarded for consumption in the inland parts of Europe, and partly re-shipped to other maritime countries. On the latter portion they intercept between us and the consumer, so much of the value as is absorbed in the charges attending an intermediate deposit.

Foreign goods, except some East India articles, are received in vessels of any nation.

Our ships may be sold and neutralized there, with exceptions of one or two privileges, which somewhat lessen their value.

*Denmark* lays considerable duties on our tobacco and rice, carried in their own vessels, and half as much more, if carried in ours; but the exact amount of these duties is not perfectly known here. They lay such as amount to prohibitions on our indigo and corn.

*Sweden* receives favorably our grains and meals, salted provisions, indigo, and whale oil.

They subject our rice to duties of sixteen mills the pound weight, carried in their own vessels, and of forty per cent additional on that, or twenty-two and four-tenths mills, carried in ours or any others. Being thus rendered too dear as an article of common food, little of it is consumed with them. They consume some of our tobaccos, which they take circuitously through Great Britain, levying heavy duties on them also; their duties of entry, town duties, and excise, being 4.34 dollars the hundred weight, if carried in their own vessels, and of forty per cent on that additional, if carried in our own or any other vessels.

They prohibit altogether our bread, fish, pot and pearl ashes, flax-seed, tar, pitch, and turpentine, wood, (except oak timber and masts) and all foreign manufactures.

Under so many restrictions and prohibitions, our navigation with them is reduced to almost nothing.

With our neighbors, an order of things much harder presents itself.

*Spain* and *Portugal* refuse, to all those parts of America which they govern, all direct intercourse with any people but themselves. The commodities in mutual demand between them and their neighbors, must be carried to be exchanged in some port of the dominant country, and the transportation between that and the subject state, must be in a domestic bottom.

*France,* by a standing law, permits her West India possessions to receive directly our vegetables, live provisions, horses, wood, tar, pitch, turpentine, rice, and maize, and prohibits our other bread stuff; but a suspension of this prohibition having been left to the colonial legislatures, in times of scarcity, it was formerly suspended occasionally, but latterly without interruption.

Our fish and salted provisions (except pork) are received in their islands under a duty of three colonial livres the quintal, and our vessels are as free as their own to carry our commodities thither, and to bring away rum and molasses.

*Great Britain* admits in her islands our vegetables, live provisions, horses, wood, tar, pitch, and turpentine, rice and bread stuff, by a proclamation of her executive, limited always to the term of a year, but hitherto renewed from year to year. She prohibits our salted fish and other salted provisions. She does not permit our vessels to carry thither our own produce. Her vessels alone may take it from us, and bring in exchange rum, molasses, sugar, coffee, cocoa-nuts, ginger, and pimento. There are, indeed, some freedoms in the island of Dominica, but, under such circumstances, as to be little used by us. In the British continental colonies, and in Newfoundland, all our productions are prohibited, and our vessels forbidden to enter their ports. Their governors, however, in times of distress, have power to permit a temporary importation of certain articles in their own bottoms, but not in ours.

Our citizens cannot reside as merchants or factors within any of the British plantations, this being expressly prohibited by the same statute of 12 Car. 2, c. 18, commonly called the navigation act.

In the *Danish American* possessions a duty of 5 per cent is levied on our corn, corn meal, rice, tobacco, wood, salted fish, indigo, horses, mules and live stock, and of 10 per cent on our flour, salted pork and beef, tar, pitch and turpentine.

In the American islands of the *United Netherlands* and *Sweden,* our vessels and produce are received, subject to duties, not so heavy as to have been complained of; but they are heavier in the Dutch possessions on the continent.

To sum up these restrictions, so far as they are important:

FIRST. In Europe—

Our bread stuff is at most times under prohibitory duties in England, and considerably dutied on re-exportation from Spain to her colonies.

Our tobaccos are heavily dutied in England, Sweden and France, and prohibited in Spain and Portugal.

Our rice is heavily dutied in England and Sweden, and prohibited in Portugal.

Our fish and salted provisions are prohibited in England, and under prohibitory duties in France.

Our whale oils are prohibited in England and Portugal.

And our vessels are denied naturalization in England, and of late in France.

SECOND. In the West Indies—

All intercourse is prohibited with the possessions of Spain and Portugal.

Our salted provisions and fish are prohibited by England.

Our salted pork and bread stuff (except maize) are received under temporary laws only, in the dominions of France, and our salted fish pays there a weighty duty.

THIRD. In the article of navigation—

Our own carriage of our own tobacco is heavily dutied in Sweden, and lately in France.

We can carry no article, not of our own production, to the British ports in Europe. Nor even our own produce to her American possessions.

Such being the restrictions on the commerce and navigation of the United States; the question is, in what way they may best be removed, modified or counteracted?

As to commerce, two methods occur. 1. By friendly arrangements with the several nations with whom these restrictions exist: Or, 2. By the separate act of our own legislatures for countervailing their effects.

There can be no doubt but that of these two, friendly arrangement is the most eligible. Instead of embarrassing commerce under piles of regulating laws, duties and prohibitions, could it be relieved from all its shackles in all parts of the world, could every country be employed in producing that which nature has best fitted it to produce, and each be free to exchange with others mutual surpluses for mutual wants, the greatest mass possible would then be produced of those things which contribute to human life and human happiness; the numbers of mankind would be increased, and their condition bettered.

Would even a single nation begin with the United States this system of free commerce, it would be advisable to begin it with that nation; since it is one by one only that it can be extended to all. Where the circumstances of either party render it expedient to levy a revenue, by way of impost, on commerce, its freedom might be modified, in that particular, by mutual and equivalent measures, preserving it entire in all others.

Some nations, not yet ripe for free commerce in all its extent, might still be willing to mollify its restrictions and regulations for us, in proportion to the advantages which an intercourse with us might offer. Particularly they may concur with us in reciprocating the duties to be levied on each side, or in compensating any excess of duty by equivalent advantages of another nature. Our commerce is certainly of a character to entitle it to favor in most countries. The commodities we offer are either necessaries of life, or materials for manufacture, or convenient subjects of revenue; and we take in exchange, either manufactures, when they have received the last finish of art and industry, or mere luxuries. Such customers may reasonably expect welcome and friendly treatment at every market. Customers, too, whose demands, increasing with their wealth and population, must very shortly give full employment to the whole industry of any nation whatever, in any line of supply they may get into the habit of calling for from it.

But should any nation, contrary to our wishes, suppose it may better find its advantage by continuing its system of prohibitions, duties and regulations, it behooves us to protect our citizens, their commerce and navigation, by counter prohibitions, duties and regulations, also. Free commerce and navigation are not to be given in exchange for restrictions and vexations; nor are they likely to produce a relaxation of them.

Our navigation involves still higher considerations. As a branch of industry, it is valuable, but as a resource of defence, essential.

Its value, as a branch of industry, is enhanced by the dependence of so many other branches on it. In times of general peace it multiplies competitors for employment in transportation, and so keeps that at its proper level; and in times of war, that is to say, when those nations who may be our principal carriers, shall be at war with each other, if we have not within ourselves the means of transportation, our produce must be exported in belligerent vessels, at the increased expense of war-freight and insurance, and the articles which will not bear that, must perish on our hands.

But it is as a resource of defence that our navigation will admit neither neglect nor forbearance. The position and circumstances of the United States leave them nothing to fear on their land-board, and nothing to desire beyond their present rights. But on their seaboard, they are open to injury, and they have there, too, a commerce which must be protected. This can only be done by possessing a respectable body of citizen-seamen, and of artists and establishments in readiness for ship-building.

Were the ocean, which is the common property of all, open to the industry of all, so that every person and vessel should be free to take employment wherever it could be found, the United States would certainly not set the example of appropriating to themselves, exclusively, any portion of the common stock of occupation. They would rely on the enterprise and activity of their citizens for a due participation of the benefits of the seafaring business, and for keeping the marine class of citizens equal to their object. But if particular nations grasp at undue shares, and, more especially, if they seize on the means of the United States, to convert them into aliment for their own strength, and withdraw them entirely from the support of those to whom they belong, defensive and protecting measures become necessary on the part of the nation whose marine resources are thus invaded; or it will be disarmed of its defence; its productions will lie at the mercy of the nation which has posssesed itself exclusively of the means of carrying them, and its politics may be influenced by those who command its commerce. The carriage of our own commodities, if once established in another channel, cannot be resumed in the moment we may desire. If we lose the seamen and artists whom it now occupies, we lose the present means of marine defence, and time will be requisite to raise up others, when disgrace or losses shall bring home to our feelings the error of having abandoned them. The materials for maintaining our due share of navigation, are ours in abundance. And, as to the mode of using them, we have only to adopt the principles of those who put us on the defensive, or others equivalent and better fitted to our circumstances.

The following principles, being founded in reciprocity, appear perfectly just, and to offer no cause of complaint to any nation:

1. Where a nation imposes high duties on our productions, or prohibits them altogether, it may be proper for us to do the same by theirs; first burdening or excluding those productions which they bring here, in competition with our own of the same kind; selecting next, such manufactures as we take from them in greatest quantity, and which, at the same time, we could the soonest furnish to ourselves, or obtain from other countries; imposing on them duties lighter at first, but heavier and heavier afterwards, as other channels of supply open. Such duties having the effect of indirect encouragement to domestic manufactures of the same kind, may induce the manufacturer to come himself into these States, where cheaper subsistence, equal laws, and a vent of his wares, free of duty, may ensure him the highest profits from his skill and industry. And here, it would be in the power of the State governments to co-operate essentially, by opening the resources of encouragement which are under their control, extending them liberally to artists in those particular branches of manufacture for which their soil, climate, population and other circumstances have matured them, and fostering the precious efforts and progress of *household* manufacture, by some patronage suited to the nature of its objects, guided by the local informations they possess, and guarded against abuse by their presence and attentions.

The oppressions on our agriculture, in foreign ports, would thus be made the occasion of relieving it from a dependence on the councils and conduct of others, and of promoting arts, manufactures and population at home.

2. Where a nation refuses permission to our merchants and factors to reside within certain parts of their dominions, we may, if it should be thought expedient, refuse residence to theirs in any and every part of ours, or modify their transactions.

3. Where a nation refuses to receive in our vessels any productions but our own, we may refuse to receive, in theirs, any but their own productions. The first and second clauses of the bill reported by the committee, are well formed to effect this object.

4. Where a nation refuses to consider any vessel as ours which has not been built within our territories, we should refuse to consider as theirs, any vessel not built within their territories.

5. Where a nation refuses to our vessels the carriage even of our own productions, to certain countries under their domination, we might refuse to theirs of every description, the carriage of the same productions to the same countries. But as justice and good neighborhood would dictate that those who have no part in imposing the restriction on us, should not be the victims of measures adopted to defeat its effect, it may be proper to confine the restriction to vessels owned or navigated by any subjects of the same dominant power, other than the inhabitants of the country to which the said productions are to be carried. And to prevent all inconvenience to the said inhabitants, and to our own, by too sudden a check on the means of transportation, we may continue to admit the vessels marked for future exclusion, on an advanced tonnage, and for such length of time only, as may be supposed necessary to provide against that inconvenience.

The establishment of some of these principles by Great Britain, alone, has already lost us in our commerce with that country and its possessions, between eight and nine hundred vessels of near 40,000 tons burden, according to statements from official materials, in which they have confidence. This involves a proportional loss of seamen, shipwrights, and ship-building, and is too serious a loss to admit forbearance of some effectual remedy.

It is true we must expect some inconvenience in practice from the establishment of discriminating duties. But in this, as in so many other cases, we are left to choose between two evils. These inconveniences are nothing when weighed against the loss of wealth and loss of force, which will follow our perseverance in the plan of indiscrimination. When once it shall be perceived that we are either in the system or in the habit of giving equal advantages to those who extinguish our commerce and navigation by duties and prohibitions, as to those who treat both with liberality and justice, liberality and justice will be converted by all into duties and prohibitions. It is not to the moderation and justice of others we are to trust for fair and equal access to market with our productions, or for our due share in the transportation of them; but to our own means of independence, and the firm will to use them. Nor do the inconveniences of discrimination merit consideration. Not one of the nations before mentioned, perhaps not a commercial nation on earth, is without them. In our case one distinction alone will suffice: that is to say, between nations who favor our productions and navigation, and those who do not favor them. One set of moderate duties, say the present duties, for the first, and a fixed advance on these as to some articles, and prohibitions as to others, for the last.

Still, it must be repeated that friendly arrangements are preferable with all who will come into them; and that we should carry into such arrangements all the liberality and spirit of accommodation which the nature of the case will admit.

France has, of her own accord, proposed negotiations for improving, by a new treaty on fair and equal principles, the commercial relations of the two countries. But her internal disturbances have hitherto prevented the prosecution of them to effect, though we have had repeated assurances of a continuance of the disposition.

Proposals of friendly arrangement have been made on our part, by the present government, to that of Great Britain, as the message states; but, being already on as good a footing in law, and a better in fact, than the most favored nation, they have not, as yet, discovered any disposition to have it meddled with.

We have no reason to conclude that friendly arrangements would be declined by the other nations, with whom we have such commercial intercourse as may render them important. In the meanwhile, it would rest with the wisdom of Congress to determine whether, as to those nations, they will not surcease *ex parte* regulations, on the reasonable presumption that they will concur in doing whatever justice and moderation dictate should be done.

## EXPLANATION OF THE ORIGIN OF THE PRINCIPLE THAT "FREE BOTTOMS MAKE FREE GOODS"

December 20, 1793

A doubt being entertained whether the use of the word *modern,* as applied to the *law of nations* in the President's proclamation, be not inconsistent with ground afterwards taken in a letter to Genet, I will state the matter while it is fresh in my mind—beginning it from an early period.

It cannot be denied that according to the general law of nations, the goods of an enemy are lawful prize in the bottom of a friend, and the goods of a friend privileged in the bottom of an enemy; or in other words, that *the goods follow the owner*. The inconvenience of this principle in subjecting neutral vessels to vexatious searches at sea, has for more than a century rendered it usual for nations to substitute a *conventional* principle *that the goods shall follow the bottom,* instead of the *natural* one before mentioned. France has done it in all her treaties; so I believe had Spain, before the American Revolution. Britain had not done it. When that war had involved those powers, Russia, foreseeing that her commerce would be much harassed by the British ships, engaged Denmark, Sweden, and Portugal to arm, and to declare that the conventional principle should be observed by the powers at war, towards neutrals, and that they would make common cause against the party who should violate it; declaring expressly, at the same time, that that Convention should be in force only during the war then existing. Holland acceded to the Convention, and Britain instantly attacked her. But the other neutral powers did not think proper to comply with their stipulation of making common cause. France declared at once that she would conform to the conventional principle. This in fact imposed no new obligation on her, for she was already bound by her treaties with all those powers to observe that principle. Spain made the same declaration. Congress gave similar orders to their vessels; but Congress afterwards gave instructions to their ministers abroad not to engage them in any future combination of powers for the general enforcement of the conventional principle that goods should follow the bottom, as this might at some time or other engage them in a war for other nations; but to introduce the principle separately with every nation by the treaties they were authorized to make with each. It had been already done with France and Holland, and it was afterwards done with Prussia, and made a regular part in every treaty they proposed to others. After the war, Great Britain established it between herself and France. When she engaged in the present war with France, it was thought extremely desirable for us to get this principle admitted by her, and hoping that as she had acceded to it in one instance, she might be induced to admit it as a principle now settled by the common consent of nations (for every nation, belligerent or neutral, had stipulated it on one or more occasions), that she might be induced to consider it as now become a *conventional* law of nations, I proposed to insert the word *modern* in the proclamation, to open upon her the idea that we should require the acquiescence in that principle as the condition of our remaining in peace. It was thought desirable by the other gentlemen; but having no expectation of any effect from it, they acquiesced in the insertion of the word, merely to gratify me. I had another view, which I did not mention to them, because I apprehended it would occasion the loss of the word.

By the ancient law of nations, *e.g.*, in the time of the Romans, the furnishing a limited aid of troops, though stipulated, was deemed a cause of war. In latter times, it is admitted not to be a cause of war. This is one of the improvements in the law of nations. I thought we might conclude, by parity of reasoning, that the guaranteeing a limited portion of territory, in a stipulated case, might not, by the modern law of nations, be a cause of war. I therefore meant by the introduction of that word, to lay the foundation of the execution of our guarantee, by way of negotiation with England. The word was, therefore, introduced, and a strong letter was written to Mr. Pinckney to observe to Great Britain that we were bound by our treaties with the other belligerent powers to observe certain principles during this war: that we were willing to observe the same principles towards her; and indeed, that we considered it as essential to proceed by the same rule to all, and to propose to her to select those articles concerning our conduct in a case of our neutrality from any one of our treaties which she pleased; or that we would take those from her own treaty with France, and make a temporary Convention of them for the term of the present war; and he was instructed to press this strongly. I told Genet that we had done this; but instead of giving us time to work our principles into effect by negotiation, he immediately took occasion in a letter, to threaten that if we did not resent the conduct of the British in taking French property in American bottoms, and protect their goods by *effectual measures* (meaning by arms), he would give direction that the principle of our treaty of goods following the bottom, should be disregarded. He was, at the same time, in the habit of keeping our goods taken in British bottoms; so that they were to take the gaining alternative of each principle, and give us the losing one. It became necessary to oppose this in the answer to his letter, and it was impossible to do it soundly, but by placing it on its true ground, to wit: that the law of nations established as a general rule that *goods should follow the owner,* and that the making them *follow the vessel* was an exception depending on special conventions only in those cases where the Convention had been made: that the exception had been established by us in our treaties with France, Holland, and Prussia, and that we should endeavor to extend it to England, Spain, and other powers; but that till it was done, we had no right to make war for the enforcement of it. He thus obliged us to abandon in the first moment the ground we were endeavoring to gain, that is to say, his ground against England and Spain, and to take the very ground of England and Spain against him. This was my private reason for proposing the term *modern* in the proclamation; that it might reserve us a ground to obtain the very things he wanted. But the world, who knew nothing of these private reasons, were to understand by the expression the *modern law of nations,* that law with all the improvements and mollifications of it which an advancement of civilization in *modern* times had introduced. It does not mean strictly anything which is not a part of the *law of nations* in *modern* times, and therefore could not be inconsistent with the ground taken in the letter to Genet, which was that of the *law of nations,* and by no means could be equivalent to a declaration by the President of the specific principle, that *goods should follow the bottom.*

# *Chapter VI*

# THE NATIONAL CAPITAL

## OPINION UPON THE QUESTION WHETHER THE PRESIDENT SHOULD VETO THE BILL, DECLARING THAT THE SEAT OF GOVERNMENT SHALL BE TRANSFERRED TO THE POTOMAC, IN THE YEAR 1790

July 15, 1790

[Secretary of State Jefferson to President Washington:

I have formed an opinion, quite satisfactory to myself, that the adjournments of Congress may be by law, as well as by resolution, without touching the constitution. I am now copying fair what I had written yesterday on the subject & will have the honor of laying it before you by ten o'clock. The address to the President contains a very full digest of all the arguments urged against the bill on the point of unconstitutionality on the floor of Congress. It was fully combated on that ground, in the committee of the whole, & on the third reading. The majority (a Southern one) overruled the objection, as a majority (a Northern one) had overruled the same objection the last session on the Susquehanna residence bill. So that two majorities, in two different sessions, & from different ends of the Union have overruled the objection, and may be fairly supposed to have declared the sense of the whole Union. I shall not lose a moment in laying before you my thoughts on the subject. I have the honor to be with the most respectful esteem, Sir, Your most obedient & most humble serv$^{t}$.[1]]

A Bill having passed the two houses of Congress, and being now before the President, declaring that the seat of the federal government shall be transferred to the Potowmac in the year 1790, that the session of Congress next ensuing the present shall be held at Philadelphia, to which place the offices shall be transferred before the 1st of December next, a writer in a public paper of July 13 has urged on the consideration of the President that the constitution has given to the two houses of Congress the exclusive right to

[1] MS. in National Archives, Records of the Department of State, Misc. Letters. The text of the "Opinion" in Ford, V, 205-210, is not accurate.

adjourn themselves, that the will of the President mixed with theirs in a decision of this kind would be an inoperative ingredient, repugnant to the constitution, and that he ought not to permit them to part, in a single instance, with their constitutional rights: consequently that he ought to negative the bill.

That is now to be considered:

Every man, and every body of men on earth, possesses the right of self-government. They receive it with their being from the hand of nature. Individuals exercise it by their single will; collections of men by that of their majority; for the law of the *majority* is the natural law of every society of men. When a certain description of men are to transact together a particular business, the times and places of their meeting and separating depend on their own will; they make a part of the natural right of self-government. This, like all other natural rights, may be abridged or modified in its exercise by their own consent, or by the law of those who depute them, if they meet in the right of others; but as far as it is not abridged or modified, they retain it as a natural right, and may exercise them in what form they please, either exclusively by themselves, or in association with others, or by others altogether, as they shall agree.

Each house of Congress possesses this natural right of governing itself, and, consequently, of fixing its own times and places of meeting, so far as it has not been abridged by the law of those who employ them, that is to say, by the Constitution. This act manifestly considers them as possessing this right of course, and therefore has nowhere given it to them. In the several different passages where it touches this right, it treats it as an existing thing, not as one called into existence by them. To evince this, every passage of the constitution shall be quoted, where the right of adjournment is touched; and it will be seen that no one of them pretends to give that right; that, on the contrary, everyone is evidently introduced either to enlarge the right where it would be too narrow, to restrain it where, in its natural and full exercise, it might be too large, and lead to inconvenience, to defend it from the latitude of its own phrases, where these were not meant to comprehend it, or to provide for its exercise by others, when they cannot exercise it themselves.

"A majority of each house shall constitute a quorum to do business; but a smaller number may adjourn from day to day, and may be authorized to compel the attendance of absent members." Art. 1, Sec. 5. A majority of every collection of men being naturally necessary to constitute its will, and it being frequently to happen that a majority is not assembled, it was necessary to enlarge the natural right by giving to "a smaller number than a majority" a right to compel the attendance of the absent members, and, in the meantime, to adjourn from day to day. This clause, then, does not pretend to give to a majority a right which it knew that majority would have of themselves, but to a number *less than a majority,* a right to which it knew that lesser number could not have of themselves.

"Neither house, during the session of Congress, shall, without the consent of the other, adjourn for more than three days, nor to any other place than that in which the two houses shall be sitting." Ibid. Each house exercising separately its natural right to meet when and where it should think best, it might happen that the two houses would separate either in time or place, which would be inconvenient. It was necessary, therefore, to keep them together by restraining their natural right of deciding on separate times and places, and by requiring a concurrence of will.

But, as it might happen that obstinacy, or a difference of object, might prevent this concurrence, it goes on to take from them, in that instance, the right of adjournment altogether, and to transfer it to another, by declaring, Art. 2, Sec. 3, that "in case of disagreement between the two houses, with respect to the time of adjournment, the President may adjourn them to such time as he shall think proper."

These clauses, then, do not import a gift, to the two houses, of a general right of adjournment, which it was known they would have without that gift, but to restrain or abrogate the right it was known they would have, in an instance where, exercised in its full extent, it might lead to inconvenience, and to give that right to another who would not naturally have had it. It also gives to the President a right, which he otherwise would not have had, "to convene both houses, or either of them, on extraordinary occasions." Thus substituting the will of another, where they are not in a situation to exercise their own.

"Every order, resolution, or vote, to which the concurrence of the Senate and House of Representatives may be necessary (except on a question of adjournment), shall be presented to the President for his approbation, &c." Art. 1, Sec. 7. The latitude of the general words here used would have subjected the natural right of adjournment of the two houses to the will of the President, which was not intended. They therefore expressly "except questions of adjournment" out of their operation. They do not here give a right of adjournment, which it was known would exist without their gift, but they defend the existing right against the latitude of their own phrases, in a case where there was no good reason to abridge it. The exception admits they will have the right of adjournment, without pointing out the source from which they will derive it.

These are all the passages of the constitution (one only excepted, which shall be presently cited) where the right of adjournment is touched; and it is evident that none of these are introduced to give that right; but everyone supposes it to be existing, and provides some specific modification for cases where either a defeat in the natural right, or a too full use of it, would occasion inconvenience.

The right of adjournment, then, is not given by the constitution, and consequently it may be modified by law without interfering with that instrument. It is a natural right, and, like all other natural rights, may be abridged or regulated in its exercise by law; and the concurrence of the third branch in any law regulating its exercise is so efficient an ingredient in that law, that the right cannot be otherwise exercised but after a repeal by a new law. The express terms of the constitution itself show that this right may be modified *by law,* when, in Art. 1, Sec. 4 (the only remaining passage on the subject not yet quoted), it says, "The Congress shall assemble at least once in every year, and such meeting shall be the first Monday in December, unless they shall, *by law,* appoint a different day." Then another day may be appointed *by law;* and the President's assent is an efficient ingredient in that law. Nay further, they cannot adjourn over the first Monday of December but by *a law.* This is another constitutional abridgment of their natural right of adjournment; and completing our review of all the clauses in the constitution which touch that right, authorizes us to say no part of that instrument gives it; and that the houses hold it, not from the constitution, but from nature.

A consequence of this is, that the houses may, by a joint resolution, remove themselves from place to place, because it is a part of their right of self-government; but that as the right of self-government does not comprehend the government of others, the two houses cannot, by a joint resolution of their majorities only, remove the executive and judiciary from place to place. These branches possessing also the rights of self-government from nature, cannot be controlled in the exercise of them but by a law, passed in the forms of the constitution. The clause of the bill in question, therefore, was necessary to be put into the form of a law, and to be submitted to the President, so far as it proposes to effect the removal of the Executive and Judiciary to Philadelphia. So far as respects the removal of the present houses of legislation thither, it was not necessary to be submitted to the President; but such a submission is not repugnant to the constitution. On the contrary, if he concurs, it will so far fix the next session of Congress at Philadelphia that it cannot be changed but by a regular law.

The sense of Congress itself is always respectable authority. It has been given very remarkably on the present subject. The address to the President in the paper of the 13th is a complete digest of all the arguments urged on the floor of the Representatives against the constitutionality of the bill now before the President; and they were overruled by a majority of that house, comprehending the delegation of all the States south of the Hudson, except South Carolina. At the last session of Congress, when the bill for remaining a certain term at New York, and then removing to Susquehanna or Germantown was objected to on the same ground, the objection was overruled by a majority comprehending the delegations of the northern half of the union with that of South Carolina. So that the sense of every State in the union has been expressed, by its delegation, against this objection South Carolina excepted, and excepting also Rhode Island, which has never yet had a delegation in place to vote on the question. In both these instances, the Senate concurred with the majority of the Representatives. The sense of the two houses is stronger authority in this case, as it is given against their own supposed privilege.

It would be as tedious, as it is unnecessary, to take up and discuss one by one, the objections proposed in the paper of July 13. Every one of them is founded on the supposition that the two houses hold their right of adjournment from the constitution. This error being corrected, the objections founded on it fall of themselves.

It would also be work of mere supererogation to show that, granting what this writer takes for granted (that the President's assent would be an inoperative ingredient, because excluded by the constitution, as he says), yet the particular views of the writer would be frustrated, for on every hypothesis of what the President may do, Congress must go to Philadelphia. 1. If he assents to the bill, that assent makes good law of the part relative to the Patomac; and the part for holding the next session at Philadelphia is good, either as an ordinance, or a vote of the two houses, containing a complete declaration of their will in a case where it is competent to the object; so that they must go to Philadelphia in that case. 2. If he dissents from the bill it annuls the part relative to the Patomac; but as to the clause for adjourning to Philadelphia, his dissent being as inefficient as his assent, it remains a good ordinance or vote, of the two houses for going thither, and consequently they must go in this case also. 3. If the President withholds his will out of the bill altogether, by a ten days' silence, then the part relative to the Patomac becomes a good law without his will, and that relative to Philadelphia is good also, either as a law, or an ordinance, or a vote of the two houses; and consequently in this case also they go to Philadelphia.

## OPINION ON PROCEEDINGS TO BE HAD UNDER THE RESIDENCE ACT

November 29, 1790

A territory not exceeding ten miles square (or, I presume, one hundred square miles in any form) to be located by metes and bounds.

Three commissioners to be appointed. I suppose them not entitled to any salary.

[If they live near the place they may, in some instances, be influenced by self interest, and partialities; but they will push the work with zeal. If they are from a distance, and northwardly, they will be more impartial, but may affect delays.]

The commissioners to purchase or accept "such quantity of land on the east side of the river as the President shall deem *proper for the United States," viz.,* for the federal Capitol, the offices, the President's house and gardens, the town house, market house, public walks and hospital. For the President's house, offices and gardens, I should think two squares should be consolidated. For the Capitol and offices, one square. For the market, one square. For the public walks, nine squares consolidated.

The expression "such quantity of land as the President shall deem *proper for the United States,"* is vague. It may therefore be extended to the acceptance or purchase of land enough for the town; and I have no doubt it is the wish, and perhaps expectation. In that case, it will be to be laid out in lots and streets. I should propose these to be at right angles, as in Philadelphia, and that no street be narrower than one hundred feet, with foot ways of fifteen feet. Where a street is long and level, it might be one hundred and twenty feet wide. I should prefer squares of at least two hundred yards every way, which will be about eight acres each.

The commissioners should have some taste in architecture, because they may have to decide between different plans.

They will, however, be subject to the President's direction in every point.

When the President shall have made up his mind as to the spot for the town, would there be any impropriety in his saying to the neighboring land holders, "I will fix the town here if you will join and purchase and give the lands." They may well afford it by the increase of value it will give to their own circumjacent lands.

The lots to be sold out in breadths of fifty feet; their depths to extend to the diagonal of the square.

I doubt much whether the obligation to build the houses at a given distance from the street, contributes to its beauty. It produces a disgusting monotony; all persons make this complaint against Philadelphia. The contrary practice varies the appearance, and is much more convenient to the inhabitants.

In Paris it is forbidden to build a house beyond a given height; and it is admitted to be a good restriction. It keeps down the price of ground, keeps the houses low and convenient, and the streets light and airy. Fires are much more manageable where houses are low.

# OPINION RELATIVE TO LOCATING THE TEN MILE SQUARE FOR THE FEDERAL GOVERNMENT, AND BUILDING THE FEDERAL CITY

March 11, 1791

Objects which may merit the attention of the President, at Georgetown.

The commissioners to be called into action.

Deeds of cession to be taken from the land-holders.

Site of the capitol and President's house to be determined on.

Proclamation completing the location of the territory, and fixing the site of the capitol.

Town to be laid off. Squares of reserve are to be decided on for the capitol, President's house, offices of government, townhouse, prison, market, and public walks.

Other squares for present sale designated.

Terms of sale to be settled. As there is not as yet a town legislature, and things may be done before there is one to prevent them, which yet it would be desirable to prevent, it would seem justifiable and expedient that the President should form a capitulary of such regulations as he may think necessary to be observed, until there shall be a town legislature to undertake this office; such capitulary to be indented, signed, sealed, and recorded, according to the laws of conveyance in Maryland. And to be referred to in every deed for conveyance of the lots to purchasers, so as to make a part thereof. The same thing might be effected, by inserting special covenants for every regulation in every deed; but the former method is the shortest. I cannot help again suggesting here one regulation formerly suggested, to wit: To provide for the extinguishment of fires, and the openness and convenience of the town, by prohibiting houses of excessive height. And making it unlawful to build on anyone's purchase any house with more than two floors between the common level of the earth and the eaves, nor with any other floor in the roof than one at the eaves. To consider in what way the contracts for the public buildings shall be made, and whether as many bricks should not be made this summer as may employ brick-layers in the beginning of the season of 1792, till more can be made in that season.

With respect to the amendment of the location so as to include Bladensburgh, I am of opinion it may be done with the consent of the legislature of Maryland, and that that consent may be so far counted on, as to render it expedient to declare the location at once.

The location A B C D A having been once made, I consider as obligatory and unalterable, but by consent of parties, except so far as was necessary to render it practicable by a correction of the beginning. That correction might be lawfully made either by stopping at the river, or at the spring of Hunting creek, or by lengthening the course from the court-house so that the second course should strike the mouth of Hunting creek. I am of opinion, therefore, that the beginning at the mouth of Hunting creek, is legally justifiable. But I would advise the location E F G H E to be hazarded so as to include Bladensburgh, because it is a better location, and I think will certainly be confirmed by Maryland. That State will necessarily have to pass another act confirming whatever location shall be made, because her former act authorized the delegates *then* in office, to convey the lands. But as they were not located, no conveyance has been made, and those persons are now out of

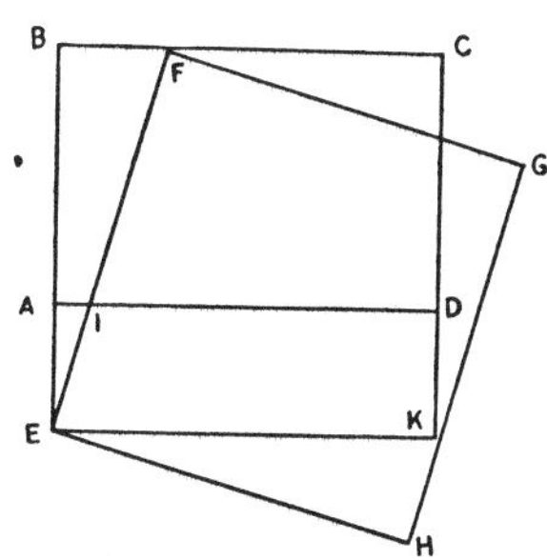


office, and dispersed. Suppose the non-concurrence of Maryland should defeat the location E F G H E, it can only be done on this principle, that the first location A B C D A was valid, and unalterable, but by mutual consent. Then their non-concurrence will re-establish the first location A B C D A, and the second location will be good for the part E I D K E without their concurrence, and this will place us where we should be were we now to complete the location E B C K E. Consequently, the experiment of an amendment proposed can lose nothing, and may gain, and probably will gain, the better location.

When I say it can lose nothing, I count as nothing, the triangle A I E, which would be in neither of the locations. Perhaps this might be taken in afterwards, either with or without the consent of Virginia.

## OPINION RELATIVE TO THE DEMOLITION OF MR. CARROLL'S HOUSE BY MAJOR L'ENFANT, IN LAYING OUT THE FEDERAL CITY

December 11, 1791

Observations on Major L'Enfant's letter of December 7th, 1791, to the President, justifying his demolition of the house of Mr. Carroll, of Duddington:

He says that "Mr. Carroll erected his house partly on a main street, and altogether on ground to which the public had a more immediate title than himself could claim." When blaming Mr. Carroll, then, he considers this as a street; but when justifying himself, he considers it not yet as a street, for to account for his not having pointed out to Carroll a situation where he might build, he says, "The President had not yet sanctioned the plan for the distribution of the city, not determined if he would approve the situation of the several areas proposed to him in that plan for public use, and that I would have been highly to be blamed to have anticipated his opinion thereon." This latter exculpation is solid; the first is without foundation. The plan of the city has not yet been definitely determined by the President. Sales to individuals, or partition decide the plan as far as these sales or partitions go. A deed with the whole plan annexed, executed by the President, and recorded, will ultimately fix it. But till a sale, or partition, or deed, it is open to alteration. Consequently, there is as yet no such thing as a street, except adjacent to the lots actually sold or divided; the erection of a house in any part of the ground cannot as yet be a nuisance in law. Mr. Carroll is tenant in common of the soil with the public, and the erection of a house by a tenant in common on the common property, is no nuisance. Mr. Carroll has acted imprudently, intemperately, foolishly; but he has not acted illegally. There must be an establishment of the streets, before his house can become a nuisance in the eye of the law. Therefore, till that establishment, neither Major L'Enfant, nor the commissioners, would have had a right to demolish his house, without his consent.

The Major says he had as much right to pull down a house, as to cut down a tree.

This is true, if he has received no authority to do either, but still there will be this difference: To cut down a tree or to demolish a house in the soil of another, is a trespass; but the cutting a tree, in this country, is so slight a trespass, that a man would be thought litigious who should prosecute it; if he prosecuted civilly, a jury would give small damages; if criminally, the judge would not inflict imprisonment, nor impose but a small fine. But the demolition of a house is so gross a trespass, that any man would prosecute it; if civilly, a jury would give great damages; if criminally, the judge would punish heavily by fine and imprisonment. In the present case, if Carroll was to bring a civil action, the jury would probably punish his folly by small damages; but if he were to prosecute criminally, the judge would as probably vindicate the insult on the laws, and the breach of the peace, by heavy fines and imprisonment. So that if Major L'Enfant is right in saying he had as much authority to pull down a house as to cut down a tree, still he would feel a difference in the punishment of the law.

But is he right in saying he had as much authority to pull down a house as to cut down a tree? I do not know what have been the authorities given him expressly or by *implication,* but I can very readily conceive that the authorities which he has received, whether from the President or from the commissioners, whether verbal or written, may have gone to the demolition of trees, and not houses. I am sure he has received no authority, either from the President or commissioners, either expressly or by implication, to pull down houses. An order to him to mark on the ground the lines of the streets and lots, might imply an order to remove trees or *small* obstructions, *where they insuperably prevented his operations;* but a person must know little of geometry who could not, in an open field, designate streets and lots, even where a line passed through a house, without pulling the house down.

In truth, the blame on Major L'Enfant, is for having pulled down the house, of his own authority, and when he had reason to believe he was in opposition to the sentiments of the President; and his fault is aggravated by its having been done to gratify private resentment against Mr. Carroll, and most probably not because it was necessary; and the style in which he writes the justification of his act, shows that a continuation of the same resentment renders him still unable to acquiesce under the authority from which he has been reproved.

He desires a line of demarcation between his office, and that of the commissioners.

What should be this line? and who is to draw it? If we consider the matter under the *act of Congress* only, the President has authority only to name the commissioners, and to approve or disapprove certain proceedings of theirs. They have the whole executive power, and stand between the President and the subordinate agents. In this view, they may employ or dismiss, order and countermand, take on themselves such parts of the execution as they please, and assign other parts to subordinate agents. Consequently, under the *act of Congress,* their will is the line of demarcation between subordinate agents, while no such line can exist between themselves and their agents. Under the deed from the proprietors to the President, his powers are much more ample. I do not accurately recollect the tenor of the deed; but I am pretty sure it was such as to put much more ample power into the hands of the President, and to commit to him the whole execution of whatever is to be done under the deed; and this goes particularly to the laying out the town: so that as to this, the President is certainly authorized to draw the line of demarcation between L'Enfant and the commissioners. But I believe there is no necessity for it, as far as I have been able to judge, from conversations and consultations with the commissioners. I think they are disposed to follow implicitly the will of the President, whenever they can find it out; but L'Enfant's letters do not breathe the same moderation or acquiescence; and I think it would be much safer to say to him, "the orders of the commissioners are your line of demarcation," than by attempting to define his powers, to give him a line where he may meet with the commissioners foot to foot, and chicane and raise opposition to their orders whenever he thinks they pass his line. I confess, that on a view of L'Enfant's proceedings and letters latterly, I am thoroughly persuaded that, to render him useful, his temper must be subdued; and that the only means of preventing his giving constant trouble to the President, is to submit him to the unlimited control of the commissioners; we know the discretion and forbearance with which they will exercise it.

## PROGRAM OF COMPETITION FOR THE UNITED STATES CAPITOL[1]

March 14, 1792

WASHINGTON, IN THE TERRITORY OF COLUMBIA

*A Premium*

of a lot in the city, to be designated by impartial judges, and $500, or a medal of that value, at the option of the party, will be given by the Commissioners of Federal Buildings to persons who, before the 15th day of July, 1792, shall produce them the most approved plan, if adopted by them for a Capitol to be erected in the city, and $250 or a medal for the plan deemed next in merit to the one they shall adopt; the building to be of brick and to contain the following compartments, to wit:

A conference room } Sufficient to accommodate 300 persons each<br>
A room for Representatives }<br>
A lobby or antechamber to the latter<br>
A Senate room of 1,200 square feet of area<br>
An antechamber and lobby to the latter<br>
} These rooms to be of full elevation.

Twelve rooms of 600 square feet area each for committee rooms and clerks, to be of half the elevation of the former.

Drawings will be expected of the ground plats, elevation of each front, and sections through the building in such directions as may be necessary to

[1] This draft was prepared and finally approved by Jefferson as Secretary of State, but signed by the Commissioners of the Territory of Columbia. It is both interesting and important as the first "Program of Competition" for public buildings of the United States.

explain the material, structure, and an estimate of the cubic feet of the brick work composing the whole mass of the walls.

THOS. JOHNSON
DD. STUART
DANL. CARROLL, *Commissioners*

*March 14,* 1792

---

[At the same time, on March 14, an advertisement was issued for plans for the President's house [2]:]

WASHINGTON, IN THE TERRITORY OF COLUMBIA [3]

*A Premium*

of Five Hundred Dollars, or a Medal of that value at the option of the party, will be given by the Commissioners of the Federal Buildings to the person who, before the fifteenth day of July next, shall produce to them the most approved PLAN adopted by them for a PRESIDENT'S HOUSE to be erected in this City. The site of the building, if the artist will attend to it, will of course influence the aspect and outline of his plan; and its destination will point out to him the number, size and distribution of the apartments. It will be a recommendation of any plan, if the central part of it may be detached, and erected for the present, with the appearance of a complete whole, and be capable of admitting the additional parts in the future if they shall be wanting. Drawings will be expected of the ground plats, elevation of each front and Sections through the building, in such direction as may be necessary to explain the material, structure, and an estimate of the cubic feet of brick-work composing the whole mass of the walls.

THE COMMISSIONERS

[2] Jefferson entered the competition anonymously; his design is reproduced above.
[3] On September 9, 1791, the Commissioners decided that the federal District should be called "The Territory of Columbia" and the federal City "The City of Washington."

*Chapter VII*

# THE WESTERN TERRITORIES

## PLAN FOR THE TEMPORARY GOVERNMENT OF THE WESTERN TERRITORY [1]

March 1, 1784

The Committee appointed to prepare a plan for the temporary government of the Western Territory, have agreed to the following resolutions:

*Resolved,* That the territory ceded or to be ceded by individual States to the United States, whensoever the same shall have been purchased of the Indian inhabitants, and offered for sale by the United States, shall be formed into distinct States, bounded in the following manner, as nearly as such cessions will admit—that is to say: northwardly and southwardly by parallels of latitude, so that each State shall comprehend, from south to north, two degrees of latitude, beginning to count from the completion of thirty-one degrees north of the equator; but any territory northwardly of the forty-seventh degree shall make part of the State next below; and eastwardly and westwardly they shall be bounded, those on the Mississippi by that river on one side, and the meridian of the lowest point of the rapids of Ohio on the other; and those adjoining on the east by the same meridian on their western side, and on their eastern by the meridian of the western cape of the mouth of the Great Kanawha and the territory eastward of this last meridian, between the Ohio, Lake Erie, and Pennsylvania, shall be one State.

That the settlers within the territory so to be purchased and offered for sale, shall, either on their own petition, or on the order of Congress, receive authority from them, with appointments of time and place for their free males, of full age, to meet together for the purpose of establishing a temporary government, to adopt the constitution and laws of any one of these

[1] Jefferson drew up this draft as chairman of a committee to prepare a plan for the government of the Northwestern Territory which Virginia ceded to the national government; Congress accepted the land on March 1, 1784.

States, so that such laws nevertheless shall be subject to alteration by their ordinary legislature; and to erect, subject to a like alteration, counties or townships for the election of members for their legislature.

That such temporary government shall only continue in force in any State until it shall have acquired twenty thousand free inhabitants; when, giving due proof thereof to Congress, they shall receive from them authority, with appointments of time and place, to call a convention of representatives to establish a permanent constitution and government for themselves: Provided, That both the temporary and permanent governments be established on these principles as their basis: 1. [That they shall forever remain a part of the United States of America;] 2. That, in their persons, property, and territory, they shall be subject to the Government of the United States in Congress assembled, and to the Articles of Confederation in all those cases in which the original States shall be so subject; 3. That they shall be subject to pay a part of the federal debts contracted or to be contracted, to be apportioned on them by Congress according to the same common rule and measure by which apportionments thereof shall be made on the other States; 4. That their respective governments shall be in republican forms, and shall admit no person to be a citizen who holds any hereditary title; 5. That after the year 1800 of the Christian era there shall be neither slavery nor involuntary servitude in any of the said States, otherwise than in punishment of crimes, whereof the party shall have been duly convicted to have been personally guilty.

That whensoever any of the said States shall have, of free inhabitants, as many as shall then be in any one of the least numerous of the thirteen original States, such State shall be admitted by its delegates into the Congress of the United States on an equal footing with the said original States; after which the assent of two-thirds of the United States in Congress assembled shall be requisite in all those cases wherein, by the Confederation, the assent of nine States is now required: Provided, The consent of nine States to such admission may be obtained according to the eleventh of the Articles of Confederation. Until such admission by their delegates into Congress, any of the said States, after the establishment of their temporary government, shall have authority to keep a sitting member in Congress, with right of debating but not of voting.

That the territory northward of the forty-fifth degree, that is to say, of the completion of forty-five degrees from the equator, and extending to the Lake of the Woods, shall be called SYLVANIA.

That of the territory under the forty-fifth and forty-fourth degrees, that which lies westward of Lake Michigan, shall be called MICHIGANIA; and that which is eastward thereof, within the peninsula formed by the lakes and waters of Michigan, Huron, St. Clair, and Erie, shall be called CHER-

RONESUS, and shall include any part of the peninsula which may extend above the forty-fifth degree.

Of the territory under the forty-third and forty-second degrees, that to the westward, through which the Assenisipi or Rock River runs, shall be called ASSENISIPIA; and that to the eastward, in which are the fountains of the Muskingum, the two Miamies of the Ohio, the Wabash, the Illinois, the Miami of the Lake, and Sandusky rivers, shall be called METROPOTAMIA.

Of the territory which lies under the forty-first and fortieth degrees, the western, through which the river Illinois runs, shall be called ILLINOIA; that next adjoining to the eastward, SARATOGA; and that between this last and Pennsylvania, and extending from the Ohio to Lake Erie, shall be called WASHINGTON.

Of the territory which lies under the thirty-ninth and thirty-eighth degrees, to which shall be added so much of the point of land within the fork of the Ohio and Mississippi as lies under the thirty-seventh degree, that to the westward, within and adjacent to which are the confluences of the rivers Wabash, Shawanee, Tanissee, Ohio, Illinois, Mississippi, and Missouri, shall be called POLYPOTAMIA; and that to the eastward, further up the Ohio, otherwise called the Pelisipi, shall be called PELISIPIA.

That the preceding articles shall be formed into a charter of compact, shall be duly executed by the President of the United States in Congress assembled, under his hand and the seal of the United States, shall be promulgated, and shall stand as fundamental constitutions between the thirteen original States and those newly described, unalterable but by the joint consent of the United States in Congress assembled, and of the particular State within which such alteration is proposed to be made.

## GOVERNMENT FOR THE WESTERN TERRITORY[1]

March 22, 1784

The Committee to whom was recommitted the report of a plan for a temporary government of the Western territory have agreed to the following resolutions.

Resolved, that so much of the territory ceded or to be ceded by individual states to the United States as is already purchased or shall be purchased of the Indian inhabitants and offered for sale by Congress, shall be divided into distinct states, in the following manner, as nearly as such cessions will admit;

[1] Jefferson's original report of March 1 (see pages 236-238) did not satisfy Congress and so he rewrote it in the above form; after amendment, it was adopted on April 23, 1784. This document, although it was superseded by the Northwest Ordinance of 1787, contains the basic provisions of that Ordinance and ranks as one of Jefferson's greatest state papers.

that is to say, by parallels of latitude, so that each state shall comprehend from South to North two degrees of latitude beginning to count from the completion of thirty-one degrees North of the Equator; and by meridians of longitude, one of which shall pass through the lowest point of the rapids of Ohio, and the other through the Western Cape of the mouth of the Great Kanhaway, but the territory Eastward of this last meridian, between the Ohio, Lake Erie, and Pennsylvania shall be one state, whatsoever may be its comprehension of latitude. That which may lie beyond the completion of the 45th degree between the said meridians shall make part of the state adjoining it on the South, and that part of the Ohio which is between the same meridians coinciding nearly with the parallel of 39° shall be substituted so far in lieu of that parallel as a boundary line.

That the settlers on any territory so purchased and offered for sale shall, either on their own petition, or on the order of Congress, receive authority from them with appointments of time and place for their free males of full age, within the limits of their state to meet together for the purpose of establishing a temporary government, to adopt the constitution and laws of any one of the original states, so that such laws nevertheless shall be subject to alteration by their ordinary legislature; and to erect, subject to a like alteration, counties or townships for the election of members for their legislature.

That such temporary government shall only continue in force in any state until it shall have acquired 20,000 free inhabitants, when giving due proof thereof to Congress, they shall receive from them authority with appointment of time and place to call a convention of representatives to establish a permanent Constitution and Government for themselves. Provided that both the temporary and permanent governments be established on these principles as their basis. 1. That they shall forever remain a part of this confederacy of the United States of America. 2. That in their persons, property and territory they shall be subject to the Government of the United States in Congress assembled, and to the articles of Confederation in all those cases in which the original states shall be so subject. 3. That they shall be subject to pay a part of the federal debts contracted or to be contracted, to be apportioned on them by Congress, according to the same common rule and measure, by which apportionments thereof shall be made on the other states. 4. That their respective Governments shall be in republican forms and shall admit no person to be a citizen who holds any hereditary title. 5. That after the year 1800 of the Christian era, there shall be neither slavery nor involuntary servitude in any of the said states, otherwise than in punishment of crimes whereof the party shall have been convicted to have been personally guilty.

That whensoever any of the said states shall have, of free inhabitants, as many as shall then be in any one the least numerous, of the thirteen original states, such state shall be admitted by its delegates into the Congress of the United States on an equal footing with the said original states: provided nine States agree to such admission according to the reservation of the 11th of the articles of Confederation, and in order to adopt the said articles of Confederation to the state of Congress when its numbers shall be thus increased, it shall be proposed to the legislatures of the states originally parties thereto, to require the assent of two thirds of the United States in Congress assembled in all those cases wherein by the said articles the assent of nine states is now required; which being agreed to by them shall be binding on the new states. Until such admission by their delegates into Congress, any of the said states after the establishment of their temporary government shall have authority to keep a sitting member in Congress, with a right of debating, but not of voting.

That the preceding articles shall be formed into a charter of compact, shall be duly executed by the president of the United States in Congress assembled, under his hand and the seal of the United States, shall be promulgated and shall stand as fundamental constitutions between the thirteen original states and each of the several states now newly described, unalterable but by the joint consent of the United States in Congress assembled, and of the particular state within which such alteration is proposed to be made.

That measures not inconsistent with the principles of the Confederation and necessary for the preservation of peace and good order among the settlers in any of the said new states until they shall assume a temporary Government as aforesaid, may from time to time be taken by the United States in Congress assembled.

## SPAIN AND THE MISSISSIPPI

March 18, 1792

The appointment of Mr. Carmichael and Mr. Short, as commissioners to negotiate, with the court of Spain, a treaty or convention relative to the navigation of the Mississippi, and which perhaps may be extended to other interests, rendering it necessary that the subjects to be treated of should be developed, and the conditions of arrangement explained:

The Secretary of State reports to the President of the United States the following observations on the subjects of negotiation between the United States of America and the court of Spain, to be communicated by way of instruction to the commissioners of the United States, appointed as before mentioned, to manage that negotiation.

These subjects are,

I. Boundary.

II. The navigation of the Mississippi.

III. Commerce.

1. As to boundary, that between Georgia and Florida is the only one which will need any explanation. Spain sets up a claim to possessions within the State of Georgia, founded on her having rescued them by force from the British during the late war. The following view of the subject seems to admit no reply:

The several States now comprising the United States of America, were, from their first establishment, separate and distinct societies, dependent on no other society of men whatever. They continued at the head of their respective governments the executive magistrate who presided over the one they had left, and thereby secured, in effect, a constant amity with the nation. In this stage of their government their several boundaries were fixed; and particularly the southern boundary of Georgia, the only one now in question, was established at the 31st degree of latitude from the Apalachicola westwardly; and the western boundary, originally the Pacific ocean, was, by the treaty of Paris, reduced to the middle of the Mississippi. The part which our chief magistrate took in a war, waged against us by the nation among whom he resided, obliged us to discontinue him, and to name one within every State. In the course of this war we were joined by France as an ally, and by Spain and Holland as associates; having a common enemy, each sought that common enemy wherever they could find him. France, on our invitation, landed a large army within our territories, continued it with us two years, and aided us in recovering sundry places from the possession of the enemy. But she did not pretend to keep possession of the places rescued. Spain entered into the remote western part of our territory, dislodged the common enemy from several of the posts they held therein, to the annoyance of Spain; and perhaps thought it necessary to remain in some of them, as the only means of preventing their return. We, in like manner, dislodged them from several posts in the same western territory, to wit: Vincennes, Cahokia, Kaskaskia, &c., rescued the inhabitants, and retained constantly afterwards both them and the territory under our possession and government. At the conclusion of the war, Great Britain, on the 30th of November, 1782, by treaty acknowledged our independence, and our boundary, to wit: the Mississippi to the west, and the completion of the 31st degree, &c. to the south. In her treaty with Spain, concluded seven weeks afterwards, to wit, January 20th, 1783, she ceded to her the two Floridas, which had been defined in the proclamation of 1763, and Minorca; and by the eighth article of the treaty, Spain agreed to restore, *without compensation,* all the territories conquered by her, and not included in the treaty, either under the head of cessions or restitutions, that is to say, all except Minorca and the Floridas. According to this stipulation, Spain was expressly bound to have delivered up the possessions she had taken within the limits of Georgia, to Great Britain, if they were conquests on Great Britain, who was to deliver them over to the United States; or rather, she should have delivered them to the United States themselves, as standing *quoad hoc* in the place of Great Britain. And she was bound by natural rights to deliver them to the same United States on a much stronger ground, as the real and only proprietors of those places which she had taken possession of in a moment of danger, without having had any cause of war with the United States, to whom they belonged, and without having declared any; but, on the contrary, conducting herself in other respects as a friend and associate. *Vattel,* 1. 3, 122.

It is an established principle, that conquest gives only an inchoate treaty of peace, which does not become perfect till confirmed by the treaty of peace, and by a renunciation or abandonment by the former proprietor. Had Great Britain been that former proprietor, she was so far from confirming to Spain the right to the territory of Georgia, invaded by Spain, that she expressly relinquished to the United States any right that might remain in her; and afterwards completed that relinquishment, by procuring and consolidating with it the agreement of Spain herself to restore such territory without compensation. It is still more palpable, that a war existing between two nations, as Spain and Great Britain, could give to neither the right to seize and appropriate the territory of a third, which is even neutral, much less which is an associate in the war, as the United States were with Spain. See, on this subject, *Grotius,* 1. 3, c. 6, § 26. *Puffendorf,* 1. 8, c. 17, § 23. *Vattel,* 1. 3, § 197, 198.

On the conclusion of the general peace, the United States lost no time in requiring from Spain an evacuation of their territory. This has been hitherto delayed by means which we need not explain to that court, but which have been equally contrary to our right and to our consent.

Should Spain pretend, as has been intimated, that there was a secret article of treaty between the United States and Great Britain, agreeing, if at the close of the war the latter should retain the Floridas, that then the southern boundary of Georgia should be the completion of the 32d degree of latitude, the commissioners may safely deny all knowledge of the fact, and refuse conference on any such postulatum. Or, should they find it necessary to enter into any argument on the subject, they will of course do it hypothetically; and in that way may justly say, on the part of the United States; suppose that the United States, exhausted by a bloody and expensive war with Great Britain, might have been willing to have purchased peace by relinquishing, under a particular contingency, a small part of their territory, it does not follow that the same United States, recruited and better organized, must relinquish the same territory to Spain without striking a blow. The United States, too, have irrevocably put it out of their power to do it, by a new constitution, which guarantees every State against the invasion of its territory. A disastrous war, indeed, might, by necessity, supersede this stipulation (as necessity is above all law), and oblige them to abandon a part of a State; but nothing short of this can justify or obtain such an abandonment.

The southern limits of Georgia depend chiefly on,

1. The charter of Carolina to the lords proprietors, in 1663, extending southwardly to the river Matheo, now called St. John, supposed in the charter to be in latitude 31, and so west in a direct line as far as the South Sea. See the charter in 4th [1] Memoires de l'Amerique, 554.

2. On the proclamation of the British King, in 1763, establishing the boundary between Georgia and the two Floridas to begin on the Mississippi, in thirty-one degrees of latitude north of the equator, and running eastwardly to the Appalachicola; thence, along the said river to the mouth of the Flint; thence, in a direct line, to the source of St. Mary's river, and down the same to the ocean. This proclamation will be found in Postlethwayte voce "British America."

3. On the treaties between the United States and Great Britain, of November 30, 1782, and September 3, 1783, repeating and confirming these ancient boundaries,—

There was an intermediate transaction, to wit: a convention concluded at the Pardo, in 1739, whereby it was agreed that Ministers Plenipotentiary should be immediately appointed by Spain and Great Britain for settling the limits of Florida and Carolina. The convention is to be found in the collections of treaties. But the proceedings of the Plenipotentiaries are unknown here. *Qu.* If it was on that occasion that the southern boundary of Carolina was transferred from the latitude of Matheo or St. John's river further north to the St. Mary's? Or was it the proclamation of 1763, which first removed this boundary? [If the commissioners can procure in Spain a copy of whatever was agreed on in consequence of the convention of the Pardo, it is a desirable State paper here.]

To this demonstration of our rights may be added the explicit declaration of the court of Spain, that she would accede to them. This took place in conversations and correspondence thereon between Mr. Jay, Minister Plenipotentiary for the United States at the court at Madrid, the Marquis de La Fayette, and the Count de Florida Blanca. Monsieur de La Fayette, in his letter of February 19, 1783, to the Count de Florida Blanca, states the result of their conversations on limits in these words: "With respect to limits, his

[1] Mr. Short is desired to purchase this book at Amsterdam, or Paris, as he may not find it at Madrid, and when it shall have answered the purposes of this mission, let it be sent here for the use of the Secretary of State's office.—T. J.

Catholic Majesty has adopted those that are determined by the preliminaries of the 30th of November, between the United States and the court of London." The Count de Florida Blanca, in his answer of February 22d, to M. de La Fayette, says, "although it is his Majesty's intention to abide for the present by the limits established by the treaty of the 30th of November, 1782, between the English and the Americans, the King intends to inform himself particularly whether it can be in any ways inconvenient or prejudicial to settle that affair amicably with the United States"; and M. de La Fayette, in his letter of the same day to Mr. Jay, wherein he had inserted the preceding, says, "on receiving the answer of the Count de Florida Blanca (to wit: his answer, before mentioned, to M. de La Fayette), I desired an explanation respecting the addition that relates to the limits. I was answered, that it was a fixed principle to abide by the limits established by the treaty between the English and the Americans; that his remark related only to mere unimportant details, which he wished to receive from the Spanish commandants, which would be amicably regulated, and *would by no means oppose the general principle.* I asked him, before the Ambassador of France [M. de Montmorin], whether he would give me his word of honor for it; he assured me he would, and that I might engage it to the United States." See the report sent herewith.

II.—The navigation of the Mississippi.

Our right to navigate that river, from its source to where our southern boundary strikes it, is not questioned. It is from that point downwards, only, that the exclusive navigation is claimed by Spain; that is to say, where she holds the country on both sides, to wit: Louisiana on the west, and Florida on the east.

Our right to participate in the navigation of that part of the river, also, is to be considered, under

1. The Treaty of Paris of 1763,
2. The Revolution Treaty of 1782-3.
3. The law of nature and nations.

1. The war of 1755-1763, was carried on jointly by Great Britain and the thirteen colonies, now the United States of America, against France and Spain. At the peace which was negotiated by our common magistrate, a right was secured to the subjects of Great Britain (the common designation of all those under his government) to navigate the Mississippi in its whole breadth and length, from its source to the sea, and expressly that part which is between the island of New Orleans and the right bank of the river, as well as the passage both in and out of its mouth; and that the vessels should not be stopped, visited, or subjected to the payment of any duty whatsoever. These are the words of the treaty, article VII. Florida was at the same time ceded by Spain, and its extent westwardly was fixed to the lakes Pont-

chartrain and Maurepas, and the river Mississippi; and Spain received soon after from France a cession of the island of New Orleans, and all the country she held westward of the Mississippi, subject of course to our right of navigating between that country and the island previously granted to us by France. This right was not parcelled out to us in severalty, that is to say, to each the exclusive navigation of so much of the river as was adjacent to our several shores—in which way it would have been useless to all—but it was placed on that footing on which alone it could be worth anything, to wit: as a right to all to navigate the whole length of the river in common. The import of the terms and the reason of the thing prove it was a right of common in the whole, and not a several right to each of a particular part. To which may be added the evidence of the stipulation itself, that we should navigate between New Orleans and the western bank, which, being adjacent to none of our States, could be held by us only as a right of common. Such was the nature of our right to navigate the Mississippi, as far as established by the treaty of Paris.

2. In the course of the Revolutionary war, in which the thirteen colonies, Spain, and France, were opposed to Great Britain, Spain took possession of several posts held by the British in Florida. It is unnecessary to inquire whether the possession of half a dozen posts scattered through a country of seven or eight hundred miles extent, could be considered as the possession and conquest of that country. If it was, it gave still but an inchoate right, as was before explained, which could not be perfected but by the relinquishment of the former possession at the close of the war; but certainly it could not be considered as a conquest *of the river,* even against Great Britain, since the possession of the shores, to wit, of the island of New Orleans on the one side, and Louisiana on the other, having undergone no change, the right in the water would remain the same, if considered only in its relation to them; and if considered as a distinct right, independent of the shores, then no naval victories obtained by Spain over Great Britain, in the course of the war, gave her the color of conquest over any water which the British fleet could enter. Still less can she be considered as having conquered the river, as against the United States, with whom she was not at war. We had a common right of navigation in the part of the river between Florida, the island of New Orleans, and the western bank, and nothing which passed between Spain and Great Britain, either during the war, or at its conclusion, could lessen that right. Accordingly, at the treaty of November, 1782, Great Britain confirmed the rights of the United States to the navigation of the river, from its source to its mouth, and in January, 1783, completed the right of Spain to the territory of Florida, by an absolute relinquishment of all her rights in it. This relinquishment could not include the navigation held by the United States in their own right, because this right existed in them-

selves only, and was not in Great Britain. If it added anything to the rights of Spain respecting the river between the eastern and western banks, it could only be that portion of right which Great Britain had retained to herself in the treaty with the United States, held seven weeks before, to wit, a right of using it in common with the United States.

So that as by the treaty of 1763, the United States had obtained a common right of navigating the whole river from its source to its mouth, so by the treaty of 1782, that common right was confirmed to them by the only power who could pretend claims against them, founded on the state of war; nor has that common right been transferred to Spain by either conquest or cession.

But our right is built on ground still broader and more unquestionable, to wit:

3. On the law of nature and nations.

If we appeal to this, as we feel it written on the heart of man, what sentiment is written in deeper characters than that the ocean is free to all men, and their rivers to all their inhabitants? Is there a man, savage or civilized, unbiased by habit, who does not feel and attest this truth? Accordingly, in all tracts of country united under the same political society, we find this natural right universally acknowledged and protected by laying the navigable rivers open to all their inhabitants. When their rivers enter the limits of another society, if the right of the upper inhabitants to descend the stream is in any case obstructed, it is an act of force by a stronger society against a weaker, condemned by the judgment of mankind. The late case of Antwerp and the Scheldt was a striking proof of a general union of sentiment on this point; as it is believed that Amsterdam had scarcely an advocate out of Holland, and even there its pretensions were advocated on the ground of treaties, and not of natural right. (The commissioners would do well to examine thoroughly what was written on this occasion.) The commissioners will be able perhaps to find, either in the practice or the pretensions of Spain, as to the Dauro, Tagus, and Guadiana, some acknowledgments of this principle on the part of that nation. This sentiment of right in favor of the upper inhabitants must become stronger in the proportion which their extent of country bears to the lower. The United States hold 600,000 square miles of habitable territory on the Mississippi and its branches, and this river and its branches afford many thousands of miles of navigable waters penetrating this territory in all its parts. The inhabitable grounds of Spain below our boundary and bordering on the river, which alone can pretend any fear of being incommoded by our use of the river, are not the thousandth part of that extent. This vast portion of the territory of the United States has no other outlet for its productions, and these productions are of the bulkiest kind. And in truth, their passage down the river may not only be innocent, as to the Spanish subjects on the river, but cannot fail to enrich them far beyond their present condition. The real interests then of all the inhabitants, upper and lower, concur in fact with their rights.

If we appeal to the law of nature and nations, as expressed by writers on the subject, it is agreed by them, that, were the river, where it passes between Florida and Louisiana, the exclusive right of Spain, still an innocent passage along it is a natural right in those inhabiting its borders above. It would indeed be what those writers call an imperfect right, because the modification of its exercise depends in a considerable degree on the conveniency of the nation through which they are to pass. But it is still a right as real as any other right, however well-defined; and were it to be refused, or to be so shackled by regulations, not necessary for the peace or safety of its inhabitants, as to render its use impracticable to us, it would then be an injury, of which we should be entitled to demand redress. The right of the upper inhabitants to use this navigation is the counterpart to that of those possessing the shore below, and founded in the same natural relations with the soil and water. And the line at which their rights meet is to be advanced or withdrawn, so as to equalize the inconveniences resulting to each party from the exercise of the right by the other. This estimate is to be fairly made with a mutual disposition to make equal sacrifices, and the numbers on each side are to have their due weight in the estimate. Spain holds so very small a tract of habitable land on either side below our boundary, that it may in fact be considered as a strait of the sea; for though it is eighty leagues from our boundary to the mouth of the river, yet it is only here and there in spots and slips that the land rises above the level of the water in times of inundation. There are, then, and ever must be, so few inhabitants on her part of the river, that the freest use of its navigation may be admitted to us without their annoyance. For authorities on this subject, see Grot. l. 2. c. 2 § 11, 12, 13, c. 3. § 7, 8, 12. Puffendorf, l. 3. c. 3. § 3, 4, 5, 6. Wolff's Inst. § 310, 311, 312. Vattel, l. 1. § 292. l. 2. § 123 to 139.

It is essential to the interests of both parties that the navigation of the river be free to both, on the footing on which it was defined by the treaty of Paris, *viz.:* through its whole breadth. The channel of the Mississippi is remarkably winding, crossing and recrossing perpetually from one side to the other of the general bed of the river. Within the elbows thus made by the channel, there is generally an eddy setting upwards, and it is by taking advantage of these eddies, and constantly crossing from one to another of them, that boats are enabled to ascend the river. Without this right the whole river would be impracticable both to the Americans and Spaniards.

It is a principle that the right to a thing gives a right to the means, without which it could not be used, that is to say, that the means follow their end. Thus, a right to navigate a river, draws to it a right to moor vessels to its shores, to land on them in cases of distress, or for other necessary purposes, &c. This principle is founded in natural reason, is evidenced by the common sense of mankind, and declared by the writers before quoted. See Grot. l. 2. c. 2. § 15. Puffend. l. 3. c. 3. § 8. Vattel, l. 2. § 129.

The Roman law, which, like other municipal laws, placed the navigation of their rivers on the footing of nature, as to their own citizens, by declaring them public,[2] (*flumina publica sunt, hoc est populi Romani,* Inst. 2. t. 1. § 2), declared also that the right to the use of the shores was incident to that of the water. Ibid, § 1, 3, 4, 5. The laws of every country probably do the same. This must have been so understood between France and Great Britain, at the treaty of Paris, when a right was ceded to British subjects to navigate the whole river, and expressly that part between the island of New Orleans and the western bank, without stipulating a word about the use of the shores, though both of them belonged then to France, and were to belong immediately to Spain. Had not the use of the shores been considered as incident to that of the water, it would have been expressly stipulated; since its necessity was too obvious to have escaped either party. Accordingly, all British subjects used the shores habitually for the purposes necessary to the navigation of the river; and when a Spanish Governor undertook at one time to forbid this, and even cut loose the vessels fastening to their shores, a British frigate went immediately, moored itself to the shore opposite to the town of New Orleans, and set out guards with orders to fire on such as might attempt to disturb her moorings. The Governor acquiesced, the right was constantly exercised afterwards, and no interruption ever offered.

This incidental right extends even beyond the shores, when circumstances render it necessary to the exercise of the principal right; as, in the case of a vessel damaged, where the mere shore could not be a safe deposit for her cargo till she could be repaired, she may remove it into safe ground off the river. The Roman law shall be quoted here too, because it gives a good idea both of the extent and the limitations of this right. Ins. l. 2. t. 1. § 4. [3] *Riparum quoque usus publicus est, ut volunt jura gentium, sicut et ipsius fluminis usus publicus est. Itaque et navigium ad ripes appellere, et funes de arboribus ibi natis religare, et navis onera in his locis reponere, liberum quique est sicuti nec per flumen ipsum navigare quisquam prohibetur.* And again, § 5, [4] *littorum quoque usus publicus, sive juri gentium est, ut et ipsius*

[2] Rivers belong to the public, that is to say to the Roman people.—T. J.

[3] "The use of the banks belongs also to the public by the laws of nations, as the use of the river itself does. Therefore, everyone is free to moor his vessel to the bank, to fasten his cables to the trees growing on it, to deposit the cargo of his vessel in those places in like manner as everyone is free to navigate the river itself."—T. J.

[4] "The use of the shores also belongs to the public, or is under the law of nations, as is that

*maris et ob id data est facultas volentibus, casas ibi sibi componere, in quas se recipere possint,* &c. Again, § 1. [5] *Nemo igitur ad littora maris accedere prohibitur; veluti deambulare aut navem appellere, sic tamen ut a villis, id est domiciliis monumentisque ibi positis, et ab edificiis abstineat, nec iis damnum inferat.*

Among incidental rights are those of having pilots, buoys, beacons, land-marks, light-houses, &c., to guide the navigators. The establishment of these at joint expense, and under joint regulations, may be the subject of a future convention. In the meantime, both should be free to have their own, and refuse those of the other, both as to use and expense.

Very peculiar circumstances attending the river Mississippi, require that the incidental right of accommodation on the shore, which needs only occasional exercise on other rivers, should be habitual and constant on this. Sea vessels cannot navigate that river, nor the river vessels go to sea. The navigation would be useless then without an entrepôt where these vessels might safely deposit their own cargoes, and take those left by the others; and where warehouses and keepers might be constantly established for the safeguard of the cargoes. It is admitted, indeed, that the incidental right thus extended into the territory of the bordering inhabitants, is liable to stricter modifications in proportion as it interferes with their territorial right. But the inconveniences of both parties are still to have their weight, and reason and moderation on both sides are to draw the line between them. As to this, we count much on the liberality of Spain, on her concurrence in opinion with us, that it is for the interest of both parties to remove completely this germ of discord from between us, and draw our friendship as close as circumstances proclaim that it should be, and on the considerations which make it palpable that a convenient spot placed under our exclusive occupation, and exempted from the jurisdiction and police of their government, is far more likely to preserve peace than a mere free port, where eternal altercations would keep us in eternal ill humor with each other. The policy of this measure, and indeed of a much larger concession, having been formerly sketched in a paper of July 12th, 1790, sent to the commissioners severally, they are now referred to that.

If this be agreed to, the manner of fixing on that extra territorial spot becomes highly interesting. The most desirable to us, would be a permission to send commissioners to choose such spot, below the town of New Orleans, as they should find most convenient.

If this be refused, it would be better now to fix on the spot. Our informa-

of the sea itself. Therefore, it is, that those who choose, have a right to build huts there, into which they may betake themselves."—T. J.

[5] "Nobody, therefore, is prohibited from landing on the sea shore, walking there, or mooring their vessel there, so nevertheless that they keep out of the villas, that is, the habitations, monuments, and public buildings, erected there, and do them no injury."—T. J.

tion is, that the whole country below the town, and for sixty miles above it, on the western shore, is low, marshy, and subject to such deep inundation for many miles from the river, that if capable of being reclaimed at all by banking, it would still never afford an entrepôt sufficiently safe; that on the eastern side the only lands below the town, not subject to inundation, are at the Detour aux Anglais, or English Turn, the highest part of which, is that whereon the fort St. Marie formerly stood. Even this is said to have been raised by art, and to be very little above the level of the inundations. This spot then is what we would fix on, if obliged now to decide, with from one to as many square miles of the circumjacent lands as can be obtained, and comprehending expressly the shores above and below the site of the fort as far as possible. But as to the spot itself, the limits, and even whether it shall be extra territorial, or only a free port, and what regulations it shall be laid under, the convenience of that Government is entitled to so much respect and attention on our part, that the arrangement must be left to the management of the commissioners, who will doubtless use their best efforts to obtain all they can for us.

The worst footing on which the determination of the ground could be placed, would be a reference to joint commissioners; because their disagreement, a very probable, nay, a certain event, would undo the whole convention, and leave us exactly where we now are. Unless indeed they will engage to us, in case of such disagreement, the highest ground at the Detour aux Anglais, of convenient extent, including the landings and harbor thereto adjacent. This would ensure us that ground, unless better could be found and mutually preferred, and close the delay of right under which we have so long labored for peace-sake.

It will probably be urged, because it was urged on a former occasion, that, if Spain *grants* to us the right of navigating the Mississippi, other nations will become entitled to it by virtue of treaties giving them the rights of the *most favored nation*.

Two answers may be given to this:

1. When those treaties were made, no nations could be under contemplation but those then existing, or those at most who might exist under similar circumstances. America did not then exist as a nation; and the circumstances of her position and commerce, are so totally dissimilar to everything then known, that the treaties of that day were not adapted to any such being. They would better fit even China than America; because, as a manufacturing nation, China resembles Europe more. When we solicited France to admit our whale oils into her ports, though she had excluded all foreign whale oils, her minister made the objection now under consideration, and the foregoing answer was given. It was found to be solid; and the whale oils of the United States are in consequence admitted, though those of Portugal and

the Hanse towns, and of all other nations, are excluded. Again, when France and England were negotiating their late treaty of commerce, the great dissimilitude of our commerce (which furnishes raw materials to employ the industry of others, in exchange for articles whereon industry has been exhausted) from the commerce of the European nations (which furnishes things ready wrought only) was suggested to the attention of both negotiators, and that they should keep their nations free to make particular arrangements with ours, by communicating to each other only the rights of the most favored European nation. Each was separately sensible of the importance of the distinction; and as soon as it was proposed by the one, it was acceded to by the other, and the word *European* was inserted in their treaty. It may fairly be considered then as the rational and received interpretation of the diplomatic term, *"gentis amicissimæ,"* that it has not in view a nation unknown in many cases at the time of using the term, and so dissimilar in all cases as to furnish no ground of just reclamation to any nation.

But the decisive answer is, that Spain does not grant us the navigation of the river. We have an inherent right to it; and she may repel the demand of any other nation by candidly stating her act to have been, what in truth it is, a recognition only, and not a grant.

If Spain apprehends that other nations may claim access to our ports in the Mississippi, under their treaties with us, giving them a right to come and trade in all our ports, though we would not choose to insert an express stipulation against them, yet we shall think ourselves justified to acquiesce in fact, under any regulations Spain may from time to time establish against their admission.

Should Spain renew another objection, which she relied much on before that the English at the Revolution treaty could not cede to us what Spain had taken from them by conquest, and what of course they did not possess themselves, the preceding observations furnish sufficient matter for refutation.

To conclude the subjects of boundary and navigation, each of the following conditions is to be considered by the commissioners as a sine qua non.

1. That our southern boundary remain established at the completion of thirty-one degrees of latitude on the Mississippi, and so on to the ocean, as has been before described, and our western one along the middle of the channel of the Mississippi, however that channel may vary, as it is constantly varying, and that Spain cease to occupy or to exercise jurisdiction in any part northward or eastward of these boundaries.

2. That our right be acknowledged of navigating the Mississippi, in its whole breadth and length, from its source to the sea, as established by the treaty of 1763.

3. That neither the vessels, cargoes, or the persons on board, be stopped,

visited, or subjected to the payment of any duty whatsoever; or, if a visit must be permitted, that it be under such restrictions as to produce the least possible inconvenience. But it should be altogether avoided, if possible, as the parent of perpetual broils.

4. That such conveniences be allowed us ashore, as may render our right of navigation practicable and under such regulations as may bona fide respect the preservation of peace and order alone, and may not have in object to embarrass our navigation, or raise a revenue on it. While the substance of this article is made a sine qua non, the modifications of it are left altogether to the discretion and management of the commissioners.

We might add, as a fifth sine qua non, that no phrase should be admitted in the treaty which could express or imply that we take the navigation of the Mississippi as a *grant* from Spain. But, however disagreeable it would be to subscribe to such a sentiment, yet, were the conclusion of a treaty to hang on that single objection, it would be expedient to waive it, and to meet, at a future day, the consequences of any resumption they may pretend to make, rather than at present, those of a separation without coming to any agreement.

We know not whether Spain has it in idea to ask a compensation for the ascertainment of our right.

1. In the first place, she cannot in reason ask a compensation for yielding what we have a right to, that is to say, the navigation of the river, and the conveniences incident to it of natural right.

2. In the second place, we have a claim on Spain for indemnification for nine years' exclusion from that navigation, and a reimbursement of the heavy duties (not less for the most part than 15 per cent on extravagant valuations) levied on the commodities she has permitted to pass to New Orleans. The relinquishment of this will be no unworthy equivalent for any accommodations she may indulge us with, beyond the line of our strict right. And this claim is to be brought into view in proper time and manner, merely to be abandoned in consideration of such accommodations. We have nothing else to give in exchange. For as to territory, we have neither the right nor the disposition to alienate an inch of what belongs to any member of our Union. Such a proposition, therefore, is totally inadmissible, and not to be treated of for a moment.

3. On the former conferences on the navigation of the Mississippi, Spain chose to blend with it the subject of commerce; and, accordingly, specific propositions thereon passed between the negotiators. Her object, then, was to obtain our renunciation of the navigation, and to hold out commercial arrangements, perhaps as a lure to us; perhaps, however, she might then, and may now, really set a value on commercial arrangements with us, and may receive them as a consideration for accommodating us in the naviga-

tion; or, may wish for them, to have the appearance of receiving a consideration. Commercial arrangements, if acceptable in themselves, will not be the less so if coupled with those relating to navigation and boundary. We have only to take care that they be acceptable in themselves.

There are two principles which may be proposed as the basis of a commercial treaty: 1. That of exchanging the privileges of *native citizens;* or,

2. Those of *the most favored nation.*

1. With the nations holding important possessions in America, we are ready to exchange the rights of native citizens, provided they be extended through the whole possessions of both parties, but the propositions of Spain, made on the former occasion, (a copy of which accompanies this,) were, that we should give their merchants, vessels, and productions, the privilege of native merchants, vessels, and productions, through the whole of our possessions, and they give the same to ours only in Spain and the Canaries. This is inadmissible, because unequal; and, as we believe that Spain is not ripe for an equal exchange on this basis, we avoid proposing it.

2. Though treaties, which merely exchange the rights of the most favored nations, are not without all inconvenience, yet they have their conveniences also. It is an important one, that they leave each party free to make what internal regulations they please, and to give what preferences they find expedient to native merchants, vessels, and productions. And as we already have treaties on this basis, with France, Holland, Sweden, and Prussia, the two former of which are perpetual, it will be but small additional embarrassment to extend it to Spain. On the contrary, we are sensible it is right to place that nation on the most favored footing, whether we have a treaty with them or not, and it can do us no harm to secure by treaty a reciprocation of the right.

Of the four treaties before mentioned, either the French or the Prussian might be taken as a model. But it would be useless to propose the Prussian; because we have already supposed that Spain would never consent to those articles which give to each party access to all the dominions of the other; and, without this equivalent, we would not agree to tie our own hands so materially in war, as would be done by the 23d article, which renounces the right of fitting out privateers, or of capturing merchant vessels. The French treaty, therefore, is proposed as the model. In this, however, the following changes are to be made.

We should be admitted to all the dominions of Spain, to which any other foreign nation is, or may be admitted.

Article 5 being an exemption from a particular duty in France, will of course be omitted, as inapplicable to Spain.

Article 8 to be omitted, as unnecessary with Morocco, and inefficacious, and little honorable with any of the Barbary powers. But it may furnish occasion to sound Spain on the project of a convention of the powers at war with the Barbary States, to keep up, by rotation, a constant cruise of a given force on their coasts, till they shall be compelled to renounce forever, and against all nations, their predatory practices. Perhaps the infidelities of the Algerines to their treaty of peace with Spain, though the latter does not choose to break openly, may induce her to subsidize *us* to cruise against them with a given force.

Article 9 and 10, concerning fisheries, to be omitted, as inapplicable.

Article 11. The first paragraph of this article, respecting the *droit d'aubaine,* to be omitted; that law being supposed peculiar to France.

Article 17, giving asylum in the ports of either to the armed vessels of the other, with the prizes taken from the enemies of that other, must be qualified as it is in the 19th article of the Prussian treaty; as the stipulation in the latter part of the article, "that no shelter or refuge shall be given in the ports of the one to such as shall have made prize on the subjects of the other of the parties," would forbid us in case of a war between France and Spain, to give shelter in our ports to prizes made by the latter on the former, while the first part of the article would oblige us to shelter those made by the former on the latter—a very dangerous covenant, and which ought never to be repeated in any other instance.

Article 29. Consuls should be received in all the ports at which the vessels of either party may be received.

Article 30, concerning free ports in Europe and America. Free ports in the Spanish possessions in America, and particularly at the Havana, San Domingo, in the island of that name, and St. John of Porto Rico, are more to be desired than expected. It can, therefore, only be recommended to the best endeavors of the commissioners to obtain them. It will be something to obtain for our vessels, flour, &c., admission to those ports during their pleasure. In like manner, if they could be prevailed on to re-establish our right of cutting log-wood in the bay of Campeachy, on the footing on which it stood before the treaty of 1763, it would be desirable, and not endanger, to us, any contest with the English, who, by the Revolution treaty, are restrained to the south-eastern parts of Yucatan.

Article 31. The *act* of ratification, on our part, may require a twelvemonth from the date of the treaty, as the Senate meets regularly but once a year; and to return it to Madrid, for exchange, may require four months more. It would be better, indeed, if Spain would send her ratification to be exchanged by her representative here.

The treaty must not exceed twelve or fifteen years' duration, except the clauses relating to boundary, and the navigation of the Mississippi, which must be perpetual and final. Indeed, these two subjects had better be in a separate instrument.

There might have been mentioned a third species of arrangement, that of making special agreements on every special subject of commerce, and of setting a tariff of duty to be paid on each side, on every particular article; but this would require in our commissioners a very minute knowledge of our commerce, as it is impossible to foresee every proposition of this kind which might be brought into discussion, and to prepare them for it by information and instruction from hence. Our commerce, too, is, as yet, rather in a course of experiment, and the channels in which it will ultimately flow, are not sufficiently known to enable us to provide for it by special agreement. Nor have the exigencies of our new government, as yet, so far developed themselves, as that we can know to what degree we may or must have recourse to commerce for the purposes of revenue. No common consideration, therefore, ought to induce us, as yet, to arrangements of this kind. Perhaps nothing should do it with any nation, short of the privileges of natives in all their possessions, foreign and domestic.

It were to be wished, indeed, that some positively favorable stipulations respecting our grain, flour, and fish, could be obtained, even on our giving reciprocal advantages to some other commodities of Spain, say her wines and brandies.

But, 1st. If we quit the ground of the *most favored nation,* as to certain articles for our convenience, Spain may insist on doing the same for other articles for her convenience, and thus our commissioners will get themselves on the ground of a treaty of *detail,* for which they will not be prepared.

2d. If we grant favor to the wines and brandies of Spain, then Portugal and France will demand the same; and in order to create an equivalent, Portugal may lay a duty on our fish and grain, and France, a prohibition on our whale oils, the removal of which will be proposed as an equivalent.

This much, however, as to grain and flour, may be attempted. There has, not long since, been a considerable duty laid on them in Spain. This was while a treaty on the subject of commerce was pending between us and Spain, as that court considers the matter. It is not generally thought right to change the state of things pending a treaty concerning them. On this consideration, and on the motive of cultivating our friendship, perhaps the commissioners may induce them to restore this commodity to the footing on which it was, on opening the conferences with Mr. Gardoqui, on the 26th day of July, 1785. If Spain says, "do the same by your tonnage on our vessels," the answer may be, that our foreign tonnage affects Spain very little, and other nations very much; where as the duty on flour in Spain affects us very much, and other nations very little. Consequently, there would be no equality in reciprocal relinquishment, as there had been none in the reciprocal innovation; and Spain, by insisting on this, would, in fact, only be aiding the interests of her rival nations, to whom we should be forced to extend the same indulgence. At the time of opening the conferences, too, we had, as yet, not erected any system; our government itself being not yet erected. Innovation then was unavoidable on our part, if it be innovation to establish a system. We did it on fair and general ground; on ground favorable to Spain. But they had a system, and, therefore, innovation was avoidable on their part.

It is known to the commissioners that we found it expedient to ask the interposition of France, lately, to bring on this settlement of our boundary, and the navigation of the Mississippi. How far that interposition has contributed to produce it, is uncertain. But we have reason to believe that her further interference would not produce an agreeable effect on Spain. The commissioners, therefore, are to avoid all further communications on the subject with the ministers of France, giving them such explanations as may preserve their good dispositions. But if, ultimately, they shall find themselves unable to bring Spain to agreement on the subject of the navigation and boundary, the interposition of France, as a mutual friend, and the guarantee of our limits, is then to be asked, in whatever light Spain may choose to consider it.

Should the negotiations on the subject of navigation and boundary assume, at any time, an unhopeful aspect, it may be proper that Spain should be given to understand, that, if they are discontinued without coming to any agreement, the Government of the United States cannot be responsible for the longer forbearance of their western inhabitants. At the same time the abandonment of the negotiation should be so managed as that, without engaging us to a further suspension of the exercise of our rights, we may not be committed to resume them on the instant. The present turbid situation of Europe cannot leave us long without a safe occasion of resuming our territory and navigation, and of carving for ourselves those conveniences, on the shores, which may facilitate and protect the latter effectually and permanently.

We had a right to expect that, pending a negotiation, all things would have remained in *statu quo,* and that Spain would not have proceeded to possess herself of other parts of our territory. But she has lately taken and fortified a new post on the Walnut hills, above the mouth of the Yazoo river, and far above the 31st degree. This garrison ought to have been instantly dislodged; but for our wish to be in friendship with Spain, and our confidence in her assurances "to bide by the limits established in our treaty with England," complaints of this unfriendly and uncandid procedure may be brought forward or not, as the commissioners shall see expedient.

# INSTRUCTIONS TO ANDREW MICHAUD FOR EXPLORING THE WESTERN BOUNDARY

January, 1793

Sundry persons having subscribed certain sums of money for your encouragement to explore the country along the Missouri, and thence westwardly to the Pacific ocean, having submitted the plan of the enterprise to the directors of the American Philosophical Society, and the society having accepted of the trust, they proceed to give you the following instructions:

They observe to you that the chief objects of your journey are to find the shortest and most convenient route of communication between the United States and the Pacific ocean, within the temperate latitudes, and to learn such particulars as can be obtained of the country through which it passes, its productions, inhabitants, and other interesting circumstances. As a channel of communication between these States and the Pacific ocean, the Missouri, so far as it extends, presents itself under circumstances of unquestioned preference. It has, therefore, been declared as a fundamental object of the subscription (not to be dispensed with) that this river shall be considered and explored as a part of the communication sought for. To the neighborhood of this river, therefore, that is to say, to the town of Kaskaskia, the society will procure you a conveyance in company with the Indians of that town now in Philadelphia.

From thence you will cross the Mississippi and pass by land to the nearest part of the Missouri above the Spanish settlements, that you may avoid the risk of being stopped.

You will then pursue such of the largest streams of that river as shall lead by the shortest way and the lowest latitudes to the Pacific ocean. When, pursuing those streams, you shall find yourself at the point from whence you may get by the shortest and most convenient route to some principal river of the Pacific ocean, you are to proceed to such river, and pursue its course to the ocean. It would seem by the latest maps as if a river called Oregon, interlocked with the Missouri for a considerable distance, and entered the Pacific ocean not far southward of Nootka Sound. But the society are aware that these maps are not to be trusted so far as to be the ground of any positive instruction to you. They therefore only mention the fact, leaving to yourself to verify it, or to follow such other as you shall find to be the real truth.

You will in the course of your journey, take notice of the country you pass through, its general face, soil, rivers, mountains, its productions—animal, vegetable, and mineral—so far as they may be new to us, and may also be useful or very curious; the latitudes of places or material for calculating it by such simple methods as your situation may admit you to practice, the names, members, and dwellings of the inhabitants, and such particulars as you can learn of their history, connection with each other, languages, manners, state of society, and of the arts and commerce among them.

Under the head of animal history, that of the mammoth is particularly recommended to your inquiries, as it is also to learn whether the Lama or Paca of Peru, is found in those parts of this continent, or how far north they come.

The method of preserving your observations is left to yourself, according to the means which shall be in your power. It is only suggested that the noting them on the skin might be best for such as may be the most important, and that further details may be committed to the bark of the paper-birch, a substance which may not excite suspicions among the Indians, and little liable to injury from wet or other common accidents. By the means of the same substance you may perhaps find opportunities, from time to time, of communicating to the society information of your progress, and of the particulars you shall have noted.

When you shall have reached the Pacific ocean, if you find yourself within convenient distance of any settlement of Europeans, go to them, commit to writing a narrative of your journey and observations, and take the best measure you can for conveying it thence to the society by sea.

Return by the same, or some other route, as you shall think likely to fulfil with most satisfaction and certainty the objects of your mission, furnishing yourself with the best proofs the nature of the case will admit of the reality and extent of your progress. Whether this shall be by certificates from Europeans settled on the western coast of America, or by what other means, must depend on circumstances. Ignorance of the country through which you are to pass, and confidence in your judgment, zeal, and discretion, prevent the society from attempting more minute instructions, and even from exacting rigorous observance of those already given, except, indeed, what is the first of all objects, that you seek for and pursue that route which shall form the shortest and most convenient communication between the higher parts of the Missouri and the Pacific ocean.

It is strongly recommended to you to expose yourself in no case to unnecessary dangers, whether such as might affect your health or your personal safety, and to consider this not merely as your personal concern, but as the injunction of science in general, which expects its enlargement from your inquiries, and of the inhabitants of the United States in particular, to whom your report will open new fields and subjects of commerce, intercourse, and observation.

If you reach the Pacific ocean and return, the society assign to you all the benefits of the subscription before mentioned. If you reach the waters only which run into that ocean, the society reserve to themselves the apportionment of the reward according to the conditions expressed in the subscription. If you do not reach even those waters they refuse all reward, and reclaim the money you may have received here under the subscription.

They will expect you to return to the city of Philadelphia to give in to them a full narrative of your journey and observations, and to answer the inquiries they shall make of you, still reserving to yourself the benefit arising from the publication of such parts of them as are in the said subscription reserved to you.

## THE LIMITS AND BOUNDS OF LOUISIANA [1]

September 7, 1803

### AN EXAMINATION INTO THE BOUNDARIES OF LOUISIANA

The French having for a century and a half been in possession of Canada, and its inhabitants penetrating to the remote waters communicating with the St. Laurence, they learned of the Indians that, in the neighborhood of those waters, arose a great river, called the Missisipi [*sic*], running due South to the sea, and through a fine country unpossessed by any white nation. In 1673 the Sieurs Joliet and Marquette, two Canadians, undertook to explore it, descended the Missisipi as far as the river Arkansa, in 33° and returned to Canada. Their account of it inflamed the enterprise of M. de la Salle, who in 1675, went to France to solicit authority to explore the Missisipi. He obtained it, returned to Canada, and in 1680 went as far as the river Illinois, on the lower part of which he built and garrisoned a fort called Crevecoeur, and sent the father Hennepin with 2 men to push his discoveries down the Mis̃ipi as far as he could; and, as preparatory to a more formal essay, going himself Northwardly. Hennepin descended the Mis̃ipi to the ocean, and returned with the information collected, to the Illinois. In 1682 La Sale and Tonti undertook their expedition; went down the river with 60 men, named

[1] On December 30, 1817, Jefferson sent this manuscript to the American Philosophical Society in Philadelphia, together with a letter to Peter S. Du Ponceau, the Corresponding Secretary of the Society, explaining the circumstances under which it was written: "While on the subject of Louisiana, I have thought I had better commit to you also an historical Memoir of my own respecting the important question of its limits. When we first made the purchase, we knew little of its extent, having never before been interested to enquire into it. Possessing then in my library every thing respecting America which I had been able to collect by unremitting researches, during my residence in Europe particularly, and generally through my life, I availed myself of the leisure of my succeeding autumnal recess from Washington, to bring together every thing which my collection furnished on the subject of its boundary. The result was the Memoire I now send you, copies of which were furnished to our Ministers at Paris and Madrid, for their information as to the extent of territory claimed under our purchase."

The original is in the archives of the American Historical Society. It was published in 1904, by Houghton Mifflin & Co., under the title: *Documents Relating to the Purchase & Exploration of Louisiana.*

The spelling of proper names is retained as in the original.

the country Louisiana, built a fort in the Chickasaw country, 60 leagues below the Ohio, which they called Prudhomme, reached the ocean, and returned to Canada the ensuing year 1683.

La Sale then went to France, to obtain the means of going thence to the Mišipi directly by sea. In the mean time some Canadians descend the river, and settle near its mouth, and along the coast Eastwardly, to the island of Massacre, opposite Mobile. The government of France, entering at once into the view of extending an united possession along the St. Laurence and Mišipi, from sea to sea equips la Sale with 4 vessels, on board of which were 280 persons, of whom 100 were officers and soldiers furnished with all necessaries. He sailed in July 1684 from Rochelle, and missing the mouth of the Missisipi, landed February 18, 1685, in the Bay of St. Bernard to the West of it. Here he takes possession, makes two successive establishments, building and garrisoning forts at each, the second of which was called St. Louis.

The Chevalier Tonti, about this time, sets out from Canada in quest of La Sale, whom he supposed to be then on the Mišipi, descends with 40 men to the mouth of the river, reconnoitres the coast 20 leagues East and West; finding nothing of La Sale, he ascends the river, builds a house on the river Arkansa, and leaves 10 men in it, which becomes a permanent settlement, and he returns to Canada.

In 1686 La Sale attempts to penetrate from fort St. Louis to the Illinois by land, but is obliged to return. In 1687 he makes another attempt with 17 men, and is murdered on the way by some of his own people. Cavelier, brother of La Sale, undertakes the same enterprise with 7 men; they find the house on the Arkansa built by Tonti, with only two men remaining in it; they leave a third, strike the Mišipi, and reach Canada. Tonti descends the river a second time, finds two Frenchmen who had separated from Cavelier settled at the Coroas, and returns to the Illinois.

In 1689 a war commenced between France and Spain, which continuing till the treaty of Ryswick in 1697 suspended the aids of France to her colony: but in 1698 D'Iberville was sent as its governor with recruits. He discovers the mouths of the Mišipi, and settles his new recruits at Isle Massacre, which he calls Isle Dauphine, and at Mobile, where they find the Canadians who had settled there in 1683. Spain had, during the war, to wit, in 1696 taken a counter-post at Pensacola.

The result from these facts is that France had formal and actual possession of the coast from Mobile to the bay of St. Bernard, and from the mouth of the Mišipi up into the country as far as the river Illinois. The nearest Spanish settlements at this time were on the River Panuco, to the West, 100 leagues from the Mišipi, and at Pensacola, to the East . . . leagues distant. There does not appear as yet indeed to have been any formal declaration of the limits of Louisiana: but the practice of nations, on making discoveries in America, has sanctioned a principle that "when a nation takes possession of any extent of sea-coast, that possession is understood as extending into the interior country to the sources of the rivers emptying within that coast, to all their branches, and the country they cover." I. Mem. de l'Amerique 116. It was in support of this principle of virtual and declared possession, that France entered into the war of 1755 against Great Britain, whose settlements began now to reach the Eastern waters of the Misipi, and who opposed the claim of France, not on a denial of this principle, but on a prior possession taken and declared by repeated charters, through the space of an hundred years preceding, as extending from sea to sea. France then had possession of the Misipi, and all the waters running into it, and of the sea coast and all its rivers and territories on them from Mobile to the bay of St. Bernard. The river Perdido, midway between the adversary possessions of Mobile and Pensacola, became afterwards the settled boundary between Spain and France, in the East, and the Rio Norte, or Bravo, midway between the bay of St. Bernard and the river Panuco, the then nearest settlement of Spain, was considered by France, if not by Spain, and on the same fair grounds as in the other quarter, as the boundary between them in the West. Besides being midway between the actual possessions of the two nations, that river formed a natural and well marked boundary, extending very far into the country Northwardly. And accordingly we find by several [2] maps, some of them published by authority of the French government, and some Spanish maps, that France claimed to that river. This claim has not been abridged, as far as is known, by any public treaty; and those which are secret, if any such have taken place, cannot bind nations having no notice of them, and succeeding fairly to the rights of France, as publicly avowed and believed to exist.[3]

But the extent of Louisiana into the interior country is not left merely on the principle of its dependency on the coast into which its waters disembogue: not on the settlements extending up its great rivers, the Misipi, the Missouri, and the Illinois; but on an authoritative and public document announcing its extent, and making a temporary disposition of it. This is the Letter patent of September 14, 1712, by which Louis XIV grants to the Sieur Anthony Crozat the exclusive commerce of that country for 15 years. The following extracts from it ascertain the extent of the country.

[2] I possess three ancient maps which mark the Rio bravo and it's Eastern branch as the dividing boundary between Louisiana and Mexico. 1. Moll's map of the West Indies and adjacent countries. 2. Moll's map of Louisiana etc. published in 1720 in which the South Western parts of Louisiana are said to be copied from a French map published in Paris in 1718, and 3. Homann's Spanish map of Louisiana of about the same date.—T. J.

[3] To this may be added the verbal declaration of the French Commissioner to those of the U.S. on the delivery of possession, that his positive instructions from his government were to take possession to the Rio Bravo.—T. J.

"Louis by the grace of god, king of France and Navarre to all &c.

"The care we have always had to procure the welfare and advantage of our subjects having induced us &c. to seek for all possible opportunities of enlarging and extending the trade of our American colonies, we did, in the year 1683 give our orders to undertake a discovery of the countries and lands which are situated in the Northern part of America, between New France and New Mexico: and the Sieur de la Sale, to whom we committed that enterprise, having had success enough to confirm a belief that communication might be settled from *New France to the gulph of Mexico,* by means of large rivers; this obliged us, immediately after the peace of Ryswick, to give orders for the establishing a colony there, and maintaining a garrison, *which has kept and preserved the possession we had taken in the very year 1683* of the lands, coasts and islands which are situated in the gulph of Mexico, between Carolina on the East, and Old and New Mexico on the West. But a new war having broke out in Europe shortly after, there was no possibility till now, of reaping from that new colony the advantages that might have been expected from thence &c. And whereas upon the information we have received, concerning the disposition and situation of the *said countries known at present by the name of the province of Louisiana,* we are of opinion that there may be established therein a considerable commerce &c. we have resolved to grant the commerce of the country of Louisiana to the Sieur Anthony Crozat &c. For these reasons &c. we, by these presents, signed by our hand, have appointed, and do appoint the said Sieur Crozat to carry on a trade in all the lands possessed by us, and bounded by New Mexico, and by the lands of the English of Carolina, all the establishment, ports, havens, rivers, and principally the port and haven of the Isle Dauphine, heretofore called Massacre, the *river of St. Louis, heretofore called Missisipi,* from the edge of the sea as far as the [4] Illinois; together with *the river St. Philip, heretofore called the Missourys,* and of *St. Jerome, heretofore called Ouabache,* with *all the countries, territories, lakes within land, and the rivers which fall directly or indirectly* into that part of the river St. Louis."

THE ARTICLES. I. Our pleasure is that all the aforesaid *lands, countries, streams, rivers and islands* be, and remain *comprised under the name of the government of Louisiana,* which shall be dependent upon the general government of New France, to which it is subordinate: and further that all the lands which we possess from the Illinois be united &c. to the general government of New France, and become part thereof &c.' [here follow 15 other articles relating to commerce only] "Given at Fontainebleau the 14th day of September in the year of grace 1712 and of our reign the 70th. Louis. By the king. Phelipeaux."

Here then is a solemn and public declaration sufficiently special to shew that all the waters running directly or indirectly into the Mis̃ipi, and the

[4] The French and Spaniards called by the name of *the Illinois,* or Illinois country, the whole country on both sides of the Upper Mis̃ipi. That on the Eastern side was called East Illinois, that on the West side West Illinois.—T. J.

country embraced by them, are held and acted on by France, under the name of the province of Louisiana; and is a full and unequivocal supplement, if any supplement were necessary, to the titles derived, 1, from the actual settlements on the river and its waters, 2, from the possession of the coast, and 3, from the principle which annexes to it all the depending waters. The treaties of Ryswick, in 1697, where France and Spain were adversary powers, and those of Utrecht in 1713, and Rastadt in 1714, where they were allies, by their silence, as well as by their provisions, as to these countries, must be considered as sanctioning the rights of France to this province: to which add the progress made by France, undisturbed and unquestioned, by Spain, in extending her settlements *ad libitum* within them, till 1763. It is true that in 1715 some Spaniards made small settlements at the Assinais, and Adais, and in 1722 attempted one on the Missouri. The last was prevented by the Indians, and the former were connived at by the Agents of France to favor a smuggling commerce with New Mexico. But these contraband encroachments cannot weigh as evidence of ownership against the possession taken by France 30 years before, and the solemn establishment of boundary by Louis XIV.

War breaking out between them in 1718, the French took Pensacola; the Spaniards retook it, but the French recovered and retained it till the peace in 1719 when it was restored to Spain; and from this epoch the river Perdido has been the acknowledged and undisturbed boundary between Louisiana and Florida.

The boundaries of Louisiana then, as held by France, were the sea-coast and islands from the river Perdido to the Rio Norte or Bravo, then up the Rio Bravo to its source; thence to the highlands encompassing the waters of the Mišipi, and along those highlands round the heads of the Missouri and Mišipi and their waters to where those highlands assume the name of the Alleganey or Apalachian mountains, thence along those mountains, and the highlands encompassing the waters of the Mobile, to the source of the Perdido, and down that to the ocean.

In opposition to these claims, both of France and Spain, were those of the then English colonies, now the U.S. whose charters extended from sea to sea, and consequently covered all Louisiana and Mexico, above the parallel of latitude which formed the Southern boundary of Georgia. These adversary claims were settled by the war of 1755-1763 and the treaty of Paris which closed it, and which made the Mišipi and Iberville the Western limit of the English possessions, and thenceforward the Eastern limit of Louisiana.

This war had begun between France and England, Spain being unconcerned in the grounds of it. In the beginning, France had sensibly the advantage, but after awhile its successes were signally on the side of England. In 1762 Spain entered into it as a volunteer and ally of France. Great Britain immediately attacked and took the town of Havanna, and an important portion of the island of Cuba; which imminently endangering the continental possessions of Spain within the gulf, and her communication with them, negociations for peace were very soon set on foot. Great Britain, in exchange for her conquest in Cuba, required Florida, and that part of Louisiana from the Perdido to the Iberville. Besides the just sympathy which France felt for Spain, who had sustained this incalculable loss by friendly endeavors to aid her, she was bound by the family compact, lately renewed, Article XVIII, "to consider the interests of Spain as her own, and to share in its losses and advantages." A considerable change too had taken place in the minds of the government of France, against the possession of distant colonies, which could not be protected but by a great navy. France therefore, by a secret treaty, November 3, 1762 (being the same day on which they publicly signed the preliminary articles with Great Britain), consented to cede all Louisiana to Spain, in order to enable her, by the sacrifice of such part of it as she thought proper, to ransom Cuba, and to indemnify her for the loss of Florida, required also by Great Britain to make up the equivalent. The portion of Louisiana from Iberville to Perdido therefore, ceded to Great Britain by the definitive treaty of February 10, 1763, did in substance move from Spain to Great Britain, although France, as not having publicly conveyed it to Spain, was the formal conveyor to England. Yet she acted herein merely as the friend and agent of Spain, who was become in truth the real proprietor of all Louisiana. The importance of seeing this translation in its true light will hereafter appear.

England immediately laid off this portion of Louisiana, with so much of Florida as laid West of the Apalachicola, into a separate government, to which she gave the name of West Florida; and the residue of Florida into another government, to which she gave the name of East Florida. And Spain, now proprietor of Louisiana, and of course free to curtail its future boundary to the Westward, according to her own convenience, extended the limits and jurisdiction of New Mexico to the waters of the river Mexicana inclusively. But this cannot disprove the former extent of Louisiana, as it had been held and ceded by France; but was done in virtue of the right ceded by France.

The war of 1775-1783 began between Great Britain and the U.S. but France and Spain at length became parties to it. By the treaty of Paris of 1783 which terminated it, Great Britain was constrained to restore to Spain Florida, and the territory East of the Iberville, which she had received at the close of the former was in exchange for Cuba. If the portion of Louisiana comprised in it had really moved from France, then the restitution of the portion between Iberville and Perdido should have been to France, and that of Florida only to Spain. But as the whole had moved substantially from Spain, the whole was restored to her. On re-entering into possession August 18, 1769, she continued the English annexation of the Eastern portion of Louisiana with a part of Florida, under the name of West Florida; restoring however the whole to the jurisdiction of the Governor of Louisiana, residing at New Orleans: and in public[5] instruments, as well as in common parlance that portion has been spoken of under the names of Louisiana, or of West Florida indifferently.

The nation of France had seen with considerable dissatisfaction the separation of Louisiana from the mother country. That province had ever been viewed by it with great partiality. It was inhabited by their relations and fellow citizens: and they considered Spain, in the immensity of her possessions, as not entitled to such a sacrifice from France. Besides she had now got back both Florida and Cuba: and there was no justice in her continuing to retain Louisiana, which had been ceded to her only as an indemnification for the loss of one, and the means of getting back the other. As soon therefore as the successful administration of the first Consul of France had raised her into a condition for re-demanding from other nations what she deemed her rights, Spain was required to make restitution of Louisiana, under the friendly cover indeed of an exchange, but its inequality shews it was but a cover. The real grounds of restitution required that it should not be mutilated, but full and entire as she received it. For what had she ever given for it? She was completely replaced in her ancient possessions. On what just ground then could she propose to retain any portion of the equivalent ceded only as an indemnity for them? Accordingly a complete retro-cession was provided for the treaty of St. Ildefonso of October 1, 1800, by definitions studiously formed to reach every thing which had been ceded to or for her by France. By that instrument she re-cedes to France the colony or province of Louisiana, with the same extent, 1, that it now has in the hands of Spain, 2, that it had when France possessed it, and 3, such as it ought to be after the treaties passed subsequently between Spain and other powers. That is 1, she is to recede the ancient country of Louisiana, as it is now recovered back into the hands of Spain and held by her under the name of Louisiana, or West Florida, or Mexico, or by whatever other names she or other powers may since have chosen to designate certain parts of it, or to sever it by overlapping Mexico on its West, and West Florida on its Eastern quarter: she is to recede the *thing*, as it is in her hands, unaffected by new names. To make it still plainer, she is to retrocede it 2dly with the same extent that it had when France possessed it. Now France never possessed it one day with any less extent than from the Perdido to the Rio Norte, and inland to the sources of all its rivers. The whole of this extent she transferred on the same day by two treaties of equal date, to wit, all Westward of the

[5] One of these was deposited in the office of state.—T. J.

Misipi and Iberville to Spain, and all Eastward to Great Britain. But, of the Eastern portion, Spain having since recovered back all below 31° of latitude, that, with the Western side, composes Louisiana, as now in the hands of Spain, and as it had been possessed by France. But, not to disturb the right of the U.S. to the portion North of 31° and to shew that it was only so much of the Louisiana held by France, as *was now in the hands of Spain,* it is expressly limited 3dly to be such as it ought to be after the treaties passed *subsequently* between Spain and other powers. *Subsequently* to what? To the cession of the country by France. When was that session? November 3, 1762, and February 10, 1763. What are the treaties subsequent to this? Those affecting the limits of Louisiana are the treaty of September 3, 1783, with Great Britain, and that of October 27, 1795, with the U.S. The former was a restitution, by Great Britain to Spain, of Florida, and the portion of Louisiana from the Perdido to the Iberville: and consequently, *after this treaty,* the extent of Louisiana *ought to be,* as again consolidated to the Perdido. But inasmuch as by the latter of these two treaties, Spain had confirmed to the U.S. a degree of latitude [from 32° to 31°] which she had long contended to be an unceded part of Louisiana, and consequently not within the limits of the U.S., therefore by this provision, that right is saved to the U.S. and the extent of Eastern Louisiana, *after this treaty, ought to be* only to the latitude of 31°.

Should it be alleged that this confirmation of the diminutions of Louisiana by treaties subsequent to its alienation by France, goes to the treaty of 1763 with Great Britain also; the answer is that this treaty was *simultaneous* with the alienation, and not subsequent to it, and therefore could not be within the scope of this definition. The confirmation too is in favor of treaties made *by Spain,* with other nations. That with Great Britain is by *France and Spain.* But it might also be justly observed that Louisiana was not lessened in its dimensions by that treaty; it was only divided, the Eastern portion thereof transferred to Great Britain, the Western to Spain; who might new-name a part of it West Florida, and a part Mexico, for their internal purposes, as they pleased; but when the portion newly called West Florida came back to *the hands of Spain,* it was still a part of ancient Louisiana, *as possessed by France, as now in the hands of Spain,* and unalienated by subsequent treaties of Spain with other powers.

On the whole, the intention of the treaty of St. Ildefonso is clearly this. France had in 1763 generously ceded all Louisiana to, or for Spain. Spain consented that the Eastern portion of it, below Georgia, together with her Florida, should go to recover Cuba. Afterwards however, in another war, by the arms of France and of the U.S. (for Spain came in late, and then did little more than waste her resources on the rock of Gibraltar) she recovers back, and has secured to her, her ancient Florida, and the Eastern portion of Louisiana, below Georgia. The treaty of St. Ildefonso therefore meant to review this whole transaction, and to restore France and Spain to the *Status quo* prior to the war of 1755-63. Spain being now in possession of her original colonies of Florida and Cuba, it was just, and was meant, that France should also be reinstated in Louisiana, so far as Spain, while it was in her hands, had not transferred portions of it by permanent alienations to other powers. She confined her reclamation therefore to the part of her ancient possession which was in the hands of Spain, not touching the portions which had been validly transferred to the U.S.

If Spain then were not to deliver the country from the Iberville and Mis̃ipi to the Perdido, this would not be delivering Louisiana with the extent it had when France possessed it, and before it had ever been dismembered: nor with the extent it *now* has in the hands of Spain, since it has been restored to its ancient and integral form: nor such as it ought to be after the treaty subsequently passed with England in 1783. And we trust that these definitions are too exact and unequivocal, and Spain too just, to admit any doubt of what we are entitled to demand, and she bound to deliver.

Whatever Louisiana was, as retroceded by Spain to France, such exactly it is, as ceded by France to the U.S. by the treaty of Paris of April 30, 1803.

P.S. The Northern Boundary of Louisiana, Coterminous with the Possessions of England.

January 15, 1804

The limits of Louisiana have been spoken of in the preceding statement, as if those established to the West and North, by the charter of Louis XIV remained still unaltered. In the West they are so, as already explained. But, in the North, a material change has taken place. With this however it was unnecessary to complicate our subject, while considering the interest of Spain alone: because the possessions of Great Britain, and not of Spain, are coterminous with Louisiana on its Northern boundary. We will now therefore proceed to examine the state of that boundary, as between Great Britain and the U.S.

Disputes having arisen between Great Britain and France as to the limits between Canada and Louisiana on the one side, and the countries of the Hudson's bay, and North Western companies on the other, it was agreed by the treaty of Utrecht (1713) Art. X, that "Commissaries should be forthwith named by each party to determine the limits between the bay of Hudson and the places appertaining to the French, and to describe and settle the boundaries between the other British and French colonies in those parts" these Commissaries accordingly fixed the Northern boundaries of Canada and Louisiana, by a line beginning on the Atlantic, at a Cape or Promontory in 58°-30′ N. Lat. thence South Westwardly to the lake Misgosink, or Mistasin, thence farther S.W. to the lat. of 49° North from the Equator, and along that line indefinitely. [Hutchins' topographical description of Louisiana, page 7.] Thus the Northern boundary of Canada and Louisiana became fixed, and the latter particularly became changed to the parallel of 49° from the Equator, instead of the highlands inclosing the Northern waters running directly or indirectly into the Mišipi, as settled by Louis XIV. Canada being, by the peace of 1763 transferred to England, its Southern boundary was settled by the treaty of 1783 with the U.S. along the St. Croix and highlands bounding the Southern waters of the St. Laurence, the 45th degree of latitude to the water communication between the lakes, and along that communication to the lake of the woods; whence the line of the U.S. was to run due West, till it should strike the Missisipi. Now, according to the maps of that time, and particularly Mitchell's [6] on which the boundary of 1783 was predicated, the line of 49° passes through the Southern part of the lake of the Woods: and the North Western point of the lake of the Woods, as observed by Thompson, Astronomer to the North West company, is in Lat. 49°-37′. [McKenzie's 2 voyage chapter 13.] At that lake therefore the English negotiators ceased to pursue the water communication, because, South of the latitude of that lake, they owned nothing: and to have followed the water line further Northwardly, would have broken in upon the continuity of their Southern boundary. Canada was thus closed to the West, by its Northern and Southern limits meeting in a point in the lake of the Woods. It was at that time believed that the Missisipi, heading North of 49° would have been intersected by that line of latitude, and our possessions consequently closed. But subsequent information rendered it probable that that river did not extend so far North; (it is now said only to 47°.38′) and consequently that there was an unclosed space between its source and the lake of the woods. Without undertaking to decide what were the limits dividing Great Britain and Spain in that quarter, we concluded it would be safest to settle, as occasions should offer, our boundary there with both nations, on the principle of "*valeat quantum valere potest*" with each. Having to form a convention with England for ascertaining our limits in the North Eastern quarter, we took that occasion for closing, as far as depended on her right, the vacancy in our North Western angle; and therefore proposed it to her. While negociations were going on at London for this purpose, an opportunity occurred of our acquiring Louisiana: and the stipulations being promptly concluded, a treaty for that acquisition was actually signed at Paris twelve days before that of London was concluded. But this treaty was not known to the negociators of either party at London; nor could the rights acquired by it, be effected by arrangements instituted and compleated there

[6] The identical map used by the negociators, with their MS. marks on it, is deposited in the office of state.—T. J.

merely for the purpose of explaining and supplying the provisions in the treaty of 1783. In result, this acquisition rendered these explanations unnecessary, and the Vth article respecting them merely nugatory. For England holding nothing in that quarter Southward of 49° the line proposed in the Vth article, from the North Western point of the lake of the Woods Southwardly to the nearest source of the Mis̃ipi, is through a country, not belonging to her, but now to the U.S. Consequently the consent of no other nation can now be necessary to authorize it. It may be run, or not, and in any direction which suits ourselves. It has become a merely municipal object respecting the line of division which we may chuse to establish between two of our territories. It follows then that the Vth Article of the Convention of London of May 12, 1803, should be expunged, as nugatory; and that instead of it, should be substituted one declaring that the dividing line between Lousiana and the British possessions adjacent to it, shall be from the North Western point of the Lake of the Woods, along the water edge Westwardly to its intersection with the parallel of 49°. North from the Equator, then along that parallel (as established by the treaty of Utrecht between Great Britain and France) until it shall meet the limits of the Spanish province next adjacent. And it would be desirable to agree further that, if that parallel shall, in any part, intersect any waters of the Missouri, then the dividing line shall pass round all those waters to the North until it shall again fall into the same parallel, or meet the limits of the Spanish province next adjacent. Or, unapprised that Spain has any right as far North as that, and Westward of Louisiana, it may be as well to leave the extent of the boundary of 49° indefinite, as was done on the former occasion.

# *Chapter VIII*

# POLITICS AND POLITICAL THEORY

## THE NEED FOR REBELLION[1]

January 30, 1787

Those characters, wherein fear predominates over hope, may . . . conclude too hastily, that nature has formed man insusceptible of any other government than that of force, a conclusion not founded in truth nor experience. Societies exist under three forms, sufficiently distinguishable. 1. Without government, as among our Indians. 2. Under governments, wherein the will of everyone has a just influence; as is the case in England, in a slight degree, and in our States, in a great one. 3. Under governments of force; as is the case in all other monarchies, and in most of the other republics. To have an idea of the curse of existence under these last, they must be seen. It is a government of wolves over sheep. It is a problem, not clear in my mind, that the first condition is not the best. But I believe it to be inconsistent with any great degree of population. The second state has a great deal of good in it. The mass of mankind under that, enjoys a precious degree of liberty and happiness. It has its evils, too; the principal of which is the turbulence to which it is subject. But weigh this against the oppressions of monarchy, and it becomes nothing. *Malo periculosam libertatem quam quietam servitutem.* Even this evil is productive of good. It prevents the degeneracy of government, and nourishes a general attention to the public affairs. I hold it, that a little rebellion, now and then, is a good thing, and as necessary in the political world as storms in the physical. Unsuccessful rebellions, indeed, generally establish the encroachments on the rights of the people, which have produced them. An observation of this truth should render honest republican governors so mild in their punishment of rebellions, as not to discourage them too much. It is a medicine necessary for the sound health of government.

[1] Letter to James Madison.

# CONFLICT WTH HAMILTON[1]

September 9, 1792

I now take the liberty of proceeding to that part of your letter wherein you notice the internal dissensions which have taken place within our government, and their disagreeable effect on its movements. That such dissensions have taken place is certain, and even among those who are nearest to you in the administration. To no one have they given deeper concern than myself; to no one equal mortification at being myself a part of them. Though I take to myself no more than my share of the general observations of your letter, yet I am so desirous ever that you should know the whole truth, and believe no more than the truth, that I am glad to seize every occasion of developing to you whatever I do or think relative to the government; and shall, therefore, ask permission to be more lengthy now than the occasion particularly calls for, or could otherwise perhaps justify.

When I embarked in the government, it was with a determination to intermeddle not at all with the Legislature, and as little as possible with my co-departments. The first and only instance of variance from the former part of my resolution, I was duped into by the Secretary of the Treasury, and made a tool for forwarding his schemes, not then sufficiently understood by me; and of all the errors of my political life, this has occasioned me the deepest regret. It has ever been my purpose to explain this to you, when, from being actors on the scene, we shall have become uninterested spectators only. The second part of my resolution has been religiously observed with the War Department; and as to that of the Treasury, has never been further swerved from than by the mere enunciation of my sentiments in conversation, and chiefly among those who, expressing the same sentiments, drew mine from me. If it has been supposed that I have ever intrigued among the members of the Legislature to defeat the plans of the Secretary of the Treasury, it is contrary to all truth. As I never had the desire to influence the members, so neither had I any other means than my friendships, which I valued too highly to risk by usurpation on their freedom of judgment, and the conscientious pursuit of their own sense of duty. That I have utterly, in my private conversations, disapproved of the system of the Secretary of the Treasury, I acknowledge and avow; and this was not merely a speculative difference. His system flowed from principles adverse to liberty, and was calculated to undermine and demolish the Republic, by creating an influence of his department over the members of the Legislature. I saw this influence actually produced, and its first fruits to be the establishment of the great outlines of his project by the votes of the very persons who, having swallowed

[1] Letter to President Washington.

his bait, were laying themselves out to profit by his plans; and that had these persons withdrawn, as those interested in a question ever should, the vote of the disinterested majority was clearly the reverse of what they made it. These were no longer the votes then of the representatives of the people, but of deserters from the rights and interests of the people; and it was impossible to consider their decisions, which had nothing in view but to enrich themselves, as the measures of the fair majority, which ought always to be respected. If, what was actually doing, begat uneasiness in those who wished for virtuous government, what was further proposed was not less threatening to the friends of the Constitution. For, in a report on the subject of manufactures (still to be acted on), it was expressly assumed that the General Government has a right to exercise all powers which may be for the *general welfare,* that is to say, all the legitimate powers of government; since no government has a legitimate right to do what is not for the welfare of the governed. There was, indeed, a sham limitation of the universality of this power *to cases where money is to be employed.* But about what is it that money cannot be employed? Thus the object of these plans, taken together, is to draw all the powers of government into the hands of the general Legislature, to establish means for corrupting a sufficient corps in that Legislature to divide the honest votes, and preponderate, by their own, the scale which suited, and to have the corps under the command of the Secretary of the Treasury, for the purpose of subverting, step by step, the principles of the Constitution which he has so often declared to be a thing of nothing, which must be changed. Such views might have justified something more than mere expressions of dissent, beyond which, nevertheless, I never went. Has abstinence from the department, committed to me, been equally observed by him? To say nothing of other interferences equally known, in the case of the two nations, with which we have the most intimate connections, France and England, my system was to give some satisfactory distinctions to the former, of little cost to us, in return for the solid advantages yielded us by them; and to have met the English with some restrictions which might induce them to abate their severities against our commerce. I have always supposed this coincided with your sentiments. Yet the Secretary of the Treasury, by his cabals with members of the Legislature, and by high-toned declamations on other occasions, has forced down his own system, which was exactly the reverse. He undertook, of his own authority, the conferences with the ministers of those two nations, and was, on every consultation, provided with some report of a conversation with the one or the other of them, adapted to his views. These views, thus made to prevail, their execution fell, of course, to me; and I can safely appeal to you, who have seen all my letters and proceedings, whether I have not carried them into execution as sincerely as if they had been my own, though I ever considered them as inconsistent with the honor and interest of our country. That they have been inconsistent with our interest is but too fatally proved by the stab to our navigation given by the French. So that if the question be by whose fault is it that Colonel Hamilton and myself have not drawn together? the answer will depend on that to two other questions, whose principles of administration best justify, by their purity, conscientious adherence? and which of us has, notwithstanding, stepped farthest into the control of the department of the other?

To this justification of opinions, expressed in the way of conversation, against the views of Colonel Hamilton, I beg leave to add some notice of his late charges against me in Fenno's Gazette; for neither the style, matter, nor venom of the pieces alluded to, can leave a doubt of their author. Spelling my name and character at full length to the public, while he conceals his own under the signature of "An American," he charges me, 1st. With having written letters from Europe to my friends to oppose the present Constitution, while depending. 2d. With a desire of not paying the public debt. 3d. With setting up a paper to decry and slander the government. 1st. The first charge is most false. No man in the United States, I suppose, approved of every tittle in the Constitution: no one, I believe, approved more of it than I did, and more of it was certainly disapproved by my accuser than by me, and of its parts most vitally republican. Of this the few letters I wrote on the subject (not half a dozen I believe) will be a proof; and for my own satisfaction and justification, I must tax you with the reading of them when I return to where they are. You will there see that my objection to the Constitution was, that it wanted a bill of rights securing freedom of religion, freedom of the press, freedom from standing armies, trial by jury, and a constant habeas corpus act. Colonel Hamilton's was, that it wanted a king and house of lords. The sense of America has approved my objection and added the bill of rights, not the king and lords. I also thought a longer term of service, insusceptible of renewal, would have made a President more independent. My country has thought otherwise, I have acquiesced implicitly. He wishes the General Government should have power to make laws binding the States in all cases whatsoever. Our country has thought otherwise: has he acquiesced? Notwithstanding my wish for a bill of rights, my letters strongly urged the adoption of the Constitution, by nine States at least, to secure the good it contained. I at first thought that the best method of securing the bill of rights would be for four States to hold off till such a bill should be agreed to. But the moment I saw Mr. Hancock's proposition to pass the Constitution as it stood, and give perpetual instructions to the representatives of every State to insist on a bill of rights, I acknowledged the superiority of his plan, and advocated universal adoption. 2d. The second charge is equally untrue. My whole correspondence while in France, and every word, letter and act on the subject, since my return, prove that no man is more ardently intent to see the public debt soon and sacredly paid off than I am. This exactly marks the difference between Colonel Hamilton's views and mine, that I would wish the debt paid tomorrow; he wishes it never to be paid, but always to be a thing wherewith to corrupt and manage the Legislature. 3d. I have never enquired what number of sons, relatives and friends of Senators, Representatives, printers or other useful partisans Colonel Hamilton has provided for among the hundred clerks of his department, the thousand excisemen, at his nod, and spread over the Union; nor could ever have imagined that the man who has the shuffling of millions backwards and forwards from paper into money and money into paper, from Europe to America, and America to Europe, the dealing out of treasury secrets among his friends in what time and measure he pleases, and who never slips an occasion of making friends with his means, that such an one, I say, would have brought forward a charge against me for having appointed the poet, Freneau, translating clerk to my office, with a salary of 250 dollars a year. That fact stands thus. While the government was at New York I was applied to on behalf of Freneau to know if there was any place within my department to which he could be appointed. I answered there were but four clerkships, all of which I found full, and continued without any change. When we removed to Philadelphia, Mr. Pintard, the translating clerk, did not choose to remove with us. His office then became vacant. I was again applied to there for Freneau, and had no hesitation to promise the clerkship for him. I cannot recollect whether it was at the same time, or afterwards, that I was told he had a thought of setting up a newspaper there. But whether then, or afterwards, I considered it a circumstance of some value, as it might enable me to do, what I had long wished to have done, that is, to have the material parts of the Leyden Gazette brought under your eye, and that of the public, in order to possess yourself and them of a juster view of the affairs of Europe than could be obtained from any other public source. This I had ineffectually attempted through the press of Mr. Fenno, while in New York, selecting and translating passages myself at first, then having it done by Mr. Pintard, the translating clerk, but they found their way too slowly into Mr. Fenno's papers. Mr. Bache essayed it for me in Philadelphia, but his being a daily paper, did not circulate sufficiently in the other States. He even tried, at my request, the plan of a weekly paper of recapitulation from his daily paper, in hopes that that might go into the other States, but in this too we failed. Freneau, as translating clerk, and the printer of a periodical paper likely to circulate through the States (uniting in one person the parts of Pintard and Fenno), revived my hopes that the thing could at length be effected. On the establishment of his paper, therefore, I furnished him with the Leyden Gazette, with an expression of my wish that he could always translate and publish the material intelligence they contained, and have continued to furnish them from time to time, as regularly as I received them. But as to any other direction or indication of my wish how his press should be conducted, what sort of intelligence he should give, what essays encourage, I can protest, in the presence of heaven, that I never did by myself, or any other, or indirectly, say a syllable, nor attempt any kind of influence. I can further protest, in the same awful presence, that I never did, by myself, or any other, directly or indirectly, write, dictate or procure any one sentence or sentiment to be inserted *in his, or any other gazette,* to which my name was not affixed or that of my office. I surely need not except here a thing so foreign to the present subject as a little paragraph about our Algerine captives, which I put once into Fenno's paper. Freneau's proposition to publish a paper, having been about the time that the writings of Publicola, and the discourses on Davila, had a good deal excited the public attention, I took for granted from Freneau's character, which had been marked as that of a good whig, that he would give free place to pieces written against the aristocratical and monarchical principles these papers had inculcated. This having been in my mind, it is likely enough I may have expressed it in conversation with others, though I do not recollect that I did. To Freneau I think I could not, because I had still seen him but once, and that was at a public table, at breakfast, at Mrs. Elsworth's, as I passed through New York the last year. And I can safely declare that my expectations looked only to the chastisement of the aristocratical and monarchical writers, and not to any criticisms on the proceedings of government. Colonel Hamilton can see no motive for any appointment, but that of making a convenient partizan. But you, Sir, who have received from me recommendations of a Rittenhouse, Barlow, Paine, will believe that talents and science are sufficient motives with me in appointments to which they are fitted; and that Freneau, as a man of genius, might find a preference in my eye to be a translating clerk, and make good title to the little aids I could give him as the editor of a gazette, by procuring subscriptions to his paper, as I did some before it appeared, and as I have with pleasure done for the labors of other men of genius. I hold it to be one of the distinguishing excellences of elective over hereditary successions, that the talents which nature has provided in sufficient proportion, should be selected by the society for the government of their affairs, rather than that this should be transmitted through the loins of knaves and fools, passing from the debauches of the table to those of the bed. Colonel Hamilton, alias "Plain Facts," says, that Freneau's salary began before he resided in Philadelphia. I do not know what quibble he may have in reserve on the word "residence." He may mean to include under that idea the removal of his family; for I believe he removed himself, before his family did, to Philadelphia. But no act of mine gave commencement to his salary before he so far took up his abode in Philadelphia, as to be sufficiently in readiness for the duties of the office. As to the merits or demerits of his paper, they certainly concern me not. He and Fenno are rivals for the public favor. The one courts them by flattery, the other by censure, and I believe it will be admitted that the one has been as servile, as the other severe. But is not the dignity, and even decency of government committed, when one of its principal ministers enlists himself as an anonymous writer or paragraphist for either the one or the other of them? No government ought to be without censors; and where the press is free, no one ever will. If virtuous, it need not fear the fair operation of attack and defence. Nature has given to man no other means of sifting out the truth, either in religion, law, or politics. I think it as honorable to the government neither to know, nor notice, its sycophants or censors, as it would be undignified and criminal to pamper the former and persecute the latter. So much for the past, a word now of the future.

When I came into this office, it was with a resolution to retire from it as soon as I could with decency. It pretty early appeared to me that the proper moment would be the first of those epochs at which the Constitution seems to have contemplated a periodical change or renewal of the public servants. In this I was confirmed by your resolution respecting the same period; from which, however, I am happy in hoping you have departed. I look to that period with the longing of a wave-worn mariner, who has at length the land in view, and shall count the days and hours which still lie between me and it. In the meanwhile, my main object will be to wind up the business of my office, avoiding as much as possible all new enterprise. With the affairs of the Legislature, as I never did intermeddle, so I certainly shall not now begin. I am more desirous to predispose everything for the repose to which I am withdrawing, than expose it to be disturbed by newspaper contests. If these however cannot be avoided altogether, yet a regard for your quiet will be a sufficient motive for my deferring it till I become merely a private citizen, when the propriety or impropriety of what I may say or do, may fall on myself alone. I may then, too, avoid the charge of misapplying that time which now, belonging to those who employ me, should be wholly devoted to their service. If my own justification, or the interests of the republic shall require it, I reserve to myself the right of then appealing to my country, subscribing my name to whatever I write, and using with freedom and truth the facts and names necessary to place the cause in its just form before that tribunal. To a thorough disregard of the honors and emoluments of office, I join as great a value for the esteem of my countrymen, and conscious of having merited it by an integrity which cannot be reproached, and by an enthusiastic devotion to their rights and liberty, I will not suffer my retirement to be clouded by the slanders of a man whose history, from the moment at which history can stoop to notice him, is a tissue of machinations against the liberty of the country which has not only received and given him bread, but heaped its honors on his head. Still, however, I repeat the hope that it will not be necessary to make such an appeal. Though little known to the people of America, I believe, that as far as I am known, it is not as an enemy to the Republic, nor an intriguer against it, nor a waster of its revenue, nor prostitutor of it to the purposes of corruption, as the "American" represents me; and I confide that yourself are satisfied that as to dissensions in the newspapers, not a syllable of them has ever proceeded from me, and that no cabals or intrigues of mine have produced those in the Legislature, and I hope I may promise both to you and myself, that none will receive aliment from me during the short space I have to remain in office, which will find ample employment in closing the present business of the department.

Observing that letters written at Mount Vernon on the Monday, and arriving at Richmond on the Wednesday, reach me on Saturday, I have now the honor to mention that the 22d instant will be the last of our post days that I shall be here, and consequently that no letter from you after the 17th, will find me here. Soon after that I shall have the honor of receiving at Mount Vernon your orders for Philadelphia, and of there also delivering you the little matter which occurs to me as proper for the opening of Congress, exclusive of what has been recommended in former speeches, and not yet acted on. In the meantime and ever I am, with great and sincere affection and respect, dear Sir, your most obedient, and most humble servant.

## NOTES ON PARTY POLICY [1]

1793

### AGENDA

Divide the Treasury department.
Abolish the bank.
Repeal the Excise law and let states raise the money.
Lower impost.
Treasurer to pay and receive cash not bills.
Repeal irredeemable quality and borrow at 4 per cent.
Exclude paper holders.
Condemn report of [Hamilton's report on foreign loans, January 3, 1793].

[1] These notes formed a sort of platform of the newly created Jeffersonian (Republican, now Democratic) party.

## CONCILIATION WITH THE FEDERALISTS [1]

### 1803

Federalism returning to reason, tho' not to good manners. No matter. Decency will come in turn, when outrages on it are found to reflect only on those who commit them.

The symptom of returning reason to those pitiable maniacs is the following paragraph in the N. York evening post of May 24, where, speaking of the removal of Mr. Rogers, the naval officer, a revolutionary tory, an Englishman and not even a citizen, till the expectation of office suggested to him the expediency of becoming one, and of the appointment of Mr. Osgood, a member of the Old Congress and President of its board of treasury, and postmaster general under the administration of General Washington, Mr. Coleman says "The Democrats have not long since had the imprudence and *contempt of truth* to declare, that, notwithstanding the removals, the Federalists hold still a great number of offices than they do themselves. In answer to which we have sometimes replied that, in point of value there was no comparison, and that every office of any value, *in this city* at least, if not in the U.S. except one, had been transferred to the Jeffersonian sect, and that one is now gone." And then he goes on with his usual scurrilities against the chief magistrate of his country, which shall not be here repeated; and with references to the President's reply to the New Haven remonstrance. I remember that in that reply it was asked whether it is political intolerance for the majority to claim a *proportionate share* in the direction of the public affairs? And, if a *due participation* of office is a matter of right, how is it to be obtained but by some removals, when nearly the whole offices of the U.S. are monopolized by a particular political sect? The reasonableness of this claim of *due proportion* of office was felt by every candid man at the first blush. But it did not accord with the feelings of Federalists. Nothing but a continuance in their monopoly of office could satisfy them: and, on the removal of the first individual, the whole band opened on the violation of their sanctuary of office, as if a general sweep had been made of every Federalist within its pale. After much uproar however repeated on every single re-

[1] Jefferson sent this article to Levi Lincoln, his Attorney-General, with the following note, written on June 1, 1803: "On reading a paragraph in the N. Y. Evening Post, I took up my pen to write a squib on it: but the subject ran away with me till I found I had written a treatise. It is one on which I have a great desire to reconcile the parties among the republicans . . . The interest I take in the question made me willing to hazard a few lines for the press, although I have through life scrupulously refrained from it; inasmuch that this is but the second instance of my being willing to depart from my rule. I have written it under the character of a Massachusetts citizen, with a view to its appearing in a paper there. The Chronicle I suppose is most read, but how to get it there [faded] of the evidence of my handwriting. Think of this if you please; correct the paper also to make it what it should be, and we will talk of it the first time we meet. Friendly salutations, and religious silence about it.

moval, not finding in the President that want of nerve which with atheism, hypocrisy, malice, &c &c 'c, they have so liberally lent him, but that on the contrary, regardless of their barking he proceeded steadily towards his object of restoring to the excluded republicans some participation in office, they find it expedient to lower their tone a little. They can now bear to talk themselves on an *equal number,* instead of a monopoly of offices. This is well, as a first symptom; and we hope, in the progress of convalescence, they will become able to bear the idea of a *due proportion.* On this ground we are ready to compromise with them: and I ask what is their due proportion? I suppose the relative numbers of the two parties will be thought to fix it; and that, judging from the elections, we over-rate the Federalists at one third or fourth of the whole mass of our citizens. In a few states, say New Hampshire, Massachusetts, and Connecticut, they have a greater proportion; but in the others much less. By Mr. Coleman's expression that every office in this city [New York] is transferred to the Jeffersonian sect, it seems expected that the distribution of office, in every town and county taken by itself is to be in proportion to its party division. This is impossible. It is questionable whether the scale of proportion can even be known and preserved in individual states, and whether we must not be contented with considering all the states as forming a single mass. I am not qualified to say, taking the state of New York by itself, how its parties are proportioned either in numbers or in offices. But I think it probable that, if Mr. Coleman will extend his views beyond the limits of the city, through the whole state, he will find his brethren possessing much more than their *due share* of office. I invite him to this examination, and doubt not that the republicans of New York will attend to his statements, and correct them if erroneous.

Confining myself to my own state, that I may speak only of what I know, I can assure Mr. Coleman that we are far below our *just proportion.* The Roll of offices published by Congress at their session before the last, informs me that in the revenue department alone of Massachusetts, there are 183 officers; of whom 33 are appointed by the President. Of these he has removed 7 either on the principle of participation, or because they were active, bitter and indecent opposers of the existing legislature and Executive. I will name them that I may be corrected if I am wrong, not meaning willfully to misstate anything. They were, Lee of Penobscot, Head of Waldoborough, Tuck and Whittermore of Gloucester, Tyng of Newburyport, Fosdyck of Portland, and Pickman of Salem. There have been two or three other removals in this state, but we have understood they were for misconduct. In Boston alone are about 30 revenue officers dependent on the collector, who, with the naval officer, surveyor and revenue inspectors, receive under the general government between 40 and 50,000 D. a year, the whole weight of whose numbers, patronage and connections is actively exerted in opposition to that government, and renders the issue of the Boston election always doubtful; when, if shifted into the scale which is in support of the government, there would no longer be any question, and Boston, one of the great cities of the U.S. would arrange herself, at her proper post, under the banners of the Union. And at the head of this massive phalanx is a character, otherwise respectable and meritorious; but certainly not so when leading processions and joining in dinners, where toasts the most insulting and outrageous against the President personally and other constituted authorities, and calculated to excite seditious combinations against the authority of the union, are drank with riotous acclamations within and announced with the law of cannon without. If Mr. Coleman counts the continuance of this gentleman in office among the proofs of the intolerance of the President, I can furnish him more such. In the judiciary department we had imagined, that the judges being federal, republican attorneys and marshals would be appointed to mollify in the execution what is rigorously decreed; and that republicans might find in our courts some of that protection which flows from fellow-feeling, while their opponents enjoy that which the laws are made to pronounce. In some of the states this has been done. But here I see Mr. Bradford still holding the office of marshal, to execute federally what the judges shall federally decree: an office too of great patronage and influence in this state, and acting with all its dependencies heavily in our elections. While in the expressions of my opinion I yield sincere respect to the authorities of my country, due to their own worth, as well as to the will of the nation establishing them, yet I am free to declare my opinion, that they are wrong in retaining this person in office. I respect his private character; but his political bias unfits him for qualifying that of the court. In the post-offices of Massachusetts are about 200 officers. I know not how many may have been removed by the postmaster General, but judging by the sound in the federal papers, which is never below truth, I should conjecture a very small proportion indeed. It should be observed too that these offices are solely within the gift and removal of the Post Master General, the President and Senate having nothing to do with them.

Hitherto I have spoken of the Federalists as if they were a homogeneous body, but this is not the truth. Under that name lurks the heretical sect of monarchists. Afraid to wear their own name they creep under the mantle of federalism, and the federalists, like sheep, permit the fox to take shelter among them, when pursued by the dogs. These men have no right to office. If a monarchist be in office anywhere, and it be known to the President, the oath he has taken to support the constitution imperiously requires the instantaneous dismission of such officer; and I should hold the President highly criminal if he permitted such to remain. To appoint a monarchist to conduct the affairs of a republic, is like appointing an atheist to the priesthood, but as to the real Federalists, I take them to my bosom as brothers: I view them as honest men, friends to the present constitution. Our difference has been about measures only, which now having passed away should no longer divide us. It was how we should treat France for the injuries offered us. They thought the occasion called for Armies and navies, that we should burthen ourselves with taxes, and our posterity with debts at exorbitant interest: that we should pass alien and sedition laws, punishing men with exile without trial by jury, and usurping the regulation of the press, exclusively belonging to the state governments. We thought some of these measures inexpedient, others unconstitutional. They, however, were the majority, they carried their opinions into effect, and we submitted. The measures themselves are now done with, except the debts contracted, which we are honestly proceeding to pay off. Why then should we longer be opposed to each other? I confess myself of opinion that this portion of our fellow-citizens should have a just participation of office, and am far from concurring with those who advocate a general sweep, without discriminating between Federalist and Monarchist. Should not these recollect their own complaints against the late administration for proscribing them from all public trust? And shall we now be so inconsistent as to act ourselves on the very principle we then so highly condemned! To countenance the anti-social doctrine that a minority has no rights? Never let *us* do wrong, because our opponents did so. Let us, rather, by doing right, shew them what they ought to have done, and establish a rule the dictates of reason and conscience, rather than of the angry passions.

If the Federalists will amalgamate with us on these terms, let us receive them, and once more unite our country into one mass. But, as they seem to hold off with a remarkable repugnance, I agree that in the meantime both justice and safety require a due proportion of office in republican hands. Whether it is best to effect this by a single stroke, or to await the operation of deaths, resignations, and removals for delinquency, for virulent opposition, and monarchism, I am not satisfied: but am willing to leave it to the constitutional authorities, who, though they proceeded slower than I have expected, yet are probably better judges than I am of the comparative merits of the two methods. The course they seem to have preferred tends more perhaps to allay the passions which so unpleasantly divide and disquiet us; and trusted as they are, with the care of the public happiness, they are bound so to modify jarring principles as to affect that happiness as far as the state of things will admit. This seems too to be a fair ground of compromise between the extremes of opinion, even among republicans, some of whom think there should be a general removal, and others none at all. The latter opinion, I am told, is much entertained in the southern states. Still I think it will be useful to go into the examination of the question which party holds an over-proportion of office? And I therefore, again invite Mr. Coleman to take the field for the state of New York, not doubting that some champion there will enter the lists for the opposite interest. In my own state the fact is so obvious that I believe no Federalists here will undertake to question it. Should anyone however appear, he will certainly find persons able and ready to confront him with facts.

"FAIR PLAY"

## ARISTOCRACY AND LIBERTY[1]

October 28, 1813

The passage you quote from Theognis, I think has an ethical rather than a political object.[2] The whole piece is a moral *exhortation,* παραινεςις, and this passage particularly seems to be a reproof to man, who, while with his domestic animals he is curious to improve the race, by employing always the finest male, pays no attention to the improvement of his own race, but intermarries with the vicious, the ugly, or the old, for considerations of wealth or ambition. It is in conformity with the principle adopted afterwards by the Pythagoreans, and expressed by Ocellus in another form; "περι δε τῆς ἐκ των αλληλων ανθρωπων γενεσεως, etc.—ουχ ηδουησενεκα η μιξις" which, as literally as intelligibility will admit, may be thus translated: "concerning the interprocreation of men, how, and of whom it shall be, in a perfect manner, and according to the laws of modesty and sanctity, conjointly, this is what I think right. First to lay it down that we do not commix for the sake of pleasure, but of the procreation of children. For the powers, the organs and desires for coition have not been given by God to man for the sake of pleasure, but for the procreation of the race. For as it were incongruous, for a mortal born to partake of divine life, the immortality of the race being taken away, God fulfilled the purpose by making the generations uninterrupted and continuous. This, therefore, we are especially to lay down as a principle, that coition is not for the sake of pleasure." But nature, not trusting to this moral and abstract motive, seems to have provided more securely for the perpetuation of the species, by making it the effect of the *oestrum*

[1] Letter to John Adams.

[2] On July 9, 1813, Adams wrote to Jefferson, mentioning a book of moral sentences from the ancient Greek poets: "In one of the oldest of them, I read in Greek, that I cannot repeat, a couplet, the sense of which was: 'Nobility in men is worth as much as it is in horses, asses, or rams; but the meanest blooded puppy in the world, if he gets a little money, is as good a man as the best of them.' Yet birth and wealth together have prevailed over virtue and talents in all ages. The many will acknowledge no other *αριστοι*."

On September 15, 1813, Adams wrote him again: "I asked you in a former letter how far advanced we were in the science of aristocracy since Theognis' Stallions, Jacks and Rams? Have not Chancellor Livingston and Major General Humphreys introduced an hereditary aristocracy of Merino Sheep? How shall we get rid of this aristocracy? It is entailed upon us forever. And an aristocracy of land jobbers and stock jobbers is equally and irremediably entailed upon us, to endless generations." Jefferson's reply is given above.

implanted in the constitution of both sexes. And not only has the commerce of love been indulged on this unhallowed impulse, but made subservient also to wealth and ambition by marriage, without regard to the beauty, the healthiness, the understanding, or virtue of the subject from which we are to breed. The selecting the best male for a Harem of well chosen females also, which Theognis seems to recommend from the example of our sheep and asses, would doubtless improve the human, as it does the brute animal, and produce a race of veritable αριςτοι. For experience proves, that the moral and physical qualities of man, whether good or evil, are transmissible in a certain degree from father to son. But I suspect that the equal rights of men will rise up against this privileged Solomon and his Harem, and oblige us to continue acquiescence under the "Αμαυρωςις γενεος αςτων" which Theognis complains of, and to content ourselves with the accidental aristoi produced by the fortuitous concourse of breeders. For I agree with you that there is a natural aristocracy among men. The grounds of this are virtue and talents. Formerly, bodily powers gave place among the aristoi. But since the invention of gunpowder has armed the weak as well as the strong with missile death, bodily strength, like beauty, good humor, politeness and other accomplishments, has become but an auxiliary ground of distinction. There is also an artificial aristocracy, founded on wealth and birth, without either virtue or talents; for with these it would belong to the first class. The natural aristocracy I consider as the most precious gift of nature, for the instruction, the trusts, and government of society. And indeed, it would have been inconsistent in creation to have formed man for the social state, and not to have provided virtue and wisdom enough to manage the concerns of the society. May we not even say, that that form of government is the best, which provides the most effectually for a pure selection of these natural aristoi into the offices of government? The artificial aristocracy is a mischievous ingredient in government, and provision should be made to prevent its ascendency. On the question, what is the best provision, you and I differ; but we differ as rational friends, using the free exercise of our own reason, and mutually indulging its errors. You think it best to put the pseudo-aristoi into a separate chamber of legislation, where they may be hindered from doing mischief by their co-ordinate branches, and where, also, they may be a protection to wealth against the Agrarian and plundering enterprises of the majority of the people. I think that to give them power in order to prevent them from doing mischief, is arming them for it, and increasing instead of remedying the evil. For if the co-ordinate branches can arrest their action, so may they that of the co-ordinates. Mischief may be done negatively as well as positively. Of this, a cabal in the Senate of the United States has furnished many proofs. Nor do I believe them necessary to protect the wealthy; because enough of these will find their way into every branch of the legislation, to protect themselves. From fifteen to twenty legislatures of our own, in action for thirty years past, have proved that no fears of an equalization of property are to be apprehended from them. I think the best remedy is exactly that provided by all our constitutions, to leave to the citizens the free election and separation of the aristoi from the pseudo-aristoi, of the wheat from the chaff. In general they will elect the really good and wise. In some instances, wealth may corrupt, and birth blind them; but not in sufficient degree to endanger the society.

It is probable that our difference of opinion may, in some measure, be produced by a difference of character in those among whom we live. From what I have seen of Massachusetts and Connecticut myself, and still more from what I have heard, and the character given of the former by yourself (vol. 1, page 111), who know them so much better, there seems to be in those two States a traditionary reverence for certain families, which has rendered the offices of the government nearly hereditary in those families. I presume that from an early period of your history, members of those families happening to possess virtue and talents, have honestly exercised them for the good of the people, and by their services have endeared their names to them. In coupling Connecticut with you, I mean it politically only, not morally. For having made the Bible the common law of their land, they seem to have modeled their morality on the story of Jacob and Laban. But although this hereditary succession to office with you, may, in some degree, be founded in real family merit, yet in a much higher degree, it has proceeded from your strict alliance of Church and State. These families are canonised in the eyes of the people on common principles, "you tickle me, and I will tickle you." In Virginia we have nothing of this. Our clergy, before the revolution, having been secured against rivalship by fixed salaries, did not give themselves the trouble of acquiring influence over the people. Of wealth, there were great accumulations in particular families, handed down from generation to generation, under the English law of entails. But the only object of ambition for the wealthy was a seat in the King's Council. All their court then was paid to the crown and its creatures; and they Philipised in all collisions between the King and the people. Hence they were unpopular; and that unpopularity continues attached to their names. A Randolph, a Carter, or a Burwell must have great personal superiority over a common competitor to be elected by the people even at this day. At the first session of our legislature after the Declaration of Independence, we passed a law abolishing entails. And this was followed by one abolishing the privilege of primogeniture, and dividing the lands of intestates equally among all their children, or other representatives. These laws, drawn by myself, laid the axe to the foot of pseudo-aristocracy. And had another which I prepared been adopted by the legislature, our work would have been complete. It was a bill for the more general diffusion of learning. This proposed to divide every county into wards of five or six miles square, like your townships; to establish in each ward a free school for reading, writing and common arithmetic; to provide for the annual selection of the best subjects from these schools, who might receive, at the public expense, a higher degree of education at a district school; and from these district schools to select a certain number of the most promising subjects, to be completed at an University, where all the useful sciences should be taught. Worth and genius would thus have been sought out from every condition of life, and completely prepared by education for defeating the competition of wealth and birth for public trusts. My proposition had, for a further object, to impart to these wards those portions of self-government for which they are best qualified, by confiding to them the care of their poor, their roads, police, elections, the nomination of jurors, administration of justice in small cases, elementary exercises of militia; in short, to have made them little republics, with a warden at the head of each, for all those concerns which, being under their eye, they would better manage than the larger republics of the county or State. A general call of ward meetings by their wardens on the same day through the State, would at any time produce the genuine sense of the people on any required point, and would enable the State to act in mass, as your people have so often done, and with so much effect by their town meetings. The law for religious freedom, which made a part of this system, having put down the aristocracy of the clergy, and restored to the citizen the freedom of the mind, and those of entails and descents nurturing an equality of condition among them, this on education would have raised the mass of the people to the high ground of moral respectability necessary to their own safety, and to orderly government; and would have completed the great object of qualifying them to select the veritable aristoi, for the trusts of government, to the exclusion of the pseudalists; and the same Theognis who has furnished the epigraphs of your two letters, assures us that "Ουδεμιαν πω, Κυρν', αγαθοι πολιν ωλεςαν ανδρες." Although this law has not yet been acted on but in a small and inefficient degree, it is still considered as before the legislature, with other bills of the revised code, not yet taken up, and I have great hope that some patriotic spirit will, at a favorable moment, call it up, and make it the key-stone of the arch of our government.

With respect to aristocracy, we should further consider, that before the establishment of the American States, nothing was known to history but the man of the old world, crowded within limits either small or overcharged, and steeped in the vices which that situation generates. A government adapted to such men would be one thing; but a very different one, that for the man of these States. Here everyone may have land to labor for himself, if he chooses; or, preferring the exercise of any other industry, may exact for it such compensation as not only to afford a comfortable subsistence, but wherewith to provide for a cessation from labor in old age. Everyone, by his property, or by his satisfactory situation, is interested in the support of law and order. And such men may safely and advantageously reserve to themselves a wholesome control over their public affairs, and a degree of freedom, which, in the hands of the *canaille* of the cities of Europe, would be instantly perverted to the demolition and destruction of everything public and private. The history of the last twenty-five years of France, and of the last forty years in America, nay of its last two hundred years, proves the truth of both parts of this observation.

But even in Europe a change has sensibly taken place in the mind of man. Science had liberated the ideas of those who read and reflect, and the American example had kindled feelings of right in the people. An insurrection has consequently begun, of science, talents, and courage, against rank and birth, which have fallen into contempt. It has failed in its first effort, because the mobs of the cities, the instrument used for its accomplishment, debased by ignorance, poverty, and vice, could not be restrained to rational action. But the world will recover from the panic of this first catastrophe. Science is progressive, and talents and enterprise on the alert. Resort may be had to the people of the country, a more governable power from their principles and subordination; and rank, and birth, and tinsel-aristocracy will finally shrink into insignificance, even there. This, however, we have no right to meddle with. It suffices for us, if the moral and physical condition of our own citizens qualifies them to select the able and good for the direction of their government, with a recurrence of elections at such short periods as will enable them to displace an unfaithful servant, before the mischief he meditates may be irremediable.

I have thus stated my opinion on a point on which we differ, not with a view to controversy, for we are both too old to change opinions which are the result of a long life of inquiry and reflection; but on the suggestions of a former letter of yours, that we ought not to die before we have explained ourselves to each other. We acted in perfect harmony, through a long and perilous contest for our liberty and independence. A constitution has been acquired, which, though neither of us thinks perfect, yet both consider as competent to render our fellow citizens the happiest and the securest on whom the sun has ever shone. If we do not think exactly alike as to its imperfections, it matters little to our country, which, after devoting to it long lives of disinterested labor, we have delivered over to our successors in life, who will be able to take care of it and of themselves.

Of the pamphlet on aristocracy which has been sent to you, or who may be its author, I have heard nothing but through your letter. If the person you suspect, it may be known from the quaint, mystical, and hyperbolical ideas, involved in affected, new-tangled and pedantic terms which stamp his writings. Whatever it be, I hope your quiet is not to be affected at this day by the rudeness or intemperance of scribblers; but that you may continue in tranquillity to live and to rejoice in the prosperity of our country, until it shall be your own wish to take your seat among the aristoi who have gone before you. Ever and affectionately yours.

## GOVERNMENT BY THE PEOPLE[1]

July 12, 1816

SIR: I duly received your favor of June the 13th, with the copy of the letters on the calling a convention, on which you are pleased to ask my opinion. I have not been in the habit of mysterious reserve on any subject, nor of buttoning up my opinions within my own doublet. On the contrary, while in public service especially, I thought the public entitled to frankness, and intimately to know whom they employed. But I am now retired: I resign myself, as a passenger, with confidence to those at present at the helm, and ask but for rest, peace and good will. The question you propose, on equal representation, has become a party one, in which I wish to take no public share. Yet, if it be asked for your own satisfaction only, and not to be quoted before the public, I have no motive to withhold it, and the less from you, as it coincides with your own. At the birth of our republic, I committed that opinion to the world, in the draught of a constitution annexed to the "Notes on Virginia," in which a provision was inserted for a representation permanently equal. The infancy of the subject at that moment, and our inexperience of self-government, occasioned gross departures in that draught from genuine republican canons. In truth, the abuses of monarchy had so much filled all the space of political contemplation, that we imagined everything republican which was not monarchy. We had not yet penetrated to the mother principle, that "governments are republican only in proportion as they embody the will of their people, and execute it." Hence, our first constitutions had really no leading principles in them. But experience and reflection have but more and more confirmed me in the particular importance of the equal representation then proposed. On that point, then, I am entirely in sentiment with your letters; and only lament that a copy-right of your pamphlet prevents their appearance in the newspapers, where alone they would be generally read, and produce general effect. The present vacancy too, of other matter, would give them place in every paper, and bring the question home to every man's conscience.

But inequality of representation in both Houses of our legislature, is not

[1] Letter to Samuel Kercheval.

the only republican heresy in this first essay of our revolutionary patriots at forming a constitution. For let it be agreed that a government is republican in proportion as every member composing it has his equal voice in the direction of its concerns (not indeed in person, which would be impracticable beyond the limits of a city, or small township, but), by representatives chosen by himself, and responsible to him at short periods, and let us bring to the test of this canon every branch of our constitution.

In the legislature, the House of Representatives is chosen by less than half the people, and not at all in proportion to those who do choose. The Senate are still more disproportionate, and for long terms of irresponsibility. In the Executive, the Governor is entirely independent of the choice of the people, and of their control; his Council equally so, and at best but a fifth wheel to a wagon. In the Judiciary, the judges of the highest courts are dependent on none but themselves. In England, where judges were named and removable at the will of an hereditary executive, from which branch most misrule was feared, and has flowed, it was a great point gained, by fixing them for life, to make them independent of that executive. But in a government founded on the public will, this principle operates in an opposite direction, and against that will. There, too, they were still removable on a concurrence of the executive and legislative branches. But we have made them independent of the nation itself. They are irremovable, but by their own body, for any depravities of conduct, and even by their own body for the imbecilities of dotage. The justices of the inferior courts are self-chosen, are for life, and perpetuate their own body in succession forever, so that a faction once possessing themselves of the bench of a county, can never be broken up, but hold their county in chains, forever indissoluble. Yet these justices are the real executive as well as judiciary, in all our minor and most ordinary concerns. They tax us at will; fill the office of sheriff, the most important of all the executive officers of the county; name nearly all our military leaders, which leaders, once named, are removable but by themselves. The juries, our judges of all fact, and of law when they choose it, are not selected by the people, nor amenable to them. They are chosen by an officer named by the court and executive. Chosen, did I say? Picked up by the sheriff from the loungings of the court yard, after everything respectable has retired from it. Where then is our republicanism to be found? Not in our constitution certainly, but merely in the spirit of our people. That would oblige even a despot to govern us republicanly. Owing to this spirit, and to nothing in the form of our constitution, all things have gone well. But this fact, so triumphantly misquoted by the enemies of reformation, is not the fruit of our constitution, but has prevailed in spite of it. Our functionaries have done well, because generally honest men. If any were not so, they feared to show it.

But it will be said, it is easier to find faults than to amend them. I do not think their amendment so difficult as is pretended. Only lay down true principles, and adhere to them inflexibly. Do not be frightened into their surrender by the alarms of the timid, or the croakings of wealth against the ascendency of the people. If experience be called for, appeal to that of our fifteen or twenty governments for forty years, and show me where the people have done half the mischief in these forty years, that a single despot would have done in a single year; or show half the riots and rebellions, the crimes and the punishments, which have taken place in any single nation, under kingly government, during the same period. The true foundation of republican government is the equal right of every citizen, in his person and property, and in their management. Try by this, as a tally, every provision of our constitution, and see if it hangs directly on the will of the people. Reduce your legislature to a convenient number for full, but orderly discussion. Let every man who fights or pays, exercise his just and equal right in their election. Submit them to approbation or rejection at short intervals. Let the executive be chosen in the same way, and for the same term, by those whose agent he is to be; and leave no screen of a council behind which to skulk from responsibility. It has been thought that the people are not competent electors of judges *learned in the law*. But I do not know that this is true, and, if doubtful, we should follow principle. In this, as in many other elections, they would be guided by reputation, which would not err oftener, perhaps, than the present mode of appointment. In one State of the Union, at least, it has long been tried, and with the most satisfactory success. The judges of Connecticut have been chosen by the people every six months, for nearly two centuries, and I believe there has hardly ever been an instance of change; so powerful is the curb of incessant responsibility. If prejudice, however, derived from a monarchical institution, is still to prevail against the vital elective principle of our own, and if the existing example among ourselves of periodical election of judges by the people be still mistrusted, let us at least not adopt the evil, and reject the good, of the English precedent; let us retain amovability on the concurrence of the executive and legislative branches, and nomination by the executive alone. Nomination to office is an executive function. To give it to the legislature, as we do, is a violation of the principle of the separation of powers. It swerves the members from correctness, by temptations to intrigue for office themselves, and to a corrupt barter of votes; and destroys responsibility by dividing it among a multitude. By leaving nomination in its proper place, among executive functions, the principle of the distribution of power is preserved, and responsibility weighs with its heaviest force on a single head.

The organization of our county administrations may be thought more difficult. But follow principle, and the knot unties itself. Divide the counties into wards of such size as that every citizen can attend, when called on, and act in person. Ascribe to them the government of their wards in all things relating to themselves exclusively. A justice, chosen by themselves, in each, a constable, a military company, a patrol, a school, the care of their own poor, their own portion of the public roads, the choice of one or more jurors to serve in some court, and the delivery, within their own wards, of their own votes for all elective officers of higher sphere, will relieve the county administration of nearly all its business, will have it better done, and by making every citizen an acting member of the government, and in the offices nearest and most interesting to him, will attach him by his strongest feelings to the independence of his country, and its republican constitution. The justices thus chosen by every ward, would constitute the county court, would do its judiciary business, direct roads and bridges, levy county and poor rates, and administer all the matters of common interest to the whole country. These wards, called townships in New England, are the vital principle of their governments, and have proved themselves the wisest invention ever devised by the wit of man for the perfect exercise of self-government, and for its preservation. We should thus marshal our government into, 1, the general federal republic, for all concerns foreign and federal; 2, that of the State, for what relates to our own citizens exclusively; 3, the county republics, for the duties and concerns of the county; and 4, the ward republics, for the small, and yet numerous and interesting concerns of the neighborhood; and in government, as well as in every other business of life, it is by division and subdivision of duties alone, that all matters, great and small, can be managed to perfection. And the whole is cemented by giving to every citizen, personally, a part in the administration of the public affairs.

The sum of these amendments is, 1. General suffrage. 2. Equal representation in the legislature. 3. An executive chosen by the people. 4. Judges elective or amovable. 5. Justices, jurors, and sheriffs elective. 6. Ward divisions. And 7. Periodical amendments of the constitution.

I have thrown out these as loose heads of amendment, for consideration and correction; and their object is to secure self-government by the republicanism of our constitution, as well as by the spirit of the people; and to nourish and perpetuate that spirit. I am not among those who fear the people. They, and not the rich, are our dependence for continued freedom. And to preserve their independence, we must not let our rulers load us with perpetual debt. We must make our election between *economy and liberty,* or *profusion and servitude.* If we run into such debts, as that we must be taxed in our meat and in our drink, in our necessaries and our comforts, in our labors and our amusements, for our callings and our creeds, as the people of England are, our people, like them, must come to labor sixteen hours in the twenty-four, give the earnings of fifteen of these to the government for their debts and daily expenses; and the sixteenth being insufficient to afford us bread, we must live, as they now do, on oatmeal and potatoes; have no time to think, no means of calling the mismanagers to account; but be glad to obtain subsistence by hiring ourselves to rivet their chains on the necks of our fellow-sufferers. Our land-holders, too, like theirs, retaining indeed the title and stewardship of estates called theirs, but held really in trust for the treasury, must wander, like theirs, in foreign countries, and be contented with penury, obscurity, exile, and the glory of the nation. This example reads to us the salutary lesson, that private fortunes are destroyed by public as well as by private extravagance. And this is the tendency of all human governments. A departure from principle in one instance becomes a precedent for a second; that second for a third; and so on, till the bulk of the society is reduced to be mere automatons of misery, to have no sensibilities left but for sinning and suffering. Then begins, indeed, the *bellum omnium in omnia,* which some philosophers observing to be so general in this world, have mistaken it for the natural, instead of the abusive state of man. And the fore horse of this frightful team is public debt. Taxation follows that, and in its train wretchedness and oppression.

Some men look at constitutions with sanctimonious reverence, and deem them like the ark of the covenant, too sacred to be touched. They ascribe to the men of the preceding age a wisdom more than human, and suppose what they did to be beyond amendment. I knew that age well; I belonged to it, and labored with it. It deserved well of its country. It was very like the present, but without the experience of the present; and forty years of experience in government is worth a century of book-reading; and this they would say themselves, were they to rise from the dead. I am certainly not an advocate for frequent and untried changes in laws and constitutions. I think moderate imperfections had better be borne with; because, when once known, we accommodate ourselves to them, and find practical means of correcting their ill effects. But I know also, that laws and institutions must go hand in hand with the progress of the human mind. As that becomes more developed, more enlightened, as new discoveries are made, new truths disclosed, and manners and opinions change with the change of circumstances, institutions must advance also, and keep pace with the times. We might as well require a man to wear still the coat which fitted him when a boy, as civilized society to remain ever under the regimen of their barbarous ancestors. It is this preposterous idea which has lately deluged Europe in blood. Their monarchs, instead of wisely yielding to the gradual change of circumstances, of favoring progressive accommodation to progressive improvement, have clung to old abuses, entrenched themselves behind steady habits, and obliged their subjects to seek through blood and violence rash and ruinous innovations, which, had they been referred to the peaceful deliberations and collected wisdom of the nation, would have been put into acceptable and salutary forms. Let us follow no such examples, nor weakly believe that one generation is not as capable as another of taking care of itself, and of ordering its own affairs. Let us, as our sister States have done, avail ourselves of our reason and experience, to correct the crude essays of our first and unexperienced, although wise, virtuous, and well-meaning councils. And lastly, let us provide in our constitution for its revision at stated periods. What these periods should be, nature herself indicates. By the European tables of mortality, of the adults living at any one moment of time, a majority will be dead in about nineteen years. At the end of that period then, a new majority is come into place; or, in other words, a new generation. Each generation is as independent of the one preceding, as that was of all which had gone before. It has then, like them, a right to choose for itself the form of government it believes most promotive of its own happiness; consequently, to accommodate to the circumstances in which it finds itself, that received from its predecessors; and it is for the peace and good of mankind, that a solemn opportunity of doing this every nineteen or twenty years, should be provided by the constitution; so that it may be handed on, with periodical repairs, from generation to generation, to the end of time, if anything human can so long endure. It is now forty years since the constitution of Virginia was formed. The same tables inform us, that, within that period, two-thirds of the adults then living are now dead. Have then the remaining third, even if they had the wish, the right to hold in obedience to their will, and to laws heretofore made by them, the other two-thirds, who, with themselves, compose the present mass of adults? If they have not, who has? The dead? But the dead have no rights. They are nothing; and nothing cannot own something. Where there is no substance, there can be no accident. This corporeal globe, and everything upon it, belong to its present corporeal inhabitants, during their generation. They alone have a right to direct what is the concern of themselves alone, and to declare the law of that direction; and this declaration can only be made by their majority. That majority, then, has a right to depute representatives to a convention, and to make the constitution what they think will be the best for themselves. But how collect their voice? This is the real difficulty. If invited by private authority, or county or district meetings, these divisions are so large that few will attend; and their voice will be imperfectly, or falsely pronounced. Here, then, would be one of the advantages of the ward divisions I have proposed. The mayor of every ward, on a question like the present, would call his ward together, take the simple yea or nay of its members, convey these to the county court, who would hand on those of all its wards to the proper general authority; and the voice of the whole people would be thus fairly, full, and peaceably expressed, discussed, and decided by the common reason of the society. If this avenue

: shut to the call of sufferance, it will make itself heard through that of ›rce, and we shall go on, as other nations are doing, in the endless circle f oppression, rebellion, reformation; and oppression, rebellion, reformation, gain; and so on forever.

These, Sir, are my opinions of the governments we see among men, and f the principles by which alone we may prevent our own from falling into he same dreadful track. I have given them at greater length than your letter :alled for. But I cannot say things by halves; and I confide them to your ionor, so to use them as to preserve me from the gridiron of the public ›apers. If you shall approve and enforce them, as you have done that of equal epresentation, they may do some good. If not, keep them to yourself as the ffusions of withered age and useless time. I shall, with not the less truth, ssure you of my great respect and consideration.

## ORIGINS OF SELF-GOVERNMENT[1]

June 5, 1824

DEAR AND VENERABLE SIR: I am much indebted for your kind letter of February the 29th, and for your valuable volume on the English constitution. I have read this with pleasure and much approbation, and think it has deduced the constitution of the English nation from its rightful root, the Anglo-Saxon. It is really wonderful, that so many able and learned men should have failed in their attempts to define it with correctness. No wonder then, that Paine, who thought more than he read, should have credited the great authorities who have declared, that the will of parliament is the constitution of England. So Marbois, before the French revolution, observed to me, that the Almanac Royal was the constitution of France. Your derivation of it from the Anglo-Saxons, seems to be made on legitimate principles. Having driven out the former inhabitants of that part of the island called England, they became aborigines as to you, and your lineal ancestors. They doubtless had a constitution; and although they have not left it in a written formula, to the precise text of which you may always appeal, yet they have left fragments of their history and laws, from which it may be inferred with considerable certainty. Whatever their history and laws show to have been practised with approbation, we may presume was permitted by their constitution; whatever was not so practised, was not permitted. And although this constitution was violated and set at naught by Norman force, yet force cannot change right. A perpetual claim was kept up by the nation, by their perpetual demand of a restoration of their Saxon laws, which shows they were never relinquished by the will of the nation. In the pullings and haulings

[1] Letter to Major John Cartwright.

for these ancient rights, between the nation, and its kings of the races of Plantagenets, Tudors and Stuarts, there was sometimes gain, and sometimes loss, until the final re-conquest of their rights from the Stuarts. The destitution and expulsion of this race broke the thread of pretended inheritance, extinguished all regal usurpations, and the nation re-entered into all its rights; and although in their bill of rights they specifically reclaimed some only, yet the omission of the others was no renunciation of the right to assume their exercise also, whenever occasion should occur. The new King received no rights or powers, but those expressly granted to him. It has ever appeared to me, that the difference between the whig and the tory of England is, that the whig deduces his rights from the Anglo-Saxon source, and the tory from the Norman. And Hume, the great apostle of toryism, says, in so many words, note AA to chapter 42, that, in the reign of the Stuarts, "it was the people who encroached upon the sovereign, not the sovereign who attempted, as is pretended, to usurp upon the people." This supposes the Norman usurpations to be rights in his successors. And again, C, 159, "the commons established a principle, which is noble in itself, and seems specious, but is belied by all history and experience, *that the people are the origin of all just power.*" And where else will this degenerate son of science, this traitor to his fellow men, find the origin of *just* powers, if not in the majority of the society? Will it be in the minority? Or in an individual of that minority?

Our Revolution commenced on more favorable ground. It presented us an album on which we were free to write what we pleased. We had no occasion to search into musty records, to hunt up royal parchments, or to investigate the laws and institutions of a semi-barbarous ancestry. We appealed to those of nature, and found them engraved on our hearts. Yet we did not avail ourselves of all the advantages of our position. We had never been permitted to exercise self-government. When forced to assume it, we were novices in its science. Its principles and forms had entered little into our former education. We established however some, although not all its important principles. The constitutions of most of our States assert, that all power is inherent in the people; that they may exercise it by themselves, in all cases to which they think themselves competent (as in electing their functionaries executive and legislative, and deciding by a jury of themselves, in all judiciary cases in which any fact is involved), or they may act by representatives, freely and equally chosen; that it is their right and duty to be at all times armed; that they are entitled to freedom of person, freedom of religion, freedom of property, and freedom of the press. In the structure of our legislatures, we think experience has proved the benefit of subjecting questions to two separate bodies of deliberants; but in constituting these, natural right has been mistaken, some making one of these bodies, and some both, the representatives of property instead of persons; whereas the double deliberation might be as well obtained without any violation of true principle, either by requiring a greater age in one of the bodies, or by electing a proper number of representatives of persons, dividing them by lots into two chambers, and renewing the division at frequent intervals, in order to break up all cabals. Virginia, of which I am myself a native and resident, was not only the first of the States, but, I believe I may say, the first of the nations of the earth, which assembled its wise men peaceably together to form a fundamental constitution, to commit it to writing, and place it among their archives, where everyone should be free to appeal to its text. But this act was very imperfect. The other States, as they proceeded successively to the same work, made successive improvements; and several of them, still further corrected by experience, have, by conventions, still further amended their first forms. My own State has gone on so far with its *première ébauche;* but it is now proposing to call a convention for amendment. Among other improvements, I hope they will adopt the subdivision of our counties into wards. The former may be estimated at an average of twenty-four miles square; the latter should be about six miles square each, and would answer to the hundreds of your Saxon Alfred. In each of these might be, 1st. An elementary school; 2d. A company of militia, with its officers; 3d. A justice of the peace and constable; 4th. Each ward should take care of their own poor; 5th. Their own roads; 6th. Their own police; 7th. Elect within themselves one or more jurors to attend the courts of justice; and 8th. Give in at their Folk-house, their votes for all functionaries reserved to their election. Each ward would thus be a small republic within itself, and every man in the State would thus become an acting member of the common government, transacting in person a great portion of its rights and duties, subordinate indeed, yet important, and entirely within his competence. The wit of man cannot devise a more solid basis for a free, durable and well-administered republic.

With respect to our State and federal governments, I do not think their relations correctly understood by foreigners. They generally suppose the former subordinate to the latter. But this is not the case. They are co-ordinate departments of one simple and integral whole. To the State governments are reserved all legislation and administration, in affairs which concern their own citizens only, and to the federal government is given whatever concerns foreigners, or the citizens of other States; these functions alone being made federal. The one is the domestic, the other the foreign branch of the same government; neither having control over the other, but within its own department. There are one or two exceptions only to this partition of power. But, you may ask, if the two departments should claim each the same subject of power, where is the common umpire to decide ultimately between them? In cases of little importance or urgency, the prudence of both parties will keep them aloof from the questionable ground; but if it can neither be avoided nor compromised, a convention of the States must be called, to ascribe the doubtful power to that department which they may think best. You will perceive by these details, that we have not yet so far perfected our constitutions as to venture to make them unchangeable. But still, in their present state, we consider them not otherwise changeable than by the authority of the people, on a special election of representatives for that purpose expressly: they are until then the *lex legum.*

But can they be made unchangeable? Can one generation bind another, and all others, in succession forever? I think not. The Creator has made the earth for the living, not the dead. Rights and powers can only belong to persons, not to things, not to mere matter, unendowed with will. The dead are not even things. The particles of matter which composed their bodies, make part now of the bodies of other animals, vegetables, or minerals, of a thousand forms. To what then are attached the rights and powers they held while in the form of men? A generation may bind itself as long as its majority continues in life; when that has disappeared, another majority is in place, holds all the rights and powers their predecessors once held, and may change their laws and institutions to suit themselves. Nothing then is unchangeable but the inherent and unalienable rights of man.

I was glad to find in your book a formal contradiction, at length, of the judiciary usurpation of legislative powers; for such the judges have usurped in their repeated decisions, that Christianity is a part of the common law. The proof of the contrary, which you have adduced, is incontrovertible; to wit, that the common law existed while the Anglo-Saxons were yet Pagans, at a time when they had never yet heard the name of Christ pronounced, or knew that such a character had ever existed. But it may amuse you, to show when, and by what means, they stole this law in upon us. In a case of *quare impedit* in the Year-book 34, H, 6, folio 38, (anno 1458,) a question was made, how far the ecclesiastical law was to be respected in a common law court? And Prisot, Chief Justice, gives his opinion in these words: *"A tiel leis qu' ils de seint église ont en* ancien scripture, *covient à nous à donner crédence; car ceo common ley sur quels touts manners leis sont fondés. Et auxy, Sir, nous sumus oblègés de conustre lour ley de saint église; et semblablement ils sont obligés de conustre nostre ley. Et, Sir, si poit apperer or à nous que l'evesque ad fait come un ordinary fera en tiel cas, adong nous devons cee adjuger bon, ou auterment nemy,"* &c. See S. C. Fitzh. Abr. Qu. imp. 89, Bro. Abr. Qu. imp. 12. Finch in his first book, c. 3, is the first afterwards who quotes this case and mistakes it thus: "To such laws of the church as have warrant in *holy scripture,* our law giveth credence." And cites Prisot; mistranslating *"ancien scripture,"* into *"holy scripture."* Whereas Prisot palpably says, "to such laws as those of holy church have in *ancient writing,* it is proper for us to give credence," to wit, to their *ancient written* laws. This was in 1613, a century and a half after the dictum of Prisot. Wingate, in 1658, erects this false translation into a maxim of the common law, copying the words of Finch, but citing Prisot, Wing. Max. 3. And Sheppard, title, "Religion," in 1675, copies the same mistranslation, quoting the Y. B. Finch and Wingate. Hale expresses it in these words: "Christianity is parcel of the laws of England." 1 Ventr. 293, 3 Keb. 607. But he quotes no authority. By these echoings and re-echoings from one to another, it had become so established in 1728, that in the case of the King *vs.* Woolston, 2 Stra. 834, the court would not suffer it to be debated, whether to write against Christianity was punishable in the temporal court at common law? Wood, therefore, 409, ventures still to vary the phrase, and say, that all blasphemy and profaneness are offences by the common law; and cites 2 Stra. Then Blackstone, in 1763, IV. 59, repeats the words of Hale, that "Christianity is part of the laws of England," citing Ventris and Strange. And finally, Lord Mansfield, with a little qualification, in Evans' case, in 1767, says, that "the essential principles of revealed religion are part of the common law." Thus ingulphing Bible, Testament and all into the common law, without citing any authority. And thus we find this chain of authorities hanging link by link, one upon another, and all ultimately on one and the same hook, and that a mistranslation of the words *"ancien scripture,"* used by Prisot. Finch quotes Prisot; Wingate does the same. Sheppard quotes Prisot, Finch and Wingate. Hale cites nobody. The court in Woolston's case, cites Hale. Wood cites Woolston's case. Blackstone quotes Woolston's case and Hale. And Lord Mansfield, like Hale, ventures it on his own authority. Here I might defy the best-read lawyer to produce another scrip of authority for this judiciary forgery; and I might go on further to show, how some of the Anglo-Saxon priests interpolated into the text of Alfred's laws, the 20th, 21st, 22d, and 23d chapters of Exodus, and the 15th of the Acts of the Apostles, from 23d to the 29th verses. But this would lead my pen and your patience too far. What a conspiracy this, between Church and State! Sing Tantarara, rogues all, rogues all! Sing Tantarara, rogues all!

## *Chapter IX*

# GOVERNMENT AND ADMINISTRATION

## NOTES OF RULES FOR THE CONTINENTAL CONGRESS[1]

July, 1776

No person to read printed papers.

Every colony present, unless divided, to be counted.

No person to vote unless present when question put.

No person to walk while question putting.

Every person to sit while not speaking.

Orders of day at 12 o'clock.

Amendments first proposed to be first put.

Committee or officers to be named before ballot.

Call of the house every morning. Absentees to be noted and returned to Convention.

No members to be absent without leave of house or written order of Convention on pain of being returned to Convention.

## REPORT ON CEREMONIAL FOR GENERAL WASHINGTON[2]

December, 1783

1. The President and members are to be seated and covered, and the Secretary to be standing by the side of the President.

2. The arrival of the General is to be announced by the messenger to the Secretary, who is thereupon to introduce the General, attended by his aids, into the Hall of Congress.

[1] Jefferson made these notes when he was a member of the committee to draw up the rules and regulations. The rules, based on these notes, were adopted on July 17, 1776.

[2] Jefferson wrote this Report as a member of a committee appointed by Congress to make arrangements for General Washington's last public reception, on December 22, 1783.

3. The General, being conducted to a chair by the Secretary, is to be seated with an aid on each side standing, and the Secretary is to resume his place.

4. After a proper time for the arrangement of spectators, silence is to be ordered by the Secretary if necessary, and the President is to address the General in the following words. "Sir; The United States in Congress assembled are prepared to receive your communications." Whereupon the General is to arise and address Congress; after which he is to deliver his commission and a copy of his address to the President.

5. The General having resumed his place, the President is to deliver the answer to Congress, which the General is to receive standing.

6. The President having finished, the Secretary is to deliver the General a copy of the answer, and the General is then to take his leave. When the General rises to make his address, and also when he retires, he is to bow to Congress, which they are to return by uncovering without bowing.

## OPINION ON THE BILL APPORTIONING REPRESENTATION

April 4, 1792

The Constitution has declared that representatives and direct taxes shall be apportioned among the several States according to their respective numbers. That the number of representatives shall not exceed one for every 30,000, but each State shall have at least one representative, and until such enumeration shall be made, the State of New Hampshire shall be entitled to choose 3, Massachusetts 2.

The bill for apportioning representatives among the several States, without explaining any principle at all, which may show its conformity with the constitution, to guide future apportionments, says, that New Hampshire shall have 3 members, Massachusetts 16, &c. We are, therefore, to find by experiment what has been the principle of the bill; to do which, it is proper to state the federal or representable numbers of each State, and the numbers allotted to them by the bill. They are as follows:

| | | MEMBERS |
|---|---|---|
| Vermont | 85,532 | 3 |
| New Hampshire | 141,823 | 5 |
| Massachusetts | 475,327 | 16 |
| Rhode Island | 68,444 | 2 |
| Connecticut | 285,941 | 8 |
| New York | 352,915 | 11 |
| New Jersey | 179,556 | 6 |
| Pennsylvania | 432,880 | 14 |
| Delaware | 55,538 | 2 |
| Maryland | 278,513 | 9 |

| | | MEMBERS |
|---|---|---|
| Virginia | 630,558 | 21 |
| Kentucky | 68,705 | 2 |
| North Carolina | 353,521 | 11 |
| South Carolina | 206,236 | 6 |
| Georgia | 70,843 | 2 |
| | 3,636,312 | 120 |

It happens that this representation, whether tried as between great and small States, or as between north and south, yields, in the present instance, a tolerably just result; and, consequently, could not be objected to on that ground, if it were obtained by the process prescribed in the Constitution; but if obtained by any process out of that, it becomes arbitrary and inadmissible.

The 1st member of the clause of the Constitution above cited is express, that representatives shall be apportioned among the several States according to their *respective numbers*. That is to say, they shall be apportioned by some common ratio—for proportion, and ratio, are equivalent words; and, in the definition of *proportion among numbers,* that they have a ratio common to all, or in other words, a common divisor. Now, trial will show that there is no common ratio, or divisor, which, applied to the numbers of each State, will give to them the number of representatives allotted in this bill. For trying the several ratios of 29, 30, 31, 32, 33, the allotments would be as follows:

| | *29* | *30* | *31* | *32* | *33* | THE BILL |
|---|---|---|---|---|---|---|
| Vermont | 2 | 2 | 2 | 2 | 2 | 3 |
| New Hampshire | 4 | 4 | 4 | 4 | 4 | 5 |
| Massachusetts | 16 | 15 | 15 | 14 | 14 | 16 |
| Rhode Island | 2 | 2 | 2 | 2 | 2 | 2 |
| Connecticut | 8 | 7 | 7 | 7 | 7 | 8 |
| New York | 12 | 11 | 11 | 11 | 10 | 11 |
| New Jersey | 6 | 5 | 5 | 5 | 5 | 6 |
| Pennsylvania | 14 | 14 | 13 | 13 | 13 | 14 |
| Delaware | 1 | 1 | 1 | 1 | 1 | 2 |
| Maryland | 9 | 9 | 8 | 8 | 8 | 9 |
| Virginia | 21 | 21 | 20 | 19 | 19 | 21 |
| Kentucky | 2 | 2 | 2 | 2 | 2 | 2 |
| North Carolina | 12 | 11 | 11 | 11 | 10 | 12 |
| South Carolina | 7 | 6 | 6 | 6 | 6 | 7 |
| Georgia | 2 | 2 | 2 | 2 | 2 | 2 |
| | 118 | 112 | 109 | 107 | 105 | 120 |

Then the bill reverses the constitutional precept, because, by it, representatives are *not* apportioned among the several States, according to their respective numbers.

It will be said that, though, for taxes, there may always be found a divisor which will apportion them among the States according to numbers exactly, without leaving any remainder, yet, for *representatives,* there can be no such common ratio, or divisor, which, applied to the several numbers, will divide them exactly, without a remainder or fraction. I answer, then, that taxes must be divided *exactly,* and representatives *as nearly* as the *nearest ratio* will admit; and the fractions must be neglected, because the Constitution calls absolutely that there be an *apportionment or common ratio,* and if any fractions result from the operation, it has left them unprovided for. In fact it could not but foresee that such fractions would result, and it meant to submit to them. It knew they would be in favor of one part of the Union at one time, and of another at another, so as, in the end, to balance occasional irregularities. But instead of such a *single* common ratio, or uniform divisor, as prescribed by the Constitution, the bill has applied *two ratios,* at least, to the different States, to wit, that of 30,026 to the seven following: Rhode Island, New York, Pennsylvania, Maryland, Virginia, Kentucky and Georgia; and that of 27,770 to the eight others, namely: Vermont, New Hampshire, Massachusetts, Connecticut, New Jersey, Delaware, North Carolina, and South Carolina, as follows:

| | | | | | |
|---|---|---|---|---|---|
| Rhode Island | 68,444 | divided by | 30,026 | gives | 2 |
| New York | 352,915 | " | " | " | 11 |
| Pennsylvania | 432,880 | " | " | " | 14 |
| Maryland | 278,513 | " | " | " | 9 |
| Virginia | 630,558 | " | " | " | 21 |
| Kentucky | 58,705 | " | " | " | 2 |
| Georgia | 70,843 | " | " | " | 2 |
| Vermont | 85,532 | divided by | 27,770 | gives | 3 |
| New Hampshire | 141,823 | " | " | " | 5 |
| Massachusetts | 475,327 | " | " | " | 16 |
| Connecticut | 235,941 | " | " | " | 8 |
| New Jersey | 179,556 | " | " | " | 6 |
| Delaware | 55,538 | " | " | " | 2 |
| North Carolina | 353,521 | " | " | " | 12 |
| South Carolina | 206,236 | " | " | " | 7 |

And if *two* ratios be applied, then *fifteen* may, and the distribution become arbitrary, instead of being apportioned to numbers. Another member of the clause of the Constitution which has been cited, says "the number of representatives shall not exceed one for every 30,000, but each State shall have at least one representative." This last phrase proves that it had no contemplation that all fractions, or *numbers below the common ratio* were to be unrepresented; and it provides especially that in the case of a State whose whole number shall be below the common ratio, one representative shall be given to it. This is the single instance where it allows representation to any smaller number than the common ratio, and by providing especially for it in this, shews it was understood that, without special provision, the smaller number would in this case, be involved in the general principle. The first phrase of the above citations, that "the number of representatives shall not exceed one for every 30,000, is violated by this bill which has given to eight States a number exceeding one for every 30,000, to wit, one for every 27,770.

In answer to this, it is said that this phrase may mean either the 30,000 *in each State,* or the 30,000 *in the whole Union,* and that in the latter case it serves only to find the amount of the whole representation; which, in the present state of population, is 120 members. Suppose the phrase might bear both meanings, which will common sense apply to it? Which did the universal understanding of our country apply to it? Which did the Senate and Representatives apply to it during the pendency of the first bill, and even till an advanced stage of this second bill, when an ingenious gentleman found out the doctrine of fractions, a doctrine so difficult and inobvious, as to be rejected at first sight by the very persons who afterwards became its most zealous advocates?

The phrase stands in the midst of a number of others, every one of which relates to States in their separate capacity. Will not plain common sense then, understand it, like the rest of its context, to relate to States in their separate capacities?

But if the phrase of one for 30,000 is only meant to give the aggregate of representatives, and not at all to influence their apportionment among the States, then the 120 being once found, in order to apportion them, we must recur to the former rule which does it according to the numbers of *the respective States;* and we must take the *nearest common divisor,* as the ratio of distribution, that is to say, that divisor which, applied to every State, gives to them such numbers as, added together, come nearest to 120. This nearest common ratio will be found to be 28,658, and will distribute 119 of the 120 members, leaving only a single residuary one. It will be found too to place 96,648 fractional numbers in the eight northernmost States, and 106,582 in the seven southernmost. The following table shows it:

| | | RATIO, 28,658 | FRACTION |
|---|---|---|---|
| Vermont | 85,832 | 2 | 27,816 |
| New Hampshire | 141,823 | 4 | 26,391 |
| Massachusetts | 475,327 | 16 | 13,599 |
| Rhode Island | 68,444 | 2 | 10,728 |

| | RATIO, 28,658 | | FRACTION | |
|---|---|---|---|---|
| Connecticut | 235,941 | 8 | 5,077 | |
| New York | 352,915 | 12 | 6,619 | |
| New Jersey | 119,856 | 6 | 6,408 | |
| Pennsylvania | 432,880 | 15 | 10 | 96,648 |
| Delaware | 55,538 | 1 | 26,680 | |
| Maryland | 278,503 | 9 | 18,191 | |
| Virginia | 630,558 | 21 | 24,540 | |
| Kentucky | 68,705 | 2 | 10,989 | |
| North Carolina | 353,521 | 12 | 7,225 | |
| South Carolina | 206,236 | 7 | 4,230 | |
| Virginia | 70,843 | 2 | 23,137 | 105,582 |
| | 3,636,312 | 119 | 202,230 | 202,230 |

Whatever may have been the intention, the effect of neglecting the nearest divisor, (which leaves but one residuary member,) and adopting a distant one (which leaves eight), is merely to take a member from New York and Pennsylvania, each, and give them to Vermont and New Hampshire. But it will be said, this is giving more than one for 30,000. True, but has it not been just said that the one for 30,000 is prescribed only to fix the aggregate number, and that we are not to mind it when we come to apportion them among the States? That for this we must recur to the former rule which distributes them according to the numbers in each State? Besides does not the bill itself apportion among seven of the States by the ratio of 27,770? which is much more than one for 30,000.

Where a phrase is susceptible of two meanings, we ought certainly to adopt that which will bring upon us the fewest inconveniences. Let us weigh those resulting from both constructions.

From that giving to each State a member for every 30,000 in that State results the single inconvenience that there may be large portions unrepresented, but it being a mere hazard on which State this will fall, hazard will equalize it in the long run. From the others result exactly the same inconvenience. A thousand cases may be imagined to prove it. Take one. Suppose eight of the States had 45,000 inhabitants each, and the other seven 44,999 each, that is to say each one less than each of the others. The aggregate would be 674,993, and the number of representatives at one for 30,000 of the aggregate, would be 22. Then, after giving one member to each State, distribute the seven residuary members among the seven highest fractions, and though the difference of population be only an unit, the representation would be the double.

| | | | FRACTIONS |
|---|---|---|---|
| 1st. | 45,000 | 2 | 15,000 |
| 2d. | 45,000 | 2 | 15,000 |
| 3d. | 45,000 | 2 | 15,000 |
| 4th. | 45,000 | 2 | 15,000 |
| 5th. | 45,000 | 2 | 15,000 |
| 6th. | 45,000 | 2 | 15,000 |
| 7th. | 45,000 | 2 | 15,000 |
| 8th. | 45,000 | 1 | 15,000 |
| 9th. | 44,999 | 1 | 14,999 |
| 10th. | 44,999 | 1 | 14,999 |
| 11th. | 44,999 | 1 | 14,999 |
| 12th. | 44,999 | 1 | 14,999 |
| 13th. | 44,999 | 1 | 14,999 |
| 14th. | 44,999 | 1 | 14,999 |
| 15th. | 44,999 | 1 | 14,999 |
| | 674,993 | 22 | |

Here a single inhabitant the more would count as 30,000. Nor is this case imaginable, only it will resemble the real one whenever the fractions happen to be pretty equal through the whole States. The numbers of our census happen by accident to give the fractions all very small, or very great, so as to produce the strongest case of inequality that could possibly have occurred, and which may never occur again. The probability is that the fractions will generally descend gradually from 29,999 to 1. The inconvenience then of large unrepresented fractions attends both constructions; and while the most obvious construction is liable to no other, that of the bill incurs many and grievous ones.

1. If you permit the large fraction in one State to choose a representative for one of the small fractions in another State, you take from the latter its election, which constitutes real representation, and substitute a virtual representation of the disfranchised fractions, and the tendency of the doctrine of virtual representation has been too well discussed and appreciated by reasoning and resistance on a former great occasion to need development now.

2. The bill does not say that it has given the residuary representatives *to the greatest fraction;* though in fact it has done so. It seems to have avoided establishing that into a rule, lest it might not suit on another occasion. Perhaps it may be found the next time more convenient to distribute them *among the smaller States;* at another time *among the larger States;* at other times according to any other crotchet which ingenuity may invent, and the combinations of the day give strength to carry; or they may do it arbitrarily by open bargains and cabal. In short this construction introduces into Con-

gress a scramble, or a vendue for the surplus members. It generates waste of time, hot blood, and may at some time, when the passions are high, extend a disagreement between the two Houses, to the perpetual loss of the thing, as happens now in the Pennsylvania assembly; whereas the other construction reduces the apportionment always to an arithmetical operation, about which no two men can ever possibly differ.

3. It leaves in full force the violation of the precept which declares that representatives shall be *apportioned* among the States according to their numbers, *i.e.,* by some common ratio.

Viewing this bill either as a *violation of the constitution,* or as giving an *inconvenient exposition of its words,* is it a case wherein the President ought to interpose his negative? I think it is.

1. The non-user of his negative begins already to excite a belief that no President will ever venture to use it; and has, consequently, begotten a desire to raise up barriers in the State legislatures against Congress, throwing off the control of the constitution.

2. It can never be used more pleasingly to the public, than in the protection of the constitution.

3. No invasions of the constitution are fundamentally so dangerous as the tricks played on their own numbers, apportionment, and other circumstances respecting themselves, and affecting their legal qualifications to legislate for the union.

4. The majorities by which this bill has been carried (to wit: of one in the Senate and two in the Representatives) show how divided the opinions were there.

5. The whole of both houses admit the constitution will bear the other exposition, whereas the minorities in both deny it will bear that of the bill.

6. The application of any one ratio is intelligible to the people, and will, therefore be approved, whereas the complex operations of this bill will never be comprehended by them, and though they may acquiesce, they cannot approve what they do not understand.

## METHODS OF CONDUCTING PRESIDENTIAL BUSINESS

November 6, 1801

### CIRCULAR TO THE HEADS OF THE DEPARTMENTS

DEAR SIR: Coming all of us into executive office, new, and unfamiliar with the course of business previously practised, it was not to be expected we should, in the first outset, adopt in every part a line of proceeding so perfect as to admit no amendment. The mode and degrees of communication, particularly between the Presidents and heads of departments, have not been practised exactly on the same scale in all of them. Yet it would certainly be more safe and satisfactory for ourselves as well as the public, that not only the best, but also an uniform course of proceeding as to manner and degree, should be observed. Having been a member of the first administration under Gen. Washington, I can state with exactness what our course then was. Letters of business came addressed sometimes to the President, but most frequently to the heads of departments. If addressed to himself, he referred them to the proper department to be acted on: if to one of the secretaries, the letter, if it required no answer, was communicated to the President, simply for his information. If an answer was requisite, the secretary of the department communicated the letter and his proposed answer to the President. Generally they were simply sent back after perusal, which signified his approbation. Sometimes he returned them with an informal note, suggesting an alteration or a query. If a doubt of any importance arose, he reserved it for conference. By this means, he was always in accurate possession of all facts and proceedings in every part of the Union, and to whatsoever department they related; he formed a central point for the different branches; preserved an unity of object and action among them; exercised that participation in the suggestion of affairs which his office made incumbent on him; and met himself the due responsibility for whatever was done. During Mr. Adams' administration, his long and habitual absences from the seat of government, rendered this kind of communication impracticable, removed him from any share in the transaction of affairs, and parcelled out the government, in fact, among four independent heads, drawing sometimes in opposite directions. That the former is preferable to the latter course, cannot be doubted. It gave, indeed, to the heads of departments the trouble of making up, once a day, a packet of all their communications for the perusal of the President; it commonly also retarded one day their despatches by mail. But in pressing cases, this injury was prevented by presenting that case singly for immediate attention; and it produced us in return the benefit of his sanction for every act we did. Whether any change of circumstances may render a change in this procedure necessary, a little experience will show us. But I cannot withhold recommending to heads of departments, that we should adopt this course for the present, leaving any necessary modifications of it to time and trial. I am sure my conduct must have proved, better than a thousand declarations would, that my confidence in those whom I am so happy as to have associated with me, is unlimited, unqualified and unabated. I am well satisfied that everything goes on with a wisdom and rectitude which I could not improve. If I had the universe to choose from, I could not change one of my associates to my better satisfaction. My sole motives are those before expressed, as governing the first administration in chalking out the rules of their proceeding; adding to them only a sense of obligation imposed on me by the public will, to meet personally the duties to which they have appointed me. If this mode of proceeding shall meet the approbation of the heads of departments, it may go into execution without giving them the trouble of an answer; if any other can be suggested which would answer our views and add less to their labors, that will be a sufficient reason for my preferring it to my own proposition, to the substance of which only, and not the form, I attach any importance.

## NOTE ON POLITICAL APPOINTMENTS[1]

Probably March, 1801

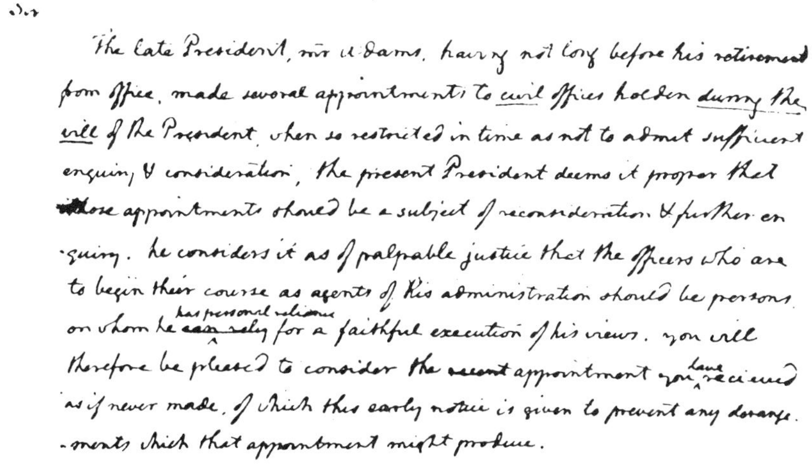

Sir

The late President, mr Adams, having not long before his retirement from office, made several appointments to civil offices holden during the will of the President, when so restricted in time as not to admit sufficient enquiry & consideration, the present President deems it proper that those appointments should be a subject of reconsideration & further enquiry. he considers it as of palpable justice that the officers who are to begin their course as agents of his administration should be persons on whom he ~~can rely~~ has personal reliance for a faithful execution of his views. you will therefore be pleased to consider the ~~recent~~ appointment you have received as if never made, of which this early notice is given to prevent any derangements which that appointment might produce.

## THE PRESIDENT AND STATE GOVERNORS[2]

July 11, 1801

DEAR SIR: As to the mode of correspondence between the general and particular executives, I do not think myself a good judge. Not because my position gives me any prejudice on the occasion; for if it be possible to be certainly conscious of anything, I am conscious of feeling no difference between writing to the highest and lowest being on earth; but because I have ever thought that forms should yield to whatever should facilitate business. Comparing the two governments together, it is observable that in all those cases where the independent or reserved rights of the States are in question, the two executives, if they are to act together, must be exactly co-ordinate; they

[1] MS. in National Archives, Records of Department of State.
[2] Letter to James Monroe, Governor of Virginia.

are, in these cases, each the supreme head of an independent government. In other cases, to wit, those transferred by the Constitution to the General Government, the general executive is certainly pre-ordinate; *e.g.*, in a question respecting the militia, and others easily to be recollected. Were there, therefore, to be a stiff adherence to etiquette, I should say that in the former cases the correspondence should be between the two heads, and that in the latter, the Governor must be subject to receive orders from the war department as any other subordinate officer would. And were it observed that either party set up unjustifiable pretensions, perhaps the other might be right in opposing them by a tenaciousness of his own rigorous rights. But I think the practice in General Washington's administration was most friendly to business, and was absolutely equal; sometimes he wrote to the Governors, and sometimes the heads of departments wrote. If a letter is to be on a general subject, I see no reason why the President should not write; but if it is to go into details, these being known only to the head of the department, it is better he should write directly. Otherwise, the correspondence must involve circuities. If this be practised promiscuously in both classes of cases, each party setting examples of neglecting etiquette, both will stand on equal ground, and convenience alone will dictate through whom any particular communication is to be made. On the whole, I think a free correspondence best, and shall never hesitate to write myself to the Governors, in every federal case, where the occasion presents itself to me particularly. Accept assurances of my sincere and constant affection and respect.

## NOTE ON THE DEPOSIT OF PUBLIC PAPERS[1]

December 29, 1801

SIR: Having no confidence that the office of the private secretary of the President of the U.S. will ever be a regular and safe deposit for public papers or that due attention will ever be paid on their transmission from one Secretary or President to another, I have, since I have been in office, sent every paper, which I deem merely public, and coming to my hands, to be deposited in one of the offices of the heads of departments; so that I shall never add a single paper to those constituting the records of the President's office; nor, should any accident happen to me, will there be any papers in my possession which ought to go into any public office. I make the selection regularly as I go along, retaining in my own possession only my private papers, or such as, relating to public subjects, were meant still to be personally confidential for myself. Mr. Meredith the late treasurer, in obedience to the law which

[1] National Archives, MS. Misc. Letters, Department of State.

directs the Treasurer's accounts to be transmitted to and remain with the President, having transmitted his accounts, I send them to you to be deposited for safe keeping in the domestic branch of the office of Secretary of State, which I suppose to be the proper one. Accept assurances of my affectionate esteem and high respect.

TO THE SECRETARY OF STATE.

## RULES OF ETIQUETTE IN WASHINGTON

November [?], 1803

i. In order to bring the members of society together in the first instance, the custom of the country has established that residents shall pay the first visit to strangers, and, among strangers, first comers to later comers, foreign and domestic; the character of stranger ceasing after the first visits. To this rule there is a single exception. Foreign ministers, from the necessity of making themselves known, pay the first visit to the ministers of the nation, which is returned.

ii. When brought together in society, all are perfectly equal, whether foreign or domestic, titled or untitled, in or out of office.

All other observances are but exemplifications of these two principles.

I. 1st. The families of foreign ministers, arriving at the seat of government, receive the first visit from those of the national ministers, as from all other residents.

2d. Members of the Legislature and of the Judiciary, independent of their offices, have a right as strangers to receive the first visit.

II. 1st. No title being admitted here, those of foreigners give no precedence.

2d. Differences of grade among diplomatic members, give no precedence.

3d. At public ceremonies, to which the government invites the presence of foreign ministers and their families, a convenient seat or station will be provided for them, with any other strangers invited and the families of the national ministers, each taking place as they arrive, and without any precedence.

4th. To maintain the principle of equality, or of pêle mêle, and prevent the growth of precedence out of courtesy, the members of the Executive will practice at their own houses, and recommend an adherence to the ancient usage of the country, of gentlemen in mass giving precedence to the ladies in mass, in passing from one apartment where they are assembled into another.

# CIRCULAR LETTER REFUSING TO MEDDLE WITH APPOINTMENTS

March, 1809

The friendship which has long subsisted between the President of the United States [1] and myself gave me reason to expect, on my retirement from office, that I might often receive applications to interpose with him on behalf of persons desiring appointments. Such an abuse of his dispositions towards me would necessarily lead to the loss of them, and to the transforming me from the character of a friend to that of an unreasonable and troublesome solicitor. It therefore became necessary for me to lay down as a law for my future conduct never to interpose in any case, either with him or the heads of departments (from whom it must go to him) in any application whatever for office. To this rule I must scrupulously adhere, for were I to depart from it in a single instance I could no longer plead it with truth to my friends in excuse for my not complying with their requests. I hope therefore that the declining it in the present, as in every other case, will be ascribed to its true cause, the obligation of this general law, and not to any disinclination existing in this particular case; and still less to an unwillingness to be useful to my friends on all occasions not forbidden by a special impropriety.

# THE EXECUTIVE [2]

January 26, 1811

When our present government was first established, we had many doubts on this question [the preference of a plural over a singular executive], and many leanings towards a supreme executive counsel. It happened that at that time the experiment of such an one was commenced in France, while the single executive was under trial here. We watched the motions and effects of these two rival plans, with an interest and anxiety proportioned to the importance of a choice between them. The experiment in France failed after a short course, and not from any circumstance peculiar to the times or nation, but from those internal jealousies and dissensions in the Director, which will ever arise among men equal in power, without a principal to decide and control their differences. We had tried a similar experiment in 1784, by establishing a committee of the States, composed of a member from every State, then thirteen, to exercise the executive functions during the recess of Congress. They fell immediately into schisms and dissensions, which became at length so inveterate as to render all co-operation among them impracticable;

[1] James Madison, who succeeded Jefferson as President on March 4, 1809.

[2] Letter to Destutt de Tracy.

they dissolved themselves, abandoning the helm of government, and it continued without a head, until Congress met the ensuing winter. This was then imputed to the temper of two or three individuals; but the wise ascribed it to the nature of man.

The failure of the French Directory, and from the same cause, seems to have authorized a belief that the form of a plurality, however promising in theory, is impracticable with men constituted with the ordinary passions. While the tranquil and steady tenor of our single executive, during a course of twenty-two years of the most tempestuous times the history of the world has ever presented, gives a rational hope that this important problem is at length solved. Aided by the counsels of a cabinet of heads of departments, originally four, but now five, with whom the President consults, either singly or altogether, he has the benefit of their wisdom and information, brings their views to one centre, and produces an unity of action and direction in all the branches of the government.

The excellence of this construction of the executive power has already manifested itself here under very opposite circumstances. During the administration of our first President, his cabinet of four members was equally divided by as marked an opposition of principle as monarchism and republicanism could bring into conflict. Had that cabinet been a directory, like positive and negative quantities in algebra, the opposing wills would have balanced each other and produced a state of absolute inaction. But the President heard with calmness the opinions and reasons of each, decided the course to be pursued, and kept the government steadily in it, unaffected by the agitation. The public knew well the dissensions of the cabinet, but never had an uneasy thought on their account, because they knew also they had provided a regulating power which would keep the machine in steady movement. I speak with an intimate knowledge of these scenes, *quorum pars fui;* as I may of others of a character entirely opposite.

The third administration,[3] which was of eight years, presented an example of harmony in a cabinet of six persons,[4] to which perhaps history has furnished no parallel. There never arose, during the whole time, an instance of an unpleasant thought or word between the members. We sometimes met under differences of opinion, but scarcely ever failed, by conversing and reasoning, so to modify each other's ideas, as to produce an unanimous result. Yet, able and amicable as these members were, I am not certain this would have been the case, had each possessed equal and independent powers. Ill-defined limits of their respective departments, jealousies, trifling at first, but

[3] Jefferson's own.

[4] James Madison, Secretary of State; Albert Gallatin, Secretary of the Treasury; Henry Dearborn, Secretary of War; Levi Lincoln, Attorney-General; Gideon Granger, Postmaster-General: Robert Smith (who succeeded his brother Samuel), Secretary of the Navy.

nourished and strengthened by repetition of occasions, intrigues without doors of designing persons to build an importance to themselves on the divisions of others, might, from small beginnings, have produced persevering oppositions. But the power of decision in the President left no object for internal dissension, and external intrigue was stifled in embryo by the knowledge which incendiaries possessed, that no division they could foment would change the course of the executive power. I am not conscious that my participations in executive authority have produced any bias in favor of the single executive; because the parts I have acted have been in the subordinate, as well as superior stations, and because, if I know myself, what I have felt, and what I have wished, I know that I have never been so well pleased, as when I could shift power from my own, on the shoulders of others; nor have I ever been able to conceive how any rational being could propose happiness to himself from the exercise of power over others.

I am still, however, sensible of the solidity of your principle, that, to insure the safety of the public liberty, its depository should be subject to be changed with the greatest ease possible, and without suspending or disturbing for a moment the movements of the machine of government. You apprehend that a single executive, with eminence of talent, and destitution of principle, equal to the object, might, by usurpation, render his powers hereditary. Yet I think history furnishes as many examples of a single usurper arising out of a government by a plurality, as of temporary trusts of power in a single hand rendered permanent by usurpation. I do not believe, therefore, that this danger is lessened in the hands of a plural executive. Perhaps it is greatly increased, by the state of inefficiency to which they are liable from feuds and divisions among themselves. The conservative body you propose might be so constituted, as, while it would be an admirable sedative in a variety of smaller cases, might also be a valuable sentinel and check on the liberticide views of an ambitious individual. I am friendly to this idea.

But the true barriers of our liberty in this country are our State governments; and the wisest conservative power ever contrived by man, is that of which our Revolution and present government found us possessed. Seventeen distinct States, amalgamated into one as to their foreign concerns, but single and independent as to their internal administration, regularly organized with a legislature and governor resting on the choice of the people, and enlightened by a free press, can never be so fascinated by the arts of one man, as to submit voluntarily to his usurpation. Nor can they be constrained to it by any force he can possess. While that may paralyze the single State in which it happens to be encamped, sixteen others, spread over a country of two thousand miles diameter, rise up on every side, ready organized for deliberation by a constitutional legislature, and for action by their governor, constitutionally the commander of the militia of the State, that is to say, of every man in it able to bear arms; and that militia, too, regularly formed into regiments and battalions, into infantry, cavalry and artillery, trained under officers general and subordinate, legally appointed, always in readiness, and to whom they are already in habits of obedience. The republican government of France was lost without a struggle, because the party of *"un et indivisible"* had prevailed; no provincial organizations existed to which the people might rally under authority of the laws, the seats of the directory were virtually vacant, and a small force sufficed to turn the legislature out of their chamber, and to salute its leader chief of the nation. But with us, sixteen out of seventeen States rising in mass, under regular organization, and legal commanders, united in object and action by their Congress, or, if that be in *duresse,* by a special convention, present such obstacles to an usurper as forever to stifle ambition in the first conception of that object

## TO THE SPEAKER AND HOUSE OF DELEGATES OF THE COMMONWEALTH OF VIRGINIA, BEING A PROTEST AGAINST INTERFERENCE OF JUDICIARY BETWEEN REPRESENTATIVE AND CONSTITUENT

1797

The petition of the subscribers, inhabitants of the counties of Amherst, Albemarle, Fluvanna, and Goochland, sheweth:

That by the constitution of this State, established from its earliest settlement, the people thereof have professed the right of being governed by laws to which they have consented by representatives chosen by themselves immediately: that in order to give to the will of the people the influence it ought to have, and the information which may enable them to exercise it usefully, it was a part of the common law, adopted as the law of this land, that their representatives, in the discharge of their functions, should be free from the cognizance or coercion of the co-ordinate branches, Judiciary and Executive; and that their communications with their constituents should of right, as of duty also, be free, full, and unawed by any: that so necessary has this intercourse been deemed in the country from which they derive principally their descent and laws, that the correspondence between the representative and constituent is privileged there to pass free of expense through the channel of the public post, and that the proceedings of the legislature have been known to be arrested and suspended at times until the Representatives could go home to their several counties and confer with their constituents.

That when, at the epoch of Independence, the constitution was formed under which we are now governed as a commonwealth, so high were the principles of representative government esteemed, that the legislature was made to consist of two branches, both of them chosen immediately by the citizens; and that general system of laws was continued which protected the relations between the representative and constituent, and guarded the functions of the former from the control of the Judiciary and Executive branches.

That when circumstances required that the ancient confederation of this with the sister States, for the government of their common concerns, should be improved into a more regular and effective form of general government, the same representative principle was preserved in the new legislature, one branch of which was to be chosen directly by the citizens of each State, and the laws and principles remained unaltered which privilege the representative functions, whether to be exercised in the State or General Government, against the cognizance and notice of the co-ordinate branches, Executive and Judiciary; and for its safe and convenient exercise, the intercommunication of the representative and constituent has been sanctioned and provided for through the channel of the public post, at the public expense.

That at the general partition of this commonwealth into districts, each of which was to choose a representative to Congress, the counties of Amherst, Albemarle, Fluvanna, and Goochland, were laid off into one district: that at the elections held for the said district, in the month of April, in the years 1795 and 1797, the electors thereof made choice of Samuel Jordan Cabell, of the county of Amherst, to be their representative in the legislature of the general government; that the said Samuel Jordan Cabell accepted the office, repaired at the due periods to the legislature of the General Government, exercised his functions there as became a worthy member, and as a good and dutiful representative was in the habit of corresponding with many of his constituents, and communicating to us, by way of letter, information of the public proceedings, of asking and receiving our opinions and advice, and of contributing, as far as might be with right, to preserve the transactions of the general government in unison with the principles and sentiments of his constituents: that while the said Samuel J. Cabell was in the exercise of his functions as a representative from this district, and was in the course of that correspondence which his duty and the will of his constituents imposed on him, the right of thus communicating with them, deemed sacred under all the forms in which our government has hitherto existed, never questioned or infringed even by Royal judges or governors, was openly and directly violated at a Circuit court of the General Government, held at the city of Richmond, for the district of Virginia, in the month of May of this present year, 1797: that at the said court, A, B, &c., some of whom were foreigners, having been called upon to serve in the office of grand jurors before the said court, were sworn to the duties of said office in the usual forms of the law, the known limits of which duties are to make presentment of those acts of individuals which the laws have declared to be crimes or misdemeanors: that departing out of the legal limits of their said office, and availing themselves of the sanction of its cover, wickedly and contrary to their fidelity to destroy the rights of the people of this commonwealth, and the fundamental principles of representative government, they made a presentment of the act of the said Samuel J. Cabell, in writing letters to his constituents in the following words, to wit: "We, of the grand jury of the United States, for the district of Virginia, present as a real evil, the circular letters of several members of the late Congress, and particularly letters with the signature of Samuel J. Cabell, endeavoring, at a time of real public danger, to disseminate unfounded calumnies against the happy government of the United States, and thereby to separate the people therefrom; and to increase or produce a foreign influence, ruinous to the peace, happiness, and independence of these United States."

That the grand jury is a part of the Judiciary, not permanent indeed, but in office, *pro hac vice* and responsible as other judges are for their actings and doings while in office: that for the Judiciary to interpose in the legislative department between the constituent and his representative, to control them in the exercise of their functions or duties towards each other, to overawe the free correspondence which exists and ought to exist between them, to dictate what communications may pass between them, and to punish all others, to put the representative into jeopardy of criminal prosecution, of vexation, expense, and punishment before the Judiciary, if his communications, public or private, do not exactly square with their ideas of fact or right, or with their designs of wrong, is to put the legislative department under the feet of the Judiciary, is to leave us, indeed, the shadow, but to take away the substance of representation, which requires essentially that the representative be as free as his constituents would be, that the same interchange of sentiment be lawful between him and them as would be lawful among themselves were they in the personal transaction of their own business; is to do away the influence of the people over the proceedings of their representatives by excluding from their knowledge, by the terror of punishment, all but such information or misinformation as may suit their own views; and is the more vitally dangerous when it is considered that grand jurors are selected by officers nominated and holding their places at the will of the Executive: that they are exposed to influence from the judges who are nominated immediately by the Executive, and who, although holding permanently their commissions as judges, yet from the career of additional office and emolument *actually* opened to them of late, whether *constitutionally* or not, are under all those motives which interest or ambition inspire, of courting the favor of that branch from which appointments flow: that grand juries are frequently composed in part of bystanders, often foreigners, of foreign attachments and interests, and little knowledge of the laws they are most improperly called to decide on; and finally, is to give to the Judiciary, and through them to the Executive, a complete preponderance over the legislature, rendering ineffectual that wise and cautious distribution of powers made by the constitution between the three branches, and subordinating to the other two that branch which most immediately depends on the people themselves, and is responsible to them at short periods.

That independently of these considerations of a constitutional nature, the right of free correspondence between citizen and citizen on their joint interests, public or private, and under whatsoever laws these interests arise, is a natural right of every individual citizen, not the gift of municipal law, but among the objects for the protection of which municipal laws are instituted: that so far as the attempt to take away this natural right of free correspondence is an offence against the privileges of the legislative house, of which the said Samuel J. Cabell is a member, it is left to that house, entrusted with the preservation of its own privileges, to vindicate its immunities against the encroachments and usurpations of a co-ordinate branch; but so far as it is an infraction of our individual rights as citizens by other citizens of our own State, the judicature of this commonwealth is solely competent to its cognizance, no other possessing any powers of redress: that the commonwealth retains all its judiciary cognizances not expressly alienated in the grant of powers to the United States as expressed in their constitution: that that constitution alienates only those enumerated in itself, or arising under laws or treaties of the United States made in conformity with its own tenor; but the right of free correspondence is not claimed under that constitution nor the laws or treaties derived from it, but as a natural right, placed originally under the protection of our municipal laws, and retained under the cognizance of our own courts.

Your petitioners further observe that though this crime may not be specifically defined and denominated by any particular statute, yet it is a crime, and of the highest and most alarming nature; that the constitution of this commonwealth, aware it would sometimes happen that deep and dangerous crimes, pronounced as such in the heart of every friend to his country and its free constitution, would often escape the definitions of the law, and yet ought not to escape its punishments, fearing at the same time to entrust such undescribed offences to the discretion of ordinary juries and judges, has reserved the same to the cognizance of the body of the commonwealth acting by their representatives in general assembly, for which purpose provision is made by the constitution in the following words, to wit: "The Governor, when he is out of office, and *others* offending against the State, either by maladministration, corruption, *or other means* by which the safety of the State may be endangered, shall be impeachable by the House of Delegates. Such impeachment to be prosecuted by the Attorney General or such other person or persons as the house may appoint in the general court, according to the laws of the land. If found guilty, he or they shall be either forever disabled to hold any office under government, or removed from such offices *pro tempore,* or subjected to such pains or penalties as the law shall direct."

Considering then the House of Delegates as the standing inquest of the whole commonwealth so established by the constitution, that its jurisdiction as such extends over all persons within its limits, and that no pale, no sanctuary has been erected against their jurisdiction to protect offenders who have committed crimes against the laws of the commonwealth and rights of its citizens: that the crime committed by the said grand jurors is of that high and extraordinary character for which the constitution has provided extraordinary procedure: that though the violation of right falls in the first instance on us, your petitioners and the representative chosen immediately by us, yet in principle and consequence it extends to all our fellow-citizens, whose safety is passed away whenever their representatives are placed, in the exercise of their functions, under the direction and coercion of either of the other departments of government, and one of their most interesting rights is lost when that of a free communication of sentiment by speaking or writing is suppressed: We, your petitioners, therefore pray that you will be pleased to take your constitutional cognizance of the premises, and institute such proceedings for impeaching and punishing the said A, B, &c., as may secure to the citizens of this commonwealth their constitutional right: that their representatives shall in the exercise of their functions be free and independent of the other departments of government, may guard that full intercourse between them and their constituents which the nature of their relations and the laws of the land establish, may save to them the natural right of communicating their sentiments to one another by speaking and writing, and may serve as a terror to others attempting hereafter to subvert those rights and the fundamental principles of our constitution, to exclude the people from all direct influence over the government they have established by reducing that branch of the legislature which they choose directly, to a subordination under those over whom they have but an indirect, distant, and feeble control.

And your petitioners further submit to the wisdom of the two houses of assembly whether the safety of the citizens of this commonwealth in their persons, their property, their laws, and government, does not require that the capacity to act in the important office of a juror, grand or petty, civil or criminal, should be restrained in future to native citizens of the United States, or such as were citizens at the date of the treaty of peace which closed our revolutionary war, and whether the ignorance of our laws and natural partiality to the countries of their birth are not reasonable causes for declaring this to be one of the rights incommunicable in future to adoptive citizens.

We, therefore, your petitioners, relying with entire confidence on the wisdom and patriotism of our representatives in General assembly, clothed preëminently with all the powers of the people which have not been reserved to themselves, or enumerated in the grant to the General Government delegated to maintain all their rights and relations not expressly and exclusively transferred to other jurisdictions, and stationed as sentinels to observe with watchfulness and oppose with firmness all movements tending to destroy the equilibrium of our excellent but complicated machine of government, invoke from you that redress of our violated rights which the freedom and safety of our common country calls for. We denounce to you a great crime, wicked in its purpose, and mortal in its consequences unless prevented, committed by citizens of this commonwealth against the body of their country. If we have erred in conceiving the redress provided by the law, we commit the subject to the superior wisdom of this house to devise and pursue such proceedings as they shall think best; and we, as in duty bound, shall ever pray, &c.

## SUPREME COURT OPINIONS [1]

October 27, 1822

There is a subject respecting the practice of the court of which you are a member, which has long weighed on my mind, on which I have long thought I would write to you, and which I will take this opportunity of doing. It is in truth a delicate undertaking, and yet such is my opinion of your candor and devotedness to the Constitution, in its true spirit, that I am sure I shall meet your approbation in unbosoming myself to you. The subject of my uneasiness is the habitual mode of making up and delivering the opinions of the supreme court of the U.S.

You know that from the earliest ages of the English law, from the date of the year-books, at least, to the end of the II[d] George, the judges of England, in all but self-evident cases, delivered their opinions seriatim, with the reasons and authorities which governed their decisions. If they sometimes consulted together, and gave a general opinion, it was so rarely as not to excite either alarm or notice. Besides the light which their separate arguments threw on the subject, and the instruction communicated by their several modes of reasoning, it shewed whether the judges were unanimous or divided, and gave accordingly more or less weight to the judgment as a precedent. It sometimes happened too that when there were three opinions

[1] Letter to William Johnson. Johnson was an associate justice of the U.S. Supreme Court, appointed by Jefferson in 1804.

against one, the reasoning of the one was so much the most cogent as to become afterwards the law of the land. When Lord Mansfield came to the bench he introduced the habit of caucusing opinions. The judges met at their chambers, or elsewhere, secluded from the presence of the public, and made up what was to be delivered as the opinion of the court. On the retirement of Mansfield, Lord Kenyon put an end to the practice, and the judges returned to that of seriatim opinions, and practice it habitually to this day, I believe. I am not acquainted with the late reporters, do not possess them, and state the fact from the information of others.

To come now to ourselves, I know nothing of what is done in other states, but in this our great and good Mr. Pendleton was, after the revolution, placed at the head of the court of Appeals. He adored Lord Mansfield, and considered him as the greatest luminary of law that any age had ever produced, and he introduced into the court over which he presided, Mansfield's practice of making up opinions in secret and delivering them as the Oracles of the court, in mass. Judge Roane, when he came to that bench, broke up the practice, refused to hatch judgments, in conclave, or to let others deliver opinions for him. At what time the seriatim opinions ceased in the supreme court of the U.S., I am not informed. They continued I know to the end of the 3d Dalls in 1800. Later than which I have no Reporter of that court.

About that time the present C[hief] J[ustice] came to the bench. Whether he carried the practice of Mr. Pendleton to it, or who, or when I do not know; but I understand from others it is now the habit of the court, and I suppose it true from the cases sometimes reported in the newspapers, and others which I casually see, wherein I observe that the opinions were uniformly prepared in private. Some of these cases too have been of such importance, of such difficulty, and the decisions so grating to a portion of the public as to have merited the fullest explanation from every judge seriatim, of the reasons which had produced such convictions on his mind. It was interesting to the public to know whether these decisions were really unanimous, or might not perhaps be of 4 against 3 and consequently prevailing by the preponderance of one voice only. The Judges holding their offices for life are under two responsibilities only. 1. Impeachment. 2. Individual reputation. But this practice compleatly withdraws them from both. For nobody knows what opinion any individual member gave in any case, nor even that he who delivers the opinion, concurred in it himself. Be the opinion therefore ever so impeachable, having been done in the dark it can be proved on no one.

As to the 2d guarantee, personal reputation, it is shielded compleatly. The practice is certainly convenient for the lazy, the modest and the incompetent. It saves them the trouble of developing their opinion methodically and even of making up an opinion at all. That of seriatim argument shews whether every judge has taken the trouble of understanding the case, of investigating it minutely, and of forming an opinion for himself, instead of pinning it on another's sleeve. It would certainly be right to abandon this practice in order to give to our citizens one and all, that confidence in their judges which must be so desirable to the judges themselves, and so important to the cement of the union. During the administration of General Washington, and while E. Randolph was Attorney General, he was required by Congress to digest the judiciary laws into a single one, with such amendments as might be thought proper. He prepared a section requiring the Judges to give their opinions seriatim, in writing, to be recorded in a distinct volume. Other business prevented this bill from being taken up, and it passed off, but such a volume would have been the best possible book of reports, and the better, as unincumbered with the hired sophisms and perversions of Counsel.

## THE USURPATION OF SUPREME COURT[1]

June 12, 1823

You request me confidentially, to examine the question, whether the Supreme Court has advanced beyond its constitutional limits, and trespassed on those of the State authorities? I do not undertake, my dear Sir, because I am unable. Age and the wane of mind consequent on it, had disqualified me from investigations so severe, and researches so laborious. And it is the less necessary in this case, as having been already done by others with a logic and learning to which I could add nothing. On the decision of the case of Cohen *vs.* The State of Virginia, in the Supreme Court of the United States, in March, 1821, Judge Roane, under the signature of Algernon Sidney, wrote for the Enquirer a series of papers on the law of that case. I considered these papers maturely as they came out, and confess that they appeared to me to pulverize every word which had been delivered by Judge Marshall, of the extra-judicial part of his opinion; and all was extra-judicial, except the decision that the act of Congress had not purported to give to the corporation of Washington the authority claimed by their lottery law, of controlling the laws of the States within the States themselves. But unable to claim that case, he could not let it go entirely, but went on gratuitously to prove, that notwithstanding the eleventh amendment of the constitution, a State *could* be brought as a defendant, to the bar of his court; and again, that Congress might authorize a corporation of its territory to exercise legislation within a State, and paramount to the laws of that State.

I cite the sum and result only of his doctrines, according to the impression made on my mind at the time, and still remaining. If not strictly accurate in circumstance, it is so in substance. This doctrine was so completely refuted

[1] Letter to William Johnson.

by Roane, that if he can be answered, I surrender human reason as a vain and useless faculty, given to bewilder, and not to guide us. And I mention this particular case as one only of several, because it gave occasion to that thorough examination of the constitutional limits between the General and State jurisdictions, which you have asked for. There were two other writers in the same paper, under the signatures of Fletcher of Saltoun, and Somers, who, in a few essays, presented some very luminous and striking views of the question. And there was a particular paper which recapitulated all the cases in which it was thought the federal court had usurped on the State jurisdictions. These essays will be found in the Enquirers of 1821, from May the 10th to July the 13th. It is not in my present power to send them to you, but if Ritchie can furnish them, I will procure and forward them. If they had been read in the other States, as they were here, I think they would have left, there as here, no dissentients from their doctrine. The subject was taken up by our legislature of 1821-'22, and two draughts of remonstrances were prepared and discussed. As well as I remember, there was no difference of opinion as to the matter of right; but there was as to the expediency of a remonstrance at that time, the general mind of the States being then under extraordinary excitement by the Missouri question; and it was dropped on that consideration. But this case is not dead, it only sleepeth. The Indian Chief said he did not go to war for every petty injury by itself, but put it into his pouch, and when that was full, he then made war. Thank Heaven, we have provided a more peaceable and rational mode of redress.

This practice of Judge Marshall, of travelling out of his case to prescribe what the law would be in a moot case not before the court, is very irregular and very censurable. I recollect another instance, and the more particularly, perhaps, because it in some measure bore on myself. Among the midnight appointments of Mr. Adams, were commissions to some federal justices of the peace for Alexandria. These were signed and sealed by him, but not delivered. I found them on the table of the department of State, on my entrance into office, and forbade their delivery. Marbury, named in one of them, applied to the Supreme Court for a mandamus to the Secretary of State (Mr. Madison) to deliver the commission intended for him. The court determined at once, that being an original process, they had no cognizance of it; and therefore the question before them was ended. But the Chief Justice went on to lay down what the law would be, had they jurisdiction of the case, to wit: that they should command the delivery. The object was clearly to instruct any other court having the jurisdiction, what they should do if Marbury should apply to them. Besides the impropriety of this gratuitous interference, could anything exceed the perversion of law? For if there is any principle of law never yet contradicted it is that delivery is one of the essentials to the validity of the deed. Although signed and sealed, yet as long as it remains in the hands of the party himself, it is in *fieri* only, it is not a deed, and can be made so only by its delivery. In the hands of a third person it may be made an escrow. But whatever is in the executive offices is certainly deemed to be in the hands of the President; and in this case, was actually in my hands, because, when I countermanded them, there was as yet no Secretary of State. Yet this case of Marbury and Madison is continually cited by bench and bar, as if it were settled law, without any animadversion on its being merely an *obiter* dissertation of the Chief Justice.

It may be impracticable to lay down any general formula of words which shall decide at once, and with precision, in every case, this limit of jurisdiction. But there are two canons which will guide us safely in most of the cases. 1st. The capital and leading object of the constitution was to leave with the States all authorities which respected their own citizens only, and to transfer to the United States those which respected citizens of foreign or other States: to make us several as to ourselves, but one as to all others. In the latter case, then, constructions should lean to the general jurisdiction, if the words will bear it; and in favor of the States in the former, if possible to be so construed. And indeed, between citizens and citizens of the same State, and under their own laws, I know but a single case in which a jurisdiction is given to the General Government. That is, where anything but gold or silver is made a lawful tender, or the obligation of contracts is any otherwise impaired. The separate legislatures had so often abused that power, that the citizens themselves chose to trust it to the general, rather than to their own special authorities. 2d. On every question of construction, carry ourselves back to the time when the constitution was adopted, recollect the spirit manifested in the debates, and instead of trying what meaning may be squeezed out of the text, or invented against it, conform to the probable one in which it was passed. Let us try Cohen's case by these canons only, referring always, however, for full argument, to the essays before cited.

1. It was between a citizen and his own State, and under a law of his State. It was a domestic case, therefore, and not a foreign one.

2. Can it be believed, that under the jealousies prevailing against the General Government, at the adoption of the constitution, the States meant to surrender the authority of preserving order, of enforcing moral duties and restraining vice, within their own territory? And this is the present case, that of Cohen being under the ancient and general law of gaming. Can any good be effected by taking from the States the moral rule of their citizens, and subordinating it to the general authority, or to one of their corporations, which may justify forcing the meaning of words, hunting after possible constructions, and hanging inference on inference, from heaven to earth, like Jacob's ladder? Such an intention was impossible, and such a licentiousness of construction and inference, if exercised by both governments, as may be

done with equal right, would equally authorize both to claim all power, general and particular, and break up the foundations of the Union. Laws are made for men of ordinary understanding, and should, therefore, be construed by the ordinary rules of common sense. Their meaning is not to be sought for in metaphysical subtleties, which may make anything mean everything or nothing, at pleasure. It should be left to the sophisms of advocates, whose trade it is, to prove that a defendant is a plaintiff, though dragged into court, *torto collo,* like Bonaparte's volunteers, into the field in chains, or that a power has been given, because it ought to have been given, *et alia talia.* The States supposed that by their tenth amendment, they had secured themselves against constructive powers. They were not lessoned yet by Cohen's case, nor aware of the slipperiness of the eels of the law. I ask for no straining of words against the General Government, nor yet against the States. I believe the States can best govern our home concerns, and the General Government our foreign ones. I wish, therefore, to see maintained that wholesome distribution of powers established by the constitution for the limitation of both; and never to see all offices transferred to Washington, where, further withdrawn from the eyes of the people, they may more secretly be bought and sold as at market.

But the Chief Justice says, "there must be an ultimate arbiter somewhere." True, there must; but does that prove it is either party? The ultimate arbiter is the people of the Union, assembled by their deputies in convention, at the call of Congress, or of two-thirds of the States. Let them decide to which they mean to give an authority claimed by two of their organs. And it has been the peculiar wisdom and felicity of our constitution, to have provided this peaceable appeal, where that of other nations is at once to force.

*Chapter X*

# THE NATIONAL ECONOMY

## RICE, OLIVES, AND OTHER PLANTS[1]

July 30, 1787

Having observed that the consumption of rice in this country, and particularly in this capital, was very great, I thought it my duty to inform myself from what markets they draw their supplies, in what proportion from ours, and whether it might not be practicable to increase that proportion. This city being little concerned in foreign commerce, it is difficult to obtain information on particular branches of it in the detail. I addressed myself to the retailers of rice, and from them received a mixture of truth and error, which I was unable to sift apart in the first moment. Continuing, however, my inquiries, they produced at length this result: that the dealers here were in the habit of selling two qualities of rice, that of Carolina, with which they were supplied chiefly from England, and that of Piedmont; that the Carolina rice was long, slender, white and transparent, answers well when prepared with milk, sugar, &c., but not so well when prepared *au gras;* that that of Piedmont was shorter, thicker, and less white, but that it presented its form better when dressed *au gras,* was better tasted, and therefore preferred by good judges for those purposes; that the consumption of rice, in this form, was much the most considerable, but that the superior beauty of the Carolina rice, seducing the eye of those purchasers who are attached to appearances, the demand for it was upon the whole as great as for that of Piedmont. They supposed this difference of quality to proceed from a difference of management; that the Carolina rice was husked with an instrument that broke it more, and that less pains were taken to separate the broken from the unbroken grains, imagining that it was the broken grains which dissolved in oily preparations; that the Carolina rice costs somewhat less than that of

[1] Letter from Paris to William Drayton.

Piedmont; but that being obliged to sort the whole grains from the broken, in order to satisfy the taste of their customers, they ask and receive as much for the first quality of Carolina, when sorted, as for the rice of Piedmont; but the second and third qualities, obtained by sorting, are sold much cheaper. The objection to the Carolina rice then, being, that it crumbles in certain forms of preparation, and this supposed to be the effect of a less perfect machine for husking, I flattered myself I should be able to learn what might be the machine of Piedmont, when I should arrive at Marseilles, to which place I was to go in the course of a tour through the seaport towns of this country. At Marseilles, however, they differed as much in account of the machines, as at Paris they had differed about other circumstances. Some said it was husked between mill-stones, others between rubbers of wood in the form of mill-stones, others of cork. They concurred in one fact, however, that the machine might be seen by me, immediately on crossing the Alps. This would be an affair of three weeks. I crossed them and went through the rice country from Vercelli to Pavia, about sixty miles. I found the machine to be absolutely the same with that used in Carolina, as well as I could recollect a description which Mr. E. Rutledge had given me of it. It is on the plan of a powder mill. In some of them, indeed, they arm each pestle with an iron tooth, consisting of nine spikes hooked together, which I do not remember in the description of Mr. Rutledge. I therefore had a tooth made, which I have the honor of forwarding you with this letter; observing, at the same time, that as many of their machines are without teeth as with them, and of course, that the advantage is not very palpable. It seems to follow, then, that the rice of Lombardy (for though called Piedmont rice, it does not grow in that country but in Lombardy) is of a different species from that of Carolina; different in form, in color and in quality. We know that in Asia they have several distinct species of this grain. Monsieur Poivre, a former Governor of the Isle of France, in travelling through several countries of Asia, observed with particular attention the objects of their agriculture, and he tells us, that in Cochin-China they cultivate six several kinds of rice, which he describes, three of them requiring water, and three growing on highlands. The rice of Carolina is said to have come from Madagascar, and De Poivre tells us, it is the white rice which is cultivated there. This favors the probability of its being of a different species originally, from that of Piedmont; and time, culture and climate may have made it still more different. Under this idea, I thought it would be well to furnish you with some of the Piedmont rice, unhusked, but was told it was contrary to the laws to export it in that form. I took such measures as I could, however, to have a quantity brought out, and lest these should fail, I brought, myself, a few pounds. A part of this I have addressed to you by the way of London;

a part comes with this letter; and I shall send another parcel by some other conveyance, to prevent the danger of miscarriage. Any one of them arriving safe, may serve to put in seed, should the society think it an object. This seed too, coming from Vercelli, where the best rice is supposed to grow, is more to be depended on than what may be sent me hereafter. There is a rice from the Levant, which is considered as of a quality still different, and some think it superior to that of Piedmont. The troubles which have existed in that country for several years back, have intercepted it from the European market, so that it is become almost unknown. I procured a bag of it, however, at Marseilles, and another of the best rice of Lombardy, which are on their way to this place, and when arrived, I will forward you a quantity of each, sufficient to enable you to judge of their qualities when prepared for the table. I have also taken measures to have a quantity of it brought from the Levant, unhusked. If I succeed, it shall be forwarded in like manner. I should think it certainly advantageous to cultivate, in Carolina and Georgia, the two qualities demanded at market; because the progress of culture, with us, may soon get beyond the demand for the white rice; and because too, there is often a brisk demand for the one quality, when the market is glutted with the other. I should hope there would be no danger of losing the species of white rice, by a confusion with the other. This would be a real misfortune, as I should not hesitate to pronounce the white, upon the whole, the most precious of the two, for us.

The dry rice of Cochin-China has the reputation of being the whitest to the eye, best flavored to the taste, and most productive. It seems then to unite the good qualities of both the others known to us. Could it supplant them, it would be a great happiness, as it would enable us to get rid of those ponds of stagnant water, so fatal to human health and life. But such is the force of habit, and caprice of taste, that we could not be sure beforehand it would produce this effect. The experiment, however, is worth trying, should it only end in producing a third quality, and increasing the demand. I will endeavor to procure some to be brought from Cochin-China. The event, however, will be uncertain and distant.

I was induced, in the course of my journey through the south of France, to pay very particular attention to the objects of their culture, because the resemblance of their climate to that of the southern parts of the United States, authorizes us to presume we may adopt any of their articles of culture, which we would wish for. We should not wish for their wines, though they are good and abundant. The culture of the vine is not desirable in lands capable of producing anything else. It is a species of gambling, and of desperate gambling too, wherein, whether you make much or nothing, you are equally ruined. The middling crop alone is the saving point, and that the seasons seldom hit. Accordingly, we see much wretchedness among this class of cultivators. Wine, too, is so cheap in these countries, that a laborer with us, employed in the culture of any other article, may exchange it for wine, more and better than he could raise himself. It is a resource for a country, the whole of whose good soil is otherwise employed, and which still has some barren spots, and surplus of population to employ on them. There the vine is good, because it is something in the place of nothing. It may become a resource to us at a still earlier period; when the increase of population shall increase our productions beyond the demand for them, both at home and abroad. Instead of going on to make an useless surplus of them, we may employ our supernumerary hands on the vine. But that period is not yet arrived.

The almond tree is also so precarious, that none can depend for subsistence on its produce, but persons of capital.

The caper, though a more tender plant, is more certain in its produce, because a mound of earth of the size of a cucumber hill, thrown over the plant in the fall, protects it effectually against the cold of winter. When the danger of frost is over in the spring, they uncover it, and begin its culture. There is a great deal of this in the neighborhood of Toulon. The plants are set about eight feet apart, and yield, one year with another, about two pounds of caper each, worth on the spot sixpence sterling per pound. They require little culture, and this may be performed either with the plough or hoe. The principal work is the gathering of the fruit as it forms. Every plant must be picked every other day, from the last of June till the middle of October. But this is the work of women and children. This plant does well in any kind of soil which is dry, or even in walls where there is no soil, and it lasts the life of a man. Toulon would be the proper port to apply for them. I must observe, that the preceding details cannot be relied on with the fullest certainty, because, in the canton where this plant is cultivated, the inhabitants speak no written language, but a medley, which I could understand but very imperfectly.

The fig and mulberry are so well known in America, that nothing need be said of them. Their culture, too, is by women and children, and therefore earnestly to be desired in countries where there are slaves. In these, the women and children are often employed in labors disproportioned to their sex and age. By presenting to the master objects of culture, easier and equally beneficial, all temptation to misemploy them would be removed, and the lot of this tender part of our species be much softened. By varying, too, the articles of culture, we multiply the chances for making something, and disarm the seasons in a proportionable degree, of their calamitous effects.

The olive is a tree the least known in America, and yet the most worthy of being known. Of all the gifts of heaven to man, it is next to the most precious, if it be not the most precious. Perhaps it may claim a preference even to bread, because there is such an infinitude of vegetables, which it renders a proper and comfortable nourishment. In passing the Alps at the Col de Tende, where they are mere masses of rock, wherever there happens to be a little soil, there are a number of olive trees, and a village supported by them. Take away these trees, and the same ground in corn would not support a single family. A pound of oil, which can be bought for three or four pence sterling, is equivalent to many pounds of flesh, by the quantity of vegetables it will prepare, and render fit and comfortable food. Without this tree, the country of Provence and territory of Genoa would not support one-half, perhaps not one-third, their present inhabitants. The nature of the soil is of little consequence if it be dry. The trees are planted from fifteen to twenty feet apart, and when tolerably good, will yield fifteen or twenty pounds of oil yearly, one with another. There are trees which yield much more. They begin to render good crops at twenty years old, and last till killed by cold, which happens at some time or other, even in their best positions in France. But they put out again from their roots. In Italy, I am told, they have trees two hundred years old. They afford an easy but constant employment through the year, and require so little nourishment, that if the soil be fit for any other production, it may be cultivated among the olive trees without injuring them. The northern limits of this tree are the mountains of the Cevennes, from about the meridian of Carcassonne to the Rhone, and from thence, the Alps and Apennines as far as Genoa, I know, and how much farther I am not informed. The shelter of these mountains may be considered as equivalent to a degree and a-half of latitude, at least, because westward of the commencement of the Cevennes, there are no olive trees in 43½ or even 43 of latitude, whereas, we find them *now* on the Rhone at Pierrelatte, in 44½, and *formerly* they were at Tains, above the mouth of the Isère, in 45, sheltered by the near approach of the Cevennes and Alps, which only leave there a passage for the Rhone. Whether such a shelter exists or not in the States of South Carolina and Georgia, I know not. But this we may say, either that it exists or that it is not necessary there, because we know that they produce the orange in open air; and wherever the orange will stand at all, experience shows that the olive will stand well, being a hardier tree. Notwithstanding the great quantities of oil made in France, they have not enough for their own consumption, and therefore import from other countries. This is an article, the consumption of which will always keep pace with its production. Raise it, and it begets its own demand. Little is carried to America, because Europe has it not to spare. We, therefore, have not learned the use of it. But cover the southern States with it, and every man will become a consumer of oil, within whose reach it can be brought in point of price. If the memory of those persons is held in great respect in South Carolina who introduced there the culture of rice, a plant which sows life and death with almost equal hand, what obligations would be due to him who should introduce the olive tree, and set the example of its culture! Were the owner of slaves to view it only as the means of bettering their condition, how much would he better that by planting one of those trees for every slave he possessed! Having been myself an eye witness to the blessings which this tree sheds on the poor, I never had my wishes so kindled for the introduction of any article of new culture into our own country. South Carolina and Georgia appear to me to be the States, wherein its success, in favorable positions at least, could not be doubted, and I flattered myself it would come within the views of the society for agriculture to begin the experiments which are to prove its practicability. Carcassonne is the place from which the plants may be most certainly and cheaply obtained. They can be sent from thence by water to Bordeaux, where they may be embarked on vessels bound for Charleston. There is too little intercourse between Charleston and Marseilles to propose this as the port of exportation. I offer my services to the society for the obtaining and forwarding any number of plants which may be desired.

Before I quit the subject of climates, and the plants adapted to them, I will add, as a matter of curiosity, and of some utility too, that my journey through the southern parts of France, and the territory of Genoa, but still more the crossing of the Alps, enabled me to form a scale of the tenderer plants, and to arrange them according to their different powers of resisting cold. In passing the Alps at the Col de Tende, we cross three very high mountains successively. In ascending, we lose these plants, one after another, as we rise, and find them again in the contrary order as we descend on the other side; and this is repeated three times. Their order, proceeding from the tenderest to the hardiest, is as follows: caper, orange, palm, aloe, olive, pomegranate, walnut, fig, almond. But this must be understood of the plant only; for as to the fruit, the order is somewhat different. The caper, for example, is the tenderest plant, yet, being so easily protected, it is among the most certain in its fruit. The almond, the hardiest, loses its fruit the oftenest, on account of its forwardness. The palm, hardier than the caper and orange, never produces perfect fruit here.

I had the honor of sending you, the last year, some seeds of the sulla of Malta, or Spanish St. Foin. Lest they should have miscarried, I now pack with the rice a cannister of the same kind of seed, raised by myself. By Colonel Franks, in the month of February last, I sent a parcel of acorns of the cork oak, which I desired him to ask the favor of the Delegates of South Carolina in Congress to forward to you.

# REPORT ON COD AND WHALE FISHERIES

February 1, 1791

The Secretary of State, to whom was referred by the House of Representatives, the representation from the General Court of the Commonwealth of Massachusetts, on the subjects of the cod and whale fisheries, together with the several papers accompanying it, has had the same under consideration, and thereupon makes the following report:

The representation sets forth that, before the late war, about four thousand seamen, and about twenty-four thousand tons of shipping, were annually employed from that State, in the whale fishery, the produce whereof was about three hundred and fifty thousand pounds lawful money a year.

That, previous to the same period, the cod fishery of that State employed four thousand men, and twenty-eight thousand tons of shipping, and produced about two hundred and fifty thousand pounds a year.

That these branches of business, annihilated during the war, have been, in some degree, recovered since; but that they labor under many and heavy embarrassments, which, if not removed, or lessened, will render the fisheries every year less extensive and important.

That these embarrassments are, heavy duties on their produce abroad, and bounties on that of their competitors; and duties at home on several articles, particularly used in the fisheries.

And it asks that the duties be taken off; that bounties be given to the fishermen; and the national influence be used abroad, for obtaining better markets for their produce.

The cod and whale fisheries, carried on by different persons, from different ports, in different vessels, in different seas, and seeking different markets, agree in one circumstance, in being as unprofitable to the adventurer, as important to the public. A succinct view of their rise, progress, and present state, with different nations, may enable us to note the circumstances which have attended their prosperity, and their decline; to judge of the embarrassments which are said to oppress ours; to see whether they depend on our own will, and may, therefore, be remedied immediately by ourselves, or, whether depending on the will of others, they are without the reach of remedy from us, either directly or indirectly.

Their history being as unconnected as their practice, they shall be separately considered.

Within twenty years after the supposed discovery of Newfoundland, by the Cabots, we find that the abundance of fish on its banks, had already drawn the attention of the people of Europe. For, as early as 1517, or 1519, we are told of fifty ships being seen there at one time. The first adventurers in that fishery were the Biscayans, of Spain, the Basques and Bas-Bretons, of France, all united anciently in language, and still in habits, and in extreme poverty. The last circumstance enabled them long to retain a considerable share of the fishery. In 1577, the French had one hundred and fifty vessels there; the Spaniards had still one hundred, and the Portuguese fifty, when the English had only fifteen. The Spaniards and Portuguese seem at length to have retired silently, the French and English claiming the fishery exclusively, as an appurtenance to their adjacent colonies, and the profits being too small for nations surcharged with the precious metals proceeding from their mines.

Without materials to trace the intermediate progress, we only know that, so late as 1744, the French employed there five hundred and sixty-four ships, and twenty-seven thousand five hundred seamen, and took one million two hundred and forty-six thousand quintals of fish, which was three times the extent to which England and her colonies together, carried this fishery at that time.

The English, in the beginning of the seventeenth century, had employed, generally, about one hundred and fifty vessels in the Newfoundland fishery. About 1670 we find them reduced to eighty, and one hundred, the inhabitants of New England beginning now to supplant them. A little before this, the British Parliament perceiving that their citizens were unable to subsist on the scanty profits which sufficed for their poorer competitors, endeavored to give them some advantage by prohibiting the importation of foreign fish; and, at the close of the century, they formed some regulations for their government and protection, and remitted to them some duties. A successful war enabled them, in 1713, to force from the French a cession of the Island of Newfoundland; under these encouragements, the English and American fisheries began to thrive. In 1731 we find the English take two hundred thousand quintals of fish, and the Americans two hundred and thirty thousand, besides the refuse fish, not fit for European markets. They continue to gain ground, and the French to lose it, insomuch that, about 1755, they are said to have been on a par; and, in 1768, the French have only two hundred and fifty-nine vessels, of twenty-four thousand four hundred and twenty tons, nine thousand seven hundred and twenty-two seamen, taking two hundred thousand quintals, while America alone, for some three or four years before that, and so on, to the commencement of the late war, employed six hundred and sixty-five vessels, of twenty-five thousand six hundred and fifty tons, and four thousand four hundred and five seamen, and took from three hundred and fifty thousand to upwards of four hundred thousand quintals of fish, and England a still greater quantity, five hundred and twenty-six thousand quintals, as is said.

Spain had formally relinquished her pretensions to a participation in these fisheries, at the close of the preceding war; and, at the end of this, the adjacent continent and islands being divided between the United States, the English and French (for the last retained two small islands merely for this object), the right of fishing was appropriated to them also.

France, sensible of the necessity of balancing the power of England on the water, and, therefore, of improving every resource for raising seamen, and seeing that her fishermen could not maintain their competition without some public patronage, adopted the experiment of bounties on her own fish, and duties on that of foreign nations brought into her markets. But, notwithstanding this, her fisheries dwindle, from a change taken place, insensibly, in the character of her navigation, which, from being the most economical, is now become the most expensive. In 1786, she is said to have employed but seven thousand men in this fishery, and to have taken four hundred and twenty-six thousand quintals; and, in 1787, but six thousand men, and one hundred and twenty-eight thousand quintals. She seems not yet sensible that the unthriftiness of her fisheries proceeds from the want of economy, and not the want of markets; and that the encouragement of our fishery abridges that of a rival nation, whose power on the ocean has long threatened the loss of all balance on that element.

The plan of the English Government, since the peace, has been to prohibit all foreign fish in their markets, and they have given from eighteen to fifty thousand pounds sterling on every fishing vessel complying with certain conditions. This policy is said to have been so far successful, as to have raised the number of seamen employed in that business, in 1786, to fourteen thousand, and the quantity of fish taken, to 732,000 quintals. . . .

✦

The fisheries of the United States, annihilated during the war; their vessels, utensils, and fishermen destroyed; their markets in the Mediterranean and British America lost, and their produce dutied in those of France; their competitors enabled by bounties to meet and undersell them at the few markets remaining open, without any public aid, and, indeed, paying aids to the public;—such were the hopeless auspices under which this important business was to be resumed. Yet it was resumed, and, aided by the mere force of natural advantages, they employed, during the years 1786, 1787, 1788, and 1789, on an average, five hundred and thirty-nine vessels, of nineteen thousand one hundred and eighty-five tons, three thousand two hundred and eighty-seven seamen, and took two hundred and fifty thousand six hundred and fifty quintals of fish. . . . And an official paper . . . shows that, in the last of those years, our exportation amounted to three hundred and seventy-five thousand and twenty quintals, and thirty thousand four hundred and sixty-one barrels; deduction made of three thousand seven hundred and one quintals, and six thousand three hundred and forty-three barrels of foreign fish, received and re-exported. . . . Still, however, the calculations . . . which accompany the representation, show that the profits of the sales in the years 1787 and 1788, were too small to afford a living to the fishermen, and on those of 1789, there was such a loss as to withdraw thirty-three vessels, of the town of Marblehead alone, from the further pursuit of this business; and the apprehension is, that, without some public aid, those still remaining will continue to withdraw, and this whole commerce be engrossed by a single nation.

This rapid view of the cod fishery enables us to discern under what policy it has flourished or declined in the hands of other nations, and to mark the fact, that it is too poor a business to be left to itself, even with the nation most advantageously situated.

It will now be proper to count the advantages which aid, and the disadvantages which oppose us, in this conflict.

Our advantages are—

1. The neighborhood of the great fisheries, which permits our fishermen to bring home their fish to be salted by their wives and children.

2. The shore fisheries, so near at hand, as to enable the vessels to run into port in a storm, and so lessen the risk, for which distant nations must pay insurance.

3. The winter fisheries, which, like household manufactures employ portions of time, which would otherwise be useless.

4. The smallness of the vessels, which the shortness of the voyage enables us to employ, and which, consequently, require but a small capital.

5. The cheapness of our vessels, which do not cost above the half of the Baltic fir vessels, computing price and duration.

6. Their excellence as sea boats, which decreases the risk and quickens the return.

7. The superiority of our mariners in skill, activity, enterprise, sobriety, and order.

8. The cheapness of provisions.

9. The cheapness of casks, which, of itself, is said to be equal to an extra profit of fifteen per cent.

These advantages are of such force, that, while experience has proved that no other nation can make a mercantile profit on the Newfoundland fishery, nor can support it without national aid, we can make a living profit, if vent for our fish can be procured.

Of the disadvantages opposed to us, those which depend on ourselves, are—

Tonnage and naval duties on the vessels employed in the fishery.

Impost duties on salt.

On tea, rum, sugar, molasses, hooks, lines, and leads, duck, cordage, and cables, iron, hemp, and twine, used in the fishery; coarse woollens, worn by the fishermen, and the poll tax levied by the State on their persons. The statement No. 6, shows the amount of these, exclusive of the State tax and drawback on the fish exported, to be $5.25 per man, or $57.75 per vessel of sixty-five tons. When a business is so nearly in equilibrio that one can hardly discern whether the profit be sufficient to continue it or not, smaller sums than these suffice to turn the scale against it. To these disadvantages, add ineffectual duties on the importation of foreign fish. In justification of these last, it is urged that the foreign fish received, is in exchange for the produce of agriculture. To which it may be answered, that the thing given, is more merchantable than that received in exchange, and agriculture has too many markets to be allowed to take away those of the fisheries. It will rest, therefore, with the wisdom of the Legislature to decide, whether prohibition should not be opposed to prohibition, and high duty to high duty, on the fish of other nations; whether any, and which, of the naval and other duties may be remitted, or an equivalent given to the fisherman, in the form of a drawback, or bounty; and whether the loss of markets abroad, may not, in some degree, be compensated, by creating markets at home; to which might contribute the constituting fish a part of the military ration, in stations not too distant from navigation, a part of the necessary sea stores of vessels, and the encouraging private individuals to let the fishermen share with the cultivator, in furnishing the supplies of the table. A habit introduced from motives of patriotism, would soon be followed from motives of taste; and who will undertake to fix the limits to this demand, if it can be once excited, with a nation which doubles, and will continue to double, at very short periods?

Of the disadvantages which depend on others, are—

1. The loss of the Mediterranean markets.
2. Exclusions from the markets of some of our neighbors.
3. High duties in those of others; and,
4. Bounties to the individuals in competition with us.

The consideration of these will find its place more aptly, after a review of the condition of our whale fishery shall have led us to the same point. To this branch of the subject, therefore, we will now proceed.

The whale fishery was first brought into notice of the southern nations of Europe, in the fifteenth century, by the same Biscayans and Basques who led the way to the fishery of Newfoundland. They began it on their own coasts, but soon found that the principal residence of the whale was in the Northern seas, into which, therefore, they pursued him. In 1578 they employed twenty-five ships in that business. The Dutch and Hamburghers took it up after this, and about the middle of the seventeenth century the former employed about two hundred ships, and the latter about three hundred and fifty.

The English endeavored also to participate of it. In 1672, they offered to their own fishermen a bounty of six shillings a ton, on the oil they should bring home, and instituted, at different times, different exclusive companies, all of which failed of success. They raised their bounty, in 1733, to twenty shillings a ton, on the admeasurement of the vessel. In 1740, to thirty shillings, with a privilege to the fishermen against being impressed. The Basque fishery, supported by poverty alone, had maintained but a feeble existence, before competitors aided by the bounties of their nation, and was, in fine, annihilated by the war of 1745, at the close of which the English bounty was raised to forty shillings. From this epoch, their whale fishery went on between the limits of twenty-eight and sixty-seven vessels, till the commencement of the last war.

The Dutch, in the meantime, had declined gradually to about one hundred and thirty ships, and have, since that, fallen down to less than half that number. So that their fishery, notwithstanding a bounty of thirty florins a man, as well as that of Hamburg, is now nearly out of competition.

In 1715, the Americans began their whale fishery. They were led to it at first by the whales which presented themselves on their coasts. They attacked them there in small vessels of forty tons. As the whale, being infested, retired from the coast, they followed him farther and farther into the ocean, still enlarging their vessels with their adventures, to sixty, one hundred, and two hundred tons. Having extended their pursuit to the Western Islands, they fell in, accidentally, with the spermaceti whale, of a different species from that of Greenland, which alone had hitherto been known in commerce; more fierce and active, and whose oil and head matter was found to be more valuable, as it might be used in the interior of houses without offending the smell. The distinction now first arose between the Northern and Southern fisheries; the object of the former being the Greenland whale, which frequents the Northern coasts and seas of Europe and America; that of the latter being the spermaceti whale, which was found in the Southern seas, from the Western Islands and coast of Africa, to that of Brazil, and still on to the Falkland Islands. Here, again, within soundings, on the coast of Brazil, they found a third species of whale, which they called the black or Brazil whale, smaller than the Greenland, yielding a still less valuable oil, fit only for summer use, as it becomes opaque at 50 degrees of Fahrenheit's thermometer, while that of the spermaceti whale is limpid to 41, and of the Greenland whale to 36, of the same thermometer. It is only worth taking, therefore, when it falls in the way of the fishermen, but not worth seeking, except when they have failed of success against the spermaceti whale, in which case, this kind, easily found and taken, serves to moderate their loss.

In 1771 the Americans had one hundred and eighty-three vessels, of thirteen thousand eight hundred and twenty tons, in the Northern fishery, and one hundred and twenty-one vessels, of fourteen thousand and twenty tons, in the Southern, navigated by four thousand and fifty-nine men. At the beginning of the late war, they had one hundred and seventy-seven vessels in the Northern, and one hundred and thirty-two in the Southern fishery. At that period, our fishery being suspended, the English seized the opportunity of pushing theirs. They gave additional bounties of £500, £400, £300, £200, £100 sterling, annually, to the five ships which should take the greatest quantities of oil. The effect of which was such, as, by the year 1786, to double the quantity of common oil necessary for their own consumption. Finding, on a review of the subject, at that time, that their bounties had cost the Government £13 10*s*. sterling a man, annually, or sixty per cent on the cargoes, a part of which went consequently to ease the purchases of this article made by foreign nations, they reduced the northern bounty from forty to thirty shillings the ton of admeasurement.

They had, some little time before, turned their attention to the Southern fishery, and given very great bounties in it, and had invited the fishermen of the United States to conduct their enterprises. Under their guidance, and with such encouragement, this fishery, which had only begun with them in 1784 or 1785, was rising into value. In 1788 they increased their bounties, and the temptations to our fishermen, under the general description of *foreigners who had been employed in the whale fishery,* to pass over with their families and vessels to the British dominions, either in America or Europe, but preferably to the latter. The effect of these measures had been prepared, by our whale oils becoming subject, in their market, to the foreign duty of £18 5*s*. sterling the ton, which, being more than equal to the price of the common oil, operated as a prohibition on that, and gave to their spermaceti oil a preference over ours to that amount.

✦

The fishermen of the United States, left without resource, by the loss of their market, began to think of accepting the British invitation, and of removing, some to Nova Scotia, preferring smaller advantages in the neighborhood of their ancient country and friends, others to Great Britain, postponing country and friends to high premiums.

The Government of France could not be inattentive to these proceedings. They saw the danger of letting four or five thousand seamen, of the best in the world, be transferred to the marine strength of another nation, and carry over with them an art, which they possessed almost exclusively. To give time for a counterplan, the Marquis de Lafayette, the valuable friend and citizen of this, as well as that country, wrote to a gentleman in Boston, to dissuade the fishermen from accepting the British proposals, and to assure them that their friends in France would endeavor to do something for them. A vessel was then arrived from Halifax at Nantucket, to take off those who had proposed to remove. Two families had gone abroad, and others were going. In this moment, the letter arriving, suspended their designs. Not another went abroad, and the vessel returned to Halifax with only the two families.

The plan adopted by the French ministry, very different from that of the first mover, was to give a counter invitation to the Nantucket men to remove and settle in Dunkirk, offering them a bounty of fifty livres (between nine and ten dollars) a ton on the admeasurement of the vessels they should equip for the whale fishery, with some other advantages. Nine families only, of thirty-three persons, accepted the invitation. This was in 1785. In 1786, the ministry were led to see that their invitation would produce but little effect, and that the true means of preventing the emigration of our fishermen to the British dominions would be to enable them still to follow their calling from their native country, by giving them a new market for their oils, instead of the old one they had lost. The duties were, therefore, abated on American whale oil immediately, and a further abatement promised by the letter No. 8, and, in December, 1787, the *arrêt* No. 9 was passed.

The rival fishermen immediately endeavored to turn this measure to their own advantage, by pouring their whale oils into the markets of France, where they were enabled, by the great premiums received from their Government, perhaps, too, by extraordinary indemnifications, to undersell both the French and American fishermen. To repel this measure, France shut her ports to all foreign fish oils whatever, by the *arrêt* No. 10. The British whale fishery fell, in consequence, the ensuing year from two hundred and twenty-two to one hundred and seventy-eight ships. But this general exclusion has palsied our fishery also. On the 7th of December, 1788, therefore, by the *arrêt* No. 11, the ports of France still remaining shut to all other nations, were again opened to the produce of the whale fisheries of the United States, continuing, however, their endeavors to recover a share in this fishery themselves, by the aid of our fishermen. In 1784, 1785, 1786, they had had four ships. In 1787, three. In 1788, seventeen in the two fisheries of four thousand five hundred tons. These cost them in bounty 225,000 livres, which divided on one thousand five hundred and fifty tons of oil, the quantity they took, amounted to 145 livres (near twenty-seven dollars) the ton, and, on about one hundred natives on board the seventeen ships, (for there were one hundred and fifty Americans engaged by the voyage) came to 2,225 livres, or about 416⅔ dollars a man.

We have had, during the years 1787, 1788 and 1789, on an average, ninety-one vessels, of five thousand eight hundred and twenty tons, in the northern, and thirty-one of four thousand three hundred and ninety tons in the southern fishery. . . .

These details will enable Congress to see with what a competition we have to struggle for the continuance of this fishery, not to say its increase. Against prohibitory duties in one country, and bounties to the adventurers in both of those which are contending with each other for the same object, ours have no auxiliaries, but poverty and rigorous economy. The business, unaided, is a wretched one. The Dutch have peculiar advantages for the northern fishery, as being within six or eight days' sail of the grounds, as navigating with more economy than any other nation in Europe, their seamen content with lower wages, and their merchants with lower profit. Yet the memorial No. 13, from a committee of the whale merchants to the States General of Holland, in the year 1775, states that fourteen millions of guilders, equal to five million six hundred thousand dollars, has been lost in that fishery in forty-seven years, being about one hundred and twenty thousand dollars a year. The States General, thereupon, gave a bounty of thirty guilders a man to the fishermen. A person immediately acquainted with the British whale fishery, and whose information merits confidence, has given assurance that the ships employed in their northern fishery, in 1788, sunk £800 each, on an average, more than the amount of the produce and bounties. An English ship of three hundred tons and forty-two seamen, in this fishery, generally brings home, after a four months' voyage, twenty-five tons of oil, worth £437 10*s*. sterling; but the wages of the officers and seamen will be £400; there remain but £37 10*s*., not worth taking into account, towards the outfit and merchants' profit. These, then, must be paid by the Government; and it is on this idea that the British bounty is calculated.

Our vessels for the northern fishery average sixty-four tons, and cost, when built, fitted out, and victualled for the first voyage, about three thousand dollars. They have taken, on an average, the three last years, according to the statement No. 12, eighteen tons of oil, worth, at our market, nine hundred dollars, which are to pay all expenses, and subsist the fishermen and merchant. Our vessels for the southern fishery average one hundred and forty tons, and cost, when built, fitted out, and victualled, for their first voyage, about six thousand five hundred dollars. They have taken on an average, the three last years, according to the same statement, thirty-two tons of oil each, worth at our market three thousand two hundred dollars, which are, in like manner, to pay all expenses, and subsist the owners and navigators. These expenses are great, as the voyages are generally of twelve months' duration. No hope can arise of their condition being bettered by an augmentation of the price of oil. This is kept down by the competition of the vegetable oils, which answer the same purposes, not quite so well, but well enough to become preferable, were the price to be raised, and so well, indeed, as to be more generally used than the fish oils for lighting houses and cities.

The American whale fishery is principally followed by the inhabitants of the island of Nantucket—a sand bar of about fifteen miles long, and three broad, capable of maintaining, by its agriculture, about twenty families; but it employed in these fisheries, before the war, between five or six thousand men and boys; and, in the only harbor it possesses, it had one hundred and forty vessels, one hundred and thirty-two of which were of the larger kind, as being employed in the southern fishery. In agriculture, then, they have no resource; and, if that of their fishery cannot be pursued from their own habitations, it is natural they should seek others from which it can be followed, and preferably those where they will find a sameness of language, religion, laws, habits, and kindred. A foreign emissary has lately been among them, for the purpose of renewing the invitations to a change of situation. But, attached to their native country, they prefer continuing in it, if their continuance there can be made supportable.

This brings us to the question, what relief does the condition of this fishery require?

1. A remission of duties on the articles used for their calling.

2. A retaliating duty on foreign oils, coming to seek a competition with them in or from our ports.

3. Free markets abroad.

1. The remission of duties will stand on nearly the same ground with that to the cod fishermen.

2. The only nation whose oil is brought hither for competition with our own, makes ours pay a duty of about eighty-two dollars the ton, in their ports. Theirs is brought here, too, to be reshipped fraudulently, under our flag, into ports where it could not be received under theirs, and ought not to be covered by ours, if we mean to preserve our own admission into them.

The 3d and principal object is to find markets for the vent of oil.

Portugal, England, Holland, Sweden, Denmark, Prussia, Russia, the Hanse towns, supply themselves and something more. Spain and Italy receive supplies from England, and need the less, as their skies are clearer. France is the only country which can take our surplus, and they take principally of the common oil; as the habit is but commencing with them of ascribing a just value to spermaceti whale. Some of this, however, finds its vent there. There was, indeed, a particular interest perpetually soliciting the exclusion of our oils from their markets. The late government there saw well that what we should lose thereby would be gained by others, not by themselves. And we are to hope that the present government, as wise and friendly, will also view us, not as rivals, but as co-operators against a common rival. Friendly arrangements with them, and accommodation to mutual interest, rendered easier by friendly dispositions existing on both sides, may long secure to us this important resource for our seamen. Nor is it the interest of the fisherman alone, which calls for the cultivation of friendly arrangements with that nation; besides five-eighths of our whale oil, and two-thirds of our salted fish, they take from us one-fourth of our tobacco, three-fourths of our live stock . . . , a considerable and growing portion of our rice, great supplies, occasionally, of other grain; in 1789, which, indeed, was extraordinary, four millions of bushels of wheat, and upwards of a million of bushels of rye and barley . . . , and nearly the whole carried in our own vessels. . . . They are a free market now, and will, in time, be a valuable one for ships and ship timber, potash, and peltry.

England is the market for the greatest part of our spermaceti oil. They impose on all our oils a duty of eighteen pounds five shillings sterling the ton, which, as to the common kind, is a prohibition, as has been before observed, and, as to the spermaceti, gives a preference of theirs over ours to that amount, so as to leave, in the end, but a scanty benefit to the fishermen; and, not long since, by a change of construction, without any change of law, it was made to exclude our oils from their ports, when carried in our vessels. On some change of circumstance, it was construed back again to the reception of our oils, on paying always, however, the same duty of eighteen pounds five shillings. This serves to show that the tenure by which we hold the admission of this commodity in their markets, is as precarious as it is hard. Nor can it be announced that there is any disposition on their part to arrange this or any other commercial matter, to mutual convenience. The *ex parte* regulations which they have begun for mounting their navigation on the ruins of ours, can only be opposed by counter regulations on our part. And the loss of seamen, the natural consequence of lost and obstructed markets for our fish and oil, calls, in the first place, for serious and timely attention. It will be too late when the seaman shall have changed his vocation, or gone over to another interest. If we cannot recover and secure for him these important branches of employment, it behooves us to replace them by others equivalent. We have three nurseries for forming seamen:

1. Our coasting trade, already on a safe footing.

2. Our fisheries, which, in spite of natural advantages, give just cause of anxiety.

3. Our carrying trade, our only resource of indemnification for what we lose in the other. The produce of the United States, which is carried to foreign markets, is extremely bulky. That part of it which is now in the hands of foreigners, and which we may resume into our own, without touching the rights of those nations who have met us in fair arrangements by treaty, or the interests of those who, by their voluntary regulations, have paid so just and liberal a respect to our interests, as being measured back to them again, places both parties on as good ground, perhaps, as treaties could place them—the proportion, I say, of our carrying trade, which may be resumed without affecting either of these descriptions of nations, will find constant employment for ten thousand seamen, be worth two millions of dollars,

annually, will go on augmenting with the population of the United States, secure to us a full indemnification for the seamen we lose, and be taken wholly from those who force us to this act of self protection in navigation.

Hence, too, would follow, that their Newfoundland ships, not receiving provisions from us in their bottoms, nor permitted (by a law of their own) to receive in ours, must draw their subsistence from Europe, which would increase that part of their expenses in the proportion of four to seven, and so far operate as a duty towards restoring the level between them and us. The tables No. 2 and 12, will show the quantity of tonnage, and, consequently, the mass of seamen whose interests are in distress; and No. 17, the materials for indemnification.

If regulations exactly the counterpart of those established against us, would be ineffectual, from a difference of circumstances, other regulations equivalent can give no reasonable ground of complaint to any nation. Admitting their right of keeping their markets to themselves, ours cannot be denied of keeping our carrying trade to ourselves. And if there be anything unfriendly in this, it was in the first example.

The loss of seamen, unnoticed, would be followed by other losses in a long train. If we have no seamen, our ships will be useless, consequently our ship timber, iron, and hemp; our ship building will be at an end, ship carpenters go over to other nations, our young men have no call to the sea, our produce, carried in foreign bottoms, be saddled with war-freight and insurance in times of war; and the history of the last hundred years shows, that the nation which is our carrier has three years of war for every four years of peace. (No. 18.) We lose, during the same periods, the carriage for belligerent powers, which the neutrality of our flag would render an incalculable source of profit; we lose at this moment the carriage of our own produce to the annual amount of two millions of dollars, which, in the possible progress of the encroachment, may extend to five or six millions, the worth of the whole, with an increase in the proportion of the increase of our numbers. It is easier, as well as better, to stop this train at its entrance, than when it shall have ruined or banished whole classes of useful and industrious citizens.

It will doubtless be thought expedient that the resumption suggested should take effect so gradually, as not to endanger the loss of produce for the want of transportation; but that, in order to create transportation, the whole plan should be developed, and made known at once, that the individuals who may be disposed to lay themselves out for the carrying business, may make their calculations on a full view of all circumstances.

On the whole, the historical view we have taken of these fisheries, proves they are so poor in themselves, as to come to nothing with distant nations, who do not support them from their treasury. We have seen that the advantages of our position place our fisheries on a ground somewhat higher, such as to relieve our treasury from giving them support; but not to permit it to draw support from them, nor to dispense the government from the obligation of effectuating free markets for them; that, for the great proportion of our salted fish, for our common oil, and a part of our spermaceti oil, markets may perhaps be preserved, by friendly arrangements towards those nations whose arrangements are friendly to us, and the residue be compensated by giving to the seamen thrown out of business the certainty of employment in another branch, of which we have the sole disposal.

## OPINION AGAINST THE CONSTITUTIONALITY OF A NATIONAL BANK

February 15, 1791

The bill for establishing a National Bank undertakes among other things:

1. To form the subscribers into a corporation.

2. To enable them in their corporate capacities to receive grants of land; and so far is against the laws of *mortmain*.[1]

3. To make alien subscribers capable of holding lands; and so far is against the laws of *alienage*.

4. To transmit these lands, on the death of a proprietor, to a certain line of successors; and so far changes the course of *descents*.

5. To put the lands out of the reach of forfeiture or escheat; and so far is against the laws of *forfeiture and escheat*.

6. To transmit personal chattels to successors in a certain line; and so far is against the laws of *distribution*.

7. To give them the sole and exclusive right of banking under the national authority; and so far is against the laws of *monopoly*.

8. To communicate to them a power to make laws paramount to the laws of the States; for so they must be construed, to protect the institution from the control of the State legislatures; and so, probably, they will be construed.

I consider the foundation of the Constitution as laid on this ground: That "all powers not delegated to the United States, by the Constitution, nor prohibited by it to the States, are reserved to the States or to the people." [XIIth amendment.] To take a single step beyond the boundaries thus specially drawn around the powers of Congress, is to take possession of a boundless field of power, no longer susceptible of any definition.

The incorporation of a bank, and the powers assumed by this bill, have not, in my opinion, been delegated to the United States, by the Constitution.

[1] Though the Constitution controls the laws of mortmain so far as to permit Congress itself to hold land for certain purposes, yet not so far as to permit them to communicate a similar right to other corporate bodies.—T. J.

I. They are not among the powers specially enumerated: for these are: 1st. A power to lay taxes for the purpose of paying the debts of the United States; but no debt is paid by this bill, nor any tax laid. Were it a bill to raise money, its origination in the Senate would condemn it by the Constitution.

2d. "To borrow money." But this bill neither borrows money nor ensures the borrowing it. The proprietors of the bank will be just as free as any other money holders, to lend or not to lend their money to the public. The operation proposed in the bill, first, to lend them two millions, and then to borrow them back again, cannot change the nature of the latter act, which will still be a payment, and not a loan, call it by what name you please.

3. To "regulate commerce with foreign nations, and among the States, and with the Indian tribes." To erect a bank, and to regulate commerce, are very different acts. He who erects a bank, creates a subject of commerce in its bills; so does he who makes a bushel of wheat, or digs a dollar out of the mines; yet neither of these persons regulates commerce thereby. To make a thing which may be bought and sold, is not to prescribe regulations for buying and selling. Besides, if this was an exercise of the power of regulating commerce, it would be void, as extending as much to the internal commerce of every State, as to its external. For the power given to Congress by the Constitution does not extend to the internal regulation of the commerce of a State (that is to say of the commerce between citizen and citizen), which remain exclusively with its own legislature; but to its external commerce only, that is to say, its commerce with another State, or with foreign nations, or with the Indian tribes. Accordingly the bill does not propose the measure as a regulation of trade, but as "productive of considerable advantages to trade." Still less are these powers covered by any other of the special enumerations.

II. Nor are they within either of the general phrases, which are the two following:

1. To lay taxes to provide for the general welfare of the United States, that is to say, "to lay taxes for *the purpose* of providing for the general welfare." For the laying of taxes is the *power,* and the general welfare the *purpose* for which the power is to be exercised. They are not to lay taxes *ad libitum for any purpose they please;* but only *to pay the debts or provide for the welfare of the Union.* In like manner, they are not *to do anything they please* to provide for the general welfare, but only to *lay taxes* for that purpose. To consider the latter phrase, not as describing the purpose of the first, but as giving a distinct and independent power to do any act they please, which might be for the good of the Union, would render all the preceding and subsequent enumerations of power completely useless.

It would reduce the whole instrument to a single phrase, that of instituting a Congress with power to do whatever would be for the good of the United States; and, as they would be the sole judges of the good or evil, it would be also a power to do whatever evil they please.

It is an established rule of construction where a phrase will bear either of two meanings, to give it that which will allow some meaning to the other parts of the instrument, and not that which would render all the others useless. Certainly no such universal power was meant to be given them. It was intended to lace them up straitly within the enumerated powers, and those without which, as means, these powers could not be carried into effect. It is known that the very power now proposed *as a means* was rejected as *an end* by the Convention which formed the Constitution. A proposition was made to them to authorize Congress to open canals, and an amendatory one to empower them to incorporate. But the whole was rejected, and one of the reasons for rejection urged in debate was, that then they would have a power to erect a bank, which would render the great cities, where there were prejudices and jealousies on the subject, adverse to the reception of the Constitution.

2. The second general phrase is, "to make all laws *necessary* and proper for carrying into execution the enumerated powers." But they can all be carried into execution without a bank. A bank therefore is not *necessary,* and consequently not authorized by this phrase.

It has been urged that a bank will give great facility or convenience in the collection of taxes. Suppose this were true: yet the Constitution allows only the means which are *"necessary,"* not those which are merely "convenient" for effecting the enumerated powers. If such a latitude of construction be allowed to this phrase as to give any non-enumerated power, it will go to everyone, for there is not one which ingenuity may not torture into a *convenience* in some instance *or other,* to *someone* of so long a list of enumerated powers. It would swallow up all the delegated powers, and reduce the whole to one power, as before observed. Therefore it was that the Constitution restrained them to the *necessary* means, that is to say, to those means without which the grant of power would be nugatory.

But let us examine this convenience and see what it is. The report on this subject, page 3, states the only *general* convenience to be, the preventing the transportation and re-transportation of money between the States and the treasury, (for I pass over the increase of circulating medium, ascribed to it as a want, and which, according to my ideas of paper money, is clearly a demerit.) Every State will have to pay a sum of tax money into the treasury; and the treasury will have to pay, in every State, a part of the interest on the public debt, and salaries to the officers of government resident in that State. In most of the States there will still be a surplus of tax money to come up to the seat of government for the officers residing there. The payments of interest and salary in each State may be made by treasury orders on the State collector. This will take up the great export of the money he has collected in his State, and consequently prevent the great mass of it from being drawn out of the State. If there be a balance of commerce in favor of that State against the one in which the government resides, the surplus of taxes will be remitted by the bills of exchange drawn for that commercial balance. And so it must be if there was a bank. But if there be no balance of commerce, either direct or circuitous, all the banks in the world could not bring up the surplus of taxes, but in the form of money. Treasury orders then, and bills of exchange may prevent the displacement of the main mass of the money collected, without the aid of any bank; and where these fail, it cannot be prevented even with that aid.

Perhaps, indeed, bank bills may be a more *convenient* vehicle than treasury orders. But a little *difference* in the degree of *convenience,* cannot constitute the necessity which the constitution makes the ground for assuming any non-enumerated power.

Besides, the existing banks will, without a doubt, enter into arrangements for lending their agency, and the more favorable, as there will be a competition among them for it; whereas the bill delivers us up bound to the National Bank, who are free to refuse all arrangement, but on their own terms, and the public not free, on such refusal, to employ any other bank. That of Philadelphia, I believe, now does this business, by their post-notes, which, by an arrangement with the treasury, are paid by any State collector to whom they are presented. This expedient alone suffices to prevent the existence of that *necessity* which may justify the assumption of a non-enumerated power as a means for carrying into effect an enumerated one. The thing may be done, and has been done, and well done, without this assumption; therefore, it does not stand on that degree of *necessity* which can honestly justify it.

It may be said that a bank whose bills would have a currency all over the States, would be more convenient than one whose currency is limited to a single State. So it would be still more convenient that there should be a bank, whose bills should have a currency all over the world. But it does not follow from this superior conveniency, that there exists anywhere a power to establish such a bank; or that the world may not go on very well without it.

Can it be thought that the Constitution intended that for a shade or two of *convenience,* more or less, Congress should be authorized to break down the most ancient and fundamental laws of the several States; such as those against mortmain, the laws of alienage, the rules of descent, the acts of distribution, the laws of escheat and forfeiture, the laws of monopoly? Nothing but a necessity invincible by any other means, can justify such a prostitution of laws, which constitute the pillars of our whole system of jurisprudence. Will Congress be too straight-laced to carry the Constitution into honest effect, unless they may pass over the foundation-laws of the State government for the slightest convenience of theirs?

The negative of the President is the shield provided by the Constitution to protect against the invasions of the legislature: 1. The right of the Executive. 2. Of the Judiciary. 3. Of the States and State legislatures. The present is the case of a right remaining exclusively with the States, and consequently one of those intended by the Constitution to be placed under its protection.

It must be added, however, that unless the President's mind on a view of everything which is urged for and against this bill, is tolerably clear that it is unauthorised by the Constitution; if the pro and the con hang so even as to balance his judgment, a just respect for the wisdom of the legislature would naturally decide the balance in favor of their opinion. It is chiefly for cases where they are clearly misled by error, ambition, or interest, that the Constitution has placed a check in the negative of the President.

## FARMING [1]

December 29, 1794

And though I observe your strictures on rotations of crops, yet it appears that in this I differ from you only in words. You keep half your lands in culture, the other half at nurse; so I propose to do. Your scheme indeed requires only four years and mine six; but the proportion of labor and rest is the same. My years of rest, however, are employed, two of them in producing clover, yours in volunteer herbage. But I still understand it to be your opinion that clover is best where lands will produce them. Indeed I think that the important improvement for which the world is indebted to Young is the substitution of clover crops instead of unproductive fallows; and the demonstration that lands are more enriched by clover than by volunteer herbage or fallows; and the clover crops are highly valuable. That our red lands which are still in tolerable heart will produce fine clover I know from the experience of the last year; and indeed that of my neighbors had established the fact. And from observations on accidental plants in the fields which have been considerably harassed with corn, I believe that even these will produce clover fit for soiling of animals green. I think, therefore, I can count on the success of that improver. My third year of rest will be devoted to cowpenning, and to a trial of the buckwheat dressing. A further progress in surveying my open arable lands has shewn me that I can have seven fields in each of my farms where I expected only six; consequently that I can add

[1] Letter to John Taylor. Taylor was a distinguished agriculturist and a pioneer in various agricultural improvements. In 1812 he published his *Arator,* the first original agricultural work ever published by a man of the South; the book popularized the four-field system, deep plowing, manuring, and other agricultural advances.

more to the portion of rest and ameliorating crops. I have doubted on a question on which I am sure you can advise me well, whether I had better give this newly acquired year as an addition to the continuance of my clover, or throw it with some improving crop between two of my crops of grain, as for instance between my corn and rye. I strongly incline to the latter, because I am not satisfied that one cleansing crop in seven years will be sufficient; and indeed I think it important to separate my exhausting crops by alternations of amelioraters. With this view I think to try an experiment of what Judge Parker informs me he practises. That is, to turn in my wheat stubble the instant the grain is off, and sow turnips to be fed out by the sheep. But whether this will answer in our fields which are harassed, I do not know. We have been in the habit of sowing only our freshest lands in turnips, hence a presumption that wearied lands will not bring them. But Young's making turnips to be fed on by sheep the basis of his improvement of poor lands, affords evidence that though they may not bring great crops, they will bring them in a sufficient degree to improve the lands. I will try that experiment, however, this year, as well as the one of buckwheat. I have also attended to another improver mentioned by you, the winter vetch, and have taken measures to get the seed of it from England, as also of the Siberian vetch which Millar greatly commends, and being a biennial might perhaps take the place of clover in lands which do not suit that. The winter vetch I suspect may be advantageously thrown in between crops, as it gives a choice to use it as green feed in the spring if fodder be run short, or to turn it in as a green-dressing. My rotation, with these amendments, is as follows:

1. Wheat, followed the same year by turnips, to be fed on by the sheep.
2. Corn and potatoes mixed, and in autumn the vetch to be used as fodder in the spring if wanted, or to be turned in as a dressing.
3. Peas or potatoes, or both according to the quality of the field.
4. Rye and clover sown on it in the spring. Wheat may be substituted here for rye, when it shall be found that the second, third, fifth, and sixth fields will subsist the farm.
5. Clover.
6. Clover, and in autumn turn it in and sow the vetch.
7. Turn in the vetch in the spring, then sow buckwheat and turn that in, having hurdled off the poorest spots for cowpenning. In autumn sow wheat to begin the circle again.

I am for throwing the whole force of my husbandry on the wheat-field, because it is the only one which is to go to market to produce money. Perhaps the clover may bring in something in the form of stock. The other fields are merely for the consumption of the farm. Melilot, mentioned by you, I never heard of. The horse bean I tried this last year. It turned out nothing.

The President has tried it without success. An old English farmer of the name of Spuryear, settled in Delaware, has tried it there with good success; but he told me it would not do without being well shaded, and I think he planted it among his corn for that reason. But he acknowledged our pea was as good an ameliorator and a more valuable pulse, as being food for man as well as horse. The succory is what Young calls Chicoria Intubus. He sent some seed to the President, who gave me some, and I gave it to my neighbors to keep up till I should come home. One of them has cultivated it with great success, is very fond of it, and gave me some seed which I sowed last spring. Though the summer was favorable it came on slowly at first, but by autumn became large and strong. It did not seed that year, but will the next, and you shall be furnished with seed. I suspect it requires rich ground, and then produces a heavy crop for green feed for horses and cattle. I had poor success with my potatoes last year, not having made more than 60 or 70 bushels to the acre. But my neighbors having made good crops, I am not disheartened. The first step towards the recovery of our lands is to find substitutes for corn and bacon. I count on potatoes, clover, and sheep. The two former to feed every animal on the farm except my Negroes, and the latter to feed them, diversified with rations of salted fish and molasses, both of them wholesome, agreeable, and cheap articles of food.

For pasture I rely on the forests by day, and soiling the evening. Why could we not have a moveable airy cow house, to be set up in the middle of the field which is to be dunged, and soil our cattle in that through the summer as well as winter, keeping them constantly up and well littered? This with me, would be in the clover field of the first year, because during the second year it would be rotting, and would be spread on it in fallow the beginning of the third, but such an effort would be far above the present tyro state of my farming. The grosser barbarisms in culture which I have to encounter are more than enough for all my attentions at present. The dung-yard must be my last effort but one. The last would be irrigation. It might be thought at first view, that the interposition of these ameliorations or dressings between my crops will be too laborious, but observe that the turnips and two dressings of vetch do not cost a single ploughing. The turning the wheat-stubble for the turnips is the fallow for the corn of the succeeding year. The first sowing of vetches is on the corn (as is now practised for wheat), and the turning it in is the flush-ploughing for the crop of potatoes and peas. The second sowing of the vetch is on the wheat fallow, and the turning it in is the ploughing necessary for sowing and buckwheat. These three ameliorations, then, will cost but a harrowing each. On the subject of the drilled husbandry, I think experience has established its preference for some plants, as the turnip, pea, bean, cabbage, corn, etc., and that of the broadcast for other plants as all the bread grains and grasses, except perhaps lucerne and Saint foin in soils and climates very productive of weeds. In dry soils and climates the broadcast is better for lucerne and Saint foin, as all the south of France can testify.

## CHEAP WINE AS A SUBSTITUTE FOR WHISKEY [1]

June 3, 1807

I gave you, some time ago, a project of a more equal tariff on wines than that which now exists. But in that I yielded considerably to the faulty classification of them in our law. I have now formed one with attention, and according to the best information I possess, classing them more rigorously. I am persuaded that were the duty on cheap wines put on the same ratio with the dear, it would wonderfully enlarge the field of those who use wine, to the expulsion of whiskey. The introduction of a very cheap wine (St. George) into my neighborhood, within two years past, has quadrupled in that time the number of those who keep wine, and will ere long increase them tenfold. This would be a great gain to the treasury, and to the sobriety of our country. I will here add my tariff, wherein you will be able to choose any rate of duty you please, and to decide whether it will not, on a fit occasion, be proper for legislative attention.

## THE INTRODUCTION OF PLANTS AND FRUITS [2]

July 15, 1808

The introduction of new cultures, and especially of objects of leading importance to our comfort, is certainly worthy the attention of every government, and nothing short of the actual experiment should discourage an essay of which any hope can be entertained. Till that is made, the result is open to conjecture; and I should certainly conjecture that the sugar cane could never become an article of profitable culture in France. We have within the ancient limits of the United States, a great extent of country which brings the orange to advantage, but not a foot in which the sugar cane can be matured. France, within its former limits, has but two small spots (Olivreles and Hières) which brings the orange in open air, and *à fortiori* therefore, none proper for the cane. I should think the sugar-maple more worthy of experiment. There is no part of France of which the climate would not admit this tree. I have never seen a reason why every farmer should not have a sugar orchard, as well as an apple orchard. The supply of sugar for his family

[1] Letter to Albert Gallatin, Secretary of the Treasury.
[2] Letter to Lasteyrie.

| | COST PER GALLON | 15 PER CENT | 20 PER CENT | 25 PER CENT, BEING THE AVERAGE OF PRESENT DUTIES | 30 PER CENT | 35 PER CENT | PRESENT DUTY | PER CENT |
|---|---|---|---|---|---|---|---|---|
| Tokay, Cape, Malmese, Hock | 4.00 | 60 | 80 | 1.00 | 1.20 | 1.40 | Tokay<br>Malmesey<br>Hock | 45 cents, which is 11¼<br>58 cents, which is 14½<br>35 cents, which is 25 |
| Champagne, Burgundy, Claret,[2] Hermitage | 2.75 | 41¼ | 55 | 68¾ | 82½ | 96¼ | Champagne, Burgundy<br>Claret, Hermitage | 45 cents, which is 16½<br>35 cents, which is 12½ |
| London particular Madeira | 2.20 | 33 | 44 | 55 | 66 | 77 | | 58 cents, which is 26½ |
| All other Madeira | 1.80 | 27 | 36 | 45 | 54 | 63 | | 50 cents, which is 27½ |
| Pacharetti, Sherry | 1.50 | 22½ | 30 | 37½ | 45 | 52½ | Pacharetti<br>Sherry | 23 cents, which is 15<br>40 cents, which is 26½ |
| [3] The wines of Medoc and Grave not before mentioned, those of Pauls, Coterotie, Condrieu, Moselle. | 1.25 | 18¾ | 25 | 31¼ | 37½ | 43¾ | | 35 cents, which is 28 |
| St. Lucar and all of Portugal | 80 | 12 | 16 | 20 | 24 | 28 | St. Lucar<br>Other Spanish | 40 cents, which is 50<br>23 cents, which is 28¾ |
| Sicily, Teneriffe, Fayal, Malaga, St. George, and other western islands | 67 | 10 | 13 | 16¾ | 20 | 23 | Sicily<br>Teneriffe, &c. | 23 cents, which is 34<br>28 cents, which is 41 |
| All other wines | | | | | | | in bottles<br>in casks | 35<br>23 often 400 per cent |

[2] The term Claret should be abolished, because unknown in the country where it is made, and because indefinite here. The four crops should be enumerated here instead of Claret, and all other wines to which that appellation has been applied, should fall into the ad valorem class. The four crops are Lafitte, Latour and Margaux, in Medoc, and Hautbrion, in Grave.—T. J.

[3] Blanquefort, Calon, Leoville, Cantenac, &c., are wines of Medoc. Barsac, Sauterne, Beaume, Preignac, St. Bris, Carbonien, Langon, Podensac, &c., are of Grave. All these are of the second order, being next after the four crops.—T. J.

would require as little ground, and the process of making it as easy as that of cider. Mr. Micheaux, your botanist here, could send you plants as well as seeds, in any quantity from the United States. I have no doubt the cotton plant will succeed in some of the southern parts of France. Whether its culture will be as advantageous as those they are now engaged in, remains to be tried. We could, in the United States, make as great a variety of wines as are made in Europe, not exactly of the same kinds, but doubtless as good. Yet I have ever observed to my countrymen, who think its introduction important, that a laborer cultivating wheat, rice, tobacco, or cotton here, will be able with the proceeds, to purchase double the quantity of the wine he could make. Possibly the same quantity of land and labor in France employed on the rich produce of your Southern counties, would purchase double the quantity of the cotton they would yield there. This however may prove otherwise on trial, and therefore it is worthy the trial. In general, it is a truth that if every nation will employ itself in what it is fittest to produce, a greater quantity will be raised of the things contributing to human happiness, than if every nation attempts to raise everything it wants within itself. The limits within which the cotton plant is worth cultivating in the United States, are the Rappahanock river to the north, and the first mountains to the west. And even from the Rappahanock to the Roanoke, we only cultivate for family use, as it cannot there be afforded at market in competition with that of the more Southern region. The Mississippi country, also within the same latitudes, admits the culture of cotton.

✦

I received . . . the seeds of the bread-tree. . . . One service of this kind rendered to a nation, is worth more to them than all the victories of the most splendid pages of their history, and becomes a source of exalted pleasure to those who have been instrumental to it.[3]

## SCHEME FOR A SYSTEM OF AGRICULTURAL SOCIETIES

March, 1811

Several persons, farmers and planters of the county of Albemarle, having, during their visits and occasional meetings together, in conversations on the subjects of their agricultural pursuits, received considerable benefits from an inter-communication of their plans and processes in husbandry, they have imagined that these benefits might be usefully extended by enlarging the field of communication so as to embrace the whole dimensions of the State. Were practical and observing husbandmen in each county to form them-

[3] Letter to Giraud, May 22, 1797.

selves into a society, commit to writing themselves, or state in conversations at their meetings to be written down by others, their practices and observations, their experiences and ideas, selections from these might be made from time to time by everyone for his own use, or by the society or a committee of it, for more general purposes. By an interchange of these selections among the societies of the different counties, each might thus become possessed of the useful ideas and processes of the whole; and everyone adopt such of them as he should deem suitable to his own situation. Or to abridge the labor of such multiplied correspondences, a central society might be agreed on to which, as a common deposit, all the others should send their communications. The society thus honored by the general confidence, would doubtless feel and fulfil the duty of selecting such papers as should be worthy of entire communication, of extracting and digesting from others whatever might be useful, and of condensing their matter within such compass as might reconcile it to the reading, as well as to the purchase of the great mass of practical men. Many circumstances would recommend, for the central society, that which should be established in the county of the seat of government. The necessary relations of every county with that would afford facilities for all the transmissions which should take place between them. The annual meeting of the legislature of that place, the individuals of which would most frequently be members of their county societies, would give opportunities of informal conferences which might promote a general and useful understanding among all the societies; and presses established there offer conveniences entirely peculiar to that situation.

In a country, of whose interests agriculture forms the basis, wherein the sum of productions is limited by the quantity of the labor it possesses, and not of its lands, a more judicious employment of that labor would be a clear addition of gain to individuals as well as to the nation, now lost to both by a want of skill and information in its direction. Everyone must have seen farms otherwise equal, the one producing the double of the other by the superior culture and management of its possessor; and everyone must have under his eye numerous examples of persons setting out in life with no other possession than skill in agriculture, and speedily, by its sole exercise, acquire wealth and independence. To promote, therefore, the diffusion of this skill, and thereby to procure, with the same labor now employed, greater means of subsistence and of happiness to our fellow citizens, is the ultimate object of this Association; and towards effecting it, we consider the following particulars among those most worthy of the attention of the societies proposed.

1st. And principally the cultivation of our primary staples of wheat, tobacco, and hemp, for market.

2d. All subsidiary articles for the support of the farm, the food, the clothing and the comfort of the household, as Indian corn, rye, oats, barley, buckwheat, millet, the family of peas and beans, the whole family of grasses, turnips, potatoes, Jerusalem artichokes, and other useful roots, cotton and flax, the garden and orchard.

3d. The care and services of useful animals for the saddle or draught, for food or clothing, and the destruction of noxious quadrupeds, fowls, insects, and reptiles.

4th. Rotations of crops, and the circumstances which should govern or vary them, according to the varieties of soil, climate, and markets, of our different counties.

5th. Implements of husbandry and operations with them, among which the plough and all its kindred instruments for dividing the soil, holds the first place, and the threshing machine an important one, the simplification of which is a great desideratum. Successful examples, too, of improvement in the operations of these instruments would be an excitement to correct the slovenly and unproductive practices too generally prevalent.

6th. Farm buildings and conveniences, inclosures, roads, fuel, timber.

7th. Manures, plaster, green-dressings, fallows, and other means of ameliorating the soil.

8th. Calendars of works, showing how a given number of laborers and of draught animals are to be employed every day in the year so as to perform within themselves, and in their due time, according to the usual course of seasons, all the operations of a farm of given size. This being essential to the proportioning the labor to the size of the farm.

9th. A succinct report of the different practices of husbandry in the county, including the bad as well as the good, that those who follow the former may read and see their own condemnation in the same page which offers better examples for their adoption. It is believed that a judicious execution of this article alone, might nearly supersede every other duty of the society, inasmuch as it would present every good practice which has occurred to the mind of any cultivator of the State for imitation, and every bad one for avoidance. And the choicest processes culled from every farm, would compose a course probably near perfection.

10th. The county communications being first digested in their respective societies, a methodical and compact digest and publication of these would be the duty of the central society; and on the judicious performance of this, would in a great degree depend the utility of the institutions, and extent of improvement flowing from them.

11th. That we may not deter from becoming members, those practical and observing husbandmen whose knowledge is the most valuable, and who are mostly to be found in that portion of citizens with whom the observance of economy is necessary, all duties of every kind should be performed gratis; and to defray the expenses of the central publication alone, each member should pay at the first stated meeting of his society in every year, —— dollars, for which he should be entitled to receive a copy of the publication bound in boards.

12th. The first association of —— persons in any county notifying themselves as constituted to the central society, should be received as the society of the county making a part of the general establishment here proposed; but every county society should be free to adopt associate members, although residents of other counties, and to receive and avail the institution of communications from persons not members, whether in or out of their county.

We are far from presuming to offer this organization and these principles of constitution as complete, and worthy the implicit adoption of other societies. They are suggested only as propositions for consideration and amendment, and we shall readily accede to any others more likely to effect the purposes we have in view. We know that agricultural societies are already established in some counties; but we are not informed of their particular constitutions. We request these to be admitted into their brotherhood, and to make with them parts of one great whole. We have learned that such a society is formed or forming at the seat of our government.[1] We ask their affiliation, and give them our suffrage for the station of a central society. We promise to all our zealous co-operation in promoting the objects of the institution, and to contribute our mite in exchange for the more abundant information we shall receive from others.

For these purposes we now constitute ourselves an agricultural society of the county of Albemarle, and adopt as rules for present observance, the principles before stated.

Our further organization shall be a President, Secretary and Treasurer, to be chosen at the first stated meeting to be held in every year, by a majority of the members present, provided those present be a majority of the existing members, and to continue in office until another election shall be made.

There shall be four stated meetings in every year, to wit: on the first Mondays in January, April, July and October.

The place of meeting, and rules of the society, shall be established, revoked or altered, and new members admitted, at any of the stated meetings, by a majority of the attending members, if they be a majority of those present, not being less than one-fourth of the whole. And, lest the powers given to the greater quorum of a majority of the whole, should at any time remain unexercised from insufficient attendance, the same may be exercised by a resolution of the lesser quorum of one-fourth, passed at a stated meeting: provided it be confirmed at the next stated meeting, by either a greater or lesser quorum, and in the meantime have no force.

[1] The first national agricultural society was established at Washington, D. C. in 1809.

Those who for two whole years shall not have attended any stated meeting shall, *ipso facto,* cease to be members. And to ascertain at all times who are the existing members, the names of those attending every meeting shall be regularly entered in the journals of the society.

The President shall preside at all meetings when present, and when absent, a president *pro tempore* may be appointed for that purpose *by those present.*

## IDEAS ON FINANCE[1]

November 6, 1813

I had not expected to have troubled you again on the subject of finance; but since the date of my last, I have received from Mr. Law a letter covering a memorial on that subject, which from its tenor, I conjecture must have been before Congress at their two last sessions. This paper contains two propositions; the one for issuing treasury notes, bearing interest, and to be circulated as money; the other for the establishment of a national bank. The first was considered in my former letter; and the second shall be the subject of the present.

The scheme is for Congress to establish a national bank, suppose of thirty millions capital, of which they shall contribute ten millions in new six per cent stock, the States ten millions, and individuals ten millions, one half of the two last contributions to be of similar stock, for which the parties are to give cash to Congress; the whole, however, to be under the exclusive management of the individual subscribers, who are to name all the directors; neither Congress nor the States having any power of interference in its administration. Discounts are to be at five per cent, but the profits are expected to be seven per cent. Congress then will be paying six per cent on twenty millions, and receiving seven per cent on ten millions, being its third of the institution; so that on the ten millions cash which they receive from the States and individuals, they will, in fact, have to pay but five per cent interest. This is the bait. The charter is proposed to be for forty or fifty years, and if any future augmentations should take place, the individual proprietors are to have the privilege of being the sole subscribers for that. Congress are further allowed to issue to the amount of three millions of notes, bearing interest, which they are to receive back in payment for lands at a premium of five or ten per cent, or as subscriptions for canals, roads, and bridges, in which undertakings they are, of course, to be engaged. This is a summary of the case as I understand it; but it is very possible I may not understand it in all its parts, these schemes being always made unintelligible for the gulls who are to enter into them. The advantages and disadvantages shall

[1] Letter to John W. Eppes, Jefferson's son-in-law.

be noted promiscuously as they occur; leaving out the speculation of canals, &c., which, being an episode only in the scheme, may be omitted, to disentangle it as much as we can.

1. Congress are to receive five millions from the States (if they will enter into this partnership, which few probably will), and five millions from the individual subscribers, in exchange for ten millions of six per cent stock, one per cent of which, however, they will make on their ten millions of stock remaining in bank, and so reduce it, in effect, to a loan of ten millions at five per cent interest. This is good; but

2. They authorize this bank to throw into circulation ninety millions of dollars (three times the capital), which increases our circulating medium fifty per cent, depreciates proportionably the present value of a dollar, and raises the price of all future purchases in the same proportion.

3. This loan of ten millions at five per cent, is to be once for all, only. Neither the terms of the scheme, nor their own prudence could ever permit them to add to the circulation in the same, or any other way, for the supplies of the succeeding years of the war. These succeeding years then are to be left unprovided for, and the means of doing it in a great measure precluded.

4. The individual subscribers, on paying their own five millions of cash to Congress, become the depositories of ten millions of stock belonging to Congress, five millions belonging to the States, and five millions to themselves, say twenty millions, with which, as no one has a right ever to see their books, or to ask a question, they may choose their time for running away, after adding to their booty the proceeds of as much of their own notes as they shall be able to throw into circulation.

5. The subscribers may be one, two, or three, or more individuals (many single individuals being able to pay in the five millions), whereupon this bank oligarchy or monarchy enters the field with ninety millions of dollars, to direct and control the politics of the nation; and of the influence of these institutions on our politics, and into what scale it will be thrown, we have had abundant experience. Indeed, England herself may be the real, while her friend and trustee here shall be the nominal and sole subscriber.

6. This state of things is to be fastened on us, without the power of relief, for forty or fifty years. That is to say, the eight millions of people now existing, for the sake of receiving one dollar and twenty-five cents apiece, at five per cent interest, are to subject the fifty millions of people who are to succeed them within that term, to the payment of forty-five millions of dollars, principal and interest, which will be payable in the course of the fifty years.

7. But the great and national advantage is to be the relief of the present *scarcity of money,* which is produced and proved by,

1. The additional industry created to supply a variety of articles for the troops, ammunition, &c.

2. By the cash sent to the frontiers, and the vacuum occasioned in the trading towns by that.

3. By the late loans.

4. By the necessity of recurring to shavers with *good* paper, which the existing banks are not able to take up; and

5. By the numerous applications of bank charters, showing that an increase of circulating medium is wanting.

Let us examine these causes and proofs of the want of an increase of medium, one by one.

1. The additional industry created to supply a variety of articles for troops, ammunition, &c. Now, I had always supposed that war produced a diminution of industry, by the number of hands it withdraws from industrious pursuits for employment in arms, &c., which are totally unproductive. And if it calls for new industry in the articles of ammunition and other military supplies, the hands are borrowed from other branches on which the demand is slackened by the war; so that it is but a shifting of these hands from one pursuit to another.

2. The cash sent to the frontiers occasions a vacuum in the trading towns, which requires a new supply. Let us examine what are the calls for money to the frontiers. Not for clothing, tents, ammunition, arms, which are all bought in the trading towns. Not for provisions; for although these are bought partly in the immediate country, bank bills are more acceptable there than even in the trading towns. The pay of the army calls for some cash, but not a great deal, as bank notes are as acceptable with the military men, perhaps more so; and what cash is sent must find its way back again in exchange for the wants of the upper from the lower country. For we are not to suppose that cash stays accumulating there forever.

3. This scarcity has been occasioned by the late loans. But does the government borrow money to keep it in their coffers? Is it not instantly restored to circulation by payment for its necessary supplies? And are we to restore a vacuum of twenty millions of dollars by an emission of ninety millions?

4. The want of medium is proved by the recurrence of individuals with *good* paper to brokers at exorbitant interest; and

5. By the numerous applications to the State governments for additional banks; New York wanting eighteen millions, Pennsylvania ten millions, &c. But say more correctly, the speculators and spendthrifts of New York and Pennsylvania, but never consider them as being the States of New York and Pennsylvania. These two items shall be considered together.

It is a litigated question, whether the circulation of paper, rather than of specie, is a good or an evil. In the opinion of England and of English writers it is a good; in that of all other nations it is an evil; and excepting England and her copyist, the United States, there is not a nation existing, I believe, which tolerates a paper circulation. The experiment is going on, however, desperately in England, pretty boldly with us, and at the end of the chapter, we shall see which opinion experience approves: for I believe it to be one of those cases where mercantile clamor will bear down reason, until it is corrected by ruin. In the meantime, however, let us reason on this new call for a national bank.

After the solemn decision of Congress against the renewal of the charter of the Bank of the United States, and the grounds of that decision (the want of constitutional power), I had imagined that question at rest, and that no more applications would be made to them for the incorporation of banks. The opposition on that ground to its first establishment, the small majority by which it was overborne, and the means practiced for obtaining it, cannot be already forgotten. The law having passed, however, by a majority, its opponents, true to the sacred principle of submission to a majority, suffered the law to flow through its term without obstruction. During this, the nation had time to consider the constitutional question, and when the renewal was proposed, they condemned it, not by their representatives in Congress only, but by express instructions from different organs of their will. Here then we might stop, and consider the memorial as answered. But, setting authority apart, we will examine whether the Legislature ought to comply with it, even if they had the power.

Proceeding to reason on this subject, some principles must be premised as forming its basis. The adequate price of a thing depends on the capital and labor necessary to produce it. [In the term *capital,* I mean to include science, because capital as well as labor has been employed to acquire it.] Two things requiring the same capital and labor, should be of the same price. If a gallon of wine requires for its production the same capital and labor with a bushel of wheat, they should be expressed by the same price, derived from the application of a common measure to them. The comparative prices of things being thus to be estimated and expressed by a common measure, we may proceed to observe, that were a country so insulated as to have no commercial intercourse with any other, to confine the interchange of all its wants and supplies within itself, the amount of circulating medium, as a common measure for adjusting these exchanges, would be quite immaterial. If their circulation, for instance, were of a million of dollars, and the annual produce of their industry equivalent to ten millions of bushels of wheat, the price of a bushel of wheat might be one dollar. If, then, by a progressive coinage, their medium should be doubled, the price of a bushel of wheat might become progressively two dollars, and without inconvenience. Whatever be the proportion of the circulating medium to the value of the annual produce of industry, it may be considered as the representative of that industry. In the first case, a bushel of wheat will be represented by one dollar; in the second, by two dollars. This is well explained by Hume, and seems admitted by Adam Smith, B. 2. c. 2, 436, 441, 490. But where a nation is in a full course of interchange of wants and supplies with all others, the proportion of its medium to its produce is no longer indifferent. *Ib.* 441. To trade on equal terms, the common measure of values should be as nearly as possible on a par with that of its corresponding nations, whose medium is in a sound state; that is to say, not in an accidental state of excess or deficiency. Now, one of the great advantages of specie as a medium is, that being of universal value, it will keep itself at a general level, flowing out from where it is too high into parts where it is lower. Whereas, if the medium be of local value only, as paper money, if too little, indeed, gold and silver will flow in to supply the deficiency; but if too much, it accumulates, banishes the gold and silver not locked up in vaults and hoards, and depreciates itself; that is to say, its proportion to the annual produce of industry being raised, more of it is required to represent any particular article of produce than in the other countries. This is agreed by Smith, (B. 2. c. 2. 437,) the principal advocate for a paper circulation; but advocating it on the sole condition that it be strictly regulated. He admits, nevertheless, that "the commerce and industry of a country cannot be so secure when suspended on the Dædalian wings of paper money, as on the solid ground of gold and silver; and that in time of war, the insecurity is greatly increased, and great confusion possible where the circulation is for the greater part in paper." B. 2. c. 2. 484. But in a country where loans are uncertain, and a specie circulation the only sure resource for them, the preference of that circulation assumes a far different degree of importance, as is explained in my former letters.

The only advantage which Smith proposes by substituting paper in the room of gold and silver money, B. 2. c. 2. 434, is "to replace an expensive instrument with one much less costly, and *sometimes* equally convenient"; that is to say, page 437, "to allow the gold and silver to be sent abroad and converted into foreign goods," and to substitute paper as being a cheaper measure. But this makes no addition to the stock or capital of the nation. The coin sent out was worth as much, while in the country, as the goods imported and taking its place. It is only, then, a change of form in a part of the national capital, from that of gold and silver to other goods. He admits, too, that while a part of the goods received in exchange for the coin exported may be materials, tools and provisions for the employment of an additional industry, a part, also, may be taken back in foreign wines, silks, &c., to be consumed by idle people who produce nothing; and so far the substitution promotes prodigality, increases expense and corruption, without increasing production. So far also, then, it lessens the capital of the nation. What may be the amount which the conversion of the part exchanged for productive goods may add to the former productive mass, it is not easy to ascertain, because, as he says, page 441, "it is impossible to determine what is the proportion which the circulating money of any country bears to the whole value of the annual produce. It has been computed by different authors, from a fifth [2] to a thirtieth of that value." In the United States it must be less than in any other part of the commercial world; because the great mass of their inhabitants being in responsible circumstances, the great mass of their exchanges in the country is effected on credit, in their merchant's ledger, who supplies all their wants through the year, and at the end of it receives the produce of their farms, or other articles of their industry. It is a fact, that a farmer with a revenue of ten thousand dollars a year, may obtain all his supplies from his merchant, and liquidate them at the end of the year, by the sale of his produce to him, without the intervention of a single dollar of cash. This, then, is merely barter, and in this way of barter a great portion of the annual produce of the United States is exchanged without the intermediation of cash. We might safely, then, state our medium at the minimum of one-thirtieth. But what is one-thirtieth of the value of the annual produce of the industry of the United States? Or what is the whole value of the annual produce of the United States? An able writer and competent judge of the subject, in 1799, on as good grounds as probably could be taken, estimated it, on the then population of four and a half millions of inhabitants, to be thirty-seven and a half millions sterling, or one hundred and sixty-eight and three-fourths millions of dollars. See Cooper's *Political Arithmetic,* page 47. According to the same estimate for our present population, it will be three hundred millions of dollars, one-thirtieth of which, Smith's minimum, would be ten millions, and one-fifth, his maximum, would be sixty millions for the quantum of circulation. But suppose that instead of our needing the least circulating medium of any nation, from the circumstance before mentioned, we should place ourselves in the middle term of the calculation, to-wit: at thirty-five millions. One-fifth of this, at the least, Smith thinks should be retained in specie, which would leave twenty-eight millions of specie to be exported in exchange for other commodities; and if fifteen millions of that should be returned in productive goods, and not in articles of prodigality, that would be the amount of capital which this operation would add to the existing mass. But to what mass? Not that of the three hundred millions, which is only its gross annual produce, but to that capital of which the three hundred millions are but the annual produce. But this being gross, we may infer from it the value of the capital by considering that the rent of lands is generally fixed at one-third of the gross produce, and is

[2] The real cash or money necessary to carry on the circulation and barter of a State, is nearly one-third part of all the annual rents of the proprietors of the said State; that is, one-ninth of the whole produce of the land. Sir William Petty supposes one-tenth part of the value of the whole produce sufficient. Postlethwait, voce, Cash.—T. J.

deemed its net profit, and twenty times that its fee simple value. The profits on landed capital may, with accuracy enough for our purpose, be supposed on a par with those of other capital. This would give us then for the United States, a capital of two thousand millions, all in active employment, and exclusive of unimproved lands lying in a great degree dormant. Of this, fifteen millions would be the hundred and thirty-third part. And it is for this petty addition to the capital of the nation, this minimum of one dollar, added to one hundred and thirty-three and a third, or three-fourths per cent, that we are to give up our gold and silver medium, its intrinsic solidity, its universal value, and its saving powers in time of war, and to substitute for it paper, with all its train of evils, moral, political and physical, which I will not pretend to enumerate.

There is another authority to which we may appeal for the proper quantity of circulating medium for the United States. The old Congress, when we were estimated at about two millions of people, on a long and able discussion, June 22d, 1775, decided the sufficient quantity to be two millions of dollars, which sum they then emitted.[3] According to this, it should be eight millions, now that we are eight millions of people. This differs little from Smith's minimum of ten millions, and strengthens our respect for that estimate.

There is, indeed, a convenience in paper; its easy transmission from one place to another. But this may be mainly supplied by bills of exchange, so as to prevent any great displacement of actual coin. Two places trading together balance their dealings, for the most part, by their mutual supplies, and the debtor individuals of either may, instead of cash, remit the bills of those who are creditors in the same dealings; or may obtain them through some third place with which both have dealings. The cases would be rare where such bills could not be obtained, either directly or circuitously, and too unimportant to the nation to overweigh the train of evils flowing from paper circulation.

From eight to thirty-five millions then being our proper circulation, and two hundred millions the actual one, the memorial proposes to issue ninety millions more, because, it says, a great scarcity of money is proved by the numerous applications for banks; to wit, New York for eighteen millions, Pennsylvania ten millions, &c. The answer to this shall be quoted from Adam Smith, B. 2. c. 2. page 462; where speaking of the complaints of the trader against the Scotch bankers, who had already gone too far in their issues of paper, he says, "those traders and other undertakers having got so much assistance from banks, wished to get still more. The banks, they seem to have

[3] Within five months after this, they were compelled by the necessities of the war, to abandon the idea of emitting only an adequate circulation, and to make those necessities the sole measure of their emissions.—T. J.

thought, could extend their credits to whatever sum might be wanted, without incurring any other expense besides that of a few reams of paper. They complained of the contracted views and dastardly spirit of the directors of those banks, which did not, they said, extend their credits in proportion to the extension of the trade of the country; meaning, no doubt, by the extension of that trade, the extension of their own projects beyond what they could carry on, either *with their own capital,* or with what they had credit to borrow of private people in the usual way of bond or mortgage. The banks, they seem to have thought, were in honor bound to supply the deficiency, and to provide them with all the capital which they wanted to trade with." And again, page 470: "when bankers discovered that certain projectors were trading, not with any capital of their own, but with that which they advanced them, they endeavored to withdraw gradually, making every day greater and greater difficulties about discounting. These difficulties alarmed and enraged in the highest degree those projectors. Their own distress, of which this prudent and necessary reserve of the banks was no doubt the immediate occasion, they called the distress of the country; and this distress of the country, they said, was altogether owing to the ignorance, pusillanimity, and bad conduct of the banks, which did not give a sufficiently liberal aid to the spirited undertakings of those who exerted themselves in order to beautify, improve and enrich the country. It was the duty of the banks, they seemed to think, to lend for as long a time, and to as great an extent, as they might wish to borrow." It is, probably, the *good paper* of these projectors which the memorial says, the bank being *unable* to discount, goes into the hands of brokers, who (knowing the risk of this *good paper*) discount it at a much higher rate than legal interest, to the great distress of the enterprising adventurers, who had rather try trade on borrowed capital, than go to the plough or other laborious calling. Smith again says, page 478, "that the industry of Scotland languished for want of money to employ it, was the opinion of the famous Mr. Law. By establishing a bank of a particular kind, which, he seems to have imagined might issue paper to the amount of the whole value of all the lands in the country, he proposed to remedy this want of money. It was afterwards adopted, with some variations, by the Duke of Orleans, at that time Regent of France. The idea of the possibility of multiplying paper to almost any extent, was the real foundation of what is called the Mississippi scheme, the most extravagant project both of banking and stock jobbing, that perhaps the world ever saw. The principles upon which it was founded are explained by Mr. Law himself, in a discourse concerning money and trade, which he published in Scotland when he first proposed his project. The splendid but visionary ideas which are set forth in that and some other works upon the same principles, still continue to make an impression upon many people, and have perhaps, in part, contributed to that excess of banking which has of late been complained of both in Scotland and in other places." The Mississippi scheme, it is well known, ended in France in the bankruptcy of the public treasury, the crush of thousands and thousands of private fortunes, and scenes of desolation and distress equal to those of an invading army, burning and laying waste all before it.

At the time we were funding our national debt, we heard much about "a public debt being a public blessing"; [4] that the stock representing it was a creation of active capital for the aliment of commerce, manufactures and agriculture. This paradox was well adapted to the minds of believers in dreams, and the gulls of that size entered *bonâ fide* into it. But the art and mystery of banks is a wonderful improvement on that. It is established on the principle that "*private* debts are a public blessing." That the evidences of those private debts, called bank notes, become active capital, and aliment the whole commerce, manufacturers, and agriculture of the United States. Here are a set of people, for instance, who have bestowed on us the great blessing of running in our debt about two hundred millions of dollars, without our knowing who they are, where they are, or what property they have to pay this debt when called on; nay, who have made us so sensible of the blessings of letting them run in our debt, that we have exempted them by law from the repayment of these debts beyond a given proportion (generally estimated at one-third). And to fill up the measure of blessing, instead of paying, they receive an interest on what they owe from those to whom they owe; for all the notes, or evidences of what they owe, which we see in circulation, have been lent to somebody on an interest which is levied again on us through the medium of commerce. And they are so ready still to deal out their liberalities to us, that they are now willing to let themselves run in our debt ninety millions more, on our paying them the same premium of six or eight per cent interest, and on the same legal exemption from the repayment of more than thirty millions of the debt, when it shall be called for. But let us look at this principle in its original form, and its copy will then be equally understood. "A public debt is a public blessing." That our debt was juggled from forty-three up to eighty millions, and funded at that amount, according to this opinion was a great public blessing, because the evidences of it could be vested in commerce, and thus converted into active capital, and then the more the debt was made to be, the more active capital was created. That is to say, the creditors could now employ in commerce the money due them from the public, and make from it an annual profit of five per cent, or four millions of dollars. But observe, that the public were at the same time paying on it an interest of exactly the same amount of four millions of dollars.

[4] Jefferson is here referring to Alexander Hamilton's famous statement: "A national debt, if it is not excessive, will be to us a national blessing." Hamilton, letter to Robert Morris, April 30, 1781.

Where then is the gain to either party, which makes it a public blessing? There is no change in the state of things, but of persons only. A has a debt due to him from the public, of which he holds their certificate as evidence, and on which he is receiving an annual interest. He wishes, however, to have the money itself, and to go into business with it. B has an equal sum of money in business, but wishes now to retire, and live on the interest. He therefore gives it to A in exchange for A's certificates of public stock. Now, then, A has the money to employ in business, which B so employed before. B has the money on interest to live on, which A lived on before; and the public pays the interest to B which they paid to A before. Here is no new creation of capital, no additional money employed, nor even a change in the employment of a single dollar. The only change is of place between A and B in which we discover no creation of capital, nor public blessing. Suppose, again, the public to owe nothing. Then A not having lent his money to the public, would be in possession of it himself, and would go into business without the previous operation of selling stock. Here again, the same quantity of capital is employed as in the former case, though no public debt exists. In neither case is there any creation of active capital, nor other difference than that there is a public debt in the first case, and none in the last; and we may safely ask which of the two situations is most truly a public blessing? If, then, a *public* debt be no public blessing, we may pronounce, *à fortiori,* that a private one cannot be so. If the debt which the banking companies owe be a blessing to anybody, it is to themselves alone, who are realizing a solid interest of eight or ten per cent on it. As to the public, these companies have banished all our gold and silver medium, which, before their institution, we had without interest, which never could have perished in our hands, and would have been our salvation now in the hour of war; instead of which they have given us two hundred million of froth and bubble, on which we are to pay them heavy interest, until it shall vanish into air, as Morris' notes did. We are warranted, then, in affirming that this parody on the principle of "a public debt being a public blessing," and its mutation into the blessing of private instead of public debts, is as ridiculous as the original principle itself. In both cases, the truth is, that capital may be produced by industry, and accumulated by economy; but jugglers only will propose to create it by legerdemain tricks with paper.

I have called the actual circulation of bank paper in the United States, two hundred millions of dollars. I do not recollect where I have seen this estimate; but I retain the impression that I thought it just at the time. It may be tested, however, by a list of the banks now in the United States, and the amount of their capital. I have no means of recurring to such a list for the present day; but I turn to two lists in my possession for the years of 1803 and 1804.

| | |
|---|---|
| In 1803, there were thirty-four banks, whose capital was | $28,902,000 |
| In 1804, there were sixty-six, consequently thirty-two additional ones. Their capital is not stated, but at the average of the others (excluding the highest, that of the United States, which was of ten millions), they would be of six hundred thousand dollars each, and add | 19,200,000 |
| Making a total of | $48,102,000 |

or say of fifty millions in round numbers. Now, everyone knows the immense multiplication of these institutions since 1804. If they have only doubled, their capital will be of one hundred millions, and if trebled, as I think probable, it will be one hundred and fifty millions, on which they are at liberty to circulate treble the amount. I should sooner, therefore, believe two hundred millions to be far below than above the actual circulation. In England, by a late parliamentary document (see *Virginia Argus* of October the 18th, 1813, and other public papers of about that date), it appears that six years ago the Bank of England had twelve millions of pounds sterling in circulation, which had increased to forty-two millions in 1812, or to one hundred and eighty-nine millions of dollars. What proportion all the other banks may add to this, I do not know; if we were allowed to suppose they equal it, this would give a circulation of three hundred and seventy-eight millions, or the double of ours on a double population. But that nation is essentially commercial, ours essentially agricultural, and needing, therefore, less circulating medium, because the produce of the husbandman comes but once a year, and is then partly consumed at home, partly exchanged by barter. The dollar, which was of four shilling and sixpence sterling, was, by the same document, stated to be then six shillings and nine pence, a depreciation of exactly fifty per cent. The average price of wheat on the continent of Europe, at the commencement of its present war with England, was about a French crown, of one hundred and ten cents, the bushel. With us it was one hundred cents, and consequently we could send it there in competition with their own. That ordinary price has now doubled with us, and more than doubled in England; and although a part of this augmentation may proceed from the war demand, yet from the extraordinary nominal rise in the prices of land and labor here, both of which have nearly doubled in that period, and are still rising with every new bank, it is evident that were a general peace to take place tomorrow, and time allowed for the re-establishment of commerce, justice, and order, we could not afford to raise wheat for much less than two dollars, while the continent of Europe, having no paper circulation, and that of its specie not being augmented, would raise it at their former price of one hundred and ten cents. It follows, then, that with our redundancy of paper, we cannot, after peace, send a bushel of wheat to

Europe, unless extraordinary circumstances double its price in particular places, and that then the exporting countries of Europe could undersell us.

It is said that our paper is as good as silver, because we may have silver for it at the bank where it issues. This is not true. One, two, or three persons might have it; but a general application would soon exhaust their vaults, and leave a ruinous proportion of their paper in its intrinsic worthless form. It is a fallacious pretence, for another reason. The inhabitants of the banking cities might obtain cash for their paper, as far as the cash of the vaults would hold out, but distance puts it out of the power of the country to do this. A farmer having a note of a Boston or Charleston bank, distant hundreds of miles, has no means of calling for the cash. And while these calls are impracticable for the country, the banks have no fear of their being made from the towns; because their inhabitants are mostly on their books, and there on sufferance only, and during good behavior.

In this state of things, we are called on to add ninety millions more to the circulation. Proceeding in this career, it is infallible, that we must end where the revolutionary paper ended. Two hundred millions was the whole amount of all the emissions of the old Congress, at which point their bills ceased to circulate. We are now at that sum, but with treble the population, and of course a longer tether. Our depreciation is, as yet, but about two for one. Owing to the support its credit receives from the small reservoirs of specie in the vaults of the banks, it is impossible to say at what point their notes will stop. Nothing is necessary to effect it but a general alarm; and that may take place whenever the public shall begin to reflect on, and perceive the impossibility that the banks should repay this sum. At present, caution is inspired no farther than to keep prudent men from selling property on long payments. Let us suppose the panic to arise at three hundred millions, a point to which every session of the legislatures hasten us by long strides. Nobody dreams that they would have three hundred millions of specie to satisfy the holders of their notes. Were they even to stop now, no one supposes they have two hundred millions in cash, or even the sixty-six and two-third millions, to which amount alone the law compels them to repay. One hundred and thirty-three and one-third millions of loss, then, is thrown on the public by law; and as to the sixty-six and two-thirds, which they are legally bound to pay, and ought to have in their vaults, everyone knows there is no such amount of cash in the United States, and what would be the course with what they really have there? Their notes are refused. Cash is called for. The inhabitants of the banking towns will get what is in the vaults, until a few banks declare their insolvency; when, the general crush becoming evident, the others will withdraw even the cash they have, declare their bankruptcy at once, and leave an empty house and empty coffers for the holders of their notes. In this scramble of creditors, the country gets nothing, the towns but little. What are they to do? Bring suits? A million of creditors bring a million of suits against John Nokes and Robert Styles, wheresoever to be found? All nonsense. The loss is total. And a sum is thus swindled from our citizens, of seven times the amount of the real debt, and four times that of the fictitious one of the United States, at the close of the war. All this they will justly charge on their legislatures; but this will be poor satisfaction for the two or three hundred millions they will have lost. It is time, then, for the public functionaries to look to this. Perhaps it may not be too late. Perhaps, by giving time to the banks, they may call in and pay off their paper by degrees. But no remedy is ever to be expected while it rests with the State legislatures. Personal motive can be excited through so many avenues to their will, that, in their hands, it will continue to go on from bad to worse, until the catastrophe overwhelms us. I still believe, however, that on proper representations of the subject, a great proportion of these legislatures would cede to Congress their power of establishing banks, saving the charter rights already granted. And this should be asked, not by way of amendment to the constitution, because until three-fourths should consent, nothing could be done; but accepted from them one by one, singly, as their consent might be obtained. Any single State, even if no other should come into the measure, woud find its interest in arresting foreign bank paper immediately, and its own by degrees. Specie would flow in on them as paper disappeared. Their own banks would call in and pay off their notes gradually, and their constituents would thus be saved from the general wreck. Should the greater part of the States concede, as is expected, their power over banks to Congress, besides insuring their own safety, the paper of the non-conceding States might be so checked and circumscribed, by prohibiting its receipt in any of the conceding States, and even in the non-conceding as to duties, taxes, judgments, or other demands of the United States, or of the citizens of other States, that it would soon die of itself, and the medium of gold and silver be universally restored. This is what ought to be done. But it will not be done. *Carthago non delibitur.* The overbearing clamor of merchants, speculators, and projectors, will drive us before them with our eyes open, until, as in France, under the Mississippi bubble, our citizens will be overtaken by the crush of this baseless fabric, without other satisfaction than that of execrations on the heads of those functionaries, who, from ignorance, pusillanimity or corruption, have betrayed the fruits of their industry into the hands of projectors and swindlers.

When I speak comparatively of the paper emission of the old Congress and the present banks, let it not be imagined that I cover them under the same mantle. The object of the former was a holy one; for if ever there was a holy war, it was that which saved our liberties and gave us independence. The object of the latter, is to enrich swindlers at the expense of the honest and industrious part of the nation.

The sum of what has been said is, that pretermitting the constitutional question on the authority of Congress, and considering this application on the grounds of reason alone, it would be best that our medium should be so proportioned to our produce, as to be on a par with that of the countries with which we trade, and whose medium is in a sound state; that specie is the most perfect medium, because it will preserve its own level; because, having intrinsic and universal value, it can never die in our hands, and it is the surest resource of reliance in time of war; that the trifling economy of paper, as a cheaper medium, or its convenience for transmission, weighs nothing in opposition to the advantages of the precious metals; that it is liable to be abused, has been, is, and forever will be abused, in every country in which it is permitted; that it is already at a term of abuse in these States, which has never been reached by any other nation, France excepted, whose dreadful catastrophe should be a warning against the instrument which produced it; that we are already at ten or twenty times the due quantity of medium; insomuch, that no man knows what his property is now worth, because it is bloating while he is calculating; and still less what it will be worth when the medium shall be relieved from its present dropsical state; and that it is a palpable falsehood to say we can have specie for our paper whenever demanded. Instead, then, of yielding to the cries of scarcity of medium set up by speculators, projectors and commercial gamblers, no endeavors should be spared to begin the work of reducing it by such gradual means as may give time to private fortunes to preserve their poise, and settle down with the subsiding medium; and that, for this purpose, the States should be urged to concede to the General Government, with a saving of chartered rights, the exclusive power of establishing banks of discount for paper.

To the existence of banks of *discount* for *cash,* as on the continent of Europe, there can be no objection, because there can be no danger of abuse, and they are a convenience both to merchants and individuals. I think they should even be encouraged, by allowing them a larger than legal interest on short discounts, and tapering thence, in proportion as the term of discount is lengthened, down to legal interest on those of a year or more. Even banks of *deposit,* where cash should be lodged, and a paper acknowledgment taken out as its representative, entitled to a return of the cash on demand, would be convenient for remittances, travelling persons, &c. But, liable as its cash would be to be pilfered and robbed, and its paper to be fraudulently re-issued, or issued without deposit, it would require skilful and strict regulation. This would differ from the bank of Amsterdam, in the circumstance that the cash could be redeemed on returning the note.

When I commenced this letter to you, my dear Sir, on Mr. Law's memorial, I expected a short one would have answered that. But as I advanced, the subject branched itself before me into so many collateral questions, that even the rapid views I have taken of each have swelled the volume of my letter beyond my expectations, and, I fear, beyond your patience. Yet on a revisal of it, I find no part which has not so much bearing on the subject as to be worth merely the time of perusal. I leave it then as it is; and will add only the assurances of my constant and affectionate esteem and respect.

## PROSPECTUS ON POLITICAL ECONOMY[1]

April 6, 1816

*Prospectus.*—Political economy in modern times assumed the form of a regular science first in the hands of a political sect in France, called the Economists. They made it a branch only of a comprehensive system on the natural order of societies. Quesnai first, Gournay, Le Frosne, Turgot and Dupont de Nemours, the enlightened, philanthropic, and venerable citizen, now of the United States, led the way in these developments, and gave to our inquiries the direction they have since observed. Many sound and valuable principles established by them, have received the sanction of general approbation. Some as in the infancy of a science might be expected, have been brought into question, and have furnished occasion for much discussion. Their opinions on production, and on the proper subjects of taxation, have been particularly controverted; and whatever may be the merit of their principles of taxation, it is not wonderful they have not prevailed; not on the questioned score of correctness, but because not acceptable to the people, whose will must be the supreme law. Taxation is in fact the most difficult function of government—and that against which their citizens are most apt to be refractory. The general aim is therefore to adopt the mode most consonant with the circumstances and sentiments of the country.

Adam Smith, first in England, published a rational and systematic work on Political Economy, adopting generally the ground of the Economists, but differing on the subjects before specified. The system being novel, much argument and detail seemed then necessary to establish principles which now are assented to as soon as proposed. Hence his book, admitted to be able, and of the first degree of merit, has yet been considered as prolix and tedious.

[1] This accompanied a letter to Joseph Milligan on the subject of Jefferson's revision of the English translation of Destutt de Tracy's *A Treatise on Political Economy.* Jefferson did a thorough job of revision and correction, but he warned Milligan: "My name must in nowise appear connected with the work." Jefferson did not complete his revision and translation until 1818.

In France, John Baptist Say has the merit of producing a very superior work on the subject of political economy. His arrangement is luminous, ideas clear, style perspicuous, and the whole subject brought within half the volume of Smith's work. Add to this considerable advances in correctness and extension of principles.

The work of Senator Tracy, now announced, comes forward with all the lights of his predecessors in the science, and with the advantages of further experience, more discussion, and greater maturity of subjects. It is certainly distinguished by important traits; a cogency of logic which has never been exceeded in any work, a rigorous enchainment of ideas, and constant recurrence to it to keep it in the reader's view, a fearless pursuit of truth whithersoever it leads, and a diction so correct that not a word can be changed but for the worse; and, as happens in other cases, that the more a subject is understood, the more briefly it may be explained, he has reduced, not indeed all the details, but all the elements and the system of principles within the compass of an 8vo, of about 400 pages. Indeed we might say within two-thirds of that space, the one-third being taken up with some preliminary pieces now to be noticed.

Mr. Tracy is the author of a treatise on the Elements of Ideology, justly considered as a production of the first order in the science of our thinking faculty, or of the understanding. Considering the present work but as a second section to those Elements under the titles of Analytical Table, Supplement, and Introduction, he gives in these preliminary pieces a supplement to the Elements, shows how the present work stands on that as its basis, presents a summary view of it, and, before entering on the formation, distribution, and employment of property and personality, a question not new indeed, yet one which has not hitherto been satisfactorily settled. These investigations are very metaphysical, profound, and demonstrative, and will give satisfaction to minds in the habit of abstract speculation. Readers, however, not disposed to enter into them, after reading the summary view, entitled, "on our actions," will probably pass on at once to the commencement of the main subject of the work, which is treated of under the following heads:

Of Society.
Of Production, or the formation of our riches.
Of Value, or the measure of utility.
Of change of form, or fabrication.
Of change of place, or commerce.
Of money.
Of the distribution of our riches.
Of population.
Of the employment of our riches, or consumption.

Of public revenue, expenses and debts.

Although the work now offered is but a translation, it may be considered in some degree as the original, that having never been published in the country in which it was written. The author would there have been submitted to the unpleasant alternative either of mutilating his sentiments, where they were either free or doubtful, or of risking himself under the unsettled regimen of the press. A manuscript copy communicated to a friend here has enabled him to give it to a country which is afraid to read nothing, and which may be trusted with anything, so long as its reason remains unfettered by law.

In the translation, fidelity has been chiefly consulted. A more correct style would sometimes have given a shade of sentiment which was not the author's, and which, in a work standing in the place of the original, would have been unjust towards him. Some gallicisms have, therefore, been admitted, where a single word gives an idea which would require a whole phrase of dictionary-English. Indeed, the horrors of neologism, which startle the purist, have given no alarm to the translator. Where brevity, perspicuity, and even euphony can be promoted by the introduction of a new word, it is an improvement to the language. It is thus the English language has been brought to what it is; one half of it having been innovations, made at different times, from the Greek, Latin, French, and other languages. And is it the worse for these? Had the preposterous idea of fixing the language been adopted by our Saxon ancestors, of Pierce Plowman, of Chaucer, of Spenser, the progress of ideas must have stopped with that of the language. On the contrary, nothing is more evident than that as we advance in the knowledge of new things, and of new combinations of old ones, we must have new words to express them. Were Van Helmont, Stane, Scheele, to rise from the dead at this time, they would scarcely understand one word of their own science. Would it have been better, then, to have abandoned the science of chemistry, rather than admit innovations in its terms? What a wonderful accession of copiousness and force has the French language attained, by the innovations of the last thirty years! And what do we not owe to Shakspeare for the enrichment of the language, by his free and magical creation of words? In giving a loose to neologism, indeed, uncouth words will sometimes be offered; but the public will judge them, and receive or reject, as sense or sound shall suggest, and authors will be approved or condemned according to the use they make of this license, as they now are from their use of the present vocabulary. The claim of the present translation, however, is limited to its duties of fidelity and justice to the sense of its original; adopting the author's own word only where no term of our own language would convey his meaning.

(A NOTE COMMUNICATED TO THE EDITOR)

Our author's classification of taxes being taken from those practised in France, will scarcely be intelligible to an American reader, to whom the nature as well as names of some of them must be unknown. The taxes with which we are familiar, class themselves readily according to the basis on which they rest. 1. Capital. 2. Income. 3. Consumption. These may be considered as commensurate; consumption being generally equal to income, and Income the annual profit of capital. A government may select either of these bases for the establishment of its system of taxation, and so frame it as to reach the faculties of every member of the society, and to draw from him his equal proportion of the public contributions; and, if this be correctly obtained, it is the perfection of the function of taxation. But when once a government has assumed its basis, to select and tax special articles from either of the other classes, is double taxation. For example, if the system be established on the basis of income, and his just proportion on that scale has been already drawn from everyone, to step into the field of consumption, and tax special articles in that, as broadcloth or homespun, wine or whiskey, a coach or a wagon, is doubly taxing the same article. For that portion of income with which these articles are purchased, having already paid its tax as income, to pay another tax on the thing it purchased, is paying twice for the same thing, it is an aggrievance on the citizens who use these articles in exoneration of those who do not, contrary to the most sacred of the duties of a government, to do equal and impartial justice to all its citizens.

How far it may be the interest and the duty of all to submit to this sacrifice on other grounds, for instance, to pay for a time an impost on the importation of certain articles, in order to encourage their manufacture at home, or an excise on others injurious to the morals or health of the citizens, will depend on a series of considerations of another order, and beyond the proper limits of this note. The reader, in deciding which basis of taxation is most eligible for the local circumstances of his country, will, of course, avail himself of the weighty observations of our author.

To this a single observation shall yet be added. Whether property alone, and the whole of what each citizen possesses, shall be subject to contribution, or only its surplus after satisfying his first wants, or whether the faculties of body and mind shall contribute also from their annual earnings, is a question to be decided. But, when decided, and the principle settled, it is to be equally and fairly applied to all. To take from one, because it is thought that his own industry and that of his fathers has acquired too much, in order to spare to others, who, or whose fathers have not exercised equal industry and skill, is to violate arbitrarily the first principle of association, "the *guarantee* to everyone of a free exercise of his industry, and the fruits acquired by it.' If the overgrown wealth of an individual be deemed dangerous to the State, the best corrective is the law of equal inheritance to all in equal degree; and the better, as this enforces a law of nature, while extra-taxation violates it.

## FRENCH AND ITALIAN WINES[1]

April 8, 1817

I promised you when I should have received and tried the wines I had ordered from France and Italy to give you a note of the kinds which I should think worthy of your procurement; and this being the season for ordering them, so that they may come in the mild temperature of autumn, I now fulfil my promise.

They are the following:

*Vin blanc liquoureux d'Hermitage de M. Jourdan à Tanis.* This costs about eighty-two and a half cents a bottle put on shipboard.

*Vin de Ledarion* (in Languedoc), something of the port character but higher flavored, more delicate, less rough. I do not know its price, but probably about twenty-five cents a bottle.

*Vin de Roussillon.* The best is that of Perpignan or Rives alte of the crop of M. Durand. It costs seventy-two cents a gallon, bears bringing in a cask. If put into bottles there it costs eleven cents a bottle more than if bottled here by an inexplicable and pernicious arrangement of our tariff.

*Vin de Nice.* The crop called Bellet, of Mr. Sasterno, is the best. This is the most elegant every-day wine in the world and costs thirty-one cents the bottle. Not much being made it is little known at the general markets.

Mr. Cathalan of Marseilles is the best channel for getting the first three of these wines and a good one for the *Nice,* being in their neighborhood and knowing well who makes the crops of best quality. The *Nice* being a wine foreign to France occasions some troublesome forms. If you could get that direct from Sasterno himself at Nice, it would be better. . . .

There is still another wine to be named to you, which is the wine of Florence called *Montepulciano,* with which Mr. Appleton can best furnish you. There is a particular very best crop of it known to him and which he has usually sent to me. This costs twenty-five cents per bottle. He knows, too, from experience how to have it so bottled and packed as to ensure its bearing the passage which in the ordinary way it does not. I have imported it through him annually ten or twelve years and do not think I have lost one bottle in one hundred.

[1] Letter to James Monroe, who had recently been inaugurated President.

## DOMESTIC MANUFACTURE[1]

January 9, 1816

You tell me I am quoted by those who wish to continue our dependence on England for manufactures. There was a time when I might have been so quoted with more candor, but within the thirty years which have since elapsed, how are circumstances changed! We were then in peace. Our independent place among nations was acknowledged. A commerce which offered the raw material in exchange for the same material after receiving the last touch of industry, was worthy of welcome to all nations. It was expected that those especially to whom manufacturing industry was important, would cherish the friendship of such customers by every favor, by every inducement, and particularly cultivate their peace by every act of justice and friendship. Under this prospect the question seemed legitimate, whether with such an immensity of unimproved land, courting the hand of husbandry, the industry of agriculture, or that of manufactures, would add most to the national wealth? And the doubt was entertained on this consideration chiefly, that to the labor of the husbandman a vast addition is made by the spontaneous energies of the earth on which it is employed: for one grain of wheat committed to the earth, she renders twenty, thirty, and even fifty fold, whereas to the labor of the manufacturer nothing is added. Pounds of flax, in his hands, yield, on the contrary, but pennyweights of lace. This exchange, too, laborious as it might seem, what a field did it promise for the occupations of the ocean; what a nursery for that class of citizens who were to exercise and maintain our equal rights on that element? This was the state of things in 1785, when the "Notes on Virginia" were first printed; when, the ocean being open to all nations, and their common right in it acknowledged and exercised under regulations sanctioned by the assent and usage of all, it was thought that the doubt might claim some consideration. But who in 1785 could foresee the rapid depravity which was to render the close of that century the disgrace of the history of man? Who could have imagined that the two most distinguished in the rank of nations, for science and civilization, would have suddenly descended from that honorable eminence, and setting at defiance all those moral laws established by the Author of nature between nation and nation, as between man and man, would cover earth and sea with robberies and piracies, merely because strong enough to do it with temporal impunity; and that under this disbandment of nations from social order, we should have been despoiled of a thousand ships, and have thousands of our citizens reduced to Algerine slavery. Yet all this has taken

[1] To Benjamin Austin. This is Jefferson's famous letter in which he reverses his lifelong position on the subject of manufacturing.

place. One of these nations interdicted to our vessels all harbors of the globe without having first proceeded to some one of hers, there paid a tribute proportioned to the cargo, and obtained her license to proceed to the port of destination. The other declared them to be lawful prize if they had touched at the port, or been visited by a ship of the enemy nation. Thus were we completely excluded from the ocean.

Compare this state of things with that of '85, and say whether an opinion founded in the circumstances of that day can be fairly applied to those of the present. We have experienced what we did not then believe, that there exists both profligacy and power enough to exclude us from the field of interchange with other nations: that to be independent for the comforts of life we must fabricate them ourselves. We must now place the manufacturer by the side of the agriculturist. The former question is suppressed, or rather assumes a new form. Shall we make our own comforts, or go without them, at the will of a foreign nation? He, therefore, who is now against domestic manufacture, must be for reducing us either to dependence on that foreign nation, or to be clothed in skins, and to live like wild beasts in dens and caverns. I am not one of these; experience has taught me that manufactures are now as necessary to our independence as to our comfort; and if those who quote me as of a different opinion, will keep pace with me in purchasing nothing foreign where an equivalent of domestic fabric can be obtained, without regard to difference of price, it will not be our fault if we do not soon have a supply at home equal to our demand, and wrest that weapon of distress from the hand which has wielded it. If it shall be proposed to go beyond our own supply, the question of '85 will then recur, will our *surplus* labor be then most beneficially employed in the culture of the earth, or in the fabrications of art? We have time yet for consideration, before that question will press upon us; and the maxim to be applied will depend on the circumstances which shall then exist; for in so complicated a science as political economy, no one axiom can be laid down as wise and expedient for all times and circumstances, and for their contraries.

## PLAN FOR REDUCING THE CIRCULATING MEDIUM[1]

November 28, 1819

DEAR SIR: The distresses of our country, produced first by the flood, then by the ebb of bank paper, are such as cannot fail to engage the interposition of the legislature. Many propositions will, of course, be offered, from all of which something may probably be culled to make a good whole. I explained to you my project, when I had the pleasure of possessing you here; and I

[1] Letter to William C. Rives.

now send its outline in writing, as I believe I promised you. Although preferable things will I hope be offered, yet some twig of this may perhaps be thought worthy of being engrafted on a better stock. But I send it with no particular object or request, but to use it as you please. Suppress it, suggest it, sound opinions, or anything else, at will, only keeping my name unmentioned, for which purpose it is copied in another hand, being ever solicitous to avoid all offence which is heavily felt, when retired from the bustle and contentions of the world. If we suffer the moral of the present lesson to pass away without improvement by the eternal suppression of bank *paper,* then indeed is the condition of our country desperate, until the slow advance of public instruction shall give to our functionaries the wisdom of their station. *Vale, et tibi persuade carissimum te mihi esse.*

The plethory of circulating medium which raised the prices of everything to several times their ordinary and standard value, in which state of things many and heavy debts were contracted; and the sudden withdrawing too great a proportion of that medium, and reduction of prices far below that standard, constitute the disease under which we are now laboring, and which must end in a general revolution of property, if some remedy is not applied. That remedy is clearly a gradual reduction of the medium to its standard level, that is to say, to the level which a metallic medium will always find for itself, so as to be in equilibrio with that of the nations with which we have commerce.

To effect this,

Let the whole of the present paper medium be suspended in its circulation after a certain and not distant day.

Ascertain by proper inquiry the greatest sum of it which has at any one time been in actual circulation.

Take a certain term of years for its gradual reduction, suppose it to be five years; then let the solvent banks issue ⅚ths of that amount in new notes, to be attested by a public officer, as a security that neither more or less is issued, and to be given out in exchange for the suspended notes, and the surplus in discount.

Let ⅕th of these notes bear on their face that the bank will discharge them with specie at the end of one year; another 5th at the end of two years; a third 5th at the end of three years; and so of the 4th and 5th. They will be sure to be brought in at their respective periods of redemption.

Make it a high offence to receive or pass within this State a note of any other.

There is little doubt that our banks will agree readily to this operation; if they refuse, declare their charters forfeited by their former irregularities, and give summary process against them for the suspended notes.

The Bank of the United States will probably concur also; if not, shut their doors and join the other States in respectful, but firm applications to Congress, to concur in constituting a tribunal (a special convention, *e.g.*) for settling amicably the question of their right to institute a bank, and that also of the States to do the same.

A stay-law for the suspension of executions, and their discharge at five annual instalments, should be accommodated to these measures.

Interdict forever, to both the State and national governments, the power of establishing any paper bank; for without this interdiction, we shall have the same ebbs and flows of medium, and the same revolutions of property to go through every twenty or thirty years.

In this way the value of property, keeping pace nearly with the sum of circulating medium, will descend gradually to its proper level, at the rate of about $\frac{1}{5}$th every year, the sacrifices of what shall be sold for payment of the first instalments of debts will be moderate, and time will be given for economy and industry to come in aid of those subsequent. Certainly no nation ever before abandoned to the avarice and jugglings of private individuals to regulate, according to their own interests, the quantum of circulating medium for the nation, to inflate, by deluges of paper, the nominal prices of property, and then to buy up that property at 1*s.* in the pound, having first withdrawn the floating medium which might endanger a competition in purchase. Yet this is what has been done, and will be done, unless stayed by the protecting hand of the legislature. The evil has been produced by the error of their sanction of this ruinous machinery of banks; and justice, wisdom, duty all require that they should interpose and arrest it before the schemes of plunder and spoliation desolate the country. It is believed that harpies are already hoarding their money to commence these scenes on the separation of the legislature; and we know that lands have been already sold under the hammer for less than a year's rent.

# *Part II*

# SPEECHES

## *Chapter XI*

# ADDRESSES AND MESSAGES

## ACCEPTANCE SPEECH AS GOVERNOR

June 2, 1779

TO THE GENERAL ASSEMBLY OF VIRGINIA:

GENTLEMEN: The honor which the General Assembly have been pleased to confer on me, by calling me to the high office of Governor of this Commonwealth, demands my most grateful acknowledgments, which I desire, through you, gentlemen, to tender them with the utmost respect. In a virtuous and free State no rewards can be so pleasing to sensible minds, as those which include the approbation of our fellow-citizens. My great pain is, lest my poor endeavors should fall short of the kind expectations of my country. So far as impartiality, assiduous attention, and sincere affection to the great American cause, shall enable me to fulfil the duties of my appointment, so far as I may with confidence undertake; for all beyond, I must rely on the wise counsels of the General Assembly, and of those whom they have appointed for my aid in those duties.

To you, gentlemen, I return my particular thanks for the polite terms in which you have been pleased to notify the will of the General Assembly.

## VICE-PRESIDENTIAL INAUGURAL ADDRESS, IN THE SENATE

March 4, 1797

GENTLEMEN OF THE SENATE: Entering on the duties of the office to which I am called, I feel it incumbent on me to apologize to this honorable House for the insufficient manner in which I fear they may be discharged. At an earlier period of my life, and through some considerable portion of it, I have been a member of legislative bodies, and not altogether inattentive to the forms of their proceedings. But much time has elapsed since that: other duties have occupied my mind, and, in a great degree, it has lost its familiarity with this subject. I fear that the House will have but too frequent occasion to perceive the truth of this acknowledgment. If a diligent attention, however, will enable me to fulfil the functions now assigned me, I may promise that diligence and attention shall be sedulously employed. For one portion of my duty I shall engage with more confidence, because it will depend on my will and not on my capacity. The rules which are to govern the proceedings of this House, so far as they shall depend on me for their application, shall be applied with the most rigorous and inflexible impartiality, regarding neither persons, their views, or principles, and seeing only the abstract proposition subject to my decision. If, in forming that decision, I concur with some and differ from others, as must of necessity happen, I shall rely on the liberality and candor of those from whom I differ, to believe that I do it on pure motives.

I might here proceed, and with the greatest truth, to declare my zealous attachment to the Constitution of the United States; that I consider the union of these States as the first of blessings, and, as the first of duties, the preservation of that Constitution which secures it; but I suppose these declarations not pertinent to the occasion of entering into an office whose primary business is merely to preside over the forms of this House, and no one more sincerely prays that no accident may call me to the higher and more important functions which the Constitution eventually devolves on this office. These have been justly confided to the eminent character which has preceded me here, whose talents and integrity have been known and revered by me through a long course of years; have been the foundation of a cordial and uninterrupted friendship between us; and I devoutly pray he may be long preserved for the government, the happiness, and prosperity of our common country.

## REPLY TO THE NOTIFICATION OF ELECTION[1]

February 20, 1801

I receive, gentlemen, with profound thankfulness this testimony of confidence from the great representative council of our nation. It fills up the measure of that grateful satisfaction which had already been derived from the suffrages of my fellow-citizens themselves, designating me as one of those to whom they were willing to commit this charge, the most important of all others to them. In deciding between the candidates whom their equal

[1] A Congressional Committee, headed by Charles C. Pinckney, notified Jefferson of his election to the Presidency, which took place on February 17, 1801, in the House of Representatives.

vote presented to your choice, I am sensible that age has been respected rather than more active and useful qualifications.

I know the difficulties of the station to which I am called, and feel and acknowledge my incompetence to them. But whatsoever of understanding, whatsoever of diligence, whatsoever of justice or of affectionate concern for the happiness of man, it has pleased Providence to place within the compass of my faculties shall be called forth for the discharge of the duties confided to me, and for procuring to my fellow-citizens all the benefits which our Constitution has placed under the guardianship of the General Government.

Guided by the wisdom and patriotism of those to whom it belongs to express the legislative will of the nation, I will give to that will a faithful execution.

I pray you, gentlemen, to convey to the honorable body from which you are deputed the homage of my humble acknowledgments and the sentiments of zeal and fidelity by which I shall endeavor to merit these proofs of confidence from the nation and its Representatives; and accept yourselves my particular thanks for the obliging terms in which you have been pleased to communicate their will.

## FAREWELL SPEECH AS VICE-PRESIDENT

February 28, 1801

GENTLEMEN OF THE SENATE: To give the usual opportunity of appointing a President *pro tempore* I now propose to retire from the chair of the Senate; and as the time is near at hand, when the relations will cease which have for some time subsisted between this honorable house and myself, I beg leave, before I withdraw, to return them my grateful thanks for all the instances of attention and respect with which they have been pleased to honor me. In the discharge of my functions here, it has been my conscientious endeavor to observe impartial justice, without regard to persons or subjects: and if I have failed in impressing this on the mind of the Senate, it will be to me a circumstance of the deepest regret. I may have erred at times. No doubt I have erred. This is the law of human nature. For honest errors, however, indulgence may be hoped. I owe to truth and justice at the same time to declare that the habits of order and decorum, which so strongly characterize the proceedings of the Senate, have rendered the umpirage of their President an office of little difficulty; that in times and on questions which have severely tried the sensibilities of the House, calm and temperate discussion has rarely been disturbed by departures from order.

Should the support which I have received from the Senate, in the performance of my duties here, attend me into the new station to which the public will has transferred me, I shall consider it as commencing under the happiest auspices.

With these expressions of my dutiful regard to the Senate as a body, I ask leave to mingle my particular wishes for the health and happiness of the individuals who compose it, and to tender them my cordial and respectful adieux.

## FIRST INAUGURAL ADDRESS

March 4, 1801

FRIENDS AND FELLOW CITIZENS: Called upon to undertake the duties of the first executive office of our country, I avail myself of the presence of that portion of my fellow citizens which is here assembled, to express my grateful thanks for the favor with which they have been pleased to look toward me, to declare a sincere consciousness that the task is above my talents, and that I approach it with those anxious and awful presentiments which the greatness of the charge and the weakness of my powers so justly inspire. A rising nation, spread over a wide and fruitful land, traversing all the seas with the rich productions of their industry, engaged in commerce with nations who feel power and forget right, advancing rapidly to destinies beyond the reach of mortal eye—when I contemplate these transcendent objects, and see the honor, the happiness, and the hopes of this beloved country committed to the issue and the auspices of this day, I shrink from the contemplation, and humble myself before the magnitude of the undertaking. Utterly indeed, should I despair, did not the presence of many whom I here see remind me, that in the other high authorities provided by our constitution, I shall find resources of wisdom, of virtue, and of zeal, on which to rely under all difficulties. To you, then, gentlemen, who are charged with the sovereign functions of legislation, and to those associated with you, I look with encouragement for that guidance and support which may enable us to steer with safety the vessel in which we are all embarked amid the conflicting elements of a troubled world.

During the contest of opinion through which we have passed, the animation of discussion and of exertions has sometimes worn an aspect which might impose on strangers unused to think freely and to speak and to write what they think; but this being now decided by the voice of the nation, announced according to the rules of the constitution, all will, of course, arrange themselves under the will of the law, and unite in common efforts for the common good. All, too, will bear in mind this sacred principle, that though the will of the majority is in all cases to prevail, that will, to be rightful, must be reasonable; that the minority possess their equal rights, which equal laws must protect, and to violate which would be oppression. Let us, then, fellow-citizens, unite with one heart and one mind. Let us restore to social intercourse that harmony and affection without which liberty and even life itself are but dreary things. And let us reflect that having banished from our land that religious intolerance under which mankind so long bled and suffered, we have yet gained little if we countenance a political intolerance as despotic, as wicked, and capable of as bitter and bloody persecutions. During the throes and convulsions of the ancient world, during the agonizing spasms of infuriated man, seeking through blood and slaughter his long-lost liberty, it was not wonderful that the agitation of the billows should reach even this distant and peaceful shore; that this should be more felt and feared by some and less by others; that this should divide opinions as to measures of safety. But every difference of opinion is not a difference of principle. We have called by different names brethren of the same principle. We are all republicans—we are federalists. If there be any among us who would wish to dissolve this Union or to change its republican form, let them stand undisturbed as monuments of the safety with which error of opinion may be tolerated where reason is left free to combat it. I know, indeed, that some honest men fear that a republican government cannot be strong; that this government is not strong enough. But would the honest patriot, in the full tide of successful experiment, abandon a government which has so far kept us free and firm, on the theoretic and visionary fear that this government, the world's best hope, may by possibility want energy to preserve itself? I trust not. I believe this, on the contrary, the strongest government on earth. I believe it is the only one where every man, at the call of the laws, would fly to the standard of the law, and would meet invasions of the public order as his own personal concern. Sometimes it is said that man cannot be trusted with the government of himself. Can he, then, be trusted with the government of others? Or have we found angels in the forms of kings to govern him? Let history answer this question.

Let us, then, with courage and confidence pursue our own federal and republican principles, our attachment to our union and representative government. Kindly separated by nature and a wide ocean from the exterminating havoc of one quarter of the globe; too high-minded to endure the degradations of the others; possessing a chosen country, with room enough for our descendants to the hundredth and thousandth generation; entertaining a due sense of our equal right to the use of our own faculties, to the acquisitions of our industry, to honor and confidence from our fellow citizens, resulting not from birth but from our actions and their sense of them; enlightened by a benign religion, professed, indeed, and practiced in various forms, yet all of them including honesty, truth, temperance, gratitude, and the love of man; acknowledging and adoring an overruling Providence, which by all its dispensations proves that it delights in the happiness of man here and his greater happiness hereafter; with all these blessings, what more is necessary to make us a happy and prosperous people? Still one thing more, fellow citizens—a wise and frugal government, which shall restrain men from injuring one another, which shall leave them otherwise free to regulate their own pursuits of industry and improvement, and shall not take from the mouth of labor the bread it has earned. This is the sum of good government, and this is necessary to close the circle of our felicities.

About to enter, fellow citizens, on the exercise of duties which comprehend everything dear and valuable to you, it is proper that you should understand what I deem the essential principles of our government, and consequently those which ought to shape its administration. I will compress them within the narrowest compass they will bear, stating the general principle, but not all its limitations. Equal and exact justice to all men, of whatever state or persuasion, religious or political; peace, commerce, and honest friendship with all nations—entangling alliances with none; the support of the State governments in all their rights, as the most competent administrations for our domestic concerns and the surest bulwarks against anti-republican tendencies; the preservation of the general government in its whole constitutional vigor, as the sheet anchor of our peace at home and safety abroad; a jealous care of the right of election by the people—a mild and safe corrective of abuses which are lopped by the sword of the revolution where peaceable remedies are unprovided; absolute acquiescence in the decisions of the majority—the vital principle of republics, from which there is no appeal but to force, the vital principle and immediate parent of despotism; a well-disciplined militia—our best reliance in peace and for the first moments of war, till regulars may relieve them; the supremacy of the civil over the military authority; economy in the public expense, that labor may be lightly burdened; the honest payment of our debts and sacred preservation of the public faith; encouragement of agriculture, and of commerce as its handmaid; the diffusion of information and the arraignment of all abuses at the bar of public reason; freedom of religion; freedom of the press; freedom of person under the protection of the *habeas corpus;* and trial by juries impartially selected—these principles form the bright constellation which has gone before us, and guided our steps through an age of revolution and reformation. The wisdom of our sages and the blood of our heroes have been devoted to their attainment. They should be the creed of our political faith—the text of civil instruction—the touchstone by which to try the services of those we trust; and should we wander from them in moments of error or alarm, let us hasten to retrace our steps and to regain the road which alone leads to peace, liberty, and safety.

I repair, then, fellow citizens, to the post you have assigned me. With experience enough in subordinate offices to have seen the difficulties of this, the greatest of all, I have learned to expect that it will rarely fall to the lot of imperfect man to retire from this station with the reputation and the favor which bring him into it. Without pretensions to that high confidence reposed in our first and great revolutionary character, whose preëminent services had entitled him to the first place in his country's love, and destined for him the fairest page in the volume of faithful history, I ask so much confidence only as may give firmness and effect to the legal administration of your affairs. I shall often go wrong through defect of judgment. When right, I shall often be thought wrong by those whose positions will not command a view of the whole ground. I ask your indulgence for my own errors, which will never be intentional; and your support against the errors of others, who may condemn what they would not if seen in all its parts. The approbation implied by your suffrage is a consolation to me for the past; and my future solicitude will be to retain the good opinion of those who have bestowed it in advance, to conciliate that of others by doing them all the good in my power, and to be instrumental to the happiness and freedom of all.

Relying, then, on the patronage of your good will, I advance with obedience to the work, ready to retire from it whenever you become sensible how much better choice it is in your power to make. And may that Infinite Power which rules the destinies of the universe, lead our councils to what is best, and give them a favorable issue for your peace and prosperity.

## FIRST ANNUAL MESSAGE TO CONGRESS

December 8, 1801

FELLOW CITIZENS OF THE SENATE AND HOUSE OF REPRESENTATIVES: It is a circumstance of sincere gratification to me that on meeting the great council of our nation, I am able to announce to them, on the grounds of reasonable certainty, that the wars and troubles which have for so many years afflicted our sister nations have at length come to an end,[1] and that the communications of peace and commerce are once more opening among them. While we devoutly return thanks to the beneficent Being who has been pleased to breathe into them the spirit of conciliation and forgiveness, we are bound with peculiar gratitude to be thankful to him that our own peace has been preserved through so perilous a season, and ourselves permitted quietly to cultivate the earth and to practice and improve those arts which tend to increase our comforts. The assurances, indeed, of friendly disposition, received from all the powers with whom we have principal relations, had inspired a confidence that our peace with them would not have been dis-

[1] In February, 1801, Napoleon made peace with Austria, in March with Naples, in July with the Pope, and in October with Russia.

turbed. But a cessation of the irregularities which had affected the commerce of neutral nations, and of the irritations and injuries produced by them, cannot but add to this confidence; and strengthens, at the same time, the hope, that wrongs committed on unoffending friends, under a pressure of circumstances, will now be reviewed with candor, and will be considered as founding just claims of retribution for the past and new assurance for the future.

Among our Indian neighbors, also, a spirit of peace and friendship generally prevails; and I am happy to inform you that the continued efforts to introduce among them the implements and the practice of husbandry, and of the household arts, have not been without success; that they are becoming more and more sensible of the superiority of this dependence for clothing and subsistence over the precarious resources of hunting and fishing; and already we are able to announce, that instead of that constant diminution of their numbers, produced by their wars and their wants, some of them begin to experience an increase of population.

To this state of general peace with which we have been blessed, one only exception exists. Tripoli, the least considerable of the Barbary States, had come forward with demands unfounded either in right or in compact, and had permitted itself to denounce war, on our failure to comply before a given day. The style of the demand admitted but one answer. I sent a small squadron of frigates into the Mediterranean, with assurances to that power of our sincere desire to remain in peace, but with orders to protect our commerce against the threatened attack. The measure was seasonable and salutary. The bey had already declared war in form. His cruisers were out. Two had arrived at Gibraltar. Our commerce in the Mediterranean was blockaded, and that of the Atlantic in peril. The arrival of our squadron dispelled the danger. One of the Tripolitan cruisers having fallen in with, and engaged the small schooner *Enterprise,* commanded by Lieutenant Sterret, which had gone as a tender to our larger vessels, was captured, after a heavy slaughter of her men, without the loss of a single one on our part. The bravery exhibited by our citizens on that element, will, I trust, be a testimony to the world that it is not the want of that virtue which makes us seek their peace, but a conscientious desire to direct the energies of our nation to the multiplication of the human race, and not to its destruction. Unauthorized by the Constitution, without the sanction of Congress, to go beyond the line of defence, the vessel being disabled from committing further hostilities, was liberated with its crew. The legislature will doubtless consider whether, by authorizing measures of offence, also, they will place our force on an equal footing with that of its adversaries. I communicate all material information on this subject, that in the exercise of the important function confided by the Constitution to the legislature exclusively, their judgment may form itself on a knowledge and consideration of every circumstance of weight.

I wish I could say that our situation with all the other Barbary states was entirely satisfactory. Discovering that some delays had taken place in the performance of certain articles stipulated by us, I thought it my duty, by immediate measures for fulfilling them, to vindicate to ourselves the right of considering the effect of departure from stipulation on their side. From the papers which will be laid before you, you will be enabled to judge whether our treaties are regarded by them as fixing at all the measure of their demands, or as guarding from the exercise of force our vessels within their power; and to consider how far it will be safe and expedient to leave our affairs with them in their present posture.

I lay before you the result of the census lately taken of our inhabitants, to a conformity with which we are to reduce the ensuing rates of representation and taxation. You will perceive that the increase of numbers during the last ten years, proceeding in geometrical ratio, promises a duplication in little more than twenty-two years. We contemplate this rapid growth, and the prospect it holds up to us, not with a view to the injuries it may enable us to do to others in some future day, but to the settlement of the extensive country still remaining vacant within our limits, to the multiplications of men susceptible of happiness, educated in the love of order, habituated to self-government, and valuing its blessings above all price.

Other circumstances, combined with the increase of numbers, have produced an augmentation of revenue arising from consumption, in a ratio far beyond that of population alone, and though the changes of foreign relations now taking place so desirably for the world, may for a season affect this branch of revenue, yet, weighing all probabilities of expense, as well as of income, there is reasonable ground of confidence that we may now safely dispense with all the internal taxes, comprehending excises, stamps, auctions, licenses, carriages, and refined sugars, to which the postage on newspapers may be added, to facilitate the progress of information, and that the remaining sources of revenue will be sufficient to provide for the support of government, to pay the interest on the public debts, and to discharge the principals in shorter periods than the laws or the general expectations had contemplated. War, indeed, and untoward events, may change this prospect of things, and call for expenses which the imposts could not meet; but sound principles will not justify our taxing the industry of our fellow citizens to accumulate treasure for wars to happen we know not when, and which might not perhaps happen but from the temptations offered by that treasure.

These views, however, of reducing our burdens, are formed on the expectation that a sensible, and at the same time a salutary reduction, may take place in our habitual expenditures. For this purpose, those of the civil government, the army, and navy, will need revisal.

When we consider that this government is charged with the external and mutual relations only of these states; that the states themselves have principal care of our persons, our property, and our reputation, constituting the great field of human concerns, we may well doubt whether our organization is not too complicated, too expensive; whether offices and officers have not been multiplied unnecessarily, and sometimes injuriously to the service they were meant to promote. I will cause to be laid before you an essay toward a statement of those who, under public employment of various kinds, draw money from the treasury or from our citizens. Time has not permitted a perfect enumeration, the ramifications of office being too multiplied and remote to be completely traced in a first trial. Among those who are dependent on executive discretion, I have begun the reduction of what was deemed necessary. The expenses of diplomatic agency have been considerably diminished. The inspectors of internal revenue who were found to obstruct the accountability of the institution, have been discontinued. Several agencies created by executive authority, on salaries fixed by that also, have been suppressed, and should suggest the expediency of regulating that power by law, so as to subject its exercises to legislative inspection and sanction. Other reformations of the same kind will be pursued with that caution which is requisite in removing useless things, not to injure what is retained. But the great mass of public offices is established by law, and, therefore, by law alone can be abolished. Should the legislature think it expedient to pass this roll in review, and try all its parts by the test of public utility, they may be assured of every aid and light which executive information can yield. Considering the general tendency to multiply offices and dependencies, and to increase expense to the ultimate term of burden which the citizen can bear, it behooves us to avail ourselves of every occasion which presents itself for taking off the surcharge; that it never may be seen here that, after leaving to labor the smallest portion of its earnings on which it can subsist, government shall itself consume the residue of what it was instituted to guard.

In our care, too, of the public contributions intrusted to our direction, it would be prudent to multiply barriers against their dissipation, by appropriating specific sums to every specific purpose susceptible of definition; by disallowing all applications of money varying from the appropriation in object, or transcending it in amount; by reducing the undefined field of contingencies, and thereby circumscribing discretionary powers over money; and by bringing back to a single department all accountabilities for money where the examination may be prompt, efficacious, and uniform.

An account of the receipts and expenditures of the last year, as prepared by the Secretary of the Treasury, will as usual be laid before you. The success which has attended the late sales of the public lands, shows that with attention they may be made an important source of receipt. Among the payments, those made in discharge of the principal and interest of the national debt, will show that the public faith has been exactly maintained. To these will be added an estimate of appropriations necessary for the ensuing year. This last will of course be effected by such modifications of the systems of expense, as you shall think proper to adopt.

A statement has been formed by the Secretary of War, on mature consideration, of all the posts and stations where garrisons will be expedient, and of the number of men requisite for each garrison. The whole amount is considerably short of the present military establishment. For the surplus no particular use can be pointed out. For defence against invasion, their number is as nothing; nor is it conceived needful or safe that a standing army should be kept up in time of peace for that purpose. Uncertain as we must ever be of the particular point in our circumference where an enemy may choose to invade us, the only force which can be ready at every point and competent to oppose them, is the body of neighboring citizens as formed into a militia. On these, collected from the parts most convenient, in numbers proportioned to the invading foe, it is best to rely, not only to meet the first attack, but if it threatens to be permanent, to maintain the defence until regulars may be engaged to relieve them. These considerations render it important that we should at every session continue to amend the defects which from time to time show themselves in the laws for regulating the militia, until they are sufficiently perfect. Nor should we now or at any time separate, until we can say we have done everything for the militia which we could do were an enemy at our door.

The provisions of military stores on hand will be laid before you, that you may judge of the additions still requisite.

With respect to the extent to which our naval preparations should be carried, some difference of opinion may be expected to appear; but just attention to the circumstances of every part of the Union will doubtless reconcile all. A small force will probably continue to be wanted for actual service in the Mediterranean. Whatever annual sum beyond that you may think proper to appropriate to naval preparations, would perhaps be better employed in providing those articles which may be kept without waste or consumption, and be in readiness when any exigence calls them into use. Progress has been made, as will appear by papers now communicated, in providing materials for seventy-four gun ships as directed by law.

How far the authority given by the legislature for procuring and establishing sites for naval purposes has been perfectly understood and pursued in the execution, admits of some doubt. A statement of the expenses already incurred on that subject, shall be laid before you. I have in certain cases suspended or slackened these expenditures, that the legislature might determine whether so many yards are necessary as have been contemplated. The works at this place are among those permitted to go on; and five of the seven frigates directed to be laid up, have been brought and laid up here, where, besides the safety of their position, they are under the eye of the executive administration, as well as of its agents, and where yourselves also will be guided by your own view in the legislative provisions respecting them which may from time to time be necessary. They are preserved in such condition, as well the vessels as whatever belongs to them, as to be at all times ready for sea on a short warning. Two others are yet to be laid up so soon as they shall have received the repairs requisite to put them also into sound condition. As a superintending officer will be necessary at each yard, his duties and emoluments, hitherto fixed by the executive, will be a more proper subject for legislation. A communication will also be made of our progress in the execution of the law respecting the vessels directed to be sold.

The fortifications of our harbors, more or less advanced, present considerations of great difficulty. While some of them are on a scale sufficiently proportioned to the advantages of their position, to the efficacy of their protection, and the importance of the points within it, others are so extensive, will cost so much in their first erection, so much in their maintenance, and require such a force to garrison them, as to make it questionable what is best now to be done. A statement of those commenced or projected, of the expenses already incurred, and estimates of their future cost, so far as can be foreseen, shall be laid before you, that you may be enabled to judge whether any attention is necessary in the laws respecting this subject.

Agriculture, manufactures, commerce, and navigation, the four pillars of our prosperity, are the most thriving when left most free to individual enterprise. Protection from casual embarrassments, however, may sometimes be seasonably interposed. If in the course of your observations or inquiries they should appear to need any aid within the limits of our constitutional powers, your sense of their importance is a sufficient assurance they will occupy your attention. We cannot, indeed, but all feel an anxious solicitude for the difficulties under which our carrying trade will soon be placed. How far it can be relieved, otherwise than by time, is a subject of important consideration.

The judiciary system of the United States, and especially that portion of it recently erected, will of course present itself to the contemplation of Congress; and that they may be able to judge of the proportion which the institution bears to the business it has to perform, I have caused to be procured from the several States, and now lay before Congress, an exact statement of all the causes decided since the first establishment of the courts, and of those which were depending when additional courts and judges were brought in to their aid.

And while on the judiciary organization, it will be worthy your consideration, whether the protection of the inestimable institution of juries has been extended to all the cases involving the security of our persons and property. Their impartial selection also being essential to their value, we ought further to consider whether that is sufficiently secured in those States where they are named by a marshal depending on executive will, or designated by the court or by officers dependent on them.

I cannot omit recommending a revisal of the laws on the subject of naturalization. Considering the ordinary chances of human life, a denial of citizenship under a residence of fourteen years is a denial to a great proportion of those who ask it, and controls a policy pursued from their first settlement by many of these States, and still believed of consequence to their prosperity. And shall we refuse the unhappy fugitives from distress that hospitality which the savages of the wilderness extended to our fathers arriving in this land? Shall oppressed humanity find no asylum on this globe? The constitution, indeed, has wisely provided that, for admission to certain offices of important trust, a residence shall be required sufficient to develop character and design. But might not the general character and capabilities of a citizen be safely communicated to everyone manifesting a *bonâ fide* purpose of embarking his life and fortunes permanently with us? with restrictions, perhaps, to guard against the fraudulent usurpation of our flag; an abuse which brings so much embarrassment and loss on the genuine citizen, and so much danger to the nation of being involved in war, that no endeavor should be spared to detect and suppress it.

These, fellow citizens, are the matters respecting the state of the nation, which I have thought of importance to be submitted to your consideration at this time. Some others of less moment, or not yet ready for communication, will be the subject of separate messages. I am happy in this opportunity of committing the arduous affairs of our government to the collected wisdom of the Union. Nothing shall be wanting on my part to inform, as far as in my power, the legislative judgment, nor to carry that judgment into faithful execution. The prudence and temperance of your discussions will promote, within your own walls, that conciliation which so much befriends national conclusion; and by its example will encourage among our constituents that progress of opinion which is tending to unite them in object and in will. That all should be satisfied with any one order of things is not to be expected, but I indulge the pleasing persuasion that the great body of our citizens will cordially concur in honest and disinterested efforts, which have for their object to preserve the general and State governments in their constitutional form and equilibrium; to maintain peace abroad, and order and obedience to the laws at home; to establish principles and practices of administration favorable to the security of liberty and prosperity, and to reduce expenses to what is necessary for the useful purposes of government.

# SECOND ANNUAL MESSAGE

December 15, 1802

TO THE SENATE AND HOUSE OF REPRESENTATIVES OF THE UNITED STATES: When we assemble together, fellow citizens, to consider the state of our beloved country, our just attentions are first drawn to those pleasing circumstances which mark the goodness of that Being from whose favor they flow, and the large measure of thankfulness we owe for his bounty. Another year has come around, and finds us still blessed with peace and friendship abroad; law, order, and religion, at home; good affection and harmony with our Indian neighbors; our burdens lightened, yet our income sufficient for the public wants, and the produce of the year great beyond example. These, fellow citizens, are the circumstances under which we meet; and we remark with special satisfaction, those which, under the smiles of Providence, result from the skill, industry and order of our citizens, managing their own affairs in their own way and for their own use, unembarrassed by too much regulations, unoppressed by fiscal exactions.

On the restoration of peace in Europe, that portion of the general carrying trade which had fallen to our share during the war, was abridged by the returning competition of the belligerent powers. This was to be expected, and was just. But in addition we find in some parts of Europe monopolizing discriminations, which, in the form of duties, tend effectually to prohibit the carrying thither our own produce in our own vessels. From existing amities, and a spirit of justice, it is hoped that friendly discussion will produce a fair and adequate reciprocity. But should false calculations of interest defeat our hope, it rests with the legislature to decide whether they will meet inequalities abroad with countervailing inequalities at home, or provide for the evil in any other way.

It is with satisfaction I lay before you an act of the British Parliament anticipating this subject so far as to authorize a mutual abolition of the duties and countervailing duties permitted under the treaty of 1794. It shows on their part a spirit of justice and friendly accommodation which it is our duty and our interest to cultivate with all nations. Whether this would produce a due equality in the navigation between the two countries, is a subject for your consideration.

Another circumstance which claims attention, as directly affecting the very source of our navigation, is the defect or the evasion of the law providing for the return of seamen, and particularly of those belonging to vessels sold abroad. Numbers of them, discharged in foreign ports, have been thrown on the hands of our consuls, who, to rescue them from the dangers into which their distresses might plunge them, and save them to their country, have found it necessary in some cases to return them at the public charge.

The cession of the Spanish province of Louisiana to France, which took place in the course of the late war, will, if carried into effect, make a change in the aspect of our foreign relations which will doubtless have a just weight in any deliberations of the legislature connected with that subject.

There was reason, not long since, to apprehend that the warfare in which we were engaged with Tripoli might be taken up by some others of the Barbary powers. A reinforcement, therefore, was immediately ordered to the vessels already there. Subsequent information, however, has removed these apprehensions for the present. To secure our commerce in that sea with the smallest force competent, we have supposed it best to watch strictly the harbor of Tripoli. Still, however, the shallowness of their coast, and the want of smaller vessels on our part, has permitted some cruisers to escape unobserved; and to one of these an American vessel unfortunately fell a prey. The captain, one American seaman, and two others of color, remain prisoners with them unless exchanged under an agreement formerly made with the bashaw, to whom, on the faith of that, some of his captive subjects had been restored.

The convention with the State of Georgia has been ratified by their legislature, and a repurchase from the Creeks has been consequently made of a part of the Tallahassee county. In this purchase has been also comprehended part of the lands within the fork of Oconee and Oakmulgee rivers. The particulars of the contract will be laid before Congress so soon as they shall be in a state for communication.

In order to remove every ground of difference possible with our Indian neighbors, I have proceeded in the work of settling with them and marking the boundaries between us. That with the Choctaw nation is fixed in one part, and will be through the whole in a short time. The country to which their title had been extinguished before the revolution is sufficient to receive a very respectable population, which Congress will probably see the expediency of encouraging so soon as the limits shall be declared. We are to view this position as an outpost of the United States, surrounded by strong neighbors and distant from its support. And how far that monopoly which prevents population should here be guarded against, and actual habitation made a condition of the continuance of title, will be for your consideration. A prompt settlement, too, of all existing rights and claims within this territory, presents itself as a preliminary operation.

In that part of the Indian territory which includes Vincennes, the lines settled with the neighboring tribes fix the extinction of their title at a breadth of twenty-four leagues from east to west, and about the same length parallel with and including the Wabash. They have also ceded a tract of four miles square, including the salt springs near the mouth of the river.

In the department of finance it is with pleasure I inform you that the receipts of external duties for the last twelve months have exceeded those of any former year, and that the ratio of increase has been also greater than usual. This has enabled us to answer all the regular exigencies of government, to pay from the treasury in one year upward of eight millions of dollars, principal and interest, of the public debt, exclusive of upward of one million paid by the sale of bank stock, and making in the whole a reduction of nearly five millions and a half of principal; and to have now in the treasury four millions and a half of dollars, which are in a course of application to a further discharge of debt and current demands. Experience, too, so far, authorizes us to believe, if no extraordinary event supervenes, and the expenses which will be actually incurred shall not be greater than were contemplated by Congress at their last session, that we shall not be disappointed in the expectations then formed. But nevertheless, as the effect of peace on the amount of duties is not yet fully ascertained, it is the more necessary to practice every useful economy, and to incur no expense which may be avoided without prejudice.

The collection of the internal taxes having been completed in some of the States, the officers employed in it are of course out of commission. In others, they will be so shortly. But in a few, where the arrangement for the direct tax had been retarded, it will still be some time before the system is closed. It has not yet been thought necessary to employ the agent authorized by an act of the last session for transacting business in Europe relative to debts and loans. Nor have we used the power confided by the same act, of prolonging the foreign debts by reloans, and of redeeming, instead thereof, an equal sum of the domestic debt. Should, however, the difficulties of remittances on so large a scale render it necessary at any time, the power shall be executed, and the money thus unemployed abroad shall, in conformity with that law, be faithfully applied here in an equivalent extinction of domestic debt. When effects so salutary result from the plans you have already sanctioned, when merely by avoiding false objects of expense we are able, without a direct tax, without internal taxes, and without borrowing, to make large and effectual payments toward the discharge of our public debt and the emancipation of our posterity from that moral canker, it is an encouragement, fellow citizens, of the highest order, to proceed as we have begun, in substituting economy for taxation, and in pursuing what is useful for a nation placed as we are, rather than what is practiced by others under different circumstances. And whensoever we are destined to meet events which shall call forth all the energies of our countrymen, we have the firmest reliance on those energies, and the comfort of leaving for calls like these the extraordinary resources of loans and internal taxes. In the meantime, by payments of the principal of our debt, we are liberating, annually, portions of the external taxes, and forming from them a growing fund still further to lessen the necessity of recurring to extraordinary resources.

The usual accounts of receipts and expenditures for the last year, with an estimate of the expenses of the ensuing one, will be laid before you by the Secretary of the Treasury.

No change being deemed necessary in our military establishment, an estimate of its expenses for the ensuing year on its present footing, as also of the sums to be employed in fortifications and other objects within that department, has been prepared by the Secretary of War, and will make a part of the general estimates which will be presented to you.

Considering that our regular troops are employed for local purposes, and that the militia is our general reliance for great and sudden emergencies, you will doubtless think this institution worthy of a review, and give it those improvements of which you find it susceptible.

Estimates for the naval department, prepared by the Secretary of the Navy for another year, will in like manner be communicated with the general estimates. A small force in the Mediterranean will still be necessary to restrain the Tripoline cruisers, and the uncertain tenure of peace with some other of the Barbary powers, may eventually require that force to be augmented. The necessity of procuring some smaller vessels for that service will raise the estimate, but the difference in their maintenance will soon make it a measure of economy.

Presuming it will be deemed expedient to expend annually a sum towards providing the naval defence which our situation may require, I cannot but recommend that the first appropriations for that purpose may go to the saving what we already possess. No cares, no attentions, can preserve vessels from rapid decay which lie in water and exposed to the sun. These decays require great and constant repairs, and will consume, if continued, a great portion of the money destined to naval purposes. To avoid this waste of our resources, it is proposed to add to our navy-yard here a dock, within which our vessels may be laid up dry and under cover from the sun. Under these circumstances experience proves that works of wood will remain scarcely at all affected by time. The great abundance of running water which this situation possesses, at heights far above the level of the tide, if employed as is practised for lock navigation, furnishes the means of raising and laying up our vessels on a dry and sheltered bed. And should the measure be found useful here, similar depositories for laying up as well as for building and repairing vessels may hereafter be undertaken at other navy-yards offering the same means. The plans and estimates of the work, prepared by a person of skill and experience, will be presented to you without delay; and from this it will be seen that scarcely more than has been the cost of one vessel is necessary to save the whole, and that the annual sum to be employed toward its completion may be adapted to the views of the legislature as to naval expenditure.

To cultivate peace and maintain commerce and navigation in all their lawful enterprises; to foster our fisheries and nurseries of navigation and for the nurture of man, and protect the manufactures adapted to our circumstances; to preserve the faith of the nation by an exact discharge of its debts and contracts, expend the public money with the same care and economy we would practise with our own, and impose on our citizens no unnecessary burden; to keep in all things within the pale of our constitutional powers, and cherish the federal union as the only rock of safety—these, fellow-citizens, are the landmarks by which we are to guide ourselves in all our proceedings. By continuing to make these our rule of action, we shall endear to our countrymen the true principles of their Constitution, and promote a union of sentiment and of action equally auspicious to their happiness and safety. On my part, you may count on a cordial concurrence in every measure for the public good, and on all the information I possess which may enable you to discharge to advantage the high functions with which you are invested by your country.

## CONFIDENTIAL MESSAGE RECOMMENDING A WESTERN EXPLORING EXPEDITION

January 18, 1803

GENTLEMEN OF THE SENATE AND OF THE HOUSE OF REPRESENTATIVES: As the continuance of the act for establishing trading-houses with the Indian tribes, will be under the consideration of the legislature at its present session, I think it my duty to communicate the views which have guided me in the execution of that act, in order that you may decide on the policy of continuing it, in the present or any other form, or discontinue it altogether, if that shall, on the whole, seem most for the public good.

The Indian tribes residing within the limits of the United States, have, for a considerable time, been growing more and more uneasy at the constant diminution of the territory they occupy, although effected by their own voluntary sales; and the policy has long been gaining strength with them, of refusing absolutely all further sale, on any conditions; insomuch that, at this time, it hazards their friendship, and excites dangerous jealousies and perturbations in their minds to make any overture for the purchase of the smallest portions of their land. A very few tribes only are not yet obstinately in these dispositions. In order peaceably to counteract this policy of theirs, and to provide an extension of territory which the rapid increase of our numbers will call for, two measures are deemed expedient. First: to encourage them to abandon hunting, to apply to the raising stock, to agriculture and domestic manufactures, and thereby prove to themselves that less land and labor will maintain them in this, better than in their former mode of living. The extensive forests necessary in the hunting life will then become useless, and they will see advantage in exchanging them for the means of improving their farms and of increasing their domestic comforts. Secondly: to multiply trading-houses among them, and place within their reach those things which will contribute more to their domestic comfort than the possession of extensive but uncultivated wilds. Experience and reflection will develop to them the wisdom of exchanging what they can spare and we want, for what we can spare and they want. In leading them thus to agriculture, to manufactures, and civilization; in bringing together their and our settlements, and in preparing them ultimately to participate in the benefits of our government, I trust and believe we are acting for their greatest good. At these trading-houses we have pursued the principles of the act of Congress, which directs that the commerce shall be carried on liberally, and requires only that the capital stock shall not be diminished. We consequently undersell private traders, foreign and domestic; drive them from the competition; and thus, with the good will of the Indians, rid ourselves of a description of men who are constantly endeavoring to excite in the Indian mind suspicions, fears, and irritations toward us. A letter now enclosed, shows the effect of our competition on the operations of the traders, while the Indians, perceiving the advantage of purchasing from us, are soliciting generally our establishment of trading-houses among them. In one quarter this is particularly interesting. The legislature, reflecting on the late occurrences on the Mississippi, must be sensible how desirable it is to possess a respectable breadth of country on that river, from our southern limit to the Illinois at least, so that we may present as firm a front on that as on our eastern border. We possess what is below the Yazoo, and can probably acquire a certain breadth from the Illinois and Wabash to the Ohio; but between the Ohio and Yazoo, the country all belongs to the Chickasaws, the most friendly tribe within our limits, but the most decided against the alienation of lands. The portion of their country most important for us is exactly that which they do not inhabit. Their settlements are not on the Mississippi, but in the interior country. They have lately shown a desire to become agricultural, and this leads to the desire of buying implements and comforts. In the strengthening and gratifying of these wants, I see the only prospect of planting on the Mississippi itself, the means of its own safety. Duty has required me to submit these views to the judgment of the legislature; but as their disclosure might embarrass and defeat their effect, they are committed to the special confidence of the two houses.

While the extension of the public commerce among the Indian tribes, may deprive of that source of profit such of our citizens as are engaged in it, it might be worthy the attention of Congress, in their care of individual as well as of the general interest, to point in another direction the enterprise of these citizens, as profitably for themselves, and more usefully for the public. The river Missouri, and the Indians inhabiting it, are not as well known as is rendered desirable by their connection with the Mississippi, and consequently with us. It is, however, understood, that the country on that river is inhabited by numerous tribes, who furnish great supplies of furs and peltry to the trade of another nation, carried on in a high latitude, through an infinite number of portages and lakes, shut up by ice through a long season. The commerce on that line could bear no competition with that of the Missouri, traversing a moderate climate, offering, according to the best accounts, a continued navigation from its source, and possibly with a single portage, from the western ocean, and finding to the Atlantic a choice of channels through the Illinois or Wabash, the lakes and Hudson, through the Ohio and Susquehanna, or Potomac or James rivers, and through the Tennessee and Savannah rivers. An intelligent officer, with ten or twelve chosen men, fit for the enterprise, and willing to undertake it, taken from our posts, where they may be spared without inconvenience, might explore the whole line, even to the western ocean; have conferences with the natives on the subject of commercial intercourse; get admission among them for our traders, as others are admitted; agree on convenient deposits for an interchange of articles; and return with the information acquired, in the course of two summers. Their arms and accoutrements, some instruments of observation, and light and cheap presents for the Indians, would be all the apparatus they could carry, and with an expectation of a soldier's portion of land on their return, would constitute the whole expense. Their pay would be going on, whether here or there. While other civilized nations have encountered great expense to enlarge the boundaries of knowledge, by undertaking voyages of discovery, and for other literary purposes, in various parts and directions, our nation seems to owe to the same object, as well as to its own interests, to explore this, the only line of easy communication across the continent, and so directly traversing our own part of it. The interests of commerce place the principal object within the constitutional powers and care of Congress, and that it should incidentally advance the geographical knowledge of our own continent, can not but be an additional gratification. The nation claiming the territory, regarding this as a literary pursuit, which it is in the habit of permitting within its own dominions, would not be disposed to view it with jealousy, even if the expiring state of its interests there did not render it a matter of indifference. The appropriation of two thousand five hundred dollars, "for the purpose of extending the external commerce of the United States," while understood and considered by the executive as giving the legislative sanction, would cover the undertaking from notice, and prevent the obstructions which interested individuals might otherwise previously prepare in its way.

## THIRD ANNUAL MESSAGE

October 17, 1803

TO THE SENATE AND HOUSE OF REPRESENTATIVES OF THE UNITED STATES: In calling you together, fellow citizens, at an earlier day than was contemplated by the act of the last session of Congress, I have not been insensible to the personal inconveniences necessarily resulting from an unexpected change in your arrangements. But matters of great public concernment have rendered this call necessary, and the interest you feel in these will supersede in your minds all private considerations.

Congress witnessed, at their last session, the extraordinary agitation produced in the public mind by the suspension of our right of deposit at the port of New Orleans, no assignment of another place having been made according to treaty. They were sensible that the continuance of that privation would be more injurious to our nation than any consequences which could flow from any mode of redress, but reposing just confidence in the good faith of the government whose officer had committed the wrong, friendly and reasonable representations were resorted to, and the right of deposit was restored.

Previous, however, to this period, we had not been unaware of the danger to which our peace would be perpetually exposed while so important a key to the commerce of the western country remained under foreign power. Difficulties, too, were presenting themselves as to the navigation of other streams, which, arising within our territories, pass through those adjacent. Propositions had, therefore, been authorized for obtaining, on fair conditions, the sovereignty of New Orleans, and of other possessions in that quarter interesting to our quiet, to such extent as was deemed practicable; and the provisional appropriation of two millions of dollars, to be applied and accounted for by the President of the United States, intended as part of the price, was considered as conveying the sanction of Congress to the acquisition proposed. The enlightened government of France saw, with just discernment, the importance to both nations of such liberal arrangements as might best and permanently promote the peace, friendship, and interests of both; and the property and sovereignty of all Louisiana, which had been restored to them, have on certain conditions been transferred to the United States by instruments bearing date the 30th of April last. When these shall have received the constitutional sanction of the Senate, they will without delay be communicated to the Representatives also, for the exercise of their functions, as to those conditions which are within the powers vested by the Constitution in Congress. While the property and sovereignty of the Mississippi and its waters secure an independent outlet for the produce of the western States, and an uncontrolled navigation through their whole course, free from collision with other powers and the dangers to our peace from that source, the fertility of the country, its climate and extent, promise in due season important aids to our treasury, an ample provision for our posterity, and a wide-spread field for the blessings of freedom and equal laws.

With the wisdom of Congress it will rest to take those ulterior measures which may be necessary for the immediate occupation and temporary government of the country; for its incorporation into our Union; for rendering the change of government a blessing to our newly-adopted brethren; for securing to them the rights of conscience and of property; for confirming to the Indian inhabitants their occupancy and self-government, establishing friendly and commercial relations with them, and for ascertaining the geography of the country acquired. Such materials for your information, relative to its affairs in general, as the short space of time has permitted me to collect, will be laid before you when the subject shall be in a state for your consideration.

Another important acquisition of territory has also been made since the last session of Congress. The friendly tribe of Kaskaskia Indians with which we have never had a difference, reduced by the wars and wants of savage life to a few individuals unable to defend themselves against the neighboring tribes, has transferred its country to the United States, reserving only for its members what is sufficient to maintain them in an agricultural way. The considerations stipulated are, that we shall extend to them our patronage and protection, and give them certain annual aids in money, in implements of agriculture, and other articles of their choice. This country, among the most fertile within our limits, extending along the Mississippi from the mouth of the Illinois to and up the Ohio, though not so necessary as a barrier since the acquisition of the other bank, may yet be well worthy of being laid open to immediate settlement, as its inhabitants may descend with rapidity in support of the lower country should future circumstances expose that to foreign enterprise. As the stipulations in this treaty also involve matters within the competence of both houses only, it will be laid before Congress as soon as the Senate shall have advised its ratification.

With many other Indian tribes, improvements in agriculture and household manufacture are advancing, and with all our peace and friendship are established on grounds much firmer than heretofore. The measure adopted of establishing trading-houses among them, and of furnishing them necessaries in exchange for their commodities, at such moderated prices as leave no gain, but cover us from loss, has the most conciliatory and useful effect upon them, and is that which will best secure their peace and good will.

The small vessels authorized by Congress with a view to the Mediterranean service, have been sent into that sea, and will be able more effectually to confine the Tripoline cruisers within their harbors, and supersede the necessity of convoy to our commerce in that quarter. They will sensibly lessen the expenses of that service the ensuing year.

A further knowledge of the ground in the north-eastern and north-western angles of the United States has evinced that the boundaries established by the treaty of Paris, between the British territories and ours in those parts, were too imperfectly described to be susceptible of execution. It has therefore been thought worthy of attention, for preserving and cherishing the harmony and useful intercourse subsisting between the two nations, to remove by timely arrangements what unfavorable incidents might otherwise render a ground of future misunderstanding. A convention has therefore been entered into, which provides for a practicable demarkation of those limits to the satisfaction of both parties.

An account of the receipts and expenditures of the year ending 30th September last, with the estimates for the service of the ensuing year, will be laid before you by the Secretary of the Treasury so soon as the receipts of the last quarter shall be returned from the more distant States. It is already ascertained that the amount paid into the treasury for that year has been between eleven and twelve millions of dollars, and that the revenue accrued during the same term exceeds the sum counted on as sufficient for our current expenses, and to extinguish the public debt within the period heretofore proposed.

The amount of debt paid for the same year is about three millions one hundred thousand dollars, exclusive of interest, and making, with the payment of the preceding year, a discharge of more than eight millions and a half of dollars of the principal of that debt, besides the accruing interest; and there remain in the treasury nearly six millions of dollars. Of these, eight hundred and eighty thousand have been reserved for payment of the first instalment due under the British convention of January 8th, 1802, and two millions are what have been before mentioned as placed by Congress under the power and accountability of the president, toward the price of New Orleans and other territories acquired, which, remaining untouched, are still applicable to that object, and go in diminution of the sum to be funded for it.

Should the acquisition of Louisiana be constitutionally confirmed and carried into effect, a sum of nearly thirteen millions of dollars will then be added to our public debt, most of which is payable after fifteen years; before which term the present existing debts will all be discharged by the established operation of the sinking fund. When we contemplate the ordinary annual augmentation of imposts from increasing population and wealth, the augmentation of the same revenue by its extension to the new acquisition, and the economies which may still be introduced into our public expenditures, I cannot but hope that Congress in reviewing their resources will find means to meet the intermediate interests of this additional debt without recurring to new taxes, and applying to this object only the ordinary progression of our revenue. Its extraordinary increase in times of foreign war will be the proper and sufficient fund for any measures of safety or precaution which that state of things may render necessary in our neutral position.

Remittances for the instalments of our foreign debt having been found practicable without loss, it has not been thought expedient to use the power given by a former act of Congress of continuing them by reloans, and of redeeming instead thereof equal sums of domestic debt, although no difficulty was found in obtaining that accommodation.

The sum of fifty thousand dollars appropriated by Congress for providing gun-boats, remains unexpended. The favorable and peaceful turn of affairs on the Mississippi rendered an immediate execution of that law unnecessary, and time was desirable in order that the institution of that branch of our force might begin on models the most approved by experience. The same issue of events dispensed with a resort to the appropriation of a million and a half of dollars contemplated for purposes which were effected by happier means.

We have seen with sincere concern the flames of war lighted up again in Europe,[1] and nations with which we have the most friendly and useful relations engaged in mutual destruction. While we regret the miseries in which we see others involved let us bow with gratitude to that kind Providence which, inspiring with wisdom and moderation our late legislative councils while placed under the urgency of the greatest wrongs, guarded us from hastily entering into the sanguinary contest, and left us only to look on and to pity its ravages. These will be heaviest on those immediately engaged. Yet the nations pursuing peace will not be exempt from all evil. In the course of this conflict, let it be our endeavor, as it is our interest and desire, to cultivate the friendship of the belligerent nations by every act of justice and of incessant kindness; to receive their armed vessels with hospitality from the distresses of the sea, but to administer the means of annoyance to none; to establish in our harbors such a police as may maintain law and order; to

[1] On May 18, 1803, after one year of peace, England declared war on France.

restrain our citizens from embarking individually in a war in which their country takes no part; to punish severely those persons, citizen or alien, who shall usurp the cover of our flag for vessels not entitled to it, infecting thereby with suspicion those of real Americans, and committing us into controversies for the redress of wrongs not our own; to exact from every nation the observance, toward our vessels and citizens, of those principles and practices which all civilized people acknowledge; to merit the character of a just nation, and maintain that of an independent one, preferring every consequence to insult and habitual wrong. Congress will consider whether the existing laws enable us efficaciously to maintain this course with our citizens in all places, and with others while within the limits of our jurisdiction, and will give them the new modifications necessary for these objects. Some contraventions of right have already taken place, both within our jurisdictional limits and on the high seas. The friendly disposition of the governments from whose agents they have proceeded, as well as their wisdom and regard for justice, leave us in reasonable expectation that they will be rectified and prevented in future; and that no act will be countenanced by them which threatens to disturb our friendly intercourse. Separated by a wide ocean from the nations of Europe, and from the political interests which entangle them together, with productions and wants which render our commerce and friendship useful to them and theirs to us, it cannot be the interest of any to assail us, nor ours to disturb them. We should be most unwise, indeed, were we to cast away the singular blessings of the position in which nature has placed us, the opportunity she has endowed us with of pursuing, at a distance from foreign contentions, the paths of industry, peace, and happiness; of cultivating general friendship, and of bringing collisions of interest to the umpirage of reason rather than of force. How desirable then must it be, in a government like ours, to see its citizens adopt individually the views, the interests, and the conduct which their country should pursue, divesting themselves of those passions and partialities which tend to lessen useful friendships, and to embarrass and embroil us in the calamitous scenes of Europe. Confident, fellow citizens, that you will duly estimate the importance of neutral dispositions toward the observance of neutral conduct, that you will be sensible how much it is our duty to look on the bloody arena spread before us with commiseration indeed, but with no other wish than to see it closed, I am persuaded you will cordially cherish these dispositions in all discussions among yourselves, and in all communications with your constituents; and I anticipate with satisfaction the measures of wisdom which the great interests now committed to *you* will give you an opportunity of providing, and *myself* that of approving and carrying into execution with the fidelity I owe to my country.

# FOURTH ANNUAL MESSAGE

November 8, 1804

TO THE SENATE AND HOUSE OF REPRESENTATIVES OF THE UNITED STATES: To a people, fellow citizens, who sincerely desire the happiness and prosperity of other nations; to those who justly calculate that their own well-being is advanced by that of the nations with which they have intercourse, it will be a satisfaction to observe that the war which was lighted up in Europe a little before our last meeting has not yet extended its flames to other nations, nor been marked by the calamities which sometimes stain the footsteps of war. The irregularities too on the ocean, which generally harass the commerce of neutral nations, have, in distant parts, disturbed ours less than on former occasions. But in the American seas they have been greater from peculiar causes; and even within our harbors and jurisdiction, infringements on the authority of the laws have been committed which have called for serious attention. The friendly conduct of the governments from whose officers and subjects these acts have proceeded, in other respects and in places more under their observation and control, gives us confidence that our representations on this subject will have been properly regarded.

While noticing the irregularities committed on the ocean by others, those on our own part should not be omitted nor left unprovided for. Complaints have been received that persons residing within the United States have taken on themselves to arm merchant vessels, and to force a commerce into certain ports and countries in defiance of the laws of those countries. That individuals should undertake to wage private war, independently of the authority of their country, cannot be permitted in a well-ordered society. Its tendency to produce aggression on the laws and rights of other nations, and to endanger the peace of our own is so obvious, that I doubt not you will adopt measures for restraining it effectually in future.

Soon after the passage of the act of the last session, authorizing the establishment of a district and port of entry on the waters of the Mobile, we learnt that its object was misunderstood on the part of Spain. Candid explanations were immediately given, and assurances that, reserving our claims in that quarter as a subject of discussion and arrangement with Spain, no act was meditated, in the meantime, inconsistent with the peace and friendship existing between the two nations, and that conformably to these intentions would be the execution of the law. That government had, however, thought proper to suspend the ratification of the convention of 1802. But the explanations which would reach them soon after, and still more, the confirmation of them by the tenor of the instrument establishing the port and district, may reasonably be expected to replace them in the dispositions and views of the whole subject which originally dictated the conviction.

I have the satisfaction to inform you that the objections which had been urged by that government against the validity of our title to the country of Louisiana have been withdrawn, its exact limits, however, remaining still to be settled between us. And to this is to be added that, having prepared and delivered the stock created in execution of the convention of Paris, of April 30, 1803, in consideration of the cession of that country, we have received from the government of France an acknowledgment, in due form, of the fulfilment of that stipulation.

With the nations of Europe in general our friendship and intercourse are undisturbed, and from the governments of the belligerent powers especially we continue to receive those friendly manifestations which are justly due to an honest neutrality, and to such good offices consistent with that as we have opportunities of rendering.

The activity and success of the small force employed in the Mediterranean in the early part of the present year, the reinforcement sent into that sea, and the energy of the officers having command in the several vessels, will, I trust, by the sufferings of war, reduce the barbarians of Tripoli to the desire of peace on proper terms. Great injury, however, ensues to ourselves as well as to others interested, from the distance to which prizes must be brought for adjudication, and from the impracticability of bringing hither such as are not seaworthy.

The bey of Tunis having made requisitions unauthorized by our treaty, their rejection has produced from him some expressions of discontent. But to those who expect us to calculate whether a compliance with unjust demands will not cost us less than a war, we must leave as a question of calculation for them, also, whether to retire from unjust demands will not cost them less than a war. We can do to each other very sensible injuries by war, but the mutual advantages of peace make that the best interest of both.

Peace and intercourse with the other powers on the same coast continue on the footing on which they are established by treaty.

In pursuance of the act providing for the temporary government of Louisiana, the necessary officers for the territory of Orleans were appointed in due time, to commence the exercise of their functions on the first day of October. The distance, however, of some of them, and indispensable previous arrangements, may have retarded its commencement in some of its parts; the form of government thus provided having been considered but as temporary, and open to such improvements as further information of the circumstances of our brethren there might suggest, it will of course be subject to your consideration.

In the district of Louisiana, it has been thought best to adopt the division into subordinate districts, which had been established under its former government. These being five in number, a commanding officer has been appointed to each, according to the provision of the law, and so soon as they can be at their station, that district will also be in its due state of organization; in the meantime their places are supplied by the officers before commanding there. The functions of the governor and judges of Indiana have commenced; the government, we presume, is proceeding in its new form. The lead mines in that district offer so rich a supply of that metal, as to merit attention. The report now communicated will inform you of their state, and of the necessity of immediate inquiry into their occupation and titles.

With the Indian tribes established within our newly-acquired limits, I have deemed it necessary to open conferences for the purpose of establishing a good understanding and neighborly relations between us. So far as we have yet learned, we have reason to believe that their dispositions are generally favorable and friendly; and with these dispositions on their part, we have in our own hands means which cannot fail us for preserving their peace and friendship. By pursuing a uniform course of justice toward them, by aiding them in all the improvements which may better their condition, and especially by establishing a commerce on terms which shall be advantageous to them and only not losing to us, and so regulated as that no incendiaries of our own or any other nation may be permitted to disturb the natural effects of our just and friendly offices, we may render ourselves so necessary to their comfort and prosperity, that the protection of our citizens from their disorderly members will become their interest and their voluntary care. Instead, therefore, of an augmentation of military force proportioned to our extension of frontier, I proposed a moderate enlargement of the capital employed in that commerce, as a more effectual, economical, and humane instrument for preserving peace and good neighborhood with them.

On this side the Mississippi an important relinquishment of native title has been received from the Delawares. That tribe, desiring to extinguish in their people the spirit of hunting, and to convert superfluous lands into the means of improving what they retain, have ceded to us all the country between the Wabash and the Ohio, south of, and including the road from the rapids towards Vincennes, for which they are to receive annuities in animals and implements for agriculture, and in other necessaries. This acquisition is important, not only for its extent and fertility, but as fronting three hundred miles on the Ohio, and near half that on the Wabash. The produce of the settled countries descending those rivers, will no longer pass in review of the Indian frontier but in a small portion, and with the cession heretofore made with the Kaskaskias, nearly consolidates our possessions north of the Ohio, in a very respectable breadth, from Lake Erie to the Mississippi. The Piankeshaws having some claim to the country ceded by the Delawares, it has been thought best to quiet that by fair purchase also. So soon as the treaties on this subject shall have received their constitutional sanctions, they shall be laid before both houses.

The act of Congress of February 28th, 1803, for building and employing a number of gun-boats, is now in a course of execution to the extent there provided for. The obstacle to naval enterprise which vessels of this construction offer for our seaport towns; their utility toward supporting within our waters the authority of the laws; the promptness with which they will be manned by the seamen and militia of the place the moment they are wanting; the facility of their assembling from different parts of the coast to any point where they are required in greater force than ordinary; the economy of their maintenance and preservation from decay when not in actual service; and the competence of our finances to this defensive provision, without any new burden, are considerations which will have due weight with Congress in deciding on the expediency of adding to their number from year to year, as experience shall test their utility, until all our important harbors, by these and auxiliary means, shall be insured against insult and opposition to the laws.

No circumstance has arisen since your last session which calls for any augmentation of our regular military force. Should any improvement occur in the militia system, that will be always seasonable.

Accounts of the receipts and expenditures of the last year with estimates for the ensuing one, will as usual be laid before you.

The state of our finances continues, to fulfil our expectations. Eleven millions and a half of dollars, received in the course of the year ending on the 30th of September last, have enabled us, after meeting all the ordinary expenses of the year, to pay upward of $3,600,000 of the public debt, exclusive of interest. This payment, with those of the two preceding years, has extinguished upward of twelve millions of the principal, and a greater sum of interest, within that period; and by a proportional diminution of interest, renders already sensible the effect of the growing sum yearly applicable to the discharge of the principal.

It is also ascertained that the revenue accrued during the last year, exceeds that of the preceding; and the probable receipts of the ensuing year may safely be relied on as sufficient, with the sum already in the treasury, to meet all the current demands of the year, to discharge upward of three millions and a half of the engagements incurred under the British and French conventions, and to advance in the farther redemption of the funded debts as rapidly as had been contemplated. These, fellow citizens, are the principal matters which I have thought it necessary at this time to communicate for your consideration and attention. Some others will be laid before you in the course of the session, but in the discharge of the great duties confided to you by our country, you will take a broader view of the field of legislation. Whether the great interests of agriculture, manufactures, commerce, or navigation, can, within the pale of your constitutional powers, be aided in any of their relations; whether laws are provided in all cases where they are wanting; whether those provided are exactly what they should be; whether any abuses take place in their administration, or in that of the public revenues; whether the organization of the public agents or of the public force is perfect in all its parts; in fine, whether anything can be done to advance the general good, are questions within the limits of your functions which will necessarily occupy your attention. In these and other matters which you in your wisdom may propose for the good of our country, you may count with assurance on my hearty co-operation and faithful execution.

## SECOND INAUGURAL ADDRESS[1]

### March 4, 1805

Proceeding, fellow citizens, to that qualification which the constitution requires, before my entrance on the charge again conferred upon me, it is my duty to express the deep sense I entertain of this new proof of confidence from my fellow citizens at large, and the zeal with which it inspires me, so to conduct myself as may best satisfy their just expectations.

On taking this station on a former occasion, I declared the principles on which I believed it my duty to administer the affairs of our commonwealth. My conscience tells me that I have, on every occasion, acted up to that declaration, according to its obvious import, and to the understanding of every candid mind.

In the transaction of your foreign affairs, we have endeavored to culti-

[1] Jefferson's notes for his draft of this inaugural address:

"The former one was an exposition of the principles on which I thought it my duty to administer the government. The second, then, should naturally be a *compte rendu,* or a statement of facts showing that I have conformed to those principles. The former was *promise:* this is *performance.* Yet the nature of the occasion requires that detail should be avoided; that the most prominent heads only should be selected, and these placed in a strong light, but in as few words as possible. These heads are foreign affairs, domestic ditto, *viz.:* Taxes, Debts, Louisiana, Religion, Indians, the Press. None of these heads need any commentary but that of Indians. This is a proper topic, not only to promote the work of humanizing our citizens towards these people, but to conciliate to us the good opinion of Europe on the subject of the Indians. This, however, might have been done in half the compass it here occupies. But every respecter of science, every friend to political reformation, must have observed with indignation the hue and cry raised against philosophy and the rights of man; and it really seems as if they would be overborne, and barbarism, bigotry, and despotism, would recover the ground they have lost by the advance of the public understanding. I have thought the occasion justified some discountenance of these anti-social doctrines, some testimony against them. But not to commit myself in direct warfare on them, I have thought it best to say what is directly applied to the Indians only, but admits by inference a more general extension."

vate the friendship of all nations, and especially of those with which we have the most important relations. We have done them justice on all occasions, favored where favor was lawful, and cherished mutual interests and intercourse on fair and equal terms. We are firmly convinced, and we act on that conviction, that with nations, as with individuals, our interests soundly calculated, will ever be found inseparable from our moral duties; and history bears witness to the fact, that a just nation is taken on its word, when recourse is had to armaments and wars to bridle others.

At home, fellow citizens, you best know whether we have done well or ill. The suppression of unnecessary offices, of useless establishments and expenses, enabled us to discontinue our internal taxes. These covering our land with officers, and opening our doors to their intrusions, had already begun that process of domiciliary vexation which, once entered, is scarcely to be restrained from reaching successively every article of produce and property. If among these taxes some minor ones fell which had not been inconvenient, it was because their amount would not have paid the officers who collected them, and because, if they had any merit, the state authorities might adopt them, instead of others less approved.

The remaining revenue on the consumption of foreign articles, is paid cheerfully by those who can afford to add foreign luxuries to domestic comforts, being collected on our seaboards and frontiers only, and incorporated with the transactions of our mercantile citizens, it may be the pleasure and pride of an American to ask, what farmer, what mechanic, what laborer, ever sees a tax-gatherer of the United States? These contributions enable us to support the current expenses of the government, to fulfil contracts with foreign nations, to extinguish the native right of soil within our limits, to extend those limits, and to apply such a surplus to our public debts, as places at a short day their final redemption, and that redemption once effected, the revenue thereby liberated may, by a just repartition among the states, and a corresponding amendment of the constitution, be applied, *in time of peace,* to rivers, canals, roads, arts, manufactures, education, and other great objects within each state. *In time of war,* if injustice, by ourselves or others, must sometimes produce war, increased as the same revenue will be increased by population and consumption, and aided by other resources reserved for that crisis, it may meet within the year all the expenses of the year, without encroaching on the rights of future generations, by burdening them with the debts of the past. War will then be but a suspension of useful works, and a return to a state of peace, a return to the progress of improvement.

I have said, fellow citizens, that the income reserved had enabled us to extend our limits; but that extension may possibly pay for itself before we are called on, and in the meantime, may keep down the accruing interest; in all events, it will repay the advances we have made. I know that the acquisition of Louisiana has been disapproved by some, from a candid apprehension that the enlargement of our territory would endanger its union. But who can limit the extent to which the federative principle may operate effectively? The larger our association, the less will it be shaken by local passions; and in any view, is it not better that the opposite bank of the Mississippi should be settled by our own brethren and children, than by strangers of another family? With which shall we be most likely to live in harmony and friendly intercourse?

In matters of religion, I have considered that its free exercise is placed by the constitution independent of the powers of the general government. I have therefore undertaken, on no occasion, to prescribe the religious exercises suited to it; but have left them, as the constitution found them, under the direction and discipline of state or church authorities acknowledged by the several religious societies.

The aboriginal inhabitants of these countries I have regarded with the commiseration their history inspires. Endowed with the faculties and the rights of men, breathing an ardent love of liberty and independence, and occupying a country which left them no desire but to be undisturbed, the stream of overflowing population from other regions directed itself on these shores; without power to divert, or habits to contend against, they have been overwhelmed by the current, or driven before it; now reduced within limits too narrow for the hunter's state, humanity enjoins us to teach them agriculture and the domestic arts; to encourage them to that industry which alone can enable them to maintain their place in existence, and to prepare them in time for that state of society, which to bodily comforts adds the improvement of the mind and morals. We have therefore liberally furnished them with the implements of husbandry and household use; we have placed among them instructors in the arts of first necessity; and they are covered with the ægis of the law against aggressors from among ourselves.

But the endeavors to enlighten them on the fate which awaits their present course of life, to induce them to exercise their reason, follow its dictates, and change their pursuits with the change of circumstances, have powerful obstacles to encounter; they are combated by the habits of their bodies, prejudice of their minds, ignorance, pride, and the influence of interested and crafty individuals among them, who feel themselves something in the present order of things, and fear to become nothing in any other. These persons inculcate a sanctimonious reverence for the customs of their ancestors; that whatsoever they did, must be done through all time; that reason is a false guide, and to advance under its counsel, in their physical, moral, or political condition, is perilous innovation; that their duty is to remain as their Creator made them, ignorance being safety, and knowledge full of danger; in short, my friends, among them is seen the action and counteraction of good sense and bigotry; they, too, have their anti-philosophers, who find an interest in keeping things in their present state, who dread reformation, and exert all their faculties to maintain the ascendency of habit over the duty of improving our reason, and obeying its mandates.

In giving these outlines, I do not mean, fellow citizens, to arrogate to myself the merit of the measures; that is due, in the first place, to the reflecting character of our citizens at large, who, by the weight of public opinion, influence and strengthen the public measures; it is due to the sound discretion with which they select from among themselves those to whom they confide the legislative duties; it is due to the zeal and wisdom of the characters thus selected, who lay the foundations of public happiness in wholesome laws, the execution of which alone remains for others; and it is due to the able and faithful auxiliaries, whose patriotism has associated with me in the executive functions.

During this course of administration, and in order to disturb it, the artillery of the press has been levelled against us, charged with whatsoever its licentiousness could devise or dare. These abuses of an institution so important to freedom and science, are deeply to be regretted, inasmuch as they tend to lessen its usefulness, and to sap its safety; they might, indeed, have been corrected by the wholesome punishments reserved and provided by the laws of the several States against falsehood and defamation; but public duties more urgent press on the time of public servants, and the offenders have therefore been left to find their punishment in the public indignation.

Nor was it uninteresting to the world, that an experiment should be fairly and fully made, whether freedom of discussion, unaided by power, is not sufficient for the propagation and protection of truth—whether a government, conducting itself in the true spirit of its constitution, with zeal and purity, and doing no act which it would be unwilling the whole world should witness, can be written down by falsehood and defamation. The experiment has been tried; you have witnessed the scene; our fellow citizens have looked on, cool and collected; they saw the latent source from which these outrages proceeded; they gathered around their public functionaries, and when the constitution called them to the decision by suffrage, they pronounced their verdict, honorable to those who had served them, and consolatory to the friend of man, who believes he may be intrusted with his own affairs.

No inference is here intended, that the laws, provided by the State against false and defamatory publications, should not be enforced; he who has time, renders a service to public morals and public tranquillity, in reforming these abuses by the salutary coercions of the law; but the experiment is noted, to prove that, since truth and reason have maintained their ground against false opinions in league with false facts, the press, confined to truth, needs no other legal restraint; the public judgment will correct false reasonings and opinions, on a full hearing of all parties; and no other definite line can be drawn between the inestimable liberty of the press and its demoralizing licentiousness. If there be still improprieties which this rule would not restrain, its supplement must be sought in the censorship of public opinion.

Contemplating the union of sentiment now manifested so generally, as auguring harmony and happiness to our future course, I offer to our country sincere congratulations. With those, too, not yet rallied to the same point, the disposition to do so is gaining strength; facts are piercing through the veil drawn over them; and our doubting brethren will at length see, that the mass of their fellow citizens, with whom they cannot yet resolve to act, as to principles and measures, think as they think, and desire what they desire; that our wish, as well as theirs, is, that the public efforts may be directed honestly to the public good, that peace be cultivated, civil and religious liberty unassailed, law and order preserved, equality of rights maintained, and that state of property, equal or unequal, which results to every man from his own industry, or that of his fathers. When satisfied of these views, it is not in human nature that they should not approve and support them; in the meantime, let us cherish them with patient affection; let us do them justice, and more than justice, in all competitions of interest; and we need not doubt that truth, reason, and their own interests, will at length prevail, will gather them into the fold of their country, and will complete their entire union of opinion, which gives to a nation the blessing of harmony, and the benefit of all its strength.

I shall now enter on the duties to which my fellow citizens have again called me, and shall proceed in the spirit of those principles which they have approved. I fear not that any motives of interest may lead me astray; I am sensible of no passion which could seduce me knowingly from the path of justice; but the weakness of human nature, and the limits of my own understanding, will produce errors of judgment sometimes injurious to your interests. I shall need, therefore, all the indulgence I have heretofore experienced—the want of it will certainly not lessen with increasing years. I shall need, too, the favor of that Being in whose hands we are, who led our forefathers, as Israel of old, from their native land, and planted them in a country flowing with all the necessaries and comforts of life; who has covered our infancy with his providence, and our riper years with his wisdom and power; and to whose goodness I ask you to join with me in supplications, that he will so enlighten the minds of your servants, guide their councils, and prosper their measures, that whatsoever they do, shall result in your good, and shall secure to you the peace, friendship, and approbation of all nations.

## FIFTH ANNUAL MESSAGE

### December 3, 1805

TO THE SENATE AND HOUSE OF REPRESENTATIVES OF THE UNITED STATES: At a moment when the nations of Europe are in commotion and arming against each other, and when those with whom we have principal intercourse are engaged in the general contest, and when the countenance of some of them toward our peaceable country threatens that even that may not be unaffected by what is passing on the general theatre, a meeting of the representatives of the nation in both houses of Congress has become more than usually desirable. Coming from every section of our country, they bring with them the sentiments and the information of the whole, and will be enabled to give a direction to the public affairs which the will and wisdom of the whole will approve and support.

In taking a view of the state of our country, we in the first place notice the late affliction of two of our cities under the fatal fever which in latter times has ocasionally visited our shores. Providence in his goodness gave it an early termination on this occasion, and lessened the number of victims which have usually fallen before it. In the course of the several visitations by this disease it has appeared that it is strictly local; incident to the cities and on the tide waters only; incommunicable in the country, either by persons under the disease or by goods carried from diseased places; that its access is with the autumn, and that it disappears with the early frosts. These restrictions within narrow limits of time and space give security even to our maritime cities during three-fourths of the year, and to the country always. Although from these facts it appears unnecessary, yet to satisfy the fears of foreign nations, and cautions on their part not to be complained of in a danger whose limits are yet unknown to them, I have strictly enjoined on the officers at the head of the customs to certify with exact truth for every vessel sailing for a foreign port, the state of health respecting this fever which prevails at the place from which she sails. Under every motive from character and duty to certify the truth, I have no doubt they have faithfully executed this injunction. Much real injury has, however, been sustained from a propensity to identify with this epidemic, and to call by the same name, fevers of very different kinds, which have been known at all times and in all countries, and never have been placed among those deemed contageous. As we advance in our knowledge of this disease, as facts develop the sources from which individuals receive it, the state authorities charged with the care of the public health, and Congress with that of the general commerce, will become able to regulate with effect their respective functions in these departments. The burden of quarantines is felt at home as well as abroad; their efficacy merits examination. Although the health laws of the States should be found to need no present revisal by Congress, yet commerce claims that their attention be ever awake to them.

Since our last meeting the aspect of our foreign relations has considerably changed. Our coasts have been infested and our harbors watched by private armed vessels, some of them without commissions, some with illegal commissions, others with those of legal form but committing piratical acts beyond the authority of their commissions. They have captured in the very entrance of our harbors, as well as on the high seas, not only the vessels of our friends coming to trade with us, but our own also. They have carried them off under pretence of legal adjudication, but not daring to approach a court of justice, they have plundered and sunk them by the way, or in obscure places where no evidence could arise against them; maltreated the crews, and abandoned them in boats in the open sea or on desert shores without food or covering. These enormities appearing to be unreached by any control of their sovereigns, I found it necessary to equip a force to cruise within our own seas, to arrest all vessels of these descriptions found hovering on our coast within the limits of the Gulf Stream, and to bring the offenders in for trial as pirates.

The same system of hovering on our coasts and harbors under color of seeking enemies, has been also carried on by public armed ships, to the great annoyance and oppression of our commerce. New principles, too, have been interloped into the law of nations, founded neither in justice nor the usage or acknowledgment of nations. According to these, a belligerent takes to himself a commerce with its own enemy which it denies to a neutral, on the ground of its aiding that enemy in the war. But reason revolts at such an inconsistency, and the neutral having equal right with the belligerent to decide the question, the interest of our constituents and the duty of maintaining the authority of reason, the only umpire between just nations, impose on us the obligation of providing an effectual and determined opposition to a doctrine so injurious to the rights of peaceable nations. Indeed, the confidence we ought to have in the justice of others, still countenances the hope that a sounder view of those rights will of itself induce from every belligerent a more correct observance of them.

With Spain our negotiations for a settlement of differences have not had a satisfactory issue. Spoliations during the former war, for which she had formally acknowledged herself responsible, have been refused to be compensated, but on conditions affecting other claims in nowise connected with them. Yet the same practices are renewed in the present war, and are already of great amount. On the Mobile, our commerce passing through that river continues to be obstructed by arbitrary duties and vexatious searches. Propositions for adjusting amicably the boundaries of Louisiana have not been acceded to. While, however, the right is unsettled, we have avoided changing the state of things by taking new posts or strengthening ourselves in the disputed territories, in the hope that the other power would not, by contrary conduct, oblige us to meet their example, and endanger conflicts of authority the issue of which may not be easily controlled. But in this hope we have now reason to lessen our confidence. Inroads have been recently made into the territories of Orleans and the Mississippi, our citizens have been seized and their property plundered in the very parts of the former which had been actually delivered up by Spain, and this by the regular officers and soldiers of that government. I have therefore found it necessary at length to give orders to our troops on that frontier to be in readiness to protect our citizens, and to repel by arms any similar aggression in future. Other details, necessary for your full information of the state of things between this country and that shall be the subject of another communication.

In reviewing these injuries from some of the belligerent powers, the moderation, the firmness, and the wisdom of the legislature will be all called into action. We ought still to hope that time and a more correct estimate of interest, as well as of character, will produce the justice we are bound to expect. But should any nation deceive itself by false calculations, and disappoint that expectation, we must join in the unprofitable contest of trying which party can do the other the most harm. Some of these injuries may perhaps admit a peaceable remedy. Where that is competent it is always the most desirable. But some of them are of a nature to be met by force only, and all of them may lead to it. I cannot, therefore, but recommend such preparations as circumstances call for. The first object is to place our seaport towns out of the danger of insult. Measures have been already taken for furnishing them with heavy cannon for the service of such land batteries as may make a part of their defence against armed vessels approaching them. In aid of these it is desirable that we should have a competent number of gunboats; and the number, to be competent, must be considerable. If immediately begun, they may be in readiness for service at the opening of the next season. Whether it will be necessary to augment our land forces will be decided by occurrences probably in the course of your session. In the meantime, you will consider whether it would not be expedient, for a state of peace as well as of war, so to organize or class the militia as would enable us, on a sudden emergency, to call for the services of the younger portions, unencumbered with the old and those having families. Upward of three hundred thousand able-bodied men, between the ages of eighteen and twenty-six years, which the last census shows we may now count within our limits, will furnish a competent number for offence or defence in any point where they may be wanted, and will give time for raising regular forces after the necessity of them shall become certain; and the reducing to the early period of life all its active service cannot but be desirable to our younger citizens, of the present as well as future times, inasmuch as it engages to them in more advanced age a quiet and undisturbed repose in the bosom of their families. I cannot, then, but earnestly recommend to your early consideration the expediency of so modifying our militia system as, by a separation of the more active part from that which is less so, we may draw from it, when necessary, an efficient corps fit for real and active service, and to be called to it in regular rotation.

Considerable provision has been made, under former authorities from Congress, of materials for the construction of ships of war of seventy-four guns. These materials are on hand, subject to the further will of the legislature.

An immediate prohibition of the exportation of arms and ammunition is also submitted to your determination.

Turning from these unpleasant views of violence and wrong, I congratulate you on the liberation of our fellow citizens who were stranded on the coast of Tripoli and made prisoners of war. In a government bottomed on the will of all, the life and liberty of every individual citizen become interesting to all. In the treaty, therefore, which has concluded our warfare with that State, an article for the ransom of our citizens has been agreed to. An operation by land, by a small band of our countrymen, and others—engaged for the occasion, in conjunction with the troops of the ex-bashaw of that country, gallantly conducted by our late consul Eaton, and their successful enterprise on the city of Derne, contributed, doubtless, to the impression which produced peace; and the conclusion of this prevented opportunities of which the officers and men of our squadron destined for Tripoli would have availed themselves, to emulate the acts of valor exhibited by their brethren in the attack of the last year. Reflecting with high satisfaction on the distinguished bravery displayed whenever occasion permitted in the Mediterranean service, I think it would be a useful encouragement, as well as a just reward, to make an opening for some present promotion by enlarging our peace establishment of captains and lieutenants.

With Tunis some misunderstandings have arisen, not yet sufficiently explained, but friendly discussions with their ambassador recently arrived, and a mutual disposition to do whatever is just and reasonable, cannot fail of dissipating these; so that we may consider our peace on that coast, generally, to be on as sound a footing as it has been at any preceding time.

Still it will not be expedient to withdraw, immediately, the whole of our force from that sea.

The law for providing a naval peace establishment fixes the number of frigates which shall be kept in constant service in time of peace, and prescribes that they shall not be manned by more than two-thirds of their complement of seamen and ordinary seamen. Whether a frigate may be trusted to two-thirds only of her proper complement of men must depend on the nature of the service on which she is ordered; that may sometimes, for her safety, as well as to insure her object, require her fullest complement. In adverting to this subject, Congress will perhaps consider whether the best limitation on the executive discretion in this case would not be by the number of seamen which may be employed in the whole service, rather than by the number of vessels. Occasions oftener arise for the employment of small than of large vessels, and it would lessen risk as well as expense to be authorized to employ them of preference. The limitation suggested by the number of seamen would admit a selection of vessels best adapted to the service.

Our Indian neighbors are advancing, many of them with spirit and others beginning to engage, in the pursuits of agriculture and household manufacture. They are becoming sensible that the earth yields subsistence with less labor and more certainty than the forest, and find it their interest, from time to time, to dispose of parts of their surplus and waste lands for the means of improving those they occupy, and of subsisting their families while they are preparing their farms. Since your last session, the northern tribes have sold to us the lands between the Connecticut reserve and the former Indian boundary; and those on the Ohio, from the same boundary to the rapids, and for a considerable depth inland. The Chickasaws and Cherokees have sold us the country between and adjacent to the two districts of Tennessee, and the Creeks, the residue of their lands in the fork of Ocmulgee, up to the Ulcofauhatche. The three former purchases are important, inasmuch as they consolidate disjointed parts of our settled country, and render their intercourse secure; and the second particularly so, as with the small point on the river which we expect is by this time ceded by the Piankeshaws, it completes our possession of the whole of both banks of the Ohio, from its source to near its mouth, and the navigation of that river is thereby rendered forever safe to our citizens settled and settling on its extensive waters. The purchase from the Creeks too has been for some time particularly interesting to the State of Georgia.

The several treaties which have been mentioned will be submitted to both houses of Congress for the exercise of their respective functions.

Deputations now on their way to the seat of government, from various nations of Indians inhabiting the Missouri and other parts beyond the Mississippi, come charged with the assurances of their satisfaction with the new relations in which they are placed with us, of their disposition to cultivate our peace and friendship, and their desire to enter into commercial intercourse with us. A statement of our progress in exploring the principal rivers of that country, and of the information respecting them hitherto obtained, will be communicated so soon as we shall receive some further relations which we have reason shortly to expect.

The receipts at the treasury during the year ending the 30th day of September last, have exceeded the sum of thirteen millions of dollars, which, with not quite five millions in the treasury at the beginning of the year, have enabled us, after meeting other demands, to pay nearly two millions of the debt contracted under the British treaty and convention, upward of four millions of principal of the public debt, and four millions of interest. These payments, with those which had been made in three years and a half preceding, have extinguished of the funded debt nearly eighteen millions of principal. Congress, by their act of November 10th, 1803, authorized us to borrow one million seven hundred and fifty thousand dollars, toward meeting the claims of our citizens assumed by the convention with France. We have not, however, made use of this authority, because the sum of four millions and a half, which remained in the treasury on the same 30th day of September last, with the receipts which we may calculate on for the ensuing year, besides paying the annual sum of eight millions of dollars appropriated to the funded debts, and meeting all the current demands which may be expected, will enable us to pay the whole sum of three millions seven hundred and fifty thousand dollars assumed by the French convention, and still leaves a surplus of nearly a million of dollars at our free disposal. Should you concur in the provisions of arms and armed vessels recommended by the circumstances of the times, this surplus will furnish the means of doing so.

On this first occasion of addressing Congress, since, by the choice of my constituents, I have entered on a second term of administration, I embrace the opportunity to give this public assurance, that I will exert my best endeavors to administer faithfully the executive department, and will zealously co-operate with you in every measure which may tend to secure the liberty, property, and personal safety of our fellow citizens, and to consolidate the republican forms and principles of our government.

In the course of your session you shall receive all the aid which I can give for the despatch of the public business, and all the information necessary for your deliberations, of which the interests of our own country and the confidence reposed in us by others will admit a communication.

# SIXTH ANNUAL MESSAGE

## December 2, 1806

TO THE SENATE AND HOUSE OF REPRESENTATIVES OF THE UNITED STATES IN CONGRESS ASSEMBLED: It would have given me, fellow citizens, great satisfaction to announce in the moment of your meeting that the difficulties in our foreign relations, existing at the time of your last separation, had been amicably and justly terminated. I lost no time in taking those measures which were most likely to bring them to such a termination, by special missions charged with such powers and instructions as in the event of failure could leave no imputation on either our moderation or forbearance. The delays which have since taken place in our negotiations with the British government appears to have proceeded from causes which do not forbid the expectation that during the course of the session I may be enabled to lay before you their final issue. What will be that of the negotiations for settling our differences with Spain, nothing which had taken place at the date of the last despatches enables us to pronounce. On the western side of the Mississippi she advanced in considerable force, and took post at the settlement of Bayou Pierre, on the Red river. This village was originally settled by France, was held by her as long as she held Louisiana, and was delivered to Spain only as a part of Louisiana. Being small, insulated, and distant, it was not observed, at the moment of redelivery to France and the United States, that she continued a guard of half a dozen men which had been stationed there. A proposition, however, having been lately made by our commander-in-chief, to assume the Sabine river as a temporary line of separation between the troops of the two nations until the issue of our negotiation shall be known; this has been referred by the Spanish commandant to his superior, and in the meantime, he has withdrawn his force to the western side of the Sabine river. The correspondence on this subject, now communicated, will exhibit more particularly the present state of things in that quarter.

The nature of that country requires indispensably that an unusual proportion of the force employed there should be cavalry or mounted infantry. In order, therefore, that the commanding officer might be enabled to act with effect, I had authorized him to call on the governors of Orleans and Mississippi for a corps of five hundred volunteer cavalry. The temporary arrangement he has proposed may perhaps render this unnecessary. But I inform you with great pleasure of the promptitude with which the inhabitants of those territories have tendered their services in defence of their country. It has done honor to themselves, entitled them to the confidence of their fellow-citizens in every part of the Union, and must strengthen the general determination to protect them efficaciously under all circumstances which may occur.

Having received information that in another part of the United States a great number of private individuals were combining together, arming and organizing themselves contrary to law, to carry on military expeditions against the territories of Spain, I thought it necessary, by proclamations as well as by special orders, to take measures for preventing and suppressing this enterprise, for seizing the vessels, arms, and other means provided for it, and for arresting and bringing to justice its authors and abettors. It was due to that good faith which ought ever to be the rule of action in public as well as in private transactions; it was due to good order and regular government, that while the public force was acting strictly on the defensive and merely to protect our citizens from aggression, the criminal attempts of private individuals to decide for their country the question of peace or war, by commencing active and unauthorized hostilities, should be promptly and efficaciously suppressed.

Whether it will be necessary to enlarge our regular force will depend on the result of our negotiation with Spain; but as it is uncertain when that result will be known, the provisional measures requisite for that, and to meet any pressure intervening in that quarter, will be a subject for your early consideration.

The possession of both banks of the Mississippi reducing to a single point the defence of that river, its waters, and the country adjacent, it becomes highly necessary to provide for that point a more adequate security. Some position above its mouth, commanding the passage of the river, should be rendered sufficiently strong to cover the armed vessels which may be stationed there for defence, and in conjunction with them to present an insuperable obstacle to any force attempting to pass. The approaches to the city of New Orleans, from the eastern quarter also, will require to be examined, and more effectually guarded. For the internal support of the country, the encouragement of a strong settlement on the western side of the Mississippi, within reach of New Orleans, will be worthy the consideration of the legislature.

The gun-boats authorized by an act of the last session are so advanced that they will be ready for service in the ensuing spring. Circumstances permitted us to allow the time necessary for their more solid construction. As a much larger number will still be wanting to place our seaport towns and waters in that state of defence to which we are competent and they entitled, a similar appropriation for a further provision for them is recommended for the ensuing year.

A further appropriation will also be necessary for repairing fortifications already established, and the erection of such works as may have real effect in obstructing the approach of an enemy to our seaport towns, or their remaining before them.

In a country whose constitution is derived from the will of the people, directly expressed by their free suffrages; where the principal executive functionaries, and those of the legislature, are renewed by them at short periods; where under the characters of jurors, they exercise in person the greatest portion of the judiciary powers; where the laws are consequently so formed and administered as to bear with equal weight and favor on all, restraining no man in the pursuits of honest industry, and securing to everyone the property which that acquires, it would not be supposed that any safeguards could be needed against insurrection or enterprise on the public peace or authority. The laws, however, aware that these should not be trusted to moral restraints only, have wisely provided punishments for these crimes when committed. But would it not be salutary to give also the means of preventing their commission? Where an enterprise is meditated by private individuals against a foreign nation in amity with the United States, powers of prevention to a certain extent are given by the laws; would they not be as reasonable and useful were the enterprise preparing against the United States? While adverting to this branch of the law, it is proper to observe, that in enterprises meditated against foreign nations, the ordinary process of binding to the observance of the peace and good behavior, could it be extended to acts to be done out of the jurisdiction of the United States, would be effectual in some cases where the offender is able to keep out of sight every indication of his purpose which could draw on him the exercise of the powers now given by law.

The states on the coast of Barbary seem generally disposed at present to respect our peace and friendship; with Tunis alone some uncertainty remains. Persuaded that it is our interest to maintain our peace with them on equal terms, or not at all, I propose to send in due time a reinforcement into the Mediterranean, unless previous information shall show it to be unnecessary.

We continue to receive proofs of the growing attachment of our Indian neighbors, and of their disposition to place all their interests under the patronage of the United States. These dispositions are inspired by their confidence in our justice, and in the sincere concern we feel for their welfare; and as long as we discharge these high and honorable functions with the integrity and good faith which alone can entitle us to their continuance, we may expect to reap the just reward in their peace and friendship.

The expedition of Messrs. Lewis and Clarke, for exploring the river Missouri, and the best communication from that to the Pacific ocean, has had all the success which could have been expected. They have traced the Missouri nearly to its source, descended the Columbia to the Pacific ocean, ascertained with accuracy the geography of that interesting communication across our continent, learned the character of the country, of its commerce, and inhabitants; and it is but justice to say that Messrs. Lewis and Clarke, and their brave companions, have by this arduous service deserved well of their country.

The attempt to explore the Red river, under the direction of Mr. Freeman, though conducted with a zeal and prudence meriting entire approbation, has not been equally successful. After proceeding up it about six hundred miles, nearly as far as the French settlements had extended while the country was in their possession, our geographers were obliged to return without completing their work.

Very useful additions have also been made to our knowledge of the Mississippi by Lieutenant Pike, who has ascended to its source, and whose journal and map, giving the details of the journey, will shortly be ready for communication to both houses of Congress. Those of Messrs. Lewis and Clarke, and Freeman, will require further time to be digested and prepared. These important surveys, in addition to those before possessed, furnish materials for commencing an accurate map of the Mississippi, and its western waters. Some principal rivers, however, remain still to be explored, toward which the authorization of Congress, by moderate appropriations, will be requisite.

I congratulate you, fellow citizens, on the approach of the period at which you may interpose your authority constitutionally, to withdraw the citizens of the United States from all further participation in those violations of human rights which have been so long continued on the unoffending inhabitants of Africa, and which the morality, the reputation, and the best interests of our country, have long been eager to proscribe. Although no law you may pass can take prohibitory effect till the first day of the year one thousand eight hundred and eight, yet the intervening period is not too long to prevent, by timely notice, expeditions which cannot be completed before that day.

The receipts at the treasury during the year ending on the 30th of September last, have amounted to near fifteen millions of dollars, which have enabled us, after meeting the current demands, to pay two millions seven hundred thousand dollars of the American claims, in parts of the price of Louisiana; to pay of the funded debt upward of three millions of principal, and nearly four of interest; and in addition, to reimburse, in the course of the present month, near two millions of five and a half per cent stock. These payments and reimbursements of the funded debt, with those which have been made in four years and a half preceding, will, at the close of the present year, have extinguished upward of twenty-three millions of principal.

The duties composing the Mediterranean fund will cease by law at the end of the present season. Considering, however, that they are levied chiefly on luxuries, and that we have an impost on salt, a necessary of life, the free use of which otherwise is so important, I recommend to your consideration the suppression of the duties on salt, and the continuation of the Mediterranean fund, instead thereof, for a short time, after which that also will become unnecessary for any purpose now within contemplation.

When both of these branches of revenue shall in this way be relinquished, there will still ere long be an accumulation of moneys in the treasury beyond the instalments of public debt which we are permitted by contract to pay. They cannot, then, without a modification assented to by the public creditors, be applied to the extinguishment of this debt, and the complete liberation of our revenues—the most desirable of all objects; nor, if our peace continues, will they be wanting for any other existing purpose. The question, therefore, now comes forward,—to what other objects shall these surpluses be appropriated, and the whole surplus of impost, after the entire discharge of the public debt, and during those intervals when the purposes of war shall not call for them? Shall we suppress the impost and give that advantage to foreign over domestic manufactures? On a few articles of more general and necessary use, the suppression in due season will doubtless be right, but the great mass of the articles on which impost is paid is foreign luxuries, purchased by those only who are rich enough to afford themselves the use of them. Their patriotism would certainly prefer its continuance and application to the great purposes of the public education, roads, rivers, canals, and such other objects of public improvement as it may be thought proper to add to the constitutional enumeration of federal powers. By these operations new channels of communication will be opened between the States; the lines of separation will disappear, their interests will be identified, and their union cemented by new and indissoluble ties. Education is here placed among the articles of public care, not that it would be proposed to take its ordinary branches out of the hands of private enterprise, which manages so much better all the concerns to which it is equal; but a public institution can alone supply those sciences which, though rarely called for, are yet necessary to complete the circle, all the parts of which contribute to the improvement of the country, and some of them to its preservation. The subject is now proposed for the consideration of Congress, because, if approved by the time the State legislatures shall have deliberated on this extension of the federal trusts, and the laws shall be passed, and other arrangements made for their execution, the necessary funds will be on hand and without employment. I suppose an amendment to the constitution, by consent of the States, necessary, because the objects now recommended are not among those enumerated in the constitution, and to which it permits the public moneys to be applied.

The present consideration of a national establishment for education, particularly, is rendered proper by this circumstance also, that if Congress, approving the proposition, shall yet think it more eligible to found it on a donation of lands, they have it now in their power to endow it with those which will be among the earliest to produce the necessary income. This foundation would have the advantage of being independent on war, which may suspend other improvements by requiring for its own purposes the resources destined for them.

This, fellow citizens, is the state of the public interest at the present moment, and according to the information now possessed. But such is the situation of the nations of Europe, and such too the predicament in which we stand with some of them, that we cannot rely with certainty on the present aspect of our affairs that may change from moment to moment, during the course of your session or after you shall have separated. Our duty is, therefore, to act upon things as they are, and to make a reasonable provision for whatever they may be. Were armies to be raised whenever a speck of war is visible in our horizon, we never should have been without them. Our resources would have been exhausted on dangers which have never happened, instead of being reserved for what is really to take place. A steady, perhaps a quickened pace in preparations for the defence of our seaport towns and waters; an early settlement of the most exposed and vulnerable parts of our country; a militia so organized that its effective portions can be called to any point in the Union, or volunteers instead of them to serve a sufficient time, are means which may always be ready yet never preying on our resources until actually called into use. They will maintain the public interests while a more permanent force shall be in course of preparation. But much will depend on the promptitude with which these means can be brought into activity. If war be forced upon us in spite of our long and vain appeals to the justice of nations, rapid and vigorous movements in its outset will go far toward securing us in its course and issue, and toward throwing its burdens on those who render necessary the resort from reason to force.

The result of our negotiations, or such incidents in their course as may enable us to infer their probable issue; such further movements also on our western frontiers as may show whether war is to be pressed there while negotiation is protracted elsewhere, shall be communicated to you from time to time as they become known to me, with whatever other information I possess or may receive, which may aid your deliberations on the great national interests committed to your charge.

## SPECIAL MESSAGE

January 22, 1807

TO THE SENATE AND HOUSE OF REPRESENTATIVES OF THE UNITED STATES: Agreeably to the request of the House of Representatives, communicated in their resolution of the sixteenth instant, I proceed to state under the reserve therein expressed, information received touching an illegal combination of private individuals against the peace and safety of the Union, and a military expedition planned by them against the territories of a power in amity with the United States, with the measures I have pursued for suppressing the same.

I had for some time been in the constant expectation of receiving such further information as would have enabled me to lay before the legislature the termination as well as the beginning and progress of this scene of depravity, so far as it has been acted on the Ohio and its waters. From this the state and safety of the lower country might have been estimated on probable grounds, and the delay was indulged the rather, because no circumstance had yet made it necessary to call in the aid of the legislative functions. Information now recently communicated has brought us nearly to the period contemplated. The mass of what I have received, in the course of these transactions, is voluminous, but little has been given under the sanction of an oath, so as to constitute formal and legal evidence. It is chiefly in the form of letters, often containing such a mixture of rumors, conjectures, and suspicions, as render it difficult to sift out the real facts, and unadvisable to hazard more than general outlines, strengthened by concurrent information, or the particular credibility of the relater. In this state of the evidence, delivered sometimes too under the restriction of private confidence, neither safety nor justice will permit the exposing names, except that of the principal actor, whose guilt is placed beyond question.

Some time in the latter part of September, I received intimations that designs were in agitation in the western country, unlawful and unfriendly to the peace of the Union; and that the prime mover in these was Aaron Burr, heretofore distinguished by the favor of his country. The grounds of these intimations being inconclusive, the objects uncertain, and the fidelity of that country known to be firm, the only measure taken was to urge the informants to use their best endeavors to get further insight into the designs and proceedings of the suspected persons, and to communicate them to me.

It was not until the latter part of October, that the objects of the conspiracy began to be perceived, but still so blended and involved in mystery that nothing distinct could be singled out for pursuit. In this state of uncertainty as to the crime contemplated, the acts done, and the legal course to be pursued, I thought it best to send to the scene where these things were principally in transaction, a person, in whose integrity, understanding, and discretion, entire confidence could be reposed, with instructions to investigate the plots going on, to enter into conference (for which he had sufficient credentials) with the governors and all other officers, civil and military, and with their aid to do on the spot whatever should be necessary to discover the designs of the conspirators, arrest their means, bring their persons to punishment, and to call out the force of the country to suppress any unlawful enterprise in which it should be found they were engaged. By this time it was known that many boats were under preparation, stores of provisions collecting, and an unusual number of suspicious characters in motion on the Ohio and its waters. Besides despatching the confidential agent to that quarter, orders were at the same time sent to the governors of the Orleans and Mississippi territories, and to the commanders of the land and naval forces there, to be on their guard against surprise, and in constant readiness to resist any enterprise which might be attempted on the vessels, posts, or other objects under their care; and on the 8th of November, instructions were forwarded to General Wilkinson to hasten an accommodation with the Spanish commander on the Sabine, and as soon as that was effected, to fall back with his principal force to the hither bank of the Mississippi, for the defence of the intersecting points on that river. By a letter received from that officer on the 25th of November, but dated October 21st, we learn that a confidential agent of Aaron Burr had been deputed to him, with communications partly written in cipher and partly oral, explaining his designs, exaggerating his resources, and making such offers of emolument and command, to engage him and the army in his unlawful enterprise, as he had flattered himself would be successful. The general, with the honor of a soldier and fidelity of a good citizen, immediately despatched a trusty officer to me with information of what had passed, proceeding to establish such an understanding with the Spanish commandant on the Sabine as permitted him to withdraw his force across the Mississippi, and to enter on measures for opposing the projected enterprise.

The general's letter, which came to hand on the 25th of November, as has been mentioned, and some other information received a few days earlier, when brought together, developed Burr's general designs, different parts of which only had been revealed to different informants. It appeared that he contemplated two distinct objects, which might be carried on either jointly or separately, and either the one or the other first, as circumstances should direct. One of these was the severance of the Union of these States by the Alleghany mountains; the other, an attack on Mexico. A third object was provided, merely ostensible, to wit: the settlement of a pretended purchase of a tract of country on the Washita, claimed by a Baron Bastrop. This was to serve as the pretext for all his preparations, an allurement for such followers as really wished to acquire settlements in that country, and a cover under which to retreat in the event of final discomfiture of both branches of his real design.

He found at once that the attachment of the western country to the present Union was not to be shaken; that its dissolution could not be effected with the consent of its inhabitants, and that his resources were inadequate, as yet, to effect it by force. He took his course then at once, determined to seize on New Orleans, plunder the bank there, possess himself of the military and naval stores, and proceed on his expedition to Mexico; and to this object all his means and preparations were now directed. He collected from all the quarters where himself or his agents possessed influence, all the ardent, restless, desperate, and disaffected persons who were ready for any enterprise analogous to their characters. He seduced good and well-meaning citizens, some by assurances that he possessed the confidence of the government and was acting under its secret patronage, a pretence which obtained some credit from the state of our differences with Spain; and others by offers of land in Bastrop's claim on the Washita.

This was the state of my information of his proceedings about the last of November, at which time, therefore, it was first possible to take specific measures to meet them. The proclamation of November 27th, two days after the receipt of General Wilkinson's information, was now issued. Orders were despatched to every intersecting point on the Ohio and Mississippi, from Pittsburg to New Orleans, for the employment of such force either of the regulars or of the militia, and of such proceedings also of the civil authorities, as might enable them to seize on all the boats and stores provided for the enterprise, to arrest the persons concerned, and to suppress effectually the further progress of the enterprise. A little before the receipt of these orders in the State of Ohio, our confidential agent, who had been diligently employed in investigating the conspiracy, had acquired sufficient information to open himself to the governor of that State, and apply for the immediate exertion of the authority and power of the State to crush the combination. Governor Tiffin and the legislature, with a promptitude, an energy, and patriotic zeal, which entitle them to a distinguished place in the affection of their sister States, effected the seizure of all the boats, provisions, and other preparations within their reach, and thus gave a first blow, materially disabling the enterprise in its outset.

In Kentucky, a premature attempt to bring Burr to justice, without sufficient evidence for his conviction, had produced a popular impression in his favor, and a general disbelief of his guilt. This gave him an unfortunate opportunity of hastening his equipments. The arrival of the proclamation and orders, and the application and information of our confidential agent, at length awakened the authorities of that State to the truth, and then produced the same promptitude and energy of which the neighboring State had set the example. Under an act of their legislature of December 23d, militia was instantly ordered to different important points, and measures taken for doing whatever could yet be done. Some boats (accounts vary from five to double or treble that number) and persons (differently estimated from one to three hundred) had in the meantime passed the falls of the Ohio, to rendezvous at the mouth of the Cumberland, with others expected down that river.

Not apprized, till very late, that any boats were building on Cumberland, the effect of the proclamation had been trusted to for some time in the State of Tennessee; but on the 19th of December, similar communications and instructions with those of the neighboring States were despatched by express to the governor, and a general officer of the western division of the State, and on the 23d of December our confidential agent left Frankfort for Nashville, to put into activity the means of that State also. But by information received yesterday, I learn that on the 22d of December, Mr. Burr descended the Cumberland with two boats merely of accommodation, carrying with him from that State no quota toward his unlawful enterprise. Whether after the arrival of the proclamation, of the orders, or of our agent, any exertion which could be made by that State, or the orders of the governor of Kentucky for calling out the militia at the mouth of Cumberland, would be in time to arrest these boats, and those from the falls of the Ohio, is still doubtful.

On the whole, the fugitives from Ohio, with their associates from Cumberland, or any other place in that quarter, cannot threaten serious danger to the city of New Orleans.

By the same express of December nineteenth, orders were sent to the governors of New Orleans and Mississippi, supplementary to those which had been given on the twenty-fifth of November, to hold the militia of their territories in readiness to co-operate for their defence, with the regular troops and armed vessels then under command of General Wilkinson. Great alarm, indeed, was excited at New Orleans by the exaggerated accounts of Mr. Burr, disseminated through his emissaries, of the armies and navies he was to assemble there. General Wilkinson had arrived there himself on the 24th of November, and had immediately put into activity the resources of the place for the purpose of its defence; and on the tenth of December he was joined by his troops from the Sabine. Great zeal was shown by the inhabitants generally, the merchants of the place readily agreeing to the most laudable exertions and sacrifices for manning the armed vessels with their seamen, and the other citizens manifesting unequivocal fidelity to the Union, and a spirit of determined resistance to their expected assailants.

Surmises have been hazarded that this enterprise is to receive aid from certain foreign powers. But these surmises are without proof or probability. The wisdom of the measures sanctioned by Congress at its last session had placed us in the paths of peace and justice with the only powers with whom we had any differences, and nothing has happened since which makes it either their interest or ours to pursue another course. No change of measures has taken place on our part; none ought to take place at this time. With the one, friendly arrangement was then proposed, and the law deemed necessary on the failure of that was suspended to give time for a fair trial of the issue. With the same power, negotiation is still preferred, and provisional measures only are necessary to meet the event of rupture. While, therefore, we do not deflect in the slightest degree from the course we then assumed, and are still pursuing, with mutual consent, to restore a good understanding, we are not to impute to them practices as irreconcilable to interest as to good faith, and changing necessarily the relations of peace and justice between us to those of war. These surmises are, therefore, to be imputed to the vauntings of the author of this enterprise, to multiply his partisans by magnifying the belief of his prospects and support.

By letters from General Wilkinson, of the 14th and 18th of September, which came to hand two days after date of the resolution of the House of Representatives, that is to say, on the morning of the 18th instant, I received the important affidavit, a copy of which I now communicate, with extracts of so much of the letters as come within the scope of the resolution. By these it will be seen that of three of the principal emissaries of Mr. Burr, whom the general had caused to be apprehended, one had been liberated by *habeas corpus,* and the two others, being those particularly employed in the endeavor to corrupt the general and army of the United States, have been embarked by him for our ports in the Atlantic States, probably on the consideration that an impartial trial could not be expected during the present agitations of New Orleans, and that that city was not as yet a safe place of confinement. As soon as these persons shall arrive, they will be delivered to the custody of the law, and left to such course of trial, both as to place and process, as its functionaries may direct. The presence of the highest judicial authorities, to be assembled at this place within a few days, the means of pursuing a sounder course of proceedings here than elsewhere, and the aid of the executive means, should the judges have occasion to use them, render it equally desirable for the criminals as for the public, that being already removed from the place where they were first apprehended, the first regular arrest should take place here, and the course of proceedings receive here its proper direction.

## SPECIAL MESSAGE

### February 10, 1807

TO THE SENATE AND HOUSE OF REPRESENTATIVES OF THE UNITED STATES: In compliance with the request of the House of Representatives, expressed in their resolution of the 5th instant, I proceed to give such information as is possessed, of the effect of gun-boats in the protection and defence of harbors, of the numbers thought necessary, and of the proposed distribution of them among the ports and harbors of the United States.

Under the present circumstances, and governed by the intentions of the legislature, as manifested by their annual appropriations of money for the purposes of defence, it has been concluded to combine—1st, land batteries, furnished with heavy cannon and mortars, and established on all the points around the place favorable for preventing vessels from lying before it; 2d, movable artillery which may be carried, as an occasion may require, to points unprovided with fixed batteries; 3d, floating batteries; and 4th, gun-boats, which may oppose an enemy at its entrance and co-operate with the batteries for his expulsion.

On this subject professional men were consulted as far as we had opportunity. General Wilkinson, and the late General Gates, gave their opinions in writing, in favor of the system, as will be seen by their letters now communicated. The higher officers of the navy gave the same opinions in separate conferences, as their presence at the seat of government offered occasions of consulting them, and no difference of judgment appeared on the subjects. Those of Commodore Barron and Captain Tingey, now here, are recently furnished in writing, and transmitted herewith to the legislature.

The efficacy of gun-boats for the defence of harbors, and of other smooth and enclosed waters, may be estimated in part from that of galleys, formerly much used, but less powerful, more costly in their construction and maintenance, and requiring more men. But the gun-boat itself is believed to be in use with every modern maritime nation for the purpose of defence. In the Mediterranean, on which are several small powers, whose system like ours is peace and defence, few harbors are without this article of protection. Our own experience there of the effect of gun-boats for harbor service, is recent. Algiers is particularly known to have owed to a great provision of these vessels the safety of its city, since the epoch of their construction. Before that it had been repeatedly insulted and injured. The effect of gun-boats at present in the neighborhood of Gibraltar, is well known, and how much they were used both in the attack and defence of that place during a former war. The extensive resort to them by the two greatest naval powers in the world, on an enterprise of invasion not long since in prospect, shows their confidence in their efficacy for the purposes for which they are suited. By the northern powers of Europe, whose seas are particularly adapted to them, they are still more used. The remarkable action between the Russian flotilla of gun-boats and galleys, and a Turkish fleet of ships-of-the-line and frigates, in the Liman sea, 1788, will be readily recollected. The latter, commanded by their most celebrated admiral, were completely defeated, and several of their ships-of-the-line destroyed.

From the opinions given as to the number of gun-boats necessary for some of the principal seaports, and from a view of all the towns and ports from Orleans to Maine inclusive, entitled to protection, in proportion to their situation and circumstances, it is concluded, that to give them a due measure of protection in time of war, about two hundred gun-boats will be requisite. According to first ideas, the following would be their general distribution, liable to be varied on more mature examination, and as circumstances shall vary, that is to say:

To the Mississippi and its neighboring waters, forty gun-boats.

To Savannah and Charleston, and the harbors on each side, from St. Mary's to Currituck, twenty-five.

To the Chesapeake and its waters, twenty.

To Delaware bay and river, fifteen.

To New York, the Sound, and waters as far as Cape Cod, fifty.

To Boston and the harbors north of Cape Cod, fifty.

The flotilla assigned to these several stations, might each be under the care of a particular commandant, and the vessels composing them would, in ordinary, be distributed among the harbors within the station in proportion to their importance.

Of these boats a proper proportion would be of the larger size, such as those heretofore built, capable of navigating any seas, and of reinforcing occasionally the strength of even the most distant port when menaced with danger. The residue would be confined to their own or the neighboring harbors, would be smaller, less furnished for accommodation, and consequently less costly. Of the number supposed necessary, seventy-three are built or building, and the hundred and twenty-seven still to be provided, would cost from five to six hundred thousand dollars. Having regard to the convenience of the treasury, as well as to the resources of building, it has been thought that one half of these might be built in the present year, and the other year the next. With the legislature, however, it will rest to stop where we are, or at any further point, when they shall be of opinion that the number provided shall be sufficient for the object.

At times when Europe as well as the United States shall be at peace, it would not be proposed that more than six or eight of these vessels should be kept afloat. When Europe is in war, treble that number might be necessary to be distributed among those particular harbors which foreign vessels of war are in the habit of frequenting, for the purpose of preserving order therein.

But they would be manned, in ordinary, with only their complement for navigation, relying on the seamen and militia of the port if called into action on sudden emergency. It would be only when the United States should themselves be at war, that the whole number would be brought into actual service, and would be ready in the first moments of the war to co-operate with other means for covering at once the line of our seaports. At all times, those unemployed would be withdrawn into places not exposed to sudden enterprise, hauled up under sheds from the sun and weather, and kept in preservation with little expense for repairs or maintenance.

It must be superfluous to observe, that this species of naval armament is proposed merely for defensive operation; that it can have but little effect toward protecting our commerce in the open seas even on our coast; and still less can it become an excitement to engage in offensive maritime war, toward which it would furnish no means.

## SEVENTH ANNUAL MESSAGE

October 27, 1807

TO THE SENATE AND HOUSE OF REPRESENTATIVES OF THE UNITED STATES: Circumstances, fellow citizens, which seriously threatened the peace of our country, have made it a duty to convene you at an earlier period than usual. The love of peace, so much cherished in the bosoms of our citizens, which has so long guided the proceedings of the public councils, and induced forbearance under so many wrongs, may not insure our continuance in the quiet pursuits of industry. The many injuries and depredations committed on our commerce and navigation upon the high seas for years past, the successive innovations on those principles of public law which have been established by the reason and usage of nations as the rule of their intercourse, and the umpire and security of their rights and peace, and all the circumstances which induced the extraordinary mission to London, are already known to you. The instructions given to our ministers were framed in the sincerest spirit of amity and moderation. They accordingly proceeded, in conformity therewith, to propose arrangements which might embrace and settle all the points in difference between us, which might bring us to a mutual understanding on our neutral and national rights, and provide for a commercial intercourse on conditions of some equality. After long and fruitless endeavors to effect the purposes of their mission, and to obtain arrangements within the limits of their instructions, they concluded to sign such as could be obtained, and to send them for consideration, candidly declaring to the other negotiators, at the same time, that they were acting against their instructions, and that their government, therefore, could not be pledged for ratification. Some of the articles proposed might have been admitted on a principle of compromise, but others were too highly disadvantageous, and no sufficient provision was made against the principal source of the irritations and collisions which were constantly endangering the peace of the two nations. The question, therefore, whether a treaty should be accepted in that form could have admitted but of one decision, even had no declarations of the other party impaired our confidence in it. Still anxious not to close the door against friendly adjustment, new modifications were framed, and further concessions authorized than could before have been supposed necessary; and our ministers were instructed to resume their negotiations on these grounds. On this new reference to amicable discussion, we were reposing in confidence, when on the 22d day of June last, by a formal order from the British admiral, the frigate Chesapeake, leaving her port for distant service, was attacked by one of those vessels which had been lying in our harbors under the indulgences of hospitality, was disabled from proceeding, had several of her crew killed, and four taken away. On this outrage no commentaries are necessary. Its character has been pronounced by the indignant voice of our citizens with an emphasis and unanimity never exceeded. I immediately, by proclamation, interdicted our harbors and waters to all British armed vessels, forbade intercourse with them, and uncertain how far hostilities were intended, and the town of Norfolk, indeed, being threatened with immediate attack, a sufficient force was ordered for the protection of that place, and such other preparations commenced and pursued as the prospect rendered proper. An armed vessel of the United States was despatched with instructions to our ministers at London to call on that government for the satisfaction and security required by the outrage. A very short interval ought now to bring the answer, which shall be communicated to you as soon as received; then also, or as soon after as the public interests shall be found to admit, the unratified treaty, and the proceedings relative to it, shall be made known to you.

The aggression thus begun has been continued on the part of the British commanders, by remaining within our waters, in defiance of the authority of the country, by habitual violations of its jurisdiction, and at length by putting to death one of the persons whom they had forcibly taken from on board the Chesapeake. These aggravations necessarily lead to the policy, either of never admitting an armed vessel into our harbors, or of maintaining in every harbor such an armed force as may constrain obedience to the laws, and protect the lives and property of our citizens, against their armed guests. But the expense of such a standing force, and its inconsistence with our principles, dispense with those courtesies which would necessarily call for it, and leave us equally free to exclude the navy, as we are the army, of a foreign power, from entering our limits.

To former violations of maritime rights, another is now added of very extensive effect. The government of that nation has issued an order interdicting all trade by neutrals between ports not in amity with them; and being now at war with nearly every nation on the Atlantic and Mediterranean seas, our vessels are required to sacrifice their cargoes at the first port they touch, or to return home without the benefit of going to any other market. Under this new law of the ocean, our trade on the Mediterranean has been swept away by seizures and condemnations, and that in other seas is threatened with the same fate.

Our differences with Spain remain still unsettled; no measure having been taken on her part, since my last communication to Congress, to bring them to a close. But under a state of things which may favor a reconsideration, they have been recently pressed, and an expectation is entertained that they may now soon be brought to an issue of some sort. With their subjects on our borders, no new collisions have taken place nor seem immediately to be apprehended. To our former grounds of complaint has been added a very serious one, as you will see by the decree, a copy of which is now communicated. Whether this decree, which professes to be conformable to that of the French government of November 21st, 1806, heretofore communicated to Congress, will also be conformed to that in its construction and application in relation to the United States, had not been ascertained at the date of our last communications. These, however, gave reason to expect such a conformity.

With the other nations of Europe our harmony has been uninterrupted, and commerce and friendly intercourse have been maintained on their usual footing.

Our peace with the several States on the coast of Barbary appears as firm as at any former period, and is as likely to continue as that of any other nation.

Among our Indian neighbors in the north-western quarter, some fermentation was observed soon after the late occurrences, threatening the continuance of our peace. Messages were said to be interchanged, and tokens to be passing, which usually denote a state of restlessness among them, and the character of the agitators pointed to the sources of excitement. Measures were immediately taken for providing against that danger; instructions were given to require explanations, and with assurances of our continued friendship, to admonish the tribes to remain quiet at home, taking no part in quarrels not belonging to them. As far as we are yet informed, the tribes in our vicinity, who are most advanced in the pursuits of industry, are sincerely disposed to adhere to their friendship with us, and to their peace with all others; while those more remote do not present appearances sufficiently quiet to justify the intermission of military precaution on our part.

The great tribes on our south-western quarter, much advanced beyond the others in agriculture and household arts, appear tranquil, and identifying their views with ours, in proportion to their advancement. With the whole of these people, in every quarter, I shall continue to inculcate peace and friendship with all their neighbors, and perseverance in those occupations and pursuits which will best promote their own well-being.

The appropriations of the last session, for the defence of our seaport towns and harbors, were made under expectation that a continuance of our peace would permit us to proceed in that work according to our convenience. It has been thought better to apply the sums then given, toward the defence of New York, Charleston, and New Orleans chiefly, as most open and most likely first to need protection; and to leave places less immediately in danger to the provisions of the present session.

The gun-boats, too, already provided, have on a like principle been chiefly assigned to New York, New Orleans, and the Chesapeake. Whether our movable force on the water, so material in aid of the defensive works on the land, should be augmented in this or any other form, is left to the wisdom of the legislature. For the purpose of manning these vessels in sudden attacks on our harbors, it is a matter for consideration, whether the seamen of the United States may not justly be formed into a special militia, to be called on for tours of duty in defence of the harbors where they shall happen to be; the ordinary militia of the place furnishing that portion which may consist of landsmen.

The moment our peace was threatened, I deemed it indispensable to secure a greater provision of those articles of military stores with which our magazines were not sufficiently furnished. To have awaited a previous and special sanction by law would have lost occasions which might not be retrieved. I did not hesitate, therefore, to authorize engagements for such supplements to our existing stock as would render it adequate to the emergencies threatening us; and I trust that the legislature, feeling the same anxiety for the safety of our country, so materially advanced by this precaution, will approve, when done, what they would have seen so important to be done if then assembled. Expenses, also unprovided for, arose out of the necessity of calling all our gun-boats into actual service for the defence of our harbors; of all which accounts will be laid before you.

Whether a regular army is to be raised, and to what extent, must depend on the information so shortly expected. In the meantime, I have called on the States for quotas of militia, to be in readiness for present defence; and have, moreover, encouraged the acceptance of volunteers; and I am happy to inform you that these have offered themselves with great alacrity in every part of the Union. They are ordered to be organized, and ready at a moment's warning to proceed on any service to which they may be called, and every preparation within the executive powers has been made to insure us the benefit of early exertions.

I informed Congress at their last session of the enterprises against the public peace, which were believed to be in preparation by Aaron Burr and his associates, of the measures taken to defeat them, and to bring the offenders to justice. Their enterprises were happily defeated by the patriotic exertions of the militia wherever called into action, by the fidelity of the army, and energy of the commander-in-chief in promptly arranging the difficulties presenting themselves on the Sabine, repairing to meet those arising on the Mississippi, and dissipating, before their explosion, plots engendering there. I shall think it my duty to lay before you the proceedings and the evidence publicly exhibited on the arraignment of the principal offenders before the circuit court of Virginia. You will be enabled to judge whether the defeat was in the testimony, in the law, or in the administration of the law; and wherever it shall be found, the legislature alone can apply or originate the remedy. The framers of our constitution certainly supposed they had guarded, as well their government against destruction by treason, as their citizens against oppression, under pretence of it; and if these ends are not attained, it is of importance to inquire by what means, more effectual, they may be secured.

The accounts of the receipts of revenue, during the year ending on the thirtieth day of September last, being not yet made up, a correct statement will be hereafter transmitted from the treasury. In the meantime, it is ascertained that the receipts have amounted to near sixteen millions of dollars, which, with the five millions and a half in the treasury at the beginning of the year, have enabled us, after meeting the current demands and interest incurred, to pay more than four millions of the principal of our funded debt. These payments, with those of the preceding five and a half years, have extinguished of the funded debt twenty-five millions and a half of dollars, being the whole which could be paid or purchased within the limits of the law and of our contracts, and have left us in the treasury eight millions and a half of dollars. A portion of this sum may be considered as a commencement of accumulation of the surpluses of revenue, which, after paying the instalments of debts as they shall become payable, will remain without any specific object. It may partly, indeed, be applied toward completing the defence of the exposed points of our country, on such a scale as shall be adapted to our principles and circumstances. This object is doubtless among the first entitled to attention, in such a state of our finances, and it is one which, whether we have peace or war, will provide security where it is due. Whether what shall remain of this, with the future surpluses, may be usefully applied to purposes already authorized, or more usefully to others requiring new authorities, or how otherwise they shall be disposed of, are questions calling for the notice of Congress, unless indeed they shall be superseded by a change in our public relations now awaiting the determination of others. Whatever be that determination, it is a great consolation that it will become known at a moment when the supreme council of the nation is assembled at its post, and ready to give the aids of its wisdom and authority to whatever course the good of our country shall then call us to pursue.

Matters of minor importance will be the subjects of future communications; and nothing shall be wanting on my part which may give information or despatch to the proceedings of the legislature in the exercise of their high duties, and at a moment so interesting to the public welfare.

## SPECIAL MESSAGE

### January 20, 1808

TO THE HOUSE OF REPRESENTATIVES OF THE UNITED STATES: Some days previous to your resolution of the 13th instant, a court of inquiry had been instituted at the request of General Wilkinson, charged to make the inquiry into his conduct which the first resolution desires, and had commenced their proceedings. To the judge-advocate of that court the papers and information on that subject, transmitted to me by the House of Representatives, have been delivered, to be used according to the rules and powers of that court.

The request of a communication of any information, which may have been received at any time since the establishment of the present government, touching combinations with foreign nations for dismembering the Union, or the corrupt receipt of money by any officer of the United States from the agents of foreign governments, can be complied with but in a partial degree.

It is well understood that, in the first or second year of the presidency of General Washington, information was given to him relating to certain combinations with the agents of a foreign government for the dismemberment of the Union; which combinations had taken place before the establishment of the present federal government. This information, however, is believed never to have been deposited in any public office, or left in that of the president's secretary, these having been duly examined, but to have been considered as personally confidential, and, therefore, retained among his private papers. A communication from the governor of Virginia to General Washington, is found in the office of the president's secretary, which, although not strictly within the terms of the request of the House of Representatives, is communicated, inasmuch as it may throw some light on the subjects of the correspondence of that time, between certain foreign agents and citizens of the United States.

In the first or second year of the administration of President Adams, Andrew Ellicott, then employed in designating, in conjunction with the Spanish authorities, the boundaries between the territories of the United States and Spain, under the treaty with that nation, communicated to the executive of the United States papers and information respecting the subjects of the present inquiry, which were deposited in the office of State. Copies of these are now transmitted to the House of Representatives, except of a single letter and a reference from the said Andrew Ellicott, which being expressly desired to be kept secret, is therefore not communicated, but its contents can be obtained from himself in a more legal form, and directions have been given to summon him to appear as a witness before the court of inquiry.

A paper "on the commerce of Louisiana," bearing date of the 18th of April, 1798, is found in the office of State, supposed to have been communicated by Mr. Daniel Clark, of New Orleans, then a subject of Spain, and now of the House of Representatives of the United States, stating certain commercial transactions of General Wilkinson, in New Orleans; an extract from this is now communicated, because it contains facts which may have some bearing on the questions relating to him.

The destruction of the war-office, by fire, in the close of 1800, involved all information it contained at that date.

The papers already described, therefore, constitute the whole information on the subjects, deposited in the public offices, during the preceding administrations, as far as has yet been found; but it cannot be affirmed that there may be no others, because, the papers of the office being filed, for the most part, alphabetically, unless aided by the suggestion of any particular name which may have given such information, nothing short of a careful examination of the papers in the offices generally, could authorize such affirmation.

About a twelvemonth after I came to the administration of the government, Mr. Clark gave some verbal information to myself, as well as to the Secretary of State, relating to the same combinations for the dismemberment of the Union. He was listened to freely, and he then delivered the letter of Governor Gagoso, addressed to himself, of which a copy is now communicated. After his return to New Orleans, he forwarded to the Secretary of State other papers, with a request that, after perusal, they should be burned. This, however, was not done, and he was so informed by the Secretary of State, and that they would be held subject to his order. These papers have not yet been found in the office. A letter, therefore, has been addressed to the former chief clerk, who may, perhaps, give information respecting them. As far as our memories enable us to say, they related only to the combinations before spoken of, and not at all to the corrupt receipt of money by any officer of the United States; consequently, they respected what was considered as a dead matter, known to the preceding administrations, and offering nothing new to call for investigations, which those nearest the dates of the transactions had not thought proper to institute.

In the course of the communications made to me on the subject of the conspiracy of Aaron Burr, I sometimes received letters, some of them anonymous, some under names true or false, expressing suspicions and insinuations against General Wilkinson. But one only of them, and that anonymous, specified any particular fact, and that fact was one of those which had already been communicated to a former administration.

No other information within the purview of the request of the house is known to have been received by any department of the government from the establishment of the present federal government. That which has recently been communicated to the House of Representatives, and by them to me, is the first direct testimony ever made known to me, charging General Wilkinson with the corrupt receipt of money; and the House of Representatives may be assured that the duties which this information devolves on me shall be exercised with rigorous impartiality. Should any want of power in the court to compel the rendering of testimony, obstruct that full and impartial inquiry, which alone can establish guilt or innocence, and satisfy justice, the legislative authority only will be competent to the remedy.

## EIGHTH ANNUAL MESSAGE

November 8, 1808

TO THE SENATE AND HOUSE OF REPRESENTATIVES OF THE UNITED STATES: It would have been a source, fellow citizens, of much gratification, if our last communications from Europe had enabled me to inform you that the belligerent nations, whose disregard of neutral rights has been so destructive to our commerce, had become awakened to the duty and true policy of revoking their unrighteous edicts. That no means might be omitted to produce this salutary effect, I lost no time in availing myself of the act authorizing a suspension, in whole or in part, of the several embargo laws. Our ministers at London and Paris were instructed to explain to the respective governments there, our disposition to exercise the authority in such manner as would withdraw the pretext on which the aggressions were originally founded, and open the way for a renewal of that commercial intercourse which it was alleged on all sides had been reluctantly obstructed. As each of those governments had pledged its readiness to concur in renouncing a measure which reached its adversary through the incontestable rights of neutrals only, and as the measure had been assumed by each as a retaliation for an asserted acquiescence in the aggressions of the other, it was reasonably expected that the occasion would have been seized by both for evincing the sincerity of their profession, and for restoring to the commerce of the United States its legitimate freedom. The instructions to our ministers with respect to the different belligerents were necessarily modified with reference to their different circumstances, and to the condition annexed by law to the executive power of suspension, requiring a degree of security to our commerce which would not result from a repeal of the decrees of France. Instead of a pledge, therefore, of a suspension of the embargo as to her in case of such a repeal, it was presumed that a sufficient inducement might be found in other considerations, and particularly in the change produced by a compliance with our just demands by one belligerent, and a refusal by the other, in the relations between the other and the United States. To Great Britain, whose power on the ocean is so ascendant, it was deemed not inconsistent with that condition to state explicitly, that on her rescinding her orders in relation to the United States their trade would be opened with her, and remain shut to her enemy, in case of his failure to rescind his decrees also. From France no answer has been received, nor any indication that the requisite change in her decrees is contemplated. The favorable reception of the proposition to Great Britain was the less to be doubted, as her orders of council had not only been referred for their vindication to an acquiescence on the part of the United States no longer to be pretended, but as the arrangement proposed, while it resisted the illegal decrees of France, involved, moreover, substantially, the precise advantages professedly aimed at by the British orders. The arrangement has nevertheless been rejected.

This candid and liberal experiment having thus failed, and no other event having occurred on which a suspension of the embargo by the executive was authorized, it necessarily remains in the extent originally given to it. We have the satisfaction, however, to reflect, that in return for the privations by the measure, and which our fellow citizens in general have borne with patriotism, it has had the important effects of saving our mariners and our vast mercantile property, as well as of affording time for prosecuting the defensive and provisional measures called for by the occasion. It has demonstrated to foreign nations the moderation and firmness which govern our councils, and to our citizens the necessity of uniting in support of the laws and the rights of their country, and has thus long frustrated those usurpations and spoliations which, if resisted, involve war; if submitted to, sacrificed a vital principle of our national independence.

Under a continuance of the belligerent measures which, in defiance of laws which consecrate the rights of neutrals, overspread the ocean with danger, it will rest with the wisdom of Congress to decide on the course best adapted to such a state of things; and bringing with them, as they do, from every part of the Union, the sentiments of our constituents, my confidence is strengthened, that in forming this decision they will, with an unerring regard to the essential rights and interests of the nation, weigh and compare the painful alternatives out of which a choice is to be made. Nor should I do justice to the virtues which on other occasions have marked the character of our fellow citizens, if I did not cherish an equal confidence that the alternative chosen, whatever it may be, will be maintained with all the fortitude and patriotism which the crisis ought to inspire.

The documents containing the correspondences on the subject of the foreign edicts against our commerce, with the instructions given to our ministers at London and Paris, are now laid before you.

The communications made to Congress at their last session explained the posture in which the close of the discussion relating to the attack by a British ship of war on the frigate Chesapeake left a subject on which the nation had manifested so honorable a sensibility. Every view of what had passed authorized a belief that immediate steps would be taken by the British government for redressing a wrong, which, the more it was investigated, appeared the more clearly to require what had not been provided for in the special mission. It is found that no steps have been taken for the purpose. On the contrary, it will be seen, in the documents laid before you, that the inadmissible preliminary which obstructed the adjustment is still adhered to; and, moreover, that it is now brought into connection with the distinct and irrelative case of the orders in council. The instructions which had been given to our ministers at London with a view to facilitate, if necessary, the reparation claimed by the United States, are included in the documents communicated.

Our relations with the other powers of Europe have undergone no material changes since your last session. The important negotiations with Spain, which had been alternately suspended and resumed, necessarily experience a pause under the extraordinary and interesting crisis which distinguished her internal situation.

With the Barbary powers we continue in harmony, with the exception of an unjustifiable proceeding of the dey of Algiers toward our consul to that regency. Its character and circumstances are now laid before you, and will enable you to decide how far it may, either now or hereafter, call for any measures not within the limits of the executive authority.

With our Indian neighbors the public peace has been steadily maintained. Some instances of individual wrong have, as at other times, taken place, but in nowise implicating the will of the nation. Beyond the Mississippi, the Iowas, the Sacs, and the Alabamas, have delivered up for trial and punishment individuals from among themselves accused of murdering citizens of the United States. On this side of the Mississippi, the Creeks are exerting themselves to arrest offenders of the same kind; and the Choctaws have manifested their readiness and desire for amicable and just arrangements respecting depredations committed by disorderly persons of their tribe. And, generally, from a conviction that we consider them as part of ourselves, and cherish with sincerity their rights and interests, the attachment of the Indian tribes is gaining strength daily—is extending from the nearer to the more remote, and will amply requite us for the justice and friendship practised towards them. Husbandry and household manufacture are advancing among them, more rapidly with the southern than the northern tribes, from circumstances of soil and climate; and one of the two great divisions of the Cherokee nation have now under consideration to solicit the citizenship of the United States, and to be identified with us in laws and government, in such progressive manner as we shall think best.

In consequence of the appropriations of the last session of Congress for the security of our seaport towns and harbors, such works of defence have been erected as seemed to be called for by the situation of the several places, their relative importance, and the scale of expense indicated by the amount of the appropriation. These works will chiefly be finished in the course of the present season, except at New York and New Orleans, where most was to be done; and although a great proportion of the last appropriation has been expended on the former place, yet some further views will be submitted to Congress for rendering its security entirely adequate against naval enterprise. A view of what has been done at the several places, and of what is proposed to be done, shall be communicated as soon as the several reports are received.

Of the gun-boats authorized by the act of December last, it has been thought necessary to build only one hundred and three in the present year. These, with those before possessed, are sufficient for the harbors and waters exposed, and the residue will require little time for their construction when it is deemed necessary.

Under the act of the last session for raising an additional military force, so many officers were immediately appointed as were necessary for carrying on the business of recruiting, and in proportion as it advanced, others have been added. We have reason to believe their success has been satisfactory, although such returns have not yet been received as enable me to present to you a statement of the numbers engaged.

I have not thought it necessary in the course of the last season to call for any general detachments of militia or volunteers under the law passed for that purpose. For the ensuing season, however, they will require to be in readiness should their services be wanted. Some small and special detachments have been necessary to maintain the laws of embargo on that portion of our northern frontier which offered peculiar facilities for evasion, but these were replaced as soon as it could be done by bodies of new recruits. By the aid of these, and of the armed vessels called into actual service in other quarters, the spirit of disobedience and abuse which manifested itself early, and with sensible effect while we were unprepared to meet it, has been considerably repressed.

Considering the extraordinary character of the times in which we live, our attention should unremittingly be fixed on the safety of our country. For a people who are free, and who mean to remain so, a well-organized and armed militia is their best security. It is, therefore, incumbent on us, at every meeting, to revise the condition of the militia, and to ask ourselves if it is prepared to repel a powerful enemy at every point of our territories exposed to invasion. Some of the States have paid a laudable attention to this object; but every degree of neglect is to be found among others. Congress alone have power to produce a uniform state of preparation in this great organ of defence; the interests which they so deeply feel in their own and their country's security will present this as among the most important objects of their deliberation.

Under the acts of March 11th and April 23d, respecting arms, the difficulty of procuring them from abroad, during the present situation and dispositions of Europe, induced us to direct our whole efforts to the means of internal supply. The public factories have, therefore, been enlarged, additional machineries erected, and in proportion as artificers can be found or formed, their effect, already more than doubled, may be increased so as to keep pace with the yearly increase of the militia. The annual sums appropriated by the latter act, have been directed to the encouragement of private factories of arms, and contracts have been entered into with individual undertakers to nearly the amount of the first year's appropriation.

The suspension of our foreign commerce, produced by the injustice of the belligerent powers, and the consequent losses and sacrifices of our citizens, are subjects of just concern. The situation into which we have thus been forced, has impelled us to apply a portion of our industry and capital to internal manufactures and improvements. The extent of this conversion is daily increasing, and little doubt remains that the establishments formed and forming will—under the auspices of cheaper materials and subsistence, the freedom of labor from taxation with us, and of protecting duties and prohibitions—become permanent. The commerce with the Indians, too, within our own boundaries, is likely to receive abundant aliment from the same internal source, and will secure to them peace and the progress of civilization, undisturbed by practices hostile to both.

The accounts of the receipts and expenditures during the year ending on the 30th day of September last, being not yet made up, a correct statement will hereafter be transmitted from the Treasury. In the meantime, it is ascertained that the receipts have amounted to near eighteen millions of dollars, which, with the eight millions and a half in the treasury at the beginning of the year, have enabled us, after meeting the current demands and interest incurred, to pay two millions three hundred thousand dollars of the principal of our funded debt, and left us in the treasury, on that day, near fourteen millions of dollars. Of these, five millions three hundred and fifty thousand dollars will be necessary to pay what will be due on the first day of January next, which will complete the reimbursement of the eight per cent stock. These payments, with those made in the six years and a half preceding, will have extinguished thirty-three millions five hundred and eighty thousand dollars of the principal of the funded debt, being the whole which could be paid or purchased within the limits of the law and our contracts; and the amount of principal thus discharged will have liberated the revenue from about two millions of dollars of interest, and added that sum annually to the disposable surplus. The probable accumulation of the surpluses of revenue beyond what can be applied to the payment of the public debt, whenever the freedom and safety of our commerce shall be restored, merits the consideration of Congress. Shall it lie unproductive in the public vaults? Shall the revenue be reduced? Or shall it rather be appropriated to the improvements of roads, canals, rivers, education, and other great foundations of prosperity and union, under the powers which Congress may already possess, or such amendment of the constitution as may be approved by the States? While uncertain of the course of things, the time may be advantageously employed in obtaining the powers necessary for a system of improvement, should that be thought best.

Availing myself of this the last occasion which will occur of addressing the two houses of the legislature at their meeting, I cannot omit the expression of my sincere gratitude for the repeated proofs of confidence manifested to me by themselves and their predecessors since my call to the administration, and the many indulgences experienced at their hands. The same grateful acknowledgments are due to my fellow citizens generally, whose support has been my great encouragement under all embarrassments. In the transaction of their business I cannot have escaped error. It is incident to our imperfect nature. But I may say with truth, my errors have been of the understanding, not of intention; and that the advancement of their rights and interests has been the constant motive for every measure. On these considerations I solicit their indulgence. Looking forward with anxiety to their future destinies, I trust that, in their steady character unshaken by difficulties, in their love of liberty, obedience to law, and support of the public authorities, I see a sure guaranty of the permanence of our republic; and retiring from the charge of their affairs, I carry with me the consolation of a firm persuasion that Heaven has in store for our beloved country long ages to come of prosperity and happiness.

## TO THE INHABITANTS OF ALBEMARLE COUNTY, VA.

April 3, 1809

Returning to the scenes of my birth and early life, to the society of those with whom I was raised, and who have been ever dear to me, I receive, fellow-citizens and neighbors, with inexpressible pleasure, the cordial welcome you were so good as to give me. Long absent on duties which the history of a wonderful era made incumbent on those called to them, the pomp, the turmoil, the bustle and splendor of office; have drawn but deeper sighs for the tranquil and irresponsible occupations of private life, for the enjoyment of an affectionate intercourse with you, my neighbors and friends, and the endearments of family love, which nature has given us all, as the sweetner of every hour. For these I gladly lay down the distressing burthen of power, and seek, with my fellow-citizens, repose and safety under the watchful cares, the labors and perplexities of younger and abler minds. The anxieties you express to administer to my happiness, do, of themselves, confer that happiness; and the measure will be complete, if any endeavors to fulfil my duties in the several public stations to which I have been called, have obtained for me the approbation of my country. The part which I have acted on the theatre of public life, has been before them; and to their sentence I submit it; but the testimony of my native county, of the individuals who have known me in private life, to my conduct in its various duties and relations, is the more grateful, as proceeding from eye-witnesses and observers, from triers of the vicinage. Of you, then, my neighbors, I may ask, in the face of the world, "Whose ox have I taken, or whom have I defrauded? Whom have I oppressed, or of whose hand have I received a bribe to blind mine eyes therewith?" On your verdict I rest with conscious security. Your wishes for my happiness are received with just sensibility, and I offer sincere prayers for your own welfare and prosperity.

## SPEECH ON LAFAYETTE[1]

October, 1824

I will avail myself of this occasion, my beloved neighbors and friends, to thank you for the kindness which now, and at all times, I have received at

[1] In October, 1824, Lafayette visited his old friend Jefferson at Monticello and on that occasion the citizens of near-by Charlottesville gave him a banquet. Jefferson then delivered the

your hands. Born and bred among your fathers, led by their partiality into the line of public life, I labored in fellowship with them through that arduous struggle which, freeing us from foreign bondage, established us in the rights of self-government; rights which have blessed ourselves, and will bless, in their sequence, all the nations of the earth. In this contest, all did our utmost, and, as none could do more, none had pretensions to superior merit.

I joy, my friends, in your joy, inspired by the visit of this our ancient and distinguished leader and benefactor. His deeds in the war of independence you have heard and read. They are known to you and embalmed in your memories, and in the pages of faithful history. His deeds, in the peace which followed that war, are perhaps not known to you; but I can attest them. When I was stationed in his country, for the purpose of cementing its friendship with ours, and of advancing our mutual interests, this friend of both, was my most powerful auxiliary and advocate. He made our cause his own, as in truth it was that of his native country also. His influence and connections there were great. All doors of all departments were open to him at all times; to me, only formally and at appointed times. In truth, I only held the nail, he drove it. Honor him then, as your benefactor in peace, as well as in war.

My friends, I am old, long in the disuse of making speeches, and without voice to utter them. In this feeble state, the exhausted powers of life leave little within my competence for your service. If, with the aid of my younger and abler coadjutors, I can still contribute anything to advance the Institution, within whose walls we are now mingling manifestations to this our guest, it will be, as it ever has been, cheerfully and zealously bestowed. And could I live to see it once enjoy the patronage and cherishment of our public authorities with undivided voice, I should die without a doubt of the future fortunes of my native State, and in the consoling contemplation of the happy influence of this institution on its character, its virtue, its prosperity, and safety.

To these effusions for the cradle and land of my birth, I add, for our nation at large, the aspirations of a heart warm with the love of country; whose invocations to heaven for its indissoluble union, will be fervent and unremitting while the pulse of life continues to beat, and, when that ceases, it will expire in prayers for the eternal duration of its freedom and prosperity.

above address—or rather, it was delivered for him, from written notes which he handed to a proxy at the table: "I am old, long in the disuse of making speeches, and without voice to utter them." He was then in his 82d year. This is his last public address.

## *Chapter XII*

# ADDRESSES TO INDIANS

## TO BROTHER JOHN BAPTIST DE COIGNE

June, 1781

BROTHER JOHN BAPTIST DE COIGNE: I am very much pleased with the visit you have made us, and particularly that it has happened when the wise men from all parts of our country were assembled together in council, and had an opportunity of hearing the friendly discourse you held to me. We are all sensible of your friendship, and of the services you have rendered, and I now, for my countrymen, return you thanks, and, most particularly, for your assistance to the garrison which was besieged by the hostile Indians. I hope it will please the great being above to continue you long in life, in health and in friendship to us; and that your son will afterwards succeed you in wisdom, in good disposition, and in power over your people. I consider the name you have given as particularly honorable to me, but I value it the more as it proves your attachment to my country. We, like you, are Americans, born in the same land, and having the same interests. I have carefully attended to the figures represented on the skins, and to their explanation, and shall always keep them hanging on the walls in remembrance of you and your nation. I have joined with you sincerely in smoking the pipe of peace; it is a good old custom handed down by your ancestors, and as such I respect and join in it with reverence. I hope we shall long continue to smoke in friendship together. You find us, brother, engaged in war with a powerful nation. Our forefathers were Englishmen, inhabitants of a little island beyond the great water, and, being distressed for land, they came and settled here. As long as we were young and weak, the English whom we had left behind, made us carry all our wealth to their country, to enrich them; and, not satisfied with this, they at length began to say we were their slaves, and should do whatever they ordered us. We were now grown up and felt ourselves strong, we knew we were free as they were, that we came here of our own accord and not at their biddance, and were determined to be free as long as we should exist. For this reason they made war on us. They have now waged that war six years, and have not yet won more land from us than will serve to bury the warriors they have lost. Your old father, the king of France, has joined us in the war, and done many good things for us. We are bound forever to love him, and wish you to love him, brother, because he is a good and true friend to us. The Spaniards have also joined us, and other powerful nations are now entering into the war to punish the robberies and violences the English have committed on them. The English stand alone, without a friend to support them, hated by all mankind because they are proud and unjust. This quarrel, when it first began, was a family quarrel between us and the English, who were then our brothers. We, therefore, did not wish you to engage in it at all. We are strong enough of ourselves without wasting your blood in fighting our battles. The English, knowing this, have been always suing to the Indians to help them fight. We do not wish you to take up the hatchet. We love and esteem you. We wish you to multiply and be strong. The English, on the other hand, wish to set you and us to cutting one another's throats, that when we are dead they may take all our land. It is better for you not to join in this quarrel, unless the English have killed any of your warriors or done you any other injury. If they have, you have a right to go to war with them, and revenge the injury, and we have none to restrain you. Any free nation has a right to punish those who have done them an injury. I say the same, brother, as to the Indians who treat you ill. While I advise you, like an affectionate friend, to avoid unnecessary war, I do not assume the right of restraining you from punishing your enemies. If the English have injured you, as they have injured the French and Spaniards, do like them and join us in the war. General Clarke will receive you and show you the way to their towns. But if they have not injured you, it is better for you to lie still and be quiet. This is the advice which has been always given by the great council of the Americans. We must give the same, because we are but one of thirteen nations, who have agreed to act and speak together. These nations keep a council of wise men always sitting together, and each of us separately follow their advice. They have the care of all the people and the lands between the Ohio and Mississippi, and will see that no wrong be committed on them. The French settled at Kaskaskias, St. Vincennes, and the Cohos, are subject to that council, and they will punish them if they do you any injury. If you will make known to me any just cause of complaint against them, I will represent it to the great council at Philadelphia, and have justice done you.

Our good friend, your father, the King of France, does not lay any claim to them. Their misconduct should not be imputed to him. He gave them up to the English the last war, and we have taken them from the English.

The Americans alone have a right to maintain justice in all the lands on this side the Mississippi,—on the other side the Spaniards rule. You complain, brother, of the want of goods for the use of your people. We know that your wants are great, notwithstanding we have done everything in our power to supply them, and have often grieved for you. The path from hence to Kaskaskias is long and dangerous; goods cannot be carried to you in that way. New Orleans has been the only place from which we could get goods for you. We have bought a great deal there; but I am afraid not so much of them have come to you as we intended. Some of them have been sold of necessity to buy provisions for our posts. Some have been embezzled by our own drunken and roguish people. Some have been taken by the Indians and many by the English.

The Spaniards, having now taken all the English posts on the Mississippi, have opened that channel free for our commerce, and we are in hopes of getting goods for you from them. I will not boast to you, brother, as the English do, nor promise more than we shall be able to fulfil. I will tell you honestly, what indeed your own good sense will tell you, that a nation at war cannot buy so many goods as when in peace. We do not make so many things to send over the great waters to buy goods, as we made and shall make again in time of peace. When we buy those goods, the English take many of them, as they are coming to us over the great water. What we get in safe, are to be divided among many, because we have a great many soldiers, whom we must clothe. The remainder we send to our brothers the Indians, and in going, a great deal of it is stolen or lost. These are the plain reasons why you cannot get so much from us in war as in peace. But peace is not far off. The English cannot hold out long, because all the world is against them. When that takes place, brother, there will not be an Englishman left on this side the great water. What will those foolish nations then do, who have made us their enemies, sided with the English, and laughed at you for not being as wicked as themselves? They are clothed for a day, and will be naked forever after; while you, who have submitted to short inconvenience, will be well supplied through the rest of your lives. Their friends will be gone and their enemies left behind; but your friends will be here, and will make you strong against all your enemies. For the present you shall have a share of what little goods we can get. We will order some immediately up the Mississippi for you and for us. If they be little, you will submit to suffer a little as your brothers do for a short time. And when we shall have beaten our enemies and forced them to make peace, we will share more plentifully. General Clarke will furnish you with ammunition to serve till we can get some from New Orleans. I must recommend to you particular attention to him. He is our great, good, and trusty warrior; and we have put everything under his care beyond the Alleghanies. He will advise you in all difficulties, and redress your wrongs. Do what he tells you, and you will be sure to do right. You ask us to send schoolmasters to educate your son and the sons of your people. We desire above all things, brother, to instruct you in whatever we know ourselves. We wish to learn you all our arts and to make you wise and wealthy. As soon as there is peace we shall be able to send you the best of schoolmasters; but while the war is raging, I am afraid it will not be practicable. It shall be done, however, before your son is of an age to receive instruction.

This, brother, is what I had to say to you. Repeat it from me to all your people, and to our friends, the Kickapoos, Peorias, Piankeshaws and Wyattanons. I will give you a commission to show them how much we esteem you. Hold fast the chain of friendship which binds us together, keep it bright as the sun, and let them, you and us, live together in perpetual love.

## SPEECHES OF JOHN BAPTIST DE COIGNE, CHIEF OF THE WABASH AND ILLINOIS INDIANS, AND OTHER INDIAN CHIEFS

Thomas Jefferson has the honor to send to the President the speech of De Coigne, written at length from his notes very exactly. He thinks he can assure the President that not a sentiment delivered by the French interpreter is omitted, nor a single one inserted which was not expressed. It differs often from what the English interpreter delivered, because he varied much from the other, who alone was regarded by Thomas Jefferson.

February 1, 1793. The President having addressed the chiefs of the Wabash and Illinois Indians, John Baptist De Coigne, chief of Kaskaskia, spoke as follows:

FATHER: I am about to open to you my heart. I salute first the Great Spirit, the Master of life, and then you.

I present you a black pipe on the death of chiefs who have come here and died in your bed. It is the calumet of the dead—take it and smoke it in remembrance of them. The dead pray you to listen to the living, and to be their friends. They are gone, we cannot recall them. Let us then be contented; for, as you have said, tomorrow, perhaps, it may be our turn. Take then their pipe, and as I have spoken for the dead, let me now address you for the living. [He delivered the black pipe.]

[Here Three-Legs, a Piankeshaw chief, came forward and carried round a white pipe, from which everyone smoked.]

John Baptist De Coigne spoke again:

*Father,*—The sky is now cleared. I am about to open my heart to you again. I do it in the presence of the Great Spirit, and I pray you to attend.

You have heard the words of our father, General Putnam. We opened our hearts to him, we made peace with him, and he has told you what we said.

This pipe is white, I pray you to consider it as of the Wyattanons, Piankeshaws, and the people of Eel river. The English at Detroit are very jealous of our father. I have used my best endeavors to keep all the red men in friendship with you, but they have drawn over the one-half, while I have kept the other. Be friendly then to those I have kept.

I have long known you, General Washington, the Congress, Jefferson, Sinclair. I have labored constantly for you to preserve peace.

You see your children on this side [pointing to the friends of the dead chief], they are now orphans. Take care, then, of the orphans of our dead friends.

*Father,*—Your people of Kentucky are like mosquitoes, and try to destroy the red men. The red men are like mosquitoes also, and try to injure the people of Kentucky. But I look to you as to a good being. Order your people to be just. They are always trying to get our lands. They come on our lands, they hunt on them; kill our game, and kill us. Keep them then on one side of the line, and us on the other. Listen, father, to what we say, and protect the nations of the Wabash and Mississippi in their lands.

The English have often spoken to me, but I shut my ears to them. I despise their money, it is nothing to me. I am attached to my lands. I love to eat in tranquillity, and not like a bird on a bough.

The Piankeshaws, Wyattanons, Wiaws, and all the Indians of the Mississippi and Wabash, pray you to open your heart and ears to them, and as you befriend them, to give them Captain Prior for their father. We love him, men, women, and children of us. He has always been friendly to us, always taken care of us, and you cannot give us a better proof of your friendship than in leaving him with us.

[Here Three-Legs handed round the white pipe to be smoked.] De Coigne, then, taking a third pipe, proceeded:

This pipe, my father, is sent you by the great chief of all the Wiaws, called Crooked-Legs. He is old, infirm, and cannot walk, therefore is not come. But he prays you to be his friend, and to take care of his people. He tells you there are many red people jealous of you, but you need not fear them. If he could have walked he would have come; but he is old and sick, and cannot walk. The English have a sugar mouth, but Crooked-Legs would never listen to them. They threatened us to send the red men to cut off him and his people, and they sent the red men who threatened to do it, unless he would join the English. But he would not join them.

The chiefs of the Wabash, father, pray you to listen. They send you this pipe from afar. Keep your children quiet at the Falls of Ohio. We know you are the head of all. We appeal to you. Keep the Americans on one side of the Ohio, from the falls downwards, and us on the other; that we may have something to live on according to your agreement in the treaty which you have. And do not take from the French the lands we have given them.

Old Crooked-Legs sends you this pipe [here he presented it], and he prays you to send him Captain Prior for his father, for he is old, and you ought to do this for him.

*Father,*—I pray you to listen. So far I have spoken for others, and now will speak for myself. I am of Kaskaskia, and have always been a good American from my youth upwards. Yet the Kentuckians take my lands, eat my stock, steal my horses, kill my game, and abuse our persons. I come far with all these people. My nation is not numerous. No people can fight against you, father, but the Great God himself. All the red men together cannot do it; but have pity on us. I am now old. Do not let the Kentuckians take my lands nor injure me, but give me a line to them to let me alone.

*Father,*—The Wyattanons, Piankeshaws, Peorias, Powtewatamies, Mosquitoes, Kaskaskias, have now made a road to you. It is broad and white. Take care of it then, and keep it open.

*Father,*—You are powerful. You said you would wipe away our tears. We thank you for this. Be firm, and take care of your children.

The hatchet has been long buried. I have been always for peace. I have done what I could, given all the money I had to procure it.

The half of my heart, father, is black. I brought the Peorias to you. Half of them are dead. I fear they will say it was my fault; but, father, I look upon you, my heart is white again, and I smile.

The Shawanee, the Delawares, and the English, are always persuading us to take up the hatchet against you, but I have been always deaf to their words. [Here he gave a belt.]

Great Joseph who came with us is dead. Have compassion on his niece, his son-in-law, and his chiefs [pointing to them]. It is a dead man who speaks to you, father; accept, therefore, these black beads. [Here he presented several strands of dark colored beads.] I have now seen General Washington, I salute and regard him next after the Great Spirit.

Como, a Powtewatamy chief, then said, that as the President had already been long detained, and the hour was advanced, he would resume what he had to say at another day.

Shawas, the Little Doe, a Kickapoo chief, though very sick, had attended the conference, and now carried the pipe round to be smoked. He then addressed the President.

*Father,*—I am still very ill, and unable to speak. I am a Kickapoo, and drink of the waters of the Wabash and Mississippi. I have been to the

Wabash and treatied with General Putnam, and I came not to do ill, but to make peace. Send to us Captain Prior to be our father, and no other. He possesses all our love.

*Father,*—I am too ill to speak. You will not forget what the others have said.

*February* 2.—The day being cloudy, the Indians did not choose to meet.

*February* 4.—The morning was cloudy, they gave notice that if it should clear up they would attend at the President's at 2 o'clock. Accordingly, the clouds having broke away about noon, they attended a little after 2, except Shawas and another, who were sick, and one woman.

Como, a Powtewatamy chief, spoke.

*Father,*—I am opening my heart to speak to you, open yours to receive my words. I first address you from a dead chief, who when he was about to die, called us up to him and charged us never to part with our lands. So I have done for you, my children, and so do you for yours. For what have we come so far? Not to ruin our nation, nor yet that we might carry goods home to our women and children; but to procure them lasting good, to open a road between them and the whites, solicit our father to send Captain Prior to us. He has taken good care of us, and we all love him.

Now, Father, I address you for our young people, but there remains not much to say, for I spoke to you through General Putnam, and you have what I said on paper. I have buried the hatchet forever, so must your children. I speak the truth, and you must believe me. We all pray you to send Captain Prior to us, because he has been so very kind to us all. [Here he delivered strands of dark colored beads.]

*Father,*—Hear me and believe me. I speak the truth, and from my heart; receive my words then into yours. I am come from afar for the good of my women and children, for their present and future good. When I was at home in the midst of them, my heart sunk within me, I saw no hope for them. The heavens were gloomy and lowering, and I could not tell why. But General Putnam spoke to us, and called us together. I rejoiced to hear him, and determined immediately to come and see my father. Father, I am happy to see you. The heavens have cleared away, the day is bright, and I rejoice to hear your voice. These beads [holding up a bundle of white strands] are a road between us. Take you hold at one end, I will at the other, and hold it fast. I will visit this road every day, and sweep it clean. If any blood be on it, I will cover it up; if stumps, I will cut them out. Should your children and mine meet in this road they shall shake hands and be good friends. Some of the Indians who belong to the English will be trying to sow harm between us, but we must be on our guard and prevent it.

*Father,*—I love the land on which I was born, the trees which cover it, and the grass growing on it. It feeds us well. I am not come here to ask gifts. I am young, and by hunting on my own land, can kill what I want and feed my women and children in plenty. I come not to beg. But if any of your traders would wish to come among us, let them come. For who will hurt them? Nobody, I will be there before them.

*Father,*—I take you by the hand with all my heart. I will never forget you; do not you forget me.

[Here he delivered the bundle of white strands.]

The Little Beaver, a Wyattanon, on the behalf of Crooked-Legs, handed round the pipe, and then spoke.

*Father,*—Listen now to me as you have done to others. I am not a very great chief; I am a chief of war, and leader of the young people.

*Father,*—I wished much to hear you; you have spoken comfort to us, and I am happy to have heard it. The sun has shone out, and all is well. This makes us think it was the Great Spirit speaking truth through you. Do then what you have said, restrain your people if they do wrong, as we will ours if they do wrong.

*Father,*—We gave to our friend (Prior) who came with us, our name of Wyattanon, and he gave us his name of American. We are now Americans, give him then unto us as a father. He has loved us and taken care of us. He had pity on our women and children, and fed them. Do not forget to grant us this request. You told us to live in quiet, and to do right. We will do what you desire, and let Prior come to us.

Now that we have come so far to hear you, write a line to your people to keep the river open between us, that we may go down in safety, and that our women and children may work in peace. When I go back, I will bear to them good tidings, and our young men will no longer hunt in fear for the support of our women and children.

*Father,*—All of us who have heard you are made happy, all are in the same sentiment with me, all are satisfied. Be assured that, when we return, the Indians and Americans will be one people, will hunt, and play, and laugh together. For me, I never will depart one step from Prior. We are come from afar to make a stable peace, to look forward to our future good. Do not refuse what we solicit, we will never forget you.

Here I will cease. The father of life might otherwise think I babbled too much, and so might you. I finish then, in giving you this pipe. It is my own, and from myself alone. I am but a warrior. I give it to you to smoke in. Let its fumes ascend to the Great Spirit in heaven.

[He delivered the pipe to the President.]

The wife of the soldier, a Wyattanon, speaks:

*Father,*—I take you by the hand with all my heart because you have spoken comfort to us. I am but a woman, yet you must listen.

The village chiefs, and chiefs of war, have opened their bodies and laid naked their hearts to you. Let them too see your heart and listen to them.

We have come, men and women, from afar to beseech you to let no one take our lands. That is one of our children [pointing to General Putnam]. It was he who persuaded us to come. We thought he spoke the truth, we came, and we hope that good will come of it.

*Father,*—We know you are strong, have pity on us. Be firm in your words. They have given us courage. The father of life has opened our hearts on both sides for good.

He who was to have spoken to you is dead, Great Joseph. If he had lived you would have heard a good man, and good words flowing from his mouth. He was my uncle, and it has fallen to me to speak for him. But I am ignorant. Excuse, then, these words, it is but a woman who speaks.

[She delivers white strands.]

Three-Legs, a Piankeshaw, spoke.

I speak for a young chief whom I have lost here. He came to speak to you, father, but he had not that happiness. He died. I am not a village chief, but only a chief of war.

We are come to seek all our good, and to be firm in it. If our father is firm, we will be so. It was a dark and gloomy day in which I lost my young chief. The master of life saw that he was good, and called him to himself. We must submit to his will. [He gave a black strand.] I pray you all who are present to say, as one man, that our peace is firm, and to let it be firm. Listen to us if you love us. We live on the river on one side, and shall be happy to see Captain Prior on the other, and to have a lasting peace. Here is our father Putnam. He heard me speak at Au Porte. If I am false let him say so.

My land is but small. If any more be taken from us, I will come again to you and complain, for we shall not be able to live. Have pity on us, father. You have many red children there, and they have little whereon to live. Leave them land enough to labor, to hunt, and to live on, and the lands which we have given to the French, let them be to them forever.

*Father,*—We are very poor, we have traders among us, but they will sell too dear. We have not the means of supplying our wants at such prices. Encourage your traders then to come, and to bring us guns, powder, and other necessaries, and send Captain Prior also to us.

[He gave a string of white beads.] De Coigne spoke:

Jefferson, I have seen you before, and we have spoken together. Sinclair, we have opened our hearts to one another. Putnam, we did the same at Au Porte.

*Father,*—You have heard these three speak of me, and you know my character. The times are gloomy in my town. We have no commander, no soldier, no priest. Have you no concern for us, father? If you have, put a magistrate with us to keep the peace. I cannot live so. I am of French blood. When there are no priests among us we think that all is not well. When I was small we had priests, now that I am old we have none; am I to forget, then, how to pray? Have pity on me and grant what I ask. I have spoken on your behalf to all the nations. I am a friend to all, and hurt none. For what are we on this earth? But as a small and tender plant of corn; even as nothing. God has made this earth for you as well as for us; we are then but as one family, and if anyone strikes you, it is as if he had struck us. If any nation strikes you, father, we will let you know what nation it is.

*Father,*—We fear the Kentuckians. They are headstrong, and do us great wrong. They are not content to come on our lands, to hunt on them, to steal and destroy our stocks, as the Shawanee and Delawares do, but they go further, and abuse our persons. Forbid them to do so. Sinclair, you know that the Shawanee and Delawares came from the Spanish side of the river, destroyed our corn, and killed our cattle. We cannot live if things go so.

*Father,*—You are rich, you have all things at command, you want for nothing, you promised to wipe away our tears. I commend our women and children to your care.

[He gave strands of white beads.]

The President then assured them that he would take in consideration what they had said, and would give them an answer on another day; whereupon the conference ended for the present.

## TO THE MIAMIS, POWTEWATAMIES, AND WEEAUKS

January 7, 1802

BROTHERS AND FRIENDS OF THE MIAMIS, POWTEWATAMIES, AND WEEAUKS: I receive with great satisfaction the visit you have been so kind as to make us at this place, and I thank the Great Spirit who has conducted you to us in health and safety. It is well that friends should sometimes meet, open their minds mutually, and renew the chain of affection. Made by the same Great Spirit, and living in the same land with our brothers, the red men, we consider ourselves as of the same family; we wish to live with them as one people, and to cherish their interests as our own. The evils which of necessity encompass the life of man are sufficiently numerous. Why should we add to them by voluntarily distressing and destroying one another? Peace, brothers, is better than war. In a long and bloody war, we lose many friends, and gain nothing. Let us then live in peace and friendship together, doing to each other all the good we can. The wise and good on both sides desire this, and we must take care that the foolish and wicked among us shall not prevent it. On our part, we shall endeavor in all things to be just and generous towards you, and to aid you in meeting those difficulties which a change of circumstances is bringing on. We shall, with great pleasure, see your people become disposed to cultivate the earth, to raise herds of the useful animals, and to spin and weave, for their food and clothing. These resources are certain; they will never disappoint you: while those of hunting may fail, and expose your women and children to the miseries of hunger and cold. We will with pleasure furnish you with implements for the most necessary arts, and with persons who may instruct you how to make and use them.

I consider it as fortunate that you have made your visit at this time, when our wise men from the sixteen States are collected together in council, who being equally disposed to befriend you, can strengthen our hands in the good we all wish to render you.

The several matters you opened to us in your speech the other day, and those on which you have since conversed with the Secretary of War, have been duly considered by us. He will now deliver answers, and you are to consider what he says, as if said by myself, and that what we promise we shall faithfully perform.

## TO THE DELAWARE AND SHAWANEE NATIONS

February 10, 1802

BROTHERS OF THE DELAWARE AND SHAWANEE NATIONS: I thank the Great Spirit that he has conducted you hither in health and safety, and that we have an opportunity of renewing our amity, and of holding friendly conference together. It is a circumstance of great satisfaction to us that we are in peace and good understanding with all our red brethren, and that we discover in them the same disposition to continue so which we feel ourselves. It is our earnest desire to merit, and possess their affections, by rendering them strict justice, prohibiting injury from others, aiding their endeavors to learn the culture of the earth, and to raise useful animals, and befriending them as good neighbors, and in every other way in our power. By mutual endeavors to do good to each other, the happiness of both will be better promoted than by efforts of mutual destruction. We are all created by the same Great Spirit; children of the same family. Why should we not live then as brothers ought to do?

I am peculiarly gratified by receiving the visit of some of your most ancient and greatest warriors, of whom I have heard much good. It is a long journey which they have taken at their age, and in this season, and I consider it as a proof that their affections for us are sincere and strong. I hope that the young men, who have come with them, to make acquaintance with us, judging our dispositions towards them by what they see themselves, and not what they may hear from others, will go hand in hand with us, through life, in the cultivation of mutual peace, friendship, and good offices.

The speech which the Blackhoof delivered us, in behalf of your nation, has been duly considered. The answer to all its particulars will now be delivered you by the Secretary of War. Whatever he shall say, you may consider as if said by myself, and that what he promises our nation will perform.

## TO BROTHER HANDSOME LAKE

November 3, 1802

BROTHER HANDSOME LAKE: I have received the message in writing which you sent me through Captain Irvine, our confidential agent, placed near you for the purpose of communicating and transacting between us, whatever may be useful for both nations. I am happy to learn you have been so far favored by the Divine spirit as to be made sensible of those things which are for your good and that of your people, and of those which are hurtful to you; and particularly that you and they see the ruinous effects which the abuse of spirituous liquors have produced upon them. It has weakened their bodies, enervated their minds, exposed them to hunger, cold, nakedness, and poverty, kept them in perpetual broils, and reduced their population. I do not wonder then, brother, at your censures, not only on your own people, who have voluntarily gone into these fatal habits, but on all the nations of white people who have supplied their calls for this article. But these nations have done to you only what they do among themselves. They have sold what individuals wish to buy, leaving to everyone to be the guardian of his own health and happiness. Spirituous liquors are not in themselves bad, they are often found to be an excellent medicine for the sick; it is the improper and intemperate use of them, by those in health, which makes them injurious. But as you find that your people cannot refrain from an ill use of them, I greatly applaud your resolution not to use them at all. We have too affectionate a concern for your happiness to place the paltry gain on the sale of these articles in competition with the injury they do you. And as it is the desire of your nation, that no spirits should be sent among them, I am authorized by the great council of the United States to prohibit them. I will sincerely coöperate with your wise men in any proper measures for this purpose, which shall be agreeable to them.

You remind me, brother, of what I said to you, when you visited me the last winter, that the lands you then held would remain yours, and shall never go from you but when you should be disposed to sell. This I now repeat, and will ever abide by. We, indeed, are always ready to buy land; but we will never ask but when you wish to sell; and our laws, in order to protect you against imposition, have forbidden individuals to purchase lands from you; and have rendered it necessary, when you desire to sell, even to a State, that an agent from the United States should attend the sale, see that your consent is freely given, a satisfactory price paid, and report to us what has been done, for our approbation. This was done in the late case of which you complain. The deputies of your nation came forward, in all the forms which we have been used to consider as evidence of the will of your nation. They proposed to sell to the State of New York certain parcels of land, of small extent, and detached from the body of your other lands; the State of New York was desirous to buy. I sent an agent, in whom we could trust, to see that your consent was free, and the sale fair. All was reported to be free and fair. The lands were your property. The right to sell is one of the rights of property. To forbid you the exercise of that right would be a wrong to your nation. Nor do I think, brother, that the sale of lands is, under all circumstances, injurious to your people. While they depended on hunting, the more extensive the forest around them, the more game they would yield. But going into a state of agriculture, it may be as advantageous to a society, as it is to an individual, who has more land than he can improve, to sell a part, and lay out the money in stocks and implements of agriculture, for the better improvement of the residue. A little land well stocked and improved, will yield more than a great deal without stock or improvement. I hope, therefore, that on further reflection, you will see this transaction in a more favorable light, both as it concerns the interest of your nation, and the exercise of that superintending care which I am sincerely anxious to employ for their subsistence and happiness. Go on then, brother, in the great reformation you have undertaken. Persuade our red brethren then to be sober, and to cultivate their lands; and their women to spin and weave for their families. You will soon see your women and children well fed and clothed, your men living happily in peace and plenty, and your numbers increasing from year to year. It will be a great glory to you to have been the instrument of so happy a change, and your children's children, from generation to generation, will repeat your name with love and gratitude forever. In all your enterprises for the good of your people, you may count with confidence on the aid and protection of the United States, and on the sincerity and zeal with which I am myself animated in the furthering of this humane work. You are our brethren of the same land; we wish your prosperity as brethren should do. Farewell.

# TO THE MIAMIS AND DELAWARES

## January 8, 1803

BROTHERS MIAMIS AND DELAWARES: I am happy to see you here, to take you by the hand, and to renew the assurances of our friendship. The journey which you have taken is long; but it leads to a right understanding of what either of us may have misunderstood; it will be useful for all. For, living in the same land, it is best for us all that we should live together in peace, friendship, and good neighborhood.

I have taken into serious consideration the several subjects on which you spoke to me the other day, and will now proceed to answer them severally.

You know, brothers, that, in ancient times, your former fathers the French settled at Vincennes, and lived and traded with your ancestors, and that those ancestors ceded to the French a tract of country, on the Wabash river, seventy leagues broad, and extending in length from Point Coupee to the mouth of White river. The French, at the close of a war between them and the English, ceded this country to the English; who, at the close of a war between them and us, ceded it to us. The remembrance of these transactions is well preserved among the white people; they have been acknowledged in a deed signed by your fathers; and you also, we suppose, must have heard it from them. Sincerely desirous to live in peace and brotherhood with you, and that the hatchet of war may never again be lifted, we thought it prudent to remove from between us whatever might at any time produce misunderstanding. The unmarked state of our boundaries, and mutual trespasses on each other's lands, for want of their being known to all our people, have at times threatened our peace. We therefore instructed Governor Harrison to call a meeting of the chiefs of all the Indian nations around Vincennes, and to propose that we should settle and mark the boundary between us. The chiefs of these nations met. They appeared to think hard that we should claim the whole of what their ancestors had ceded and sold to the white men, and proposed to mark off for us from Point Coupee to the mouth of White river, a breadth of twenty-four leagues only, instead of seventy. His offer was a little more than a third of our right. But the desire of being in peace and friendship with you, and of doing nothing which should distress you, prevailed in our minds, and we agreed to it. This was the act of the several nations, original owners of the soil, and by men duly authorized by the body of those nations. You, brothers, seem not to have been satisfied with it. But it is a rule in all countries that what is done by the body of a nation must be submitted to by all its members. We have no right to alter, on a partial deputation, what we have settled by treaty with the body of the nations concerned. The lines too, which are agreed on, are to be run and marked in the presence of your chiefs, who will see that they are fairly run. Your nations were so sensible of the moderation of our conduct towards them, that they voluntarily offered to lend us forever the salt springs, and four miles square of land near the mouth of the Wabash, without price. But we wish nothing without price. And we propose to make a reasonable addition to the annuity we pay to the owners.

You complain that our people buy your lands individually, and settle and hunt on them without leave. To convince you of the care we have taken to guard you against the injuries and arts of interested individuals, I now will give you a copy of a law, of our great council the Congress, forbidding individuals to buy lands from you, or to settle or hunt on your lands; and making them liable to severe punishment. And if you will at any time seize such individuals, and deliver them to any officer of the United States, they will be punished according to law.

We have long been sensible, brothers, of the great injury you receive from an immoderate use of spirituous liquors; and although it be profitable to us to make and sell these liquors, yet we value more the preservation of your health and happiness. Heretofore we apprehended you would be displeased, were we to withhold them from you. But leaving it to be your desire, we have taken measures to prevent their being carried into your country; and we sincerely rejoice at this proof of your wisdom. Instead of spending the produce of your hunting in purchasing this pernicious drink, which produces poverty, broils and murders, it will now be employed in procuring food and clothing for your families, and increasing instead of diminishing your numbers.

You have proposed, brothers, that we should deduct from your next year's annuity, the expenses of your journey here; but this would be an exactness we do not practise with our red brethren. We will bear with satisfaction the expenses of your journey, and of whatever is necessary for your personal comfort; and will not, by deducting them, lessen the amount of the necessaries which your women and children are to receive the next year.

From the same good will towards you, we shall be pleased to see you making progress in raising stock and grain, and making clothes for yourselves. A little labor in this way, performed at home and at ease, will go further towards feeding and clothing you, than a great deal of labor in hunting wild beasts.

In answer to your request of a smith to be stationed in some place convenient to you, I can inform you that Mr. Wells, our agent, is authorized to make such establishments, and also to furnish you with implements of husbandry and manufacture, whenever you shall be determined to use them. The particulars on this subject, as well as of some others mentioned in your speech, and in the written speech you brought me from Buckangalah and others, will be communicated and settled with you by the Secretary at War. And I shall pray you in your return, to be the bearers to your countrymen and friends of assurances of my sincere friendship, and that our nation wishes to befriend them in everything useful, and to protect them against all injuries committed by lawless persons from among our citizens, either on their lands, their lives or their property.

## TO THE CHOCTAW NATION

December 17, 1803

BROTHERS OF THE CHOCTAW NATION: We have long heard of your nation as a numerous, peaceable, and friendly people; but this is the first visit we have had from its great men at the seat of our government. I welcome you here; am glad to take you by the hand, and to assure you, for your nation, that we are their friends. Born in the same land, we ought to live as brothers, doing to each other all the good we can, and not listening to wicked men, who may endeavor to make us enemies. By living in peace, we can help and prosper one another; by waging war, we can kill and destroy many on both sides; but those who survive will not be the happier for that. Then, brothers, let it forever be peace and good neighborhood between us. Our seventeen States compose a great and growing nation. Their children are as the leaves of the trees, which the winds are spreading over the forest. But we are just also. We take from no nation what belongs to it. Our growing numbers make us always willing to buy lands from our red brethren, when they are willing to sell. But be assured we never mean to disturb them in their possessions. On the contrary, the lines established between us by mutual consent, shall be sacredly preserved, and will protect your lands from all encroachments by our own people or any others. We will give you a copy of the law, made by our great Council, for punishing our people, who may encroach on your lands, or injure you otherwise. Carry it with you to your homes, and preserve it, as the shield which we spread over you, to protect your land, your property and persons.

It is at the request which you sent me in September, signed by Puckshanublee and other chiefs, and which you now repeat, that I listen to your proposition to sell us lands. You say you owe a great debt to your merchants, that you have nothing to pay it with but lands, and you pray us to take lands, and pay your debt. The sum you have occasion for, brothers, is a very great one. We have never yet paid as much to any of our red brethren for the purchase of lands. You propose to us some on the Tombigbee, and some on the Mississippi. Those on the Mississippi suit us well. We wish to have establishments on that river, as resting places for our boats, to furnish them provisions, and to receive our people who fall sick on the way to or from New Orleans, which is now ours. In that quarter, therefore, we are willing to purchase as much as you will spare. But as to the manner in which the line shall be run, we are not judges of it here, nor qualified to make any bargain. But we will appoint persons hereafter to treat with you on the spot, who, knowing the country and quality of the lands, will be better able to agree with you on a line which will give us a just equivalent for the sum of money you want paid.

You have spoken, brothers, of the lands which your fathers formerly sold and marked off to the English, and which they ceded to us with the rest of the country they held here; and you say that, though you do not know whether your fathers were paid for them, you have marked the line over again for us, and do not ask repayment. It has always been the custom, brothers, when lands were bought of the red men, to pay for them immediately, and none of us have ever seen an example of such a debt remaining unpaid. It is to satisfy their immediate wants that the red men have usually sold lands; and in such a case, they would not let the debt be unpaid. The presumption from custom then is strong; so it is also from the great length of time since your fathers sold these lands. But we have, moreover, been informed by persons now living, and who assisted the English in making the purchase, that the price was paid at the time. Were it otherwise, as it was their contract, it would be their debt, not ours.

I rejoice, brothers, to hear you propose to become cultivators of the earth for the maintenance of your families. Be assured you will support them better and with less labor, by raising stock and bread, and by spinning and weaving clothes, than by hunting. A little land cultivated, and a little labor, will procure more provisions than the most successful hunt; and a woman will clothe more by spinning and weaving, than a man by hunting. Compared with you, we are but as of yesterday in this land. Yet see how much more we have multiplied by industry, and the exercise of that reason which you possess in common with us. Follow then our example, brethren, and we will aid you with great pleasure.

The clothes and other necessaries which we sent you the last year, were, as you supposed, a present from us. We never meant to ask land or any other payment for them; and the store which we sent on, was at your request also; and to accommodate you with necessaries at a reasonable price, you wished of course to have it on your land; but the land would continue yours, not ours.

As to the removal of the store, the interpreter, and the agent, and any other matters you may wish to speak about, the Secretary at War will enter into explanations with you, and whatever he says, you may consider as said by myself, and what he promises you will be faithfully performed.

I am glad, brothers, you are willing to go and visit some other parts of our country. Carriages shall be ready to convey you, and you shall be taken care of on your journey; and when you shall have returned here and rested yourselves to your own mind, you shall be sent home by land. We had provided for your coming by land, and were sorry for the mistake which carried you to Savannah instead of Augusta, and exposed you to the risks of a voyage by sea. Had any accident happened to you, though we could not help it, it would have been a cause of great mourning to us. But we thank the Great Spirit who took care of you on the ocean, and brought you safe and in good health to the seat of our great Council; and we hope His care will accompany and protect you, on your journey and return home; and that He will preserve and prosper your nation in all its just pursuits.

## TO THE WHITE-HAIRS, CHIEFS, AND WARRIORS OF THE OSAGE NATION

MY CHILDREN, WHITE-HAIRS, CHIEFS, AND WARRIORS OF THE OSAGE NATION: I repeat to you assurances of the satisfaction it gives me to receive you here. Besides the labor of such a journey, the confidence you have shown in the honor and friendship of my countrymen is peculiarly gratifying, and I hope you have seen that your confidence was justly placed, that you have found yourselves, since you crossed the Mississippi, among brothers and friends, with whom you were as safe as at home.

*My Children,*—I sincerely weep with you over the graves of your chiefs and friends, who fell by the hands of their enemies lately descending the Osage river. Had they been prisoners, and living, we would have recovered them. But no voice can awake the dead; no power undo what is done. On this side the Mississippi, where our government has been long established, and our authority organized, our friends visiting us are safe. We hope it will not be long before our voice will be heard and our arm respected, by those who meditate to injure our friends on the other side of that river. In the meantime, Governor Harrison will be directed to take proper measures to inquire into the circumstances of the transaction, to report them to us for consideration, and for the further measures they may require.

*My Children,*—By late arrangements with France and Spain, we now take their place as your neighbors, friends, and fathers; and we hope you will have no cause to regret the change. It is so long since our forefathers came from beyond the great water, that we have lost the memory of it, and seem to have grown out of this land, as you have done. Never more will you have occasion to change your fathers. We are all now of one family, born in the same land, and bound to live as brothers; and the strangers from beyond the great water are gone from among us. The Great Spirit has given you strength, and has given us strength; not that we might hurt one another, but to do each other all the good in our power. Our dwellings, indeed, are very far apart, but not too far to carry on commerce and useful intercourse. You have furs and peltries which we want, and we have clothes and other useful things which you want. Let us employ ourselves, then, in mutually accommodating each other. To begin this on our part, it was necessary to know what nations inhabited the great country called Louisiana, which embraces all the waters of the Mississippi and Missouri, what number of peltries they could furnish, what quantities and kind of merchandize they would require, where would be the deposits most convenient for them, and to make an exact map of all those waters. For this purpose I sent a beloved man, Captain Lewis, one of my own household, to learn something of the people with whom we are now united, to let you know we were your friends, to invite you to come and see us, and to tell us how we can be useful to you. I thank you for the readiness with which you have listened to his voice, and for the favor you have showed him in his passage up the Missouri. I hope your countrymen will favor and protect him as far as they extend. On his return we shall hear what he has seen and learnt, and proceed to establish trading houses where our red brethren shall think best, and to exchange commodities with them on terms with which they will be satisfied.

With the same views I had prepared another party to go up the Red River to its source, thence to the source of the Arkansas, and down it to its mouth. But I will now give orders that they shall only go a small distance up the Red River this season, and return to tell us what they have seen, and that they shall not set out for the head of that river till the ensuing spring, when you will be at home, and will, I hope, guide and guard them in their journey. I also propose the next year to send another small party up the river of the Kansas to its source, thence to the head of the river of the Panis, and down to its mouth; and others up the rivers on the north side of the Missouri. For guides along these rivers, we must make arrangements with the nations inhabiting them.

*My Children,*—I was sorry to learn that a schism had taken place in your nation, and that a part of your people had withdrawn with the Great-Track to the Arkansas river. We will send an agent to them, and will use our best offices to induce them to return, and to live in union with you. We wish to make them also our friends, and to make that friendship, and the weight it may give us with them, useful to you and them.

We propose, my children, immediately to establish an agent to reside with you, who will speak to you our words, and convey yours to us, who will be the guardian of our peace and friendship, convey truths from one to the other, dissipate all falsehoods which might tend to alienate and divide us, and maintain a good understanding and friendship between us. As the distance is too great for you to come often and tell us your wants, you will tell them to him on the spot, and he will convey them to us in writing, so that we shall be sure that they come from you. Through the intervention of such an agent we shall hope that our friendship will forever be preserved. No wrong will ever be done you by our nation, and we trust that yours will do none to us. And should ungovernable individuals commit unauthorized outrage on either side, let them be duly punished; or if they escape, let us make to each other the best satisfaction the case admits, and not let our peace be broken by bad men. For all people have some bad men among them, whom no laws can restrain.

As you have taken so long a journey to see your father, we wish you not to return till you shall have visited our country and towns toward the sea coast. This will be new and satisfactory to you, and it will give you the same knowledge of the country on this side the Mississippi, which we are endeavoring to acquire of that on the other side, by sending trusty persons to explore them. We propose to do in your country only what we are desirous you should do in ours. We will provide accommodations for your journey, for your comfort while engaged in it, and for your return in safety to your own country, carrying with you those proofs of esteem with which we distinguish our friends, and shall particularly distinguish you. On your return tell your people that I take them all by the hand; that I become their father hereafter; that they shall know our nation only as friends and benefactors; that we have no views upon them but to carry on a commerce useful to them and us; to keep them in peace with their neighbors, that their children may multiply, may grow up and live to a good old age, and their women no more fear the tomahawk of any enemy.

My children, these are my words, carry them to your nation, keep them in your memories, and our friendship in your hearts, and may the Great Spirit look down upon us and cover us with the mantle of his love.

## TO THE CHIEFS OF FOXES, SACS, AND PAUTEWATAMIES[1]

January, 1805 (?)

MY FRIENDS AND CHILDREN, CHIEFS OF FOXES, SACS AND PAUTEWATAMIES: We have long known each other by hearsay, our people have had some inter-

[1] MS. in National Archives: Records of the office of Indian Affairs, Secretary of War, Letter Book "B."

course together, but this is the first time that our friends the Sacs and Foxes have visited us at the Seat of Government. I take you all by the hand of friendship, and give you a hearty welcome. I think the Great Spirit who has inspired you with a desire to come and see us, and who has protected you through the journey and brought you safely to the residence of your friends, and I hope he will have you constantly in his safe keeping and restore you in good health to your stations and families.

*My Friends and Children,* born in the same land, and approaching every day nearer and nearer one another as neighbours, we should live together as one family, in peace and friendship, doing to each other all the good we can. Our nation is numerous and strong; but we wish to be just to all: and particularly to be kind and useful to all our red children. We propose as fast as we can do it, to establish factories among them to supply them with the necessaries they want, and to receive their furs and peltries in exchange. We want no profit in this business. We shall ask from them only what everything costs us, and give for their furs and peltries whatever we can get for them again. I am persuaded that in doing this we can make your situation better than it is; and we have no other motive for doing it.

*My Friends and Children,* I am endeavoring to persuade all the nations of red men to live in peace and friendship with one another as brethren of the same family ought to do. How much better is it for neighbours to help than to hurt one another— How much happier must it make them. If you will cease to make war on one another, if you will live in friendship with all mankind, you can employ all your time in providing food and clothing for yourselves and your families,—your men will not be destroyed in war, and your women and children will lie down to sleep in their cabins, without fear of being surprised by their enemy and killed or carried away. Your numbers will be increased instead of diminishing, and you will live in plenty and in quiet. Look at your brethren in the South. They have been for some time following my advice, they have left off wars, they are increasing in their numbers, are learning to clothe and provide for their families as we do, and you see the proofs of it in such of them as you happened to find here.

*My Children,* we are strong, we are numerous as the Stars in the Heavens, and we are all gun-men, yet we live in peace and friendship with all Nations and all Nations esteem and honor us because we are peaceable and just. Be you then peaceable and just also; take each other by the hand and hold it fast. if ever bad men among your neighbours should do you wrong and their Nations refuse you justice, apply to the beloved man whom we shall place nearest to you; he will go to the offending Nation and endeavour to obtain right and preserve peace. If ever bad men among yourselves injure your neighbours be always ready to do justice. It is always honorable in those who have done wrong to acknowledge and make amends for it; and it is the only way in which peace can be maintained among men. Remember then my advice, my Children, carry it home to your people and tell them that we wish as a true father should do, that we may all live together as one household, and that before they strike one another, they should come to their father and let him endeavour to make up the quarrel.

*My Children,* you have come a long journey to see us. You have now reached to where the waters are constantly rising and falling every day, but you are still distant from the sea. I very much desire that you should not stop here, but go on and see your brethren as far as the edge of the great water. I am persuaded you have so far seen that every man by the way has received you as his brothers, and has been ready to do you all the kindnesses in his power. You will see the same thing quite to the sea shore; and I wish you therefore to go and visit our Great Cities in that quarter, and see how many friends and brothers you have here. I wish you to see all you can and to tell your people all you see; because I am sure the more they know of us, the more they will be our hearty friends. I invite you therefore to pay a visit to Baltimore, Philadelphia, New York and the cities still beyond that if you should be willing to go further. We will provide carriages to convey you, and a person to go with you and to see that you want for nothing; by the time you come back the snows on the mountains will be melted, and the ice in the rivers broken up, and you will be wishing to set out on your return home.

*My Children,* I have long desired to see you. I have now opened my heart to you; let my words sink into your hearts and never be forgotten. If ever lying people or bad spirits should raise up clouds between us, call to mind what I have said and what you have seen yourselves. Be sure there are some lying spirits between us; let us come together as friends, and explain to each other what is misrepresented or misunderstood, the clouds will fly away like the morning Fog, and the Sun of friendship appear and shine forever bright and clear between us.

*My Children,* It may happen that while you are here, occasion may arise to talk about many things which I do not now particularly mention: The Secretary at War will always be ready to talk with you and you are to consider whatever he says as said by myself. He will also take care of you and see that you are furnished with all comforts here.

## TO THE CHIEFS OF THE CHICKASAW NATION, MINGHEY, MATAHA, AND TISHOHOTANA

March 7, 1805

MY CHILDREN, CHIEFS OF THE CHICKASAW NATION, MINGHEY, MATAHA, AND TISHOHOTANA: I am happy to receive you at the seat of the government of the twenty-two nations, and to take you by the hand. Your friendship to the Americans has long been known to me. Our fathers have told us that your nation never spilled the blood of an American, and we have seen you fighting by our side and cementing our friendship by mixing our blood in battle against the same enemies. I rejoice, therefore, that the Great Spirit has covered you with his protection through so long a journey and so inclement a season, and brought you safe to the dwelling of a father who wishes well to all his red children, and to you especially. It would have been also pleasing to have received the other chiefs who had proposed to come with you, and to have known and become known to them, had it been convenient for them to come. I have long wished to see the beloved men of your nation, to renew the friendly conferences of former times, to assure them that we remain constant in our attachment to them, and to prove it by our good offices.

Your country, like all those on this side the Mississippi, has no longer game sufficient to maintain yourselves, your women and children, comfortably by hunting. We, therefore, wish to see you undertake the cultivation of the earth, to raise cattle, corn, and cotton, to feed and clothe your people. A little labor in the earth will produce more food than the best hunts you can now make, and the women will spin and weave more clothing than the men can procure by hunting. We shall very willingly assist you in this course by furnishing you with the necessary tools and implements, and with persons to instruct you in the use of them.

We have been told that you have contracted a great debt to some British traders, which gives you uneasiness, and which you honestly wish to pay by the sale of some of your lands. Whenever you raise food from the earth, and make your own clothing, you will find that you have a great deal of land more than you can cultivate or make useful, and that it will be better for you to sell some of that, to pay your debts, and to have something over to be paid to you annually to aid you in feeding and clothing yourselves. Your lands are your own, my children, they shall never be taken from you by our people or any others. You will be free to keep or to sell as yourselves shall think most for your own good. If at this time you think it will be better for you to dispose of some of them to pay your debts, and to help your people to improve the rest, we are willing to buy on reasonable terms. Our people multiply so fast that it will suit us to buy as much as you wish to sell, but only according to your good will. We have lately obtained from the French and Spaniards all the country beyond the Mississippi called Louisiana, in which there is a great deal of land unoccupied by any red men. But it is very far off, and we would prefer giving you lands there, or money and goods as you like best, for such parts of your land on this side the Mississippi as you are disposed to part with. Should you have anything to say on this subject now, or at any future time, we shall be always ready to listen to you.

I am obliged, within a few days, to set out on a long journey; but I wish you to stay and rest yourselves according to your own convenience. The Secretary at War will take care of you, will have you supplied with whatever you may have occasion for, and will provide for your return at your own pleasure. And I hope you will carry to your countrymen assurances of the sincere friendship of the United States to them, and that we shall always be disposed to render them all the service in our power. This, my children, is all I had proposed to say at this time.

## TO THE CHOCTAW NATION

March 13, 1805

MY CHILDREN: I learn with great satisfaction that you have leased to us three stations of one mile square each on the road from Chickasaws to Natchez, and one on the Pearl river; and you desire me to send you a paper under my own hand to show to your warriors that these lands are not sold but lent. I now accordingly declare that the property in those lands remains in your nation, that they are lent to us for a rent of four hundred pounds weight of powder annually, and that your nation has a right to take them back at their pleasure; and this paper now signed by my own hand will be evidence of these things to future generations. We will, according to your desire, settle but one white family on each section, and take care that they conduct themselves peaceably and friendly toward you; or being made known to me that they do otherwise they shall be removed. They will be placed there merely for the accommodation of our paper carriers and travellers.

*My children,* you have asked whether I did not promise to send you ploughs to enable you to improve in husbandry? I did promise it and immediately sent the ploughs; but by a mistake in forwarding them, they were delayed some time before we knew of it. You must, however, have received them before this time.

You ask if I did not promise to send your deputation ten rifles for yourselves and other deserving warriors? I did not promise it. You said they would be acceptable, but I said nothing in reply. But although I did not promise, yet to show my good will to you, I will send you the rifles.

You ask if we will allow commissions to you according to your rank and medals and commissions to such chiefs as you may appoint to assist in the government of your country? It has not been a custom with us to give commissions to our friends among the red men; and it is a new thing. We will take it into consideration. We wish to do what is agreeable to you, if we find we can do it with prudence.

We shall be willing to give medals to a certain number of distinguished chiefs who aid you in the government of your country, and who manifest dispositions to preserve peace and friendship between your nation and ours. We wish you, therefore, to recommend such to us.

*My children,* persevere in your friendship to the United States. We will never injure you nor permit you to be injured by any white people, and we trust you will take care that none of our people are injured by yours. Encourage among you the cultivation of the earth, raising of cattle, spinning and weaving, and we will assist you in it. With plenty of food and clothing you will raise many children, multiply, be strong and happy. May the Great Spirit protect and prosper you in all your just pursuits. Farewell.

## TO McINTOSH AND THE CHIEFS OF THE CREEK NATION[1]

November 2, 1805

FRIEND MC INTOSH AND CHIEFS OF THE CREEK NATION: I am glad to receive your visit at the Seat of our Government, and to take you by the hand of friendship as our neighbours and children. I thank the Great Spirit who has brought you safely through so long a journey, and who I hope will continue his protection, and restore you safely to your friends.

It is now 15 years since the Great Chiefs of your Nation met us at New York in the time of our first President Washington. Our friend Cornell and myself were at that meeting. We then laid the foundation of that peace and friendship which has bound us together ever since, and which I hope will continue to bind us forever. We have endeavoured from that time by all the ways in our power, to promote your prosperity and happiness, and especially by encouraging you to cultivate the earth, raise stock, make clothing, for the support and comfort of yourselves, women and children. A

[1] MS. in National Archives: Records of the Office of Indian Affairs, Secretary of War, Letter Book "B."

little land cultivated in corn and cotton will go further in providing sustenance and clothing for your people, than the most extensive range of country can furnish by hunting: and I learn with great pleasure from our beloved man, Col. Hawkins, the progress you have made in these arts of first necessity. Instead of decreasing numbers from year to year as heretofore, you will find in this new mode of life, that every year will add to your numbers: And we shall see it with pleasure, because we consider it as multiplying our friends. You will certainly find your interest in selling from time to time portions of your waste and useless lands, to enable you to procure stock and utensils for your farms, to improve them, and in the meantime to maintain your families—but your lands are your own, my Children, we will protect your right in them not only against others, but against our own people. We prove this to you by the expensive establishment of Fort Wilkinson. We are a growing people, therefore whenever you wish to sell lands, we shall be ready to buy; but only in compliance with your own free will. When we treated at Fort Wilkinson, for the lands in the Fork of Oconee and Ocmulgee, we wished to have obtained the whole lands from River to river; because neither your cattle nor ours regard a marked line. They trespass on both side and this produces trespasses by men. The same considerations urged us to renew this subject lately, when we authorized our beloved man Col. Hawkins and Gen[l] Meriwether to endeavour to extend the purchase to Ocmulgee River, that we might have a plain boundary, a water path which our people could not trespass across through ignorance and raise ill blood between us. You agreed to sell, my Children, but at such a price as the Great Council of our Nation could not listen to. Nothing like that price was ever before asked or given in any of the purchases we have ever made from your neighbours. Look back on all the purchases made by the former Government of the English, at all those which have been made in later times, no instance can be produced of half that price ever given; no profits you make from them can justify it. For this reason, my friends and Children, and that we might not seem to part in an unkind way, I invited some of your distinguished Chiefs to come here and renew the chain of friendship, to talk over this subject and see if we can not conclude it. Your Nation, by their Agreement of the last year, shewed they were willing to part with the land, so that it only remains to see whether we cannot agree upon a reasonable price.

You have heard, my friends and Children, that we have purchased the Country called Louisiana from the French, who had purchased it from the Spaniards. Our Possessions now, therefore, extend all around our Indian neighbours: and it is become indispensable for us to have roads from one part to another and particularly from this place through Georgia to New

Orleans. Among the Nations of White people it is deemed a matter of right for the people of one Nation to have a free and innocent passage through the country of another, injuring nothing as they pass and paying for the subsistence they ask for on the road. To you, my friends and Children, we are willing to pay not only for the subsistence we ask for on the Road, but for the right to pass along it. On our part we undertake that those who pass along it shall do no wrong to your people, and if your bad people do wrong to our Passengers, we are confident that you will use your best endeavours to punish them; and if you do your best, we ask no more: We shall not hold you accountable for what you cannot prevent.

I am persuaded that your people who shall settle on the road, and furnish Travellers with provisions and lodging, will soon see the advantage and that the road will be speedily settled by them through its whole length so that Travellers will pass in comfort and safety.

On both of these subjects, my friends and Children, the lands of Ocmulgee and the road I have authorized the Secretary at War to confer with you, and to see whether we cannot come to an Agreement which our Great Council will approve.

Having mentioned Louisiana, I will also mention the information I have received that lies have been circulated among you, my friends and Children, by people whom it does not suit to speak truth. You have been told that we should not long remain masters of Louisiana. On this point, my Children, I wish to place your minds ever at rest. While the Sun shines in Heaven Louisiana will remain United with us. We are too strong for it to be taken from us, we are too wise to give it up—and who is to take it from us? I do not love to boast, my Children, but you, friend Cornell, have in former times seen the parts of our Country, besides those that you and your brethren have now come through. You know something more of our numbers and characters. Look at us, and then look at your neighbours on the other side, and judge which side ought to be afraid of the other. We have so far lived in uninterrupted peace and friendship with all our neighbours; not because we fear them, but because we believe men are happier in peace than war. We have never done them an injury, and we hope and believe they will not think it their interest to do us such an injury as might make it necessary for us to relinquish the state of peace. We recommend to you also, my friends and Children, the same peaceable demeanor towards all Nations and we assure you that you shall always find in us faithful friends and patrons.

## TO THE CHIEFS OF THE OSAGES, MISSOURIS, KANSAS, OTTOS, PANIS, AGOWAS, AND SIOUX [1]

January 4, 1806

MY FRIENDS AND CHILDREN, CHIEFS OF THE OSAGES, MISSOURIS, KANSAS, OTTOS, PANIS, AGOWAS, AND SIOUX: I take you by the hand of friendship and give you a hearty welcome to the Seat of Government of the United States. The journey you have undertaken to visit your fathers on this side of our Island, is a long one, and your having undertaken it is a proof that you desired to become acquainted with us. I thank the great Spirit that he has protected you through the journey and brought you safely to the residence of your friends, and I hope he will have you constantly in his safe keeping and restore you in good health to your Nations and families.

*My Friends and Children,* We are descended from the old Nations which live beyond the Great Water, but we and our forefathers have been so long here, that we seem like you to have grown out of this land. We consider ourselves no longer as of the old Nations beyond the Great Water, but as united in one family with our red brethren here. The French, the English, the Spaniards, have now agreed with us to retire from all the country which you and we hold between Canada and Mexico, and never more to return to it. And remember the words I now speak to you, my Children, they are never to return again. We are become as numerous as the leaves of the trees, and, tho' we do not boast, we do not fear any nation. We are now your fathers, and you should not loose by the change. As soon as Spain had agreed to withdraw from all the waters of the Missouri and Mississippi, I felt the desire of becoming acquainted with all my Red Children beyond the Mississippi, and of uniting them with us as we have done [with] those on this side of that River, in the bonds of peace and friendship. I wish to learn what we could do to benefit them by furnishing them the necessaries they want in exchange for their furs and peltries. I therefore sent our beloved man, Capt. Lewis, one of my own family, to go up the Missouri River, to get acquainted with all the Indian Nations in its neighborhood, to take them by the hand, deliver my talks to them, and to tell us in what way we could be useful to them. Some of you who are here have seen him and heard his words. You have taken him by the hand and been friendly to him. My Children, I thank you for the services you rendered him, and for your attention to his words. When he returns he will tell us when we should establish Factories to be convenient to you all, and what we must send to them. In establishing a trade with you we desire to make no profit. We shall ask

[1] MS. in National Archives: Records of the Office of Indian Affairs, Secretary of War, Letter Book "B."

from you only what every thing costs us, and give you for your furs and pelts whatever we can get for them. Be assured you shall find your advantages in this change of your friends. It will take us some time to be in readiness to supply your wants, but in the mean while and till Capt. Lewis returns, the traders who have heretofore furnished you will continue so.

*My Friends and Children,* I have now an important advice to give you, I have already told you that you are all my children, and I wish you to live in peace and friendship with one another as brethren of the same family ought to do. How much better is it for neighbours to help than to hurt one another. How much happier must it make them. If you will cease to make war on one another, if you will live in friendship with all mankind, you can employ all your time in providing food and clothing for yourselves and your families; your men will not be destroyed in war; and your women and children will lie down to sleep in their cabins without fear of being surprised by their enemies and killed or carried away. Your numbers will be increased instead of diminishing, and you will live in plenty and in quiet.

*My Children,* I have given this advice to all your red brethren on this side the Mississippi;—they are following it;—they are increasing in their numbers, and learning to clothe and provide for their families as we do, and you see the proofs of it in such of them as you happened to find here. My Children, we are strong, we are numerous as the Stars in the Heavens, and we are all gun-men, yet we live in peace with all Nations, and all Nations esteem and honor us because we are peaceable and just. Be you then peaceable and just also; take each other by the hand and hold it fast. If ever bad men among your neighbours should do you wrong, and their Nation refuse you justice, apply to the beloved man whom we shall place nearest to you; he will go to the offending Nation and endeavour to obtain right and preserve peace. If ever bad men among you yourselves injure your neighbours, be always ready to do justice. It is always honorable in those who have done wrong to acknowledge and make amends for it; and it is the only way in which peace can be maintained among men. Remember then my advice, my Children, carry it home to your people, and tell them that from the day we became father to them, we wish, as a true father should do, that we may all live together as one household, and that before they strike one another, they should come to their father and let him endeavour to make up the quarrel.

*My Children,* you come from the other side of our Great Island, from where the Sun sets to see your new friends at the Sun-rising. You have now arrived where the waters are constantly rising and falling every day, but you are still distant from the sea. I very much desire that you should not stop here but go on and see your brethren as far as the edge of the Great Water. I am persuaded you have so far seen that every man by the way has received you as his brothers, and has been ready to do you all the kindnesses in his power. You will see the same thing quite to the sea shore; and I wish you therefore to go and visit our Great Cities in that quarter, and see how many friends and Brothers you have here. You will then have travelled a long line from West to East, and if you had time to go from North to South, from Canada to Florida, you would find it as long in that direction, and all the people as sincerely your friends. I wish you, my Children, to see all you can, and to tell your people all you see; because I am sure the more they know of us, the more they will be our hearty friends. I invite you therefore to pay a visit to Baltimore, Philadelphia, New York, and the cities still beyond that, if you should be willing to go further. We will provide carriages to convey you, and a person to go with you and to see that you want for nothing. By the time you come back, the snow will be melted on the Mountains, the Ice in the rivers broken up, and you will be wishing to set out on your return home.

*My Children,* I have long desired to see you: I have now opened my heart to you: let my words sink into your hearts and never be forgotten. If ever lying people or bad spirits should raise up clouds between us, call to mind what I have said and what you have seen yourselves. Be sure there are some lying spirits between us:—Let us come together as friends and explain to each other what is misrepresented or misunderstood, the clouds will fly away like the morning fog and the Sun of friendship appear and shine forever, bright and clear between us.

*My Children,* it may happen that while you are here, occasion may arise to talk about many things which I do not now particularly mention. The Secretary at War will always be ready to talk to you. And you are to consider whatever he says as said by myself. He will also take care of you and see that you are furnished with all the comforts here.

## TO THE CHIEFS OF THE CHEROKEE NATION

January 10, 1806

MY FRIENDS AND CHILDREN, CHIEFLY OF THE CHEROKEE NATION: Having now finished our business and finished it I hope to mutual satisfaction, I cannot take leave of you without expressing the satisfaction I have received from your visit. I see with my own eyes that the endeavors we have been making to encourage and lead you in the way of improving your situation have not been unsuccessful; it has been like grain sown in good ground, producing abundantly. You are becoming farmers, learning the use of the plough and the hoe, enclosing your grounds and employing that labor in their cultivation which you formerly employed in hunting and in war; and

I see handsome specimens of cotton cloth raised, spun and woven by yourselves. You are also raising cattle and hogs for your food, and horses to assist your labors. Go on, my children, in the same way and be assured the further you advance in it the happier and more respectable you will be.

Our brethren, whom you have happened to meet here from the West and Northwest, have enabled you to compare your situation now with what it was formerly. They also make the comparison, and they see how far you are ahead of them, and seeing what you are they are encouraged to do as you have done. You will find your next want to be mills to grind your corn, which by relieving your women from the loss of time in beating it into meal, will enable them to spin and weave more. When a man has enclosed and improved his farm, builds a good house on it and raised plentiful stocks of animals, he will wish when he dies that these things shall go to his wife and children, whom he loves more than he does his other relations, and for whom he will work with pleasure during his life. You will, therefore, find it necessary to establish laws for this. When a man has property, earned by his own labor, he will not like to see another come and take it from him because he happens to be stronger, or else to defend it by spilling blood. You will find it necessary then to appoint good men, as judges, to decide contests between man and man, according to reason and to the rules you shall establish. If you wish to be aided by our counsel and experience in these things we shall always be ready to assist you with our advice.

*My children,* it is unnecessary for me to advise you against spending all your time and labor in warring with and destroying your fellow-men, and wasting your own members. You already see the folly and iniquity of it. Your young men, however, are not yet sufficiently sensible of it. Some of them cross the Mississippi to go and destroy people who have never done them an injury. My children, this is wrong and must not be; if we permit them to cross the Mississippi to war with the Indians on the other side of that river, we must let those Indians cross the river to take revenge on you. I say again, this must not be. The Mississippi now belongs to us. It must not be a river of blood. It is now the water-path along which all our people of Natchez, St. Louis, Indiana, Ohio, Tennessee, Kentucky and the western parts of Pennsylvania and Virginia are constantly passing with their property, to and from New Orleans. Young men going to war are not easily restrained. Finding our people on the river they will rob them, perhaps kill them. This would bring on a war between us and you. It is better to stop this in time by forbidding your young men to go across the river to make war. If they go to visit or to live with Cherokees on the other side of the river we shall not object to that. That country is ours. We will permit them to live in it.

*My children,* this is what I wished to say to you. To go on in learning to cultivate the earth and to avoid war. If any of your neighbors injure you, our beloved men whom we place with you will endeavor to obtain justice for you and we will support them in it. If any of your bad people injure your neighbors, be ready to acknowledge it and to do them justice. It is more honorable to repair a wrong than to persist in it. Tell all your chiefs, your men, women and children, that I take them by the hand and hold it fast. That I am their father, wish their happiness and well-being, and am always ready to promote their good.

*My children,* I thank you for your visit and pray to the Great Spirit who made us all and planted us all in this land to live together like brothers that He will conduct you safely to your homes, and grant you to find your families and your friends in good health.

## TO THE RICARA NATION[1]

1806

MY FRIENDS AND CHILDREN OF THE RICARA NATION: It gave me great pleasure to see your beloved Chief arrive here on a visit to his White Brothers of the United States of America. I took him by the hand with affection,—I considered him as bringing to me the assurances of your friendship, and that you were willing to become of one family with us. Wishing to see as much as he could of his new Brethren, he consented to go on towards the sea as far as Baltimore and Philadelphia. He found nothing but kindness and good will wherever he passed. On his return to this place, he was taken sick;—everything we could do to help him was done, but it pleased the Great Spirit to take him from among us. We buried him among our own deceased friends and relations. We shed many tears over his grave, and we now mingle our affections with yours on the loss of this beloved Chief. But death must happen to all men; and his time was come.

*My Friends and Children,* We are descended from the old Nations which live beyond the Great Water; but we and our forefathers have been so long here that we seem like you to have grown out of this land. We consider ourselves no longer as of the old Nations beyond the Great Water, but as united in one family with our Red Brethren here. The French, the English, the Spaniards, have now agreed with us to retire from all the Country which you and we hold between Canada and Mexico, and never more to return to it. And remember the words I now speak to you, my Children, they are never to return again. We are become as numerous as the leaves of the trees,

[1] MS. in National Archives: Records of the Office of Indian Affairs, Secretary of War, Letter Book "B."

and though we do not boast, we do not fear any Nation. We are now your fathers, and you shall not lose by the change. As soon as Spain had agreed to withdraw from all the waters of the Missouri and Mississippi, I felt the desire of becoming acquainted with all my Red Children beyond the Mississippi, and of uniting them with us, as we have done there on this side of that River, in the bonds of peace and friendship. I wished to learn what we could do to benefit them, by furnishing them the necessaries they want in exchange for their furs and peltries. I therefore sent our beloved man, Capt. Lewis, one of my own family, to go up the Missouri River, to get acquainted with all the Indian Nations in its neighborhood, to take them by the hand, deliver my talks to them, and to inform us in what way we could be useful to them. You saw him and heard his words. You took him by the hand, were friendly to him. My Children, I thank you for the services you rendered him, and your attention to his words. When he returns he will tell us when we should establish factories to be convenient to you all, and what we must send to them. In establishing a trade with you, we desire to make no profit. We shall ask from you only what every thing costs us, and give you for your furs and peltries whatever we can get for them again. Be assured you shall find your advantage in this change of your friends. It will take us some time to be in readiness to supply your wants, but in the mean while and till Capt. Lewis returns, the traders who have heretofore furnished you will continue to do so.

*My Friends and Children,* I have now an important advice to give you. I have already told you that you are all my children, and I wish you to live in peace and friendship with one another as Brethren of the same family ought to do. How much better is it for neighbours to help than to hurt one another; how much happier must it make them. If you will cease to make war on one another, if you will live in friendship with all mankind, you can employ all your time in providing food and clothing for yourselves and your families; your men will not be destroyed in war, and your women and children will lie down to sleep in their cabins without fear of being surprised by their enemies, and killed or carried away. Your numbers will be increased instead of diminishing, and you will live in plenty and in quiet. My Children, I have given this advice to all your red brethren, on this side of the Mississippi; they are beginning to follow it. They are increasing in their numbers, and are learning to clothe and provide for their families as we do. My Children, we are strong; we are numerous as the stars in the heavens and we are all gun-men, yet we live in peace and friendship with all Nations; and all Nations esteem and honor us because we are peaceable and just. Be you then peaceable and just also, take each other by the hand and hold it fast. If ever bad men among your neighbours should do you wrong, and their Nation refuse you justice, apply to the beloved man whom we shall place nearest to you; he will go to the offending Nation, and endeavor to obtain right and preserve peace; if ever bad men among ourselves injure your neighbours, be always ready to do justice. It is always honorable in those who have done wrong, to acknowledge and make amends for it; and it is the only way in which peace can be maintained among men.

*My Children,* I have now opened my heart to you; let my words sink into your hearts and never be forgotten. If ever lying people or bad spirits should raise up clouds between us, call to mind what I have said. Be sure there are some lying spirits between us—let us come together as friends and explain to each other what is misrepresented or misunderstood. The clouds will fly away like the morning fog and the sun of friendship appear and shine forever bright and clear between us.

## TO THE CHIEFS AND PEOPLE OF THE MANDAM NATION [1]

1806

MY FRIENDS AND CHILDREN: I should have received with great satisfaction at the seat of our Government, some of your Chiefs, with those of the Osages, Ricaras, Missouris, Panis and others who have lately visited us. They would have seen with their own eyes proofs of the friendship which myself and all their white brethren of these United States bear them, of our desire to live in peace with them, and to render them all the services in our power. But the journey is long; liable to many accidents; and therefore not to be insisted on between friends. At some future time, perhaps I shall have the pleasure of seeing some of you here. I consider you as the first Nation beyond the Mississippi, which we became acquainted with through our beloved man, Capt. Lewis, who passed a winter with you. You received him as a friend,—were kind to him;—and I now thank you for all the services you rendered him and his people.

*My Friends and Children,* We are descended [the same as the talk to the Ricara Nation]. . . .

## TO THE CHIEFS AND PEOPLE OF THE MANDAM NATION [2]

1806 (?)

MY SON, THE LITTLE BEAR, CHIEF OF THE CHIPPEWAY NATION: I will now give a separate answer to the speech which you delivered to me separately. The

[1] MS. in National Archives: Records of the Office of Indian Affairs, Secretary of War, Letter Book "B."

[2] MS. in National Archives: Records of the Office of Indian Affairs, Secretary of War, Letter Book "B."

Secretary at War has explained to you our assent to the exchange of lands which you propose with a particular individual and this shall be put into writing.

He has also explained to you the difficulties we find in getting Smiths and Carpenters, who are honest and capable men to go and live among you, and that we shall continue to use our best endeavors for this.

We will take care that there be always someone with you who shall teach you how to plough and cultivate your lands; and we are now taking measures for supporting the establishment of the school at Detroit, where we wish you to send your young lads to learn agriculture and useful trades and your young girls to learn to spin, weave, sew and other household arts, and to learn to speak our language, that in time we may all be able to converse with one another and not meet as we have done here, seven or eight languages together and be like dead men, unable to hold conversation with one another.

The Secretary at War has told you that the sum of five hundred dollars shall be laid out for you and my other red children in that part of the country in domestic animals and implements of husbandry, to assist them in cultivating and stocking their farms and that two hundred dollars of the Chippeway annuity for this year shall now be paid to you.

This, my Son, is what I have to say in answer to your speech; and I hope, you will see in it satisfactory proofs of my good will to your nation and of my great personal esteem for yourself.

## TO THE WOLF AND PEOPLE OF THE MANDAM NATION

December 30, 1806

MY CHILDREN, THE WOLF AND PEOPLE OF THE MANDAM NATION: I take you by the hand of friendship and give you a hearty welcome to the seat of the government of the United States. The journey which you have taken to visit your fathers on this side of our island is a long one, and your having undertaken it is a proof that you desired to become acquainted with us. I thank the Great Spirit that he has protected you through the journey and brought you safely to the residence of your friends, and I hope He will have you constantly in his safe keeping, and restore you in good health to your nations and families.

*My friends and children,* we are descended from the old nations which live beyond the great water, but we and our forefathers have been so long here that we seem like you to have grown out of this land. We consider ourselves no longer of the old nations beyond the great water, but as united in one family with our red brethren here. The French, the English, the

Spaniards, have now agreed with us to retire from all the country which you and we hold between Canada and Mexico, and never more to return to it. And remember the words I now speak to you, my children, they are never to return again. We are now your fathers; and you shall not lose by the change. As soon as Spain had agreed to withdraw from all the waters of the Missouri and Mississippi, I felt the desire of becoming acquainted with all my red children beyond the Mississippi, and of uniting them with us as we have those on this side of that river, in the bonds of peace and friendship. I wished to learn what we could do to benefit them by furnishing them the necessaries they want in exchange for their furs and peltries. I therefore sent our beloved man, Captain Lewis, one of my own family, to go up the Missouri river to get acquainted with all the Indian nations in its neighborhood, to take them by the hand, deliver my talks to them, and to inform us in what way we could be useful to them. Your nation received him kindly, you have taken him by the hand and been friendly to him. My children, I thank you for the services you rendered him, and for your attention to his words. He will now tell us where we should establish trading houses to be convenient to you all, and what we must send to them.

*My friends and children,* I have now an important advice to give you. I have already told you that you and all the red men are my children, and I wish you to live in peace and friendship with one another as brethren of the same family ought to do. How much better is it for neighbors to help than to hurt one another; how much happier must it make them. If you will cease to make war on one another, if you will live in friendship with all mankind, you can employ all your time in providing food and clothing for yourselves and your families. Your men will not be destroyed in war, and your women and children will lie down to sleep in their cabins without fear of being surprised by their enemies and killed or carried away. Your numbers will be increased instead of diminishing, and you will live in plenty and in quiet. My children, I have given this advice to all your red brethren on this side of the Mississippi; they are following it, they are increasing in their numbers, are learning to clothe and provide for their families as we do. Remember then my advice, my children, carry it home to your people, and tell them that from the day that they have become all of the same family, from the day that we became father to them all, we wish, as a true father should do, that we may all live together as one household, and that before they strike one another, they should go to their father and let him endeavor to make up the quarrel.

*My children,* you are come from the other side of our great island, from where the sun sets, to see your new friends at the sun rising. You have now arrived where the waters are constantly rising and falling every day, but you are still distant from the sea. I very much desire that you should not stop here, but go and see your brethren as far as the edge of the great water. I am persuaded you have so far seen that every man by the way has received you as his brothers, and has been ready to do you all the kindness in his power. You will see the same thing quite to the sea shore; and I wish you, therefore, to go and visit our great cities in that quarter, and see how many friends and brothers you have here. You will then have travelled a long line from west to east, and if you had time to go from north to south, from Canada to Florida, you would find it as long in that direction, and all the people as sincerely your friends. I wish you, my children, to see all you can, and to tell your people all you see; because I am sure the more they know of us, the more they will be our hearty friends. I invite you, therefore, to pay a visit to Baltimore, Philadelphia, New York, and the cities still beyond that, if you are willing to go further. We will provide carriages to convey you and a person to go with you to see that you want for nothing. By the time you come back the snows will be melted on the mountains, the ice in the rivers broken up, and you will be wishing to set out on your return home.

*My children,* I have long desired to see you; I have now opened my heart to you, let my words sink into your hearts and never be forgotten. If ever lying people or bad spirits should raise up clouds between us, call to mind what I have said, and what you have seen yourselves. Be sure there are some lying spirits between us; let us come together as friends and explain to each other what is misrepresented or misunderstood, the clouds will fly away like morning fog, and the sun of friendship appear and shine forever bright and clear between us.

*My children,* it may happen that while you are here occasion may arise to talk about many things which I do not now particularly mention. The Secretary at War will always be ready to talk with you, and you are to consider whatever he says as said by myself. He will also take care of you and see that you are furnished with all comforts here.

## TO THE CHIEFS OF THE OSAGE NATION

December 31, 1806

MY CHILDREN, CHIEFS OF THE OSAGE NATION: I welcome you sincerely to the seat of the government of the United States. The journey you have taken is long and fatiguing, and proved your desire to become acquainted with your new brothers of this country. I thank the master of life, who has preserved you by the way and brought you safely here. I hope you have found yourselves, through the whole journey, among brothers and friends, who have used you kindly, and convinced you they wish to live always in peace and harmony with you.

*My children,* your forefathers have doubtless handed it down to you that in ancient times the French were the fathers of all the red men in the country called Louisiana, that is to say, all the country on the Mississippi and on all its western waters. In the days of your fathers France ceded that country to the Spaniards and they became your fathers; but six years ago they restored it to France and France ceded it to us, and we are now become your fathers and brothers; and be assured you will have no cause to regret the change. It is so long since our forefathers came from beyond the great water, that we have lost the memory of it, and seem to have grown out of this land as you have done. Never more will you have occasion to change your fathers. We are all now of one family, born in the same land, and bound to live as brothers, and to have nothing more to do with the strangers who live beyond the great water. The Great Spirit has given you strength and has given us strength, not that we should hurt one another, but to do each other all the good in our power. Our dwellings indeed are very far apart, but not too far to carry on commerce and useful intercourse. You have furs and peltries which we want, and we have clothes and other useful things which you want. Let us employ ourselves, then, in making exchanges of these articles useful to both. In order to prepare ourselves for this commerce with our new children, we have found it necessary to send some of our trusty men up the different rivers of Louisiana, to see what nations live upon them, what number of peltries they can furnish, what quantities and kinds of merchandize they want, and where are the places most convenient to establish trading houses with them. With this view we sent a party to the head of the Missouri and the great water beyond that, who are just returned. We sent another party up the Red river, and we propose, the ensuing spring, to send one up the Arkansas as far as its head. This party will consist, like the others, of between twenty and thirty persons. I shall instruct them to call and see you at your towns, to talk with my son the Big Track, who, as well as yourselves and your people, will I hope receive them kindly, protect them and give them all the information they can as to the people on the same river above you. When they return they will be able to tell us how we can best establish a trade with you, and how otherwise we can be useful to them.

*My children,* I was sorry to learn that a difference had arisen among the people of your nation, and that a part of them had separated and removed to a great distance on the Arkansas. This is a family quarrel with which I do not pretend to intermeddle. Both parties are my children, and I wish equally well to both. But it would give me great pleasure if they could again reunite, because a nation, while it holds together, is strong against its enemies, but, breaking into parts, it is easily destroyed. However I hope you will at least make friends again, and cherish peace and brotherly love with one another. If I can be useful in restoring friendship between you, I shall do it with great pleasure. It is my wish that all my red children live together as one family, that when differences arise among them, their old men should meet together and settle them with justice and in peace. In this way your women and children will live in safety, your nation will increase and be strong.

As you have taken so long a journey to see your fathers, we wish you not to return till you have visited our country and towns towards the sea coast. This will be new and satisfactory to you, and it will give you the same knowledge of the country on this side of the Mississippi, which we are endeavoring to acquire of that on the other side, by sending trusty persons to explore them. We propose to do in your country only what we are desirous you should do in ours. We will provide accommodations for your journey, for your comfort while engaged in it, and for your return in safety to your own country, carrying with you those proofs of esteem with which we distinguish our friends, and shall particularly distinguish you. On your return, tell your chief, the Big Track, and all your people, that I take them by the hand, that I become their father hereafter, that they shall know our nation only as friends and benefactors, that we have no views upon them but to carry on a commerce useful to them and us, to keep them in peace with their neighbors, that their children may multiply, may grow up and live to a good old age, and their women no longer fear the tomahawk of any enemy.

*My children,* these are my words, carry them to your nation, keep them in your memories and our friendship in your hearts, and may the Great Spirit look down upon us and cover us with the mantle of his love.

## TO THE CHIEFS OF THE SHAWANEE NATION

February 19, 1807

MY CHILDREN, CHIEFS OF THE SHAWANEE NATION: I have listened to the speeches of the Blackhoof, Blackbeard, and the other head chiefs of the Shawanese, and have considered them well. As all these speeches relate to the public affairs of your nation, I will answer them together.

You express a wish to have your lands laid off separately to yourselves, that you may know what is your own, may have a fixed place to live on, of which you may not be deprived after you shall have built on it, and improved it; you would rather that this should be towards Fort Wayne, and to include the three reserves; you ask a strong writing from us, declaring your right, and observe that the writing you had was taken from you by the Delawares.

After the close of our war with the English, we wished to establish peace and friendship with our Indian neighbors also. In order to do this, the first thing necessary was to fix a firm boundary between them and us, that there might be no trespasses across that by either party. Not knowing then what parts on our border belonged to each Indian nation particularly, we thought it safest to get all those in the north to join in one treaty, and to settle a general boundary line between them and us. We did not intermeddle as to the lines dividing them one from another, because this was their concern, not ours. We therefore met the chiefs of the Wyandots, Delawares, Shawanees, Ottawas, Chippewas, Powtewatamies, Miamis, Eel-Rivers, Weeauks, Kickapoos, Piankeshaws, and Kaskaskies, at Greeneville, and agreed on a general boundary which was to divide their lands from those of the whites, making only some particular reserves, for the establishment of trade and intercourse with them. This treaty was eleven years ago, as Blackbeard has said. Since that, some of them have thought it for their advantage to sell us portions of their lands, which has changed the boundaries in some parts; but their rights in the residue remain as they were, and must always be settled among themselves. If the Shawanese and Delawares, and their other neighbors, choose to settle the boundaries between their respective tribes, and to have them marked and recorded in our books, we will mark them as they shall agree among themselves, and will give them strong writings declaring the separate right of each. After which, we will protect each tribe in its respective lands, as well as against other tribes who might attempt to take them from them, as against our own people. The writing which you say the Delawares took from you, must have been the copy of the treaty of Greeneville. We will give you another copy to be kept by your nation.

With respect to the reserves, you know they were made for the purpose of establishing convenient stations for trade and intercourse with the tribes within whose boundaries they are. And as circumstances shall render it expedient to make these establishments, it is for your interest, as well as ours, that the possession of these stations should enable us to make them.

You complain that Blue-jacket, and a part of your people at Greeneville, cheat you in the distribution of your annuity, and take more of it than their just share. It will be difficult to remedy this evil while your nation is living in different settlements. We will, however, direct our agent to enquire, and inform us what are your numbers in each of your settlements, and will then divide the annuities between the settlements justly, according to their numbers. And if we can be of any service in bringing you all together into one place, we will willingly assist you for that purpose. Perhaps your visit to the settlement of your people on the Mississippi under the Flute may assist towards gathering them all into one place from which they may never again remove.

You say that you like our mode of living, that you wish to live as we do, to raise a plenty of food for your children, and to bring them up in good principles; that you adopt our mode of living, and ourselves as your brothers. My children, I rejoice to hear this; it is the wisest resolution you have ever formed, to raise corn and domestic animals, by the culture of the earth, and to let your women spin and weave clothes for you all, instead of depending for these on hunting. Be assured that half the labor and hardships you go through to provide your families by hunting, with food and clothing, if employed in a farm would feed and clothe them better. When the white people first came to this land, they were few, and you were many: now we are many, and you few; and why? because, by cultivating the earth, we produce plenty to raise our children, while yours, during a part of every year, suffer for want of food, are forced to eat unwholesome things, are exposed to the weather in your hunting camps, get diseases and die. Hence it is that your numbers lessen.

You ask for instruction in our manner of living, for carpenters and blacksmiths. My children, you shall have them. We will do everything in our power to teach you to take care of your wives and children, that you may multiply and be strong. We are sincerely your friends and brothers, we are as unwilling to see your blood spilt in war, as our own. Therefore, we encourage you to live in peace with all nations, that your women and children may live without danger, and without fear. The greatest honor of a man is in doing good to his fellow men, not in destroying them. We have placed Mr. Kirk among you, who will have other persons under him to teach you how to manage farms, and to make clothes for yourselves; and we expect you will put some of your young people to work with the carpenters and smiths we place among you, that they may learn the trades. In this way only can you have a number of tradesmen sufficient for all your people.

You wish me to name to you the person authorized to speak to you in our name, that you may know whom to believe, and not be deceived by impostors. My children, Governor Harrison is the person we authorize to talk to you in our name. You may depend on his advice, and that it comes from us. He stands between you and us, to convey with truth whatever either of us wishes to say to the other.

*My children,* I wish you a safe return to your friends and families, that you may retain your resolution of learning to live in our way, that it may give health and comfort to your families, and add members to your nation. In me you will always find a sincere and true friend.

## TO KITCHAO GEBOWAY

February 27, 1808

MY SON KITCHAO GEBOWAY: I have received the speech which you sent me through General Gansevoort from Albany on the 13th of this month, and now return you my answer. It would have given me great pleasure to have been able to converse with and understand you, when you visited me at Washington; but the want of an interpreter rendered that impossible.

*My son,* tell your nation, the Chippewas, that I take them by the hand, and consider them as a part of the great family of the United States, which extends to the great Lakes and the Lake of the Woods, northwardly, and from the rising to the setting sun; that the United States wish to live in peace with them, to consider them as a part of themselves, to establish a commerce with them, as advantageous to the Chippewas as they can make it, and in all cases to render them every service in our power. We shall never ask them to enter into our quarrels, nor to spill their blood in fighting our enemies. My son, in visiting this quarter of the United States, you have seen a part of our country, and some of our people from East to West. If you had travelled also from North to South, you would have seen it the same. You see that we are as numerous as the leaves of the trees, that we are strong enough to fight our own battles, and too strong to fear any enemy. When, therefore, we wish you to live in peace with all people, red and white, we wish it because it is for your good, and because it is our desire that your women and children shall live in safety, not fearing the tomahawk of any enemy, that they may learn to raise food enough to support their families, and that your nation may multiply and be strong. If any white men advise you to go to war for them, it is a proof they are too weak to defend themselves, that they are in truth your enemies, wishing to sacrifice you to save themselves; and when they shall be driven away, my son, what is to become of the red men who may join in their battles? Take the advice then of a father, and meddle not in the quarrels of the white people, should any war take place between them; but stay at home in peace, taking care of your wives and children. In that case not a hair of your heads shall be touched. Never will we do you an injury unprovoked, or disturb you in your towns or lands by any violence.

*My son,* I confirm everything which your father, Governor Hull, said to you at Detroit on my part: and in all your difficulties and dangers apply to him, and take his advice. If some of your principal chiefs will pay me a visit at Washington, I shall be very happy to receive them, to smoke the pipe of friendship with them, to take them by the hand and never to let go their friendship. They shall see that I want nothing from them but their good will, and to do them all the good in my power.

*My son,* the Secretary at War will comply with your request in giving you a chief's coat with epaulettes, and a stand of the colors of the United States, to plant in your town, to let all the world see that you are a part of the family of the United States.

*My son,* I wish you a pleasant journey, and a safe return to your family and friends.

## TO THE CHIEFS OF THE OTTAWAS, CHIPPEWAS, POWTEWATTAMIES, WYANDOTS, AND SENECAS OF SANDUSKY

April 22, 1808

MY CHILDREN: I received your message of July last, and I am glad of the opportunity it gives me of explaining to you the sentiments of the government of the United States towards you.

Many among you must remember the time when we were governed by the British nation, and the war by which we separated ourselves from them. Your old men must remember also that while we were under that government we were constantly kept at war with the red men our neighbors. Many of these took side in the English war against us; so that after we had made peace with the English, ill blood remained between us for some time; and it was not till the treaty of Greeneville that we could come to a solid peace and perfect good understanding with all our Indian neighbors. This being once done and fixed lines drawn between them and us, laying off their lands to themselves, and ours to ourselves, so that each might know their own, and nothing disturb our future peace, we have from that moment, my children, looked upon you heartily as our brothers, and as a part of ourselves. We saw that your game was becoming too scarce to support you, and that unless we could persuade you to cultivate the earth, to raise the tame animals, and to spin and weave clothes for yourselves as we do, you would disappear from the earth. To encourage you, therefore, to save yourselves has been our constant object; and we have hoped that the day would come when every man among you would have his own farm laid off to himself as we have, would maintain his family by labor as we do, and would make one people with us. But in all these things you have been free to do as you please; your lands are your own; your right to them shall never be violated by us; they are yours to keep or to sell as you please. Whenever you find it your interest to dispose of a part to enable you to improve the rest, and to support your families in the meantime, we are willing to buy, because our people increase fast. When a want of land in a particular place induces us to ask you to sell, still you are always free to say "No," and it will never disturb our friendship for you. We will never be angry with others for exercising their own rights according to what they think their own interests. You say you were told at Swan's Creek, that if you would not let us have lands, we should be angry with you, and would force you. Those, my children, who told you so, said what was false, and what never had been said or thought of by us. We never meant to control your free will; we never will do it. I will explain to you the ground of our late application to you for lands. You know that the posts of Detroit and Mackinac have very little lands belonging to them. It is for your interest as well as ours that these posts should be maintained for the purposes of our trade with one another. We were desirous therefore to purchase as much land around them as would enable us to have sufficient settlements there to support the posts; and that this might be so laid off as to join with our possessions on Lake Erie. But we expressly instructed our beloved man, Governor Hull, not to press you beyond your own convenience, nor to buy more than you would spare with good will. He accordingly left you to your own inclinations, using no threats whatever, as you tell me in your message. You agreed to let us have a part of what we wished to buy. We are contented with it, my children. We find no fault with you for what you did not do, but thank you for what you did.

You complain, my children, that your annuities are not regularly paid, that the goods delivered you are often bad in kind, that they sometimes arrive damaged, and are dear, and that you would rather receive them in money. You shall have them in money. We had no interest in laying out your money in goods for you.

It cost us considerable trouble in the purchase and transportation, and as we could not be everywhere with them to take care of them ourselves, we could not prevent their being injured sometimes by accident, sometimes by carelessness. To pay money therefore, is more convenient to us, and as it will please you better, it shall be done.

I am now, my children, to address you on a very serious subject, one which greatly concerns your happiness. Open your ears, therefore, let my words sink deeply into your bosoms, and never forget them. For be assured that I will not, and that I will fulfil them to their uttermost import. We have for some time had a misunderstanding with the English, and we do not yet know whether it will end in peace or in war. But in either case, my children, do you remain quiet at home, taking no part in these quarrels. We do not wish you to shed your blood in our battles. We are able to fight them ourselves. And if others press you to take part against us, it is because they are weak, not able to protect themselves nor you. Consider well then what you do. Since we have freed ourselves from the English government, and made our peace with our Indian neighbors, we have cultivated that peace with sincerity and affection. We have done them such favors as were in our power, and promoted their interest and peace wherever we could. We consider them now as a part of ourselves, and we look to their welfare as our own. But if there be among you any nation whom no benefits can attach, no good offices on our part can convert into faithful friends, if relinquishing their permanent connection with us for the fugitive presents or promises of others, they shall prefer our enmity to our friendship, and engage in war against us, that nation must abandon forever the land of their fathers. No nation rejecting our friendship, and commencing wanton and unprovoked war against us, shall ever after remain within our reach; it shall never be in their power to strike us a second time. These words, my children, may appear harsh; but they are spoken in kindness; they are intended to warn you beforehand of the ruin into which those will rush, who shall once break the chain of friendship with us. You know they are not spoken from fear. We fear no nation. We love yours. We wish you to live forever in peace with all men, and in brotherly affection with us; to be with us as one family; to take care of your women and children, feed and clothe them well, multiply and be strong with your friends and your enemies.

*My children,* I salute you with fatherly concern for your welfare.

## TO THE CHIEFS OF THE UPPER CHEROKEES

May 4, 1808

MY CHILDREN, CHIEFS OF THE UPPER CHEROKEES: I am glad to see you at the seat of government, to take you by the hand, and to assure you in person of the friendship of the United States towards all their red children, and of their desire to extend, to them all, their protection of good offices. The journey you have come is a long one, and the object expressed in our conference of the other day is important. I have listened to it with attention, and given it the consideration it deserves. You complain that you do not receive your just proportion of the annuities we pay your nation; that the chiefs of the lower towns take for them more than their share. My children, this distribution is made by the authority of the Cherokee nation, and according to their own rules over which we have no control. We do our duty in delivering the annuities to the head men of the nation, and we pretend to no authority over them, to no right of directing how they are to be distributed. But we will instruct our agent, Colonel Meigs, to exhort the chiefs to do justice to all the parts of their nation in the distribution of these annuities, and to endeavor that every town shall have its due share. We would willingly pay these annuities in money, which could be more equally divided, if the nation would prefer that, and if we can be assured that the money will not be laid out in strong drink instead of necessaries for your wives and children. We wish to do whatever will best secure your people from suffering for want of clothes or food. It is these wants which bring sickness and death into your families, and prevent you from multiplying as we do. In answer to your question relating to the lands we have purchased from your nation at different times, I inform you that the payments have for the most part been made in money, which has been left, as the annuities are, to the discharge of your debts, and to distribute according to the rules of the nation.

You propose, my children, that your nation shall be divided into two, and that your part, the upper Cherokees, shall be separated from the lower by a fixed boundary, shall be placed under the government of the United States, become citizens thereof, and be ruled by our laws; in fine, to be our brothers instead of our children. My children, I shall rejoice to see the day when the red men, our neighbors, become truly one people with us, enjoying all the rights and privileges we do, and living in peace and plenty as we do, without any one to make them afraid, to injure their persons, or to take their property without being punished for it according to fixed laws. But are you prepared for this? Have you the resolution to leave off hunting for your living, to lay off a farm for each family to itself, to live by industry, the men working that farm with their hands, raising stock, or learning trades as we do, and the women spinning and weaving clothes for their husbands and children? All this is necessary before our laws can suit you or be of any use to you. However, let your people take this matter into consideration. If they think themselves prepared for becoming citizens of the United States, for living in subjection to laws and under their protection as we do, let them consult the lower towns, come with them to an agreement of separation by a fixed boundary, and send to this place a few of the chiefs they have most confidence in, with powers to arrange with us regulations concerning the protection of their persons, punishment of crimes, assigning to each family their separate farms, directing how these shall go to the family as they die one after another, in what manner they shall be governed, and all other particulars necessary for their happiness in their new condition. On our part I will ask the assistance of our great council, the Congress, whose authority is necessary to give validity to these arrangements, and who wish nothing more sincerely than to render your condition secure and happy. Should the principal part of your people determine to adopt this alteration, and a smaller part still choose to continue the hunter's life, it may facilitate the settlement among yourselves to be told that we will give to those leave to go, if they choose it, and settle on our lands beyond the Mississippi, where some Cherokees are already settled, and where game is plenty, and we will take measures for establishing a store there among them, where they may obtain necessaries in exchange for their pel-ries, and we will still continue to be their friends there as much as here.

*My children,* carry these words to your people, advise with Colonel Meigs n your proceedings, ask him to inform me from time to time how you go on, and I will further advise you in what may be necessary. Tell your people I take them all by the hand; that I leave them free to do as they choose, and that whatever choice they make, I will still be their friend and father.

## TO COLONEL LOUIS COOK AND JACOB FRANCIS OF THE ST. REGIS INDIANS

May 5, 1808

MY CHILDREN: I take you by the hand, and all the people of St. Regis within the limits of the United States, and I desire to speak to them through you. A great misunderstanding has taken place between the English and the United States, and although we desire to live in peace with all the world and unmolested, yet it is not quite certain whether this difference will end in peace or war. Should war take place, do you, my children, remain at home in peace, taking care of your wives and children. You have no concern in our quarrel, take therefore no part in it. We do not wish you to spill your blood in our battles. We can fight them ourselves. Say the same to your red brethren everywhere, let them remain neutral and quiet, and we will never disturb them. Should the English insist on their taking up the hatchet against us, if they choose rather to break up their settlements and come over to live in peace with us, we will find other settlements for them, and they shall become our children. The red nations who shall remain in peace with the United States, shall forever find them true friends and fathers. Those who commence against them an unprovoked war, must expect their lasting enmity.

*My children,* I wish you well, and a safe return to your own country.

## TO THE DELAWARE CHIEF, CAPTAIN ARMSTRONG

December 2, 1808

TO THE DELAWARE CHIEF, CAPTAIN ARMSTRONG: I have received your letter of October 20th, wherein you express a wish to obtain a deed for the thirteen sections of lands reserved for the Delawares in the State of Ohio, by an act of Congress. I accordingly now send you an authentic deed designating the thirteen sections, and signed by the Secretary of the Treasury, who was authorized for this purpose by the act of Congress. Under this you are free to settle on the lands when you please, and to occupy them according to your own rules. You cannot, indeed, sell them to the white citizens of the United States. Knowing how liable you would be to be cheated and deceived, were we to permit our citizens to purchase your lands, our government acting as your friends and patrons, and desirous of guarding your interests against the frauds that would surround you, does not permit white persons to purchase your lands from you. In every other way they are yours, free to be used as you please; and their possession will be protected and guaranteed to you by the United States. I salute you and my children, the Delawares, with friendship.

## TO THE MIAMIS, POWTEWATAMIES, DELAWARES, AND CHIPPEWAYS

December 21, 1808

MY CHILDREN: Some of you are old enough to remember, and the youngest have heard from their fathers, that the country was formerly governed by the English. While they governed it there were constant wars between the white and the red people. To such a height was the hatred of both parties carried that they thought it no crime to kill one another in cold blood whenever they had an opportunity. This spirit led many of the Indians to take side against us in the war; and at the close of it the English made peace for themselves, and left the Indians to get out of it as well as they could. It was not till twelve years after that we were able by the treaty of Greeneville to close our wars with all our red neighbors. From that moment, my children, the policy of this country towards you has been entirely changed. General Washington, our first President, began a line of just and friendly conduct towards you. Mr. Adams, the second, continued it; and from the moment I came into the administration I have looked upon you with the same good will as my own fellow citizens, have considered your interests as our interests, and peace and friendship as a blessing to us all. Seeing with sincere regret that your people were wasting away, believing that this proceeded from your frequent wars, and the destructive use of spirituous liquors, and scanty supplies of food, I have inculcated peace with all your neighbors, have endeavored to prevent the introduction of spirituous liquors among you, and pressed on you to rely for food on the culture of the earth more than on hunting. On the contrary, my children, the English persuade you to hunt, they supply you with spirituous liquors, and are now endeavoring to engage you to join them in the war against us, should a war take place. You possess reason, my children, as we do, and you will judge for yourselves which of us advise you as friends. The course they advise has worn you down to your present numbers, but temperance, peace and agriculture will raise you up to be what your forefathers were, will prepare you to possess property, to wish to live under regular laws, to join us in our government, to mix with us in society, and your blood and ours united will spread again over the great island.

*My children,* this is the last time I shall speak to you as your father, it is the last counsel I shall give. I am now too old to watch over the extensive concerns of the seventeen States and their territories. I have, therefore, requested my fellow citizens to permit me to retire, to live with my family and to choose another chief and another father for you, and in a short time I shall retire and resign into his hands the care of your and our concerns. Be assured, my children, that he will have the same friendly disposition towards you which I have had, and that you will find in him a true and affectionate father. Entertain, therefore, no uneasiness on account of this change, for there will be no change as to you. Indeed, my children, this is now the disposition towards you of all our people. They look upon you as brethren, born in the same land, and having the same interests. In your journey to this place you have seen many of them. I am certain they have received you as brothers and been ready to show you every kindness. You will see the same on the road by which you will return; and were you to pass from north to south, or east to west in any part of the United States, you would find yourselves always among friends. Tell this, therefore, to your people on your return home, assure them that no change will ever take place in our dispositions towards them; deliver to them my adieux and my prayers to the Great Spirit for their happiness, tell them that during my administration I have held their hand fast in mine, that I will put it into the hand of their new father, who will hold it as I have done.

## TO LITTLE TURTLE, CHIEF OF THE MIAMIS

MY SON: It is always with pleasure that I receive you here and take you by the hand, and that tc the assurances of friendship to your nation I can add those of my personal respect and esteem for you. Our confidence in your friendship has been the stronger, as your enlarged understanding could not fail to see the advantages resulting to your nation as well as to us from a mutual good understanding. We ask nothing from them but their peace and good will, and it is a sincere solicitude for their welfare which has induced us, from time to time, to warn them of the decay of their nation by continuing to rely on the chase for food, after the deer and buffalo are become too scanty to subsist them, and to press them before they are reduced too low, to begin the culture of the earth and the raising of domestic animals. A little of their land in corn and cattle will feed them much better than the whole of it in deer and buffalo, in their present scarce state, and they will be scarcer every year. I have, therefore, always believed it an act of friendship to our red brethren whenever they wished to sell a portion of their lands, to be ready to buy whether we wanted them or not, because the price enables them to improve the lands they retain, and turning their industry from hunting to agriculture, the same exertions will support them more plentifully.

You inform me, my son, that your nation claims all the land on the Wabash and the Miami of the Lake and their waters, and that a small portion of that which was sold to us by the Ottawas, Wyandots, and other tribes of Michigan belonged to you. My son, it is difficult for us to know the exact boundaries which divide the lands of the several Indian tribes, and indeed it appears often that they do not know themselves, or cannot agree about them. I have long thought it desirable that they should settle their boundaries with one another, and let them be written on paper and preserved by them and by us, to prevent disputes among themselves. The tribes who made that sale certainly claim the lands on both sides of the Miami, some distance up from the mouth, as they have since granted us two roads from the rapids to the Miami, the one eastwardly to the line of the treaty of Fort Industry, and the other south eastwardly to the line of the treaty of Greeneville. I observe, moreover, that in the late conveyance of lands on the White River branch of the Wabash, to the Delawares, the Powtewatamies join you in the conveyance, which is an acknowledgment that all the lands on the waters of the Wabash do not belong to the Miamis alone. If, however, the Ottawas and others who sold to us had no right themselves, they could convey none to us, and we acknowledge we cannot acquire lands by buying them of those who have no title themselves. This question cannot be determined here, where we have no means of inquiring from those who have knowledge of the facts. We will instruct Governor Hull to collect the evidence from both parties, and from others, and to report it to us. And if it shall appear that the lands belonged to you and not to those who sold them, be assured we will do you full justice. We ask your friendship and confidence no longer than we shall merit it by our justice. On this subject, therefore, my son, your mind may be tranquil. You have an opportunity of producing before Governor Hull all the evidences of your right, and they shall be fairly weighed against the opposite claims.

*My son,* I salute your nation with constant friendship, and assure you of my particular esteem.

## TO MANCHOL, THE GREAT WAR CHIEF OF THE POWTEWATAMIES

MY SON: I am happy to receive you at the seat of Government of the United States, to take you and your nation by the hand, and to welcome you to this place. It has long been my desire to see the distinguished men of the Powtewatamies, and to give them the same assurances of friendship and good will which I have given to all my other red children. I wish to see them living in plenty and prosperity, beginning to cultivate the earth and raise domestic animals for their comfortable subsistence. In this way they will raise up young people in abundance to succeed to the old, and to keep their nation strong. For this reason I recommend to them to live in peace with all men, and not, by destroying one another, to make the whole race of red men disappear from the land.

You say, my son, that you have engaged in a war with the Osages, and that the war club is now in your hand for that purpose; but you do not tell me for what cause you are waging war with the Osages. I have never heard that they have crossed the Mississippi and attacked your villages, killed your women and children, or destroyed the game on your lands. What is the injury then which they have done you and for which you wish to cross the Mississippi and to destroy them? If they have done you no wrong, have you a right to make war upon innocent and unoffending people? Be assured that the Great Spirit will not approve of this,—He did not make men strong that they might destroy all other men. If your young people think that in this way they will acquire honor as great warriors, they are mistaken. Nobody can acquire honor by doing what is wrong.

You say, my son, that it is not the wish of my red children to meddle in the wars between the whites, nor that we should meddle in the wars among our red children. If your wars in no wise affect our rights, or our relations with those on whom you make war, we do not meddle with them but by way of advice, as your father and friend submitting it to your own consideration. But, my son, your war parties cannot pass from your towns to the country of the Osages, nor can the Osages come to revenge themselves on your towns without traversing extensively a country which is ours. They must cross the Mississippi which is always covered with our boats, our people and property. All the produce of the western parts of Pennsylvania, Virginia, Kentucky, Ohio, Indiana, Tennessee, and Louisiana, goes down the river Mississippi to New Orleans. It cannot be indifferent to us that this should be exposed to danger from unruly young men going to war. Our interests require that the Mississippi shall be a river of peace, not to be crossed by men seeking to shed blood. We have a right then to say that no war parties shall cross our river or our country without our consent. The

Sacs and Foxes, besides the country from the Illinois to the Wisconsin on the east side of the Mississippi, ceded to us the country on the west side of the Mississippi, between that river and the Missouri, for about one hundred miles up each. The Osages have ceded to us all the country from the south side of the Missouri to the Arkansas, more than two hundred miles up each river. Surely, my son, we are justifiable in so far meddling with your wars as to say that, in carrying them on neither the Osages nor you must cross that country which is ours, to get at one another, and in doing so to endanger our people and our property, and to stain our land with blood; and friendship requires that we should give you this warning.

*My son,* I wish you to consider this subject maturely, and to tell your nation that I request them to consider it also. I am ready to do them every favor in my power, and to give them every aid, but not aids to carry war across our territory. Do not suppose that in refusing this I am not your friend. If I were your enemy, what could I do better than to encourage you in tomahawking one another till not a man should be left. Neither must you suppose this to proceed from partiality to the Osages. You are nearer to me than the Osages, and on that account I should be more ready to do you good offices. But my desire to keep you in peace arises from my sincere wish to see you happy and prosperous, increasing in numbers, supplying your families plentifully with food and clothing, and relieving them from the constant chance of being destroyed by their enemies.

*My son,* the Secretary at War will give to you those tokens of our good will by which we manifest our friendship to the distinguished men among our red children who visit us. Be assured that I shall set a great value on your friendship; and convey for me to your nation assurances that I wish nothing more than their welfare. You shall return by the way of Baltimore and Philadelphia as you desire. I wish you to see as many of your brothers of the United States as you can. You will find them all to be your friends, and that they will receive you hospitably.

## TO BEAVER, THE HEAD WARRIOR OF THE DELAWARES

December 21, 1808

MY SON: I am glad to see you here to take you by the hand. I am the friend of your nation, and sincerely wish them well. I shall now speak to them as their friend, and advise them for their good.

I have read your speech to the Secretary at War, and considered it maturely. You therein say that after the conclusion of the treaty of Greeneville, the Wapanakies and other tribes of Indians mutually agreed to maintain peace among themselves and with the United States. This, my son, was wise, and I entirely approve of it. And I equally commend you for what you further say, that yours and the other tribes have constantly maintained the articles of peace with us, and have ceased to listen to bad advice. I hope, my son, that you will continue in this good line of conduct, and I assure you the United States will forever religiously observe the treaty on their part, not only because they have agreed to it, but because they esteem you; they wish you well, and would endeavor to promote your welfare even if there were no treaty; and rejoicing that you have ceased to listen to bad advice, they hope you will listen to that which is good.

*My son,* you say that the Osage nation has refused to be at peace with your nation or any others; that they have refused the offers of peace, and extended their aggressions to all people. This is all new to me. I never heard of an Osage coming to war on this side of the Mississippi. Have they attacked your towns, killed your people, or destroyed your game? Tell me in what year they did this? or what is the aggression they have committed on yours and the other tribes on this side the Mississippi? But if they have defended themselves and their country, when your tribes have gone over to destroy them, they have only done what brave men ought to do, and what just men ought never to have forced them to do. Your having committed one wrong on them gives you no right to commit a second; and be assured, my son, that the Almighty Spirit which is above will not look down with indifference on your going to war against his children on the other side the Mississippi, who have never come to attack you. He is their father as well as your father, and He did not make the Osages to be destroyed by you. I tell you that if you make war unjustly on the Osages, He will punish your nation for it. He will send upon your nation famine, sickness, or the tomahawk of a stronger nation, who will cut you off from the land. Consider this thing well, then, before it is too late, and before you strike. His hand is uplifted over your heads, and His stroke will follow yours. My son, I tell you these things because I wish your nation well. I wish them to become a peaceable, prosperous, and happy nation; and if this war against the Osages concerned yourselves alone, I would confine myself to giving you advice, and leave it to yourselves to profit by it. But this war deeply concerns the United States. Between you and the Osages is a country of many hundred miles extent belonging to the United States. Between you also is the Mississippi, the river of peace. On this river are floating the boats, the people, and all the produce of the western States of the Union. This commerce must not be exposed to the alarm of war parties crossing the river, nor must a path of blood be made across our country. What we say to you, my son, we say also to the Osages. We tell them that armed bands of warriors, entering on the lands or waters of the United States without our consent, are the enemies of the United States. If, therefore, considerations of your own welfare are not sufficient to restrain you from this unauthorized war, let me warn you on the part of the United States to respect their rights, not to violate their territory.

You request, my son, to be informed of our warfares, that you may be enabled to inform your nation on your return. We are yet at peace, and shall continue so, if the injustice of the other nations will permit us. The war beyond the water is universal. We wish to keep it out of our island. But should we go to war, we wish our red children to take no part in it. We are able to fight our own battles, and we know that our red children cannot afford to spill their blood in our quarrels. Therefore, we do not ask it, but wish them to remain home in quiet, taking care of themselves and their families.

You complain that the white people in your neighborhood have stolen a number of your horses. My son, the Secretary of War will take measures for inquiring into the truth of this, and if it so appears, justice shall be done you.

The two swords which you ask shall be given to you; and we shall be happy to give you every other proof that we esteem you personally, my son, and shall always be ready to do anything which may advance your comfort and happiness. I hope you will deliver to your nation the words I have spoken to you, and assure them that in everything which can promote their welfare and prosperity they shall ever find me their true and faithful friend and father, that I hold them fast by the hand of friendship, which I hope they will not force me to let go.

## TO CAPTAIN HENDRICK, THE DELAWARES, MOHICCONS, AND MUNRIES

MY SON AND MY CHILDREN: I am glad to see you here to receive your salutations, and to return them by taking you by the hand, and renewing to you the assurances of my friendship. I learn with pleasure that the Miamis and Powtawatamies have given you some of their lands on the White River to live on and that you propose to gather there your scattered tribes, and to dwell on it all your days.

The picture which you have drawn, my son, of the increase of our numbers and the decrease of yours is just, the causes are very plain, and the remedy depends on yourselves alone. You have lived by hunting the deer and buffalo—all these have been driven westward; you have sold out on the sea-board and moved westwardly in pursuit of them. As they became scarce there, your food has failed you; you have been a part of every year without food, except the roots and other unwholesome things you could find in the forest. Scanty and unwholesome food produce diseases and death among your children, and hence you have raised few and your numbers have decreased. Frequent wars, too, and the abuse of spirituous liquors, have assisted in lessening your numbers. The whites, on the other hand, are in the habit of cultivating the earth, of raising stocks of cattle, hogs, and other domestic animals, in much greater numbers than they could kill of deer and buffalo. Having always a plenty of food and clothing they raise abundance of children, they double their numbers every twenty years, the new swarms are continually advancing upon the country like flocks of pigeons, and so they will continue to do. Now, my children, if we wanted to diminish our numbers, we would give up the culture of the earth, pursue the deer and buffalo, and be always at war; this would soon reduce us to be as few as you are, and if you wish to increase your numbers you must give up the deer and buffalo, live in peace, and cultivate the earth. You see then, my children, that it depends on yourselves alone to become a numerous and great people. Let me entreat you, therefore, on the lands now given you to begin to give every man a farm; let him enclose it, cultivate it, build a warm house on it, and when he dies, let it belong to his wife and children after him. Nothing is so easy as to learn to cultivate the earth; all your women understand it, and to make it easier, we are always ready to teach you how to make ploughs, hoes, and necessary utensils. If the men will take the labor of the earth from the women they will learn to spin and weave and to clothe their families. In this way you will also raise many children, you will double your numbers every twenty years, and soon fill the land your friends have given you, and your children will never be tempted to sell the spot on which they have been born, raised, have labored and called their own. When once you have property, you will want laws and magistrates to protect your property and persons, and to punish those among you who commit crimes. You will find that our laws are good for this purpose; you will wish to live under them, you will unite yourselves with us, join in our great councils and form one people with us, and we shall all be Americans; you will mix with us by marriage, your blood will run in our veins, and will spread with us over this great island. Instead, then, my children, of the gloomy prospect you have drawn of your total disappearance from the face of the earth, which is true, if you continue to hunt the deer and buffalo and go to war, you see what a brilliant aspect is offered to your future history, if you give up war and hunting. Adopt the culture of the earth and raise domestic animals; you see how from a small family you may become a great nation by adopting the course which from the small beginning you describe has made us a great nation.

*My children,* I will give you a paper declaring your right to hold, against all persons, the lands given you by the Miamis and Powtewatamies, and that you never can sell them without their consent. But I must tell you that if ever they and you agree to sell, no paper which I can give you can prevent your doing what you please with your own. The only way to prevent this is to give to every one of your people a farm, which shall belong to him and his family, and which the nation shall have no right to take from them and sell; in this way alone can you ensure the lands to your descendants through all generations, and that it shall never be sold from under their feet. It is not the keeping your lands which will keep your people alive on them after the deer and buffalo shall have left them; it is the cultivating them alone which can do that. The hundredth part in corn and cattle will support you better than the whole in deer and buffalo.

*My son Hendrick,* deliver these words to your people. I have spoken to them plainly, that they may see what is before them, and that it is in their own power to go on dwindling to nothing, or to become again a great people. It is for this reason I wish them to live in peace with all people, to teach their young men to love agriculture, rather than war and hunting. Let these words sink deep in their hearts, and let them often repeat them and consider them. Tell them that I hold them fast by the hand, and that I will ever be their friend to advise and to assist them in following the true path to their future happiness.

## TO KITCHAO GEBOWAY

MY SON: I am happy to receive your visit at the seat of our government, and to repeat to you the assurances of my friendly dispositions towards your nation. I am the more pleased to see you again, as at your last visit we could not converse together for want of an interpreter. This difficulty is now removed by the presence of Mr. Ryley. I approve of your disposition, my son, to live at peace with all the world. It is what we wish all our red children to do, and to consider themselves as brethren of the same family, and forming with us but one nation. The Great Spirit did not make men that they might destroy one another, but doing to each other all the good in their power, and thus filling the land with happiness instead of misery and murder. This is the way in which we wish all our red children to live with one another, and with us; and this is what I wish you to say to your nation from me, when you deliver to them what I said to you the last winter. I am sorry you have not been able to carry it to them; they would have seen by that, that you came here as the friend of your own nation, and of all your red brethren. My son, I take by the hand the young man, the son of your friend, whom you brought with you. He is now young, and

I hope will live to be old, and through his life will be steadfast in encouraging his nation to live in peace and friendship with their white brethren of the United States.

The Secretary at War will provide for your journey back, and your father Governor Hull will be glad to see you on your way. He will always give good advice to your nation in my name, and will guide them in the paths of peace and friendship with all men.

## TO THE DEPUTIES OF THE CHEROKEE UPPER TOWNS

January 9, 1809

MY CHILDREN: I have maturely considered the speeches you have delivered me, and will now give you answers to the several matters they contain.

You inform me of your anxious desires to engage in the industrious pursuits of agriculture and civilized life. That finding it impracticable to induce the nation at large to join in this, you wish a line of separation to be established between the upper and lower towns, so as to include all the waters of the Hiwassee in your part, and that having thus contracted your society within narrower limits, you propose within these to begin the establishment of fixed laws and of regular government. You say that the lower towns are satisfied with the division you propose; and on these several matters you ask my advice and aid.

With respect to the line of division beween yourselves and the lower towns, it must rest on the joint consent of both parties. The one you propose seems moderate, reasonable, and well defined. We are willing to recognize those on each side of that line as distinct societies, and if our aid shall be necessary to mark it more plainly than nature has done, you shall have it. I think with you, that on this reduced scale it will be more easy for you to introduce the regular administration of laws.

In proceeding to the establishment of laws, you wish to adopt them from ours, and such only for the present as suit your present condition; chiefly, indeed, those for the punishment of crimes, and the protection of property. But who is to determine which of our laws suit your condition, and shall be in force with you? All of you being equally free, no one has a right to say what shall be law for the others. Our way is to put these questions to the vote, and to consider that as law for which the majority votes. The fool has as great a right to express his opinion by vote as the wise, because he is equally free, and equally master of himself. But as it would be inconvenient for all your men to meet in one place, would it not be better for every town to do as we do, that is to say, choose by the vote of the majority of the town and of the country people nearer to that than to any other town, one, two, three, or more, according to the size of the town, of those whom each voter thinks the wisest and honestest men of their place, and let these meet together and agree which of our laws suit them. But these men know nothing of our laws; how then can they know which to adopt. Let them associate in their council our beloved man living with them, Colonel Meigs, and he will tell them what our law is on any point they desire. He will inform them, also, of our methods of doing business in our councils, so as to preserve order, and to obtain the vote of every member fairly. This council can make a law for giving to every head of a famliy a separate parcel of land, which, when he has built upon and improved, it shall belong to him and his descendants forever, and which the nation itself shall have no right to sell from under his feet; they will determine, too, what punishment shall be inflicted for every crime. In our States, generally, we punish murder only by death, and all other crimes by solitary confinement in a prison.

But when you shall have adopted laws, who are to execute them? Perhaps it may be best to permit every town and the settlers in its neighborhood attached to it, to select some of their best men, by a majority of its votes, to be judges in all differences, and to execute the law according to their own judgment. Your council of representatives will decide on this or such other mode as may best suit you. I suggest these things, my children, for the consideration of the upper towns of your nation, to be decided on as they think best; and I sincerely wish you may succeed in your laudable endeavors to save the remains of your nation by adopting industrious occupations and a government of regular law. In this you may always rely on the counsel and assistance of the government of the United States. Deliver these words to your people in my name, and assure them of my friendship.

## TO THE DEPUTIES OF THE CHEROKEES OF THE UPPER AND LOWER TOWNS

January 9, 1809

MY CHILDREN: I understand from the speeches which you have delivered me, that there is a difference of disposition among the people of both parts of your nation, some of them desiring to remain on their lands, to betake themselves to agriculture, and the industrious occupations of civilized life, while others, retaining their attachment to the hunter life, and having little game on their present lands, are desirous to remove across the Mississippi, to some of the vacant lands of the United States, where game is abundant. I am pleased to find so many disposed to ensure, by the cultivation of the earth, a plentiful subsistence for their families, and to improve their minds by education; but I do not blame those who, having been brought up from their infancy to the pursuit of game, desire still to follow it to distant countries. I know how difficult it is for men to change the habits in which they have been raised. The United States, my children, are the friends of both parties, and as far as can reasonably be asked, they will be willing to satisfy the wishes of both. Those who remain may be assured of our patronage, our aid, and good neighborhood; those who wish to remove, are permitted to send an exploring party to reconnoitre the country on the waters of the Arkansas and White rivers, and the higher up the better, as they will be the longer unapproached by our settlements, which will begin at the mouths of those rivers. The regular districts of the government of St. Louis are already laid off to the St. Francis. When this party shall have found a tract of country suiting the emigrants, and not claimed by other Indians, we will arrange with them and you the exchange of that for a just portion of the country they leave, and to a part of which proportioned to their numbers they have a right. Every aid towards their removal, and what will be necessary for them there, will then be freely administered to them, and when established in their new settlements, we shall still consider them as our children, give them the benefit of exchanging their peltries for what they want at our factories, and always hold them firmly by the hand.

I will now, my children, proceed to answer your kind address on my retiring from the government. Sensible that I am become too old to watch over the extensive concerns of the seventeen States and their territories, I requested my fellow citizens to permit me to retire, to live with my family, and to choose another President for themselves and father for you. They have done so; and in a short time I shall retire, and resign into his hands the care of your and our concerns. Be assured, my children, that he will have the same friendly dispositions towards you which I have had, and that you will find in him a true and affectionate father. Indeed, this is now the disposition of all our people towards you; they look upon you as brethren, born in the same land, and having the same interests. Tell your people, therefore, to entertain no uneasiness on account of this change, for there will be no change as to them. Deliver to them my adieux, and my prayers to the Great Spirit for their happiness. Tell them that during my administration I have held their hand fast in mine, and that I will put it into the hand of their new father, who will hold it as I have done.

## TO THE CHIEFS OF THE WYANDOTS, OTTAWAS, CHIPPEWAS, POWTEWATAMIES, AND SHAWANESE

January 10, 1809

MY CHILDREN: This is the first time I have had the pleasure of seeing the distinguished men of our neighbors the Wyandots, Ottawas and Chippewas, at the seat of our government. I welcome you to it as well as the Powtewatamies and Shawanese, and thank the Great Spirit for having conducted you hither in safety and health. I take you and your people by the hand and salute you as my children; I consider all my red children as forming one family with the whites, born in the same land with them, and bound to live like brethren, in peace, friendship and good neighborhood. In former times, my children, we were not our own masters, but were governed by the English. Then we were often at war with our neighbors. Ill blood was raised and kept up between us, and in the war in which we threw off the English government, many of the red people, mistaking their brothers and real friends, took sides with the English government against us; and it was not till many years after we made peace with the English, that the treaty of Greeneville closed our last wars with our Indian neighbors. From that time, my children, we have looked on you as a part of ourselves, and have cherished your prosperity as our own. We saw that these things were wasting away your numbers to nothing; that the intemperate use of ardent spirits produced poverty, trouble and murders among you; your wars with one another were lessening your numbers, and attachment to the hunter life, after game had nearly left you, produced famine, sickness and deaths among you in the scarce season of every year. It has been our endeavor, therefore, like true fathers and brothers, to withhold strong liquors from you, to keep you in peace with one another, and to encourage and aid you in the culture of the earth, and raising domestic animals, to take the place of the wild ones. This we have done, my children, because we are your friends, and wish you well. If we feared you, if we were your enemies, we should have furnished you plentifully with whiskey, let the men destroy one another in perpetual wars, and the women and children waste away for want of food, and remain insensible that they could raise it out of the earth. We have been told, my children, that some of you have been doubting whether we or the English were your truest friends. What do the English do for you? They furnish you with plenty of whiskey, to keep you in idleness, drunkenness and poverty; and they are now exciting you to join them in war against us, if war should take place between them and us. But we tell you to stay at home in quiet, to take no part in quarrels which do not concern you. The English are now at war with all the world but us, and it is not yet known whether they will not force us also into it. They are strong on the water, but weak on the land. We live on the land and we fear them not. We are able to fight our own battles; therefore we do not ask you to spill your blood in our quarrels, much less do we wish to be forced to spill it with our own hands. You have travelled through our country from the lakes to the tide waters. You have seen our numbers in that direction, and were you to pass along the sea shore you would find them much greater. You know the English numbers, their scattered forts and string of people, along the borders of the lakes and the St. Lawrence, how long do you think it will take us to sweep them out of the country? and when they are swept away, what is to become of those who join them in their war against us? My children, if you love the land in which you were born, if you wish to inhabit the earth which covers the bones of your fathers, take no part in the war between the English and us, if we should have war. Never will we do an unjust act towards you. On the contrary, we wish to befriend you in every possible way; but the tribe which shall begin an unprovoked war against us, we will extirpate from the earth, or drive to such a distance as that they shall never again be able to strike us. I tell you these things, my children, not to make you afraid. I know you are brave men and therefore cannot fear. But you are also wise men and prudent men. I say it, therefore, that, in your wisdom and prudence, you may look forward. That you may go to the graves of your fathers and say, "fathers, shall we abandon you?" That you may look in the faces of your wives and children and ask, "shall we expose these our own flesh and blood to perish from want in a distant country and have our race and name extinguished from the face of the earth?" Think of these things, my children, as wise men, and as men loving their fathers, their wives and children, and the name and memory of their nation. I repeat, that we will never do an unjust act towards you. On the contrary, we wish you to live in peace, to increase in numbers, to learn to labor as we do, and furnish food for your increasing numbers, when the game shall have left you. We wish to see you possessed of property, and protecting it by regular laws. In time, you will be as we are; you will become one people with us. Your blood will mix with ours; and will spread, with ours, over this great island. Hold fast then, my children, the chain of friendship which binds us together, and join us in keeping it forever bright and unbroken.

I invite you to come here, my children, that you might hear with your own ears, the words of your father; that you might see with your own eyes, the sincere disposition of the United States towards you. In your journey to this place you have seen great numbers of your white brothers; you have been received by them as brothers, have been treated kindly and hospitably, and you have seen and can tell your people that their hearts are now sincerely with you. This is the first time I have ever addressed your chiefs, in person, at the seat of Government,—it will also be the last. Sensible that I am become too old to watch over the extensive concerns of the seventeen States and their territories, I requested my fellow citizens to permit me to retire to live with my family, and to choose another President for themselves, and father for you. They have done so; and in a short time I shall retire and resign into his hands the care of your and our concerns. Be assured, my children, that he will have the same friendly dispositions towards you which I have had, and that you will find in him a true and affectionate father. Indeed this is now the disposition of all our people towards you; they look upon you as brethren, born in the same land, and having the same interests. Tell your people, therefore, to entertain no uneasiness on account of this change, for there will be no change as to them. Deliver to them my adieus, and my prayers to the Great Spirit for their happiness. Tell them that during my administration, I have held their hand fast in mine; and that I will put it into the hand of their new father, who will hold it as I have done.

## TO THE CHIEFS OF THE OTTAWAS, CHIPPEWAS, POWTEWATAMIES, SHAWANESE AND WYANDOTS

January 18, 1809

MY CHILDREN: I have considered the speech you have delivered me, and will now make answer to it. You have gone back to ancient times, and given a true history of the uses made of you by the French, who first inhabited your country, and afterwards by the English; and how they used you as dogs to set upon those whom they wanted to destroy. They kept the hatchet always in your hand, exposing you to be killed in their quarrels, and then gave you whiskey that you might quarrel and kill one another. I am glad you understand these things, and are determined no more to fight their battles. We shall never wish you to fight ours, but to stay at home in peace and take care of yourselves. You still wish, however, to keep up a correspondence with the English, because you say your young people find an advantage in it. The less you have to do with them the better, because all their endeavors will be, as you know, to persuade you to go to war for them. If they owe you for lands, they ought to pay you once for all and be done with it. With respect to your people on the English side of the water, should we have war with the English, let them remain neutral and we shall not disturb them; but if the English should endeavor to force them into the war, you would do well to receive them and let them live with you till we can clear the way for them to go back again, which will not take long.

You ask me what passed between this Government and the Little Turtle, the chiefs of the Chippewas, Powtewatamies, Shawanese, Ottawas, Isaac Williams, the Crane and the Delawares, at their visits to the seat of this Government many years ago. Those visits were in the time of my predecessors, so that I did not hear their speeches, and they did not leave them in writing. It is not in my power, therefore, to tell you what they were. But I can assure you that when the Little Turtle visited me, and in like manner when the chiefs of other tribes have visited me, not one word was ever said to the prejudice of the other Indians. I have no reason to believe they wished to speak to me in that way, but if they did, they knew I would not listen to them, and therefore did not do it. My advice to them all has been constantly to live in peace and friendship with one another, to begin to cultivate the earth, to raise domestic animals, and leave off the use of ardent spirits: in short, precisely what I have said to yourselves.

You ask whether the treaties at Swan's creek, and those of the last fall, and the fall before, were made by my desire. I will explain the subject to you. We consider your lands as belonging fully to yourselves, and that we have no right to purchase them but with your own free consent. Whenever you wish to sell, we are willing to buy, although it may be lands which we do not immediately want. We believe it to be for your benefit to sell a part of your lands for annuities, which may enable you to improve farms, and in the meantime to support yourselves. While you keep such large tracts of country, the few deer which remain tempt you to continue hunters, and are yet not enough to maintain you plentifully through the year. A small part of the land cultivated in corn, with the cattle, hogs, and sheep it would enable you to raise, would maintain you better through the year, than the whole does in game. A thorough persuasion, therefore, that it is better for you to turn your surplus lands from time to time into money, induces us to buy when you desire to sell. On this principle, at the treaty of Swan's creek we purchased the slip of land which laid between what you sold to the Connecticut company and our former lines. We had no particular desire to buy it, but were told that it would be convenient to you to sell that parcel, and therefore we bought it.

The lands which were purchased of you near Detroit the last fall and the fall before, we did wish to purchase, provided you were willing freely to sell. At Detroit, you know, we keep a garrison to watch the English, and to protect the factory we established there, to carry on trade with you. It is very desirable for us, therefore, to obtain so much land in the neighborhood as would receive settlers sufficient to raise provisions for the garrison, and to strengthen the garrison if attacked by the English. But still we instructed Governor Hull, however much we wished to get some land there, not to press it on you if you were not entirely willing to accommodate us. The settlement of our people there will be a great advantage to you if you become cultivators of the earth. You saw the Cherokees who were here when you arrived, my children. These were wealthy men, and became wealthy merely by living near our settlements. Their mother towns of Chota and Chilowee, are but twelve miles from our principal town of Knoxville. The Cherokees there have good farms, good houses, and abundance of cattle and horses. If a family raises more cattle or corn than they want for their own use, instead of letting it be eaten by their own lazy people who will not work, they carry it to Knoxville, sell it to our people, and purchase with the money clothes and other comforts for themselves. Our settlements around Detroit will give you the same advantages. If you become farmers and raise cattle, hogs, sheep, fowls, and such things to spare, you can immediately exchange them for clothing and other necessaries. I am satisfied, therefore, my children, that the accommodating us with that land was as beneficial to you as to us. But, notwithstanding, I believe it to be better for you to sell your surplus lands from time to time; yet I repeat to you the assurances that although we may go so far, sometimes, as to say we would be willing to buy such a piece of land, yet we will never press you to sell, until you shall desire yourselves to sell it.

I have thus, my children, answered the particulars of your speech. I have done it with truth and an open heart, and I hope it will be satisfactory to you.

## TO THE CHIEFS OF THE OTTAWAS, CHIPPEWAS, POWTEWATAMIES, WYANDOTS, AND SHAWANESE

January 31, 1809

MY CHILDREN: I have considered the speech you have delivered me, and I will now give you an answer to it.

You have told us on former occasions of certain promises made to you at the treaty of Greeneville, by General Wayne, respecting certain lands whereon you and your friends live. But when we looked into the treaty of Greeneville, we found no such promises there; and as it is our custom to put all our agreements into writing, that they may never be forgotten or mistaken, we concluded no such promises had been made. But you now explain that the chiefs of the Wyandots near Detroit did not arrive at Greeneville till after the treaty was signed—that they then convinced General Wayne that provision ought to be made for securing to them possession of the lands they lived on, so long as they and their descendants shall choose to live on them, and that he agreed to it. Of this, besides other evidence, you now produce the belt of wampum reserved by you, in memory of it, the counter-belt given us having probably been destroyed in the fire which consumed our war office in the year 1800. Such evidence, therefore, being now produced as induces a belief of the agreement, it shall be committed to writing, according to what has passed between the Secretary at War and yourselves; and we will also put into writing what has passed respecting the reserves for the Indians, and you shall have a copy of these writings which shall be firm and good to you forever.

You complain that white people go on your lands and settle without your consent. This is entirely against our will, and I earnestly desire you, my children, as soon as any intruder of the whites sets down on your lands, that you will not delay a moment to inform our agent, who will always be instructed in the measures to be taken for their immediate removal; and I desire you to do this, on your return, as to the intruders you now complain of.

The Secretary at War has explained to you the circumstances which attended the running the boundary line near Sandusky, under the treaty at Swan's creek, so as to satisfy you that no variation of it was intended; and you may be assured that when we proceed to run the lines for the roads granted us the last fall, you shall have notice, in order that your chiefs may attend and see it fairly done.

For these roads, with which your nations have been so friendly as to accommodate us, and which you wished us to accept as a present, I return you my thanks, and I accept them; and I request you, on our part, to accept as a token of our good will, the sum of a thousand dollars, of which five hundred dollars will be paid you here. And we shall be happy if you can employ this sum to your benefit or comfort in any way. Our settlements are now extending so much in every direction, that we shall be obliged to ask roads from our Indian brethren, that we may pass conveniently from one settlement to another, for which we will always gladly pay them the full value.

You have been informed, as you desired, of the exact amount of your annuities.

I have thus, my children, answered all the parts of your speech, and I have done it sincerely and with good will to you. I have not filled you with whiskey, as the English do, to make you promise, or give up what is against your interest, when out of your senses. I have listened to your complaints and proposals, I have found them reasonable, and I have given you the answers which a just and a reasonable nation ought to do. And this you may be assured is the way in which we shall always do business with you, because we do not consider you as another nation, but as a part of us, living indeed under your own laws, but having the same interests with us. I hope you will tell these things to your people, and that they will sink deep into their minds.

## *Chapter XIII*

# REPLIES TO ADDRESSES

## TO THE GENERAL ASSEMBLY OF RHODE ISLAND AND PROVIDENCE PLANTATIONS

May 26, 1801

I return my grateful thanks to the General Assembly of the State of Rhode Island and Providence Plantations, for the congratulations which, on behalf of themselves and their constituents, they have been pleased to express on my election to the Chief Magistracy of the United States; and I learn with pleasure their approbation of the principles declared by me on that occasion; principles which flowed sincerely from the heart and judgment, and which, with sincerity, will be pursued. While acting on them, I ask only to be judged with truth and candor.

To preserve the peace of our fellow citizens, promote their prosperity and happiness, reunite opinion, cultivate a spirit of candor, moderation, charity, and forbearance towards one another, are objects calling for the efforts and sacrifices of every good man and patriot. Our religion enjoins it; our happiness demands it; and no sacrifice is requisite but of passions hostile to both.

It is a momentous truth, and happily of universal impression on the public mind, that our safety rests on the preservation of our Union. Our citizens have wisely formed themselves into one nation as to others, and several States as among themselves. To the united nation belongs our external and mutual relations; to each State severally the care of our persons, our property, our reputation, and religious freedom. This wise distribution, if carefully preserved, will prove, I trust from example, that while smaller governments are better adapted to the ordinary objects of society, larger confederations more effectually secure independence and the preservation of republican government.

I am sensible of the great interest which your State justly feels in the prosperity of commerce. It is of vital interest also to States more agricultural, whose produce, without commerce, could not be exchanged. As the handmaid of agriculture therefore, commerce will be cherished by me both from principle and duty.

Accept, I beseech you, for the General Assembly of the State of Rhode Island and Providence Plantations, the homage of my high consideration and respect, and I pray God to have them always in his safe and holy keeping.

## TO ELIAS SHIPMAN AND OTHERS, A COMMITTEE OF THE MERCHANTS OF NEW HAVEN

July 12, 1801

GENTLEMEN: I have received the remonstrance you were pleased to address to me, on the appointment of Samuel Bishop to the office of collector of New Haven, lately vacated by the death of David Austin. The right of our fellow citizens to represent to the public functionaries their opinion on proceedings interesting to them, is unquestionably a constitutional right, often useful, sometimes necessary, and will always be respectfully acknowledged by me.

Of the various executives duties, no one excites more anxious concern than that of placing the interests of our fellow citizens in the hands of honest men, with understandings sufficient for their stations. No duty, at the same time, is more difficult to fulfil. The knowledge of characters possessed by a single individual is, of necessity, limited. To seek out the best through the whole Union, we must resort to other information, which, from the best of men, acting disinterestedly and with the purest motives, is sometimes incorrect. In the case of Samuel Bishop, however, the subject of your remonstrance, time was taken, information was sought, and such obtained as could leave no room for doubt of his fitness. From private sources it was learned that his understanding was sound, his integrity pure, his character unstained. And the offices confided to him within his own State, are public evidences of the estimation in which he is held by the State in general, and the city and township particularly in which he lives. He is said to be the town clerk, a justice of the peace, mayor of the city of New Haven, an office held at the will of the legislature, chief judge of the court of common pleas for New Haven county, a court of high criminal and civil jurisdiction wherein most causes are decided without the right of appeal or review, and sole judge of the court of probates, wherein he singly decides all questions of wills, settlement of estates, testate and intestate, appoints guardians, settles their accounts, and in fact has under his jurisdiction and care all the property real and personal of persons dying. The two last offices, in the annual gift of the legislature, were given to him in May last. Is it possible that the man to whom the legislature of Connecticut has so recently committed trusts of such difficulty and magnitude, is "unfit to be the collector of the district of New Haven," though acknowledged in the same writing, to have obtained all this confidence "by a long life of usefulness"? It is objected, indeed, in the remonstrance, that he is seventy-seven years of age; but at a much more advanced age, our Franklin was the ornament of human nature. He may not be able to perform in person, all the details of his office; but if he gives us the benefit of his understanding, his integrity, his watchfulness, and takes care that all the details are well performed by himself or his necessary assistants, all public purposes will be answered. The remonstrance, indeed, does not allege that the office *has been* illy conducted, but only apprehends that it *will be* so. Should this happen in event, be assured I will do in it what shall be just and necessary for the public service. In the meantime, he should be tried without being prejudged.

The removal, as it is called, of Mr. Goodrich, forms another subject of complaint. Declarations by myself in favor of *political tolerance,* exhortations to *harmony* and affection in social intercourse, and to respect for the *equal rights* of the minority, have, on certain occasions, been quoted and misconstrued into assurances that the tenure of offices was to be undisturbed. But could candor apply such a construction? It is not indeed in the remonstrance that we find it; but it leads to the explanations which that calls for. When it is considered, that during the late administration, those who were not of a particular sect of politics were excluded from all office; when, by a steady pursuit of this measure, nearly the whole offices of the United States were monopolized by that sect; when the public sentiment at length declared itself, and burst open the doors of honor and confidence to those whose opinions they more approved, was it to be imagined that this monopoly of office was still to be continued in the hands of the minority? Does it violate their *equal rights*, to assert some rights in the majority also? Is it *political intolerance* to claim a proportionate share in the direction of the public affairs? Can they not *harmonize* in society unless they have everything in their own hands? If the will of the nation, manifested by their various elections, calls for an administration of government according with the opinions of those elected; if, for the fulfilment of that will, displacements are necessary, with whom can they so justly begin as with persons appointed in the last moments of an administration, not for its own aid, but to begin a career at the same time with their successors, by whom they had never been approved, and who could scarcely expect from them a cordial cooperation? Mr. Goodrich was one of these. Was it proper for him to place himself in office, without knowing whether those whose agent he was to be would have confidence in his agency? Can the preference of another, as the successor to Mr. Austin, be candidly called a removal of Mr. Goodrich? If a due participation of office is a matter of right, how are vacancies to be obtained? Those by death are few; by resignation, none. Can any other mode than that of removal be proposed? This is a painful office; but it is made my duty, and I meet it as such. I proceed in the operation with deliberation and inquiry, that it may injure the best men least, and effect the purposes of justice and public utility with the least private distress; that it may be thrown, as much as possible, on delinquency, on oppression, on intolerance, on anti-revolutionary adherence to our enemies.

The remonstrance laments "that a change in the administration must produce a change in the subordinate officers"; in other words, that it should be deemed necessary for all officers to think with their principal? But on whom does this imputation bear? On those who have excluded from office every shade of opinion which was not theirs? Or on those who have been so excluded? I lament sincerely that unessential differences of opinion should ever have been deemed sufficient to interdict half the society from the rights and the blessings of self-government, to proscribe them as unworthy of every trust. It would have been to me a circumstance of great relief, had I found a moderate participation of office in the hands of the majority. I would gladly have left to time and accident to raise them to their just share. But their total exclusion calls for prompter corrections. I shall correct the procedure; but that done, return with joy to that state of things, when the only questions concerning a candidate shall be, is he honest? Is he capable? Is he faithful to the Constitution?

I tender you the homage of my high respect.

## TO MESSRS. NEHEMIAH DODGE, EPHRAIM ROBBINS, AND STEPHEN S. NELSON, A COMMITTEE OF THE DANBURY BAPTIST ASSOCIATION, IN THE STATE OF CONNECTICUT

January 1, 1802

GENTLEMEN: The affectionate sentiments of esteem and approbation which you are so good as to express towards me, on behalf of the Danbury Baptist Association, give me the highest satisfaction. My duties dictate a faithful and zealous pursuit of the interests of my constituents, and in proportion as they are persuaded of my fidelity to those duties, the discharge of them becomes more and more pleasing.

Believing with you that religion is a matter which lies solely between man and his God, that he owes account to none other for his faith or his worship, that the legislative powers of government reach actions only, and not opinions, I contemplate with sovereign reverence that act of the whole American people which declared that their legislature should "make no law respecting an establishment of religion, or prohibiting the free exercise thereof," thus building a wall of separation between church and State. Adhering to this expression of the supreme will of the nation in behalf of the rights of conscience, I shall see with sincere satisfaction the progress of those sentiments which tend to restore to man all his natural rights, convinced he has no natural right in opposition to his social duties.

I reciprocate your kind prayers for the protection and blessing of the common Father and Creator of man, and tender you for yourselves and your religious association, assurances of my high respect and esteem.

## TO WILLIAM JUDD, ESQUIRE, CHAIRMAN

November 15, 1802

Expressions of confidence from the respectable description of my fellow citizens, in whose name you have been pleased to address me, are received with that cordial satisfaction which kindred principles and sentiments naturally inspire.

The proceedings which they approve were sincerely intended for the general good; and if, as we hope, they should in event produce it, they will be indebted for it to the wisdom of our legislative councils, and of those distinguished fellow laborers whom the laws have permitted me to associate in the general administration.

Exercising that discretion which the constitution has confided to me in the choice of public agents, I have been sensible, on the one hand, of the justice done to those who have been systematically excluded from the service of their country, and attentive, on the other, to restore justice in such a way as might least affect the sympathies and the tranquillity of the public mind. Deaths, resignations, delinquencies, malignant and active opposition to the order of things established by the will of the nation, will, it is believed, within a moderate space of time, make room for a just participation in the management of the public affairs; and that being once effected, future changes at the helm will be viewed with tranquillity by those in subordinate station.

Every wish of my heart will be completely gratified when that portion of my fellow citizens which has been misled as to the character of our measures and principles, shall, by their salutary effects, be corrected in their opinions, and joining with good will the great mass of their fellow citizens, consolidate an union which cannot be too much cherished.

I pray you, Sir, to accept for yourself, and for the general meeting of the Republicans of the State of Connecticut at New Haven, whose sentiments you have been so good as to convey to me, assurances of my high consideration and respect.

## TO THE LEGISLATURE OF THE STATE OF TENNESSEE

December 24, 1803

Amidst the anxieties which are felt for the favorable issue of measures adopted for promoting the public good, it is a consolation to meet the approbation of those on whose behalf they are instituted. I shall certainly endeavor to merit a continuance of the good opinion which the legislature of Tennessee have been pleased to express in their address of the 8th November, by a zealous attention to the interests of my constituents; and shall count on a candid indulgence whenever untoward events may happen to disappoint well-founded expectations.

In availing our western brethren of those circumstances which occur for promoting their interests, we only perform that duty which we owe to every portion of the Union, under occurrences equally favorable; and, impressed with the inconveniences to which the citizens of Tennessee are subjected by a want of contiguity in the portions composing their State, I shall be ready to do for their relief, whatever the general legislature may authorize, and justice to our neighbors permit.

The acquisition of Louisiana, although more immediately beneficial to the western States, by securing for their produce a certain market, not subject to interruption by officers over whom we have no control, yet is also deeply interesting to the maritime portion of our country, inasmuch as by giving the exclusive navigation of the Mississippi, it avoids the burthens and sufferings of a war, which conflicting interests on that river would inevitably have produced at no distant period. It opens, too, a fertile region for the future establishments in the progress of that multiplication so rapidly taking place in all parts.

I have seen with great satisfaction the promptitude with which the first portions of your militia repaired to the standard of their country. It was deemed best to provide a force equal to any event which might arise out of the transaction, and especially to the preservation of order, among our newly-associated brethren, in the first moments of their transition from one authority to another. I tender to the legislature of Tennessee assurances of my high respect and consideration.

## TO THE PRESIDENT OF THE SENATE, AND SPEAKER OF THE HOUSE OF REPRESENTATIVES OF MASSACHUSETTS

February 14, 1807

GENTLEMEN: I acknowledge, in the first moment it has been in my power, the receipt of your joint letter of January 26th, with the address of the two branches of legislature of Massachusetts, expressing their approbation of the proceedings of our government. This declaration cannot fail to give particular and general satisfaction to our fellow citizens, and to produce wholesome effects at home and abroad. The remarkable union of sentiment which pervaded nearly the whole of the States and territories composing our nation, was such, indeed, as to inspire a just confidence in the course we had to pursue. Yet something was sensibly wanting to fill up the measure of our happiness, while a member so important, so esteemed as Massachusetts, had not yet declared its participation in the common sentiment. That it is now done, will be a subject of mutual congratulation.

I am sensible that the terms in which you have been pleased to make this communication, are not merely those of official duty. I feel how much I am indebted to the kind and friendly disposition they manifest; and I cherish them as proofs of an esteem highly valued.

Permit me, through you, to return to the two branches of the legislature the enclosed answer, and accept the assurances of my esteem and high consideration.

## TO THE TWO BRANCHES OF THE LEGISLATURE OF MASSACHUSETTS

February 14, 1807

It is with sincere pleasure that I receive, from the two branches of the legislature of Massachusetts, an address, expressive of their satisfaction with the administration of our government. The approbation of my constituents is truly the most valued reward for any services it has fallen to my lot to render them—their confidence and esteem, the greatest consolation of my life. The measures which you have been pleased particularly to note, I have believed to have been for the best interests of our country. But far from assuming their merit to myself, they belong first, to a wise and patriotic legislature, which has given them the form and sanction of law, and next, to my faithful and able fellow-laborers in the Executive administration.

The progression of sentiment in the great body of our fellow citizens of Massachusetts, and the increasing support of their opinion, I have seen with satisfaction, and was ever confident I should see; persuaded that an enlightened people, whenever they should view impartially the course we have pursued, could never wish that our measures should have been reversed; could never desire that the expenses of the government should have been increased, taxes multiplied, debt accumulated, wars undertaken, and the tomahawk and scalping knife left in the hands of our neighbors, rather than the hoe and plough. In whatever tended to strengthen the republican features of our constitution, we could not fail to expect from Massachusetts, the cradle of our revolutionary principles, an ultimate concurrence; and cultivating the peace of nations, with justice and prudence, we yet were always confident that, whenever our rights would be to be vindicated against the aggression of foreign foes, or the machinations of internal conspirators, the people of Massachusetts, so prominent in the military achievements which placed our country in the right of self-government, would never be found wanting in their duty to the calls of their country, or the requisitions of their government.

During the term, which yet remains, of my continuance in the station assigned me, your confidence shall not be disappointed, so far as faithful endeavors for your service can merit it.

I feel with particular sensibility your kind expressions towards myself personally; and I pray that that Providence in whose hand are the nations of the earth, may continue towards ours his fostering care, and bestow on yourselves the blessings of His protection and favor.

## TO MESSRS. THOMAS, ELLICOT, AND OTHERS

November 13, 1807

FRIENDS AND FELLOW CITIZENS: I thank you for the address you have kindly presented me, on behalf of that portion of the Society of Friends of which you are the representatives, and I learn with satisfaction their approbation of the principles which have influenced the councils of the general government in their decisions on several important subjects confided to them.

The desire to preserve our country from the calamities and ravages of war, by cultivating a disposition, and pursuing a conduct, conciliatory and friendly to all nations, has been sincerely entertained and faithfully followed. It was dictated by the principles of humanity, the precepts of the gospel, and the general wish of our country, and it was not to be doubted that the Society of Friends, with whom it is a *religious* principle, would sanction it by their support.

The same philanthropic motives have directed the public endeavors to ameliorate the condition of the Indian natives, by introducing among them a knowledge of agriculture and some of the mechanic arts, by encouraging them to resort to these as more certain, and less laborious resources for subsistence than the chase; and by withholding from them the pernicious supplies of ardent spirits. They are our brethren, our neighbors; they may be valuable friends, and troublesome enemies. Both duty and interest then enjoin, that we should extend to them the blessings of civilized life, and prepare their minds for becoming useful members of the American family. In this important work I owe to your society an acknowledgment that we have felt the benefits of their zealous co-operation, and approved its judicious direction towards producing among those people habits of industry, comfortable subsistence, and civilized usages, as preparatory to religious instruction and the cultivation of letters.

Whatever may have been the circumstances which influenced our forefathers to permit the introduction of personal bondage into any part of these States, and to participate in the wrongs committed on an unoffending quarter of the globe, we may rejoice that such circumstances, and such a sense of them, exist no longer. It is honorable to the nation at large that their legislature availed themselves of the first practicable moment for arresting the progress of this great moral and political error; and I sincerely pray with you, my friends, that all the members of the human family may, in the time prescribed by the Father of us all, find themselves securely established in the enjoyment of life, liberty, and happiness.

## TO CAPTAIN JOHN THOMAS

November 18, 1807

SIR: I received on the 14th instant your favor of August 31, and I beg you to assure my fellow citizens of the Baptist church of Newhope meeting-house, that I learn with great satisfaction their approbation of the principles which have guided the present administration of the government. To cherish and maintain the rights and liberties of our citizens, and to ward from them the burthens, the miseries, and the crimes of war, by a just and friendly conduct towards all nations, were among the most obvious and important duties of those to whom the management of their public interests have been confided; and happy shall we be if a conduct guided by these views on our part, shall secure to us a reciprocation of peace and justice from other nations.

Among the most inestimable of our blessings, also, is that you so justly particularize, of liberty to worship our Creator in the way we think most agreeable to his will; a liberty deemed in other counties incompatible with good government, and yet proved by our experience to be its best support.

Your confidence in my dispositions to befriend every human right is highly grateful to me, and is rendered the more so by a consciousness that these dispositions have been sincerely entertained and pursued. I am thankful for the kindness expressed towards me personally, and pray you to return to the society in whose name you have addressed me, my best wishes for their happiness and prosperity; and to accept for yourself assurances of my great esteem and respect.

## TO HIS EXCELLENCY GOVERNOR SMITH

December 1, 1807

SIR: The Secretary of State has communicated to me your letter to him of the 14th of November, covering the resolutions of the General Assembly of Vermont of the 4th of the same month.

The sentiments expressed by the General Assembly of Vermont on the late hostile attack on the *Chesapeake* by the *Leopard* ship-of-war,[1] as well as on other violations of our maritime and territorial rights, are worthy of their known patriotism; and their readiness to rally around the constituted authorities of their country, and to support its rights with their lives and fortunes, is the more honorable to them as exposed by their position, in front of the contest. The issue of the present misunderstandings cannot now be foreseen; but the measures adopted for their settlement have been sincerely directed to maintain the rights, the honor, the peace of our country; and the approbation of them expressed by the General Assembly is to me a confirmation of their correctness.

The confidence they are pleased to declare in my personal care of the public interests, is highly gratifying to me, and gives a new claim to everything which zeal can effect for their service.

I beg leave to tender to the General Assembly of Vermont, and to yourself, the assurances of my high consideration and respect.

## TO THE LEGISLATURE OF VERMONT

December 10, 1807

I received in due season the *address* of the Legislature of Vermont, bearing date the 5th of November 1806, in which, with their approbation of the general course of my administration, they were so good as to express their desire that I would consent to be proposed again, to the public voice, on the expiration of my present term of office. Entertaining, as I do, for the legislature of Vermont those sentiments of high respect which would have prompted an immediate answer, I was certain, nevertheless, they would ap-

[1] On June 22, 1807, the British frigate *Leopard* fired on the American frigate *Chesapeake* outside Chesapeake Bay, and inflicted 21 casualties. The incident brought the two countries to the verge of war.

prove a delay which had for its object to avoid a premature agitation of the public mind, on a subject so interesting as the election of a chief magistrate.

That I should lay down my charge at a proper period, is as much a duty as to have borne it faithfully. If some termination to the services of the chief magistrate be not fixed by the constitution, or supplied by practice, his office, nominally for years, will, in fact, become for life; and history shows how easily that degenerates into an inheritance. Believing that a representative government, responsible at short periods of election, is that which produces the greatest sum of happiness to mankind, I feel it a duty to do no act which shall essentially impair that principle; and I should unwillingly be the person who, disregarding the sound precedent set by an illustrious predecessor, should furnish the first example of prolongation beyond the second term of office.

Truth, also, requires me to add, that I am sensible of that decline which advancing years bring on; and feeling their physical, I ought not to doubt their mental effect. Happy if I am the first to perceive and to obey this admonition of nature, and to solicit a retreat from cares too great for the wearied faculties of age.

For the approbation which the legislature of Vermont has been pleased to express of the principles and measures pursued in the management of their affairs, I am sincerely thankful; and should I be so fortunate as to carry into retirement the equal approbation and good will of my fellow citizens generally, it will be the comfort of my future days, and will close a service of forty years with the only reward it ever wished.

[Jefferson also received addresses, approving his administration, from Georgia, December 6th, 1806; from Rhode Island, February 27th, 1807; from New York, March 13th, 1807; from Pennsylvania, March 13th, 1807; and from Maryland, January 3d, 1807. To all of them he replied in the same way that he did to Vermont.]

## TO THE REPRESENTATIVES OF THE PEOPLE OF NEW JERSEY IN THEIR LEGISLATURE

December 10, 1807

The sentiments, fellow citizens, which you are pleased to express in your address of the 4th inst., of attachment and esteem for the general government, and of confidence and approbation of those who direct its councils, cannot but be pleasing to the friends of union generally, and give a new claim on all those who direct the public affairs, for everything which zeal can effect for the good of their country.

It is indeed to be deplored that distant as we are from the storms and convulsions which agitate the European world, the pursuit of an honest neutrality, beyond the reach of reproach, has been insufficient to secure to us the certain enjoyment of peace with those whose interests as well as ours would be promoted by it. What will be the issue of present misunderstandings cannot as yet be foreseen; but the measures adopted for their settlement have been sincerely directed to maintain the rights, the honor, and the peace of our country. Should they fail, the ardor of our citizens to obey the summons of their country, and the offer which you attest, of their lives and fortunes in its support, are worthy of their patriotism, and are pledges of our safety.

The suppression of the late conspiracy by the hand of the people, uplifted to destroy it whenever it reared its head, manifests their fitness for self-government, and the power of a nation, of which every individual feels that his own will is a part of the public authority.

The effect of the public contributions in reducing the national debt, and liberating our resources from the canker of interest, has been so far salutary, and encourages us to continue in the same course; or, if necessarily interrupted, to resume it as soon as practicable.

I perceive with sincere pleasure that my conduct in the chief magistracy has so far met your approbation, that my continuance in that office, after its present term, would be acceptable to you. But that I should lay down my charge at a proper period is as much a duty as to have borne it faithfully. If some termination to the services of the chief magistrate be not fixed by the constitution, or supplied by practice, his office, nominally for years, will, in fact, become for life, and history shows how easily that degenerates into an inheritance. Believing that a representative government, responsible at short periods of election, is that which produces the greatest sum of happiness to mankind, I feel it a duty to do no act which shall essentially impair that principle; and I should unwillingly be the person who, disregarding the sound precedent set by an illustrious predecessor, should furnish the first example of prolongation beyond the second term of office.

Truth also obliges me to add, that I am sensible of that decline which advancing years bring on, and feeling their physical, I ought not to doubt their mental effect. Happy if I am the first to perceive and to obey this admonition of nature, and to solicit a retreat from cares too great for the wearied faculties of age.

Declining a re-election on grounds which cannot but be approved, I am sincerely thankful for the approbation which the Legislature of New Jersey are pleased to manifest of the principles and measures pursued in the management of their affairs; and should I be so fortunate as to carry into retirement the equal approbation and good will of my fellow citizens generally, it will be the comfort of my future days, and will close a service of forty years with the only reward it ever wished.

## TO THE TAMMANY SOCIETY OF THE CITY OF WASHINGTON

December 14, 1807

The appearances for some time past, threatening our peace, fellow citizens, have justly excited a general anxiety; and I have been happy to receive from every quarter of the Union the most satisfactory assurances of fidelity to our country, and of devotion to the support of its rights. Your concurrence in these sentiments, expressed in the address you have been pleased to present me, is a proof of your patriotism, and of that firm spirit which constitutes the ultimate appeal of nations. What will be the issue of present misunderstandings, is, as yet, unknown. But, willing ourselves to do justice to others, we ought to expect it from them. If any among us view erroneously the rights which late events have brought into question, let us hope that they will be corrected by the further investigation of reason; but, at all events, that they will acquiesce in what their country shall authoritatively decide, and arrange themselves faithfully under the banners of the law.

Your approbation of the measures which have been pursued, is a pleasing confirmation of their correctness; and, with particular thankfulness for the kind expressions of your address towards myself personally, I reciprocate sincere wishes for your welfare.

## TO MESSRS. ABNER WATKINS AND BERNARD TODD

December 21, 1807

I have duly received, fellow citizens, the address of October 21st, which you have been so kind as to forward me on the part of the society of Baptists, of the Appomattox Association, and it is with great satisfaction when I learn from my constituents that the measures pursued in the administration of their affairs, during the time I have occupied the presidential chair, have met their approbation. Of the wisdom of these measures, it belongs to others to judge; that they have always been dictated by a desire to do what should be most for the public good, I may conscientiously affirm. Believing that a definite period of retiring from this station will tend materially to secure our elective form of government; and sensible, too, of that decline which advancing years bring on, I have felt it a duty to withdraw at the close of my present term of office; and to strengthen by practice a principle which I deem salutary. That others may be found whose talents and integrity render them proper deposits of the public liberty and interests, and who have made themselves known by their eminent services, we can all affirm, of our personal knowledge. To us it will belong, fellow citizens, when their country shall have called them to its helm, to give them our support while there, to facilitate their honest efforts for the public good, even where other measures might seem to us more direct, to strengthen the arm of our country by union under them, and to reserve ourselves for judging them at the constitutional period of election.

I pray you to tender to your society, of which you are a committee, my thanks for the indulgence with which they have viewed my conduct, with the assurance of my high respect, and to accept yourselves my friendly and respectful salutations.

## TO THE GENERAL ASSEMBLY OF NORTH CAROLINA

January 10, 1808

The wrongs our country has suffered, fellow citizens, by violations of those moral rules which the Author of our nature has implanted in man as the law of his nature, to govern him in his associated, as well as individual character, have been such as justly to excite the sensibilities you express, and a deep abhorrence at indications threatening a substitution of power for right in the intercourse between nations. Not less worthy of your indignation have been the machinations of parricides who have endeavored to bring into danger the union of these States, and to subvert, for the purposes of inordinate ambition, a government founded in the will of its citizens, and directed to no object but their happiness.

I learn, with the liveliest sentiments of gratitude and respect, your approbation of my conduct, in the various charges which my country has been pleased to confide to me at different times; and especially that the administration of our public affairs, since my accession to the chief magistracy, has been so far satisfactory, that my continuance in that office after its present term, would be acceptable to you. But, that I should lay down my charge at a proper period, is as much a duty as to have borne it faithfully. If some termination to the services of the chief magistrate be not fixed by the constitution, or supplied by practice, his office, nominally for years, will in fact become for life; and history shows how easily that degenerates into an inheritance. Believing that a representative government, responsible at short periods of election, is that which produces the greatest sum of happiness to mankind, I feel it a duty to do no act which shall essentially impair that principle; and I should unwillingly be the person who, disregarding the sound precedent set by an illustrious predecessor, should furnish the first example of prolongation beyond the second term of office.

Truth also obliges me to add, that I am sensible of that decline which advancing years bring on; and feeling their physical, I ought not to doubt their mental effect. Happy if I am the first to perceive and obey this admonition of nature, and to solicit a retreat from cares too great for the wearied faculties of age.

Declining a re-election on grounds which cannot but be approved, it will be the great comfort of my future days, and the satisfactory reward of a service of forty years, to carry into retirement such testimonies as you have been pleased to give, of the approbation and good will of my fellow citizens generally. And I supplicate the Being in whose hands we all are, to preserve our country in freedom and independence, and to bestow on yourselves the blessings of his favor.

## TO THE SOCIETY OF TAMMANY, OR COLUMBIAN ORDER, NO. 1, OF THE CITY OF NEW YORK

February 29, 1808

I have received your address, fellow citizens, and, thankful for the expressions so personally gratifying to myself, I contemplate with high satisfaction the ardent spirit it breathes of love to our country, and of devotion to its liberty and independence. The crisis in which it is placed, cannot but be unwelcome to those who love peace, yet spurn at a tame submission to wrong. So fortunately remote from the theatre of European contests, and carefully avoiding to implicate ourselves in them, we had a right to hope for an exemption from the calamities which have afflicted the contending nations, and to be permitted unoffendingly to pursue paths of industry and peace.

But the ocean, which, like the air, is the common birth-right of mankind, is arbitrarily wrested from us, and maxims consecrated by time, by usage, and by an universal sense of right, are trampled on by superior force. To give time for this demoralizing tempest to pass over, one measure only remained which might cover our beloved country from its overwhelming fury: an appeal to the deliberate understanding of our fellow citizens in a cessation of all intercourse with the belligerent nations, until it can be resumed under the protection of a returning sense of the moral obligations which constitute a law for nations as well as individuals. There can be no question, in a mind truly American, whether it is best to send our citizens and property into certain captivity, and then wage war for their recovery, or to keep them at home, and to turn seriously to that policy which plants the manufacturer and the husbandman side by side, and establishes at the door of everyone that exchange of mutual labors and comforts, which we have hitherto sought in distant regions, and under perpetual risk of broils with them. Between these alternatives your address has soundly decided, and I doubt not your aid, and that of every real and faithful citizen, towards carrying into effect the measures of your country, and enforcing the sacred principle, that in opposing foreign wrong there must be but one mind.

I receive with sensibility your kind prayers for my future happiness, and I supplicate a protecting providence to watch over your own and our country's freedom and welfare.

## TO THE DELEGATES OF THE DEMOCRATIC REPUBLICANS OF THE CITY OF PHILADELPHIA, IN GENERAL WARD COMMITTEE ASSEMBLED

May 25, 1808

The epoch, fellow citizens, into which our lot has fallen, has indeed been fruitful of events, which require vigilance, and embarrass deliberation. That during such a period of difficulty, and amidst the perils surrounding us, the public measures which have been pursued should meet your approbation, is a source of great satisfaction. It was not expected in this age, that nations so honorably distinguished by their advances in science and civilization, would suddenly cast away the esteem they had merited from the world, and, revolting from the empire of morality, assume a character in history, which all the tears of their posterity will never wash from its pages. But during this delirium of the warring powers, the ocean having become a field of lawless violence, a suspension of our navigation for a time was equally necessary to avoid contest, or enter it with advantage. This measure will, indeed, produce some temporary inconvenience; but promises lasting good by promoting among ourselves the establishment of manufactures hitherto sought abroad, at the risk of collisions no longer regulated by the laws of reason or morality.

It is to be lamented that any of our citizens, not thinking with the mass of the nation as to the principles of our government, or of its administration, and seeing all its proceedings with a prejudiced eye, should so misconceive and misrepresent our situation as to encourage aggressions from foreign nations. Our expectation is, that their distempered views will be understood by others as they are by ourselves; but should wars be the consequence of these delusions, and the errors of our dissatisfied citizens find atonement only in the blood of their sounder brethren, we must meet it as an evil necessarily flowing from that liberty of speaking and writing which guards our other liberties; and I have entire confidence in the assurances that your ardor will

be animated, in the conflicts brought on, by considerations of the necessity, honor, and justice of our cause.

I sincerely thank you, fellow citizens, for the concern you so kindly express for my future happiness. It is a high and abundant reward for endeavors to be useful; and I supplicate the care of Providence over the well-being of yourselves and our beloved country.

## TO THE LEGISLATURE, COUNCIL, AND HOUSE OF REPRESENTATIVES OF THE TERRITORY OF ORLEANS

June 18, 1808

I received, fellow citizens, with a just sensibility, the expressions of esteem and approbation, communicated in your kind address of the 29th of March, and am thankful for them. The motives which have led to my retirement from office were dictated by a sense of duty, and will, I trust, be approved by my fellow citizens generally.

It is, indeed, a source of real concern that an impartial neutrality scrupulously observed towards the belligerent nations of Europe, has not been sufficient to protect us against encroachments on our rights; and, although deprecating war, should no alternative be presented us but disgraceful submission to unlawful pretensions, I have entire confidence in your assurances that you will cheerfully submit to whatever sacrifices and privations may be necessary for vindicating the rights, the honor, and independence of our nation.

Far from a disposition to avail ourselves of the peculiar situation of any belligerent nation to ask concessions incompatible with their rights, with justice, or reciprocity, we have never proposed to any the sacrifice of a single right; and in consideration of existing circumstances, we have ever been willing, where our duty to other nations permitted us, to relax for a time, and in some cases, that strictness of right which the laws of nature, the acknowledgments of the civilized world, and the equality and independence of nations entitle us to. Should, therefore, excessive and continued injury compel at length a resort to the means of self-redress, we are strong in the consciousness that no wrong committed on our part, no precipitancy in repelling the wrongs committed by others, no want of moderation in our exactions of voluntary justice, but undeniable aggressions on us, and the avowed purpose of continuing them, will have produced a recurrence so little consonant with our principles or inclinations.

To carry with me into retirement the approbation and esteem of my fellow citizens, will, indeed, be the highest reward they can confer on me, and certainly the only one I have ever desired. I invoke the favor of heaven, fellow citizens, towards yourselves and our beloved country.

## TO THE LEGISLATURE OF NEW HAMPSHIRE

August 2, 1808

In the review, fellow citizens, which, in your address of the 14th of June, you have taken of the measures pursued since I have been charged with their direction, I read with great satisfaction and thankfulness, the approbation you have bestowed on them; and I feel it an ample reward for any services I may have been able to render.

The present moment is certainly eventful, and one which peculiarly requires that the bond of confederation connecting us as a nation should receive all the strength which unanimity between the national councils and the State legislatures can give it.

The depredations committed on our vessels and property on the high seas, the violences to the persons of our citizens employed on that element, had long been the subject of remonstrance and complaint, when, instead of reparation, new declarations of wrong are issued, subjecting our navigation to general plunder. In this state of things our first duty was to withdraw our sea-faring citizens and property from abroad, and to keep at home resources so valuable at all times, and so essential, if resort must ultimately be had to force.

It gave us time, too, to make a last appeal to the reason and reputation of nations. In the meanwhile I see with satisfaction that this measure of self-denial is approved and supported by the great body of our real citizens; that they meet with cheerfulness the temporary privations it occasions, and are preparing with spirit to provide for themselves those comforts and conveniences of life, for which it would be unwise evermore to recur to distant countries. How long this course may be preferable to a more serious appeal, must depend for decision on the wisdom of the legislature; unless, indeed, a return to established principles should remove the existing obstacles to a peaceable intercourse with foreign nations. In every event, fellow citizens, my confidence is entire that your resolution to maintain our national independence and sovereignty will be as firm as it has been forbearing; and looking back on our history, I am assured by the past, that its future pages will present nothing unworthy of the former.

I am happy that you approve of the motives of my retirement. I shall carry into it ardent prayers for the welfare of my country, and the sincerest wishes for that of yourselves personally.

## TO HIS EXCELLENCY GOVERNOR LANGDON

August 2, 1808

I received in due time your favor of June 24th, covering the address of the House of Representatives and Senate of New Hampshire, and I ask leave, through the same channel, to return the enclosed answer, to be communicated to them in whatever way you think most acceptable. Highly gratified by this approbation of the legislature of your State, as it respects myself personally, the moment at which it is expressed gives it peculiar value as a public document. It is the testimony of a respectable legislature in favor of a measure submitting our fellow citizens to some present sufferings to preserve them from future and greater, and cannot fail to strengthen the disposition to maintain it which I am happy to perceive is so general. I tender you my affectionate salutations, and with every wish for your health and happiness, the assurance of my high respect and consideration.[1]

## TO THE HONORABLE JOSEPH ALSTON, SPEAKER OF THE HOUSE OF REPRESENTATIVES OF SOUTH CAROLINA

August 4, 1808

SIR: I have duly received your letter of July 6th, covering the resolutions of the legislature of South Carolina of June 29th, and I see in those resolutions a new manifestation of the national spirit of which South Carolina has given so many proofs. It is the more exemplary, as it is certain that no State sacrifices more by the operation of a measure which, whether to avoid war, or to prepare for it, has been deemed equally necessary. The unanimity too

[1] To His Excellency Governor Langdon (private), August 2, 1808:

MY DEAR SIR: The enclosed are formal, and for the public; but in sending them to you I cannot omit the occasion of indulging my friendship in a more familiar way, and of recalling myself to your recollection. How much have I wished to have had you still with us through the years of my employment at Washington. I have seen with great pleasure the moderation and circumspection with which you have been kind enough to act under my letter of May 6th, and I have been highly gratified with the late general expressions of public sentiment in favor of a measure which alone could have saved us from immediate war, and give time to call home eighty millions of property, twenty or thirty thousand seamen, and two thousand vessels. These are now nearly at home, and furnish a great capital, much of which will go into manufactures and seamen to man a fleet of privateers, whenever our citizens shall prefer war to a longer continuance of the embargo. Perhaps, however, the whale of the ocean may be tired of the solitude it has made on that element, and return to honest principles, and his brother robber on the land may see that, as to us, the grapes are sour. I think one war enough for the life of one man; and you and I have gone through one which at least may lessen our impatience to embark in another. Still, if it becomes necessary, we must meet it like men, old men indeed, but yet good for something. But whether in peace or war, may you have as many years of life as you desire, with health and prosperity to make them happy years. I salute you with constant affection and great esteem and respect.

of these resolutions, does peculiar honor to those individuals, who differing from the mass of their fellow citizens in their opinions of government, yet forget all differences when the rights of their country are in question; who when it is assailed by foreign wrong, and menaced with the evils of war, instead of encouraging enemies by forebodings of weakness and division, present to them one common and undivided front. Persuaded that the sentiments expressed in these resolutions are a true specimen of those entertained by the great mass of our fellow citizens, we may regret the evils which a contrary opinion in others may produce, but we cannot fear the result of any trial they may put us to.

I receive with particular gratification assurances of approbation from the legislature of South Carolina, and will not cease in my endeavors to merit a continuance of it. I pray you to accept my salutations and assurances of great respect and consideration.

## TO THE INHABITANTS OF THE TOWN OF BOSTON, NEWBURYPORT, AND PROVIDENCE, IN LEGAL TOWN MEETING ASSEMBLED

August 26, 1808

Your representation and request were received on the 22d inst., and have been considered with the attention due to every expression of the sentiments and feelings of so respectable a body of my fellow citizens. No person has seen, with more concern than myself, the inconveniences brought on our country in general by the circumstances of the times in which we happen to live; times to which the history of nations presents no parallel. For years we have been looking as spectators on our brethren of Europe, afflicted by all those evils which necessarily follow an abandonment of the moral rules which bind men and nations together. Connected with them in friendship and commerce, we have happily so far kept aloof from their calamitous conflicts, by a steady observance of justice towards all, by much forbearance and multiplied sacrifices. At length, however, all regard to the rights of others having been thrown aside, the belligerent powers have beset the highway of commercial intercourse with edicts which, taken together, expose our commerce and mariners, under almost every destination, a prey to their fleets and armies. Each party, indeed, would admit our commerce with themselves, with the view of associating us in their war against the other. But we have wished war with neither. Under these circumstances were passed the laws of which you complain, by those delegated to exercise the powers of legislation for you, with every sympathy of a common interest in exercising them faithfully. In reviewing these measures, therefore, we should advert to the difficulties out of which a choice was of necessity to be made. To have submitted our rightful commerce to prohibitions and tributary exactions from others, would have been to surrender our independence. To resist them by arms was war, without consulting the state of things or the choice of the nation. The alternative preferred by the legislature of suspending a commerce placed under such unexampled difficulties, besides saving to our citizens their property, and our mariners to their country, has the peculiar advantage of giving time to the belligerent nations to revise a conduct as contrary to their interests as it is to our rights.

"In the event of such peace, or suspension of hostilities between the belligerent powers of Europe, or of such change in their measures affecting neutral commerce, as may render that of the United States sufficiently safe, in the judgment of the President," he is authorized to suspend the embargo. But no peace or suspension of hostilities, no change of measures affecting neutral commerce, is known to have taken place. The orders of England, and the decrees of France and Spain, existing at the date of these laws, are still unrepealed, as far as we know. In Spain, indeed, a contest for the government appears to have arisen; but of its course or prospects we have no information on which prudence would undertake a hasty change in our policy, even were the authority of the Executive competent to such a decision.

You desire that, in this defect of power, Congress may be specially convened. It is unnecessary to examine the evidence or the character of the facts which are supposed to dictate such a call; because you will be sensible, on an attention to dates, that the legal period of their meeting is as early as, in this extensive country, they could be fully convened by a special call.

I should, with great willingness, have executed the wishes of the inhabitants of the town of Boston, Newburyport, and Providence, had peace, or a repeal of the obnoxious edicts, or other charges, produced the case in which alone the laws have given me that authority; and so many motives of justice and interest lead to such changes, that we ought continually to expect them. But while these edicts remain, the legislature alone can prescribe the course to be pursued.

## TO A PORTION OF THE CITIZENS OF BOSTON

SIR: I have duly received the address of that portion of the citizens of [Boston] who have declared their approbation of the present suspension of our commerce, and their dissent from the representation of those of the same place, who wished its removal. A division of sentiment was not unexpected. On no question can a perfect unanimity be hoped, or certainly it would have been on that between war and embargo, the only alternatives presented to our choice. For the general capture of our vessels would have been war on one side, which reason and interest would repel by war and reprisal on our part.

Of the several interests composing those of the United States, that of manufactures would of course prefer to war a state of nonintercourse, so favorable to their rapid growth and prosperity. Agriculture, although sensibly feeling the loss of market for its produce, would find many aggravations in a state of war. Commerce and navigation, or that portion which is foreign, in the inactivity to which they are reduced by the present state of things, certainly experience their full share in the general inconvenience; but whether war would to them be a preferable alternative, is a question their patriotism would never hastily propose. It is to be regretted, however, that overlooking the real sources of their sufferings, the British and French edicts, which constitute the actual blockade of our foreign commerce and navigation, they have, with too little reflection, imputed them to laws which have saved them from greater, and have preserved for our own use our vessels, property and seamen, instead of adding them to the strength of those with whom we might eventually have to contend.

The embargo, giving time to the belligerent powers to revise their unjust proceedings, and to listen to the dictates of justice, of interest and reputation, which equally urge the correction of their wrongs, has availed our country of the only honorable expedient for avoiding war; and should a repeal of these edicts supersede the cause for it, our commercial brethren will become sensible that it has consulted their interests, however against their own will. It will be unfortunate for their country if, in the meantime, these their expressions of impatience should have the effect of prolonging the very sufferings which have produced them, by exciting a fallacious hope that we may, under any pressure, relinquish our equal right of navigating the ocean, go to such ports only as others may prescribe, and there pay the tributary exactions they may impose; an abandonment of national independence and of essential rights, revolting to every manly sentiment. While these edicts are in force, no American can ever consent to a return of peaceable intercourse with those who maintain them.

I am happy, in the approach of the period when the feelings and the wisdom of the nation will be collected in their representatives assembled together. To them are committed our rights, to them our wrongs are known, and they will pronounce the remedy they call for; and I hear with pleasure from all, as well those who approve, as who disapprove of the present measures, assurances of an implicit acquiescence in their enunciation of the general will.

I beg leave through you to communicate this answer to the address on which your signature held the first place, and to add the assurances of my respect.

## TO THE MEMBERS OF THE BALTIMORE BAPTIST ASSOCIATION

October 17, 1808

I receive with great pleasure the friendly address of the Baltimore Baptist Association, and am sensible how much I am indebted to the kind dispositions which dictated it.

In our early struggles for liberty, religious freedom could not fail to become a primary object. All men felt the right, and a just animation to obtain it was exhibited by all. I was one only among the many who befriended its establishment, and am entitled but in common with others to a portion of that approbation which follows the fulfilment of a duty.

Excited by wrongs to reject a foreign government which directed our concerns according to its own interests, and not to ours, the principles which justified us were obvious to all understandings, they were imprinted in the breast of every human being; and Providence ever pleases to direct the issue of our contest in favor of that side where justice was. Since this happy separation, our nation has wisely avoided entangling itself in the system of European interests, has taken no side between its rival powers, attached itself to none of its ever-changing confederacies. Their peace is desirable; and you do me justice in saying that to preserve and secure this, has been the constant aim of my administration. The difficulties which involve it, however, are now at their ultimate term, and what will be their issue, time alone will disclose. But be it what it may, a recollection of our former vassalage in religion and civil government, will unite the zeal of every heart, and the energy of every hand, to preserve that independence in both which, under the favor of heaven, a disinterested devotion to the public cause first achieved, and a disinterested sacrifice of private interests will now maintain.

I am happy in your approbation of my reasons for determining to retire from a station, in which the favor of my fellow citizens has so long continued and supported me: I return your kind prayers with supplications to the same almighty Being for your future welfare and that of our beloved country.

## TO THE MEMBERS OF THE KETOCTON BAPTIST ASSOCIATION

October 18, 1808

I received with great pleasure the affectionate address of the Ketocton Baptist Association, and am sensible how much I am indebted to the kind dispositions which dictated it.

In our early struggles for liberty, religious freedom could not fail to become a primary object. All men felt the right, and a just animation to obtain it was excited in all. And although your favor selected me as the organ of your petition to abolish the religious denomination of a privileged church, yet I was but one of the many who befriended its object, and am entitled but in common with them to a portion of that approbation which follows the fulfilment of a duty.

The views you express of the conduct of the belligerent powers are as correct as they are afflicting to the lovers of justice and humanity. Those moral principles and conventional usages which have heretofore been the bond of civilized nations, which have so often preserved their peace by furnishing common rules for the measure of their rights, have now given way to force, the law of Barbarians, and the nineteenth century dawns with the Vandalism of the fifth. Nothing has been spared on our part to preserve the peace of our country, during this distempered state of the world. But the difficulties which involve it are now at their ultimate term, and what will be their issue, time alone will disclose. But be that what it may, a recollection of our former vassalage in religion and civil government will unite the zeal of every heart, and the energy of every hand, to preserve that independence in both, which, under the favor of heaven, a disinterested devotion to the public cause first achieved, and a disinterested sacrifice of private interests will now maintain.

I am happy in your approbation of my reasons for determining to retire from a station in which the favor of my fellow citizens has so long continued and supported me; and I return your kind prayers by supplications to the same Almighty being for your future welfare, and that of our beloved country.

## TO THE GENERAL MEETING OF CORRESPONDENCE OF THE SIX BAPTIST ASSOCIATIONS REPRESENTED AT CHESTERFIELD, VIRGINIA

November 21, 1808

Thank you, fellow citizens, for your affectionate address, and I receive with satisfaction your approbation of my motives for retirement. In reviewing the history of the times through which we have passed, no portion of it gives greater satisfaction, on reflection, than that which presents the efforts of the friends of religious freedom, and the success with which they were crowned. We have solved by fair experiment, the great and interesting question whether freedom of religion is compatible with order in government, and obedience to the laws. And we have experienced the quiet as well as the comfort which results from leaving everyone to profess freely and openly those principles of religion which are the inductions of his own reason, and the serious convictions of his own inquiries.

It is a source of great contentment to me to learn that the measures which have been pursued in the administration of your affairs have met your approbation. Too often we have had but a choice among difficulties; and this situation characterizes remarkably the present moment. But, fellow citizens, if we are faithful to our country, if we acquiesce, with good will, in the decisions of the majority, and the nation moves in mass in the same direction, although it may not be that which every individual thinks best, we have nothing to fear from any quarter.

I thank you sincerely for your kind wishes for my welfare, and with equal sincerity implore the favor of a protecting Providence for yourselves.

## TO TABER FITCH, ESQ., CHAIRMAN

November 21, 1808

SIR: I have received with great pleasure the address of the republicans of the State of Connecticut, and am particularly sensible of the kindness with which they have viewed my conduct in the direction of their affairs. Having myself highly approved the example of an illustrious predecessor, in voluntarily retiring from a trust, which, if too long continued in the same hands, might become a subject of reasonable uneasiness and apprehension, I could not mistake my own duty when placed in a similar situation.

Our experience so far, has satisfactorily manifested the competence of a republican government to maintain and promote the best interests of its citizens; and every future year, I doubt not, will contribute to settle a question on which reason, and a knowledge of the character and circumstances of our fellow citizens, could never admit a doubt, and much less condemn them as fit subjects to be consigned to the dominion of wealth and force. Although under the pressure of serious evils at this moment, the governments of the other hemisphere cannot boast a more favorable situation. We certainly do not wish to exchange our difficulties for the sanguinary distresses of our fellow men beyond the water. In a state of the world unparalleled in times past, and never again to be expected, according to human probabilities, no form of government has, so far, better shielded its citizens from the prevailing afflictions. By withdrawing awhile from the ocean we have suffered some loss; but we have gathered home our immense capital. Exposed to foreign depredation, we have saved our seamen from the jails of Europe, and gained time to prepare for the defence of our country. The questions of submission, of war, or embargo, are now before our country as unembarrassed as at first. Submission and tribute, if that be our choice, will be no baser now than at the date of the embargo. But if, as I trust, that idea be spurned, we may now decide on the other alternatives of war and embargo, with the advantage of possessing all the means which have been rescued from the grasp of capture. These advantages certainly justify the approbation of the embargo declared in your address, and I have no doubt will ensure that of every candid citizen, who will correctly trace the consequences of any other course.

I thank you for the kind concern you are pleased to express for my future happiness, and offer my sincere prayers for your welfare and prosperity.

## TO THE YOUNG REPUBLICANS OF PITTSBURGH AND ITS VICINITIES

December 2, 1808

The sentiments which you express in your address of October 27th, of attachment to the rights of your country, of your determination to support them with your lives and fortunes, and of disregard of the inconveniences which must be encountered in resisting insult and aggression, are honorable to yourselves, and encouraging to your country. They are particularly solacing to those who, having labored faithfully in establishing the right of self-government, see in the rising generation, into whose hands it is passing, that purity of principle, and energy of character, which will protect and preserve it through their day, and deliver it over to their sons as they receive it from their fathers. The measure of a temporary suspension of commerce was adopted to cover us from greater evils. It has rescued from capture an important capital, and our seamen from the jails of Europe. It has given time to prepare for defence, and has shown to the aggressors of Europe that evil, as well as good actions, recoil on the doers. If these evils have involved our inoffending neighbors also, towards whom we have not a sentiment but of friendship and useful intercourse, it results from that state of violence by which the interests of the American hemisphere are directed to the objects of Europe. Endowed by nature with a system of interests and connections of its own, it is drawn from these by the unnatural bonds which enchain its different parts to the conflicting interests and fortunes of another world, and render its inhabitants strangers and enemies, to their neighbors and mutual friends.

Believing that the happiness of mankind is best promoted by the useful pursuits of peace, that on these alone a stable prosperity can be founded, that the evils of war are great in their endurance, and have a long reckoning for ages to come, I have used my best endeavors to keep our country uncommitted in the troubles which afflict Europe, and which assail us on every side. Whether this can be done longer, is to be doubted. I am happy that so far my conduct meets the approbation of my fellow citizens. It is the highest reward I can receive for my endeavors to serve them; and I am particularly thankful to yourselves for the kind expressions of esteem and confidence, and tender my best wishes for your personal happiness and prosperity.

## TO THE SOCIETY OF THE METHODIST EPISCOPAL CHURCH AT PITTSBURGH, PENNSYLVANIA

December 9, 1808

I am much indebted, fellow citizens, for your friendly address of November 20th, and gratified by its expressions of personal regard to myself. Having ever been an advocate for the freedom of religious opinion and exercise, from no person, certainly, was an abridgment of these sacred rights to be apprehended less than from myself.

In justice, too, to our excellent constitution, it ought to be observed, that it has not placed our religious rights under the power of any public functionary. The power, therefore, was wanting, not less than the will, to injure these rights.

The times in which we live, fellow citizens, are indeed times of trouble, such as no age has yet seen, or perhaps will ever see again. To avoid their calamitous influence, has been our duty and endeavor, and to effect it, great sacrifices of our citizens have been necessary. They have seen that these necessities were forced by the wrongs of others, and they have met them with the zeal which the crisis called for. What course we are finally to take, cannot yet be foreseen; but reading, reflecting, and examining for yourselves, you will find your public functionaries, according to the best of their judgments, directing your affairs, without passion or partiality, with a single view to your rights and best interests. And it is the approbation of those who so read, reflect, and examine for themselves, which is so truly consoling to the persons charged with the guidance of your affairs. For that portion of your approbation which you are pleased to bestow on my conduct, I am truly thankful, and I offer my sincere prayers for your welfare, and a happy issue of our country from the difficulties impending over it.

## TO THE ELECTORS OF THE COUNTY OF ONTARIO, IN THE STATE OF NEW YORK

December 13, 1808

The wrongs which we have sustained, fellow citizens, from the belligerent powers of Europe, and of which you have taken so just a view in your address, received by me on the 27th of the last month, could not fail to excite in the bosoms of freemen the sentiments of high indignation expressed by you. The love of peace had long induced us to bear with these aggressions, and the hope of a return to a spirit of justice had encouraged us to persevere in endeavors at amicable adjustment. Their outrages, however, have at length forced us to suspend all intercourse with them, to gather home our resources, and to prepare for whatever may happen. Your approbation of these measures is gratifying to your public functionaries, and the readiness you express to encounter the privations and sacrifices which these aggressions occasion, is honorable to yourselves. The legislature of the nation now assembled together, will decide how long the state of non-intercourse may be preferable to a more serious appeal. The decided support which you tender either of the present, or such other measures as they shall adopt for the good of the Union, and the pledge of your lives, your fortunes and honor for that purpose, are calculated to inspire them with firmness in their deliberations, and an assurance that the result will be supported by their country. The confidence you are so good as to express in the conduct of the administration, is highly gratifying to them, and encourages a perseverance in their best endeavors for the public good. That these may issue in effecting your happiness, and the peace and prosperity of our country, is my sincere prayer.

## TO THE CITIZENS OF THE CITY AND COUNTY OF PHILADELPHIA, IN TOWN-MEETING ASSEMBLED

February 3, 1809

In the resolutions and address which you have been pleased to present to me, I recognize with great satisfaction the sentiments of faithful citizens, devoted to the maintenance of the rights of their country, to the sacred bond which unites these States together, and rallying round their government in support of its laws. After the intolerable assault on our maritime rights, by the declarations of the belligerent powers, that we should navigate the ocean only as they should permit, the recall of our seamen, recovery of our property abroad, and putting ourselves into a state of defence, should perseverance on their parts force us to the last appeal, were duties to first obligation. No other course was left us but to reduce our navigation within the limits they dictated, and to hold even that subject to such further restrictions as their interests or will should prescribe. To this no friend to the independence of his country should submit.

Your resolution to aid in bringing to justice all violators of the laws of their country, and particularly of the embargo laws, and to be ready at all times to assist in carrying them into effect, is worthy of the patriotism which distinguishes the city and county of Philadelphia. This voluntary support of laws, formed by persons of our own choice, distinguishes peculiarly the minds capable of self-government. The contrary spirit is anarchy, which of necessity produces despotism. It is from the supporters of regular government only that the pledge of life, fortune, and honor is worthy of confidence.

I learn with great satisfaction your approbation of the several measures passed by the government, and enumerated in your address. For the advantages flowing from them you are indebted principally to a wise and patriotic legislature, and to the able and inestimable coadjutors with whom it has been my good fortune to be associated in the direction of your affairs. That these measures may be productive of the ends intended, must be the wish of every friend of his country; and the belief that everything has been done to preserve our peace, secure the rights of our fellow citizens, and to promote their best interests, will be a consolation under every situation to which the great disposer of events may destine us.

Your approbation of the motives for my retirement from the station so long confided to me, is a confirmation of their correctness. In no office can rotation be more expedient; and none less admits the indulgence of age. I am peculiarly sensible of your kind wishes for my happiness in the tranquillity of retirement. Nothing will contribute more to it than the hope of carrying with me the approbation of my fellow citizens, of the endeavors which I have faithfully exerted to be useful to them. To the all-protecting favor of heaven I commit yourselves and our common country.

## TO THE LEGISLATURE OF THE STATE OF GEORGIA

February 3, 1809

The address which the Legislature of Georgia, the immediate organ of the will of their constituents, has been pleased to present to me, is received with that high satisfaction which the approbation of so respectable a State is calculated to inspire. During the unexampled contest which has so long afflicted Europe, which has prostrated all the laws which have hitherto been deemed sacred among nations, and have so long constituted the rule of their intercourse, we had vainly hoped that our distance from the scene of carnage, and the invariable justice with which we have conducted ourselves towards all parties, would shield us from its baleful effects. But that commerce indispensably necessary for the exchange of the produce of this great agricultural country for the things which we want, increased by a temporary succession to the commerce of other nations, as being ourselves the only neutrals, has brought us into contact with the lawless belligerents in every sea, and threatens to involve us in the vortex of their contests. The privations for the want of a vent for our produce, have been the unavoidable result of the edicts of the belligerent powers. Should the measure adopted in consequence of them, and which meets your approbation, still save the lives and property of our brethren from the insults and rapacity of these powers, it will be a fortunate addition to the other benefits derived from it. On the other hand, should our present embarrassments eventuate in war, I am satisfied that the State of Georgia will zealously emulate her sister States in supporting the government of their choice, and in maintaining the rights and interests of the nation. Our soil, our industry, and our numbers, with the bravery which will be engaged in the cause, can never leave us without resources to maintain such a contest.

To no events which can concern the future welfare of my country, can I ever become an indifferent spectator; her prosperity will be my joy, her calamities my affliction.

Thankful for the indulgence with which my conduct has been viewed by the Legislature of Georgia, and for the kind expressions of their good will, I supplicate the favor of heaven towards them and our beloved country.

## TO THE SOCIETY OF THE METHODIST EPISCOPAL CHURCH AT NEW LONDON, CONNECTICUT

February 4, 1809

The approbation you are so good as to express of the measures which have been recommended and pursued during the course of my administration of the national concerns, is highly acceptable. The approving voice of our fellow citizens, for endeavors to be useful, is the greatest of all earthly rewards.

No provision in our constitution ought to be dearer to man than that which protects the rights of conscience against the enterprises of the civil authority. It has not left the religion of its citizens under the power of its public functionaries, were it possible that any of these should consider a conquest over the consciences of men either attainable or applicable to any desirable purpose. To me no information could be more welcome than that the minutes of the several religious societies should prove, of late, larger additions than have been usual, to their several associations, and I trust that the whole course of my life has proved me a sincere friend to religious as well as civil liberty.

I thank you for your affectionate good wishes for my future happiness. Retirement has become essential to it; and one of its best consolations will be to witness the advancement of my country in all those pursuits and acquisitions which constitute the character of a wise and virtuous nation; and I offer sincere prayers to heaven that its benediction may attend yourselves, our country and all its sons.

## TO THE GENERAL ASSEMBLY OF VIRGINIA

February 16, 1809

I receive with peculiar sensibility the affectionate address of the General Assembly of my native State, on my approaching retirement from the office with which I have been honored by the nation at large. Having been one of those who entered into public life at the commencement of an æra the most extraordinary which the history of man has ever yet presented to his contemplation, I claim nothing more, for the part I have acted in it, than a common merit of having, with others, faithfully endeavored to do my duty in the several stations allotted me. In the measures which you are pleased particularly to approve, I have been aided by the wisdom and patriotism of the national legislature, and the talents and virtues of the able coadjutors with whom it has been my happiness to be associated, and to whose valuable and faithful services I with pleasure and gratitude bear witness.

From the moment that to preserve our rights a change of government became necessary, no doubt could be entertained that a republican form was most consonant with reason, with right, with the freedom of man, and with the character and situation of our fellow citizens. To the sincere spirit of republicanism are naturally associated the love of country, devotion to its liberty, its rights, and its honor. Our preference to that form of government has been so far justified by its success, and the prosperity with which it has blessed us. In no portion of the earth were life, liberty and property ever so securely held; and it is with infinite satisfaction that withdrawing from the active scenes of life, I see the sacred design of these blessings committed to those who are sensible of their value and determined to defend thm.

It would have been a great consolation to have left the nation under the assurance of continued peace. Nothing has been spared to effect it; and at no other period of history would such efforts have failed to ensure it. For neither belligerent pretends to have been injured by us, or can say that we have in any instance departed from the most faithful neutrality; and certainly none will charge us with a want of forbearance.

In the desire of peace, but in full confidence of safety from our unity, our position, and our resources, I shall retire into the bosom of my native State, endeared to me by every tie which can attach the human heart. The assurances of your approbation, and that my conduct has given satisfaction to my fellow citizens generally, will be an important ingredient in my future happiness; and that the supreme ruler of the universe may have our country under his special care, will be among the latest of my prayers.

## TO THE CITIZENS OF WILMINGTON AND ITS VICINITY, IN TOWN-MEETING ASSEMBLED

February 16, 1809

The resolutions which have been entered into by the citizens of Wilmington and its vicinity, are worthy of the well-known patriotism of that place.

The storm which with little intermission has been raging for so many years, which has immolated the ancient dynasties and institutions of Europe, and prostrated the principles of public law heretofore respected, has hitherto been felt but in a secondary degree by us. But threatening at length to involve us in its vortex, it is time for all good citizens to rally round the constituted authorities by a public expression of their determination to support the laws and government of their choice, and to frown into silence all disorganizing movements. Strong in our numbers, our position and resources, we can never be endangered but by schisms at home. It has been the anxious care of the government to preserve the United States from this destructive contest; but whether it can yet be done depends on a return to reason by those who have so long rejected its dictates. On our part, there is no doubt of a continuance of the same desire to conduct the nation quietly through the political storms prevailing, and to lead it in safety through the perils with which we are menaced by the ambition of foreign nations.

I am thankful for the great indulgence with which you have viewed the measures of my administration. Of their wisdom others must judge; but I may truly say they have been pursued with honest intentions, unbiased by any personal or interested views. It is a consolation to know that the motives for my retirement are approved; and although I withdraw from public functions, I shall continue an anxious spectator of passing events, and offer to heaven my constant prayers for the preservation of our republic, and especially of those its best principles which secure to all its citizens a perfect equality of rights.

## TO JOHN GASSAWAY, ESQ.

February 17, 1809

SIR: I have duly received the resolutions of the republican citizens of Annapolis and Anne-Arundel county, of the 4th inst., which you were so kind as to forward to me.

That the aggressions and injuries of the belligerent nations have been the real obstructions which have interrupted our commerce, and now threaten our peace, and that the embargo laws were salutary and indispensably necessary to meet those obstructions, are truths as evident to every candid man, as it is worthy of every good citizen to declare his reprobation of that system of opposition which goes to an avowed and practical resistance of these laws. To such a resistance I trust that the patriotism of our faithful citizens in no section of the Union will give any countenance. Where the law of majority ceases to be acknowledged, there government ends, the law of the strongest takes its place, and life and property are his who can take them.

I receive with particular pleasure and thankfulness the testimony of the republican citizens of Annapolis and Anne-Arundel, in favor of the course of proceedings during my administration of the public affairs. And I can truly say, in their words, that they have been conducted with the purest regard and devotion to the interests of the people and the national safety and honor; and I pray you, with my acknowledgments for these favorable sentiments, to accept the assurances of my high respect and consideration.

## TO CAPTAIN JOSEPH ——, JR.

February 17, 1809

SIR: The resolutions entered into at a meeting of the officers of the Legionary Brigade of the 1st Division of Massachusetts militia, on the 31st ult., which you have been pleased to forward to me, breathe that spirit of fidelity to our common country which must ever be peculiarly the spirit of its militia, and which renders that the safest and last reliance of a republican nation. The perils with which we have been for some time environed, have been such as ought to have induced every faithful citizen to unite in support of the rights of his country, laying aside little differences, political or personal, till they might be indulged without hazarding the safety of our country. Assailed in our essential rights by two of the most powerful nations on the globe, we have remonstrated, negotiated, and at length retired to the last stand, in the hope of peaceably preserving our rights. In this extremity I have entire confidence that no part of *the people* in any section of the Union, will desert the banners of their country, and co-operate with the enemies who are threatening its existence. The subscribing officers of the legionary brigade have furnished an honorable example of declaring their attachment to the constitution, the laws, and the union of the States, that they will at the call of law, rally around the standard of their country, and protect its constitution, laws, right and liberties, against all foes. I thank them, in the name of their country, for these patriotic resolutions, the pledge of support they tender will lead them to no more than the honor of a soldier and fidelity of a citizen would of itself require. I salute yourself and the subscribing offices with esteem and respect.

## TO THE REPUBLICAN YOUNG MEN OF NEW LONDON, BENJAMIN HEMPSTEAD CHAIRMAN

February 24, 1809

The approbation which you are pleased to express of my past administration, is highly gratifying to me. That in a free government there should be differences of opinion as to public measures and the conduct of those who direct them, is to be expected. It is much, however, to be lamented, that these differences should be indulged at a crisis which calls for the undivided councils and energies of our country, and in a form calculated to encourage our enemies in the refusal of justice, and to force their country into war as the only resource for obtaining it.

You do justice to the government in believing that their utmost endeavors have been used to steer us clear of wars with other nations, and honor to yourselves in declaring that if these endeavors prove ineffectual, and your country is called upon to defend its rights and injured honor by an appeal to arms, you will be ready for the contest, and will meet our enemies at the threshold of our country. While prudence will endeavor to avoid this issue, bravery will prepare to meet it.

I thank you, fellow citizens, for your kind expressions of regard for myself, and prayers for my future happiness, and I join in supplications to that Almighty Being who has heretofore guarded our councils, still to continue his gracious benedictions towards our country, and that yourselves may be under the protection of his divine favor.

## TO THE REPUBLICANS OF LOUDOUN COUNTY, CONVENED AT LEESBURG, FEBRUARY 13, 1809

February 24, 1809

The measures lately pursued in preference either to war or an ignominious surrender of our rights as an independent people, have undoubtedly produced the beneficial effects of saving our property and seamen, of lengthening the term of our peace, and of giving time for defensive preparations. Other efficacious results would probably have been produced, in a much higher degree, had not the measures been counteracted by unworthy passions. It is still possible that the blessings of peace may be continued to us, should sounder calculations of interest induce a return to justice by the aggressive nations. But should we be disappointed in what ought to be so justly expected, the solemn pledge of life and fortune in vindication of our violated rights received from yourselves as well as from other citizens, leaves us without apprehension as to the issue of any contest into which we may be forced.

I thank you particularly for the approbation you manifest of my conduct and motives, and the kind concern you express for my future happiness, and I beg leave to tender you my best wishes and assurances of respect.

## TO GOVERNOR TOMPKINS

February 24, 1809

SIR: I received, a few days ago, your Excellency's favor of the 9th inst., covering the patriotic resolutions of the Legislature of New York, of the 3d. The times do certainly render it incumbent on all good citizens, attached to the rights and honor of their country, to bury in oblivion all internal differences, and rally around the standard of their country in opposition to the outrages of foreign nations. All attempts to enfeeble and destroy the exertions of the General Government, in vindication of our national rights, or to loosen the bands of union by alienating the affections of the people, or opposing the authority of the laws at so eventful a period, merit the discountenance of all.

The confidence which the Legislature expresses in the national administration is highly consolatory, and their determination to support the just rights of their country with their lives and fortunes, are worthy of the high character of the State of New York.

By all, I trust, the union of these States will ever be considered as the palladium of their safety, their prosperity and glory, and all attempts to sever it will be frowned on with reprobation and abhorrence. And I have equal confidence, that all moved by the sacred principles of liberty and patriotism will prepare themselves for any crisis we may be able to meet, and will be ready to co-operate with each other, and with the constituted authorities, in resisting and repelling the aggressions of foreign nations.

The Legislature may be assured that every exertion will be used to put the United States in the best condition of defence, that we may be fully prepared to meet the dangers which menace the peace of our country. I avail myself with pleasure of every occasion to tender to your Excellency the assurances of my high respect and consideration.

## TO GENERAL JAMES ROBERTSON

February 24, 1809

SIR: I have duly received your letter covering the resolutions of the citizens of West Tennessee, assembled in the town of Nashville. Every friend of his country must feel the regret and indignation they so laudably express at the unjust and unprecedented measures adopted by the belligerent powers of Europe, violating our maritime rights as a free and independent nation, and compelling us for their preservation to resort to measures the effects of which we must all feel. And all must see with pleasure their honorable declaration against receding from the grounds taken with regard to the belligerent nations, and their reprobation of the surrender of any essential points in difference between us and those nations.

Should the embargo be continued, or a non-intercourse be substituted, it is pleasing to know that our fellow citizens will afford every aid in their power to render it effectual; and if war must at length be resorted to, I have entire confidence in their declarations, that as citizen soldiers they will be ready at the call of their country to prove to their enemies that they know how to value and defend their rights.

I am happy to learn their approbation of the measures adopted by the General Government in relation to Great Britain and France, and particularly thankful for the satisfaction they express with the course I have pursued in the discharge of the arduous duties which devolved on me as chief magistrate of the United States.

I pray you to accept for yourself and them the assurances of my great respect and consideration.

## TO THE REPUBLICANS OF THE COUNTY OF NIAGARA, CONVENED AT CLARENCE ON THE 26TH OF JANUARY, 1809

February 24, 1809

The eventful crisis in our national affairs so truly portrayed in your very friendly address, has justly excited your serious attention. The nations of the earth prostrated at the foot of power, the ocean submitted to the despotism of a single nation, the laws of nature and the usages which have hitherto regulated the intercourse of nations and interposed some restraint between power and right, now totally disregarded. Such is the state of things when the United States are left single-handed to maintain the rights of neutrals, and the principles of public right against a warring world. Under these circumstances, it is a great consolation to receive the assurances of our faithful citizens that they will unite their destiny with their government, will rally under the banners of their country, and with their lives and fortunes, defend and support their civil and religious rights. This declaration, too, is the more honorable from those whose frontier residence will expose them particularly to the inroads of a foe.

I receive with great pleasure your approbation of the impartial neutrality we have so invariably pursued, and of the trying measure of embargo rendered necessary by the belligerent edicts, which has saved our seamen and our property, has given us time to prepare for vindicating our honor and preserving our national independence, and has excited the spirit of manufacturing for ourselves those things which, though we raised the raw material, we have hitherto sought from other countries at the risk of war and rapine.

I thank you for your kind wishes for my future happiness in retiring from public life to the bosom of my family. Nothing will contribute more to it than the assurance that my fellow citizens approve of my endeavors to serve them, and the hope that we shall be continued in the blessings we have enjoyed under the favor of Heaven.

## TO CAPTAIN QUIN MORTON

February 24, 1809

SIR: I have duly received your favor tendering the service of fifty citizens of Tennessee as a company of volunteer riflemen. There are two acts of Congress which regulate the acceptances of these tenders; that of the last year (1808) is for a service of six months, and authorizes the governors to accept; and that of 1807, for a service of twelve months, authorizing the President to accept, who has delegated that power to the governors of the several States. Under whichever of these, therefore, your tender was meant to be made, I must pray you to repeat it to the governor of the State; expressing, at the same time, my great satisfaction at the readiness and patriotism with which I see my fellow citizens resort to the standard of their country when danger threatens it. Accept for your company my thanks on the public behalf, and for yourself the assurances of my respect.

## TO THE TAMMANY SOCIETY OR COLUMBIAN ORDER OF THE CITY OF WASHINGTON

March 2, 1809

The observations are but too just which are made in your friendly address, on the origin and progress of those abuses of public confidence and power which have so often terminated in a suppression of the rights of the people, and the mere aggrandizement and emolument of their oppressors. Taught by these truths, and aware of the tendency of power to degenerate into abuse, the worthies of our own country have secured its independence by the establishment of a constitution and form of government for our nation, calculated to prevent as well as to correct abuse.

Beyond the great water the torch of discord has been long lighted up, and long and unremitting have been the endeavors of the belligerents to immerge us in the evils they were inflicting on each other, and to make us parties in their quarrels. Whether it will be possible much longer to escape these evils, is difficult to decide; but you do me justice in believing that no efforts on my part have been spared to effect this purpose, and to preserve for our nation the blessings of peace.

I learn with sincere pleasure that the measures I have pursued in directing the affairs of our nation have met with approbation. Their sole object has certainly been the good of my fellow citizens, which sometimes may have been mistaken, but never intentionally disregarded. This approbation is the more valued as being the spontaneous effusion of the feelings of those who have lived in the same city with myself, and having examined carefully and even jealously my conduct through every passing day, bear testimony to their belief in its fidelity.

I am happy, in my retirement, to carry with me your esteem and your prayers for my health, peace and happiness; and I sincerely supplicate Heaven that your own personal welfare may long make a part of the general prosperity of a great, a free, and a happy people.

## TO THE CITIZENS OF WASHINGTON

March 4, 1809

I received with peculiar gratification the affectionate address of the citizens of Washington, and in the patriotic sentiments it expresses, I see the true character of the national metropolis.

The station which we occupy among the nations of the earth is honorable, but awful. Trusted with the destinies of this solitary republic of the world, the only monument of human rights, and the sole depository of the sacred fire of freedom and self-government, from hence it is to be lighted up in other regions of the earth, if other regions of the earth shall ever become susceptible of its benign influence. All mankind ought then, with us, to rejoice in its prosperous, and sympathize in its adverse fortunes, as involving everything dear to man. And to what sacrifices of interest, or convenience, ought not these considerations to animate us? To what compromises of opinion and inclination, to maintain harmony and union among ourselves, and to preserve from all danger this hallowed ark of human hope and happiness. That differences of opinion should arise among men, on politics, on religion, and on every other topic of human inquiry, and that these should be freely expressed in a country where all our faculties are free, is to be expected. But these valuable privileges are much prevented when permitted to disturb the harmony of social intercourse, and to lessen the tolerance of opinion. To the honor of society here, it has been characterized by a just and generous liberality, and an indulgence of those affections which, without regard to political creeds, constitute the happiness of life. That the improvement of this city must proceed with sure and steady steps, follows from its many obvious advantages, and from the enterprizing spirit of its inhabitants, which promises to render it the fairest seat of wealth and science.

It is very gratifying to me that the general course of my administration is approved by my fellow citizens, and particularly that the motives of my retirement are satisfactory. I part with the powers entrusted to me by my country, as with a burthen of heavy bearing; but it is with sincere regret that I part with the society in which I have lived here. It has been the source of much happiness to me during my residence at the seat of government, and I owe it much for its kind dispositions. I shall ever feel a high interest in the prosperity of the city, and an affectionate attachment to its inhabitants.

## TO THE REPUBLICANS OF GEORGETOWN

March 8, 1809

The affectionate address of the republicans of Georgetown on my retirement from public duty, is received with sincere pleasure. In the review of my political life, which they so indulgently take, if it be found that I have done my duty as other faithful citizens have done, it is all the merit I claim. Our lot has been cast on an awful period of human history. The contest which began with us, which ushered in the dawn of our national existence and led us through various and trying scenes, was for everything dear to free-born man. The principles on which we engaged, of which the charter of our independence is the record, were sanctioned by the laws of our being, and we but obeyed them in pursuing undeviatingly the course they called for. It issued finally in that inestimable state of freedom which alone can ensure to man the enjoyment of his equal rights. From the moment which sealed our peace and independence, our nation has wisely pursued the paths of peace and justice. During the period in which I have been charged with its concerns, no effort has been spared to exempt us from the wrongs and the rapacity of foreign nations, and with you I feel assured that no American will hesitate to rally round the standard of his insulted country, in defence of that freedom and independence achieved by the wisdom of sages, and consecrated by the blood of heroes.

The favorable testimony of those among whom I have lived, and lived happily as a fellow citizen, as a neighbor, and in the various relations of social life, will enliven the days of my retirement, and be felt and cherished with affection and gratitude.

I thank you, fellow citizens, for your kind prayers for my future happiness. I shall ever retain a lively sense of your friendly attentions, and continue to pray for your prosperity and well being.

## TO STEPHEN CROSS, ESQ., TOPSHAM

March 28, 1809

To the delegates from the various towns in the county of Essex and commonwealth of Massachusetts, assembled on the 20th of February, at Topsham.

The receipt of your kind address in the last moments of the session of Congress, will, I trust, offer a just apology for this late acknowledgment of it. I am very sensible of the indulgence with which you are so good as to review the measures of my late administration, and I feel for that indulgence the sentiments of gratitude it so justly calls for. The stand which has been made on behalf of our seamen enslaved and incarcerated in foreign ships, and against the prostration of our rights on the ocean under laws of nature acknowledged by all civilized nations, was an effort due to the protection of our commerce, and to that portion of our fellow citizens engaged in the pursuits of navigation. The opposition of the same portion to the vindication of their peculiar rights, has been as wonderful as the loyalty of their agricultural brethren in the assertion of them has been disinterested and meritorious. If the honor of the nation can be forgotten, whether the abandonment of the right of navigating the ocean may not be compensated by exemption from the wars it would produce, may be a question for our future councils, which the disclaimer of our navigating citizens may, if continued, relieve from the embarrassment of their rights.

Sincerely and affectionately attached to our national constitution, as the ark of our safety, and grand palladium of our peace and happiness, I learn with pleasure that the number of those in the county of Essex, who read and think for themselves, is great, and constituted of men who will never surrender but with their lives, the invaluable liberties achieved by their fathers. Their elevated minds put all to the hazard for a three penny duty on tea, by the same nation which now exacts a tribute equal to the value of half our exported produce.

I thank you, fellow citizens, for the kind interest you take in my future happiness, and I sincerely supplicate that overruling providence which governs the destinies of men and nations, to dispense his choicest blessings on yourselves and our beloved country.

## TO THE REPUBLICAN MECHANICS OF THE TOWN OF LEESBURG AND ITS VICINITY, ASSEMBLED ON THE 27TH OF FEBRUARY LAST

March 29, 1809

The receipt of your kind address in the last moments of the session of Congress, will, I trust, offer a just apology for its late acknowledgment.

Your friendly salutations on the close of my public life, and approbation of the motives which dictated my retirement, are received with great satisfaction.

That there should be a contrariety of opinions respecting the public agents and their measures, and more especially respecting that which recently suspended our commerce and produced temporary privations, is ever to be expected among free men; and I am happy to find you are in the number of those who are satisfied that the course pursued was marked out by our country's interest, and called for by her dearest rights. While the principles of our constitution give just latitude to inquiry, every citizen faithful to it will, with you, deem embodied expressions of discontent, and open outrages of law and patriotism, as dishonorable as they are injurious; and there is reason to believe that had the efforts of the government against the innovations and tyranny of the belligerent powers been unopposed among ourselves, they would have been more effectual towards the establishment of our rights.

Unconscious of partiality between the different callings of my fellow citizens, I trust that a fair review of my attention to the interests of commerce in particular, in every station of my political life, will afford sufficient proofs of my just estimation of its importance in the social system. What has produced our present difficulties, and what will have produced the impending war, if that is to be our lot? Our efforts to save the rights of commerce and navigation. From these, solely and exclusively, the whole of our present dangers flow.

With just reprobations of the resistance made or menaced against the laws of our country, I applaud your patriotic resolution to meet hostility to them with the energy and dignity of freemen; and thankful for your solicitude for my health and happiness, I salute you with affectionate sentiments of respect.

## TO THE FRIENDS OF THE ADMINISTRATION OF THE UNITED STATES IN BRISTOL COUNTY, RHODE ISLAND

March 29, 1809

The receipt of your friendly address in the last moments of the session of Congress, will, I trust, offer a just apology for its late acknowledgment.

We have certainly cause to rejoice that since the waves of affliction and peril, raised from the storm of war by the rival belligerents of Europe, have undulated on our shores, the councils of the nation have been able to preserve it from the numerous evils which have awfully menaced, and otherwise might have fallen upon us. How long we may yet retain this desirable position is difficult to be foreseen. But confident I am that as long as it can be done consistently with the honor and interest of our country, it will be maintained by those to whom you have confided the helm of government. A surer pledge for this cannot be found than in the public and private virtues of the successor to the chair of government, which you so justly recognize. Your reflections are certainly correct on the importance of a good administration in a republican government, towards securing to us our dearest rights, and the practical enjoinment of all our liberties; and such an one can never fail to give consolation to the friends of free government, and mortification to its enemies. In retiring from the duties of my late station, I have the consolation of knowing that such is the character of those into whose hands they are transferred, and of a conviction that all will be done for us which wisdom and virtue can do.

I thank you, fellow citizens, for the kind sentiments of your address, and am particularly gratified by your approbation of the course I have pursued; and I pray heaven to keep you under its holy favor.

## TO THE DEMOCRATIC REPUBLICAN DELEGATES FROM THE TOWNSHIPS OF WASHINGTON COUNTY, IN PENNSYLVANIA, CONVENED ON THE 21ST OF FEBRUARY, 1809

March 31, 1809

The satisfaction you express, fellow citizens, that my endeavors have been unremitting to preserve the peace and independence of our country, and that a faithful neutrality has been observed towards all the contending powers, is highly grateful to me; and there can be no doubt that in any common times they would have saved us from the present embarrassments, thrown in the way of our national prosperity by the rival powers.

It is true that the embargo laws have not had all the effect in bringing the powers of Europe to a sense of justice, which a more faithful observance of them might have produced. Yet they have had the important effects of saving our seamen and property, of giving time to prepare for defence; and they will produce the further inestimable advantage of turning the attention and enterprise of our fellow citizens, and the patronage of our State legislatures, to the establishment of useful manufactures in our country. They will have hastened the day when an equilibrium between the occupations of agriculture, manufactures, and commerce, shall simplify our foreign concerns to the exchange only of that surplus which we cannot consume for those articles of reasonable comfort or convenience which we cannot produce.

Our lot has been cast, by the favor of heaven, in a country and under circumstances, highly auspicious to our peace and prosperity, and where no pretence can arise for the degrading and oppressive establishments of Europe. It is our happiness that honorable distinctions flow only from public approbation; and that finds no object in titled dignitaries and pageants. Let us then, fellow citizens, endeavor carefully to guard this happy state of things, by keeping a watchful eye over the disaffection of wealth and ambition to the republican principles of our constitution, and by sacrificing all our local and personal interests to the cultivation of the Union, and maintenance of the authority of the laws.

My warmest thanks are due to you, fellow citizens, for the affectionate sentiments expressed in your address, and my prayers will ever be offered for your welfare and happiness.

## TO THE CITIZENS OF ALLEGANY COUNTY, IN MARYLAND

March 31, 1809

The sentiments of attachment, respect, and esteem, expressed in your address of the 20th ult., have been read with pleasure, and would sooner have received my thanks, but for the mass of business engrossing the last moments of a session of Congress. I am gratified by your approbation of our efforts for the general good, and our endeavors to promote the best interests of our country, and to place them on a basis firm and lasting. The measures respecting our intercourse with foreign nations were the result, as you suppose, of a choice between two evils, either to call and keep at home our seamen and property, or suffer them to be taken under the edicts of the belligerent powers. How a difference of opinion could arise between these alternatives is still difficult to explain on any acknowledged ground; and I am persuaded, with you, that when the storm and agitation characterizing the present moment shall have subsided, when passion and prejudice shall have yielded to reason its usurped place, and especially when posterity shall pass its sentence on the present times, justice will be rendered to the course which has been pursued. To the advantages derived from the choice which was made will be added the improvements and discoveries made and making in the arts, and the establishments in domestic manufacture, the effects whereof will be permanent and diffused through our wide-extended continent. That we may live to behold the storm which seems to threaten us, pass like a summer's cloud away, and that yourselves may continue to enjoy all the blessings of peace and prosperity, is my fervent prayer.

## TO THE REPUBLICAN CITIZENS OF WASHINGTON COUNTY, MARYLAND, ASSEMBLED AT HAGERSTOWN ON THE 6TH INSTANT.

March 31, 1809

The affectionate sentiments you express on my retirement from the high office conferred upon me by my country, are gratefully received and acknowledged with thankfulness. Your approbation of the various measures which have been pursued, cannot but be highly consolatory to myself, and encouraging to future functionaries, who will see that their honest endeavors for the public good will receive due credit with their constituents. That the great and leading measure respecting our foreign intercourse was the most salutary alternative, and preferable to the submission of our rights as a free and independent republic, or to a war at that period, cannot be doubted by candid minds. Great and good effects have certainly flowed from it, and greater would have been produced, had they not been, in some degree, frustrated by unfaithful citizens.

If, in my retirement to the humble station of a private citizen, I am accompanied with the esteem and approbation of my fellow citizens, trophies obtained by the blood-stained steel, or the tattered flags of the tented field, will never be envied. The care of human life and happiness, and not their destruction, is the first and only legitimate object of good government.

I salute you, fellow citizens, with every wish for your welfare, and the perpetual duration of our government, in all the purity of its republican principles.

## TO JAMES HOCHIE, ESQ., PRESIDENT OF THE ANCIENT PLYMOUTH SOCIETY OF NEW LONDON

April 2, 1809

SIR: I have duly received your favor of March 17th, covering resolutions of the Ancient Plymouth Society of New London, approving my conduct, as well during the period of my late administration, as the preceding portion of my public services.

Our lot has been cast in times which called for the best exertions of all our citizens to recover and preserve the rights which nature had given them; and we may say with truth, that the mass of our fellow citizens have performed with zeal and effect the duties called for. If I have been fortunate enough to give satisfaction in the performance of those allotted to me by our country, I find an ample reward in the assurances of that satisfaction. Possessed of the blessing of self-government, and of such a portion of civil liberty as no other civilized nation enjoys, it now behooves us to guard and preserve them by a continuance of the sacrifices and exertions by which they were acquired, and especially to nourish that union which is their sole guarantee. I pray you to accept for yourself and your associates the assurances of my high consideration and respect.

## TO HIS EXCELLENCY GOVERNOR WRIGHT [1]

April 3, 1809

DEAR SIR: Your friendly note of March 3d, was delivered to me on that day. You know the pressure of the last moments of a session of Congress, and can judge of that of my own departure from Washington, and of my first attentions here. This must excuse my late acknowledgment of your note. The assurances of your approbation of the course I have observed are highly flattering, and the more so, as you have been sometimes an eye-witness and long of the vicinage of the public councils. The testimony of my fellow citizens, and especially of one who, having been himself in the high departments, to the means of information united the qualifications to judge, is a consolation which will sweeten the residue of my life. The fog which arose in the east in the last moments of my service, will doubtless clear away and expose under a stronger light the rocks and shoals which have threatened us with danger. It is impossible the good citizens of the east should not see the agency of England, the tools she employs among them, and the criminal arts and falsehoods of which they have been the dupes. I still trust and pray that

[1] Robert Wright, Governor of Maryland.

our union may be perpetual, and I beg you to accept the assurances of my high esteem and respect.

## TO THE LEGISLATURE OF THE STATE OF NEW YORK

April 12, 1809

I receive with respect and gratitude, from the Legislature of New York, on my retirement from the office of chief magistrate of the United States, the assurances of their esteem, and of their satisfaction with the services I have endeavored to render. The welfare of my fellow citizens, and the perpetuation of our republican institutions, having been the governing principles of my public life, the favorable testimony borne by the Legislature of a State so respectable as that of New York, gives me the highest consolation. And this is much strengthened by an intimate conviction that the same principles will govern the conduct of my successor, whose talents, and eminent services, are a certain pledge that the confidence in him expressed by the Legislature of New York, will never be disappointed.

Sole depositories of the remains of human liberty, our duty to ourselves, to posterity, and to mankind, call on us by every motive which is sacred or honorable, to watch over the safety of our beloved country during the troubles which agitate and convulse the residue of the world, and to sacrifice to that all personal and local considerations. While the boasted energies of monarchy have yielded to easy conquest the people they were to protect, should our fabric of freedom suffer no more than the slight agitations we have experienced, it will be an useful lesson to the friends as well as the enemies of self-government. That it may stand the shocks of time and accident, and that your own may make a distinguished part of the mass of prosperity it may dispense, will be my latest prayer.

## TO THE REPUBLICANS OF QUEEN ANNE'S COUNTY

April 13, 1809

I have received, fellow citizens, your farewell address, with those sentiments of respect and satisfaction which its very friendly terms are calculated to inspire. With the consciousness of having endeavored to serve my fellow citizens according to their best interests, these testimonies of their good will are the sole and highest remuneration my heart has ever desired.

I am sensible of the indulgence with which you review the measures which have been pursued; and approving our sincere endeavors to observe a strict neutrality with respect to foreign powers. It is with reason you observe that, if hostilities must succeed, we shall have the consolation that justice will be on our side. War has been avoided from a due sense of the miseries, and the demoralization it produces, and of the superior blessings of a state of peace and friendship with all mankind. But peace on our part, and war from others, would neither be for our happiness or honor; and should the lawless violences of the belligerent powers render it necessary to return their hostilities, no nation has less to fear from a foreign enemy.

I thank you, fellow citizens, for your very kind wishes for my happiness, and pray you to accept the assurances of my cordial esteem, and grateful sense of your favor.

## TO THE MEMBERS OF THE BAPTIST CHURCH OF BUCK MOUNTAIN IN ALBEMARLE

April 13, 1809

I thank you, my friends and neighbors, for your kind congratulations on my return to my native home, and on the opportunities it will give me of enjoying, amidst your affections, the comforts of retirement and rest. Your approbation of my conduct is the more valued as you have best known me, and is an ample reward for any services I may have rendered. We have acted together from the origin to the end of a memorable revolution, and we have contributed, each in the line allotted us, our endeavors to render its issue a permanent blessing to our country. That our social intercourse may, to the evening of our days, be cheered and cemented by witnessing the freedom and happiness for which we have labored, will be my constant prayer. Accept the offering of my affectionate esteem and respect.

## TO JONATHAN LOW, ESQ., HARTFORD, CONNECTICUT

April 13, 1809

SIR: I received on the 6th instant your favor covering the resolutions of the general meeting of the republicans of the State of Connecticut who had been convened at Hartford; and I see with pleasure the spirit they breathe. They express with truth the wrongs we have sustained, the forbearance we have exercised, and the duty of rallying round the constituted authorities, for the protection of our Union. Surrounded by such difficulties and dangers, it is really deplorable that any should be found among ourselves vindicating the conduct of the aggressors; co-operating with them in multiplying embarrassments to their own country, and encouraging disobedience to the laws provided for its safety. But a spirit which should go further, and countenance the advocates for a dissolution of the Union, and for setting in hostile array one portion of our citizens against another, would require to be viewed under a more serious aspect. It would prove indeed that it is high time for every friend to his country, in a firm and decided manner, to express his sentiments of the measures which government has adopted to avert the impending evils, unhesitatingly to pledge himself for the support of the laws, liberties and independence of his country; and, with the general meeting of the republicans of Connecticut, to resolve that, for the preservation of the Union, the support and enforcement of the laws, and for the resistance and repulsion of every enemy, they will hold themselves in readiness, and put at stake, if necessary, their lives and fortunes, on the pledge of their sacred honor.

With my thanks for the mark of attention in making this communication, I pray you to accept for yourself and my respectable fellow citizens from whom it proceeds, the assurance of my high consideration, and my prayers for their welfare.

## TO THE TAMMANY SOCIETY OF THE CITY OF BALTIMORE

May 25, 1809

Your free and cordial salutations in my retirement are received, fellow citizens, with great pleasure, and the happiness of that retirement is much heightened by assurances of satisfaction with the course I have pursued in the transaction of the public affairs, and that the confidence my fellow citizens were pleased to repose in me, has not been disappointed.

Great sacrifices of interest have certainly been made by our nation under the difficulties latterly forced upon us by transatlantic powers. But every candid and reflecting mind must agree with you, that while these were temporary and bloodless, they were calculated to avoid permanent subjection to foreign law and tribute, relinquishment of independent rights, and the burthens, the havoc, and desolations of war. That these will be ultimately avoided, we have now some reason to hope; and the successful example of recalling nations to the practice of justice by peaceable appeals to their interests, will doubtless have salutary effects on our future course. As a countervail, too, to our short-lived sacrifices, when these shall no longer be felt, we shall permanently retain the benefit they have prompted, of fabricating for our own use the materials of our own growth, heretofore carried to the work-houses of Europe, to be wrought and returned to us.

The hope you express that my successor will continue in the same system of measures, is guaranteed, as far as future circumstances will permit, by his enlightened and zealous participation in them heretofore, and by the happy pacification he is now effecting for us. Your wishes for my future happiness are very thankfully felt, and returned by the sincerest desires that yourselves may experience the favors of the great dispenser of all good.

*Part III*

# BOOKS, JOURNALS, AND ESSAYS

## *Chapter XIV*

# NOTES ON THE STATE OF VIRGINIA

1781-1785

**NOTES on the ſtate of VIRGINIA;**

**written in the year 1781,[1] ſomewhat corrected and enlarged in the winter of 1782, for the uſe of a Foreigner of diſtinction, in anſwer to certain queries propoſed by him reſpecting**

1. Its boundaries - - -
2. Rivers - - - -
3. Sea ports - - - -
4. Mountains - - -
5. Caſcades and caverns - -
6. Productions mineral, vegetable and animal -
7. Climate - - -
8. Population - - -
9. Military force - - -
10. Marine force - - -
11. Aborigines - - -
12. Counties and towns - -
13. Conſtitution - - -
14. Laws - - -
15. Colleges, buildings, and roads -
16. Proceedings as to tories - -
17. Religion - - -
18. Manners - - - -
19. Manufactures - - -
20. Subjects of commerce - -
21. Weights, Meaſures and Money -
22. Public revenue and expences - -
23. Hiſtories, memorials, and ſtate-papers -

---

**MDCCLXXXII.**

[1] Jefferson published a limited and anonymous edition of 200 copies in Paris in 1785. A French edition came out in 1786, a London one in 1787, a Philadelphia one in 1788, a German one (Leipzig) in 1789. Subsequently the book went through numerous editions.

## QUERY I

### *An exact description of the limits and boundaries of the State of Virginia*

*Virginia* is bounded on the east by the Atlantic; on the north by a line of latitude crossing the eastern shore through Watkin's Point, being about 37° 57′ north latitude; from thence by a straight line to Cinquac, near the mouth of Potomac; thence by the Potomac, which is common to Virginia and Maryland, to the first fountain of its northern branch; thence by a meridian line, passing through that fountain till it intersects a line running east and west, in latitude 39° 43′ 42.4″ which divides Maryland from Pennsylvania, and which was marked by Messrs. Mason and Dixon; thence by that line, and a continuation of it westwardly to the completion of five degrees of longitude from the eastern boundary of Pennsylvania, in the same latitude, and thence by a meridian line to the Ohio; on the west by the Ohio and Mississippi, to latitude 36° 30′ north, and on the south by the line of latitude last mentioned. By admeasurements through nearly the whole of this last line, and supplying the unmeasured parts from good data, the Atlantic and Mississippi are found in this latitude to be seven hundred and fifty-eight miles distant, equal to 30° 38′ of longitude, reckoning fifty-five miles and three thousand one hundred and forty-four feet to the degree. This being our comprehension of longitude, that of our latitude, taken between this and Mason and Dixon's line, is 3° 13′ 42.4″ equal to two hundred and twenty-three and one-third miles, supposing a degree of a great circle to be sixty-nine miles, eight hundred and sixty-four feet, as computed by Cassina. These boundaries include an area somewhat triangular of one hundred and twenty-one thousand five hundred and twenty-five square miles, whereof seventy-nine thousand six hundred and fifty lie westward of the Alleghany mountains, and fifty-seven thousand and thirty-four westward of the meridian of the mouth of the Great Kanhaway. This State is therefore one-third larger than the islands of Great Britain and Ireland, which are reckoned at eighty-eight thousand three hundred and fifty-seven square miles.

These limits result from, 1. The ancient charters from the crown of England. 2. The grant of Maryland to the Lord Baltimore, and the subsequent determinations of the British court as to the extent of that grant. 3. The grant of Pennsylvania to William Penn, and a compact between the general assemblies of the commonwealths of Virginia and Pennsylvania as to the extent of that grant. 4. The grant of Carolina, and actual location of its northern boundary, by consent of both parties. 5. The treaty of Paris of 1763. 6. The confirmation of the charters of the neighboring States by the convention of *Virginia* at the time of constituting their commonwealth. 7. The cession made by *Virginia* to Congress of all the lands to which they had title on the north side of the Ohio.

## QUERY II

*A notice of its rivers, rivulets, and how far they are navigable*

An inspection of a map of *Virginia,* will give a better idea of the geography of its rivers, than any description in writing. Their navigation may be imperfectly noted.

*Roanoke,* so far as it lies within the State, is nowhere navigable but for canoes, or light batteaux; and even for these in such detached parcels as to have prevented the inhabitants from availing themselves of it at all.

*James River,* and its waters, afford navigation as follows:

The whole of *Elizabeth River,* the lowest of those which run into James River, is a harbor, and would contain upwards of three hundred ships. The channel is from one hundred and fifty to two hundred fathoms wide, and at common flood tide affords eighteen feet water to Norfolk. The Stafford, a sixty gun ship, went there, lightening herself to cross the bar at Sowel's Point. The Fier Rodrigue, pierced for sixty-four guns, and carrying fifty, went there without lightening. Craney Island, at the mouth of this river, commands its channel tolerably well.

*Nansemond River* is navigable to Sleepy Hole for vessels of two hundred and fifty tons; to Suffolk for those of one hundred tons; and to Milner's for those of twenty-five.

*Pagan Creek* affords eight or ten feet water to Smithfield, which admits vessels of twenty tons.

*Chickahominy* has at its mouth a bar, on which is only twelve feet water at common flood tide. Vessels passing that, may go eight miles up the river; those of ten feet draught may go four miles further, and those of six tons burden twenty miles further.

*Appamattox* may be navigated as far as Broadways, by any vessel which has crossed Harrison's bar in James River; it keeps eight or ten feet water a mile or two higher up to Fisher's bar, and four feet on that and upwards to Petersburg, where all navigation ceases.

*James River* itself affords a harbor for vessels of any size in Hampton Road, but not in safety through the whole winter; and there is navigable water for them as far as Mulberry Island. A forty gun ship goes to Jamestown, and, lightening herself, may pass Harrison's bar; on which there is only fifteen feet water. Vessels of two hundred and fifty tons may go to Warwick; those of one hundred and twenty-five go to Rocket's, a mile below Richmond; from thence is about seven feet water to Richmond; and about the centre of the town, four feet and a half, where the navigation is interrupted by falls, which in a course of six miles, descend about eighty-eight feet perpendicular; above these it is resumed in canoes and batteaux, and is prosecuted safely and advantageously to within ten miles of the Blue Ridge and even through the Blue Ridge a ton weight has been brought and the expense would not be great, when compared with its object, to open a tolerable navigation up Jackson's river and Carpenter's creek, to within twenty-five miles of Howard's creek of Green Briar, both of which have then water enough to float vessels into the Great Kanhaway. In some future state of population I think it possible that its navigation may also be made to interlock with that of the Potomac, and through that to communicate by a short portage with the Ohio. It is to be noted that this river is called in the maps *James River,* only to its confluence with the Rivanna; thence to the Blue Ridge it is called the Fluvanna; and thence to its source Jackson's river. But in common speech, it is called James River to its source.

The *Rivanna,* a branch of James River, is navigable for canoes and batteaux to its intersection with the South-West mountains, which is about twenty-two miles; and may easily be opened to navigation through these mountains to its fork above Charlottesville.

*York River,* at Yorktown, affords the best harbor in the State for vessels of the largest size. The river there narrows to the width of a mile, and is contained within very high banks, close under which vessels may ride. It holds four fathom water at high tide for twenty-five miles above York to the mouth of Poropotank, where the river is a mile and a half wide, and the channel only seventy-five fathom, and passing under a high bank. At the confluence of *Pamunkey* and *Mattapony,* it is reduced to three fathom depth, which continues up Pamunkey to Cumberland, where the width is one hundred yards, and up Mattapony to within two miles of Frazier's ferry, where it becomes two and a half fathom deep, and holds that about five miles. Pamunkey is then capable of navigation for loaded flats to Brockman's bridge, fifty miles above Hanover town, and Mattapony to Downer's bridge, seventy miles above its mouth.

*Piankatank,* the little rivers making out of *Mobjack Bay* and those of the eastern shore, receive only very small vessels, and these can but enter them.

*Rappahannock* affords four fathom water to Hobb's hole, and two fathom from thence to Fredericksburg.

*Potomac* is seven and a half miles wide at the mouth; four and a half at Nomony bay; three at Aquia; one and a half at Hallowing point; one and a quarter at Alexandria. Its soundings are seven fathom at the mouth; five at St. George's island; four and a half at Lower Matchodic; three at Swan's point, and thence up to Alexandria; thence ten feet water to the falls, which are thirteen miles above Alexandria. These falls are fifteen miles in length, and of very great descent, and the navigation above them for batteaux and canoes is so much interrupted as to be little used. It is, however, used in a small degree up the Cohongoronta branch as far as fort Cumberland, which was at the mouth of Willis's creek; and is capable, at no great expense, of being rendered very practicable. The Shenandoah branch interlocks with James river about the Blue Ridge, and may perhaps in future be opened.

The *Mississippi* will be one of the principal channels of future commerce for the country westward of the Alleghany. From the mouth of this river to where it receives the Ohio, is one thousand miles by water, but only five hundred by land, passing through the Chickasaw country. From the mouth of the Ohio to that of the Missouri, is two hundred and thirty miles by water, and one hundred and forty by land, from thence to the mouth of the Illinois river, is about twenty-five miles. The Mississippi, below the mouth of the Missouri, is always muddy, and abounding with sand bars, which frequently change their places. However, it carries fifteen feet water to the mouth of the Ohio, to which place it is from one and a half to two miles wide, and thence to Kaskaskia from one mile to a mile and a quarter wide. Its current is so rapid, that it never can be stemmed by the force of the wind alone, acting on sails. Any vessel, however, navigated with oars, may come up at any time, and receive much aid from the wind. A batteau passes from the mouth of Ohio to the mouth of Mississippi in three weeks, and is from two to three months getting up again. During its floods, which are periodical as those of the Nile, the largest vessels may pass down it, if their steerage can be insured. These floods begin in April, and the river returns into its banks early in August. The inundation extends further on the western than eastern side, covering the lands in some places for fifty miles from its banks. Above the mouth of the Missouri it becomes much such a river as the Ohio, like it clear and gentle in its current, not quite so wide, the period of its floods nearly the same, but not rising to so great a height. The streets of the village at Cohoes are not more than ten feet above the ordinary level of the water, and yet were never overflowed. Its bed deepens every year. Cohoes, in the memory of many people now living, was insulated by every flood of the river. What was the eastern channel has now become a lake, nine miles in length and one in width, into which the river at this day never flows. This river yields turtle of a peculiar kind, perch, trout, gar, pike, mullets, herrings, carp, spatula-fish of fifty pounds weight, cat-fish of one hundred pounds weight, buffalo fish, and sturgeon. Alligators or crocodiles have been seen as high up as the Acansas. It also abounds in herons, cranes, ducks, brant, geese, and swans. Its passage is commanded by a fort established by this State, five miles below the mouth of the Ohio, and ten miles above the Carolina boundary.

The Missouri, since the treaty of Paris, the Illinois and northern branches of the Ohio, since the cession to Congress, are no longer within our limits. Yet having been so heretofore, and still opening to us channels of extensive communication with the western and north-western country, they shall be noted in their order.

The *Missouri* is, in fact, the principal river, contributing more to the common stream than does the Mississippi, even after its junction with the Illinois. It is remarkably cold, muddy, and rapid. Its overflowings are considerable. They happen during the months of June and July. Their commencement being so much later than those of the Mississippi, would induce a belief that the sources of the Missouri are northward of those of the Mississippi, unless we suppose that the cold increases again with the ascent of the land from the Mississippi westwardly. That this ascent is great, is proved by the rapidity of the river. Six miles above the mouth, it is brought within the compass of a quarter of a mile's width; yet the Spanish merchants at Pancore, or St. Louis, say they go two thousand miles up it. It heads far westward of the Rio Norte, or North River. There is, in the villages of Kaskaskia, Cohoes, and St. Vincennes, no inconsiderable quantity of plate, said to have been plundered during the last war by the Indians from the churches and private houses of Santa Fé, on the North river, and brought to the villages for sale. From the mouth of the Ohio to Santa Fé are forty days journey, or about one thousand miles. What is the shortest distance between the navigable waters of the Missouri, and those of the North river, or how far this is navigable above Santa Fé, I could never learn. From Santa Fé to its mouth in the Gulf of Mexico is about twelve hundred miles. The road from New Orleans to Mexico crosses this river at the post of Rio Norte, eight hundred miles below Santa Fé, and from this post to New Orleans is about twelve hundred miles; thus making two thousand miles between Santa Fé and New Orleans, passing down the North river, Red river, and Mississippi; whereas it is two thousand two hundred and thirty through the Missouri and Mississippi. From the same post of Rio Norte, passing near the mines of La Sierra and Laiguana, which are between the North river, and the river Salina to Sartilla, is three hundred and seventy-five miles, and from thence, passing the mines of Charcas, Zaccatecas, and Potosi, to the city of Mexico, is three hundred and seventy-five miles; in all, one thousand five hundred and fifty miles from Santa Fé to the city of Mexico. From New Orleans to the city of Mexico is about one thousand nine hundred and fifty miles; the roads after setting out from the Red river, near Natchitoches, keeping generally parallel with the coast, and about two hundred miles from it, till it enters the city of Mexico.

The *Illinois* is a fine river, clear, gentle, and without rapids; insomuch that it is navigable for batteaux to its source. From thence is a portage of two miles only to the Chicago, which affords a batteau navigation of sixteen miles to its entrance into lake Michigan. The Illinois, about ten miles above its mouth, is three hundred yards wide.

The *Kaskaskia* is one hundred yards wide at its entrance into the Mississippi, and preserves that breadth to the Buffalo plains, seventy miles above. So far, also, it is navigable for loaded batteaux, and perhaps much further. It is not rapid.

The *Ohio* is the most beautiful river on earth. Its current gentle, waters clear, and bosom smooth and unbroken by rocks and rapids, a single instance only excepted.

It is one-quarter of a mile wide at Fort Pitt, five hundred yards at the mouth of the Great Kanhaway, one mile and twenty-five poles at Louisville, one-quarter of a mile on the rapids three or four miles below Louisville, half a mile where the low country begins, which is twenty miles above Green river, a mile and a quarter at the receipt of the Tennessee, and a mile wide at the mouth.

Its length, as measured according to its meanders by Captain Hutchins, is as follows:

From Fort Pitt

| | | | |
|---|---|---|---|
| To Log's Town | 18½ | Two Creeks | 21¾ |
| Big Beaver Creek | 10¾ | Long Reach | 53¾ |
| Little Beaver Creek | 13½ | Eng Long Reach | 16½ |
| Yellow Creek | 11¾ | Muskingum | 25½ |

| | | | |
|---|---|---|---|
| Little Kanhaway | 12¼ | Kentucky | 44¼ |
| Hockhocking | 16 | Rapids | 77¼ |
| Great Kanhaway | 82½ | Low Country | 155¾ |
| Guiandot | 43¾ | Buffalo River | 64½ |
| Sandy Creek | 14½ | Wabash | 97¼ |
| Sioto | 48¼ | Big Cave | 42¾ |
| Little Miami | 126¼ | Shawanee River | 52½ |
| Licking Creek | 8 | Cherokee River | 13 |
| Great Miami | 26¾ | Massac | 11 |
| Big Bones | 32½ | Mississippi | 46 |
| | | | 1188 |

In common winter and spring tides it affords fifteen feet water to Louisville, ten feet to Le Tarte's rapids, forty miles above the mouth of the great Kanhaway, and a sufficiency at all times for light batteaux and canoes to Fort Pitt. The rapids are in latitude 38° 8′. The inundations of this river begin about the last of March, and subside in July. During these, a first-rate man-of-war may be carried from Louisville to New Orleans, if the sudden turns of the river and the strength of its current will admit a safe steerage. The rapids at Louisville descend about thirty feet in a length of a mile and a half. The bed of the river there is a solid rock, and is divided by an island into two branches, the southern of which is about two hundred yards wide, and is dry four months in the year. The bed of the northern branch is worn into channels by the constant course of the water, and attrition of the pebble stones carried on with that, so as to be passable for batteaux through the greater part of the year. Yet it is thought that the southern arm may be the most easily opened for constant navigation. The rise of the waters in these rapids does not exceed ten or twelve feet. A part of this island is so high as to have been never overflowed, and to command the settlement at Louisville, which is opposite to it. The fort, however, is situated at the head of the falls. The ground on the south side rises very gradually.

The *Tennessee,* Cherokee, or Hogohege river, is six hundred yards wide at its mouth, a quarter of a mile at the mouth of Holston, and two hundred yards at Chotee, which is twenty miles above Holston, and three hundred miles above the mouth of the Tennessee. This river crosses the southern boundary of Virginia, fifty-eight miles from the Mississippi. Its current is moderate. It is navigable for loaded boats of any burden to the Muscle shoals, where the river passes through the Cumberland mountain. These shoals are six or eight miles long, passable downwards for loaded canoes, but not upwards, unless there be a swell in the river. Above these the navigation for loaded canoes and batteaux continues to the Long island. This river has its inundations also. Above the Chickamogga towns is a whirlpool called the Sucking-pot, which takes in trunks of trees or boats, and throws them out again half a mile below. It is avoided by keeping very close to the bank, on the south side. There are but a few miles portage between a branch of this river and the navigable waters of the river Mobile, which runs into the Gulf of Mexico.

*Cumberland,* or Shawanee river, intersects the boundary between Virginia and

North Carolina sixty-seven miles from the Mississippi, and again one hundred and ninety-eight miles from the same river, a little above the entrance of Obey's river into the Cumberland. Its Clear fork crosses the same boundary about three hundred miles from the Mississippi. Cumberland is a very gentle stream, navigable for loaded batteaux eight hundred miles, without interruption; then intervene some rapids of fifteen miles in length, after which it is again navigable seventy miles upwards, which brings you within ten miles of the Cumberland mountains. It is about one hundred and twenty yards wide through its whole course, from the head of its navigation to its mouth.

The *Wabash* is a very beautiful river, four hundred yards wide at the mouth, and three hundred at St. Vincennes, which is a post one hundred miles above the mouth, in a direct line. Within this space there are two small rapids, which give very little obstruction to the navigation. It is four hundred yards wide at the mouth, and navigable thirty leagues upwards for canoes and small boats. From the mouth of Maple river to that of Eel river is about eighty miles in a direct line, the river continuing navigable, and from one to two hundred yards in width. The Eel river is one hundred and fifty yards wide, and affords at all times navigation for periaguas, to within eighteen miles of the Miami of the Lake. The Wabash, from the mouth of Eel river to Little river, a distance of fifty miles direct, is interrupted with frequent rapids and shoals, which obstruct the navigation, except in a swell. Little river affords navigation during a swell to within three miles of the Miami, which thence affords a similar navigation into Lake Erie, one hundred miles distant in a direct line. The Wabash overflows periodically in correspondence with the Ohio, and in some places two leagues from its banks.

*Green River* is navigable for loaded batteaux at all times fifty miles upwards; but it is then interrupted by impassable rapids, above which the navigation again commences and continues good thirty or forty miles to the mouth of Barren river.

*Kentucky River* is ninety yards wide at the mouth, and also at Boonsborough, eighty miles above. It affords a navigation for loaded batteaux one hundred and eighty miles in a direct line, in the winter tides.

The *Great Miami* of the Ohio, is two hundred yards wide at the mouth. At the Piccawee towns, seventy-five miles above, it is reduced to thirty yards; it is, nevertheless, navigable for loaded canoes fifty miles above these towns. The portage from its western branch into the Miami of Lake Erie, is five miles; that from its eastern branch into Sandusky river, is of nine miles.

*Salt River* is at all times navigable for loaded batteaux seventy or eighty miles. It is eighty yards wide at its mouth, and keeps that width to its fork, twenty-five miles above.

The *Little Miami* of the Ohio, is sixty or seventy yards wide at its mouth, sixty miles to its source, and affords no navigation.

The *Sioto* is two hundred and fifty yards wide at its mouth, which is in latitude 38° 22′, and at the Saltlick towns, two hundred miles above the mouth, it is yet one hundred yards wide. To these towns it is navigable for loaded batteaux, and its eastern branch affords navigation almost to its source.

*Great Sandy River* is about sixty yards wide, and navigable sixty miles for loaded batteaux.

*Guiandot* is about the width of the river last mentioned, but is more rapid. It may be navigated by canoes sixty miles.

The *Great Kanhaway* is a river of considerable note for the fertility of its lands, and still more, as leading towards the head waters of James river. Nevertheless, it is doubtful whether its great and numerous rapids will admit a navigation, but at an expense to which it will require ages to render its inhabitants equal. The great obstacles begin at what are called the Great Falls, ninety miles above the mouth, below which are only five or six rapids, and these passable, with some difficulty, even at low water. From the falls to the mouth of Greenbriar is one hundred miles, and thence to the lead mines one hundred and twenty. It is two hundred and eighty yards wide at its mouth.

*Hockhocking* is eighty yards wide at its mouth, and yields navigation for loaded batteaux to the Press-place, sixty miles above its mouth.

The *Little Kanhaway* is one hundred and fifty yards wide at the mouth. It yields a navigation of ten miles only. Perhaps its northern branch, called Junius' creek, which interlocks with the western of Monongahela, may one day admit a shorter passage from the latter into the Ohio.

The *Muskingum* is two hundred and eighty yards wide at its mouth, and two hundred yards at the lower Indian towns, one hundred and fifty miles upwards. It is navigable for small batteaux to within one mile of a navigable part of Cuyahoga river, which runs into Lake Erie.

At Fort Pitt the river Ohio loses its name, branching into the Monongahela and Alleghany.

The *Monongahela* is four hundred yards wide at its mouth. From thence is twelve or fifteen miles to the mouth of Yohogany, where it is three hundred yards wide. Thence to Redstone by water is fifty miles, by land thirty. Then to the mouth of Cheat river by water forty miles, by land twenty-eight, the width continuing at three hundred yards, and the navigation good for boats. Thence the width is about two hundred yards to the western fork, fifty miles higher, and the navigation frequently interrupted by rapids, which, however, with a swell of two or three feet, become very passable for boats. It then admits light boats, except in dry seasons, sixty-five miles further to the head of Tygart's valley, presenting only some small rapids and falls of one or two feet perpendicular, and lessening in its width to twenty yards. The *Western fork* is navigable in the winter ten or fifteen miles towards the northern of the Little Kanhaway, and will admit a good wagon road to it. The *Yohogany* is the principal branch of this river. It passes through the Laurel mountain, about thirty miles from its mouth; is so far from three hundred to one hundred and fifty yards wide, and the navigation much obstructed in dry weather by rapids and shoals. In its passage through the mountain it makes very great falls, admitting no navigation for ten miles to the Turkey Foot. Thence to the Great Crossing, about twenty miles, it is again navigable, except in dry seasons, and at this place is two hundred yards wide. The sources of this river are divided from those of the Potomac by the Alleghany mountain.

From the falls, where it intersects the Laurel mountain, to Fort Cumberland, the head of the navigation on the Potomac, is forty miles of very mountainous road. Willis' creek, at the mouth of which was Fort Cumberland, is thirty or forty yards wide, but affords no navigation as yet. *Cheat* river, another considerable branch of the Monongahela, is two hundred yards wide at its mouth, and one hundred yards at the *Dunkard's* settlement, fifty miles higher. It is navigable for boats, except in dry seasons. The boundary between Virginia and Pennsylvania crosses it about three or four miles above its mouth.

The *Alleghany* river, with a slight swell, affords navigation for light batteaux to Venango, at the mouth of French Creek, where it is two hundred yards wide, and is practised even to Le Bœuf, from whence there is a portage of fifteen miles to Presque Isle on the Lake Erie.

The country watered by the Mississippi and its eastern branches, constitutes five-eighths of the United States, two of which five-eighths are occupied by the Ohio and its waters; the residuary streams which run into the Gulf of Mexico, the Atlantic, and the St. Lawrence, water the remaining three-eighths.

Before we quit the subject of the western waters, we will take a view of their principal connections with the Atlantic. These are three; the Hudson river, the Potomac, and the Mississippi itself. Down the last will pass all heavy commodities. But the navigation through the Gulf of Mexico is so dangerous, and that up the Mississippi so difficult and tedious, that it is thought probable that European merchandise will not return through that channel. It is most likely that flour, timber, and other heavy articles will be floated on rafts, which will themselves be an article for sale as well as their loading, the navigators returning by land, or in light batteaux. There will, therefore, be a competition between the Hudson and Potomac rivers for the residue of the commerce of all the country westward of Lake Erie, on the waters of the lakes, of the Ohio, and upper parts of the Mississippi. To go to New York, that part of the trade which comes from the lakes or their waters, must first be brought into Lake Erie. Between Lake Superior and its waters and Huron, are the rapids of St. Mary, which will permit boats to pass, but not larger vessels. Lakes Huron and Michigan afford communication with Lake Erie by vessels of eight feet draught. That part of the trade which comes from the waters of the Mississippi must pass from them through some portage into the waters of the lakes. The portage from the Illinois river into a water of Michigan is of one mile only. From the Wabash, Miami, Muskingum, or Alleghany, are portages into the waters of Lake Erie, of from one to fifteen miles. When the commodities are brought into, and have passed through Lake Erie, there is between that and Ontario an interruption by the falls of Niagara, where the portage is of eight miles; and between Ontario and the Hudson river are portages at the falls of Onondago, a little above Oswego, of a quarter of a mile; from Wood creek to the Mohawks river two miles; at the little falls of the Mohawks river half a mile; and from Schenectady to Albany sixteen miles. Besides the increase of expense occasioned by frequent change of carriage, there is an increased risk of pillage produced by committing merchandise to a greater number of hands successively. The Potomac offers itself under the following circumstances: For the trade of the lakes and their waters westward of Lake Erie, when it shall have entered that lake, it must coast along its southern shore, on account of the number and excellence of its harbors; the northern, though shortest, having few harbors, and these unsafe. Having reached Cuyahoga, to proceed on to New York it will have eight hundred and twenty-five miles and five portages; whereas it is but four hundred and twenty-five miles to Alexandria, its emporium on the Potomac, if it turns into the Cuyahoga, and passes through that, Big Beaver, Ohio, Yohogany (or Monongahela and Cheat), and Potomac, and there are but two portages; the first of which, between Cuyahoga and Beaver, may be removed by uniting the sources of these waters, which are lakes in the neighborhood of each other, and in a champaign country; the other from the waters of Ohio to Potomac will be from fifteen to forty miles, according to the trouble which shall be taken to approach the two navigations. For the trade of the Ohio, or that which shall come into it from its own waters or the Mississippi, it is nearer through the Potomac to Alexandria than to New York by five hundred and eighty miles, and it is interrupted by one portage only. There is another circumstance of difference too. The lakes themselves never freeze, but the communications between them freeze, and the Hudson river is itself shut up by the ice three months in the year; whereas the channel to the Chesapeake leads directly into a warmer climate. The southern parts of it very rarely freeze at all, and whenever the northern do, it is so near the sources of the rivers, that the frequent floods to which they are there liable, break up the ice immediately, so that vessels may pass through the whole winter, subject only to accidental and short delays. Add to all this, that in case of war with our neighbors, the Anglo-Americans or the Indians, the route to New York becomes a frontier through almost its whole length, and all commerce through it ceases from that moment. But the channel to New York is already known to practice, whereas the upper waters of the Ohio and the Potomac, and the great falls of the latter, are yet to be cleared of their fixed obstructions. (A.)

## QUERY III

*A notice of the best Seaports of the State, and how big are the vessels they can receive?*

Having no ports but our rivers and creeks, this *Query* has been answered under the preceding one.

## QUERY IV

*A notice of its Mountains*

For the particular geography of our mountains I must refer to Fry and Jefferson's map of Virginia; and to Evans' analysis of this map of America, for a more philosophical view of them than is to be found in any other work. It is worthy of notice, that our mountains are not solitary and scattered confusedly over the face of the country; but that they commence at about one hundred and fifty miles from the sea-coast, are disposed in ridges, one behind another, running nearly parallel with the sea-coast, though rather approaching it as they advance north-eastwardly. To the south-west, as the tract of country between the sea-coast and the Mississippi becomes narrower, the mountains converge into a single ridge, which, as it approaches the Gulf of Mexico, subsides into plain country, and gives rise to some of the waters of that gulf, and particularly to a river called the Apalachicola, probably from the Apalachies, an Indian nation formerly residing on it. Hence the mountains giving rise to that river, and seen from its various parts, were called the Appalachian mountains, being in fact the end or termination only of the great ridges passing through the continent. European geographers, however, extended the name northwardly as far as the mountains extended; some giving it, after their separation into different ridges, to the Blue Ridge, others to the North Mountain, others to the Alleghany, others to the Laurel Ridge, as may be seen by their different maps. But the fact I believe is, that none of these ridges were ever known by that name to the inhabitants, either native or emigrant, but as they saw them so called in European maps. In the same direction, generally, are the veins of limestone, coal, and other minerals hitherto discovered; and so range the falls of our great rivers. But the courses of the great rivers are at right angles with these. James and Potomac penetrate through all the ridges of mountains eastward of the Alleghany; that is, broken by no water course. It is in fact the spine of the country between the Atlantic on one side, and the Mississippi and St. Lawrence on the other. The passage of the Potomac through the Blue Ridge is, perhaps, one of the most stupendous scenes in nature. You stand on a very high point of land. On your right comes up the Shenandoah, having ranged along the foot of the mountain an hundred miles to seek a vent. On your left approaches the Potomac, in quest of a passage also. In the moment of their junction, they rush together against the mountain, rend it asunder, and pass off to the sea. The first glance of this scene hurries our senses into the opinion, that this earth has been created in time, that the mountains were formed first, that the rivers began to flow afterwards, that in this place, particularly, they have been dammed up by the Blue Ridge of mountains, and have formed an ocean which filled the whole valley; that continuing to rise they have at length broken over at this spot, and have torn the mountain down from its summit to its base. The piles of rock on each hand, but particularly on the Shenandoah, the evident marks of their disrupture and avulsion from their beds by the most powerful agents of nature, corroborate the impression. But the distant finishing which nature has given to the picture, is of a very different character. It is a true contrast to the foreground. It is as placid and delightful as that is wild and tremendous. For the mountain being cloven asunder, she presents to your eye, through the cleft, a small catch of smooth blue horizon, at an infinite distance in the plain country, inviting you, as it were, from the riot and tumult roaring around, to pass through the breach and participate of the calm below. Here the eye ultimately composes itself; and that way, too, the road happens actually to lead. You cross the Potomac above the junction, pass along its side through the base of the mountain for three miles, its terrible precipices hanging in fragments over you, and within about twenty miles reach Fredericktown, and the fine country round that. This scene is worth a voyage across the Atlantic. Yet here, as in the neighborhood of the Natural Bridge, are people who have passed their lives within half a dozen miles, and have never been to survey these monuments of a war between rivers and mountains, which must have shaken the earth itself to its centre. (B.)

The height of our mountains has not yet been estimated with any degree of exactness. The Alleghany being the great ridge which divides the waters of the Atlantic from those of the Mississippi, its summit is doubtless more elevated above the ocean than that of any other mountain. But its relative height, compared with the base on which it stands, is not so great as that of some others, the country rising behind the successive ridges like the steps of stairs. The mountains of the Blue Ridge, and of these the Peaks of Otter, are thought to be of a greater height, measured from their base, than any others in our country, and perhaps in North America. From data, which may found a tolerable conjecture, we suppose the highest peak to be about four thousand feet perpendicular, which is not a fifth part of the height of the mountains of South America, nor one-third of the height which would be necessary in our latitude to preserve ice in the open air unmelted through the year. The ridge of mountains next beyond the Blue Ridge, called by us the North mountain, is of the greatest extent; for which reason they were named by the Indians the endless mountains.

A substance supposed to be Pumice, found floating on the Mississippi, has induced a conjecture that there is a volcano on some of its waters; and as these are mostly known to their sources, except the Missouri, our expectations of verifying the conjecture would of course be led to the mountains which divide the waters of the Mexican Gulf from those of the South Sea; but no volcano having ever yet been known at such a distance from the sea, we must rather suppose that this floating substance has been erroneously deemed Pumice.

## QUERY V

### *Its Cascades and Caverns*

The only remarkable cascade in this country is that of the Falling Spring in Augusta. It is a water of James' river where it is called Jackson's river, rising in the warm spring mountains, about twenty miles south west of the warm spring, and flowing into that valley. About three-quarters of a mile from its source it falls over a rock two hundred feet into the valley below. The sheet of water is broken in its breadth by the rock, in two or three places, but not at all in its height. Between the sheet and the rock, at the bottom, you may walk across dry. This cataract will bear no comparison with that of Niagara as to the quantity of water composing it; the sheet being only twelve or fifteen feet wide above and somewhat more spread below; but it is half as high again, the latter being only one hundred and fifty-six feet, according to the mensuration made by order of M. Vaudreuil, Governor of Canada, and one hundred and thirty according to a more recent account.

In the lime-stone country there are many caverns of very considerable extent. The most noted is called Madison's Cave, and is on the north side of the Blue Ridge, near the intersection of the Rockingham and Augusta line with the south fork of the southern river of Shenandoah. It is in a hill of about two hundred feet perpendicular height, the ascent of which, on one side, is so steep that you may pitch a biscuit from its summit into the river which washes its base. The entrance of the cave is, in this side, about two-thirds of the way up. It extends into the earth about three hundred feet, branching into subordinate caverns, sometimes ascending a little, but more generally descending, and at length terminates, in two different places, at basons of water of unknown extent, and which I should judge to be nearly on a level with the water of the river; however, I do not think they are formed by refluent water from that, because they are never turbid; because they do not rise and fall in correspondence with that in times of flood or of drought; and because the water is always cool. It is probably one of the many reservoirs with which the interior parts of the earth are supposed to abound, and yield supplies to the fountains of water, distinguished from others only by being accessible. The vault of this cave is of solid lime-stone, from twenty to forty or fifty feet high; through which water is continually percolating. This, trickling down the sides of the cave, has incrusted them over in the form of elegant drapery; and dripping from the top of the vault generates on that and on the base below, stalactites of a conical form, some of which have met and formed massive columns.

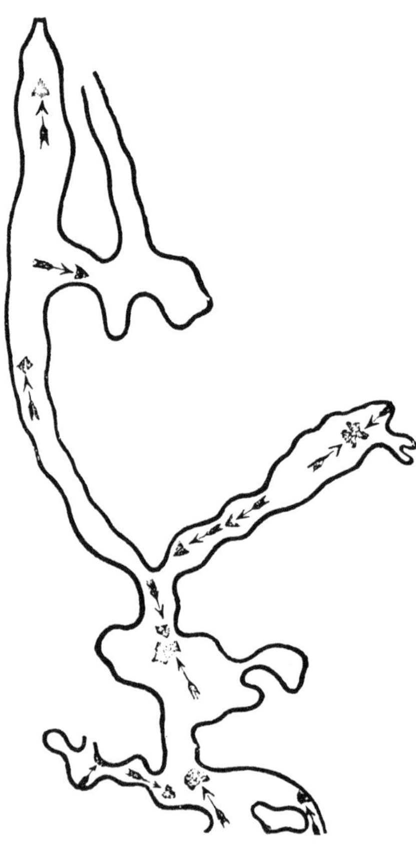

An eye draught of Madison's cave on a scale of 67 feet to the inch. The arrows show where it descends or ascends.

Another of these caves is near the north mountain, in the county of Frederic, on the lands of Mr. Zane. The entrance into this is on the top of an extensive ridge. You descend thirty or forty feet, as into a well, from whence the cave extends, nearly horizontally, four hundred feet into the earth, preserving a breadth of from twenty to fifty feet, and a height of from five to twelve feet. After entering this cave a few feet, the mercury, which in the open air was 50°, rose to 57° of Fahrenheit's thermometer, answering to 11° of Reaumur's, and it continued at that to the remotest parts of the cave. The uniform temperature of the cellars of the observatory of Paris, which are ninety feet deep, and of all subterraneous cavities of any depth, where no chemical agencies may be supposed to produce a factitious heat, has been found to be 10° of Reaumur, equal to 54½° of Fahrenheit. The temperature of the cave above mentioned so nearly corresponds with this, that the difference may be ascribed to a difference of instruments.

At the Panther gap, in the ridge which divides the waters of the Crow and the Calf pasture, is what is called the *Blowing Cave.* It is in the side of a hill, is of about one hundred feet diameter, and emits constantly a current of air of such force as to keep the weeds prostrate to the distance of twenty yards before it. This current is strongest in dry, frosty weather, and in long spells of rain weakest. Regular inspirations and expirations of air, by caverns and fissures, have been probably enough accounted for by supposing them combined with intermitting fountains; as they must of course inhale air while their reservoirs are emptying themselves, and again emit it while they are filling. But a constant issue of air, only varying in its force as the weather is drier or damper, will require a new hypothesis. There is another blowing cave in the Cumberland mountain, about a mile from where it crosses the Carolina line. All we know of this is, that it is not constant, and that a fountain of water issues from it.

The *Natural Bridge,* the most sublime of nature's works, though not comprehended under the present head, must not be pretermitted. It is on the ascent of a hill, which seems to have been cloven through its length by some great convulsion. The fissure, just at the bridge, is, by some admeasurements, two hundred and seventy feet deep, by others only two hundred and five. It is about forty-five feet wide at the bottom and ninety feet at the top; this of course determines the length of the bridge, and its height from the water. Its breadth in the middle is about sixty feet, but more at the ends, and the thickness of the mass, at the summit of the arch, about forty feet. A part of this thickness is constituted by a coat of earth, which gives growth to many large trees. The residue, with the hill on both sides, is one solid rock of lime-stone. The arch approaches the semi-elliptical form; but the larger axis of the ellipsis, which would be the cord of the arch, is many times longer than the transverse. Though the sides of this bridge are provided in some parts with a parapet of fixed rocks, yet few men have resolution to walk to them, and look over into the abyss. You involuntarily fall on your hands and feet, creep to the parapet, and peep over it. Looking down from this height about a minute, gave me a violent head-ache. If the view from the top be painful and intolerable, that from below is delightful in an equal extreme. It is impossible for the emotions arising from the sublime to be felt beyond what they are here; so beautiful an arch, so elevated, so light, and springing as it were up to heaven! the rapture of the spectator is really indescribable! The fissure continuing narrow, deep, and straight, for a considerable distance above and below the bridge, opens a short but very pleasing view of the North mountain on one side and the Blue Ridge on the other, at the distance each of them of about five miles. This bridge is in the county of Rockbridge, to which it has given name, and affords a public and commodious passage over a valley which cannot be crossed elsewhere for a considerable distance. The stream passing under it is called Cedar-creek. It is a water of James' river, and sufficient in the driest seasons to turn a grist-mill, though its fountain is not more than two miles above.[1]

## QUERY VI

*A notice of the mines and other subterraneous riches; its trees, plants, fruits, &c.*

I knew a single instance of gold found in this State. It was interspersed in small specks through a lump of ore of about four pounds weight, which yielded seventeen pennyweights of gold, of extraordinary ductility. This ore was found on the north side of Rappahanock, about four miles below the falls. I never heard of any other indication of gold in its neighborhood.

On the Great Kanhaway, opposite to the mouth of Cripple creek, and about twenty-five miles from our southern boundary, in the county of Montgomery, are mines of lead. The metal is mixed, sometimes with earth, and sometimes with rock, which requires the force of gunpowder to open it; and is accompanied with a portion of silver too small to be worth separation under any process hitherto attempted there. The proportion yielded is from fifty to eighty pounds of pure metal from one hundred pounds of washed ore. The most common is that of sixty to one hundred pounds. The veins are sometimes most flattering, at others they disappear suddenly and totally. They enter the side of the hill and proceed horizontally. Two of them are wrought at present by the public, the

[1] Don Ulloa mentions a break, similar to this, in the province of Angaraez, in South America. It is from sixteen to twenty-two feet wide, one hundred and eleven feet deep, and of 1.3 miles continuance, English measure. Its breadth at top is not sensibly greater than at bottom. But the following fact is remarkable, and will furnish some light for conjecturing the probable origin of our natural bridge. "*Esta caxa, ó cauce está cortada en péna viva con tanta precision, que las desigualdades del un lado entrantes, corresponden á las del otro lado salientes, como si aquella altura se hubiese abierto expresamente, con sus bueltas y tortuosidades, para darle transito á los aguas por entre los dos morallones que la forman; siendo tal su igualdad, que si llegasen á juntarse se endentarian uno con otro sin dextar hueco.*" Not. Amer. ii. § 10. Don Ulloa inclines to the opinion that this channel has been effected by the wearing of the water which runs through it, rather than that the mountain should have been broken open by any convulsion of nature. But if it had been worn by the running of water, would not the rocks which form the sides, have been worn plain? or if, meeting in some parts with veins of harder stone, the water had left prominences on the one side, would not the same cause have sometimes, or perhaps generally, occasioned prominences on the other side also? Yet Don Ulloa tells us, that on the other side there are always corresponding cavities, and that these tally with the prominences so perfectly, that, were the two sides to come together they would fit in all their indentures, without leaving any void. I think that this does not resemble the effect of running water, but looks rather as if the two sides had parted asunder. The sides of the break, over which is the natural bridge of Virginia, consisting of a veiny rock which yields to time, the correspondence between the salient and re-entering inequalities, if it existed at all, has now disappeared. This break has the advantage of the one described by Don Ulloa in its finest circumstance; no portion in that instance having held together, during the separation of the other parts, so as to form a bridge over the abyss.—T. J.

best of which is one hundred yards under the hill. These would employ about fifty laborers to advantage. We have not, however, more than thirty generally, and these cultivate their own corn. They have produced sixty tons of lead in the year; but the general quantity is from twenty to twenty-five tons. The present furnace is a mile from the ore bank and on the opposite side of the river. The ore is first wagoned to the river, a quarter of a mile, then laden on board of canoes and carried across the river, which is there about two hundred yards wide, and then again taken into wagons and carried to the furnace. This mode was originally adopted that they might avail themselves of a good situation on a creek for a pounding mill; but it would be easy to have the furnace and pounding mill on the same side of the river, which would yield water, without any dam, by a canal of about half a mile in length. From the furnace the lead is transported one hundred and thirty miles along a good road, leading through the peaks of Otter to Lynch's ferry, or Winston's on James' river, from whence it is carried by water about the same distance to Westham. This land carriage may be greatly shortened, by delivering the lead on James' river, above the Blue Ridge, from whence a ton weight has been brought on two canoes. The Great Kanhaway has considerable falls in the neighborhood of the mines. About seven miles below are three falls, of three or four feet perpendicular each; and three miles above is a rapid of three miles continuance, which has been compared in its descent to the great falls of James' river. Yet it is the opinion, that they may be laid open for useful navigation, so as to reduce very much the portage between the Kanhaway and James' river.

A valuable lead mine is said to have been lately discovered in Cumberland, below the mouth of Red river. The greatest, however, known in the western country, are on the Mississippi, extending from the mouth of Rock river one hundred and fifty miles upwards. These are not wrought, the lead used in that country being from the banks on the Spanish side of the Mississippi, opposite to Kaskaskia.

A mine of copper was once opened in the county of Amherst, on the north side of James' river, and another in the opposite country, on the south side. However, either from bad management or the poverty of the veins, they were discontinued. We are told of a rich mine of native copper on the Ouabache, below the upper Wiaw.

The mines of iron worked at present are Callaway's, Ross's, and Ballendine's, on the south side of James' river; Old's on the north side, in Albemarle; Miller's in Augusta, and Zane's in Frederic. These two last are in the valley between the Blue Ridge and North mountain. Callaway's, Ross's, Miller's, and Zane's make about one hundred and fifty tons of bar iron each, in the year. Ross's makes also about sixteen hundred tons of pig iron annually; Ballendine's one thousand; Callaway's, Miller's, and Zane's, about six hundred each. Besides these, a forge of Mr. Hunter's, at Fredericksburg, makes about three hundred tons a year of bar iron, from pigs imported from Maryland; and Taylor's forge on Neapsco of Potomac, works in the same way, but to what extent I am not informed. The indications of iron in other places are numerous, and dispersed through all the middle country. The toughness of the cast iron of Ross's and Zane's furnaces is very remarkable. Pots and other utensils, cast thinner than usual, of this iron, may be safely thrown into, or out of the wagons in which they are transported. Salt-pans made of the same, and no longer wanted for that purpose, cannot be broken up, in order to be melted again, unless previously drilled in many parts.

In the western country, we are told of iron mines between the Muskingum and Ohio; of others on Kentucky, between the Cumberland and Barren rivers, between Cumberland and Tennessee, on Reedy creek, near the Long Island, and on Chesnut creek, a branch of the Great Kanhaway, near where it crosses the Carolina line. What are called the iron banks, on the Mississippi, are believed, by a good judge, to have no iron in them. In general, from what is hitherto known of that country, it seems to want iron.

Considerable quantities of black lead are taken occasionally for use from Winterham in the county of Amelia. I am not able, however, to give a particular state of the mine. There is no work established at it; those who want, going and procuring it for themselves.

The country on James' river, from fifteen to twenty miles above Richmond, and for several miles northward and southward, is replete with mineral coal of a very excellent quality. Being in the hands of many proprietors, pits have been opened, and, before the interruption of our commerce, were worked to an extent equal to the demand.

In the western country coal is known to be in so many places, as to have induced an opinion, that the whole tract between the Laurel mountain, Mississippi, and Ohio, yields coal. It is also known in many places on the north side of the Ohio. The coal at Pittsburg is of very superior quality. A bed of it at that place has been a-fire since the year 1765. Another coal-hill on the Pike-run of Monongahela has been a-fire ten years; yet it has burnt away about twenty yards only.

I have known one instance of an emerald found in this country. Amethysts have been frequent, and crystals common; yet not in such numbers any of them as to be worth seeking.

There is very good marble, and in very great abundance, on James' river, at the mouth of Rockfish. The samples I have seen, were some of them of a white as pure as one might expect to find on the surface of the earth; but most of them were variegated with red, blue, and purple. None of it has been ever worked. It forms a very large precipice, which hangs over a navigable part of the river. It is said there is marble at Kentucky.

But one vein of limestone is known below the Blue Ridge. Its first appearance, in our country, is in Prince William, two miles below the Pignut ridge of mountains; thence it passes on nearly parallel with that, and crosses the Rivanna about five miles below it, where it is called the South-west ridge. It then crosses Hard-ware, above the mouth of Hudson's creek, James' river at the mouth of Rockfish, at the marble quarry before spoken of, probably runs up that river to where it appears again at Ross's iron-works, and so passes off south-westwardly by Flat Creek of Otter river. It is never more than one hundred yards wide. From the Blue Ridge westwardly, the whole country seems to be founded on a rock of limestone, besides infinite quantities on the surface, both loose and fixed. This is cut into beds, which range, as the mountains and sea-coast do, from south-west to north-east, the lamina of each bed declining from the horizon towards a parallelism with the axis of the earth. Being struck with this observation, I made, with a quadrant, a great number of trials on the angles of their declination, and found them to vary from 22° to 60°; but averaging all my trials, the result was within one-third of a degree of the elevation of the pole or latitude of the place, and much the greatest part of them taken separately were little different from that; by which it appears, that these lamina are, in the main, parallel with the axis of the earth. In some instances, indeed, I found them perpendicular, and even reclining the other way; but these were extremely rare, and always attended with signs of convulsion, or other circumstances of singularity, which admitted a possibility of removal from their original position. These trials were made between Madison's cave and the Potomac. We hear of limestone on the Mississippi and Ohio, and in all the mountainous country between the eastern and western waters, not on the mountains themselves, but occupying the valleys between them.

Near the eastern foot of the North mountain are immense bodies of *Schist,* containing impressions of shells in a variety of forms. I have received petrified shells of very different kinds from the first sources of Kentucky, which bear no resemblance to any I have ever seen on the tide-waters. It is said that shells are found in the Andes, in South America, fifteen thousand feet above the level of the ocean. This is considered by many, both of the learned and unlearned, as a proof of an universal deluge. To the many considerations opposing this opinion, the following may be added: The atmosphere, and all its contents, whether of water, air, or other matter, gravitate to the earth; that is to say, they have weight. Experience tells us, that the weight of all these together never exceeds that of a column of mercury of thirty-one inches height, which is equal to one of rain water of thirty-five feet high. If the whole contents of the atmosphere, then, were water, instead of what they are, it would cover the globe but thirty-five feet deep; but as these waters, as they fell, would run into the seas, the superficial measure of which is to that of the dry parts of the globe, as two to one, the seas would be raised only fifty-two and a half feet above their present level, and of course would overflow the lands to that height only. In Virginia this would be a very small proportion even of the champaign country, the banks of our tide-waters being frequently, if not generally, of a greater height. Deluges beyond this extent, then, as for instance, to the North mountain or to Kentucky, seem out of the laws of nature. But within it they may have taken place to a greater or less degree, in proportion to the combination of natural causes which may be supposed to have produced them. History renders probably some instances of a partial deluge in the country lying round the Mediterranean sea. It has been often [2] supposed, and it is not unlikely, that that sea was once a lake. While

[2] 2 Buffon Époques, 96.—T. J.

such, let us admit an extraordinary collection of the waters of the atmosphere from the other parts of the globe to have been discharged over that and the countries whose waters run into it. Or without supposing it a lake, admit such an extraordinary collection of the waters of the atmosphere, and an influx from the Atlantic ocean, forced by long-continued western winds. The lake, or that sea, may thus have been so raised as to overflow the low lands adjacent to it, as those of Egypt and Armenia, which, according to a tradition of the Egyptians and Hebrews, were overflowed about two thousand three hundred years before the Christian era; those of Attica, said to have been overflowed in the time of Ogyges, about five hundred years later; and those of Thessaly, in the time of Deucalion, still three hundred years posterior. But such deluges as these will not account for the shells found in the higher lands. A second opinion has been entertained, which is, that in times anterior to the records either of history or tradition, the bed of the ocean, the principal residence of the shelled tribe, has, by some great convulsion of nature, been heaved to the heights at which we now find shells and other marine animals. The favorers of this opinion do well to suppose the great events on which it rests to have taken place beyond all the eras of history; for within these, certainly, none such are to be found; and we may venture to say farther, that no fact has taken place, either in our own days, or in the thousands of years recorded in history, which proves the existence of any natural agents, within or without the bowels of the earth, of force sufficient to heave, to the height of fifteen thousand feet, such masses as the Andes. The difference between the power necessary to produce such an effect, and that which shuffled together the different parts of Calabria in our days, is so immense, that from the existence of the latter, we are not authorized to infer that of the former.

M. de Voltaire has suggested a third solution of this difficulty. (Quest. Encycl. Coquilles.) He cites an instance in Touraine, where, in the space of eighty years, a particular spot of earth had been twice metamorphosed into soft stone, which had become hard when employed in building. In this stone shells of various kinds were produced, discoverable at first only with a microscope, but afterwards growing with the stone. From this fact, I suppose, he would have us infer, that, besides the usual process for generating shells by the elaboration of earth and water in animal vessels, nature may have provided an equivalent operation, by passing the same materials through the pores of calcareous earth and stones; as we see calcareous drop-stones generating every day, by the percolation of water through lime-stone, and new marble forming in the quarries from which the old has been taken out. And it might be asked, whether is it more difficult for nature to shoot the calcareous juice into the form of a shell, than other juices into the forms of crystals, plants, animals, according to the construction of the vessels through which they pass? There is a wonder somewhere. Is it greatest on this branch of the dilemma; on that which supposes the existence of a power, of which we have no evidence in any other case; or on the first, which requires us to believe the creation of a body of water and its subsequent annihilation? The establishment of the instance, cited by M. de Voltaire, of the growth of shells unattached to animal bodies, would have been that of his theory. But he has not established it. He has not even left it on ground so respectable as to have rendered it an object of inquiry to the *literati* of his own country. Abandoning this fact, therefore, the three hypotheses are equally unsatisfactory; and we must be contented to acknowledge, that this great phenomenon is as yet unsolved. Ignorance is preferable to error; and he is less remote from the truth who believes nothing, than he who believes what is wrong.

There is great abundance (more especially when you approach the mountains) of stone, white, blue, brown, &c., fit for the chisel, good mill-stone, such also as stands the fire, and slate stone. We are told of flint, fit for gun-flints, on the Meherrin in Brunswick, on the Mississippi between the mouth of the Ohio and Kaskaskia, and on others of the western waters. Isinglass or mica is in several places; loadstone also; and an Asbestos of a ligneous texture, is sometimes to be met with.

Marle abounds generally. A clay, of which, like the Sturbridge in England, bricks are made, which will resist long the violent action of fire, has been found on Tuckahoe creek of James' river, and no doubt will be found in other places. Chalk is said to be in Botetourt and Bedford. In the latter county is some earth believed to be gypseous. Ochres are found in various parts.

In the lime-stone country are many caves, the earthy floors of which are impregnated with nitre. On Rich creek, a branch of the Great Kanhaway, about sixty miles below the lead mines, is a very large one, about twenty yards wide, and entering a hill a quarter or half a mile. The vault is of rock, from nine to fifteen or twenty feet above the floor. A Mr. Lynch, who gives me this account, undertook to extract the nitre. Besides a coat of the salt which had formed on the vault and floor, he found the earth highly impregnated to the depth of seven feet in some places, and generally of three, every bushel yielding on an average three pounds of nitre. Mr. Lynch having made about ten hundred pounds of the salt from it, consigned it to some others, who have since made ten thousand pounds. They have done this by pursuing the cave into the hill, never trying a second time the earth they have once exhausted, to see how far or soon it receives another impregnation. At least fifty of these caves are worked on the Greenbriar. There are many of them known on Cumberland river.

The country westward of the Alleghany abounds with springs of common salt. The most remarkable we have heard of are at Bullet's-lick, the Big-bones, the Blue-licks, and on the north fork of Holston. The area of Bullet's-lick is of many acres. Digging the earth to the depth of three feet the water begins to boil up, and the deeper you go and the drier the weather, the stronger is the brine. A thousand gallons of water yield from a bushel to a bushel and a half of salt, which is about eighty pounds of water to one pound of salt. So that sea-water is more than three times as strong as that of these springs. A salt spring has been lately discovered at the Turkey foot on Yohogany, by which river it is overflowed, except at very low water. Its merit is not yet known. Dunning's lick is also as yet untried, but it is supposed to be the best on this side the Ohio. The salt springs on the margin of the Onondago lake are said to give a saline taste to the waters of the lake.

There are several medicinal springs, some of which are indubitably efficacious, while others seem to owe their reputation as much to fancy and change of air and regimen, as to their real virtues. None of them having undergone a chemical analysis in skilful hands, nor been so far the subject of observations as to have produced a reduction into classes of the disorders which they relieve; it is in my power to give little more than an enumeration of them.

The most efficacious of these are two springs in Augusta near the first sources of James' river, where it is called Jackson's river. They rise near the foot of the ridge of mountains generally called the Warm spring mountains, but in the maps Jackson's mountains. The one distinguished by the name of the Warm spring, and the other of the Hot spring. The Warm spring issues with a very bold stream, sufficient to work a grist mill and to keep the waters of its basin, which is thirty feet in diameter, at the vital warmth, *viz.* 96° of Fahrenheit's thermometer. The matter with which these waters is allied is very volatile; its smell indicates it to be sulphureous, as also does the circumstance of its turning silver black. They relieve rheumatisms. Other complaints also of very different natures have been removed or lessened by them. It rains here four or five days in every week.

The *Hot spring* is about six miles from the Warm, is much smaller, and has been so hot as to have boiled an egg. Some believe its degree of heat to be lessened. It raises the mercury in Fahrenheit's thermometer to 112 degrees, which is fever heat. It sometimes relieves where the Warm fails. A fountain of common water, issuing within a few inches of its margin, gives it a singular appearance. Comparing the temperature of these with that of the Hot springs of Kamschatka, of which Krachininnikow gives an account, the difference is very great, the latter raising the mercury to 200° which is within 12° of boiling water. These springs are very much resorted to in spite of a total want of accommodation for the sick. Their waters are strongest in the hottest months, which occasions their being visited in July and August principally.

The Sweet springs are in the county of Botetourt, at the eastern foot of the Alleghany, about forty-two miles from the Warm springs. They are still less known. Having been found to relieve cases in which the others had been ineffectually tried, it is probable their composition is different. They are different also in their temperature, being as cold as common water; which is not mentioned, however, as a proof of a distinct impregnation. This is among the first sources of James' river.

On Potomac river, in Berkley county, above the North mountain, are medicinal springs, much more frequented than those of Augusta. Their powers, however, are less, the waters weakly mineralized, and scarcely warm. They are more visited, because situated in a fertile, plentiful, and populous country, better provided with accommodations, always safe from the Indians, and nearest to the more populous States.

In Louisa county, on the head waters of the South Ann branch of York river, are springs of some medicinal virtue. They are not much used however. There is a weak chalybeate at Richmond; and many others in various parts of the country, which are of too little worth, or too little note, to be enumerated after those before mentioned.

We are told of a sulphur spring on Howard's creek of Greenbriar, and another at Boonsborough on Kentucky.

In the low grounds of the Great Kanhaway, seven miles above the mouth of Elk river, and sixty-seven above that of the Kanhaway itself, is a hole in the earth of the capacity of thirty or forty gallons, from which issues constantly a bituminous vapor, in so strong a current as to give to the sand about its orifice the motion which it has in a boiling spring. On presenting a lighted candle or torch within eighteen inches of the hole it flames up in a column of eighteen inches in diameter, and four or five feet height, which sometimes burns out within twenty minutes, and at other times has been known to continue three days, and then has been still left burning. The flame is unsteady, of the density of that of burning spirits, and smells like burning pit coal. Water sometimes collects in the basin, which is remarkably cold, and is kept in ebullition by the vapor issuing through it. If the vapor be fired in that state, the water soon becomes so warm that the hand cannot bear it, and evaporates wholly in a short time. This, with the circumjacent lands, is the property of His Excellency General Washington and of General Lewis.

There is a similar one on Sandy river, the flame of which is a column of about twelve inches diameter, and three feet high. General Clarke, who informs me of it, kindled the vapor, staid about an hour, and left it burning.

The mention of uncommon springs leads me to that of Syphon fountains. There is one of these near the intersection of the Lord Fairfax's boundary with the North mountain, not far from Brock's gap, on the stream of which is a grist mill, which grinds two bushel of grain at every flood of the spring; another near Cow-pasture river, a mile and a half below its confluence with the Bull-pasture river, and sixteen or seventeen miles from Hot springs, which intermits once in every twelve hours; one also near the mouth of the north Holston.

After these may be mentioned the *Natural Well,* on the lands of a Mr. Lewis in Frederick county. It is somewhat larger than a common well; the water rises in it as near the surface of the earth as in the neighboring artificial wells, and is of a depth as yet unknown. It is said there is a current in it tending sensibly downwards. If this be true, it probably feeds some fountain, of which it is the natural reservoir, distinguished from others, like that of Madison's cave, by being accessible. It is used with a bucket and windlass as an ordinary well.

A complete catalogue of the trees, plants, fruits, &c., is probably not desired. I will sketch out those which would principally attract notice, as being first, Medicinal; second, Esculent; third, Ornamental; or four, useful for fabrication; adding the Linnæan to the popular names, as the latter might not convey precise information to a foreigner. I shall confine myself too to native plants.

1. Senna. Cassia ligustrina.
Arsmart. Polygonum Sagittatum.
Clivers, or goose-grass. Galium spurium.
Lobelia of several species.
Palma Christi. Ricinus.
(3) Jamestown weed. Datura Stramonium.
Mallow. Malva rotundafolia.
Syrian mallow. Hibiscus moschentos.
Hibiscus Virginicus.
Indian mallow. Sida rhombifolia.
Sida abutilon.
Virginia marshmallow. Napæa hermaphrodita.
Napæa dioica.
Indian physic. Spiria trifoliata.
Euphorbia Ipecacuanhæ.
Pleurisy root. Asclepias decumbens.
Virginia snake-root. Aristolochia serpentaria.
Black snake-root. Actæ racemosa.
Seneca rattlesnake-root. Polygala Senega.
Valerian. Valeriana locusta radiata.
Gentiana, Saponaria, Villosa & Centaurium.
Ginseng. Panax quinquefolium.
Angelica. Angelica sylvestris.
Cassava. Jatropha urens.
2. Tuckahoe. Lycoperdon tuber.
Jerusalem artichoke. Helianthus tuberosus.
Long potatoes. Convolvulas batatas.
Granadillas. Maycocks, Maracocks, Passiflora incarnata.
Panic. Panicum of many species.
Indian millet. Holcus laxus.
Indian millet. Holcus striosus.
Wild oat. Zizania aquaticia.
Wild pea. Dolichos of Clayton.
Lupine. Lupinus perennis.
Wild hop. Humulus lupulus.
Wild cherry. Prunus Virginiana.
Cherokee plum. Prunus sylvestris fructu majori. Clayton.
Wild plum. Prunus sylvestris fructu minori. Clayton.
Wild crab apple. Pyrus coronaria.
Red mulberry. Morus rubra.
Persimmon. Diospiros Virginiana.
Sugar maple. Acer saccarinum.
Scaly bark hiccory. Juglans alba cortice squamoso. Clayton.
Common hiccory. Juglans alba, fructu minore rancido. Clayton.
Paccan, or Illinois nut. Not described by Linnæus, Millar, or Clayton. Were I to venture to describe this, speaking of the fruit from memory, and of the leaf from plants of two years' growth, I should specify it as Juglans alba, foliolis lanceolatis, acuminatus, serratis, tomentosis, fructu minore, ovato, compresso, vix insculpto, dulci, putamine tenerrimo. It grows on the Illinois, Wabash, Ohio, and Mississippi. It is spoken of by Don Ulloa under the name of Pacanos, in his Noticias Americanas. Entret. 6.
Black walnut. Juglans nigra.
White walnut. Juglans alba.
Chesnut. Fagus castanea.
Chinquapin. Fagus pumila.
Hazlenut. Corylus avellana.
Grapes. Vitis. Various kinds; though only three described by Clayton.
Scarlet strawberries. Fragaria Virginiana of Millar.
Whortleberries. Vaccinium uliginosum.
Wild gooseberries. Ribes grossularia.
Cranberries. Vaccinium oxycoccos.
Black raspberries. Rubus occidentalis.
Blackberries. Rubus fructicosus.
Dewberries. Rubus cæsius.
Cloudberries. Rubus Chamæmorus.
3. Plane tree. Platanus occidentalis.
Poplar. Liriodendron tulipifera.
Populus heterophylla.
Black poplar. Populus nigra.
Aspen. Populus tremula.
Linden, or lime. Telia Americana.
Red flowering maple. Acer rubrum.
Horse-chesnut, or buck's-eye. Æsculus pavia.
Catalpa. Bignonia catalpa.
Umbrella. Magnolia tripetala.
Swamp laurel. Magnolia glauca.

Cucumber-tree. Magnolia acuminata.
Portugal bay. Laurus indica.
Red bay. Laurus borbonia.
Dwarf-rose bay. Rhododendron maximum.
Laurel of the western country. Qu. species?
Wild pimento. Laurus benzoin.
Sassafras. Laurus sassafras.
Locust. Robinia pseudo-acacia.
Honey-locust. Gleditsia. 1. 6
Dogwood. Cornus florida.
Fringe, or snow-drop tree. Chionanthus Virginica.
Barberry. Barberis vulgaris.
Redbud, or Judas-tree. Cercis Canadensis.
Holly. Ilex aquifolium.
Cockspur hawthorn. Cratægus coccinea.
Spindle-tree. Euonymus Europæus.
Evergreen spindle-tree. Euonymus Americanus.
Itea Virginica.
Elder. Sambucus nigra.
Papaw. Annona triloba.
Candleberry myrtle. Myrica cerifera.
Dwarf laurel. Kalmia angustifolia, Kalmia latifolia (called ivy with us).
Ivy. Hedera quinquefolia.
Trumpet honeysuckle. Lonicera sempervirens
Upright honeysuckle. Azalea nudiflora.
Yellow jasmine. Bignonia sempervirens.
Calycanthus floridus.
American aloe. Agave Virginica.
Sumach. Rhus. Qu. species?
Poke. Phytolacca decandra.
Long moss. Tillandsia Usneoides.
4. Reed. Aruudo phragmitis.
Virginia hemp. Acnida cannabina.
Flax. Linum Virginianum.
Black, or pitch-pine. Pinus tæda.
White pine. Pinus strobus.
Yellow pine. Pinus Virginica.
Spruce pine. Pinus foliis singularibus. Clayton.
Hemlock spruce Fir. Pinus Canadensis.
Abor vitæ. Thuya occidentalis.
Juniper. Juniperus Virginica (called cedar with us).
Cypress. Cupressus disticha.
White cedar. Cupressus Thyoides.
Black oak. Quercus nigra.
White oak. Quercus alba.
Red oak. Quercus rubra.
Willow oak. Quercus phellos.
Chesnut oak. Quercus prinus.
Black jack oak. Quercus aquatica. Clayton.
Ground oak. Quercus pumila. Clayton.
Live oak. Quercus Virginiana. Millar.
Black birch. Betula nigra.
White birch. Betula alba.
Beach. Fagus sylvatica.
Ash. Fraxinus Americana.
Fraxinus Novæ Angliæ. Millar.
Elm. Ulmus Americana.
Willow. Salix. Qu. species?
Sweet gum. Liquidambar styraciflua.

The following were found in Virginia when first visited by the English; but it is not said whether of spontaneous growth, or by cultivation only. Most probably they were natives of more southern climates, and handed along the continent from one nation to another of the savages.

Tobacco. Nicotiana.
Maize. Zea mays.
Round potatoes. Solanum tuberosum.
Pumpkins. Cucurbita pepo.
Cymlings. Cucurbita verrucosa.
Squashes. Cucurbita melopepo.

There is an infinitude of other plants and flowers, for an enumeration and scientific description of which I must refer to the Flora Virginica of our great botanist, Dr. Clayton, published by Gronovius at Leyden, in 1762. This accurate observer was a native and resident of this State, passed a long life in exploring and describing its plants, and is supposed to have enlarged the botanical catalogue as much as almost any man who has lived.

Besides these plants, which are native, our *farms* produce wheat, rye, barley, oats, buck-wheat, broom corn, and Indian corn. The climate suits rice well enough, wherever the lands do. Tobacco, hemp, flax, and cotton, are staple commodities. Indigo yields two cuttings. The silk-worm is a native, and the mulberry, proper for its food, grows kindly.

We cultivate, also, potatoes, both the long and the round, turnips, carrots, parsnips, pumpkins, and ground nuts (Arachis.) Our grasses are lucerne, st. foin, burnet, timothy, ray, and orchard grass; red, white, and yellow clover; greensward, blue grass, and crab grass.

The *gardens* yield musk-melons, water-melons, tomatoes, okra, pomegranates, figs, and the esculant plants of Europe.

The *orchards* produce apples, pears, cherries, quinces, peaches, nectarines, apricots, almonds, and plums.

Our quadrupeds have been mostly described by Linnæus and Mons. de Buffon. Of these the mammoth, or big buffalo, as called by the Indians, must certainly have been the largest. Their tradition is, that he was carnivorous, and still exists in the northern parts of America. A delegation of warriors from the Delaware tribe having visited the Governor of Virginia, during the revolution, on matters of business, after these had been discussed and settled in council, the Governor asked them some questions relative to their country, and among others, what they knew or had heard of the animal whose bones were found at the Saltlicks on the Ohio. Their chief speaker immediately put himself into an attitude of oratory, and with a pomp suited to what he conceived the elevation of his subject, informed him that it was a tradition handed down from their fathers, "That in ancient times a herd of these tremendous animals came to the Big-bone licks, and began an universal destruction of the bear, deer, elks, buffaloes, and other animals which had been created for the use of the Indians; that the Great Man above, looking down and seeing this, was so enraged that he seized his lightning, descended on the earth, seated himself on a neighboring mountain, on a rock of which his seat and the print of his feet are still to be seen, and hurled his bolts among them till the whole were slaughtered, except the big bull, who presenting his forehead to the shafts, shook them off as they fell; but missing one at length, it wounded him in the side; whereon, springing round, he bounded over the Ohio, over the Wabash, the Illinois, and finally over the great lakes, where he is living at this day." It is well known, that on the Ohio, and in many parts of America further north, tusks, grinders, and skeletons of unparalleled magnitude, are found in great numbers, some lying on the surface of the earth, and some a little below it. A Mr. Stanley, taken prisoner near the mouth of the Tennessee, relates, that after being transferred through several tribes, from one to another, he was at length carried over the mountains west of the Missouri to a river which runs westwardly; that these bones abounded there, and that the natives described to him the animal to which they belonged as still existing in the northern parts of their country; from which description he judged it to be an elephant. Bones of the same kind have been lately found, some feet below the surface of the earth, in salines opened on the North Holston, a branch of the Tennessee, about the latitude of 36½° north. From the accounts published in Europe, I suppose it to be decided that these are of the same kind with those found in Siberia. Instances are mentioned of like animal remains found in the more southern climates of both hemispheres; but they are either so loosely mentioned as to leave a doubt of the fact, so inaccurately described as not to authorize the classing them with the great northern bones, or so rare as to found a suspicion that they have been carried thither as curiosities from the northern regions. So that, on the whole, there seem to be no certain vestiges of the existence of this animal farther south than the salines just mentioned. It is remarkable that the tusks and skeletons have been ascribed by the naturalists of Europe to the elephant, while the grinders have been given to the hippopotamus, or river horse. Yet it is acknowledged, that the tusks and skeletons are much larger than those of the elephant, and the grinders many times greater than those of the hippopotamus, and essentially different in form. Wherever these grinders are found, there also we find the tusks and skeleton; but no skeleton of the hippopotamus nor grinders of the elephant. It will not be said that the hippopotamus and elephant came always to the same spot, the former to deposit his grinders, and the latter his tusks and skeleton. For what became of the parts not deposited there? We must agree then, that these remains belong to each other, that they are of one and the same animal, that this was not a hippopotamus, because the hippopotamus had no tusks, nor such a frame, and because the grinders differ in their size as well as in the number and form of their points. That this was not an elephant, I think ascertained by proofs equally decisive. I will not avail myself of the authority of the celebrated[3] anatomist, who, from an examination of the form and structure of the tusks, has declared they were essentially different from those of the elephant; because another[4] anatomist, equally celebrated, has declared, on a like examination, that they are precisely the same. Between two such authorities I will suppose this circumstance equivocal. But, 1. The skeleton of the mammoth (for so the incognitum has been called) bespeaks an animal of five or six times the cubic volume of the elephant, as Mons. de Buffon has admitted. 2. The grinders are five times as large, are square, and the grinding surface studded with four or five rows of blunt points; whereas those of the elephant are broad and thin, and their grinding surface flat. 3. I have never heard an instance, and suppose there has been none, of the grinder of an elephant being found in America. 4. From the known temperature and constitution of the elephant, he could never have existed in those regions where the remains of the mammoth have been found. The elephant is a native only of the torrid zone and its vicinities; if, with the assistance of warm apartments and warm clothing, he has been preserved in the temperate climates of Europe, it has only been for a small portion of what would have been his natural period, and no instance of his multiplication in them has ever been

[3] Hunter.—T. J.

[4] D'Aubenton.—T. J.

known. But no bones of the mammoth, as I have before observed, have been ever found further south than the salines of Holston, and they have been found as far north as the Arctic circle. Those, therefore, who are of opinion that the elephant and mammoth are the same, must believe, 1. That the elephant known to us can exist and multiply in the frozen zone; or, 2. That an eternal fire may once have warmed those regions, and since abandoned them, of which, however, the globe exhibits no unequivocal indications; or, 3. That the obliquity of the ecliptic, when these elephants lived, was so great as to include within the tropics all those regions in which the bones are found; the tropics being, as is before observed, the natural limits of habitation for the elephant. But if it be admitted that this obliquity has really decreased, and we adopt the highest rate of decrease yet pretended, that is, of one minute in a century, to transfer the northern tropic to the Arctic circle, would carry the existence of these supposed elephants two hundred and fifty thousand years back; a period far beyond our conception of the duration of animal bones less exposed to the open air than these are in many instances. Besides, though these regions would then be supposed within the tropics, yet their winters would have been too severe for the sensibility of the elephant. They would have had, too, but one day and one night in the year, a circumstance to which we have no reason to suppose the nature of the elephant fitted. However, it has been demonstrated, that, if a variation of obliquity in the ecliptic takes place at all, it is vibratory, and never exceeds the limits of nine degrees, which is not sufficient to bring these bones within the tropics. One of these hypotheses, or some other equally voluntary and inadmissible to cautious philosophy, must be adopted to support the opinion that these are the bones of the elephant. For my own part, I find it easier to believe that an animal may have existed, resembling the elephant in his tusks, and general anatomy, while his nature was in other respects extremely different. From the 30th degree of south latitude to the 30th degree of north, are nearly the limits which nature has fixed for the existence and multiplication of the elephant known to us. Proceeding thence northwardly to 36½ degrees, we enter those assigned to the mammoth. The farther we advance north, the more their vestiges multiply as far as the earth has been explored in that direction; and it is as probable as otherwise, that this progression continues to the pole itself, if land extends so far. The centre of the frozen zone, then, may be the acmé of their vigor, as that of the torrid is of the elephant. Thus nature seems to have drawn a belt of separation between these two tremendous animals, whose breadth, indeed, is not precisely known, though at present we may suppose it about 6½ degrees of latitude; to have assigned to the elephant the regions south of these confines, and those north to the mammoth, founding the constitution of the one in her extreme of heat, and that of the other in the extreme of cold. When the Creator has therefore separated their nature as far as the extent of the scale of animal life allowed to this planet would permit, it seems perverse to declare it the same, from a partial resemblance of their tusks and bones. But to whatever animal we ascribe these remains, it is certain such a one has existed in America, and that it has been the largest of all terrestrial beings. It should have sufficed to have rescued the earth it inhabited, and the atmosphere it breathed, from the imputation of impotence in the conception and nourishment of animal life on a large scale; to have stifled, in its birth, the opinion of a writer, the most learned, too, of all others in the science of animal history, that in the new world, *"La nature vivante est beaucoup moins agissante, beaucoup moins forte:"* [5] that nature is less active, less energetic on one side of the globe than she is on the other. As if both sides were not warmed by the same genial sun; as if a soil of the same chemical composition was less capable of elaboration into animal nutriment; as if the fruits and grains from that soil and sun yielded a less rich chyle, gave less extension to the solids and fluids of the body, or produced sooner in the cartilages, membranes, and fibres, that rigidity which restrains all further extension, and terminates animal growth. The truth is, that a pigmy and a Patagonian, a mouse and a mammoth, derive their dimensions from the same nutritive juices. The difference of increment depends on circumstances unsearchable to beings with our capacities. Every race of animals seems to have received from their Maker certain laws of extension at the time of their formation. Their elaborate organs were formed to produce this, while proper obstacles were opposed to its further progress. Below these limits they cannot fall, nor rise above them. What intermediate station they shall take may depend on soil, on climate, on food, on a careful choice of breeders. But all the manna of heaven would never raise the mouse to the bulk of the mammoth.

The opinion advanced by the Count de Buffon,[6] is 1. That the animals common both to the old and new world are smaller in the latter. 2. That those peculiar to the new are on a smaller scale. 3. That those which have been domesticated in both have degenerated in America; and 4. That on the whole it exhibits fewer species. And the reason he thinks is, that the heats of America are less; that more waters are spread over its surface by nature, and fewer of these drained off by the hand of man. In other words, that *heat* is friendly, and *moisture* adverse to the production and development of large quadrupeds. I will not meet this hypothesis on its first doubtful ground, whether the climate of America be comparatively more humid? Because we are not furnished with observations sufficient to decide this question. And though, till it be decided, we are as free to deny as others are to affirm the fact, yet for a moment let it be supposed. The hypothesis, after this supposition, proceeds to another; that *moisture* is unfriendly to animal growth. The truth of this is inscrutable to us by reasonings *à priori*. Nature has hidden from us her *modus agendi*. Our only appeal on such questions is to experience; and I think that experience is against the supposition. It is by the assistance of *heat* and *moisture* that vegetables are elaborated from the elements of earth, air, water, and fire. We accordingly see the more humid climates produce the greater quantity of vegetables. Vegetables are mediately or immediately the food of every animal; and in proportion to the quantity of food, we see animals not only multiplied in their numbers, but improved in their bulk, as far as the laws of their nature will admit. Of this opin-

[5] Buffon, xviii. 112 edit. Paris, 1764.—T. J. [6] Buffon, xviii. 100, 156.—T. J.

ion is the Count de Buffon himself in another part of his work; [7] "*en general il paroit ques les pays un peu* froids *conviennent mieux á nos boeufs que les pays chauds, et qu'ils sont d'autant plus gross et plus grands que le climat est plus* humide *et plus abondans en paturages. Les boeufs de Danemarck, de la Podolie, de l'Ulkraine et de la Tartarie qu habitent les Calmouques sont les plus grands de tous.*" Here then a race of animals, and one of the largest too, has been increased in its dimensions by *cold* and *moisture,* in direct opposition to the hypothesis, which supposes that these two circumstances diminish animal bulk, and that it is their contraries *heat* and *dryness* which enlarge it. But when we appeal to experience we are not to rest satisfied with a single fact. Let us, therefore, try our question on more general ground. Let us take two portions of the earth, Europe and America for instance, sufficiently extensive to give operation to general causes; let us consider the circumstances peculiar to each, and observe their effect on animal nature. America, running through the torrid as well as temperate zone, has more *heat* collectively taken, than Europe. But Europe, according to our hypothesis, is the *dryest.* They are equally adapted then to animal productions; each being endowed with one of those causes which befriend animal growth, and with one which opposes it. If it be thought unequal to compare Europe with America, which is so much larger, I answer, not more so than to compare America with the whole world. Besides, the purpose of the comparison is to try an hypothesis, which makes the size of animals depend on the *heat* and *moisture* of climate. If, therefore, we take a region so extensive as to comprehend a sensible distinction of climate, and so extensive too as that local accidents, or the intercourse of animals on its borders, may not materially affect the size of those in its interior parts, we shall comply with those conditions which the hypothesis may reasonably demand. The objection would be the weaker in the present case, because any intercourse of animals which may take place on the confines of Europe and Asia, is to the advantage of the former, Asia producing certainly larger animals than Europe. Let us then take a comparative view of the quadrupeds of Europe and America, presenting them to the eye in three different tables, in one of which shall be enumerated those found in both countries; in a second, those found in one only; in a third, those which have been domesticated in both. To facilitate the comparison, let those of each table be arranged in gradation according to their sizes, from the greatest to the smallest, so far as their sizes can be conjectured. The weights of the large animals shall be expressed in the English avoirdupois and its decimals; those of the smaller, in the same ounce and its decimals. Those which are marked thus *, are actual weights of particular subjects, deemed among the largest of their species. Those marked thus †, are furnished by judicious persons, well acquainted with the species, and saying, from conjecture only, what the largest individual they had seen would probably have weighed. The other weights are taken from Messrs. Buffon and D'Aubenton, and are of such subjects as came casually to their hands for dissection. This circumstance must be remembered where their weights and mine stand opposed; the latter being stated

[7] viii. 134.—T. J.

not to produce a conclusion in favor of the American species, but to justify a suspension of opinion until we are better informed, and a suspicion, in the meantime, that there is no uniform difference in favor of either; which is all I pretend.

### A COMPARATIVE VIEW OF THE QUADRUPEDS OF EUROPE AND OF AMERICA

#### I. Aboriginals of Both

| | EUROPE LB. | AMERICA LB. |
|---|---|---|
| Mammoth | | |
| Buffalo. Bison | | * 1800 |
| White Bear. Ours blanc | | |
| Carribou. Renne | | |
| Bear. Ours | 153.7 | * 410 |
| Elk. Elan. Original palmated | | |
| Red deer. Cerf | 288.8 | * 273 |
| Fallow Deer. Daim | 167.8 | |
| Wolf. Loup | 69.8 | |
| Roe. Chevreuil | 56.7 | |
| Glutton. Glouton. Carcajou | | |
| Wild cat. Chat sauvage | | † 30 |
| Lynx. Loup cervier | 25. | |
| Beaver. Castor | 18.5 | * 45 |
| Badger Blaireau | 13.6 | |
| Red fox. Renard | 13.5 | |
| Gray fox. Isatis | | |
| Otter. Loutre | 8.9 | † 12 |
| Monax. Marmotte | 6.5 | |
| Vison. Fouine | 2.8 | |
| Hedgehog. Herisson | 2.2 | |
| Marten. Marte | 1.9 | † 6 |
| | OZ. | |
| Water rat. Rat d'eau | 7.5 | |
| Weasel. Belette | 2.2 | OZ. |
| Flying squirrel. Polatouche | 2.2 | † 4 |
| Shrew moseu Musaraigne | 1. | |

#### II. Aboriginals of One Only

| *Europe* | | *America* | |
|---|---|---|---|
| | LB. | | LB. |
| Sanglier. Wild boar | 280. | Tapir | 534. |
| Mouflon. Wild sheep | 56. | Elk, round horned | † 450. |
| Bouquetin. Wild goat | | Puma | |
| Lievre. Hare | 7.6 | Jaguar | 218. |
| Lapin. Rabbit | 3.4 | Cabiai | 109. |
| Putois. Polecat | 3.3 | Tamanoir | 109. |
| Genette | 3.1 | Tammandua | 65.4 |
| Desman. Muskrat | OZ. | Cougar of North-America | 75. |
| Ecureuil. Squirrel | 12. | Cougar of South-America | 59.4 |

| *Europe* | LB. | *America* | LB. |
|---|---|---|---|
| Hermine. Ermin | 8.2 | Ocelot | |
| Rat. Rat | 7.5 | Pecari | 46.3 |
| Loirs | 3.1 | Jaguaret | 43.6 |
| Lerot. Dormouse | 1.8 | Alco | |
| Taupe. Mole | 1.2 | Lama | |
| Hampster | .6 | Paco | |
| Zisel | | Paca | 32.7 |
| Leming | | Serval | |
| Souris. Mouse | .6 | Sloth. Unau | 27.25 |
| | | Saricovienne | |
| | | Kincajou | |
| | | Tatou Kabassou | 21.8 |
| | | Urson. Urchin | |
| | | Raccoon. Raton | 16.5 |
| | | Coati | |
| | | Coendou | 16.3 |
| | | Sloth. Aï | 13. |
| | | Sapajou Ouarini | |
| | | Sapajou Coaita | 9.8 |
| | | Tatou Encubert | |
| | | Tatou Apar | |
| | | Tatou Cachica | 7. |
| | | Little Coendou | 6.5 |
| | | Opossum. Sarigu | |
| | | Tapeti | |
| | | Margay | |
| | | Crabier | |
| | | Agouti | 4.2 |
| | | Sapajou Saï | 3.5 |
| | | Tatou Cirquinçon | |
| | | Tatou Tatouate | 3.3 |
| | | Mouffette Squash | |
| | | Mouffette Chinche | |
| | | Mouffette Conepate | |
| | | Scunk | |
| | | Mouffette. Zorilla | |
| | | Whabus. Hare. Rabbit. | |
| | | Aperea | |
| | | Akouchi | |
| | | Ondatra. Muskrat | |
| | | Pilori | |
| | | Great gray squirrel | † 2.7 |
| | | Fox squirrel of Virginia | † 2.625 |
| | | Surikate | 2. |
| | | Mink | † 2. |
| | | Sapajou. Sajou | 1.8 |
| | | Indian pig. Cochon d'Inde | 1.6 |
| | | Sapajou Saïmiri | 1.5 |

| America | LB. |
|---|---|
| Phalanger | |
| Coqualain | |
| Lesser gray squirrel | † 1.5 |
| Black squirrel | † 1.5 |
| Red squirrel | 10.oz. |
| Sagoin Saki | |
| Sagoin Pinche | |
| Sagoin Tamarin | oz. |
| Sagoin Ouistiti | 4.4 |
| Sagoin Marakine | |
| Sagoin Mico | |
| Cayopollin | |
| Fourmillier | |
| Marmose | |
| Sarigue of Cayenne | |
| Tucan | |
| Red mole | oz. |
| Ground squirrel | 4. |

III. Domesticated in Both

| | EUROPE LB. | AMERICA LB. |
|---|---|---|
| Cow | 765. | * 2500 |
| Horse | | * 1366 |
| Ass | | |
| Hog | | * 1200 |
| Sheep | | * 125 |
| Goat | | * 80 |
| Dog | 67.6 | |
| Cat | 7. | |

I have not inserted in the first table the Phoca,[8] nor leather-winged bat, because the one living half the year in the water, and the other being a winged animal, the individuals of each species may visit both continents.

Of the animals in the first table, Monsieur de Buffon himself informs us, [xxvii. 130, xxx. 213,] that the beaver, the otter, and shrew mouse, though of the same species, are larger in America than in Europe. This should therefore have corrected the generality of his expressions, xviii. 145, and elsewhere, that the animals common to the two countries, are considerably less in America than in Europe, *"et cela sans aucune exception."* He tells us too, [Quadrup. viii. 334, edit. Paris 1777,] that on examining a bear from America, he remarked no difference, *"dans* la forme *de cet ours d'Amerique comparé a celui d'Europe,"*

[8] It is said that this animal is seldom seen above thirty miles from shore, or beyond the 56th degree of latitude. The interjacent islands between Asia and America admit his passing from one continent to the other without exceeding these bounds. And in fact, travellers tell us that these islands are places of principal resort for them, and especially in the season of bringing forth their young.—T. J.

but adds from Bartram's journal, that an American bear weighed four hundred pounds, English, equal to three hundred and sixty-seven pounds French; whereas we find the European bear examined by Mons. D'Aubenton [xvii. 82], weighed but one hundred and forty-one pounds French. That the palmated elk is larger in America than in Europe, we are informed by Kalm,[9] a naturalist, who visited the former by public appointment, for the express purpose of examining the subjects of natural history. In this fact Pennant concurs with him. [Barrington's Miscellanies.] The same Kalm tells us[10] that the black moose, or renne of America, is as high as a tall horse; and Catesby,[11] that it is about the bigness of a middle-sized ox. The same account of their size has been given me by many who have seen them. But Monsieur D'Aubenton says[12] that the renne of Europe is about the size of a red deer. The weasel is larger in America than in Europe, as may be seen by comparing its dimensions as reported by Monsieur D'Aubenton[13] and Kalm. The latter tells us,[14] that the lynx, badger, red fox, and flying squirrel, are the *same* in America as in Europe; by which expression I understand, they are the same in all material circumstances, in size as well as others; for if they were smaller, they would differ from the European. Our gray fox is, by Catesby's account,[15] little different in size and shape from the European fox. I presume he means the red fox of Europe, as does Kalm, where he says,[16] that in size "they do not quite come up to our foxes." For proceeding next to the red fox of America, he says, "they are entirely the same with the European sort"; which shows he had in view one European sort only, which was the red. So that the result of their testimony is, that the American gray fox is somewhat less than the European red; which is equally true of the gray fox of Europe, as may be seen by comparing the measures of the Count de Buffon and Monseiur D'Aubenton.[17] The white bear of America is as large as that of Europe. The bones of the mammoth which has been found in America, are as large as those found in the old world. It may be asked, why I insert the mammoth, as if it still existed? I ask in return, why I should omit it, as if it did not exist? Such is the economy of nature, that no instance can be produced, of her having permitted any one race of her animals to become extinct; of her having formed any link in her great work so weak as to be broken. To add to this, the traditionary testimony of the Indians, that this animal still exists in the northern and western parts of America, would be adding the light of a taper to that of the meridian sun. Those parts still remain in their aboriginal state, unexplored and undisturbed by us, or by others for us. He may as well exist there now, as he did formerly where we find his bones. If he be a carnivorous animal, as some anatomists have conjectured, and the Indians affirm, his

[9] I. 233, Lon. 1772.—T. J.
[10] Ib. 233.—T. J.
[11] I. xxvii.—T. J.
[12] XXIV. 162.—T. J.
[13] XV. 42—T. J.
[14] I. 359. I. 48, 221, 251. II. 52.—T. J.
[15] II. 78.—T. J.
[16] I. 220.—T. J.
[17] XXVII. 63. XIV. 119. Harris, II. 387. Buffon, Quad. IX. 1.—T. J.

early retirement may be accounted for from the general destruction of the wild game by the Indians, which commences in the first instant of their connection with us, for the purpose of purchasing match-coats, hatchets, and firelocks, with their skins. There remain then the buffalo, red deer, fallow deer, wolf, roe, glutton, wild cat, monax, bison, hedgehog, marten, and water-rat, of the comparative sizes of which we have not sufficient testimony. It does not appear that Messieurs de Buffon and D'Aubenton have measured, weighed, or seen those of America. It is said of some of them, by some travellers, that they are smaller than the European. But who were these travellers? Have they not been men of a very different description from those who have laid open to us the other three quarters of the world? Was natural history the object of their travels? Did they measure or weigh the animals they speak of? or did they not judge of them by sight, or perhaps even from report only? Were they acquainted with the animals of their own country, with which they undertake to compare them? Have they not been so ignorant as often to mistake the species? A true answer to these questions would probably lighten their authority, so as to render it insufficient for the foundation of an hypothesis. How unripe we yet are, for an accurate comparison of the animals of the two countries, will appear from the work of Monsieur de Buffon. The ideas we should have formed of the sizes of some animals, from the information he had received at his first publications concerning them, are very different from what his subsequent communications give us. And indeed his candor in this can never be too much praised. One sentence of his book must do him immortal honor. *"J'aime autant une personne qui me releve d'une erreur, qu'une autre qui m'apprend une verité parce qu'en effet une erreur corrigée est une verité."* [18] He seems to have thought the cabiai he first exclaimed wanted little of its full growth. *"Il n'etoit pas encore tout-a-fait adulte."* [19] Yet he weighed but forty-six and a half pounds, and he found afterwards,[20] that these animals, when full grown, weigh one hundred pounds. He had supposed, from the examination of a jaguar,[21] said to be two years old, which weighed but sixteen pounds twelve ounces, that when he should have acquired his full growth, he would not be larger than a middle-sized dog. But a subsequent account [22] raises his weight to two hundred pounds. Further information will, doubtless, produce further corrections. The wonder is, not that there is yet something in this great work to correct, but that there is so little. The result of this view then is, that of twenty-six quadrupeds common to both countries, seven are said to be larger in America, seven of equal size, and twelve not sufficiently examined. So that the first table impeaches the first member of the assertion, that of the animals common to both countries, the American are smallest, *"et cela sans aucune exception."* It shows it is not just, in all the latitude in which its author has advanced it, and probably not to such a degree as to found a distinction between the two countries.

[18] Quad. IX. 158.—T. J.
[19] XXV. 184.—T. J.
[20] Quad. IX. 132.—T. J.
[21] XIX. 2.—T. J.
[22] Quad. IX. 41.—T. J.

Proceeding to the second table, which arranges the animals found in one of the two countries only, Monsieur de Buffon observes, that the tapir, the elephant of America, is but of the size of a small cow. To preserve our comparison, I will add, that the wild boar, the elephant of Europe, is little more than half that size. I have made an elk with round or cylindrical horns an animal of America, and peculiar to it; because I have seen many of them myself, and more of their horns; and because I can say, from the best information, that, in Virginia, this kind of elk has abounded much, and still exists in smaller numbers; and I could never learn that the palmated kind had been seen here at all. I suppose this confined to the more northern latitudes.[23] I have made our hare or rabbit peculiar, believing it to be different from both the European animals of those denominations, and calling it therefore by its Algonquin name, Whabus, to keep it distinct from these. Kalm is of the same opinion.[24] I have enumerated the squirrels according to our own knowledge, derived from daily sight of them, because I am not able to reconcile with that the European appellations and descriptions. I have heard of other species, but they have never come within my own notice. These, I think, are the only instances in which I have departed from the authority of Monsieur de Buffon in the construction of this table. I take him for my ground work, because I think him the best informed of any naturalist who has ever written. The result is, that there are

[23] The descriptions of Theodat, Denys and La Honton, cited by Monsieur de Buffon, under the article Elan, authorize the supposition, that the flat-horned elk is found in the northern parts of America. It has not however extended to our latitudes. On the other hand, I could never learn that the round-horned elk has been seen further north than the Hudson's river. This agrees with the former elk in its general character, being, like that, when compared with a deer, very much larger, its ears longer, broader, and thicker in proportion, its hair much longer, neck and tail shorter, having a dewlap before the breast (caruncula gutturalis Linnæi) a white spot often, if not always, of a foot diameter, on the hinder part of the buttocks round the tail; its gait a trot, and attended with a rattling of the hoofs; but distinguished from that decisively by its horns, which are not palmated, but round and pointed. This is the animal described by Catesby as the Cervus major Americanus, the stag of America, le Cerf de l'Amerique. But it differs from the Cervus as totally as does the palmated elk from the dama. And in fact it seems to stand in the same relation to the palmated elk, as the red deer does to the fallow. It has abounded in Virginia, has been seen, within my knowledge, on the eastern side of the Blue Ridge since the year 1765, is now common beyond those mountains, has been often brought to us and tamed, and its horns are in the hands of many. I should designate it as the "*Alces Americanus cornibus teretibus.*" It were to be wished, that naturalists, who are acquainted with the renne and elk of Europe, and who may hereafter visit the northern parts of America, would examine well the animals called there by the names of gray and black moose, caribou, original and elk. Monsieur de Buffon has done what could be done from the materials in his hands, toward clearing up the confusion introduced by the loose application of these names among the animals they are meant to designate. He reduces the whole to the renne and flat-horned elk. From all the information I have been able to collect, I strongly suspect they will be found to cover three, if not four distinct species of animals. I have seen skins of a moose, and of the caribou: they differ more from each other, and from that of the round-horned elk, than I ever saw two skins differ which belonged to different individuals of any wild species. These differences are in the color, length, and coarseness of the hair, and in the size, texture, and marks of the skin. Perhaps it will be found that there is, 1, the moose, black and gray, the former being said to be the male, and the latter the female; 2, the caribou or renne; 3, the flat-horned elk, or original; 4, the round-horned elk. Should this last, though possessing so nearly the characters of the elk, be found to be the same with the Cerf d'Ardennes or Brandhitz of Germany, still there will remain the three species first enumerated.—T. J.

[24] Kalm II. 340, I. 82.—T. J.

eighteen quadrupeds peculiar to Europe; more than four times as many, to wit, seventy four, peculiar to America; that the [25] first of these seventy-four weighs more than the whole column of Europeans; and consequently this second table disproves the second member of the assertion, that the animals peculiar to the new world are on a smaller scale, so far as that assertion relied on European animals for support; and it is in full opposition to the theory which makes the animal volume to depend on the circumstances of *heat* and *moisture*.

The third table comprehends those quadrupeds only which are domestic in both countries. That some of these, in some parts of America, have become less than their original stock, is doubtless true; and the reason is very obvious. In a thinly-peopled country, the spontaneous productions of the forests, and waste fields, are sufficient to support indifferently the domestic animals of the farmer, with a very little aid from him, in the severest and scarcest season. He therefore finds it more convenient to receive them from the hand of nature in that indifferent state, than to keep up their size by a care and nourishment which would cost him much labor. If, on this low fare, these animals dwindle, it is no more than they do in those parts of Europe where the poverty of the soil, or the poverty of the owner, reduces them to the same scanty subsistence. It is the uniform effect of one and the same cause, whether acting on this or that side of the globe. It would be erring, therefore, against this rule of philosophy, which teaches us to ascribe like effects to like causes, should we impute this diminution of size in America to any imbecility or want of uniformity in the operations of nature. It may be affirmed with truth, that, in those countries, and with those individuals in America, where necessity or curiosity has produced equal attention, as in Europe, to the nourishment of animals, the horses, cattle, sheep, and hogs, of the one continent are as large as those of the other. There are particular instances, well attested, where individuals of this country have imported good breeders from England, and have improved their size by care in the course of some years. To make a fair comparison between the two countries, it will not answer to bring together animals of what might be deemed the middle or ordinary size of their species; because an error in judging of that middle or ordinary size, would vary the result of the comparison. Thus Mons. D'Aubenton [26] considers a horse of 4 feet five inches high and 400lb. weight French, equal to 4 feet 8.6 inches and 436lb. English, as a middle-sized horse. Such a one is deemed a small horse in America. The extremes must therefore be resorted to. The same anatomist [27] dissected a horse of 5 feet 9 inches height, French measure, equal to 6 feet 1.7 English. This is near 6 inches higher than any horse I have seen; and could it be supposed that I had seen the largest

[25] The Tapir is the largest of the animals peculiar to America. I collect his weight thus: Monsieur de Buffon says, XXIII. 274, that he is of the size of a Zebu, or a small cow. He gives us the measures of a Zebu, ib. 4, as taken by himself, *viz.* five feet seven inches from the muzzle to the root of the tail, and five feet one inch circumference behind the fore-legs. A bull, measuring in the same way six feet nine inches and five feet two inches, weighed six hundred pounds, VIII. 153. The Zebu then, and of course the Tapir, would weigh about five hundred pounds. But one individual of every species of European peculiars would probably weigh less than four hundred pounds. These are French measures and weights.—T. J.

[26] VII. 432.—T. J.

[27] VII. 474.—T. J.

horses in America, the conclusion would be, that ours have diminished, or that we have bred from a smaller stock. In Connecticut and Rhode Island, where the climate is favorable to the production of grass, bullocks have been slaughtered which weighed 2,500, 2,200, and 2,100 lbs. nett; and those of 1,800 lbs. have been frequent. I have seen a hog[28] weigh 1,050 lbs. after the blood, bowels, and hair had been taken from him. Before he was killed, an attempt was made to weigh him with a pair of steel yards, graduated to 1,200 lbs., but he weighed more. Yet this hog was probably not within fifty generations of the European stock. I am well informed of another which weighed 1,100 lbs. gross. Asses have been still more neglected than any other domestic animal in America. They are neither fed or housed in the most rigorous season of the year. Yet they are larger than those measured by Mons. D'Aubenton,[29] of 3 feet 7¼ inches, 3 feet 4 inches, and 3 feet 2½ inches, the latter weighing only 215.8 lbs. These sizes, I suppose, have been produced by the same negligence in Europe, which has produced a like diminution here. Where care has been taken of them on that side of the water, they have been raised to a size bordering on that of the horse; not by the *heat* and *dryness* of the climate, but by good food and shelter. Goats have been also much neglected in America. Yet they are very prolific here, bearing twice or three times a year, and from one to five kids at a birth. Mons. de Buffon has been sensible of a difference in this circumstance in favor of America.[30] But what are their greatest weights, I cannot say. A large sheep here weighs 100 lbs. I observe Mons. D'Aubenton calls a ram of 62 lbs. one of the middle size.[31] But to say what are the extremes of growth in these and the other domestic animals of America, would require information of which no one individual is possessed. The weights actually known and stated in the third table preceding will suffice to show, that we may conclude on probable grounds, that, with equal food and care, the climate of America will preserve the races of domestic animals as large as the European stock from which they are derived; and, consequently, that the third member of Mons. de Buffon's assertion that the domestic animals are subject to degeneration from the climate of America, is as probably wrong as the first and second were certainly so.

That the last part of it is erroneous, which affirms that the species of American quadrupeds are comparatively few, is evident from the tables taken together. By these it appears that there are an hundred species aboriginal in America. Mons. de Buffon supposes about double that number existing on the whole earth.[32] Of these Europe, Asia, and Africa, furnish suppose one hundred and twenty-six; that is, the twenty-six common to Europe and America, and about one hundred which are not in America at all. The American species, then, are to those of the rest of the earth, as one hundred to one hundred and twenty-six, or four to five. But the residue of the earth being double the extent of America, the exact proportion would have been but as four to eight.

Hitherto I have considered this hypothesis as applied to brute animals only,

[28] In Williamsburg, April, 1769.—T. J.

[29] VIII. 48, 55, 66.—T. J.

[30] XVIII. 96.—T. J.

[31] IX. 41.—T. J.

[32] XXX. 219.—T. J.

and not in its extension to the man of America, whether aboriginal or transplanted. It is the opinion of Mons. de Buffon that the former furnishes no exception to it.[33]

*"Quoique le sauvage du nouveau monde soit à peu près de même stature que l'homme de notre monde, cela ne suffit pas pour qu'il puisse faire une exception au fait général du rapetissement de la nature vivante dans tout ce continent; le sauvage est foible et petit par les organes de la génération; il n'a ni poil, ni barbe, and nulle ardeur pour sa femelle. Quoique plus léger que l'Européen, parce qu'il a plus d'habitude à courir, il est cependant beaucoup moins fort de corps; il est aussi bien moins sensible, et cependant plus craintif et plus lâche; il n'a nulle vivacité, nulle activité dans l'ame; celle du corps est moins un exercise, un mouvement volontaire qu'une nécessité d'action causée par le besoin; ôtez lui la faim et la soif, vous détruirez en même tems le principe actif de tous ses mouvemens; il demeurera stupidement en repos sur ses jambes ou couché pendant des jours entiers. Il ne faut pas aller chercher plus loin à cause de la vie dispersée des sauvages et de leur éloignement pour la société; la plus précieuse étincelle du feu de la nature leur a été refusée; ils manquent d'ardeur pour leur femelle, et par consequent d'amour pour leur semblables; ne connoissant pas l'attachment le plus vif, le plus tendre de tous, leurs autres sentimens de ce genre, sont froids et languissans; ils aiment foiblement leurs pères et leurs enfans; la société la plus intime de toutes, celle de la même famille, n'a donc chez eux que de foibles liens; la société d'une famille à l'autre n'en a point de tout; dès lors nulle réunion, nulle république, nulle état social. La physique de l'amour fait chez eux le moral des mœurs; leur cœur est glacé, leur societé et leur empire dur. Ils ne regardent leurs femmes que comme des servantes de peine ou des bêtes de somme qu'ils chargent, sans ménagement, du fardeau de leur chasse, et qu'ils forcent, sans pitié, sans reconnoissance, à des ouvrages qui souvent sont au dessus de leurs forces; ils n'ont que peu d'enfans; ils en ont peu de soin; tout se ressent de leur premier defaut; ils sont indifférents parce qu'ils sont peu puissants, et cette indifference pour le sexe est la tache originelle qui flétrit la nature, qui l'empeche de s'épanouir, et qui detruisant les germes de la vie, coupe en même temps la racine de société. L'homme ne fait donc point d'exception ici. La nature en lui refusant les puissances de l'amour l'a plus maltraité et plus rapetissé qu'aucun des animaux."*

An afflicting picture, indeed, which for the honor of human nature, I am glad to believe has no original. Of the Indian of South America I know nothing; for I would not honor with the appellation of knowledge, what I derive from the fables published of them. These I believe to be just as true as the fables of Æsop. This belief is founded on what I have seen of man, white, red, and black, and what has been written of him by authors, enlightened themselves, and writing among an enlightened people. The Indian of North America being more within our reach, I can speak of him somewhat from my own knowledge, but more from the information of others better acquainted with him, and on whose truth and judgment I can rely. From these sources I am able to say, in contradiction to this representation, that he is neither more defective in ardor, nor more impotent with his female, than the white reduced to the same diet and exercise; that he is brave, when an enterprise depends on bravery; educa-

[33] XVIII. 146.—T. J.

tion with him making the point of honor consist in the destruction of an enemy by stratagem, and in the preservation of his own person free from injury; or, perhaps, this is nature, while it is education which teaches us to [34] honor force more than finesse; that he will defend himself against a host of enemies, always choosing to be killed, rather than to surrender,[35] though it be to the whites, who he knows will treat him well; that in other situations, also, he meets death with more deliberation, and endures tortures with a firmness unknown almost to religious enthusiasm with us; that he is affectionate to his children, careful of them, and indulgent in the extreme; that his affections comprehend his other connections, weakening, as with us, from circle to circle, as they recede from the centre; that his friendships are strong and faithful to the uttermost [36] extremity; that his sensibility is keen, even the warriors weeping most bitterly on the loss of their children, though in general they endeavor to appear superior to human events; that his vivacity and activity of mind is equal to ours in the

[34] *Sol Rodomonte sprezza di venire*
*Se non, dove la via meno è ficura.* (ARISTO, 14, 117.)—T. J.

[35] In so judicious an author as Don Ulloa, and one to whom we are indebted for the most precise information we have of South America, I did not expect to find such assertions as the following: *"Los Indios vencidos son los mas cobardes y pusilanimes que se pueden vér: Se hacen inöcentes, le humillan hasta el desprecio, disculpan su inconsiderado arrojo, y con las suplicas y los ruegos dán seguras pruebas de su pusilanimidad. ó lo que resieren las historias de la Conquista, sobre sus grandes acciones, es en un sendito figurado, ó el caracter de estas gentes no es ahora segun era entonces; pero lo que no tiene duda es, que las Naciones de la parte Septentrional subsisten en la misma libertad que siempre han tenido, sin haber sido sojuzgados por algon Principe extrano, y que viven segun su régimen y costumbres de toda la vida, sin que haya habido motivo para que muden de caracter; y en estos se vé lo mismo, que sucede en los Peru, y de toda la América Meridional, reducidos, y que nunca lo han estado."* Noticias Americanas, Entretenimiento xviii. § 1. Don Ulloa here admits, that the authors who have described the Indians of South America, before they were enslaved, had represented them as a brave people, and therefore seems to have suspected that the cowardice which he had observed in those of the present race might be the effect of subjugation. But, supposing the Indians of North America to be cowards also, he concludes the ancestors of those of South America to have been so too, and, therefore, that those authors have given fictions for truth. He was probably not acquainted himself with the Indians of North America, and had formed his opinion from hear-say. Great numbers of French, of English, and of Americans, are perfectly acquainted with these people. Had he had an opportunity of inquiring of any of these, they would have told him, that there never was an instance known of an Indian begging his life when in the power of his enemies; on the contrary, that he courts death by every possible insult and provocation. His reasoning, then, would have been reversed thus: "Since the present Indian of North America is brave, and authors tell us that the ancestors of those of South America were brave also, it must follow that the cowardice of their descendants is the effect of subjugation and ill treatment." For he observes, ib. §. 27, that *"los obrages los aniquillan por la inhumanidad con que les trata."*—T. J.

[36] A remarkable instance of this appeared in the case of the late Colonel Byrd, who was sent to the Cherokee nation to transact some business with them. It happened that some of our disorderly people had just killed one or two of that nation. It was therefore proposed in the council of the Cherokees that Colonel Byrd should be put to death, in revenge for the loss of their countrymen. Among them was a chief named Silòuee, who, on some former occasion, had contracted an acquaintance and friendship with Colonel Byrd. He came to him every night in his tent, and told him not to be afraid, they should not kill him. After many days' deliberation, however, the determination was, contrary to Silòuee's expectation, that Byrd should be put to death, and some warriors were despatched as executioners. Silòuee attended them, and when they entered the tent, he threw himself between them and Byrd, and said to the warriors, "This man is my friend; before you get at him, you must kill me." On which they returned, and the council respected the principle so much as to recede from their determination.—T. J.

same situation; hence his eagerness for hunting, and for games of chance. The women are submitted to unjust drudgery. This I believe is the case with every barbarous people. With such, force is law. The stronger sex imposes on the weaker. It is civilization alone which replaces women in the enjoyment of their natural equality. That first teaches us to subdue the selfish passions, and to respect those rights in others which we value in ourselves. Were we in equal barbarism, our females would be equal drudges. The man with them is less strong than with us, but their women stronger than ours; and both for the same obvious reason; because our man and their woman is habituated to labor, and formed by it. With both races the sex which is indulged with ease is the least athletic. An Indian man is small in the hand and wrist, for the same reason for which a sailor is large and strong in the arms and shoulders, and a porter in the legs and thighs. They raise fewer children than we do. The causes of this are to be found, not in a difference of nature, but of circumstance. The women very frequently attending the men in their parties of war and of hunting, child-bearing becomes extremely inconvenient to them. It is said, therefore, that they have learned the practice of procuring abortion by the use of some vegetable; and that it even extends to prevent conception for a considerable time after. During these parties they are exposed to numerous hazards, to excessive exertions, to the greatest extremities of hunger. Even at their homes the nation depends for food, through a certain part of every year, on the gleanings of the forest; that is, they experience a famine once in every year. With all animals, if the female be badly fed, or not fed at all, her young perish; and if both male and female be reduced to like want, generation becomes less active, less productive. To the obstacles, then, of want and hazard, which nature has opposed to the multiplication of wild animals, for the purpose of restraining their numbers within certain bounds, those of labor and of voluntary abortion are added with the Indian. No wonder, then, if they multiply less than we do. Where food is regularly supplied, a single farm will show more of cattle, than a whole country of forests can of buffaloes. The same Indian women, when married to white traders, who feed them and their children plentifully and regularly, who exempt them from excessive drudgery, who keep them stationary and unexposed to accident, produce and raise as many children as the white women. Instances are known, under these circumstances, of their rearing a dozen children. An inhuman practice once prevailed in this country, of making slaves of the Indians. It is a fact well known with us, that the Indian women so enslaved produced and raised as numerous families as either the whites or blacks among whom they lived. It has been said that Indians have less hair than the whites, except on the head. But this is a fact of which fair proof can scarcely be had. With them it is disgraceful to be hairy on the body. They say it likens them to hogs. They therefore pluck the hair as fast as it appears. But the traders who marry their women, and prevail on them to discontinue this practice, say, that nature is the same with them as with the whites. Nor, if the fact be true, is the consequence necessary which has been drawn from it. Negroes have notoriously less hair than the whites; yet they are more ardent. But if cold and moisture be the agents of nature for diminishing the races of animals, how comes she all at once to suspend their operation as to the physical man of the new world, whom the Count acknowledges to be *"à peu près de même stature que l'homme de notre monde,"* and to let loose their influence on his moral faculties? How has this "combination of the elements and other physical causes, so contrary to the enlargement of animal nature in this new world, these obstacles to the development and formation of great germs,"[37] been arrested and suspended, so as to permit the human body to acquire its just dimensions, and by what inconceivable process has their action been directed on his mind alone? To judge of the truth of this, to form a just estimate of their genius and mental powers, more facts are wanting, and great allowance to be made for those circumstances of their situation which call for a display of particular talents only. This done, we shall probably find that they are formed in mind as well as in body, on the same module with the[38] *"Homo sapiens Europæus."* The principles of their society forbidding all compulsion, they are to be led to duty and to enterprise by personal influence and persuasion. Hence eloquence in council, bravery and address in war, become the foundations of all consequence with them. To these acquirements all their faculties are directed. Of their bravery and address in war we have multiplied proofs, because we have been the subjects on which they were exercised. Of their eminence in oratory we have fewer examples, because it is displayed chiefly in their own councils. Some, however, we have, of very superior lustre. I may challenge the whole orations of Demosthenes and Cicero, and of any more eminent orator, if Europe has furnished more eminent, to produce a single passage, superior to the speech of Logan, a Mingo chief, to Lord Dunmore, then governor of this State. And as a testimony of their talents in this line, I beg leave to introduce it, first stating the incidents necessary for understanding it.

In the spring of the year 1774, a robbery was committed by some Indians on certain land-adventurers on the river Ohio. The whites in that quarter, according to their custom, undertook to punish this outrage in a summary way. Captain Michael Cresap, and a certain Daniel Greathouse, leading on these parties, surprised, at different times, travelling and hunting parties of the Indians, having their women and children with them, and murdered many. Among these were unfortunately the family of Logan, a chief celebrated in peace and war, and long distinguished as the friend of the whites. This unworthy return provoked his vengeance. He accordingly signalized himself in the war which ensued. In the autumn of the same year a decisive battle was fought at the mouth of the Great Kanhaway, between the collected forces of the Shawanese, Mingoes and Delawares, and a detachment of the Virginia militia. The Indians were defeated and sued for peace. Logan, however, disdained to be seen among the suppliants. But lest the sincerity of a treaty should be disturbed, from which so distinguished a chief absented himself, he sent, by a messenger, the following speech, to be delivered to Lord Dunmore.

"I appeal to any white man to say, if ever he entered Logan's cabin hungry,

[37] XVIII. 146.—T. J.

[38] Linn. Syst. Definition of a Man.—T. J.

and he gave him not meat; if ever he came cold and naked, and he clothed him not. During the course of the last long and bloody war Logan remained idle in his cabin, an advocate for peace. Such was my love for the whites, that my countrymen pointed as they passed, and said, 'Logan is the friend of white men.' I had even thought to have lived with you, but for the injuries of one man. Colonel Cresap, the last spring, in cold blood, and unprovoked, murdered all the relations of Logan, not even sparing my women and children. There runs not a drop of my blood in the veins of any living creature. This called on me for revenge. I have sought it: I have killed many: I have fully glutted my vengeance: for my country I rejoice at the beams of peace. But do not harbor a thought that mine is the joy of fear. Logan never felt fear. He will not turn on his heel to save his life. Who is there to mourn for Logan?—Not one." [39]

[39] Philadelphia, December 31, 1797.

DEAR SIR: Mr. Tazewell has communicated to me the inquiries you have been so kind as to make, relative to a passage in the "Notes on Virginia," which has lately excited some newspaper publications. I feel, with great sensibility, the interest you take in this business, and with pleasure, go into explanations with one whose objects I know to be truth and justice alone. Had Mr. Martin thought proper to suggest to me, that doubts might be entertained of the transaction respecting Logan, as stated in the "Notes on Virginia," and to inquire on what grounds that statement was founded, I should have felt myself obliged by the inquiry; have informed him candidly of the grounds, and cordially have co-operated in every means of investigating the fact, and correcting whatsoever in it should be found to have been erroneous. But he chose to step at once into the newspapers, and in his publications there and the letters he wrote to me, adopted a style which forbade the respect of an answer. Sensible, however, that no act of his could absolve me from the justice due to others, as soon as I found that the story of Logan could be doubted, I determined to inquire into it as accurately as the testimony remaining, after a lapse of twenty odd years, would permit, and that the result should be made known, either in the first new edition which should be printed of the "Notes on Virginia," or by publishing an appendix. I thought that so far as that work had contributed to impeach the memory of Cresap, by handing on an erroneous charge, it was proper it should be made the vehicle of retribution. Not that I was at all the author of the injury; I had only concurred, with thousands and thousands of others, in believing a transaction on authority which merited respect. For the story of Logan is only repeated in the "Notes on Virginia," precisely as it had been current for more than a dozen years before they were published. When Lord Dunmore returned from the expedition against the Indians, in 1774, he and his officers brought the speech of Logan, and related the circumstances of it. These were so affecting, and the speech itself so fine a morsel of eloquence, that it became the theme of every conversation, in Williamsburg particularly, and generally, indeed, wheresoever any of the officers resided or resorted. I learned it in Williamsburg, I believe at Lord Dunmore's; and I find in my pocket-book of that year (1774) an entry of the narrative, as taken from the mouth of some person, whose name, however, is not noted, nor recollected, precisely in the words stated in the "Notes on Virginia." The speech was published in the Virginia Gazette of that time, (I have it myself in the volume of gazettes of that year,) and though it was the translation made by the common interpreter, and in a style by no means elegant, yet it was so admired, that it flew through all the public papers of the continent, and through the magazines and other periodical publications of Great Britain; and those who were boys at that day will now attest, that the speech of Logan used to be given them as a school exercise for repetition. It was not till about thirteen or fourteen years after the newspaper publications, that the "Notes on Virginia" were published in America. Combating, in these, the contumelious theory of certain European writers, whose celebrity gave currency and weight to their opinions, that our country from the combined effects of soil and climate, degenerated animal nature, in the general, and particularly the moral faculties of man, I considered the speech of Logan as an apt proof of the contrary, and used it as such; and I copied, verbatim, the narrative I had taken down in 1774, and the speech as it had been given us in a better translation by Lord Dunmore. I knew nothing of the Cresaps, and could not possibly have a motive to do them an injury with design. I repeated what thousands had done before, on as good authority as we have for most of the facts we learn through life, and such as,

Before we condemn the Indians of this continent as wanting genius, we must consider that letters have not yet been introduced among them. Were we to compare them in their present state with the Europeans, north of the Alps, when the Roman arms and arts first crossed those mountains, the comparison would be unequal, because, at that time, those parts of Europe were swarming with numbers; because numbers produce emulation, and multiply the chances of improvement, and one improvement begets another. Yet I may safely ask, how many good poets, how many able mathematicians, how many great inventors in arts or sciences, had Europe, north of the Alps, then produced? And it was sixteen centuries after this before a Newton could be formed. I do not

to this moment, I have seen no reason to doubt. That any body questioned it, was never suspected by me, till I saw the letter of Mr. Martin in the Baltimore paper. I endeavored then to recollect who among my contemporaries, of the same circle of society, and consequently of the same recollections, might still be alive; three and twenty years of death and dispersion had left very few. I remembered, however, that General Gibson was still living, and knew that he had been the translator of the speech. I wrote to him immediately. He, in answer, declares to me, that he was the very person sent by Lord Dunmore to the Indian town; that, after he had delivered his message there, Logan took him out to a neighboring wood; sat down with him, and rehearsing, with tears, the catastrophe of his family, gave him that speech for Lord Dunmore; that he carried it to Lord Dunmore; translated it for him; has turned to it in the Encyclopedia, as taken from the "Notes on Virginia," and finds that it was his translation I had used, with only two or three verbal variations of no importance. These, I suppose, had arisen in the course of successive copies. I cite General Gibson's letter by memory, not having it with me; but I am sure I cite it substantially right. It establishes unquestionably, that the speech of Logan is genuine; and that being established, it is Logan himself who is author of all the important facts. "Colonel Cresap," says he, "in cold blood and unprovoked, murdered all the relations of Logan, not sparing even my women and children; there runs not a drop of my blood in the veins of any living creature." The person and the fact, in all its material circumstances, are here given by Logan himself. General Gibson, indeed, says, that the title was mistaken; that Cresap was a Captain, and not a Colonel. This was Logan's mistake. He also observes, that it was on another water of the Ohio, and not on the Kanhaway, that his family was killed. This is an error which has crept into the traditionary account; but surely of little moment in the moral view of the subject. The material question is, was Logan's family murdered, and by whom? That it was murdered has not, I believe, been denied; that it was by one of the Cresaps, Logan affirms. This is a question which concerns the memories of Logan and Cresap; to the issue of which I am as indifferent as if I had never heard the name of either. I have begun and shall continue to inquire into the evidence additional to Logan's, on which the fact was founded. Little, indeed, can now be heard of, and that little dispersed and distant. If it shall appear on inquiry, that Logan has been wrong in charging Cresap with the murder of his family, I will do justice to the memory of Cresap, as far as I have contributed to the injury, by believing and repeating what others had believed and repeated before me. If, on the other hand, I find that Logan was right in his charge, I will vindicate, as far as my suffrage may go, the truth of a Chief, whose talents and misfortunes have attached to him the respect and commiseration of the world.

I have gone, my dear Sir, into this lengthy detail to satisfy a mind, in the candor and rectitude of which I have the highest confidence. So far as you may incline to use the communication for rectifying the judgments of those who are willing to see things truly as they are, you are free to use it. But I pray that no confidence which you may repose in any one, may induce you to let it go out of your hands, so as to get into a newspaper: against a contest in that field I am entirely decided. I feel extraordinary gratification, indeed, in addressing this letter to you, with whom shades of difference in political sentiment have not prevented the interchange of good opinion, nor cut off the friendly offices of society and good correspondence. This political tolerance is the more valued by me, who consider social harmony as the first of human felicities, and the happiest moments, those which are given to the effusions of the heart. Accept them sincerely, I pray you, from one who has the honor to be, with sentiments of high respect and attachment, dear Sir, your most obedient, and most humble servant.—T. J.

mean to deny that there are varieties in the race of man, distinguished by their powers both of body and mind. I believe there are, as I see to be the case in the races of other animals. I only mean to suggest a doubt, whether the bulk and faculties of animals depend on the side of the Atlantic on which their food happens to grow, or which furnishes the elements of which they are compounded? Whether nature has enlisted herself as a Cis or Trans-Atlantic partisan? I am induced to suspect there has been more eloquence than sound reasoning displayed in support of this theory; that it is one of those cases where the judgment has been seduced by a glowing pen; and whilst I render every tribute of honor and esteem to the celebrated zoologist, who has added, and is still adding, so many precious things to the treasures of science, I must doubt whether in this instance he has not cherished error also, by lending her for a moment his vivid imagination and bewitching language.

So far the Count de Buffon has carried this new theory of the tendency of nature to belittle her productions on this side the Atlantic. Its application to the race of whites transplanted from Europe, remained for the Abbé Raynal. "*On doit etre etonné* (he says) *que l'Amerique n'ait pas encore produit un bon poëte, un habile mathematicien, un homme de genie dans un seul art, ou seule science.*" Hist. Philos. p. 92, ed. Maestricht, 1774. "America has not yet produced one good poet." When we shall have existed as a people as long as the Greeks did before they produced a Homer, the Romans a Virgil, the French a Racine and Voltaire, the English a Shakespeare and Milton, should this reproach be still true, we will inquire from what unfriendly causes it has proceeded, that the other countries of Europe and quarters of the earth shall not have inscribed any name in the roll of poets.[40] But neither has America produced "one able mathematician, one man of genius in a single art or a single science." In war we have produced a Washington, whose memory will be adored while liberty shall have votaries, whose name shall triumph over time, and will in future ages assume its just station among the most celebrated worthies of the world, when that wretched philosophy shall be forgotten which would have arranged him among the degeneracies of nature. In physics we have produced a Franklin, than whom no one of the present age has made more important discoveries, nor has enriched philosophy with more, or more ingenious solutions of the phenomena of nature. We have supposed Mr. Rittenhouse second to no astronomer living; that in genius he must be the first, because he is self-taught. As an artist he has exhibited as great a proof of mechanical genius as the world has ever produced. He has not indeed made a world; but he has by imitation approached nearer its Maker than any man who has lived from the creation to this day.[41] As in philosophy and war, so in government, in oratory, in painting,

[40] Has the world as yet produced more than two poets, acknowledged to be such by all nations? An Englishman only reads Milton with delight, an Italian, Tasso, a Frenchman the Henriade; a Portuguese, Camoens; but Homer and Virgil have been the rapture of every age and nation; they are read with enthusiasm in their originals by those who can read the originals, and in translations by those who cannot.—T. J.

[41] There are various ways of keeping truth out of sight. Mr. Rittenhouse's model of the planetary system has the plagiary application of an Orrery; and the quadrant invented by Godfrey, an American also, and with the aid of which the European nations traverse the globe, is called Hadley's quadrant.—T. J.

in the plastic art, we might show that America, though but a child of yesterday, has already given hopeful proofs of genius, as well as of the nobler kinds, which arouse the best feelings of man, which call him into action, which substantiate his freedom, and conduct him to happiness, as of the subordinate, which serve to amuse him only. We therefore suppose, that this reproach is as unjust as it is unkind: and that, of the geniuses which adorn the present age, America contributes its full share. For comparing it with those countries where genius is most cultivated, where are the most excellent models for art, and scaffoldings for the attainment of science, as France and England for instance, we calculate thus: The United States contains three millions of inhabitants; France twenty millions; and the British islands ten. We produce a Washington, a Franklin, a Rittenhouse. France then should have half a dozen in each of these lines, and Great Britain half that number, equally eminent. It may be true that France has; we are but just becoming acquainted with her, and our acquaintance so far gives us high ideas of the genius of her inhabitants. It would be injuring too many of them to name particularly a Voltaire, a Buffon, the constellation of Encyclopedists, the Abbé Raynal himself, &c. &c. We, therefore, have reason to believe she can produce her full quota of genius. The present war having so long cut off all communication with Great Britain, we are not able to make a fair estimate of the state of science in that country. The spirit in which she wages war, is the only sample before our eyes, and that does not seem the legitimate offspring either of science or of civilization. The sun of her glory is fast descending to the horizon. Her philosophy has crossed the channel, her freedom the Atlantic, and herself seems passing to that awful dissolution whose issue is not given human foresight to scan.[42]

Having given a sketch of our minerals, vegetables, and quadrupeds, and being led by a proud theory to make a comparison of the latter with those of Europe, and to extend it to the man of America, both aboriginal and emigrant, I will proceed to the remaining articles comprehended under the present query.

Between ninety and a hundred of our birds have been described by Catesby. His drawings are better as to form and attitude than coloring, which is generally too high. They are the following:

[42] In a later edition of the Abbé Raynal's work, he has withdrawn his censure from that part of the new world inhabited by the Federo-Americans; but has left it still on the other parts. North America has always been more accessible to strangers than South. If he was mistaken then as to the former, he may be so as to the latter. The glimmerings which reach us from South America enable us to see that its inhabitants are held under the accumulated pressure of slavery, superstition and ignorance. Whenever they shall be able to rise under this weight, and to show themselves to the rest of the world, they will probably show they are like the rest of the world. We have not yet sufficient evidence that there are more lakes and fogs in South America than in other parts of the earth. As little do we know what would be their operation on the mind of man. That country has been visited by Spaniards and Portuguese chiefly, and almost exclusively. These, going from a country of the old world remarkably dry in its soil and climate, fancied there were more lakes and fogs in South America than in Europe. An inhabitant of Ireland, Sweden, or Finland would have formed the contrary opinion. Had South America then been discovered and settled by a people from a fenny country, it would probably have been represented as much drier than the old world. A patient pursuit of facts, and cautious combination and comparison of them, is the drudgery to which man is subjected by his Maker, if he wishes to attain sure knowledge.—T. J.

| LINNÆAN DESIGNATION | CATESBY'S DESIGNATION | | POPULAR NAMES | BUFFON OISEAUX |
|---|---|---|---|---|
| Lanius tyrannus | Muscicapa coronâ rubrâ | 1.55 | Tyrant. Field martin | 8.398 |
| Vultur aura | Buteo specie Gallo-pavonis | 1. 6 | Turkey buzzard | 1.246 |
| Falco leucocephalus | Aquila capite albo | 1. 1 | Bald eagle | 1.138 |
| Falco sparverius | Accipiter minor | 1. 5 | Little hawk. Sparrow hawk | |
| Falco columbarious | Accipiter palumbarius | 1. 3 | Pigeon hawk | 1.338 |
| Falco furcatus | Accipiter caudâ furcatâ | 1. 4 | Forked tail hawk | 1.286.312 |
| | Accipiter piscatorius | 1. 2 | Fishing hawk | 1.199 |
| Strix asio | Noctua aurita minor | 1. 7 | Little owl | 1.141 |
| Psittacus Caroliniensis | Psittacus Caroliniensus | 1.11 | Parrot of Carolina. Parroquet | 11.383 |
| Corvus cristatus | Pica glandaria, eærulea, cristata | 1.15 | Blue jay | 5.164 |
| Oriolus Baltimore | Icterus ex aureo nigroque varius | 1.48 | Baltimore bird | 5.318 |
| Oriolus spurius | Icterus minor | 1.49 | Bastard Baltimore | 5.321 |
| Gracula quiscula | Monedula purpurea | 1.12 | Purple jackdaw. Crow blackbird | 5.134 |
| Cuculus Americanus | Cuculus Caroliniensis | 1. 9 | Carolina cuckow | 12.62 |
| Picus principalis | Picus maximus rostro albo | 1.16 | White bill woodpecker | 13.69 |
| Picus pileatus | Picus niger maximus, capite rubro | 1.17 | Larger red-crested woodpecker | 13.72 |
| Picus erythrocephalus | Picus capite toto rubro | 1.20 | Red headed woodpecker | 13.83 |
| Picus ouratus | Picus major alis aureis | 1.18 | Gold winged woodpecker. Yucker | 13.59 |
| Picus Carolinus | Picus ventre rubro | 1.19 | Red-bellied woodpecker | 13.105 |
| Picus pubescens | Picus varius minimus | 1.21 | Smallest spotted woodpecker | 13.113 |
| Picus villosus | Picus medius quasi-villosus | 1.19 | Hairy woodpecker. Spec. woodpecker | 13.111 |
| Picus varius | Picus varius minor ventre luteo | 1.21 | Yellow-bellied woodpecker | 13.115 |
| Sitta Europæa | { Sitta capite nigro | 1.22 | Nuthatch | 10.213 |
| | { Sitta capite fusco | 1.22 | Small Nuthatch | 10.214 |
| Alcedo alcyon | Ispida | 1.69 | Kingfisher | 13.310 |
| Certhia pinus | Parus Americanus lutescens | 1.61 | Pine-Creeper | 9.433 |
| Trochilus colubris | Mellivora avis Caroliniensis | 1.65 | Humming bird | 11.16 |
| Anas Canadensis | Anser Canadensis | 1.92 | Wild goose | 17.122 |
| Anas bucephala | Anas minor purpureo capite | 1.95 | Buffel's-head duck | 17.356 |

| LINNÆAN DESIGNATION | CATESBY'S DESIGNATION | | POPULAR NAMES | BUFFON OISEAUX |
|---|---|---|---|---|
| Anas rustica | Anas minor ex albo & fusco vario | 1.98 | Little brown duck | 17.413 |
| Anas discors. β | Querquedula Americana variegata | 1.10 | White face teal | 17.403 |
| Anas discors. β | Querquedula Americana fusca | 1.99 | Blue wing teal | 17.405 |
| Anas sponsa | Anas Americanus cristatus elegans | 1.97 | Summer duck | 17.351 |
| | Anas Americanus lato rostro | 1.96 | Blue wing shoveler | 17.275 |
| Mergus cucullatus | Anas cristatus | 1.94 | Round crested duck | 15.437 |
| Columbus podiceps | Prodicipes minor rostro vario | 1.91 | Pied bill dopchick | 15.383 |
| Ardea Herodias | Ardea cristata maxima Americana | 3.10 | Largest crested heron | 14.113 |
| Ardea violacea | Ardea stellaris cristata Americana | 1.79 | Crested bittern | 14.134 |
| Ardea cærulea | Ardea cærulea | 1.76 | Blue heron. Crane | 14.131 |
| Ardea virescens | Ardea stellaris minima | 1.80 | Small bittern | 14.142 |
| Ardea æquinoctialis | Ardea alba minor Caroliniensis | 1.77 | Little white heron | 14.136 |
| | Ardea stellaris Americana | 1.78 | Brown bittern. Indian hen | 14.175 |
| Tantalus loculator | Pelicanus Americanus | 1.81 | Wood pelican | 13.403 |
| Tantalus alber | Numenius albus | 1.82 | White curlew | 15.62 |
| Tantalus fuscus | Numenius fuscus | 1.83 | Brown curlew | 15.64 |
| Charadrius vociferus | Pluvialis vociferus | 1.71 | Chattering plover. Kildee | 15.151 |
| Hæmatopus ostralegus | Hæmatopus | 1.85 | Oyster-catcher | 15.185 |
| Rallus Virginianus | Gallinula Americana | 1.70 | Soree. Ral-bird | 15.256 |
| Meleagris Gallopavo | Gallopava Sylvestris | xliv. | Wild Turkey | 3.187.229 |
| Tetrao Virginianus | Perdix Sylvestris Virginiana | 3.12 | American partridge. American quail | 4.237 |
| | Urgallus minor, or kind of Lagopus | 3. 1 | Pheasant. Mountain partridge | 3.409 |
| Columba passerina | Turtur minimus guttatus | 1.26 | Ground dove | 4.404 |
| Columba migratorio | Palumbus migratorius | 1.23 | Pigeon of passage. Wild pigeon | 4.351 |
| Columba Caroliniensis | Turtur Caroliniensis | 1.24 | Turtle. Turtle dove | 4.401 |
| Alauda alpestris | Alauda gutture flavo | 1.32 | Lark. Sky lark | 9.79 |
| Alauda magna | Alauda magna | 1.33 | Field lark. Large lark | 6.59 |
| | Sturnus niger allis superné rubentibus | 1.13 | Red wing. Starling. Marsh blackbird | 5.293 |
| Tardus migratorius | Turdus pilaris migratorius | 1.29 | Fieldfare of Carolina. Robin redbreast | {5.426 9.257 |
| Tardus rufus | Turdus rufus | 1.28 | Fox colored thrush. Thrush | 5.449 |

| Linnæus | Catesby | | English name | Buffon |
|---|---|---|---|---|
| Tardus polyglottos | Turdus minor cinereo albus non maculatus | 1.27 | Mocking bird | 5.451 |
| | Turdus minimus | 1.31 | Little thrush | 5.400 |
| Ampelis garrulus. β | Garrulus Caroliniensis | 1.46 | Chatterer | 6.162 |
| Loxia Cardinalis | Coccothranstes rubra | 1.38 | Red bird. Virginia nightingale | 6.185 |
| Loxia Cærulea | Coccothranstes cærulea | 1.39 | Blue gross beak | 8.125 |
| Emberiza hyemalis | Passer nivalis | 1.36 | Snow bird | 8.47 |
| Emberiza Oryzivora | Hortulanus Caroliniensis | 1.14 | Rice bird | 8.49 |
| Emberiza Ciris | Fringilla tricolor | 1.44 | Painted finch | 7.247 |
| Tanagra cyanea | Linaria cærulea | 1.45 | Blue linnet | 7.122 |
| | Passerculus | 1.35 | Little sparrow | 7.120 |
| | Passer fuscus | 1.34 | Cowpen bird | 7.196 |
| Fringilla erythrophthalma | Passer niger oculis rubris | 1.34 | Towne bird | 7.201 |
| Fringilla tristis | Carduelis Americanus | 1.43 | American goldfinch. Lettuce bird | 7.297 |
| | Fringilla purpurea | 1.41 | Purple finch | 8.129 |
| Muscicapa crinita | Muscicapa cristata ventre luteo | 1.52 | Crested flycatcher | 8.379 |
| Muscicapa rubra | Muscicapa rubra | 1.56 | Summer red bird | 8.410 |
| Muscicapa ruticilla | Ruticilla Americana | 1.67 | Red start | {8.349 9.259 |
| Muscicapa Caroliniensis | Muscicapa vertice nigro | 1.66 | Cat bird | 8.372 |
| | Muscicapa nigrescens | 1.53 | Black cap flycatcher | 8.341 |
| | Muscicapa fusca | 1.54 | Little brown flycatcher | 8.344 |
| | Muscicapa oculis rubris | 1.54 | Red-eyed flycatcher | 8.337 |
| Motacilla Sialis | Rubicula Americana cærulea | 1.47 | Blue bird | 9.308 |
| Motacilla regulus | Regulus cristatus | 3.13 | Wren | 10.58 |
| Motacilla trochilus. β | Oenanthe Americana pectore luteo | 1.50 | Yellow breasted chat | 6.96 |
| Parus bicolor | Parus cristatus | 1.57 | Crested titmouse | 10.181 |
| Parus Americanus | Parus fringillaris | 1.64 | Finch creeper | 9.442 |
| Parus Virginianus | Parus uropygeo luteo | 1.58 | Yellow rump | 10.184 |
| | Parus cucullo nigro | 1.60 | Hooded titmouse | 10.183 |
| | Parus Americanus gutture luteo | 1.62 | Yellow throated creeper | |
| | Parus Caroliniensis | 1.63 | Yellow titmouse | 9.431 |
| Hirundo Pelasgia | Hirundo cauda aculeata Americana | 3. 8 | American swallow | 12.478 |
| Hirundo purpurea | Hirundo purpurea | 1.51 | Purple marten. House marten | 12.445 |
| Caprimulgus Éuropæus. α | Caprimulgus | 1. 8 | Goatsucker. Great bat | 12.243 |
| Caprimulgus Éuropæus. β | Caprimulgus minor Americanus | 3.16 | Whip poor Will | 12.246 |

Besides these, we have,

The Royston crow. Corvus cornix.
Crane. Ardea Canadensis.
House swallow. Hirundo rustica.
Ground swallow. Hirundo riparia.
Greatest gray eagle.
Smaller turkey buzzard, with a feathered head.
Greatest owl, or night hawk.
Wet hawk, which feeds flying.
Raven.
Water Pelican of the Mississippi, whose pouch holds a peck.
Swan.
Loon.
Cormorant.
Duck and mallard.
Widgeon.
Sheldrach, or Canvas back.
The Black head.
Ballcoot.
Sprigtail.
Didapper, or dopchick
Spoon-billed duck.
Water-witch.
Water-pheasant.
Mow-bird.
Blue Peter.
Water Wagtail.
Yellow-legged Snipe.
Squatting Snipe.
Small Plover.
Whistling Plover.
Woodcock.
Red bird, with black head, wings and tail.

And doubtless many others which have not yet been described and classed.

To this catalogue of our indigenous animals, I will add a short account of an anomaly of nature, taking place sometimes in the race of negroes brought from Africa, who, though black themselves, have, in rare instances, white children, called Albinos. I have known four of these myself, and have faithful accounts of three others. The circumstances in which all the individuals agree are these. They are of a pallid cadaverous white, untinged with red, without any colored spots or seams; their hair of the same kind of white, short, coarse, and curled as is that of the negro; all of them well formed, strong, healthy, perfect in their senses, except that of sight, and born of parents who had no mixture of white blood. Three of these Albinos were sisters, having two other full sisters, who were black. The youngest of the three was killed by lightning, at twelve years of age. The eldest died at about 27 years of age, in child-bed, with her second child. The middle one is now alive, in health, and has issue, as the eldest had, by a black man, which issue was black. They are uncommonly shrewd, quick in their apprehensions and in reply. Their eyes are in a perpetual tremulous vibration, very weak, and much affected by the sun; but they see much better in the night than we do. They are of the property of Colonel Skipwith, of Cumberland. The fourth is a negro woman, whose parents came from Guinea, and had three other children, who were of their own color. She is freckled, her eye-sight so weak that she is obliged to wear a bonnet in the summer; but it is better in the night than day. She had an Albino child by a black man. It died at the age of a few weeks. These were the property of Col. Carter, of Albemarle. A sixth instance is a woman the property of a Mr. Butler, near Petersburg. She is stout and robust, has issue a daughter, jet black, by a black man. I am not informed as to her eye-sight. The seventh instance is of a male belonging to a Mr. Lee of Cumberland. His eyes are tremulous and weak. He is tall of stature, and now advanced in years. He is the only male of the Albinos which have come within my information. Whatever be the cause of the disease in the skin, or in its coloring matter, which produces this change, it seems more incident to the female than male sex. To these I may add the mention of a negro man within my own knowledge, born black, and of black parents; on whose chin, when a boy, a white spot appeared. This continued to increase till he became a man, by which time it had extended over his chin, lips, one cheek, the under jaw, and neck on that side. It is of the Albino white, without any mixture of red, and has for several years been stationary. He is robust and healthy, and the change of color was not accompanied with any sensible disease, either general or topical.

Of our fish and insects there has been nothing like a full description or collection. More of them are described in Catesby than in any other work. Many also are to be found in Sir Hans Sloane's Jamaica, as being common to that and this country. The honey-bee is not a native of our continent. Marcgrave, indeed, mentions a species of honey-bee in Brazil. But this has no sting, and is therefore different from the one we have, which resembles perfectly that of Europe. The Indians concur with us in the tradition that it was brought from Europe; but when, and by whom, we know not. The bees have generally extended themselves into the country, a little in advance of the white settlers. The Indians, therefore, call them the white man's fly, and consider their approach as indicating the approach of the settlements of the whites. A question here occurs, How far northwardly have these insects been found? That they are unknown in Lapland, I infer from Scheffer's information, that the Laplanders eat the pine bark, prepared in a certain way, instead of those things sweetened with sugar. *"Hoc comedunt pro rebus saccharo conditis."* Scheff. Lapp. c. 18. Certainly if they had honey, it would be a better substitute for sugar than any preparation of the pine bark. Kalm tells us [43] the honey-bee cannot live through the winter in Canada. They furnish then an additional fact first observed by the Count de Buffon, and which has thrown such a blaze of light on the field of natural history, that no animals are found in both continents, but those which are able to bear the cold of those regions where they probably join.

## QUERY VII

*A notice of all that can increase the progress of Human Knowledge*

Under the latitude of this query, I will presume it not improper nor unacceptable to furnish some data for estimating the climate of Virginia. Journals of observations on the quantity of rain, and degree of heat, being lengthy, confused, and too minute to produce general and distinct ideas, I have taken five years' observations, to wit, from 1772 to 1777, made in Williamsburg and its neighborhood, have reduced them to an average for every month in the year,

[43] I. 126.—T. J.

and stated those averages in the following table, adding an analytical view of the winds during the same period.

The rains of every month, (as of January, for instance,) through the whole period of years, were added separately, and an average drawn from them. The coolest and warmest point of the same day in each year of the period, were added separately, and an average of the greatest cold and greatest heat of that day was formed. From the averages of every day in the month, a general average was formed. The point from which the wind blew, was observed two or three times in every day. These observations, in the month of January, for instance, through the whole period, amounted to three hundred and thirty-seven. At seventy-three of these, the wind was from the north; forty-seven from the north-east, &c. So that it will be easy to see in what proportion each wind usually prevails in each month; or, taking the whole year, the total of observations through the whole period having been three thousand six hundred and ninety-eight, it will be observed that six hundred and eleven of them were from the north, five hundred and fifty-eight from the north-east, &c.

| | FALL OF RAIN, ETC., IN INCHES | LEAST AND GREATEST DAILY HEAT, BY FAHRENHEIT'S THERMOMETER | WINDS | | | | | | | | |
|---|---|---|---|---|---|---|---|---|---|---|---|
| | | | N. | N.E. | E. | S.E. | S. | S.W. | W. | N.W. | TOTAL |
| Jan. | 3.192 | 38½ to 44 | 73 | 47 | 32 | 10 | 11 | 78 | 40 | 46 | 337 |
| Feb. | 2.049 | 41 .. 47½ | 61 | 52 | 24 | 11 | 4 | 63 | 30 | 31 | 276 |
| March | 3.95 | 48 .. 54½ | 49 | 44 | 38 | 28 | 14 | 83 | 29 | 33 | 318 |
| April | 3.68 | 56 .. 62½ | 35 | 44 | 54 | 19 | 9 | 58 | 18 | 20 | 257 |
| May | 2.871 | 63 .. 70½ | 27 | 36 | 62 | 23 | 7 | 74 | 32 | 20 | 281 |
| June | 3.751 | 71½ .. 78¼ | 22 | 34 | 43 | 24 | 13 | 81 | 25 | 25 | 267 |
| July | 4.497 | 77 .. 82½ | 41 | 44 | 75 | 15 | 7 | 95 | 32 | 19 | 328 |
| August | 9.153 | 76¼ .. 81 | 43 | 52 | 40 | 30 | 9 | 103 | 27 | 30 | 334 |
| Sept. | 4.761 | 69½ .. 74¼ | 70 | 60 | 51 | 18 | 10 | 81 | 18 | 37 | 345 |
| Oct. | 3.633 | 61¼ .. 66½ | 52 | 77 | 64 | 15 | 6 | 56 | 23 | 34 | 327 |
| Nov. | 2.617 | 47¾ .. 53½ | 74 | 21 | 20 | 14 | 9 | 63 | 35 | 58 | 294 |
| Dec. | 2.877 | 43 .. 48¾ | 64 | 37 | 18 | 16 | 10 | 91 | 42 | 56 | 334 |
| Total | 47.038 | 8 A.M. to 4 P.M. | 611 | 548 | 521 | 223 | 109 | 926 | 351 | 409 | 3,698 |

Though by this table it appears we have on an average forty-seven inches of rain annually, which is considerably more than usually falls in Europe, yet from the information I have collected, I suppose we have a much greater proportion of sunshine here than there. Perhaps it will be found, there are twice as many cloudy days in the middle parts of Europe, as in the United States of America. I mention the middle parts of Europe, because my information does not extend to its northern or southern parts.

In an extensive country, it will of course be expected that the climate is not the same in all its parts. It is remarkable, that proceeding on the same parallel of latitude westwardly, the climate becomes colder in like manner as when you proceed northwardly. This continues to be the case till you attain the summit of the Alleghany, which is the highest land between the ocean and the Mississippi. From thence, descending in the same latitude to the Mississippi, the change reverses; and, if we may believe travellers, it becomes warmer there than it is in the same latitude on the sea-side. Their testimony is strengthened by the vegetables and animals which subsist and multiply there naturally, and do not on the sea-coast. Thus Catalpas grow spontaneously on the Mississippi, as far as the latitude of 37°, and reeds as far as 38°. Parroquets even winter on the Scioto, in the 39th degree of latitude. In the summer of 1779, when the thermometer was at 90° at Monticello, and 96° at Williamsburg, it was 110° at Kaskaskia. Perhaps the mountain, which overhangs this village on the north side, may, by its reflection, have contributed somewhat to produce this heat. The difference of temperature of the air at the sea-coast, or on the Chesapeake bay, and at the Alleghany, has not been ascertained; but contemporary observations, made at Williamsburg, or in its neighborhood, and at Monticello, which is on the most eastern ridge of the mountains, called the South-West, where they are intersected by the Rivanna, have furnished a ratio by which that difference may in some degree be conjectured. These observations make the difference between Williamsburg and the nearest mountains, at the position before mentioned, to be on an average 6⅓° of Fahrenheit's thermometer. Some allowance, however, is to be made for the difference of latitude between these two places, the latter being 38° 8′ 17″, which is 52′ 22″ north of the former. By contemporary observations of between five and six weeks, the averaged and almost unvaried difference of the height of mercury in the barometer, at those two places, was .784 of an inch, the atmosphere at Monticello being so much the lightest, that is to say, about one-thirty-seventh of its whole weight. It should be observed, however, that the hill of Monticello is of five hundred feet perpendicular height above the river which washes its base. This position being nearly central between our northern and southern boundaries, and between the bay and Alleghany, may be considered as furnishing the best average of the temperature of our climate. Williamsburg is much too near the south-eastern corner to give a fair idea of our general temperature.

But a more remarkable difference is in the winds which prevail in the different parts of the country. The following table exhibits a comparative view of the winds prevailing at Williamsburg, and at Monticello. It is formed by reducing nine months' observations at Monticello to four principal points, to wit, the north-east, south-east, south-west, and north-west; these points being perpendicular to, or parallel with our coast, mountains, and rivers; and by reducing in like manner, an equal number of observations, to wit, four hundred and twenty-one from the preceding table of winds at Williamsburg, taking them proportionably from every point:

| | N.E. | S.E. | S.W. | N.W. | TOTAL |
|---|---|---|---|---|---|
| Williamsburg | 127 | 61 | 132 | 101 | 421 |
| Monticello | 32 | 91 | 126 | 172 | 421 |

By this it may be seen that the south-west wind prevails equally at both places; that the north-east is, next to this, the principal wind towards the sea-coast, and the north-west is the predominant wind at the mountains. The difference between these two winds to sensation, and in fact, is very great. The north-east is loaded with vapor, insomuch, that the salt-makers have found that their crystals would not shoot while that blows; it brings a distressing chill, and is heavy and oppressive to the spirits. The north-west is dry, cooling, elastic, and animating. The eastern and south-eastern breezes come on generally in the afternoon. They have advanced into the country very sensibly within the memory of people now living. They formerly did not penetrate far above Williamsburg. They are now frequent at Richmond, and every now and then reach the mountains. They deposit most of their moisture, however, before they get that far. As the lands become more cleared, it is probable they will extend still further westward.

Going out into the open air, in the temperate, and warm months of the year, we often meet with bodies of warm air, which passing by us in two or three seconds, do not afford time to the most sensible thermometer to seize their temperature. Judging from my feelings only, I think they approach the ordinary heat of the human body. Some of them, perhaps, go a little beyond it. They are of about twenty to thirty feet diameter horizontally. Of their height we have no experience, but probably they are globular volumes wafted or rolled along with the wind. But whence taken, where found, or how generated? They are not to be ascribed to volcanoes, because we have none. They do not happen in the winter when the farmers kindle large fires in clearing up their grounds. They are not confined to the spring season, when we have fires which traverse whole counties, consuming the leaves which have fallen from the trees. And they are too frequent and general to be ascribed to accidental fires. I am persuaded their cause must be sought for in the atmosphere itself, to aid us in which I know but of these constant circumstances: a dry air; a temperature as warm, at least, as that of the spring or autumn; and a moderate current of wind. They are most frequent about sun-set; rare in the middle parts of the day; and I do not recollect having ever met with them in the morning.

The variation in the weight of our atmosphere, as indicated by the barometer, is not equal to two inches of mercury. During twelve months' observation at Williamsburg, the extremes 29 and 30.86 inches, the difference being 1.86 of an inch; and in nine months, during which the height of the mercury was noted at Monticello, the extremes were 28.48 and 29.69 inches, the variation being 1.21 of an inch. A gentleman, who has observed his barometer many years, assures me it has never varied two inches. Contemporary observations made at Monticello and Williamsburg, proved the variations in the weight of air to be simultaneous and corresponding in these two places.

Our changes from heat to cold, and cold to heat, are very sudden and great. The mercury in Fahrenheit's thermometer has been known to descend from 92° to 47° in thirteen hours.

It was taken for granted, that the preceding table of average heat will not give a false idea on this subject, as it proposes to state only the ordinary heat and cold of each month, and not those which are extraordinary. At Williamsburg, in August 1766, the mercury in Fahrenheit's thermometer was at 98°, corresponding with 29⅓ of Reaumur. At the same place in January 1780, it was 6°, corresponding with 11½ below zero of Reaumur. I believe[44] these may be considered to be nearly the extremes of heat and cold in that part of the country. The latter may most certainly, as that time York river, at Yorktown, was frozen over, so that people walked across it; a circumstance which proves it to have been colder than the winter of 1740, 1741, usually called the cold winter, when York river did not freeze over at that place. In the same season of 1780, Chesapeake bay was solid, from its head to the mouth of Potomac. At Annapolis, where it is 5¼ miles over between the nearest points of land, the ice was from five to seven inches thick quite across, so that loaded carriages went over on it. Those, our extremes of heat and cold, of 6° and 98°, were indeed very distressing to us, and were thought to put the extent of the human constitution to considerable trial. Yet a Siberian would have considered them as scarcely a sensible variation. At Jenniseitz in that country, in latitude 58° 27′, we are told that the cold in 1735 sunk the mercury by Fahrenheit's scale to 126° below nothing; and the inhabitants of the same country use stove rooms two or three times a week, in which they stay two hours at a time, the atmosphere of which raises the mercury to 135° above nothing. Late experiments show that the human body will exist in rooms heated to 140° of Reaumur, equal to 347° of Fahrenheit's, and 135° above boiling water. The hottest point of the twenty-four hours is about four o'clock, P. M., and the dawn of day the coldest.

The access of frost in autumn, and its recess the spring, do not seem to depend merely on the degree of cold; much less on the air's being at the freezing point. White frosts are frequent when the thermometer is at 47°, have killed young plants of Indian corn at 48°, and have been known at 54°. Black frost, and even ice, have been produced at 38½°, which is 6½ degrees above the freezing point. That other circumstances must be combined with this cold to produce frost, is evident from this also, on the higher parts of mountains, where it is absolutely colder than in the plains on which they stand, frosts do not appear so early by a considerable space of time in autumn, and go off sooner in the spring, than in the plains. I have known frosts so severe as to kill the hickory trees round about Monticello, and yet not injure the tender fruit blossoms then in bloom on the top and higher parts of the mountain; and in the course of forty years, during which it had been settled, there have been but two instances of a general loss of fruit on it; while in the circumjacent country, the fruit has escaped but twice in the last seven years. The plants of tobacco, which grow from the roots of those which have been cut off in the summer, are frequently green here at Christmas. This privilege against the frost is undoubtedly combined with the want of dew on the mountains. That the dew is very rare on their higher parts, I may say with certainty, from twelve years' observations, having scarcely ever, during that time, seen an unequivocal proof of its existence on them at all during summer. Severe frosts

[44] At Paris, in 1753, the mercury in Reaumur's thermometer was at 30½ above zero, and in 1776, it was at 16 below zero. The extremities of heat and cold therefore at Paris, are greater than at Williamsburg, which is in the hottest part of Virginia.—T. J.

in the depth of winter prove that the region of dews extends higher in that season than the tops of the mountains; but certainly, in the summer season, the vapors, by the time they attain that height, are so attenuated as not to subside and form a dew when the sun retires.

The weavil has not yet ascended the high mountains.

A more satisfactory estimate of our climate to some, may perhaps be formed, by noting the plants which grow here, subject, however, to be killed by our severest colds. These are the fig, pomegranate, artichoke, and European walnut. In mild winters, lettuce and endive require no shelter; but, generally, they need a slight covering. I do not know that the want of long moss, reed, myrtle, swamp laurel, holly, and cypress, in the upper country proceeds from a greater degree of cold, nor that they were ever killed with any degree of cold, nor that they were ever killed with any degree of cold in the lower country. The aloe lived in Williamsburg, in the open air, through the severe winter of 1779, 1780.

A change in our climate, however, is taking place very sensibly. Both heats and colds are become much more moderate within the memory even of the middle-aged. Snows are less frequent and less deep. They do not often lie, below the mountains, more than one, two, or three days, and very rarely a week. They are remembered to have been formerly frequent, deep, and of long continuance. The elderly inform me, the earth used to be covered with snow about three months in every year. The rivers, which then seldom failed to freeze over in the course of the winter, scarcely ever do so now. This change has produced an unfortunate fluctuation between heat and cold, in the spring of the year, which is very fatal to fruits. From the year 1741 to 1769, an interval of twenty-eight years, there was no instance of fruit killed by the frost in the neighborhood of Monticello. An intense cold, produced by constant snows, kept the buds locked up till the sun could obtain, in the spring of the year, so fixed an ascendency as to dissolve those snows, and protect the buds, during their development, from every danger of returning cold. The accumulated snows of the winter remaining to be dissolved all together in the spring, produced those overflowings of our rivers, so frequent then, and so rare now.

Having had occasion to mention the particular situation of Monticello for other purposes, I will just take notice that its elevation affords an opportunity of seeing a phenomenon which is rare at land, though frequent at sea. The seamen call it *looming*. Philosophy is as yet in the rear of the seamen, for so far from having accounted for it, she has not given it a name. Its principal effect is to make distant objects appear larger, in opposition to the general law of vision, by which they are diminished. I knew an instance, at Yorktown, from whence the water prospect eastwardly is without termination, wherein a canoe with three men, at a great distance was taken for a ship with its three masts. I am little acquainted with the phenomenon as it shows itself at sea; but at Monticello it is familiar. There is a solitary mountain about forty miles off in the South, whose natural shape, as presented to view there, is a regular cone; but by the effect of looming, it sometimes subsides almost totally in the horizon; sometimes it rises more acute and more elevated; sometimes it is hemispherical;

and sometimes its sides are perpendicular, its top flat, and as broad as its base. In short, it assumes at times the most whimsical shapes, and all these perhaps successively in the same morning. The blue ridge of mountains comes into view, in the north-east, at about one hundred miles distance, and approaching in a direct line, passes by within twenty miles, and goes off to the south-west. This phenomenon begins to show itself on these mountains, at about fifty miles distance, and continues beyond that as far as they are seen. I remark no particular state, either in the weight, moisture, or heat of the atmosphere, necessary to produce this. The only constant circumstances are its appearance in the morning only, and on objects at least forty or fifty miles distant. In this latter circumstance, if not in both, it differs from the looming on the water. Refraction will not account for the metamorphosis. That only changes the proportions of length and breadth, base and altitude, preserving the general outlines. Thus it may make a circle appear elliptical, raise or depress a cone, but by none of its laws, as yet developed, will it make a circle appear a square, or a cone a sphere.

## QUERY VIII

### *The number of its inhabitants*

The table on page 624 shows the number of persons imported for the establishment of our colony in its infant state, and the census of inhabitants at different periods, extracted from our historians and public records, as particularly as I have had opportunities and leisure to examine them. Successive lines in the same year show successive periods of time in that year. I have stated the census in two different columns, the whole inhabitants having been sometimes numbered, and sometimes the *tythes* only. This term, with us, includes the free males above sixteen years of age, and slaves above that age of both sexes. A further examination of our records would render this history of our population much more satisfactory and perfect, by furnishing a greater number of intermediate terms. These, however, which are here stated will enable us to calculate, with a considerable degree of precision, the rate at which we have increased. During the infancy of the colony, while numbers were small, wars, importations, and other accidental circumstances render the progression fluctuating and irregular. By the year 1654, however, it becomes tolerably uniform, importations having in a great measure ceased from the dissolution of the company, and the inhabitants become too numerous to be sensibly affected by Indian wars. Beginning at that period, therefore, we find that from thence to the year 1772, our tythes had increased from 7,209 to 153,000. The whole term being of one hundred and eighteen years, yields a duplication once in every twenty-seven and a quarter years. The intermediate enumerations taken in 1700, 1748, and 1759, furnish proofs of the uniformity of this progression. Should this rate of increase continue, we shall have between six and seven millions of inhabitants within ninety-five years. If we suppose our country to be bounded, at some future day, by the meridian of the mouth of the Great Kanhaway, (within which it has been before conjectured, are 64,461 square miles) there will then be one hundred inhabitants for every square mile, which is nearly the state of population in the British Islands.

| YEARS | SETTLERS IMPORTED | CENSUS OF INHABITANTS | CENSUS OF TYTHES |
|---|---|---|---|
| 1607 | 100 | .... | .... |
| .. | .... | 40 | .... |
| .. | 120 | .... | .... |
| 1608 | .... | 130 | .... |
| .. | 70 | .... | .... |
| 1609 | .... | 490 | .... |
| .. | 16 | .... | .... |
| .. | .... | 60 | .... |
| 1610 | 150 | .... | .... |
| .. | .... | 200 | .... |
| 1611 | 3 ship loads. | .... | .... |
| .. | 300 | .... | .... |
| 1612 | 80 | .... | .... |
| 1617 | .... | 400 | .... |
| 1618 | 200 | .... | .... |
| .. | 40 | .... | .... |
| .. | .... | 600 | .... |
| 1619 | 1,216 | .... | .... |
| 1621 | 1,300 | .... | .... |
| 1622 | .... | 3,800 | .... |
| .. | .... | 2,500 | .... |
| 1628 | .... | 3,000 | .... |
| 1632 | .... | .... | 2,000 |
| 1644 | .... | .... | 4,822 |
| 1645 | .... | .... | 5,000 |
| 1652 | .... | .... | 7,000 |
| 1654 | .... | .... | 7,209 |
| 1700 | .... | .... | 22,000 |
| 1748 | .... | .... | 82,100 |
| 1759 | .... | .... | 105,000 |
| 1772 | .... | .... | 153,000 |
| 1782 | .... | 567,614 | .... |

Here I will beg leave to propose a doubt. The present desire of America is to produce rapid population by as great importations of foreigners as possible. But is this founded in good policy? The advantage proposed is the multiplication of numbers. Now let us suppose (for example only) that, in this state, we could double our numbers in one year by the importation of foreigners; and this is a greater accession than the most sanguine advocate for emigration has a right to expect. Then I say, beginning with a double stock, we shall attain any given degree of population only twenty-seven years, and three months sooner than if we proceed on our single stock. If we propose four millions and a half as a competent population for this State, we should be fifty-four and a half years attaining it, could we at once double our numbers; and eighty-one and three quarter years, if we rely on natural propagation, as may be seen by the following table:

| | PROCEEDING ON OUR PRESENT STOCK | PROCEEDING ON A DOUBLE STOCK |
|---|---|---|
| 1781 | 567,614 | 1,135,228 |
| 1808¼ | 1,135,228 | 2,270,456 |
| 1835½ | 2,270,456 | 4,540,912 |
| 1862¾ | 4,540,912 | |

In the first column are stated periods of twenty-seven and a quarter years; in the second are our numbers at each period, as they will be if we proceed on our actual stock; and in the third are what they would be, at the same periods, were we to set out from the double of our present stock. I have taken the term of four million and a half of inhabitants for example's sake only. Yet I am persuaded it is a greater number than the country spoken of, considering how much inarable land it contains, can clothe and feed without a material change in the quality of their diet. But are there no inconveniences to be thrown into the scale against the advantage expected from a multiplication of numbers by the importation of foreigners? It is for the happiness of those united in society to harmonize as much as possible in matters which they must of necessity transact together. Civil government being the sole object of forming societies, its administration must be conducted by common consent. Every species of government has its specific principles. Ours perhaps are more peculiar than those of any other in the universe. It is a composition of the freest principles of the English constitution, with others derived from natural right and natural reason. To these nothing can be more opposed than the maxims of absolute monarchies. Yet from such we are to expect the greatest number of emigrants. They will bring with them the principles of the governments they leave, imbibed in their early youth; or, if able to throw them off, it will be in exchange for an unbounded licentiousness, passing, as is usual, from one extreme to another. It would be a miracle were they to stop precisely at the point of temperate liberty. These principles, with their language, they will transmit to their children. In proportion to their numbers, they will share with us the legislation. They will infuse into it their spirit, warp and bias its directions, and render it a heterogenious, incoherent, distracted mass. I may appeal to experience, during the present contest, for a verification of these conjectures. But, if they be not certain in event, are they not possible, are they not probable? Is it not safer to wait with patience twenty-seven years and three months longer, for the attainment of any degree of population desired or expected? May not our government be more homogeneous, more peaceable, more durable? Suppose twenty millions of republican Americans thrown all of a sudden into France, what would be the condition of that kingdom? If it would be more turbulent, less happy, less strong, we may believe that the addition of half a million of foreigners to our present numbers would produce a similar effect here. If they come of themselves they are entitled to all the rights of citizenship; but I doubt the expediency of inviting them by extraordinary encouragements. I mean not that these doubts should be extended to the importation of useful artificers. The policy of that measure depends on very different considerations. Spare no expense in obtaining them. They will after a while go to the plough and the hoe; but, in the mean time, they will teach us something we do not know. It is not so in agriculture. The indifferent state of that among us does not proceed from a want of knowledge merely; it is from our having such quantities of land to waste as we please. In Europe the object is to make the most of their land, labor being abundant; here it is to make the most of our labor, land being abundant.

It will be proper to explain how the numbers for the year 1782 have been obtained; as it was not from a perfect census of the inhabitants. It will at the same time develope the proportion between the free inhabitants and slaves. The following return of taxable articles for that year was given in.

53,289 free males above twenty-one years of age.
211,698 slaves of all ages and sexes.
23,766 not distinguished in the returns, but said to be tytheable slaves.
195,439 horses.
609,734 cattle.
5,126 wheels of riding-carriages.
191 taverns.

There were no returns from the eight counties of Lincoln, Jefferson, Fayette, Monongahela, Yohogania, Ohio, Northampton, and York. To find the number of slaves which should have been returned instead of the 23,766 tytheables, we must mention that some observations on a former census had given reason to believe that the numbers above and below sixteen years of age were equal. The double of this number, therefore, to wit, 47,532 must be added to 211,698, which will give us 259,230 slaves of all ages and sexes. To find the number of free inhabitants we must repeat the observation that those above and below sixteen are nearly equal. But as the number 53,289 omits the males below sixteen and twenty-one we must supply them from conjecture. On a former experiment it had appeared that about one-third of our militia, that is, of the males between sixteen and fifty, were unmarried. Knowing how early marriage takes place here, we shall not be far wrong in supposing that the unmarried part of our militia are those between sixteen and twenty-one. If there be young men who do not marry till after twenty-one, there are many who marry before that age. But as men above fifty were not included in the militia, we will suppose the unmarried, or those between sixteen and twenty-one, to be one-fourth of the whole number above sixteen, then we have the following calculation:

53,289 free males above twenty-one years of age.
17,763 free males between sixteen and twenty-one.

17,052 free males under sixteen.
142,104 free males of all ages.

---

284,208 free inhabitants of all ages.
259,230 slaves of all ages.

---

543,438 inhabitants, exclusive of the eight counties from which were no returns. In these eight counties in the years 1779 and 1780, were 3,161 militia. Say then,

3,161 free males above the age of sixteen.
3,161 free males under sixteen.
6,322 free females.

---

12,644 free inhabitants in these eight counties. To find the number of slaves, say, as 284,208 to 259,230, so is 12,644 to 11,532. Adding the third of these numbers to the first, and the fourth to the second, we have,

296,852 free inhabitants.
270,762 slaves.

---

567,614 inhabitants of every age, sex and condition. But 296,852, the number of free inhabitants, are to 270,762, the number of slaves, nearly as 11 to 10. Under the mild treatment our slaves experience, and their wholesome, though coarse food, this blot in our country increases as fast, or faster than the whites. During the regal government we had at one time obtained a law which imposed such a duty on the importation of slaves as amounted nearly to a prohibition, when one inconsiderate assembly, placed under a peculiarity of circumstance, repealed the law. This repeal met a joyful sanction from the then reigning sovereign, and no devices, no expedients, which could ever be attempted by subsequent assemblies, and they seldom met without attempting them, could succeed in getting the royal assent to a renewal of the duty. In the very first session held under the republican government, the assembly passed a law for the perpetual prohibition of the importation of slaves. This will in some measure stop the increase of this great political and moral evil, while the minds of our citizens may be ripening for a complete emancipation of human nature.

## QUERY IX

*The number and condition of the Militia and Regular Troops, and their Pay*

The following is a state of the militia, taken from returns of 1780 and 1781, except in those counties marked with an asterisk, the returns from which are somewhat older.

Every able-bodied freeman, between the ages of sixteen and fifty, is enrolled in the militia. Those of every county are formed into companies, and these again into one or more battalions, according to the numbers in the county. They are commanded by colonels, and other subordinate officers, as in the regular service. In every county is a county-lieutenant, who commands the whole militia of his county, but ranks only as a colonel in the field. We have no general officers always existing. These are appointed occasionally, when an invasion or insurrection happens, and their commission determines with the occasion. The governor is head of the military, as well as civil power. The law requires every militia-man to provide himself with the arms usual in the regular

| SITUATION | COUNTIES | MILITIA |
|---|---|---|
| Westward of the Alleghany. 4,458 | Lincoln | 600 |
| | Jefferson | 300 |
| | Fayette | 156 |
| | Ohio | . . |
| | Monongalia | * 1,000 |
| | Washington | * 829 |
| | Montgomery | 1,071 |
| | Greenbriar | 502 |
| Between the Alleghany and Blue Ridge. 7,673 | Hampshire | 930 |
| | Berkeley | * 1,100 |
| | Frederick | 1,143 |
| | Shenando | * 925 |
| | Rockingham | 875 |
| | Augusta | 1,375 |
| | Rockbridge | * 625 |
| | Boutetourt | * 700 |
| Between the Blue Ridge and Tide Waters. 18,828 | Loudoun | 1,746 |
| | Faquier | 1,078 |
| | Culpepper | 1,513 |
| | Spotsylvania | 480 |
| | Orange | * 600 |
| | Louisa | 603 |
| | Goochland | * 550 |
| | Fluvanna | * 296 |
| | Albemarle | 873 |
| | Amherst | 896 |
| | Buckingham | * 625 |
| | Bedford | 1,300 |
| | Henry | 1,004 |
| | Pittsylvania | * 725 |
| | Halifax | * 1,139 |
| | Charlotte | 612 |
| | Prince Edward | 589 |
| | Cumberland | 408 |
| | Powhatan | 330 |
| | Amelia | * 1,125 |
| | Lunenburg | 677 |
| | Mecklenburg | 1,100 |
| | Brunswick | 559 |

| SITUATION | | COUNTIES | MILITIA |
|---|---|---|---|
| On the Tide Waters, and in that Parallel. 19,012 | Between James River and Carolina. 6,959 | Greensville | 500 |
| | | Dinwiddie | * 750 |
| | | Chesterfield | 665 |
| | | Prince George | 328 |
| | | Surrey | 380 |
| | | Sussex | * 700 |
| | | Southampton | 874 |
| | | Isle of White | * 600 |
| | | Nansemond | * 644 |
| | | Norfolk | * 880 |
| | | Prince Anne | * 594 |
| | Between James & York rivers. 3,009 | Henrico | 619 |
| | | Hanover | 706 |
| | | New Kent | * 418 |
| | | Charles City | 286 |
| | | James City | 235 |
| | | Williamsburgh | 129 |
| | | York | * 244 |
| | | Warwick | * 100 |
| | | Elizabeth City | 182 |
| | Bet. York & Rappa-hannock. 3,269 | Caroline | 805 |
| | | King William | 436 |
| | | King and Queen | 500 |
| | | Essex | 468 |
| | | Middlesex | * 210 |
| | | Gloucester | 850 |
| | Betw'n Rappahannock and Powtomac. 4,137 | Fairfax | 652 |
| | | Prince William | 614 |
| | | Stafford | * 500 |
| | | King George | 483 |
| | | Richmond | 412 |
| | | Westmoreland | 544 |
| | | Northumberland | 630 |
| | | Lancaster | 332 |
| | East'n shore. 1,638 | Accomac | * 1,208 |
| | | Northampton | * 430 |
| | Whole Militia of the State | | 49,971 |

service. But this injunction was always indifferently complied with, and the arms they had, have been so frequently called for to arm the regulars, that in the lower parts of the country they are entirely disarmed. In the middle country a fourth or fifth part of them may have such firelocks as they had provided to destroy the noxious animals which infest their farms; and on the western side of the Blue ridge they are generally armed with rifles. The pay of our militia, as well as of our regulars, is that of the continental regulars. The condition of our regulars, of whom we have none but continentals, and part of a battalion of state troops, is so constantly on the change, that a state of it at this day would not be its state a month hence. It is much the same with the condition of the other continental troops, which is well enough known.

## QUERY X

### *The Marine*

Before the present invasion of this State by the British, under the command of General Phillips, we had three vessels of sixteen guns, one of fourteen, five small gallies, and two or three armed boats. They were generally so badly manned as seldom to be in a condition for service. Since the perfect possession of our rivers assumed by the enemy, I believe we are left with a single armed boat only.

## QUERY XI

### *A description of the Indians established in that State*

When the first effectual settlement of our colony was made, which was in 1607, the country from the sea-coast to the mountains, and from the Potomac to the most southern waters of James' river, was occupied by upwards of forty different tribes of Indians. Of these the *Powhatans,* the *Mannahoacs,* and *Monacans,* were the most powerful. Those between the seacoast and falls of the rivers, were in amity with one another, and attached to the *Powhatans* as their link of union. Those between the falls of the rivers and the mountains, were divided into two confederacies; the tribes inhabiting the head waters of Potomac and Rappahannock, being attached to the *Mannahoacs;* and those on the upper parts of James' river to the *Monacans.* But the *Monacans* and their friends were in amity with the *Mannahoacs* and their friends, and waged joint and perpetual war against the *Powhatans.* We are told that the *Powhatans, Mannahoacs,* and *Monacans,* spoke languages so radically different, that interpreters were necessary when they transacted business. Hence we may conjecture, that this was not the case between all the tribes, and, probably, that each spoke the language of the nation to which it was attached; which we know to have been the case in many particular instances. Very possibly there may have been anciently three different stocks, each of which multiplying in a long course of time, had separated into so many little societies. This practice results from the circumstance of their having never submitted themselves to any laws, any coercive power, any shadow of government. Their only controls are their manners, and that moral sense of right and wrong, which, like the sense of tasting and feeling in every man, makes a part of his nature. An offence against these is punished by contempt, by exclusion from society, or, where the case is serious, as that of murder, by the individuals whom it concerns. Imperfect as this species

NORTH

WEST

## MANNAHOACS

| | TRIBES | COUNTRY | CF. TOWNS | WARRIORS 1669 |
|---|---|---|---|---|
| Between Patowmac and Rappahannoc. | Whonkenties. | Fauquier. | | |
| | Tegninaties. | Culpepper. | | |
| | Ontponies. | Orange. | | |
| | Tauxitanians. | Fauquier. | | |
| | Hassinungaes. | Culpepper. | | |
| Bet. Rappahannoc & York. | Stegarakies. | Orange. | | |
| | Shackakonies. | Spotsylvania. | | |
| | Manahoacs. | Stafford. | | |
| | | Spotsylvania. | | |
| | **MONACANS** | | | |
| Between York and James. | Monacans. | James river, above the falls. | Fork of James river. | 30 |
| | Monasiccapanoes. | Louisa. | | |
| | | Fluvanna. | | |
| Between James & Carolina. | Monahassanoes. | Bedford. | | |
| | | Buckingham. | | |
| | Massinacacs. | Cumberland. | | |
| | Mohemenchoes. | Powhatan. | | |
| Eastern shore. | | | | |

## POWHATANS

| TRIBES | COUNTRY | CHIEF TOWNS | WARRIORS 1607 | WARRIORS 1669 | |
|---|---|---|---|---|---|
| Tauxenents. | Fairfax. | About Gen. Washington's. | 40 | | |
| Patówomekes. | Stafford. King George. | Pawtomac cr. | 200 | | |
| Cuttatawomans. | King George. | About Lamb creek. | 20 | 60 | By the name of Matchotics, U. Matchodic, Nanzaticos, Nanzatico, Appomatox, Matox. |
| Pissasecs. | King George. Richmond. | Above Leeds Town. | .. | | |
| Onaumanients. | Westmoreland. | Nomony river. | 100 | | |
| Rappahànocs. | Richmond co. | Rappahanoc creek. | 100 | 30 | |
| Moàughtacunds. | Lancaster. Richmond. | Moratico river. | 80 | 40 | By the name of Totuskeys |
| Secacaconies. | Northumberland. | Coan river. | 30 | | |
| Wighcocòmicoes. | Northumberland. | Wicocomico river. | 130 | 70 | |
| Cuttatawomans. | Lancaster. | Corotoman. | 30 | | |
| Nantaughtacunds. | Essex. Caroline. | Port Tobacco creek. | 150 | 60 | |
| Màttapomènts. | Mattapony river. | . . . . . . . . | 30 | 20 | |
| Pamùnkies. | King William. | Romuncock. | 300 | 50 | |
| Wèrowocòmicos. | Gloucester. | About Rosewell. | 40 | | |
| Payànkatonks. | Piankatank river. | Turk's Ferry. Grimesby. | 55 | | |
| Youghtanunds. | Pamunkey river. | . . . . . . . . | 60 | | |
| Chickahòminies. | Chickahominy r. | Orapaks. | 250 | 60 | |
| Powhatàns. | Henrico. | Powhatan. Mayo's. | 40 | 10 | |
| Arrowhàtocs. | Henrico. | Arrohatocs. | 30 | | |
| Wèanocs. | Charles city. | Weynoke. | 100 | 15 | |
| Paspahèghes. | Charles city. James city. | Sandy-Point. | 40 | | |
| Chiskiacs. | York. | Chiskiac. | 45 | 15 | |
| Kecoughtáns. | Elizabeth city. | Roscows. | 20 | | |
| Appamàttocs. | Chesterfield. | Bermuda Hundred. | 60 | 50 | |
| Quiocohànoes. | Surry. | About Upp. Chipoak. | 25 | 3 Pohics | |
| Wàrrasqueaks. | Isle of Wight. | Warrasqueoc. | .. | | |
| Nasamónds. | Nansamond. | A't mouth W. branch. | 200 | 45 | |
| Chèsapeaks. | Princess Anne. | About Lynhaven riv. | 100 | | |
| Accohanocs. | Accom. Northampton. | Accohanoc river. | 40 | | |
| Accomàcks. | Northampton. | About Cheriton's. | 80 | | |

| | 1699 |
|---|---|
| Nottoways. | .. |
| Meherrics. | 90 |
| Tuteloes. | 50 |

EAST

SOUTH

of coercion may seem, crimes are very rare among them; insomuch that were it made a question, whether no law, as among the savage Americans, or too much law, as among the civilized Europeans, submits man to the greatest evil, one who has seen both conditions of existence would pronounce it to be the last; and that the sheep are happier of themselves, than under care of the wolves. It will be said, that great societies cannot exist without government. The savages, therefore, break them into small ones.

The territories of the *Powhatan* confederacy, south of the Potomac, comprehended about eight thousand square miles, thirty tribes, and two thousand four hundred warriors. Captain Smith tells us, that within sixty miles of Jamestown were five thousand people, of whom one thousand five hundred were warriors. From this we find the proportion of their warriors to their whole inhabitants, was as three to ten. The *Powhatan* confederacy, then, would consist of about eight thousand inhabitants, which was one for every square mile; being about the twentieth part of our present population in the same territory, and the hundredth of that of the British islands.

Besides these were the *Nottoways,* living on Nottoway river, the *Meherrins* and *Tuteloes* on Meherrin river, who were connected with the Indians of Carolina, probably with the Chowanocs.

The preceding table contains a state of these several tribes, according to their confederacies and geographical situation, with their numbers when we first became acquainted with them, where these numbers are known. The numbers of some of them are again stated as they were in the year 1669, when an attempt was made by assembly to enumerate them. Probably the enumeration is imperfect, and in some measure conjectural, and that a farther search into the records would furnish many more particulars. What would be the melancholy sequel of their history, may, however, be argued from the census of 1669; by which we discover that the tribes therein enumerated were, in the space of sixty-two years, reduced to about one-third of their former numbers. Spirituous liquors, the small-pox, war, and an abridgement of territory to a people who lived principally on the spontaneous productions of nature, had committed terrible havoc among them, which generation, under the obstacles opposed to it among them, was not likely to make good. That the lands of this country were taken from them by conquest, is not so general a truth as is supposed. I find in our historians and records, repeated proofs of purchase, which cover a considerable part of the lower country; and many more would doubtless be found on further search. The upper country, we know, has been acquired altogether by purchases made in the most unexceptional form.

Westward of all these tribes, beyond the mountains, and extending to the great lakes, were the *Maſſawomees,* a most powerful confederacy, who harassed unremittingly the *Powhatans* and *Manahoacs.* These were probably the ancestors of tribes known at present by the name of the *Six Nations.*

Very little can now be discovered of the subsequent history of these tribes severally. The *Chickahominies* removed about the year 1661, to Mattapony river. Their chief, with one from each of the Pamunkies and Mattaponies, attended the treaty of Albany in 1685. This seems to have been the last chapter in their history. They retained, however, their separate name so late as 1705, and were at length blended with the Pamunkies and Mattaponies, and exist at present only under their names. There remain of the *Mattaponies* three or four men only, and have more negro than Indian blood in them. They have lost their language, have reduced themselves, by voluntary sales, to about fifty acres of land, which lie on the river of their own name, and have from time to time, been joining the Pamunkies, from whom they are distant but ten miles. The *Pamunkies* are reduced to about ten or twelve men, tolerably pure from mixture with other colors. The older ones among them preserve their language in a small degree, which are the last vestiges on earth, as far as we know, of the Powhatan language. They have about three hundred acres of very fertile land, on Pamunkey river, so encompassed by water that a gate shuts in the whole. Of the *Nottoways,* not a male is left. A few women constitute the remains of that tribe. They are seated on Nottoway river, in Southampton country, on very fertile lands. At a very early period, certain lands were marked out and appropriated to these tribes, and were kept from encroachment by the authority of the laws. They have usually had trustees appointed, whose duty was to watch over their interests, and guard them from insult and injury.

The *Monacans* and their friends, better known latterly by the name of *Tuscaroras,* were probably connected with the Massawomecs, or Five Nations. For though we are[45] told their languages were so different that the intervention of interpreters was necessary between them, yet do we also[46] learn that the Erigas, a nation formerly inhabiting on the Ohio, were of the same original stock with the Five Nations, and that they partook also of the Tuscarora language. Their dialects might, by long separation, have become so unlike as to be unintelligible to one another. We know that in 1712, the Five Nations received the Tuscaroras into their confederacy, and made them the Sixth Nation. They received the Meherrins and Tuteloes also into their protection; and it is most probable, that the remains of many other of the tribes, of whom we find no particular account, retired westwardly in like manner, and were incorporated with one or the other of the western tribes. (5).

I know of no such thing existing as an Indian monument; for I would not honor with that name arrow points, stone hatchets, stone pipes, and half-shapen images. Of labor on the large scale, I think there is no remain as respectable as would be a common ditch for the draining of lands; unless indeed it would be the barrows, of which many are to be found all over this country. These are of different sizes, some of them constructed of earth, and some of loose stones. That they were repositories of the dead, has been obvious to all; but on what particular occasion constructed, was a matter of doubt. Some have thought they covered the bones of those who have fallen in battles fought on the spot of interment. Some ascribed them to the custom, said to prevail among the Indians, of collecting, at certain periods, the bones of all their dead, wheresoever deposited at the time of death. Others again supposed them the general sepulchres for towns, conjectured to have been on or near these grounds; and this

[45] Smith.—T. J.

[46] Evans.—T. J.

opinion was supported by the quality of the lands in which they are found, (those constructed of earth being generally in the softest and most fertile meadow-grounds on river sides,) and by a tradition, said to be handed down from the aboriginal Indians, that, when they settled in a town, the first person who died was placed erect, and earth put about him, so as to cover and support him; that when another died, a narrow passage was dug to the first, the second reclined against him, and the cover of earth replaced, and so on. There being one of these in my neighborhood, I wished to satisfy myself whether any, and which of these opinions were just. For this purpose I determined to open and examine it thoroughly. It was situated on the low grounds of the Rivanna, about two miles above its principal fork, and opposite to some hills, on which had been an Indian town. It was of a spheroidical form, of about forty feet diameter at the base, and had been of about twelve feet altitude, though now reduced by the plough to seven and a half, having been under cultivation about a dozen years. Before this it was covered with trees of twelve inches diameter, and round the base was an excavation of five feet depth and width, from whence the earth had been taken of which the hillock was formed. I first dug superficially in several parts of it, and came to collections of human bones, at different depths, from six inches to three feet below the surface. These were lying in the utmost confusion, some vertical, some oblique, some horizontal, and directed to every point of the compass, entangled and held together in clusters by the earth. Bones of the most distant parts were found together, as, for instance, the small bones of the foot in the hollow of a scull; many sculls would sometimes be in contact, lying on the face, on the side, on the back, top or bottom, so as, on the whole, to give the idea of bones emptied promiscuously from a bag or a basket, and covered over with earth, without any attention to their order. The bones of which the greatest numbers remained, were sculls, jaw-bones, teeth, the bones of the arms, thighs, legs, feet and hands. A few ribs remained, some vertebræ of the neck and spine, without their processes, and one instance only of the [47] bone which serves as a base to the vertebral column. The sculls were so tender, that they generally fell to pieces on being touched. The other bones were stronger. There were some teeth which were judged to be smaller than those of an adult; a scull, which on a slight view, appeared to be that of an infant, but it fell to pieces on being taken out, so as to prevent satisfactory examination; a rib, and a fragment of the under-jaw of a person about half grown; another rib of an infant; and a part of the jaw of a child, which had not cut its teeth. This last furnishing the most decisive proof of the burial of children here, I was particular in my attention to it. It was part of the right half of the under-jaw. The processes, by which it was attenuated to the temporal bones, were entire, and the bone itself firm to where it had been broken off, which, as nearly as I could judge, was about the place of the eye-tooth. Its upper edge, wherein would have been the sockets of the teeth, was perfectly smooth. Measuring it with that of an adult, by placing their hinder processes together, its broken end extended to the penultimate grinder of the

[47] The *os sacrum*.—T. J.

adult. This bone was white, all the others of a sand color. The bones of infants being soft, they probably decay sooner, which might be the cause so few were found here. I proceeded then to make a perpendicular cut through the body of the barrow, that I might examine its internal structure. This passed about three feet from its centre, was opened to the former surface of the earth, and was wide enough for a man to walk through and examine its sides. At the bottom, that is, on the level of the circumjacent plain, I found bones; above these a few stones, brought from a cliff a quarter of a mile off, and from the river one-eighth of a mile off; then a large interval of earth, then a stratum of bones, and so on. At one end of the section were four strata of bones plainly distinguishable; at the other, three; the strata in one part not ranging with those in another. The bones nearest the surface were least decayed. No holes were discovered in any of them, as if made with bullets, arrows, or other weapons. I conjectured that in this barrow might have been a thousand skeletons. Everyone will readily seize the circumstances above related, which militate against the opinion, that it covered the bones only of persons fallen in battle; and against the tradition also, which would make it the common sepulchre of a town, in which the bodies were placed upright, and touching each other. Appearances certainly indicate that it has derived both origin and growth from the accustomary collection of bones, and deposition of them together; that the first collection had been deposited on the common surface of the earth, a few stones put over it, and then a covering of earth, that the second had been laid on this, had covered more or less of it in proportion to the number of bones, and was then also covered with earth; and so on. The following are the particular circumstances which give it this aspect. 1. The number of bones. 2. Their confused position. 3. Their being in different strata. 4. The strata in one part having no correspondence with those in another. 5. The different states of decay in these strata, which seem to indicate a difference in the time of inhumation. 6. The existence of infant bones among them.

But on whatever occasion they may have been made, they are of considerable notoriety among the Indians; for a party passing, about thirty years ago, through the part of the country where this barrow is, went through the woods directly to it, without any instructions or inquiry, and having staid about it for some time, with expressions which were construed to be those of sorrow, they returned to the high road, which they had left about half a dozen miles to pay this visit, and pursued their journey. There is another barrow much resembling this, in the low grounds of the south branch of Shenandoah, where it is crossed by the road leading from the Rockfish gap to Staunton. Both of these have, within these dozen years, been cleared of their trees and put under cultivation, are much reduced in their height, and spread in width, by the plough, and will probably disappear in time. There is another on a hill in the Blue Ridge of mountains, a few miles north of Wood's gap, which is made up of small stones thrown together. This has been opened and found to contain human bones, as the others do. There are also many others in other parts of the country.

Great question has arisen from whence came those aboriginals of America? Discoveries, long ago made, were sufficient to show that the passage from Europe to America was always practicable, even to the imperfect navigation of ancient times. In going from Norway to Iceland, from Iceland to Greenland, from Greenland to Labrador, the first traject is the widest; and this having been practised from the earliest times of which we have any account of that part of the earth, it is not difficult to suppose that the subsequent trajects may have been sometimes passed. Again, the late discoveries of Captain Cook, coasting from Kamschatka to California, have proved that if the two continents of Asia and America be separated at all, it is only by a narrow strait. So that from this side also, inhabitants may have passed into America; and the resemblance between the Indians of America and the eastern inhabitants of Asia, would induce us to conjecture, that the former are the descendants of the latter, or the latter of the former; excepting indeed the Esquimaux, who, from the same circumstance of resemblance, and from identity of language must be derived from the Greenlanders, and these probably from some of the northern parts of the old continent. A knowledge of their several languages would be the most certain evidence of their derivation which could be produced. In fact, it is the best proof of the affinity of nations which ever can be referred to. How many ages have elapsed since the English, the Dutch, the Germans, the Swiss, the Norwegians, Danes and Swedes have separated from their common stock? Yet how many more must elapse before the proofs of their common origin, which exist in their several languages, will disappear? It is to be lamented then, very much to be lamented, that we have suffered so many of the Indian tribes already to extinguish, without our having previously collected and deposited in the records of literature, the general rudiments at least of the languages they spoke. Were vocabularies formed of all the languages spoken in North and South America, preserving their appellations of the most common objects in nature, of those which must be present to every nation barbarous or civilized, with the inflections of their nouns and verbs, their principles of regimen and concord, and these deposited in all the public libraries, it would furnish opportunities to those skilled in the languages of the old world to compare them with these, now, or at any future time, and hence to construct the best evidence of the derivation of this part of the human race.

But imperfect as is our knowledge of the tongues spoken in America, it suffices to discover the following remarkable fact: Arranging them under the radical ones to which they may be palpably traced, and doing the same by those of the red men of Asia, there will be found probably twenty in America, for one in Asia, of those radical languages, so called because if they were ever the same they have lost all resemblance to one another. A separation into dialects may be the work of a few ages only, but for two dialects to recede from one another till they have lost all vestiges of their common origin, must require an immense course of time; perhaps not less than many people give to the age of the earth. A greater number of those radical changes of language having taken place among the red men of America, proves them of greater antiquity than those of Asia.

Northward and Westward of the United States

| TRIBES | CROGHAN 1759 | BOUQUET 1764 | HUTCHINS 1768 | WHERE THEY RESIDE |
|---|---|---|---|---|
| Oswegatchies | .... | .... | 100 | At Swagatchy, on the river St. Laurence. |
| Connasedagoes | .... | | 300 | Near Montreal. |
| Cohunnewagoes | .... | 200 | | |
| Orondocs | .... | .... | 100 | Near Trois Rivieres. |
| Abenakies | .... | 350 | 150 | Near Trois Rivieres. |
| Little Alkonkins | .... | .... | 100 | Near Trois Rivieres. |
| Michmacs | .... | 700 | .... | River St. Laurence. |
| Amelistes | .... | 550 | .... | River St. Laurence. |
| Chalas | .... | 130 | .... | River St. Laurence. |
| Nipissins | .... | 400 | .... | Towards the heads of the Ottawas river. |
| Algonquins | .... | 300 | .... | Towards the heads of the Ottawas river. |
| Round Heads | .... | 2,500 | .... | Riviere aux Tetes boules, on the east side of Lake Superior. |
| Messasagues | .... | 2,000 | .... | Lakes Huron and Superior. |
| Christianaux—Kris | .... | 3,000 | .... | Lake Christianaux. |
| Assinaboes | .... | 1,500 | .... | Lake Assinaboes. |
| Blancs, or Barbus | .... | 1,500 | .... | |
| Sioux of the Meadows | | 2,500 | | |
| Sioux of the Woods | 10,000 | 1,800 | 10,000 | On the heads of the Mississippi and westward of that river. |
| Sioux | | .... | | |
| Ajoues | .... | 1,100 | .... | North of the Padoucas. |
| Panis—White | .... | 2,000 | .... | South of the Missouri. |
| Panis—Freckled | .... | 1,709 | .... | South of the Missouri. |
| Padoucas | .... | 500 | .... | South of the Missouri. |
| Grandes-Eaux | .... | 1,000 | .... | |
| Canses | .... | 1,600 | .... | South of the Missouri. |
| Osages | .... | 600 | .... | South of the Missouri. |
| Missouris | 400 | 3,000 | .... | On the river Missouri. |
| Arkansas | .... | 2,000 | .... | On the River Arkansas. |
| Caouitas | .... | 700 | .... | East of the Alibamous. |

| | TRIBES | CROGHAN 1759 | BOUQUET 1764 | HUTCHINS 1768 | DODGE 1779 | WHERE THEY RESIDE |
|---|---|---|---|---|---|---|
| Within the limits of the United States | Mohocks | .... | .... | 160 | 100 | Mohocks river. |
| | Onèidas | .... | .... | 300 | 400 | East side of Oneida Lake and head branches of Susquehanna. |
| | Tuscoròras | .... | .... | 200 | | Between the Oneidas and Onondagoes. |
| | Onondàgoes | .... | 1,550 | 260 | 230 | Near Onondago Lake. |
| | Cayùgas | .... | .... | 200 | 220 | On the Cayuga Lake, near the north branch of Susquehanna. |
| | Senecas | .... | .... | 1,000 | 650 | On the waters of Susquehanna, of Ontario, and the heads of the Ohio. |
| | Aughquàgahs | .... | .... | 150 | .... | East branch of Susquehanna, and on Aughquagah. |
| | Nànticoes | .... | .... | 100 | .... | Utsanango, Chaghnet, and Owegy, on the east branch of Susquehanna. |
| | Mohiccons | .... | .... | 100 | .... | In the same parts. |
| | Conòies | .... | .... | 30 | .... | In the same parts. |
| | Sapòonies | .... | .... | 30 | .... | At Diahago and other villages up the north branch of Susquehanna. |
| | Mùnsies | .... | .... | 150 | *150 | At Diahago and other villages up the north branch of Susquehanna. |
| | Delawares, or Linnelinopies | .... | .... | 150 | *500 | At Diahago and other villages up the north branch of Susquehanna. |
| | Delawares, or Linnelinopies | 600 | 600 | 600 | | Between Ohio and Lake Erie and the branches of Beaver creek, Cayahoga and Muskingum. |
| | Shàwanees | 500 | 400 | 300 | 300 | Sioto and the branches of Muskingum. |
| | Mingoes | .... | .... | .... | 60 | On a branch of Sioto. |
| | Mohìccons | .... | .... | | *60 | |
| | Cohunnewagos | .... | .... | 300 | .... | Near Sandusky. |
| | Wyandots | 300 | 300 | | 180 | |
| | Wyandots | | .... | 250 | | Near Fort St. Joseph's and Detroit. |
| | Twightwees | 300 | .... | 250 | .... | Miami river near Fort Miami. |
| | Miamis | .... | 350 | ... | 300 | Miami river, about Fort St. Joseph. |
| | Ouiàtonons | 200 | 400 | 300 | *400 | On the banks of the Wabash, near Fort Ouiatonon. |
| | Piànkishas | 300 | 250 | 300 | *400 | On the banks of the Wabash, near Fort Ouiatonon. |
| | Shákirs | .... | .... | 200 | .... | On the banks of the Wabash, near Fort Ouiatonon. |

| | | | | | | |
|---|---|---|---|---|---|---|
| Within the limits of the United States | Kaskaskias | .... | | 300 | .... | Near Kaskaskia. |
| | Illinois | 400 | 600 | 300 | .... | Near Cahokia. Query, If not the same with the Mitchigamis? |
| | Piorias | .... | 800 | .... | .... | On the Illinois river, called Pianrias, but supposed to mean Piorias. |
| | Ponteòtamies | .... | 350 | 300 | 450 | Near Fort St. Joseph's and Fort Detroit. |
| | Ottawas | .... | .... | 550 | *300 | Near Fort St. Joseph's and Fort Detroit. |
| | Chippawas | .... | .... | 200 | .... | On Saguinam bay of Lake Huron |
| | Ottawas | .... | .... | | .... | On Saguinam bay of Lake Huron. |
| | Chippawas | .... | .... | 400 | .... | Near Michillimackinac. |
| | Ottawas | 2,000 | 5,900 | 250 | 5,450 | Near Michillimackinac. |
| | | | | | | Near Fort St. Mary's on Lake Superior. |
| | Chippawas | .... | | 400 | .... | Several other villages along the banks of Lake Superior. Numbers unknown. |
| | Chippawas | .... | .... | .... | .... | Near Puans bay on Lake Michigan. |
| | Shakies | 200 | 400 | 550 | .... | Near Puans bay on Lake Michigan. |
| | Mynonàmies | .... | .... | .... | .... | Near Puans bay on Lake Michigan. |
| | Ouisconsings | .... | 550 | .... | .... | Ouisconsing river. |
| | Kickapous | 600 | 300 | .... | 250 | |
| | Otogamies—Foxes | .... | .... | .... | .... | |
| | Màscoutens | .... | 500 | | .... | On Lake Michigan, and between that and the Mississippi. |
| | Miscòthins | .... | .... | 4,000 | .... | |
| | Outimacs | .... | .... | .... | .... | |
| | Musquakies | 200 | 250 | .... | 250 | |
| | Sioux. Eastern | .... | .... | .... | 500 | On the eastern heads of the Mississippi, and the islands of Lake Superior. |
| | | | | GALPHIN 1678 | | |
| | Cherokees | 1,500 | 2,500 | 3,000 | .... | Western parts of North Carolina. |
| | Chickasaws | .... | 750 | 500 | .... | Western parts of Georgia. |
| | Catawbas | .... | 150 | .... | .... | On the Catawba river in South Carolina. |
| | Chacktaws | 2,000 | 4,500 | 6,000 | .... | Western parts of Georgia. |
| | Upper Creeks | .... | .... | 3,000 | .... | Western parts of Georgia. |
| | Lower Creeks | .... | 1,180 | | .... | |
| | Natchez | .... | 150 | .... | .... | |
| | Alibamous | .... | 600 | .... | .... | Alabama river, in the western parts of Georgia. |

I will now proceed to state the nations and numbers of the Aborigines which still exist in a respectable and independent form. And as their undefined boundaries would render it difficult to specify those only which may be within any certain limits, and it may not be unacceptable to present a more general view of them, I will reduce within the form of a catalogue all those within, and circumjacent to, the United States, whose names and numbers have come to my notice. These are taken from four different lists, the first of which was given in the year 1759 to General Stanwix by George Croghan, deputy agent for Indian affairs under Sir William Johnson; the second was drawn up by a French trader of considerable note, resident among the Indians many years, and annexed to Colonel Bouquet's printed account of his expedition in 1764. The third was made out by Captain Hutchins, who visited most of the tribes, by order, for the purpose of learning their numbers, in 1768; and the fourth by John Dodge, an Indian trader, in 1779, except the numbers marked *, which are from other information. [See table on pages 637-639.]

The following tribes are also mentioned:

| | Tribe | Number | Location |
|---|---|---|---|
| Croghan's Catal. | Lezar | 400 | From the mouth of Ohio to the mouth of Wabash |
| | Webings | 200 | On the Mississippi below the Shakies |
| | Ousasoys<br>Grand Tuc | 4,000 | On White Creek, a branch of the Mississippi |
| | Linways | 1,000 | On the Mississippi |
| Bouquet's | Les Puans | 700 | Near Puans Bay |
| | Folle Avoine | 350 | Near Puans Bay |
| | Ouanakina | 300 | Conjectured to be tribes of the Creeks |
| | Chiakanessou | 350 | |
| | Machecous | 800 | |
| | Souikilas | 200 | |
| Dodge's | Minneamis | 2,000 | North-west of Lake Michigan, to the heads of Mississippi, and up to Lake Superior |
| | Piankishas<br>Mascoutins<br>Vermillions | 800 | On and near the Wabash toward the Illinois |

But apprehending these might be different appellations for some of the tribes already enumerated, I have not inserted them in the table, but state them separately as worthy of further inquiry. The variations observable in numbering the same tribe may sometimes be ascribed to imperfect information, and sometimes to a greater or less comprehension of settlements under the same name. (7)

## QUERY XII

*A notice of the counties, cities, townships, and villages*

The counties have been enumerated under Query IX. They are seventy-four in number, of very unequal size and population. Of these thirty-five are on the tide waters, or in that parallel; twenty-three are in the midlands, between the tide waters and Blue Ridge of mountains; eight between the Blue Ridge and Alleghany; and eight westward of the Alleghany.

The State, by another division, is formed into parishes, many of which are commensurate with the counties; but sometimes a county comprehends more than one parish, and sometimes a parish more than one county. This division had relation to the religion of the State, a portion of the Anglican church, with a fixed salary, having been heretofore established in each parish. The care of the poor was another object of the parochial division.

We have no townships. Our country being much intersected with navigable waters, and trade brought generally to our doors, instead of our being obliged to go in quest of it, has probably been one of the causes why we have no towns of any consequence. Williamsburg, which, till the year 1780, was the seat of our government, never contained above 1,800 inhabitants; and Norfolk, the most populous town we ever had, contained but 6,000. Our towns, but more properly our villages and hamlets, are as follows:

On *James River* and its waters, Norfolk, Portsmouth, Hampton, Suffolk, Smithfield, Williamsburg, Petersburg, Richmond, the seat of our government, Manchester, Charlottesville, New London.

On *York River* and its waters, York, Newcastle, Hanover.

On *Rappahannock*, Urbanna, Port-Royal, Fredericksburg, Falmouth.

On *Potomac* and its waters, Dumfries, Colchester, Alexandria, Winchester, Staunton.

On *Ohio*, Louisville.

There are other places at which, like some of the foregoing, the *laws* have said there shall be towns; but *nature* has said there shall not, and they remain unworthy of enumeration. *Norfolk* will probably be the emporium for all the trade of the Chesapeake bay and its waters; and a canal of eight or ten miles will bring to it all that of Albemarle sound and its waters. Secondary to this place, are the towns at the head of the tide waters, to wit, Petersburg on Appomattox; Richmond on James river; Newcastle on York river; Alexandria on Potomac, and Baltimore on Patapsco. From these the distribution will be to subordinate situations in the country. Accidental circumstances, however, may control the indications of nature, and in no instance do they do it more frequently than in the rise and fall of towns.

## QUERY XIII

### *The constitution of the State and its several charters*

Queen Elizabeth by her letters patent, bearing date March 25, 1584, licensed Sir Walter Raleigh to search for remote heathen lands, not inhabited by Christian people, and granted to him in fee simple, all the soil within two hundred leagues of the places where his people should, within six years, make their dwellings or abidings; reserving only to herself and her successors, their allegiance and one-fifth part of all the gold and silver ore they should obtain. Sir Walter immediately sent out two ships, which visited Wococon island in

North Carolina, and the next year despatched seven with one hundred and seven men, who settled in Roanoke island, about latitude 35° 50′. Here Okisko, king of the Weopomeiocs, in a full council of his people is said to have acknowledged himself the homager of the Queen of England, and, after her, of Sir Walter Raleigh. A supply of fifty men were sent in 1586, and one hundred and fifty in 1587. With these last Sir Walter sent a governor, appointed him twelve assistants, gave them a charter of incorporation, and instructed them to settle on Chesapeake bay. They landed, however, at Hatorask. In 1588, when a fleet was ready to sail with a new supply of colonists and necessaries, they were detained by the Queen to assist against the Spanish armada. Sir Walter having now expended £40,000 in these enterprises, obstructed occasionally by the crown without a shilling of aid from it, was under a necessity of engaging others to adventure their money. He, therefore, by deed bearing date the 7th of March, 1589, by the name of Sir Walter Raleigh, Chief Governor of Assamàcomòc, (probably Acomàc,) alias Wingadacoia, alias Virginia, granted to Thomas Smith and others, in consideration of their adventuring certain sums of money, liberty to trade to this new country free from all customs and taxes for seven years, excepting the fifth part of the gold and silver ore to be obtained; and stipulated with them and the other assistants, then in Virginia, that he would confirm the deed of incorporation which he had given in 1587, with all the prerogatives, jurisdictions, royalties and privileges granted to him by the Queen. Sir Walter, at different times, sent five other adventurers hither, the last of which was in 1602; for in 1603 he was attainted and put into close imprisonment, which put an end to his cares over his infant colony. What was the particular fate of the colonists he had before sent and seated, has never been known; whether they were murdered, or incorporated with the savages.

Some gentlemen and merchants, supposing that by the attainder of Sir Walter Raleigh the grant to him was forfeited, not inquiring over carefully whether the sentence of an English court could affect lands not within the jurisdiction of that court, petitioned king James for a new grant of Virginia to them. He accordingly executed a grant to Sir Thomas Gates and others, bearing date the 9th of March, 1607, under which, in the same year, a settlement was effected at Jamestown, and ever after maintained. Of this grant, however, no particular notice need be taken, as it was superseded by letters patent of the same king, of May 23, 1609, to the Earl of Salisbury and others, incorporating them by the name of "The Treasurer and company of Adventurers and Planters of the City of London for the first colony in Virginia," granting to them and their successors all the lands in Virginia from Point Comfort along the sea-coast, to the northward two hundred miles, and from the same point along the sea-coast to the southward two hundred miles, and all the space from this precinct on the sea-coast up into the land, west and north-west, from sea to sea, and the islands within one hundred miles of it, with all the communities, jurisdictions, royalties, privileges, franchises, and pre-eminencies, within the same, and thereto and thereabouts, by sea and land, appertaining in as ample manner as had before been granted to any adventurer; to be held of the king and his successors, in common soccage, yielding one-fifth part of the gold and silver ore to be therein found, for all manner of services; establishing a counsel in England for the direction of the enterprise, the members of which were to be chosen and displaced by the voice of the majority of the company and adventurers, and were to have the nomination and revocation of governors, officers, and ministers, which by them should be thought needful for the colony, the power of establishing laws and forms of government and magistracy, obligatory not only within the colony, but also on the seas in going and coming to and from it; authorizing them to carry thither any persons who should consent to go, freeing them forever from all taxes and impositions on any goods or merchandise on importations into the colony, or exportation out of it, except the five per cent due for custom on all goods imported into the British dominions, according to the ancient trade of merchants; which five per cent only being paid they might, within thirteen months, re-export the same goods into foreign parts, without any custom, tax, or other duty, to the king or any of his officers, or deputies; with powers of waging war against those who should annoy them; giving to the inhabitants of the colony all the rights of natural subjects, as if born and abiding in England; and declaring that these letters should be construed, in all doubtful parts, in such manner as should be most for the benefit of the grantees.

Afterwards on the 12th of March, 1612, by other letters patent, the king added to his former grants, all islands in any part of the ocean between the 30th and 41st degrees of latitude, and within three hundred leagues of any of the parts before granted to the treasurer and company, not being possessed or inhabited by any other Christian prince or state, nor within the limits of the northern colony.

In pursuance of the authorities given to the company by these charters, and more especially of that part in the charter of 1609, which authorized them to establish a form of government, they on the 24th of July, 1621, by charter under their common seal, declared that from thenceforward there should be two supreme councils in Virginia, the one to be called the council of state, to be placed and displaced by the treasurer, council in England, and company from time to time, whose office was to be that of assisting and advising the governor; the other to be called the general assembly, to be convened by the governor once yearly or oftener, which was to consist of the council of state, and two burgesses out of every town, hundred, or plantation, to be respectively chosen by the inhabitants. In this all matters were to be decided by the greater part of the votes present; reserving to the governor a negative voice; and they were to have power to treat, consult, and conclude all emergent occasions concerning the public weal, and to make laws for the behoof and government of the colony, imitating and following the laws and policy of England as nearly as might be; providing that these laws should have no force till ratified in a general court of the company in England, and returned under their common seal; and declaring that, after the government of the colony should be well framed and settled, no orders of the council in England should bind the colony unless ratified in the said general assembly. The king and company quarrelled, and by a mixture of law and force, the latter were ousted of all their rights without retribution, after having expended one hundred thousand pounds in establishing the colony, without the smallest aid from government. King James suspended their powers by proclamation of July 15, 1624, and Charles I. took the government into his own hands. Both sides had their partisans in the colony, but, in truth, the people of the colony in general thought themselves little concerned in the dispute. There being three parties interested in these several charters, what passed between the first and second, it was thought could not affect the third. If the king seized on the powers of the company, they only passed into other hands, without increase or diminution, while the rights of the people remained as they were. But they did not remain so long. The northern parts of their country were granted away to the lords Baltimore and Fairfax; the first of these obtaining also the rights of separate jurisdiction and government. And in 1650 the parliament, considering itself as standing in the place of their deposed king, and as having succeeded to all his powers, without as well as within the realm, began to assume a right over the colonies, passing an act for inhibiting their trade with foreign nations. This succession to the exercise of kingly authority gave the first color for parliamentary interference with the colonies, and produced that fatal precedent which they continued to follow, after they had retired, in other respects, within their proper functions. When this colony, therefore, which still maintained its opposition to Cromwell and the parliament, was induced in 1651 to lay down their arms, they previously secured their most essential rights by a solemn convention, which, having never seen in print, I will here insert literally from the records.

"ARTICLES agreed on and concluded at James Cittie in Virginia for the surrendering and settling of that plantation under the obedience and government of the commonwealth of England by the commissioners of the Councill of State by authoritie of the parliamt of England, and by the Grand assembly of the Governour, Councill, and Burgesses of that countrey.

"First it is agreed and consted that the plantation of Virginia, and all the inhabitants thereof, shall be and remain in due obedience and subjection to the Commonwealth of England, according to the laws there established, and that this submission and subscription bee acknowledged a voluntary act not forced nor constrained by a conquest upon the countrey, and that they shall have and enjoy such freedoms and priviledges as belong to the free borne people of England, and that the former government by the Commissions and Instructions be void and null.

"2ly. That the Grand assembly as formerly shall convene and transact the affairs of Virginia, wherein nothing is to be acted or done contrairie to the government of the Commonwealth of England and the lawes there established.

"3ly. That there shall be a full and totall remission and indempnitie of all acts, words, or writeings done or spoken against the parliament of England in relation to the same.

"4ly. That Virginia shall have and enjoy the antient bounds and lymitts granted by the charters of the former kings, and that we shall seek a new charter from the parliament to that purpose against any that have intrencht upon the rights thereof.

"5ly. That all the pattents of land granted under the colony seal by any of the precedent governours shall be and remaine in their full force and strength.

"6ly. That the priviledge of haveing ffiftie acres of land for every person transported in that collonie shall continue as formerly granted.

"7ly. That the people of Virginia have free trade as the people of England do enjoy to all places and with all nations according to the lawes of that commonwealth, and that Virginia shall enjoy all priviledges equall with any English plantations in America.

"8ly. That Virginia shall be free from all taxes, customs and impositions whatsoever, and none to be imposed on them without consent of the Grand assembly; and soe that neither fforts nor castle bee erected or garrisons maintained without their consent.

"9ly. That noe charge shall be required from this country in respect of this present ffleet.

"10ly. That for the future settlement of the countrey in their due obedience, the engagement shall be tendred to all the inhabitants according to act of parliament made to that purpose, that all persons who shall refuse to subscribe the said engagement, shall have a yeare's time if they please to remove themselves and their estates out of Virginia, and in the meantime during the said yeare to have equall justice as formerly.

"11ly. That the use of the booke of common prayer shall be permitted for one yeare ensueinge with referrence to the consent of the major part of the parishes, provided that those which relate to kingshipp or that government be not used publiquely, and the continuance of ministers in their places, they not misdemeaning themselves, and the payment of their accustomed dues and agreements made with them respectively shall be left as they now stand dureing this ensueing yeare.

"12ly. That no man's cattell shall be questioned as the companies, unless such as have been entrusted with them or have disposed of them without order.

"13ly. That all ammunition, powder and armes, other than for private use, shall be delivered up, securitie being given to make satisfaction for it.

"14ly. That all goods allreadie brought hither by the Dutch or others which are now on shoar shall be free from surprizall.

"15ly. That the quittrents granted unto us by the late kinge for seaven yeares bee confirmed.

"16ly. That the commissioners for the parliament subscribeing these articles engage themselves and the honour of parliament for the full performance thereof; and that the present governour, and the councill, and the burgesses do likewise subscribe and engage the whole collony on their parts.

RICHARD BENNETT.—Seale.
WILLIAM CLAIBORNE.—Seale.
EDMOND CURTIS.—Seale.

"Theise articles were signed and sealed by the Commissioners of the Councill of state for the Commonwealth of England the twelveth day of March 1651."

Then follow the articles stipulated by the governor and council, which relate merely to their own persons and property, and then the ensuing instrument:

"An act of indempnitie made att the surrender of the countrey.

"Whereas, by the authoritie of the parliament wee the commissioners appointed by the councill of state authorized thereto, having brought a ffleet and force before

James cittie in Virginia to reduce that collonie under the obedience of the commonwealth of England, and finding force raised by the Governour and countrey to make opposition against the said ffleet, whereby assured danger appearinge of the ruine and destruction of the plantation, for prevention whereof the burgesses of all the severall plantations being called to advise and assist therein, uppon long and serious debate, and in sad contemplation of the great miseries and certain destruction which were soe neerely hovering over the whole countrey; Wee the said Commissioners have thought fitt and condescending and granted to signe and confirme under our hands, seales and by our oath, Articles bearinge date with theise presents, and do further declare that by the authoritie of the parliament and commonwealth of England derived unto us their commissioners, that according to the articles in generall wee have granted an act of indempnitie and oblivion to all the inhabitants of this collonie from all words, actions, or writings that have been spoken, acted or writt against the parliament or commonwealth of England or any other person from the beginning of the world to this daye. And this we have done that all the inhabitants of the collonie may live quietly and securely under the commonwealth of England. And we do promise that the parliament and commonwealth of England shall confirm and make good all those transactions of ours. Witness our hands and seales this 12th of Marcn 1651.

RICHARD BENNETT.—Seale.
WILLIAM CLAIBORNE.—Seale.
EDMOND CURTIS.—Seale.

The colony supposed, that, by this solemn convention, entered into with arms in their hands, they had secured the ancient limits [48] of their country, its free trade,[49] its exemption from taxation [50] but by their own assembly, and exclusion of military force [51] from among them. Yet in every of these points was this convention violated by subsequent kings and parliaments, and other infractions of their constitution, equally dangerous committed. Their general assembly, which was composed of the council of state and burgesses, sitting together and deciding by plurality of voices, was split into two houses, by which the council obtained a separate negative on their laws. Appeals from their supreme court, which had been fixed by law in their general assembly, were arbitrarily revoked to England, to be there heard before the king and council. Instead of four hundred miles on the seacoast, they were reduced, in the space of thirty years, to about one hundred miles. Their trade with foreigners was totally suppressed, and when carried to Great Britain, was there loaded with imposts. It is unnecessary, however, to glean up the several instances of injury, as scattered through American and British history, and the more especially as, by passing on to the accession of the present king, we shall find specimens of them all, aggravated, multiplied and crowded within a small compass of time, so as to evince a fixed design of considering our rights natural, conventional and chartered as mere nullities. The following is an epitome of the first sixteen years of his reign: The colonies were taxed internally and externally; their essential interests sacrificed to individuals in Great Britain; their legislatures suspended; charters annulled; trials by juries taken away; their persons subjected

[48] Art. 4.—T. J.
[49] Art. 7.—T. J.
[50] Art. 8.—T. J.
[51] Art. 8.—T. J.

to transportation across the Atlantic, and to trial before foreign judicatories; their supplications for redress thought beneath answer; themselves published as cowards in the councils of their mother country and courts of Europe; armed troops sent among them to enforce submission to these violences; and actual hostilities commenced against them. No alternative was presented but resistance, or unconditional submission. Between these could be no hesitation. They closed in the appeal to arms. They declared themselves independent states. They confederated together into one great republic; thus securing to every State the benefit of an union of their whole force. In each State separately a new form of government was established. Of ours particularly the following are the outlines: The executive powers are lodged in the hands of a governor, chosen annually, and incapable of acting more then three years in seven. He is assisted by a council of eight members. The judiciary powers are divided among several courts, as will be hereafter explained. Legislation is exercised by two houses of assembly, the one called the house of Delegates, composed of two members from each county, chosen annually by the citizens, possessing an estate for life in one hundred acres of uninhabited land, or twenty-five acres with a house on it, or in a house or lot in some town: the other called the Senate, consisting of twenty-four members, chosen quadrennially by the same electors, who for this purpose are distributed into twenty-four districts. The concurrence of both houses is necessary to the passage of a law. They have the appointment of the governor and council, the judges of the superior courts, auditors, attorney-general, treasurer, register of the land office, and delegates to Congress. As the dismemberment of the State had never had its confirmation, but, on the contrary, had always been the subject of protestation and complaint, that it might never be in our own power to raise scruples on that subject, or to disturb the harmony of our new confederacy, the grants to Maryland, Pennsylvania, and the two Carolinas, were ratified.

This constitution was formed when we were new and unexperienced in the science of government. It was the first, too, which was formed in the whole United States. No wonder then that time and trial have discovered very capital defects in it.

1. The majority of the men in the State, who pay and fight for its support, are unrepresented in the legislature, the roll of freeholders entitled to vote not including generally the half of those on the roll of the militia, or of the tax-gatherers.

2. Among those who share the representation, the shares are very unequal. Thus the county of Warwick, with only one hundred fighting men, has an equal representation with the county of Loudon, which has one thousand seven hundred and forty-six. So that every man in Warwick has as much influence in the government as seventeen men in Loudon. But lest it should be thought that an equal interspersion of small among large counties, through the whole State, may prevent any danger of injury to particular parts of it, we will divide it into districts, and show the proportions of land, of fighting men, and of representation in each:

| | SQUARE MILES | FIGHTING MEN | DELE-GATES | SENATORS |
|---|---|---|---|---|
| Between the sea-coast and falls of the rivers | [52] 11,205 | 19,012 | 71 | 12 |
| Between the falls of the rivers and the Blue Ridge mountains | 18,759 | 18,828 | 46 | 8 |
| Between the Blue Ridge and the Alleghany | 11,911 | 7,673 | 16 | 2 |
| Between the Alleghany and Ohio | [53] 79,650 | 4,458 | 16 | 2 |
| Total | 121,525 | 49,971 | 149 | 24 |

An inspection of this table will supply the place of commentaries on it. It will appear at once that nineteen thousand men, living below the falls of the rivers, possess half the senate, and want four members only of possessing a majority of the house of delegates; a want more than supplied by the vicinity of their situation to the seat of government, and of course the greater degree of convenience and punctuality with which their members may and will attend in the legislature. These nineteen thousand, therefore, living in one part of the country, give law to upwards of thirty thousand living in another, and appoint all their chief officers, executive and judiciary. From the difference of their situation and circumstances, their interests will often be very different.

3. The senate is, by its constitution, too homogenous with the house of delegates. Being chosen by the same electors, at the same time, and out of the same subjects, the choice falls of course on men of the same description. The purpose of establishing different houses of legislation is to introduce the influence of different interests or different principles. Thus in Great Britain it is said their constitution relies on the house of commons for honesty, and the lords for wisdom; which would be a rational reliance, if honesty were to be bought with money, and if wisdom were hereditary. In some of the American States, the delegates and senators are so chosen, as that the first represent the persons, and the second the property of the State. But with us, wealth and wisdom have equal chance for admission into both houses. We do not, therefore, derive from the separation of our legislature into two houses, those benefits which a proper complication of principles are capable of producing, and those which alone can compensate the evils which may be produced by their dissensions.

4. All the powers of government, legislative, executive, and judiciary, result to the legislative body. The concentrating these in the same hands is precisely the definition of despotic government. It will be no alleviation that these powers will be exercised by a plurality of hands, and not by a single one. One hundred and seventy-three despots would surely be as oppressive as one. Let those who doubt it turn their eyes on the republic of Venice. As little will it avail us that they are chosen by ourselves. An *elective despotism* was not the government we fought for, but one which should not only be founded on free principles,

[52] Of these 542 are on the eastern shore.—T. J.

[53] Of these, 22,616 are eastward of the meridian of the north of the Great Kanhaway.—T. J.

but in which the powers of government should be so divided and balanced among several bodies of magistracy, as that no one could transcend their legal limits, without being effectually checked and restrained by the others. For this reason that convention which passed the ordinance of government, laid its foundation on this basis, that the legislative, executive, and judiciary departments should be separate and distinct, so that no person should exercise the powers of more than one of them at the same time. But no barrier was provided between these several powers. The judiciary and executive members were left dependent on the legislative, for their subsistence in office, and some of them for their continuance in it. If, therefore, the legislature assumes executive and judiciary powers, no opposition is likely to be made; nor, if made, can it be effectual; because in that case they may put their proceedings into the form of an act of assembly, which will render them obligatory on the other branches. They have, accordingly, in many instances, decided rights which should have been left to judiciary controversy; and the direction of the executive, during the whole time of their session, is becoming habitual and familiar. And this is done with no ill intention. The views of the present members are perfectly upright. When they are led out of their regular province, it is by art in others, and inadvertence in themselves. And this will probably be the case for some time to come. But it will not be a very long time. Mankind soon learn to make interested uses of every right and power which they possess, or may assume. The public money and public liberty, intended to have been deposited with three branches of magistracy, but found inadvertently to be in the hands of one only, will soon be discovered to be sources of wealth and dominion to those who hold them; distinguished, too, by this tempting circumstance, that they are the instrument, as well as the object of acquisition. With money we will get men, said Cæsar, and with men we will get money. Nor should our assembly be deluded by the integrity of their own purposes, and conclude that these unlimited powers will never be abused, because themselves are not disposed to abuse them. They should look forward to a time, and that not a distant one, when a corruption in this, as in the country from which we derive our origin, will have seized the heads of government, and be spread by them through the body of the people; when they will purchase the voices of the people, and make them pay the price. Human nature is the same on every side of the Atlantic, and will be alike influenced by the same causes. The time to guard against corruption and tyranny, is before they shall have gotten hold of us. It is better to keep the wolf out of the fold, than to trust to drawing his teeth and talons after he shall have entered. To render these considerations the more cogent, we must observe in addition:

5. That the ordinary legislature may alter the constitution itself. On the discontinuance of assemblies, it became necessary to substitute in their place some other body, competent to the ordinary business of government, and to the calling forth the powers of the State for the maintenance of our opposition to Great Britain. Conventions were therefore introduced, consisting of two delegates from each county, meeting together and forming one house, on the plan

of the former house of burgesses, to whose places they succeeded. These were at first chosen anew for every particular session. But in March 1775, they recommended to the people to choose a convention, which should continue in office a year. This was done, accordingly, in April 1775, and in the July following that convention passed an ordinance for the election of delegates in the month of April annually. It is well known, that in July 1775, a separation from Great Britain and establishment of republican government, had never yet entered into any person's mind. A convention, therefore, chosen under that ordinance, cannot be said to have been chosen for the purposes which certainly did not exist in the minds of those who passed it. Under this ordinance, at the annual election in April 1776, a convention for the year was chosen. Independence, and the establishment of a new form of government, were not even yet the objects of the people at large. One extract from the pamphlet called Common Sense had appeared in the Virginia papers in February, and copies of the pamphlet itself had got in a few hands. But the idea had not been opened to the mass of the people in April, much less can it be said that they had made up their minds in its favor.

So that the electors of April 1776, no more than the legislators of July 1775, not thinking of independence and a permanent republic, could not mean to vest in these delegates powers of establishing them, or any authorities other than those of the ordinary legislature. So far as a temporary organization of government was necessary to render our opposition energetic, so far their organization was valid. But they received in their creation no power but what were given to every legislature before and since. They could not, therefore, pass an act transcendent to the powers of other legislatures. If the present assembly pass an act, and declare it shall be irrevocable by subsequent assemblies, the declaration is merely void, and the act repealable, as other acts are. So far, and no farther authorized, they organized the government by the ordinance entitled a constitution or form of government. It pretends to no higher authority than the other ordinances of the same session; it does not say that it shall be perpetual; that it shall be unalterable by other legislatures; that it shall be transcendent above the powers of those who they knew would have equal power with themselves. Not only the silence of the instrument is a proof they thought it would be alterable, but their own practice also; for this very convention, meeting as a house of delegates in general assembly with the Senate in the autumn of that year, passed acts of assembly in contradiction to their ordinance of government; and every assembly from that time to this has done the same. I am safe, therefore, in the position that the constitution itself is alterable by the ordinary legislature. Though this opinion seems founded on the first elements of common sense, yet is the contrary maintained by some persons. 1. Because, say they, the conventions were vested with every power necessary to make effectual opposition to Great Britain. But to complete this argument, they must go on, and say further, that effectual opposition could not be made to Great Britain without establishing a form of government perpetual and unalterable by the legislature; which is not true. An opposition which at some time or other was to come to an end, could not need a perpetual institution to carry it on; and a government amendable as its defects should be discovered, was as likely to make effectual resistance, as one that should be unalterably wrong. Besides, the assemblies were as much vested with all powers requisite for resistance as the conventions were. If, therefore, these powers included that of modelling the form of government in the one case, they did so in the other. The assemblies then as well as the conventions may model the government; that is, they may alter the ordinance of government. 2. They urge, that if the convention had meant that this instrument should be alterable, as their other ordinances were, they would have called it an ordinance; but they have called it a *constitution,* which, ex vi termini, means "an act above the power of the ordinary legislature." I answer that *constitutio, constitutium, statutum, lex,* are convertible terms. "*Constitutio* dicitur jus quod a principe conditure." "*Constitutium,* quod ab imperatoribus rescriptum statutumve est." "*Statutum,* idem quod lex." Calvini Lexicon juridicum. *Constitution* and *statute* were originally terms of the [54] civil law, and from thence introduced by ecclesiastics into the English law. Thus in the statute 25 Hen. VIII. c. 19, §. 1, "*Constitutions* and *ordinances*" are used as synonymous. The term *constitution* has many other significations in physics and politics; but in jurisprudence, whenever it is applied to any act of the legislature, it invariably means a statute, law, or ordinance, which is the present case. No inference then of a different meaning can be drawn from the adoption of this title; on the contrary, we might conclude that, by their affixing to it a term synonymous with ordinance or statute. But of what consequence is their meaning, where their power is denied? If they meant to do more than they had power to do, did this give them power? It is not the name, but the authority that renders an act obligatory. Lord Coke says, "an article of the statute, 11 R. II. c. 5, that no person should attempt to revoke any ordinance then made, is repealed, for that such restraint is against the jurisdiction and power of the parliament." 4. Inst. 42. And again, "though divers parliaments have attempted to restrain subsequent parliaments, yet could they never effect it; for the latter parliament hath ever power to abrogate, suspend, qualify, explain, or make void the former in the whole or in any part thereof, notwithstanding any words of restraint, prohibition, or penalty, in the former; for it is a maxim in the laws of the parliament, *quod leges posteriores priores contrarias abrogant.*" 4. Inst. 43. To get rid of the magic supposed to be in the word *constitution,* let us translate it into its definition as given by those who think it above the power of the law; and let us suppose the convention, instead of saying, "We the ordinary legislature, establish a *constitution,*" had said, "We the ordinary legislature, establish an act *above the power of the ordinary legislature.*" Does not this expose the absurdity of the attempt? 3. But, say they, the people have acquiesced, and this has given it an authority superior to the laws. It is true that the people did not rebel against it; and was that a time for the people to rise in rebellion? Should a

[54] To bid, to set, was the ancient legislative word of the English. Ll. Hlotharri and Eadrici. Ll. Inæ. Ll. Eadwerdi. Ll. Aathelstani.—T. J.

prudent acquiescence, at a critical time, be construed into a confirmation of every illegal thing done during that period? Besides, why should they rebel? At an annual election they had chosen delegates for the year, to exercise the ordinary powers of legislation, and to manage the great contest in which they were engaged. These delegates thought the contest would be best managed by an organized government. They therefore, among others, passed an ordinance of government. They did not presume to call it perpetual and unalterable. They well knew they had no power to make it so; that our choice of them had been for no such purpose, and at a time when we could have no such purpose in contemplation. Had an unalterable form of government been meditated, perhaps we should have chosen a different set of people. There was no cause then for the people to rise in rebellion. But to what dangerous lengths will this argument lead? Did the acquiescence of the colonies under the various acts of power exercised by Great Britain in our infant State, confirm these acts, and so far invest them with the authority of the people as to render them unalterable, and our present resistance wrong? On every unauthoritative exercise of power by the legislature must the people rise in rebellion, or their silence be construed into a surrender of that power to them? If so, how many rebellions should we have had already? One certainly for every session of assembly. The other States in the union have been of opinion that to render a form of government unalterable by ordinary acts of assembly, the people must delegate persons with special powers. They have accordingly chosen special conventions to form and fix their governments. The individuals then who maintain the contrary opinion in this country, should have the modesty to suppose it possible that they may be wrong, and the rest of America right. But if there be only a possibility of their being wrong, if only a plausible doubt remains of the validity of the ordinance of government, is it not better to remove that doubt by placing it on a bottom which none will dispute? If they be right we shall only have the unnecessary trouble of meeting once in convention. If they be wrong, they expose us to the hazard of having no fundamental rights at all. True it is, this is no time for deliberating on forms of government. While an enemy is within our bowels, the first object is to expel him. But when this shall be done, when peace shall be established, and leisure given us for intrenching within good forms, the rights for which we have bled, let no man be found indolent enough to decline a little more trouble for placing them beyond the reach of question. If anything more be requisite to produce a conviction of the expediency of calling a convention at a proper season to fix our form of government, let it be the reflection:

6. That the assembly exercises a power of determining the quorum of their own body which may legislate for us. After the establishment of the new form they adhered to the *Lex majoris partis,* founded in [55] common law as well as common right. It is the [56] natural law of every assembly of men, whose numbers are not fixed by any other law. They continued for some time to require

[55] Bro. abr. Corporations, 31, 34. Hakewell, 93.—T. J.
[56] Puff. Off. hom. 1. 2, c. 6, §. 12.—T. J.

the presence of a majority of their whole number, to pass an act. But the British parliament fixes its own quorum; our former assemblies fixed their own quorum; and one precedent in favor of power is stronger than an hundred against it. The house of delegates, therefore, have [57] lately voted that, during the present dangerous invasion, forty members shall be a house to proceed to business. They have been moved to this by the fear of not being able to collect a house. But this danger could not authorize them to call that a house which was none; and if they may fix it at one number, they may at another, till it loses its fundamental character of being a representative body. As this vote expires with the present invasion, it is probable the former rule will be permitted to revive; because at present no ill is meant. The power, however, of fixing their own quorum has been avowed, and a precedent set. From forty it may be reduced to four, and from four to one; from a house to a committee, from a committee to a chairman or speaker, and thus an oligarchy or monarchy be substituted under forms supposed to be regular. *"Omnia mala exempla ex bonis orta sunt; sed ubi imperium ad ignaros aut minus bonos pervenit, novum illud exemplum ab dignis et idoneis adindignos et non idoneos fertur."* When, therefore, it is considered, that there is no legal obstacle to the assumption by the assembly of all the powers legislative, executive, and judiciary, and that these may come to the hands of the smallest rag of delegation, surely the people will say, and their representatives, while yet they have honest representatives, will advise them to say, that they will not acknowledge as laws any acts not considered and assented to by the major part of their delegates.

In enumerating the defects of the constitution, it would be wrong to count among them what is only the error of particular persons. In December 1776, our circumstances being much distressed, it was proposed in the house of delegates to create a *dictator,* invested with every power legislative, executive, and judiciary, civil and military, of life and of death, over our persons and over our properties; and in June 1781, again under calamity, the same proposition was repeated, and wanted a few votes only of being passed. One who entered into this contest from a pure love of liberty, and a sense of injured rights, who determined to make every sacrifice, and to meet every danger, for the re-establishment of those rights on a firm basis, who did not mean to expend his blood and substance for the wretched purpose of changing this matter for that, but to place the powers of governing him in a plurality of hands of his own choice, so that the corrupt will of no one man might in future oppress him, must stand confounded and dismayed when he is told, that a considerable portion of that plurality had mediated the surrender of them into a single hand, and, in lieu of a limited monarchy, to deliver him over to a despotic one! How must we find his efforts and sacrifices abused and baffled, if he may still, by a single vote, be laid prostrate at the feet of one man! In God's name, from whence have they derived this power? Is it from our ancient laws? None such can be produced. Is it from any principle in our new constitution expressed or implied? Every lineament expressed or implied, is in full opposition to it.

[57] June 4, 1781.—T. J.

Its fundamental principle is, that the State shall be governed as a commonwealth. It provides a republican organization, proscribes under the name of *prerogative* the exercise of all powers undefined by the laws; places on this basis the whole system of our laws; and by consolidating them together, chooses that they should be left to stand or fall together, never providing for any circumstances, nor admitting that such could arise, wherein either should be suspended; no, not for a moment. Our ancient laws expressly declare, that those who are but delegates themselves shall not delegate to others powers which require judgment and integrity in their exercise. Or was this proposition moved on a supposed right in the movers, of abandoning their posts in a moment of distress? The same laws forbid the abandonment of that post, even on ordinary occasions; and much more a transfer of their powers into other hands and other forms, without consulting the people. They never admit the idea that these, like sheep or cattle, may be given from hand to hand without an appeal to their own will. Was it from the necessity of the case? Necessities which dissolve a government, do not convey its authority to an oligarchy or a monarchy. They throw back, into the hands of the people, the powers they had delegated, and leave them as individuals to shift for themselves. A leader may offer, but not impose himself, nor be imposed on them. Much less can their necks be submitted to his sword, their breath to be held at his will or caprice. The necessity which should operate these tremendous effects should at least be palpable and irresistible. Yet in both instances, where it was feared, or pretended with us, it was belied by the event. It was belied, too, by the preceding experience of our sister States, several of whom had grappled through greater difficulties without abandoning their forms of government. When the proposition was first made, Massachusetts had found even the government of committees sufficient to carry them through an invasion. But we at the time of that proposition, were under no invasion. When the second was made, there had been added to this example those of Rhode Island, New York, New Jersey, and Pennsylvania, in all of which the republican form had been found equal to the task of carrying them through the severest trials. In this State alone did there exist so little virtue, that fear was to be fixed in the hearts of the people, and to become the motive of their exertions, and principle of their government? The very thought alone was treason against the people; was treason against mankind in general; as rivetting forever the chains which bow down their necks, by giving to their oppressors a proof, which they would have trumpeted through the universe, of the imbecility of republican government, in times of pressing danger, to shield them from harm. Those who assume the right of giving away the reins of government in any case, must be sure that the herd, whom they hand on to the rods and hatchet of the dictator, will lay their necks on the block when he shall nod to them. But if our assemblies supposed such a recognition in the people, I hope they mistook their character. I am of opinion, that the government, instead of being braced and invigorated for greater exertions under their difficulties, would have been thrown back upon the bungling machinery of county committees for administration, till a convention could have been called, and its wheels again set into regular motion. What a cruel moment was this for creating such an embarrassment, for putting to the proof the attachment of our countrymen to republican government! Those who meant well, of the advocates of this measure, (and most of them meant well, for I know them personally, had been their fellow-laborer in the common cause, and had often proved the purity of their principles,) had been seduced in their judgment by the example of an ancient republic, whose constitution and circumstances were fundamentally different. They had sought this precedent in the history of Rome, where alone it was to be found, and where at length, too, it had proved fatal. They had taken it from a republic rent by the most bitter factions and tumults, where the government was of a heavy-handed unfeeling aristocracy, over a people ferocious, and rendered desperate by poverty and wretchedness; tumults which could not be allayed under the most trying circumstances, but by the omnipotent hand of a single despot. Their constitution, therefore, allowed a temporary tyrant to be erected, under the name of a dictator; and that temporary tyrant, after a few examples, became perpetual. They misapplied this precedent to a people mild in their dispositions, patient under their trial, united for the public liberty, and affectionate to their leaders. But if from the constitution of the Roman government there resulted to their senate a power of submitting all their rights to the will of one man, does it follow that the assembly of Virginia have the same authority? What clause in our constitution has substituted that of Rome, by way of residuary provision, for all cases not otherwise provided for? Or if they may step *ad libitum* into any other form of government for precedents to rule us by, for what oppression may not a precedent be found in this world of the *ballum omnium in omnia?* Searching for the foundations of this proposition, I can find none which may pretend a color of right or reason, but the defect before developed, that there being no barrier between the legislative, executive, and judiciary departments, the legislature may seize the whole; that having seized it, and possessing a right to fix their own quorum, they may reduce that quorum to one, whom they may call a chairman, speaker, dictator, or by any other name they please. Our situation is indeed perilous, and I hope my countrymen will be sensible of it, and will apply, at a proper season, the proper remedy; which is a convention to fix the constitution, to amend its defects, to bind up the several branches of government by certain laws, which, when they transgress, their acts shall become nullities; to render unnecessary an appeal to the people, or in other words a rebellion, on every infraction of their rights, on the peril that their acquiescence shall be construed into an intention to surrender those rights.

## QUERY XIV

*The administration of justice and the description of the laws*

The State is divided into counties. In every county are appointed magistrates, called justices of the peace, usually from eight to thirty or forty in number, in proportion to the size of the county, of the most discreet and honest inhabitants. They are nominated by their fellows, but commissioned by the governor, and act without reward. These magistrates have jurisdiction both criminal and civil. If the question before them be a question of law only, they decide on it themselves; but if it be of fact, or of fact and law combined, it must be referred to a jury. In the latter case, of a combination of law and fact, it is usual for the jurors to decide the fact, and to refer the law arising on it to the decision of the judges. But this division of the subject lies with their discretion only. And if the question relate to any point of public liberty, or if it be one of those in which the judges may be suspected of bias, the jury undertake to decide both law and fact. If they be mistaken, a decision against right, which is casual only, is less dangerous to the State, and less afflicting to the loser, than one which makes part of a regular and uniform system. In truth, it is better to toss up cross and pile in a cause, than to refer it to a judge whose mind is warped by any motive whatever, in that particular case. But the common sense of twelve honest men gives still a better chance of just decision, than the hazard of cross and pile. These judges execute their process by the sheriff or coroner of the county, or by constables of their own appointment. If any free person commit an offence against the commonwealth, if it be below the degree of felony, he is bound by a justice to appear before their court, to answer it on an indictment or information. If it amount to felony, he is committed to jail; a court of these justices is called; if they on examination think him guilty, they send him to the jail of the general court, before which court he is to be tried first by a grand jury of twenty-four, of whom thirteen must concur in opinion; if they find him guilty, he is then tried by a jury of twelve men of the county where the offence was committed, and by their verdict, which must be unanimous, he is acquitted or condemned without appeal. If the criminal be a slave, the trial by the county court is final. In every case, however, except that of high treason, there resides in the governor a power of pardon. In high treason the pardon can only flow from the general assembly. In civil matters these justices have jurisdiction in all cases of whatever value, not appertaining to the department of the admiralty. This jurisdiction is twofold. If the matter in dispute be of less value than four dollars and one-sixth, a single member may try it at any time and place within his county, and may award execution on the goods of the party cast. If it be of that or greater value, it is determinable before the county court, which consists of four at the least of those justices and assembles at the court-house of the county on a certain day in every month. From their determination, if the matter be of the value of ten pounds sterling, or concern the title or bounds of lands, an appeal lies to one of the superior courts.

There are three or four superior courts, to wit, the high court of chancery, the general court, and the court of admiralty. The first and second of these receive appeals from the county courts, and also have original jurisdiction, where the subject of controversy is of the value of ten pounds sterling; or where it concerns the title or bounds of lands. The jurisdiction of the admiralty is original altogether. The high court of chancery is composed of three judges, the general court of five, and the court of admiralty of three. The two first hold their sessions at Richmond at stated times, the chancery twice in the year, and the general court twice for business civil and criminal, and twice more for criminal only. The court of admiralty sits at Williamsburg whenever a controversy arises.

There is one supreme court, called the court of appeals, composed of the judges of the three superior courts, assembling twice a year at stated times at Richmond. This court receives appeals in all civil cases from each of the superior courts, and determines them finally. But it has no original jurisdiction.

If a controversy arise between two foreigners of a nation in alliance with the United States, it is decided by the Consul for their State, or, if both parties choose it, by the ordinary courts of justice. If one of the parties only be such a foreigner, it is triable before the courts of justice of the country. But if it shall have been instituted in a county court, the foreigner may remove it into the general court, or court of chancery, who are to determine it at their first sessions, as they must also do if it be originally commenced before them. In cases of life and death, such foreigners have a right to be tried by a jury, the one-half foreigners, the other natives.

All public accounts are settled with a board of auditors, consisting of three members appointed by the general assembly, any two of whom may act. But an individual, dissatisfied with the determination of that board, may carry his case into the proper superior court.

A description of the laws.

The general assembly was constituted, as has been already shown, by letters-patent of March the 9th, 1607, in the fourth year of the reign of James the first. The laws of England seem to have been adopted by consent of the settlers, which might easily enough be done whilst they were few and living all together. Of such adoption, however, we have no other proof than their practice till the year 1661, when they were expressly adopted by an act of the assembly, except so far as "a difference of condition" rendered them inapplicable. Under this adoption, the rule, in our courts of judicature was, that the common law of England, and the general statutes previous to the fourth of James, were in force here; but that no subsequent statutes were, *unless we were named in them,* said the judges and other partisans of the crown, but *named or not named,* said those who reflected freely. It will be unnecessary to attempt a description of the laws of England, as that may be found in English publications. To those which were established here, by the adoption of the legislature, have been since added a number of acts of assembly passed during the monarchy, and ordinances of convention and acts of assembly enacted since the establishment of the republic. The following variations from the British model are perhaps worthy of being specified:

Debtors unable to pay their debts, and making faithful delivery of their whole effects, are released from confinement, and their persons forever discharged from restraint for such previous debts; but any property they may afterwards acquire will be subject to their creditors.

The poor unable to support themselves, are maintained by an assessment on the tytheable persons in their parish. This assessment is levied and administered by twelve persons in each parish, called vestrymen, originally chosen by the housekeepers of the parish, but afterwards filling vacancies in their own body by their own choice. These are usually the most discreet farmers, so distributed through their parish, that every part of it may be under the immediate eye of some one of them. They are well acquainted with the details and economy of private life, and they find sufficient inducements to execute their charge well, in their philanthropy, in the approbation of their neighbors, and the distinction which that gives them. The poor who have neither property, friends, nor strength to labor, are boarded in the houses of good farmers, to whom a stipulated sum is annually paid. To those who are able to help themselves a little, or have friends from whom they derive some succors, inadequate however to their full maintenance, supplementary aids are given which enable them to live comfortably in their own houses, or in the houses of their friends. Vagabonds without visible property or vocation, are placed in work houses, where they are well clothed, fed, lodged, and made to labor. Nearly the same method of providing for the poor prevails through all our States; and from Savannah to Portsmouth you will seldom meet a beggar. In the large towns, indeed, they sometimes present themselves. These are usually foreigners, who have never obtained a settlement in any parish. I never yet saw a native American begging in the streets or highways. A subsistence is easily gained here, and if, by misfortunes, they are thrown on the charities of the world, those provided by their own country are so comfortable and so certain, that they never think of relinquishing them to become strolling beggars. Their situation too, when sick, in the family of a good farmer, where every member is emulous to do them kind offices, where they are visited by all the neighbors, who bring them the little rarities which their sickly appetites may crave, and who take by rotation the nightly watch over them, when their condition requires it, is without comparison better than in a general hospital, where the sick, the dying and the dead are crammed together in the same rooms, and often in the same beds. The disadvantages, inseparable from general hospitals, are such as can never be counterpoised by all the regularities of medicine and regimen. Nature and kind nursing save a much greater proportion in our plain way, at a smaller expense, and with less abuse. One branch only of hospital institution is wanting with us; that is, a general establishment for those laboring under difficult cases of chirurgery. The aids of this art are not equivocal. But an able chirurgeon cannot be had in every parish. Such a receptacle should therefore be provided for those patients; but no others should be admitted.

Marriages must be solemnized either on special license, granted by the first magistrate of the county, on proof of the consent of the parent or guardian of either party under age, or after solemn publication, on three several Sundays, at some place of religious worship, in the parishes where the parties reside.

The act of solemnization may be by the minister of any society of Christians, who shall have been previously licensed for this purpose by the court of the county. Quakers and Menonists, however, are exempted from all these conditions, and marriage among them is to be solemnized by the society itself.

A foreigner of any nation, not in open war with us, becomes naturalized by removing to the State to reside, and taking an oath of fidelity; and thereupon acquires every right of a native citizen; and citizens may divest themselves of that character, by declaring, by solemn deed, or in open court, that they mean to expatriate themselves, and no longer to be citizens of this State.

Conveyances of land must be registered in the court of the county wherein they lie, or in the general court, or they are void, as to creditors, and subsequent purchasers.

Slaves pass by descent and dower as lands do. Where the descent is from a parent, the heir is bound to pay an equal share of their value in money to each of their brothers and sisters.

Slaves, as well as lands, were entailable during the monarchy; but, by an act of the first republican assembly, all donees in tail, present and future, were vested with the absolute dominion of the entailed subject.

Bills of exchange, being protested, carry ten per cent interest from their date.

No person is allowed, in any other case, to take more than five per cent per annum simple interest for the loan of moneys.

Gaming debts are made void, and moneys actually paid to discharge such debts (if they exceed forty shillings) may be recovered by the payer within three months, or by any other person afterwards.

Tobacco, flour, beef, pork, tar, pitch, and turpentine, must be inspected by persons publicly appointed, before they can be exported.

The erecting iron-works and mills is encouraged by many privileges; with necessary cautions however to prevent their dams from obstructing the navigation of the water-courses. The general assembly have on several occasions shown a great desire to encourage the opening the great falls of James and Potomac rivers. As yet, however, neither of these have been effected.

The laws have also descended to the preservation and improvement of the races of useful animals, such as horses, cattle, deer; to the extirpation of those which are noxious, as wolves, squirrels, crows, blackbirds; and to the guarding our citizens against infectious disorders, by obliging suspected vessels coming into the State, to perform quarantine, and by regulating the conduct of persons having such disorders within the State.

The mode of acquiring lands, in the earliest times of our settlement, was by petition to the general assembly. If the lands prayed for were already cleared of the Indian title, and the assembly thought the prayer reasonable, they passed the property by their vote to the petitioner. But if they had not yet been ceded by the Indians, it was necessary that the petitioner should previously purchase their right. This purchase the assembly verified, by inquiries of the Indian proprietors; and being satisfied of its reality and fairness, proceeded further to examine the reasonableness of the petition, and its consistence with policy; and according to the result, either granted or rejected the petition. The company also sometimes, though very rarely, granted lands, independently of the general assembly. As the colony increased, and individual applications for land multiplied, it was found to give too much occupation to the general assembly to inquire into and execute the grant in every special case. They therefore thought it better to establish general rules, according to which all grants should be made, and to leave to the governor the execution of them, under these rules. This they did by what have been usually called the land laws, amending them from time to time, as their defects were developed. According to these laws, when an individual wished a portion of unappropriated land, he was to locate and survey it by a public officer, appointed for that purpose; its breadth was to bear a certain proportion to its length: the grant was to be executed by the governor; and the lands were to be improved in a certain manner, within a given time. From these regulations there resulted to the State a sole and exclusive power of taking conveyances of the Indian right of soil; since, according to them an Indian conveyance alone could give no right to an individual, which the laws would acknowledge. The State, or the crown, thereafter, made general purchases of the Indians from time to time, and the governor parcelled them out by special grants, conformable to the rules before described, which it was not in his power, or in that of the crown, to dispense with. Grants, unaccompanied by their proper legal circumstances, were set aside regularly by *fiere facias,* or by bill in chancery. Since the establishment of our new government, this order of things is but little changed. An individual, wishing to appropriate to himself lands still unappropriated by any other, pays to the public treasurer a sum of money proportioned to the quantity he wants. He carries the treasurer's receipt to the auditors of public accounts, who thereupon debit the treasurer with the sum, and order the register of the land-office to give the party a warrant for his land. With this warrant from the register, he goes to the surveyor of the county where the land lies on which he has cast his eye. The surveyor lays it off for him, gives him its exact description, in the form of a certificate, which certificate he returns to the land office, where a grant is made out, and is signed by the governor. This vests in him a perfect dominion in his lands, transmissible to whom he pleases by deed or will, or by descent to his heirs, if he die intestate.

Many of the laws which were in force during the monarchy being relative merely to that form of government, or inculcating principles inconsistent with republicanism, the first assembly which met after the establishment of the commonwealth appointed a committee to revise the whole code, to reduce it into proper form and volume, and report it to the assembly. This work has been executed by three gentlemen, and reported; but probably will not be taken up till a restoration of peace shall leave to the legislature leisure to go through such a work.

The plan of the revisal was this. The common law of England, by which is meant, that part of the English law which was anterior to the date of the oldest statutes extant, is made the basis of the work. It was thought dangerous to attempt to reduce it to a text; it was therefore left to be collected from the usual monuments of it. Necessary alterations in that, and so much of the whole body of the British statutes, and of acts of assembly, as were thought proper to be retained, were digested into one hundred and twenty-six new acts, in which simplicity of style was aimed at, as far as was safe. The following are the most remarkable alterations proposed:

To change the rules of descent, so as that the lands of any person dying intestate shall be divisible equally among all his children, or other representatives, in equal degree.

To make slaves distributable among the next of kin, as other movables.

To have all public expenses, whether of the general treasury, or of a parish or county, (as for the maintenance of the poor, building bridges, court-houses, &c.,) supplied by assessment on the citizens, in proportion to their property.

To hire undertakers for keeping the public roads in repair, and indemnify individuals through whose lands new roads shall be opened.

To define with precision the rules whereby aliens should become citizens, and citizens make themselves aliens.

To establish religious freedom on the broadest bottom.

To emancipate all slaves born after the passing the act. The bill reported by the revisers does not itself contain this proposition; but an amendment containing it was prepared, to be offered to the legislature whenever the bill should be taken up, and farther directing, that they should continue with their parents to a certain age, then to be brought up, at the public expense, to tillage, arts, or sciences, according to their geniuses, till the females should be eighteen, and the males twenty-one years of age, when they should be colonized to such place as the circumstances of the time should render most proper, sending them out with arms, implements of household and of the handicraft arts, seeds, pairs of the useful domestic animals, &c., to declare them a free and independent people, and extend to them our alliance and protection, till they have acquired strength; and to send vessels at the same time to other parts of the world for an equal number of white inhabitants; to induce them to migrate hither, proper encouragements were to be proposed. It will probably be asked, Why not retain and incorporate the blacks into the State, and thus save the expense of supplying by importation of white settlers, the vacancies they will leave? Deep-rooted prejudices entertained by the whites; ten thousand recollections, by the blacks, of the injuries they have sustained; new provocations; the real distinctions which nature has made; and many other circumstances, will divide us into parties, and produce convulsions, which will probably never end but in the extermination of the one or the other race. To these objections, which are political, may be added others, which are physical and moral. The first difference which strikes us is that of color. Whether the black of the negro resides in the reticular membrane between the skin and scarf-skin, or in the scarf-skin itself; whether it proceeds from the color of the blood, the color of the bile, or from that of some other secretion, the difference is fixed in nature, and is as real as if its seat and cause were better known to us. And is this difference of no importance? Is it not the foundation of a greater or less share of beauty in the two races? Are not the fine mixtures of red and white, the expressions of every passion by greater or less suffusions of color in the one, preferable to that eternal monotony, which reigns in the countenances, that immovable veil of black which covers the emotions of the other race? Add to these, flowing hair, a more elegant symmetry of form, their own judgment in favor of the whites, declared by their preference of them, as uniformly as is the preference of the Oranootan for the black woman over those of his own species. The circumstance of superior beauty, is thought worthy attention in the propagation of our horses, dogs, and other domestic animals; why not in that of man? Besides those of color, figure, and hair, there are other physical distinctions proving a difference of race. They have less hair on the face and body. They secrete less by the kidneys, and more by the glands of the skin, which gives them a very strong and disagreeable odor. This greater degree of transpiration, renders them more tolerant of heat, and less so of cold than the whites. Perhaps, too, a difference of structure in the pulminary apparatus, which a late ingenious[58] experimentalist has discovered to be the principal regulator of animal heat, may have disabled them from extricating, in the act of inspiration, so much of that fluid from the outer air, or obliged them in expiration, to part with more of it. They seem to require less sleep. A black after hard labor through the day, will be induced by the slightest amusements to sit up till midnight, or later, though knowing he must be out with the first dawn of the morning. They are at least as brave, and more adventuresome. But this may perhaps proceed from a want of forethought, which prevents their seeing a danger till it be present. When present, they do not go through it with more coolness or steadiness than the whites. They are more ardent after their female; but love seems with them to be more an eager desire, than a tender delicate mixture of sentiment and sensation. Their griefs are transient. Those numberless afflictions, which render it doubtful whether heaven has given life to us in mercy or in wrath, are less felt, and sooner forgotten with them. In general, their existence appears to participate more of sensation than reflection. To this must be ascribed their disposition to sleep when abstracted from their diversions, and unemployed in labor. An animal whose body is at rest, and who does not reflect, must be disposed to sleep of course. Comparing them by their faculties of memory, reason, and imagination, it appears to me that in memory they are equal to the whites; in reason much inferior, as I think one could scarcely be found capable of tracing and comprehending the investigations of Euclid; and that in imagination they are dull, tasteless, and anomalous. It would be unfair to follow them to Africa for this investigation. We will consider them here, on the same stage with the whites, and where the facts are not apocryphal on which a judgment is to be formed. It will be right to make great allowances for the difference of condition, of education, of conversation, of the sphere in which they move. Many millions of them have been brought

[58] Crawford.—T. J.

to, and born in America. Most of them, indeed, have been confined to tillage, to their own homes, and their own society; yet many have been so situated, that they might have availed themselves of the conversation of their masters; many have been brought up to the handicraft arts, and from that circumstance have always been associated with the whites. Some have been liberally educated, and all have lived in countries where the arts and sciences are cultivated to a considerable degree, and all have had before their eyes samples of the best works from abroad. The Indians, with no advantages of this kind, will often carve figures on their pipes not destitute of design and merit. They will crayon out an animal, a plant, or a country, so as to prove the existence of a germ in their minds which only wants cultivation. They astonish you with strokes of the most sublime oratory; such as prove their reason and sentiment strong, their imagination glowing and elevated. But never yet could I find that a black had uttered a thought above the level of plain narration; never saw even an elementary trait of painting or sculpture. In music they are more generally gifted than the whites with accurate ears for tune and time, and they have been found capable of imagining a small catch.[59] Whether they will be equal to the composition of a more extensive run of melody, or of complicated harmony, is yet to be proved. Misery is often the parent of the most affecting touches in poetry. Among the blacks is misery enough, God knows, but no poetry. Love is the peculiar œstrum of the poet. Their love is ardent, but it kindles the senses only, not the imagination. Religion, indeed, has produced a Phyllis Whately; but it could not produce a poet. The compositions published under her name are below the dignity of criticism. The heroes of the Dunciad are to her, as Hercules to the author of that poem. Ignatius Sancho has approached nearer to merit in composition; yet his letters do more honor to the heart than the head. They breathe the purest effusions of friendship and general philanthropy, and show how great a degree of the latter may be compounded with strong religious zeal. He is often happy in the turn of his compliments, and his style is easy and familiar, except when he affects a Shandean fabrication of words. But his imagination is wild and extravagant, escapes incessantly from every restraint of reason and taste, and, in the course of its vagaries, leaves a tract of thought as incoherent and eccentric, as is the course of a meteor through the sky. His subjects should often have led him to a process of sober reasoning; yet we find him always substituting sentiment for demonstration. Upon the whole, though we admit him to the first place among those of his own color who have presented themselves to the public judgment, yet when we compare him with the writers of the race among whom he lived and particularly with the epistolary class in which he has taken his own stand, we are compelled to enrol him at the bottom of the column. This criticism supposes the letters published under his name to be genuine, and to have received amendment from no other hand; points which would not be of easy investigation. The improvement of the blacks in body and mind, in the first instance

[59] The instrument proper to them is the Banjar, which they brought hither from Africa, and which is the original of the guitar, its chords being precisely the four lower chords of the guitar.—T. J.

of their mixture with the whites, has been observed by everyone, and proves that their inferiority is not the effect merely of their condition of life. We know that among the Romans, about the Augustan age especially, the condition of their slaves was much more deplorable than that of the blacks on the continent of America. The two sexes were confined in separate apartments, because to raise a child cost the master more than to buy one. Cato, for a very restricted indulgence to his slaves in this particular,[60] took from them a certain price. But in this country the slaves multiply as fast as the free inhabitants. Their situation and manners place the commerce between the two sexes almost without restraint. The same Cato, on a principle of economy, always sold his sick and superannuated slaves. He gives it as a standing precept to a master visiting his farm, to sell his old oxen, old wagons, old tools, old and diseased servants, and everything else become useless. *"Vendat boves vetulos, plaustrum vetus, feramenta vetera, servum senem, servum morbosum, et si quid aliud supersit vendat."* Cato de re rusticâ, c. 2. The American slaves cannot enumerate this among the injuries and insults they receive. It was the common practice to expose in the island Aesculapius, in the Tyber, diseased slaves whose cure was like to become tedious.[61] The emperor Claudius, by an edict, gave freedom to such of them as should recover, and first declared that if any person chose to kill rather than to expose them, it should not be deemed homicide. The exposing them is a crime of which no instance has existed with us; and were it to be followed by death, it would be punished capitally. We are told of a certain Vedius Pollio, who, in the presence of Augustus, would have given a slave as food to his fish, for having broken a glass. With the Romans, the regular method of taking the evidence of their slaves was under torture. Here it has been thought better never to resort to their evidence. When a master was murdered, all his slaves, in the same house, or within hearing, were condemned to death. Here punishment falls on the guilty only, and as precise proof is required against him as against a freeman. Yet notwithstanding these and other discouraging circumstances among the Romans, their slaves were often their rarest artists. They excelled too in science, insomuch as to be usually employed as tutors to their master's children. Epictetus, Terence, and Phædrus, were slaves. But they were of the race of whites. It is not their condition then, but nature, which has produced the distinction. Whether further observation will or will not verify the conjecture, that nature has been less bountiful to them in the endowments of the head, I believe that in those of the heart she will be found to have done them justice. That disposition to theft with which they have been branded, must be ascribed to their situation, and not to any depravity of the moral sense. The man in whose favor no laws of property exist, probably feels himself less bound to respect those made in favor of others. When arguing for ourselves, we lay it down as a fundamental, that laws, to be just, must give a reciprocation of right; that, without this, they are mere arbitrary rules of conduct, founded in force, and not in conscience; and it is a problem

60 *Tous doulous etaxen örismenou nomesmatos homilein tais therapainsin.* (Plutarch. Cato.) —T. J.

61 Suet. Claud. 25.—T. J.

which I give to the master to solve, whether the religious precepts against the violation of property were not framed for him as well as his slave? And whether the slave may not as justifiably take a little from one who has taken all from him, as he may slay one who would slay him? That a change in the relations in which a man is placed should change his ideas of moral right or wrong, is neither new, nor peculiar to the color of the blacks. Homer tells us it was so two thousand six hundred years ago.

> *"Emisu, ger t' aretes apoainutai euruopa Zeus*
> *Haneros, eut' an min kata doulion ema elesin.*
> Odd. 17, 323.

> Jove fix'd it certain, that whatever day
> Makes man a slave, takes half his worth away.

But the slaves of which Homer speaks were whites. Notwithstanding these considerations which must weaken their respect for the laws of property, we find among them numerous instances of the most rigid integrity, and as many as among their better instructed masters, of benevolence, gratitude, and unshaken fidelity. The opinion that they are inferior in the faculties of reason and imagination, must be hazarded with great diffidence. To justify a general conclusion, requires many observations, even where the subject may be submitted to the anatomical knife, to optical glasses, to analysis by fire or by solvents. How much more then where it is a faculty, not a substance, we are examining; where it eludes the research of all the senses; where the conditions of its existence are various and variously combined; where the effects of those which are present or absent bid defiance to calculation; let me add too, as a circumstance of great tenderness, where our conclusion would degrade a whole race of men from the rank in the scale of beings which their Creator may perhaps have given them. To our reproach it must be said, that though for a century and a half we have had under our eyes the races of black and of red men, they have never yet been viewed by us as subjects of natural history. I advance it, therefore, as a suspicion only, that the blacks, whether originally a distinct race, or made distinct by time and circumstances, are inferior to the whites in the endowments both of body and mind. It is not against experience to suppose that different species of the same genus, or varieties of the same species, may possess different qualifications. Will not a lover of natural history then, one who views the gradations in all the races of animals with the eye of philosophy, excuse an effort to keep those in the department of man as distinct as nature has formed them? This unfortunate difference of color, and perhaps of faculty, is a powerful obstacle to the emancipation of these people. Many of their advocates, while they wish to vindicate the liberty of human nature, are anxious also to preserve its dignity and beauty. Some of these, embarrassed by the question, "What further is to be done with them?" join themselves in opposition with those who are actuated by sordid avarice only. Among the Romans emancipation required but one effort. The slave, when made free, might mix with, without staining the blood of his master. But with us a second is necessary, unknown to history. When freed, he is to be removed beyond the reach of mixture.

The revised code further proposes to proportion crimes and punishments. This is attempted on the following scale:

I. Crimes whose punishment extends to LIFE.

1. High treason. Death by hanging.
   Forfeiture of lands and goods to the commonwealth.
2. Petty treason. Death by hanging. Dissection.
   Forfeiture of half the lands and goods to the representatives of the party slain.
3. Murder.
   1. By poison. Death by poison.
      Forfeiture of one-half, as before.
   2. In duel. Death by hanging. Gibbeting, if the challenger.
      Forfeiture of one-half as before, unless it be the party challenged, then the forfeiture is to the commonwealth.
   3. In any other way. Death by hanging.
      Forfeiture of one-half as before.
4. Manslaughter. The second offence is murder.

II. Crimes whose punishment goes to LIMB.

1. Rape } Dismemberment.
2. Sodomy }
3. Maiming } Retaliation, and the forfeiture of half of the lands and goods to the sufferer.
4. Disfiguring }

III. Crimes punishable by LABOR.

| | | |
|---|---|---|
| 1. Manslaughter, 1st offence. | Labor VII. years for the public. | Forfeiture of half, as in murder. |
| 2. Counterfeiting money. | Labor VI. years | Forfeiture of lands and goods to the commonwealth. |
| 3. Arson.<br>4. Asportation of vessels. | Labor V. years | Reparation three-fold. |
| 5. Robbery.<br>6. Burglary. | Labor IV. years | Reparation double. |
| 7. House-breaking.<br>8. Horse-stealing. | Labor III. years | Reparation. |
| 9. Grand larceny. | Labor II. years | Reparation. Pillory. |
| 10. Petty larceny. | Labor I. year | Reparation. Pillory. |
| 11. Pretensions to witchcraft, &c. | Ducking. | Stripes. |
| 12. Excusable homicide.<br>13. Suicide.<br>14. Apostasy. Heresy. | To be pitied, not punished. | |

Pardon and privilege of clergy are proposed to be abolished; but if the verdict be against the defendant, the court in their discretion may allow a new trial. No attainder to cause a corruption of blood, or forfeiture of dower. Slaves guilty of offences punishable in others by labor, to be transported to Africa, or elsewhere, as the circumstances of the time admit, there to be continued in slavery. A rigorous regimen proposed for those condemned to labor.

Another object of the revisal is, to diffuse knowledge more generally through the mass of the people. This bill proposes to lay off every county into small districts of five or six miles square, called hundreds, and in each of them to establish a school for teaching, reading, writing, and arithmetic. The tutor to be supported by the hundred, and every person in it entitled to send their children three years gratis, and as much longer as they please, paying for it. These schools to be under a visitor who is annually to choose the boy of best genius in the school, of those whose parents are too poor to give them further education, and to send him forward to one of the grammar schools, of which twenty are proposed to be erected in different parts of the country, for teaching Greek, Latin, Geography, and the higher branches of numerical arithmetic. Of the boys thus sent in one year, trial is to be made at the grammar schools one or two years, and the best genius of the whole selected, and continued six years, and the residue dismissed. By this means twenty of the best geniuses will be raked from the rubbish annually, and be instructed, at the public expense, so far as the grammar schools go. At the end of six years instruction, one half are to be discontinued (from among whom the grammar schools will probably be supplied with future masters); and the other half, who are to be chosen for the superiority of their parts and disposition, are to be sent and continued three years in the study of such sciences as they shall choose, at William and Mary college, the plan of which is proposed to be enlarged, as will be hereafter explained, and extended to all the useful sciences. The ultimate result of the whole scheme of education would be the teaching all the children of the State reading, writing, and common arithmetic; turning out ten annually, of superior genius, well taught in Greek, Latin, Geography, and the higher branches of arithmetic; turning out ten others annually, of still superior parts, who, to those branches of learning, shall have added such of the sciences as their genius shall have led them to; the furnishing to the wealthier part of the people convenient schools at which their children may be educated at their own expense. The general objects of this law are to provide an education adapted to the years, to the capacity, and the condition of everyone, and directed to their freedom and happiness. Specific details were not proper for the law. These must be the business of the visitors entrusted with its execution. The first stage of this education being the schools of the hundreds, wherein the great mass of the people will receive their instruction, the principal foundations of future order will be laid here. Instead, therefore, of putting the Bible and Testament into the hands of the children at an age when their judgments are not sufficiently matured for religious inquiries, their memories may here be stored with the most useful facts from Grecian, Roman, European and American history. The first elements of morality too may be instilled into their minds; such as, when further developed as their judgments advance in strength, may teach them how to work out their own greatest happiness, by showing them that it does not depend on the condition of life in which chance has placed them, but is always the result of a good conscience, good health, occupation, and freedom in all just pursuits. Those whom either the wealth of their parents or the adoption of the State shall destine to higher degrees of learning, will go on to the grammar schools, which constitute the next stage, there to be instructed in the languages. The learning Greek and Latin, I am told, is going into disuse in Europe. I know not what their manners and occupations may call for; but it would be very ill-judged in us to follow their example in this instance. There is a certain period of life, say from eight to fifteen or sixteen years of age, when the mind like the body is not yet firm enough for laborious and close operations. If applied to such, it falls an early victim to premature exertion; exhibiting, indeed, at first, in these young and tender subjects, the flattering appearance of their being men while they are yet children, but ending in reducing them to be children when they should be men. The memory is then most susceptible and tenacious of impressions; and the learning of languages being chiefly a work of memory, it seems precisely fitted to the powers of this period, which is long enough too for acquiring the most useful languages, ancient and modern. I do not pretend that language is science. It is only an instrument for the attainment of science. But that time is not lost which is employed in providing tools for future operation; more especially as in this case the books put into the hands of the youth for this purpose may be such as will at the same time impress their minds with useful facts and good principles. If this period be suffered to pass in idleness, the mind becomes lethargic and impotent, as would the body it inhabits if unexercised during the same time. The sympathy between body and mind during their rise, progress and decline, is too strict and obvious to endanger our being missed while we reason from the one to the other. As soon as they are of sufficient age, it is supposed they will be sent on from the grammar schools to the university, which constitutes our third and last stage, there to study those sciences which may be adapted to their views. By that part of our plan which prescribes the selection of the youths of genius from among the classes of the poor, we hope to avail the State of those talents which nature has sown as liberally among the poor as the rich, but which perish without use, if not sought for and cultivated. But of the views of this law none is more important, none more legitimate, than that of rendering the people the safe, as they are the ultimate, guardians of their own liberty. For this purpose the reading in the first stage, where *they* will receive their whole education, is proposed, as has been said, to be chiefly historical. History, by apprizing them of the past, will enable them to judge of the future; it will avail them of the experience of other times and other nations; it will qualify them as judges of the actions and designs of men; it will enable them to know ambition under every disguise it may assume; and knowing it, to defeat its views. In every government on earth is some trace of human weakness, some germ of corruption and degeneracy, which cunning will discover, and wickedness insensibly open, cultivate and improve. Every government degenerates when trusted to the rulers of the people alone. The people themselves therefore are its only safe depositories. And to render even them safe, their minds must be improved to a certain degree. This indeed is not all that is necessary, though it be essentially necessary. An amendment of our constitution must here come in aid of the public education. The influence over government must be shared among all the people. If every individual which composes their mass participates of the ultimate authority, the government will be safe; because the corrupting the whole mass will exceed any private resources of wealth; and public ones cannot be provided but by levies on the people. In this case every man would have to pay his own price. The government of Great Britain has been corrupted, because but one man in ten has a right to vote for members of parliament. The sellers of the government, therefore, get nine-tenths of their price clear. It has been thought that corruption is restrained by confining the right of suffrage to a few of the wealthier of the people; but it would be more effectually restrained by an extension of that right to such numbers as would bid defiance to the means of corruption.

Lastly, it is proposed, by a bill in this revisal, to begin a public library and gallery, by laying out a certain sum annually in books, paintings, and statues.

## QUERY XV

*The Colleges and Public Establishments, the Roads, Buildings, &c.*

The college of William and Mary is the only public seminary of learning in this State. It was founded in the time of king William and queen Mary, who granted to it twenty thousand acres of land, and a penny a pound duty on certain tobaccoes exported from Virginia and Maryland, which had been levied by the statute of 25 Car. II. The assembly also gave it, by temporary laws, a duty on liquors imported, and skins and furs exported. From these resources it received upwards of three thousand pounds *communibus annis.* The buildings are of brick, sufficient for an indifferent accommodation of perhaps an hundred students. By its charter it was to be under the government of twenty visitors, who were to be its legislators, and to have a president and six professors, who were incorporated. It was allowed a representative in the general assembly. Under this charter, a professorship of the Greek and Latin languages, a professorship of mathematics, one of moral philosophy, and two of divinity, were established. To these were annexed, for a sixth professorship, a considerable donation by Mr. Boyle, of England, for the instruction of the Indians, and their conversion to Christianity. This was called the professorship of Brafferton, from an estate of that name in England, purchased with the monies given. The admission of the learners of Latin and Greek filled the college with children. This rendering it disagreeable and degrading to young gentlemen already prepared for entering on the sciences, they were discouraged from resorting to it, and thus the schools for mathematics and moral philosophy, which might have been of some service, became of very little. The revenues, too, were exhausted in accommodating those who came only to acquire the rudiments of science. After the present revolution, the visitors, having no power to change those circumstances in the constitution of the college which were fixed by the charter, and being therefore confined in the number of the professorships, undertook to change the objects of the professorships. They excluded the two schools for divinity, and that for the Greek and Latin languages, and substituted others; so that at present they stand thus:

A Professorship for Law and Police;
Anatomy and Medicine;
Natural Philosophy and Mathematics;
Moral Philosophy, the Law of Nature and Nations, the Fine Arts;
Modern Languages;
For the Brafferton.

And it is proposed, so soon as the legislature shall have leisure to take up this subject, to desire authority from them to increase the number of professorships, as well for the purpose of subdividing those already instituted, as of adding others for other branches of science. To the professorships usually established in the universities of Europe, it would seem proper to add one for the ancient languages and literature of the north, on account of their connection with our own language, laws, customs, and history. The purposes of the Brafferton institution would be better answered by maintaining a perpetual mission among the Indian tribes, the object of which, besides instructing them in the principles of Christianity, as the founder requires, should be to collect their traditions, laws, customs, languages, and other circumstances which might lead to a discovery of their relation with one another, or descent from other nations. When these objects are accomplished with one tribe, the missionary might pass on to another.

The roads are under the government of the county courts, subject to be controlled by the general court. They order new roads to be opened wherever they think them necessary. The inhabitants of the county are by them laid off into precincts, to each of which they allot a convenient portion of the public roads to be kept in repair. Such bridges as may be built without the assistance of artificers, they are to build. If the stream be such as to require a bridge of regular workmanship, the court employs workmen to build it, at the expense of the whole county. If it be too great for the county, application is made to the general assembly, who authorize individuals to build it, and to take a fixed toll from all passengers, or give sanction to such other proposition as to them appears reasonable.

Ferries are admitted only at such places as are particularly pointed out by law, and the rates of ferriage are fixed.

Taverns are licensed by the courts, who fix their rates from time to time.

The private buildings are very rarely constructed of stone or brick, much the greatest portion being of scantling and boards, plastered with lime. It is impossible to devise things more ugly, uncomfortable, and happily more perishable. There are two or three plans, on one of which, according to its size, most of the houses in the State are built. The poorest people build huts of logs, laid horizontally in pens, stopping the interstices with mud. These are warmer in winter, and cooler in summer, than the more expensive construction of scantling and plank. The wealthy are attentive to the raising of vegetables, but very little so to fruits. The poorer people attend to neither, living principally on milk and animal diet. This is the more inexcusable, as the climate requires indispensably a free use of vegetable food, for health as well as comfort, and is very friendly to the raising of fruits. The only public buildings worthy mention are the capitol, the palace, the college, and the hospital for lunatics, all of them in Williamsburg, heretofore the seat of our government. The capitol is a light and airy structure, with a portico in front of two orders, the lower of which, being Doric, is tolerably just in its proportions and ornaments, save only that the intercolonations are too large. The upper is Ionic, much too small for that on which it is mounted, its ornaments not proper to the order, nor proportioned within themselves. It is crowned with a pediment, which is too high for its span. Yet, on the whole, it is the most pleasing piece of architecture we have. The palace is not handsome without, but it is spacious and commodious within, is prettily situated, and with the grounds annexed to it, is capable of being made an elegant seat. The college and hospital are rude, misshapen piles, which, but that they have roofs, would be taken for brick-kilns. There are no other public buildings but churches and court-houses, in which no attempts are made at elegance. Indeed, it would not be easy to execute such an attempt, as a workman could scarcely be found capable of drawing an order. The genius of architecture seems to have shed its maledictions over this land. Buildings are often erected, by individuals, of considerable expense. To give these symmetry and taste, would not increase their cost. It would only change the arrangement of the materials, the form and combination of the members. This would often cost less than the burthen of barbarous ornaments with which these buildings are sometimes charged. But the first principles of the art are unknown, and there exists scarcely a model among us sufficiently chaste to give an idea of them. Architecture being one of the fine arts, and as such within the department of a professor of the college, according to the new arrangement, perhaps a spark may fall on some young subjects of natural taste, kindle up their genius, and produce a reformation in this elegant and useful art. But all we shall do in this way will produce no permanent improvement to our country, while the unhappy prejudice prevails that houses of brick or stone are less wholesome than those of wood. A dew is often observed on the walls of the former in rainy weather, and the most obvious solution is, that the rain has penetrated through these walls. The following facts, however, are sufficient to prove the error of this solution: 1. This dew upon the walls appears when there is no rain, if the state of the atmosphere be moist. 2. It appears upon the partition as well as the exterior walls. 3. So, also, on pavements of brick or stone. 4. It is more copious in proportion as the walls are thicker; the reverse of which ought to be the case, if this hypothesis were just. If cold water be poured into a vessel of stone, or glass, a dew forms instantly on the outside; but if it be poured into a vessel of wood, there is no such appearance. It is not supposed, in the first case, that the water has exuded through the glass, but that it is precipitated from the circumambient air; as the humid particles of vapor, passing from the boiler of an alembic through its refrigerant, are precipitated from the air, in which they are suspended, on the internal surface of the refrigerant. Walls of brick and stone act as the refrigerant in this instance. They are sufficiently cold to condense and precipitate the moisture suspended in the air of the room, when it is heavily charged therewith. But walls of wood are not so. The question then is, whether the air in which this moisture is left floating, or that which is deprived of it, be most wholesome? In both cases the remedy is easy. A little fire kindled in the room, whenever the air is damp, prevents the precipitation on the walls; and this practice, found healthy in the warmest as well as coldest seasons, is as necessary in a wooden as in a stone or brick house. I do not mean to say, that the rain never penetrates through walls of brick. On the contrary, I have seen instances of it. But with us it is only through the northern and eastern walls of the house, after a north-easterly storm, this being the only one which continues long enough to force through the walls. This, however, happens too rarely to give a just character of unwholesomeness to such houses. In a house, the walls of which are of well-burnt brick and good mortar, I have seen the rain penetrate through but twice in a dozen or fifteen years. The inhabitants of Europe, who dwell chiefly in houses of stone or brick, are surely as healthy as those of Virginia. These houses have the advantage, too, of being warmer in winter and cooler in summer than those of wood; of being cheaper in their first construction, where lime is convenient, and infinitely more durable. The latter consideration renders it of great importance to eradicate this prejudice from the minds of our countrymen. A country whose buildings are of wood, can never increase in its improvements to any considerable degree. Their duration is highly estimated at fifty years. Every half century then our country becomes a *tabula rasa,* whereon we have to set out anew, as in the first moment of seating it. Whereas when buildings are of durable materials, every new edifice is an actual and permanent acquisition to the State, adding to its value as well as to its ornament.

## QUERY XVI

*The measures taken with regard to the estates and possessions of the Rebels, commonly called Tories*

A tory has been properly defined to be a traitor in thought but not in deed. The only description, by which the laws have endeavored to come at them, was that of non-jurors, or persons refusing to take the oath of fidelity to the State. Persons of this description were at one time subjected to double taxation, at another to treble, and lastly were allowed retribution, and placed on a level with good citizens. It may be mentioned as a proof, both of the lenity of our government, and unanimity of its inhabitants, that though this war has now raged near seven years, not a single execution for treason has taken place.

Under this query I will state the measures which have been adopted as to

British property, the owners of which stand on a much fairer footing than the tories. By our laws, the same as the English as in this respect, no alien can hold lands, nor alien enemy maintain an action for money, or other movable thing. Lands acquired or held by aliens become forfeited to the State; and, on an action by an alien enemy to recover money, or other movable property, the defendant may plead that he is an alien enemy. This extinguishes his right in the hands of the debtor or holder of his movable property. By our separation from Great Britain, British subjects became aliens, and being at war, they were alien enemies. Their lands were of course forfeited, and their debts irrecoverable. The assembly, however, passed laws at various times, for saving their property. They first sequestered their lands, slaves, and other property on their farms in the hands of commissioners, who were mostly the confidential friends or agents of the owners, and directed their clear profits to be paid into the treasury; and they gave leave to all persons owing debts to British subjects to pay them also into the treasury. The monies so to be brought in were declared to remain the property of the British subject, and if used by the State, were to be repaid, unless an improper conduct in Great Britain should render a detention of it reasonable. Depreciation had at that time, though unacknowledged and unperceived by the whigs, begun in some small degree. Great sums of money were paid in by debtors. At a later period, the assembly, adhering to the political principles which forbid an alien to hold lands in the State, ordered all British property to be sold; and, become sensible of the real progress of depreciation, and of the losses which would thence occur, if not guarded against, they ordered that the proceeds of the sales should be converted into their then worth in tobacco, subject to the future direction of the legislature. This act has left the question of retribution more problematical. In May, 1780, another act took away the permission to pay into the public treasury debts due to British subjects.

## QUERY XVII

*The different religions received into that State*

The first settlers in this country were emigrants from England, of the English Church, just at a point of time when it was flushed with complete victory over the religious of all other persuasions. Possessed, as they became, of the powers of making, administering, and executing the laws, they showed equal intolerance in this country with their Presbyterian brethren, who had emigrated to the northern government. The poor Quakers were flying from persecution in England. They cast their eyes on these new countries as asylums of civil and religious freedom; but they found them free only for the reigning sect. Several acts of the Virginia assembly of 1659, 1662, and 1693, had made it penal in parents to refuse to have their children baptized; had prohibited the unlawful assembling of Quakers; had made it penal for any master of a vessel to bring a Quaker into the State; had ordered those already here, and such as should come thereafter, to be imprisoned till they should abjure the country; provided a milder punishment for their first and second return, but death for their third; had inhibited all persons from suffering their meetings in or near their houses, entertaining them individually, or disposing of books which supported their tenets. If no execution took place here, as did in New England, it was not owing to the moderation of the church, or spirit of the legislature, as may be inferred from the law itself; but to historical circumstances which have not been handed down to us. The Anglicans retained full possession of the country about a century. Other opinions began then to creep in, and the great care of the government to support their own church, having begotten an equal degree of indolence in its clergy, two-thirds of the people had become dissenters at the commencement of the present revolution. The laws, indeed, were still oppressive on them, but the spirit of the one party had subsided into moderation, and of the other had risen to a degree of determination which commanded respect.

The present state of our laws on the subject of religion is this. The convention of May 1776, in their declaration of rights, declared it to be a truth, and a natural right, that the exercise of religion should be free; but when they proceeded to form on that declaration the ordinance of government, instead of taking up every principle declared in the bill of rights, and guarding it by legislative sanction, they passed over that which asserted our religious rights, leaving them as they found them. The same convention, however, when they met as a member of the general assembly in October, 1776, repealed all *acts of Parliament* which had rendered criminal the maintaining any opinions in matters of religion, the forbearing to repair to church, and the exercising any mode of worship; and suspended the laws giving salaries to the clergy, which suspension was made perpetual in October, 1779. Statutory oppressions in religion being thus wiped away, we remain at present under those only imposed by the common law, or by our own acts of assembly. At the common law, *heresy* was a capital offence, punishable by burning. Its definition was left to the ecclesiastical judges, before whom the conviction was, till the statute of the 1 El. c. 1 circumscribed it, by declaring, that nothing should be deemed heresy, but what had been so determined by authority of the canonical scriptures, or by one of the four first general councils, or by other council, having for the grounds of their declaration the express and plain words of the scriptures. Heresy, thus circumscribed, being an offence against the common law, our act of assembly of October 1777, c. 17, gives cognizance of it to the general court, by declaring that the jurisdiction of that court shall be general in all matters at the common law. The execution is by the writ *De haeretico comburendo*. By our own act of assembly of 1705, c. 30, if a person brought up in the Christian religion denies the being of a God, or the Trinity, or asserts there are more gods than one, or denies the Christian religion to be true, or the scriptures to be of divine authority, he is punishable on the first offence by incapacity to hold any office or employment ecclesiastical, civil, or military; on the second by disability to sue, to take any gift or legacy, to be guardian, executor, or administrator, and by three years' imprisonment without bail. A father's right to the custody of his own children being founded in law on his right of guardianship, this being taken away, they may of course be severed from him, and put by the authority of a court into more orthodox hands. This is a summary view of that religious slavery under which a people have been willing to remain, who have lavished their lives and fortunes for the establishment of their civil freedom. [62] The error seems not sufficiently eradicated, that the operations of the mind, as well as the acts of the body, are subject to the coercion of the laws. But our rulers can have no authority over such natural rights, only as we have submitted to them. The rights of conscience we never submitted, we could not submit. We are answerable for them to our God. The legitimate powers of government extend to such acts only as are injurious to others. But it does me no injury for my neighbor to say there are twenty gods, or no God. It neither picks my pocket nor breaks my leg. If it be said, his testimony in a court of justice cannot be relied on, reject it then, and be the stigma on him. Constraint may make him worse by making him a hypocrite, but it will never make him a truer man. It may fix him obstinately in his errors, but will not cure them. Reason and free inquiry are the only effectual agents against error. Give a loose to them, they will support the true religion by bringing every false one to their tribunal, to the test of their investigation. They are the natural enemies of error, and of error only. Had not the Roman government permitted free inquiry, Christianity could never have been introduced. Had not free inquiry been indulged at the era of the reformation, the corruptions of Christianity could not have been purged away. If it be restrained now, the present corruptions will be protected, and new ones encouraged. Was the government to prescribe to us our medicine and diet, our bodies would be in such keeping as our souls are now. Thus in France the emetic was once forbidden as a medicine, and the potato as an article of food. Government is just as infallible, too, when it fixes systems in physics. Galileo was sent to the Inquisition for affirming that the earth was a sphere; the government had declared it to be as flat as a trencher, and Galileo was obliged to abjure his error. This error, however, at length prevailed, the earth became a globe, and Descartes declared it was whirled round its axis by a vortex. The government in which he lived was wise enough to see that this was no question of civil jurisdiction, or we should all have been involved by authority in vortices. In fact, the vortices have been exploded, and the Newtonian principle of gravitation is now more firmly established, on the basis of reason, than it would be were the government to step in, and to make it an article of necessary faith. Reason and experiment have been indulged, and error has fled before them. It is error alone which needs the support of government. Truth can stand by itself. Subject opinion to coercion: whom will you make your inquisitors? Fallible men; men governed by bad passions, by private as well as public reasons. And why subject it to coercion? To produce uniformity. But is uniformity of opinion desirable? No more than of face and stature. Introduce the bed of Procrustes then, and as there is danger that the large men may beat the small, make us all of a size, by lopping the former and stretching the latter. Difference of opinion is advantageous in religion. The

[62] *Furneaux passim.*—T. J.

several sects perform the office of a *censor morum* over such other. Is uniformity attainable? Millions of innocent men, women, and children, since the introduction of Christianity, have been burnt, tortured, fined, imprisoned; yet we have not advanced one inch towards uniformity. What has been the effect of coercion? To make one half the world fools, and the other half hypocrites. To support roguery and error all over the earth. Let us reflect that it is inhabited by a thousand millions of people. That these profess probably a thousand different systems of religion. That ours is but one of that thousand. That if there be but one right, and ours that one, we should wish to see the nine hundred and ninety-nine wandering sects gathered into the fold of truth. But against such a majority we cannot effect this by force. Reason and persuasion are the only practicable instruments. To make way for these, free inquiry must be indulged; and how can we wish others to indulge it while we refuse it ourselves. But every State, says an inquisitor, has established some religion. No two, say I, have established the same. Is this a proof of the infallibility of establishments? Our sister States of Pennsylvania and New York, however, have long subsisted without any establishment at all. The experiment was new and doubtful when they made it. It has answered beyond conception. They flourish infinitely. Religion is well supported; of various kinds, indeed, but all good enough; all sufficient to preserve peace and order; or if a sect arises, whose tenets would subvert morals, good sense has fair play, and reasons and laughs it out of doors, without suffering the State to be troubled with it. They do not hang more malefactors than we do. They are not more disturbed with religious dissensions. On the contrary, their harmony is unparalleled, and can be ascribed to nothing but their unbounded tolerance, because there is no other circumstance in which they differ from every nation on earth. They have made the happy discovery, that the way to silence religious disputes, is to take no notice of them. Let us too give this experiment fair play, and get rid, while we may, of those tyrannical laws. It is true, we are as yet secured against them by the spirit of the times. I doubt whether the people of this country would suffer an execution for heresy, or a three years' imprisonment for not comprehending the mysteries of the Trinity. But is the spirit of the people an infallible, a permanent reliance? Is it government? Is this the kind of protection we receive in return for the rights we give up? Besides, the spirit of the times may alter, will alter. Our rulers will become corrupt, our people careless. A single zealot may commence persecutor, and better men be his victims. It can never be too often repeated, that the time for fixing every essential right on a legal basis is while our rulers are honest, and ourselves united. From the conclusion of this war we shall be going down hill. It will not then be necessary to resort every moment to the people for support. They will be forgotten, therefore, and their rights disregarded. They will forget themselves, but in the sole faculty of making money, and will never think of uniting to effect a due respect for their rights. The shackles, therefore, which shall not be knocked off at the conclusion of this war, will remain on us long, will be made heavier and heavier, till our rights shall revive or expire in a convulsion.

## QUERY XVIII

*The particular customs and manners that may happen to be received in that State*

It is difficult to determine on the standard by which the manners of a nation may be tried, whether *catholic* or *particular*. It is more difficult for a native to bring to that standard the manners of his own nation, familiarized to him by habit. There must doubtless be an unhappy influence on the manners of our people produced by the existence of slavery among us. The whole commerce between master and slave is a perpetual exercise of the most boisterous passions, the most unremitting despotism on the one part, and degrading submissions on the other. Our children see this, and learn to imitate it; for man is an imitative animal. This quality is the germ of all education in him. From his cradle to his grave he is learning to do what he sees others do. If a parent could find no motive either in his philanthropy or his self-love, for restraining the intemperance of passion towards his slave, it should always be a sufficient one that his child is present. But generally it is not sufficient. The parent storms, the child looks on, catches the lineaments of wrath, puts on the same airs in the circle of smaller slaves, gives a loose to the worst of passions, and thus nursed, educated, and daily exercised in tyranny, cannot but be stamped by it with odious peculiarities. The man must be a prodigy who can retain his manners and morals undepraved by such circumstances. And with what execration should the statesman be loaded, who, permitting one half the citizens thus to trample on the rights of the other, transforms those into despots, and these into enemies, destroys the morals of the one part, and the *amor patriae* of the other. For if a slave can have a country in this world, it must be any other in preference to that in which he is born to live and labor for another; in which he must lock up the faculties of his nature, contribute as far as depends on his individual endeavors to the evanishment of the human race, or entail his own miserable condition on the endless generations proceeding from him. With the morals of the people, their industry also is destroyed. For in a warm climate, no man will labor for himself who can make another labor for him. This is so true, that of the proprietors of slaves a very small proportion indeed are ever seen to labor. And can the liberties of a nation be thought secure when we have removed their only firm basis, a conviction in the minds of the people that these liberties are of the gift of God? That they are not to be violated but with his wrath? Indeed I tremble for my country when I reflect that God is just; that his justice cannot sleep forever; that considering numbers, nature and natural means only, a revolution of the wheel of fortune, an exchange of situation is among possible events; that it may become probable by supernatural interference! The Almighty has no attribute which can take side with us in such a contest. But it is impossible to be temperate and to pursue this subject through the various considerations of policy, of morals, of history natural and civil. We must be contented to hope they will force their way into everyone's mind. I think a change already perceptible, since the origin of the present revolution. The spirit of the master is abating, that of the slave rising from the dust, his condition mollifying, the way I hope preparing, under the auspices of heaven, for a total emancipation, and that this is disposed, in the order of events, to be with the consent of the masters, rather than by their extirpation.

## QUERY XIX

*The present state of manufactures, commerce, interior and exterior trade*

We never had an interior trade of any importance. Our exterior commerce has suffered very much from the beginning of the present contest. During this time we have manufactured within our families the most necessary articles of clothing. Those of cotton will bear some comparison with the same kinds of manufacture in Europe; but those of wool, flax and hemp are very coarse, unsightly, and unpleasant; and such is our attachment to agriculture, and such our preference for foreign manufactures, that be it wise or unwise, our people will certainly return as soon as they can, to the raising raw materials, and exchanging them for finer manufactures than they are able to execute themselves.

The political economists of Europe have established it as a principle, that every State should endeavor to manufacture for itself; and this principle, like many others, we transfer to America, without calculating the difference of circumstance which should often produce a difference of result. In Europe the lands are either cultivated, or locked up against the cultivator. Manufacture must therefore be resorted to of necessity not of choice, to support the surplus of their people. But we have an immensity of land courting the industry of the husbandman. Is it best then that all our citizens should be employed in its improvement, or that one half should be called off from that to exercise manufactures and handicraft arts for the other? Those who labor in the earth are the chosen people of God, if ever He had a chosen people, whose breasts He has made His peculiar deposit for substantial and genuine virtue. It is the focus in which he keeps alive that sacred fire, which otherwise might escape from the face of the earth. Corruption of morals in the mass of cultivators is a phenomenon of which no age nor nation has furnished an example. It is the mark set on those, who, not looking up to heaven, to their own soil and industry, as does the husbandman, for their subsistence, depend for it on casualties and caprice of customers. Dependence begets subservience and venality, suffocates the germ of virtue, and prepares fit tools for the designs of ambition. This, the natural progress and consequence of the arts, has sometimes perhaps been retarded by accidental circumstances; but, generally speaking, the proportion which the aggregate of the other classes of citizens bears in any State to that of its husbandmen, is the proportion of its unsound to its healthy parts, and is a good enough barometer whereby to measure its degree of corruption. While we have land to labor then, let us never wish to see our citizens occupied at a work-bench, or twirling a distaff. Carpenters, masons, smiths, are wanting in husbandry; but, for the general operations of manufacture, let our workshops remain in Europe. It is better to carry provisions and materials to workmen there, than bring them to the provisions and materials, and with them their manners and principles. The loss by the transportation of commodities across the Atlantic will be made up in happiness and permanence of government. The mobs of great cities add just so much to the support of pure government, as sores do to the strength of the human body. It is the manners and spirit of a people which preserve a republic in vigor. A degeneracy in these is a canker which soon eats to the heart of its laws and constitution.

## QUERY XX

*A notice of the commercial productions particular to the State, and of those objects which the inhabitants are obliged to get from Europe and from other parts of the world*

Before the present war we exported, *communibus annis,* according to the best information I can get, nearly as follows:

| ARTICLES | QUANTITY | PRICE IN DOLLARS | AMOUNT IN DOLLARS |
|---|---|---|---|
| Tobacco | 55,000 hhds. of 1,000 lbs. | at 30d. per hhd. | $1,650,000 |
| Wheat | 800,000 bushels. | at 5-6d. per bush. | 666,666⅔ |
| Indian corn | 600,000 " | at ⅓d. per bush. | 200,000 |
| Shipping | ....... | ...... | 100,000 |
| Masts, planks, scantling, shingles, staves | ....... | ...... | 66,666⅔ |
| Tar, pitch, turpentine | 30,000 barrels. | at 1⅓d. per bbl. | 40,000 |
| Peltry, *viz.*, skins of deer, beavers, otters, musk rats, raccoons, foxes | 180 hhds. of 600 lbs. | at 5-12d. per lb. | 42,000 |
| Pork | 4,000 barrels. | at 10d. per bbl. | 40,000 |
| Flax-seed, hemp, cotton | ....... | ...... | 8,000 |
| Pit coal, pig iron | ....... | ...... | 6,666⅔ |
| Peas | 5,000 bushels. | at ⅔d. per bush. | 3,333⅓ |
| Beef | 1,000 barrels. | at 3⅓d. per bbl. | 3,333⅓ |
| Sturgeon, white shad, herring | ....... | ...... | 3,333⅓ |
| Brandy from peaches and apples, and whiskey | ....... | ...... | 1,666⅔ |
| Horses | ....... | ...... | 1,666⅔ |
| | ....... | ...... | [63] $2,833,333⅓ |

In the year 1758 we exported seventy thousand hogsheads of tobacco, which was the greatest quantity ever produced in this country in one year. But its culture was fast declining at the commencement of this war and that of wheat taken its place; and it must continue to decline on the return of peace. I suspect that the change in the temperature of our climate has become sensible to that plant, which to be good, requires an extraordinary degree of heat. But it requires still more indispensably an uncommon fertility of soil; and the price which it commands at market will not enable the planter to produce this by manure. Was the supply still to depend on Virginia and Maryland alone as its culture becomes more difficult, the price would rise so as to enable the

[63] This sum is equal to £850,000; Virginia money, 607,142 guineas.—T. J.

planter to surmount those difficulties and to live. But the western country on the Mississippi, and the midlands of Georgia, having fresh and fertile lands in abundance, and a hotter sun, will be able to undersell these two States, and will oblige them to abandon the raising of tobacco altogether. And a happy obligation for them it will be. It is a culture productive of infinite wretchedness. Those employed in it are in a continual state of exertion beyond the power of nature to support. Little food of any kind is raised by them; so that the men and animals on these farms are badly fed, and the earth is rapidly impoverished. The cultivation of wheat is the reverse in every circumstance. Besides clothing the earth with herbage, and preserving its fertility, it feeds the laborers plentifully, requires from them only a moderate toil, except in the season of harvest, raises great numbers of animals for food and service, and diffuses plenty and happiness among the whole. We find it easier to make an hundred bushels of wheat than a thousand weight of tobacco, and they are worth more when made. The weavil indeed is a formidable obstacle to the cultivation of this grain with us. But principles are already known which must lead to a remedy. Thus a certain degree of heat, to wit, that of the common air in summer, is necessary to hatch the eggs. If subterranean granaries, or others, therefore, can be contrived below that temperature, the evil will be cured by cold. A degree of heat beyond that which hatches the egg we know will kill it. But in aiming at this we easily run into that which produced putrefaction. To produce putrefaction, however, three agents are requisite, heat, moisture, and the external air. If the absence of any one of these be secured, the other two may safely be admitted. Heat is the one we want. Moisture then, or external air, must be excluded. The former has been done by exposing the grain in kilns to the action of fire, which produces heat, and extracts moisture at the same time; the latter, by putting the grain into hogsheads, covering it with a coating of lime, and heading it up. In this situation its bulk produced a heat sufficient to kill the eggs; the moisture is suffered to remain indeed, but the external air is excluded. A nicer operation yet has been attempted; that is, to produce an intermediate temperature of heat between that which kills the egg, and that which produces putrefaction. The threshing the grain as soon as it is cut, and laying it in its chaff in large heaps, has been found very nearly to hit this temperature, though not perfectly, nor always. The heap generates heat sufficient to kill most of the eggs, whilst the chaff commonly restrains it from rising into putrefaction. But all these methods abridge too much the quantity which the farmer can manage, and enable other countries to undersell him, which are not infested with this insect. There is still a desideratum then to give with us decisive triumph to this branch of agriculture over that of tobacco. The culture of wheat by enlarging our pasture, will render the Arabian horse an article of very considerable profit. Experience has shown that ours is the particular climate of America where he may be raised without degeneracy. Southwardly the heat of the sun occasions a deficiency of pasture, and northwardly the winters are too cold for the short and fine hair, the particular sensibility and constitution of that race. Animals transplanted into unfriendly climates, either change their nature and acquire new senses against the new difficulties in which they are placed, or they multiply poorly and become extinct. A good foundation is laid for their propagation here by our possessing already great numbers of horses of that blood, and by a decided taste and preference for them established among the people. Their patience of heat without injury, their superior wind, fit them better in this and the more southern climates even for the drudgeries of the plough and wagon. Northwardly they will become an object only to persons of taste and fortune, for the saddle and light carriages. To those, and for these uses, their fleetness and beauty will recommend them. Besides these there will be other valuable substitutes when the cultivation of tobacco shall be discontinued such as cotton in the eastern parts of the State, and hemp and flax in the western.

It is not easy to say what are the articles either of necessity, comfort, or luxury, which we cannot raise, and which we therefore shall be under a necessity of importing from abroad, as everything hardier than the olive, and as hardy as the fig, may be raised here in the open air. Sugar, coffee and tea, indeed, are not between these limits; and habit having placed them among the necessaries of life with the wealthy part of our citizens, as long as these habits remain we must go for them to those countries which are able to furnish them.

## QUERY XXI

*The weights, measures and the currency of the hard money Some details relating to exchange with Europe*

Our weights and measures are the same which are fixed by acts of parliament in England. How it has happened that in this as well as the other American States the nominal value of coin was made to differ from what it was in the country we had left, and to differ among ourselves too, I am not able to say with certainty. I find that in 1631 our house of burgesses desired of the privy council in England, a coin debased to twenty-five per cent; that in 1645 they forbid dealing by barter for tobacco, and established the Spanish piece of eight at six shillings, as the standard of their currency; that in 1655 they changed it to five shillings sterling. In 1680 they sent an address to the king, in consequence of which, by proclamation in 1683, he fixed the value of French crowns, rix dollars, and pieces of eight, at six shillings, and the coin of New England at one shilling. That in 1710, 1714, 1727, and 1762, other regulations were made, which will be better presented to the eye stated in the form of the table on page 682.

The first symptom of the depreciation of our present paper money, was that of silver dollars selling at six shillings, which had before been worth but five shilling and ninepence. The assembly thereupon raised them by law to six shillings. As the dollar is now likely to become the money-unit of America, as it passes at this rate in some of our sister States, and as it facilitates their computation in pounds and shillings, &c., converso, this seems to be more convenient than its former denomination. But as this particular coin now stands higher

| | 1710 | 1714 | 1727 | 1762 |
|---|---|---|---|---|
| Guineas | .... | 26s. | | |
| British gold coin not milled, gold coin of Spain and France, chequins, Arabian gold, moidores of Portugal | .... | 5s. dwt. | | |
| Coined gold of the empire | .... | 5s. dwt. | .... | 4s. 3d. dwt. |
| English milled silver money, in proportion to the crown, at | .... | 5s. 10d. | 6s. 3d. | |
| Pieces of eight of Mexico, Seville & Pillar, ducatoons of Flanders, French ecus, or silver Louis, crusados of Portugal | 3¾d. dwt. | .... | 4d. dwt. | |
| Peru pieces, cross dollars, and old rix dollars of the empire | 3½d. dwt. | .... | 3¾d. dwt. | |
| Old British silver coin not milled | .... | 3¾d. dwt. | | |

than any other in the proportion of one hundred and thirty-three and a half to one hundred and twenty-five, or sixteen to fifteen, it will be necessary to raise the others in proportion.

## QUERY XXII

### *The public Income and expenses*

The nominal amount of these varying constantly and rapidly, with the constant and rapid depreciation of our paper money, it becomes impracticable to say what they are. We find ourselves cheated in every essay by the depreciation intervening between the declaration of the tax and its actual receipt. It will therefore be more satisfactory to consider what our income may be when we shall find means of collecting what our people may spare. I should estimate the whole taxable property of this State at an hundred millions of dollars, or thirty millions of pounds, our money. One per cent on this, compared with anything we ever yet paid, would be deemed a very heavy tax. Yet I think that those who manage well, and use reasonable economy, could pay one and a half per cent, and maintain their household comfortably in the meantime, without aliening any part of their principal, and that the people would submit to this willingly for the purpose of supporting their present contest. We may say, then, that we could raise, from one million to one million and a half of dollars annually, that is from three hundred to four hundred and fifty thousand pounds, Virginia money.

Of our expenses it is equally difficult to give an exact state, and for the same reason. They are mostly stated in paper money, which varying continually, the legislature endeavors at every session, by new corrections, to adapt the nominal sums to the value it is wished they would bear. I will state them, therefore, in real coin, at the point at which they endeavor to keep them:

| | DOLLARS |
|---|---|
| The annual expenses of the general assembly are about | 20,000 |
| The governor | 3,333⅓ |

| | DOLLARS |
|---|---|
| The council of state | 10,666⅔ |
| Their clerks | 1,166⅔ |
| Eleven judges | 11,000 |
| The clerk of the chancery | 666⅔ |
| The attorney general | 1,000 |
| Three auditors and a solicitor | 5,333⅓ |
| Their clerks | 2,000 |
| The treasurer | 2,000 |
| His clerks | 2,000 |
| The keeper of the public jail | 1,000 |
| The public printer | 1,666⅔ |
| Clerks of the inferior courts | 43,333⅓ |
| Public levy; this is chiefly for the expenses of criminal justice | 40,000 |
| County levy, for bridges, court-houses, prisons, &c. | 40,000 |
| Members of Congress | 7,000 |
| Quota of the federal civil list, supposed one-sixth of about $78,000 | 13,000 |
| Expenses of collecting, six per cent on the above | 12,310 |
| The clergy receive only voluntary contributions; suppose them on an average one-eighth of a dollar a tythe on 200,000 tythes | 25,000 |
| Contingencies, to make round numbers not far from truth | 7,523⅓ |
| | $250,000 |

or 53,571 guineas. This estimate is exclusive of the military expense. That varies with the force actually employed, and in time of peace will probably be little or nothing. It is exclusive also of the public debts, which are growing while I am writing, and cannot therefore be now fixed. So it is of the maintenance of the poor, which being merely a matter of charity cannot be deemed expended in the administration of government. And if we strike out the $25,000 for the services of the clergy, which neither makes part of that administration, more than what is paid to physicians, or lawyers, and being voluntary, is either much or nothing as everyone pleases, it leaves $225,000, equal to 48,208 guineas, the real cost of the apparatus of government with us. This divided among the actual inhabitants of our country, comes to about two-fifths of a dollar, twenty-one pence sterling, or forty-two sols, the price which each pays annually for the protection of the residue of his property, and the other advantages of a free government. The public revenues of Great Britain divided in like manner on its inhabitants would be sixteen times greater. Deducting even the double of the expenses of government, as before estimated, from the million and a half of dollars which we before supposed might be annually paid without distress, we may conclude that this State can contribute one million of dollars annually towards supporting the federal army, paying the federal debt, building a federal navy, or opening roads, clearing rivers, forming safe ports, and other useful works.

To this estimate of our abilities, let me add a word as to the application of them. If, when cleared of the present contest, and of the debts with which that will charge us, we come to measure force hereafter with any European power. Such events are devoutly to be deprecated. Young as we are, and with such a country before us to fill with people and with happiness, we should point in that direction the whole generative force of nature, wasting none of it in efforts of mutual destruction. It should be our endeavor to cultivate the peace and friendship of every nation, even of that which has injured us most, when we shall have carried our point against her. Our interest will be to throw open the doors of commerce, and to knock off all its shackles, giving perfect freedom to all persons for the vent of whatever they may chuse to bring into our ports, and asking the same in theirs. Never was so much false arithmetic employed on any subject, as that which has been employed to persuade nations that it is their interest to go to war. Were the money which it has cost to gain, at the close of a long war, a little town, or a little territory, the right to cut wood here, or to catch fish there, expended in improving what they already possess, in making roads, opening rivers, building ports, improving the arts, and finding employment for their idle poor, it would render them much stronger, much wealthier and happier. This I hope will be our wisdom. And, perhaps, to remove as much as possible the occasions of making war, it might be better for us to abandon the ocean altogether, that being the element whereon we shall be principally exposed to jostle with other nations; to leave to others to bring what we shall want, and to carry what we can spare. This would make us invulnerable to Europe, by offering none of our property to their prize, and would turn all our citizens to the cultivation of the earth; and, I repeat it again, cultivators of the earth are the most virtuous and independent citizens. It might be time enough to seek employment for them at sea, when the land no longer offers it. But the actual habits of our countrymen attach them to commerce. They will exercise it for themselves. Wars then must sometimes be our lot; and all the wise can do, will be to avoid that half of them which would be produced by our own follies and our own acts of injustice; and to make for the other half the best preparations we can. Of what nature should these be? A land army would be useless for offence, and not the best nor safest instrument of defence. For either of these purposes, the sea is the field on which we should meet an European enemy. On that element it is necessary we should possess some power. To aim at such a navy as the greater nations of Europe possess, would be a foolish and wicked waste of the energies of our countrymen. It would be to pull on our own heads that load of military expense which makes the European laborer go supperless to bed, and moistens his bread with the sweat of his brows. It will be enough if we enable ourselves to prevent insults from those nations of Europe which are weak on the sea, because circumstances exist, which render even the stronger ones weak as to us. Providence has placed their richest and most defenceless possessions at our door; has obliged their most precious commerce to pass, as it were, in review before us. To protect this, or to assail, a small part only of their naval force will ever be risked across the Atlantic. The dangers to which the elements expose them here are too well known, and the greater dangers to which they would be exposed at home were any general calamity to involve their whole fleet. They can attack us by detachment only; and it will suffice to make ourselves equal to what they may detach. Even a smaller force than they may detach will be rendered equal or superior by the quickness with which any check may be repaired with us, while losses with them will be irreparable till too late. A small naval force then is sufficient for us, and a small one is necessary. What this should be, I will not undertake to say. I will only say, it should by no means be so great as we are able to make it. Suppose the million of dollars, or three hundred thousand pounds, which Virginia could annually spare without distress, to be applied to the creating a navy. A single year's contribution would build, equip, man, and send to sea a force which should carry three hundred guns. The rest of the confederacy, exerting themselves in the same proportion, would equip in the same time fifteen hundred guns more. So that one year's contributions would set up a navy of eighteen hundred guns. The British ships of the line average seventy-six guns; their frigates thirty-eight. Eighteen hundred guns then would form a fleet of thirty ships, eighteen of which might be of the line, and twelve frigates. Allowing eight men, the British average, for every gun, their annual expense, including subsistence, clothing, pay, and ordinary repairs, would be about $1,280 for every gun, or $2,304,000 for the whole. I state this only as one year's possible exertion, without deciding whether more or less than a year's exertion should be thus applied.

The value of our lands and slaves, taken conjunctly, doubles in about twenty years. This arises from the multiplication of our slaves, from the extension of culture, and increased demand for lands. The amount of what may be raised will of course rise in the same proportion.

## QUERY XXIII

*The histories of the State, the memorials published in its name in the time of its being a colony, and the pamphlets relating to its interior or exterior affairs present or ancient*

Captain Smith, who next to Sir Walter Raleigh may be considered as the founder of our colony, has written its history, from the first adventures to it, till the year 1624. He was a member of the council, and afterwards president of the colony; and to his efforts principally may be ascribed its support against the opposition of the natives. He was honest, sensible, and well informed; but his style is barbarous and uncouth. His history, however, is almost the only source from which we derive any knowledge of the infancy of our State.

The reverend William Stith, a native of Virginia, and president of its college, has also written the history of the same period, in a large octavo volume of small print. He was a man of classical learning, and very exact, but of no taste in style. He is inelegant, therefore, and his details often too minute to be tolerable, even to a native of the country, whose history he writes.

Beverley, a native also, has run into the other extreme, he has comprised our history from the first propositions of Sir Walter Raleigh to the year 1700, in the hundredth part of the space which Stith employs for the fourth part of the period.

Sir Walter Keith has taken it up at its earliest period, and continued it to the year 1725. He is agreeable enough in style, and passes over events of little importance. Of course he is short and would be preferred by a foreigner.

During the regal government, some contest arose on the exaction of an illegal fee by governor Dinwiddie, and doubtless there were others on other occasions not at present recollected. It is supposed that these are not sufficiently interesting to a foreigner to merit a detail.

The petition of the council and burgesses of Virginia to the king, their memorials to the lords, and remonstrance to the commons in the year 1764, began the present contest; and these having proved ineffectual to prevent the passage of the stamp-act, the resolutions of the house of burgesses of 1765 were passed declaring the independence of the people of Virginia of the parliament of Great Britain, in matters of taxation. From that time till the declaration of independence by Congress in 1776, their journals are filled with assertions of the public rights.

The pamphlets published in this State on the controverted question, were:

1766, An Inquiry into the rights of the British Colonies, by Richard Bland.

1769, The Monitor's Letters, by Dr. Arthur Lee.

1774, A summary View of the rights of British America.[64]

1774, Considerations, &c., by Robert Carter Nicholas.

Since the declaration of independence this State has had no controversy with any other, except with that of Pennsylvania, on their common boundary. Some papers on this subject passed between the executive and legislative bodies of the two States, the result of which was a happy accommodation of their rights.

To this account of our historians, memorials, and pamphlets, it may not be unuseful to add a chronological catalogue of American state-papers, as far as I have been able to collect their titles. It is far from being either complete or correct. Where the title alone, and not the paper itself, has come under my observation, I cannot answer for the exactness of the date. Sometimes I have not been able to find any date at all, and sometimes have not been satisfied that such a paper exists. An extensive collection of papers of this description has been for some time in a course of preparation by a gentleman[65] fully equal to the task, and from whom, therefore, we may hope ere long to receive it. In the meantime accept this as the result of my labors, and as closing the tedious detail which you have so undesignedly drawn upon yourself.

| | |
|---|---|
| 1496, Mar. 5<br>11. H. 7 | Pro Johanne Caboto et filiis suis super terra incognita investiganda. 12. Ry. 595. 3. Hakl. 4. 2. Mem. A. 409. |
| 1498, Feb. 3<br>13. H. 7 | Billa signata anno 13. Henrici septimi. 3. Hakluyt's voiages 5. |
| 1502, Dec. 19<br>18. H. 7 | De potestatibus ad terras incognitas investigandum. 13. Rymer. 37. |

[64] By the author of these notes.—T. J.

[65] Mr. Hazard.—T. J.

| | |
|---|---|
| Commission de François I. à Jacques Catier pour l'establissement du Canada. L'Escarbot. 397. 2. Mem. Am. 416. | 1540, Oct. 17 |
| An act against the exaction of money, or any other thing, by any officer for license to traffique into Iseland and New-foundland, made in An. 2. Edwardi sexti. 3. Hakl. 131. | 1548, 2. E. 6 |
| The letters-patent granted by her Majestie to Sir Humphrey Gilbert, knight, for the inhabiting and planting of our people in America. 3. Hakl. 135. | 1578, June 11<br>20. El |
| Letters-patent of Queen Elizabeth to Adrian Gilbert and others, to discover the northwest passage to China. 3. Hakl. 96. | 1583, Feb. 6 |
| The letters-patent granted by the Queen's majestie to M. Walter Raleigh, now knight, for the discovering and planting of new lands and countries, to continue the space of six years and no more. 3. Hakl. 243. | 1584, Mar. 25<br>26 El |
| An assignment by Sir Walter Raleigh for continuing the action of inhabiting and planting his people in Virginia. Hakl. 1st. ed. publ. in 1589. p. 815. | Mar. 7, 31. El |
| Lettres de Lieutenant General de l'Acadie et pays circonvoisins pour le Sieur de Monts. L'Escarbot. 417. | 1603, Nov. 8 |
| Letters-patent to Sir Thomas Gates, Sir George Somers and others of America. Stith. Apend. No. 1. | 1606, Apr. 10<br>4. Jac. 1 |
| An ordinance and constitution enlarging the council of the two colonies in Virginia and America, and augmenting their authority, M. S. | 1607, Mar. 9<br>4. Jac. 1 |
| The second charter to the treasurer and company for Virginia, erecting them into a body politick. Stith. Ap. 2. | 1609, May 23<br>7. Jac. 1 |
| Letters-patents to the E. of Northampton, granting part of the island of Newfoundland. 1. Harris. 861. | 1610, Apr. 10<br>Jac. 1 |
| A third charter to the treasurer and company for Virginia. Stith. Ap. 3. | 1611, Mar. 12<br>9. Jac. 1 |
| A commission to Sir Walter Raleigh. Qu. | 1617, Jac. 1 |
| Commissio specialis concernens le garbling herbæ Nocotianæ. 17. Rym. 190. | 1620, Apr. 7<br>18. Jac. 1 |
| A proclamation for restraint of the disordered trading of tobacco. 17. Rym. 233. | 1620, June 29<br>18. Jac. 1 |
| A grant of New-England to the council of Plymouth. | 1620, Nov. 3<br>Jac. 1 |
| An ordinance and constitution of the treasurer, council and company in England, for a council of state and general assembly in Virginia. Stith. Ap. 4. | 1621, July 24<br>Jac. 1 |
| A grant of Nova Scotia to Sir William Alexander. 2. Mem. de l'Amerique. 193. | 1621, Sep. 10<br>20 Jac. 1 |
| A proclamation prohibiting interloping and disorderly trading to New England in America. 17. Rym. 416. | 1622, Nov. 6<br>20 Jac. 1 |
| De commissione speciali Willelmo Jones militi directa. 17. Rym. 490. | 1623, May 9<br>21 Jac. 1 |
| A grant to Sir Edmund Ployden, of New Albion. Mentioned in Smith's examination. 82. | 1623 |
| De commissione Henrico vicecomiti Mandevill et aliis. 17. Rym. 609. | 1624, July 15<br>22. Jac. 1 |
| De commissione speciali concernenti gubernationem in Virginia. 17. Rym. 618. | 1624, Aug. 26<br>22 Jac. 1 |

| | |
|---|---|
| 1624, Sep. 29 22 Jac. 1 | A proclamation concerning tobacco. 17. Rym. 621. |
| 1624, Nov. 9 22 Jac. 1 | De concessione demiss, Edwardo Ditchfield et aliis. 17. Rym. 633. |
| 1625, Mar. 2 22 Jac. 1 | A proclamation for the utter prohibiting the importation and use of all tobacco which is not of the proper growth of the colony of Virginia and the Somer islands, or one of them. 17. Rym. 668. |
| 1625, Mar. 4 1 Car. 1 | De commissione directa Georgio Yardeley militi et aliis. 18. Rym. 311. |
| 1625, Apr. 9 1 Car. 1 | Proclamatio de herba Nicotianâ. 18. Rym. 19. |
| 1625, May 13 1 Car. 1 | A proclamation for settlinge the plantation of Virginia. 18. Rym. 72. |
| 1625, July 12 | A grant of the soil, barony, and domains of Nova Scotia to Sir Wm. Alexander of Minstrie. 2. Mem. Am. 226. |
| 1626, Jan. 31 2 Car. 1 | Commissio directa a Johanni Wolstenholme militi et aliis. 18. Rym. 831. |
| 1626, Feb. 17 2 Car. 1 | A proclamation touching tobacco. Rym. 848. |
| 1627, Mar. 19 qu? 2 Car. 1 | A grant of Massachusetts bay by the council of Plymouth to Sir Henry Roswell and others. |
| 1627, Mar. 26 3 Car. 1 | De concessione commissionis specialis proconcilio in Virginia. 18. Rym. 980. |
| 1627, Mar. 30 3 Car. 1 | De proclamatione de signatione de tobacco. 18. Rym. 886. |
| 1627, Aug. 9 3 Car. 1 | De proclamatione pro ordinatione de tobacco. 18. Rym. 920. |
| 1628, Mar. 4 3 Car. 1 | A confirmation of the grant of Massachusetts bay by the crown. |
| 1629, Aug. 19 | The capitulation of Quebec. Champlain pert. 2. 216. 2. Mem. Am. 489. |
| 1630, Jan. 6 5 Car. 1 | A proclamation concerning tobacco. 19. Rym. 235. |
| 1630, Apr. 30 | Conveyance of Nova Scotia (Port-royal excepted) by Sir William Alexander to Sir Claude St. Etienne Lord of la Tour and of Uarre and to his son Sir Charles de St. Etienne Lord of St. Denniscourt, on condition that they continue subjects to the king of Scotland under the great seal of Scotland. |
| 1630-31, Nov. 24: 6 Car. 1 | A proclamation forbidding the disorderly trading with the savages in New England in America, especially the furnishing the natives in those and other parts of America by the English with weapons and habiliments of warre. 19. Ry. 210. 3. Rushw. 82. |
| 1630, Dec. 5 6 Car. 1 | A proclamation prohibiting the selling arms, &c. to the savages in America. Mentioned 3. Rushw. 75. |
| 1630, Car. 1 | A grant of Connecticut by the council of Plymouth to the E. of Warwick. |
| 1630, Car. 1 | A confirmation by the crown of the grant of Connecticut [said to be in the petty-bag office in England.] |
| 1631, Mar. 19 6 Car. 1 | A conveiance of Connecticut by the E. of Warwick to Lord Say, and Seal, and others. Smith's examination, Appendix No. 1. |
| 1631, June 27 7 Car. 1 | A special commission to Edward, Earle of Dorsett, and others, for the better plantation of the colony of Virginia. 19. Ry. 301. |

| | |
|---|---|
| Litere continentes promissionem regis ad tradenum castrum et habitationem de Kebec in Canada ad regem Francorum. 19. Ry. 303. | 1632, June 29<br>7 Car. 1 |
| Traité entre le roy Louis XIII. et Charles roi d'Angleterre pour la restitution de la nouvelle France, la Cadie et Canada et des navires et merchandises pris de part et d'autrie. Fait a St. Germain. 19. Ry. 361. 2. Mem. Am. 5. | 1632, Mar. 29<br>8 Car. 1 |
| A grant of Maryland to Cæcilius Calvert, baron of Baltimore in Ireland. | 1632, June 20<br>8 Car. 1 |
| A petition of the planters of Virginia against the grant to lord Baltimore. | 1633, July 3<br>9 Car. 1 |
| Order of council upon the dispute between the Virginia planters and lord Baltimore. Votes of repres. Pennsylvania. V. | 1633, July 3 |
| A proclamation to prevent abuses growing by the unordered retailing of tobacco. Mentioned 3. Rushw. 191. | 1633, Aug. 13<br>9 Car. 1 |
| A special commission to Thomas Young to search, discover and find out what ports are not yet inhabited in Virginia and America and other parts thereunto adjoining. 19. Ry. 472. | 1633, Sept. 23<br>9 Car. 1 |
| A proclamation for preventing of the abuses growing by the unordered retailing of tobacco. 19. Ry. 474. | 1633, Oct. 13<br>9 Car. 1 |
| A proclamation restraining the abusive venting of tobacco. 19. Rym. 522. | 1633, Mar. 13<br>Cer. 1 |
| A proclamation concerning the landing of tobacco, and also forbidding the planting thereof in the king's dominions. 19. Ry. 553. | 1634, May 19<br>10 Car. 1 |
| A commission to the Archbishop of Canterbury and 11 others, for governing the American colonies. | 1634, Car. 1 |
| A commission concerning tobacco. M S. | 1634, June 19<br>10 Car. 1 |
| A commission from Lord Say, and Seal, and others, to John Winthrop to be governor of Connecticut. Smith's App. | 1635, July 18<br>11 Car. 1 |
| A grant to Duke Hamilton. | 1635, Car. 1 |
| De commissione speciali Johanni Harvey militi to pro meliori regemine coloniae in Virginia. 20. Ry. 3. | 1636, Apr. 2<br>12 Car. 1 |
| A proclamation concerning tobacco. Title in 3. Rush. 617. | 1637, Mar. 14<br>Car. 1 |
| De commissione speciali Georgio domino Goring et aliis concessâ concernente venditionem de tobacco absque licentiâ regiâ. 20. Ry. 116. | 1636-7, Mar. 16. 12 Car. 1 |
| A proclamation against disorderly transporting his Majesty's subjects to the plantations within the parts of America. 20. Ry. 143. 3. Rush. 409. | 1637, Apr. 30<br>13 Car. 1 |
| An order of the privy council to stay 8 ships now in the Thames from going to New England. 3. Rush. 409. | 1637, May 1<br>13 Car. 1 |
| A warrant of the Lord Admiral to stop unconformable ministers from going beyond the sea. 3. Rush. 410. | 1637, Car. 1 |
| Order of council upon Claiborne's petition against Lord Baltimore. Votes of representatives of Pennsylvania. vi. | 1638, Apr. 4<br>Car. 1 |
| An order of the king and council that the attorney general draw up a proclamation to prohibit transportation of passengers to New England without license. 3. Rush. 718. | 1638, Apr. 6<br>14 Car. 1 |
| A proclamation to restrain the transporting of passengers and provisions to New England without license. 20. Ry. 223. | 1638, May 1<br>14 Car. 1 |

| | |
|---|---|
| 1639, Mar. 25 Car. 1 | A proclamation concerning tobacco. Title 4. Rush. 1060. |
| 1639, Aug. 19 15 Car. 1 | A proclamation declaring his majesty's pleasure to continue his commission and letters patents for licensing retailers of tobacco. 20. Ry. 348. |
| 1639, Dec. 16 15 Car. 1 | De commissione speciali Henrico Ashton armigero ét aliis ad amovendum Henricum Hawley gubernatorem de Barbadoes. 20. Rym. 357. |
| 1639, Car. 1 | A proclamation concerning retailers of tobacco. 4. Rush. 966. |
| 1641, Aug. 9 17 Car. 1 | De constitutione gubernatoris et concilii pro Virginia. 20. Ry. 484. |
| 1643, Car. 1 | Articles of union and confederacy entered into by Massachusetts, Plymouth, Connecticut and New-haven. 1. Neale. 223. |
| 1644, Car. 1 | Deed from George Fenwick to the old Connecticut jurisdiction. |
| | An ordinance of the lords and commons assembled in parliament, for exempting from custom and imposition all commodities exported for, or imported from New England, which has been very prosperous and without any public charge to this State, and is likely to prove very happy for the propagation of the gospel in those parts. Tit. in Amer. library 90.5. No date. But seems by the neighbouring articles to have been in 1644. |
| 1644, June 20 Car. 2 | An act for charging of tobacco brought from New England with custom and excise. Title in American library. 99. 8. |
| 1644, Aug. 1 Car. 2 | An act for the advancing and regulating the trade of this commonwealth. Tit. in Amer. libr. 99. 9. |
| Sep. 18 1 Car. 2 | Grant of the Northern neck of Virginia to Lord Hopton, Lord Jermyn, Lord Culpepper, Sir John Berkley, Sir William Moreton, Sir Dudley Wyatt, and Thomas Culpepper. |
| 1650, Oct. 3 2 Car. 2 | An act prohibiting trade with the Barbadoes, Virginia, Bermudas and Antego Scobell's Acts. 1027. |
| 1650, Car. 2 | A declaration of Lord Willoughby, governor of Barbadoes, and of his council, against an act of parliament of 3d of October, 1650. 4. Polit. register. 2. cited from 4 Neal. hist. of the Puritans. App. No. 12 but not there. |
| 1650, Car. 2 | A final settlement of boundaries between the Dutch New Netherlands and Connecticut. |
| 1651, Sept. 26 3 Car. 2 | Instructions for Captain Robert Dennis, Mr. Richard Bennet, Mr. Thomas Stagge, and Captain William Claibourn, appointed commissioners for the reducing of Virginia and the inhabitants thereof to their due obedience to the commonwealth of England. 1 Thurloe's state papers, 197. |
| 1651, Oct. 9 8 Car. 2 | An act for increase of shipping and encouragement of the navigation of this nation. Scobell's acts, 1449. |
| 1651-2, Mar. 12. 4 Car. 2 | Articles agreed on and concluded at James citie in Virginia for the surrendering and settling of that plantation under the obedience and government of the commonwealth of England, by the commissioners of the council of state, by authoritie of the parliament of England, and by the grand assembly of the governor, council, and burgesse of that state. M. S. [Ante. p. 206.] |
| 1651-2, Mar. 12. 4 Car. 1 | An act of indempnitie made at the surrender of the country [of Virginia.] [Ante p. 206.] |
| 1654, Aug. 16 | Capitulation de Port Royal. Mem. Am. 507. |

A proclamation of the protector relating to Jamaica. 3 Thurl. 75. | 1655, Car. 2

The protector to the commissioners of Maryland. A letter. 4 Thurl. 55. | 1655, Sep. 26 7 Car. 2

An instrument made at the council of Jamaica, Oct. 8, 1655, for the better carrying on of affairs there. 4 Thurl. 17. | 1655, Oct. 8 7 Car. 2

Treaty of Westminster between France and England. 6. corps diplom. part 2. p. 121. 2 Mem. Am. 10. | 1655, Nov. 3

The assembly at Barbadoes to the protector. 4 Thurl. 651. | 1656, Mar. 27 8 Car. 2

A grant by Cromwell to Sir Charles de Saint Etienne, a baron of Scotland, Crowne and Temple. A French translation of it. 2 Mem. Am. 511. | 1656, Aug. 9

A paper concerning the advancement of trade, 5 Thurl. 80. | 1656, Car. 2

A brief narration of the English rights to the Northern parts of America. 5 Thurl. 81. | 1656, Car. 2

Mr. R. Bennet and Mr. S. Matthew to Secretary Thurlow. 5 Thurl. 482. | 1656, Oct. 10 8 Car. 2

Objections against the Lord Baltimore's patent, and reasons why the government of Maryland should not be put into his hands. 5 Thurl. 482. | 1656, Oct. 10 8 Car. 2

A paper relating to Maryland. 5 Thurl. 483. | 1656, Oct. 10 8 Car. 2

A breviet of the proceedings of the lord Baltimore and his officers and compliers in Maryland, against the authority of the parliament of the commonwealth of England and against his highness the lord protector's authority, laws and government. 5 Thurl. 486. | 1656, Oct. 10 8 Car. 2

The assembly of Virginia to secretary Thurlow. 5 Thurl. 497. | 1656, Oct. 15 8 Car. 2

The governor of Barbadoes to the protector. 6 Thurl. 69. | 1657, Apr. 4 9 Car. 2

Petition of the general court at Hartford upon Connecticut for charter. Smith's exam. App. 4. | 1661, Car. 2

Charter of the colony of Connecticut. Smith's exam. App. 6. | 1662, Apr. 23 14 Car. 2

The first charter granted by Charles II. to the proprietaries of Carolina, to wit, to the Earl of Clarendon, Duke of Albemarle, Lord Craven, Lord Berkeley, Lord Ashley, Sir George Carteret, Sir William Berkeley, and Sir John Colleton. 4 Mem. Am. 554. | 1662-2, Mar. 24 Apr. 4. 15 C. 2

The concessions and agreement of the lords proprietors of the province of New Cæsarea, or New Jersey, to and with all and every of the adventurers and all such as shall settle or plant there. Smith's New Jersey. App. 1. | 1664, Feb. 10

A grant of the colony of New York to the Duke of York. | 1664, Mar. 12 20 Car. 2

A commission to Colonel Nichols and others to settle disputes in New England. Hutch. Hist. Mass. Bay, App. 537. | 1664, Apr. 26 16 Car. 2

The commission to Sir Robert Carre and others to put the Duke of York in possession of New York, New Jersey, and all other lands thereunto appertaining. | 1664, Apr. 26

Sir Robert Carre and others proclamation to the inhabitants of New York, New Jersey, &c. Smith's N. J. 36.

| | |
|---|---|
| 1664, June 23 24. 16 Car. 2 | Deeds of lease and release of New Jersey by the Duke of York to Lord Berkeley and Sir George Carteret. |
| | A conveiance of the Delaware counties to William Penn. |
| 1664, Aug. 19-29, 20-30, 24 Aug. 25. Sept. 4. | Letters between Stuyvesant and Colonel Nichols on the English right. Smith's N. J. 37—42. |
| 1664, Aug. 27 | Treaty between the English and Dutch for the surrender of the New Netherlands. Sm. N. J. 42. |
| Sept. 3 | Nicoll's commission to Sir. Robert Carre to reduce the Dutch on Delaware bay. Sm. N. J. 47. |
| | Instructions to Sir Robert Carre for reducing of Delaware bay and settling the people there under his majesty's obedience. Sm. N. J. 47. |
| 1664, Oct. 1 | Articles of capitulation between Sir Robert Carre and the Dutch and Swedes on Delaware bay and Delaware river. Sm. N. J. 49. |
| 1664, Dec. 1 16 Car. 2 | The determination of the commissioners of the boundary between the Duke of York and Connecticut. Sm. Ex. Ap. 9. |
| 1664 | The New Haven case. Smith's Ex. Ap. 20. |
| 1665, June 13 24. 17 Car. 2 | The second charter granted by Charles II. to the same proprietors of Carolina. 4. Mem. Am. 586. |
| 1666, Jan. 26 | Declaration de guerre par la France contre l'Angleterre. 3 Mem. Am. 123. |
| 1666, Feb. 9. 17 Car. 2 | Declaration of war by the king of England against the king of France. |
| 1667, July 31 | The treaty of peace between France and England made at Breda. 7 Corps, Dipl. part 1. p. 51 2. Mem. Am. 32. |
| 1667, July 31 | The treaty of peace and alliance between England and the United Provinces made at Breda. 7. Cor. Dip. p. 1. d. 44. 2. Mem. Am. 40. |
| 1667-8, Feb. 17 | Acte de la cession de l'Acadie au roi de France. 2. Mem. Am. 40. |
| 1668, April 21 | Directions from the governor and council of New York for a better settlement of the government on Delaware. Sm. N. J. 51. |
| 1668 | Lovelace's order for customs at the Hoarkills. Sm. N. J. 55. |
| 16- May 8 21 Car. 2 | A confirmation of the grant of the northern neck of Virginia to the Earl of St. Albans, Lord Berkeley, Sir William Moreton and John Tretheway. |
| 1672 | Incorporation of the town of Newcastle or Amstell. |
| 1673, Feb. 25 25 Car. 2 | A demise of the colony of Virginia to the Earl of Arlington and Lord Culpepper for 31 years. M S. |
| 1673-4 | Treaty at London between king Charles II. and the Dutch. Article VI. |
| | Remonstrance against the two grants of Charles II. of Northern and Southern Virginia. Ment[d]. Beverley 65. |
| 1674, July 13 | Sir George Carteret's instructions to Governor Carteret. |
| 1674, Nov. 9 | Governor Andros's proclamation on taking possession of Newcastle for the Duke of York. Sm. N. J. 78. |
| 1675, Oct. 1 27 Car. 2 | A proclamation for prohibiting the importation of commodities of Europe into any of his majesty's plantations in Africa, Asia, or America, which were not laden in England; and for putting all other laws relating to the trade of the plantations in effectual execution. |

| | |
|---|---|
| The concessions and agreements of the proprietors, freeholders and inhabitants of the province of West New Jersey in America. Sm. N. J. App. 2. | 1676, Mar. 3 |
| A deed quintipartite for the division of New Jersey. | 1676, July 1 |
| Letter from the proprietors of New Jersey to Richard Hartshorne. Sm. N. J. 80. | 1676, Aug. 18 |
| Proprietors instructions to James Wasse and Richard Hartshorne. Sm. N. J. 83. | |
| The charter of king Charles II. to his subjects of Virginia. M S. | 1676, Oct. 10<br>28 Car. 2 |
| Cautionary epistle from the trustees of Byllinge's part of New Jersey. Sm. N. J. 84. | 1676 |
| Indian deed for the lands between Rankokos creek and Timber creek, in New Jersey. | 1677, Sept. 10 |
| Indian deed for lands from Oldman's creek to Timber creek, in New Jersey. | 1677, Sept. 27 |
| Indian deed for the lands from Rankokos creek to Assunpink creek, in New Jersey. | 1677, Oct. 10 |
| The will of Sir George Carteret, sole proprieter of East Jersey ordering the same to be sold. | 1678, Dec. 5 |
| An order of the king in council for the better encouragement of all his majesty's subjects in their trade to his majesty's plantations, and for the better information of all his majesty's loving subjects in these matters—Lond. Gaz. No. 1596. Title in Amer. library. 134. 6. | 1680, Feb. 16 |
| Arguments against the customs demanded in West New Jersey by the governor of New York, addressed to the Duke's commissioners. Sm. N. J. 117. | 1680 |
| Extracts of proceedings of the committee of trade and plantations; copies of letters, reports, &c., between the board of trade, Mr. Penn, Lord Baltimore and Sir John Werden, in the behalf of the Duke of York and the settlement of the Pennsylvania boundaries by the L. C. J. North. Votes of Repr. Pennsyl. vii-xiii. | 1680, June 14. 23. 25<br>Oct. 16.<br>Nov. 4. 8 11. 18. 20 23.<br>Dec. 16.<br>1680-1, Jan. 15. 22.<br>Feb. 24. |
| A grant of Pennsylvania to William Penn. Votes of Represen. Pennsyl. xviii. | 1631, Mar. 4<br>Car. 2 |
| The king's declaration to the inhabitants and planters of the province of Pennsylvania. Vo. Repr. Penn. xxiv. | 1681, Apr. 2 |
| Certain conditions or concessions agreed upon by William Penn, proprietary and governor of Pennsylvania, and those who are the adventurers and purchasers in the same province. Votes of Rep. Pennsyl. xxiv. | 1681, July 11 |
| Fundamental laws of the province of West New Jersey. Sm. N. J. 126. | 1681, Nov. 9 |
| The methods of the commissioners for settling and regulation of lands in New Jersey. Sm. N. J. 130. | 1681-2, Jan. 14 |
| Indentures of lease and release by the executors of Sir George Carteret to William Penn and 11 others, conveying East Jersey. | 1681-2, F. 1 2 |
| The Duke of York's fresh grant of East New Jersey to the 24 proprietors. | 1682, Mar. 14 |

1682, Apr. 25 The frame of the government of the province of Pennsylvania, in America. Votes of Repr. Penn. xxvii.

1682, Aug. 21 The Duke of York's deed for Pennsylvania. Vo. Repr. Penn. xxxv.

1682, Aug. 24 The Duke of York's deed for the feoffment of Newcastle and twelve miles circle to William Penn. Vo. Repr. Penn.

1682, Aug. 24 The Duke of York's deed of feoffment of a tract of land 12 miles south from Newcastle to the Whorekills, to William Penn. Vo. Repr. Penn. xxxvii.

1682, Nov. 27
34 Car. 2 A commission to Thomas Lord Culpepper to be lieutenant and governor-general of Virginia. M. S.

1682, 10th mon. 6th day An act of union for annexing and uniting of the counties of Newcastle, Jones's and Whorekill's, alias Deal, to the province of Pennsylvania, and of naturalization of all foreigners in the province and counties aforesaid.

1682, Dec. 6 An act of settlement.

1683, Apr. 2 The frame of the government of the province of Pennsylvania and territories thereunto annexed in America.

1685, Mar. 17
Aug. 18, 26
Sept. 2
Oct. 8, 17, 31
Nov. 7 Proceedings of the committee of trade and Plantations in the dispute between Lord Baltimore and Mr. Penn. Vo. R. P. xiii-xviii. { 1683, Apr. 17. 27. May 30. June 12. 1684, Feb. 12. July 2, 16, 23, Sept. 30. Dec. 9.

1683, July 17 A commission by the proprietors of East New Jersey to Robert Barclay to be governor. Sm. N. J. 166.

1683, July 26
35 Car. 2 An order of council for issuing a quo warranto against the charter of the colony of the Massachusetts bay in New England, with his majesty's declaration that in case the said corporation of Massachusetts bay shall before prosecution had upon the same quo warranto make a full submission and entire resignation to his royal pleasure, he will then regulate their charter in such a manner as shall be for his service and the good of that colony. Title in American library. 139, 6.

1683, Sept. 28
35 Car. 2 A commission to Lord Howard of Effingham to be lieutenant and governor general of Virginia. M S.

1684, May 3 The humble address of the chief governor, council and representatives of the island of Nevis, in the West Indies, presented to his majesty by Colonel Netheway and Captain Jefferson, at Windsor, May 3, 1684. Title in Amer. libr. 142. 3. cites Lond. Gaz. No. 1927.

1684, Aug. 2 A treaty with the Indians at Albany.

1686, Nov. 16 A treaty of neutrality for America between France and England. 7 Corps Dipl. part 2, p. 44. 2. Mem. Am. 40.

1687, Jan. 20 By the king, a proclamation for the more effectual reducing and suppressing of pirates and privateers in America, as well on the sea as on the land in great numbers, committing frequent robberies and piracies, which hath occasioned a great prejudice and obstruction to trade and commerce, and given a great scandal and disturbance to our government in those parts. Title Amer. libr. 147. 2. cites Lond. Gaz. No. 2315.

1687, Feb. 12 Constitution of the council of proprietors of West Jersey. Smith's N. Jersev. 199.

A confirmation of the grant of the Northern neck of Virginia to Lord Culpepper. 1687, qu. Sept. 27. 4. Jac. 2

Governor Coxe's declaration to the council of proprietors of West Jersey. Sm. N. J. 190. 1687, Sept. 5

Provisional treaty of Whitehall concerning America between France and England. 2 Mem. de l'Am. 89. 1687, Dec. 16

Governor Coxe's narrative relating to the division line, directed to the council of proprietors of West Jersey. Sm. App. No. 4. 1687

The representation of the council of proprietors of West Jersey to Governor Burnet. Smith. App. No. 5. 1687

The remonstrance and petition of the inhabitants of East New Jersey to the king. Sm. App. No. 8.

The memorial of the proprietors of East New Jersey to the Lords of trade. Sm. App. No. 9.

Agreement of the line of partition between East and West New Jersey. Smith's N. J. 196. 1778, Sept. 5

Conveyance of the government of West Jersey and territories, by Dr. Coxe, to the West Jersey society. 1691

A charter granted by King William and Queen Mary to the inhabitants of the province of Massachusetts bay, in New England. 2 Mem. de l'Am. 593. 1691, Oct. 7

The frame of government of the province of Pennsylvania and the territories thereunto belonging, passed by Gov. Markham. Nov. 7, 1696. 1696, Nov. 7

The treaty of peace between France and England, made at Ryswick. 7 Corps Dipl. part 2. p. 399. 2 Mem. Am. 89. 1697, Sept. 20

The opinion and answer of the Lords of trade to the memorial of the proprietors of East N. Jersey. Sm. App. No. 10. 1699, July 5

The memorial of the proprietors of East New Jersey to the Lords of trade. Sm. App. No. 11. 1700, Jan. 15

The petition of the proprietors of East and West New Jersey to the Lords justices of England. Sm. App. No. 12.

A confirmation of the boundary between the colonies of New York and Connecticut, by the crown. 1700, W. 3

The memorial of the proprietors of East and West New Jersey to the king. Sm. App. No. 14. 1701, Aug. 12

Representation of the Lords of trade to the Lords justices. Sm. App. No. 18. 1701, Oct. 2

A treaty with the Indians. 1701

Report of Lords of trade to king William, of draughts of a commission and instructions for a governor of N. Jersey. Sm. N. J. 262. 1701-2, Jan. 6

Surrender from the proprietors of E. and W. N. Jersey, of their pretended right of government to her majesty Queen Anne. Sm. N. J. 211. 1702, Apr. 15

The Queen's acceptance of the surrender of government of East and West Jersey. Sm. N. J. 219. 1702, Apr. 17

Instructions to lord Cornbury. Sm. N. J. 230. 1702, Nov. 16

A commission from Queen Anne to Lord Cornbury, to be captain general and governor in chief of New Jersey. Sm. N. J. 220. 1702, Dec. 5

| | |
|---|---|
| 1703, June 27 | Recognition by the council of proprietors of the true boundary of the deeds of Sept. 10, and Oct. 10, 1677, (New Jersey.) Sm. N. J. 96. |
| 1703 | Indian deeds for the lands above the falls of the Delaware in West Jersey. |
| | Indian deed for the lands at the head of Rankokus river, in West Jersey. |
| 1704, June 18 | A proclamation by Queen Anne, for settling and ascertaining the current rates of foreign coins in America. Sm. N. J. 281. |
| 1705, May 3 | Additional instructions to Lord Cornbury. Sm. N. S. 235. |
| 1707, May 3 | Additional instructions to Lord Cornbury. Sm. N. J. 258. |
| 1707, Nov. 20 | Additional instructions to Lord Cornbury. Sm. N. J. 259. |
| 1707 | An answer by the council of proprietors for the western division of N. Jersey, to questions proposed to them by Lord Cornbury. Sm. N. J. 285. |
| 1708-9, Feb. 28 | Instructions to Colonel Vetch in his negotiations with the governors of America. Sm. N. J. 364. |
| 1708-9, Feb. 28 | Instructions to the governor of New Jersey and New York. Sm. J. 361. |
| 1710, Aug. | Earl of Dartmouth's letter to governor Hunter. |
| 1711, Apr. 22 | Premiers propositions de la France. 6. Lamberty, 669, 2 Mem. Am. 341. |
| 1711, Oct. 8 | Réponses de la France aux demandes préliminaries de la Grande Bretagne. 6 Lamb. 681. 2 Mem. Amer. 344. |
| 1711, Sept. 27 / Oct. 8 | Demandes préliminaries plus particulieres de la Grande-Bretagne, avec les réponses. 2 Mem. de l'Am. 346. |
| 1711, Sept. 27 / Oct. 8 | L'acceptation de la part de la Grande-Bretagne. 2 Mem. Am. 356. |
| 1711, Dec. 23 | The Queen's instructions to the Bishop of Bristol and Earl of Stafford, her plenipotentiaries, to treat for a general peace. 6 Lamberty, 744. 2. Mem. Am. 358. |
| 1712, May 24 / June 10 | A memorial of Mr. St. John to the Marquis de Torci, with regard to North America, to commerce, and to the suspension of arms. 7. Recueil de Lamberty 161, 2 Mem. de l'Amer. 376. |
| 1712, June 10 | Réponse du roi de France au memoire de Londres. 7. Lamberty, p. 163. 2. Mem. Am. 380. |
| 1712, Aug. 19 | Traité pour une suspension d'armes entre Louis XIV. roi de France, and Anne, reign de la Grande-Bretagne, fait à Paris. 8. Corps Diplom. part 1. p. 308. 2. Mem. d'Am. 104. |
| 1712, Sept. 10 | Offers of France to England, demands of England, and the answers of France. 7. Rec. de Lamb. 461. 2 Mem. Am. 390. |
| 1713, Mar. 31 / April 11 | Traité de paix et d'amitié entre Louis XIV. roi de France, et Anne, reine de la Grande-Bretagne, fait à Utrecht. 15 Corps Diplomatique de Dumont, 339. id. Latin. 2 Actes et memoires de la pais d'Utrecht, 457. id. Lat. Fr. 2. Mem. Am. 113. |
| 1713, Mar. 31 / April 11 | Traité de navigation et de commerce entre Louis XIV. roi de France, et Anne, reine de la Grande-Bretagne. Fait à Utrecht. 8 Corps Dipl. part 1. p. 345. 2 Mem. de l'Am. 137. |
| 1726 | A treaty with the Indians. |
| 1728. Jan. | The petition of the representatives of the province of New Jersey, to have a distinct governor. Sm. N. J. 421. |

| | |
|---|---|
| Deed of release by the government of Connecticut to that of New York. | 1732, G. 2. |
| The charter granted by George II. for Georgia. 4. Mem. de l'Am. 617. | 1732, June 9 20. 5 Geo. 2 |
| Petition of Lord Fairfax, that a commission might issue for running and marking the dividing line between his district and the province of Virginia. | 1733 |
| Order of the king in council for commissioners to survey and settle the said dividing line between the proprietary and royal territory. | 1733, Nov. 29 |
| Report of the Lords of trade relating to the separating the government of the province of New Jersey from New York. Sm. N. J. 423. | 1736, Aug. 5 |
| Survey and report of the commissioners appointed on the part of the crown to settle the line between the crown and Lord Fairfax. | 1737, Aug. 10 |
| Survey and report of the commissioners appointed on the part of Lord Fairfax to settle the line between the crown and him. | 1737, Aug. 11 |
| Order of reference of the surveys between the crown and Lord Fairfax to the council for plantation affairs. | 1738, Dec. 21 |
| Treaty with the Indians of the six nations at Lancaster. | 1744, June |
| Report of the council for plantation affairs, fixing the head springs of Rappahanoc and Potomac, and a commission to extend the line. | 1745, Apr. 6 |
| Order of the king in council confirming the said report of the council for plantation affairs. | 1745, Apr. 11 |
| Articles préliminaries pour parvenir à la paix, signés à Aix-la-Chapelle entre les ministres de France, de la Grande-Bretagne, et des Provinces-Unies des Pays-Bas. 2 Mem. de l'Am. 159. | 1748, Apr. 30 |
| Declaration des ministres de France, de la Grande-Bretagne, et des Provinces-Unies des Pays-Bas, pour rectifier les articles I. et II. des préliminaries. 2. Mem. Am. 165. | 1748, May 21 |
| The general and definitive treaty of peace concluded at Aix-la-Chapelle. Lon. Mag. 1748. 503. French 2. Mem. Am. 169. | 1748, Oct. 7-18. 22. G. 2 |
| A treaty with the Indians. | 1754 |
| A conference between governor Bernard and Indian nations at Burlington. Sm. N. J. 449. | 1758, Aug. 7 |
| A conference between governor Denny, governor Bernard, and others, and Indian nations at Easton. Sm. N. J. 455. | 1758, Oct. 8 |
| The capitulation of Niagara. | 1759, July 25 33. G. 2 |
| The king's proclamation promising lands to soldiers. | 175- |
| The definitive treaty concluded at Paris. Lon. Mag. 1763. 149. | 1763, Feb. 10 3. G. 3 |
| A proclamation for regulating the cessions made by the last treaty of peace. Guth. Geogr. Gram. 623. | 1763, Oct. 7 G. 3 |
| The king's proclamation against settling on any lands on the waters westward of the Alleghany. | 1763 |
| Deed from the six nations of Indians to William Trent, and others, for lands betwixt the Ohio and Monongahela. View of the title to Indiana. Phil. Steiner and Cist. 1776. | 1768, Nov. 3 |
| Deed from the six nations of Indians to the crown for certain lands and settling a boundary. M S. | 1768, Nov. 5 |

## *Chapter XV*

# A MANUAL OF PARLIAMENTARY PRACTICE

1800 [1]

## PREFACE

The Constitution of the United States, establishing a Legislature for the Union under certain forms, authorizes each branch of it "to determine the rules of its own proceedings." The Senate have accordingly formed some rules for its own government: but those going only to few cases, they have referred to the decision of their President, without debate and without appeal, all questions of order arising either under their own rules, or where they have provided none. This places under the discretion of the President a very extensive field of decision, and one which, irregularly exercised, would have a powerful effect on the proceedings and determinations of the House. The President must feel, weightily and seriously, this confidence in his discretion: and the necessity of recurring, for its government, to some known system of rules, that he may neither leave himself free to indulge caprice or passion, nor open to the imputation of them. But to what system of rules is he to recur, as supplementary to those of the Senate? To this there can be but one answer: to the systems of regulations adopted by the government of some one of the parliamentary bodies within these States, or of that which has served as a prototype to most of them. This last is the model which we have studied; while we are little acquainted with the modifications of it in our several States. It is deposited, too, in publications possessed by many, and open to all. Its rules are probably as wisely constructed for governing the debates of a considerative body, and obtaining its true sense, as any which can become known to us; and the acquiescence of the Senate hitherto under the references to them, has given them the sanction of their approbation.

Considering, therefore, the law of proceedings in the Senate as composed of the precepts of the Constitution, the regulations of the Senate, and where these are silent, of the rules of Parliament, I have here endeavored to collect and digest so much of these as is called for in ordinary practice, collating the parliamentary with the senatorial rules, both where they agree and where they vary. I have done this, as well to have them at hand for my own government, as to

[1] It was published by Samuel Harrison Smith, in Washington, D. C., in 1801.

deposit with the Senate the standard by which I judge and am willing to be judged. I could not doubt the necessity of quoting the sources of my information; among which Mr. Hatsel's most valuable book is pre-eminent; but as he has only treated some general heads, I have been obliged to recur to other authorities, in support of a number of common rules of practice to which his plan did not descend. Sometimes each authority cited supports the whole passage. Sometimes it rests on all taken together. Sometimes the authority goes only to a part of the text, the residue being inferred from known rules and principles. For some of the most familiar forms, no written authority is or can be quoted; no writer having supposed it necessary to repeat what all were presumed to know. The statement of these must rest on their notoriety.

I am aware, that authorities can often be produced in opposition to the rules which I lay down as parliamentary. An attention to dates will generally remove their weight. The proceedings of Parliament in ancient times, and for a long while, were crude, multiform, and embarrassing. They have been, however, constantly advancing towards uniformity and accuracy; and have now obtained a degree of aptitude to their object, beyond which little is to be desired or expected.

Yet I am far from the presumption of believing, that I may not have mistaken the parliamentary practice in some cases; and especially in those minor forms, which, being practised daily, are supposed known to everybody, and therefore have not been committed to writing. Our resources in this quarter of the globe, for obtaining information on that part of the subject, are not perfect. But I have begun a sketch, which those who come after me will successively correct and fill up, till a code of rules shall be formed for the use of the Senate, the effects of which may be accuracy in business, economy of time, order, uniformity, and impartiality.

NOTE

The rules and practices peculiar to the Senate are printed in small type. Those of Parliament are in large.

## IMPORTANCE OF RULES [2]

### SECTION I

#### THE IMPORTANCE OF ADHERING TO RULES

Mr. Onslow, the ablest among the Speakers of the House of Commons, used to say, "It was a maxim he had often heard when he was a young man, from old and experienced members, that nothing tended more to throw power into

[2] Letter to George Wythe:

Philadelphia, February 28, 1800

MY DEAR SIR: I know how precious your time is, and how exclusively you devote it to the duties of your office, yet I venture to ask a few hours or minutes of it on motives of public service, as well as private friendship. I will explain the occasion of the application. You recollect enough of the old Congress to remember that their mode of managing the business of the House was not only unparliamentary, but that the forms were so awkward and inconvenient that it was impossible sometimes to get at the true sense of the majority. The House the hands of administration and those who acted with the majority of the House of Commons, than a neglect of, or departure from, the rules of proceeding; that these forms, as instituted by our ancestors, operated as a check, and control, on the actions of the majority; and that they were, in many instances, a shelter and protection to the minority, against the attempts of power."

So far the maxim is certainly true, and is founded in good sense, that as it is always in the power of the majority, by their numbers, to stop any improper measures proposed on the part of their opponents, the only weapons by which the minority can defend themselves against similar attempts from those in power, are the forms and rules of proceeding, which have been adopted as they were found necessary from time to time, and are become the law of the house; by a strict adherence to which, the weaker party can only be protected from those irregularities and abuses which these forms were intended to check, and which the wantonness of power is but too often apt to suggest to large and successful majorities.—2 *Hats.* 171, 172.

And whether these forms be in all cases the most rational or not, is really not of so great importance. It is much more material that there should be a rule to go by, than what that rule is; that there may be a uniformity of proceeding in business, not subject to the caprice of the Speaker, or captiousness of the mem-

of Representatives of the United States are now pretty much in the same situation. In the Senate it is in our power to get into a better way; our ground is this: The Senate have established a few rules for their government, and have subjected the decisions on these and on *all other points of order* without debate, and without appeal, to the judgment of their President, he, for his own sake, as well as theirs, must prefer recurring to some system of rules ready formed; and there can be no question that the Parliamentary rules are the best known to us for managing the debates, and obtaining the sense of a deliberative body. I have therefore made them my rule of decision, rejecting those of the old Congress altogether, and it gives entire satisfaction to the Senate; insomuch that we shall not only have a good system there, but probably, by the example of its effects, produce a conformity in the other branch. But in the course of this business I find perplexities, having for twenty years been out of deliberative bodies, and become rusty as to many points of proceeding; and so little has the Parliamentary branch of the law been attended to, that I not only find no person here, but not even a book to aid me. I had, at an early period of life, read a good deal on the subject, and common-placed what I read. This common-place has been my pillar; but there are many questions of practice on which that is silent, some of them are so minute indeed, and belong too much to every-day's practice, that they have never been thought worthy of being written down, yet from desuetude they have slipped my memory. You will see by the enclosed paper what they are. I know with what pain you write: therefore I have left a margin in which you can write a simple negative or affirmative opposite every position, or perhaps, with as little trouble, correct the text by striking out or interlining. This is what I have earnestly to solicit from you, and I would not have given you the trouble if I had had any other resource. But you are, in fact, the only spark of Parliamentary science now remaining to us. I am the more anxious, because I have been forming a manual of Parliamentary law which I mean to deposit with the Senate as the standard by which I judge, and am willing to be judged. Though I should be opposed to its being printed, yet it may be done perhaps without my consent; and in that case I should be sorry indeed should it go out with errors that a Tyro should not have committed. And yet it is precisely those to which I am most exposed. I am less afraid as to important matters, because for them I have printed authorities; but it is those small matters of daily practice, which twenty years ago were familiar to me, but have in that time escaped my memory. I hope under these circumstances you will pardon the trouble I propose to you in the enclosed paper. I am not pressed in time, so that your leisure will be sufficient for me. Accept the salutations of grateful and sincere friendship and attachment, and many prayers for your health and happiness from, Dear Sir,

Yours affectionately.

[T. J.]

bers. It is very material that order, decency, and regularity be preserved in a dignified public body.—2 *Hats.* 149. And in 1698 the Lords say the reasonableness of what is desired is never considered by us, for we are bound to consider nothing but what is usual. Matters of form are essential to government, and 'tis of consequence to be in the right. All the reason for forms is custom, and the law of forms is practice; the reason is quite out of doors. Some particular customs may not be grounded on reason, and no good account can be given of them; and yet many nations are zealous for them; and Englishmen are as zealous as any others to pursue their old forms and methods.—4 *Hats.* 258.

## SECTION II

### LEGISLATURE

All legislative powers herein granted shall be vested in a Congress of the United States, which shall consist of a Senate and House of Representatives.—*Constitution of the United States,* Art. I. Sec. 1.

The Senators and Representatives shall receive a compensation for their services, to be ascertained by law, and paid out of the treasury of the United States. *Const. U. S.,* Art. I. Sec. 6.

For the powers of Congress, see the following Articles and Sections of the Constitution of the United States:—Art. I. Sec. 4, 7, 8, 9.—Art. II. Sec. 1, 2.—Art. III. Sec. 3.—Art. IV. Sec. 1, 3, 5.—And all Amendments.

## SECTION III

### PRIVILEGE

The privileges of the members of Parliament, from small and obscure beginnings, have been advancing for centuries, with a firm and never-yielding pace. Claims seem to have been brought forward from time to time, and repeated till some example of their admission enabled them to build law on that example. We can only, therefore, state the point of progression at which they now are. It is now acknowledged, 1st. That they are at all times exempted from question elsewhere, for anything said in their own house: that during the time of privilege, 2d. Neither a member himself, his wife,[3] or his servants, [*familiares sui*] for any matter of their own, may be[4] arrested on mesne process, in any civil suit: 3d. Nor be detained under execution, though levied before the time of privilege: 4th. Nor impleaded, cited or subpœnaed, in any court: 5th. Nor summoned as a witness or juror: 6th. Nor may their lands or goods be distrained: 7th. Nor their persons assaulted, or characters traduced. And the period of time, covered by privilege, before and after the session, with the practice of short prorogations under the connivance of the Crown, amounts in fact to a perpetual protection against the course of justice. In one instance, indeed, it has been relaxed by 10 *G.* 3, c. 50, which permits judiciary proceedings to go on against

[3] Order of the House of Commons, 1663, July 16.—T. J.
[4] Elsynge, 217; 1 Hats. 21; 1 Grey's Deb. 133.—T. J.

them. That these privileges must be continually progressive, seems to result from their rejecting all definition of them; the doctrine being, that "their dignity and independence are preserved by keeping their privileges indefinite"; and that "the maxims upon which they proceed, together with the method of proceeding, rest entirely in their own breast, and are not defined and ascertained by any particular stated laws."—1 *Blackstone,* 163, 164.

It was probably from this view of the encroaching character of privilege, that the framers of our Constitution, in their care to provide that the laws shall bind equally on all, and especially that those who make them shall not be exempt themselves from their operation, have only privileged "Senators and Representatives" themselves from the single act of arrest in all cases except treason, felony, and breach of the peace, during their attendance at the session of their respective Houses, and in going to and returning from the same, and from being questioned in any other place for any speech or debate in either House.—Const. U.S. Art. I. Sec. 6. Under the general authority "to make all laws necessary and proper for carrying into execution the powers given them," Const. U.S. Art. II. Sec. 8, they may provide by law the details which may be necessary for giving full effect to the enjoyment of this privilege. No such law being as yet made, it seems to stand at present on the following ground:—1. The act of arrest is void, *ab initio,* 2 Stra. 989.—2. The member arrested may be discharged on motion, 1 Bl. 166. 2. Stra. 990; or by Habeas Corpus under the Federal or State authority, as the case may be; or by a writ of privilege out of the Chancery, 2 Stra. 989, in those States which have adopted that part of the laws of England.—Orders of the House of Com. 1550, Feb. 20.—3. The arrest being unlawful, is a trespass for which the officer and others concerned are liable to action or indictment in the ordinary courts of justice, as in other cases of unauthorized arrest.—4. The court before which the process is returnable, is bound to act as in other cases of unauthorized proceeding, and liable also, as in other similar cases, to have their proceedings stayed or corrected by the Superior Courts.

The time necessary for going to and returning from Congress not being defined, it will of course be judged of in every particular case by those who will have to decide the case.

While privilege was understood in England to extend, as it does here, only to exemption from arrest *eundo, morando, et redeundo,* the House of Commons themselves decided that "a convenient time was to be understood."—1580—1 *Hats.* 99, 100. Nor is the law so strict in point of time as to require the party to set out immediately on his return, but allows him time to settle his private affairs, and to prepare for his journey; and does not even scan his road very nicely, nor forfeit his protection for a little deviation from that which is most direct; some necessity perhaps constraining him to it.—2 *Stra.* 986, 987.

This privilege from arrest, privileges of course against all process, the disobedience is punishable by an attachment of the person; as a subpœna ad respondendum, or testificandum, or a summons on a jury; and with reason, because a member has superior duties to perform in another place.

When a Representative is withdrawn from his seat by summons, the 47,700 people whom he represents lose their voice in debate and vote, as they do in his voluntary absence: when a Senator is withdrawn by summons, his State loses half its voice in debate and vote, as it does in his voluntary absence. The enormous disparity of evil admits no comparison.

So far there will probably be no difference of opinion as to the privileges of the two Houses of Congress; but in the following cases it is otherwise. In Dec. 1795, the House of Representatives committed two persons of the names of Randall and Whitney, for attempting to corrupt the integrity of certain members, which they considered as a contempt and breach of the privileges of the House and the facts being proved, Whitney was detained in confinement a fortnight, and Randall three weeks, and was reprimanded by the Speaker. In March, 1796, the House of Representatives voted a challenge given to a member of their House, to be a breach of the privileges of the House; but satisfactory apologies and acknowledgments being made, no further proceedings were had. The Editor of the Aurora having in his paper of Feb. 19, 1800, inserted some paragraphs defamatory to the Senate, and failed in his appearance, he was ordered to be committed. In debating the legality of this order, it was insisted in support of it, that every man, by the law of nature, and every body of men, possesses the right of self-defence; that all public functionaries are essentially invested with the powers of self-preservation; that they have an inherent right to do all acts necessary to keep themselves in a condition to discharge the trusts confided to them; that whenever authorities are given, the means of carrying them into execution are given by necessary implication; that thus we see the British Parliament exercise the right of punishing contempts; all the State Legislatures exercise the same power; and every Court does the same; that if we have it not, we sit at the mercy of every intruder who may enter our doors or gallery, and by noise and tumult render proceeding in business impracticable; that if our tranquillity is to be perpetually disturbed by newspaper defamation, it will not be possible to exercise our functions with the requisite coolness and deliberation; and that we must therefore have a power to punish these disturbers of our peace and proceedings. To this it was answered, that the Parliament and Courts of England have cognizance of contempts by the express provisions of their laws; that the State Legislatures have equal authority, because their powers are plenary; they represent their constituents completely, and possess all their powers, except such as their Constitutions have expressly denied them; that the Courts of the several States have the same powers by the laws of their States, and those of the Federal Government by the same State laws, adopted in each State by a law of Congress; that none of these bodies, therefore, derive those powers from natural or necessary right, but from express law; that Congress have no such natural or necessary power, nor any powers but such as are given them by the Constitution; that that has given them directly exemption from personal arrest, exemption from question elsewhere for what is said in the House, and power over their own members and proceedings; for these, no further law is necessary, the Constitution being the law; that, moreover, by that article of the Constitution which authorizes them "to make all laws necessary and proper for carrying into execution the powers vested by the Constitution in them," they may provide by law for an undisturbed exercise of their functions, *e.g.*, for the punishment of contempts, of affrays or tumults in their presence, &c.; but, till the law be made, it does not exist; and does not exist, from their own neglect; that in the meantime, however, they are not unprotected, the ordinary magistrates and courts of law being open and competent to punish all unjustifiable disturbances or defamations, and even their own sergeant, who may appoint deputies ad libitum to aid him, 3 *Grey*, 59, 147, 255, is equal to the smallest disturbances; that, in requiring a previous law, the Constitution had regard to the inviolability of the citizen as well as of the member; as, should one House, in the regular form of a bill, aim at too broad privileges, it may be checked by the other, and both by the President; and also as, the law being promulgated, the citizen will know how to avoid offence. But if one branch may assume its own privileges without control; if it may do it on the spur of the occasion, conceal the law in its own breast, and after the fact committed make its sentence both the law and the judgment on that fact; if the offence is to be kept undefined, and to be declared only ex re nata, and according to the passions of the moment, and there be no limitation either in the manner or measure of the punishment, the condition of the citizen will be perilous indeed. Which of these doctrines is to prevail, time will decide. Where there is no fixed law, the judgment on any particular case is the law of that single case only, and dies with it. When a new and even a similar case arises, the judgment which is to make, and at the same time apply, the law, is open to question and consideration, as are all new laws. Perhaps Congress, in the meantime, in their care for the safety of the citizens, as well as that for their own protection, may declare by law what is necessary and proper to enable them to carry into execution the powers vested in them, and thereby hang up a rule for the inspection of all, which may direct the conduct of the citizen, and at the same time test the judgments they shall themselves pronounce in their own case.

Privilege from arrest takes place by force of the election; and before a return be made, a member elected may be named of a committee, and is to every intent a member, except that he cannot vote until he is sworn.—*Memor.* 107, 108.—*D'Ewes,* 642. *col.* 2. 653. *col.* 1.—*Pet. Miscel. Parl.* 119; *Lex. Parl. c.* 23; 2 *Hats.* 22. 62.

Every man must, at his peril, take notice who are members of either House returned of record.—*Lex. Parl.* 23, 4—*Inst.* 24.

On complaint of a breach of privilege, the party may either be summoned, or sent for in custody of the sergeant.—1 *Grey,* 88, 95.

The privilege of a member is the privilege of the House. If the member waive it without leave, it is a ground for punishing him, but cannot in effect waive the privilege of the House.—*Grey,* 140. 222.

For any speech or debate in either House, they shall not be questioned in any other place.—*Const. U.S.,* Art. I. Sec. 6. *S. P. protest of Commons to James I.* 1621. 2 *Rapin.* No. 54 p. 211, 212. But this is restrained to things done in the House in a Parliamentary course, 1 *Rush,* 663.—For he is not to have privilege contra morem parliamentarium, to exceed the bounds and limits of his place and duty.—*Com.* p.

If an offence be committed by a member in the House, of which the House has cognizance, it is an infringement of their right for any person or court to take notice of it, till the House has punished the offender, or referred him to a due course.—*Lex. Parl.* 63.

Privilege is in the power of the House, and is a restraint to the proceeding of inferior courts; but not of the House itself.—2 *Nalson,* 450; 2 *Grey,* 399. For whatever is spoken in the House, is subject to the censure of the House; and offences of this kind have been severely punished, by calling the person to the bar to make submission, committing him to the Tower, expelling the House, &c.—*Scob.* 72; *Lex. Parl. c.* 22.

It is a breach of order, for the Speaker to refuse to put a question which is in order.—*Hats.* 175, 176; 5 *Grey,* 133.

And even in cases of treason, felony, and breach of the peace, to which privilege does not extend as to substance; yet, in Parliament, a member is privileged as to the mode of proceeding. The case is first to be laid before the House, that it may judge of the fact, and of the grounds of the accusation, and how far forth the manner of the trial may concern their privilege. Otherwise it would be in the power of other branches of the government, and even of every private man, under pretences of treason, &c., to take any man from his service in the House; and so as many, one after another, as would make the House what he pleaseth.—*Decision of the Commons on the King's declaring Sir John Hotham a traitor*—4 *Rushw.* 586. So when a member stood indicted of felony, it was adjudged that he ought to remain of the House till conviction. For it may be any man's case, who is guiltless, to be accused and indicted of felony, or the like crime.—23 *El.* 1580.—*D'Ewes,* 283, *col.* 1.—*Lex. Parl.* 133.

When it is found necessary for the public service to put a member under arrest, or when, on any public inquiry, matter comes out which may lead to affect the person of a member, it is the practice immediately to acquaint the House, that they may know the reasons for such a proceeding, and take such steps as they think proper.—2 *Hats.* 259. Of which, see many examples.—2 *Hats.* 256, 257, 258. But the communication is subsequent to the arrest.—1 *Blackst.* 167.

It is highly expedient, says Hatsell, for the due preservation of the privileges of the separate branches of the Legislature, that neither should encroach on the other, or interfere in any matter depending before them, so as to preclude, or even influence, that freedom of debate, which is essential to a free council. They are, therefore, not to take notice of any bills or other matters depending, or of votes that have been given, or of speeches that have been held, by the members of either of the other branches of the Legislature, until the same have been communicated to them in the usual Parliamentary manner.—2 *Hats.* 252; 4 *Inst.* 15; *Seld. Jud.* 63. Thus the King's taking notice of the bill for suppressing soldiers depending before the House, his proposing a provisional clause for a bill before it was presented to him by the two Houses, his expressing displeasure against some persons for matters moved in Parliament during the debate and preparation of a bill, were breaches of privilege.—2 *Nalson,* 743. And in 1783, December 17, it was declared a breach of fundamental privileges, &c. to report any opinion or pretended opinion of the King, on any bill or proceeding depending in either House of Parliament, with a view to influence the votes of the members.—2 *Hats.* 251, 6.

## SECTION IV

### ELECTIONS

The times, places, and manner of holding elections for Senators and Representatives, shall be prescribed in each State by the Legislature thereof; but the Congress may at any time by law make or alter such regulations, except as to the place of choosing Senators.—*Const. U.S.* Art. I. Sec. 4.

Each House shall be the judge of the elections, returns, and qualifications of its own members.—*Const. U.S.* Art. I. Sec. 5.

## SECTION V

### QUALIFICATIONS

The Senate of the United States shall be composed of two Senators from each State, chosen by the Legislature thereof, for six years; and each Senator shall have one vote.

Immediately after they shall be assembled, in consequence of the first election, they shall be divided as equally as may be into three classes. The seats of the Senators of the first class shall be vacated at the end of the second year; of the second class, at the expiration of the fourth year; and of the third class, at the expiration of the sixth year; so that one-third may be chosen every second year; and if vacancies happen, by resignation or otherwise, during the recess of the Legislature of any State, the Executive thereof may make temporary appointments, until the next meeting of the Legislature, which shall then fill such vacancies.

No person shall be a Senator, who shall not have attained to the age of thirty years, and been nine years a citizen of the United States, and who shall not, when elected, be an inhabitant of that State for which he shall be chosen.—*Const. U.S.* Art. I. Sec. 3.

The House of Representatives shall be composed of members chosen every second year by the people of the several States; and the electors in each State shall have the qualifications requisite for electors of the most numerous branch of the State Legislature.

No person shall be a Representative who shall not have attained to the age of twenty-five years, and been seven years a citizen of the United States, and who shall not, when elected, be an inhabitant of that State in which he shall be chosen.

Representatives and direct taxes shall be apportioned among the several States which may be included within this Union, according to their respective numbers, which shall be determined by adding to the whole number of free persons, including those bound to service for a term of years, and excluding Indians not taxed, three-fifths of all other persons. The actual enumeration shall be made within three years after the first meeting of Congress of the United States, and within every subsequent term of ten years, in such manner as they shall by law direct. The number of Representatives shall not exceed one for every thirty thousand; but each State shall have at least one Representative. *Const. U.S.* Art. I. Sec. 2.

The provisional apportionments of Representatives made in the Constitution in 1787, and afterwards by Congress, were as follows:

| | 1787 | 1793 | 1801 | 1813 |
|---|---|---|---|---|
| New Hampshire | 3 | 4 | 5 | 6 |
| Massachusetts | 8 | 14 | 17 | 20 |
| Rhode Island | 1 | 2 | 2 | 2 |
| Connecticut | 5 | 7 | 7 | 7 |
| Vermont | | 2 | 6 | 6 |
| New York | 6 | 10 | 17 | 27 |
| New Jersey | 4 | 5 | 6 | 6 |
| Pennsylvania | 8 | 13 | 18 | 23 |
| Delaware | 1 | 1 | 1 | 2 |
| Maryland | 6 | 8 | 9 | 9 |
| Virginia | 10 | 19 | 22 | 23 |
| Kentucky | | 2 | 3 | 10 |
| Tennessee | | | 1 | 6 |
| North Carolina | 5 | 10 | 12 | 13 |
| South Carolina | 5 | 6 | 8 | 9 |
| Georgia | 3 | 2 | 4 | 6 |
| Ohio | | | | 6 |

When vacancies happen in the representation from any State, the executive authority thereof shall issue writs of election to fill such vacancies.—*Const. U.S.* Art. I. Sec. 2.

No Senator or Representative shall, during the time for which he was elected, be appointed to any civil office under the authority of the United States, which shall have been created, or the emoluments whereof shall have been increased during such time; and no person holding any office under the United States shall be a member of either house during his continuance in office.—*Const. U.S.* Art. I. Sec. 6.

## SECTION VI

### QUORUM

A majority of each House shall constitute a quorum to do business; but a smaller number may adjourn from day to day, and may be authorized to compel the attendance of absent members, in such manner, and under such penalties, as each house may provide.—*Const. U.S.* Art. I. Sec. 5.

In general, the chair is not to be taken till a quorum for business is present; unless, after due waiting, such a quorum be despaired of, when the chair may be taken, and the House adjourned. And whenever, during business, it is observed that a quorum is not present, any member may call for the House to be counted; and being found deficient, business is suspended.—2 *Hats.* 125, 126.

The President having taken the chair, and a quorum being present, the journal of the preceding day shall be read to the end, that any mistake may be corrected that shall have been made in the entries.—*Rules of the Senate,* 1.

## SECTION VII

### CALL OF THE HOUSE

On a call of the House, each person rises up as he is called, and answereth; the absentees are then only noted, but no excuse to be made till the House be fully called over. Then the absentees are called a second time, and if still absent, excuses are to be heard.—*Ord H. of C.* 92.

They rise that their persons may be recognized; the voice, in such a crowd, being an inefficient verification of their presence. But in so small a body as the Senate of the United States, the trouble of rising cannot be necessary.

Orders for calls on different days may subsist at the same time.—2 *Hats.* 72.

## SECTION VIII

### ABSENCE

No member shall absent himself from the service of the Senate without leave of the Senate first obtained. And in case a less number than a quorum of the Senate shall convene, they are hereby authorized to send the sergeant-at-arms, or any other person or persons by them authorized, for any or all absent members, as the majority of such members present shall agree, at the expense of such absent members respectively, unless such excuse for non-attendance shall be made, as the Senate, when a quorum is convened, shall judge sufficient, and in that case the expense shall be paid out of the contingent fund. And this rule shall apply as well to the first convention of the Senate, at the legal time of meeting, as to each day of the session, after the hour is arrived to which the Senate stood adjourned.—*Rule* 19.

## SECTION IX

### SPEAKER

The Vice-President of the United States shall be President of the Senate, but shall have no vote unless they be equally divided.—*Const. U.S.* Art. 1. Sec. 3.

The Senate shall choose their other officers, and also a President pro tempore in the absence of the Vice-President, or when he shall exercise the office of President of the United States.—*Const. U.S.* Art. I. Sec. 3.

The House of Representatives shall choose their Speaker and other officers.—*Const. U.S. Art.* I. Sec. 3.

When but one person is proposed, and no objection made, it has not been usual in Parliament to put any question to the House; but without a question, the members proposing him, conduct him to the chair. But if there be objection, or another proposed, a question is put by the clerk.—2 *Hats.* 168. As are also questions of adjournment.—6 *Grey,* 406. Where the House debated and exchanged messages and answers with the King for a week, without a Speaker, till they were prorogued. They have done it de die in diem for 14 days.—1 *Chand.* 331, 335.

In the Senate, a President pro tempore, in the absence of the Vice-President, is proposed and chosen by ballot. His office is understood to be determined on the Vice-President's appearing and taking the chair, or at the meeting of the Senate after the first recess.—*Vide Rule* 23.

Where the Speaker has been ill, other Speakers pro tempore have been appointed. Instances of this are, 1 *H.* 4, Sir John Cheney, and for Sir William Sturton, and in 15 *H.* 6, Sir John Tyrrell, in 1656, Jan. 27; 1658, Mar. 9; 1659, Jan. 13.

Sir Job Charlton ill, Seymour chosen, 1673, Feb. 18.
Seymour being ill, Sir Robert Sawyer chosen, 1678, April 15.
Sawyer being ill, Seymour chosen,
} Not merely pro tempore.—1 *Chand.* 169, 276, 7.

Thorpe in execution, a new Speaker chosen—31 *H.* VI.—3 *Grey,* 11; and March 14, 1694, Sir John Trevor chosen. There have been no later instances.—2 *Hats.* 161.—4 *Inst.*—8 *Lex. Parl.* 263.

A Speaker may be removed at the will of the House, and a Speaker pro tempore appointed.—2 *Grey,* 186; 5 *Grey,* 134.

## SECTION X

### ADDRESS

The President shall, from time to time, give to the Congress information of the state of the Union, and recommend to their consideration such measures as he shall judge necessary and expedient.—*Const. U.S.* Art. II. Sec. 3.

A joint address from both Houses of Parliament is read by the Speaker of the House of Lords. It may be attended by both Houses in a body, or by a committee from each House, or by the two Speakers only. An address of the House of Commons only may be presented by the whole House, or by the Speaker,—9 *Grey,* 473; 1 *Chandler,* 298, 301; or by such particular members as are of the Privy Council.—2 *Hats.* 278.

## SECTION XI

### COMMITTEES

Standing committees, as of privileges and elections, &c., are usually appointed at the first meeting, to continue through the session. The person first named is generally permitted to act as chairman. But this is a matter of courtesy; every committee having a right to elect their own chairman, who presides over them, puts questions, and reports their proceedings to the House.—4 *Inst.* 11, 12; *Scob.* 7; 1 *Grey,* 112.

At these committees the members are to speak standing, and not sitting, though there is reason to conjecture it was formerly otherwise.—*D'Ewes,* 630, *col.* 1; 4 *Parl. Hist.* 440; 2 *Hats.* 77.

Their proceedings are not to be published, as they are of no force till confirmed by the House.—*Rushw. part* 3, *vol.* 2, 74; 3 *Grey,* 401; *Scob.* 39. Nor can they receive a petition but through the House.—9 *Grey,* 412.

When a committee is charged with an inquiry, if a member prove to be involved, they cannot proceed against him, but must make a special report to the House; whereupon the member is heard in his place, or at the bar, or a special authority is given to the committee to inquire concerning him.—9 *Grey,* 523.

So soon as the House sits, and a committee is notified of it, the chairman is in duty bound to rise instantly, and the members to attend the service of the House.—2 *Nals.* 19.

It appears, that on joint committee of the Lords and Commons, each committee acted integrally in the following instances;—7 *Grey,* 261, 278, 286, 338; 1 *Chandler,* 357, 462. In the following instances it does not appear whether they did or not: 6 *Grey,* 129; 7 *Grey,* 213, 229, 321.

## SECTION XII

### COMMITTEE OF THE WHOLE

The speech, messages, and other matters of great concernment, are usually referred to a committee of the whole House—6 *Grey,* 311, where general principles are digested in the form of resolutions, which are debated and amended till they get into a shape which meets the approbation of a majority. These being reported and confirmed by the House, are then referred to one or more select committees, according as the subject divides itself into one or more bills.—*Scob.* 36, 44. Propositions for any charge on the people are especially to be first made in a committee of the whole.—3 *Hats.* 127. The sense of the whole is better taken in committee, because in all committees everyone speaks as often as he pleases.—*Scob.* 49. They generally acquiesce in the chairman named by the Speaker; but, as well as all other committees, have a right to elect one, some member, by consent, putting the question.—*Scob.* 36; 3 *Grey,* 301. The form of going from the House into committee, is for the Speaker on motion, to put the question that the House do now resolve itself into a committee of the whole, to take under consideration such a matter, naming it. If determined in the affirmative, he leaves the chair, and takes a seat elsewhere, as any other member; and the person appointed chairman seats himself at the clerk's table.—*Scob.* 36. Their quorum is the same as that of the House; and if a defect happens, the chairman, on a motion and question, rises, the Speaker resumes the chair, and the chairman can make no other report than to inform the House of the cause of their dissolution. If a message is announced during a committee, the Speaker takes the chair, and receives it, because the committee cannot.—2 *Hats.* 125, 126.

In a committee of the whole, the tellers, on a division, differing as to numbers, great heats and confusion arose, and dangers of a decision by the sword. The Speaker took the chair, the mace was forcibly laid on the table; whereupon, the members retiring to their places, the Speaker told the House "he had taken the chair without an order, to bring the House into order." Some excepted against it; but it was generally approved as the only expedient to suppress the disorder. And every member was required, standing up in his place, to engage that he would proceed no further, in consequence of what had happened in the grand committee, which was done.—3 *Grey,* 139.

A committee of the whole being broken up in disorder, and the chair resumed by the Speaker without an order, the House was adjourned. The next day the committee was considered as thereby dissolved, and the subject again before the House; and it was decided in the House, without returning into committee.—3 *Grey,* 130.

No previous question can be put in a committee; nor can this committee adjourn as others may; but if their business is unfinished, they rise on a question, the House is resumed, and the chairman reports that the committee of the whole have, according to order, had under their consideration such a matter, and have made progress therein; but not having time to go through the same, have directed him to ask leave to sit again. Whereupon, a question is put on their having leave, and on the time when the House will again resolve itself into a committee.—*Scob.* 38. But if they have gone through the matter referred to them, a member moves that the committee may rise, and the chairman report their proceedings to the House; which being resolved, the chairman rises, the Speaker resumes the chair, the chairman informs him that the committee have gone through the business referred to them, and that he is ready to make report when the House shall think proper to receive it. If the House have time to receive it, there is usually a cry of "Now, Now," whereupon he makes the report; but if it be late, the cry is, "Tomorrow, Tomorrow," or, "On Monday," &c., or a motion is made to that effect, and a question put, that it be received tomorrow, &c.—*Scob.* 38.

In other things the rules of proceedings are to be the same as in the House.—*Scob.* 39.

## SECTION XIII

### EXAMINATION OF WITNESSES

Common fame is a good ground for the House to proceed by inquiry, and even to accusation.—*Resolution of the House of Commons,* 1 *Car.* 1, 1625; *Rush. Lex. Parl.* 115; 1 *Grey,* 16. 22. 92; 8 *Grey,* 21. 23. 27. 45.

Witnesses are not to be produced but where the House has previously instituted an inquiry, 2 *Hats.* 102, nor then are orders for their attendance given blank.—3 *Grey,* 51. The process is a summons from the House.—4 *Hats.* 255. 258.

When any person is examined before a committee, or at the bar of the House, any member wishing to ask the person a question, must address it to the Speaker or chairman, who repeats the question to the person, or says to him, "You hear the question, answer it." But if the propriety of the question be objected to, the Speaker directs the witness, counsel, and parties to withdraw; for no question can be moved, or put, or debated, while they are there.—2 *Hats.* 108. Sometimes the questions are previously settled in writing before the witness enters.—2 *Hats.* 106, 107; 8 *Grey,* 64. The questions asked must be entered in the journals.—3 *Grey,* 81. But the testimony given in answer before the House is never written down; but before a committee it must be for the information of the House, who are not present to hear it.—7 *Grey,* 52, 334.

If either House have occasion for the presence of a person in custody of the other, they ask the other their leave that he may be brought up to them in custody.—3 *Hats.* 52.

A member, in his place, gives information to the House of what he knows of any matter under hearing at the bar.—*Jour. H. of C.,* Jan. 22, 1744, 5.

Either House may request, but not command, the attendance of a member of the other. They are to make the request by message to the other House, and to express clearly the purpose of attendance, that no improper subject of examination may be tendered to him. The House then gives leave to the member to attend, if he choose it; waiting first to know from the member himself whether he chooses to attend, till which they do not take the message into consideration. But when the Peers are sitting as a court of Criminal Judicature, they may order attendance; unless where it be a case of impeachment by the Commons. There it is to be a request.—3 *Hats.* 17; 9 *Grey,* 306, 406; 10 *Grey,* 133.

Counsel are to be heard only on private, not on public bills; and on such points of law only as the House shall direct.—19 *Grey,* 61.

## SECTION XIV

### ARRANGEMENT OF BUSINESS

The Speaker is not precisely bound to any rules as to what bills or other matter shall be first taken up, but is left to his own discretion, unless the House on a question decide to take up a particular subject.—*Hakew.* 136.

A settled order of business is, however, necessary for the government of the presiding person, and to restrain individual members from calling up favorite measures, or matters under their special patronage, out of their just turn. It is useful also for directing the discretion of the House, when they are moved to take up a particular matter, to the prejudice of others having a priority of right to their attention in the general order of business.

In Senate, the bills and other papers which are in possession of the House, and in a state to be acted upon, are arranged every morning, and brought on in the following order:

1. Bills ready for a second reading are read, that they may be referred to committees, and so be put under way. But if, on their being read, no motion is made for commitment, they are then laid on the table in the general file, to be taken up in their just turn.

2. After twelve o'clock, bills ready for it are put on their passage.

3. Reports in possession of the House which offer grounds for a bill, are to be taken up, that the bill may be ordered in.

4. Bills or other matters before the House, and unfinished on the preceding day, whether taken up in turn, or on special order, are entitled to be resumed and passed on through their present stage.

5. These matters being despatched, for preparing and expediting business, the general file of bills and other papers is then taken up, and each article of it is brought on according to its seniority, reckoned by the date of its first introduction to the House. Reports on bills belong to the dates of their bills.

In this way we do not waste our time in debating what shall be taken up: we do one thing at a time, follow up a subject while it is fresh, and till it is done with; clear the House of business, gradatim as it is brought on, and prevent, to a certain degree, its immense accumulation towards the close of the session.

Arrangement, however, can only take hold of matters in possession of the House. New matter may be moved at any time, when no question is before the House. Such are original motions, and reports on bills. Such are, bills from the other House, which are received at all times, and receive their first reading as soon as the question then before the House is disposed of; and bills brought in on leave, which are read first whenever presented. So, messages from the other House respecting amendments to bills, are taken up as soon as the House is clear of a question, unless they require to be printed for better consideration. Orders of the day may be called for, even when another question is before the House.

## SECTION XV

### ORDER

Each House may determine the rules of its proceedings; punish its members for disorderly behavior, and, with the concurrence of two-thirds, expel a member.—*Const.* I. 5.

In Parliament, "instances make order," *per Speaker Onslow,* 2 *Hats.* 144; but what is done only by one Parliament, cannot be called custom of Parliament: *by Prynne,* 1 *Grey,* 52.

## SECTION XVI

### ORDER RESPECTING PAPERS

The Clerk is to let no journals, records, accounts, or papers, be taken from the table, or out of his custody.—2 *Hats.* 193, 194.

Mr. Prynne having, at a committee of the whole, amended a mistake in a bill, without order or knowledge of the committee, was reprimanded. 1 *Chand.* 77.

A bill being missing, the House resolved, that a protestation should be made and subscribed by the members, "before Almighty God and this honorable House, that neither myself nor any other, to my knowledge, have taken away, or do at this present conceal a bill entitled," &c.—5 *Grey,* 202.

After a bill is engrossed, it is put into the Speaker's hands, and he is not to let anyone have it to look into.—*Town. col.* 209.

## SECTION XVII

### ORDER IN DEBATE

When the Speaker is seated in his chair, every member is to sit in his place. —*Scob.* 6; *Grey,* 403.

When any member means to speak, he is to stand up in his place, uncovered, and to address himself, not to the House, or any particular member, but to the Speaker, who calls him by his name, that the House may take notice who it is that speaks.—*Scob.* 6; *D'Ewes,* 487, *col.* 1; 2 *Hats.* 77; 4 *Grey,* 66; 8 *Grey,* 108. But members who are indisposed may be indulged to speak sitting.—3 *Hats.* 75, 77; 1 *Grey,* 195.

In Senate, every member, when he speaks, shall address the chair, standing in his place; and when he has finished, shall sit down.—*Rule* 3.

When a member stands up to speak, no question is to be put; but he is to be heard, unless the House overrule him.—4 *Grey,* 390; 5 *Grey,* 6, 143.

If two or more rise to speak nearly together, the Speaker determines who was first up, and calls him by name; whereupon he proceeds, unless he voluntarily sits down, and gives way to the other. But sometimes the House does not acquiesce in the Speaker's decision; in which case, the question is put, "which member was first up?"—2 *Hats.* 76; *Scob.* 7; *D'Ewes,* 434, *col.* 1, 2.

In the Senate of the United States, the President's decision is without appeal. Their rule is in these words:—*When two members rise at the same time, the President shall name the person to speak; but in all cases,* the member who shall first rise and address the chair, shall speak first.—*Rule* 5.

No man can speak more than once to the same bill, on the same day; or even on another day, if the debate be adjourned. But if it be read more than once, in the same day, he may speak once at every reading.—*Co.* 12, 116; *Hakew.* 148; *Scob.* 58; 2 *Hats.* 75. Even a change of opinion does not give a right to be heard a second time.—*Smyth. Comw. L.* 2. *c.* 3; *Arcan. Parl.* 17.

The corresponding rule of the Senate is in these words:—No member shall speak more than twice in any one debate on the same day, without leave of the Senate.— *Rule* 4.

But he may be permitted to speak again to clear a matter of fact.—3 *Grey,* 357,416. Or merely to explain himself, 3 *Hats.* 73, in some material part of his speech, *ib.* 75; or to the manner or words of the question, keeping himself to that only, and not travelling into the merits of it, *Memorials in Hakew.* 29; or to the orders of the House, if they be transgressed, keeping within that line, and falling into the matter itself.—*Mem. Hakew,* 30, 31.

But if the Speaker rises to speak, the member standing up ought to sit down, that he may be first heard. *Town. col.* 205; *Hale. Parl.* 133; *Mem. in Hakew.* 30, 31. Nevertheless, though the Speaker may of right speak to matters of order, and be first heard, he is restrained from speaking on any other subject, except where the House have occasion for facts within his knowledge: then he may, with their leave, state the matter of fact.—3 *Grey,* 38.

No one is to speak impertinently or beside the question, superfluously or tediously.—*Scob.* 31, 33; 2 *Hats.* 166, 168; *Hale Parl.* 133.

No person is to use indecent language against the proceedings of the House, no prior determination of which is to be reflected on by any member unless he means to conclude with a motion to rescind it.—2 *Hats.* 169, 170; *Rushw.* p. 3. v. 1. fol. 42. But while a proposition is under consideration, is still in fieri, though it has even been reported by a committee, reflections on it are no reflections on the House.—9 *Grey,* 308.

No person in speaking, is to mention a member then present by his name; but to describe him by his seat in the House, or who spoke last or on the other side of the question, &c. *Mem. in Hawk.*—3 *Smyth's Comw, L.* 2. *c.* 3; nor to digress from the matter to fall upon the person.—*Scob.* 31; *Hale, Parl.* 133; 2 *Hats.* 166, by speaking, reviling, nipping, or unmannerly words against a particular member. *Smyth's Comw. L.* 2. *c.* 3. The consequence of a measure may be reprobated in strong terms; but to arraign the motives of those who propose or advocate it, is a personality, and against order. Qui digreditur a materia ad personam, Mr. Speaker ought to suppress.—*Ord. Com.* 1604, Apr. 19.

When a member shall be called to order he shall sit down, until the President shall have determined whether he is in order or not.—*Rule* 16.

No member shall speak to another, or otherwise interrupt the business of the Senate, or read any printed paper while the Journals or public papers are reading, or when any member is speaking in any debate.—*Rule* 2.

No one is to disturb another in his speech, by hissing, coughing, spitting,—6 *Grey,* 332; *Scob.* 8; *D'Ewes,* 332, *col.* 1; nor stand up to interrupt him,—*Town. col.* 205; *Mem. in Hakew.* 31; nor to pass between the Speaker and the speaking member; nor to go across the House,—*Scob.* 6; or to walk up and down it; or to take books or papers from the table, or write there.—2 *Hats.* 171.

Nevertheless, if a member finds it is not the inclination of the House to hear him, and that, by conversation or any other noise, they endeavor to drown his voice, it is the most prudent way to submit to the pleasure of the House, and sit down; for it scarcely ever happens that they are guilty of this piece of ill manners without sufficient reason, or inattentive to a member who says any thing worth their hearing.—2 *Hats.* 77, 78.

If repeated calls do not produce order, the Speaker may call by his name any member obstinately persisting in irregularity; whereupon the House may require the member to withdraw. He is then to be heard in exculpation and to withdraw. Then the Speaker states the offence committed, and the House considers the degree of punishment they will inflict.—2 *Hats.* 169, 7, 8, 172.

For instances of assaults and affrays in the House of Commons, and the proceedings thereon, see 1 *Pet. Misc.* 82; 3 *Grey,* 128; 4 *Grey,* 328; 5 *Grey,* 38; 26 *Grey,* 204; 10 *Grey,* 8. Whenever warm words or an assault have passed between the members, the House, for the protection of their members, requires them to declare in their place not to prosecute any quarrel,—3 *Grey,* 128, 293; 5

*Grey,* 289; or orders them to attend the Speaker, who is to accommodate their differences, and to report to the House,—3 *Grey,* 419; and they are put under restraint, if they refuse, or until they do.—9 *Grey,* 234, 312.

Disorderly words are not to be noticed till the member has finished his speech.—5 *Grey,* 356; 6 *Grey,* 60. Then the person objecting to them, and desiring them to be taken down by the clerk at the table, must repeat them. The Speaker then may direct the clerk to take them down in his minutes. But if he thinks them not disorderly, he delays the direction. If the call becomes pretty general, he orders the clerk to take them down, as stated by the objecting member. They are then part of his minutes, and when read to the offending member, he may deny they were his words, and the House must then decide by a question, whether they are his words or not. Then the member may justify them, or explain the sense in which he used them, or apologize. If the House is satisfied, no further proceeding is necessary. But if two members still insist to take the sense of the House, the member must withdraw before that question is stated, and then the sense of the House is to be taken.—2 *Hats.* 199; 4 *Grey,* 170; 6 *Grey,* 59. When any member has spoken, or other business intervened, after offensive words spoken, they cannot be taken notice of for censure. And this is for the common security of all, and to prevent mistakes, which must happen, if words are not taken down immediately. Formerly, they might be taken down at any time the same day.—2 *Hats.* 196; *Mem. in Hakew.* 71; 3 Grey, 48; 9 *Grey,* 514.

Disorderly words spoken in a committee, must be written down as in the House; but the committee can only report them to the House for animadversion.—6 *Grey,* 46.

The rule of the Senate says,—If a member be called to order for words spoken, the exceptionable words shall be immediately taken down in writing, that the President may be better enabled to judge.—*Rule* 17.

In Parliament, to speak irreverently or seditiously against the King, is against order.—*Smyth's Comw. L.* 2, *c.* 3; 2 *Hats.* 170.

It is a breach of order in debate to notice what has been said on the same subject in the other House, or the particular votes or majorities on it there; because the opinion of each House should be left to its own independency, not to be influenced by the proceedings of the other; and the quoting them might beget reflections leading to a misunderstanding between the two Houses.—8 *Grey,* 22.

Neither House can exercise any authority over a member or officer of the other, but should complain to the House of which he is, and leave the punishment to them. Where the complaint is of words disrespectfully spoken by a member of another House, it is difficult to obtain punishment, because of the rules supposed necessary to be observed (as to the immediate noting down of words) for the security of members. Therefore it is the duty of the House, and more particularly of the Speaker, to interfere immediately, and not to permit expressions to go unnoticed, which may give a ground of complaint to the other House, and introduce proceedings and mutual accusations between the two Houses, which can hardly be terminated without difficulty and disorder.—3 *Hats.* 51.

No member may be present when a bill, or any business concerning himself, is debating; nor is any member to speak to the merits of it till he withdraws.—2 *Hats.* 219. The rule is, that if a charge against a member arise out of a report of a committee, or examination of witnesses in the House, as the member knows from that to what points he is to direct his exculpation, he may be heard to those points before any question is moved or stated against them. He is then to be heard, and withdraw before any question is moved. But if the question itself is the charge, as for breach of order, or matter arising in debate, there the matter must be stated; that is, the question must be moved, himself heard, and then to withdraw.—2 *Hats.* 121, 122.

Where the private interests of a member are concerned in a bill or question, he is to withdraw. And where such an interest has appeared, his voice has been disallowed, even after a division. In a case so contrary not only to the laws of decency, but to the fundamental principles of the social compact, which denies to any man to be a judge in his own cause, it is for the honor of the House that this rule of immemorial observance should be strictly adhered to.—2 *Hats.* 119, 121; 6 *Grey,* 368.

No member is to come into the House with his head covered, nor to remove from one place to the other with his hat on, nor is to put on his hat in coming in, or removing, until he be sit down in his place.—*Scob.* 6.

A question of order may be adjourned to give time to look into precedents.—2 *Hats.* 118.

In the Senate of the United States, every question of order is to be decided by the President, without debate; but if there be a doubt in his mind, he may call for the sense of the Senate.—*Rule* 16.

In Parliament, all decisions of the Speaker may be controlled by the House.—3 *Grey,* 319.

## SECTION XVIII

### ORDERS OF THE HOUSE

Of right, the door of the House ought not to be shut, but to be kept by porters, or sergeants-at-arms, assigned for that purpose.—*Mod. ten. Parl.* 23.

By the rule of the Senate, on motion made and seconded to shut the doors of the Senate, on the discussion of any business which may in the opinion of a member, require secrecy, the President shall direct the gallery to be cleared; and during the discussion of such motion the door shall remain shut.—*Rule* 28.

No motion shall be deemed in order, to admit any person or persons whatever within the doors of the Senate-chamber, to present any petition, memorial, or address, or to hear any such read.—*Rule* 29.

The only case where a member has a right to insist on anything, is where he calls for the execution of a subsisting order of the House. Here, there having been already a resolution, any member has a right to insist that the Speaker, or any other whose duty it is, shall carry it into execution; and no debate or delay can be had on it. Thus any member has a right to have the House or gallery cleared of strangers, an order existing for that purpose; or to have the House told when there is not a quorum present.—2 *Hats.* 87, 129. How far an order of the House is binding, see *Hakew.* 392.

But where an order is made that any particular matter be taken up on a particular day, there a question is to be put when it is called for, Whether the House will now proceed to that matter? Where orders of the day are on important or interesting matter, they ought not to be proceeded on till an hour at which the House is usually full—(*which in Senate is at noon.*)

Orders of the day may be discharged at any time, and a new one made for a different day.—3 *Grey,* 48, 313.

When a session is drawing to a close, and the important bills are all brought in, the House, in order to prevent interruption by further unimportant bills, sometimes come to a resolution, that no new bill be brought in, except it be sent from the other House.—3 *Grey,* 156.

All orders of the House determine with the session; and one taken under such an order may, after the session is ended, be discharged on a Habeas Corpus. —*Raym.* 120; *Jacob's L. D. by Ruffhead; Parliament,* 1 *Lev.* 165, *Prichard's case.*

Where the Constitution authorizes each House to determine the rule of its proceedings, it must mean in those cases, legislative, executive, or judiciary, submitted to them by the Constitution, or in something relating to these, and necessary towards their execution. But orders and resolutions are sometimes entered in their journals, having no relation to these, such as acceptances of invitations to attend orations, to take part in processions, &c. These must be understood to be merely conventional among those who are willing to participate in the ceremony, and are therefore, perhaps, improperly placed among the records of the House.

## SECTION XIX

### PETITIONS

A petition prays something. A remonstrance has no prayer.—1 *Grey,* 58.

Petitions must be subscribed by the petitioners, *Scob.* 87; *L. Parl. c.* 22; 9 *Grey,* 362, unless they are attending, 1 *Grey,* 401, or unable to sign, and averred by a member.—3 *Grey,* 418. But a petition not subscribed, but which the member presenting it affirmed to be all in the handwriting of the petitioner, and his name written in the beginning, was, on the question, (March 14, 1800,) received by the Senate. The averment of a member, or somebody without doors, that they know the handwriting of the petitioners, is necessary, if it be questioned.—6 *Grey,* 36. It must be presented by a member, not by the petitioners, and must be opened by him, holding it in his hand.—10 *Grey,* 57.

Before any petition or memorial, addressed to the Senate, shall be received and read at the table, whether the same shall be introduced by the President or a member, a brief statement of the contents of the petition or memorial shall verbally be made by the introducer.—*Rule* 21.

Regularly a motion for receiving it must be made and seconded, and a question put, Whether it shall be received? But a cry from the House of "Received," or even its silence, dispenses with the formality of this question: it is then to be read at the table, and disposed of.

## SECTION XX

### MOTIONS

When a motion has been made, it is not to be put to the question, or debated, until it is seconded.—*Scob.* 21.

The Senate say, No motion shall be debated until the same shall be seconded.—*Rule* 6.

It is then, and not till then, in possession of the House. It is to be put into writing, if the House or Speaker require it, and must be read to the House by the Speaker, as often as any member desires it for his information.—2 *Hats.* 82.

The rule of the Senate is, When a motion shall be made and seconded, it shall be reduced to writing, if desired by the President or any member, delivered in at the table, and read by the President before the same shall be debated.—*Rule* 7.

It might be asked, whether a motion for adjournment, or for the orders of the day, can be made by one member while another is speaking? It cannot. When two members offer to speak, he who rose first is to be heard, and it is a breach of order in another to interrupt him, unless by calling him to order if he departs from it. And the question of order being decided, he is still to be heard through. A call for adjournment, or for the order of the day, or for the question, by gentlemen from their seats, is not a motion. No motion can be made without arising and addressing the chair. Such calls are themselves breaches of order, which, though the member who has risen may respect as an expression of impatience of the House against farther debate, yet, if he chooses, he has a right to go on.

## SECTION XXI

### RESOLUTIONS

When the House commands, it is by an "order." But facts, principles, their own opinions and purposes, are expressed in the form of resolutions.

A resolution for an allowance of money to the clerks being moved, it was objected to as not in order, and so ruled by the chair. But on appeal to the Senate, (*i.e.*, a call for their sense by the President, on account of doubt in his mind, according to Rule 16), the decision was overruled.—*Journ. Sen.*, June 1, 1796. I presume the doubt was, whether an allowance of money could be made otherwise than by bill.

## SECTION XXII

### BILLS

Every bill shall receive three readings previous to its being passed; and the President shall give notice at each, whether it be the first, second, or third; which readings shall be on three different days, unless the Senate unanimously direct otherwise, or unless by a joint vote of both Houses, or the expiration of their term, the session is to be closed within three days.—*Rule* 13.

## SECTION XXIII

### BILLS, LEAVE TO BRING IN

One day's notice, at least, shall be given of an intended motion for leave to bring in a bill.—*Rule* 12.

When a member desires to bring a bill on any subject, he states to the House, in general terms, the causes for doing it, and concludes by moving for leave to bring in a bill, entitled, &c. Leave being given, on the question, a committee is appointed to prepare and bring in the bill. The mover and seconder are always appointed on this committee, and one or more in addition.—*Hakew.* 132; *Scob.* 40.

It is to be presented fairly written, without any erasure or interlineation; or the Speaker may refuse it.—*Scob.* 31; 1 *Grey,* 82, 84.

## SECTION XXIV

### BILLS, FIRST READING

When a bill is first presented, the clerk reads it at the table, and hands it to the Speaker, who, rising, states to the House the title of the bill; that this is the first time of reading it; and the question will be, Whether it shall be read a second time? Then, sitting down, to give an opening for objections; if none be made, he rises again, and puts the question, Whether it shall be read a second time?—*Hakew.* 137, 141. A bill cannot be amended at the first reading,—6 *Grey,* 286; nor is it usual for it to be opposed then, but it may be done and rejected.—*D'Ewes,* 335, *col.* 1; 3 *Hats.* 198.

## SECTION XXV

### BILLS, SECOND READING

The second reading must regularly be on another day.—*Hakew.* 143. It is done by the clerk at the table, who then hands it to the Speaker. The Speaker, rising, states to the House the title of the bill, that this is the second time of reading it, and that the question will be, Whether it shall be committed, or engrossed and read a third time? But if the bill came from the other House, as it always comes engrossed, he states that the question will be, Whether it shall be read a third time? And before he has so reported the state of the bill, no one is to speak to it.—*Hakew.* 143, 146.

In the Senate of the United States, the President reports the title of the bill, that this is the second time of reading it, that it is now to be considered as in a committee of the whole, and the question will be, Whether it shall be read a third time? or, that it may be referred to a special committee.

## SECTION XXVI

### BILLS, COMMITMENT

If, on motion and question, it be decided that the bill shall be committed, it may then be moved to be referred to a committee of the whole House, or to a special committee. If the latter, the Speaker proceeds to name the committee. Any member also may name a single person, and the clerk is to write him down as of the committee. But the House have a controlling power over the names and number, if a question be moved against anyone; and may in any case put in and put out whom they please.

Those who take exceptions to some particulars in the bill, are to be of the committee. But none who speak directly against the body of the bill. For he that would totally destroy, would not amend it.—*Hakew.* 146; *Town. col.* 208; *D'Ewes,* 634, *col.* 2; *Scob.* 47; or, as is said, 5 *Grey,* 145, the child is not to be put to a nurse that cares not for it.—6 *Grey,* 373. It is therefore a constant rule, "that no man is to be employed in any matter who has declared himself against it." And when any member who is against the bill, hears himself named of its committee, he ought to ask to be excused. Thus, March 6, 1606, Mr. Hadley was, on the question being put, excused from being of a committee, declaring himself to be against the matter itself.—*Scob.* 48.

No bill shall be committed or amended until it shall have been twice read, after which it may be referred to a committee.—*Rule* 14.

All committees shall be appointed by ballot, and a plurality of voices shall make a choice.—*Rule* 15.

The clerk may deliver the bill to any member of the committee.—*Town. col.* 138. But it is usual to deliver it to him who is first named.

In some cases, the House has ordered the committee to withdraw immediately into the committee-chamber, and act on and bring back the bill, sitting the House.—*Scob.* 48.

A committee meets when and where they please, if the House has not ordered time and place for them.—6 *Grey,* 370. But they can only act when together, and not by separate consultation and consent; nothing being the report of the committee, but what has been agreed to in committee, actually assembled.

A majority of the committee constitutes a quorum for business.—*Elsynge's method of passing bills,* 11.

Any member of the House may be present at any select committee, but cannot vote, and must give place to all of the committee, and must sit below them. —*Elsynge,* 12; *Scob.* 49.

But in 1626, April 24th, the House of Commons resolved that though any members may be present at the examination of witnesses, they may not be at the debate, disposition, or penning of the business by the select committee.—4 *Hats.* 124.

The committee have full power over the bill or other paper committed to them, except that they cannot change the title or subject.—8 *Grey,* 228.

The paper before a committee, whether select or of the whole, may be a bill, resolutions, draught of an address, &c., and it may either originate with them, or be referred to them. In every case, the whole paper is read first by the clerk, and then by the chairman, by paragraphs, *Scob.* 49, pausing at the end of each paragraph, and putting questions, for amending, if proposed. In the case of resolutions on distinct subjects, originating with themselves, a question is put on each separately, as amended, or unamended, and no final question on the whole.—3 *Hats.* 276. But if they relate to the same subject, a question is put on the whole. If it be a bill, draught of an address, or other paper originating with them, they proceed by paragraphs, putting questions for amending, either by inserting or striking out, if proposed; but no question on agreeing to the paragraphs separately. This is reserved to the close, when a question is put on the whole for agreeing to it as amended or unamended. But if it be a paper referred to them, they proceed to put questions of amendment, if proposed, but no final question on the whole; because all parts of the paper having been adopted by the House, stand, of course, unless altered, or struck out by a vote. Even if they are opposed to the whole paper, and think it cannot be made good by amendments, they cannot reject it, but must report it back to the House without amendments, and there make their opposition.

The natural order in considering and amending any paper is, to begin at the beginning, and proceed through it by paragraphs; and this order is so strictly adhered to in Parliament, that, when a latter part has been amended, you cannot recur back and make any alteration in a former part.—2 *Hats.* 90. In numerous assemblies, this restraint is, doubtless, important.

But in the Senate of the United States, though in the main we consider and amend the paragraphs in their natural order, yet recurrences are indulged; and they seem, on the whole, in that small body, to produce advantages overweighing their inconveniences.

To this natural order of beginning at the beginning, there is a single exception found in Parliamentary usage. When a bill is taken up in committee, or on its second reading, they postpone the preamble, till the other parts of the bill are gone through. The reason is, that on consideration of the body of the bill, such alterations may therein be made, as may also occasion the alteration of the preamble.—*Scob.* 50; 7 *Grey,* 431.

On this head, the following case occurred in the Senate, March 6, 1800. A resolution which had no preamble, having been already amended by the House, so that a few words only of the original remained in it, a motion was made to prefix a preamble, which, having an aspect very different from the resolution, the mover intimated that he should afterwards propose a correspondent amendment in the body of the resolution. It was objected that a preamble could not be taken up till the body of the resolution is done with. But the preamble was received; because we are in fact through the body of the resolution, we have amended that as far as amendments have been offered, and indeed till little of the original is left. It is the proper time, therefore, to consider a preamble; and whether the one offered be consistent with the resolution, is for the House to determine. The mover, indeed, has intimated that he shall offer a subsequent proposition for the body of the resolution; but the House is not in possession of it; it remains in his breast, and may be withheld. The rules of the House can only operate on what is before them. The practice of the Senate, too, allows recurrences backwards and forwards for the purpose of amendments, not permitting amendments in a subsequent, to preclude those in a prior part, or *a converso*.

When the committee is through the whole, a member moves that the committee may rise, and the chairman report the paper to the House, with or without amendments, as the case may be. 2 *Hats*. 289, 292; *Scob*. 53; 2 *Hats*. 290; 8 *Scob*. 50.

When a vote is once passed in a committee, it cannot be altered but by the House, their votes being binding on themselves.—1607, June 4.

The committee may not erase, interline, or blot the bill itself; but must, in a paper by itself, set down the amendments, stating the words that are to be inserted or omitted, *Scob*. 50; and where, by reference to the page, line, and word of the bill.—*Scob*. 50.

## SECTION XXVII

### REPORT OF COMMITTEE

The chairman of the committee, standing in his place, informs the House that the committee, to whom was referred such a bill, have, according to order, had the same under consideration, and have directed him to report the same without any amendment, or with sundry amendments (as the case may be), which he is ready to do when the House pleases to receive it. And he, or any other, may move that it be now received. But the cry of "now, now," from the House, generally dispenses with the formality of a motion and question. He then reads the amendments, with the coherence in the bill, and opens the alterations, and the reasons of the committee for such amendment, until he has gone through the whole. He then delivers it at the clerk's table, where the amendments reported are read by the clerk, without the coherence; whereupon the papers lie upon the table, till the House, at his convenience, shall take up the report.—*Scob*. 52; *Hakew*. 148.

The report being made, the committee is dissolved, and can act no more without a new power.—*Scob*. 51. But it may be revived by a vote, and the same matter recommitted to them.—4 *Grey*, 361.

## SECTION XXVIII

### BILL, RECOMMITMENT

After a bill has been committed and reported, it ought not, in an ordinary course, to be recommitted. But in cases of importance, and for special reasons, it is sometimes recommitted, and usually to the same committee. *Hakew.* 151. If a report be committed before agreed to in the House, what has passed in the committee is of no validity; the whole question is again before the committee, and a new resolution must be again moved, as if nothing had passed.—3 *Hats.* 131, note.

In Senate, January, 1800, the salvage bill was recommitted three times after the committment.

A particular clause of a bill may be committed without the whole bill,—3 *Hats.* 131; or so much of a paper to one, and so much to another committee.

## SECTION XXIX

### BILL, REPORT TAKEN UP

When the report of a paper, originating with a committee, is taken up by the House, they proceed exactly as in committee. Here, as in committee, when the paragraphs have, on distinct questions, been agreed to *seriatim,*—5 *Grey,* 365; 6 *Grey,* 368; 8 *Grey,* 47, 104, 360; 1 *Torbuck's deb.* 124; 3 *Hats.* 348,—no question need be put on the whole report.—5 *Grey,* 381.

On taking up a bill reported with amendments, the amendments only are read by the clerk. The Speaker then reads the first, and puts it to the question, and so on till the whole are adopted or rejected, before any other amendment be admitted, except it be an amendment to an amendment.—*Elsynge's Mem.* 23. When through the amendments of the committee, the Speaker pauses, and gives time for amendments to be proposed in the House to the body of the bill; as he does also if it has been reported without amendments; putting no question but on amendments proposed; and when through the whole, he puts the question, Whether the bill shall be read the third time?

## SECTION XXX

### QUASI-COMMITTEE

If, on the motion and question, the bill be not committed, or if no proposition for commitment be made, then the proceedings in the Senate of United States and in Parliament are totally different. The former shall be first stated.

The 20th rule of the Senate says, "All bills, on a second reading, shall first be considered by the Senate in the same manner as if the Senate were in a committee of the whole, before they shall be taken up and proceeded on by the Senate agreeably to the standing rules, unless otherwise ordered"; that is to say, unless ordered to be referred to a special committee.

The proceeding of the Senate, as in committee of the whole, or in quasi-committee, are precisely as in a real committee of the whole, taking no questions but on amendments. When through the whole, they consider the quasi-committee as risen, the House resumed, without any motion, question, or resolution to that effect, and the President reports, that "the House, acting as in committee of the whole, have had under consideration the bill entitled, &c., and have made sundry amendments, which he will now report to the House." The bill is then before them, as it would have been if reported from a committee, and questions are regularly to be put again on every amendment: which being gone through, the President pauses to give time to the House to propose amendments to the body of the bill, and when through, puts the question, whether it shall be read a third time?

After progress in amending a bill in quasi-committee, a motion may be made to refer it to a special committee. If the motion prevails, it is equivalent in effect to the several votes that the committee rise, the House resume itself, discharge the committee of the whole, and refer the bill to a special committee. In that case, the amendments already made fall. But if the motion fails, the quasi-committee stands in *statu quo*.

How far does this 20th rule subject the House, when in quasi-committee, to the laws which regulate the proceedings of a committee of the whole? The particulars, in which these differ from proceedings in the House, are the following:—1. In a committee, every member may speak as often as he pleases.—2. The votes of a committee may be rejected or altered when reported to the House.—3. A committee, even of the whole, cannot refer any matter to another committee.—4. In a committee, no previous question can be taken: the only means to avoid an improper discussion, is to move that the committee rise; and if it be apprehended that the same discussion will be attempted on returning into committee, the House can discharge them, and proceed itself on the business, keeping down the improper discussion by the previous question.—5. A committee cannot punish a breach of order, in the House, or in the gallery,—9 *Grey,* 113; it can only rise and report it to the House, who may proceed to punish.

The 1st and 2d of these peculiarities attach to the quasi-committee of the Senate, as every day's practice proves; and seem to be the only ones to which the 20th rule meant to subject them: for it continues to be a House, and therefore, though it acts in some respects as a committee, in others it preserves its character as a House.—Thus, 3d, It is in the daily habit of referring its business to a special committee—4th. It admits the previous question: if it did not, it would have no means of preventing an improper discussion; not being able, as the committee is, to avoid it by returning into the House: for the moment it would resume the same subject there, the 20th rule declares it again a quasi-committee.—5th. It would doubtless exercise its powers as a House on any breach of order.—6th. It takes a question by Yea and Nay, as the House does.—7th. It receives messages from the President and the other House.—8th. In the midst of a debate, it receives a motion to adjourn, and adjourns as a House, not as a committee.

## SECTION XXXI

### BILL, SECOND READING IN THE HOUSE

In Parliament, after the bill has been read a second time, if, on the motion and question, it be not committed, or if no proposition for commitment be made, the Speaker reads it by paragraphs, pausing between each, but putting no questions but on amendments proposed; and when through the whole, he puts the question, Whether it shall be read the third time? if it came from the other House. Or, if originating with themselves, Whether it shall be engrossed and read a third time? The Speaker reads sitting, but rises to put a question. The clerk stands while he reads.

But the Senate of the United States is so much in the habit of making many and material amendments at the third reading, that it has become the practice not to engross a bill till it has passed. An irregular and dangerous practice; because, in this way, the paper which passes the Senate is not that which goes to the other House; and that which goes to the other House as the act of the Senate, has never been seen in Senate. In reducing numerous, difficult, and illegible amendments into the text, the secretary may, with the most innocent intentions, commit errors which can never again be corrected.

The bill being now as perfect as its friends can make it, this is the proper stage for those, fundamentally opposed, to make their own attack. All attempts at other periods are with disjointed efforts; because many who do not expect to be in favor of the bill, ultimately, are willing to let it go on to its perfect state, to take time to examine it themselves, and to hear what can be said for it; knowing that, after all, they have sufficient opportunities of giving it their veto. Its two last stages, therefore, are reserved for this, that is to say, on the question, Whether it shall be engrossed and read a third time? and, lastly, Whether it shall pass? The first of these is usually the most interesting contest; because then the whole subject is new and engaging, and the minds of the members having not yet been declared by any trying vote, the issue is the more doubtful. In this stage, therefore, is the main trial of strength between its friends and opponents; and it behooves everyone to make up his mind decisively for this question, or he loses the main battle; and accident and management may, and often do, prevent a successful rallying on the next and last question, Whether it shall pass?

When the bill is engrossed, the title is to be endorsed on the back, and not within the bill.—*Hakew.* 250.

## SECTION XXXII

### READING PAPERS

Where papers are laid before the House, or referred to a committee, every member has a right to have them once read at the table, before he can be compelled to vote on them. But it is a great, though common error, to suppose that he has a right, *toties quoties,* to have acts, journals, accounts, or papers, on the table, read independently of the will of the House. The delay and interruption which this might be made to produce, evince the impossibility of the existence of such a right. There is indeed so manifest a propriety of permitting every member to have as much information as possible on every question on which he is to vote, that when he desires the reading, if it be seen that it is really for information, and not for delay, the Speaker directs it to be read without putting a question, if no one objects. But if objected to, a question must be put.—2 *Hats.* 117, 118.

It is equally an error to suppose, that any member has a right, without a question put, to lay a book or paper on the table, and have it read, on suggesting that it contains matter infringing on the privileges of the House.—2 *Hats.* 117, 118.

For the same reason, a member has not a right to read a paper in his place, if it be objected to, without leave of the House. But this rigor is never exercised but where there is an intentional or gross abuse of the time and patience of the House.

A member has not a right even to read his own speech, committed to writing, without leave. This also is to prevent an abuse of time; and therefore is not refused, but where that is intended.—2 *Grey,* 227.

A report of a committee of the Senate on a bill from the House of Representatives being under consideration, on motion that the report of the committee of the House of Representatives on the same bill be read in the Senate, it passed in the negative.—Feb. 28, 1793.

Formerly, when papers were referred to a committee, they used to be first read; but of late, only the titles; unless a member insists they shall be read, and then nobody can oppose it.—2 *Hats.* 117.

## SECTION XXXIII

### PRIVILEGED QUESTIONS

While a question is before the Senate, no motion shall be received unless for an amendment, for the previous question, or for postponing the main question, or to commit it, or to adjourn.—Rule 8.

It is no possession of a bill, unless it be delivered to the clerk to be read, or the Speaker reads the title.—*Lex. Parl.* 274; *Elsynge, Mem.* 85; *Ord. House Commons,* 64.

It is a general rule, that the question first moved and seconded shall be first put.—*Scob.* 28, 22; 2 *Hats.* 81. But this rule gives way to what may be called privileged questions; and the privileged questions are of different grades among themselves.

A motion to adjourn, simply takes place of all others; for otherwise the House might be kept sitting against its will, and indefinitely. Yet this motion cannot be received after another question is actually put, and while the House is engaged in voting.

Orders of the day take place of all other questions, except for adjournment. That is to say, the question which is the subject of an order, is made a privileged one, *pro hac vice*. The order is a repeal of the general rule as to this special case. When any member moves, therefore, for the orders of the day to be read, no further debate is permitted on the question which was before the House; for if the debate might proceed, it might continue through the day, and defeat the order. This motion, to entitle it to precedence, must be for the orders generally, and not for any particular one; and if it be carried on the question, "Whether the House will now proceed to the orders of the day?" they must be read and proceeded on in the course in which they stand.—2 *Hats*. 83. For priority of order gives priority of right, which cannot be taken away but by another special order.

After these there are other privileged questions, which will require considerable explanation.

It is proper that every Parliamentary assembly should have certain forms of questions, so adapted as to enable them fitly to dispose of every proposition which can be made to them. Such are, 1. The previous question: 2. To postpone indefinitely: 3. To adjourn to a definite day: 4. To lie on the table: 5. To commit: 6. To amend. The proper occasion for each of these questions should be understood.

1. When a proposition is moved, which it is useless or inexpedient now to express or discuss, the previous question has been introduced for suppressing, for that time, the motion and its discussion.—3 *Hats*. 188, 189.

2. But as the previous question gets rid of it only for that day, and the same proposition may recur the next day, if they wish to suppress it for the whole of that session, they postpone it indefinitely.—3 *Hats*. 183. This quashes the proposition for that session, as an indefinite adjournment is a dissolution, or the continuance of a suit sine die is a discontinuance of it.

3. When a motion is made which it will be proper to act on, but information is wanted, or something more pressing claims the present time, the question or debate is adjourned to such a day within the session as will answer the views of the House.—2 *Hats*. 81. And those who have spoken before, may not speak again when the adjourned debate is resumed.—2 *Hats*. 73. Sometimes, however, this has been abusively used, by adjourning it to a day beyond the session, to get rid of it altogether, as would be done by an indefinite postponement.

4. When the House has something else which claims its present attention, but would be willing to reserve in their power to take up a proposition whenever it shall suit them, they order it to lie on their table. It may then be called for at any time.

5. If the proposition will want more amendment and digestion than the formalities of the House will conveniently admit, they refer it to a committee.

6. But if the proposition be well digested, and may need but few and simple amendments, and especially if these be of leading consequence, they then proceed to consider and amend it themselves.

The Senate, in their practice, vary from this regular gradation of forms. Their practice, comparatively with that of Parliament, stands thus:

| For the Parliamentary, | The Senate uses, |
|---|---|
| Postmt. indefinite. | —Postmt. to a day beyond the session. |
| Adjournment, | —Postmt. to a day within the session. |
| Laying on the table. | Postponement indefinite.<br>Laying on the table. |

In their 8th Rule, therefore, which declares, that while a question is before the Senate, no motion shall be received, unless it be for the previous question, or to postpone, commit or amend the main question, the term postponement must be understood according to their broad use of it, and not in its Parliamentary sense. Their rule then establishes as privileged questions, the previous question, postponement, commitment, and amendment.

But it may be asked, Have these questions any privilege among themselves? or are they so equal that the common principle of the "first moved, first put," takes place among them? This will need explanation. Their competitions may be as follows:

1. Prev. Qu. and Postpone / Commit / Amend
2. Postpone and Prev. Qu. / Commit / Amend
3. Commit and Prev. Qu. / Postpone / Amend
4. Amend and Prev. Qu. / Postpone / Commit

In the 1st, 2d, and 3d classes, and the 1st member of the 4th class, the rule "first moved, first put," takes place.

In the 1st class, where the previous question is first moved, the effect is peculiar; for it not only prevents the after motion to postpone or commit from being put to question before it, but also from being put after it. For if the previous question be decided affirmatively, to wit, that the main question shall *now* be put, it would of course be against the decision to postpone or commit. And if it be decided negatively, to wit, that the main question shall not now be put, this puts the House out of possession of the main question, and consequently there is nothing before them to postpone or commit. So that neither voting for nor against the previous question will enable the advocates for postponing or committing to get at their object. Whether it may be amended, shall be examined hereafter.

2d class.—If postponement be decided affirmatively, the proposition is removed from before the House, and consequently there is no ground for the previous question, commitment, or amendment. But if decided negatively, that it shall not be postponed, the main question may then be suppressed by the previous question, or may be committed or amended.

The 3d class is subject to the same observations as the 2d.

The 4th class.—Amendment of the main question first moved, and afterwards the previous question, the question of amendment shall be first put.

Amendment and postponement competing, postponement is first put, as the equivalent proposition to adjourn the main question would be in Parliament. The reason is, that the question for amendment is not suppressed by postponing or adjourning the main question, but remains before the House whenever the main question is resumed; and it might be that the occasion for other urgent business might go by, and be lost by length of debate on the amendment, if the House had it not in their power to postpone the whole subject.

Amendment and commitment. The question for committing, though last moved, shall be first put; because in truth it facilitates and befriends the motion to amend. *Scobell* is express:— "On a motion to amend a bill, anyone may, notwithstanding, move to commit it, and the question for commitment shall be first put."—*Scob.* 46.

We have hitherto considered the case of two or more of the privileged questions contending for privilege between themselves, when both were moved on the original or main question; but now let us suppose one of them to be moved, not on the original primary question, but on the secondary one, *e.g.*

Suppose a motion to postpone, commit, or amend the main question, and that it be moved to suppress that motion by putting the previous question on it. This is not allowed, because it would embarrass questions too much to allow them to be piled on one another several stories high; and the same result may be had in a more simple way, by deciding against the postponement, commitment, or amendment.—2 *Hats.* 81, 2, 3, 4.

Suppose a motion for the previous question, or commitment or amendment of the main question, and that it be then moved to postpone the motion for the previous question, or for commitment or amendment of the main question: 1. It would be absurd to postpone the previous question, commitment, or amendment, alone, and thus separate the appendage from its principal; yet it must be postponed separately from the original, if at all, because the 8th rule of the Senate says, that when a main question is before the House, no motion shall be received but to commit, amend, or pre-question the original question, which is the parliamentary doctrine; therefore, the motion to postpone the secondary motion for the previous question, or for committing or amending, cannot be received: 2. This is a piling of questions one on another, which, to avoid embarrassment, is not allowed: 3. The same result may be had more simply, by voting against the previous question, commitment, or amendment.

Suppose a commitment moved, of a motion for the previous question, or to postpone, or amend.

The 1st, 2d, and 3d reasons before stated, all hold good against this.

Suppose an amendment moved to a motion for the previous question? Answer: The previous question cannot be amended. Parliamentary usage, as well as the 9th rule of the Senate, has fixed its form to be, "Shall the main question be now put?" *i.e.,* at this instant. And as the present instant is but one, it can admit of no modification. To change it to tomorrow, or any other moment, is without example and without utility. But suppose a motion to amend a motion for postponement, as to one day instead of another, or to a special instead of indefinite time. The useful character of amendment gives it a privilege of attaching itself to a secondary privileged motion. That is, we may amend a postponement of a main question. So we may amend a commitment of a main question, as by adding, for example, "with instruction to inquire," &c. In like manner, if an amendment be moved to an amendment, it is admitted. But it would not be admitted in another degree, to wit, to amend an amendment to an amendment of a main question. This would lead to too much embarrassment. The line must be drawn somewhere; and usage has drawn it after the amendment to the amendment. The same result must be sought by deciding against the amendment to the amendment, and then moving it again as it was wished to be amended. In this form it becomes only an amendment to an amendment.

*In filling a blank with a sum, the largest sum shall be first put to the question, by the* 18*th Rule of the Senate,* contrary to the rule of Parliament, which privileges the smallest sum and longest time.—5 *Grey,* 179; 2 *Hats.* 8, 83; 3 *Hats.* 132, 133. And this is considered to be not in the form of an amendment to the question, but as alternative or successive originals. In all cases of time or number, we must consider whether the larger comprehends the lesser, as in a question to what day a postponement shall be, the number of a committee, amount of a fine, term of an imprisonment, term of irredeemability of a loan, or the *terminus in quem* in any other case. Then the question must begin *a maximo.* Or whether the lesser includes the greater, as in question on the limitation of the rate of interest, on what day the session shall be closed by adjournment, on what day the next shall commence, when an act shall commence, or the *terminus a quo* in any other case, where the question must begin *a minimo.* The object being not to begin at that extreme, which, and more, being within every man's wish, no one could negative it, and yet, if we should vote in the affirmative, every question for more would be precluded; but at that extreme which would unite few, and then to advance or recede till you get to a number which will unite a bare majority.—3 *Grey,* 376, 384, 385. "The fair question in this case is not that to which and more all will agree, whether there shall be addition to the question."—1 *Grey,* 365.

Another exception to the rule of priority is, when a motion has been made to strike out or agree to a paragraph. Motions to amend it are to be put to the question, before a vote is taken on striking out, or agreeing to the whole paragraph.

But there are several questions, which, being incidental to every one, will take place of every one, privileged or not; to wit, a question of order arising out of any other question, must be decided before that question.—2 *Hats.* 88.

A matter of privilege arising out of any question, or from a quarrel between two members, or any other cause, supersedes the consideration of the original question, and must first be disposed of.—2 *Hats.* 88.

Reading papers relative to the question before the House. This question must be put before the principal one.—2 *Hats.* 88.

Leave asked to withdraw a motion. The rule of Parliament being, that a motion made and seconded is in possession of the House, and cannot be withdrawn without leave, the very terms of the rule imply that leave may be given, and, consequently, may be asked and put to the question.

## SECTION XXXIV

### THE PREVIOUS QUESTION

When any question is before the House, any member may move a previous question, "Whether that question (called the main question) shall now be put?" If it pass in the affirmative, then the main question is to be put immediately, and no man may speak anything further to it, either to add or alter.—*Memor. in Hakew.* 28; 4 *Grey,* 27.

The previous question being moved and seconded, the question from the chair shall be, "Shall the main question be now put?" and if the nays prevail, the main question shall not then be put.—*Rule* 9.

This kind of question is understood by Mr. Hatsell to have been introduced in 1604.—2 *Hats.* 80. Sir Henry Vane introduced it.—2 *Grey,* 113, 114; 3 *Grey,* 384. When the question was put in this form, "Shall the main question be put?" a determination in the negative suppressed the main question during the session; but since the words "now put" are used, they exclude it for the present only. Formerly, indeed, only till the present debate was over; 4 *Grey,* 43; but now for that day and no longer.—2 *Grey,* 113, 114.

Before the question, "Whether the main question shall now be put?" any person might formerly have spoken to the main question, because otherwise he would be precluded from speaking to it at all.—*Mem. in Hakew.* 28.

The proper occasion for the previous question is, when a subject is brought forward of a delicate nature as to high personages, &c., or the discussion of which may call forth observations which might be of injurious consequences. Then the previous question is proposed, and, in the modern usage, the discussion of the main question is suspended, and the debate confined to the previous question. The use of it has been extended abusively to other cases; but in these, it is an embarrassing procedure: its uses would be as well answered by other more simple Parliamentary forms, and therefore it should not be favored, but restricted within as narrow limits as possible.

Whether a main question may be amended after the previous question on it has been moved and seconded? 2 *Hatsell,* 88, says, If the previous question had been moved and seconded, and also proposed from the chair, (by which he means, stated by the Speaker for debate,) it has been doubted whether an amendment can be admitted to the main question. He thinks it may, after the previous question moved and seconded; but not after it has been proposed from the chair.

In this case he thinks the friends to the amendment must vote that the main question be not now put, and then move their amended question, which being made new by the amendment, is no longer the same which has been just suppressed, and therefore may be proposed as a new one. But this proceeding certainly endangers the main question, by dividing its friends, some of whom may choose it unamended, rather than lose it altogether; while others of them may vote, as Hatsell advises, that the main question be not now put, with a view to move it again in an amended form. The enemies of the main question by this manœuvre to the previous question, get the enemies to the amendment added to them on the first vote, and throw the friends of the main question under the embarrassment of rallying again as they can. To support his opinion, too, he makes the deciding circumstance, whether an amendment may or may not be made, to be, that the previous question has been proposed from the chair. But as the rule is, that the House is in possession of a question as soon as it is moved and seconded, it cannot be more than possessed of it by its being also proposed from the chair. It may be said, indeed, that the object of the previous question being to get rid of a question, which it is not expedient should be discussed, this object may be defeated by moving to amend, and, in the discussion of that motion, involving the subject of the main question. But so may the object of the previous question be defeated by moving the amended question, as Mr. Hatsell proposes, after the decision against putting the original question. He acknowledges, too, that the practice has been to admit previous amendment, and only cites a few late instances to the contrary. On the whole, I should think it best to decide it *ab inconvenienti;* to wit, Which is most inconvenient, to put it in the power of one side of the House to defeat a proposition by hastily moving the previous question, and thus forcing the main question to be put amended? or to put it in the power of the other side to force on, incidentally at least, a discussion which would be better avoided? Perhaps the last is the least inconvenience; inasmuch as the Speaker, by confining the discussion rigorously to the amendment only, may prevent their going into the main question; and inasmuch also, as so great a proportion of the cases, in which the previous question is called for, are fair and proper subjects of public discussion, and ought not to be obstructed by a formality introduced for questions of a peculiar character.

## SECTION XXXV

### AMENDMENTS

On an amendment being moved, a member who has spoken to the main question may speak again to the amendment.—*Scob.* 23.

If an amendment be proposed inconsistent with one already agreed to, it is a fit ground for its rejection by the House; but not within the competence of the Speaker to suppress, as if it were against order. For, were he permitted to draw questions of consistence within the vortex of order, he might usurp a negative on important modifications, and suppress instead of subserving the legislative will.

Amendments may be made so as totally to alter the nature of the proposition; and it is a way of getting rid of a proposition, by making it bear a sense different from what was intended by the movers, so that they vote against it themselves.—2 *Hats.* 79; 4, 82, 84. A new bill may be ingrafted, by way of amendment, on the words, "Be it enacted," &c.—1 *Grey,* 190, 192.

If it be proposed to amend by leaving out certain words, it may be moved as an amendment to this amendment, to leave out a part of the words of the amendment, which is equivalent to leaving them in the bill.—2 *Hats.* 80, 9. The Parliamentary question is always, Whether the words shall stand part of the bill?

When it is proposed to amend by inserting a paragraph, or part of one, the friends of the paragraph may make it as perfect as they can, by amendments, before the question is put for inserting it. If it be received, it cannot be amended afterwards, in the same stage, because the House has, on a vote, agreed to it in that form. In like manner, if it is proposed to amend by striking out a paragraph, the friends of the paragraph are first to make it as perfect as they can by amendments, before the question is put for striking it out. If, on the question, it be retained, it cannot be amended afterwards; because a vote against striking out is equivalent to a vote agreeing to it in that form.

When it is moved to amend, by striking out certain words and inserting others, the manner of stating the question is, first to read the whole passage to be amended, as it stands at present; then the words proposed to be struck out; next those to be inserted; and lastly, the whole passage, as it will be when amended. And the question, if desired, is then to be divided, and put first on striking out. If carried, it is next on inserting the words proposed. If that be lost, it may be moved to insert others.—2 *Hats.* 80, 7.

A motion is made to amend by striking out certain words, and inserting others in their place, which is negatived. Then it is moved to strike out the same words, and to insert others of a tenor entirely different from those first proposed. It is negatived. Then it is moved to strike out the same words and insert nothing, which is agreed to. All this is admissible; because to strike out and insert A, is one proposition. To strike out and insert B, is a different proposition. And to strike out and insert nothing is still different. And the rejection of one proposition does not preclude the offering a different one. Nor would it change the case were the first motion divided by putting the question first on striking out, and that negatived. For as putting the whole motion to the question at once would not have precluded, the putting the half of it cannot do it.[5]

[5] In a case of division of the question, and a decision against striking out, I advance, doubtingly, the opinion here expressed. I find no authority either way; and I know it may be viewed under a different aspect. It may be thought, that having decided separately not to strike out the passage, the same question for striking out cannot be put over again, though with a view to a different insertion. Still I think it more reasonable and convenient to consider the striking out and insertion as forming one proposition; but should readily yield to any evidence that the contrary is the practice in Parliament.—T. J.

But if it had been carried affirmatively to strike out the words and to insert A, it could not afterwards be permitted to strike out A and insert B. The mover of B should have notified, while the insertion of A was under debate, that he would move to insert B. In which case, those who preferred it would join in rejecting A.

After A is inserted, however, it may be moved to strike out a portion of the original paragraph, comprehending A, provided the coherence to be struck out be so substantial as to make this effectively a different proposition. For then it is resolved into the common case of striking out a paragraph after amending it. Nor does anything forbid a new insertion, instead of A and its coherence.

In Senate, January 25, 1798, a motion to postpone, until the second Tuesday in February, some amendments proposed to the Constitution. The words, "until the second Tuesday in February," were struck out by way of amendment. Then it was moved to add, "until the first day of June." Objected, that it was not in order, as the question should first be put on the longest time; therefore, a shorter time decided against, a longer cannot be put to question. It was answered, that this rule takes place only in filling blanks for time. But when a specific time stands part of a motion, that may be struck out as well as any other part of the motion; and when struck out, a motion may be received to insert any other. In fact, it is not till they are struck out, and a blank for the time thereby produced, that the rule can begin to operate, by receiving all the propositions for different times, and putting the questions successively on the longest. Otherwise, it would be in the power of the mover, by inserting originally a short time, to preclude the possibility of a longer. For, till the short time is struck out, you cannot insert a longer; and if, after it is struck out, you cannot do it, then it cannot be done at all. Suppose the first motion has been to amend by striking out "the second Tuesday in February," and inserting, instead thereof, "the first of June." It would have been regular then to divide the question, by proposing first the question to strike out and then that to insert. Now, this is precisely the effect of the present proceeding; only, instead of one motion and two questions, there are two motions and two questions to effect it; the motion being divided as well as the question.

When the matter contained in two bills might be better put into one, the manner is to reject the one, and incorporate its matter into another bill by way of amendment. So, if the matter of one bill would be better distributed into two, any part may be struck out by way of amendment, and put into a new bill. If a section is to be transposed, a question must be put on striking it out where it stands, and another for inserting it in the place desired.

A bill passed by the one House, with blanks. These may be filled up by the other, by way of amendments, returned to the first, as such, and passed.—3 *Hats.* 83.

The number prefixed to the section of a bill being merely a marginal indication, and no part of the text of the bill, the clerk regulates that; the House or committee is only to amend the text.

# SECTION XXXVI

## DIVISION OF THE QUESTION

If a question contain more parts than one, it may be divided into two or more questions.—*Mem. in Hakew.* 29. But not as the right of an individual member, but with the consent of the House. For who is to decide whether a question is complicated or not? where it is complicated? into how many propositions it may be divided? The fact is, that the only mode of separating a complicated question is by moving amendments to it; and these must be decided by the House on a question, unless the House orders it to be divided: as on the question, Dec. 2, 1640, making void the election of the Knights of Worcester, on a motion it was resolved to make two questions of it, to wit, one on each Knight.—2 *Hats.* 85, 86. So, wherever there are several names in a question, they may be divided, and put one by one.—9 *Grey,* 444. So, 1729, April 17, on an objection that a question was complicated, it was separated by amendment.—2 *Hats.* 79. 5.

The soundness of these observations will be evident from the embarrassments produced by the 10th rule of the Senate, which says, "If the question in debate contain several points, any member may have the same divided."

1798, May 30, the alien bill in quasi-committee. To a section and proviso in the original, had been added two new provisos by way of amendment. On a motion to strike out the section as amended, the question was desired to be divided. To do this, it must be put first on striking out either the former proviso, or some distinct member of the section. But when nothing remains but the last member of the section, and the provisos, they cannot be divided so as to put the last member to question by itself; for the provisos might thus be left standing alone as exceptions to a rule when the rule is taken away: or the new provisos might be left to a second question, after having been decided on once before at the same reading; which is contrary to rule. But the question must be on striking out the last member of the section as amended. This sweeps away the exceptions with the rule, and relieves from inconsistence. A question to be divisible, must comprehend points so distinct and entire, that one of them being taken away, the other may stand entire. But a proviso or exception, with an enacting clause, does not contain an entire point or proposition.

May 31. The same bill being before the Senate. There was a proviso, that the bill should not extend, 1. To any foreign minister; nor, 2. To any person to whom the President should give a passport; nor, 3. To any alien merchant, conforming himself to such regulations as the President shall prescribe; and division of the question into its simplest elements was called for. It was divided into four parts, the 4th taking in the words "conforming himself," &c. It was objected, that the words "any alien merchant" could not be separated from their modifying words "conforming," &c., because these words, if left by themselves, contain no substantive idea, will make no sense. But admitting that the divisions of a paragraph into separate questions must be so made as that each part may stand by itself, yet the House having, on the question, retained the first two divisions, the words "any alien merchant" may be struck out, and their modifying words will then attach themselves to the preceding description of persons, and become a modification of that description.

When a question is divided, after the question on the 1st member, the 2d is open to debate and amendment: because it is a known rule, that a person may rise and speak at any time before the question has been completely decided by putting the negative, as well as the affirmative side. But the question is not completely put when the vote has been taken on the first member only. One half of the question, both affirmative and negative, still remains to be put.—See *Executive Journ.*, June 25, 1795. The same decision by President Adams.

## SECTION XXXVII

### CO-EXISTING QUESTIONS

It may be asked whether the House can be in possession of two motions or propositions at the same time? So that, one of them being decided, the other goes to question without being moved anew? The answer must be special. When a question is interrupted by a vote of adjournment, it is thereby removed from before the House; and does not stand *ipso facto* before them at their next meeting, but must come forward in the usual way: so, when it is interrupted by the order of the day. Such other privileged questions also as dispose of the main question (*e.g.*, the previous question, the postponement, or commitment) remove it from before the House. But it is only suspended by a motion to amend, to withdraw, to read papers, or by a question of order or privilege, and stands again before the House when these are decided. None but the class of privileged questions can be brought forward while there is another question before the House; the rule being, that when a motion has been made and seconded no other can be received except it be a privileged one.

## SECTION XXXVIII

### EQUIVALENT QUESTIONS

If, on a question for rejection, a bill be retained, it passes of course to its next reading.—*Hakew.* 141. *Scob.* 42, and a question for a second reading determined negatively, is a rejection without farther question.—4 *Grey,* 149. And see *Elsynge's Memor.* 42, in what case questions are to be taken for rejection.

Where questions are perfectly equivalent, so that the negative of the one amounts to the affirmative of the other, and leaves no other alternative, the decision of the one concludes necessarily the other.—4 *Grey,* 157. Thus the negative of striking out amounts to the affirmative of agreeing; and therefore to put a question on agreeing after that on striking out, would be to put the same question in effect twice over. Not so in questions of amendments between the two Houses. A motion to recede being negatived, does not amount to a positive vote to insist, because there is another alternative, to wit, to adhere.

A bill originating in one House, is passed by the other with an amendment. A motion in the originating House, to agree to the amendment, is negatived. Do these result from this vote of disagreement? or must the question on disagreement be expressly voted? The questions respecting amendments from another House are, 1st. To agree: 2d. Disagree: 3d. Recede: 4th. Insist: 5th. Adhere.

| | |
|---|---|
| 1st. To agree.<br>2d. To disagree. | Either of these concludes the other necessarily, for the positive of either is exactly the equivalent of the negative of the other, and no other alternative remains. On either motion, amendments to the amendment may be proposed; *e.g.*, if it be moved to disagree, those who are for the amendment have a right to propose amendments, and to make it as perfect as they can, before the question of disagreeing is put. |
| 3d. To recede.<br>4th. To insist.<br>5th. To adhere. | You may then either insist or adhere. You may then either recede or adhere. You may then either recede or insist. Consequently, the negative of these is not equivalent to a positive vote the other way. It does not raise so necessary an implication as may authorize the secretary by inference to enter another vote; for two alternatives still remain, either of which may be adopted by the House. |

## SECTION XXXIX

### THE QUESTION

The question is to be put first on the affirmative, and then on the negative side.

After the Speaker has put the affirmative part of the question, any member who has not spoken before the question, may rise and speak before the negative be put. Because it is no full question till the negative part be put.—*Scob.* 23; *Hats.* 73.

But in small matters, and which are of course, such as receiving petitions, reports, withdrawing motions, reading papers, &c., the Speaker most commonly supposes the consent of the House, where no objection is expressed, and does not give them the trouble of putting the question formally.—*Scob.* 22; 2 *Hats.* 87. 2. 87; 5 *Grey,* 129; 9 *Grey,* 301.

## SECTION XL

### BILL, THIRD READING

To prevent bills from being passed by surprise, the House, by a standing order, directs that they shall not be put on their passage before a fixed hour, naming one at which the House is commonly full.—*Hakew.* 153.

The usage of the Senate is, not to put bills on their passage till noon.

A bill reported and passed to the third reading, cannot on that day be read the third time and passed. Because this would be to pass on two readings on the same day. At the third reading, the clerk reads the bill, and delivers it to the Speaker, who states the title, that it is the third time of reading the bill, and that the question will be, Whether it shall pass? Formerly, the Speaker, or those who prepared a bill, prepared also a breviate or summary statement of its contents, which the Speaker read when he declared the state of the bill at the several readings. Sometimes, however, he read the bill itself, especially on its passage.—*Hakew.* 136, 137, 153; *Coke,* 22, 115. Latterly, instead of this, he, at the third reading, states the whole contents of the bill, verbatim; only instead of reading the formal parts, "be it enacted," &c., he states that "the preamble recites so and so; the first section enacts, that, &c.; the second section enacts," &c.

But in the Senate of the United States, both of these formalities are dispensed with; the breviate presenting but an imperfect view of the bill, and being capable of being made to present a false one; and the full statement being a useless waste of time, immediately after a full reading by the clerk; and especially as every member has a printed copy in his hand.

A bill, on the third reading, is not to be committed for the matter or body thereof; but, to receive some particular clause or proviso, it hath been sometimes suffered, but as a thing very unusual.—*Hakew.* 156; thus, 27 *El.* 1584, a bill was committed on the third reading, having been formerly committed on the second; but it is declared not usual.—*D'Ewes,* 137, *col.* 2. 414. *col.* 2.

When an essential provision has been omitted, rather than erase the bill, and render it suspicious, they add a clause on a separate paper, engrossed and called a rider, which is read, and put to the question three times.—*Elsynge's Memorials,* 59; 6 *Grey,* 335; 1 *Blackst.* 183. For examples of riders, see 3 *Hats.* 121, 122, 124, 126. Everyone is at liberty to bring in a rider without asking leave.—10 *Grey,* 52.

It is laid down as a general rule, that amendments proposed at the second reading shall be twice read, and those proposed at the third reading thrice read; as also all amendments from the other House.—*Town. col.* 19, 23, 24, 25, 26, 27, 28.

It is with great, and almost invincible reluctance, that amendments are admitted at this reading, which occasion erasures or interlineations. Sometimes the proviso has been cut off from a bill; sometimes erased.—9 *Grey,* 513.

This is the proper stage for filling up blanks; for if filled up before, and now altered by erasure, it would be peculiarly unsafe.

At this reading, the bill is debated afresh, and for the most part is more spoken to, at this time, than on any of the former readings.—*Hakew.* 153.

The debate on the question, Whether it should be read a third time? has discovered to its friends and opponents the arguments on which each side relies, and which of these appear to have influence with the House; they have had time to meet them with new arguments, and to put their old ones into new shapes. The former vote has tried the strength of the first opinion, and furnished grounds to estimate the issue; and the question now offered for its passage, is the last occasion which is ever to be offered for carrying or rejecting it.

When the debate is ended, the Speaker, holding the bill in his hand, puts the question for its passage, by saying, "Gentlemen, all you who are of opinion that this bill shall pass, say ay"; and after the answer of ayes, "All those of the contrary opinion, say no."—*Hakew.* 154.

After the bill has passed, there can be no further alteration of it in any point.—*Hakew.* 159.

## SECTION XLI

### DIVISION OF THE HOUSE

The affirmative and negative of the question having been both put and answered, the Speaker declares whether the yeas or nays have it by the sound, if he be himself satisfied, and it stands as the judgment of the House. But if he be not himself satisfied which voice is the greater, or if, before any other member comes into the House, or before any new motion is made, (for it is too late after that,) any member shall rise and declare himself dissatisfied with the Speaker's decision, then the Speaker is to divide the House.—*Scob.* 24; 2 *Hats.* 140.

When the House of Commons is divided, the one party goes forth, and the other remains in the House. This has made it important which go forth, and which remain; because the latter gain all the indolent, the indifferent, and inattentive. Their general rule, therefore, is, that those who give their vote for the preservation of the orders of the House shall stay in, and those who are for introducing any new matter, or alteration, or proceeding contrary to the established course, are to go out. But this rule is subject to many exceptions and modifications.—2 *Rush.* p. 3, fol. 92; *Scob.* 43, 52; *Co.* 12, 116; *D'Ewes,* 505, *col.* 1; *Mem. in Hakew.* 25, 29; as will appear by the following statement of who go forth.

| | |
|---|---|
| Petition that it be received [6] / Read | Ayes. |
| Lie on the table / Rejected after refusal to lie on the table | Noes. |
| Referred to a committee, or farther proceeding | Ayes. |
| Bill, that it be brought in / Read 1st or 2d time / Engrossed or read 3d time / Proceeding on every other stage / Committed | Ayes. |
| To a committee of the whole | Noes. |
| To a select committee | Ayes. |
| Report of a bill to lie on table | Noes. |

[6] Noes.—9 Grey, 365.—T. J.

| | | |
|---|---|---|
| Be *now* read<br>Be taken into consideration three months hence | Ayes. | 50 P. J.<br>251. |
| Amendments be read a 2d time | Noes. | |
| Clause offered on report of bill be read 2d time<br>For receiving a clause<br>With amendments be engrossed | Ayes. | 334 |
| That a bill be now read a 3d time | Noes. | 398 |
| Receive a rider<br>Pass<br>Be printed | Ayes. | 260<br>259 |
| Committees. That A take the chair<br>To agree to the whole or any part of report<br>That the House do *now* resolve into a committee<br>Speaker. That he now leave the chair, after order to go into committee<br>That he issue warrant for a new visit<br>Member. That none be absent without leave | Noes. | 291 |
| Witness. That he be further examined | Ayes. | 344 |
| Previous questions | Noes. | |
| Blanks. That they be filled with the largest sum<br>Amendments. That words stand part of | Ayes. | |
| Lords. That their amendments be read a 2d time | Ayes. | |
| Messenger be received<br>Orders of the day to be now read, if before 2 o'clock | Ayes. | |
| If after 2 o'clock | Noes. | |
| Adjournment till the next sitting day if before 4 o'clock | Ayes. | |
| If after 4 o'clock | Noes. | |
| Over a sitting day, (unless a previous resolution) | Ayes. | |
| Over the 30th January | Noes. | |
| For sitting on Sunday, or any other day not being a sitting day | Ayes. | |

The one party being gone forth, the Speaker names two tellers from the affirmative, and two from the negative side, who first count those sitting in the House, and report the number to the Speaker. Then they place themselves within the door, two on each side, and count those who went forth, as they come in, and report the number to the speaker.—*Mem. in Hakew.* 26.

A mistake in the report of the tellers may be rectified after the report made.—2 *Hats.* 145. Note.

But, in both Houses of Congress, all those intricacies are avoided. The ayes first rise, and are counted, standing in their places, by the President or Speaker. Then they sit, and the noes rise, and are counted in like manner.

In Senate, if they be equally divided, the Vice-President announces his opinion, which decides.

The Constitution, however, has directed that "the yeas and nays of the members of either House, on any question, shall, at the desire of one-fifth of those present, be entered on the journal." And again, that in all cases of re-considering a bill disapproved by the President, and returned with his objections, "the votes of both Houses shall be determined by the yeas and nays, and the names of the persons voting for and against the bill, shall be entered on the journals of each House respectively."

By the 11th rule of the Senate, when the yeas and nays shall be called for by one-fifth of the members present, each member called upon shall, unless for special reasons he be excused by the Senate, declare openly, and without debate, his assent or dissent to the question. In taking the yeas and nays, and upon the call of the House, the names of the members shall be taken alphabetically.

When it is proposed to take a vote by yeas and nays, the President or Speaker states that "The question is whether, *e.g.*, the bill shall pass? That it is proposed that the yeas and nays shall be entered on the journal. Those, therefore, who desire it will rise." If he finds and declares that one-fifth have risen, he then states, that "those who are of opinion that the bill shall pass, are to answer in the affirmative, those of the contrary opinion, in the negative." The clerk then calls over the names alphabetically, notes the yea or nay of each, and gives the list to the President or Speaker, who declares the result. In Senate, if there be an equal division, the Secretary calls on the Vice-President, who notes his affirmative or negative, which becomes the decision of the House.

In the House of Commons, every member must give his vote the one way or the other.—*Scob.* 24. As it is not permitted to anyone to withdraw who is in the House when the question is put, nor is anyone to be told in the division who was not in when the question was put.—2 *Hats.* 140.

This last position is always true when the vote is by yeas and nays; where the negative as well as the affirmative of the question is stated by the President at the same time, and the vote of both sides begins and proceeds *pari passu.* It is true, also, when the question is put in the usual way, if the negative has also been put. But if it has not, the member entering, or any other member may speak, and even propose amendments, by which the debate may be opened again, and the question greatly deferred. And, as some who have answered ay, may have been changed by the new arguments, the affirmative must be put over again. If, then, the member entering may, by speaking a few words, occasion a repetition of the question, it would be useless to deny it on his simple call for it.

While the House is telling, no member may speak, or move out of his place; for, if any mistake be suspected, it must be told again.—*Mem. in Hakew.* 26; 2 *Hats.* 143.

If any difficulty arises in point of order, during the division, the Speaker is to decide peremptorily, subject to the future censure of the House, if irregular. He sometimes permits old experienced members to assist him with their advice, which they do sitting in their seats, covered to avoid the appearance of debate; but this can only be with the Speaker's leave, else the division might last several hours.—2 *Hats.* 143.

The voice of the majority decides. For the *lex majoris partis* is the law of all councils, elections, &c., where not otherwise expressly provided.—*Hakew.* 93. But if the House be equally divided, *"semper presumatur pro negante":* that is, the former law is not to be changed but by a majority.—*Towns. col.* 134.

But, in the Senate of the United States, the Vice-President decides, when the House is divided.—*Const. U. S.,* Art. I. Sec. 2.

When, from counting the House, on a division, it appears that there is not a quorum, the matter continues exactly in the state in which it was before the division, and must be resumed at that point on any future day.—2 *Hats.* 126.

1606, May 1, on a question whether a member having said Yea, may afterwards sit and change his opinion? a precedent was remembered by the Speaker, of Mr. Morris, attorney of the wards, in 39 *Eliz.,* who in like case changed his opinion.—*Mem. in Hakew.* 27.

## SECTION XLII

### TITLE

After the bill has passed, and not before, the title may be amended, and is to be fixed by a question; and the bill is then sent to the other House.

## SECTION XLIII

### RE-CONSIDERATION

When a question has been once made and carried in the affirmative or negative, it shall be in order for any member of the majority to move for the re-consideration thereof.—*Rule* 22.

1798, Jan. A bill on its second reading, being amended, and on the question, whether it shall be read a third time negatived, was restored by a decision to re-consider the question. Here the votes of negative and re-consideration, like positive and negative quantities in equation, destroy one another, and are as if they were expunged from the journals. Consequently the bill is open for amendment, just so far as it was the moment preceding the question for the third reading. That is to say, all parts of the bill are open for amendment, except those on which votes have been already taken in its present stage. So also may it be re-committed.

The rule permitting a re-consideration of a question affixing to it no limitation of time or circumstance, it may be asked whether there is no limitation? If, after the vote, the paper on which it has passed has been parted with, there can be no re-consideration: as if a vote has been for the passage of a bill, and the bill has been sent to the other House. But where the paper remains, as on a bill rejected, when, or under what circumstances, does it cease to be susceptible of re-consideration? This remains to be settled, unless a sense that the right of re-consideration is a right to waste the time of the House in repeated agitations of the same question, so that it shall never know when a question is done with should induce them to reform this anomalous proceeding.

In Parliament, a question once carried, cannot be questioned again, at the same session; but must stand as the judgment of the House.—*Towns. col.* 67; *Memor. in Hakew.* 33. And a bill once rejected, another of the same substance cannot be brought in again the same session.—*Hakew.* 158; 6 *Grey,* 392. But this does not extend to prevent putting the same questions in different stages of a bill; because every stage of a bill submits the whole and every part of it to the opinion of the House, as open for amendment, either by insertion or omission, though the same amendment has been accepted or rejected in a former stage. So in reports of committees, *e.g.,* report of an address, the same question is before the House, and open for free discussion.—*Towns. col.* 26; 2 *Hats.* 98, 100, 101. So, orders of the House, or instructions to committees may be discharged. So a bill begun in one House, sent to the other, and there rejected, may be renewed again in that other, passed, and sent back.—*Ib.* 92; 3 *Hats.* 161. Or if, instead of being rejected, they read it once, and lay it aside, and put it off a month, they may offer in another to the same effect, with the same or a different title.—*Hakew.* 97, 98.

Divers expedients are used to correct the effects of this rule; as, by passing an explanatory act, if anything has been omitted or ill-expressed, 3 *Hats.* 278; or an act to enforce, and make more effectual an act, &c., or to rectify mistakes in an act, &c.; or a committee on one bill may be instructed to receive a clause to rectify the mistakes of another. Thus, June 24, 1685, a clause was inserted in a bill for rectifying a mistake committed by a clerk in engrossing a bill of reply.—2 *Hats.* 194. 6. Or the session may be closed for one, two, three, or more days, and a new one commenced. But then all matters depending must be finished, or they fall, and are to begin *de novo.*—2 *Hats.* 94, 98. Or a part of the subject may be taken up by another bill, or taken up in a different way.—6 *Grey,* 316.

And in cases of the last magnitude, this rule has not been so strictly and verbally observed as to stop indispensable proceedings altogether.—2 *Hats.* 92, 98. Thus, when the address on the preliminaries of peace, in 1782, had been lost by a majority of one; on account of the importance of the question, and smallness of the majority, the same question in substance, though with words not in the first, and which might change the opinions of some members, was brought on again and carried: as the motives for it were thought to outweigh the objections of form.—2 *Hats.* 99, 100.

A second bill may be passed, to continue an act of the same session; or to enlarge the time limited for its execution.—2 *Hats.* 95, 98. This is not in contradiction to the first act.

## SECTION XLIV

### BILLS SENT TO THE OTHER HOUSE

All bills passed in the Senate, shall before they are sent to the House of Representatives, be examined by the committees respectively who brought in such bills, or to whom the same have been last committed in Senate.—*Rule* 23.

A bill from the other House is sometimes ordered to lie on the table.—2 *Hats.* 97.

When bills, passed in one House and sent to the other, are grounded on special facts requiring proof, it is usual, either by message, or at a conference, to ask the grounds and evidence; and this evidence, whether arising out of papers, or from the examination of witnesses, is immediately communicated.—3 *Hats.* 48.

## SECTION XLV

### AMENDMENTS BETWEEN THE HOUSES

When either House, *e.g.*, the House of Commons, sends a bill to the other, the other may pass it with amendments. The regular progression in this case is, that the Commons disagree to the amendment; the Lords insist on it; the Commons insist on their disagreement; the Lords adhere to their amendment; the Commons adhere to their disagreement. The term of insisting may be repeated as often as they choose, to keep the question open. But the first adherence by either renders it necessary for the other side to recede or adhere also; when the matter is usually suffered to fall.—10 *Grey,* 148. Latterly, however, there are instances of their having gone to a second adherence. There must be an absolute conclusion of the subject somewhere, or otherwise transactions between the Houses would be endless.—3 *Hats.* 268, 270. The term of insisting, we are told by Sir John Trevor, was then [1679] newly introduced into Parliamentary usage, by the Lords.—7 *Grey,* 94. It was certainly a happy innovation, as it multiplies the opportunities of trying modifications which may bring the House to a concurrence. Either House, however, is free to pass over the term of insisting, and to adhere in the first instance.—10 *Grey,* 146. But it is not respectful to the other. In the ordinary Parliamentary course, there are two free conferences at least before adherence.—10 *Grey,* 147.

Either House may recede from its amendment, and agree to the bill; or recede from their disagreement to the amendment, and agree to the same absolutely, or with an amendment. For here the disagreement and receding destroy one another, and the subject stands as before the disagreement.—*Elsynge,* 23, 27; 9 *Grey,* 476.

But the House cannot recede from or insist on, its own amendment with an amendment, for the same reason that it cannot send to the other House an amendment to its own act after it has passed the act. They may modify an amendment from the other House by ingrafting an amendment on it, because they have never assented to it; but they cannot amend their own amendment, because they have, on the question, passed it in that form; 9 *Grey,* 353; 10 *Grey,* 240. In Senate, March 29, 1798. Nor where one House has adhered to their amendment, and the other agrees with an amendment, can the first House depart from the form which they have fixed by an adherence.

In the case of a money bill, the Lords' proposed amendments became, by delay, confessedly necessary. The Commons, however, refused them, as infringing on their privilege as to money bills, but they offered themselves to add to the bill a proviso to the same effect, which had no coherence with the Lords' amendments, and urged, that it was an expedient warranted by precedent, and not unparliamentary in a case become impracticable, and irremediable in any other way.—3 *Hats.* 256, 266, 270, 271. But the Lords refused and the bill was lost, 1 *Chand.* 288. A like case, 1 *Chand.* 311. So the Commons resolve, that it is unparliamentary to strike out at a conference anything in a bill which hath been agreed and passed by both Houses, 6 *Grey,* 274; 1 *Chand.* 312.

A motion to amend an amendment from the other House, takes precedence of a motion to agree or disagree.

A bill originating in one House, is passed by the other with an amendment. The originating House agrees to their amendment with an amendment. The other may agree to their amendment with an amendment; that being only in the second and not the third degree. For, as to the amending House, the first amendment with which they passed the bill is a part of its text; it is the only text they have agreed to. The amendment to that text by the originating House, therefore, is only in the 1st degree, and the amendment to that again by the amending House is only in the 2d, to wit, an amendment to an amendment, and so admissible. Just so when, on a bill from the originating House, the other, at its 2d reading, makes an amendment; on the 3d reading, this amendment is become the text of the bill, and if an amendment to it be moved, an amendment to that amendment may also be moved, as being only in the second degree.

## SECTION XLVI

### CONFERENCES

It is on the occasion of amendments between the Houses that conferences are usually asked; but they may be asked in all cases of difference of opinion between the two Houses on matters depending between them. The request of a conference, however, must always be by the House which is possessed of the papers.—3 *Hats.* 71; 1 *Grey,* 435; 4 *Hats.* 3, 43.

Conferences may be either simple or free. At a conference simply, written reasons are prepared by the House asking it, and they are read and delivered without debate, to the managers of the other House at the conference; but are not then to be answered.—3 *Grey,* 144. The other House then, if satisfied, vote the reasons satisfactory, or say nothing; if not satisfied, they resolve them not satisfactory, and ask a conference on the subject of the last conference, where they read and deliver in like manner written answers to those reasons.—3 *Grey,* 183. They are meant chiefly to record the justification of each House to the nation at large, and to posterity, and in proof that the miscarriage of a necessary measure is not imputable to them.—3 *Grey*, 255. At free conferences, the managers discuss *viva voce* and freely, and interchange propositions for such modifications as may be made in a Parliamentary way, and may bring the sense of the two houses together. And each party reports in writing to their respective Houses the substance of what is said on both sides, and it is entered in their journals.—6 *Grey*, 220; 3 *Hats*. 280. (*Vide Joint Rules*, 1.) This report cannot be amended or altered as that of a committee may be.—*Journ. Senate*, May 24, 1796.

A conference may be asked, before the House asking it has come to a resolution of disagreement, insisting or adhering.—3 *Hats*. 269, 341. In which case the papers are not left with the other conferees, but are brought back to be the foundation of the vote to be given. And this is the most reasonable and respectful proceeding. For, as was urged by the Lords on a particular occasion, "it is held vain, and below the wisdom of Parliament, to reason or argue against fixed resolutions, and upon terms of impossibility to persuade."—3 *Hats*. 226. So the Commons say "an adherence is never delivered at a free conference, which implies debate."—10 *Grey*, 147. And on another occasion, the Lords made it an objection that the Commons had asked a free conference after they had made resolutions of adhering. It was then affirmed, however, on the part of the Commons, that nothing was more Parliamentary than to proceed with free conferences after adhering; 3 *Hats*. 269; and we do in fact see instances of conference or of free conference, asked after the resolution of disagreeing.—3 *Hats*. 251, 253, 260, 286, 291, 316, 349, of insisting, *ib*. 280, 296, 299, 319, 322, 355, of adhering, 269, 270, 283, 300; and even of a second or final adherence.—3 *Hats*. 270. And in all cases of conference asked after a vote of disagreement, &c., the conferees of the House asking it are to leave the papers with the conferees of the other; and in one case where they refused to receive them, they were left on the table in the conference chamber.—3 *Hats*. 271, 317, 323, 354; 10 *Grey*, 146. The Commons affirm, that it is usual to have two free conferences or more before either House proceeds to adhere, because, before that time, the Houses have not had the full opportunity of making replies to one another's arguments, and, to adhere so suddenly and unexpectedly, excludes all possibility of offering expedients.—4 *Hats*. 330.

After a free conference the usage is to proceed with free conferences, and not to return again to a conference.—3 *Hats*. 270; 9 *Grey*, 229.

After a conference denied, a free conference may be asked.—1 *Grey*, 45.

When a conference is asked, the subject of it must be expressed, or the conference not agreed to.—*Ord. H. Com*. 89; 1 *Grey*, 425; 7 *Grey*, 31. They are sometimes asked to inquire concerning an offence or default of a member of the other House, 6 *Grey*, 181; 1 *Chand*. 304; or the failure of the other House to present to the King a bill passed by both Houses, 8 *Grey*, 302; or on information received, and relating to the safety of the nation, 10 *Grey*, 171, or when the methods of Parliament are thought by the one House to have been departed from by the other, a conference is asked to come to a right understanding thereon.—10 *Grey,* 148. So, when an unparliamentary message has been sent, instead of answering it, they ask a conference.—3 *Grey,* 155. Formerly, an address, or articles of impeachment, or a bill with amendments, or a vote of the House, or concurrence in a vote, or a message from the King, were sometimes communicated by way of conference.—7 *Grey,* 128, 300, 387; 7 *Grey,* 80; 8 *Grey,* 210, 255; 1 *Torbuck's Deb.* 278; 10 *Grey,* 293; 1 *Chandler,* 49, 287. But this is not modern practice.—8 *Grey,* 255.

A conference has been asked after the first reading of a bill.—1 *Grey,* 194. This is a singular instance. During the time of a conference, the House can do no business. As soon as the names of the managers are called over, and they are gone to the conference, the Speaker leaves the chair, without any question, and resumes it in the return of the managers. It is the same while the managers of an impeachment are at the House of Lords.—4 *Hats.* 47, 209, 288.

## SECTION XLVII

### MESSAGES

Messages between the Houses are to be sent only while both Houses are sitting.—3 *Hats.* 15. They are received during a debate, without adjourning the debate.—3 *Hats.* 22.

In Senate, the messengers are introduced in any state of business, except—1. While a question is putting. 2. While the yeas and nays are calling. 3. While the ballots are calling. The first case is short: the second and third are cases where any interruption might occasion errors difficult to be corrected.—So arranged, June 15th, 1798.

In the House of Representatives, as in Parliament, if the House be in a committee when a messenger attends, the Speaker takes the chair to receive the message, and then quits it to return into a committee, without any question or interruption.—4 *Grey,* 226.

Messengers are not saluted by the members, but by the Speaker, for the House.—2 *Grey,* 253, 274.

If messengers commit an error in delivering their messages, they may be admitted, or called in, to correct their message.—4 *Grey,* 41. Accordingly, March 13, 1800, the Senate having made two amendments to a bill from the House of Representatives, their secretary, by mistake, delivered one only; which being inadmissible by itself, that House disagreed, and notified the Senate of their disagreement. This produced a discovery of the mistake. The secretary was sent to the other House to correct his mistake, the correction was received, and the two amendments acted on *de novo.*

As soon as the messenger, who has brought bills from the other House, has retired, the Speaker holds the bills in his hand, and acquaints the House, "That the other House have, by their messenger, sent certain bills," and then reads their titles, and delivers them to the clerk to be safely kept till they shall be called for to be read.—*Hakew.* 178.

It is not the usage for one House to inform the other by what numbers a bill has passed.—10 *Grey,* 150. Yet they have sometimes recommended a bill as of great importance to the consideration of the House to which it is sent.—3 *Hats.* 25. Nor when they have rejected a bill from the other House, do they give notice of it; but it passes sub-silentio to prevent unbecoming altercation.—1 *Black.* 133.

But in Congress the rejection is notified by message to the House in which the bill originated.

A question is never asked by the one House of the other by way of message, but only at a conference; for this is an interrogatory, not a message.—3 *Grey,* 151, 181.

When a bill is sent by one House to the other, and is neglected, they may send a message to remind them of it.—3 *Hats.* 25; 5 *Grey,* 154. But if it be mere inattention, it is better to have it done informally, by communications between the Speakers, or members of the two Houses.

Where the subject of a message is of a nature that it can properly be communicated to both Houses of Parliament, it is expected that this communication should be made to both on the same day. But where a message was accompanied with an original declaration, signed by the party, to which the message referred, its being sent to one House was not noticed by the other, because the declaration, being original, could not possibly be sent to both Houses at the same time.—2 *Hats.* 260, 261, 262.

The King having sent original letters to the Commons, afterwards desires they may be returned, that he may communicate them to the Lords.—1 *Chandler,* 303.

## SECTION XLVIII

### ASSENT

The House which has received a bill, and passed it, may present it for the King's assent, and ought to do it, though they have not by message notified to the other their passage of it. Yet the notifying by message is a form which ought to be observed between the two Houses, from motives of respect and good understanding.—3 *Hats.* 242. Were the bill to be withheld from being presented to the King, it would be an infringement of the rules of Parliament.—2 *Hats.* 242.

When a bill has passed both Houses of Congress, the House last acting on it notifies its passage to the other, and delivers the bill to the joint committee of enrolment, who see that it is truly enrolled in parchment. When the bill is enrolled, it is not to be written in paragraphs, but solidly and all of a piece, that the blanks within the paragraphs may not give room for forgery.—9 *Grey,* 143. It is then put in the hands of the clerk of the House of Representatives, to have it signed by the Speaker. The clerk then brings it by way of message to the Senate, to be signed by their President. The secretary of the Senate returns it to the committee of enrolment, who present it to the President of the United States. If he approves, he signs and deposits it among the rolls in the office of the Secretary of State, and notifies by message the House in which it originated, that he has approved and signed it; of which that

House informs the other by message. If the President disapproves, he is to return it, with his objections, to the House in which it shall have originated; who are to enter the objections at large on their journal, and proceed to reconsider it. If, after such reconsideration, two-thirds of the House shall agree to pass the bill, it shall be sent, together with the President's objections, to the other House, by which it shall likewise be reconsidered, and if approved by two-thirds of that House, it shall become a law. If any bill shall not be returned by the President within ten days (Sundays excepted) after it shall have been presented to him, the same shall be a law, in like manner as if he had signed it, unless the Congress, by their adjournment, prevent its return; in which case it shall not be a law.—*Const. U. S.* Art. I. Sec. 7.

Every order, resolution, or vote, to which the concurrence of the Senate and the House of Representatives may be necessary, (except on a question of adjournment,) shall be presented to the President of the United States, and before the same shall take effect, shall be approved by him, or, being disapproved by him, shall be re-passed by two-thirds of the Senate and House of Representatives, according to the rules and limitations prescribed in the case of a bill.—*Const. U. S.,* Art. I. Sec. 7.

## SECTION XLIX

### JOURNALS

Each House shall keep a journal of its proceedings, and from time to time publish the same, excepting such parts as may, in their judgment, require secrecy.—*Const.,* I. 5, 3.

Every vote of Senate shall be entered on the journal, and a brief statement of the contents of each petition, memorial, or paper, presented to the Senate, be also inserted on the journal.—*Rule* 24.

The proceedings of the Senate, when not acting as in a committee of the House, shall be entered on the journals, as concisely as possible, care being taken to detail a true account of the proceedings.—*Rule* 26.

The titles of bills, and such part thereof only as shall be affected by proposed amendments, shall be inserted on the journals.—*Rule* 27.

If a question is interrupted by a vote to adjourn, or to proceed to the orders of the day, the original question is never printed in the journal, it never having been a vote, nor introductory to any vote; but when suppressed by the previous question, the first question must be stated, in order to introduce, and make intelligible, the second.—2 *Hats.* 83.

So also, when a question is postponed, adjourned, or laid on the table, the original question, though not yet a vote, must be expressed in the journals; because it makes part of the vote of postponement, adjourning, or laying on the table.

Where amendments are made to a question, those amendments are not printed in the journals, separated from the question; but only the question as finally agreed to by the House. The rule of entering in the journals only what the House has agreed to, is founded in great prudence and good sense; as there may be many questions proposed which it may be improper to publish to the world, in the form in which they are made.—2 *Hats.* 85.

In both Houses of Congress, all questions whereon the yeas and nays are desired by one-fifth of the members present, whether decided affirmatively or negatively, must be entered on the journals.—*Const.* I. 5, 3.

The first order for printing the votes of the House of Commons, was October 30, 1685.—1 *Chandler,* 387.

Some judges have been of opinion, that the journals of the House of Commons are no records, but remembrances. But this is no law.—*Cob.* 110, 111; *Lex. Parl.* 114, 115; *Jour. H. C.* Mar. 17, 1592; *Hale Parl.* 105. For the Lords, in their House, have power of judicature; the Commons, in their House, have power of judicature; and both Houses together have power of judicature; and the book of the clerk of the House of Commons is a record, as is affirmed by act of Parliament.—6 *H.* 8. *c.* 16; *Inst.* 23, 24; and every member of the House of Commons has a judicial place.—4 *Inst.* 15. As records, they are open to every person; and a printed vote of either House is sufficient ground for the other to notice it. Either may appoint a committee to inspect the journals of the other, and report what has been done by the other in any particular case.—2 *Hats.* 261; 3 *Hats.* 27, 30. Every member has a right to see the journals, and to take and publish votes from them. Being a record, everyone may see and publish them.—6 *Grey,* 118, 119.

On information of a mis-entry or omission of an entry in the journal, a committee may be appointed to examine and rectify it, and report it to the House.—2 *Hats.* 194, 5.

## SECTION L

### ADJOURNMENT

The two Houses of Parliament have the sole, separate, and independent power of adjourning, each their respective Houses. The King has no authority to adjourn them; he can only signify his desire, and it is in the wisdom and prudence of either House to comply with his requisition, or not, as they see fitting. —2 *Hats.* 332; 1 *Blackstone,* 186; 5 *Grey,* 122.

By the Constitution of the United States, a smaller number than a majority may adjourn from day to day.—I. 5. But neither House, during the session of Congress, shall, without the consent of the other, adjourn for more than three days, nor to any other place than that in which the two Houses shall be sitting.—I. 5. The President may, on extraordinary occasions, convene both Houses, or either of them, and in case of disagreement between them, with respect to the time of adjournment, he may adjourn them to such time as he shall think proper.—*Const.* II. 3.

A motion to adjourn simply, cannot be amended as by adding, "To a particular day." But must be put simply, "That this House do now adjourn?" and if carried in the affirmative, it is adjourned to the next sitting day, unless it has come to a previous resolution, "That at its rising, it will adjourn to a particular day"; and then the House is adjourned to that day.—2 *Hats.* 82.

Where it is convenient that the business of the House be suspended for a short time, as for a conference presently to be held, &c., it adjourns during pleasure.—2 *Hats.* 305. Or for a quarter of an hour.—5 *Grey,* 331.

If a question be put for adjournment, it is no adjournment till the Speaker pronounces it.—5 *Grey,* 137. And from courtesy and respect, no member leaves his place till the Speaker has passed on.

## SECTION LI

### A SESSION

Parliament have three modes of separation, to wit, by adjournment, by prorogation, by dissolution by the King, or by the efflux of the term for which they were elected. Prorogation or dissolution constitutes there what is called a session; provided some act has passed. In this case, all matters depending before them are discontinued, and at their next meeting are to be taken up *de novo,* if taken up at all.—1 *Blackstone,* 186. Adjournment, which is by themselves, is no more than a continuance of the session from one day to another, or for a fortnight, a month, &c., *ad libitum.* All matters depending remain in *statu quo,* and when they meet again, be the term ever so distant, are resumed without any fresh commencement, at the point at which they were left.—1 *Lev.* 165; *Lex. Parl. c.* 2; 1 *Ro. Rep.* 29; 4 *Inst.* 7, 27, 28; *Hut.* 61; 1 *Mod.* 152; *Ruffh. Jac. L. Dict. Parliaments; Blackstone,* 186. Their whole session is considered in law but as one day, and has relation to the first day thereof.—*Bro. Abro. Parliament,* 86.

Committees may be appointed to sit during a recess by adjournment, but not by prorogation.—5 *Grey,* 374; 9 *Grey,* 350; 1 *Chandler,* 50. Neither House can continue any portion of itself in any Parliamentary function, beyond the end of the session, without the consent of the other two branches. When done, it is by a bill constituting them commissioners for the particular purpose.

Congress separate in two ways only, to wit, by adjournment or dissolution by the efflux of their time. What then constitutes a session with them? A dissolution certainly closes one session, and the meeting of the new Congress begins another. The Constitution authorizes the President, "On extraordinary occasions, to convene both Houses, or either of them."—Art. I. Sec. 3. If convened by the President's proclamation, this must begin a new session, and of course determine the preceding one to have been a session. So, if it meets under the clause of the Constitution, which says, "The Congress shall assemble, at least once in every year, and such meeting shall be on the first Monday in December, unless they shall by law appoint a different day,"—I. 4,—this must begin a new session. For even if the last adjournment was to this day, the act of adjournment is merged in the higher authority of the Constitution, and the meeting will be under that and not under their adjournment. So far we have fixed landmarks for determining sessions. In other cases, it is declared by the joint vote authorizing the President of the Senate and the Speaker to close the session on a fixed day, which is usually in the following form, "Resolved, by the Senate and House of Representatives, that the President of the Senate and the Speaker of the House of Representatives, be authorized to close the present session, by adjourning their respective Houses on the —— day of ——."

When it was said above, that all matters depending before Parliament were discontinued by the determination of the session, it was not meant for judiciary cases, depending before the House of Lords, such as impeachments, appeals, and writs of error. These stand continued of course to the next session.—*Raym.* 120, 381; *Ruffh. Jac. L. D. Parliament.*

Impeachments stand in like manner continued before the Senate of the United States.

## SECTION LII

### TREATIES

The President of the United States has power, by and with the advice and consent of the Senate, to make treaties, provided two-thirds of the Senators present concur.—*Const. U. S.* Art. II. Sec. 2.

Resolved, That all confidential communications, made by the President of the United States to the Senate, shall be, by the members thereof, kept inviolably secret; and that all treaties, which may hereafter be laid before the Senate, shall also be kept secret, until the Senate shall, by their resolution, take off the injunction of secrecy.—*Dec. 22d,* 1804.

Treaties are legislative acts. A treaty is a law of the land. It differs from other laws only as it must have the consent of a foreign nation, being but a contract with respect to that nation. In all countries, I believe, except England, treaties are made by the legislative power; and there, also, if they touch the laws of the land, they must be approved by Parliament. Ware *vs.* Hilton.—3 *Dallas's Rep.* 199. It is acknowledged, for instance, that the King of Great Britain cannot, by a treaty, make a citizen of an alien.—*Vattel, b.* 1, *c.* 19, *sec.* 214. An act of Parliament was necessary to validate the American treaty of 1783. And abundant examples of such acts can be cited. In the case of the treaty of Utrecht, in 1712, the commercial articles required the concurrence of Parliament. But a bill brought in for that purpose was rejected. France, the other contracting party, suffered these articles, in practice, to be not insisted on, and adhered to the rest of the treaty.—4 *Russell's Hist. Mod. Europe,* 457; 2 *Smollet,* 242, 246.

By the Constitution of the United States, this department of legislation is confined to two branches only, of the ordinary Legislature; the President originating, and Senate having a negative. To what subject this power extends, has not been defined in detail by the Constitution; nor are we entirely agreed among ourselves. 1. It is admitted that it must concern the foreign nation, party to the contract, or it would be a mere nullity *res inter alias acta.* 2. By the general power to make treaties, the Constitution must have intended to comprehend only those objects which are usually regulated by treaty, and cannot be otherwise regulated. 3. It must have meant to except out of these the rights reserved to the States; for surely the President and Senate cannot do by treaty what the whole government is interdicted from doing in any way. 4. And also to except those subjects of legislation in which it gave a participation to the House of Representatives. This last exception is denied by some, on the ground that it would leave very little matter for the treaty power to work on.

The less the better say others. The Constitution thought it wise to restrain the Executive and Senate from entangling and embroiling our affairs with those of Europe. Besides, as the negotiations are carried on by the Executive alone, the subjecting to the ratification of the Representatives such articles as are within their participation, is no more inconvenient than to the Senate. But the ground of this exemption is denied as unfounded. For examine, *e.g.,* the treaty of commerce with France, and it will be found that out of thirty-one articles, there are not more than small portions of two or three of them which would not still remain as subjects of treaties, untouched by these exceptions.

Treaties being declared, equally with the laws of the United States, to be the supreme law of the land, it is understood that an act of the Legislature alone can declare them infringed and rescinded. This was accordingly the process adopted in the case of France, 1798.

It has been the usage of the Executive, when it communicates a treaty to the Senate for their ratification, to communicate also the correspondence of the negotiations. This having been omitted in the case of the Prussian treaty, was asked by a vote of the House of February 12, 1800, and was obtained. And in December, 1800, the Convention of that year, between the United States and France, with the report of the negotiations by the Envoys, but not their instructions, being laid before the Senate, the instructions were asked for, and communicated by the President.

The mode of voting on questions of ratification is by nominal call.

Resolved, as a standing rule, That whenever a treaty shall be laid before the Senate for ratification, it shall be read a first time for information only; when no motion to reject, ratify, or modify the whole or any part, shall be received.

That its second reading shall be for consideration; and on a subsequent day, when it shall be taken up as in a committee of the whole, and everyone shall be free to move a question on any particular article in this form: "Will the Senate advise and consent to the ratification of this article?" or to propose amendments thereto, either by inserting or leaving out words, in which last case the question shall be, "Shall the words stand part of the article?" And in every of the said cases, the concurrence of two-thirds of the Senators present shall be required to decide affirmatively. And when through the whole, the proceedings shall be stated to the House, and questions be again severally put thereon for confirmation, or new ones proposed, requiring in like manner a concurrence of two-thirds for whatever. is retained or inserted.

That the votes so confirmed shall, by the House or a committee thereof, be reduced into the form of a ratification with or without modifications, as may have been decided, and shall be proposed on a subsequent day, when everyone shall again be free to move amendments, either by inserting or leaving out words; in which last case the question shall be, "Shall the words stand part of the resolution?" And in both cases the concurrence of two-thirds shall be requisite to carry the affirmative; as well as on the final question to advise and consent to the ratification in the form agreed to.—*Rule of Jan.* 6, 1801.

Resolved, That when any question may have been decided by the Senate, in which two-thirds of the members present are necessary to carry the affirmative, any member who voted on that side which prevailed in the question may be at liberty to move for a reconsideration; and a motion for reconsideration shall be decided by a majority of votes.—*Rule of Feb.* 3, 1801.

## SECTION LIII

### IMPEACHMENT

The House of Representatives shall have the sole power of impeachment.—*Const. U. S.* Art. I. Sec. 3.

The Senate shall have the sole power to try all impeachments. When sitting for that purpose, they shall be on oath or affirmation. When the President of the United States is tried, the Chief Justice shall preside; and no person shall be convicted without the concurrence of two-thirds of the members present. Judgment, in cases of impeachment, shall not extend further than to removal from office, and disqualification to hold and enjoy any office of honor, trust, or profit, under the United States. But the party convicted shall nevertheless be liable and subject to indictment, trial, judgment, and punishment, according to law.—*Const. U. S.* Art. I. Sec. 3.

The President, Vice-President, and all civil officers of the United States, shall be removed from office on impeachment for, and conviction of, treason, bribery, or other high crimes and misdemeanors.—*Const. U. S.* Art. II. Sec. 4.

The trial of crimes, except in cases of impeachment, shall be by jury.—*Const. U. S.* Art. III. Sec. 2.

These are the provisions of the Constitution of the United States on the subject of impeachments. The following is a sketch on some of the principles and practices of England on the same subject.

*Jurisdiction.*—The Lords cannot impeach any to themselves, nor join in the accusation, because they are judges.—*Seld. Judic. in Parl.* 12, 63. Nor can they proceed against a commoner, but on complaint of the Commons.—*Ib.* 84. The Lords may not, by the law, try a commoner for capital offence, on the information of the King, or a private person; because the accused is entitled to a trial by his peers generally; but on accusation by the House of Commons, they may proceed against the delinquent, of whatsoever degree, and whatsoever be the nature of the offence; for there they do not assume to themselves trial at common law. The Commons are then instead of a jury, and the judgment is given on their demand, which is instead of a verdict. So the Lords do only judge but not try the delinquent.—*Ib.* 6, 7. But Wooddeson denies that a commoner can now be charged capitally before the Lords, even by the Commons; and cites Fitzharris's case, 1681, impeached of high treason, where the Lords remitted the prosecution to the inferior court.—8 *Grey's Deb.* 325, 6, 7; 2 *Wooddeson,* 601, 576; 3 *Seld.* 1610, 1619, 1641; 4 *Black.* 257; 3 *Seld.* 1604. 1618, 9. 1656.

*Accusation.*—The Commons, as the grand inquest of the nation, become suitors for penal justice.—2 *Woodd.* 597; 6 *Grey,* 356. The general course is to pass a resolution, containing a criminal charge against the supposed delinquent, and then to direct some member to impeach him by oral accusation, at the bar of the House of Lords, in the name of the Commons. The person signifies, that the articles will be exhibited, and desires that the delinquent may be sequestered from his seat, or be committed, or that the Peers will take order for his appearance.—*Sachev. Trial.* 325; 2 *Woodd.* 602, 605; *Lords' Journ.* 3 June, 1701; 1 *Wms.* 616; *Grey,* 324.

*Process.*—If the party do not appear, proclamations are to be issued giving him a day to appear. On their return they are strictly examined. If any error be found in them, a new proclamation issues, giving a short day. If he appear not, his goods may be arrested, and they may proceed.—*Seld. Jud.* 98, 99.

*Articles.*—The accusation (article) of the Commons, is substituted in place of an indictment. Thus, by the usage of Parliament, an impeachment for writing or speaking the particular words, need not be specified.—*Sach. Tr.* 325; 2 *Woodd.* 602, 605; *Lords' Journ.* 3 June, 1701; 1 *Wms.* 616.

*Appearance*—If he appears, and the case be capital, he answers in custody; though not if the accusation be general. He is not to be committed but on special accusations. If it be for a misdemeanor only, he answers a Lord in his place, a Commoner at the bar, and not in custody, unless, on the answer, the Lords find cause to commit him till he finds sureties to attend, and lest he should fly.—*Seld. Jud.* 98, 99. A copy of the articles is given him, and a day fixed for his answer.—*T. Ray;* 1 *Rushw.* 268; *Fost.* 232. 1 *Clar. Hist. of the Reb.* 379. On a misdemeanor, his appearance may be in person, or he may answer in writing, or by attorney.—*Seld. Jud.* 100. The general rule on accusation for a misdemeanor is, that in such a state of liberty or restraint as the party is when the Commons complain of him, in such he is to answer. *Seld. Jud.* 101. If previously committed by the Commons, he answers as a prisoner. But this may be called, in some sort, *judicium parium suorum.*—*Seld. Jud.* In misdemeanors, the party has a right to counsel by the common law; but not in capital cases.—*Jud. Seld.* 102-5.

*Answer.*—The answer need not observe great strictness of form. He may plead guilty as to part, and defend as to the residue; or, saving all exceptions, deny the whole, or give a particular answer to each article separately.—1 *Rush.* 274; 2 *Rush.* 1374; 12 *Parl. Hist.* 442; 3 *Lords' Journ.* 13 Nov. 1643; 2 *Woodd.* 607. But he cannot plead a pardon in bar to the impeachment.—2 *Woodd.* 618; 2 *St. Tr.* 735.

*Replication, rejoinder, &c.*—There may be a replication, rejoinder, &c.—*Seld. Jud.* 114; 8 *Grey's Deb.* 233; *Sach. Tr.* 15; *Journ. House of Commons,* 6 March, 1640, 1.

*Witnesses.*—The practice is to swear the witnesses in open House, and then examine them there: or a committee may be named, who shall examine them in committee either on interrogatories agreed on in the House, or such as the committee, in their discretion, shall demand.—*Seld. Jud.* 120. 123.

*Jury.*—In the case of Alice Pierce, 1 *R.* 2. a jury was empanelled for her trial before a committee.—*Seld. Jud.* 123. But this was on a complaint, not an impeachment by the Commons.—*Seld. Jud.* 163. It must also have been for a misdemeanor only, as the Lords Spiritual sat in the case, which they do on misdemeanors, but not in capital cases.—*Seld. Jud.* 148. The judgment was a forfeiture of all her lands and goods.—*Seld. Jud.* 188. This, Selden says, is the only jury he finds recorded in Parliament for misdemeanors; but he makes no doubt if the delinquent doth put himself on the trial of his country, a jury ought to be empanelled: and he adds, that it is not so on impeachment by the Commons; for they are in *oco proprio,* and here no jury ought to be empanelled.—*Ib.* 124. The Lord Berkley, 6 *E.* 3, was arranged for the murder of, *L.* 2, on an information on the part of the King, and not on impeachment of the Commons; for then they had been *patria sua.* He waived his peerage, and was tried by a jury of Gloucestershire and Warwickshire.—*Ib.* 125. In one, 1 *H.* 7, the Common protest that they are not to be considered as parties to any judgment given, or hereafter to be given in Parliament.—*Ib.* 133. They have been generally, and more justly considered, as is before stated, as the grand jury. For the conceit of Selden is certainly not accurate, that they are the *patria sua* of the accused, and that the Lords do only judge, but not try. It is undeniable that they do try. For they examine witnesses as to the facts, and acquit or condemn according to their own belief of them. And Lord Hale says, "the Peers are judges of law as well as of fact."—2 *Hale, P. C.* 275. Consequently of fact as well as of law.

*Presence of Commons.*—The Commons are to be present at the examination of witnesses.—*Seld. Jud.* 124. Indeed, they are to attend throughout, either as a committee of the whole House; or otherwise, at discretion, appoint managers to conduct the proofs.—*Rushw. Tr. of Straff.* 37; *Com. journ.* 4 *Feb.* 1709, 10; 2 *Wood.* 614. And judgment is not to be given till they demand it.—*Seld. Jud.* 124. But they are not to be present on impeachment when the Lords consider of the answer or proofs, and determine of their judgment. Their presence, however, is necessary at the answer and judgment in cases capital.—*Ib.* 58, 159; as well as not capital, 162. The Lords debate the judgment among themselves. Then the vote is first taken on the question of guilty or not guilty; and if they convict, the question, or particular sentence, is out of that which seemeth to be most generally agreed on.—*Seld. Jud.* 167; 2 *Woodd.* 612.

*Judgment.*—Judgments in Parliament, for death, have been strictly guided *per legem terræ,* which they cannot alter; and not at all according to their discretion. They can neither admit any part of the legal judgment, nor add to it. Their sentence must be *secundum, non ultra legem.*—*Seld. Jud.* 168, 169, 170, 171. This trial, though it varies in external ceremony, yet differs not in essentials from criminal prosecutions before inferior courts. The same rules of evidence, the same legal notions of crimes and punishments, prevail. For impeachments were not framed to alter the law, but to carry it into more effectual execution against two powerful delinquents. The judgment, therefore, is to be such as is warranted by legal principles or precedents.—6 *Stra. Tr.* 14; 2 *Woodd.* 611. The Chancellor gives judgments in misdemeanors; the Lord High Steward, formerly, in cases of life and death.—*Seld. Jud.* 180. But now the Steward is deemed not necessary.—*Fost.* 144; 1 *Woodd.* 613. In misdemeanors, the greatest corporal punishment hath been imprisonment.—*Seld. Jud.* 184. The King's assent is necessary in capital judgments, (but 2 *Woodd.* 614. contra.) but not in misdemeanors.—*Seld. Jud.* 136.

*Continuance.*—An impeachment is not discontinued by the dissolution of Parliament; but may be resumed by the new Parliament.—*T. Ray.* 383; 5 *Com. Journ.* 23 Dec. 1790; *Lords' Journ.* May 16, 1791; 2 *Woodd.* 618.

## *Chapter XVI*

# MEMORANDA OF TRAVELS IN EUROPE

## MEMORANDA TAKEN ON A JOURNEY FROM PARIS INTO THE SOUTHERN PARTS OF FRANCE, AND NORTHERN OF ITALY, IN THE YEAR 1787

March 3-June 10, 1787

CHAMPAGNE. March 3. *Sens* to *Vermanton*. The face of the country is in large hills, not too steep for the plough, somewhat resembling the Elk hill, and Beaver-dam hills of Virginia. The soil is generally a rich mulatto loam, with a mixture of coarse sand and some loose stone. The plains of the Yonne are of the same color. The plains are in corn, the hills in vineyard, but the wine not good. There are a few apple trees, but none of any other kind, and no inclosures. No cattle, sheep, or swine; fine mules.

Few châteaux; no farm-houses, all the people being gathered in villages. Are they thus collected by that dogma of their religion, which makes them believe, that to keep the Creator in good humor with his own works, they must mumble a mass every day? Certain it is, that they are less happy and less virtuous in villages, than they would be insulated with their families on the grounds they cultivate. The people are illy clothed. Perhaps they have put on their worst clothes at this moment, as it is raining. But I observe women and children carrying heavy burthens, and laboring with the hoe. This is an unequivocal indication of extreme poverty. Men, in a civilized country, never expose their wives and children to labor above their force and sex, as long as their own labor can protect them from it. I see few beggars. Probably this is the effect of a police.

BURGUNDY. March 4. *Lucy le bois. Cussy les forges. Rouvray. Maison-neuve. Vitteaux. La Chaleure. Pont de Panis. Dijon.* The hills are higher and more abrupt. The soil, a good red loam and sand, mixed with more or less grit, small stone, and sometimes rock. All in corn. Some forest wood here and there, broom, whins and holly, and a few inclosures of quick hedge. Now and then a flock of sheep.

The people are well clothed, but it is Sunday. They have the appearance of being well fed. The Château de Sevigny, near Cussy les forges, is a charming situation. Between Maison-neuve and Vitteaux the road leads through an avenue of trees, eight American miles long, in a right line. It is impossible to paint the ennui of this avenue. On the summits of the hills which border the valley in which Vitteaux is, there is a parapet of rock, twenty, thirty, or forty feet perpendicular, which crowns the hills. The tops are nearly level, and appear to be covered with earth. Very singular. Great masses of rock in the hills between la Chaleure and Pont de Panis, and a conical hill in the approach to the last place.

*Dijon.* The tavern price of a bottle of the best wine (*e.g.,* of Vaune) is four livres. The best round potatoes here I ever saw. They have begun a canal thirty feet wide, which is to lead into the Saone at ——. It is fed by springs. They are not allowed to take any water out of the riviere d'Ouche, which runs through this place, on account of the mills on that river. They talk of making a canal to the Seine, the nearest navigable part of which at present is fifteen leagues from hence. They have very light wagons here for the transportation of their wine. They are long and narrow; the fore wheels as high as the hind. Two pieces of wine are drawn by one horse in one of these wagons. The road in this part of the country is divided into portions of forty or fifty feet by stones, numbered, which mark the task of the laborers.

March 7 and 8. From *la Baraque* to *Chagny.* On the left are plains which extend to the Saone, on the right the ridge of mountains called the Cote. The plains are of a reddish-brown, rich loam, mixed with much small stone. The Cote has for its basis a solid rock, on which is about a foot of soil and small stone, in equal quantities, the soil red and of middling quality. The plains are in corn; the Cote in vines. The former have no inclosures, the latter is in small ones of dry stone wall. There is a good deal of forest. Some small herds of small cattle and sheep. Fine mules, which come from Provence. and cost twenty louis. They break them at two years old, and they last to thirty.

The corn lands here rent for about fifteen livres the arpent. They are now planting, pruning, and sticking their vines. When a new vineyard is made, they plant the vines in gutters about four feet apart. As the vines advance, they lay them down. They put out new shoots, and fill all the intermediate space, till all trace of order is lost. They have ultimately about one foot square to each vine. They begin to yield good profit at five or six years old, and last one hundred, or one hundred and fifty years. A vigneron at Voulenay carried me into his vineyard, which was of about ten arpents. He told me that some years it produced him sixty pieces of wine, and some, not more than three pieces. The latter is the most advantageous produce, because the wine is better in quality, and higher in price in proportion as less is made, and the expenses at the same time diminish in the same proportion. Whereas, when much is made, the expenses are increased, while the price and quality become less. In very plentiful years, they often give one half the wine for casks to contain the other half. The cask for two hundred and fifty bottles, costs six livres in scarce years, and ten in plentiful. The Feuillette is of one hundred and twenty-five bottles, the Piece of two hundred and fifty, and the Queue or Botte, of five hundred. An arpent rents at from twenty to sixty livres. A farmer of ten arpents has about three laborers engaged by the year. He pays four louis to a man, and half as much to a woman, and feeds them. He kills one hog, and salts it, which is all the meat used in the family during the year. Their ordinary food is bread and vegetables. At Pommard and Voulenay, I observed them eating good wheat bread; at Meursault, rye. I asked the reason of this difference. They told me that the white wines fail in quality much oftener than the red, and remain on hand. The farmer, therefore, cannot afford to feed his laborers so well. At Meursault, only white wines are made, because there is too much stone for the red. On such slight circumstances depends the condition of man! The wines which have given such celebrity to Burgundy, grow only on the Cote, an extent of about five leagues long, and half a league wide. They begin at Chambertin, and go through Vougeau, Romanie, Veaune, Nuys, Beaune, Pommard, Voulenay, Meursault, and end at Monrachet. Those of the two last are white, the others red. Chambertin, Vougeau and Neaune are strongest, and will bear transportation and keeping. They sell, therefore, on the spot for twelve hundred livres the queue, which is forty-eight sous the bottle. Voulenay is the best of the other reds, equal in flavor to Chambertin, &c., but being lighter, will not keep, and therefore sells for not more than three hundred livres the queue, which is twelve sous the bottle. It ripens sooner than they do, and consequently is better for those who wish to broach at a year old. In like manner of the white wines, and for the same reason, Monrachet sells for twelve hundred livres the queue (forty-eight sous the bottle), and Meursault of the best quality, *viz.,* the Goutte d'or, at only one hundred and fifty livres (six sous the bottle). It is remarkable, that the best of each kind, that is, of the red and white, is made at the extremities of the line, to wit, at Chambertin and Monrachet. It is pretended that the adjoining vineyards produce the same qualities, but that belonging to obscure individuals, they have not obtained a name, and therefore sell as other wines. The aspect of the Cote is a little south of east. The western side is also covered with vines, and is apparently of the same soil, yet the wines are of the coarsest kinds. Such, too, are those which are produced in the plains; but there the soil is richer and less strong. Vougeau is the property of the monks of Citeaux, and produces about two hundred pieces. Monrachet contains about fifty arpents, and produces, one year with another, about one hundred and twenty pieces. It belongs to two proprietors only, Monsieur de Clarmont, who leases to some wine merchants, and the Marquis de Sarsnet, of Dijon, whose part is farmed to a Monsieur de la Tour, whose family for many generations have had the farm. The best wines are carried to Paris by land. The transportation costs thirty-six livres the piece. The more indifferent go by water. Bottles cost four and a half sous each.

March 9. *Chalons. Sennecy. Tournus. St. Albin. Macon.* On the left are the fine plains of the Saone; on the right, high lands, rather waving than hilly, sometimes sloping gently to the plains, sometimes dropping down in precipices, and occasionally broken into beautiful valleys by the streams which run into the Saone. The plains are a dark rich loam, in pasture and corn; the heights more or less red or reddish, always gritty, of middling quality only, their sides in vines, and their summits in corn. The vineyards are inclosed with dry stone walls, and there are some quick hedges in the corn grounds. The cattle are few and indifferent. There are some good oxen, however. They draw by the head. Few sheep, and small. A good deal of wood lands.

I passed three times the canal called le Charollois, which they are opening from Chalons on the Saone to Dijon on the Loire. It passes near Chagny, and will be twenty-three leagues long. They have worked on it three years, and will finish it in four more. It will re-animate the languishing commerce of Champagne and Burgundy, by furnishing a water transportation for their wines to Nantes, which also will receive new consequence by becoming the emporium of that commerce. At some distance on the right are high mountains, which probably form the separation between the waters of the Saone and Loire. Met a malefactor in the hands of one of the Marechausée; perhaps a dove in the talons of the hawk. The people begin now to be in separate establishments, and not in villages. Houses are mostly covered with tile.

BEAUJOLOIS. *Maison blanche. St. George. Château de Laye-Epinaye.* The face of the country is like that from Chalons to Macon. The plains are a dark rich loam, the hills a red loam of middling quality, mixed generally with more or less coarse sand and grit, and a great deal of small stone. Very little forest. The vineyards are mostly inclosed with dry stone wall. A few small cattle and sheep. Here, as in Burgundy, the cattle are all white.

This is the richest country I ever beheld. It is about ten or twelve leagues in length, and three, four, or five in breadth; at least, that part of it which is under the eye of the traveller. It extends from the top of a ridge of mountains, running parallel with the Saone, and sloping down to the plains of that river, scarcely any where too steep for the plough. The whole is thick set with farm-houses, chateaux, and the Bastides of the inhabitants of Lyons. The people live separately, and not in villages. The hill sides are in vine and corn; the plains in corn and pasture. The lands are farmed either for money, or on half-stocks. The rents of the corn lands, farmed for money, are about ten or twelve livres the arpent. A farmer takes, perhaps, about one hundred and fifty arpents, for three, six, or nine years. The first year they are in corn; the second in other small grain, with which he sows red clover. The third is for the clover. The spontaneous pasturage is of green sward, which they call fromenteau. When lands are rented on half-stocks, the cattle, sheep, &c., are furnished by the landlord. They are valued, and must be left of equal value. The increase of these, as well as the produce of the farm, is divided equally. These leases are only from year to year. They have a method of mixing beautifully the culture of vines, trees, and corn. Rows of fruit trees are planted about twenty feet apart. Between the trees, in the row, they plant vines four feet apart, and espalier them. The intervals are sowed alternately in corn, so as to be one year in corn, the next in pasture, the third in corn, the fourth in pasture, &c. One hundred toises of vines in length, yield generally about four pieces of wine. In Dauphiné, I am told, they plant vines only at the roots of the trees, and let them cover the whole trees. But this spoils both the wine and the fruit. Their wine when distilled, yields but one-third its quantity in brandy. The wages of a laboring man here, are five louis; of a woman, one half. The women do not work with the hoe; they only weed the vines, the corn, &c., and spin. They speak a Patois very difficult to understand. I passed some time at the Château de Laye-Epinaye. Monsieur de Laye has a seignory of about fifteen thousand arpents, in pasture, corn, vines, and wood. He has over this, as is usual, a certain jurisdiction, both criminal and civil. But this extends only to the first crude examination, which is before his judges. The subject is referred for final examination and decision, to the regular judicatures of the country. The Seigneur is keeper of the peace on his domains. He is therefore subject to the expenses of maintaining it. A criminal prosecuted to sentence and execution, costs M. de Laye about five thousand livres. This is so burthensome to the Seigneurs, that they are slack in criminal prosecutions. A good effect from a bad cause. Through all Champagne, Burgundy, and the Beaujolois, the husbandry seems good, except that they manure too little. This proceeds from the shortness of their leases. The people of Burgundy and Beaujolois are well clothed, and have the appearance of being well fed. But they experience all the oppressions which result from the nature of the general government, and from that of their particular tenures, and of the seignorial government to which they are subject. What a cruel reflection, that a rich country cannot long be a free one. M. de Laye has a Diana and Endymion, a very superior morsel of sculpture by Michael Angelo Slodtz, done in 1740. The wild gooseberry is in leaf; the wild pear and sweet briar in bud.

*Lyons.* There are some feeble remains here, of an amphitheatre of two hundred feet diameter, and of an aqueduct in brick. The Pont d'Ainay has nine arches of forty feet from centre to centre. The piers are of six feet. The almond is in bloom.

DAUPHINÉ. From *St. Fond* to *Mornas.* March 15, 16, 17, 18. The Rhone makes extensive plains, which lie chiefly on the eastern side, and are often in two stages. Those of Montelimart are three or four miles wide, and rather good. Sometimes, as in the neighborhood of Vienne, the hills come in precipices to the river, resembling then very much our Susquehanna and its hills, except that the Susquehanna is ten times as wide as the Rhone. The highlands are often very level. The soil, both of hill and plain, where there is soil, is generally tinged, more or less, with red. The hills are sometimes mere masses of rock, sometimes a mixture of loose stone and earth. The plains are always stony, and, as often as otherwise, covered perfectly with a coat of round stones, of the size of the fist, so as to resemble the remains of inundations, from which all the soil has been carried away. Sometimes they are middling good, sometimes barren. In the neighborhood of Lyons, there is more corn than wine. Towards Tains, more wine than corn. From thence, the plains, where best, are in corn, clover, almonds, mulberries, walnuts; where there is still some earth, they are in corn, almonds, and oaks. The hills are in vines. There is a good deal of forest-wood near Lyons, but not much afterwards. Scarcely any inclosures.

There are a few small sheep before we reach Tains; there the number increases.

Nature never formed a country of more savage aspect, than that on both sides the Rhone. A huge torrent, rushes like an arrow between high precipices, often of massive rock, at other times of loose stone, with but little earth. Yet has the hand of man subdued this savage scene, by planting corn where there is a little fertility, trees where there is still less, and vines where there is none. On the whole, it assumes a romantic, picturesque, and pleasing air. The hills on the opposite side of the river, being high, steep, and laid up in terraces, are of a singular appearance. Where the hills are quite in waste, they are covered with broom, whins, box, and some clusters of small pines. The high mountains of Dauphiné and Languedoc are now covered with snow. The almond is in general bloom, and the willow putting out its leaf. There were formerly olives at Pains; but a great cold, some years ago, killed them, and they have not been replanted. I am told at Montelimart, that an almond tree yields about three livres profit a year. Supposing them three toises apart, there will be one hundred to the arpent, which gives three hundred livres a year, besides the corn growing on the same ground. A league below Vienne, on the opposite side of the river, is Cote Rotie. It is a string of broken hills, extending a league on the river, from the village of Ampuys to the town of Condrieux. The soil is white, tinged a little, sometimes, with yellow, sometimes with red, stony, poor, and laid up in terraces. Those parts of the hills only, which look to the sun at mid-day, or the earlier hours of the afternoon, produce wines of the first quality. Seven hundred vines, three feet apart, yield a feuillette, which is about two and a half pieces, to the arpent. The best red wine is produced at the upper end, in the neighborhood of Ampuys; the best white, next to Condrieux. They sell of the first quality and last vintage, at one hundred and fifty livres the piece, equal to twelve sous the bottle. Transportation to Paris is sixty livres, and the bottle four sous; so it may be delivered at Paris in bottles, at twenty sous. When old, it costs ten or eleven louis the piece. There is a quality which keeps well, bears transportation, and cannot be drunk under four years. Another must be drunk at a year old. They are equal in flavor and price.

The wine called Hermitage is made on the hills impending over the village of Tains; on one of which is the hermitage, which gives name to the hills for about two miles, and to the wine made on them. There are but three of those hills which produce wine of the first quality, and of these, the middle regions only. They are about three hundred feet perpendicular height, three-quarters of a mile in length, and have a southern aspect. The soil is scarcely tinged red, consists of small rotten stone, and is, where the best wine is made, without any perceptible mixture of earth. It is in sloping terraces. They use a little dung. An homme de vignes, which consists of seven hundred plants, three feet apart, yields generally about three quarters of a piece, which is nearly four pieces to the arpent. When new, the piece is sold at about two hundred and twenty-five livres; when old, at three hundred. It cannot be drunk under four years, and improves fastest in a hot situation. There is so little white made in proportion to the red, that it is difficult to buy it separate. They make the white sell the red. If bought separately, it is from fifteen to sixteen louis the piece, new, and three livres the bottle, old. To give quality to the red, they mix one eighth of white grapes. Portage to Paris is seventy-two livres the piece, weighing six hundred pounds. There are but about one thousand pieces of both red and white, of the first quality, made annually. Vineyards are never rented here, nor are laborers in the vineyard hired by the year. They leave buds proportioned to the strength of the vine; sometimes as much as fifteen inches. The last hermit died in 1751.

In the neighborhood of Montelimart, and below that, they plant vines in rows, six, eight, or ten feet apart, and two feet asunder in the row, filling the intervals with corn. Sometimes the vines are in double rows, two feet apart. I saw single asses in ploughs proportioned to their strength. There are few chateaux in this province. The people, too, are mostly gathered into villages. There are, however, some scattering farm houses. These are made either of mud, or of round stone and mud. They make inclosures also, in both those ways. Day laborers receive sixteen or eighteen sous the day, and feed themselves. Those by the year receive, men three louis, women half that, and are fed. They rarely eat meat; a single hog salted, being the year's stock for a family. But they have plenty of cheese, eggs, potatoes and other vegetables, and walnut oil with their salad. It is a trade here, to gather dung along the road for their vines. This proves they have few cattle. I have seen neither hares nor partridges since I left Paris, nor wild fowl on any of the rivers. The roads from Lyons to St. Rambert, are neither paved nor gravelled. After that, they are coated with broken flint. The ferry boats on the Rhone and the Isere, are moved by the stream, and very rapidly. On each side of the river is a moveable stage, one end of which is on an axle and two wheels, which, according to the tide, can be advanced or withdrawn, so as to apply to the gunwale of the boat. The Prætorian palace at Vienne is forty-four feet wide, of the Corinthian order, four columns in front, and four in flank. It was begun in the year 400, and finished by Charlemagne. The Sepulchral pyramid, a little way out of the town, has an order for its basement, the pedestal of which, from point to point of its cap, is twenty-four feet one inch. At each angle, is a column, engaged one fourth in the wall. The circumference of the three fourths disengaged, is four feet four inches; consequently, the diameter is twenty-three inches. The base of the column indicates it to be Ionic, but the capitals are not formed. The cornice, too, is a bastard Ionic, without modillions or dentils. Between the columns, on each side, is an arch of eight feet four inches, opening with a pilaster on each side of it. On the top of the basement is a zocle, in the plane of the frieze below. On that is the pyramid, its base in the plane of the collarino of the pilaster below. The pyramid is a little truncated on its top. This monument is inedited.

March 18th. *Principality of Orange.* The plains on the Rhone here are two or three leagues wide, reddish, good, in corn, clover, almonds, olives. No forests. Here begins the country of olives, there being very few till we enter this principality. They are the only tree which I see planted among vines. Thyme grows wild here on the hills. Asses, very small, sell here for two or three louis. The high hills in Dauphiné are covered with snow. The remains of the Roman aqueduct are of brick: a fine piece of Mosaic, still on its bed, forming the floor of a cellar. Twenty feet of it still visible. They are taking down the circular wall of the amphitheatre to pave a road.

March 19th to 23d. LANGUEDOC. *Pont St. Esprit. Bagnols. Connault. Valignieres. Remoulins. St. Gervasy. Nismes. Pont d'Arles.* To Remoulins, there is a mixture of hill and dale. Thence to Nismes, hills on the right, on the left, plains extending to the Rhone and the sea. The hills are rocky. Where there is soil, it is reddish and poor. The plains, generally reddish and good, but stony. When you approach the Rhone, going to Arles, the soil becomes a dark gray loam with some sand, and very good. The culture is corn, clover, St. foin, olives, vines, mulberries, willow, and some almonds. There is no forest. The hills are inclosed in dry stone wall. Many sheep.

From the summit of the first hill, after leaving Pont St. Esprit, there is a beautiful view of the bridge at about two miles distance, and a fine landscape of the country both ways. From thence, an excellent road, judiciously conducted, through very romantic scenes. In one part, descending the face of a hill, it is laid out in serpentine, and not zigzag, to ease the descent. In others, it passes through a winding meadow, from fifty to one hundred yards, walled, as it were, on both sides, by hills of rock; and at length issues into plain country. The waste hills are covered with thyme, box, and chene-vert. Where the body of the mountains has a surface of soil, the summit has sometimes a crown of rock, as observed in Champagne. At Nismes, the earth is full of limestone. The horses are shorn. They are now pruning the olive. A very good tree produces sixty pounds of olives, which yield fifteen pounds of oil: the best quality sells at twelve sous the pound, retail, and ten sous, wholesale. The high hills of Languedoc still covered with snow. The horse chestnut and mulberry are leafing; apple trees and peas blossoming. The first butterfly I have seen. After the vernal equinox, they are often six or eight months without rain. Many separate farm houses, numbers of people in rags, and abundance of beggars. The mine of wheat, weighing thirty pounds, costs four livres and ten sous. Wheat bread, three sous the pound. Vin ordinaire, good, and of a strong body, two or three sous the bottle. Oranges, one sou a piece. They are nearly finishing at Nismes, a great mill, worked by a steam engine, which pumps water from a lower into an upper cistern, from whence two overshot wheels are supplied, each of which turns two pair of stones. The upper cistern being once filled with water, it passes through the wheels into the lower one, from whence it is returned to the upper by the pumps. A stream of water of one quarter or one half inch diameter, supplies the waste of evaporation, absorption, &c. This is furnished from a well by a horse. The arches of the Pont St. Esprit are of eighty-eight feet. Wild figs, very flourishing, grow out of the joints of the Pont du Gard. The fountain of Nismes is so deep, that a stone was thirteen seconds descending from the surface to the bottom.

March 24th. From *Nismes* to *Arles.* The plains extending from Nismes to the Rhone, in the direction of Arles, are broken in one place by a skirt of low hills. They are red and stony at first, but as you approach the Rhone, they are of a dark gray mould, with a little sand, and very good. They are in corn and clover, vines, olives, almonds, mulberries, and willow. There are some sheep, no wood, no inclosures.

The high hills of Languedoc are covered with snow. At an ancient church, in the suburbs of Arles, are some hundreds of ancient stone coffins, along the road side. The ground is thence called les champs elysées. In a vault in a church, are some curiously wrought, and in a back yard are many ancient statues, inscriptions, &c. Within the town, are a part of two Corinthian columns, and of the pediment with which they were crowned, very rich, having belonged to the ancient capitol of the place. But the principal monument here, is an amphitheatre, the external portico of which is tolerably complete. How many porticoes there were, cannot be seen: but at one of the principal gates, there are still five, measuring, from out to in, seventy-eight feet ten inches, the vault diminishing inwards. There are sixty-four arches, each of which is, from centre to centre, twenty feet six inches. Of course, the diameter is of four hundred and thirty-eight feet; or of four hundred and fifty feet, if we suppose the four principal arches a little larger than the rest. The ground-floor is supported on innumerable vaults. The first story, externally, has a tall pedestal, like a pilaster, between every two arches: the upper story, a column, the base of which would indicate it Corinthian. Every column is truncated as low as the impost of the arch, but the arches are all entire. The whole of the upper entablature is gone, and of the attic, if there was one. Not a single seat of the internal is visible. The whole of the inside, and nearly the whole of the outside, is masked by buildings. It is supposed there are one thousand inhabitants within the amphitheatre. The walls are more entire and firm than those of the amphitheatre at Nismes. I suspect its plan and distribution to have been very different from that.

*Terrasson.* The plains of the Rhone from Arles to this place, are a league or two wide: the mould is of a dark gray, good, in corn and lucerne. Neither wood, nor inclosures. Many sheep.

*St. Remis.* From Terrasson to St. Remis, is a plain of a league or two wide, bordered by broken hills of massive rock. It is gray and stony, mostly in olives. Some almonds, mulberries, willows, vines, corn, and lucerne. Many sheep. No forest, nor inclosures.

A laboring man's wages here, are one hundred and fifty livres, a woman's half, and fed. Two hundred and eighty pounds of wheat sell for forty-two livres. They make no butter here. It costs, when brought, fifteen sous the pound. Oil is ten sous the pound. Tolerably good olive trees yield, one with another, about twenty pounds of oil. An olive tree must be twenty years old before it has paid its own expenses. It lasts forever. In 1765, it was so cold, that the Rhone was frozen over at Arles for two months. In 1767, there was a cold spell of a week, which killed all the olive trees. From being fine weather, in one hour there was ice hard enough to bear a horse. It killed people on the road. The old roots of the olive trees put out again. Olive grounds sell for twenty-four livres a tree, and lease at twenty-four sous the tree. The trees are fifteen pieds apart. But lucerne is a more profitable culture. An arpent yields one hundred quintals of hay a year, worth three livres the quintal. It is cut four or five times a year. It is sowed in the broadcast, and lasts five or six years. An arpent of ground for corn, rents at from thirty to thirty-six livres. Their leases are for six or nine years. They plant willow for fire-wood, and for hoops to their casks. It seldom rains here in summer. There are some chateaux, many separate farm-houses, good, and ornamented in the small way, so as to show that the tenant's whole time is not occupied in procuring physical necessaries.

March 25th. *Orgon. Pontroyal. St. Cannat.* From Orgon to Pontroyal, after quitting the plains of the Rhone, the country seems still to be a plain, cut into compartments by chains of mountains of massive rock, running through it in various directions. From Pontroyal to St. Cannat, the land lies rather in basins. The soil is very various, gray and clay, gray and stony, red and stony; sometimes good, sometimes middling, often barren. We find some golden willows. Towards Pontroyal, the hills begin to be in vines, and afterwards, in some pasture of green sward and clover. About Orgon are some inclosures of quick set, others of conical yews planted close. Towards St. Cannat, they begin to be of stone.

The high mountains are covered with snow. Some separate farm-houses of mud. Near Pontroyal is a canal for watering the country; one branch goes to Terrasson, the other to Arles.

March 25th, 26th, 27th, 28th. *Aix.* The country is waving in vines, pasture of green sward and clover, much inclosed with stone, and abounding with sheep.

On approaching Aix, the valley which opens from thence towards the mouth of the Rhone and the sea, is rich and beautiful; a perfect grove of olive trees, mixed among which are corn, lucerne, and vines. The waste grounds throw out thyme and lavender. Wheat bread is three sous the pound. Cow's milk sixteen sous the quart, sheep's milk six sous, butter of sheep's milk twenty sous the pound. Oil, of the best quality, is twelve sous the pound, and sixteen sous if it be virgin oil. This is what runs from the olive when put into the press, spontaneously; afterwards they are forced by the press and by hot water. Dung costs ten sous the one hundred pounds. Their fire-wood is chene-vert and willow. The latter is lopped every three years. An ass sells for from one to three louis; the best mules for thirty louis. The best asses will carry two hundred pounds; the best horses three hundred pounds; the best mules six hundred pounds. The temperature of the mineral waters of Aix, is 90° of Farenheit's thermometer, at the spout. A mule eats half as much as a horse. The allowance to an ass for the day, is a handful of bran mixed with straw. The price of mutton and beef, about six and a half sous the pound. The beef comes from Auvergne, and is poor and bad. The mutton is small, but of excellent flavor. The wages of a laboring man are one hundred and fifty livres the year, a woman's sixty to sixty-six livres, and fed. Their bread is half wheat, half rye, made once in three or four weeks, to prevent too great a consumption. In the morning, they eat bread with an anchovy, or an onion. Their dinner in the middle of the day, is bread, soup, and vegetables. Their supper the same. With their vegetables, they have always oil and vinegar. The oil costs about eight sous the pound. They drink what is called piquette. This is made after the grapes are pressed, by pouring hot water on the pumice. On Sunday they have meat and wine. Their wood for building comes mostly from the Alps, down the Durance and Rhone. A stick of pine fifty feet long, girting sixty feet and three inches at one end, and three feet three inches at the other, costs, delivered here, from fifty-four to sixty livres. Sixty pounds of wheat cost seven livres. One of their little asses will travel with his burthen about five or six leagues a day, and day by day; a mule from six to eight leagues.[1]

March 29. *Marseilles.* The country is hilly, intersected by chains of hills and mountains of massive rock. The soil is reddish, stony, and indifferent where best. Wherever there is any soil, it is covered with olives. Among these are corn, vines, some lucerne, mulberry, some almonds and willow. Neither inclosures, nor forest. A very few sheep.

On the road I saw one of those little whirlwinds which we have in Virginia, also some gullied hill sides. The people are in separate establishments. Ten morning observations of the thermometer, from the 20th to the 31st of March inclusive, made at Nismes, St. Renny, Aix and Marseilles, give me an average of 52½ and 46° and 61, for the greatest and least morning heats. Nine afternoon observations, yield an average of 62⅔ and 57° and 66°, the greatest and least. The longest day here, from sunrise to sunset, is fifteen hours and fourteen minutes; the shortest is eight hours and forty-six minutes; the latitude being ——. There are no tides in the Mediterranean. It is observed to me, that the olive tree grows no where more than thirty leagues distant from that sea. I suppose, however, that both Spain and Portugal furnish proofs to the contrary, and doubt its truth as to Asia, Africa, and America. They are six or eight months at a time, here, without rain. The most delicate figs known in Europe, are those growing about this place, called figues Marcelloises, or les veritables Marcelloises, to distinguish them from others of inferior quality growing here. These keep any length of time. All others exude a sugar in the spring of the year, and become sour. The only process for preserving them, is drying them in the sun, without putting any thing to them whatever. They sell at fifteen sous the pound, while there are others as cheap as five sous the pound. I meet here a small dried grape from Smyrna without a seed. There are few of the plants growing in this neighborhood. The best grape for drying known here, is called des Panses. They are very large, with a thick skin and much juice. They are best against a wall of southern aspect, as their abundance of juice requires a great deal of sun to dry it. Pretty good fig trees are about the size of the apricot tree, and yield about twenty pounds of figs when dry, each. But the largest will yield the value of a louis. They are some-

[1] It is twenty American miles from Aix to Marseilles, and they call it five leagues. Their league, then, is of four American miles.—T. J.

times fifteen inches in diameter. It is said the Marseilles fig degenerates when transported into any other part of the country. The leaves of the mulberry tree will sell for about three livres, the purchaser gathering them. The caper is a creeping plant. It is killed to the roots every winter. In the spring it puts out branches, which creep to the distance of three feet from the centre. The fruit forms on the stem, as that extends itself, and must be gathered every day as it forms. This is the work of women. The pistache grows in this neighborhood also, but not very good. They eat them in their milky state. Monsieur de Bergasse has a wine cellar two hundred and forty pieds long, in which are one hundred and twenty tons, of from fifty to one hundred pieces each. These tons are twelve pieds diameter; the staves four inches thick, the heading two and a half pouces thick. The temperature of his cellar is of 9½ of Reaumur. The best method of packing wine, when bottled, is to lay the bottles on their side, and cover them with sand. The 2nd of April, the young figs are formed; the 4th we have Windsor beans. They have had asparagus ever since the middle of March. The 5th, I see strawberries and the Guelder rose in blossom. To preserve the raisin, it is first dipped into ley and then dried in the sun. The aloe grows in the open ground. I measured a mule, not the largest, five feet and two inches high. Marseilles is in an amphitheatre, at the mouth of the Vaune, surrounded by high mountains of naked rock, distant two or three leagues. The country within that amphitheatre is a mixture of small hills, valleys and plains. The latter are naturally rich. The hills and valleys are forced into production. Looking from the Chateau de Notre dame de la garde, it would seem as if there was a Bastide for every arpent. The plain land sells for one hundred louis the caterelle, which is less than an acre. The ground of the arsenal in Marseilles, sold for from fifteen to forty louis the square verge, being nearly the square yard English. In the fields open to the sea, they are obliged to plant rows of canes, every here and there, to break the force of the wind. Saw at the Chateau Borelli, pumps worked by the wind.

April 6. From *Marseilles* to *Aubagne*. A valley on the Vaune, bordered on each side by high mountains of massive rock, on which are only some small pines. The interjacent valley is of small hills, valleys and plains, reddish, gravelly, and originally poor, but fertilized by art, and covered with corn, vines, olives, figs, almonds, mulberries, lucerne and clover. The river is twelve or fifteen feet wide, one or two feet deep and rapid.

From *Aubagne* to *Cuges, Beausset, Toulon.* The road quitting the Vaune and its wealthy valley, a little after Aubagne, enters those mountains of rock, and is engaged with them about a dozen miles. Then it passes six or eight miles through a country still very hilly and stony, but laid up in terraces, covered with olives, vines and corn. It then follows for two or three miles, a hollow between two of those high mountains, which has been found or made by a small stream. The mountains then, reclining a little from their perpendicular, and presenting a coat of soil, reddish and tolerably good, have given place to the little village of Olioules, in the gardens of which are oranges in the open ground. It continues hilly till we enter the plain of Toulon. On different parts of this road there are figs in the open fields. At Cuges, is a plain of about three-fourths of a mile in diameter, surrounded by high mountains of rock. In this, the caper is principally cultivated. The soil is mulatto, gravelly, and of middling quality, or rather indifferent. The plants are set in quincunx, about eight feet apart. They have been covered during winter by a hill of earth a foot high. They are now inclosing, pruning and ploughing them.

*Toulon.* From Olioules to Toulon, the figs are in the open fields. Some of them have stems of fifteen inches diameter. They generally fork near the ground, but sometimes have a single stem of five feet long. They are as large as apricot trees. The olive trees of this day's journey are about the size of large apple trees. The people are in separate establishments. Toulon is in a valley at the mouth of the Goutier, a little river of the size of the Vaune; surrounded by high mountains of naked rock, leaving some space between them and the sea. This space is hilly, reddish, gravelly, and of middling quality, in olives, vines, corn, almonds, figs and capers. The capers are planted eight feet apart. A bush yields, one year with another, two pounds, worth twelve sous the pound. Every plant then, yields twenty-four sous, equal to one shilling sterling. An acre containing six hundred and seventy-six plants, would yield thirty-three pounds sixteen shillings sterling. The fruit is gathered by women, who can gather about twelve pounds a day. They begin to gather about the last of June, and end about the middle of October. Each plant must be picked every day. These plants grow equally well in the best or worst soil, or even in the walls where there is no soil. They will last the life of a man or longer. The heat is so great at Toulon in summer, as to occasion very great cracks in the earth. Where the caper is in a soil that will admit it, they plough it. They have peas here through the winter, sheltering them occasionally; and they have had them ever since the 25th of March without shelter.

April 6. *Hières.* This is a plain of two or three miles diameter, bounded by the sea on one side, and mountains of rock on the other. The soil is reddish, gravelly, tolerably good and well watered. It is in olives, mulberries, vines, figs, corn, and some flax. There are also some cherry trees. From Hières to the sea, which is two or three miles, is a grove of orange trees, olives, and mulberries. The largest orange tree is of two feet diameter one way, and one foot the other (for the section of all the larger ones would be an oval, not a round), and about twenty feet high. Such a tree will yield about six thousand oranges a year. The garden of M. Fille has fifteen thousand six hundred orange trees. Some years they yield forty thousand livres, some only ten thousand; but generally about twenty-five thousand. The trees are from eight to ten feet apart. They are blossoming and bearing all the year, flowers and fruit in every stage, at the same time. But the best fruit is that which is gathered in April and May. Hières is a village of about five thousand inhabitants, at the foot of a mountain which covers it from the north, and from which extends a plain of two or three miles to the sea shore. It has no port. Here are palm trees twenty or thirty feet high, but they bear no fruit. There is also a botanical garden kept by the King. Considerable salt ponds here. Hières is six miles from the public road. It is built on a narrow spur of the mountain. The streets in every direction are steep, in steps of stairs, and about eight feet wide. No carriage of any kind can enter it. The wealthiest inhabitants use *chaises à porteurs.* But there are few wealthy, the bulk of the inhabitants being laborers of the earth. At a league's distance in the sea, is an island on which is the Château de Géans, belonging to the Marquis de Pontoives; there is a cause-way leading to it. The cold of the last November killed the leaves of a great number of the orange trees, and some of the trees themselves.

From Hières to *Cuers, Pignans, Luc,* is mostly a plain, with mountains on each hand, at a mile or two distance. The soil is generally reddish, and the latter part very red and good. The growth is, olives, figs, vines, mulberries, corn, clover, and lucerne. The olive trees are from three to four feet in diameter. There are hedges of pomegranates, sweetbriar, and broom. A great deal of thyme growing wild. There are some inclosures of stone; some sheep and goats.

April 9th. From Luc to *Vidauban, Muy, Frejus,* the road leads through valleys, and crosses occasionally the mountains which separate them. The valleys are tolerably good, always red and stony, gravelly or gritty. Their produce as before. The mountains are barren.

*Lesterelle, Napoule.* Eighteen miles of ascent and descent, of a very high mountain. Its growth, where capable of any, two-leaved pine, very small, and some chene-vert.

*Antibes, Nice.* From Napoule, the road is generally near the sea, passing over little hills or strings of valleys, the soil stony, and much below mediocrity in its quality. Here and there, is a good plain.

There is snow on the high mountains. The first frogs I have heard, are of this day (the 9th.) At Antibes are oranges in the open ground, but in small inclosures; palm trees also. From thence to the Var, are the largest fig trees and olive trees I have seen. The fig trees are eighteen inches in diameter, and six feet, stem; the olives, sometimes six feet in diameter, and as large heads as the largest low ground apple trees. This tree was but a shrub where I first fell in with it, and has become larger and larger to this place. The people are mostly in villages. The several provinces, and even cantons are distinguished by the form of the women's hats, so that one may know of what canton a woman is, by her hat.

*Nice.* The pine bur is used here for kindling fires. The people are in separate establishments. With respect to the orange, there seems to be no climate on this side of the Alps, sufficiently mild in itself to preserve it without shelter. At Olioules, they are between two high mountains; at Hières, covered on the north by a very high mountain; at Antibes and Nice, covered by mountains, and also within small high enclosures. Quere. To trace the true line from east to west, which forms the northern and natural limit of that fruit? Saw an elder tree (sambucus) near Nice, fifteen inches in diameter, and eight feet stem. The wine made in this neighborhood is good, though not of the first quality. There are one thousand mules, loaded with merchandise, which pass every week between Nice and Turin, counting those coming as well as going.

April 13th. *Scarena. Sospello.* There are no orange trees after we leave the environs of Nice. We lose the olive after rising a little above the village of Scarena, on Mount Braus, and find it again on the other side, a little before we get down to Sospello. But wherever there is soil enough, it is terraced, and in corn. The waste parts are either in two-leaved pine and thyme, or of absolutely naked rock. Sospello is on a little torrent, called Bevera, which runs into the river Roia, at the mouth of which is Ventimiglia. The olive trees on the mountain are now loaded with fruit; while some at Sospello are in blossom. Firewood here and at Scarena costs fifteen sous the quintal.

April 14th. *Ciandola. Tende.* In crossing Mount Brois we lose the olive tree after getting to a certain height, and find it again on the other side at the village of Breglio. Here we come to the river Roia, which, after receiving the branch on which is Sospello, leads to the sea at Ventimiglia. The Roia is about twelve yards wide, and abounds with speckled trout. Were a road made from Breglio, along the side of the Roia, to Ventimiglia, it might turn the commerce of Turin to this last place instead of Nice; because it would avoid the mountains of Braus and Brois, leaving only that of Tende; that is to say, it would avoid more than half the difficulties of the passage. Further on, we come to the Château di Saorgio, where a scene is presented, the most singular and picturesque I ever saw. The castle and village seem hanging to a cloud in front. On the right, is a mountain cloven through, to let pass a gurgling stream; on the left, a river, over which is thrown a magnificent bridge. The whole forms a basin, the sides of which are shagged with rocks, olive trees, vines, herds, &c. Near here I saw a tub wheel without a ream; the trunk descended from the top of the water fall to the wheel, in a direct line, but with the usual inclination. The produce along this passage, is most generally olives, except on the heights as before observed; also corn, vines, mulberries, figs, cherries, and walnuts. They have cows, goats, and sheep. In passing on towards Tende, olives fail us ultimately at the village of Fontan, and there the chesnut trees begin in good quantity. Ciandola consists of only two houses, both taverns. Tende is a very inconsiderable village, in which they have not yet the luxury of glass windows; nor in any of the villages on this passage have they yet the fashion of powdering the hair. Common stone and limestone are so abundant, that the apartments of every story are vaulted with stone, to save wood.

April 15th. *Limone. Coni.* I see abundance of limestone as far as the earth is uncovered with snow; *i.e.,* within half or three-quarters of an hour's walk of the top. The snows descend much lower on the eastern than the western side. Wherever there is soil, there is corn quite to the commencement of the snows, and I suppose under them also. The waste parts are in two-leaved pine, lavender and thyme. From the foot of the mountain to Coni, the road follows a branch of the Po, the plains of which begin narrow, and widen at length into a general plain country, bounded on one side by the Alps. They are good, dark colored, sometimes tinged with red, and in pasture, corn, mulberries, and some almonds. The hill sides bordering these plains are reddish, and where they admit of it, are in corn; but this is seldom. They are mostly in chesnut, and often absolutely barren. The whole of the plains are plentifully watered from the river, as is much of the hill side. A great deal of golden willow all along the rivers, on the whole of this passage through the Alps. The southern parts of France, but still more the passage through the Alps, enable one to form a scale of the tenderer plants, arranging them according to their several powers of resisting cold. Ascending three different mountains, Braus, Brois, and Tende, they disappear one after another; and descending on the other side, they show themselves again one after another. This is their order, from the tenderest to the hardiest. Caper, orange, palm, aloe, olive, pomegranate, walnut, fig, almond. But this must be understood of the plant; for as to the fruit, the order is somewhat different. The caper, for example, is the tenderest plant, yet being so easily protected, it is the most certain in its fruit. The almond, the hardiest plant, loses its fruit the oftenest, on account of its forwardness. The palm, hardier than the caper and the orange, never produces perfect fruit in these parts. Coni is a considerable town, and pretty well built. It is walled.

April 16th. *Centale. Savigliano. Racconigi. Poerino. Turin.* The Alps, as far as they are in view from north to south, show the gradation of climate, by the line which terminates the snows lying on them. This line begins at their foot northwardly, and rises, as they pass on to the south, so as to be half way up their sides on the most southern undulations of the mountain, now in view. From the mountains to Turin, we see no tree tenderer than the walnut. Of these, as well as of almonds and mulberries, there are a few; somewhat more of vines, but most generally, willows and poplars. Corn is sowed with all these. They mix with them also clover and small grass. The country is a general plain; the soil dark, and sometimes, though rarely, reddish. It is rich, and much infested with wild onions. At Racconigi, I see the tops and shocks of maize, which prove it is cultivated here; but it can be in small quantities only, because I observe very little ground, but what has already something else in it. Here and there are small patches prepared, I suppose, for maize. They have a method of planting the vine, which I have not seen before. At intervals of about eight feet, they plant from two to six plants of vine in a cluster. At each cluster they fix a forked staff, the plane of the prongs of the fork at a right angle with the row of vines. Athwart these prongs they lash another staff, like a handspike, about eight feet long, horizontally, seven or eight feet from the ground. Of course, it crosses the rows at right angles. The vines are brought from the foot of the fork up to this cross piece, turned over it, and conducted along over the next, the next, and so on, as far as they will extend, the whole forming an arbor eight feet wide and high, and of the whole length of the row, little interrupted by the stems of the vines, which being close around the fork, pass up through hoops, so as to occupy a space only of smaller diameter. All the buildings in this country are of brick, sometimes covered with plaster, sometimes not. There is a very large and handsome bridge of seven arches, over the torrent of Sangone. We cross the Po, in swinging batteaux. Two are placed side by side, and kept together by a plank floor, common to both, and lying on the gunwales. The carriage drives on this, without taking out any of the horses. About one hundred and fifty yards up the river, is a fixed stake, and a rope tied to it, the other end of which is made fast to one side of the batteaux, so as to throw them oblique to the current. The stream then acting on them, as on an inclined plane, forces them cross the current in the portion of a circle of which the rope is the radius. To support the rope in its whole length, there are two intermediate canoes, about fifty yards apart, in the heads of which are short masts. To the top of these, the rope is lashed, the canoes being free otherwise to concur with the general vibration, in their smaller arcs of circles. The Po is there about fifty yards wide, and about one hundred in the neighborhood of Turin.

April 17th, 18th. *Turin.* The first nightingale I have heard this year, is today (18th.) There is a red wine of Nebiule made in the neighborhood, which is very singular. It is about as sweet as the silky Madeira, as astringent on the palate as Bourdeaux, and as brisk as Champagne. It is a pleasing wine. At Moncaglieri, about six miles from Turin, on the right side of the Po, begins a ridge of mountains, which, following the Po by Turin, after some distance, spreads wide, and forms the duchy of Montferrat. The soil is mostly red, and in vines, affording a wine called Montferrat, which is thick and strong.

April 19th. *Settimo. Chivasco. Ciliano. S. Germano. Vercelli.* The country continues plain and rich, the soil black. The culture, corn, pasture, maize, vines, mulberries, walnuts, some willow and poplar. The maize bears a very small proportion to the small grain. The earth is formed into ridges from three to four feet wide, and the maize sowed in the broadcast on the higher parts of the ridge, so as to cover a third or half of the whole surface. It is sowed late in May. This country is plentifully and beautifully watered at present. Much of it is by torrents which are dry in summer. These torrents make a great deal of waste ground, covering it with sand and stones. These wastes are sometimes planted in trees, sometimes quite unemployed. They make hedges of willows, by setting the plants from one to three feet apart. When they are grown to the height of eight or ten feet, they bend them down, and interlace them one with another. I do not see any of these, however, which are become old. Probably, therefore, they soon die. The women here smite on the anvil, and work with the maul and spade. The people of this country are ill dressed in comparison with those of France, and there are more spots of uncultivated ground. The plough here is made with a single handle, which is a beam twelve feet long, six inches in diameter below, and tapered to about two inches at the upper end. They use goads for the oxen, not whips. The first swallows I have seen, are today. There is a wine called Gatina, made in the neighborhood of Vercelli, both red and white. The latter resembles Calcavallo. There is also a red wine of Salusola which is esteemed. It is very light. In the neighborhood of Vercelli begin the rice fields. The water with which they are watered is very dear. They do not permit rice to be sown within two miles of the cities on account of the insalubrity. Notwithstanding this, when the water is drawn off the fields in August, the whole country is subject to agues and fevers. They estimate that the same measure of ground yields three times as much rice as wheat, and with half the labor. They are now sowing. As soon as sowed, they let on the water, two or three inches deep. After six weeks, or two months, they draw it off to weed; then let it on again, and it remains till August, when it is drawn off, about three or four weeks before the grain is ripe. In September they cut it. It is first threshed, then beaten in the mortar to separate the husk, then by different siftings it is separated into three qualities. Twelve rupes, equal to three hundred pounds of twelve ounces each, sell for sixteen livres, money of Piedmont, where the livre is exactly the shilling of England. Twelve rupes of maize sell for nine livres. The machine for separating the husk is thus made. In the axis of a water wheel are a number of arms inserted, which, as they revolve, catches each the cog of a pestle, lifts it to a certain height, and lets it fall again. These pestles are five and a quarter inches square, ten feet long, and at their lower end formed into a truncated cone of three inches diameter, where cut off. The conical part is covered with iron. The pestles are ten and a half inches apart in the clear. They pass through two horizontal beams, which string them, as it were, together, and while the mortises in the beams are so loose as to let the pestles work vertically, it restrains them to that motion. There is a mortar of wood, twelve or fifteen inches deep, under each pestle, covered with a board, the hole of which is only large enough to let the pestle pass freely. There are two arms in the axis for every pestle, so that the pestle gives two strokes for every revolution of the wheel. Poggio, a muleteer, who passes every week between Vercelli and Genoa, will smuggle a sack of rough rice for me to Genoa; it being death to export it in that form. They have good cattle, and in good number, mostly cream-colored; and some middle-sized sheep. The streams furnish speckled trout.

April 20th. *Novara. Buffalora. Sedriano. Milan.* From Vercelli to Novara the fields are all in rice, and now mostly under water. The dams separating the several water-plats, or ponds, are set in willow. At Novara there are some figs in the gardens, in situations well protected. From Novara to the Ticino, it is mostly stony and waste, grown up in broom. From Ticino to Milan, it is all in corn. Among the corn are willows, principally a good many mulberries, some walnuts, and here and there an almond. The country still a plain, the soil black and rich, except between Novara and the Ticino, as before mentioned. There is very fine pasture round Vercelli and Novara to the distance of two miles, within which rice is not permitted. We cross the Sisto on the same kind of vibrating or pendulum boat as on the Po. The river is eighty or ninety yards wide; the rope fastened to an island two hundred yards above, and supported by five intermediate canoes. It is about one and a half inches in diameter. On these rivers they use a short oar of twelve feet long, the flat end of which is hooped with iron, shooting out a prong at each corner, so that it may be used occasionally as a setting pole. There is snow on the Apennines, near Genoa. They have still another method here of planting the vine. Along rows of trees, they lash poles from tree to tree. Between the trees are set vines, which, passing over the pole, are carried on to the pole of the next tree, whose vines are in like manner brought to this, and twined together, thus forming the intervals between the rows of trees alternately into arbors and open space. They have another method also of making quick set hedges. Willows are planted from one to two feet apart, and interlaced, so that every one is crossed by three or four others.

April 21st, 22d. *Milan*. Figs and pomegranates grow here unsheltered, as I am told. I saw none, and therefore suppose them rare. They had formerly olives; but a great cold in 1709 killed them, and they have not been replanted. Among a great many houses painted *al fresco,* the Casa Roma and Casa Candiani, by Appiani, and Casa Belgioiosa, by Martin, are superior. In the second is a small cabinet, the ceiling of which is in small hexagons, within which are cameos and heads painted alternately, no two the same. The salon of the Casa Belgioiosa is superior to anything I have ever seen. The mixture called Scaiola, of which they make their walls and floors, is so like the finest marble as to be scarcely distinguishable from it. The nights of the 20th and 21st instant the rice ponds froze half an inch thick. Drouths of two or three months are not uncommon here in summer. About five years ago, there was such a hail as to kill cats. The Count del Verme tells me of a pendulum odometer for the wheel of a carriage. Leases here are mostly for nine years. Wheat costs a louis d'or the one hundred and forty pounds. A laboring man receives sixty livres, and is fed and lodged. The trade of this country is principally rice, raw silk, and cheese.

April 23d. *Casino,* five miles from Milan. I examined another rice-beater of six pestles. They are eight feet nine inches long. Their ends, instead of being a truncated cone, have nine teeth of iron, bound closely together. Each tooth is a double pyramid, joined at the base. When put together, they stand with the upper ends placed in contact, so as to form them into one great cone, and the lower ends diverging. The upper are socketed into the end of the pestle, and the lower, when a little blunted by use, are not unlike the jaw teeth of the mammoth, with their studs. They say here, that pestles armed with these teeth, clean the rice faster, and break it less. The mortar, too, is of stone, which is supposed as good as wood, and more durable. One half of these pestles are always up. They rise about twenty-one inches, and each makes thirty-eight strokes in a minute; one hundred pounds of rough rice is put into the six mortars, and beaten somewhat less than a quarter of an hour. It is then taken out, put into a sifter of four feet diameter, suspended horizontally; sifted there; shifted into another of the same size; sifted there; returned to the mortars; beaten little more than a quarter of an hour; sifted again; and it is finished. The six pestles will clear four thousand pounds in twenty-four hours. The pound here is twenty-eight ounces; the ounce equal to that of Paris. The best rice requires half an hour's boiling; a more indifferent kind, somewhat less. To sow the rice, they first plough the ground, then level it with a drag harrow, and let on the water; when the earth has become soft, they smoothe it with a shovel under the water, and then sow the rice in the water.

*Rozzano*. Parmesan cheese. It is supposed this was formerly made at Parma, and took its name thence, but none is made there now. It is made through all the country extending from Milan for one hundred and fifty miles. The most is made about Lodi. The making of butter being connected with that of making cheese, both must be described together. There are, in the stables I saw, eighty-five cows, fed on hay and grass, not on grain. They are milked twice in twenty-four hours, ten cows yielding at the two milkings a brenta of milk, which is twenty-four of our gallons. The night's milk is scummed in the morning at daybreak, when the cows are milked again, and the new milk mixed with the old. In three hours, the whole mass is scummed a second time, the milk remaining in a kettle for cheese, and the cream being put into a cylindrical churn, shaped like a grindstone, eighteen inches radius, and fourteen inches thick. In this churn, there are three staves pointing inwardly, endwise, to break the current of the milk. Through its centre passes an iron axis, with a handle at each end. It is turned about an hour and a half by two men till the butter is produced. Then they pour off the buttermilk, and put in some water which they agitate backwards and forwards about a minute, and pour it off. They take out the butter, press it with their hands into loaves, and stamp it. It has no other washing. Sixteen American gallons of milk yield fifteen pounds of butter, which sell at twenty-four sous the pound.

The milk, which, after being scummed as before, had been put into a copper kettle, receives its due quantity of rennet, and is gently warmed, if the season requires it. In about four hours it becomes a slip. Then the whey begins to separate. A little of it is taken out. The curd is then thoroughly broken by a machine like a chocolate mill. A quarter of an ounce of saffron is put to seven brenta of milk, to give color to the cheese. The kettle is then moved over the hearth, and heated by a quick fire till the curd is hard enough, being broken into small lumps by continued stirring. It is moved off the fire, most of the whey taken out, the curd compressed into a globe by the hand, a linen cloth slipped under it, and it is drawn out in that. A loose hoop is then laid on a bench, and the curd, as wrapped in the linen, is put into the hoop; it is a little pressed by the hand, the hoop drawn tight and made fast. A board two inches thick is laid on it, and a stone on that of about twenty pounds weight. In an hour, the whey is run off, and the cheese finished. They sprinkle a little salt on it every other day in summer, and every day in winter, for six weeks. Seven brentas of milk make a cheese of fifty pounds, which requires six months to ripen, and is then dried to forty-five pounds. It sells on the spot for eighty-eight livres the one hundred pounds. There are now one hundred and fifty cheeses in this dairy. They are nineteen inches diameter, and six inches thick. They make a cheese a day in summer, and two in three days, or one in two days, in winter.

The whey is put back into the kettle, the butter-milk poured into it, and of this, they make a poor cheese for the country people. The whey of this is given to the hogs. Eight men suffice to keep the cows, and to do all the business of this dairy. Mascarponi, a kind of curd, is made by pouring some buttermilk into cream, which is thereby curdled, and is then pressed into a linen cloth.

The ice-houses at Rozzano are dug about fifteen feet deep, and twenty feet diameter, and poles are driven down all round. A conical thatched roof is then put over them, fifteen feet high, and pieces of wood are laid at the bottom, to keep the ice out of the water which drips from it, and goes off by a sink. Straw is laid on this wood, and then the house filled with ice, always putting straw between the ice and the walls, and covering ultimately with straw. About a third is lost by melting. Snow gives the most delicate flavor to creams; but ice is the most powerful congealer, and lasts longest. A tuft of trees surrounds these ice-houses.

Round Milan, to the distance of five miles, are corn, pasture, gardens, mulberries, willows, and vines. For in this State, rice ponds are not permitted within five miles of the cities.

*Binasco. Pavia.* Near Cassino the rice ponds begin, and continue to within five miles of Pavia, the whole ground being in rice, pasture, and willows. The pasture is in the rice grounds which are resting. In the neighborhood of Pavia, again, are corn, pasture, &c., as round Milan. They gave me green peas at Pavia.

April 24th. *Voghera. Tortona. Novi.* From Pavia to Novi, corn, pasture, vines, mulberries, willows; but no rice. The country continues plain, except that the Apennines are approaching on the left. The soil, always good, is dark till we approach Novi, and then red. We cross the Po where it is three hundred yards wide, in a pendulum boat. The rope is fastened on one side of the river, three hundred yards above, and supported by eight intermediate canoes, with little masts in them to give a greater elevation to the rope. We pass in eleven minutes. Women, girls, and boys are working with the hoe, and breaking the clods with mauls.

April 25th. *Voltaggio. Campo-Marone. Genoa.* At Novi, the Apennines begin to rise. Their growth of timber is oak, tall, small and knotty, and chesnut. We soon lose the walnut, ascending, and find it again, about one-fourth of the way down, on the south side. About half way down, we find figs and vines, which continue fine and in great abundance. The Apennines are mostly covered with soil, and are in corn, pasture, mulberries, and figs, in the parts before indicated. About half way from their foot to Genoa, at Campo-Marone, we find again the olive tree. Hence the produce becomes mixed, of all the kinds before mentioned. The method of sowing the Indian corn at Campo-Marone, is as follows: With a hoe shaped like the blade of a trowel, two feet long, and six inches broad at its upper end, pointed below, and a little curved, they make a trench. In that, they drop the grains six inches apart. Then two feet from that, they make another trench, throwing the earth they take out of that on the grain of the last one, with a singular slight and quickness; and so through the whole piece. The last trench is filled with the earth adjoining.

April 26th. *Genoa.* Strawberries at Genoa. Scaffold poles for the upper parts of a wall, as for the third story, rest on the window sills of the story below. Slate is used here for paving, for steps, for stairs (the rise as well as tread), and for fixed Venetian blinds. At the Palazzo Marcello Durazzo, benches with straight legs, and bottoms of cane. At the Palazzo del prencipe Lomellino, at Sestri, a phaeton with a canopy. At the former, tables folding into one plane. At Nervi they have peas, strawberries, &c., all the year round. The gardens of the Count Durazzo at Nervi, exhibit as rich a mixture of the *utile dulci,* as I ever saw. All the environs in Genoa, are in olives, figs, oranges, mulberries, corn, and garden stuff. Aloes in many places, but they never flower.

April 28th. *Noli.* The Apennines and Alps appear to me, to be one and the same continued ridge of mountains, separating everywhere the waters of the Adriatic Gulf from those of the Mediterranean. Where it forms an elbow, touching the Mediterranean, as a smaller circle touches a larger, within which it is inscribed, in the manner of a tangent, the name changes from Alps to Apennines. It is the beginning of the Apennines which constitutes the State of Genoa, the mountains there generally falling down in barren naked precipices into the sea. Wherever there is soil on the lower parts, it is principally in olives and figs, in vines also, mulberries, and corn. Where there are hollows well protected, there are oranges. This is the case at Golfo de Laspeze, Sestri, Bugiasco, Nervi, Genoa, Pegli, Savona, Finale, Oneglia (where there are abundance), St. Remo, Ventimiglia, Mantone, and Monaco. Noli, into which I was obliged to put, by a change of wind, is forty miles from Genoa. There are twelve hundred inhabitants in the village, and many separate houses round about. One of the precipices hanging over the sea is covered with aloes. But neither here, nor anywhere else I have been, could I procure satisfactory information that they ever flower. The current of testimony is to the contrary. Noli furnishes many fishermen. Paths penetrate up into the mountains in several directions, about three-fourths of a mile; but these are practicable only for asses and mules. I saw no cattle nor sheep in the settlement. The wine they make, is white and indifferent. A curious cruet for oil and vinegar in one piece, I saw here. A bishop resides here, whose revenue is two thousand livres, equal to sixty-six guineas. I heard a nightingale here.

April 29th. *Albenga.* In walking along the shore from Louano to this place, I saw no appearance of shells. The tops of the mountains are covered with snow, while there are olive trees, &c. on the lower parts. I do not remember to have seen assigned anywhere, the cause of the apparent color of the sea. Its water is generally clear and colorless, if taken up and viewed in a glass. That of the Mediterranean is remarkably so. Yet in the mass, it assumes, *by reflection,* the color of the sky or atmosphere, black, green, blue, according to the state of the weather. If any person wished to retire from his acquaintance, to live absolutely unknown, and yet in the midst of physical enjoyments, it should be in some of the little villages of this coast, where air, water and earth concur to offer what each has, most precious. Here are nightingales, beccaficas, ortolans, pheasants, partridges, quails, a superb climate, and the power of changing it from summer to winter at any moment, by ascending the mountains. The earth furnishes wine, oil, figs, oranges, and every production of the garden, in every season. The sea yields lobsters, crabs, oysters, thunny, sardines, anchovies, &c. Ortolans sell at this time, at thirty sous, equal to one shilling sterling, the dozen. At this season, they must be fattened. Through the whole of my route from Marseilles, I observe they plant a great deal of cane or reed, which is convenient while growing, as a cover from the cold and boisterous winds, and when cut, it serves for espaliers to vines, peas, &c. Through Piedmont, Lombardy, the Milanese, and Genoese, the garden bean is a great article of culture; almost as much so as corn. At Albenga, is a rich plain opening from between two ridges of mountains, triangularly, to the sea, and of several miles extent. Its growth is olives, figs, mulberries, vines, corn, and beans. There is some pasture. A bishop resides here, whose revenue is forty thousand livres. This place is said to be rendered unhealthy in summer, by the river which passes through the valley.

April 30th. *Oneglia.* The wind continuing contrary, I took mules at Albenga for Oneglia. Along this tract are many of the tree called carroubier, being a species of locust. It is the ceratonia siliqua of Linnæus. Its pods furnish food for horses, and also for the poor, in time of scarcity. It abounds in Naples and Spain. Oneglia and Port Maurice, which are within a mile of each other, are considerable places, and in a rich country. At St. Remo, are abundance of oranges and lemons, and some palm trees.

May 1st. *Ventimiglia. Menton. Monaco. Nice.* At Bordighera, between Ventimiglia and Menton, are extensive plantations of palms, on the hill as well as in the plain. They bring fruit, but it does not ripen. Something is made of the midrib, which is in great demand at Rome, on the Palm Sunday, and which renders this tree profitable here. From Menton to Monaco, there is more good land, and extensive groves of oranges and lemons. Orange water sells here at forty sous, equal to sixteen pence sterling, the American quart. The distances on this coast, are, from Laspeze, at the eastern end of the territories of Genoa, to Genoa, fifty-five miles, geometrical; to Savona, thirty; Albenga, thirty; Oneglia, twenty; Ventimiglia, twenty-five; Monaco, ten; Nice, ten; in the whole, one hundred and eighty miles. A superb road might be made along the margin of the sea from Laspeze, where the champaign country of Italy opens, to Nice, where the Alps go off northwardly, and the post roads of France begin; and it might even follow the margin of the sea quite to Cette. By this road, travellers would enter Italy without crossing the Alps, and all the little insulated villages of the Genoese would communicate together, and in time form one continued village along that road.

May 3d. *Luc. Brignolles. Tourves. Pourcieux. La Galiniere.* Long, small mountains, very rocky, the soil reddish from bad to middling; in olives, grapes, mulberries, vines and corn. Brignolles is in an extensive plain, between two ridges of mountains, and along a water course which continues to Tourves. Thence to Pourcieux we cross a mountain, low and easy. The country is rocky and poor. To La Galiniere are waving grounds, bounded by mountains of rock at a little distance. There are some inclosures of dry wall from Luc to La Galiniere; also, sheep and hogs. There is snow on the high mountains. I see no plums in the vicinities of Brignolles; which makes me conjecture that the celebrated plum of that name, is not derived from this place.

May 8. *Orgon. Avignon. Vaucluse.* Orgon is on the Durance. From thence, its plain opens till it becomes common with that of the Rhone; so that from Orgon to Avignon is entirely a plain of rich dark loam, which is in willows, mulberries, vines, corn and pasture. A very few figs. I see no olives in this plain. Probably the cold winds have too much power here. From the Bac de Nova (where we cross the Durance) to Avignon, is about nine American miles; and from the same Bac to Vaucluse, eleven miles. In the valley of Vaucluse, and on the hills impending over it, are olive trees. The stream issuing from the fountain of Vaucluse is about twenty yards wide, four or five feet deep, and of such rapidity that it could not be stemmed by a canoe. They are now mowing hay, and gathering mulberry leaves. The high mountains just back of Vaucluse are covered with snow. Fine trout in the stream of Vaucluse, and the valley abounds peculiarly with nightingales. The vin blanc de M. de Rochequde of Avignon, resembles dry Lisbon. He sells it at six years old for twenty-two sous the bottle, the price of the bottle, &c., included.

*Avignon. Remoulins.* Some good plains, but generally hills, stony and poor. In olives, mulberries, vines and corn. Where it is waste the growth is, chenevert, box, furze, thyme and rosemary.

May 10. *Nismes. Lunel.* Hills on the right, plains on the left. The soil reddish, a little stony, and of middling quality. The produce, olives, mulberries, vines, corn, St. foin. No wood and few inclosures. Lunel is famous for its vin de muscat blanc, thence called Lunel, or vin muscat de Lunel. It is made from the raisin muscat, without fermenting the grain in the hopper. When fermented it makes a red muscat, taking the tinge from the dissolution of the skin of the grape, which injures the quality. When a red muscat is required, they prefer coloring it with a little Alicant wine. But the white is best. The piece of two hundred and forty bottles, after being properly drawn off from its lees, and ready for bottling, costs from one hundred and twenty to two hundred livres, the first quality and last vintage. It cannot be bought old, the demand being sufficient to take it all the first year. They are not more than from fifty to one hundred pieces a year, made of this first quality. A *setterie* yields about one piece, and my informer supposes there are about two setteries in an arpent. Portage to Paris by land is fifteen livres the quintal. The best *recoltes* are those of M. Bouquet and M. Tremoulet. The vines are in rows four feet apart, every way.

May 11. *Montpelier.* Snow on the Cevennes, still visible from here. With respect to the muscat grape, of which the wine is made, there are two kinds, the red and the white. The first has a red skin, but a white juice. If it be fermented in the *cuve,* the coloring matter which resides in the skin is imparted to the wine. If not fermented in the cuve, the wine is white. Of the white grape, only a white wine can be made. The species of St. foin cultivated here by the name of sparsette, is the hedysarum onobryches. They cultivate a great deal of madder (garance) rubia tinctorum here, which is said to be immensely profitable. Monsieur de Gouan tells me that the pine, of which they use the burs for fuel, is the pinus sativus, being two leaved. They use for an edging to the borders of their gardens, the santolina, which they call garderobe. I find the yellow clover here, in a garden; and the large pigeon succeeding well, confined in a house.

May 12. *Frontignan.* Some tolerably good plains in olives, vines, corn, St. foin, and lucerne. A great proportion of the hills are waste. There are some inclosures of stone, and some sheep. The first four years of madder are unproductive; the fifth and sixth yield the whole value of the land. Then it must be renewed. The sparsette is the common or true St. foin. It lasts about five years; in the best land it is cut twice, in May and September, and yields three thousand pounds of dry hay to the setterie the first cutting, and five hundred pounds the second. The setterie is of seventy-five *dextres en tout sens,* supposed about two arpents. Lucerne is the best of all forage; it is sowed here in the broadcast, and lasts about twelve or fourteen years. It is cut four times a year, and yields six thousand pounds of dry hay at the four cuttings, to the setterie. The territory in which the vin muscat de Frontignan is made, is about a league of three thousand toises long, and one-fourth of a league broad. The soil is reddish and stony, often as much stone as soil. On the left, it is a plain, on the right, hills. There are made about one thousand pieces (of two hundred and fifty bottles each) annually, of which six hundred are of the first quality, made on the coteaux. Of these, Madame Soubeinan makes two hundred, Monsieur Reboulle, ninety, Monsieur Lambert, médicin de la faculté de Montpelier, sixty, Monsieur Thomas, notaire, fifty, Monsieur Argilliers, fifty, Monsieur Audibert, forty; equal to four hundred and ninety; and there are some small proprietors who make small quantities. The first quality is sold, brut, for one hundred and twenty livres the piece; but it is then thick, and must have a winter and the fouet to render it potable and brilliant. The fouet is like a chocolate mill, the handle of iron, the brush of stiff hair. In bottles, this wine costs twenty-four sous, the bottles, &c., included. It is potable the April after it is made, is best that year, and after ten years begins to have a pitchy taste, resembling it to Malaga. It is not permitted to ferment more than half a day, because it would not be so liquorish. The best color, and its natural one, is the amber. By force of whipping, it is made white, but loses flavor. There are but two or three pieces a year of red muscat made; there being but one vineyard of the red grape, which belongs to a baker called Pascal. This sells in bottles at thirty sous, the bottle included. Rondelle, negociant en vin, Porte St. Bernard, fauxbourg St. Germains, Paris, buys three hundred pieces of the first quality every year. The coteaux yield about half a piece to the setterie, the plains a whole piece. The inferior quality is not at all esteemed. It is bought by the merchants of Cette, as is also the wine of Béziers, and sold by them for Frontignan of the first quality. They sell thirty thousand pieces a year under that name. The town of Frontignan marks its casks with a hot iron: an individual of that place having two casks emptied, was offered forty livres for the empty cask by a merchant of Cette. The town of Frontignan contains about two thousand inhabitants; it is almost on the level of the ocean. Transportation to Paris is fifteen livres the quintal, and takes fifteen days. The price of packages is about eight livres eight sous the one hundred bottles. A setterie of good vineyard sells for from three hundred and fifty to five hundred livres, and rents for fifty livres. A laboring man hires at one hundred and fifty livres the year, and is fed and lodged; a woman at half as much. Wheat sells at ten livres the setterie, which weighs one hundred pounds, poids de table. They make some Indian corn here, which is eaten by the poor. The olives do not extend northward of this into the country, above twelve or fifteen leagues. In general, the olive country in Languedoc is about fifteen leagues broad. More of the waste lands between Frontignan and Mirval are capable of culture; but it is a marshy country, very subject to fever and ague, and generally unhealthy. Thence arises, as is said, a want of hands.

*Cette*. There are in this town about ten thousand inhabitants. Its principal commerce is wine; it furnishes great quantities of grape pomice for making verdigrise. They have a very growing commerce; but it is kept under by the privileges of Marseilles.

May 13. *Agde*. On the right of the Etang de Tau, are plains of some width, then hills, in olives, vines, mulberry, corn and pasture. On the left, a narrow sand bar separating the Etang from the sea, along which it is proposed to make a road from Cette to Agde. In this case, the post would lead from Montpelier, by Cette and Agde, to Béziers, being leveller, and an hour, or an hour and a half nearer. Agde contains six or eight thousand inhabitants.

May 14. *Béziers*. Rich plains in corn, St. foin and pasture; hills at a little distance to the right, in olives; the soil both of hill and plain is red, going from Agde to Béziers. But at Béziers the country becomes hilly, and is in olives, St. foin, pasture, some vines and mulberries.

May 15. *Béziers. Argilies. Le Saumal*. From Argilies to Saumal are considerable plantations of vines. Those on the red hills to the right, are said to produce good wine. No wood, no inclosures. There are sheep and good cattle. The Pyrenees are covered with snow. I am told they are so in certain parts all the year. The canal of Languedoc, along which I now travel, is six toises wide at bottom, and ten toises at the surface of the water, which is one toise deep. The barks which navigate it are seventy and eighty feet long, and seventeen or eighteen feet wide. They are drawn by one horse, and worked by two hands, one of which is generally a woman. The locks are mostly kept by women, but the necessary operations are much too laborious for them. The encroachments by the men, on the offices proper for the women, is a great derangement in the order of things. Men are shoemakers, tailors, upholsterers, stay-makers, mantua-makers, cooks, housekeepers, house-cleaners, bed-makers, they coiffe the ladies, and bring them to bed: the women, therefore, to live, are obliged to undertake the offices which they abandon. They become porters, carters, reapers, sailors, lock-keepers, smitters on the anvil, cultivators of the earth, &c. Can we wonder, if such of them as have a little beauty, prefer easier courses to get their livelihood, as long as that beauty lasts? Ladies who employ men in the offices which should be reserved for their sex, are they not bawds in effect? For every man whom they thus employ, some girl, whose place he has thus taken, is driven to whoredom. The passage of the eight locks at Béziers, that is, from the opening of the first to the last gate, took one hour and thirty-three minutes. The bark in which I go, is about thirty-five feet long, drawn by one horse, and goes from two to three geographical miles an hour. The canal yields abundance of carp and eel. I see also small fish resembling our perch and chub. Some plants of white clover and some of yellow, on the banks of the canal near Capestan; santolina also, and a great deal of yellow iris. Met a raft of about three hundred and fifty beams, forty feet long, and twelve or thirteen inches in diameter, formed into fourteen rafts, tacked together. The extensive and numerous fields of St. foin in general bloom, are beautiful.

May 16th. *Le Saumal. Marseillette.* May 17th. *Marseillette. Carcassonne.* From Saumal to Carcassonne, we have always the river Aube close on our left. This river runs in the valley between the Cevennes and Pyrenees, serving as the common receptacle for both their waters. It is from fifty to one hundred and fifty yards wide, always rapid, rocky, and insusceptible of navigation. The canal passes in the side of hills made by that river, overlooks the river itself, and its plains, and has its prospect ultimately terminated, on one side, by mountains of rock overtopped by the Pyrenees, on the other, by small mountains, sometimes of rock, sometimes of soil, overtopped by the Cevennes. Marseillette is on a ridge, which separates the river Aube from the Etang de Marseillette. The canal, in its approach to this village, passes the ridge, and rides along the front, overlooking the Etang, and the plains on its border; and having passed the village, re-crosses the ridge, and resumes its general ground in front of the Aube. The land is in corn, St. foin, pasture, vines, mulberries, willows, and olives.

May 18th. *Carcassonne. Castelnaudari.* Opposite to Carcassonne, the canal receives the river Fresquel, about thirty yards wide, which is its substantial supply of water from hence to Béziers. From Béziers to Agde, the river Orb furnishes it, and the Eraut, from Agde to the Etang de Thau. By means of ecluse ronde at Agde, the waters of the Eraut can be thrown towards Béziers, to aid those of the Orb, as far as the ecluse de Porcaraigne, nine geometrical miles. Where the Fresquel enters the canal, there is, on the opposite side, a waste, to let off the superfluous waters. The horseway is continued over this waste, by a bridge of stone of eighteen arches. I observe them fishing in the canal, with a skimming net of about fifteen feet diameter, with which they tell me they catch carp. Flax in blossom. Neither strawberries nor peas yet at Carcassonne. The Windsor bean just come to table. From the ecluse de la Lande we see the last olive trees near a métairie, or farm house, called la Lande. On a review of what I have seen and heard of this tree, the following seem to be its northern limits. Beginning on the Atlantic, at the Pyrenees, and along them to the meridian of la Lande, or of Carcassonne; up that meridian to the Cevennes, as they begin just there to raise themselves high enough to afford it shelter. Along the Cevennes, to the parallel of forty-five degrees of latitude, and along that parallel (crossing the Rhone near the mouth of the Isere) to the Alps; thence along the Alps and Apennines, to what parallel of latitude I know not. Yet here the tracing of the line becomes the most interesting. For from the Atlantic, so far, we see this production the effect of shelter and latitude combined. But where does it venture to launch forth unprotected by shelter, and by the mere force of latitude alone? Where for instance does its northern limits cross the Adriatic? I learn that the olive tree resists cold to eight degrees of Reaumur below the freezing point, which corresponds to fourteen above zero of Fahrenheit; and that the orange resists to four degrees below freezing of Reaumur, which is twenty-three degrees above zero of Fahrenheit.

May 19th. *Castelnaudari. St. Feriol. Escamaze. Lampy.* Some sheep and cattle; no inclosures. St. Feriol, Escamaze, and Lampy are in the montagnes noires. The country almost entirely waste. Some of it in shrubbery. The voute d'Escamaze is of one hundred and thirty-five yards. Round about Castelnaudari, the country is hilly, as it has been constantly from Béziers; it is very rich. Where it is plain, or nearly plain, the soil is black; in general, however, it is hilly and reddish, and in corn. They cultivate a great deal of Indian corn here, which they call millet; it is planted but not yet up.

May 20th. *Castelnaudari. Naurouze. Villefranche. Baziege.* At Naurouze, is the highest ground which the canal had to pass, between the two seas. It became necessary then to find water still higher to bring it here. The river Fresquel heading by its two principal branches in the montagnes noires, a considerable distance off to the eastward, the springs of the most western one were brought together, and conducted to Naurouze, where its waters are divided, part furnishing the canal towards the ocean, the rest towards the Mediterranean, as far as the ecluse de Fresquel, where, as has been before noted, the Lampy branch, and the Alzau, under the name of the Fresquel, enter.

May 20th. They have found that a lock of six pieds is best; however, eight pieds is well enough. Beyond this, it is bad. Monsieur Pin tells me of a lock of thirty pieds, made in Sweden, of which it is impossible to open the gates. They therefore divided it into four locks. The small gates of the locks of this canal, have six square pieds of surface. They tried the machinery of the jack for opening them. They were more easily opened, but very subject to be deranged, however strongly made. They returned therefore to the original wooden screw, which is excessively slow and laborious. I calculate that five minutes are lost at every basin by this screw, which, on the whole number of basis, is one eighth of the time necessary to navigate the canal; and of course, if a method of lifting the gate at one stroke could be found, it would reduce the passage from eight to seven days, and the freight equally. I suggested to Monsieur Pin and others, a quadrantal gate, turning on a pivot, and lifted by a lever like a pump handle, aided by a windlass and cord, if necessary. He will try it, and inform me of the success. The price of transportation from Cette to Bourdeaux, through the canal and Garonne is —— the quintal; round by the straits of Gibraltar is ——. Two hundred and forty barks, the largest of twenty-two hundred quintals (or say, in general, of one hundred tons) suffice to perform the business of this canal, which is stationary, having neither increased nor diminished for many years. When pressed, they can pass and repass between Toulouse and Béziers in fourteen days; but sixteen is the common period. The canal is navigated ten and a half months of the year; the other month and a half being necessary to lay it dry, cleanse it and repair the works. This is done in July and August, when there would, perhaps, be a want of water.

May 21st. *Baziege. Toulouse.* The country continues hilly, but very rich. It is in mulberries, willows, some vines, corn, maize, pasture, beans, flax. A great number of chateaux and good houses, in the neighborhood of the canal. The people partly in farm houses, partly in villages. I suspect the farm houses are occupied by the farmers, while the laborers (who are mostly by the day) reside in the villages. Neither strawberries nor peas yet at Baziege or Toulouse. Near the latter, are some fields of yellow clover.

At Toulouse the canal ends. It has four communications with the Mediterranean. 1. Through the ponds of Thau, Frontignan, Palavas, Maguelone, and Manjo, the canal de la Radela Aiguesmortes, le canal des Salines de Pecair, and the arm of the Rhone called Bras de fer, which ends at Fourgues, opposite to Arles, and thence down the Rhone. 2. At Cette, by a canal of a few hundred toises, leading out of the Etang de Thau into the sea. The vessels pass the Etang, through a length of nine thousand toises, with sails. 3. At Agde, by the river Eraut, twenty-five hundred toises. It has but five or six pieds of water at its mouth. It is joined to the canal at the upper part of this communication, by a branch of a canal two hundred and seventy toises long. 4. At Narbonne, by a canal they are now opening, which leads from the great canal near the aqueduct of the river Cesse, twenty-six hundred toises, into the Aude. This new canal will have five lock-basins of about twelve pieds fall, each. Then you are to cross the Aude very obliquely, and descend a branch of it six thousand toises, through four lock-basins to Narbonne, and from Narbonne down the same branch, twelve hundred toises into the Etang de Sigen, across that Etang four thousand toises, issuing at an inlet, called Grau de la nouvelle, into the Gulph of Lyons. But only vessels of thirty or forty tons can enter this inlet. Of these four communications, that of Cette only, leads to a deep sea-port, because the exit is there by a canal, and not a river. Those by the Rhone, Eraut, and Aude, are blocked up by bars at the mouths of those rivers. It is remarkable, that all the rivers running into the Mediterranean, are obstructed at their entrance by bars and shallows, which often change their position. This is the case with the Nile, Tyber, the Po, the Lez, le Lyoron, the Orbe, the Gly, the Tech, the Tet, &c. Indeed, the formation of these bars seems not confined to the mouths of the rivers, though it takes place at them, more certainly. Along almost the whole of the coast, from Marseilles towards the Pyrenees, banks of sand are thrown up, parallel with the coast, which have insulated portions of the sea, that is, formed them into etangs, ponds, or sounds, through which here and there, narrow and shallow inlets only, are preserved by the currents of the rivers. These sounds fill up in time, with the mud and sand deposited in them by the rivers. Thus the Etang de Vendres, navigated formerly by vessels of sixty tons, is now nearly filled up by the mud and sand of the Aude. The Vistre and Vidourle which formerly emptied themselves into the Gulf of Lyons, are now received by the Etangs de Manjo and Aiguesmortes, that is to say, the part of the Gulf of Lyons which formerly received, and still receives those rivers, is now cut off from the sea by a bar of sand, which has been thrown up in it, and has formed it into sounds. Other proofs that the land gains there on the sea, are, that the towns of St. Gilles and Notre dame d'asposts, formerly sea ports, are now far from the sea, and that Aiguesmortes, where are still to be seen the iron rings to which vessels were formerly moored, and where St. Louis embarked for Palestine, has now in its vicinities, only ponds which cannot be navigated, and communicates with the sea by an inlet, called Grau du roy, through which only fishing barks can pass. It is pretty well established, that all the Delta of Egypt has been formed by the depositions of the Nile, and the alluvions of the sea, and it is probable that that operation is still going on. Has this peculiarity of the Mediterranean any connection with the scantiness of its tides, which even at the equinoxes, are of two or three feet only?

The communication from the western end of the canal to the ocean is by the river Garonne. This is navigated by flat boats of eight hundred quintals, when the water is well; but when it is scanty, these boats carry only two hundred quintals till they get to the mouth of the Tarn. It has been proposed to open a canal that far, from Toulouse, along the right side of the river.

May 22d. *Toulouse.* 23d. *Agen.* 24th. *Castres. Bourdeaux.* The Garonne and rivers emptying into it, make extensive and rich plains, which are in mulberries, willows, corn, maize, pasture, beans and flax. The hills are in corn, maize, beans, and a considerable proportion of vines. There seems to be as much maize as corn in this country. Of the latter, there is more rye than wheat. The maize is now up, and about three inches high. It is sowed in rows two feet, or two and a half feet apart, and is pretty thick in the row. Doubtless they mean to thin it. There is a great deal of forage they call farouche. It is a species of red trefoil, with few leaves, a very coarse stalk, and a cylindrical blossom of two inches in length, and three quarters of an inch in diameter, consisting of floscules, exactly as does that of the red clover. It seems to be a coarse food, but very plentiful. They say it is for their oxen. These are very fine, large, and cream-colored. The services of the farm, and of transportation, are performed chiefly by them. There are a few horses and asses, but no mules. Even in the city of Bourdeaux, we see scarcely any beasts of draught but oxen. When we cross the Garonne at Langon, we find the plains entirely of sand and gravel, and they continue so to Bourdeaux. Where they are capable of anything, they are in vines, which are in rows, four, five, or six feet apart, and sometimes more. Near Langon is Saulerne, where the best white wines of Bourdeaux are made. The waste lands are in fern, furze, shrubbery, and dwarf trees. The farmers live on their farms. At Agen, Castres, Bourdeaux, strawberries and peas are now brought to table, so that the country on the canal of Languedoc seems to have later seasons than that east and west of it. What can be the cause? To the eastward, the protection of the Cevennes makes the warm season advance sooner. Does the neighborhood of the Mediterranean co-operate? And does that of the ocean mollify and advance the season to the westward? There are ortolans at Agen, but none at Bourdeaux. The buildings on the canal and the Garonne are mostly of brick, the size of the bricks the same with that of the ancient Roman brick, as seen in the remains of their buildings in this country. In those of a circus at Bourdeaux, considerable portions of which are standing, I measured the bricks, and found them nineteen or twenty inches long, eleven or twelve inches wide, and from one and a half to two inches thick; their texture as fine, compact, and solid as that of porcelain. The bricks now made, though of the same dimensions, are not so fine. They are burnt in a kind of furnace, and make excellent work. The elm tree shows itself at Bourdeaux, peculiarly proper for being spread flat for arbors. Many are done in this way on the quay des Charterons. Strawberries, peas, and cherries at Bourdeaux.

May 24th, 25th, 26th, 27th, 28th. *Bourdeaux.* The cantons in which the most celebrated wines of Bourdeaux are made, are Medoc down the river, Grave adjoining the city, and the parishes next above; all on the same side of the river. In the first is made red wine principally, in the two last, white. In Medoc, they plant the vines in cross rows of three and a half pieds. They keep them so low, that poles extended along the rows one way, horizontally, about fifteen or eighteen inches above the ground, serve to tie the vines to, and leave the cross row open to the plough. In Grave, they set the plants in quincunx, *i.e.,* in equilateral triangles of three and a half pieds every side; and they stick a pole of six or eight feet high to every vine, separately. The vine stock is sometimes three or four feet high. They find these two methods equal in culture, duration, quantity and quality. The former, however, admits the alternative of tending by hand or with the plough. The grafting of the vine, though a critical operation, is practised with success. When the graft has taken, they bend it into the earth, and let it take root above the scar. They begin to yield an indifferent wine at three years old, but not a good one till twenty-five years, nor after eighty, when they begin to yield less, and worse, and must be renewed. They give three or four workings in the year, each worth seventy, or seventy-five livres the journal, which is of eight hundred and forty square toises, and contains about three thousand plants. They dung a little in Medoc and Grave, because of the poverty of the soil; but very little, as more would affect the wine. The journal yields, *communibus annis,* about three pieces (of two hundred and forty or two hundred and fifty bottles each). The vineyards of first quality are all worked by their proprietors. Those of the second rent for three hundred livres the journal, those of the third at two hundred livres. They employ a kind of overseer at four or five hundred livres the year, finding him lodging and drink; but he feeds himself. He superintends and directs, though he is expected to work but little. If the proprietor has a garden, the overseer tends that. They never hire laborers by the year. The day wages for a man are thirty sous, a woman's fifteen sous, feeding themselves. The women make the bundles of sarment, weed, pull off the snails, tie the vines, and gather the grapes. During the vintage, they are paid high and fed well.

Of red wines, there are four vineyards of the first quality, *viz.*, 1. Château Margau, belonging to the Marquis d'Agicourt, who makes about one hundred and fifty tons, of one thousand bottles each. He has engaged to Jernon, a merchant. 2. La Tour de Segur, en Saint Lambert, belonging to Monsieur Miresmenil, who makes one hundred and twenty-five tons. 3. Hautbrion, belonging two thirds to M. le Comte de Femelle, who has engaged to Barton, a merchant; the other third to the Comte de Toulouse, at Toulouse. The whole is seventy-five tons. 4. Château de la Fite, belonging to the President Pichard, at Bourdeaux, who makes one hundred and seventy-five tons. The wines of the three first are not in perfection till four years old; those of De la Fite, being somewhat lighter, are good at three years, that is, the crop of 1786 is good in the spring of 1789. These growths of the year 1783 sell now at two thousand livres the ton; those of 1784, on account of the superior quality of that vintage, sell at twenty-four hundred livres; those of 1785, at eighteen hundred livres; those of 1786, at eighteen hundred livres, though they had sold at first for only fifteen hundred livres. Red wines of the second quality, are Rozan, Dabbadie or Lionville, la Rose, Quirouen, Durfort; in all eight hundred tons, which sell at one thousand livres, new. The third class are, Calons, Mouton, Gassie, Arboete, Pontette, de Ferme, Candale; in all two thousand tons, at eight or nine hundred livres. After these, they are reckoned common wines, and sell from five hundred livres down to one hundred and twenty livres the ton. All red wines decline after a certain age, losing color, flavor and body. Those of Bourdeaux begin to decline at about seven years old.

Of white wines, those made in the canton of Grave are most esteemed at Bourdeaux. The best crops are, 1. Pontac, which formerly belonged to M. de Pontac, but now to M. de Lamont. He makes forty tons, which sell at four hundred livres, new. 2. St. Brise, belonging to M. de Pontac; thirty tons, at three hundred and fifty livres. 3. De Carbonius, belonging to the Benedictine monks, who make fifty tons, and never selling till three or four years old, get eight hundred livres the ton. Those made in the three parishes next above Grave, and more esteemed at Paris, are, 1. Sauterne. The best crop belonging to M. Diquem at Bourdeaux, or to M. de Salus, his son-in-law; one hundred and fifty tons, at three hundred livres, new, and six hundred livres, old. The next best crop is M. de Filotte's; one hundred tons, sold at the same price. 2. Prignac. The best is the President du Roy's, at Bourdeaux. He makes one hundred and seventy-five tons, which sell at three hundred livres, new, and six hundred livres, old. Those of 1784, for their extraordinary quality, sell at eight hundred livres. 3 Barsac. The best belongs to the President Pichard, who makes one hundred and fifty tons, at two hundred and eighty livres, new, and six hundred livres, old. Sauterne is the pleasantest; next Prignac, and lastly Barsac; but Barsac is the strongest; next Prignac, and lastly Sauterne; and all stronger than Grave. There are other good crops made in the same parishes of Sauterne, Prignac, and Barsac; but none as good as these. There is a virgin wine, which, though made of a red grape, is of a light rose color, because, being made without pressure, the coloring matter of the skin does not mix with the juice. There are other white wines, from the preceding prices down to seventy-five livres. In general, the white wines keep longest. They will be in perfection till fifteen or twenty years of age. The best vintage now to be bought, is of 1784; both of red and white. There has been no other good year since 1779.

The celebrated vineyards before mentioned are plains, as is generally the canton of Medoc, and that of the Grave. The soil of Hautbrion, particularly, which I examined, is a sand, in which is near as much round gravel or small stone, and very little loam; and this is the general soil of Medoc. That of Pontac, which I examined also, is a little different. It is clayey, with a fourth or fifth of fine rotten stone; and at two feet depth it becomes all a rotten stone. M. de Lamont tells me he has a kind of grape without seeds, which I did not formerly suppose to exist; but I saw at Marseilles dried raisins from Smyrna without seeds. I saw in his farm at Pontac some plants of white clover, and a good deal of yellow; also some small peach trees in the open ground. The principal English wine merchants at Bourdeaux are, Jemon, Barton, Johnston, Foster, Skinner, Copinger and McCartey; the chief French wine merchants are, Feger, Nerac, Bruneau, Jauge, and du Verget. Desgrands, a wine broker, tells me they never mix the wines of first quality; but that they mix the inferior ones to improve them. The smallest wines make the best brandy. They yield about a fifth or sixth.

May 28th, 29th. From Bourdeaux to Blaye, the country near the river is hilly, chiefly in vines, some corn, some pasture; further out, are plains, boggy and waste. The soil, in both cases, clay and grit. Some sheep on the waste. To Etauliere, we have sometimes boggy plains, sometimes waving grounds and sandy, always poor, generally waste, in fern and furze, with some corn however, interspersed. To Mirambeau and St. Genis, it is hilly, poor, and mostly waste. There are some corn and maize however, and better trees than usual. Towards Pons, it becomes a little red, mostly rotten stone. There are vines, corn, and maize, which is up. At Pons we approach the Clarenton; the country becomes better, a blackish mould mixed with a rotten chalky stone; a great many vines, corn, maize, and farouche. From Lajart to Saintes and Rochefort, the soil is reddish, its foundation a chalky rock, at about a foot depth; in vines, corn, maize, clover, lucerne, and pasture. There are more and better trees than I have seen in all my journey; a great many apple and cherry trees; fine cattle and many sheep. May 30th. From Rochefort to le Rochex, it is sometimes hilly and red, with a chalky foundation, middling good; in corn, pasture, and some waste; sometimes it is reclaimed marsh, in clover and corn, except the parts accessible to the tide, which are in wild grass. About Rochelle, it is a low plain. Towards Usseau, and half way to Marans, level highlands, red, mixed with an equal quantity of broken chalk; mostly in vines, some corn and pasture; then to Marans and half way to St. Hermines, it is reclaimed marsh, dark, tolerably good, and all in pasture; there we rise to plains a little higher, red, with a chalky foundation, boundless to the eye, and altogether in corn and maize. May 31st. At St. Hermines, the country becomes very hilly, a red clay mixed with chalky stone, generally waste, in furze and broom, with some patches of corn and maize; and so it continues to Chantenay, and St. Fulgent. Through the whole of this road from Bourdeaux, are frequent hedge rows, and small patches of forest wood, not good, yet better than I had seen in the preceding part of my journey. Towards Montaigu, the soil mends a little; the cultivated parts in corn and pasture, the uncultivated in broom. It is in very small inclosures of ditch and quickset. On approaching the Loire to Nantes, the country is leveller; the soil from Rochelle to this place, may be said to have been sometimes red, but oftener grey, and always on a chalky foundation. The last census, of about 1770, made one hundred and twenty thousand inhabitants at Nantes. They conjecture there are now one hundred and fifty thousand, which equals it to Bourdeaux. June 1st, 2d. The country from Nantes to L'Orient is very hilly and poor, the soil grey; nearly half is waste, in furze and broom, among which is some poor grass. The cultivated parts are in corn, some maize, a good many apple trees; no vines. All is in small inclosures of quick hedge and ditch. There are patches and hedge-rows of forest wood, not quite deserving the name of timber. The people are mostly in villages; they eat rye bread, and are ragged. The villages announce a general poverty, as does every other appearance. Women smite on the anvil, and work with the hoe, and cows are yoked to labor. There are great numbers of cattle, insomuch that butter is their staple. Neither asses nor mules; yet it is said that the fine mules I have met with on my journey, are raised in Poictou. There are but few châteaux here. I observe mill ponds, and hoes with long handles. Have they not, in common with us, derived these from England, of which Bretagne is probably a colony? L'Orient is supposed to contain twenty-five thousand inhabitants. They tell me here, that to make a reasonable profit on potash and pearl ash, as bought in America, the former should sell at thirty livres, the latter thirty-six livres the quintal. Of turpentine they make no use in their vessels. Bayonne furnishes pitch enough; but tar is in demand, and ours sells well. The tower of L'Orient is sixty-five pieds above the level of the sea, one hundred and twenty pieds high, twenty-five pieds in diameter; the stairs four feet radius, and cost thirty thousand livres, besides the materials of the old tower.

June 3d, 4th, 5th. The country and productions from L'Orient to Rennes, and from Rennes to Nantes, are precisely similar to those from Nantes to L'Orient. About Rennes, it is somewhat leveller, perhaps less poor, and almost entirely in pasture. The soil always grey. Some small separate houses which seem to be the residence of laborers, or very small farmers; the walls frequently of mud, and the roofs generally covered with slate. Great plantations of walnut, and frequently of pine. Some apple trees and sweet briar still in bloom, and broom generally so. I have heard no nightingale since the last day of May. There are gates in this country made in such a manner, that the top rail of the gate overshoots backwards the hind post, so as to counterpoise the gate, and prevent its swagging.

*Nantes.* Vessels of eight feet draught only, can come to Nantes. Those which are larger, lie at Point Boeuf, ten leagues below Nantes, and five leagues above the mouth of the river. There is a continued navigation from Nantes to Paris, through the Loire, the canal de Briare and the Seine. Carolina rice is preferred to that of Lombardy for the Guinea trade, because it requires less water to boil it.

June 6th, 7th, 8th. *Nantes. Ancenis. Angers. Tours.* Ascending the Loire from Nantes, the road, as far as Angers, leads over the hills, which are grey, oftener below than above mediocrity, and in corn, pasture, vines, some maize, flax, and hemp. There are no waste lands. About the limits of Bretagne and Anjou, which are between Loriottiere and St. George, the lands change for the better. Here and there, we get views of the plains on the Loire, of some extent, and good appearance, in corn and pasture. After passing Angers, the road is raised out of the reach of inundations, so as at the same time, to ward them off from the interior plains. It passes generally along the river side; but sometimes leads through the plains, which, after we pass Angers, become extensive and good, in corn, pasture, some maize, hemp, flax, peas, and beans; many willows, also poplars and walnuts. The flax is near ripe. Sweet briar in general bloom. Some broom here still, on which the cattle and sheep browse in winter and spring, when they have no other green food; and the hogs eat the blossoms and pods, in spring and summer. This blossom, though disagreeable when smelt in a small quantity, is of delicious fragrance when there is a whole field of it. There are some considerable vineyards in the river plains, just before we reach Les trois volées, (which is at the one hundred and thirty-sixth mile stone) and after that, where the hills on the left come into view, they are mostly in vines. Their soil is clayey and stony, a little reddish, and of southern aspect. The hills on the other side of the river, looking to the north, are not in vines. There is very good wine made on these hills; not equal indeed to the Bourdeaux of best quality, but to that of good quality, and like it. It is a great article of exportation from Anjou and Touraine, and probably is sold abroad, under the name of Bourdeaux. They are now mowing the first crop of hay. All along both hills of the Loire, is a mass of white stone, not durable, growing black with time, and so soft, that the people cut their houses out of the solid, with all the partitions, chimneys, doors, &c. The hill sides resemble cony burrows, full of inhabitants. The borders of the Loire, are almost a continued village. There are many châteaux; many cattle, sheep, and horses; some asses.

Tours is at the one hundred and nineteenth mile stone. Being desirous of inquiring here into a fact stated by Voltaire, in his Questions Encyclopédiques, articles Coquilles, relative to the growth of shells unconnected with animal bodies, at the Château of Monsieur de la Sauvagiere, near Tours, I called on Monsieur Gentil, premier secretaire de l'Intendance, to whom the Intendant had written on my behalf, at the request of the Marquis de Chastellux. I stated to him the fact as advanced by Voltaire, and found he was, of all men, the best to whom I could have addressed myself. He told me he had been in correspondence with Voltaire on that very subject, and was perfectly acquainted with Monsieur de la Sauvagiere, and the Faluniere where the fact is said to have taken place. It is at the Château de Grillemont, six leagues from Tours, on the road to Bourdeaux, belonging now to Monsieur d'Orcai. He says, that de la Sauvagiere was a man of truth, and might be relied on for whatever facts he stated as of his own observations; but that he was overcharged with imagination, which, in matters of opinion and theory, often led him beyond his facts; that this feature in his character had appeared principally in what he wrote on the antiquities of Touraine; but that, as to the fact in question, he believed him. That he himself, indeed, had not watched the same identical shells, as Sauvagiere had done, growing from small to great; but that he had often seen such masses of those shells of all sizes, from a point to a full size, as to carry conviction to his mind that they were in the act of growing; that he had once made a collection of shells for the Emperor's cabinet, reserving duplicates of them for himself; and that these afforded proofs of the same fact; that he afterwards gave those duplicates to a Monsieur du Verget, a physician of Tours, of great science and candor, who was collecting on a larger scale, and who was perfectly in sentiment with Monsieur de la Sauvagiere, that not only the Faluniere, but many other places about Tours, would convince any unbiased observer, that shells are a fruit of the earth, spontaneously produced; and he gave me a copy of de la Sauvagiere's Recueil de Dissertations, presented by the author wherein is one Sur la vegetation spontanée des coquilles du Château des Places. So far, I repeat from him. What are we to conclude? That we have not materials enough yet, to form any conclusion. The fact stated by Sauvagiere is not against any law of nature, and is therefore possible; but it is so little analogous to her habitual processes, that, if true, it would be extraordinary; that to command our belief, therefore, there should be such a suite of observations, as that their untruth would be more extraordinary than the existence of the fact they affirm. The bark of trees, the skin of fruits and animals, the feathers of birds, receive their growth and nutriment from the internal circulation of a juice through the vessels of the individual they cover. We conclude from analogy, then, that the shells of the testaceous tribe, receive also their growth from a like internal circulation. If it be urged, that this does not exclude the possibility of a like shell being produced by the passage of a fluid through the pores of the circumjacent body, whether of earth, stone, or water; I answer, that it is not within the usual economy of nature, to use two processes for one species of production. While I withhold my assent, however, from this hypothesis, I must deny it to every other I have ever seen, by which their authors pretend to account for the origin of shells in high places. Some of these are against the laws of nature, and therefore impossible; and others are built on positions more difficult to assent to, than that of de la Sauvagiere. They all suppose the shells to have covered submarine animals, and have then to answer the question, How came they fifteen thousand feet above the level of the sea? And they answer it, by demanding what cannot be conceded. One, therefore, who had rather have no opinion than a false one, will suppose this question one of those beyond the investigation of human sagacity; or wait till further and fuller observations enable him to decide it.

*Chanteloup.* I heard a nightingale today at Chanteloup. The gardener says, it is the male who alone sings, while the female sits; and that when the young are hatched, he also ceases. In the border at Chanteloup, is an ingenious contrivance to hide the projecting steps of a stair-case. Three steps were of necessity to project into the boudoir: they are therefore made triangular steps; and instead of being rested on the floor, as usual, they are made fast at their broad end to the stair door, swinging out and in, with that. When it shuts, it runs them under the other steps; when open, it brings them out to their proper place. In the kitchen garden, are three pumps, worked by one horse. The pumps are placed in an equilateral triangle, each side of which is of about thirty-five feet. In the centre is a post, ten or twelve feet high, and one foot in diameter. In the top of this, enters the bent end of a lever, of about twelve or fifteen feet long, with a swingle tree at the other end. About three feet from the bent end, it receives on a pin, three horizontal bars of iron, which at their other end lay hold of one corner of a quadrantal crank (like a bell crank) moving in a vertical plane, to the other corner of which is hooked the vertical handle of the pump. The crank turns on its point as a centre, by a pin or pivot passing through it. The horse moving the lever horizontally in a circle, every point of the lever describes a horizontal circle. That which receives the three bars, describes a circle of six feet in diameter. It gives a stroke then of six feet to the handle of each pump, at each revolution.

*Blois. Orleans.* June 9, 10. At Blois, the road leaves the river, and traverses the hills, which are mostly reddish, sometimes gray, good enough, in vines, corn, St. foin. From Orleans to the river Juines, at Estampes, it is a continued plain of corn, and St. foin, tolerably good, sometimes gray, sometimes red. From Estampes to Estrechy, the country is mountainous and rocky, resembling that of Fontainebleau. Quere. If it may not be the same vein?

## A TOUR TO SOME OF THE GARDENS OF ENGLAND

### March-April, 1786

[Memorandums made on a tour to some of the gardens in England, described by Whateley in his book on gardening.]

While his descriptions, in point of style, are models of perfect elegance and classical correctness, they are as remarkable for their exactness. I always walked over the gardens with his book in my hand, examined with attention the particular spots he described, found them so justly characterized by him as to be easily recognized, and saw with wonder, that his fine imagination had never been able to seduce him from the truth. My inquiries were directed chiefly to such practical things as might enable me to estimate the expense of making and maintaining a garden in that style. My journey was in the months of March and April, 1786.

*Chiswick.*—Belongs to Duke of Devonshire. A garden about six acres;—the octagonal dome has an ill effect, both within and without: the garden shows still too much of art. An obelisk of very ill effect; another in the middle of a pond useless.

*Hampton-Court.*—Old fashioned. Clipt yews grown wild.

*Twickenham.*—Pope's original garden, three and a half acres. Sir Wm. Stanhope added one and a half acre. This is a long narrow slip, grass and trees in the middle, walk all around. Now Sir Wellbore Ellis's. Obelisk at bottom of Pope's garden, as monument to his mother. Inscription, "Ah! Editha, matrum optima, mulierum amantissima, Vale." The house about thirty yards from the Thames: the ground shelves gently to the water side; on the back of the house passes the street, and beyond that the garden. The grotto is under the street, and goes out level to the water. In the centre of the garden a mound with a spiral walk round it. A rookery.

*Esher-Place.*—The house in a bottom near the river; on the other side the ground rises pretty much. The road by which we come to the house forms a dividing line in the middle of the front; on the right are heights, rising one beyond and above another, with clumps of trees; on the farthest a temple. A hollow filled up with a clump of trees, the tallest in the bottom, so that the top is quite flat. On the left the ground descends. Clumps of trees, the clumps on each hand balance finely—a most lovely mixture of concave and convex. The garden is of about forty-five acres, besides the park which joins. Belongs to Lady Frances Pelham.

*Claremont.*—Lord Clive's. Nothing remarkable.

*Paynshill.*—Mr. Hopkins. Three hundred and twenty-three acres, garden and park all in one. Well described by Whateley. Grotto said to have cost £7,000. Whateley says one of the bridges is of stone, but both now are of wood, the lower sixty feet high: there is too much evergreen. The dwelling-house built by Hopkins, ill-situated: he has not been there in five years. He lived there four years while building the present house. It is not finished; its architecture is incorrect. A Doric temple, beautiful.

*Woburn.*—Belongs to Lord Peters. Lord Loughborough is the present tenant for two lives. Four people to the farm, four to the pleasure garden, four to the kitchen garden. All are intermixed, the pleasure garden being merely a highly-ornamented walk through and round the divisions of the farm and kitchen garden.

*Caversham.*—Sold by Lord Cadogan to Major Marsac. Twenty-five acres of garden, four hundred acres of park, six acres of kitchen garden. A large lawn, separated by a sunk fence from the garden, appears to be part of it. A straight, broad gravel walk passes before the front and parallel to it, terminated on the right by a Doric temple, and opening at the other end on a fine prospect. This straight walk has an ill effect. The lawn in front, which is pasture, well disposed with clumps of trees.

*Wotton.* Now belongs to the Marquis of Buckingham, son of George Grenville. The lake covers fifty acres, the river five acres, the basin fifteen acres, the little river two acres—equal to seventy-two acres of water. The lake and great river are on a level, they fall into the basin five feet below, and that again into the little river five feet lower. These waters lie in form of an L: the house is in middle of open side, fronting the angle. A walk goes round the whole, three miles in circumference, and containing within it about three hundred acres: sometimes it passes close to the water, sometimes so far off as to leave large pasture grounds between it and the water. But two hands to keep the pleasure grounds in order; much neglected. The water affords two thousand brace of carp a year. There is a Palladian bridge, of which, I think, Whateley does not speak.

*Stowe.*—Belongs to the Marquis of Buckingham, son of George Grenville, and who takes it from Lord Temple. Fifteen men and eighteen boys employed in keeping pleasure grounds. Within the walk are considerable portions separated by inclosures and used for pasture. The Egyptian pyramid is almost entirely taken down by the late Lord Temple, to erect a building there, in commemoration of Mr. Pitt, but he died before beginning it, and nothing is done to it yet. The grotto and two rotundas are taken away. There are four levels of water, receiving it one from the other. The basin contains seven acres, the lake below that ten acres. Kent's building is called the temple of Venus. The inclosure is entirely by ha-ha. At each end of the front line there is a recess like the bastion of a fort. In one of these is the temple of Friendship, in the other the temple of Venus. They are seen the one from the other, the line of sight passing, not through the garden, but through the country parallel to the line of the garden. This has a good effect. In the approach to Stowe, you are brought a mile through a straight avenue, pointing to the Corinthian arch and to the house, till you get to the arch, then you turn short to the right. The straight approach is very ill. The Corinthian arch has a very useless appearance, inasmuch as it has no pretension to any destination. Instead of being an object from the house, it is an obstacle to a very pleasing distant prospect. The Grecian valley being clear of trees, while the hill on each side is covered with them, is much deepened to appearance.

*Leasowes, in Shropshire.*—Now the property of Mr. Horne by purchase. One hundred and fifty acres within the walk. The waters small. This is not even an ornamented farm—it is only a grazing farm with a path round it, here and there a seat of board, rarely anything better. Architecture has contributed nothing. The obelisk is of brick. Shenstone had but three hundred pounds a year, and ruined himself by what he did to this farm. It is said that he died of the heart-aches which his debts occasioned him. The part next the road is of red earth, that on the further part gray. The first and second cascades are beautiful. The landscape at number eighteen, and prospect at thirty-two, are fine. The walk through the wood is umbrageous and pleasing. The whole arch of prospect may be of ninety degrees. Many of the inscriptions are lost.

*Hagley, now Lord Wescot's.*—One thousand acres: no distinction between park and garden—both blended, but more of the character of garden. Eight or nine laborers keep it in order. Between two and three hundred deer in it, some few of them red deer. They breed sometimes with the fallow. This garden occupying a descending hollow between the Clent and Witchbury hills, with the spurs from those hills, there is no level in it for a spacious water. There are, therefore, only some small ponds. From one of these there is a fine cascade; but it can only be occasionally, by opening the sluice. This is in a small, dark, deep hollow, with recesses of stone in the banks on every side. In one of these is a Venus predique, turned half round as if inviting you with her into the recess. There is another cascade seen from the portico on the bridge. The castle is triangular, with a round tower at each angle, one only entire; it seems to be between forty and fifty feet high. The ponds yield a great deal of trout. The walks are scarcely gravelled.

*Blenheim.*—Twenty-five hundred acres, of which two hundred is garden, one hundred and fifty water, twelve kitchen garden, and the rest park. Two hundred people employed to keep it in order, and to make alterations and additions. About fifty of these employed in pleasure grounds. The turf is mowed once in ten days. In summer, about two thousand fallow deer in the park, and two or three thousand sheep. The palace of Henry II. was remaining till taken down by Sarah, widow of the first Duke of Marlborough. It was on a round spot levelled by art, near what is now water, and but a little above it. The island was a part of the high road leading to the palace. Rosamond's bower was near where is now a little grove, about two hundred yards from the palace. The well is near where the bower was. The water here is very beautiful, and very grand. The cascade from the lake, a fine one; except this the garden has no great beauties. It is not laid out in fine lawns and woods, but the trees are scattered thinly over the ground, and every here and there small thickets of shrubs, in oval raised beds, cultivated, and flowers among the shrubs. The gravelled walks are broad—art appears too much. There are but a few seats in it, and nothing of architecture more dignified. There is no one striking position in it. There has been a great addition to the length of the river since Whateley wrote.

*Enfield Chase.*—One of the four lodges. Garden about sixty acres. Originally by Lord Chatham, now in the tenure of Dr. Beaver, who married the daughter of Mr. Sharpe. The lease lately renewed—not in good repair. The water very fine; would admit of great improvement by extending walks, &c., to the principal water at the bottom of the lawn.

*Moor Park.*—The lawn about thirty acres. A piece of ground up the hill of six acres. A small lake. Clumps of spruce firs. Surrounded by walk—separately inclosed—destroys unity. The property of Mr. Rous, who bought of Sir Thomas Dundas. The building superb; the principal front a Corinthian portico of four columns; in front of the wings a colonnade, Ionic, subordinate. Back front a terrace, four Corinthian pilasters. Pulling down wings of building; removing deer; wants water.

*Kew.*—Archimedes' screw for raising water. A horizontal shaft made to turn the oblique one of the screw by a patent machinery of this form:

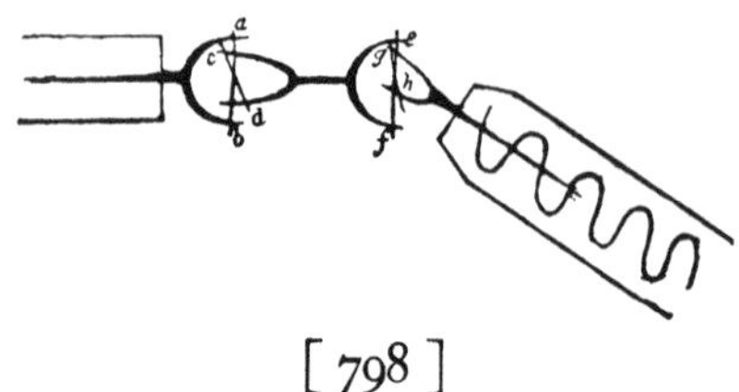

*The pieces separate.*

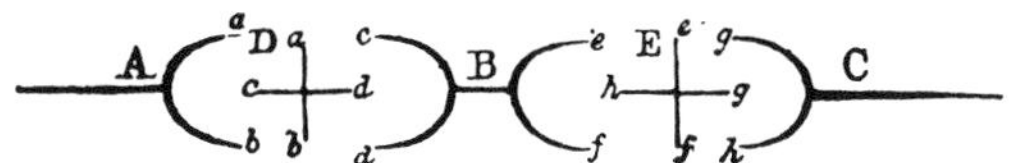


A is driven by its shank into the horizontal axis of the wheel which turns the machine.

B is an intermediate iron to connect the motion of A and C.

C is driven by its shank into the axis of the screw.

D is a cross axis, the ends, *a* and *b,* going into the corresponding holes *a* and *b* of the iron A, and the ends, *c* and *d,* going into the corresponding holes *c* and *d* of the iron B.

E is another cross axis, the ends, *e* and *f,* going into the corresponding holes *e* and *f* of the iron B, and the ends, *g* and *h,* going into the corresponding holes *g* and *h* of the iron C.

## MEMORANDUMS ON A TOUR FROM PARIS TO AMSTERDAM, STRASBURG, AND BACK TO PARIS

March 3-April 23, 1788

*Amsterdam.*—Joists of houses placed, not with their sides horizontally and perpendicularly, but diamond wise, thus: ◇ first, for greater strength: second, to arch between with brick, thus: Windows opening so that they admit air and not rain. The upper sash opens on a horizontal axis, or pins in the centre of the sides, the lower sash slides up.

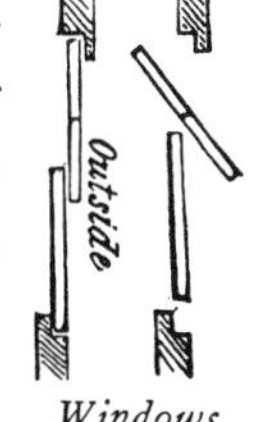


*Windows*

Manner of fixing a flag staff on the mast of a vessel: *a* is the bolt on which it turns; *b* a bolt which is taken in and out to fasten it or to let it down. When taken out, the lower end of the staff is shoved out of its case, and the upper end being heaviest brings itself down: a rope must have been previously fastened to the butt end, to pull it down again when you want to raise the flag end. Dining tables letting down with single or double leaves, so as to take the room of their thickness only with a single leaf when open, thus:

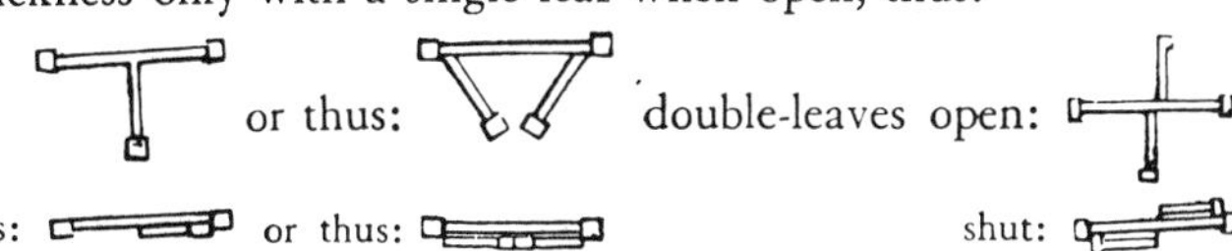

or thus: double-leaves open:

shut, thus: or thus: shut:

Peat costs about one doit each, or twelve and a half stivers the hundred. One hundred make seven cubic feet, and to keep a tolerably comfortable fire for a study or chamber, takes about six every hour and a half.

A machine for drawing light *empty* boats over a dam at Amsterdam. It is an axis in peritrochio fixed on the dam. From the dam each way is a sloping stage, the boat is presented to this, the rope of the axis made fast to it, and it is drawn up. The water on one side of the dam is about four feet higher than on the other.

The camels used for lightening ships over the Pampus will raise the ships eight feet. There are beams passing through the ship's sides, projecting to the off side of the camel and resting on it; of course that alone would keep the camel close to the ship. Besides this, there are a great number of windlasses on the camels, the ropes of which are made fast to the gunwale of the ship. The camel is shaped to the ship on the near side, and straight on the off one. When placed alongside, water is let into it so as nearly to sink it; in this state it receives the beams, &c., of the ship, and then the water is pumped out.

Wind saw mills. See the plans detailed in the moolen book which I bought. A circular foundation of brick is raised about three or four feet high, and covered with a curb or sill of wood, and has little rollers under its sill which make it turn easily on the curb. A hanging bridge projects at each end about fifteen or twenty feet beyond the circular area, thus: 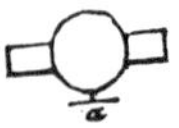 horizontally, and thus: 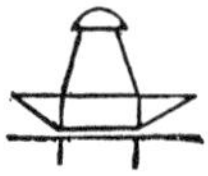 in the profile to increase the play of the timbers on the frame. The wings are at one side, as at *a;* there is a shelter over the hanging bridges, but of plank with scarce any frame, very light.

A bridge across a canal formed by two scows, which open each to the opposite shore and let boats pass.

A lanthern over the street door, which gives light equally into the antechamber and the street. It is a hexagon, and occupies the place of the middle pane of glass in the circular top of the street door.

A bridge on a canal, turning on a swivel, by which means it is arranged along the side of the canal so as not to be in the way of boats when not in use. When used, it is turned across the canal. It is, of course, a little more than double the width of the canal.

Hedges of beach, which, not losing the old leaf till the new bud pushes it off, has the effect of an evergreen as to cover.

Mr. Ameshoff, merchant at Amsterdam. The distribution of his aviary is worthy of notice. Each kind of the large birds has its coop eight feet wide and four feet deep; the middle of the front is occupied by a broad glass window, on one side of which is a door for the keeper to enter at, and on the other a little trap-door for the birds to pass in and out. The floor strewed with clean hay. Before each coop is a court of eight by sixteen feet, with wire in front and netting above, if the fowls be able to fly. For such as require it, there are bushes of evergreen growing in their court for them to lay their eggs under. The coops are frequently divided into two stories: the upper for those birds which perch, such as pigeons, &c., the lower for those which feed on the ground, as peasants, partridges, &c. The court is in common for both stories, because the birds do no injury to each other. For the water-fowl there is a pond of water passing through the courts, with a movable separation. While they are breeding they must be separate, afterwards they may come together. The small birds are some of them in a common aviary, and some in cages.

The Dutch wheel-barrow is in this form: 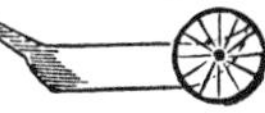 which is very convenient for loading and unloading.

Mr. Hermen Hend Damen, merchant-broker of Amsterdam, tells me that the emigrants to America come from the Palatinate down the Rhine, and take shipping from Amsterdam. Their passage is ten guineas if paid here, and eleven if paid in America. He says they might be had in any number to go to America, and settle lands as tenants on half stocks or métairies. Perhaps they would serve their employer one year as an indemnification for the passage, and then be bound to remain on his lands seven years. They would come to Amsterdam at their own expense. He thinks they would employ more than fifty acres each; but *quære,* especially if they have fifty acres for their wife also?

*Hodson.*—The best house. Stadhonderian, his son, in the government. Friendly, but old and very infirm.

*Hope.*—The first house in Amsterdam. His first object England; but it is supposed he would like to have the American business also, yet he would probably make our affairs subordinate to those of England.

*Vollenhoven.*—An excellent old house; connected with no party.

*Sapportus.*—A brother, very honest and ingenuous, well-disposed; acts for Hope, but will say with truth what he can do for us. The best person to consult with as to the best house to undertake a piece of business. He has brothers in London in business. Jacob Van Staphorst tells me there are about fourteen millions of florins, new money, placed in loans in Holland every year, being the savings of individuals out of their annual revenue, &c. Besides this, there are every year reimbursements of old loans from some quarter or other to be replaced at interest in some new loan.

1788. March 16th. Baron Steuben has been generally suspected of having suggested the first idea of the self-styled Order of Cincinnati. But Mr. Adams tells me, that in the year 1776 he had called at a tavern in the State of New York to dine, just at the moment when the British army was landing at Frog's Neck. Generals Washington, Lee, Knox and Parsons, came to the same tavern. He got into conversation with Knox. They talked of ancient history—of Fabius, who used to raise the Romans from the dust; of the present contest, &c.; and General Knox, in the course of the conversation, said he should wish for some ribbon to wear in his hat, or in his button hole, to be transmitted to his descendants as a badge and a proof that he had fought in defence of their liberties. He spoke of it in such precise terms, as showed he had revolved it in his mind before. Mr. Adams says he and Knox were standing together in the door of the tavern, and does not recollect whether General Washington and the others were near enough to hear the conversation, or were even in the room at that moment. Baron Steuben did not arrive in America till above a year after that. Mr. Adams is now fifty-three years old, *i.e.,* nine years more than I am.

It is said this house will cost four tons of silver, or forty thousand pounds sterling. The separation between the middle building and wings in the upper story has a capricious appearance, yet a pleasing one. The right wing of the house (which is the left in the plan) extends back to a great length, so as to

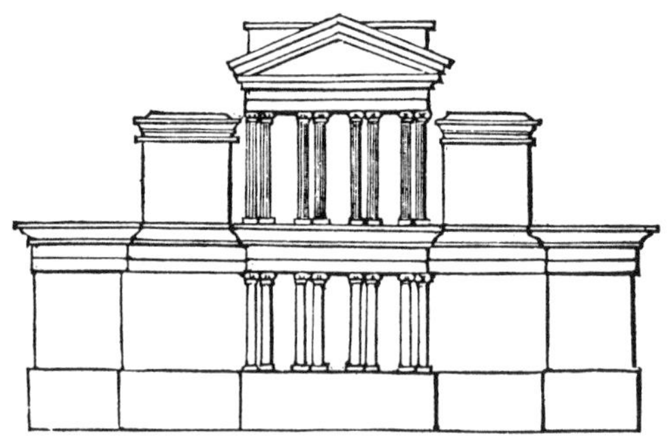

HOPE'S HOUSE, NEAR HARLAEM

make the ground plan in the form of an L. The parapet has a panel of wall, and a pannel of ballusters alternately, which lighten it. There is no portico, the columns being backed against the wall of the front.

March 30th, 31st. *Amsterdam. Utrecht. Nimeguen.* The lower parts of the Low Countries seem partly to have been gained from the sea, and partly to be made up of the plains of the Yssel, the Rhine, the Maese and the Schelde united. To Utrecht nothing but plains are seen, a rich black mould, wet, lower than the level of the waters which intersect it; almost entirely in grass; few or no farm-houses, as the business of grazing requires few laborers. The canal is lined with country houses, which bespeak the wealth and cleanliness of the country; but generally in an uncouth state, and exhibiting no regular architecture. After passing Utrecht, the hills north-east of the Rhine come into view, and gather in towards the river, till at Wyck Dursted they are within three or four miles, and at Amelengen they join the river. The plains, after passing Utrecht, become more sandy, the hills are very poor and sandy, generally waste in broom, sometimes a little corn. The plains are in corn, grass, and willow. The plantations of the latter are immense, and give it the air of an uncultivated country. There are now few châteaux; farm-houses abound, built generally of brick, and covered with tile or thatch. There are some apple-trees, but no forest; a few inclosures of willow wattling. In the gardens are hedges of beach, one foot apart, which, not losing its old leaves till they are pushed off in the spring by the young ones, gives the shelter of evergreens. The Rhine is here about three hundred yards wide, and the road to Nimeguen passing it a little below Wattelingen, leaves Hetern in sight on the left. On this side, the plains of the Rhine, the Ling, and the Waal unite. The Rhine and Waal are crossed on vibrating boats, the rope supported by a line of seven little barks.

The platform by which you go on to the ferry-boat is supported by boats. The view from the hill at Cress is sublime. It commands the Waal, and extends far up the Rhine. That also up and down the Waal from the Bellevue of Nimeguen, is very fine. The château here is pretended to have lodged Julius Cæsar. This is giving it an antiquity of at least eighteen centuries, which must be apocryphal. Some few sheep today, which were feeding in turnip patches.

April 1st. *Cranenburg. Cleves. Santen. Reynberg. Hoogstraat.* The transition from ease and opulence to extreme poverty is remarkable on crossing the line between the Dutch and Prussian territories. The soil and climate are the same; the governments alone differ. With the poverty, the fear also of slaves is visible in the faces of the Prussian subjects. There is an improvement, however, in the physiognomy, especially could it be a little brightened up. The road leads generally over the hills, but sometimes through skirts of the plains of the Rhine. These are always extensive and good. They want manure, being visibly worn down. The hills are almost always sandy, barren, uncultivated, and insusceptible of culture, covered with broom and moss; here and there a little indifferent forest, which is sometimes of beach. The plains are principally in corn; some grass and willow. There are no châteaux, nor houses that bespeak the existence even of a middle class. Universal and equal poverty overspreads the whole. In the villages, too, which seem to be falling down, the over-proportion of women is evident. The cultivators seem to live on their farms. The farm-houses are of mud, the better sort of brick; all covered over with thatch. Cleves is little more than a village. If there are shops or magazines of merchandise in it, they show little. Here and there at a window some small articles are hung up within the glass. The goose-berry beginning to leaf.

April 2d. Passed the Rhine at *Essenberg*. It is there about a quarter of a mile wide, or five hundred yards. It is crossed in a scow with sails. The wind being on the quarter, we were eight or ten minutes only in the passage. Duysberg is but a village in fact, walled in; the buildings mostly of brick. No new ones, which indicate a thriving state. I had understood that near that were remains of the encampment of Varus, in which he and his legions fell by the arms of Arminius (in the time of Tiberius I think it was), but there was not a person to be found in Duysberg who could understand either English, French, Italian, or Latin. So I could make no inquiry.

From *Duysberg* to *Düsseldorf* the road leads sometimes over the hills, sometimes through the plains of the Rhine, the quality of which are as before described. On the hills, however, are considerable groves of oak, of spontaneous growth, which seem to be of more than a century; but the soil being barren, the trees, though high, are crooked and knotty. The undergrowth is broom and moss. In the plains is corn entirely. As they are become rather sandy for grass, there are no inclosures on the Rhine at all. The houses are poor and ruinous, mostly of brick, and scantling mixed. A good deal of grape cultivated.

*Düsseldorf*. The gallery of paintings is sublime, particularly the room of Vanderwerff. The plains from Düsseldorf to Cologne are much more extensive, and go off in barren downs at some distance from the river. These downs extend far, according to appearance. They are manuring the plains with lime. A gate at the Elector's château on this road in this form. We cross at Cologne

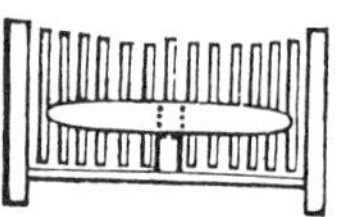

on a pendulum boat. I observe the hog of this country (Westphalia), of which the celebrated ham is made, is tall, gaunt, and with heavy lop ears. Fatted at a year old, would weigh one hundred or one hundred and twenty pounds. At two years old, two hundred pounds. Their principal food is acorns. The pork, fresh, sells at two and a half pence sterling the pound. The hams, ready made, at eight and a half pence sterling the pound. One hundred and six pounds of this country is equal to one hundred pounds of Holland. About four pounds of fine Holland salt is put on one hundred pounds of pork. It is smoked in a room which has no chimney. Well-informed people here tell me there is no other part of the world where the bacon is smoked. They do not know that we do it. Cologne is the principal market of exportation. They find that the small hog makes the sweetest meat.

*Cologne* is a sovereign city, having no territory out of its walls. It contains about sixty thousand inhabitants; appears to have much commerce, and to abound with poor. Its commerce is principally in the hands of Protestants, of whom there are about sixty houses in the city. They are extremely restricted in their operations, and otherwise oppressed in every form by the government, which is Catholic, and excessively intolerant. Their Senate, some time ago, by a majority of twenty-two to eighteen, allowed them to have a church; but it is believed this privilege will be revoked. There are about two hundred and fifty Catholic churches in the city. The Rhine is here about four hundred yards wide. This city is in 51° latitude, wanting about 6′. Here the vines begin, and it is the most northern spot on the earth on which wine is made. Their first grapes came from Orleans, since that from Alsace, Champagne, &c. It is thirty-two years only since the first vines were sent from Cassel, near Mayence, to the Cape of Good Hope, of which the Cape wine is now made. Afterwards new supplies were sent from the same quarter. That I suppose is the most southern spot on the globe where wine is made, and it is singular that the same vine should have furnished two wines as much opposed to each other in quality as in situation. I was addressed here by Mr. Damen, of Amsterdam, to Mr. Jean Jaques Peuchen, of this place, Merchant.

April 4th. *Cologne. Bonne. Andernach. Coblentz.* I saw many walnut trees today in the open fields. It would seem as if this tree and wine required the same climate. The soil begins now to be reddish, both on the hills and in the plains. Those from Cologne to Bonne extend about three miles from the river on each side; but a little above Bonne they become contracted, and continue from thence to be from one mile to nothing, comprehending both sides of the river. They are in corn, some clover and rape, and many vines. These are planted in rows three feet apart both ways. The vine is left about six or eight feet high, and stuck with poles ten or twelve feet high. To these poles they are tied in two places, at the height of about two and four feet. They are now performing this operation. The hills are generally excessively steep, a great proportion of them barren; the rest in vines principally, sometimes small patches of corn. In the plains, though rich, I observed they dung their vines plentifully; and it is observed here, as elsewhere, that the plains yield much wine, but bad. The good is furnished from the hills. The walnut, willow, and apple tree beginning to leaf.

*Andernach* is the port on the Rhine to which the famous mill-stones of Cologne are brought; the quarry, as some say, being at Mendich, three or four leagues from thence. I suppose they have been called Cologne mill-stones, because the merchants of that place having the most extensive correspondence, have usually sent them to all parts of the world. I observed great collections of them at Cologne. This is one account.

April 5. *Coblentz. Nassau.* Another account is, that these stones are cut at Triers and brought down the Moselle. I could not learn the price of them at the quarry; but I was shown a grind-stone of the same stone, five feet diameter, which cost at Triers six florins. It was of but half the thickness of a mill-stone. I supposed, therefore, that two mill-stones would cost about as much as three of these grind-stones, *i.e.,* about a guinea and a half. This country abounds with slate.

The best Moselle wines are made about fifteen leagues from hence, in an excessively mountainous country. The first quality (without any comparison) is that made on the mountain of Braunberg, adjoining to the village of Dusmond; and the best crops is that of the Baron Breidbach Burresheim, grand chambellan et grand Baillif de Coblentz. His Receveur, of the name of Mayer, lives at Dusmond. The last fine year was 1783, which sells now at fifty louis the foudre, which contains six aunes of one hundred and seventy bottles each, equal about one thousand one hundred and ten bottles. This is about twenty-two sous Tournois the bottle. In general, the Baron Burresheim's crops will sell as soon as made, say at the vintage, for one hundred and thirty, one hundred and forty, and one hundred and fifty écus the foudre (the écu is one and a half florin of Holland), say two hundred. 2. Vialen is the second quality, and sells new at one hundred and twenty écus the foudre. 3. Crach-Bispost is the third, and sells for about one hundred and five ecus. I compared Crach of 1783 with Baron Burresheim's of the same year. The latter is quite clear of acid, stronger, and very sensibly the best. 4. Selting, which sells at one hundred écus. 5. Kous-Berncastle, the fifth quality, sells at eighty or ninety. After this there is a gradation of qualities down to thirty écus. These wines must be five or six years old before they are quite ripe for drinking. One thousand plants yield a foudre of wine a year in the most plentiful vineyards. In other vineyards, it will take two thousand or two thousand and five hundred plants to yield a foudre. The culture of one thousand plants costs about one louis a year. A day's labor of a man is paid in winter twenty kreitzers (*i.e.,* one-third of a florin), in summer twenty-six; a woman's is half that. The red wines of this country are very indifferent, and will not keep. The Moselle is here from one hundred to two hundred yards wide; the Rhine three hundred to four hundred. A jessamine in the Count de Moustier's garden in leaf.

In the Elector of Treves' palace at *Coblentz,* are large rooms very well warmed by warm air conveyed from an oven below, through tubes which open into the rooms. An oil and vinegar cruet in this form:  At Coblentz we pass the river on a pendulum boat, and the road to Nassau is over tremendous hills, on which is here and there a little corn, more vines, but mostly barren. In some of these barrens are forests of beach and oak, tolerably large, but crooked and knotty; the undergrowth beach brush, broom, and moss. The soil of the plains, and of the hills where they are cultivable, is reddish. Nassau is a village the whole rents of which should not amount to more than a hundred or two guineas. Yet it gives the title of Prince to the house of Orange to which it belongs.

April 6th. *Nassau. Schwelbach. Wisbaden. Hocheim. Frankfort.* The road from Nassau to Schwelbach is over hills, or rather mountains, both high and steep; always poor, and above half of them barren in beach and oak. At Schwelbach there is some chesnut. The other parts are either in winter grain, or preparing for that of the spring. Between Schwelbach and Wisbaden we come in sight of the plains of the Rhine, which are very extensive. From hence the lands, both high and low, are very fine, in corn, vines, and fruit trees. The country has the appearance of wealth, especially in the approach to Frankfort.

April 7th. *Frankfort.* Among the poultry, I have seen no turkeys in Germany till I arrive at this place. The Stork, or Crane, is very commonly tame here. It is a miserable, dirty, ill-looking bird. The Lutheran is the reigning religion here, and is equally intolerant to the Catholic and Calvinist, excluding them from the free corps.

April 8th. *Frankfort. Hanau.* The road goes through the plains of the Maine, which are mulatto, and very fine. They are well cultivated till you pass the line between the republic and the landgraviate of Hesse, when you immediately see the effect of the difference of government, notwithstanding the tendency which the neighborhood of such a commercial town as Frankfort has to counteract the effects of tyranny in its vicinities, and to animate them in spite of oppression. In Frankfort all is life, bustle, and motion; in Hanau the silence and quiet of the mansions of the dead. Nobody is seen moving in the streets; every door is shut; no sound of the saw, the hammer, or other utensil of industry. The drum and fife is all that is heard. The streets are cleaner than a German floor, because nobody passes them. At Williamsbath, near Hanau, is a country seat of the Landgrave. There is a ruin which is clever. It presents the remains of an old castle. The ground plan is in this form: 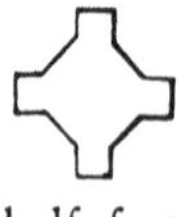 The upper story in this:  A circular room of thirty-one and a half feet diameter within. The four little square towers at the corners finish at the floor of the upper story, so as to be only platforms to walk out on. Over the circular room is a platform also, which is covered by the broken parapet which once crowned the top, but is now fallen off some parts, whilst the other parts remain. I like better, however, the form of the ruin at Hagley, in England, which was thus a centry box here, covered over with bark, so as to look exactly like the trunk of an old tree. This is a good idea; and may be of much avail in a garden. There is a hermitage in which is a good figure of a hermit in plaster, colored to the life, with a table and book before him, in the attitude of reading and contemplation. In a little cell is his bed; in another his books, some tools, &c.; in another his little provision of firewood, &c. There is a monument erected to the son of the present landgrave, in the form of a pyramid, the base of which is eighteen and a half feet. The side declines from the perpendicular about twenty-one and a half degrees. An arch is carried through it both ways so as to present a door in each side. In the middle of this, at the crossing of the two arches, is a marble monument with this inscription: "ante tempus." He died at twelve years of age. Between Hanau and Frankfort, in sight of the road, is the village of Bergen, where was fought the battle of Bergen in the war before last. Things worth noting here are: 1. A folding ladder. 2. Manner of packing china cups and saucers, the former in a circle within the latter. 3. The marks of different manufactures of china, to wit: Dresden with two swords. Hecks with a wheel with W, Frankendaal with CT (for Charles Theodore), and a crown over it. Berlin with 4. The top rail of a wagon supported by the washers on the ends of the axle-trees.

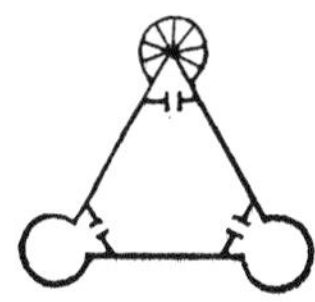

April 10th. *Frankfort. Hocheim. Mayence.* The little tyrants round about having disarmed their people, and made it very criminal to kill game, one knows when they quit the territory of Frankfort by the quantity of game which is seen. In the Republic, everybody being allowed to be armed, and to hunt on their own lands, there is very little game left in its territory. The hog hereabouts resembles extremely the little hog of Virginia. Round like that, a small head, and short upright ears. This makes the ham of Mayence so much esteemed at Paris.

We cross the Rhine at Mayence on a bridge one thousand eight hundred and forty feet long, supported by forty-seven boats. It is not in a direct line, but curved up against the stream; which may strengthen it if the difference between the upper and lower curve be sensible, if the planks of the floor be thick, well jointed together, and forming sectors of circles, so as to act on the whole as the stones of an arch. But it has by no means this appearance. Near one end, one of the boats has an axis in peritrochio, and a chain, by which it may be let drop down stream some distance, with the portion of the floor belonging to it, so as to let a vessel through. Then it is wound up again into place, and to consolidate it the more with the adjoining parts, the loose section is a little higher, and has at each end a folding stage, which folds back on it when it moves down, and when brought up again into place, these stages are folded over on the bridge. This whole operation takes but four or five minutes. In the winter the bridge is taken away entirely, on account of the ice. And then everything passes on the ice through the whole winter.

April 11th. *Mayence. Rudesheim. Johansberg. Markebrom.* The women do everything here. They dig the earth, plough, saw, cut and split wood, row, tow the batteaux, &c. In a small but dull kind of batteau, with two hands rowing with a kind of large paddle, and a square sail, but scarcely a breath of wind, we went down the river at the rate of five miles an hour, making it three and a half hours to Rudesheim. The floats of wood which go with the current only, go one mile and a half an hour. They go night and day. There are five boat-mills abreast here. Their floats seem to be about eight feet broad. The Rhine yields salmon, carp, pike, and perch, and the little rivers running into it yield speckled trout. The plains from Maintz to Rudesheim are good and in corn; the hills mostly in vines. The banks of the river are so low that, standing up in the batteau, I could generally see what was in the plains. Yet they are seldom overflowed.

Though they begin to make wine, as has been said, at Cologne, and continue it up the river indefinitely, yet it is only from Rudesheim to Hocheim that wines of the very first quality are made. The river happens there to run due east and west, so as to give its hills on that side a southern aspect. And even in this canton, it is only Hocheim, Johansberg, and Rudesheim, that are considered as of the very first quality. Johansberg is a little mountain (berg signifies mountain), whereon is a religious house, about fifteen miles below Mayence, and near the village of Vingel. It has a southern aspect, the soil a barren mulatto clay, mixed with a good deal of stone, and some slate. This wine used to be but on a par with Hocheim and Rudesheim; but the place having come to the Bishop of Fulda, he improved its culture so as to render it stronger; and since the year 1775, it sells at double the price of the other two. It has none of the acid of the Hocheim and other Rhenish wines. There are about sixty tons made in a good year, which sell, as soon as of a drinkable age, at one thousand franks each. The tun here contains seven and a-half aunes of one hundred and seventy bottles each. Rudesheim is a village of about eighteen or twenty miles below Mayence. Its fine wines are made on the hills about a mile below the village, which look to the south, and on the middle and lower parts of them. They are terraced. The soil is gray, about one-half of slate and rotten stone, the other half of barren clay, excessively steep. Just behind the village also is a little spot, called Hinder House, belonging to the Counts of Sicken and Oschstein, whereon each makes about a ton of wine of the very first quality. This spot extends from the bottom to the top of the hill. The vignerons of Rudesheim dung their vines about once in five or six years, putting a one-horse tumbrel load of dung on every twelve feet square. One thousand plants yield about four aunes in a good year. The best crops are,

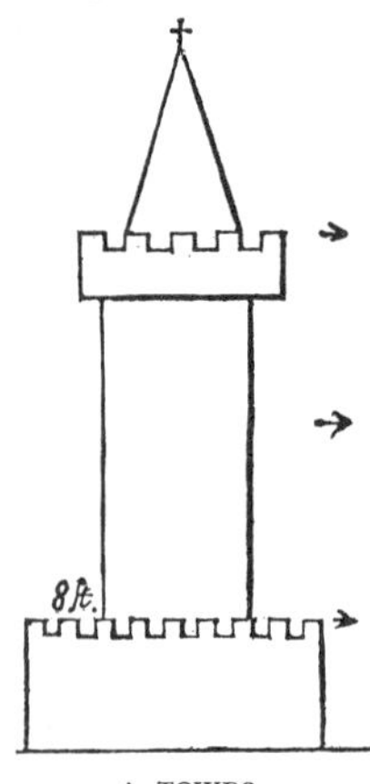

A TOWER AT RUDESHEIM

| | | |
|---|---|---|
| The Chanoines of Mayence, who make | 15 | pieces of 7½ aunes |
| Le Comte de Sicken | 6 | " " |
| Le Comte d'Oschstein | 9 | " " |
| L'Electeur de Mayence | 6 | " " |
| Le Comte de Meternisch | 6 | " " |
| Monsieur de Boze | 5 | " " |
| M. Ackerman, baliff et aubergiste des 3 couronnes | 8 | " " |
| M. Ackerman le fils, aubergiste à la couronne | 5 | " " |
| M. Lynn, aubergiste de l'ange | 5 | " " |
| Baron de Wetzel | 7 | " " |
| Convent de Mariahousen, des religieuses Benedictines | 7 | " " |
| M. Johan Yung | 8 | " " |
| M. de Rieden | 5 | " " |
| | 92 | |

These wines begin to be drinkable at about five years old. The proprietors sell them old or young, according to the prices offered, and according to their own want of money. There is always a little difference between different casks, and therefore when you choose and buy a single cask, you pay three, four, five or six hundred florins for it. They are not at all acid, and to my taste much preferable to Hocheim, though but of the same price. Hocheim is a village about three miles above Mayence, on the Maine, where it empties into the Rhine. The spot whereon the good wine is made is the hill side from the church down to the plain, a gentle slope of about a quarter of a mile wide, and extending half a mile towards Mayence. It is of south-western aspect, very poor, sometimes gray, sometimes mulatto, with a moderate mixture of small broken stone. The vines are planted three feet apart, and stuck with sticks about six feet high. The vine, too, is cut at that height. They are dunged once in three or four years. One thousand plants yield from one to two aunes a year: they begin to yield a little at three years old, and continue to one hundred years, unless sooner killed by a cold winter. Dick, keeper of the Rothen-house tavern at Frankfort, a great wine merchant, who has between three and four hundred tons of wine in his cellars, tells me that Hocheim of the year 1783, sold, as soon as it was made, at ninety florins the aune, Rudesheim of the same year, as soon as made, at one hundred and fifteen florins, and Markebronn seventy florins. But a peasant of Hocheim tells me that the best crops of Hocheim in the good years, when sold new, sell but for about thirty-two or thirty-three florins the aune; but that it is only the poorer proprietors who sell new. The fine crops are,

| | | |
|---|---|---|
| Count Ingleheim about | 10 tuns | All of these keep till about fifteen years old, before they sell, unless they are offered a very good price sooner. |
| Baron d'Alberg | 8 " | |
| Count Schimbon | 14 " | |
| The Chanoines of Mayence | 18 " | |
| Counsellor Schik de Vetsler | 15 " | |
| Convent of Jacobsberg | 8 " | |
| The Chanoine of Fechbach | 10 " | |
| The Carmelites of Frankfort | 8 " | Who only sell by the bottle in their own tavern in Frankfort. |

| | | |
|---|---|---|
| The Bailiff of Hocheim | 11 tuns | Who sells at three or four years old. |
| Zimmerman, a bourgeois | 4 " | These being poor, sell new. |
| Feldman, a carpenter | 2 " | |

Markebronn (bronn signifies a spring, and is probably of affinity with the Scotch word, burn) is a little canton in the same range of hills, adjoining to the village of Hagenheim, about three miles above Johansberg, subject to the elector of Mayence. It is a sloping hill side of southern aspect, mulatto, poor, and mixed with some stone. This yields wine of the second quality.

April 12th. *Mayence. Oppenheim. Dorms. Manheim.* On the road between Mayence and Oppenheim are three cantons, which are also esteemed as yielding wines of the second quality. These are Laudenheim, Bodenheim, and Nierstein. Laudenheim is a village about four or five miles from Mayence. Its wines are made on a steep hill side, the soil of which is gray, poor and mixed with some stone. The river there happens to make a short turn to the south-west, so as to present its hills to the south-east. Bodenheim is a village nine miles, and Nierstein another about ten or eleven miles from Mayence. Here, too, the river is north-east and south-west, so as to give the hills between these villages a south-east aspect; and at Thierstein, a valley making off, brings the face of the hill round to the south. The hills between these villages are almost perpendicular, of a vermilion red, very poor, and having as much rotten stone as earth. It is to be observed that these are the only cantons on the south side of the river which yield good wine, the hills on this side being generally exposed to the cold winds, and turned from the sun. The annexed bill of prices current, will give an idea of the estimation of these wines respectively.

With respect to the grapes in this country, there are three kinds in use for making white wine, (for I take no notice of the red wines, as being absolutely worthless.) 1. The Klemperien, of which the inferior qualities of Rhenish wines are made, and is cultivated because of its hardness. The wines of this grape descend as low as one hundred florins the tun of eight aunes. 2. The Rhysslin grape, which grows only from Hocheim down to Rudesheim. This is small and delicate, and therefore succeeds only in this chosen spot. Even at Rudesheim it yields a fine wine only in the little spot called Hinder House, before mentioned; the mass of good wines made at Rudesheim, below the village, being of the third kind of grape, which is called the Orleans grape.

To Oppenheim the plains of the Rhine and Maine are united. From that place we see the commencement of the Berg-strasse, or mountains which separate at first the plains of the Rhine and Maine, then cross the Neckar at Heidelberg, and from thence forms the separation between the plains of the Neckar and Rhine, leaving those of the Rhine about ten or twelve miles wide. These plains are sometimes black, sometimes mulatto, always rich. They are in corn, potatoes, and some willow. On the other side again, that is, on the west side, the hills keep at first close to the river. They are about one hundred and fifty, or two hundred feet high, sloping, red, good, and mostly in vines. Above Oppenheim, they begin to go off till they join the mountains of Lorraine and Alsace, which separate the waters of the Moselle and Rhine, leaving to the whole valley of the Rhine about twenty or twenty-five miles breadth. About Worms these plains are sandy, poor, and often covered only with small pine.

April 13th. *Manheim.* There is a bridge over the Rhine here, supported on thirty-nine boats, and one over the Neckar on eleven boats. The bridge over the Rhine is twenty-one and a half feet wide from rail to rail. The boats are four feet deep, fifty-two feet long, and nine feet eight inches broad. The space between boat and boat is eighteen feet ten inches. From these data the length of the bridge should be 9 ft. 8 in. + 18 ft. 10 in. × 40 = 1140 feet. In order to let vessels pass through, two boats well framed together, with their flooring, are made to fall down stream together. Here, too, they make good ham. It is fattened on round potatoes and Indian corn. The farmers smoke what is for their own use in their chimneys. When it is made for sale, and in greater quantities than the chimney will hold, they make the smoke of the chimney pass into an adjoining loft, or apartment, from which it has no issue; and here they hang their hams.

An economical curtain bedstead. The bedstead is seven feet by four feet two inches. From each leg there goes up an iron rod three-eighths of an inch in diameter. Those from the legs at the foot of the bed meeting at top as in the margin, and those from the head meeting in like manner, so that the two at the foot form one point, and the two at the head another. On these points lays an oval iron rod, whose long diameter is five feet, and short one three feet one inch. There is a hole through this rod at each end, by which it goes on firm on the point of the upright rods. Then a nut screws it down firmly. Ten breadths of stuff two feet ten inches wide, and eight feet six inches long, form the curtains. There is no top nor valance. The rings are fastened within two and a half or three inches of the top on the inside, which two and a half or three inches stand up, and are an ornament somewhat like a ruffle.

I have observed all along the Rhine that they make the oxen draw by the horns. A pair of very handsome chariot horses, large, bay, and seven years old, sell for fifty louis. One pound of beef sells for eight kreitzers, (*i.e.,* eight sixtieths of a florin;) one pound of mutton or veal, six kreitzers; one pound of pork, seven and a half kreitzers; one pound of ham, twelve kreitzers; one pound of fine wheat bread, two kreitzers; one pound of butter, twenty kreitzers; one hundred and sixty pounds of wheat, six francs; one hundred and sixty pounds of maize, five francs; one hundred and sixty pounds of potatoes, one franc; one hundred pounds of hay, one franc; a cord of wood (which is 4 4 and 6 feet), seven francs; a laborer by the day receives twenty-four kreitzers, and feeds himself. A journee or arpent of land (which is eight by two hundred steps), such as the middling plains of the Rhine, will sell for two hundred francs. There are more soldiers here than other inhabitants, to wit: six thousand soldiers and four thousand males of full age of the citizens, the whole number of whom is reckoned at twenty thousand.

April 14th. *Manheim. Dossenheim. Heidelberg. Schwetzingen Manheim.* The elector placed, in 1768, two males and five females of the Angora goat at Dossenheim, which is at the foot of the Bergstrasse mountains. He sold twenty-five last year, and has now seventy. They are removed into the mountains four leagues beyond Dossenheim. Heidelberg is on the Neckar just where it issues from the Bergstrasse mountains, occupying the first skirt of plain which it forms. The château is up the hill a considerable height. The gardens lie above the château, climbing up the mountain in terraces. This château is the most noble ruin I have ever seen, having been reduced to that state by the French in the time of Louis XIV, 1693. Nothing remains under cover but the chapel. The situation is romantic and pleasing beyond expression. It is on a great scale much like the situation of Petrarch's château, at Vaucluse, on a small one. The climate, too, is like that of Italy. The apple, the pear, cherry, peach, apricot, and almond, are all in bloom. There is a station in the garden to which the château re-echoes distinctly four syllables. The famous ton of Heidelberg was new built in 1751, and made to contain thirty foudres more than the ancient one. It is said to contain two hundred and thirty-six foudres of one thousand two hundred bottles each. I measured it, and found its length external to be twenty-eight feet ten inches; its diameter at the end twenty feet three inches; the thickness of the staves seven and a half inches; thickness of the hoops seven and a half inches; besides a great deal of external framing. There is no wine in it now. The gardens at Schwetzingen show how much money may be laid out to make an ugly thing. What is called the English quarter, however, relieves the eye from the straight rows of trees, round and square basins, which constitute the great mass of the garden. There are some tolerable morsels of Grecian architecture, and a good ruin. The Aviary, too, is clever. It consists of cells of about eight feet wide, arranged round, and looking into a circular area of about forty or fifty feet diameter. The cells have doors both of wire and glass, and have small shrubs in them. The plains of the Rhine on this side are twelve miles wide, bounded by the Bergstrasse mountains. These appear to be eight hundred or a thousand feet high; the lower part in vines, from which is made what is called the vin de Nichar; the upper in chesnut. There are some cultivated spots however, quite to the top. The plains are generally mulatto, in corn principally; they are planting potatoes in some parts, and leaving others open for maize and tobacco. Many peach and other fruit trees on the lower part of the mountain. The paths on some parts of these mountains are somewhat in the style represented in the margin.

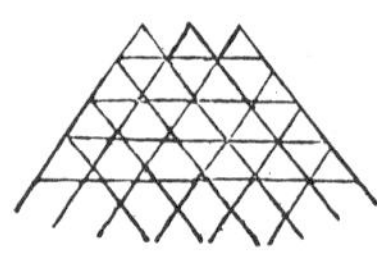

*Manheim. Kaeferthal. Manheim.* Just beyond Kaeferthal is an extensive, sandy waste, planted in pine, in which the elector has about two hundred sangliers, tamed. I saw about fifty; the heavies I am told, would weigh about three hundred pounds. They are fed on round potatoes, and range in the forest of pines. At the village of Kaeferthal is a plantation of rhubarb, begun in 1769 by a private company. It contains twenty arpents or jourries, and its culture costs about four or five hundred francs a year; it sometimes employs forty or fifty laborers at a time. The best age to sell the rhubarb at is the fifth or sixth year, but the sale being dull, they keep it sometimes to the tenth year; they find it best to let it remain in the ground. They sell about two hundred kentals a year at two or three francs a pound, and could sell double that quantity from the ground if they could find a market. The apothecaries of Francfort and of England are the principal buyers. It is in beds, resembling lettuce-beds; the plants four, five or six feet apart. When dug, a thread is passed through every piece of root, and it is hung separate in a kind of rack; when dry it is rasped; what comes off is given to the cattle.

April 15. *Manheim. Spire. Carlsruhe.* The valley preserves its width, extending on each side of the river about ten or twelve miles, but the soil loses much in its quality, becoming sandy and lean, often barren and overgrown with pine thicket. At Spire is nothing remarkable. Between that and Carlsruhe we pass the Rhine in a common skow with oars, where it is between three and four hundred yards wide. Carlsruhe is the residence of the Margrave of Baden, a sovereign prince. His château is built in the midst of a natural forest of several leagues diameter, and of the best trees I have seen in these countries: they are mostly oak, and would be deemed but indifferent in America. A great deal of money has been spent to do more harm than good to the ground—cutting a number of straight alleys through the forest. He has a pheasantry of the gold and silver kind, the latter very tame, but the former excessively shy. A little inclosure of stone, two and a half feet high and thirty feet diameter, in which are two tamed beavers. There is a pond of fifteen feet diameter in the centre, and at each end a little cell for them to retire into, which is stowed with boughs and twigs with leaves on them, which is their principal food. They eat bread also;—twice a week the water is changed. They cannot get over this wall. Some cerfs of a peculiar kind, spotted like fawns, the horns remarkably long, small and sharp, with few points. I am not sure there were more than two to each main beam, and if I saw distinctly, there came out a separate and subordinate beam from the root of each. Eight angora goats—beautiful animals—all white. This town is only an appendage of the château, and but a moderate one. It is a league from Durlach, half way between that and the river. I observe they twist the flues of their stoves in any form for ornament merely, without smoking, as thus, *e.g.*

April 16. *Carlsruhe. Rastadt. Scholhoven. Bischofheim. Kehl. Strasburg.* The valley of the Rhine still preserves its breadth, but varies in quality; sometimes a rich mulatto loam, sometimes a poor sand, covered with small pine. The culture is generally corn. It is to be noted, that through the whole of my route through the Netherlands and the valley of the Rhine, there is a little red clover every here and there, and a great deal of grape cultivated. The seed of this is sold to be made into oil. The grape is now in blossom. No inclosures. The fruit trees are generally blossoming through the whole valley. The high mountains of the Bergstrasse, as also of Alsace, are covered with snow. Within this day or two, the every-day dress of the country women here is black. Rastadt is a seat also of the Margrave of Baden. Scholhoven and Kehl are in his territory, but

not Bischofheim. I see no beggars since I entered his government, nor is the traveller obliged to ransom himself every moment by a chausée gold. The roads are excellent, and made so, I presume, out of the coffers of the prince. From Cleves till I enter the Margravate of Baden, the roads have been strung with beggars—in Hesse the most, and the road tax very heavy. We pay it cheerfully, however, through the territory of Francfort and thence up the Rhine, because fine gravelled roads are kept up; but through the Prussian, and other parts of the road below Francfort, the roads are only as made by the carriages, there not appearing to have been ever a day's work employed on them. At Strasburg we pass the Rhine on a wooden bridge.

At *Brussels and Antwerp,* the fuel is pit-coal, dug in Brabant. Through all Holland it is turf. From Cleves to Cologne it is pit-coal brought from England. They burn it in open stoves. From thence it is wood, burnt in close stoves, till you get to Strasburg, where the open chimney comes again into use.

April 16th, 17th, 18th. *Strasburg.* The vin de paille is made in the neighborhood of Colmar, in Alsace, about —— from this place. It takes its name from the circumstance of spreading the grapes on straw, where they are preserved till spring, and then made into wine. The little juice then remaining in them makes a rich sweet wine, but the dearest in the world, without being the best by any means. They charge nine florins the bottle for it in the taverns of Strasburg. It is the caprice of wealth alone which continues so losing an operation. This wine is sought because dear; while the better wine of Frontignan is rarely seen at a good table because it is cheap.

*Strasburg. Saverne. Phalsbourg.* As far as Saverne the country is in waving hills and hollows; red, rich enough; mostly in small grain, but some vines; a little stone. From Saverne to Phalsbourg we cross a considerable mountain, which takes an hour to rise it.

April 19th. *Phalsbourg. Fenestrange. Moyenvic. Nancy.* Asparagus today at Moyenvic. The country is always either mountainous or hilly; red, tolerably good, and in small grain. On the hills about Fenestrange, Moyenvic, and Nancy, are some small vineyards where a bad wine is made. No inclosures. Some good sheep, indifferent cattle, and small horses. The most forest I have seen in France, principally of beech, pretty large. The houses, as in Germany, are of scantling, filled in with wicked and mortar, and covered either with thatch or tiles. The people, too, here as there, are gathered in villages. Oxen plough here with collars and hames. The awkward figure of their mould-board leads one to consider what should be its form. The offices of the mould-board are to receive the sod after the share has cut under it, to raise it gradually, and to reverse it. The fore-end of it then, should be horizontal to enter under the sod, and the hind end perpendicular to throw it over; the intermediate surface changing gradually from the horizontal to the perpendicular. It should be as wide as the furrow, and of a length suited to the construction of the plough. The following would seem a good method of making it: Take a block, whose length, breadth and thickness, is that of your intended mould-board, suppose two and a half feet long and eight inches broad and thick. Draw the lines *a d* and *c d,* figure 1, with a saw, the toothed edge of which is straight, enter at *a* and cut on, guiding the hind part of the saw on the line *a b,* and the fore part on the line *a d,* till the saw reaches the points *c* and *d,* then enter it at *c* and cut on, guiding it by the lines *c b* and *c d* till it reaches the points *b* and *d. The* quarter, *a b c d,* will then be completely cut out, and the diagonal from *d* to *b* laid bare. The piece may now be represented as in figure 2. Then saw in transversely at every two inches till the saw reaches the line *c e,* and the diagonal *b d,* and cut out the pieces with an adze. The upper surface will thus be formed. With a gauge opened to eight inches, and guided by the lines *c e,* scribe the upper edge of the board from *d b,* cut that edge perpendicular to the face of the board, and scribe it of the proper thickness. Then form the underside by the upper, by cutting transversely with the saw and taking out the piece with an adze. As the upper edge of the wing of the share rises a little, the fore end of the board, *b c,* will rise as much from a strict horizontal position, and will throw the hind end, *e d,* exactly as much beyond the perpendicular, so as to promote the reversing of the sod. The women here, as in Germany, do all sorts of work. While one considers them as useful and rational companions, one cannot forget that they are also objects of our pleasures; nor can they ever forget it. While employed in dirt and drudgery, some tag of a ribbon, some ring, or bit of bracelet, earbob or necklace, or something of that kind, will show that the desire of pleasing is never suspended in them. It is an honorable circumstance for man, that the first moment he is at his ease, he allots the internal employments to his female partner, and takes the external on himself. And this circumstance, or its reverse, is a pretty good indication that a people are, or are not at their ease. Among the Indians, this indication fails from a particular cause: every Indian man is a soldier or warrior, and the whole body of warriors constitute a standing army, always employed in war or hunting. To support that army, there remain no laborers but the women. Here, then, is so heavy a military establishment, that the civil part of the nation is reduced to women only. But this is a barbarous perversion of the natural destination of the two sexes. Women are formed by nature for attentions, not for hard labor. A woman never forgets one of the numerous train of little offices which belong to her. A man forgets often.

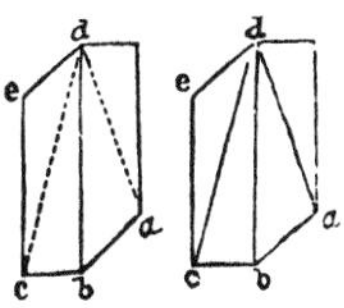

April 20th. *Nancy. Toule. Void. Ligny en Barrois. Bar le Duc. St. Dizier.* Nancy itself is a neat little town, and its environs very agreeable. The valley of the little branch of the Moselle, on which it is, is about a mile wide: the road then crossing the head-waters of the Moselle, the Maes, and the Marne, the country is very hilly, and perhaps a third of it poor and in forests of beech: the other two-thirds from poor up to middling, red, and stony. Almost entirely in corn, now and then only some vines on the hills. The Moselle at Toule is thirty or forty yards wide: the Maese near Void about half that: the Marne at St. Dizier about forty yards. They all make good plains of from a quarter of a mile to a mile wide. The hills of the Maese abound with chalk. The rocks coming down from the tops of the hills, on all the road of this day, at regular intervals like the ribs of an animal, have a very irregular appearance. Considerable flocks of sheep and asses, and, in the approach to St. Dizier, great plantations of apple and cherry trees; here and there a peach tree, all in general bloom. The roads through Lorraine are strung with beggars.

April 21st. *St. Dizier. Vitry le Français. Châlons sur Marne. Épernay.* The plains of the Marne and Sault uniting, appear boundless to the eye till we approach their confluence at Vitry, where the hills come in on the right; after that the plains are generally about a mile, mulatto, of middling quality, sometimes stony. Sometimes the ground goes off from the river so sloping, that one does not know whether to call it high or low land. The hills are mulatto also, but whitish, occasioned by the quantity of chalk which seems to constitute their universal base. They are poor, and principally in vines. The streams of water are of the color of milk, occasioned by the chalk also. No inclosures, some flocks of sheep; children gathering dung in the roads. Here and there a château; but none considerable.

April 22d. *Épernay.* The hills abound with chalk. Of this they make lime, not so strong as stone lime, and therefore to be used in greater proportion. They cut the blocks into regular forms also, like stone, and build houses of it. The common earth too, well impregnated with this, is made into mortar, moulded in the form of brick, dried in the sun, and houses built of them which last one hundred or two hundred years. The plains here are a mile wide, red, good, in corn, clover, Luzerne, St. Foin. The hills are in vines, and this being precisely the canton where the most celebrated wines of Champagne are made, details must be entered into. Remember, however, that they will always relate to the white wines, unless where the red are expressly mentioned. The reason is that their red wines, though much esteemed on the spot, are by no means esteemed elsewhere equally with their white; nor do they merit equal esteem.

A Topographical sketch of the position of the wine villages, the course of the hills, and consequently the aspect of the vine-yards.

*Soil,* meagre, mulatto clay, mixed with small broken stone, and a little hue of chalk. Very dry.

*Aspect,* may be better seen by the annexed diagram. The wine of Aij is

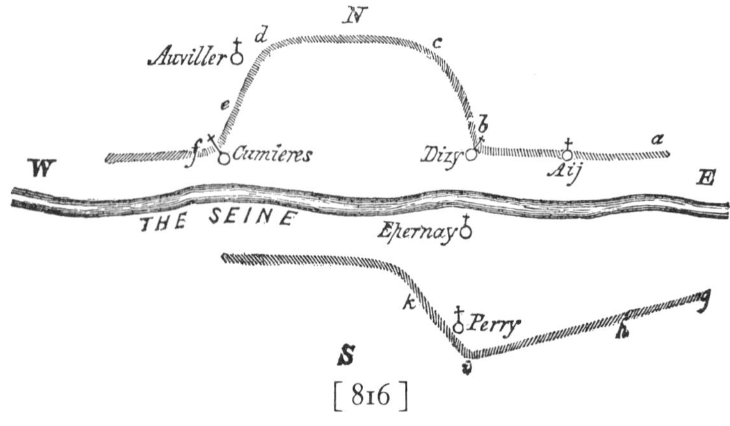

made from *a* to *b,* those of Dizij from *b* to *c,* Auvillij *d* to *e,* Cumières *e* to *f,* Épernay *g* to *h,* Perij *i* to *k*. The hills are generally about two hundred and fifty feet high. The good wine is made only in the middle region. The lower region, however, is better than the upper; because this last is exposed to cold winds, and a colder atmosphere.

*Culture.* The vines are planted two feet apart. Afterwards they are multiplied (provignés). When a stock puts out two shoots they lay them down, spread them open and cover them with earth, so as to have in the end about a plant for every square foot. For performing this operation they have a hook, of this shape, ϒ and nine inches long, which, being stuck in the ground, holds down the main stock, while the laborer separates and covers the new shoot. They leave two buds above the ground. When the vine has shot up high enough, they stick it with split sticks of oak, from an inch to an inch and a half square, and four feet long, and tie the vine to its stick with straw. These sticks cost two florins the hundred, and will last forty years. An arpent, one year with another, in the fine vineyards, gives twelve pieces, and in the inferior vineyards twenty-five pieces, of two hundred bottles each. An arpent of the first quality sells for three thousand florins, and there have been instances of seven thousand two hundred florins. The arpent contains one hundred verges, of twenty-two pieds square. The arpent of inferior quality sells at one thousand florins. They plant the vines in a hole about a foot deep, and fill that hole with good mould, to make the plant take. Otherwise it would perish. Afterwards, if ever they put dung, it is very little. During wheat harvest there is a month or six weeks that nothing is done in the vineyard, that is to say, from the 1st of August to the beginning of vintage. The vintage commences early in September, and lasts a month. A day's work of a laborer in the busiest season is twenty sous, and he feeds himself: in the least busy season it is fifteen sous. Corn lands are rented from four florins to twenty-four; but vine lands are never rented. The three façons (or workings) of an arpent cost fifteen florins. The whole year's expense of an arpent is worth one hundred florins.

*Grapes.*—The bulk of their grapes are purple, which they prefer for making even white wine. They press them very lightly, without treading or permitting them to ferment at all, for about an hour; so that it is the beginning of the running only which makes the bright wine. What follows the beginning is of a straw color, and therefore not placed on a level with the first. The last part of the juice, produced by strong pressure, is red and ordinary. They choose the bunches with as much care, to make wine of the very first quality, as if to eat. Not above one-eighth of the whole grapes will do for this purpose. The white grape, though not so fine for wine as the red, when the red can be produced, and more liable to rot in a moist season, yet grows better if the soil be excessively poor, and therefore in such a soil is preferred, or rather, is used of necessity, because there the red would not grow at all.

*Wine.*—The white wines are either mousseux, sparkling, or non-mousseux, still. The sparkling are little drunk in France, but are almost alone known and drunk in foreign countries. This makes so great a demand, and so certain a one, that it is the dearest by about an eighth, and therefore they endeavor to make all sparkling if they can. This is done by bottling in the spring, from the beginning of March till June. If it succeeds, they lose abundance of bottles, from one-tenth to one-third. This is another cause increasing the price. To make the still wine, they bottle in September. This is only done when they know from some circumstance that the wine will not be sparkling. So if the spring bottling fails to make a sparkling wine, they decant it into other bottles in the fall, and it then makes the very best still wine. In this operation, it loses from one-tenth to one-twentieth by sediment. They let it stand in the bottles in this case forty-eight hours, with only a napkin spread over their mouths, but no cork. The best sparkling wine, decanted in this manner, makes the best still wine, and which will keep much longer than that originally made still by being bottled in September. The sparkling wines lose their briskness the older they are, but they gain in quality with age to a certain length. These wines are in perfection from two to ten years old, and will even be very good to fifteen. 1766 was the best year ever known. 1775 and 1776 next to that. 1783 is the last good year, and that not to be compared with those. These wines stand icing very well.

*Aij.* M. Dorsay makes one thousand and one hundred pieces, which sell, as soon as made, at three hundred florins, and in good years four hundred florins, in the cask. I paid in his cellar, to M. Louis, his homme d'affaires, for the remains of the year 1783, three florins ten sous the bottle. Sparkling Champagne, of the same degree of excellence, would have cost four florins, (the piece and demiqueue are the same; the feuillette is one hundred bottles.) M. le Duc makes four hundred to five hundred pieces. M. de Villermont, three hundred pieces. M. Janson, two hundred and fifty pieces. All of the first quality, red and white in equal quantities.

*Auvillaij.* The Benedictine monks make one thousand pieces, red and white, but three-fourths red, both of the first quality. The king's table is supplied by them. This enables them to sell at five hundred and fifty florins the piece. Though their white is hardly as good as Dorsay's, their red is the best. L'Abbatiale, belonging to the bishop of the place, makes one thousand to twelve hundred pieces, red and white, three-fourths red, at four hundred to five hundred and fifty florins, because neighbors to the monks.

*Cumières* is all of the second quality, both red and white, at one hundred and fifty to two hundred florins the piece.

*Épernay.* Madame Jermont makes two hundred pieces at three hundred florins. M. Patelaine, one hundred and fifty pieces. M. Mare, two hundred pieces. M. Chertems, sixty pieces. M. Lauchay, fifty pieces. M. Cousin (Aubergiste de l'hôtel de Róhan à Épernay), one hundred pieces. M. Pierrot, one hundred pieces. Les Chanoines régulières d'Épernay, two hundred pieces. Mesdames les Ursulines religieuses, one hundred pieces. M. Gilette, two hundred pieces. All of the first quality; red and white in equal quantities.

*Pierrij.* M. Casotte makes five hundred pieces. M. de la Motte, three hundred pieces. M. de Failli, three hundred pieces. I tasted his wine of 1779, one of the good years. It was fine, though not equal to that of M. Dorsay, of 1783. He sells it at two florins ten sous to merchants, and three florins to individuals. Les Séminaristes, one hundred and fifty pieces. M. Hoquart, two hundred pieces. All of the first quality; white and red in equal quantities.

At Cramont, also, there are some wines of the first quality made. At Avisi also, and Aucy, Le Meni, Mareuil, Verzis-Verzenni. This last place belongs to the Marquis de Sillery. The wines are carried to Sillery, and there stored, whence they are called Vins de Sillery, though not made at Sillery.

All these wines of Épernay and Pierrij sell almost as dear as M. Dorsay's, their quality being nearly the same. There are many small proprietors who might make wine of the first quality, if they would cull their grapes, but they are too poor for this. Therefore, the proprietors before named, whose names are established, buy of the poorer ones the right to cull their vineyards, by which means they increase their quantity, as they find about one-third of the grapes will make wines of the first quality.

The lowest-priced wines of all are thirty florins the piece, red or white. They make brandy of the pumice. In very bad years, when their wines become vinegar, they are sold for six florins the piece, and made into brandy. They yield one-tenth brandy.

White Champagne is deemed good in proportion as it is silky and still. Many circumstances derange the scale of wines. The proprietor of the best vineyard, in the best year, having bad weather come upon him while he is gathering his grapes, makes a bad wine, while his neighbor, holding a more indifferent vineyard, which happens to be ingathering while the weather is good, makes a better. The M. de Casotte at Pierrij formerly was the first house. His successors, by some imperceptible change of culture, have degraded the quality of their wines. Their cellars are admirably made, being about six, eight or ten feet wide, vaulted, and extending into the ground, in a kind of labyrinth, to a prodigious distance, with an air-hole of two feet diameter every fifty feet. From the top of the vault to the surface of the earth, is from fifteen to thirty feet. I have nowhere seen cellars comparable to these. In packing their bottles, they lay on their side; then cross them at each end, they lay laths, and on these another row of bottles, heads and points; and so on. By this means, they can take out a bottle from the top, or where they will.

April 23d. *Épernay. Château Thieray. St. Jean. Meaux. Vergalant. Paris.* From Épernay to St. Jean the road leads over hills, which in the beginning are indifferent, but get better towards the last. The plains, wherever seen, are inconsiderable. After passing St. Jean, the hills become good, and the plains increase. The country about Vergalant is pretty. A skirt of a low ridge which runs in on the extensive plains of the Marne and Seine, is very picturesque. The general bloom of fruit trees proves there are more of them than I had imagined from travelling in other seasons, when they are less distinguishable at a distance from the forest trees.

## TRAVELLING NOTES FOR MR. RUTLEDGE AND MR. SHIPPEN

June 3, 1788

*General Observations.*—On arriving at a town, the first thing is to buy the plan of the town, and the book noting its curiosities. Walk round the ramparts when there are any, go the top of a steeple to have a view of the town and its environs.

When you are doubting whether a thing is worth the trouble of going to see, recollect that you will never again be so near it, that you may repent the not having seen it, but can never repent having seen it. But there is an opposite extreme too, that is, the seeing too much. A judicious selection is to be aimed at, taking care that the indolence of the moment have no influence in the decision. Take care particularly not to let the porters of churches, cabinets, &c., lead you through all the little details of their profession, which will load the memory with trifles, fatigue the attention, and waste that and your time. It is difficult to confine these people to the few objects worth seeing and remembering. They wish for your money, and suppose you give it the more willingly the more they detail to you.

When one calls in the taverns for the *vin du pays,* they give what is natural and unadulterated and cheap: when *vin étranger* is called for, it only gives a pretext for charging an extravagant price for an unwholesome stuff, very often of their own brewery. The people you will naturally see the most of will be tavern keepers, *valets de place,* and postilions. These are the hackneyed rascals of every country. Of course they must never be considered when we calculate the national character.

*Objects of attention for an American.*—1. Agriculture. Everything belonging to this art, and whatever has a near relation to it. Useful or agreeable animals which might be transported to America. Species of plants for the farmer's garden, according to the climate of the different States.

2. Mechanical arts, so far as they respect things necessary in America, and inconvenient to be transported thither ready-made, such as forges, stone quarries, boats, bridges, (very especially,) &c., &c.

3. Lighter mechanical arts, and manufactures. Some of these will be worth a superficial view; but circumstances rendering it impossible that America should become a manufacturing country during the time of any man now living, it would be a waste of attention to examine these minutely.

4. Gardens, peculiarly worth the attention of an American, because it is the country of all others where the noblest gardens may be made without expense. We have only to cut out the superabundant plants.

5. Architecture worth great attention. As we double our numbers every twenty years, we must double our houses. Besides, we build of such perishable materials, that one half of our houses must be rebuilt in every space of twenty years, so that in that time, houses are to be built for three-fourths of our inhabitants. It is, then, among the most important arts; and it is desirable to introduce taste into an art which shows so much.

6. Painting. Statuary. Too expensive for the state of wealth among us. It would be useless, therefore, and preposterous, for us to make ourselves connoisseurs in those arts. They are worth seeing, but not studying.

7. Politics of each country, well worth studying so far as respects internal affairs. Examine their influence on the happiness of the people. Take every possible occasion for entering into the houses of the laborers, and especially at the moments of their repast; see what they eat, how they are clothed, whether they are obliged to work too hard; whether the government or their landlord takes from them an unjust proportion of their labor; on what footing stands the property they call their own, their personal liberty, &c., &c.

8. Courts. To be seen as you would see the tower of London or menagerie of Versailles, with their lions, tigers, hyenas, and other beasts of prey, standing in the same relation to their fellows. A slight acquaintance with them will suffice to show you that, under the most imposing exterior, they are the weakest and worst part of mankind. Their manners, could you ape them, would not make you beloved in your own country, nor would they improve it could you introduce them there to the exclusion of that honest simplicity now prevailing in America, and worthy of being cherished.

## *Chapter XVII*

# LITERATURE AND LANGUAGE

## LOVELY PEGGY[1]

*c.* 1760's

Once more I'll tune the vocal shell
To hills and dales my passion tell,
A flame which time can never quell
  That burns for lovely Peggy. . . .

I stole a kiss the other day,
And trust me, nought but truth I say,
The fragrant breath of blooming May
  Was not so sweet as Peggy.

While bees from flow'r to flow'r shall rove,
And linnets warble through the grove,
Or stately swans the waters love,
  So long shall I love Peggy.

And when death with his pointed dart
Shall strike the blow that rives my heart,
My words shall be when I depart,
  Adieu, my lovely Peggy.

## INSCRIPTION FOR AN AFRICAN SLAVE[2]

1771

Shores there are, bless'd shores for us remain,
And favor'd isles with golden fruitage crown's
Where tufted flow'rets paint the verdant plain,

[1] These verses are in Jefferson's hand, but the authorship is not certain.
[2] Written in Jefferson's copy of the *Virginia Almanack for 1771*. Since it is not found anywhere in print, one may assume that Jefferson wrote it.

Where ev'ry breeze shall med'cine every wound.
There the stern tyrant that embitters life,
Shall vainly suppliant, spread his asking hand;
There shall we view the billow's raging strife,
Aid the kind breast, and waft his boat to land.

## HEAD-AND-HEART DIALOGUE[1]

October 26, 1786

MY DEAR MADAM: Having performed the last sad office of handing you into your carriage, at the pavillon de St. Denis, and seen the wheels get actually into motion, I turned on my heel and walked, more dead than alive, to the opposite door, where my own was awaiting me. Mr. Danquerville was missing. He was sought for, found, and dragged down stairs. We were crammed into the carriage, like recruits for the Bastille, and not having soul enough to give orders to the coachman, he presumed Paris our destination, and drove off. After a considerable interval, silence was broke, with a *"Je suis vraiment affligé du départ de ces bons gens."* This was a signal for a mutual confession of distress. We began immediately to talk of Mr. and Mrs. Cosway, of their goodness, their talents, their amiability; and, though we spoke of nothing else, we seemed hardly to have entered into the matter, when the coachman announced the rue St. Denis, and that we were opposite Mr. Danquerville's. He insisted on descending there, and traversing a short passage to his lodgings. I was carried home. Seated by my fireside, solitary and sad, the following dialogue took place between my Head and my Heart.

HEAD. Well, friend, you seem to be in a pretty trim.

HEART. I am indeed the most wretched of all earthly beings. Overwhelmed with grief, every fibre of my frame distended beyond its natural powers to bear, I would willingly meet whatever catastrophe should leave me no more to feel, or to fear.

HEAD. These are the eternal consequences of your warmth and precipitation. This is one of the scrapes into which you are ever leading us. You confess your follies, indeed; but still you hug and cherish them; and no reformation can be hoped where there is no repentance.

HEART. Oh, my friend! this is no moment to upbraid my foibles. I am rent into fragments by the force of my grief! If you have any balm, pour it into my wounds; if none, do not harrow them by new torments. Spare me in this awful moment! At any other, I will attend with patience to your admonitions.

[1] Letter to Maria Cosway.

HEAD. On the contrary, I never found that the moment of triumph, with you, was the moment of attention to my admonitions. While suffering under your follies, you may perhaps be made sensible of them, but the paroxysm over, you fancy it can never return. Harsh, therefore, as the medicine may be, it is my office to administer it. You will be pleased to remember, that when our friend Trumbull used to be telling us of the merits and talents of these good people, I never ceased whispering to you that we had no occasion for new acquaintances; that the greater their merits and talents, the more dangerous their friendship to our tranquillity, because the regret at parting would be greater.

HEART. Accordingly, Sir, this acquaintance was not the consequence of my doings. It was one of your projects, which threw us in the way of it. It was you, remember, and not I, who desired the meeting at Legrand and Motinos. I never trouble myself with domes nor arches. The Halle aux bleds might have rotted down, before I should have gone to see it. But you, forsooth, who are eternally getting us to sleep with your diagrams and crotchets, must go and examine this wonderful piece of architecture; and when you had seen it, oh! it was the most superb thing on earth! What you had seen there was worth all you had yet seen in Paris! I thought so too. But I meant it of the lady and gentleman to whom we had been presented; and not of a parcel of sticks and chips put together in pens. You, then, Sir, and not I, have been the cause of the present distress.

HEAD. It would have been happy for you if my diagrams and crotchets had gotten you to sleep on that day, as you are pleased to say they eternally do. My visit to Legrand and Motinos had public utility for its object. A market is to be built in Richmond. What a commodious plan is that of Legrand and Motinos; especially, if we put on it the noble dome of the Halle aux bleds. If such a bridge as they showed us can be thrown across the Schuylkill, at Philadelphia, the floating bridges taken up, and the navigation of that river opened, what a copious resource will be added, of wood and provisions, to warm and feed the poor of that city? While I was occupied with these objects, you were dilating with your new acquaintances, and contriving how to prevent a separation from them. Every soul of you had an engagement for the day. Yet all these were to be sacrificed, that you might dine together. Lying messengers were to be despatched into every quarter of the city, with apologies for your breach of engagement. You, particularly, had the effrontery to send word to the Duchess Danville, that on the moment we were setting out to dine with her, despatches came to hand, which required immediate attention. You wanted me to invent a more ingenious excuse; but I knew you were getting into a scrape, and I would have nothing to do with it. Well; after dinner to St. Cloud, from St. Cloud to Ruggieri's, from Ruggieri's to Krumholtz; and if the day had been as long as a Lapland summer day, you would still have contrived means among you to have filled it.

HEART. Oh! my dear friend, how you have revived me by recalling to my mind the transactions of that day! How well I remember them all, and that, when I came home at night, and looked back to the morning, it seemed to have been a month agone. Go on, then, like a kind comforter, and paint to me the day we went to St. Germains. How beautiful was every object! the Port de Reuilly, the hills along the Seine, the rainbows of the machine of Marly, the terrace of St. Germains, the châteaux, the gardens, the statues of Marly, the pavillon of Lucienne. Recollect, too, Madrid, Bagatelle, the King's garden, the Dessert. How grand the idea excited by the remains of such a column. The spiral staircase, too, was beautiful. Every moment was filled with something agreeable. The wheels of time moved on with a rapidity, of which those of our carriage gave but a faint idea. And yet, in the evening, when one took a retrospect of the day, what a mass of happiness had we travelled over! Retrace all those scenes to me, my good companion, and I will forgive the unkindness with which you were chiding me. The day we went to St. Germains was a little too warm, I think; was it not?

HEAD. Thou art the most incorrigible of all the beings that ever sinned! I reminded you of the follies of the first day, intending to deduce from thence some useful lessons for you; but instead of listening to them, you kindle at the recollection, you retrace the whole series with a fondness, which shows you want nothing, but the opportunity, to act it over again. I often told you, during its course, that you were imprudently engaging your affections, under circumstances that must have cost you a great deal of pain; that the persons, indeed, were of the greatest merit, possessing good sense, good humor, honest hearts, honest manners, and eminence in a lovely art; that the lady had, moreover, qualities and accomplishments belonging to her sex, which might form a chapter apart for her; such as music, modesty, beauty, and that softness of disposition, which is the ornament of her sex and charm of ours; but that all these considerations would increase the pang of separation; that their stay here was to be short; that you rack our whole system when you are parted from those you love, complaining that such a separation is worse than death, inasmuch as this ends our sufferings, whereas that only begins them; and that the separation would, in this instance, be the more severe, as you would probably never see them again.

HEART. But they told me they would come back again, the next year.

HEAD. But, in the meantime, see what you suffer; and their return, too, depends on so many circumstances, that if you had a grain of prudence, you would not count upon it. Upon the whole, it is improbable, and therefore you should abandon the idea of ever seeing them again.

HEART. May heaven abandon me if I do!

HEAD. Very well. Suppose, then, they come back. They are to stay two months, and, when these are expired, what is to follow? Perhaps you flatter yourself they may come to America?

HEART. God only knows what is to happen. I see nothing impossible in that supposition; and I see things wonderfully contrived sometimes, to make us happy. Where could they find such objects as in America, for the exercise of their enchanting art? especially the lady, who paints landscapes so inimitably. She wants only subjects worthy of immortality, to render her pencil immortal. The Falling Spring, the Cascade of Niagara, the passage of the Potomac through the Blue Mountains, the Natural Bridge; it is worth a voyage across the Atlantic to see these objects; much more to paint, and make them, and thereby ourselves, known to all ages. And our own dear Monticello; where has nature spread so rich a mantle under the eye? mountains, forests, rocks, river. With what majesty do we there ride above the storms! How sublime to look down into the workhouse of nature, to see her clouds, hail, snow, rain, thunder, all fabricated at our feet! and the glorious sun, when rising as if out of a distant water, just gilding the tops of the mountains, and giving life to all nature! I hope in God, no circumstance may ever make either seek an asylum from grief! With what sincere sympathy I would open every cell of my composition, to receive the effusion of their woes! I would pour my tears into their wounds; and if a drop of balm could be found on the top of the Cordilleras, or at the remotest sources of the Missouri, I would go thither myself to seek and to bring it. Deeply practised in the school of affliction, the human heart knows no joy which I have not lost, no sorrow of which I have not drunk! Fortune can present no grief of unknown form to me! Who, then, can so softly bind up the wound of another, as he who has felt the same wound himself? But heaven forbid they should ever know a sorrow! Let us turn over another leaf, for this has distracted me.

HEAD. Well. Let us put this possibility to trial then, on another point. When you consider the character which is given of our country, by the lying newspapers of London, and their credulous copiers in other countries; when you reflect that all Europe is made to believe we are a lawless banditti, in a state of absolute anarchy, cutting one another's throats, and plundering without distinction, how could you expect that any reasonable creature would venture among us?

HEART. But you and I know that all this is false: that there is not a country on earth, where there is greater tranquillity; where the laws are milder, or better obeyed; where everyone is more attentive to his own business, or meddles less with that of others; where strangers are better received, more hospitably treated, and with a more sacred respect.

HEAD. True, you and I know this, but your friends do not know it.

HEART. But they are sensible people, who think for themselves. They will ask of impartial foreigners, who have been among us, whether they saw or heard on the spot, any instance of anarchy. They will judge, too, that a people, occupied as we are, in opening rivers, digging navigable canals, making roads, building public schools, establishing academies, erecting busts and statues to our great men, protecting religious freedom, abolishing sanguinary punishments, reforming and improving our laws in general; they will judge, I say, for themselves, whether these are not the occupations of a people at their ease; whether this is not better evidence of our true state, than a London newspaper, hired to lie, and from which no truth can ever be extracted but by reversing everything it says.

HEAD. I did not begin this lecture, my friend, with a view to learn from you what America is doing. Let us return, then, to our point. I wish to make you sensible how imprudent it is to place your affections, without reserve, on objects you must so soon lose, and whose loss, when it comes, must cost you such severe pangs. Remember the last night. You knew your friends were to leave Paris today. This was enough to throw you into agonies. All night you tossed us from one side of the bed to the other; no sleep, no rest. The poor crippled wrist, too, never left one moment in the same position; now up, now down, now here, now there; was it to be wondered at, if its pains returned? The surgeon then was to be called, and to be rated as an ignoramus, because he could not divine the cause of this extraordinary change. In fine, my friend, you must mend your manners. This is not a world to live at random in, as you do. To avoid those eternal distresses, to which you are forever exposing us, you must learn to look forward, before you take a step which may interest our peace. Everything in this world is matter of calculation. Advance then with caution, the balance in your hand. Put into one scale the pleasures which any object may offer; but put fairly into the other, the pains which are to follow, and see which preponderates. The making an acquaintance, is not a matter of indifference. When a new one is proposed to you, view it all round. Consider what advantages it presents, and to what inconveniences it may expose you. Do not bite at the bait of pleasure, till you know there is no hook beneath it. The art of life is the art of avoiding pain; and he is the best pilot, who steers clearest of the rocks and shoals with which it is beset. Pleasure is always before us; but misfortune is at our side: while running after that, this arrests us. The most effectual means of being secure against pain, is to retire within ourselves, and to suffice for our own happiness. Those which depend on ourselves, are the only pleasures a wise man will count on: for nothing is ours, which another may deprive us of. Hence the inestimable value of intellectual pleasures. Ever in our power, always leading us to something new, never cloying, we ride serene and sublime above the concerns of this mortal world, contemplating truth and nature, matter and motion, the laws which bind up their existence, and that Eternal Being who made and bound them up by those laws. Let this be our employ. Leave the bustle and tumult of society to those who have not talents to occupy themselves without them. Friendship is but another name for an alliance with the follies and the misfortunes of others. Our own share of miseries is sufficient: why enter then as volunteers into those of another? Is there so little gall poured into our cup, that we must need help to drink that of our neighbor? A friend dies, or leaves us: we feel as if a limb was cut off. He is sick: we must watch over him, and participate of his pains. His fortune is shipwrecked: ours must be laid under contribution. He loses a child, a parent, or a partner: we must mourn the loss as if it were our own.

HEART. And what more sublime delight than to mingle tears with one whom the hand of heaven hath smitten! to watch over the bed of sickness, and to beguile its tedious and its painful moments! to share our bread with one to whom misfortune has left none! This world abounds indeed with misery; to lighten its burthen, we must divide it with one another. But let us now try the virtue of your mathematical balance, and as you have put into one scale the burthens of friendship, let me put its comforts into the other. When languishing then under disease, how grateful is the solace of our friends! how are we penetrated with their assiduities and attentions! how much are we supported by their encouragements and kind offices! When heaven has taken from us some object of our love, how sweet is it to have a bosom whereon to recline our heads, and into which we may pour the torrent of our tears! Grief, with such a comfort, is almost a luxury! In a life, where we are perpetually exposed to want and accident, yours is a wonderful proposition, to insulate ourselves, to retire from all aid, and to wrap ourselves in the mantle of self-sufficiency! For, assuredly, nobody will care for him who cares for nobody. But friendship is precious, not only in the shade, but in the sunshine of life; and thanks to a benevolent arrangement of things, the greater part of life is sunshine. I will recur for proof to the days we have lately passed. On these, indeed, the sun shone brightly. How gay did the face of nature appear! Hills, valleys, châteaux, gardens, rivers, every object wore its liveliest hue! Whence did they borrow it? From the presence of our charming companion. They were pleasing, because she seemed pleased. Alone, the scene would have been dull and insipid: the participation of it with her gave it relish. Let the gloomy monk, sequestered from the world, seek unsocial pleasures in the bottom of his cell! Let the sublimated philosopher grasp visionary happiness, while pursuing phantoms dressed in the garb of truth! Their supreme wisdom is supreme folly; and they mistake for happiness the mere absence of pain. Had they ever felt the solid pleasure of one generous spasm of the heart, they would exchange for it all the frigid speculations of their lives, which you have been vaunting in such elevated terms. Believe me, then, my friend, that that is a miserable arithmetic which could estimate friendship at nothing, or at less than nothing. Respect for you has induced me to enter into this discussion, and to hear principles uttered which I detest and abjure. Respect for myself now obliges me to recall you into the proper limits of your office. When nature assigned us the same habitation, she gave us over it a divided empire. To you, she allotted the field of science; to me, that of morals. When the circle is to be squared, or the orbit of a comet to be traced; when the arch of greatest strength, or the solid of least resistance, is to be investigated, take up the problem; it is yours; nature has given me no cognizance of it. In like manner, in denying to you the feelings of sympathy, of benevolence, of gratitude, of justice, of love, of friendship, she has excluded you from their control. To these, she has adapted the mechanism of the heart. Morals were too essential to the happiness of man, to be risked on the uncertain combinations of the head. She laid their foundation, therefore, in sentiment, not in science. That she gave to all, as necessary to all; this to a few only, as sufficing with a few. I know, indeed, that you pretend authority to the sovereign control of our conduct, in all its parts; and a respect for your grave saws and maxims, a desire to do what is right, has sometimes induced me to conform to your counsels. A few facts, however, which I can readily recall to your memory, will suffice to prove to you, that nature has not organized you for our moral direction. When the poor, wearied soldier whom we overtook at Chickahomony, with his pack on his back, begged us to let him get up behind our chariot, you began to calculate that the road was full of soldiers, and that if all should be taken up, our horses would fail in their journey. We drove on therefore. But, soon becoming sensible you had made me do wrong, that, though we cannot relieve all the distressed, we should relieve as many as we can, I turned about to take up the soldier; but he had entered a bye-path, and was no more to be found; and from that moment to this, I could never find him out, to ask his forgiveness. Again, when the poor woman came to ask a charity in Philadelphia, you whispered that she looked like a drunkard, and that half a dollar was enough to give her for the ale-house. Those who want the dispositions to give, easily find reasons why they ought not to give. When I sought her out afterwards, and did what I should have done at first, you know that she employed the money immediately towards placing her child at school. If our country, when pressed with wrongs at the point of the bayonet, had been governed by its heads instead of its hearts, where should we have been now? Hanging on a gallows as high as Haman's. You began to calculate, and to compare wealth and numbers:

we threw up a few pulsations of our blood; we supplied enthusiasm against wealth and numbers; we put our existence to the hazard, when the hazard seemed against us, and we saved our country: justifying, at the same time, the ways of Providence, whose precept is, to do always what is right, and leave the issue to him. In short, my friend, as far as my recollection serves me, I do not know that I ever did a good thing on your suggestion, or a dirty one without it. I do forever, then, disclaim your interference in my province. Fill paper as you please with triangles and squares: try how many ways you can hang and combine them together. I shall never envy nor control your sublime delights. But leave me to decide, when and where friendships are to be contracted. You say, I contract them at random. So you said the woman at Philadelphia was a drunkard. I receive none into my esteem, till I know they are worthy of it. Wealth, title, office, are no recommendations to my friendship. On the contrary, great good qualities are requisite to make amends for their having wealth, title, and office. You confess, that, in the present case, I could not have made a worthier choice. You only object, that I was so soon to lose them. We are not immortal ourselves, my friend; how can we expect our enjoyments to be so? We have no rose without its thorn; no pleasure without alloy. It is the law of our existence; and we must acquiesce. It is the condition annexed to all our pleasures, not by us who receive, but by him who gives them. True, this condition is pressing cruelly on me at this moment. I feel more fit for death than life. But, when I look back on the pleasures of which it is the consequence, I am conscious they were worth the price I am paying. Notwithstanding your endeavors, too, to damp my hopes, I comfort myself with expectations of their promised return. Hope is sweeter than despair; and they were too good to mean to deceive me. "In the summer," said the gentleman; but "in the spring," said the lady; and I should love her forever, were it only for that! Know, then, my friend, that I have taken these good people into my bosom; that I have lodged them in the warmest cell I could find; that I love them, and will continue to love them through life; that if fortune should dispose them on one side the globe, and me on the other, my affections shall pervade its whole mass to reach them. Knowing then my determination, attempt not to disturb it. If you can, at any time, furnish matter for their amusement, it will be the office of a good neighbor to do it. I will, in like manner, seize any occasion which may offer, to do the like good turn for you with Condorcet, Rittenhouse, Madison, La Cretelle, or any other of those worthy sons of science, whom you so justly prize.

I thought this a favorable proposition whereon to rest the issue of the dialogue. So I put an end to it by calling for my nightcap. Methinks, I hear you wish to heaven I had called a little sooner, and so spared you the ennui of such a sermon. I did not interrupt them sooner, because I was in a mood for hearing sermons. You too were the subject; and on such a thesis, I never think the theme long; not even if I am to write it, and that slowly and awkwardly, as now, with the left hand. But, that you may not be discouraged from a correspondence which begins so formidably, I will promise you, on my honor, that my future letters shall be of a reasonable length. I will even agree to express but half my esteem for you, for fear of cloying you with too full a dose. But, on your part, no curtailing. If your letters are as long as the Bible, they will appear short to me. Only let them be brimful of affection. I shall read them with the dispositions with which Arlequin, in *Les deux billets,* spelt the words *"je t'aime,"* and wished that the whole alphabet had entered into their composition.

We have had incessant rains since your departure. These make me fear for your health, as well as that you had an uncomfortable journey. The same cause has prevented me from being able to give you any account of your friends here. This voyage to Fontainebleau will probably send the Count de Moutier and the Marquis de Brehan, to America. Danquerville promised to visit me, but has not done it as yet. De la Tude comes sometimes to take family soup with me, and entertains me with anecdotes of his five and thirty years' imprisonment. How fertile is the mind of man, which can make the Bastile and dungeon of Vincennes yield interesting anecdotes! You know this was for making four verses on Madame de Pompadour. But I think you told me you did not know the verses. They were these: *"Sans esprit, sans sentiment, Sans etre belle, ni neuve, En France on peut avoir le premier amant: Pompadour en est l' épreuve."* I have read the memoir of his three escapes. As to myself, my health is good, except my wrist which mends slowly, and my mind which mends not at all, but broods constantly over your departure. The lateness of the season obliges me to decline my journey into the south of France. Present me in the most friendly terms to Mr. Cosway, and receive me into your own recollection with a partiality and warmth, proportioned not to my own poor merit, but to the sentiments of sincere affection and esteem, with which I have the honor to be, my dear Madam, your most obedient humble servant.[2]

[2] To Mrs. Cosway, October 13, 1786:

MY DEAR MADAM: Just as I had sealed the enclosed, I received a letter of a good length, dated Antwerp, with your name at the bottom. I prepared myself for a feast. I read two or three sentences; looked again at the signature to see if I had not mistaken it. It was visibly yours. Read a sentence or two more. Diable! Spelt your name distinctly. There was not a letter of it omitted. Began to read again. In fine, after reading a little and examining the signature, alternately, half a dozen times, I found that your name was to four lines only, instead of four pages. I thank you for the four lines, however, because they prove you think of me; little, indeed, but better little than none. To show how much I think of you, I send you the enclosed letter of three sheets of paper, being a history of the evening I parted with you. But how expect you should read a letter of three mortal sheets of paper? I will tell you. Divide it into six doses of half a sheet each, and every day, when the toilette begins, take a dose, that is to say, read half a sheet. By this means, it will have the only merit its length and dulness

# THOUGHTS ON ENGLISH PROSODY[1]

After 1790

Everyone knows the difference between verse and prose in his native language; nor does he need the aid of prosody to enable him to read or to repeat verse according to its just rhythm. It is the business of the poet so to arrange his words as that, repeated in their accustomed measures they shall strike the ear with that regular rhythm which constitutes verse.

It is for foreigners principally that prosody is necessary; not knowing the accustomed measures of words, they require the aid of rules to teach them those measures and to enable them to read verse so as to make themselves or others sensible of its music. I suppose that the system of rules or exceptions which constitutes Greek and Latin prosody, as shown with us, was unknown to those nations, and that it has been invented by the moderns to whom those languages were foreign. I do not mean to affirm this, however,

can aspire to, that of assisting your *coiffeuse* to procure you six good naps of sleep. I will even allow you twelve days to get through it, holding you rigorously to one condition only, that is, that at whatever hour you receive this, you do not break the seal of the enclosed till the next toilette. Of this injunction I require a sacred execution. I rest it on your friendship, and that, in your first letter, you tell me honestly whether you have honestly performed it. I send you the song I promised. Bring me in return the subject, *Jours heureux!* Were I a songster, I should sing it all to these words: "*Dans ces lieux qu'elle tarde à se rendre!*" Learn it, I pray you, and sing it with feeling. My right hand presents its devoirs to you, and sees, with great indignation, the left supplanting it in a correspondence so much valued. You will know the first moment it can resume its rights. The first exercise of them shall be addressed to you, as you had the first essay of its rival. It will yet, however, be many a day. Present my esteem to Mr. Cosway, and believe me to be yours very affectionately.

[1] An explanation of the reason for writing this essay is to be found in a letter by Jefferson to the Marquis de Chastellux, who visited Monticello in the Spring of 1782. The letter is undated, but was apparently written after his return from France, at the end of 1789:

"Among the topics of conversation which stole off like so many minutes the few hours I had the happiness of possessing you at Monticello, the measures of English verse was one. I thought it depended like Greek and Latin verse, on long and short syllables arranged into regular feet. You were of a different opinion. I did not pursue this subject after your departure, because it always presented itself with the painful recollection of a pleasure which in all human probability I was never to enjoy again. This probability like other human calculations has been set aside by events; and we have again discussed on this side the Atlantic a subject which had occupied us during some pleasing moments on the other. A daily habit of walking in the Bois de Boulogne gave me an opportunity of turning this subject in my mind and I determined to present you my thoughts on it in the form of a letter. I for some time parried the difficulties which assailed me, but at length I found they were not to be opposed, and their triumph was complete . . . I began with the design of converting you to my opinion that the arrangement of long and short syllables into regular feet constituted the harmony of English verse. I ended by discovering that you were right in denying that proposition. The next object was to find out the real circumstance which gives harmony to English poetry and laws to those who make it. I present you with the result."

In 1801 Jefferson wrote to John D. Burke: "In earlier life I was fond of it [poetry], and easily pleased. But as age and cares advanced, the powers of fancy have declined. Every year seems to have plucked a feather from her wings, till she can no longer waft one to those sublime heights to which it is necessary to accompany the poet. So much has my relish for poetry deserted me that, at present, I cannot read even Virgil with pleasure."

This Essay was first published in vol. XIX of the Memorial Edition of Jefferson's *Writings* (1904).

because you have not searched into the history of this art, nor am I at present in a situation which admits of that search. By industrious examination of the Greek and Latin verse it has been found that pronouncing certain combinations of vowels and consonants long, and certain others short, the actual arrangement of those long and short syllables, as found in their verse, constitutes a rhythm which is regular and pleasing to the ear, and that pronouncing them with any other measures, the run is unpleasing, and ceases to produce the effect of the verse. Hence it is concluded and rationally enough that the Greeks and Romans pronounced those syllables long or short in reading their verse; and as we observe in modern languages that the syllables of words have the same measures both in verse and prose, we ought to conclude that they had the same also in those ancient languages, and that we must lengthen or shorten in their prose the same syllables which we lengthen or shorten in their verse. Thus, if I meet with the word *praeteritos* in Latin prose and want to know how the Romans pronounced it, I search for it in some poet and find it in the line of Virgil, *"O mihi praeteritos referat si Jupiter annos!"* where it is evident that *prae* is long and *te* short in direct opposition to the pronunciation which we often hear. The length allowed to a syllable is called its quantity, and hence we say that the Greek and Latin languages are to be pronounced according to quantity.

Those who have undertaken to frame a prosody for the English language have taken quantity for their basis and have mounted the English poetry on Greek and Latin feet. If this foundation admits of no question the prosody of Doctor Johnson, built upon it, is perhaps the best. He comprehends under three different feet every combination of long and short syllables which he supposes can be found in English verse, to wit: 1. a long and a short, which is the trochee of the Greeks and Romans; 2. a short and a long, which is their iambus; and 3. two short and a long, which is their anapest. And he thinks that all English verse may be resolved into these feet.

It is true that in the English language some one syllable of a word is always sensibly distinguished from the others by an emphasis of pronunciation or by an accent as we call it. But I am not satisfied whether this accented syllable be pronounced longer, louder, or harder, and the others shorter, lower, or softer. I have found the nicest ears divided on the question. Thus in the word *calenture,* nobody will deny that the first syllable is pronounced more emphatically than the others; but many will deny that it is longer in pronunciation. In the second of the following verses of Pope, I think there are but two short syllables.

Oh! be thou bless'd with all that Heav'n can send
Long health, long youth, long pleasure, and a friend.

Innumerable instances like this might be produced. It seems, therefore, too much to take for the basis of a system a postulatum which one-half of mankind will deny. But the superstructure of Doctor Johnson's prosody may still be supported by substituting for its basis accent instead of quantity; and nobody will deny us the existence of accent.

In every word of more than one syllable there is some one syllable strongly distinguishable in pronunciation by its emphasis or accent.

If a word has more than two syllables it generally admits of a subordinate emphasis or accent on the alternate syllables counting backwards and forwards from the principal one, as in this verse of Milton:

Well if thrown out as supernumerary,

where the principal accent is on *nu,* but there is a lighter one on *su* and *ra* also. There are some few instances indeed wherein the subordinate accent is differently arranged, as *parisyllabic, Constantinople.* It is difficult, therefore, to introduce words of this kind into verse.

That the accent shall never be displaced from the syllable whereon usage hath established it is the fundamental law of English verse.

There are but three arrangements into which these accents can be thrown in the English language which entitled the composition to be distinguished by the name of verse. That is, 1. Where the accent falls on all the odd syllables. 2. Where it falls on all the even syllables. 3. When it falls on every third syllable. If the reason of this be asked, no other can be assigned but that it results from the nature of the sounds which compose the English language and from the construction of the human ear. So, in the infinite gradations of sounds from the lowest to the highest in the musical scale, those only give pleasure to the ear which are at the intervals we call whole tones and semitones. The reason is that it has pleased God to make us so. The English poet then must so arrange his words that their established accents shall fall regularly in one of these three orders. To aid him in this he has at his command the whole army of monosyllables which in the English language is a very numerous one. These he may accent or not, as he pleases. Thus is this verse:

'Tis júst resentment ańd becómes the brave.
—POPE

the monosyllable *and* standing between two unaccented syllables catches the accent and supports the measures. The same monosyllable serves to fill the interval between two accents in the following instance:

From úse obscúre and súbtle, bút to knów.

—MILTON

The monosyllables *with* and *in* receive the accent in one of the following instances and suffer it to pass over them in the other.

The témpted *wíth* dishónor fóul, suppósed.

—MILTON

Attémpt *with* cónfidénce, the wórk is dóne.

—HOPKINS

Which múst be mútual *ín* propórtion dúe.

—MILTON

Too múch of órnamént *in* oútward shéw.

—MILTON

The following lines afford other proofs of this license.

Yet, yét, I lóve—from Abelard it came.

—POPE

Flow, flow, my stream this devious way.

—SHENSTONE

The Greeks and Romans in like manner had a number of syllables which might in any situation be pronounced long or short without offending the ear. They had others which they could make long or short by changing their position. These were of great avail to the poets. The following is an example:

Πολλάκις ὢ πολυφάμε, τὰ μη καλὰ καλὰ πε φαυλαι.

—THEOCRITUS

'Αγες, 'Αγες βροτολοιγὲ, μιαι φόνε τει χεδιπλῆτα.

—HOMER, IL.

Μετςα δε τεμ' χε Θεοιςι, το νδ μετρόν εςτιν ἀγίςον.

—PHOCYL

where the word Ages, being used twice, the first syllable is long in the first and short in the second instance, and the second is short in the first and long in the second instance.

But though the poets have great authority over the monosyllables, yet it is not altogether absolute. The following is a proof of this:

Throúgh the dark póstern óf time lóng elápsed.

—YOUNG

It is impossible to read this without throwing the accent on the monosyllable *of* and yet the ear is shocked and revolts at this.

That species of our verse wherein the accent falls on all the odd syllables, I shall call, from that circumstance, odd or imparisyllabic verse. It is what has been heretofore called trochaic verse. To the foot which composes it, it will still be convenient and most intelligible to retain the ancient name of trochee, only remembering that by that term we do not mean a long and short syllable, but an accented and unaccented one.

That verse wherein the accent is on the even syllables may be called even or parisyllabic verse, and corresponds with what has been called iambic verse; retaining the term iambus for the name of the foot we shall thereby mean an unaccented and an accented syllable.

That verse wherein the accent falls on every third syllable, may be called trisyllabic verse; it is equivalent to what has been called anapestic; and we will still use the term anapest to express two unaccented and one accented syllable.

Accent then is, I think, the basis of English verse; and it leads us to the same threefold distribution of it to which the hypothesis of *quantity* had led Dr. Johnson. While it preserves to us the simplicity of his classification it relieves us from the doubtfulness, if not the error, on which it was founded.

### OBSERVATION ON THE THREE MEASURES

Wherever a verse should regularly begin or end with an accented syllable, that unaccented syllable may be suppressed.

Bréd 'on pláins, or bórn in válleys,
Whó would bid thóse scénes adíeu?
Stránger tó the árts of málice,
Whó would éver cóurts pursúe?
—SHENSTONE

Rúin séize thée, rúthléss kíng!
Confúsión on thy bánners wáit;
Though, fanńed by Cónquest's crímson wíng,
They móck the aír with ídle státe.
Helḿ, nor haúlberk's twísted máil,
Nor év'n thy vírtues, Týrant, sháll avaíl
To sáve thy sécret soúl from níghtly féars.
From Cámbria's cúrse, from Cámbria's téars!
—GRAY

Y̆e Shép / herds / give eár / to my láy,
And táke no more héed of my shéep;
They have nóthing to dó but to stráy;
I have nóthing to dó but to wéep.
—SHENSTONE

In the first example the unaccented syllable with which the imparisyllabic (odd) verse should end is omitted in the second and fourth lines. In the second example the unaccented syllable with which the parisyllabic (even) verse should begin is omitted in the first and fifth lines. In the third instance one of the unaccented syllables with which the trisyllabic (triple) verse should begin, is omitted in the first and second lines and in the first of the following line both are omitted:

> Únder this márble, or únder this síll
> Or únder this túrf, or é'en what you wíll
> Lies one who ne'er car'd, and still cares not a pin
> What they said, or may say, of the mortal within;
> But who, living or dying, serene still and free,
> Trusts in God that as well as he was he shall be.
>
> —POPE

An accented syllable may be prefixed to a verse which should regularly begin with an accent and added to one which should end with an accent, thus:

1. Daúntless ón his nátive sánds
   The drágon-són of Móna stánds;
   In glíttering árms and glóry drést,
   Hígh he réars his rúby crést.
   Theré the thúndering strókes begín,
   Theré the préss, and thére the dín;
   Talymalfra's rocky shore.

   —GRAY

   Theré Confúsion, Térror's chíld,
   Cónflict fiérce, and Rúin wíld,
   Ágoný, that pánts for bréath,
   Despaír, and hónoráble déath.

   —GRAY

2. Whát is this wórld? thy schóol Oh! Misséry!
   Our ónly lésson ís to leárn to súffer;
   And hé who knóws not thát, was bórn for nó*thing.*
   My cómfort ís each móment tákes awáy
   A gráin at léast fróm the dead lóad that's ón *me*
   And gíves a néarer próspect óf the gráve.

   —YOUNG

3. Says Ríchard to Thómas (and séem'd half afráid).
   "I'm thínking to márry thy místress's máid;
   Now, becaúse Mrs. Lúcy to theé is well knówn,
   I will dó't if thou bidst me, or lét it alóne."
   Said Thomás to Ríchard, "To speák my opín*ion,*
   There is nót such a bítch in King Géorge's domín*ion;*

And I fírmly beliéve, if thou knéw'st her as Í *do,*
Thou wouldst choóse out a whípping-post fírst to be tíed *to.*
She's peévish, she's thiévish, she's úgly, shé's old,
And a liár, and a fóol, and a slút, and a scóld."
Next dáy Richard hásten'd to chúrch and was wéd,
And ere níght had infórm'd her what Thómas had sáid.

—SHENSTONE

An accented syllable can never be either omitted or added without changing the character of the verse. In fact it is the number of accented syllables which determines the length of the verse. That is to say, the number of feet of which it consists.

Imparisyllabic verse being made up of trochees should regularly end with an unaccented syllable; and in that case if it be in rhyme both syllables of the foot must be rhymed. But most frequently the unaccented syllable is omitted according to the license before mentioned and then it suffices to rhyme the accented one. The following is given as a specimen of this kind of verse.

Shépherd, wóuldst thou heré obtaín
Pléasure unálloy'd with páin?
Jóy that súits the rúral sphére?
Géntle shépherd, lénd an eár.

Leárn to rélish cálm delíght
Vérdant váles and foúntains bríght;
Treés that nód o'er slóping hills,
Cavés that écho tínkling rílls.

Íf thou cánst no chárm disclóse
Ín the símplest búd that blóws;
Gó, forsake thy plaín and fóld;
Jóin the crówd, and toíl for góld.

Tránquil pleásures néver clóy;
Bánish eách tumúltuous jóy;
Áll but lóve—for lóve inspíres
Fónder wíshes, wármer fíres.

Sée, to sweeten thy repose,
The blóssom buds, the fountain flows;
Ló! to crown thy healthful board,
Áll that milk and fruits afford.

Seék no more—the rest is vain;
Pléasure ending soon in pain:
Ánguish lightly gilded o'er:
Clóse thy wish, and seek no more.

—SHENSTONE

Parisyllabic verse should regularly be composed of all iambuses; that is to say, all its even syllables should be accented. Yet it is very common for the first foot of the line to be a trochee as in this verse:

Yé who e'er lóst an ángel, píty mé!

Sometimes a trochee is found in the midst of this verse. But this is extremely rare indeed. The following, however, are instances of it taken from Milton.

To dó ought góod *néver* will bé our tásk
Behésts obéy, *wórthiest* to bé obéyed.

Than sélf-esteém, *gróunded* on júst and ríght
Leans the huge elephant the *wisest* of brutes!

In these instances it has not a good effect, but in the following it has:

This hánd is míne—*óh! whát* a hánd is hére!
So soft, souls sink into it and are lost.

When this trochee is placed at the beginning of a verse, if it be not too often repeated it produces a variety in the measure which is pleasing. The following is a specimen of the parisyllabic verse, wherein the instances of this trochee beginning the verse are noted:

*Píty* the sórrows óf a póor old mán,
  Whose trémbling límbs have bórne him tó your dóor,
Whose dáys are dwíndled tó the shórtest span;
  *Óh! give* relíef, and Heáven will bléss your stóre.

These táttered clóthes my povérty bespeák,
  These hoáry lócks proclaím my léngthen'd yéars,
And mány a fúrrow ín my gríef-worn chéek
  Has beén the chánnel to a flóod of teárs.

Yon hoúse, erécted ón the rísing gróund,
  With témpting áspect, dréw me fróm my róad;
For plénty thére a résidénce has fóund,
  And grándeur á magnifícent abóde.

*Hárd is* the fáte of thé infírm ánd póor!
  Here, as I craved a mórsel of their bréad,
A pámper'd ménial drove me fróm the dóor,
  To seék a shélter ín an húmbler shéd.

*Óh! take* me tó your hóspitáble dóme;
  *Keén blows* the wínd, and píercing ís the cóld!
*Shórt is* my pássage tó the fríendly tómb,
  For Í am póor, and mísérably óld.

*Heaven sends* misfórtunes; why should we repine?
'Tis Heaven has brought me tó the state you sée;
And your condition máy be sóon like mine,
The child of sórrow and of misery.

—MOSS

Trisyllabic verse consists altogether of anapests, that is, of feet made up of two unaccented and one accented syllable; and it does not admit a mixture of any other feet. The following is a specimen of this kind of verse:

I have found out a gift for my fair;
I have found where the wood-pigeons bréed;
But lét me that plunder forbear,
She will sáy 'twas a bárbarous déed;

For he ne'er could be true, she averr'd,
Who could rób a poor bird of its young;
And I loved her the more when I héard
Such tenderness fall from her tongue.

—SHENSTONE

The following are instances of an iambus in an anapestic verse:

Or under this turf, or ev'n what they will.

—POPE

It never was known that circular letters.

—SWIFT

They are extremely rare and are deformities, which cannot be admitted to belong to the verse, notwithstanding the authority of the writers from whom they are quoted. Indeed, the pieces from which they are taken are merely pieces of sport on which they did not mean to rest their poetical merit.

But to what class shall we give the following species of verse? "God save great Washington." It is triple verse, but the accent is on the first syllable of the foot instead of the third. Is this an attempt at dactylian verse? or shall we consider it still as anapestic, wherein either the two unaccented syllables which should begin the verse are omitted; or else the two which should end it are, in reciting, transposed to the next verse to complete the first anapest of that, as in Virgil in the following instance, the last syllable of the line belongs to the next, being amalgamated with that into one.[2]

I am not able to recollect another instance of this kind of verse and a single example cannot form a class. It is not worth while, therefore, to provide a foreigner with a critical investigation of its character.

[2] Virgil quotation not given.

## OF ELISION

The vowels only suffer elision except that "v" is also omitted in the word over and "w" in will, "h" in have. This is actually made in most cases, as it was with the Greeks. Sometimes, however, it is neglected to be done, and in those cases the reader must make it for himself, as in the following examples:

Thou yet *mightest* act the friendly part
And lass *unnoticed* from malignant right
And *fallen* to save his injur'd land
Impatient for *it is* past the promis'd hour.

He *also against* the house of God was bold
Anguish and doubt and fear and sorr*ow and* pain
Of Phlegma with *the he*roic race was joined
Damasco, or Maroc*co, or* Trebisond
All her *original* brightness, nor appear'd
*Open or* understood must be resolv'd.

## OF SYNECPHONESIS

Diphthongs are considered as forming one syllable. But vowels belonging to different syllables are sometimes forced to coalesce into a diphthong if the measure requires it. Nor is this coalescence prevented by the intervention of an "h," a "w" or a liquid. In this case the two syllables are run into one another with such rapidity as to take but the time of one.

The following are examples:

And wish th*e* avenging fight
B*e i*t so, for I submit, his doom is fair.
When wint'ry winds deform the plent*eo*us year
Droop'd their fair leaves, nor knew th*e u*nfriendly soil
The rad*ia*nt morn resumed her orient pride
While born to bring the Muse's happ*ie*r days
A patr*io*t's hand protects a poet's lays
Ye midnight lamps, ye cur*ious* homes
That eagle gen*ius*! had he let fall—

Fair fancy wept; and ech*oi*ng sighs confest
The sounding forest fluct*ua*tes in the storm
Thy greatest infl*ue*nce own
Iss*uei*ng from out the portals of the morn
What groves nor streams bestow a virt*uou*s mind
With man*y a* proof of recollected love.
With kind concern our pit*yi*ng eyes o'erflow
Lies yet a little embr*yo* unperceiv'd—

> Now Marg*are*t's curse is fall'n upon our heads
> And ev*en a* Shakespeare to her fame be born
> When min*era*l fountains vainly bear
> O how self-fettered was my grov*eli*ng soul!
> To ev*ery* sod which wraps the dead
> And beam protection on a wand*eri*ng maid
> Him or his children, ev*il he* may be sure
> Love unlibid*inou*s resigned, nor jealousy
> And left t*o he*rself, if evil thence ensue.
> Big swell'd my heart and own'd the p*owe*rful maid
> Proceeding, runs low bell*owi*ng round the hills
> Thy cherishing, thy hon*ouri*ng, and thy love
> With all its shad*owy* shapes is shown
> The shepherd's so civil y*ou ha*ve nothing to fear.

The elision of a vowel is often actually made where the coalescence before noted be more musical. Perhaps a vowel should never suffer elision when it is followed by a vowel or where only an "h," a "w" or a liquid intervenes between that and a next vowel, or in other words there should never be an elision where synecphonesis may take place. Consider the following instances:

> Full of the dear ecstatic pow'r, and sick
> Dare not th' infectious sigh; thy pleading look
> While ev'ning draws her crimson curtains round
> And fright the tim'rous game
> Fills ev'ry nerve, and pants in ev'ry vein.

> Full of the dear ecstatic power, and sick
> Dare not the infectious sigh; thy pleading look
> While evening draws her crimson curtains round
> And fright the timorous game
> Fills every nerve, and pants in every vein.

The pronunciation in these instances with the actual elision is less agreeable to my ear than by synecphonesis.

### OF RULES FOR THE ACCENT

Accent deciding the measure of English verse as quantity does that of the Latin, and rules having been formed for teaching the quantity of the Latins it would be expected that rules should also be offered for indicating to foreigners the accented syllable of every word in English. Such rules have been attempted. Were they to be so completely formed as that the rules and their necessary exceptions would reach every word in the language, they would be too great a charge on the memory and too complicated for use either in reading or conversation. In the imperfect manner in which they have been hitherto proposed they would lead into infinite errors. It is usage which has established the accent of every word, or rather I might say it has been caprice or chance, for nothing can be more arbitrary or less consistent. I am of opinion it is easier for a foreigner to learn the accent of every word individually, than the rules which would teach it. This his dictionary will teach him, if, when he recurs to it for the meaning of a word, he will recollect that he should notice also on which syllable is its accent. Or he may learn the accent by reading poetry, which differs our language from Greek and Latin, wherein you must learn their prosody in order to read their poetry. Knowing that with us the accent is on every odd syllable or on every even one or on every third, he has only to examine of which of these measures the verse is to be able to read it correctly. But how shall he distinguish the measure to which the verse belongs?

If he can find in the piece any one word the accent of which he already knows, that word will enable him to distinguish if it be parisyllabic or imparisyllabic. Let us suppose, for example, he would read the following piece:

How sleep the brave, who sink to rest,
By all their country's wishes blest!
When Spring, with dewy fingers cold,
Returns to deck their hallowed mould,
She there shall dress a *sweeter* sod
Than Fancy's feet have ever trod.
By fairy hands their knell is rung;
By forms unseen their dirge is sung;
There Honor comes, a pilgrim gray,
To bless the turf that wraps their clay;
And Freedom shall a while repair,
To dwell a weeping hermit there!

—COLLINS

He finds the word *sweeter,* the accent of which he has already learned to be on the first syllable, sweet. He observes that that is an even syllable, being the sixth of the line. He knows then that it is parisyllabic verse and from that he can accent the whole piece. If he does not already know the accent of a single word he must look in his dictionary for some one, and that will be a key to the whole piece. He should take care not to rely on the first foot of any line, because, as has been before observed, that is often a trochee even in the parisyllabic verse. Without consulting his dictionary at all, or knowing a single accent, the following observation will enable him to distinguish between these two species of verse when they are in rhyme. An odd number of syllables with a single rhyme, or an even number with a double rhyme, prove the verse to be imparisyllabic. An even number of syllables with a single rhyme, or an odd number with a double one, prove it to be parisyllabic, *e.g.:*

Learn by this unguarded lover
When your secret sighs prevail
Not to let your tongue discover
Raptures that you should conceal.
—CUNNINGHAM

He sung and hell consented
To hear the poet's prayer
Stern Proserpine relented
And gave him back the fair.
—POPE

If in thus examining the seat of the accent he finds it is alternately on an even syllable, that is to say, on the third, sixth, ninth, twelfth syllables, the verse is trisyllabic.

With her how I stray'd amid fóuntains and bowers!
Or loīter'd behińd, and collected the flowérś!
Then breathless with ardor my fair one pursued,
And to think with what kindness my garland she views'd!
But be still, my fond heart! this emōtion give o'er;
Fain wouldst thou forgēt thou must love her no more.
—SHENSTONE

It must be stated that in this kind of verse we should count backward from the last syllable, if it be a single rhyme, or the last but one if it be double; because one of the unaccented syllables which should begin the verse is so often omitted. This last syllable in the preceding example should be the twelfth. When the line is full it is acented of course. Consulting the dictionary, therefore, we find in the first line the ninth syllable accented; in the second, the sixth; in the third line the accented syllables there being alternately odd and even, to wit, the third, sixth, ninth and twelfth, we know the verse must be trisyllabic.

The foreigner then first determining the measure of the verse, may read it boldly. He will commit a few errors, indeed; let us see what they are likely to be. In imparisyllabic verse none, because that consists of trochees invariably; if an unaccented syllable happens to be prefixed to the verse, he will discover it by the number of syllables. In parisyllabic verse, when a trochee begins the verse, he will pronounce that foot wrong. This will perhaps happen once in ten lines; in some authors more, in others less. In like manner he will pronounce wrong the trochee in the middle of the line. But this he will encounter once in some hundreds of times. In the trisyllabic verse he can never commit an error if he counts from the end of the line. These imperfections are as few as a foreigner can possibly expect in the beginning; and he will reduce their number in proportion as he acquires by practice a knowledge of the accents.

The subject of accent cannot be quitted till we apprise him of another imperfection which will show itself in his reading, and which will be longer removing. Though there be accents on the first, the second or the third syllables of the foot, as has been before explained, yet is there subordination among these accents, a modulation in their tone of which it is impossible to give a precise idea in writing. This is intimately connected with the sense; and though a foreigner will readily find to what words that would give distinguished emphasis, yet nothing but habit can enable him to give actually the different shades of emphasis which his judgment would dictate to him. Even natives have very different powers as to this article. This difference exists both in the organ and the judgment. Foote is known to have read Milton so exquisitely that he received great sums of money for reading him to audiences who attended him regularly for that purpose. This difference, too, enters deeply into the merit of theatrical actors. The foreigner, therefore, must acquiesce under a want of perfection which is the lot of natives in common with himself.

We will proceed to give examples which may explain what is here meant, distinguishing the accents into four shades by these marks //// /// // / the greater number of marks denoting the strongest accents.

> Oh when the growling winds contend and all
> The sounding forest fluctuates in the storm
> To sink in warm repose, and hear the din
> Howl o'er the steady battlements, delights
> Above the luxury of vulgar sleep.
>
> —ARMSTRONG

> Life's cares are comforts; such by heav'n design'd
> He that has none, must make them or be wretched
> Cares are employments; and without employ
> The soul is on a rack, the rack of rest.
>
> —YOUNG

> O! lost to virtue, lost to manly thought,
> Lost to the noble sallies of the soul!
> Who think it solitude, to be alone.
> Communion sweet! communion large and high!
> Our reason, guardian angel, and our God!
> Then nearest these, when others most remote;
> And all, ere long, shall be remote, but these.
>
> —YOUNG

By nature's law, what may be, may be now;
There's no prerogative in human hours.
In human hearts what bolder thought can rise,
Than man's presumption on tomorrow's dawn?
Where is tomorrow? In another world.
For numbers this is certain; the reverse
Is sure to none; and yet on this perhaps,
This peradventure, infamous for lies,
As on a rock of adamant, we build
Our mountain hopes; spin out eternal schemes,
As we the fatal sisters could outspin,
And, big with life's futurities, expire.

—YOUNG

Cowards die many times before their deaths;
The valiant never taste of death but once.
Of all the wonders that I yet have heard,
It seems to me most strange that men should fear,
Seeing that death, a necessary end,
Will come when it will come.

I cannot tell what you and other men
Think of this life, but, for my single self,
I had as lief not be as live to be
In awe of such a thing as I myself.
I was born free as Cæsar, so were you;
We both have fed as well, and we can both
Endure the winter's cold as well as he.

The cloud-capp'd towers, the gorgeous palaces,
The solemn temples, the great globe itself,
Yea, all which it inherit, shall dissolve,
And, like this insubstantial pageant faded,
Leave not a rack behind.

I am far from presuming to give this accentuation as perfect. No two persons will accent the same passage alike. No person but a real adept would accent it twice alike. Perhaps two real adepts who should utter the same passage with infinite perfection yet by throwing the energy into different words might produce very different effects. I suppose that in those passages of Shakespeare, for example, no man but Garrick ever drew their full tone out of them, if I may borrow an expression from music. Let those who are disposed to criticise, therefore, try a few experiments themselves. I have essayed these short passages to let the foreigner see that the accent is not equal; that they are not to be read monotonously. I chose, too, the most pregnant passages, those wherein every word teems with latent meaning, that he might form an idea of the degrees of excellence of which this art is capable. He must not apprehend that all poets present the same difficulty. It is only the most brilliant passages. The great mass, even of good poetry, is easily enough read. Take the following examples, wherein little differences in the enunciation will not change the meaning sensibly.

Here, in cool grot and mossy cell,
We rural fays and faeries dwell;
Though rarely seen by mortal eye,
When the pale Moon, ascending high,
Darts through yon lines her quivering beams,
We frisk it near these crystal streams.

Her beams, reflected from the wave,
Afford the light our revels crave;
The turf, with daisies broider'd o'er,
Exceeds, we wot, the Parian floor;
Nor yet for artful strains we call,
But listen to the water's fall.

Would you then taste our tranquil scene,
Be sure your bosoms be serene:
Devoid of hate, devoid of strife,
Devoid of all that poisons life:
And much it 'vails you, in their place
To graft the love of human race.

And tread with awe these favor'd bowers,
Nor wound the shrubs, nor bruise the flowers;
So may your path with sweets abound;
So may your couch with rest be crown'd!
But harm betide the wayward swain,
Who dares our hallow'd haunts profane!

—SHENSTONE

To fair Fidele's grassy tomb
  Soft maids and village hinds shall bring
Each opening sweet, of earliest bloom,
  And rifle all the breathing Spring.

No wailing ghost shall dare appear
  To vest with shrieks this quiet grove,
But shepherd lads assemble here,
  And melting virgins own their love.

No wither'd witch shall here be seen,
  No goblins lead their nightly crew;
The female fays shall haunt the green,
  And dress thy grave with pearly dew;

The red-breast oft at evening hours
  Shall kindly lend his little aid,
With hoary moss, and gather'd flowers,
  To deck the ground where thou art laid.

When howling winds, and beating rain,
  In tempests shake thy sylvan cell;
Or 'midst the chase on every plain,
  The tender thought on thee shall dwell.

Each lonely scene shall thee restore,
For thee the tear be duly shed;
Belov'd, till life can charm no more
  And mourn'd, till Pity's self be dead.

—COLLINS

### OF THE LENGTH OF VERSE

Having spoken of feet which are only the constituent part of verse, it becomes necessary to say something of its larger divisions, and even of the verse itself. For what is a verse? This question naturally occurs, and it is not sufficiently answered by saying it is a whole line. Should the printer think proper to print the following passage in this manner:

῞Ως εἰπὼν οὗ παιδὸς ὀρέξατο φαίδιμος ῞Εκτωρ ἂψ δ' ὁ πάις πρὸς κόλπον ἐϋζώνοιο τιθήνης ἐκλίνθη ἰάχων, πατρὸς φίλου ὄψιν ἀτυχθείς, ταρβήσας χαλκόν τε ἰδὲ λόφου ἱππιοχαίτην, δεινὸν ἀπ' ἀκροτάτης κόρυθος νεύοντα νοήσας ἐκ δ' ἐγέλασσε πατήρ τε φίλος και πότνια μήτηρ· αὐτίκ' ἀπὸ κρατὸς κόρυθ' εἵλετο φαίδιμος ῞Εκτωρ, καὶ τὴν μὲν κατέθηκεν ἐπὶ χθονὶ παμφανόωσαν αὐτὰρ ὅ γ' ὃν φίλον υἱὸν ἐπεὶ κύσε πῆλέ τε χερσίν, εἶπεν ἐλευξάμενος Διί τ' ἄλλοισίν τε θεοῖσι· Ζεῦ ἄλλοι τε θεοί, δότε δὴ καὶ τόνδε γενέσθαι παῖδ' ἐμόν, ὡς καὶ ἐγώ περ, ἀριπρεπέα Τρώεσσιν, ὧδε βίην τ' ἀγαθὸν καὶ 'Ιλίου ἶφι ἀνάσσειν καὶ ποτέ τις εἴποι, 'πατρὸς γ' ὅδε πολλὸν ἀμείνων' ἐκ πολέμου ἀνιόντα· φέροι δ' ἔναρα βροτόεντα κτείνας δήϊον ἄνδρα, χαρείη δὲ φρένα μήτηρ. ῞Ως εἰπὼν ἀλόχοιο φίλης ἐν χερσὶν ἔθηκε παῖδ' ἑόν· ἡ δ' ἄρα μιν κηώδεϊ δέξατο κόλπῳ δακρυόεν γελάσασα· πόσις δ' ἐλέησε νοήσας, χειρί τέ μιν κατέρεξεν ἔπος τ' ἔφατ' ἔκ τ' ὀνόμαζε.

it would still be verse; it would still immortalize its author were every other syllable of his compositions lost. The poet then does not depend on the printer to give a character to his work. He has studied the human ear. He has discovered that in any rhythmical composition the ear is pleased to find at certain regular intervals a pause where it may rest, by which it may divide the composition into parts, as a piece of music is divided into bars. He contrives to mark this division by a pause in the sense or at least by an emphatical word which may force the pause so that the ear may feel the regular return of the pause. The interval then between these regular pauses constitutes a verse. In the morsel before cited this interval comprehends six feet, and though it is written in the manner of prose, yet he who can read it without pausing at every sixth foot, like him who is insensible to the charm of music, who is insensible of love or of gratitude, is an unfavored son of nature to whom she has given a faculty fewer than to others of her children, one source of pleasure the less in a world where there are none to spare. A well-organized ear makes the pause regularly whether it be printed as verse or as prose. But not only the organization of the ear but the character of the language have influence in determining the length of the verse. Otherwise the constitution of the ear being the same with all nations the verse would be of the same length in all languages, which is not the case. But the difference in language occasions the ear to be pleased with a difference of interval in the pause. The language of Homer enabled him to compose in verse of six feet; the English language cannot bear this. They may be of one, two, three, four, or five feet, as in the following examples:

One foot.

Turning
Burning
Changing
Ranging

I mourn
I sigh
I burn
I die
Let us part—
Let us part
Will you break
My poor heart?

Two feet.

Flow'ry mountains
Mossy fountains
Shady woods
Crystal floods
To me the rose
No longer glows
Ev'ry plant
Has lost its scent.

Prithee Cupid no more
Hurl thy darts at threescore
To thy girls and thy boys
Give thy pains and thy joys.

Three feet.

Farewell fear and sorrow
Pleasure till tomorrow.

Yes, ev'ry flow'r that blows
  I passed unheeded by
Till this enchanting rose
  Had fix'd my wand'ring eye.
—CUNNINGHAM

The rose though a beautiful red
  Looks faded to Phyllis's bloom;
And the breeze from the bean-flower bed
  To her breath's but a feeble perfume;
A lily I plucked in full pride
  Its freshness with hers to compare,
And foolishly thought till I try'd
  The flow'ret was equally fair.
—CUNNINGHAM

Four feet.

From the dark tremendous cell
Where the fiends of magic dwell
Now the sun hath left the skies
Daughters of Enchantment, rise!
—CUNNINGHAM

Come Hope, and to my pensive eye
Thy far foreseeing tube apply
Whose kind deception steals us o'er
The gloomy waste that lies before.
—LANGHORNE

'Mongst lords and fine ladies we shepherds are told
The dearest affections are barter'd for gold
That discord in wedlock is often their lot
While Cupid and Hymen shake hands in a cot.
—CUNNINGHAM

Here the parisyllabic alone bears one foot more.

Oh liberty! thou goddess heav'nly bright
Profuse of bliss, and pregnant with delight,

Eternal pleasures in thy presence reign,
And smiling Plenty leads thy wanton train;
Eas'd of her load subjection grows more light,
And Poverty looks cheerful in thy sight;
Thou mak'st the gloomy face of nature gay
Giv'st beauty to the sun, and pleasure to the day.

—ADDISON

The last line furnishes an instance of six feet, usually called an Alexandrian; but no piece is ever wholly in that measure. A single line only is tolerated now and then, and is never a beauty. Formerly it was thought that the language bore lines of seven feet in length, as in the following:

'Tis he whose ev'ry thought and deed by rules of virtue moves;
Whose gen'rous tongue disdains to speak the thing his heart disproves
Who never did a slander forge his neighbor's fame to wound;
Nor listen to a false report by malice whisper'd round.

—PSALM 15

But a little attention shows that there is as regular a pause at the fourth foot as at the seventh, and as verse takes its denomination from the shortest regular intervals, this is no more than an alternate verse of four and of three feet. It is, therefore, usually written as in the following stanzas of the same piece:

Who to his plighted vows and trust
  Has ever firmly stood
And, though he promise to his loss,
  He makes his promise good.

The man who by this steady course
  Has happiness ensur'd
When earth's foundations shake, will stand
  By Providence secur'd.

We may justly consider, therefore, verses of five feet as the longest the language sustains, and it is remarkable that not only this length, though the extreme, is generally the most esteemed, but that it is the only one which has dignity enough to support blank verse, that is, verse without rhyme. This is attempted in no other measure. It constitutes, therefore, the most precious part of our poetry. The poet, unfettered by rhyme, is at liberty to prune his diction of those tautologies, those feeble nothings necessary to introtrude the rhyming word. With no other trammel than that of measure he is able to condense his thoughts and images and to leave nothing but what is truly poetical. When enveloped in all the pomp and majesty of his subject he sometimes even throws off the restraint of the regular pause:

Of Man's first disobedience, and the fruit
Of that forbidden tree, whose mortal taste
Brought death into the world, and all our woe,
With loss of Eden, till one greater Man
Restore us, and regain the blissful seat,
Sing, heavenly Muse! that on the sacred top
Of Oreb, or of Sinai, didst inspire
That shepherd, who first taught the chosen seed,
In the beginning, how the Heavens and Earth
Rose out of Chaos.

They stay'd the fervid wheels, and in his hand
He took the golden compasses, prepared
In God's eternal store, to circumscribe
This universe, and all created things
One foot he centred, and the other turn'd
Round, through the vast profundity obscure
And said, "Thus far extend."

There are but two regular pauses in this whole passage of seven verses. They are constantly drowned by the majesty of the rhythm and sense. But nothing less than this can authorize such a license. Take the following proof from the same author:

Again, God said, "Let there be firmament
Amid the waters, and let it divide
The waters from the waters"; and God made
The firmament.

—MILTON 7: 261

And God said, Let there be a firmament in the midst of the waters, and let it divide the waters from the waters.
And God made the firmament.

—GENESIS I: 6

I have here placed Moses and Milton side by side, that he who can may distinguish which verse belongs to the poet. To do this he will not have the aid either of the sentiment, diction or measure of poetry. The original is so servilely copied that though it be cut into pieces of ten syllables, no pause is marked between these portions.

What proves the excellence of blank verse is that the taste lasts longer than that for rhyme. The fondness for the jingle leaves us with that for the rattles and baubles of childhood, and if we continue to read rhymed verse at a later period of life it is such only where the poet has had force enough to bring great beauties of thought and diction into this form. When young any composition pleases which unites a little sense, some imagination, and some rhythm, in doses however small. But as we advance in life these things fall off one by one, and I suspect we are left at last with only Homer and Virgil, perhaps with Homer alone. He like

Hope travels on nor quits us when we die.

Having noted the different lengths of line which the English poet may give to his verse it must be further observed that he may intermingle these in the same verse according to his fancy.

The following are selected as examples:

A tear bedews my Delia's eye,
To think yon playful kid must die;
From crystal spring, and flowery mead,
Must, in his prime of life, recede!

She tells with what delight he stood,
To trace his features in the flood;
Then skipp'd aloof with quaint amaze,
And then drew near again to gaze.

—SHENSTONE

Full many a gem of purest ray serene
  The dark unfathomed caves of ocean bear;
Full many a flower is born to blush unseen,
  And waste its sweetness on the desert air.

Some village Hampden, that, with dauntless breast,
  The little tyrant of his fields withstood,
Some mute inglorious Milton here may rest,
  Some Cromwell, guiltless of his country's blood.

—GRAY

There shall my plaintive song recount
  Dark themes of hopeless woe,
And faster than the drooping fount
  I'll teach mine eyes to flow.

There leaves, in spite of Autumn green
  Shall shade the hallow'd ground,
And Spring will there again be seen
  To call forth flowers around.

—SHENSTONE

O Health! capricious maid!
  Why dost thou shun my peaceful bower,
  Where I had hope to share thy power,
And bless thy lasting aid?

—SHENSTONE

The man whose mind, on virtue bent
Pursues some greatly good intent
  With undivided aim
Serene beholds the angry crowd
Nor can their clamors fierce and loud
  His stubborn purpose tame.

Ye gentle Bards! give ear,
  Who talk of amorous rage,
Who spoil the lily, rob the rose,
Come learn of me to weep your woes:
  "O sweet! O sweet Anne Page!"

—SHENSTONE

Too long a stranger to repose,
At length from Pain's abhorred couch I rose
  And wander'd forth alone,
To court once more the balmy breeze,
And catch the verdure of the trees,
  Ere yet their charms were flown.

—SHENSTONE

O thou, by Nature taught
To breathe her genuine thought,
In numbers warmly pure, and sweetly strong;
Who first, on mountains wild,
In Fancy, loveliest child,
Thy babe, and Pleasure's, nursed the powers of song!

—COLLINS

'Twas in a land of learning,
The Muse's favorite city,
Such pranks of late
Were play'd by a rat,
As—tempt one to be witty.

—SHENSTONE

Yet stay, O stay! celestial Pow'rs!
  And with a hand of kind regard
Dispel the boisterous storm that low'rs
  Destruction on the fav'rite bard;
O watch with me his last expiring breath
And snatch him from the arms of dark oblivious death.

—GRAY

What is grandeur, what is power?
Heavier toil, superior pain.
What the bright reward we gain?
The grateful memory of the good.

Sweet is the breath of vernal shower,
The bee's collected treasures sweet,
Sweet music's melting fall, but sweeter yet
The still small voice of gratitude.

Methinks I hear, in accents low,
The sportive, kind reply:
Poor moralist! and what art thou?
A solitary fly!
Thy joys no glittering female meets,
No hive hast thou of hoarded sweets,
No painted plumage to display;
On hasty wings thy youth is flown;
Thy sun is set, thy spring is gone—
We frolic while 'tis May.

—GRAY

Then let me rove some wild and heathy scene;
Or find some ruin, 'midst its dreary dells,
Whose walls more awful nod
By thy religious gleams.

Or, if chill blustering winds, or driving rain,
Prevent my willing feet, be mine the hut,
That, from the mountain's side,
Views wilds, and swelling floods.

—COLLINS

Though the license to intermingle the different measures admits an infinitude of combinations, yet this becomes less and less pleasing in proportion as they depart from that simplicity and regularity of which the ear is most sensible. When these are wholly or nearly neglected, as in the lyric pieces, the poet renounces one of the most fascinating charms of his art. He must then look well to his matter and supply in sublimity or other beauties the loss of regular measure. In effect these pieces are seldom read twice.

## ESSAY ON THE ANGLO-SAXON LANGUAGE [1]

1798

The importance of the Anglo-Saxon dialect toward a perfect understanding of the English language seems not to have been duly estimated by those

[1] This was first published by the University of Virginia in 1851: *An Essay Towards Facilitating Instruction in the Anglo-Saxon and Modern Dialects of the English Language.* It was

charged with the education of youth; and yet it is unquestionably the basis of our present tongue. It was a full-formed language; its frame and construction, its declension of nouns and verbs, and its syntax were peculiar to the Northern languages, and fundamentally different from those of the South. It was the language of all England, properly so called, from the Saxon possession of that country in the sixth century to the time of Henry III in the thirteenth, and was spoken pure and unmixed with any other. Although the Romans had been in possession of that country for nearly five centuries from the time of Julius Caesar, yet it was a military possession chiefly, by their soldiery alone, and with dispositions intermutually jealous and unamicable. They seemed to have aimed at no lasting settlements there, and to have had little familiar mixture with the native Britons. In this state of connection there would probably be little incorporation of the Roman into the native language, and on the subsequent evacuation of the island its traces would soon be lost altogether. And had it been otherwise, these innovations would have been carried with the natives themselves when driven into Wales by the invasion and entire occupation of the rest of the Southern portion of the island by the Anglo-Saxons.

The language of these last became that of the country from that time forth, for nearly seven centuries; and so little attention was paid among them to the Latin, that it was known to a few individuals only as a matter of science, and without any chance of transfusion into the vulgar language. We may safely repeat the affirmation, therefore, that the pure Anglo-Saxon constitutes at this day the basis of our language. That it was sufficiently copious for the purposes of society in the existing condition of arts and manners, reason alone would satisfy us from the necessity of the case. Its copiousness, too, was much favored by the latitude it allowed of combining primitive

originally sent to Sir Herbert Croft, the English etymologist, to whom Jefferson wrote on October 30, 1798:

"I was led to set a due value on the study of the Northern languages, and especially of our Anglo-Saxon, while I was a student of the law, by being obliged to recur to that source for explanation of a multitude of law-terms. A preface to Fortescue on Monarchies, written by Fortescue Aland, and afterwards premised to his volume of Reports, develops the advantages to be derived to the English student generally, and particularly the student of law, from an acquaintance with the Anglo-Saxon; and mentions the books to which the learner may have recourse for acquiring the language. I accordingly devoted some time to its study, but my busy life has not permitted me to indulge in a pursuit to which I felt great attraction. While engaged in it, however, some ideas occurred for facilitating the study by simplifying its grammar, by reducing the infinite diversities of its unfixed orthography to single and settled forms, indicating at the same time the pronunciation of the word by its correspondence with the characters and powers of the English alphabet."

In 1820 Jefferson wrote to John Adams: "In a letter . . . to Mr. Croft who sent . . . me a copy of his treatise on the English and German languages, as preliminary to an etymological dictionary he meditated, I went into explanations with him of an easy process for simplifying the study of the Anglo-Saxon, and lessening the terrors and difficulties presented by its rude alphabet."

In 1825 he confessed in a letter that the study of Anglo-Saxon "is a hobby which too often runs away with me."

words so as to produce any modification of idea desired. In this characteristic it was equal to the Greek, but it is more especially proved by the actual fact of the books they have left us in the various branches of history, geography, religion, law, and poetry. And although since the Norman conquest it has received vast additions and embellishments from the Latin, Greek, French, and Italian languages, yet these are but engraftments on its idiomatic stem; its original structure and syntax remain the same, and can be but imperfectly understood by the mere Latin scholar. Hence the necessity of making the Anglo-Saxon a regular branch of academic education. In the sixteenth and seventeenth centuries it was assiduously cultivated by a host of learned men. The names of Lambard, Parker, Spelman, Wheeloc, Wilkins, Gibson, Hickes, Thwaites, Somner, Benson, Mareschal, Elstob, deserve to be ever remembered with gratitude for the Anglo-Saxon works which they have given us through the press, the only certain means of preserving and promulgating them. For a century past this study has been too much neglected. The reason of this neglect, and its remedy, shall be the subject of some explanatory observations. These will respect—I. The Alphabet. II. Orthography. III. Pronunciation. IV. Grammar.

### I. THE ALPHABET

The Anglo-Saxon alphabet, as known to us in its printed forms, consists of twenty-six characters, about the half of which are Roman, the others of forms peculiarly Saxon. These, mixed with the others, give an aspect to the whole rugged, uncouth, and appalling to an eye accustomed to the roundness and symmetry of the Roman character. This is a first discouragement to the English student. Next, the task of learning a new alphabet, and the time and application necessary to render it easy and familiar to the reader, often decides the doubting learner against an enterprise so apparently irksome.

The earliest remains extant of Saxon writing are said to be of the seventh century; and the latest of the thirteenth. The black letter seems to have been introduced by William the Conqueror, whose laws are written in Norman French, and in that letter. The full alphabet of Roman characters was first used about the beginning of the sixteenth century. But the expression of the same sounds, by a different character did not change these sounds, nor the language which they constituted; did not make the language of Alfred a different one from that of Piers Ploughman, of Chaucer, Douglas, Spenser, and Shakespeare, any more than the second revolution, which substituted the Roman for the English black letter, made theirs a different language from that of Pope and Bolingbroke; or the writings of Shakespeare, printed in black letter, different from the same as now done in Roman type. The life of

Alfred, written in Latin and in Roman character by Asser, was reprinted by Archbishop Parker in Anglo-Saxon letters. But it is Latin still, although the words are represented by characters different from those of Asser's original. And the extracts given us by Dr. Hickes from the Greek Septuagint, in Anglo-Saxon characters, are Greek still, although the Greek sounds are represented by other types. Here then I ask, why should not this Roman character, with which we are all familiar, be substituted now for the Anglo-Saxon, by printing in the former the works already edited in the latter type? and also the manuscripts still inedited? This may be done letter for letter, and would remove entirely the first discouraging obstacle to the general study of the Anglo-Saxon.

### II. ORTHOGRAPHY

In the period during which the Anglo-Saxon alphabet was in use, reading and writing were rare arts. The highest dignitaries of the church subscribed their marks, not knowing how to write their names. Alfred himself was taught to read in his thirty-sixth year only, or, as some editions of Asser say, in his thirty-ninth. Speaking of learning in his Preface to the Pastoral of Gregory, Alfred says, "Swa clean hi was oth-fallen on Angelkin that swithe few were on behinan Humber, the hior thenung cuthon understandan on Englisc, oth furthon an errand y-write of Latin on Englisc areckon. And I ween that not many beyondan Humber nay aren; swa few hior weron that I furthon ane on lepne nay may y-thinkan be-Suthan Thames tha tha I to ric fang." Or, as literally translated into later English by Archbishop Parker, "So clean was it fallen amongst the English nation, that very few were on this side Humber which their service could understand in English, or else furthermore an epistle from Latin into English to declare. And I ween that not many beyond Humber were not. So few of them were that I also one only may not remember by South Tamise when as I to reign undertook." In this benighted state, so profoundly illiterate, few read at all, and fewer wrote: and the writer having no examples of orthography to recur to, thinking them indeed not important, had for his guide his own ideas only of the power of the letters, unpractised and indistinct as they might be. He brought together, therefore, those letters which he supposed must enter into the composition of the sound he meant to express, and was not even particular in arranging them in the order in which the sounds composing the word followed each other. Thus, *birds* was spelt brides; *grass,* gaers; *run,* yrnan; *cart,* crætt; *fresh,* fersh. They seemed to suppose, too, that a final vowel was necessary to give sound to the consonant preceding it, and they used for that purpose any vowel indifferently. A *son* was suna, sune, sunu; *mæra,* mære, mæro, mæru; *fines,* limites; *ge, ye, y, i,* are various spellings of the same prefix. The final *e* mute in English is a remain of this, as in *give, love, curse.*

The vowels were used indiscriminately also for every vowel sound. Thus,

The comparative ended in *ar, er, ir, or, ur, yr.*
The superlative ended in *ast, est, ist, ost, ust, yst.*
The participle present ended in *and, end, ind, ond, und, ynd.*
The participle past ended in *ad, ed, id, od, ud, yd.*
Other examples are, betweox, betwix, betwox, betwux, betwyx, for *betwixt;* egland, igland, ygland, for *island.*

Of this promiscuous use of the vowels we have also abundant remains still in English. For according to the powers given to our letters we often use them indifferently for the same sound, as in *bulwark, assert, stir, work, lurk, myrtle.* The single word *many,* in Anglo-Saxon, was spelt, as Dr. Hickes has observed, in twenty different ways; to wit, mænigeo, mænio, mæniu, menio, meniu, mænigo, mænego, manige, menigo, manegeo, mænegeo, menegeo, mænygeo, menigeo, manegu, mænigu, menegu, menego, menigu, manigo. To prove, indeed, that everyone spelt according to his own notions, without regard to any standard, we have only to compare different editions of the same composition. Take, for example, Alfred's Preface to Gregory's Pastoral before cited, as published in different editions:

| Swa | clæne | hio | wæs | othfeallenu | on | angelkynne | thætte | swythe | feawe |
|---|---|---|---|---|---|---|---|---|---|
| | | heo | | othfeallen | | angelcynne | that | | feawa |
| | | | | | | | | | fewa |

| wæron | behionan | Humbre | the | hiora | thenunga | cuthen | understandan | on | Englisc |
|---|---|---|---|---|---|---|---|---|---|
| | beheonan | | | hira | theninga | cuthon | understondan | | Ænglisc |
| | | | | | thenunge | | | | |

| oththe | furthum | an | ærendgewrit | of | Lædene | on | Englisc | areccan | & | ic | wene |
|---|---|---|---|---|---|---|---|---|---|---|---|
| | furthon | | ærendgewryt | | Ledene | | Ænglisc | areccean | | | |

| thaette | nauht | monige | begeondan | Humbre | næren. |
|---|---|---|---|---|---|
| that | noht | | begiondan | | nearon. |
| | naht | | | | næron. |

This unsettled orthography renders it necessary to swell the volume of the dictionaries, by giving to each word as many places in order of the alphabet as there are different modes of spelling it; and in proportion as this is omitted, the difficulty of finding the words increases on the student.

Since, then, it is apparent that the Anglo-Saxon writers had established no particular standard of orthography, but each followed arbitrarily his own mode of combining the letters, we are surely at liberty equally to adopt any mode which, establishing uniformity, may be more consonant with the power of the letters, and with the orthography of the present dialect, as established by usage. The latter attention has the advantage of exhibiting more evidently the legitimate parentage of the two dialects.

To determine what that was among the Anglo-Saxons, our means are as defective as to determine the long-agitated question what was the original pronunciation of the Greek and Latin languages. The presumption is certainly strong that in Greece and Italy, the countries occupied by those languages, their pronunciation has been handed down, by tradition, more nearly than it can be known to other countries: and the rather, as there has been no particular point of time at which those ancient languages were changed into the modern ones occupying the same grounds. They have been gradually worn down to their present forms by time, and changes of modes and circumstances. In like manner there has been no particular point of time at which the Anglo-Saxon has been changed into its present English form. The languages of Europe have generally, in like manner, undergone a gradual metamorphosis, some of them in name as well as in form. We should presume, therefore, that in those countries of Great Britain which were occupied earliest, longest, and latest by the Saxon immigrants, the pronunciation of their language has been handed down more nearly than elsewhere; and should be searched for in the provincial dialects of those countries. But the fact is, that these countries have divaricated in their dialects, so that it would be difficult to decide among them which is the most genuine. Under these doubts, therefore, we may as well take the pronunciation now in general use as the legitimate standard, and that form which it is most promotive of our object to infer the Anglo-Saxon pronunciation. It is, indeed, the forlorn hope of all aim at their probable pronunciation; for were we to regard the powers of the letters only, no human organ could articulate their uncouth jumble. We will suppose, therefore, the power of the letters to have been generally the same in Anglo-Saxon as now in English; and to produce the same sounds we will combine them, as nearly as may be, conformably with the present English orthography. This is, indeed, a most irregular and equivocal standard; but a conformity with it will bring the two dialects nearer together in sound and semblance, and facilitate the transition from the one to the other more auspiciously than a rigorous adherence to any uniform system of orthography which speculation might suggest.

I will state some instances only (referring to Dr. Hickes for more) of the unskilful and inconsistent uses of the letters by the Anglo-Saxons, in proof of the necessity of changing them, to produce, to a modern reader, the very sounds which we suppose them to have intended by their confused combinations. Their vowels, promiscuously used, as before observed, must all be freely changed to those used in corresponding words in English orthography.

| | | | |
|---|---|---|---|
| *b* sounds as | *v,* | as in | ober, *over.* |
| *c* " | *g,* | " | fic, *fig.* |
| *c* " | *j,* | " | ceole, *jowl.* |
| *c* " | *k,* | " | tacn, *token;* bacen, *baked;* cind, *kind.* |
| *c* " | *s,* | " | cedar, *cedar.* |
| *c* " | *ch,* | " | ceak, *cheek.* |
| *cg* " | *dge,* | " | bricg, *bridge.* |
| *d* " | *th,* | " | worden, or worthen; mid or mith, *with.* |
| *f* " | *v,* | " | delfan, *to delve;* yfel, *evil.* |
| *v* " | *f,* | " | vot, *foot.* |
| *g* " | *c,* | " | gamel, *camel.* |
| *g* " | *ga,* | " | gandra, *gander;* garlec, *garlic.* |
| *g* " | *ge,* | " | angel. |
| *g* " | *w,* | " | laga, *law;* agen, *own;* fugel, *fowl.* |
| *g* " | *y.* | | This is its most general power, as ge, *ye;* gear, *year;* burigan, *bury;* geoc, *yoke;* ego, *eye;* ge, *ye, y.* |
| *sc* " | *sh,* | as in | scame, *shame;* scip, *ship;* score, *shore;* scyl, *shall.* |
| *y* " | *ou,* | as in | ynce, *ounce.* |
| *x* " | *sh,* | as in | fixas, *fishes;* axan, *ashes.* |
| *x* " | *sk,* | as in | axian, *ask.* |

And finally, in the words of Dr. Hickes, "*Demum quomodo Anglo-Saxonicae voces factae sunt Anglicae mutando literas ejusdem organi, asperando lenes, et leniendo asperas, vocales, diphongos, et interdum consonantes leviter mutando, auferendo initiales et finales syllabas, prœsertim terminationem modo infinitivi, prœterea addendo, transponendo, et interponendo literas, et voces quoque syncopando, exemplis docendum est.*"

## IV. GRAMMAR

Some observations on Anglo-Saxon grammar may show how much easier that also may be rendered to the English student. Dr. Hickes may certainly be considered as the father of this branch of modern learning. He has been the great restorer of the Anglo-Saxon dialect from the oblivion into which it was fast falling. His labors in it were great, and his learning not less than his labors. His grammar may be said to be the only one we yet possess: for that edited at Oxford in 1711 is but an extract from Hickes, and the principal merit of Mrs. Elstob's is, that it is written in English, without anything original in it. Some others have been written, taken also, and almost entirely from Hickes. In his time there was too exclusive a prejudice in favor of the Greek and Latin languages. They were considered as the standards of perfection, and the endeavor generally was to force other languages to a conformity with these models. But nothing can be more radically unlike than the frames of the ancient languages, Southern and Northern, of the Greek and Latin languages, from those of the Gothic family. Of this last are the Anglo-Saxon and English; and had Dr. Hickes, instead of keeping his eye fixed on the Greek and Latin languages, as his standard, viewed the Anglo-Saxon in its conformity with the English only, he would greatly have enlarged the advantages for which we are already so much indebted to him. His labors, however, have advanced us so far on the right road, and a correct pursuit of it will be a just homage to him.

A noun is to be considered under its accidents of genders, cases, and numbers. The word gender is, in nature, synonymous with sex. To all the subjects of the animal kingdom nature has given sex, and that is twofold only, male or female, masculine or feminine. Vegetable and mineral subjects have no distinction of sex, consequently are of no gender. Words, like other inanimate things, have no sex, are of no gender. Yet in the construction of the Greek and Latin languages, and of the modern ones of the same family, their adjectives being varied in termination, and made distinctive of animal sex, in conformity with the nouns or names of animal subjects, the two real genders, which nature has established, are distinguished in these languages. But, not stopping here, they have by usage, thrown a number of unsexual subjects into the sexual classes, leaving the residuary mass to a third class, which grammarians call neutral—that is to say, of no gender or sex: and some Latin grammarians have so far lost sight of the real and natural genders as to ascribe to that language seven genders, the masculine, feminine, neuter, gender common to two, common to three, the doubtful, and the epicene; than which nothing can be more arbitrary, and nothing more useless. But the language of the Anglo-Saxons and English is based on principles totally different from those of the Greek and Latin, and is constructed on laws peculiar and idiomatic to itself. Its adjectives have no changes of termination on account of gender, number or case. Each has a single one applicable to every noun, whether it be the name of a thing having sex, or not. To ascribe gender to nouns in such a case would be to embarrass the learner with unmeaning and useless distinctions.

It will be said, *e.g.,* that a priest is of one gender, and a priestess of another; a poet of one, a poetess of another, etc.; and that therefore the words designating them must be of different genders. I say, not at all; because although the thing designated may have sex, the word designating it, like other inanimate things, has no sex, no gender. In Latin, we well know that the thing may be of one gender and the word designating it of another. See Martial vii., Epig. 17. The ascription of gender to it is artificial and arbitrary, and, in English and Anglo-Saxon, absolutely useless. Lowthe, therefore, among the most correct of our English grammarians, has justly said that in the nouns of the English language there is no other distinction of gender but that of nature, its adjectives admitting no change but of the degrees of comparison. We must guard against the conclusion of Dr. Hickes that the change of termination in the Anglo-Saxon adjectives, as god, gode, for example, is an indication of gender; this, like others of his examples of inflection, is only an instance of unsettled orthography. In the languages acknowledged to ascribe genders to their words, as Greek, Latin, Italian, Spanish, French, their dictionaries indicate the gender of every noun; but the Anglo-Saxon and English dictionaries give no such indication; a proof of the general sense that gender makes no part of the character of the noun. We may safely therefore dismiss the learning of genders from our language, whether in its ancient or modern form.

2. Our law of Cases is different. They exist in nature, according to the difference of accident they announce. No language can be without them, and it is an error to say that the Greek is without an ablative. Its ablative indeed is always like its dative; but were that sufficient to deny its existence, we might equally say that the Latins had no ablative plural, because in all nouns of every declension, their ablative plural is the same with the dative. It would be to say that to go *to* a place, or *from* a place, means the same thing. The grammarians of Port-Royal, therefore, have justly restored the ablative to Greek nouns. Our cases are generally distinguished by the aid of the prepositions *of, to, by, from,* or *with,* but sometimes also by change of termination. But these changes are not so general or difficult as to require, or to be capable of a distribution into declensions. Yet Dr. Hickes, having in view the Saxon declensions of the Latin, and ten of the Greek language, has given six, and Thwaytes seven to the Anglo-Saxon. The whole of them, however, are comprehended under the three simple canons following:

(1.) The datives and ablatives plural of all nouns end in *um.*

(2.) Of the other cases, some nouns inflect their genitive singular only, and some their nominative, accusative and vocative plural also in *s,* as in English.

(3.) Others, preserving the primitive form in their nominative and vocative singular, inflect all the other cases and numbers in *en.*

3. Numbers. Every language, as I presume, has so formed its nouns and verbs as to distinguish a single and a plurality of subjects, and all, as far as I know, have been contented with the simple distinction of singular and plural, except the Greeks, who have interposed between them a dual number, so distinctly formed by actual changes of termination and inflection, as to leave no doubt of its real distinction from the other numbers. But they do not uniformly use their dual for its appropriate purpose. The number two is often expressed plurally, and sometimes by a dual noun and plural verb. Dr. Hickes supposes the Anglo-Saxon to have a dual number also, not going through the whole vocabulary of nouns and verbs, as in Greek, but confined to two particular pronouns, *i.e., wit* and *yit,* which he translates we two, and

ye two. But Benson renders *wit* by *nos,* and does not give *yit* at all. And is it worth while to embarrass grammar with an extra distinction for two or three, or half a dozen words? And why may not *wit,* we two, and *yit,* ye two, be considered plural, as well as we three, or we four? as duo, ambo, with the Latins? We may surely say then that neither the Anglo-Saxon nor English have a dual number.

4. Verbs, moods. To the verbs in Anglo-Saxon Dr. Hickes gives six moods. The Greeks, besides the four general moods, Indicative, Subjunctive, Imperative, and Infinitive, have really an Optative mood, distinguished from the others by actual differences of termination. And some Latin grammarians, besides the Optative, have added, in that language, a Potential mood; neither of them distinguished by differences of termination or inflection. They have therefore been disallowed by later and sounder grammarians; and we may, in like manner, disembarrass our Anglo-Saxon and English from the Optatives and Potentials of Dr. Hickes.

### SUPINES AND GERUNDS

He thinks, too, that the Anglo-Saxon has supines and gerunds among its variations; accidents certainly peculiar to Latin verbs only. He considers *lufian,* to love, as the infinitive, and *to lufian,* a supine. The exclusion, therefore, of the preposition *to,* makes with him the infinitive, while we have ever considered it as the essential sign of that mood. And what all grammarians have hitherto called the infinitive, he considers as a supine or gerund. His examples are given in Anglo-Saxon and Latin, but I will add the equivalent Greek and English for illustration:

1 Mark, 24:—Come thu us to for-spillan?
Venisti nos *perditum?*
Ἠλθες ἀπολεσαι ἡμας;
*Comest thou to destroy us?*

9 Luke, I:—And he him an-wield sealed untrimness to healan, and devil-sickness ut to a-drivan.
Potestatem *curandi* infirmitates, et *ejiciendi* dæmonia.
ἐξουσιαν ἐπι παντα τὰ δαιμόνια και νοσμος θεράπευειν
*Authority over all demons, and to cure diseases.*

2. Matt., 13:—Herod seeketh that child to for-spillan.
Herodes quærit puerum ad *perdendum eum.*
Ἡροδης ζητειν τὸ παιδιον τομ ἀπολέσαι αὐτο
*Herod seeketh the child to destroy him.*

1 Luke, 77:—To sellen his folc hæle y-wit.
*Ad dandam* scientiam salutis plebi suæ.
τομ θοῦναι γνῶσιν σωτέριας τω λαῷ αὐτου.
*To give knowledge of salvation to his people.*

I ask then if ἀπολέσαι, θεράπευειν, θοῦναι, are supines or gerunds? Why then should to for-spillan, to healan, to a-drivan, to sellen, or, to destroy, to heal, to cure, to drive, to give, be necessarily supines or gerunds? The fact is only that the Latins express by these inflections, peculiar to themselves, what other languages do by their infinitives.

From these aberrations, into which our great Anglo-Saxon leader, Dr. Hickes, has been seduced by too much regard to the structure of the Greek and Latin languages and too little to their radical difference from that of the Gothic family, we have to recall our footsteps into the right way, and we shall find our path rendered smoother, plainer, and more direct to the object of profiting of the light which each dialect throws on the other. And this, even as to the English language, appears to have been the opinion of Wallis, the best of our English grammarians, who, in the preface to his English grammar, says: "Omnes ad Latinæ linguæ normam hanc nostram Anglicanam nimium exigentes multa inutilia, præcepta de nominum casibus, generibus et declinationibus, atque verborum temporibus, modis et conjugationibus, de nominum item et verborum regimine, aliisque similibus tradiderunt, quæ a lingua nostra sunt prorsus aliena, adeoque confusionem potius et obscuritatem pariunt, quam explicationi inserviunt?"

Having removed, then, this cumbrous scaffolding, erected by too much learning, and obscuring instead of enlightening our Anglo-Saxon structure, I will proceed to give a specimen of the manner in which I think might be advantageously edited any future republications of the Anglo-Saxon writings which we already possess in print, or any manuscripts which may hereafter be given to us through the medium of the press.

I take my specimen from Thwaites' Heptateuch, beginning with the 1st Chapter of Genesis. I give in one column the Anglo-Saxon text, in the Anglo-Saxon character, preserving letter for letter, the orthography of the Saxon original; in another column the same text in the Anglo-Saxon character also, spelt with a combined regard to the power of the letters, to English orthography and English pronunciation. I interline a version verbally exact, placing every English word against its Anglo-Saxon root, without regard to the change of acceptation it has undergone in time; as *e.g.*, "the earth was *idle* and empty," I Gen. 2, instead of the modern words "without form and void," and the ἀορατος και ἀκατασκεῦαστος of the LXX., leaving the ingenuity of the reader to trace the history of the change. In rendering the Anglo-Saxon into the corresponding English word, I have considered as English not only what is found in the oldest English writers, in glossaries and dictionaries, but in the Provincial dialects also, and in common parlance of unlettered people, who have preserved more of the ancient language than those whose style has been polished by education. Grammar, too, is disregarded, my principal object being to manifest the identity of the two languages. This version is rendered more uncouth by the circumstances that 1. The ordo verborum of the Anglo-Saxon is not exactly the same as the English. 2. They used much oftener the noun without the article. 3. They frequently use their oblique cases without a preposition prefixed the English very rarely. In this verbal version these omissions are to be understood.

The Anglo-Saxon writings, in this familiar form, are evidently nothing but old English; and we may join conscientiously in the exhortation of Archbishop Parker, in his preface to Asser, "Omnes qui in regni institutis addiscendis, elaboraverint, cohortabor ut *exiguo labore, seu pene nullo,* hujus sibi linguæ cognitionem acquirant?"

As we are possessed in America of the printed editions of the Anglo-Saxon writings, they furnish a fit occasion for this country to make some return to the older nations for the science for which we are indebted to them; and in this task I hope an honorable part will in time be borne by our University, for which, at an hour of life too late for anything elaborate, I hazard these imperfect hints, for consideration chiefly on a subject on which I pretend not to be profound. The publication of the inedited manuscripts which exist in the libraries of Great Britain only, must depend on the learned of that nation. Their means of science are great. They have done much, and much is yet expected from them. Nor will they disappoint us. Our means are as yet small; but the widow's mite was piously given and kindly accepted. How much would contribute to the happiness of these two nations a brotherly emulation in doing good to each other, rather than the mutual vituperations so unwisely and unjustifiably sometimes indulged in by both. And this too by men on both sides of the water, who think themselves of a superior order of understanding, and some of whom are truly of an elevation far above the ordinary stature of the human mind. No two people on earth can so much help or hurt each other. Let us then yoke ourselves jointly to the same car of mutual happiness, and vie in common efforts to do each other all the good we can—to reflect on each other the lights of mutual science particularly, and the kind affections of kindred blood. Be it our task, in the case under consideration, to reform and republish, in forms more advantageous, what we already possess, and theirs to add to the common stock the inedited treasures which have been too long buried in their depositories.

P.S. January, 1825. In the year 1818, by authority of the legislature of Virginia, a plan for the establishment of an University was prepared and proposed by them. In that plan the Anglo-Saxon language was comprehended as a part of the circle of instruction to be given to the students; and the preceding pages were then committed to writing for the use of the University. I pretend not to be an Anglo-Saxon scholar. From an early period of my studies, indeed, I have been sensible of the importance of making it a part of the regular education of our youth; and at different times, as leisure permitted, I applied myself to the study of it, with some degree of attention. But my life has been too busy in pursuits of another character to have made much proficiency in this. The leading idea which very soon impressed itself on my mind, and which has continued to prevail through the whole of my observations on the language, was, that it was nothing more than the Old English of a period of some ages earlier than that of Piers Ploughman; and under this view my cultivation of it has been continued. It was apparent to me that the labors of Dr. Hickes, and other very learned men, have been employed in a very unfortunate direction, in endeavors to give it the complicated structure of the Greek and Latin languages. I have just now received a copy of a new work, by Mr. Bosworth, on the elements of Anglo-Saxon grammar, and it quotes two other works, by Turner and Jamieson, both of great erudition, but not yet known here.

Mr. Bosworth's is, indeed, a treasure of that venerable learning. It proves the assiduity with which he has cultivated it, the profound knowledge in it which he has attained, and that he has advanced far beyond all former grammarians in the science of its structure. Yet, I own, I was disappointed on finding that in proportion as he has advanced on and beyond the footsteps of his predecessors, he has the more embarrassed the language with rules and distinctions, in imitation of the grammars of Greek and Latin; has led it still further from its genuine type of old English, and increased its difficulties by the multitude and variety of new and minute rules with which he has charged it. I had the less expected this from observations made early in the work, on "the total disregard of the Anglo-Saxons of any settled rules of orthography, their confounding the letters, using them indifferently for each other, and especially the vowels and diphthongs (p. 46), on the frequent transpositions of their letters, and the variety of ways of writing the same word by different Anglo-Saxon authors"; giving as examples, six ways of spelling the word "youth," and twenty ways of spelling "many"; observing that, in the comparative degree, the last syllable, *er,* was spelt with all the vowels indifferently; so also the syllable *est,* of the superlative degree, and so the participial terminations of *end* and *ed* (p. 54); adding many other examples of a use entirely promiscuous of the vowels, and much so of the consonants.

And in page 249 he says: "It must be evident that learning was not so common in the Saxon era as at the present time. Our ancestors, having few opportunities of literary acquirements, could not have determined upon fixed rules for orthography, any more than illiterate persons in the present day, who, having been employed in manual labor, could avail themselves of the facilities which were offered. Hence arose the differences observable in spelling the same words in Saxon." And again, in a note, p. 253, he says: "Those changes in Saxon, which are denominated dialects, appear in reality only to be the alterations observed in the progress of the language, as it gradually flowed from the Saxon, varying, or casting off many of its inflections, till it settled in the form of the present English. This progressive transformation of the Anglo-Saxon into our present form of speech will be evident by the following examples, taken from the translations of the most learned men of the age to which they are referred." And he proceeds to give specimens of the Paternosters of the years 890, 930, 1130, 1160, 1180, 1250, 1260, 1380, 1430, 1500, 1526, 1537, 1541, 1556, 1611, that is, from the time of Alfred to that of Shakespeare. These obviously prove the gradual changes of the language from the Anglo-Saxon form to that of the present English, and that there was no particular point of time at which the Anglo-Saxon was superseded by the English dialect; for dialects we may truly call them, of the same language, separated by lines of time instead of space. And these specimens prove also that the language of Alfred was, no more than that of Piers Ploughman, a different one from that we now speak.

In like manner, the language of France, cotemporary with our Anglo-Saxon, was as different from modern French, as the Anglo-Saxon from modern English; and their Romanum-rusticum, or Romain-rustique, as it was called, has changed insensibly, as our Anglo-Saxon, to the form now spoken. Yet so much of the fundamental idiom remains the same in both, that to read and understand the elder dialect, they need but a glossary for words lost by disuse.

I will make one more quotation from Mr. Bosworth, because it confirms what I have said of the scholastic bias of our early authors to place our old language in the line of Latin and Greek. "Hickes," says he, page 213, note 2, "indisputably one of the most learned of those who can be said to have examined, with a critical eye, our Saxon literature, influenced by the desire of reducing everything to some classical standard, a prejudice not uncommon in the age in which he wrote, endeavors, with greater zeal than success, to show that the writers whom he was recommending to the world (the Anglo-Saxon poets) observed the legitimate rules of Latin prosody, and measured their feet by syllabic quantity."

Notwithstanding these proofs that our author was fully aware of the unsettled and uncertain orthography of the Anglo-Saxons, and his particular observations, p. 53, 54, that "the final letters of words are often omitted," and "that the different letters suffer very frequent changes of position," he proceeds, in conformity with preceding authorities, which indeed support him, to make genders, cases, and declensions of nouns to depend on their terminating vowels, pp. 80, 81, 82, 83, 94; the formations of different parts of verbs to depend on the collocation of the letters (p. 143), and other formations (p. 181) and even regimen (p. 202) to depend on the final syllable. And this leads to such an infinitude of minute rules and observances, as are beyond the power of any human memory to retain. If, indeed, this be the true genius of the Anglo-Saxon language, then its difficulties go beyond its worth, and render a knowledge of it no longer a compensation for the time and labor its acquisition will require; and, in that case, I would recommend its abandonment in our University, as an unattainable and unprofitable pursuit.

But if, as I believe, we may consider it as merely an antiquated form of our present language, if we may throw aside the learned difficulties which mask its real character, liberate it from these foreign shackles, and proceed to apply ourselves to it with little more preparation than to Piers Plough-man, Douglas, or Chaucer, then I am persuaded its acquisition will require little time or labor, and will richly repay us by the intimate insight it will give us into the genuine structure, powers and meanings of the language we now read and speak. We shall then read Shakespeare and Milton with a superior degree of intelligence and delight, heightened by the new and delicate shades of meaning developed to us by a knowledge of the original sense of the same words.

This rejection of the learned labors of our Anglo-Saxon doctors, may be considered, perhaps, as a rebellion against science. My hope, however, is, that it may prove a revolution. Two great works, indeed, will be wanting to effect all its advantages. 1. A grammar on the simple principles of the English grammar, analogizing the idiom, the rules and principles of the one and the other, eliciting their common origin, the identity of their structure, laws and composition, and their total unlikeness to the genius of the Greek and Latin. 2. A dictionary, on the plan of Stephens or Scapula, in which the Anglo-Saxon roots should be arranged alphabetically, and the derivatives from each root, Saxon and English, entered under it in their proper order and connection. Such works as these, with new editions of the Saxon writings, on the plan I venture to propose, would show that the Anglo-Saxon is really old English, little more difficult to understand than works we possess, and read, and still call English. They would recruit and renovate the vigor of the English language, too much impaired by the neglect of its ancient constitution and dialects, and would remove, for the student, the principal difficulties of ascending to the source of the English language, the main object of what has been here proposed.

## OBSERVATIONS ON ANGLO-SAXON GRAMMAR

*Pronunciation.*—Different nations use different alphabets for expressing the sounds of their languages; and nations which use the same alphabet assign very different powers to the same characters. Hence, to enable persons to learn the language of other countries, grammars are composed explaining to what letters and combinations of them, in their own language, the letters and combinations of them in another are equivalent. The pronunciation of the living languages is deposited in records of this kind, as doubtless was that of the Greek and Latin languages, now considered as dead. These evidences of their pronunciation, however, being lost, we resort to the countries in which these languages were once spoken, and where they have been insensibly altered to what is now spoken there; and we presume that, the same alphabetical characters being still preserved there, the powers assigned to them are those handed down by tradition, with some changes, no doubt, but yet tolerably correct in the main: and that the present pronunciation of those characters by the inhabitants of the same country is better evidence of their ancient power than any other to be obtained at this day. Hence it is presumed that the pronunciation of the Greek and Roman characters, now practiced by the modern Greeks and Italians, is nearer probably to that of the ancient Greeks and Romans than the sounds assigned to the same characters by any other nation.

The Anglo-Saxon is also become a dead language. Its alphabet is preserved; but if any written evidences exist of the powers assigned to its different characters, it is unknown to me. On the contrary, I believe that the expressions of the sounds of their language by alphabetical characters had not been long and generally enough practised to settle an uniform power in each letter or combination of letters. This I infer from their infinitely diversified modes of spelling the same word. For example, the word *many* is found spelt in twenty different manners. To supply evidence, therefore, of the pronunciation of their words, we should, I think, resort to the pronunciation of the corresponding words in modern English. For as the Anglo-Saxon was insensibly changed into the present English language, it is probable the English have the pronunciation, as well as the words, by tradition. Indeed, I consider the actual pronunciation of a word by the English as better evidence of its pronunciation by their Anglo-Saxon ancestors than the multiform representation of it by letters which they have left us. The following examples will give an idea of the appeal I make to English pronunciation for the power of the Saxon letters, and sound of the Saxon words:

**The Anglo-Saxon .c in cy. cẏnꞃic was probably sounded as *k* in the corresponding Englisah words *kine, kingric.***

**ci. in cieꞅte = ch, in chest.**
**eo. in eoƿ, eoƿeꞃ = yo, in you, your.**
**" in þꞃeo, ꞅeoꝼon = e, in three, seven.**
**" in ꝼeoƿeꞃ = o, in four.**

**ea. in anꝼealꝺ, tƿẏꝼealꝺ=a, or o, in onefold, twofold.**

**ᵹe. prefix=y, in yclept, or a. in adown, along, aside, among, about, etc.**

**io. in ꞅioc, ꞅiolc, ꞅiolꝼoꞃ=i, in sick, silk, silver.**

**ꞅc in biꞅceop, juꝺeiꞅc, ꞅcomleaꞅe=sh, in bishop, Jewish, shameless.**

Those, I think, who have leisure and knowledge of the subject, could not render it a greater service than by new editions of the Saxon writings still extant, digested under four columns, whereof the first should present the text in the Saxon character and original loose orthography; the second the same text in Saxon characters reformed to modern English orthography as nearly as allowable; the third, the same text in the English character and orthography; the fourth, an English version, as literally expressed, both as to words and their arrangement, as any indulgences of grammar or of obsolete or provincial terms, would tolerate. I will exhibit the following passage from Alfred's Orosius, I. i., p. 23, as a specimen:

| 1. Saxon Orthography. | 2. Saxon Orthography reformed. | 3. English Character and Orthography. | 4. English Literal Version. |
|---|---|---|---|
| he ƿæꞅ miꝺ þæm ꝼẏꞃꞅt- | he ƿaꞅ miþ þem ꝼiꞃꞅt- | he (other) was mid them first- | he (ohtere) was with the first |
| -um mannum on þæm | -um mannum in þem | -um mannum in them | men in the |
| lanꝺe. *næꝼꝺe he | lanꝺ. naꝼꝺ he | land. nhaved he | land, nor had he |
| þeah ma þonne tƿen- | þo ma þen tƿen- | tho ma then twen- | tho' more then twen- |
| tiᵹ hꞃẏðeꞃa ⁊ tƿen- | tẏ hꞃẏðeꞃa. ⁊ tƿen- | -ty bryther, & twen- | -ty cattle, and twen- |
| tiᵹ ꞅceapa. ⁊ tƿentiᵹ | tẏ ꞅceep. ⁊ tƿentẏ | -ty sheep, & twenty | -ty sheep, and twenty |
| ꞅƿẏna. ⁊ þat lẏtle | ꞅƿine. ⁊ þat little | swine. & that little | swine. and that little |
| þat he eꞃeꝺe. he eꞃeꝺe | þat he eaꞃeꝺ he eaꞃeꝺ | that he eared, he eared | that he *eared, he eared |
| miꝺ hoꞃꞅan. ac hẏꞃa | miþ hoꞃꞅen. ac hẏꞃ | mith horsen, ac hir | with horses, but their |
| aꞃ iꞅ mæꞅt on þæm | aꞃ iꞅ moꞅt on þem | ar is most in them | rent is most in the |
| ᵹaꝼol þe þa Finnaꞅ | ᵹavel þa þe Finneꞅ | gavel tha the Fins | gavel that the Fins |
| him ᵹẏlꝺað. þæt ᵹa- | him ẏielꝺeð. þat ᵹa- | him yieldeth. that ga- | them yield. that ga- |
| ꝼol bið on ꝺeoꞃa ꝼel- | -vel beeð on ꝺeeꞃ ꝼel- | -vel beeth in deer fel- | -vel be in deer fells, |
| -lum. ⁊ on Fuᵹela ꝼe- | -lum. ⁊ on Foƿl ꝼe- | -lum, & in fowl-fea- | and in fowl fea- |
| ðeꞃum. ⁊ hƿaleꞅ | þeꞃum. ⁊ ƿhaleꞅ | -therum, & whales | -thers, and whale's |
| bane. ⁊ on þæm ꞅcip- | bone. ⁊ on þem ꞅhip- | -bone, & in them ship- | bone, and in the ship- |
| -ꞃapum þe beoð oꝼ | -ꞃopum þe beeð oꝼ | -ropum tha beeth of | -ropes that be of |
| hƿæleꞅ hẏꝺe ᵹeꞃoƿht | ƿhaleꞅ hiꝺe ẏƿꞃoᵹht. | whales hide ywrought, | whale's hide wrought |
| ⁊ oꝼ ꞅeoleꞅ :. Æᵹh- | ⁊ oꝼ ꞅealꞅ. aẏ- | & of seals : ay- | and of seals : aye- |
| -ƿilc ᵹẏlt be hẏꞅ ᵹe- | -ƿhile ẏielꝺ bẏ hiꞅ ẏ- | -while yield by his y- | -while (every one) yields by his |
| -bẏꞃꝺum. ꞅe bẏꞃꝺeꞅ- | biꞃðum. ꞅe biꞃðeꞅt | -birthum. se birthest | birth [state] the birthest [state- |
| ta ꞅceal ᵹẏlꝺan | ꞅhall ẏielꝺen | shall yield | -best] shall yield |
| ꝼiꝼtẏne meaꞃðeꞅ | ꝼiꝼteen maꞃtꞅ | fifteen marts | fifteen martin's |
| ꝼell. ⁊ ꝼiꝼ hꞃaneꞅ. ⁊ | ꝼell. ⁊ ꝼive ꞃaineꞅ. ⁊ | fell, & five rains, & | fells, and five raindeer, and |
| an beꞃan ꝼel. ⁊ tẏn | an beaꞃen ꝼell. ⁊ ten | an bearenfell, & ten | an bear's fell, and ten |
| ambꞃa ꝼeðꞃa. ⁊ be- | hampeꞃa ꝼeaþeꞃa. ⁊ | hampera feathera, & | hampers of feathers, and |
| -ꞃenne kẏꞃtel oððe | beaꞃen kiꞃtle oþ | bearen kirtle oth | bear's kirtle or |
| ẏteꞃenne. ⁊ tƿeᵹen | otteꞃen. ⁊ tƿain | otteren, & twain | otter's, and twain |
| ꞅcipꞃapaꞅ. æᵹþeꞃ | ꞅhipꞃopeꞅ. eiþeꞃ | shipropes, either | ship ropes, either |
| ꞅẏ ꞅẏxtiᵹ elne lanᵹ. | ꞅi ꞅixtẏ ellen lonᵹ. | si sixty ellen long. | is sixty ells long. |
| oþeꞃ ꞅẏ oꝼ hƿæleꞅ | oþeꞃ ꞅi oꝼ ƿhaleꞅ | other si of whales | other is of whale's |
| hẏꝺe ᵹeƿoꞃht. | hiꝺe ẏƿꞃoᵹht | hide ywrought, | hide wrought, |
| oþeꞃ oꝼ ꞅioleꞅ :. | oþeꞃ oꝼ ꞅealꞅ. | other of seals. | other of seals. |
| * ne-hæꝼꝺe contracted. | | | * ploughed. |

The dissimilitude between Saxon and English is more in appearance than in reality. It consists chiefly in the difference of character and orthography. Suppress that (as is done in the third column), represent the sounds by the English character and orthography, and it is immediately seen to be, not a different language, but the same in an earlier stage of its progression. And such editions of the Saxon writers, by removing the obstructions of character and false spelling, enabling us to give habitual and true, instead of uncouth and false sounds to words, would promote the study of the English language, by facilitating its examination in its mother state, and making us sensible of delicacies and beauties in it, unfelt but by the few who have had the courage, through piles of rubbish to seek a radical acquaintance with it.

### DECLENSIONS OF NOUNS

One of the simplifications of the study of the Anglo-Saxon which would result from a reformation of its orthography to the present English standard, would be a reduction in the number of the declensions of nouns heretofore assigned to it. The Anglo-Saxons seem to have thought some final vowel necessary to give sound to the preceding consonant, although that vowel was not itself to be sounded; and nothing being less fixed than the power of their vowels and diphthongs, they have used all the vowels indiscriminately for this purpose. Thus,

The word Son, in modern English, was spelt by them **ꞅuna, ꞅune, ꞅunu**. Free; **ꝼꞃeah, ꝼꞃeo, ꝼꞃeoh, ꝼꞃiᵹ**. Meal; mela, mele, melu. Man; man, mon. Milk; meolc, meoloc, meoluc, milc. Mickle; micel, mucel, mycel, mycle, myccle. Pepper; **peopeꞃ, peppoꞃ, pipoꞃ**.

Notwithstanding these various orthographies, all, I presume, represent the same sound, and probably that still retained by the English. For I can more easily suppose that an unlettered people used various modes of spelling the same word, than that they had so many different words to express the same thing. The *e* final of the English is a relict of the Anglo-Saxon practice of ending a word with a final vowel. A difference of orthography, therefore, and still less a mere difference of a final vowel is not sufficient to characterize a different declension of nouns. I should deem an unequivocal change in the sound necessary to constitute an inflection, and a difference in the inflections necessary to form a class of nouns into a different declension. On these principles I should reduce Thwaite's seven declensions to four, as follows:

1st declension, being Thwaite's 5th and 6th:

| | | | |
|---|---|---|---|
| ***Sing.*** | ***Nom. Acc. Voc.*** | **ƿiln** | **=ƿiln** |
| | ***Gen. Dat. Abl.*** | **ƿilne** | |
| ***Plur.*** | ***Nom.*** | **ƿilna-e-o-u** | |
| | ***Gen. Acc. Voc.*** | **ƿilna** | |
| | ***Dat. Abl.*** | **ƿilnum . .** | **ƿilnum** |

| | | | |
|---|---|---|---|
| ***Sing.*** | ***Nom. Voc. Abl.*** | **ꞅunu** | **ꞅun** |
| | ***Gen.*** | **ꞅuna** | |
| ***Plur.*** | ***Nom. Gen. Acc. Voc.*** | | |
| ***Sing.*** | ***Dat. Acc.*** | **ꞅuna. u** | |
| ***Plur.*** | ***Dat. Abl.*** | **ꞅunum . .** | **ꞅunum** |

2d declension, comprehending Thwaite's 3d and 4th:

| | Case | Anglo-Saxon | Reformed |
|---|---|---|---|
| *Sing.* | *Nom. Acc. Voc.* | anꝺᵹiꞇ | = anꝺᵹiꞇ |
| | *Dat. Abl.* | anꝺᵹiꞇe-a | |
| *Plur.* | *Gen.* | anꝺᵹiꞇa | |
| | *Acc. Voc.* | anꝺᵹiꞇu | |
| | *Nom.* | anꝺᵹiꞇn-a. o | |
| *Sing.* | *Gen.* | anꝺᵹiꞇeꞅ . | = anꝺᵹiꞇꞅ |
| | *Dat. Abl.* | anꝺᵹiꞇum . | anꝺᵹiꞇum |

| | Case | Anglo-Saxon | Reformed |
|---|---|---|---|
| *Sing.* | *Nom. Acc. Voc.* | ƿoꞃꝺ | ƿoꞃꝺ |
| *Plur.* | *Acc. Voc.* | | |
| | *Nom.* | ƿoꞃꝺe-a | |
| | *Gen.* | ƿoꞃꝺa | |
| *Sing.* | *Dat. Acc.* | ƿoꞃꝺe | |
| | *Gen.* | ƿoꞃꝺꞅ . | ƿoꞃꝺꞅ |
| *Plur.* | *Dat. Abl.* | ƿoꞃꝺum. | ƿoꞃꝺum |

3d declension, comprehending Thwaite's 1st and 7th:

| | Case | Anglo-Saxon | Reformed |
|---|---|---|---|
| *Sing.* | *Nom. Acc. Voc.* | ꞅmið | ꞅmið |
| | *Dat. Abl.* | ꞅmiðe | |
| *Plur.* | *Gen.* | ꞅmiða | |
| *Sing.* | *Gen.* | ꞅmiðeꞅ | ꞅmiðꞅ |
| *Plur.* | *Nom. Acc. Voc.* | ꞅmiðaꞅ | |
| | *Dat. Abl.* | ꞅmiððum . . | ꞅmiðum |

| | Case | Anglo-Saxon | Reformed |
|---|---|---|---|
| *Sing.* | *Nom. Acc.* | ꝼꞃeo-oh | ꝼꞃe |
| | *Dat. Abl.* | ꝼꞃeo | |
| | *Voc.* | ꝼꞃeoh | |
| *Plur.* | *Gen.* | ꝼꞃea | |
| | *Nom. Acc. Voc.* | ꝼꞃeoꞅ | =ꝼꞃeꞃ |
| *Sing.* | *Gen.* | | |
| *Plur.* | *Dat. Abl.* | ꝼꞃeum . . | ꝼꞃeum |

4th declension, being Thwaite's 2d:

| | Case | Anglo-Saxon | Reformed |
|---|---|---|---|
| *Sing.* | *Nom. Voc.* | ƿiꞇeᵹa | =ƿiꞇeᵹ |
| | *Gen. Dat. Acc. Abl.* | ƿiꞇeᵹan | ƿiꞇeᵹen |
| *Plur.* | *Nom. Acc. Voc.* | | |
| | *Gen.* | ƿiꞇeᵹena | |
| | *Dat. Abl.* | ƿiꞇeᵹum | ƿiꞇeᵹum |

In stating the declensions here the first column presents the Anglo-Saxon orthography, the varieties of which have been deemed sufficient to constitute inflections and declensions. The second column presents a reformed orthography, supposed equivalent to the other as to sound, and consequently showing that a variety in spelling where there is a sameness of sound does not constitute an inflection, or change of declination.

The four declensions, reformed to an uniform orthography, would stand thus:

| I. | | |
|---|---|---|
| *Sing.* | *Nom.* | ƿiln, ꞅun |
| | *Gen.* | |
| | *Dat.* | |
| | *Acc.* | |
| | *Voc.* | |
| | *Abl.* | |
| *Plur.* | *Nom.* | |
| | *Gen.* | |
| | *Acc.* | |
| | *Voc.* | |
| | *Dat.* | ƿilnum, ꞅunum |
| | *Abl.* | |

| II. | | |
|---|---|---|
| *Sing.* | *Nom.* | anꝺᵹiꞇ, ƿoꞃꝺ |
| | *Dat.* | |
| | *Acc.* | |
| | *Voc.* | |
| | *Abl.* | |
| *Plur.* | *Nom.* | |
| | *Gen.* | |
| | *Acc.* | |
| | *Voc.* | |
| *Sing.* | *Gen.* | anꝺᵹiꞇꞅ, ƿoꞃꝺꞅ |
| *Plur.* | *Dat.* | anꝺᵹiꞇum, ƿoꞃꝺum |
| | *Abl.* | |

| III. | | |
|---|---|---|
| *Sing.* | *Nom.* | ꞅmiꝺ, ꝼꞃe |
| | *Dat.* | |
| | *Acc.* | |
| | *Voc.* | |
| | *Abl.* | |
| *Plur.* | *Gen.* | |
| *Sing.* | *Gen.* | ꞅmiꝺꞅ, ꝼꞃeꞅ |
| *Plur.* | *Nom.* | |
| | *Acc.* | |
| | *Voc.* | |
| | *Dat.* | ꞅmiꝺum, ꝼꞃeum |
| | *Abl.* | |

| IV. | | |
|---|---|---|
| *Sing.* | *Nom.* | ƿiꞇeᵹ |
| | *Voc.* | |
| | *Gen.* | ƿiꞇeᵹen |
| | *Dat.* | |
| | *Acc.* | |
| | *Abl.* | |
| *Plur.* | *Nom.* | |
| | *Gen.* | |
| | *Acc.* | |
| | *Voc.* | |
| | *Dat.* | ƿiꞇeᵹum |
| | *Abl.* | |

In this scheme, then,

The first declension has no inflection, but for the dative and ablative plurals, which end in UM.

The second inflects its genitive singular in ꞅ, and dative and ablative plural in UM.

The third inflects its genitive, singular, nominative, accusative, and vocative plural in ꞅ; and dative and ablative plural in UM.

The fourth preserving its radical form in the nominative and vocative singular, inflects all its other cases in en, except the dative and ablative plural, which, in all the declensions, end invariably in UM.

It may be said that this is a bold proposition, amounting to a change of the language. But not so at all. What constitutes a language is a system of articulated sounds, to each of which an idea is attached. The artificial representation of these sounds on paper is a distinct thing. Surely there were languages before the invention of letters; and there are now languages never yet expressed in letters. To express the sounds of a language perfectly, every letter of its alphabet should have but a single power, and those letters only should be used whose powers successively pronounced would produce the sound required. The Italian orthography is more nearly in this state than any other with which I am acquainted; the French and English the farthest from it. Would a reformation of the orthography of the latter languages change them? If the French word *aimaient,* for example, were spelt *émé,* according to the French, or *ama,* according to the English power of those letters, would the word be changed? Or if the English word *cough* were spelt *cof,* would that change the word?

And how much more reasonable is it to reform the orthography of an illiterate people among whom the use of letters was so rare that no particular mode of spelling had yet been settled, no uniform power given to their letters, everyone being left free to express the words of the language by such combinations of letters as seemed to him to come near their sound. How little they were agreed as to the powers of their own letters, and how differently and awkwardly they combined them to produce the same sound, needs no better example than that furnished by Dr. Hickes of the short and simple sound of *many* being endeavored to be represented by twenty different combinations of letters; to wit, in English characters, mænigeo, mænio, mæniu, menio, meniu, mænigo, mænego, manige, menigo, manegeo, mænegeo, menegeo, mænygeo, menigeo, manegu, mænigu, menegu, menego, menigu, manigo. Now, would it change the word to banish all these, and give it, in their books, the orthography of *many,* in which they have all ended? And their correction in type is no more than every reader is obliged to make in his mind as he reads along; for it is impracticable for our organs to pronounce all the letters which their bungling spellers have huddled together. No one would attempt to give to each of these twenty methods of spelling *many* the distinct and different sounds which their different combinations of letters would call for. This would be to make twenty words where there surely was but one. He would probably reduce them all, wherever he met with them, to the single and simple sound of *many,* which all of them aimed to produce.

This, then, is what I would wish to have done to the reader's hand, in order to facilitate and encourage his undertaking. For remove the obstacles of uncouth spelling and unfamiliar character, and there would be little more difficulty in understanding an Anglo-Saxon writer than Burns' Poems. So as to the form of the characters of their alphabet. That may be changed without affecting the language. It is not very long since the forms of the English and French characters were changed from the black letter to the

Roman; yet the languages were not affected. Nor are they by the difference between the printed and written characters now in use. The following note, written by Ælfric, is not the less Latin because expressed in Anglo-Saxon characters:

> **Ego Ælfricus scripsi hunc Librum in monasterio Baþdonio et Sedi Brihtwoldo Preposito**

We may say truly, then, that the Anglo-Saxon language would still be the same, were it written in the characters now used in English, and its orthography conformed to that of the English; and certainly the acquisition of it to the English student would be greatly facilitated by such an operation.

## A SPECIMEN

of the

Form in Which the Anglo-Saxon Writings Still Extant Might Be Advantageously Published, for Facilitating to the English Student the Knowledge of the Anglo-Saxon Dialect

### GENESIS—Chapter I

1. On Angin y-shope God hevenan and earthan.

*In beginning shaped God heaven and earth.*

1. On Anginne gesceop God heofenan and eorthan.

2. Se earth sothelic was idle and empty, and thestre weron over there newelness broadness; and God's gost was [2] y-fared over water.

*The earth forsooth was idle and empty, and darkness were over the abyss's broadness; and God's ghost was fared over water.*

2. Seo eorthe sothlice wæs ydel & æmtig, and thoestru wæron ofer thære niwelnisse bradnisse & Godes gast was geferod ofer wæteru.

3. God cwoth tha, y-werth liht, and liht werth y-wrought.

*God quoth then were light, and light were wrought.*

3. God cwæth tha, ge-weorthe leoht; & leoht wearth ge-worht.

4. God y-saw tha that it good was, and he to-dealed that liht from tham thestrum.

4. God geseah tha thæt hit god was, and he to dælde that leoht fram tham theostrum.

[2] The prefixes *ge, ye, y, i,* being equivalent, I shall use the *y* for them all.—T. J.

*God saw then that it good was, and he dealed that light from the darkness.*

5. And het that liht day, and the thestre night. Tha was y-worden even and morowen an day.

*And hight that light day, and the darkness night. Then was wrought even and morn ane day.*

6. God cwoth tha aft, y-werth nu fastness to-mids them waterum, & to-[3]tweme the water from them waterum.

*God quoth them afer, were now fastness amidst the waters, & twain the waters from the waters.*

7. And God y-wroht the fastness, and to-twemed the water the weron under there fastness from them the weron boven there fastness; it was tha swa y-done.

*And God wrought the fastness, and twained the waters that were under the fastness from them that were aboven there fastness; it was then so done.*

8. And God het the fastness heavenan, and was tha y-wroden even & morowen other day.

*And God hight the fastness heaven, and was then wrought even & morn other day.*

9. God tha soothlic cwoth been y-gathered tha water the sind under there heavenan, and atewy dryness; it was tha swa y-done.

*God then forsooth quoth, be gathered the waters that are under the heavens, and shew dryness; it was then so done.*

10. And God y-kyed the dryness earthan, and the water y-gathering he

5. And het that leoht dæg, and tha theostra niht. Tha wæs ge-worden æfen & morgen an dæg.

6. God cwæth tha eft, gewurthe nu fæstnis tomiddes tham waterum, and totwæme tha wæteru fram tham wæterum.

7. And God geworhte tha fæstnisse, & totwæmde the wæteru the wæron under thære fæstnisse fram tham the wæron bufan thære fæstnisse; hit wæs tha swa gedon.

8. And God het tha fæstnisse heofenan, and wæs tha geworden æfen & morgen other dæg.

9. God tha sothlice cwæth, beon gegaderode tha wæteru the sind under theare heofenan, and æteowigedrignis, hit wæs tha gedon.

10. And God gecigde tha drignisse eorthan and thæra wætera gegaderunga

[3] *Twam* (tweme) signifies twain.—T. J.

het seas: God y-saw tha that it good was.

*And God called the dryness earth, and the water gathering he hight seas: God saw then that it good was.*

he het sæs. God geseah tha that hit god wæs.

11. And cwoth, sprute se earth growend gras & seed workend, and apple bear tree wæstm workend after his kin, these seed sy on him selfum over earthen; it was tha swa y-done.

*And quoth, sprout the earth growing grass & seed working, and apple bear tree fruit working after his kin, the seed be in him self over earth; it was then so done.*

11. And cwæth, spritte seo eorthe growende gær and sæd wircende, and æpplebære treow, wæstm wir cende æfter his cinne; thæs sædsig on him silfum ofer eorthan. Hit wæs tha swa gedon.

12. And se earth fortha-teah growend wort & seed bearing by hire kin; & tree westm workend, and y-whilc seed havend after his hue. God y-saw tha that it good was;

*And the earth*[4] *forth-brought growing wort & seed bearing by their kin; & tree fruit working, and ilc seed having after its hue. God saw then that it good was;*

12. And seo eorthe fortha-teah growende wirte and sæd berende be hire cinne, and treow westm wircende & gehwilc sæd hæbbende æfter his hiwe. God geseah that hat hit god was.

13. And was y-wroden even and morwen the third day.

*And was wrought even and morn the third day.*

13. And wæs gewroden æfen & morgen the thridda dæg.

14. God cwath tha sothlic, be nu liht on there heavenan fastness, and to-dealon day and niht, and been to-toknum & to-tidum, & to-dayum, & to-yearum.

*God quoth then forsooth, be now light in the heaven*[5] *fastness, and deal day and night, and be tokens & tides, & days & years.*

14. God cwæth tha sothlice, beo nu leoht on thære heofenan fæstnisse, and to ælon dæg & nihte, & beon to tacnum & to tidum & to dagum & to gearum.

15. And hi shinon on there heavenon fastness, and a-lithon tha earthan; it was tha swa y-wroden.

15. And hig scinon on thære heofenan fæstnisse and alihton tha eorthan. Hit wæs tha swa geworden.

[4] *Teon producere, fortha-teon,* forth-bring. See post v. 20, *teon,* forth; also, *ii,* 9, *fortha-teah.*—T. J.

*And they shine in the heaven fastness, and a-lighten the earth; it was then so wrought.*

16. And God y-wroht twa mickle liht, that mair liht to these days lihting, & that less liht to the niht lihting; and starran he y-wroht.

*And God wrought twa mickle lights, the more light to the days lighting, & the less light to the night lighting; and stars he wrought.*

16. And God geworhte twa micele leoht, that mare leoht, to thæs dæges lightinge, and that læsse leoht to thære nihte lihtinge; & steorran he geworhte.

17. And y-set hi on there heavenon that hi shinon over earthan,

*And set them in the heavens that they shine over earth,*

17. And gesette hig on thære heofenan, that hig scinon over eorthan.

18. And gimdon these days and these niht, and to-dealdon liht and thester. God y-saw tha that it good was.

*And govern the days and the nights, and deal light and darkness. God saw then that it good was.*

18. And gimdon thæs dæges thære nihte, & to dældon leoht and theostra. God geseah tha that hit god wæs.

19. And was y-wroden even and morwen, the fourth day.

*And was wrought even and morn, the fourth day.*

19. And wæs geworden æfen & morgen se feortha dæg.

20. God cwoth eke swilc, teon nu that water forth swimmend kin cuic in life, & flying kin over earthan under there heavenan fastness.

*God quoth* [6] *eke swilc, bring now the water forth swimming kind quick in life, & flying kind over earth under the heaven fastness.*

20. God cwæth eac swilce, teon nu tha wæteru forth swimmede cynn cuic on life, & fleogende cinn ofer eorthan under thære heofenan fæstnisse.

21. And God y-shope tha the mickelan whales and all livend fishen, and stirrendlia the tha water tugon forth on heor hiwum, and all flyend kin after heor kin; God y-saw tha that it good was;

*And God* [7] *shope then the mickle*

21. And God gesceope tha tha micelanh walas, & eall libbende fisccinn & stirigendlice, the tha wæterut ugon forth on heora hiwum, and eall fleogende cinn æfter heora cinne. God geseah tha that hit god wæs.

[5] *Fastness,* firmament.—T. J. [6] *Eac-swilc,* also.—T. J. [7] *Shope* (Bailey), for shaped.—T. J.

*whales, and all living fishes, and stirring that the water*[8] *tows forth in their* [9] *hue, and all flying kind after their kind; God saw then that it good was;*

22. And bletsed hi thus quothend, waxath and beeth y-manifold & y-fillath the sea-water and tha fuweles been y-manifold over earthan.

*And blessed them thus quothing, wax and be manifold, & fill the sea-water and the fowles be manifold over earth.*

23. And tha was y-wroughten even and morwen tha fifth day.

*And then was wrought even and morn the fifth day.*

24. God cwoth eke-swilc, lead se earth forth cuic niten on heor kin, & creepend kin and deer after heor hiwum. It was tha swa y-wroden.

*God quoth eke-swilc, lead the earth forth quick* [10] *neats in heor kin, & creeping kind and* [11] *deer after their hue. It was then so wrought.*

25. And God y-wroht there earthen deer after hir hiwum, and tha neaton, and all creepend kin on hior kin. God y-saw tha that it good was.

*And God wrought the earthen deer after their hue, and the neats, and all creeping kind in their kind. God saw then that it good was.*

26. And cwoth, [12] Uton, workan man to and-likeness, and to our y-likeness, and he sy over the fishes, and over the fowles, and over the deer, and over all y-shaft, & over all the crepend the stirreth on earthan.

22. And bletsode his thus cwethende, weaxath & beoth gemenigfilde, & gefillath thære sæ wæteru, and tha fugelas beon gemenigfilde ofer eorthan.

23. And tha wæs geworden æfen and morgen se fifta dæg.

24. God cwæth eacswilc, læde seo eorthe forth cuic nitena on heora cinne, and creopende cinn, and deor æfter heora hiwum. Hit wæs tha swa geworden.

25. And God geworhte thære eorthan deor æfter hira hiwum, & tha nitenu and eall creopende cynn on heora cynne. God geseah tha that hit good wæs.

26. And cwæth, Uton, wircean, man to andlicnisse, and to ure gelicnisse, and he sig ofer tha fixas, & ofer tha fugelas, and ofer the deor, and ofer ealle gesceafta, and ofer ealle tha creopende se stirrath on eorthan.

[8] *Verstegan—tuge,* to draw out—to lead; toga ductor (Benson).—T. J.
[9] *Hiew,* color (Versteg-Benson); it means also a hive, house, family.—T. J.
[10] *Nitena,* neat cattle.—T. J.
[11] *Deer.* Probably this was then the generic name for all the feræ or wild quadrupeds. —T. J.
[12] *Uton,* verbum hortantis, ace (Benson); come.—T. J.

*And quoth, Come, work man to likeness, and to our likeness, and he be over the fishes, and over the fowls, and over the deer, and over all creatures, & over all the creeping that stirreth on earth.*

27. God y-shope the man to his and-likeness, to Godes and-likeness he y-shope hine werhoods and wifehoods he y-shope hy.

*God shope then man to his likeness, to God's likeness he shope him, manhoods and wife-hoods he shope them.*

28. And God hy bletsed and swoth, waxeth and beeth y-manifold, and y-filleth the earthan, and y-wieldeth hy, and haveth on yourum y-wield there sea-fishes and there lyft-fowels and all neaten that stirreth over earthan.

*And God them blessed and quoth, wax and be manifold, and fill the earth, and wield them, and have in your wield the sea-fishes and the air-fowls and all neats that stirreth over earth.*

29. God cwoth tha, [13] even, I forgive you all grass and wortseed bearend over earthan, and al treewa tha the haveth seed on him selfon, heor owens kins, that hy been you to meat.

*God quoth then, even, I give you all grass and wort-seed bearing over earth, and all trees that haveth seed in himself, their own kinds, that they be you to meat.*

30. And allum neatum and all fowelkin and eallum tham the stirreth on earthan, on tham the is livend life, and hi havon hem to yreordien. It was tha swa y-done.

*And all neats and all fowl-kind, and all them that stirreth on earth, on*

27. God gesceop tha man to his andlicnisse, to Godes andlicnisse he gesceop hine, wehades and wifhades he gesceop hig.

28. And God hig bletsode and cwæth, wexath and beoth gemenigfilde, and gefillath tha eorthan and gewildath hig, and habbath on eowrum gewealde thære sæ fixas and thære lyfte fugelas & ealle nytenu the stiriath ofer eorthan.

29. God cwæth tha, Efne, Ic forgeaf eow eall gærs and wyrta sæd berende ofer eorthan, and ealle treowa tha the habbath sæd on him silfon heora agenes cynnes, that hig beon eow to mete.

30. And eallum nytenum & eallum fugelcynne and eallum tham the stiriath on eorthan, on tham the ys libbende lif, that hig habbon him to gereordienne. It was tha swa gedon.

[13] *Efne*, verily, adv. (Bailey); lo!—T. J.

*them that is living life, and they have them to feed. It was then so done.*

31. And God y-saw all the thing the he y-wroht, & he weron good. Was tha y-wroughten even and morwen se sixth day.

*And God saw all the things that he wrought, & they were good. Was then wrought even and morn the sixth day.*

31. And God y-saw ealle tha thing he geworhte, and hig wæron swithe gode. Was tha geworden æfen and mergen se sixth dæg.

## THE REVIVAL OF ANGLO-SAXON[1]

November 9, 1825

I learn from you with great pleasure, that a taste is reviving in England for the recovery of the Anglo-Saxon dialect of our language; for a mere dialect it is, as much as those of Piers Plowman, Gower, Douglas, Chaucer, Spenser, Shakspeare, Milton, for even much of Milton is already antiquated. The Anglo-Saxon is only the earliest we possess of the many shades of mutation by which the language has tapered down to its modern form. Vocabularies we need for each of these stages from Somner to Bailey, but not grammars for each or any of them. The grammar has changed so little, in the descent from the earliest to the present form, that a little observation suffices to understand its variations. We are greatly indebted to the worthies who have preserved the Anglo-Saxon form, from Doctor Hickes down to Mr. Bosworth. Had they not given to the public what we possess through the press, that dialect would by this time have been irrecoverably lost. I think it, however, a misfortune that they have endeavored to give it too much of a learned form, to mount it on all the scaffolding of the Greek and Latin, to load it with their genders, numbers, cases, declensions, conjugations, &c. Strip it of these embarrassments, vest it in the Roman type which we have adopted instead of our English black letter, reform its uncouth orthography, and assimilate its pronunciation, as much as may be, to the present English, just as we do in reading Piers Plowman or Chaucer, and with the cotemporary vocabulary for the few lost words, we understand it as we do them. For example, the Anglo-Saxon text of the Lord's prayer, as given us 6th Matthew, IX, is spelt and written thus, in the equivalent Roman type: "Faeder ure thec the eart in heafenum, si thin nama ychalgod. To becume thin rice. Gerrurthe thin willa on eartham, swa swa on heofenum. Ume doeghw amli can hlaf syle us to doeg. And forgyfus ure gyltas, swa swa we forgifath urum gyltendum. And ne ge-loedde thu us on costnunge, ae alys

[1] Letter to J. Evelyn Denison, M.P.

us of yfele." I should spell and pronounce thus: "Father our, thou tha art in heavenum, si thine name y-hallowed. Come thin ricy-y-wurth thine will on eartham, so so on heavenum: ourn daynhamlican loaf sell us today, and forgive us our guilts so so we forgiveth ourum guiltendum. And no y-lead thou us on constnunge, ac a-lease us of evil." And here it is to be observed by-the-bye, that there is but the single word "temptation" in our present version of this prayer that is not Anglo-Saxon; for the word "trespasses" taken from the French, (οφειλημαια in the original) might as well have been translated by the Anglo-Saxon "guilts."

The learned apparatus in which Dr. Hickes and his successors have muffled our Anglo-Saxon, is what has frightened us from encountering it. The simplification I propose may, on the contrary, make it a regular part of our common English education.

So little reading and writing was there among our Anglo-Saxon ancestors of that day, that they had no fixed orthography. To produce a given sound, everyone jumbled the letters together, according to his unlettered notion of their power, and all jumbled them differently, just as would be done at this day, were a dozen peasants, who have learnt the alphabet, but have never read, desired to write the Lord's prayer. Hence the varied modes of spelling by which the Anglo-Saxons meant to express the same sound. The word *many,* for example, was spelt in twenty different ways; yet we cannot suppose they were twenty different words, or that they had twenty different ways of pronouncing the same word. The Anglo-Saxon orthography, then, is not an exact representation of the sounds meant to be conveyed. We must drop in pronunciation the superfluous consonants, and give to the remaining letters their present English sound; because, not knowing the true one, the present enunciation is as likely to be right as any other, and indeed more so, and facilitates the acquisition of the language.

It is much to be wished that the publication of the present county dialects of England should go on. It will restore to us our language in all its shades of variation. It will incorporate into the present one all the riches of our ancient dialects; and what a store this will be, may be seen by running the eye over the county glossaries, and observing the words we have lost by abandonment and disuse, which in sound and sense are inferior to nothing we have retained. When these local vocabularies are published and digested together into a single one, it is probable we shall find that there is not a word in Shakspeare which is not now in use in some of the counties in England, from whence we may obtain its true sense. And what an exchange will their recovery be for the volumes of idle commentaries and conjectures with which that divine poet has been masked and metamorphosed. We shall find in him new sublimities which we had never tasted before, and find beauties in our ancient poets which are lost to us now. It is not that I am merely an enthusiast for Palæology. I set equal value on the beautiful engraftments we have borrowed from Greece and Rome, and I am equally a friend to the encouragement of a judicious neology; a language cannot be too rich. The more copious, the more susceptible of embellishment it will become. There are several things wanting to promote this improvement. To reprint the Saxon books in modern type; reform their orthography; publish in the same way the treasures still existing in manuscript. And, more than all things, we want a dictionary on the plan of Stephens or Scapula, in which the Saxon root, placed alphabetically, shall be followed by all its cognate modifications of nouns, verbs, &c., whether Anglo-Saxon, or found in the dialects of subsequent ages. We want, too, an elaborate history of the English language. In time our country may be able to co-operate with you in these labors, of common advantage, but as yet it is too much a blank, calling for other and more pressing attentions. We have too much to do in the improvements of which it is susceptible, and which are deemed more immediately useful. Literature is not yet a distinct profession with us. Now and then a strong mind arises, and at its intervals of leisure from business, emits a flash of light. But the first object of young societies is bread and covering; science is but secondary and subsequent.

I owe apology for this long letter. It must be found in the circumstance of its subject having made an interesting part in the tenor of your letter, and in my attachment to it. It is a hobby which too often runs away with me where I meant not to give up the rein. Our youth seem disposed to mount it with me, and to begin their course where mine is ending.

## GRAMMAR AND THE AMERICAN LANGUAGE[1]

August 16, 1813

Grammar . . . [has] never been a favorite with me. The scanty foundation, laid in at school, has carried me through a life of much hasty writing, more indebted for style to reading and memory, than to rules of grammar. I have been pleased to see that in all cases you appeal to usage, as the arbiter of language; and justly consider that as giving law to grammar, and not grammar to usage. I concur entirely with you in opposition to Purists, who would destroy all strength and beauty of style, by subjecting it to a rigorous compliance with their rules. Fill up all the ellipses and syllepses of Tacitus, Sallust, Livy, &c., and the elegance and force of their sententious brevity are extinguished.

*"Auferre, trucidare, rapere, falsis nominibus, imperium appellant." "Doerum injurias, diis curae." "Allieni appetens, sui profusus; ardens in*

[1] Letter to John Waldo (author of *Rudiments of English Grammar*).

*cupiditatibus; satis loquentiae, sapientiae parum." "Annibal peto pacem." "Per diem Sol non* uret *te, neque Luna per noctem."* Wire-draw these expressions by filling up the whole syntax and sense, and they become dull paraphrases on rich sentiments. We may say then truly with Quinctilian, *"Aliud est Grammaticé, aliud Latiné loqui."* I am no friend, therefore, to what is called *Purism,* but a zealous one to the *Neology* which has introduced these two words without the authority of any dictionary. I consider the one as destroying the nerve and beauty of language, while the other improves both, and adds to its copiousness. I have been not a little disappointed, and made suspicious of my own judgment, on seeing the Edinburgh Reviews, the ablest critics of the age, set their faces against the introduction of new words into the English language; they are particularly apprehensive that the writers of the United States will adulterate it. Certainly so great growing a population, spread over such an extent of country, with such a variety of climates, of productions, of arts, must enlarge their language, to make it answer its purpose of expressing all ideas, the new as well as the old. The new circumstances under which we are placed, call for new words, new phrases, and for the transfer of old words to new objects. An American dialect will therefore be formed; so will a West-Indian and Asiatic, as a Scotch and an Irish are already formed. But whether will these adulterate, or enrich the English language? Has the beautiful poetry of Burns, or his Scottish dialect, disfigured it? Did the Athenians consider the Doric, the Ionian, the Aeolic, and other dialects, as disfiguring or as beautifying their language? Did they fastidiously disavow Herodotus, Pindar, Theocritus, Sappho, Alcæus, or Grecian writers? On the contrary, they were sensible that the variety of dialects, still infinitely varied by poetical license, constituted the riches of their language, and made the Grecian Homer the first of poets, as he must ever remain, until a language equally ductile and copious shall again be spoken.

Every language has a set of terminations, which make a part of its peculiar idiom. Every root among the Greeks was permitted to vary its termination, so as to express its radical idea in the form of any one of the parts of speech; to wit, as a noun, an adjective, a verb, participle, or adverb; and each of these parts of speech again, by still varying the termination, could vary the shade of idea existing in the mind.

✦

It was not, then, the number of Grecian roots (for some other languages may have as many) which made it the most copious of the ancient languages; but the infinite diversification which each of these admitted. Let the same license be allowed in English, the roots of which, native and adopted, are perhaps more numerous, and its idiomatic terminations more various than of the Greek, and see what the language would become. Its idiomatic terminations are:

*Subst.* Gener-ation—ator; degener-acy; gener-osity—ousness—alship—alissimo; king-dom—ling; joy-ance; enjoy-er—ment; herb-age—alist; sanctuary—imony—itude; royal-ism; lamb-kin; child-hood; bishop-ric; proceedure; horseman-ship; worthi-ness.

*Adj.* Gener-ant—ative—ic—ical—able—ous—al; joy-ful—less—some; herb-y; accous-escent—ulent; child-ish; wheat-en.

*Verb.* Gener-ate—alize.

*Part.* Gener-ating—ated.

*Adv.* Gener-al—ly.

I do not pretend that this is a complete list of all the terminations of the two languages. It is as much so as a hasty recollection suggests, and the omissions are as likely to be to the disadvantage of the one as the other. If it be a full, or equally fair enumeration, the English are the double of the Greek terminations.

But there is still another source of copiousness more abundant than that of termination. It is the composition of the root, and of every member of its family, 1, with prepositions, and 2, with other words. The prepositions used in the composition of Greek words are:

✦

Now multiply each termination of a family into every preposition, and how prolific does it make each root! But the English language, besides its own prepositions, about twenty in number, which it compounds with English roots, uses those of the Greek for adopted Greek roots, and of the Latin for Latin roots. The English prepositions, with examples of their use, are a, as in a-long, a-board, a-thirst, a-clock; be, as in be-lie; mis, as in mis-hap; these being inseparable. The separable, with examples, are above-cited, afterthought, gain-say, before-hand, fore-thought, behind-hand, by-law, for-give, fro-ward, in-born, on-set, over-go, out-go, thorough-go, under-take, up-lift, with-stand. Now let us see what copiousness this would produce, were it allowed to compound every root and its family with every preposition, where both sense and sound would be in its favor. Try it on an English root, the verb "to place," Anglo Saxon *plæce,*[2] for instance, and the Greek and Latin roots, of kindred meaning, adopted in English, to wit, ϑεσις and locatio, with their prepositions.

[2] Johnson derives "place" from the French "place," an open square in a town. But its northern parentage is visible in its syno-nime *platz,* Teutonic, and *plattse,* Belgic, both of which signify locus, and the Anglo-Saxon *plæce, platea, vicus.*—T. J.

mis-place
after-place
gain-place
fore-place
hind-place
by-place
for-place
fro-place
in-place
on-place
over-place
out-place
thorough-place
under-place
up-place
with-place

amphi-thesis
ana-thesis
anti-thesis
apo-thesis
dia-thesis
ek-thesis
en-thesis
epi-thesis
cata-thesis
para-thesis
peri-thesis
pro-thesis
pros-thesis
syn-thesis
hyper-thesis
hypo-thesis

a-location
ab-location
abs-location
al-location
anti-location
circum-location
cis-location
col-location
contra-location
de-location
di-location
dis-location
e-location
ex-location
extra-location
il-location

inter-location
intro-location
juxta-location
ob-location
per-location
post-location
pre-location
preter-location
pro-location
retro-location
re-location
se-location
sub-location
super-location
trans-location
ultra-location

Some of these compounds would be new; but all present distinct meanings, and the synonisms of the three languages offer a choice of sounds to express the same meaning; add to this, that in some instances, usage has authorized the compounding an English root with a Latin preposition, as in de-place, dis-place, re-place. This example may suffice to show what the language would become, in strength, beauty, variety, and every circumstance which gives perfection to language, were it permitted freely to draw from all its legitimate sources.

The second source of composition is of one family of roots with another. The Greek avails itself of this most abundantly, and beautifully. The English once did it freely, while in its Anglo-Saxon form, *e.g.*, boc-cræft, book-craft, learning, ȝeleaf-full, right-belief-ful, orthodox. But it has lost by desuetude much of this branch of composition, which it is desirable however to resume.

If we wish to be assured from experiment of the effect of a judicious spirit of Neology, look at the French language. Even before the revolution, it was deemed much more copious than the English; at a time, too, when they had an academy which endeavored to arrest the progress of their language, by fixing it to a Dictionary, out of which no word was ever to be sought, used, or tolerated. The institution of parliamentary assemblies in 1789, for which their language had no opposite terms or phrases, as having never before needed them, first obliged them to adopt the Parliamentary vocabulary of England; and other new circumstances called for corresponding new words; until by the number of these adopted, and by the analogies for adoption which they have legitimated, I think we may say with truth that a Dictionaire Neologique of these would be half as large as the dictionary of the academy; and that at this time it is the language in which every shade of idea, distinctly perceived by the mind, may be more exactly expressed, than in any language at this day spoken by man. Yet I have no hesitation in saying that the English language is founded on a broader base, native and adopted, and capable, with the like freedom of employing its materials, of becoming superior to that in copiousness and euphony. Not indeed by holding fast to Johnson's Dictionary; not by raising a hue and cry against every word he has not licensed; but by encouraging and welcoming new compositions of its elements. Learn from Lye and Benson what the language would now have been if restrained to their vocabularies. Its enlargement must be the consequence, to a certain degree, of its transplantation from the latitude of London into every climate of the globe; and the greater the degree the more precious will it become as the organ of the development of the human mind.

These are my visions on the improvement of the English language by a free use of its faculties. To realize them would require a course of time. The example of good writers, the approbation of men of letters, the judgment of sound critics, and of none more than of the Edinburgh Reviewers, would give it a beginning, and once begun, its progress might be as rapid as it has been in France, where we see what a period of only twenty years has effected. Under the auspices of British science and example it might commence with hope. But the dread of innovation there, and especially of any example set by France, has, I fear, palsied the spirit of improvement. Here, where all is new, no innovation is feared which offers good. But we have no distinct class of literati in our country. Every man is engaged in some industrious pursuit, and science is but a secondary occupation, always subordinate to the main business of his life. Few therefore of those who are qualified, have leisure to write. In time it will be otherwise. In the meanwhile, necessity obliges us to neologize. And should the language of England continue stationary, we shall probably enlarge our employment of it, until its new character may separate it in name as well as in power, from the mother-tongue.

Although the copiousness of a language may not in strictness make a part of its grammar, yet it cannot be deemed foreign to a general course of lectures on its structure and character; and the subject having been presented to my mind by the occasion of your letter, I have indulged myself in its speculation.

## CENSORSHIP OF BOOKS[1]

April 19, 1814

I am really mortified to be told that, *in the United States of America,* a fact like this[2] can become a subject of inquiry, and of criminal inquiry too, as an offence against religion; that a question about the sale of a book can be carried before the civil magistrate. Is this then our freedom of religion? and are we to have a censor whose imprimatur shall say what books may be sold, and what we may buy? And who is thus to dogmatize religious opinions for our citizens? Whose foot is to be the measure to which ours are all to be cut or stretched? Is a priest to be our inquisitor, or shall a layman, simple as ourselves, set up his reason as the rule for what we are to read, and what we must believe? It is an insult to our citizens to question whether they are rational beings or not, and blasphemy against religion to suppose it cannot stand the test of truth and reason. If M. de Becourt's book be false in its facts, disprove them; if false in its reasoning, refute it. But, for God's sake, let us freely hear both sides, if we choose. I know little of its contents, having barely glanced over here and there a passage, and over the table of contents. From this, the Newtonian philosophy seemed the chief object of attack, the issue of which might be trusted to the strength of the two combatants; Newton certainly not needing the auxiliary arm of the government, and still less the holy author of our religion, as to what in it concerns him. I thought the work would be very innocent, and one which might be confided to the reason of any man; not likely to be much read if let alone, but, if persecuted, it will be generally read. Every man in the United States will think it a duty to buy a copy, in vindication of his right to buy, and to read what he pleases.

[1] Letter to Dufief, April 19, 1814.

[2] The sale of De Becourt's book (in French), *Sur la Création du Monde, un Système d'Organisation Primitive.*

## *Chapter XVIII*

# BIOGRAPHIC SKETCHES

## JOHN ADAMS[1]

January 30, 1787

A seven months' intimacy with him here [in Paris], and as many weeks' in London,[2] have given me opportunities of studying him closely. He is vain, irritable, and a bad calculator of the force and probable effect of the motives which govern men. This is all the ill which can possibly be said of him. He is as disinterested as the being who made him: he is profound in his views; and accurate in his judgment, except where knowledge of the world is necessary to form a judgment. He is so amiable, that I pronounce you will love him, if ever you become acquainted with him. He would be, as he was, a great man in Congress.[3]

## GEORGES L. C. BUFFON[4]

December, 1824

When I was in France, the Marquis de Chastellux carried me over to Buffon's residence in the country, and introduced me to him.

It was Buffon's practice to remain in his study till dinner time, and receive no visitors under any pretence; but his house was open and his

[1] Letter to James Madison.

[2] In March and April, 1786, Jefferson visited England, where John Adams was American Minister.

[3] In Congress, Jefferson had looked up to Adams, who was his senior by eight years. In 1809 Adams wrote to Dr. Benjamin Rush: "There has never been the smallest interruption of the personal friendship between me and Mr. Jefferson that I know of. You should remember that Jefferson was but a boy to me. . . . I am bold to say I was his preceptor in politicks and taught him everything that has been good and solid in his whole political conduct"; M.S. letter, on sale in New York on May 24 and 25: quoted in the *New York Times*, May 6, 1943.

[4] Conversation with Daniel Webster.

grounds, and a servant showed them very civilly, and invited all strangers and friends to remain to dine. We saw Buffon in the garden, but carefully avoided him; but we dined with him, and he proved himself then, as he always did, a man of extraordinary powers in conversation. He did not declaim; he was singularly agreeable.

I was introduced to him as Mr. Jefferson, who, in some notes on Virginia, had combated some of his opinions. Instead of entering into an argument, he took down his last work, presented it to me, and said, "When Mr. Jefferson shall have read this, he will be perfectly satisfied that I am right."

Being about to embark from Philadelphia for France, I observed an uncommonly large panther skin at the door of a hatter's shop. I bought it for half a Jo (sixteen dollars) on the spot, determining to carry it to France to convince Monsieur Buffon of his mistake in relation to this animal; which he had confounded with the cougar. He acknowledged his mistake, and said he would correct it in his next volume.

I attempted also to convince him of his error in relation to the common deer, and the moose of America; he having confounded our deer with the red deer of Europe, and our moose with the reindeer. I told him that our deer had horns two feet long; he replied with warmth, that if I could produce a single specimen, with horns one foot long, he would give up the question. Upon this I wrote to Virginia for the horns of one of our deer, and obtained a very good specimen, four feet long. I told him also that the reindeer could walk under the belly of our moose; but he entirely scouted the idea. Whereupon I wrote to General Sullivan of New Hampshire. I desired him to send me the bones, skin, and antlers of our moose, supposing they could easily be procured by him. Six months afterwards my agent in England advised me that General Sullivan had drawn on him for forty guineas. I had forgotten my request, and wondered why such a draft had been made, but I paid it at once. A little later came a letter from General Sullivan, setting forth the manner in which he had complied with my request. He had been obliged to raise a company of nearly twenty men, had made an excursion towards the White Hills, camping out many nights, and had at last after many difficulties caught my moose, boiled his bones in the desert, stuffed his skin and remitted him to me. This accounted for my debt and convinced Mr. Buffon.[5] He promised in his next volume to set these things right also, but he died directly afterwards.

[5] Jefferson to Buffon, October 3, 1787: "I had written to some of my friends in America, desiring they would send me such of the spoils of the moose, caribou, elk and deer, as might throw light on that class of animals; but more particularly, to send me the complete skeleton, skin and horns of the moose, in such condition as that the skin might be sewed up and stuffed, on its arrival here. I am happy to be able to present to you at this moment, the bones and skin of a moose, the horns of another individual of the same species, the horns of the caribou, the elk, the deer, the spiked horned buck, and the roebuck of America. They all come from New Hampshire and Massachusetts, and were received by me yesterday. . . . I

# ANECDOTES OF BENJAMIN FRANKLIN[1]

December, 1818

Our revolutionary process, as is well known, commenced by petitions, memorials, remonstrances, &c. from the old Congress. These were followed by a non-importation agreement, as a pacific instrument of coercion. While that was before us, and sundry exceptions, as of arms, ammunition, &c. were moved from different quarters of the house, I was sitting by Dr. Franklin and observed to him that I thought we should except books; that we ought not to exclude science, even coming from an enemy. He thought so too, and I proposed the exception, which was agreed to. Soon after it occurred that medicine should be excepted, and I suggested that also to the Doctor. "As to that," said he, "I will tell you a story. When I was in London, in such a year, there was a weekly club of physicians, of which Sir John Pringle was President, and I was invited by my friend Dr. Fothergill to attend when convenient. Their rule was to propose a thesis one week and discuss it the next. I happened there when the question to be considered was whether physicians had, on the whole, done most good or harm? The young members, particularly, having discussed it very learnedly and eloquently till the subject was exhausted, one of them observed to Sir John Pringle, that although it was not usual for the President to take part in a debate, yet they were desirous to know his opinion on the question. He said they must first tell him whether, under the appellation of physicians, they meant to include *old women,* if they did he thought they had done more good than harm, otherwise more harm than good."

The confederation of the States, while on the carpet before the old Congress, was strenuously opposed by the smaller States, under apprehensions that they would be swallowed up by the larger ones. We were long engaged in the discussion; it produced great heats, much ill humor, and intemperate declarations from some members. Dr. Franklin at length brought the debate to a close with one of his little apologues. He observed that "at the time of the union of England and Scotland, the Duke of Argyle was most violently opposed to that measure, and among other things predicted that, as the whale had swallowed Jonas, so Scotland would be swallowed by England. However," said the Doctor, "when Lord Bute came into the government, he soon brought into its administration so many of

really suspect you will find that the moose, the round-horned elk, and the American deer, are species not existing in Europe. The moose is, perhaps, of a new class. I wish these spoils, Sir, may have the merit of adding anything new to the treasures of nature, which have so fortunately come under your observation, and of which she seems to have given you the key."

[1] This accompanied a letter to Robert Walsh, December 4, 1818: "I state a few anecdotes of Dr. Franklin, within my own knowledge."

his countrymen, that it was found in event that Jonas swallowed the whale." This little story produced a *general* laugh, and restored good humor, and the article of difficulty was passed.

When Dr. Franklin went to France, on his revolutionary mission, his eminence as a philosopher, his venerable appearance, and the cause on which he was sent, rendered him extremely popular. For all ranks and conditions of men there, entered warmly into the American interest. He was, therefore, feasted and invited to all the court parties. At these he sometimes met the old Duchess of Bourbon, who, being a chess player of about his force, they very generally played together. Happening once to put her king into prize, the Doctor took it. "Ah," says she, "we do not take kings so." "We do in America," said the Doctor.

At one of these parties the emperor Joseph II then at Paris, incog., under the title of Count Falkenstein, was overlooking the game in silence, while the company was engaged in animated conversations on the American question. "How happens it M. le Comte," said the Duchess, "that while we all feel so much interest in the cause of the Americans, you say nothing for them?" "I am a king by trade," said he.

When the Declaration of Independence was under the consideration of Congress, there were two or three unlucky expressions in it which gave offence to some members. The words "Scotch and other foreign auxiliaries" excited the ire of a gentleman or two of that country. Severe strictures on the conduct of the British king, in negotiating our repeated repeals of the law which permitted the importation of slaves, were disapproved by some Southern gentlemen, whose reflections were not yet matured to the full abhorrence of that traffic. Although the offensive expressions were immediately yielded, these gentlemen continued their depredations on other parts of the instrument. I was sitting by Dr. Franklin, who perceived that I was not insensible to these mutilations. "I have made it a rule," said he, "whenever in my power, to avoid becoming the draughtsman of papers to be reviewed by a public body. I took my lesson from an incident which I will relate to you. When I was a journeyman printer, one of my companions, an apprentice hatter, having served out his time, was about to open shop for himself. His first concern was to have a handsome sign-board, with a proper inscription. He composed it in these words, 'John Thompson, *Hatter, makes* and *sells hats* for ready money,' with a figure of a hat subjoined; but he thought he would submit it to his friends for their amendments. The first he showed it to thought the word *'Hatter'* tautologous, because followed by the words 'makes hats,' which show he was a hatter. It was struck out. The next observed that the word *'makes'* might as well be omitted, because his customers would not care who made the hats. If good and to their mind, they would buy, by whomsoever made. He struck it out. A third said he thought the words *'for ready money'* were useless, as it was not the custom of the place to sell on credit. Everyone who purchased expected to pay. They were parted with, and the inscription now stood, 'John Thompson sells hats.' *'Sells hats'* says his next friend! Why nobody will expect you to give them away, what then is the use of that word? It was stricken out, and *'hats'* followed it, the rather as there was one painted on the board. So the inscription was reduced ultimately to 'John Thompson' with the figure of a hat subjoined."

The Doctor told me at Paris the two following anecdotes of the Abbé Raynal. He had a party to dine with him one day at Passy, of whom one half were Americans, the other half French, and among the last was the Abbé. During the dinner he got on his favorite theory of the degeneracy of animals, and even of man, in America, and urged it with his usual eloquence. The Doctor at length noticing the accidental stature and position of his guests, at table, "Come," says he, "M. l'Abbé, let us try this question by the fact before us. We are here one half Americans, and one half French, and it happens that the Americans have placed themselves on one side of the table, and our French friends are on the other. Let both parties rise, and we will see on which side nature has degenerated." It happened that his American guests were Carmichael, Harmer, Humphreys, and others of the finest stature and form; while those of the other side were remarkably diminutive, and the Abbé himself particularly, was a mere shrimp. He parried the appeal, however, by a complimentary admission of exceptions, among which the Doctor himself was a conspicuous one.

The Doctor and Silas Deane were in conversation one day at Passy, on the numerous errors in the Abbé's *"Histoire des deux Indes,"* when he happened to step in. After the usual salutations, Silas Deane said to him, "The Doctor and myself, Abbé, were just speaking of the errors of fact into which you have been led in your history." "Oh, no, Sir," said the Abbé, "that is impossible. I took the greatest care not to insert a single fact, for which I had not the most unquestionable authority." "Why," says Deane, "there is the story of Polly Baker, and the eloquent apology you have put into her mouth, when brought before a court of Massachusetts to suffer punishment under a law which you cite, for having had a bastard. I know there never was such a law in Massachusetts." "Be assured," said the Abbé, "you are mistaken, and that that is a true story. I do not immediately recollect indeed the particular information on which I quote it; but I am certain that I had for it unquestionable authority." Doctor Franklin, who had been for some time shaking with unrestrained laughter at the Abbé's confidence in his authority for that tale, said, "I will tell you, Abbé, the origin of that story. When I was a printer and editor of a newspaper, we were sometimes slack of news, and, to amuse our customers, I used to fill up our vacant columns with anecdotes and fables, and fancies of my own, and this of Polly Baker is a story of my making, on one of these occasions." The Abbé, without the least disconcert, exclaimed with a laugh, "Oh, very well, Doctor, I had rather relate your stories than other men's truths."

## GEORGE IV [1]

### January 11, 1789

As the character of the Prince of Wales [later George IV] is becoming interesting,[2] I have endeavored to learn what it truly is. This is less difficult in his case, than in that of other persons of his rank, because he has taken no pains to hide himself from the world. The information I most rely on, is from a person here with whom I am intimate, who divides his time between Paris and London, an Englishman by birth, of truth, sagacity and science. He is of a circle, when in London, which has had good opportunities of knowing the Prince; but he has also, himself, had special occasions of verifying their information, by his own personal observation. He happened, when last in London, to be invited to a dinner of three persons. The Prince came by chance, and made the fourth. He ate half a leg of mutton; did not taste of small dishes, because small; drank Champagne and Burgundy, as small beer during dinner, and Bourdeaux after dinner, as the rest of the company. Upon the whole, he ate as much as the other three, and drank about two bottles of wine without seeming to feel it. My informant sat next him, and being till then unknown to the Prince, personally (though not by character), and lately from France, the Prince confined his conversation almost entirely to him. Observing to the Prince that he spoke French without the least foreign accent, the Prince told him, that when very young, his father had put only French servants about him, and that it was to that circumstance he owed his pronunciation. He led him from this to give an account of his education, the total of which was the learning a little Latin. He has not a single element of Mathematics, of Natural or Moral Philosophy, or of any other science on earth, nor has the society he has kept been such as to supply the void of education. It has been that of the lowest, the most illiterate and profligate persons of the kingdom, without choice of rank or mind, and with whom the subjects of conversation are only horses, drinking-matches, bawdy houses, and in terms the most vulgar. The young nobility, who begin by associating with him, soon leave him,

[1] Letter to John Jay.

[2] It was expected that the Prince would succeed George III, who was considered to be mentally deranged. On December 4, 1788, Jefferson informed General Washington: "the lunacy of the King of England . . . is a decided fact, notwithstanding all the stuff the English papers publish about his fevers, his deliriums, &c."

disgusted with the insupportable profligacy of his society; and Mr. Fox, who has been supposed his favorite, and not over-nice in the choice of company, would never keep his company habitually. In fact, he never associated with a man of sense. He has not a single idea of justice, morality, religion, or of the rights of men, or any anxiety for the opinion of the world. He carries that indifference for fame so far, that he would probably not be hurt were he to lose his throne, provided he could be assured of having always meat, drink, horses, and women. In the article of women, nevertheless, he is become more correct, since his connection with Mrs. Fitzherbert, who is an honest and worthy woman: he is even less crapulous than he was. He had a fine person, but it is becoming coarse. He possesses good native common sense; is affable, polite, and very good humoured. Saying to my informant, on another occasion, "your friend, such a one, dined with me yesterday, and I made him damned drunk"; he replied, "I am sorry for it; I had heard that your royal highness had left off drinking": the Prince laughed, tapped him on the shoulder very good naturedly, without saying a word, or ever after showing any displeasure. The Duke of York, who was for some time cried up as the prodigy of the family, is as profligate, and of less understanding. To these particular traits, from a man of sense and truth, it would be superfluous to add the general terms of praise or blame, in which he is spoken of by other persons, in whose impartiality and penetration I have less confidence. A sample is better than a description.

## PATRICK HENRY[1]

*c.* 1811

My acquaintance with Mr. Henry commenced in the winter of 1759-60. On my way to college I passed the Christmas holidays at Colo. Dandridge's, in Hanover, to whom Mr. Henry was a near neighbor. During the festivity of the season I met him in society every day, and we became well acquainted, although I was much his junior, being then but in my 17th year and he a married man. The spring following he came to Williamsburg to obtain a license as a lawyer, and he called on me at college. He told me he had been reading law only 6 weeks. Two of the examiners, however, Peyton and John Randolph, men of great facility of temper, signed his license with

[1] Jefferson sent this sketch to William Wirt, Henry's biographer, on April 12, 1812, with the following comment: "The enclosed paper written for you a year or two ago, has laid by me with a view still to add something to it, but on reflection, I send it as it is. The additional matter contemplated respected Mr. Henry's ravenous avarice, the only passion paramount to his love of popularity. The facts I have heard on that subject are not within my own knowledge, and ought not to be hazarded but on better testimony than I possess."

This paper was first printed in *The Age* (Philadelphia), July, 1867, and criticized in the New York *World,* on August 2 and 3, 1867, by William Wirt Henry.

as much reluctance as their dispositions would permit them shew. Mr. Wythe absolutely refused. Robert C. Nicholas refused also at first, but on repeated importunities and promises of future reading, he signed. These facts I had afterwards from the gentlemen themselves, the two Randolphs acknowledging he was very ignorant of law, but that they perceived him to be a young man of genius, and did not doubt he would soon qualify himself.

He was some time after elected a representative of the county of Hanover and brought himself into public notice on the following occasion, which I think took place in 1762, or a year sooner or later. The gentlemen of this country had at that time become deeply involved in that state of indebtment which has since ended in so general a crush of their fortunes. Robinson the speaker was also Treasurer, an officer always chosen by the Assembly. He was an excellent man, liberal, friendly and rich. He had been drawn in to lend on his own account great sums of money to persons of this description, and especially those who were of the assembly. He used freely for this purpose the public money, confiding for its replacement in his own means and the securities he had taken on those loans. About this time however he became sensible that his deficit to the public was become so enormous as that a discovery must soon take place, for as yet the public had no suspicion of it. He devised therefore with his friends in the assembly a plan for a public loan office to a certain amount, from which monies might be lent on public account and on good landed security to individuals. This was accordingly brought forward in the House of Burgesses, and had it succeeded, the debts due to Robinson on these loans would have been transferred to the public, and his deficit thus completely covered. This state of things however was not yet known; but Mr. Henry attacked the scheme on other general grounds in that style of bold grand and overwhelming eloquence, for which he became so justly celebrated afterwards. He carried with him all the members of the upper counties, and left a minority composed merely of the aristocracy of the country. From this time his popularity swelled apace, and Robinson dying 4 years after, his deficit was brought to light, and discovered the true object of the proposition.

The next great occasion on which he signalised himself was that which may be considered as the dawn of the Revolution in March, 1764. The British parliament had passed resolutions preparatory to the levying a revenue on the colonies by a stamp tax. The Virginia assembly at their next session, prepared and sent to England very elaborate representations addressed in separate forms to the King, Lords and Commons, against the right to impose such taxes. The famous stamp act was, however, past in January, 1765, and in the session of the Virginia assembly of May following, Mr. Henry introduced the celebrated resolutions of that date. These were drawn by George Johnston, a lawyer of the Northern neck, a very able, logical and correct speaker. Mr. Henry moved and Johnston seconded these resolutions successively. They were opposed by Randolph, Blood, Pendleton, Nicholas, Wythe and all the old members whose influence in the house had till then been unbroken. They did it, not from any question of our rights, but on the ground that the same sentiments had been at their preceding session expressed in a more conciliatory form to which the answers were not yet received. But torrents of sublime eloquence from Mr. Henry, backed up by the solid reasoning of Johnston, prevailed. The last however, and strongest resolution was carried but by a single vote. The debate on it was most bloody. I was then but a student and was listening at the door of the lobby (for as yet there was no gallery) when Peyton Randolph, after the vote, came out of the house and said, as he entered the lobby, "By god I would have given 500 guineas for a single vote," for as this would have divided the house, the vote of Robinson, the speaker, would have rejected the resolution. Mr. Henry left town that evening and the next morning before the meeting of the house, I saw Peter Randolph, then of the council, but who had formerly been clerk in the house, for an hour or two at the clerk's table searching the old journals for a precedent while he was clerk, of a resolution of the house erased from the journals by a subsequent order of the house. Whether he found it or not I do not remember; but when the house met, a motion was made and carried to erase that resolution; and there being at that day but one printer and he entirely under the controul of the governor, I do not know that this resolution ever appeared in print. I write this from memory, but the impression made on me, at the time, was such as to fix the facts indelibly in my mind.

I came into the Legislature as a burgess for Albemarle in the winter of 1768/9 on the accession of Ld. Botetourt to the government and about 9 years after Mr. Henry had entered on the stage of public life. The exact conformity of our political opinions strengthened our friendship, and indeed, the old leaders of the house being substantially firm, we had not after this any differences of opinion in the House of Burgesses on matters of principles, though sometimes on matters of form. We were dissolved by Lord Botetourt at our first session; but all were re-elected. There being no divisions among us, occasions became very rare for any display of Mr. Henry's eloquence. In ordinary business he was a very inefficient member. He could not draw a bill on the most simple subject which would bear legal criticism, or even the ordinary criticism which looks to correctness of style and ideas, for indeed there was no accuracy of idea in his head. His imagination was copious, poetical, sublime, but vague also. He said the strongest things in the finest language, but without logic, without arrangement, desultorily. This appeared eminently and in a mortifying degree in the 1st session of the 1st Congress which met in September, 1774.

Mr. Henry and Richard Henry Lee took at once the lead in that assembly, and by the high style of their eloquence were in the first days of the session looked up to as primi inter pares. A petition to the King, an Address to the people of Great Britain, and a Memorial to the people of British America were agreed to be drawn. Lee, Henry and others were appointed for the first, and Lee, Livingston and Jay for the two last. The splendor of their debut occasioned Mr. Henry to be designated by his committee to draw the petition to the king, with which they were charged, and Mr. Lee was charged with the address to the people of England. The last was first reported. On reading it every countenance fell and a dead silence ensued for many minutes. At length, it was laid on the table for perusal and consideration till the next day when first one member, and then another arose, and paying some faint compliment to the composition observed that there were still certain considerations not expressed in it, which should properly find a place in it. At length Mr. Livingston (the governor of New Jersey) a member of the committee rose and observed that a friend of his had been sketching what he had thought might be proper for such an address, from which he thought some paragraphs might be advantageously introduced into the draught proposed: and he read an address which Mr. Jay had prepared de bene ese as it were. There was but one sentiment of admiration. The address was recommitted for amendment, and Mr. Jay's draught reported and adopted with scarce any alteration. These facts were stated to me by Mr. Pendleton and Colonel Harrison of our own delegation, except that Colonel Harrison ascribed the draught to Governor Livingston and were afterwards confirmed to me by Governor Livingston, and I will presently mention an anecdote confirmative of them from Mr. Jay and R. H. Lee themselves.

Mr. Henry's draught of a petition to the king was equally unsuccessful, and was recommitted for amendment. Mr. John Dickenson was added to the committee and a new draught prepared by him was passed.

The occasion of my learning from Mr. Jay that he was the author of the address to the people of Great Britain requires explanation by a statement of some preceding circumstances. The 2d session of the 1st Congress met on their own adjournment in May, 1775. Peyton Randolph was their president. In the mean time Lord North's conciliatory propositions came over to be laid by the Governors before their Legislatures. Lord Dunmore accordingly called that of Virginia to meet in June. This obliged P. Randolph as Speaker to return. Our other old members being at Congress, he pressed me to draw the answer to Lord North's proposition. I accordingly did so, and it passed with a little softening of some expressions for which the times were not yet ripe and wire-drawing and weakening some others to satisfy individuals. I had been appointed to go on to Congress in place of Peyton

Randolph, and proceed immediately, charged with presenting this answer to Congress. As it was the first which had been given, and the tone of it was strong the members were pleased with it hoping it would have a good effect on the answers of the other states. A Committee which had been appointed to prepare a Declaration to be published by General Washington on his arrival at the army, having reported one, it was committed, and Dickinson and myself added to the committee. On the adjournment of the house happening to go out with Governor Livingston, one of the Committee, I expressed to him my hope he would draw the Declaration. He modestly excused himself, and expressed his wish that I would do it. But urging him with considerable importunity, he at length said "You and I, sir, are but new acquaintances: what can have excited so earnest a desire on your part that I should be the Draughtsman?" "Why, sir," said I, "I have been informed you drew the Address to the people of Great Britain. I think it the first composition in the English language, and therefore am anxious this declaration should be prepared by the same pen." He replied, that I might have been "misinformed on that subject." A few days after being in conversation with R. H. Lee in Congress till a little before the meeting of the house, Mr. Jay observing us, came up, and taking R. H. Lee by a button of the coat said to him pretty sternly, "I understand, Sir, that you informed this gentleman that the Address to the people of Great Britain presented to the Committee by me was drawn by Governor Livingston." The fact was that the Committee having consisted of only Lee, Livingston, who was father-in-law of Jay and Jay himself and Lee's draught having been rejected and Jay's approved so unequivocally, his suspicions naturally fell on Lee as the author of the report; and the rather as they had daily much sparring in Congress, Lee being firm in the revolutionary measures, and Jay hanging heavily on their rear. I immediately stopped Mr. Jay, and assured him that though I had indeed been so informed, it was not by Mr. Lee, whom I had never heard utter a word on the subject.

I found Mr. Henry to be a silent and almost unmeddling member in Congress. On the original opening of that body, while general grievances were the topics, he was in his element and captivated all by his bold and splendid eloquence. But as soon as they came to specific matters, to sober reasoning and solid argumentation he had the good sense to perceive that his declamation however excellent in its proper place, had no weight at all in such an assembly as that, of cool-headed, reflecting, judicious men. He ceased therefore in a great measure to take any part in the business. He seemed indeed very tired of the place and wonderfully relieved when, by appointment of the Virginia convention to be Colonel of their 1st regiment he was permitted to leave Congress about the last of July. How he acquitted himself in his military command will be better known from others. He was relieved from his position again by being appointed Governor on the first organization of the government. After my service as his successor in the same office my appointment to Congress in 1783, mission to Europe in '84, and appointment in the new government in '89, kept us so far apart that I had no further personal knowledge of him.

Mr. Henry began his career with very little property. He acted, as I have understood, as barkeeper in the tavern at Hanover C[ourt] H[ouse] for sometime. He married very young; settled, I believe, at a place called the Roundabout in Louisa, got credit for some little store of merchandize, but very soon failed. From this he turned his views to the law, for the acquisition or practice of which however he was too lazy. Whenever the courts were closed for the winter session, he would make up a party of poor hunters of his neighborhood, would go off with them to the pinywoods of Fluvannia, and pass weeks in hunting deer, of which he was passionately fond, sleeping under a tent, before a fire, wearing the same shirt the whole time, and covering all the dirt of his dress with a hunting-shirt. He never undertook to draw pleadings if he could avoid it or to manage that part of a cause and very unwillingly engaged, but as an assistant, to speak in the cause. And the fee was an indispensable preliminary, observing to the applicant that he kept no accounts, never putting pen to paper, which was true. His powers over a jury were so irresistible that he received great fees for his services, and had the reputation of being insatiable in money. After about 10 years practice in the Country courts he came to the General court where however being totally unqualified for anything but mere jury causes, he devoted himself to these, and chiefly to the criminal business. From these poor devils it was always understood that he squeezed exorbitant fees of 50, 100 and 200. From this source he made his great profits, and they were said to be great.

His other business, exclusive of the criminal, would never, I am sure, pay the expenses of his attendance. He now purchased from Mr. Lomax the valuable estate on the waters of Smith's river, to which he afterwards removed. The purchase was on long credit and finally paid in depreciated paper not worth oak leaves. About the close of the war he engaged in the Yazoo speculation, and bought up a great deal of depreciated paper at 2/ and 2/6 in the pound to pay for it. At the close of the war, many of us wished to reopen all accounts which had been paid in depreciated money, and have them settled by the scale of depreciation, but on this he frowned most indignantly, and knowing the general indisposition of the legislature, it was considered hopeless to attempt it with such an opponent at their head as Henry.

I believe he never distinguished himself so much as on the similar question of British debts in the case of Jones and Walker. He had exerted a degree of industry in that case totally foreign to his character, and not only seemed, but had made himself really learned on the subject. Another of the great occasions on which he exhibited examples of eloquence such as probably had never been exceeded, was on the question of adopting the new constitution in 1788. To this he was most violently opposed, as is well known; and after its adoption he continued hostile to it, expressing more than any other man in the U.S. his thorough contempt and hatred of General Washington. From being the most violent of all anti-federalists however he was brought over to the new constitution by his Yazoo speculation, before mentioned. The Georgia legislature having declared that transaction fraudulent and void, the depreciated paper which he had bought up to pay for the Yazoo purchase was likely to remain on his hands worth nothing. But Hamilton's founding system came most opportunely to his relief, and suddenly raised his paper from 2/6 to 27/6 the pound. Hamilton became now his idol, and abandoning the republican advocates of the constitution, the federal government on federal principles became his political creed. General Washington flattered him by an appointment to a mission to Spain, which he declined; and by proposing to him the office of Secretary of State, on the most earnest solicitations of General Henry Lee, who pledged himself that Henry should not accept it; for General Washington knew that he was entirely unqualified for it, and moreover that his self-esteem had never suffered him to act as second to any man on earth. I had this fact from information, but that of the mission to Spain is of my own knowledge because after my retiring from the office of Secretary of State General Washington passed the papers to Mr. Henry through my hands. Mr. Henry's apostacy sunk to him to nothing in the estimation of his country. He lost at once all that influence which federalism had hoped, by cajoling him, to transfer with him to itself and a man who through a long and active life had been the idol of his country beyond anyone that ever lived, descended to the grave with less than its indifference, and verified the saying of the philosopher, that no man must be called happy till he is dead.

✦

[On August 14, 1814, Jefferson wrote to William Wirt:]

I had been intimate with Mr. Henry since the winter of 1759-60, and felt an interest in what concerned him, and I can never forget a particular exclamation of his in the debate in which he electrified his hearers. It had been urged that from certain unhappy circumstances of the colony, men of sub stantial property had contracted debts, which, if exacted suddenly, must ruin them and their families, but, with a little indulgence of time, might be paid with ease. "What, Sir!" exclaimed Mr. Henry, in animadverting on this, "is it proposed then to reclaim the spendthrift from his dissipation and extravagance, by filling his pockets with money." These expressions are indelibly impressed on my memory. He laid open with so much energy the spirit of favoritism on which the proposition was founded, and the abuses to which it would lead, that it was crushed in its birth.

## PATRICK HENRY[1]

December, 1824

Patrick Henry was originally a barkeeper. He was married very young, and going into some business, on his own account, was a bankrupt before the year was out. When I was about the age of fifteen, I left the school here, to go to college of Williamsburg. I stopped a few days at a friend's in the county of Louisa. There I first saw and became acquainted with Patrick Henry.[2] Having spent the Christmas holidays there, I proceeded to Williamsburg. Some question arose about my admission, as my preparatory studies had not been pursued at the school connected with that institution. This delayed my admission a fortnight, at which time Henry appeared in Williamsburg, and applied for a license to practice law, having commenced the study of it or subsequently to the time of my meeting him in Louisa. There were four examiners, Wythe, Pendleton, Peyton Randolph and John Randolph. Wythe and Pendleton at once rejected his application. The two Randolphs, by his importunity, were prevailed upon to sign the license; and having obtained their signatures, he applied again to Pendleton, and after much entreaty and many promises of future study, succeeded in obtaining his. He then turned out for a practising lawyer.

The first case which brought him into notice was a contested election, in which he appeared as counsel before a committee of the House of Burgesses. His second was the Parsons cause, already well known. These and similar efforts soon obtained for him so much reputation that he was elected a member of the legislature. He was as well suited to the times as any man ever was, and it is not now easy to say what we should have done without Patrick Henry. He was far before all in maintaining the spirit of the Revolution. His influence was most extensive with the members from the upper counties, and his boldness and their votes overawed and controlled the more cool or

[1] Taken from Daniel Webster, "Memorandum of Mr. Jefferson's Conversation," in *The Private Correspondence of Daniel Webster* (1857). Webster visited Jefferson at Monticello in December 1824.

[2] "During the festivity of the season, I met him in society every day, and we became well acquainted, although I was much his junior. . . . His manners had something of coarseness in them. His passion was music, dancing, and pleasantry. He excelled in the last, and it attached everyone to him." P. L. Ford, *Writings of Thomas Jefferson,* IX, 339. Henry, born in 1736, was seven years older than Jefferson.

the more timid aristocratic gentlemen of the lower part of the State. His eloquence was peculiar, if indeed it should be called eloquence; for it was impressive and sublime, beyond what can be imagined.[3] Although it was difficult when he had spoken to tell what he had said, yet, while he was speaking, it always seemed directly to the point. When he had spoken in opposition to my opinion, had produced a great effect, and I myself been highly delighted and moved, I have asked myself when he ceased: "what the d—l has he said?" I could never answer the inquiry. His person was of full size, and his manner and voice free and manly. His utterance neither very fast nor very slow. His speeches generally short, from a quarter to a half an hour. His pronunciation was vulgar and vicious, but it was forgotten while he was speaking.[4]

He was a man of very little knowledge of any sort; he read nothing, and had no books. Returning one November from Albemarle court, he borrowed of me Hume's Essays, in two volumes, saying he should have leisure in the winter for reading. In the spring he returned them, and declared he had not been able to go further than twenty or thirty pages in the first volume. He wrote almost nothing—he could not write. The resolutions of '75, which have been ascribed to him, have by many been supposed to have been written by Mr. Johnson, who acted as his second in that occasion; but if they were written by Henry himself, they are not such as to prove any power of composition.

Neither in politics nor in his profession was he a man of business; he was a man of debate only. His biographer [5] says that he read Plutarch every year. I doubt whether he ever read a volume of it in his life. His temper was excellent, and he generally observed decorum in debate. On one or two occasions I have seen him angry, and his anger was terrible; those who witnessed it, were not disposed to rouse it again. In his opinions he was yielding and practicable and not disposed to differ from his friends. In private conversation, he was agreeable and facetious, and, while in genteel society, appeared to understand all the decencies and proprieties of it; but, in his heart, he preferred low society, and sought it as often as possible. He would hunt in the pine woods of Fluvannah with overseers, and people of that description, living in a camp for a fortnight at a time without a change of raiment. I have been astonished at his command of proper language; how he attained the knowl-

[3] Jefferson, *Autobiography:* "Mr. Henry's talents as a popular orator . . . were great indeed; such as I never heard from any other man. He appeared to me to speak as Homer wrote."

[4] Henry talked like a backwoodsman "about men's *naiteral* parts being improved by *larnin* —about the *yearth*, etc." H. S. Randall, *The Life of Thomas Jefferson* (1871 ed.), I, 20.

[5] William Wirt, *Sketches of the Life and Character of Patrick Henry* (1817). Jefferson thought that this book was a mere panegyric. "It is a poor book written in bad taste, and gives so imperfect an idea of Patrick Henry, that it seems intended to show off the writer more than the subject."

edge of it. I never could find out, as he read so little [6] and conversed little with educated men. After all, it must be allowed that he was our leader in the measures of the Revolution, in Virginia. In that respect more was due to him than any other person. If we had not had him we should probably have got on pretty well, as you did, by a number of men of nearly equal talents, but he left us all far behind.

## ANDREW JACKSON [7]

December, 1824

I feel much alarmed at the prospect of seeing General Jackson President. He is one of the most unfit men I know of for such a place. He has had very little respect for laws or constitutions, and is, in fact, an able military chief. His passions are terrible. When I was President of the Senate he was a Senator; and he could never speak on account of the rashness of his feelings. I have seen him attempt it repeatedly, and as often choke with rage. His passions are no doubt cooler now; he has been much tried since I knew him, but he is a dangerous man.

## GENERAL KOSCIUSKO [8]

1. *Circumstances relating to General Kosciusko previously to his joining the American Army.* Kosciusko was born in the Grand Duchy of Sillicíania in the year 1752. His family was noble, and his patrimony considerable; circumstances which he justly appreciated, for as belonging to himself they were never matters of boasting, and rarely subjects of notice, and as the property of others only regarded as advantages when accompanied by good sense and good morals. The workings of his mind on the subject of civil liberty were early and vigorous; before he was twenty the vassalage of his serfs filled him with abhorrence, and the first act of his manhood was to break their fetters.

In the domestic quarrel between the king and the dissidents in 1761, he was too young to take a part, but the partition of Poland in 1772 (of which this quarrel was one of the pretences), engaged him in the defence of his country, and soon made him sensible of the value of military education, which he afterwards sought in the schools of Paris. It was there and while

[6] "He was the laziest man in reading I ever knew." Jefferson, *Autobiography.*

[7] Conversation with Daniel Webster.

[8] On February 21, 1798, Jefferson wrote to General Horatio Gates about General Kosciusko: "I see him often, and with great pleasure mixed with commiseration. He is as pure a son of liberty as I have ever known, and of that liberty which is to go to all, and not to the few or the rich alone."

prosecuting this object, that he first became acquainted with the name of America, and the nature of the war in which the British colonies were then engaged with the mother country. In the summer of 1776 he embarked for this country, and in October of that year was appointed by Congress a Colonel of Engineers.

2. *Services of the General during the war.* In the spring of 1777 he joined the northern army, and in July following the writer of this notice left him on Lake Champlain engaged in strengthening our works at Ticonderoga and Mount Independence. The unfortunate character of the early part of this campaign is sufficiently known. In the retreat of the American army Kosciusko was distinguished for activity and courage, and upon him devolved the choice of camps and posts and everything connected with fortifications. The last frontier taken by the army while commanded by Gen. Schuyler was on an island in the Hudson near the mouth of the Mohawk river, and within a few miles of Albany. Here Gates, who had superseded Schuyler, found the army on the —— day of August. Public feeling and opinion were strikingly affected by the arrival of this officer, who gave it a full and lasting impression by ordering the army to advance upon the enemy. The state of things at that moment are well and faithfully expressed by that distinguished officer, Col. Udney Hay, in a letter to a friend. "Fortune," says he, "as if tired of persecuting us, had began to change, and Burgoyne had suffered materially on both his flanks. But these things were not of our doing; the main army, as it was called, was hunted from post to pillar, and dared not to measure its strength with the enemy; much was wanting to reinspire it with confidence in itself, with that self-respect without which an army is but a flock of sheep, a proof of which is found in the fact, that we have thanked in general orders a detachment double the force of that of the enemy, for having dared to return their fire. From this miserable state of despondency and terror, Gates' arrival raised us, as if by magic. We began to hope and then to act. Our first step was to Stillwater, and we are now on the heights called Bhemus', looking the enemy boldly in the face. Kosciusko has selected this ground, and has covered its weak point (its right) with redoubts from the hill to the river." In front of this camp thus fortified two battles were fought, which eventuated in the retreat of the enemy and his surrender at Saratoga!

The value of Colonel Kosciusko's services during this campaign, and that of 1778, will be found in the following extract from a letter of General Gates written in the spring of 1780:

"My dear friend: After parting with you at Yorktown, I got safely to my own fireside, and without inconvenience of any kind, excepting sometimes cold toes and cold fingers. Of this sort of punishment, however, I am, it seems, to have no more, as I am destined by the Congress to command in the South. In entering on this new and (as Lee says) most difficult theatre of the war, my first thoughts have been turned to the selections of an Engineer, an Adjutant-General and a Quarter-Master-General, Kosciusko, Hay and yourself, if I can prevail upon you all, are to fill these offices, and will fill them well. The *excellent qualities* of the Pole, which no one knows better than yourself, are now acknowledged at head-quarters, and may induce others to prevent his joining us. But his promise once given, we are sure of him."

The —— of Gates, for which the preceding extract had prepared us, was given and accepted, and though no time was lost by Kosciusko, his arrival was not early enough to enable him to give his assistance to his old friend and General. But to Greene (his successor) he rendered the most important services to the last moment of the war, and which were such as drew from that officer the most lively, ardent, repeated acknowledgments, which induced Congress, in October, 1783, to bestow upon him the brevet of Brigadier General, and to pass a vote declaratory *of their high sense of his faithful and meritorous conduct.*

The war having ended, he now contemplated returning to Poland, and was determined in this measure by a letter from Prince Joseph Poniatowski, nephew of the king and generalissimo of the army. It was, however, ten years after this period (1783) before Kosciusko drew the sword on the frontiers of Cracovia.

3. *Conduct of Kosciusko in France.* When Bonaparte created the Duchy of Warsaw and bestowed it on the King of Saxony, great pains were taken to induce Kosciusko to lend himself to the frontier and support of that policy. Having withstood both the smiles and the frowns of the minister of police, a last attempt was made through the General's countrywoman and friend, the Princess Sassiche. The argument she used was founded on the condition of Poland, which, she said, no change could make worse, and that of the General which even a small change might make better. "But on this head I have a *carte blanche,* Princess," answered the General (taking her hand and leading her to her carriage), "it is the first time in my life I have wished to shorten your visit; but you shall not make me think less respectfully of you than I now do."

When these attempts had failed, a manifesto in the name of Kosciusko, dated at Warsaw and addressed to the Poles, was fabricated and published at Paris. When he complained of this abuse of his name, &c., the minister of Police advised him to go to Fontainbleau.

# MERIWETHER LEWIS[1]

April, 1813

Meriwether Lewis, late Governor of Louisiana, was born on the 18th of August, 1774, near the town of Charlottesville, in the county of Albemarle, in Virginia, of one of the distinguished families of that State. John Lewis, one of his father's uncles, was a member of the King's Council before the revolution; another of them, Fielding Lewis, married a sister of General Washington. His father, William Lewis, was the youngest of five sons of Colonel Robert Lewis of Albemarle, the fourth of whom, Charles, was one of the early patriots who stepped forward in the commencement of the revolution, and commanded one of the regiments first raised in Virginia, and placed on continental establishment. Happily situated at home with a wife and young family, and a fortune placing him at ease, he left all to aid in the liberation of his country from foreign usurpations, then first unmasking their ultimate end and aim. His good sense, integrity, bravery, enterprise and remarkable bodily powers, marked him an officer of great promise; but he unfortunately died early in the revolution. Nicholas Lewis, the second of his father's brothers, commanded a regiment of militia in the successful expedition of 1776, against the Cherokee Indians, who, seduced by the agents of the British government to take up the hatchet against us, had committed great havoc on our southern frontier, by murdering and scalping helpless women and children according to their cruel and cowardly principles of warfare. The chastisement they then received closed the history of their wars, prepared them for receiving the elements of civilization, which, zealously inculcated by the present government of the United States, have rendered them an industrious, peaceable and happy people. This member of the family of Lewises, whose bravery was so usefully proved on this occasion, was endeared to all who knew him by his inflexible probity, courteous disposition, benevolent heart, and engaging modesty and manners. He was the umpire of all the private differences of his county, selected always by both parties. He was also the guardian of Meriwether Lewis, of whom we are now to speak, and who had lost his father at an early age. He continued some years under the fostering care of a tender mother, of the respectable family of Meriwethers of the same county, and was remarkable even in his infancy for enterprise, boldness and discretion. When only eight years of age, he habitually went out, in the dead of the night, alone with his dogs, into the forest to hunt the raccoon and opossum, which, seeking their food in the night, can then only be taken. In this exercise no season or circum-

[1] This sketch accompanied a letter to Paul Allen of Philadelphia, on April 13, 1813, in reply to a request for information about the famous explorer.

stance could obstruct his purpose, plunging through the winter's snows and frozen streams in pursuit of his object. At thirteen, he was put to the Latin school, and continued at that until eighteen, when he returned to his mother, and entered on the cares of his farm, having, as well as a younger brother, been left by his father with a competency for all the correct and comfortable purposes of temperate life. His talent for observation, which had led him to an accurate knowledge of the plants and animals of his own county, would have distinguished him as a farmer; but at the age of twenty, yielding to the ardor of youth, and a passion for more dazzling pursuits, he engaged as a volunteer in the body of militia which were called out by General Washington, on occasion of the discontents produced by the excise taxes in the western parts of the United States; and from that situation he was removed to the regular service as a lieutenant in the line. At twenty-three he was promoted to a captaincy; and always attracting the first attention where punctuality and fidelity were requisite, he was appointed paymaster to his regiment. About this time a circumstance occurred which, leading to the transaction which is the subject of this book, will justify a recurrence to its original idea. While I resided in Paris, John Ledyard of Connecticut arrived there, well known in the United States for energy of body and mind. He had accompanied Captain Cook in his voyage to the Pacific ocean, and distinguished himself on that voyage by his intrepidity. Being of a roaming disposition, he was now panting for some new enterprise. His immediate object at Paris was to engage a mercantile company in the fur trade of the western coast of America, in which, however, he failed. I then proposed to him to go by land to Kamschatka, cross in some of the Russian vessels to Nootka Sound, fall down into the latitude of the Missouri, and penetrate to and through that to the United States. He eagerly seized the idea, and only asked to be assured of the permission of the Russian government. I interested in obtaining that M. de Simoulin, M. P. of the Empress at Paris, but more especially the Baron de Grimm, M. P. of Saxe-Gotha, her more special agent and correspondent there, in matters not immediately diplomatic. Her permission was obtained, and an assurance of protection while the course of the voyage should be through her territories. Ledyard set out from Paris and arrived at St. Petersburg after the Empress had left that place to pass the winter (I think) at Moscow. His finances not permitting him to make unnecessary stay at St. Petersburg, he left it with a passport from one of the ministers, and at two hundred miles from Kamschatka, was obliged to take up his winter quarters. He was preparing in the spring to resume his journey, when he was arrested by an officer of the Empress, who, by this time, had changed her mind, and forbidden his proceeding. He was put into a close carriage and conveyed day and night, without ever stopping, till they reached Poland, where he was set down and left to himself. The fatigue of this journey broke down his constitution, and when he returned to Paris, his bodily strength was much impaired. His mind, however, remained firm; and after this he undertook the journey to Egypt. I received a letter from him, full of sanguine hopes, dated at Cairo, the 15th of November, 1788, the day before he was to set out for the head of the Nile, on which day, however, he ended his career and life; and thus failed the first attempt to explore the western part of our northern continent.

In 1792 I proposed to the A. P. S., that we should set on foot a subscription to engage some competent person to explore that region in the opposite direction, that is, by ascending the Missouri, crossing the Stony mountains, and descending the nearest river to the Pacific. Captain Lewis being then stationed at Charlottesville on the recruiting service, warmly solicited me to obtain for him the execution of that object. I told him it was proposed that the person engaged should be attended by a single companion only, to avoid exciting alarm among the Indians. This did not deter him. But Mr. André Michaux, a professed botanist, author of the *"Flora Boreali-Americana,"* and of the *"Histoire des chenes, d'Amerique,"* offering his services, they were accepted. He received his instructions, and when he had reached Kentucky in the prosecution of his journey, he was overtaken by an order from the minister of France then at Philadelphia, to relinquish the expedition, and to pursue elsewhere the Botanical inquiries on which he was employed by that government; and thus failed the second attempt for exploring that region.

In 1803, the act for establishing trading houses with the Indian tribes being about to expire, some modifications of it were recommended to Congress by a confidential message of January 18th, and an extension of its views to the Indians on the Missouri. In order to prepare the way, the message proposed the sending an exploring party to trace the Missouri to its source, to cross the highlands and follow the best water communication which offered itself from thence to the Pacific ocean. Congress approved the proposition, and voted a sum of money for carrying it into execution. Captain Lewis, who had then been near two years with me as private secretary, immediately renewed his solicitations to have the direction of the party. I had now had opportunities of knowing him intimately. Of courage undaunted, possessing a firmness and perseverance of purpose which nothing but impossibilities could divert from its direction, careful as a father of those committed to his charge, yet steady in the maintenance of order and discipline, intimate with the Indian character, customs and principles. Habituated to the hunting life, guarded by exact observation of the vegetables and animals of his own country, against losing time in the description of objects already possessed, honest, disinterested, liberal, of sound understanding, and a fidelity to truth so scrupulous that whatever he should report would be as certain as if seen by ourselves, with all these qualifications as if selected and implanted by nature in one body, for this express purpose, I could have no hesitation in confiding the enterprise to him. To fill up the measure desired, he wanted nothing but a greater familiarity with the technical language of the natural sciences, and readiness in the astronomical observations necessary for the geography of his route. To acquire these he repaired immediately to Philadelphia, and placed himself under the tutorage of the distinguished professors of that place, who, with a zeal and emulation, enkindled by an ardent devotion to science, communicated to him freely the information requisite for the purposes of the journey. While attending to at Lancaster, the fabrication of the arms with which he chose that his men should be provided, he had the benefit of daily communication with Mr. Andrew Ellicott, whose experience in astronomical observation and practice of it in the woods, enabled him to apprize Captain Lewis of the wants and difficulties he would encounter, and of the substitutes and resources offered by a woodland and uninhabited country. Deeming it necessary he should have some person with him of known competence to the direction of the enterprise, and to whom he might confide it, in the event of accident to himself, he proposed William Clarke, brother of General George Rogers Clarke, who was approved, and with that view received a commission of captain.

In April, 1803, a draught of his instructions was sent to Captain Lewis, and on the 20th of June they were signed in the following form:

"To Meriwether Lewis, Esquire, Captain of the 1st regiment of infantry of the United States of America:

"Your situation as Secretary of the President of the United States has made you acquainted with the objects of my confidential message of January 18th, 1803, to the legislature; you have seen the act they passed, which, though expressed in general terms, was meant to sanction those objects, and you are appointed to carry them into execution.

"Instruments for ascertaining by celestial observations, the geography of the country through which you will pass, have been already provided. Light articles for barter and presents among the Indians, arms for your attendants, say for from ten to twelve men, boats, tents and other travelling apparatus, with ammunition, medicine, surgical instruments and provisions, you will have prepared with such aids as the Secretary at War can yield in his departments; and from him also you will receive authority to engage among our troops, by voluntary agreement, the number of attendants above mentioned, over whom you, as their commanding officer, are invested with all the powers the laws give in such a case.

"As your movements while within the limits of the United States will be better directed by occasional communications, adapted to circumstances as they arise, they will not be noticed here. What follows will respect your proceedings after your departure from the United States.

"Your mission has been communicated to the ministers here from France, Spain and Great Britain, and through them to their governments; and such assurances given them as to its objects, as we trust will satisfy them. The country of Louisiana having been ceded by Spain to France, the passport you have from the minister of France, the representative of the present sovereign of that country, will be a protection with all its subjects; and that from the minister of England will entitle you to the friendly aid of any traders of that allegiance with whom you may happen to meet.

"The object of your mission is to explore the Missouri river, and such principal streams of it, as, by its course and communication with the waters of the Pacific ocean, whether the Columbia, Oregon, Colorado, or any other river, may offer the most direct and practicable water communication across the continent for the purposes of commerce.

"Beginning at the mouth of the Missouri, you will take observations of latitude and longitude at all remarkable points on the river, and especially at the mouths of rivers, at rapids, at islands, and other places and objects distinguished by such natural marks and characters of a durable kind as that they may with certainty be recognized hereafter. The courses of the river between these points of observation may be supplied by the compass, the log-line and by time, corrected by the observations themselves. The variations of the compass too, in different places, should be noticed.

"The interesting points of the portage between the heads of the Missouri, and of the water offering the best communication with the Pacific ocean, should also be fixed by observation, and the course of that water to the ocean, in the same manner as that of the Missouri.

"Your observations are to be taken with great pains and accuracy, to be entered distinctly and intelligibly for others as well as yourself, to comprehend all the elements necessary, with the aid of the usual tables, to fix the latitude and longitude of the places at which they were taken, and are to be rendered to the war office, for the purpose of having the calculations made concurrently by proper persons within the United States. Several copies of these as well as of your other notes should be made at leisure times, and put into the care of the most trust-worthy of your attendants, to guard, by multiplying them, against the accidental losses to which they will be exposed. A further guard would be that one of these copies be on the paper of the birch, as less liable to injury from damp than common paper.

"The commerce which may be carried on with the people inhabiting the line you will pursue, renders a knowledge of those people important. You will, therefore, endeavor to make yourself acquainted, as far as a diligent pursuit of your journey shall admit, with the names of the nations and their numbers; the extent of their possessions; their relations with other tribes or nations; their language, traditions, monuments; their ordinary occupations in agriculture, fishing, hunting, war, arts, and the implements for these; their food, clothing and domestic accommodations; the diseases prevalent among them, and the remedies they use; moral and physical circumstances which distinguish them from the tribes we know; peculiarities in their laws, customs and dispositions; and articles of commerce they may need or furnish, and to what extent; and, considering the interest which every nation has in extending and strengthening the authority of reason and justice among the people around them, it will be useful to acquire what knowledge you can of the state of morality, religion, and information among them, as it may better enable those who may endeavor to civilize and instruct them, to adopt their measures to the existing notions and practices of those on whom they are to operate.

"Other objects worthy of notice will be, the soil and face of the country, its growth and vegetable productions, especially those not of the United States, the animals of the country generally, and especially those not known in the United States; the remains and accounts of any which may be deemed rare or extinct; the mineral productions of every kind, but particularly metals, lime-stone, pit-coal and salt-petre; salines and mineral waters, noting the temperature of the last, and such circumstances as may indicate their character; volcanic appearances; climate, as characterized by the thermometer, by the proportion of rainy, cloudy, and clear days, by lightning, hail, snow, ice, by the access and recess of frost, by the winds prevailing at different seasons, the dates at which particular plants put forth or lose their flower or leaf, times of appearance of particular birds, reptiles or insects.

"Although your route will be along the channel of the Missouri, yet you will endeavor to inform yourself, by inquiry, of the character and extent of the country watered by its branches, and especially on its southern side. The north river, or Rio Bravo, which runs into the Gulf of Mexico, and the north river, or Rio Colorado, which runs into the Gulf of California, are understood to be the principal streams heading opposite to the waters of the Missouri, and running southwardly. Whether the dividing grounds between the Missouri and them are mountains or flat lands, what are their distance from the Missouri, the character of the intermediate country, and the people inhabiting it, are worthy of particular inquiry. The northern waters of the Missouri are less to be inquired after, because they have been ascertained to a considerable degree, and are still in a course of ascertainment by English traders and travellers. But if you can learn anything certain of the most northern source of the Mississippi, and of its position relatively to the lake of the woods, it will be interesting to us. Some account, too, of the path of the Canadian traders from the Mississippi, at the mouth of the Ouisconsing to where it strikes the Missouri, and of the soil and rivers in its course, is desirable.

"In all your intercourse with the natives, treat them in the most friendly and conciliatory manner which their own conduct will admit; allay all jealousies as to the object of your journey, satisfy them of its innocence; make them acquainted with the position, extent, character, peaceable and commercial dispositions of the United States, of our wish to be neighborly, friendly and useful to them, and of our dispositions to a commercial intercourse with them; confer with them on the points most convenient as mutual emporiums, and the articles of most desirable interchange for them and us. If a few of their influential chiefs within practicable distance, wish to visit us, arrange such a visit with them, and furnish them with authority to call on our officers, on their entering the United States, to have them conveyed to this place at the public expense. If any of them should wish to have some of their young people brought up with us, and taught such arts as may be useful to them, we will receive, instruct, and take care of them. Such a mission, whether of influential chiefs or of young people, would give some security to your own party. Carry with you some matter of the kine pox; inform those of them with whom you may be, of its efficacy as a preservative from the small pox; and instruct and encourage them in the use of it. This may be especially done wherever you winter.

"As it is impossible for us to foresee in what manner you will be received by those people, whether with hospitality or hostility, so is it impossible to prescribe the exact degree of perseverance with which you are to pursue your journey. We value too much the lives of citizens to offer them to probable destruction. Your numbers will be sufficient to secure you against the unauthorized opposition of individuals or of small parties; but if a superior force, authorized or not authorized by a nation, should be arrayed against your further passage, and inflexibly determined to arrest it, you must decline its farther pursuit, and return. In the loss of yourselves, we should lose also the information you will have acquired. By returning safely with that, you may enable us to renew the essay with better calculated means. To your own discretion, therefore, must be left the degree of danger you may risk, and the point at which you should decline, only saying we wish you to err on the side of your safety, and to bring us back your party safe, even if it be with less information.

"Should you reach the Pacific ocean, inform yourself of the circumstances which may decide whether the furs of those parts may not be collected as advantageously at the head of the Missouri (convenient as is supposed to the waters of the Colorado and Oregon or Columbia), as at Nootka Sound, or any other point of that coast; and that trade be consequently conducted through the Missouri and United States more beneficially than by the circumnavigation now practised.

"As far up the Missouri as the white settlements extend, an intercourse will probably be found to exist between them and the Spanish posts of St. Louis opposite Cahokia, or St. Genevieve opposite Kaskaskia. From still further up the river, the traders may furnish a conveyance for letters. Beyond that, you may perhaps be able to engage Indians to bring letters for the government to Cahokia or Kaskaskia, on promising that they shall there receive such special compensation as you shall have stipulated with them. Avail yourself of these means to communicate to us, at seasonable intervals, a copy of your journal, notes, and observations, of every kind, putting into cypher whatever might do injury if betrayed.

"On your arrival on that coast, endeavor to learn if there be any post within your reach frequented by the sea vessels of any nation, and to send two of your trusty people back by sea, in such way as shall appear practicable, with a copy of your notes; and should you be of opinion that the return of your party by the way they went will be imminently dangerous, then ship the whole, and return by sea, by the way either of Cape Horn or the Cape of Good Hope, as you shall be able. As you will be without money, clothes, or provisions, you must endeavor to use the credit of the United States to obtain them, for which purpose open letters of credit shall be furnished you, authorizing you to draw on the executive of the United States, or any of its officers, in any part of the world, on which draughts can be disposed of, and to apply with our recommendations to the consuls, agents, merchants, or citizens of any nation with which we have intercourse, assuring them in our name, that any aids they may furnish you, shall be honorably repaid, and on demand. Our consuls, Thomas Hewes at Batavia in Java, William Buchanan in the Isles of France and Bourbon, and John Elmslie at the Cape of Good Hope, will be able to supply your necessities by draughts on us.

"Should you find it safe to return by the way you go, after sending two of your party round by sea, or with your whole party, if no conveyance by sea can be found, do so; making such observations on your return, as may serve to supply, correct, or confirm those made on your outward journey.

"On re-entering the United States and reaching a place of safety, discharge any of your attendants who may desire and deserve it, procuring for them immediate payment of all arrears of pay and clothing which may have incurred since their departure, and assure them that they shall be recommended to the liberality of the legislature for the grant of a soldier's portion of land each, as proposed in my message to Congress; and repair yourself with your papers to the seat of government.

"To provide in the accident of your death, against anarchy, dispersion and the consequent danger to your party, and total failure of the enterprise, you are hereby authorized, by any instrument signed and written in your own hand, to name the person among them who shall succeed to the command on your decease, and by like instruments to change the nomination from time to time as further experience of the characters accompanying you shall point out superior fitness; and all the powers and authorities given to yourself are, in the event of your death, transferred to, and vested in the successor so named, with further power to him, and his successors in like manner, to name each his successor, who, on the death of his predecessor, shall be invested with all the powers and authorities given to yourself.

"Given under my hand at the city of Washington, this 20th day of June, 1803.

"THOMAS JEFFERSON, President of the U. States of America."

While these things were going on here, the country of Louisiana, lately ceded by Spain to France, had been the subject of negotiation between us and this last power; and had actually been transferred to us by treaties executed at Paris on the 30th of April. This information, received about the 1st day of July, increased infinitely the interest we felt in the expedition, and lessened the apprehensions of interruption from other powers. Everything in this quarter being now prepared, Captain Lewis left Washington on the 5th of July, 1803, and proceeded to Pittsburg, where other articles had been ordered to be provided for him. The men, too, were to be selected from the military stations on the Ohio. Delays of preparation, difficulties of navigation down the Ohio, and other untoward obstructions, retarded his arrival at Cahokia until the season was so far advanced as to render it prudent to suspend his entering the Missouri before the ice should break up in the succeeding spring. From this time his journal, now published, will give the history of his journey to and from the Pacific ocean, until his return to St. Louis on the 23d of September, 1806. Never did a similar event excite more joy through the United States.

The humblest of its citizens had taken a lively interest in the issue of this journey, and looked forward with impatience for the information it would furnish. Their anxieties, too, for the safety of the corps had been kept in a state of excitement by lugubrious rumors, circulated from time to time on uncertain authorities, and uncontradicted by letters or other direct information from the time they had left the Mandan towns on their ascent up the river in April of the preceding year, 1805, until their actual return to St. Louis.

It was the middle of Feb. 1807, before Capt. Lewis with his companion Clarke reached the city of Washington, where Congress was then in session. That body granted to the two chiefs and their followers, the donation of lands which they had been encouraged to expect in reward of their toils and dangers. Capt. Lewis was soon after appointed Governor of Louisiana, and Capt. Clarke a General of its militia, and agent of the United States for Indian affairs in that department.

A considerable time intervened before the Governor's arrival at St. Louis. He found the territory distracted by feuds and contentions among the officers of the government, and the people themselves divided by these into factions and parties. He determined at once to take no sides with either, but to use every endeavor to conciliate and harmonize them. The even-handed justice he administered to all soon established a respect for his person and authority, and perseverance and time wore down animosities, and reunited the citizens again into one family.

Governor Lewis had from early life been subject to hypocondriac affections. It was a constitutional disposition in all the nearer branches of the family of his name, and was more immediately inherited by him from his father. They had not, however, been so strong as to give uneasiness to his family. While he lived with me in Washington, I observed at times sensible depressions of mind, but knowing their constitutional source, I estimated their course by what I had seen in the family. During his western expedition, the constant exertion which that required of all the faculties of body and mind, suspended these distressing affections; but after his establishment at St. Louis in sedentary occupations, they returned upon him with redoubled vigor, and began seriously to alarm his friends. He was in a paroxysm of one of these when his affairs rendered it necessary for him to go to Washington. He proceeded to the Chickasaw bluffs, where he arrived on the 15th of September, 1809, with a view of continuing his journey thence by water. Mr. Neely, agent of the United States with the Chickasaw Indians, arriving there two days after, found him extremely indisposed, and betraying at times some symptoms of a derangement of mind. The rumors of a war with England, and apprehensions that he might lose the papers he was bringing on, among which were the vouchers of his public accounts, and the journals and papers of his western expedition, induced him here to change his mind, and to take his course by land through the Chickasaw country. Although he appeared somewhat relieved, Mr. Neely kindly determined to accompany and watch over him. Unfortunately, at their encampment, after having passed the Tennessee one day's journey, they lost two horses, which obliging Mr. Neely to halt for their recovery, the Governor proceeded under a promise to wait for him at the house of the first white inhabitant on his road. He stopped at the house of a Mr. Grinder, who, not being at home, his wife, alarmed at the symptoms of derangement she discovered, gave him up the house, and retired to rest herself in an out-house; the Governor's and Neely's servants lodging in another. About 3 o'clock in the night he did the deed which plunged his friends into affliction, and deprived his country of one of her most valued citizens, whose valor and intelligence would have been now employed in avenging the wrongs of his country, and in emulating by land the splendid deeds which have honored her arms on the ocean. It lost, too, to the nation the benefit of receiving from his own hand the narrative now offered them of his sufferings and successes in endeavoring to extend for them the boundaries of science, and to present to their knowledge that vast and fertile country which their sons are destined to fill with arts, with science, with freedom and happiness.

To this melancholy close of the life of one whom posterity will declare not to have lived in vain, I have only to add that all the facts I have stated, are either known to myself, or communicated by his family or others, for whose truth I have no hesitation to make myself responsible; and I conclude with tendering you the assurances of my respect and consideration.

## JAMES MONROE [1]

October 5, 1781

DEAR SIR: The bearer hereof Colo. James Monroe who served some time as an officer in the American army and as such distinguished himself in the affair of Princetown as well as on other occasions, having resumed his studies, comes to Europe to complete them. Being a citizen of this state, of abilities, [judg]ment & fortune, and my particular friend, I take the liberty of making him known to you, that should any circumstances render your patronage & protection as necessary as they would be always agreeable to him, you may be assured they are bestowed on one fully worthy of them.

He will be able to give you a particular detail of American affairs, and especially of the prospect we have thrô' the aid of our father of France of making captives of L$^{d}$ Cornwallis & his army of the recovery of Georgia & South Carolina, and the possibility that Charlestown itself will be opened to us.

I have the honour to be with the most profound respect & esteem D$^{r}$ Sir,
Your most obed$^{t}$ & most humble se$^{nt}$.

[1] Letter to Benjamin Franklin. MS. in possession of Mr. Stuart W. Jackson, of Montclair, N. J., by whose courtesy it is here printed.

Jefferson's high opinion of Monroe, whom he trained and profoundly influenced, continued throughout his life. In 1786 he wrote to W. T. Franklin that Monroe "is a man whose soul might be turned wrong side outwards, without discovering a blemish to the world." In 1819, when Monroe was President, Jefferson said that he would "willingly put both soul and body" into Monroe's pocket.

## NAPOLEON

July 5, 1814

The Attila of the age dethroned, the ruthless destroyer of ten millions of the human race, whose thirst for blood appeared unquenchable, the great oppressor of the rights and liberties of the world, shut up within the circle of a little island of the Mediterranean, and dwindled to the condition of an humble and degraded pensioner on the bounty of those he had most injured. How miserably, how meanly, has he closed his inflated career! What a sample of the bathos will his history present! He should have perished on the swords of his enemies, under the walls of Paris.

But Bonaparte was a lion in the field only. In civil life, a cold-blooded, calculating, unprincipled usurper, without a virtue; no statesman, knowing nothing of commerce, political economy, or civil government, and supplying ignorance by bold presumption. I had supposed him a great man until his entrance into the Assembly *des cinq cens,* eighteen Brumaire (au. 8). From that date, however, I set him down as a great scoundrel only.[1]

I grieve for France; although it cannot be denied that by the afflictions with which she wantonly and wickedly overwhelmed other nations, she has merited severe reprisals. For it is no excuse to lay the enormities to the wretch who led to them, and who has been the author of more misery and suffering to the world, than any being who ever lived before him. After destroying the liberties of his country, he has exhausted all its resources, physical and moral, to indulge his own maniac ambition, his own tyrannical and overbearing spirit. His sufferings cannot be too great.[2]

## JACQUES NECKER[3]

June 17, 1789

Nature bestowed on Mr. Neckar an ardent passion for glory, without, at the same time, granting him those qualities required for its pursuit by direct means. The union of a fruitful imagination, with a limited talent, with which she has endowed him, is always incompatable with those faculties of the mind which qualify their possessor to penetrate, to combine, and to comprehend all the relations of objects.

He had probably learned in Geneva, his native country, the influence which riches exercise on the success of ambition, without having recourse

[1] Letter to John Adams.

[2] Letter to Albert Gallatin, October 16, 1815.

[3] This sketch of Jacques Necker accompanied a letter to John Jay, dated Paris, June 17, 1789.

to the school of Paris, where he arrived about the twenty-eighth year of his age. A personal affair with his brother, in which the chiefs of the republic conducted themselves unjustly towards him, the circumstances of which, moreover, exposed him to ridicule, determined him to forsake his country. On taking his leave, he assured his mother that he would make a great fortune at Paris. On his arrival, he engaged himself as clerk, at a salary of six hundred livres, with the banker Thelusson, a man of extreme harshness in his intercourse with his dependents. The same cause which obliged other clerks to abandon the service of Thelusson, determined Neckar to continue in it. By submitting to the brutality of his master with a servile resignation, whilst, at the same time, he devoted the most unremitting attention to his business, he recommended himself to his confidence, and was taken into partnership. Ordinary abilities only, were requisite to avail him of the multitude of favorable circumstances, which, before he entered into the administration, built up a fortune of six millions of livres. He owed much of his good fortune to his connections with the Abbé Terrai, of whose ignorance he did not scruple to profit. His riches, his profession, his table, and a virtuous, reasonable and well-informed wife, procured him the acquaintance of many persons of distinction, among whom were many men of letters, who celebrated his knowledge and wisdom.

The wise and just principles by which Turgot aimed to correct the abuses of the administration, not having been received with favor, he seized the occasion to flatter ignorance and malignity, by publishing his work against the freedom of the corn trade. He had published, two years before, an eulogy on Colbert. Both these productions exhibited the limited capacity of a banker, and, in no degree, the enlarged views of a statesman. Not at all delicate in the choice of his means, he succeeded to his wish in his object, which was the establishing himself in public opinion. Elevated by a secret cabal, to the direction of the finances, he began by refusing the salaries of his office. He affected a spirit of economy and austerity, which imposed even on foreign nations, and showed the possibility of making war without laying new taxes. Such, at least, was his boast; but, in reality, they have been increased under his administration, about twenty millions, partly by a secret augmentation of the *bailles* and of the poll-tax, partly by some versifications of the *twentieths,* and partly by the natural progression, which is tested by the amount of taxes on consumption, the necessary result of the successive increase of population, of riches, and of expensive tastes.

All these circumstances reared for him an astonishing reputation, which his fall has consecrated. People will not reflect, that, in the short period of his ministry, he had more than doubled his fortune. Not that he had peculated on the public treasury; his good sense and pride forbade a resort to this manœuvre of weak minds; but by resorting to loans and the costly operations of the bank, to provide the funds of war, and being still connected with the house to which he addressed himself for much the greater part of his negotiations. They have not remarked that his great principles of economy have nothing more than a false show, and that the loans resorted to, in order to avoid the imposition of taxes, have been the source of the mischief which has reduced the finances to their present alarming condition.

As to his *compte rendu;* he has been forgiven the nauseous panegyric which he has passed upon himself, and the affection of introducing his wife into it, for the purpose of praising her: and we are spared the trouble of examining his false calculations. M. de Calonnes has undertaken this investigation. Without being able to vindicate himself, he has already begun to unmask his antagonist, and he promises to do it effectually.

Necessity has recalled this man to the ministry; and it must be confessed that he is beyond comparison a less mischievous minister than his predecessors. I would compare him to a steward, who, by his management, does not entirely ruin his master, but who enriches himself at his expense. The desire of glory should inspire him as much as possible with the energy requisite for the public business. There is every likelihood that his ministry will not endure long enough to cause it to feel the effects of his false principles of administration; and it is he alone who is able, if anyone can, to preserve order in the finances, until the reform is effected which we hope from the assembling of the States General. In the meantime the public estimation of his talents and virtue is not so high as it has been. There are persons who pretend that he is more firmly established in public opinion than he ever was. They deceive themselves. The ambitious desire he has always manifested of getting again into the administration, his work on the importance of religious opinions, and the memoires of M. de Calonnes, have greatly impaired his reputation.

## MADAME NECKER[1]

December, 1824

Madame Necker was a very sincere and excellent woman, but she was not very pleasant in conversation, for she was subject to what in Virginia we call the "Budge," that is, she was very nervous and fidgety. She could rarely remain long in the same place, or converse long on the same subject. I have known her get up from table five or six times in the course of the dinner, and walk up and down her salon to compose herself.

[1] Conversation with Daniel Webster. Madame Necker was the wife of Jacques Necker and the mother of the famous Madame de Staël.

## PEYTON RANDOLPH

July, 1816

Peyton Randolph was the eldest son of Sir John Randolph, of Virginia, a barrister at law, and an eminent practitioner at the bar of the General Court. Peyton was educated at the College of William and Mary in Williamsburg, and thence went to England, and studied law at the Temple. At his return he intermarried with Elizabeth Harrison, sister of the afterwards Governor Harrison, entered into practice in the General Court, was afterwards appointed the king's Attorney General for the colony, and became a representative in the House of Burgesses (then so called) for the city of Williamsburg

Governor Dinwiddie having, about this period, introduced the exaction of a new fee on his signature of grants for lands, without the sanction of any law, the House of Burgesses remonstrated against it, and sent Peyton Randolph to England, as their agent to oppose it before the king and council. The interest of the governor, as usual, prevailed against that of the colony, and his new exaction was confirmed by the king.

After Braddock's defeat on the Monongahela, in 1755, the incursions of the Indians on our frontiers spread panic and dismay through the whole country, insomuch that it was scarcely possible to procure men, either as regulars or militia, to go against them. To counteract this terror and to set good example, a number of the wealthiest individuals of the colony, and the highest standing in it, in public as well as in their private relations, associated under obligations to furnish each of them two able-bodied men, at their own expense, to form themselves into a regiment under the denomination of the Virginia Blues, to join the colonial force on the frontier, and place themselves under its commander, George Washington, then a colonel. They appointed William Byrd, a member of the council, colonel of the regiment, and Peyton Randolph, I think, had also some command. But the original associators had more the will than the power of becoming effective soldiers. Born and bred in the lap of wealth, all the habits of their lives were of ease, indolence and indulgence. Such men were little fitted to sleep under tents, and often without them, to be exposed to all the intemperances of the seasons, to swim rivers, range the woods, climb mountains, wade morasses, to skulk behind trees, and contend as sharp shooters with the savages of the wilderness, who in all the scenes and exercises would be in their natural element. Accordingly, the commander was more embarrassed with their care, than reinforced by their service. They had the good fortune to see no enemy, and to return at the end of the campaign rewarded by the favor of the public for this proof of their generous patriotism and good will.

When afterwards, in 1764, on the proposal of the Stamp Act, the House of Burgesses determined to send an address against it to the king, and memorials to the Houses of Lord and Commons, Peyton Randolph, George Wythe, and (I think) Robert C. Nicholas, were appointed to draw these papers. That to the king was by Peyton Randolph, and the memorial to the Commons was by George Wythe. It was on the ground of these papers that those gentlemen opposed the famous resolutions of Mr. Henry in 1765, to wit, that the principles of these resolutions had been asserted and maintained in the address and memorials of the year before, to which an answer was yet to be expected

On the death of the speaker, Robinson, in 1766, Peyton Randolph was elected speaker. He resigned his office of Attorney General, in which he was succeeded by his brother Randolph, father of the late Edmund Randolph, and retired from the bar. He now devoted himself solely to his duties as a legislator, and although sound in his principles, and going steadily with us in opposition to the British usurpations, he, with the other older members, yielded the lead to the younger, only tempering their ardor, and so far moderating their pace as to prevent their going too far in advance of the public sentiment.

On the establishment of a committee by the legislature, to correspond with the other colonies, he was named their chairman, and their first proposition to the other colonies was to appoint similar committees, who might consider the expediency of calling a general Congress of deputies in order to procure a harmony of procedure among the whole. This produced the call of the first Congress, to which he was chosen a delegate, by the House of Burgesses, and of which he was appointed, by that Congress, its president.

On the receipt of what was called Lord North's conciliatory proposition, in 1775, Lord Dunmore called the General Assembly and laid it before them. Peyton Randolph quitted the chair of Congress, in which he was succeeded by Mr. Hancock, and repaired to that of the House which had deputed him. Anxious about the tone and spirit of the answer which should be given (because being the first it might have effect on those of the other colonies), and supposing that a younger pen would be more likely to come up to the feelings of the body he had left, he requested me to draw the answer, and steadily supported and carried it through the House, with a few softenings only from the more timid members.

After the adjournment of the House of Burgesses he returned to Congress, and died there of an apoplexy, on the 22d of October following, aged, as I should conjecture, about fifty years.

He was indeed a most excellent man; and none was ever more beloved and respected by his friends. Somewhat cold and coy towards strangers, but of the sweetest affability when ripened into acquaintance. Of attic pleasantry in conversation, always good humored and conciliatory. With a sound and logical head, he was well read in the law; and his opinions when consulted, were highly regarded, presenting always a learned and sound view of the subject, but generally, too, a listlessness to go into its thorough development; for being heavy and inert in body, he was rather too indolent and careless for business, which occasioned him to get a smaller proportion of it at the bar than his abilities would otherwise have commanded. Indeed, after his appointment as Attorney General, he did not seem to court, nor scarcely to welcome business. In that office he considered himself equally charged with the rights of the colony as with those of the crown; and in criminal prosecutions exaggerating nothing, he aimed at a candid and just state of the transaction, believing it more a duty to save an innocent than to convict a guilty man. Although not eloquent, his matter was so substantial that no man commanded more attention, which, joined with a sense of his great worth, gave him a weight in the House of Burgesses which few ever attained. He was liberal in his expenses, but correct also, so as not to be involved in pecuniary embarrassments; and with a heart always open to the amiable sensibilities of our nature, he did as many good acts as could have been done with his fortune, without injuriously impairing his means of continuing them. He left no issue, and gave his fortune to his widow and nephew, the late Edmund Randolph.

## GENERAL GEORGE WASHINGTON[1]

January 2, 1814

I think I knew General Washington intimately and thoroughly; and were I called on to delineate his character, it should be in terms like these.

His mind was great and powerful, without being of the very first order; his penetration strong, though not so acute as that of a Newton, Bacon, or Locke; and as far as he saw, no judgment was ever sounder.[2] It was slow in operation, being little aided by invention or imagination, but sure in conclusion. Hence the common remark of his officers, of the advantage he derived from councils of war, where hearing all suggestions, he selected whatever was best; and certainly no General ever planned his battles more judiciously. But if deranged during the course of the action, if any member of his plan was dislocated by sudden circumstances, he was slow in readjustment. The consequence was, that he often failed in the field, and rarely against an enemy in station, as at Boston and York. He was in-

[1] Letter to Dr. Walter Jones.

[2] "He errs as other men do, but errs with integrity." Letter to W. B. Giles, 1795.

capable of fear, meeting personal dangers with the calmest unconcern. Perhaps the strongest feature in his character was prudence, never acting until every circumstance, every consideration, was maturely weighed; refraining if he saw a doubt, but, when once decided, going through with his purpose, whatever obstacles opposed. His integrity was most pure, his justice the most inflexible I have ever known, no motives of interest or consanguinity, of friendship or hatred, being able to bias his decision. He was, indeed, in every sense of the words, a wise, a good, and a great man. His temper was naturally high toned; but reflection and resolution had obtained a firm and habitual ascendency over it. If ever, however, it broke its bonds, he was most tremendous in his wrath. In his expenses he was honorable, but exact; liberal in contributions to whatever promised utility; but frowning and unyielding on all visionary projects, and all unworthy calls on his charity. His heart was not warm in its affections; but he exactly calculated every man's value, and gave him a solid esteem proportioned to it. His person, you know, was fine, his stature exactly what one would wish, his deportment easy, erect and noble; the best horseman of his age, and the most graceful figure that could be seen on horseback. Although in the circle of his friends, where he might be unreserved with safety, he took a free share in conversation, his colloquial talents were not above mediocrity, possessing neither copiousness of ideas, nor fluency of words. In public, when called on for a sudden opinion, he was unready, short and embarrassed. Yet he wrote readily, rather diffusely, in an easy and correct style. This he had acquired by conversation with the world, for his education was merely reading, writing and common arithmetic, to which he added surveying at a later day. His time was employed in action chiefly, reading little, and that only in agriculture and English history. His correspondence became necessarily extensive, and, with journalizing his agricultural proceedings, occupied most of his leisure hours within doors. On the whole, his character was, in its mass, perfect, in nothing bad, in few points indifferent; and it may truly be said, that never did nature and fortune combine more perfectly to make a man great, and to place him in the same constellation with whatever worthies have merited from man an everlasting remembrance. For his was the singular destiny and merit, of leading the armies of his country successfully through an arduous war, for the establishment of its independence; of conducting its councils through the birth of a government, new in its forms and principles, until it had settled down into a quiet and orderly train; and of scrupulously obeying the laws through the whole of his career, civil and military, of which the history of the world furnishes no other example.

How, then, can it be perilous for you to take such a man on your shoulders? I am satisfied the great body of republicans think of him as I do.

We were, indeed, dissatisfied with him on his ratification of the British treaty. But this was short lived. We knew his honesty, the wiles with which he was encompassed, and that age had already began to relax the firmness of his purposes; and I am convinced he is more deeply seated in the love and gratitude of the republicans, than in the Pharisaical homage of the federal monarchists. For he was no monarchist from preference of his judgment. The soundness of that gave him correct views of the rights of man, and his severe justice devoted him to them. He has often declared to me that he considered our new constitution as an experiment on the practicability of republican government, and with what dose of liberty man could be trusted for his own good; that he was determined the experiment should have a fair trial, and would lose the last drop of his blood in support of it. And these declarations he repeated to me the oftener and more pointedly, because he knew my suspicions of Colonel Hamilton's views, and probably had heard from him the same declarations which I had, to wit, "that the British constitution, with its unequal representation, corruption and other existing abuses, was the most perfect government which had ever been established on earth, and that a reformation of those abuses would make it an impracticable government." I do believe that General Washington had not a firm confidence in the durability of our government. He was naturally distrustful of men, and inclined to gloomy apprehensions; and I was ever persuaded that a belief that we must at length end in something like a British constitution, had some weight in his adoption of the ceremonies of levees, birth-days, pompous meetings with Congress, and other forms of the same character, calculated to prepare us gradually for a change which he believed possible, and to let it come on with as little shock as might be to the public mind.

These are my opinions of General Washington, which I would vouch at the judgment seat of God, having been formed on an acquaintance of thirty years. I served with him in the Virginia legislature from 1769 to the Revolutionary war, and again, a short time in Congress, until he left us to take command of the army. During the war and after it we corresponded occasionally, and in the four years of my continuance in the office of Secretary of State, our intercourse was daily, confidential and cordial. After I retired from that office, great and malignant pains were taken by our federal monarchists, and not entirely without effect, to make him view me as a theorist, holding French principles of government, which would lead infallibly to licentiousness and anarchy. And to this he listened the more easily, from my known disapprobation of the British treaty. I never saw him afterwards, or these malignant insinuations should have been dissipated before his just judgment, as mists before the sun. I felt on his death, with my countrymen, that "verily a great man hath fallen this day in Israel."

# GEORGE WYTHE[1]

August 31, 1820

George Wythe was born about the year 1727, or 1728, of a respectable family in the County of Elizabeth City, on the shores of the Chesapeake. He inherited, from his father, a fortune sufficient for independence and ease. He had not the benefit of a regular education in the schools, but acquired a good one of himself, and without assistance; insomuch, as to become the best Latin and Greek scholar in the State. It is said, that while reading the Greek Testament, his mother held an English one, to aid him in rendering the Greek text conformably with that. He also acquired, by his own reading, a good knowledge of Mathematics, and of Natural and Moral Philosophy. He engaged in the study of the law under the direction of a Mr. Lewis, of that profession, and went early to the bar of the General Court, then occupied by men of great ability, learning, and dignity in their profession. He soon became eminent among them, and, in process of time, the first at the bar, taking into consideration his superior learning, correct elocution, and logical style of reasoning; for in pleading he never indulged himself with an useless or declamatory thought or word; and became as distinguished by correctness and purity of conduct in his profession, as he was by his industry and fidelity to those who employed him. He was early elected to the House of Representatives, then called the House of Burgesses, and continued in it until the Revolution. On the first dawn of that, instead of higgling on half-way pinciples, as others did who feared to follow their reason, he took his stand on the solid ground that the only link of political union between us and Great Britain, was the identity of our Executive; that that nation and its Parliament had no more authority over us, than we had over them, and that we were co-ordinàte nations with Great Britain and Hanover.

In 1774, he was a member of a Committee of the House of Burgesses, appointed to prepare a Petition to the King, a Memorial to the House of Lords, and a Remonstrance to the House of Commons, on the subject of the proposed Stamp Act. He was made draughtsman of the last, and, following his own principles, he so far overwent the timid hesitations of his colleagues, that his draught was subjected by them to material modifications; and, when the famous Resolutions of Mr. Henry, in 1775, were proposed, it was not on any difference of principle that they were opposed by Wythe, Randolph, Pendleton, Nicholas, Bland, and other worthies, who had

[1] This sketch was the result of a request made by John Saunderson, who wanted materials for a biography of Wythe. Jefferson sent him "these scanty outlines" with an apology for his inability to go into greater detail about a man who was his "most affectionate friend" for more than forty years.

long been the habitual leaders of the House; but because those papers of the preceding session had already expressed the same sentiments and assertions of right, and that an answer to them was yet to be expected.

In August, 1775, he was appointed a member of Congress, and in 1776, signed the Declaration of Independence, of which he had, in debate, been an eminent supporter. And subsequently, in the same year, he was appointed, by the Legislature of Virginia, one of a Committee to revise the laws of the State, as well of British as of Colonial enactment, and to prepare bills for re-enacting them, with such alterations as the change in the form and principles of the government, and other circumstances, required; and of this work, he executed the period commencing with the revolution in England, and ending with the establishment of the new government here; excepting the Acts for regulating descents, for religious freedom, and for proportioning crimes and punishments. In 1777, he was chosen Speaker of the House of Delegates, being of distinguished learning in Parliamentary law and proceedings; and towards the end of the same year, he was appointed one of the three Chancellors, to whom that department of the Judiciary was confided, on the first organization of the new government. On a subsequent change of the form of that court, he was appointed sole Chancellor, in which office he continued to act until his death, which happened in June, 1806, about the seventy-eighth or seventy-ninth year of his age.

Mr. Wythe had been twice married: first, I believe, to a daughter of Mr. Lewis, with whom he had studied law, and afterwards to a Miss Taliaferro, of a wealthy and respectable family in the neighborhood of Williamsburg; by neither of whom did he leave issue.

No man ever left behind him a character more venerated than George Wythe. His virtue was of the purest tint; his integrity inflexible, and his justice exact; of warm patriotism, and, devoted as he was to liberty, and the natural and equal rights of man, he might truly be called the Cato of his country, without the avarice of the Roman; for a more disinterested person never lived. Temperance and regularity in all his habits, gave him general good health, and his unaffected modesty and suavity of manners endeared him to everyone. He was of easy elocution, his language chaste, methodical in the arrangement of his matter, learned and logical in the use of it, and of great urbanity in debate; not quick of apprehension, but, with a little time, profound in penetration, and sound in conclusion. In his philosophy he was firm, and neither troubling, nor perhaps trusting, anyone with his religious creed, he left the world to the conclusion, that that religion must be good which could produce a life of such exemplary virtue.

His stature was of the middle size, well formed and proportioned, and the features of his face were manly, comely, and engaging. Such was George Wythe, the honor of his own, and the model of future times.

*Part IV*

# RELIGION, SCIENCE, AND PHILOSOPHY

# *Chapter XIX*

# RELIGION

## CHRISTIANITY AND THE COMMON LAW[1]

*c.* 1765

*Common-place Book:*[2]

873. In Quare impedit, in C. B. 34, H. 6, fo. 38, the defendant, Bishop of Lincoln, pleads that the church of the plaintiff became void by the death of the incumbent, that the pl. and I.S. each pretending a right, presented two several clerks; that the church being thus rendered litigious, he was not obliged, by the *Ecclesiastical law* to admit either, until an inquisition *de jure patronatus,* in the ecclesiastical court: that, by the same law, this inquisition was to be at the suit of either claimant, and was not *ex-officio* to be instituted by the bishop, and at his proper costs; that neither party had desired such an inquisition; that six months passed whereon it belonged to him of right to present as on a lapse, which he had done. The pl. demurred. A question was, How far the *Ecclesiastical law* was to be respected in this matter by the common law court? And Prisot C. 5, in the course of his argument, uses this expression, *"A tiels leis que ils de seint église ont en* ancien scripture, *covient à nous à donner crédence, car ceo common ley sur quel touts manners leis sont fondés. Et auxy, Sir, nous*

[1] On February 10, 1814, Jefferson wrote to Thomas Cooper: "I promised you a sample from my common-place book, of the pious disposition of the English judges, to connive at the frauds of the clergy, a disposition which has even rendered them faithful allies in practice. When I was a student of the law, now half a century ago, after getting through Coke Littleton, whose matter cannot be abridged, I was in the habit of abridging and common-placing what I read meriting it, and of sometimes mixing my own reflections on the subject. I now enclose you the extract from these entries which I promised. They were written at a time of life when I was bold in the pursuit of knowledge, never fearing to follow truth and reason to whatever results they lead, and bearding every authority which stood in their way. This must be the apology, if you find the conclusions bolder than historical facts and principles will warrant."

[2] A complete modern edition is that by Gilbert Chinard, *The Commonplace Book of Thomas Jefferson. A Repertory of His Ideas on Government* (1926).

*sumus obligés de conustre lour ley de saint église. Et semblablement ils sont obligés de conustre nostre ley, et, Sir, si poit apperer or à nous que liévesque ad fait comme un ordinary fera en tiel cas, adonq nous devons ceo adjuger bon, ou autrement nemy,"* &c. It does not appear that judgment was given. Y. B. ubi supra. S. C. Fitzh. abr. Qu. imp. 89. Bro. abr. Qu. imp. 12. Finch mis-states this in the following manner: "To such laws of the church as have warrant in *Holy Scripture,* our law giveth credence," and cites the above case, and the words of Prisot in the margin. Finch's law. B. 1, ch. 3, published 1613. Here we find *"ancien scripture"* converted into "Holy Scripture," whereas it can only mean the *ancient written* laws of the church. It cannot mean the Scriptures, 1st, because the *"ancien scripture"* must then be understood as meaning the *"Old* Testament" or Bible, in opposition to the *"New* Testament," and to the exclusion of that, which would be absurd and contrary to the wish of those who cite this passage to prove that the Scriptures, or Christianity, is a part of the common law. 2. Because Prisot says, *"Ceo [est] common ley, sur quel touts manners leis sont fondés."* Now, it is true that the ecclesiastical law, so far as admitted in England, derives its authority from the common law. But it would not be true that the Scriptures so derive their authority. 3. The whole case and arguments show that the question was how far the Ecclesiastical law in general should be respected in a common law court. And in Bro. abr. of this case, Littleton says, *"Les juges del common ley prendra conusans quid est* lax ecclesiæ, *vel admiralitatis, et trujus modi."* 4. Because the particular part of the Ecclesiastical law then in question, to wit, the right of the patron to present to his advowson, was not founded on the law of God, but subject to the modification of the lawgiver, and so could not introduce any such general position as Finch pretends. Yet Wingate [in 1658] thinks proper to erect this false quotation into a maxim of the common law, expressing it in the very words of Finch, but citing Prisot, wing. max. 3. Next comes Sheppard, [in 1675], who states it in the same words of Finch, and quotes the Year-Book, Finch and Wingate. 3. Shepp. abr. tit. Religion. In the case of the King *v.* Taylor, Sir Matthew Hale lays it down in these words, "Christianity is parcel of the laws of England." 1 Ventr. 293, 3 Keb. 607. But he quotes no authority, resting it on his own, which was good in all cases in which his mind received no bias from his bigotry, his superstitions, his visions about sorceries, demons, &c. The power of these over him is exemplified in his hanging of the witches. So strong was this doctrine become in 1728, by additions and repetitions from one another, that in the case of the King *v.* Woolston, the court would not suffer it to be debated, whether to write against Christianity was punishable in the temporal courts at common law, saying it had been so settled in Taylor's case, ante 2, stra. 834; therefore, Wood, in his Institute, lays it down that all blasphemy and profaneness are offences by the *common law,* and cites Strange ubi supra. Wood 409. And Blackstone [about 1763] repeats, in the words of Sir Matthew Hale, that "Christianity is part of the laws of England," citing Ventris and Strange ubi supra. 4. Blackst. 59. Lord Mansfield qualifies it a little by saying that "The essential principles of revealed religion are part of the common law." In the case of the Chamberlain of London *v.* Evans, 1767. But he cites no authority, and leaves us at our peril to find out what, in the opinion of the judge, and according to the measure of his foot or his faith, are those essential principles of revealed religion obligatory on us as a part of the common law.

Thus we find this string of authorities, when examined to the beginning, all hanging on the same hook, a perverted expression of Prisot's, or on one another, or nobody. Thus Finch quotes Prisot; Wingate also; Sheppard quotes Prisot, Finch and Wingate; Hale cites nobody; the court in Woolston's case cite Hale; Wood cites Woolston's case; Blackstone that and Hale; and Lord Mansfield, like Hale, ventures it on his own authority. In the earlier ages of the law, as in the year-books, for instance, we do not expect much recurrence to authorities by the judges, because in those days there were few or none such made public. But in latter times we take no judge's word for what the law is, further than he is warranted by the authorities he appeals to. His decision may bind the unfortunate individual who happens to be the particular subject of it; but it cannot alter the law. Though the common law may be termed *"Lex non Scripta,"* yet the same Hale tells us "when I call those parts of our laws *Leges non Scriptæ,* I do not mean as if those laws were only oral, or communicated from the former ages to the latter merely by word. For all those laws have their several monuments in writing, whereby they are transferred from one age to another, and without which they would soon lose all kind of certainty. They are for the most part extant in records of pleas, proceedings, and jüdgments, in books of reports and judicial decisions, in tractates of learned men's arguments and opinions, preserved from ancient times and still extant in writing." Hale's H. c. d. 22. Authorities for what is common law may therefore be as well cited, as for any part of the Lex Scripta, and there is no better instance of the necessity of holding the judges and writers to a declaration of their authorities than the present; where we detect them endeavoring to make law where they found none, and to submit us at one stroke to a whole system, no particle of which has its foundation in the common law. For we know that the common law is that system of law which was introduced by the Saxons on their settlement in England, and altered from time to time by proper legislative authority from that time to the date of Magna Charta, which terminates the period of the common law, or lex non scripta, and commences that of the statute law, or Lex Scripta. This settlement took place about the middle of the fifth century. But Christianity was not introduced till the seventh century; the conversion of the first christian king of the Heptarchy having taken place about the year 598, and that of the last about 686. Here, then, was a space of two hundred years, during which the common law was in existence, and Christianity no part of it. If it ever was adopted, therefore, into the common law, it must have been between the introduction of Christianity and the date of the Magna Charta. But of the laws of this period we have a tolerable collection by Lambard and Wilkins, probably not perfect, but neither very defective; and if anyone chooses to build a doctrine on any law of that period, supposed to have been lost, it is incumbent on him to prove it to have existed, and what were its contents. These were so far alterations of the common law, and became themselves a part of it. But none of these adopt Christianity as a part of the common law. If, therefore, from the settlement of the Saxons to the introduction of Christianity among them, that system of religion could not be a part of the common law, because they were not yet Christians, and if, having their laws from that period to the close of the common law, we are all able to find among them no such act of adoption, we may safely affirm (though contradicted by all the judges and writers on earth) that Christianity neither is, nor ever was a part of the common law. Another cogent proof of this truth is drawn from the silence of certain writers on the common law. Bracton gives us a very complete and scientific treatise of the whole body of the common law. He wrote this about the close of the reign of Henry III, a very few years after the date of the Magna Charta. We consider this book as the more valuable, as it was written about the time which divides the common and statute law, and therefore gives us the former in its ultimate state. Bracton, too, was an ecclesiastic, and would certainly not have failed to inform us of the adoption of Christianity as a part of the common law, had any such adoption ever taken place. But no word of his, which intimates anything like it, has ever been cited. Fleta and Britton, who wrote in the succeeding reign (of Edward I), are equally silent. So also is Glanvil, an earlier writer than any of them, (*viz.:* temp. H. 2.) but his subject perhaps might not have led him to mention it. Justice Fortescue Aland, who possessed more Saxon learning than all the judges and writers before mentioned put together, places this subject on more limited ground. Speaking of the laws of the Saxon kings, he says, "the ten commandments were made part of their laws, and consequently were *once* part of the law of England; so that to break any of the ten commandments was then esteemed a breach of the common law, of England; and why it is not so now, perhaps it may be difficult to give a good reason." Preface to Fortescue Aland's reports, xvii. Had he proposed to state with more minuteness how much of the scriptures had been made a part of the common law, he might have added that in the laws of Alfred, where he found the ten commandments, two or three other chapters of Exodus are copied almost verbatim. But the adoption of a part proves rather a rejection of the rest, as municipal law. We might as well say that the Newtonian system of philosophy is a part of the common law, as that the Christian religion is. The truth is that Christianity and Newtonianism being reason and verity itself, in the opinion of all but infidels and Cartesians, they are protected under the wings of the common law from the dominion of other sects, but not erected into dominion over them. An eminent Spanish physician affirmed that the lancet had slain more men than the sword. Doctor Sangrado, on the contrary, affirmed that with plentiful bleedings, and draughts of warm water, every disease was to be cured. The common law protects both opinions, but enacts neither into law. See post. 879.

879. Howard, in his Contumes Anglo-Normandes, 1.87, notices the falsification of the laws of Alfred, by prefixing to them four chapters of the Jewish law, to wit: the 20th, 21st, 22d and 23d chapters of Exodus, to which he might have added the 15th chapter of the Acts of the Apostles, v. 23, and precepts from other parts of the scripture. These he calls a *hors d'œuvre* of some pious copyist. This awkward monkish fabrication makes the preface to Alfred's genuine laws stand in the body of the work, and the very words of Alfred himself prove the fraud; for he declares, in that preface, that he has collected these laws from those of Ina, of Offa, Aethelbert and his ancestors, saying nothing of any of them being taken from the Scriptures. It is still more certainly proved by the inconsistencies it occasions. For example, the Jewish legislator Exodus xxi. 12, 13, 14, (copied by the Pseudo Alfred § 13,) makes murder, with the Jews, death. But Alfred himself, Le. xxvi., punishes it by a fine only, called a Weregild, proportioned to the condition of the person killed. It is remarkable that Hume (append. 1 to his History) examining this article of the laws of Alfred, without perceiving the fraud, puzzles himself with accounting for the inconsistency it had introduced. To strike a pregnant woman so that she die is death by Exodus, xxi. 22, 23, and Pseud. Alfr. § 18; but by the laws of Alfred ix., pays a Weregild for both woman and child. To smite out an eye, or a tooth, Exod. xxi. 24-27. Pseud. Alfr. § 19, 20, if of a servant by his master, is freedom to the servant; in every other case retaliation. But by Alfr. Le. xl. a fixed indemnification is paid. Theft of an ox, or a sheep, by the Jewish law, Exod. xxii. 1, was repaid five-fold for the ox and four-fold for the sheep; by the Pseudograph § 24, the ox double, the sheep four-fold; but by Alfred Le. xvi., he who stole a cow and a calf was to repay the worth of the cow and 40l for the calf. Goring by an ox was the death of the ox, and the flesh not to be eaten. Exod. xxi. 28. Pseud. Alfr. § 21 by Alfred Le. xxiv., the wounded person had the ox. The Pseudograph makes municipal laws of

the ten commandments, § 1-10, regulates concubinage, § 12, makes it death to strike or to curse father or mother, § 14, 15, gives an eye for an eye, tooth for a tooth, hand for hand, foot for foot, burning for burning, wound for wound, strife for strife, § 19; sells the thief to repay his theft, § 24; obliges the fornicator to marry the woman he has lain with, § 29; forbids interest on money, § 35; makes the laws of bailment, § 28, very different from what Lord Holt delivers in Coggs *v.* Bernard, ante 92, and what Sir William Jones tells us they were; and punishes witchcraft with death, § 30, which Sir Matthew Hale, 1 H. P. C. B. 1, ch. 33, declares was not a felony before the Stat. 1, Jac. 12. It was under that statute, and not this forgery, that he hung Rose Cullendar and Amy Duny, 16 Car. 2. (1662,) on whose trial he declared "that there were such creatures as witches he made no doubt at all; for first the Scripture had affirmed so much, secondly the wisdom of all nations had provided laws against such persons, and such hath been the judgment of this kingdom, as appears by that act of Parliament which hath provided punishment proportionable to the quality of the offence." And we must certainly allow greater weight to this position that "it was no felony till James' Statute," laid down deliberately in his H. P. C., a work which he wrote to be printed, finished, and transcribed for the press in his life time, than to the hasty scripture that "at *common law* witchcraft was punished with death as heresy, by writ de Heretico Comburendo" in his Methodical Summary of the P. C. p. 6, a work "not intended for the press, not fitted for it, and which he declared himself he had never read over since it was written"; Pref. Unless we understand his meaning in that to be that witchcraft could not be punished at common law as witchcraft, but as heresy. In either sense, however, it is a denial of this pretended law of Alfred. Now, all men of reading know that these pretended laws of homicide, concubinage, theft, retaliation, compulsory marriage, usury, bailment, and others which might have been cited, from the Pseudograph, were never the laws of England, not even in Alfred's time; and of course that it is a forgery. Yet palpable as it must be to every lawyer, the English judges have piously avoided lifting the veil under which it was shrouded. In truth, the alliance between Church and State in England has ever made their judges accomplices in the frauds of the clergy; and even bolder than they are. For instead of being contented with these four surreptitious chapters of Exodus, they have taken the whole leap, and declared at once that the whole Bible and Testament in a lump, make a part of the common law; ante 873: the first judicial declaration of which was by this same Sir Matthew Hale. And thus they incorporate into the English code laws made for the Jews alone, and the precepts of the gospel, intended by their benevolent author as obligatory only in *foro concientiae;* and they arm the whole with the coercions of municipal law. In doing this, too, they have not even used the Connecticut caution of declaring, as is done in their blue laws, that the laws of God shall be the laws of their land, except where their own contradict them; but they swallow the yea and nay together. Finally, in answer to Fortescue Aland's question why the ten commandments should not now be a part of the common law of England? we may say they are not because they never were made so by legislative authority, the document which has imposed that doubt on him being a manifest forgery.

## NOTES ON RELIGION[1]

October, 1776 (?)

Sabellians. Christian heretics. That there is but one person in the Godhead. That the "Word" and holy spirit are only virtues, emanations or functions of the deity.

Sorcinians. Christian heretics. That the Father is the one only god. That the Word is no more than an expression of the godhead and had not existed from all eternity; that Jesus Christ was god no otherwise than by his superiority above all creatures who were put in subjection to him by the father. That he was not a mediator, but sent to be a pattern of conduct to men. That the punishments of hell are not eternal.

Arminians. They think with the Romish church (against the Calvinists) that there is an universal grace given to all men, and that man is always *free* and at liberty to receive or reject grace. That God creates men free, that his justice would not permit him to punish men for crimes they are predestinated to commit. They admit the presence of god, but distinguish between fore-knowing and predestinating. All the fathers before St. Austin were of this opinion. The church of England founded her article of predestination on his authority.

Arians. Christian heretics. They avow there was a time when the Son was not, that he was created in time mutable in nature, and like the angels liable to sin; they deny the three persons in the trinity to be of the same essence. Erasmus and Grotius were Arians.

Apollinarians. Christian heretics. They affirm there was but one nature in Christ, that his body as well as soul was impassive and immortal, and that his birth, death, and resurrection was only in appearance.

Macedonians. Christian heretics. They teach that the Holy ghost was a mere creature, but superior in excellence to the Angels. See Broughton,

[1] These are, literally, "notes," intended to be used in speeches and petitions in the Virginia House of Delegates, particularly in connection with the disestablishment of the Episcopal church. The date is not certain; Jefferson dated the manuscript: "scraps early in the revolution." In the original the "Notes" are frequently abbreviated; in this text the full spelling is given.

verbo "Heretics," an enumeration of 48 sects of Christians pronounced Heretics.

Locke's system of Christianity is this: Adam was created happy and immortal; but his happiness was to have been *Earthly* and *Earthly* immortality. By *sin* he lost this—so that he became subject to total death (like that of brutes) to the crosses and unhappiness of this life. At the intercession however of the son of god this sentence was in part remitted. A life conformable to the law was to restore them again to immortality. And moreover to them who *believed* their *faith* was to be counted for righteousness. Not that faith without works was to save them; St. James, c. 2 says expressly the contrary; and all make the fundamental pillars of Christianity to be faith and *repentance*. So that a reformation of life (included under *repentance*) was essential, and defects in this would be made up by their *faith; i.e.*, their faith should be counted for righteousness. As to that part of mankind who never had the gospel preached to them, they are 1. Jews.—2. Pagans, or Gentiles. The Jews had the law of works revealed to them. By this therefore they were to be saved: and a lively faith in God's promises to send the Messiah would supply small defects. 2. The Gentiles. St. Paul says—Romans 2, 13, "the Gentiles have the law written in their hearts," *i.e.*, the law of nature: to which adding a *faith* in God and his attributes that on their repentance he would pardon them, they also would be justified. This then explains the text "there is no other *name* under heaven by which a man may be saved," *i.e.*, the defects in good works shall not be supplied by a faith in Mahomet Foe [?] or any other except Christ.

The fundamentals of Christianity as found in the gospels are 1. Faith, 2. Repentance. That faith is every[where] explained to be a belief that Jesus was the Messiah who had been promised. Repentance was to be proved sincerely by good works. The advantages accruing to mankind from our Saviour's mission are these.

1. The knowledge of one god only.

2. A clear knowledge of their duty, or system of morality, delivered on such authority as to give it sanction.

3. The outward forms of religious worship wanted to be purged of that farcical pomp and nonsense with which they were loaded.

4. An inducement to a pious life, by revealing clearly a future existence in bliss, and that it was to be the reward of the virtuous.

The Epistles were written to persons *already Christians*. A person might be a Christian then before they were written. Consequently the fundamentals of Christianity were to be found in the preaching of our Saviour, which is related in the gospels. These fundamentals are to be found in the epistles dropped here and there, and promiscuously mixed with other truths. But these other truths are not to be made fundamentals. They serve for edification indeed and explaining to us matters in worship and morality, but being written occasionally it will readily be seen that their explanations are adapted to the notions and customs of the people they were written to. But yet every sentence in them (though the writers were inspired) must not be taken up and made a fundamental, without assent to which a man is not to be admitted a member of the Christian church here, or to his kingdom hereafter. The Apostles creed was by them taken to contain all things necessary to salvation, and consequently to a communion.

Shaftesbury *Charact.* As the Ancients tolerated visionaries and enthusiasts of all kinds so they permitted a free scope to philosophy as a balance. As the Pythagoreans and latter Platonists joined with the superstition of their times the Epicureans and Academicks were allowed all the use of wit and railery against it. Thus matters were balanced; reason had play and science flourished. These contrarieties produced harmony. Superstition and enthusiasm thus let alone never raged to bloodshed, persecution, &c. But now a new sort of policy, which considers the future lives and happiness of men rather than the present, has taught to distress one another, and raised an antipathy which if temporal interest could ever do now *uniformity* of opinion, a hopeful project! is looked on as the only remedy against this evil and is made the very object of government itself. If magistracy had vouchsafed to interpose thus in other sciences, we should have as bad logic, mathematics and philosophy as we have divinity in countries where the law settles orthodoxy.

Suppose the state should take into head that there should be an uniformity of countenance. Men would be obliged to put an artificial bump or swelling here, a patch there &c., but this would be merely hypocritical, or if the alternative was given of wearing a mask 99/100ths must immediately mask. Would this add to the beauty of nature? Why otherwise in opinions? In the middle ages of Christianity opposition to the State opinions was hushed. The consequence was, Christianity became loaded with all the Romish follies. Nothing but free argument, raillery and even ridicule will preserve the purity of religion. 2 Cor. I. 24. the apostles declare they had no dominion over the faith.

A heretic is an impugner of fundamentals. What are fundamentals? The protestants will say those doctrines which are clearly and precisely delivered in the holy Scriptures. Dr. Vaterland would say the Trinity. But how far this character of being clearly delivered will suit the doctrine of the trinity I leave others to determine. It is nowhere expressly declared by any of the earliest fathers, and was never affirmed or taught by the Church before the Council of Nice (Chillingas Pref. # 18. 33). Iraneaus says "who are the clean? those who go on firmly, believing in the Father and in the Son." The fundamental doctrine or the firmness of the Christian faith in this early age then was to believe in the *Father and Son*. Constantine wrote to Arius and Alexander treating the question "as vain foolish and impertinent as a dispute of words without sense which none could explain nor any comprehend, &c." This line is commended by Eusebius (*Vit. Constant.* I r. c. 64 &c.) and Socrates (*Hist. Eccles.* 1. i. c. 7) as excellent, admirable and full of wisdom. 2 *Middleton*. 115. remarks on the story of St. John and [illegible] *"Le saint concil (de Nièce anno 630) ayant defini que le fils de dieu est de même substance que son père et qu'il est eternel comme lui, composa une Simbole* (the Nicene creed) *ou il explique la divinité du* père et du fils *et qu'il finit par ces paroles 'dont le rêgne n'aura point de fin,' car la doctrine que regarde le* Saint Esprit *ne fut ajoutée que dans le second concile tenu contre les erreurs des Macedoniens, où ces questions furent agitées."* Zonaras *par Coussin*. Ann. 330. The second council meant by *Zonaras* was that of Constantinople ann. 381. *D'hist. Prim. Xty.* pref. XXXVIII. 2d app. to pref. 49. The Council of Antioch [ ] expressly affirms of our Saviour όυκ ἐστιν ὁμουσιος that he was not consubstantial to the father. The Council of Nice affirmed the direct contrary. *D'hist. Prim. Xty. Pref.* CXXV.

Episcopy. Gr. Επιςκοπος Lat. Episcopus. Ital. Vescovo. Fr. Evesque. Saxon, Byscop. Bishop (overseer). The epistles of Paul to Timothy and Titus are relied on (together with Tradition) for the Apostolic institution of bishops.

As to tradition, if we are Protestants we reject all tradition, and rely on the scripture alone, for that is the essence and common principle of all the protestant churches. As to Scripture I Tim. 3. 2. "a bishop must be blameless &c." Επισκοπος v. 8; "likewise must the deacons be grave &c. Διακονος" (ministers). C. 5. v. 6, he calls Timothy a "minister, Διακονος"; C. 4. v. 14. "neglect not the gift that is in thee, which was given thee by prophecy with the laying on the hands of the presbytery, πρεσβυτεριου"; C. 5. "rebuke not an elder. Πρεσβυτεροι," 5:17;—"let the elders that rule well," &c., Πρεσβυτεροι, 5.19; "against an elder (Πρεσβυτερος) receive not an accusation." 5.22. "lay hands suddenly on no man, χειρας ἐπιτίθει." 6. 11. He calls Timothy man of God ἄνθρωπε τοῦ θεοῦ, 2. Tim. 1.6. "stir up the gift of god, which is in thee, by the putting on of *my* hands επιθεσεως των χειρων" but ante c. 4. v. 14, he said it was by the hands of the presbytery. This imposition of hands then was some ceremony or custom frequently repeated, and certainly is a good proof that Timothy was ordained by the elders (and consequently that they might ordain) as that it was by Paul. I. II. Paul calls himself "a preacher," "an apostle," "a teacher." "κηρνε, και αποστολος και διδασκαλος." Here he designates himself by several synonyms as he had before done Timothy. Does this prove that synonym authorizes a different order of ecclesiastics. 4. 5. "do the work of an Evangelist, make full proof of thy ministry" "ἐργου ποιησουεὐαγγελιστου, την διακονιαν σου πληροφορελιστος."

Timothy then is called "επισκοπος, διακονος, ευαγγελιστος, ανθρωπος θεου." 4.11. He tells Timothy to bring Mark with him, for "he is profitable to me for the ministry." διακονιαν. Epistle to Titus. 1. 1, he calls himself "a servant of god." δουλοσ θεου. 1.5. "For this cause left I thee in Crete that thou shouldst set in order the things that are wanting, and ordain (καταστησης) *elders* in every city, as I had appointed thee." If any be blameless, the husband of one wife, having faithful children, not accused of riot or unruly, for a *bishop* must be blameless as the steward of god &c. Here then it appears that as the elders appointed the bishops, so the bishops appointed the elders, *i.e.,* they are synonyms. Again when telling Titus to appoint *elders* in every city he tells him what kind of men they must be, for said he a bishop must be &c., so that in the same sentence he calls elders bishops. 3.10 "a man that is an *heretic* after the first and second admonition, reject, 'αίρετικον.'" James 5. 14. "is any sick among you? Let him call for the elders (πρεσβυτερος) of the church, and let them pray over him, anointing him with oil in the name of the lord."

Another plea for Episcopal government in Religion in England is its similarity to the political government by a king. No bishop, no king. This then with us is a plea for government by a presbytery which resembles republican government.

The clergy have ever seen this. The bishops were always mere tools of the crown.

The Presbyterian spirit is known to be so congenial with friendly liberty, that the patriots after the restoration finding that the humour of people was running too strongly to exalt the prerogative of the crown promoted the dissenting interest as a check and balance, and thus was produced the Toleration Act.

St. Peter gave the title of *clergy* to all god's people till Pope Higinus [2] and the succeeding prelates took it from them and appropriated it to priests only. 1 Milt. 230.

Origen, being yet a layman, expounded the scriptures publickly and was therein defended by Alexander of Jerusalem and Theodotn of Caesarea producing in his behalf divers examples that the privilege of teaching was anciently permitted to laymen. The first Nicene council called in the assistance of many learned lay brethren. ib. 230.

Bishops were elected by the hands of the whole church. Ignatius (the most ancient of the extant fathers) writing to the Philadelphians says "that it belongs to them as to the church of god to chuse a bishop." Camden in his description of Scotland says "that over all the world bishops had no certain diocese till pope Dionysius [3] about the year 268 did cut them out, and that

[2] Higinus, or Hyginus, son of a Greek philosopher, was Pope from 136 to *c.* 140 A.D.
[3] Dionysius was Pope from 269 to 274 A.D.

the bishops of Scotland extended their function in what place soever they came, indifferently till temp. Malcolm 3. 1070."

Cyprian, epist. 68. says "the people chiefly hath power either of chusing worthy or refusing unworthy bishops the council of Nice contrary to the African churches exorts them to chuse orthodox bishops in the place of the dead." 1 Milt. 254.

Nicephorus Phocas the Greek emperor Ann. 1000 first enacted that no bishops should be chosen without his will. Ignatius in his epistle to those of Tra [illegible] confesseth that the presbyters are his fellow-sellers and fellow henchers and Cyprian in the 6. 4. 52. epistle calls the presbyters, "his compresbyters" yet he was a bishop. A modern bishop to be moulded into a primitive one must be elected by the people, undiocest, unrevenued, unlorded. 1. Milt. 255. From the dissensions among sects themselves arises necessarily a right of chusing and necessity of deliberating to which we will conform but if we chuse for ourselves, we must allow others to chuse also, and to reciprocally [sic]. This establishes religious liberty.

Why require those things in order to ecclesiastical communion which Christ does not require in order to life eternal? How can that be the church of Christ which excludes such persons from its communion as he will one day receive into the kingdom of heaven.

The arms of a religious society or church are exhortations, admonitions and advice, and ultimately expulsion or excommunication. This last is the utmost limit of power.

How far does the duty of toleration extend?

1. No church is bound by the duty of toleration to retain within her bosom obstinate offenders against her laws.
2. We have no right to prejudice another in his *civil* enjoyments because he is of another church. If any man err from the right way, it is his own misfortune, no injury to thee; nor therefore art thou to punish him in the things of this life because thou supposeth he will be miserable in that which is to come—on the contrary according to the spirit of the gospel, charity, bounty, liberality is due to him.

Each church being free, no one can have jurisdiction over another one, not even when the civil magistrate joins it. It neither acquires the right of the sword by the magistrate's coming to it, nor does it lose the rights of instruction or excommunication by his going from it. It cannot by the accession of any new member acquire jurisdiction over those who do not accede. He brings only himself, having no power to bring others. Suppose for instance two churches, one of Arminians another of Calvinists in Constantinople, has either any right over the other? Will it be said the orthodox one has? Every church is to itself orthodox; to *others* erroneous or heretical.

No man complains of his neighbor for ill management of his affairs, for an error in sowing his land, or marrying his daughter, for consuming his substance in taverns, pulling down building &c. in all these he has his liberty: but if he do not frequent the church, or there conform to ceremonies, there is an immediate uproar.

The care of every man's soul belongs to himself. But what if he neglect the care of it? Well what if he neglect the care of his health or estate, which more nearly relate to the state. Will the magistrate make a law that he shall not be poor or sick? Laws provide against injury from others; but not from ourselves. God himself will not save men against their wills.

If I be marching on with my utmost vigour in that way which according to the sacred geography leads to Jerusalem straight, why am I beaten and ill used by others because my hair is not of the right cut; because I have not been dressed right, because I eat flesh on the road, because I avoid certain by-ways which seem to lead into briars, because among several paths I take that which seems shortest and cleanest, because I avoid travellers less grave and keep company with others who are more sour and austere, or because I follow a guide crowned with a mitre and cloathed in white, yet these are the frivolous things which keep Christians at war.

If the magistrate command me to bring my commodity to a publick store house I bring it because he can indemnify me if he erred and I thereby lose it; but what indemnification can he give one for the kingdom of heaven?

I cannot give up my guidance to the magistrates, because he knows no more of the way to heaven than I do, and is less concerned to direct me right than I am to go right. If the Jews had followed their Kings, among so many, what number would have led them to idolatry? Consider the vicissitudes among the Emperors, Arians, Athana &c. or among our princes. H. 8. E. 6. Mary. Elizabeth. *Locke's* Works 2d vol.

Why persecute for difference in religious opinion?

1. For love to the person.

2. Because of tendency of these opinions to dis [illegible].

1. When I see them persecute their nearest connection and acquaintance for gross vices, I shall believe it may proceed from love. Till they do this I appeal to their own consciences if they will examine, wh. they do not find some other principle.

2. Because of tendency. Why not then level persecution at the crimes you fear will be introduced? Burn or hang the adulterer, cheat &c. Or exclude them from offices. Strange should be so zealous against things which tend to produce immorality and yet so indulgent to the immorality when produced. These moral vices all men acknowledge to be diametrically against Christianity and obstructive of salvation of souls, but the fantastical points for which we generally persecute are often very questionable; as we may be

assured by the very different conclusions of people. Our Savior chose not to propagate his religion by temporal punishments or civil incapacitation, if he had, it was in his almighty power. But he chose to extend it by its influence on reason, there by shewing to others how they should proceed.

The commonwealth is "a Society of men constituted for protecting their civil interests."

*Civil interests* are "life, health, indolency of body, liberty and property." That the magistrate's jurisdictions extends only to civil rights appears from these considerations.

1. The magistrate has no power but what the people gave.

The people have not given him the care of souls because they could not, they could not, because no man has *right* to abandon the care of his salvation to another.

No man has *power* to let another prescribe his faith. Faith is not faith without believing. No man can conform his faith to the dictates of another. The life and essence of religion consists in the internal persuasion or belief of the mind. External forms of worship, when against our belief are hypocrisy and impiety. Rom. 14. 23. "he that doubteth is damned, if he eat, because he eateth not of faith: for whatsoever is not of faith, is sin."

2. If it be said the magistrate may make use of arguments and so draw the heterodox to truth, I answer, every man has a commission to admonish, exhort, convince another of error.

12. [?] A church is "a *voluntary* society of men, joining themselves together of their own accord, in order to the public worshipping of god in such a manner as they judge acceptable to him and effectual to the salvation of their souls." It is *voluntary* because no man is *by nature* bound to any church. The hope of salvation is the cause of his entering into it. If he find anything wrong in it, he should be as free to go out as he was to come in.

13. What is the power of that church. As it is a society it must have some laws for its regulation. Time and place of meeting. Admitting and excluding members &c. Must be regulation but as it was a spontaneous joining of members, it follows that its laws extend to its own members only, not to those of any other voluntary society, for then by the same rule some other voluntary society might usurp power over them.

Christ has said "wheresoever 2 or 3 are gathered together in his name he will be in the midst of them." This is his definition of a society. He does not make it essential that a bishop or presbyter govern them. Without them it suffices for the salvation of souls.

Compulsion in religion is distinguished peculiarly from compulsion in every other thing. I may grow rich by art I am compelled to follow, I may recover health by medicines I am compelled to take against my own judgment, but I cannot be saved by a worship I disbelieve and abhor.

Whatsoever is lawful in the Commonwealth, or permitted to the subject in ordinary way, cannot be forbidden to him for religious uses: and whatsoever is prejudicial to the Commonwealth in their ordinary uses and therefore prohibited by the laws, ought not to be permitted to churches in their sacred rites. For instance it is unlawful in the ordinary course of things or in a private house to murder a child. It should not be permitted any sect then to sacrifice children: it is ordinarily lawful (or temporarily lawful) to kill calves or lambs. They may therefore be religiously sacrificed, but if the good of the state required a temporary suspension of killing lambs, as during a siege, sacrifices of them may then be rightfully suspended also. This is the true extent of toleration.

Truth will do well enough if left to shift for herself. She seldom has received much aid from the power of great men to whom she is rarely known and seldom welcome. She has no need of force to procure entrance into the minds of men. Error indeed has often prevailed by the assistance of power or force. Truth is the proper and sufficient antagonist to error. If anything pass in a religious meeting seditiously and contrary to the public peace, let it be punished in the same manner and no otherwise than as if it had happened in a fair or market. These meetings ought not to be sanctuaries for faction and flagitiousness.

Locke denies toleration to those who entertain opinions contrary to those moral rules necessary for the preservation of society; as for instance, that faith is not to be kept with those of another persuasion, that Kings excommunicated forfeit their crowns, that dominion is founded in grace, or that obedience is due to some foreign prince, or who will not own and teach the duty of tolerating all men in matters of religion, or who deny the existence of a god (it was a great thing to go so far—as he himself says of the parliament who framed the act of toleration but where he stopped short we may go on).[4]

He says "neither Pagan nor Mahomedan nor Jew ought to be excluded from the civil rights of the Commonwealth because of his religion." Shall we suffer a Pagan to deal with us and not suffer him to pray to his god? Why have Christians been distinguished above all people who have ever lived, for persecutions? Is it because it is the genius of their religion? No, its genius is the reverse. It is the refusing *toleration* to those of a different opinion which has produced all the bustles and wars on account of religion. It was the misfortune of mankind that during the darker centuries the Christian priests following their ambition and avarice combining with the magistrate

[4] Will not his own excellent rule be sufficient here too; to punish these as civil offences, *e.g.*, to assert that a foreign prince has power within this Commonwealth is a misdemeanor. The other opinions may be despised. Perhaps the single thing and which may be required to others before toleration to them would be an oath that they would allow toleration to others.—T. J.

to divide the spoils of the people, could establish the notion that schismatics might be ousted of their possessions and destroyed. This notion we have not yet cleared ourselves from. In this case no wonder the oppressed should rebel, and they will continue to rebel and raise disturbance until their civil rights are full restored to them and all partial distinctions, exclusions and incapacitations removed.

## A BILL FOR ESTABLISHING RELIGIOUS FREEDOM[1]

1779

SECTION I. Well aware that the opinions and belief of men depend on their own will, but follow involuntarily the evidence proposed to their minds; that Almighty God hath created the mind free, and manifested his supreme will that free it shall remain by making it altogether insusceptible of restraint; that all attempts to influence it by temporal punishments, or burthens, or by civil incapacitations, tend only to beget habits of hypocrisy and meanness, and are a departure from the plan of the holy author of our religion, who being lord both of body and mind, yet choose not to propagate it by coercions on either, as was in his Almighty power to do, but to exalt it by its influence on reason alone; that the impious presumption of legislature and ruler, civil as well as ecclesiastical, who, being themselves but fallible and uninspired men, have assumed dominion over the faith of others, setting up their own opinions and modes of thinking as the only true and infallible, and as such endeavoring to impose them on others, hath established and maintained false religions over the greatest part of the world and through all time: That to compel a man to furnish contributions of money for the propagation of opinions which he disbelieves and abhors, is sinful and tyrannical; that even the forcing him to support this or that teacher of his own religious persuasion, is depriving him of the comfortable liberty of giving his contributions to the particular pastor whose morals he would make his pattern, and whose powers he feels most persuasive to righteousness; and is withdrawing from the ministry those temporary rewards, which proceeding from an approbation of their personal conduct, are an additional incitement to earnest and unremitting labours for the instruction of mankind;

[1] This constitutes Ch. LXXXII of the *Report of the Revisors*. The bill was introduced into the Virginia Assembly on June 13, 1779, and aroused so much opposition that its passage was delayed until 1786, when it was adopted with certain changes.

Jefferson considered this bill one of his major achievements; before he died, he asked that it be engraved on his tombstone that he was its author. Together with the Declaration of Independence, this bill does, indeed, rank as one of the great foundation stones of the American republic. It established religious freedom—the greatest of all freedoms—and toleration in Virginia, the most populous and influential American State, and served as a model for the rest of the country.

The bill was printed in Paris, in 1786, both in English and in French.

that our civil rights have no dependance on our religious opinions, any more than our opinions in physics or geometry; and therefore the proscribing any citizen as unworthy the public confidence by laying upon him an incapacity of being called to offices of trust or emolument, unless he profess or renounce this or that religious opinion, is depriving him injudiciously of those privileges and advantages to which, in common with his fellow-citizens, he has a natural right; that it tends also to corrupt the principles of that very religion it is meant to encourage, by bribing with a monopoly of worldly honours and emoluments, those who will externally profess and conform to it; that though indeed these are criminals who do not withstand such temptation, yet neither are those innocent who lay the bait in their way; that the opinions of men are not the object of civil government, nor under its jurisdiction; that to suffer the civil magistrate to intrude his powers into the field of opinion and to restrain the profession or propagation of principles on supposition of their ill tendency is a dangerous fallacy, which at once destroys all religious liberty, because he being of course judge of that tendency will make his opinions the rule of judgment, and approve or condemn the sentiments of others only as they shall square with or suffer from his own; that it is time enough for the rightful purposes of civil government for its officers to interfere when principles break out into overt acts against peace and good order; and finally, that truth is great and will prevail if left to herself; that she is the proper and sufficient antagonist to error, and has nothing to fear from the conflict unless by human interposition disarmed of her natural weapons, free argument and debate; errors ceasing to be dangerous when it is permitted freely to contradict them.

SECTION II. We the General Assembly of Virginia do enact that no man shall be compelled to frequent or support any religious worship, place, or ministry whatsoever, nor shall be enforced, restrained, molested, or burthened in his body or goods, or shall otherwise suffer, on account of his religious opinions or belief; but that all men shall be free to profess, and by argument to maintain, their opinions in matters of religion, and that the same shall in no wise diminish, enlarge, or affect their civil capacities.

SECTION III. And though we well know that this Assembly, elected by the people for their ordinary purposes of legislation only, have no power to restrain the acts of succeeding Assemblies, constituted with powers equal to our own, and that therefore to declare this act to be irrevocable would be of no effect in law; yet we are free to declare, and do declare, that the rights hereby asserted are of the natural rights of mankind, and that if any act shall be hereafter passed to repeal the present or to narrow its operations, such act will be an infringement of natural right.

## SYLLABUS OF AN ESTIMATE OF THE MERIT OF THE DOCTRINES OF JESUS, COMPARED WITH THOSE OF OTHERS [1]

April, 1803

In a comparative view of the Ethics of the enlightened nations of antiquity, of the Jews and of Jesus, no notice should be taken of the corruptions of reason among the ancients, to wit, the idolatry and superstition of the vulgar, nor of the corruptions of Christianity by the learned among its professors.

Let a just view be taken of the moral principles inculcated by the most esteemed of the sects of ancient philosophy, or of their individuals; particularly Pythagoras, Socrates, Epicurus, Cicero, Epictetus, Seneca, Antoninus.

I. Philosophers. 1. Their precepts related chiefly to ourselves, and the government of those passions which, unrestrained, would disturb our tranquillity of mind.[2] In this branch of philosophy they were really great.

2. In developing our duties to others, they were short and defective. They embraced, indeed, the circles of kindred and friends, and inculcated patriotism, or the love of our country in the aggregate, as a primary obligation; towards our neighbors and countrymen they taught justice, but scarcely viewed them as within the circle of benevolence. Still less have they inculcated peace, charity, and love to our fellow-men, or embraced with benevolence the whole family of mankind.

II. Jews. 1. Their system was Deism; that is, the belief in one only God. But their ideas of him and of his attributes were degrading and injurious.

2. Their Ethics were not only imperfect, but often irreconcilable with the sound dictates of reason and morality, as they respect intercourse with those around us; and repulsive and anti-social, as respecting other nations. They needed reformation, therefore, in an eminent degree.

[1] This paper was written after many discussions with Dr. Benjamin Rush in 1798 and 1799. Jefferson promised to write down his views and for the next four years he frequently thought about the subject. He finally jotted down his thoughts in the form of the above syllabus, which he sent to Dr. Rush on April 21, 1803, with the request that it be kept confidential. This paper was kept secret during Jefferson's lifetime. Apart from Dr. Rush, only two or three other persons, among them John Adams, ever saw it. After Rush's death, Jefferson requested the Rush family to return the syllabus. In his letter accompanying the syllabus, Jefferson stated his religious faith: "To the corruptions of Christianity I am indeed opposed; but not to the genuine precepts of Jesus himself. I am a Christian, in the only sense in which he wished anyone to be; sincerely attached to his doctrines, in preference to all others; ascribing to himself every *human* excellence; and believing he never claimed any other."

[2] To explain, I will exhibit the heads of Seneca's and Cicero's philosophical works, the most extensive of any we have received from the ancients. Of ten heads in Seneca, seven relate to ourselves, *viz., de ira consolatio, de tranquillitate, de constantia sapientis, de otio sapientis, de vita beata, de brevitate vitae;* two relate to others, *de clementia, de beneficiis;* and one relates to the government of the world, *de providentia.* Of eleven tracts of Cicero, five respect ourselves, *viz., de finibus, Tusculana, academica, paradoxa, de senectute;* one, *de officiis,* relates partly to ourselves, partly to others; one, *de amicitia* relates to others; and four are on different subjects, to wit, *de natura deorum, de divinatione, de fato,* and *somnium Scipionis.*—T. J.

III. Jesus. In this state of things among the Jews, Jesus appeared. His parentage was obscure; his condition poor; his education null; his natural endowments great; his life correct and innocent; he was meek, benevolent, patient, firm, disinterested, and of the sublimest eloquence.

The disadvantages under which his doctrines appear are remarkable.

1. Like Socrates and Epictetus, he wrote nothing himself.

2. But he had not, like them, a Xenophon or an Arrian to write for him. I name not Plato, who only used the name of Socrates to cover the whimsies of his own brain. On the contrary, all the learned of his country, entrenched in its power and riches, were opposed to him, lest his labors should undermine their advantages; and the committing to writing of his life and doctrines fell on unlettered and ignorant men; who wrote, too, from memory, and not till long after the transactions had passed.

3. According to the ordinary fate of those who attempt to enlighten and reform mankind, he fell an early victim to the jealousy and combination of the altar and the throne, at about thirty-three years of age, his reason having not yet attained the maximum of its energy, nor the course of his preaching, which was but of three years at most, presented occasions for developing a complete system of morals.

4. Hence the doctrines which he really delivered were defective as a whole, and fragments only of what he did deliver have come to us mutilated, misstated, and often unintelligible.

5. They have been still more disfigured by the corruptions of schismatizing followers, who have found an interest in sophisticating and perverting the simple doctrines he taught, by engrafting on them the mysticisms of a Grecian sophist, frittering them into subtleties, and obscuring them with jargon, until they have caused good men to reject the whole in disgust, and to view Jesus himself as an impostor.

Notwithstanding these disadvantages, a system of morals is presented to us, which, if filled up in the style and spirit of the rich fragments he left us, would be the most perfect and sublime that has ever been taught by man.

The question of his being a member of the Godhead, or in direct communication with it, claimed for him by some of his followers, and denied by others, is foreign to the present view, which is merely an estimate of the intrinsic merits of his doctrines.

1. He corrected the Deism of the Jews, confirming them in their belief of one only God, and giving them juster notions of his attributes and government.

2. His moral doctrines, relating to kindred and friends, were more pure and perfect than those of the most correct of the philosophers, and greatly more so than those of the Jews; and they went far beyond both in inculcat-

ing universal philanthropy not only to kindred and friends, to neighbors and countrymen, but to all mankind, gathering all into one family, under the bonds of love, charity, peace, common wants and common aids. A development of this head will evince the peculiar superiority of the system of Jesus over all others.

3. The precepts of philosophy, and of the Hebrew code, laid hold of actions only. He pushed his scrutinies into the heart of man; erected his tribunal in the region of his thoughts, and purified the waters at the fountain head.

4. He taught, emphatically, the doctrines of a future state, which was either doubted, or disbelieved by the Jews; and wielded it with efficacy, as an important incentive, supplementary to the other motives to moral conduct.

## THE PRINCIPLES OF JESUS[1]

October 13, 1813

To compare the morals of the Old, with those of the New Testament, would require an attentive study of the former, a search through all its books for its precepts, and through all its history for its practices, and the principles they prove. As commentaries, too, on these the philosophy of the Hebrews must be inquired into, their Mishna, their Gemara, Cabbala, Jezirah, Sohar, Cosri, and their Talmud, must be examined and understood, in order to do them full justice. Brucker [History of Philosophy], it would seem, has gone deeply into these repositories of their ethics, and Enfield his epitomizer, concludes in these words: "Ethics were so little understood among the Jews, that in their whole compilation called the Talmud, there is only one treatise on moral subjects. Their books of morals chiefly consisted in a minute enumeration of duties. From the law of Moses were deduced six hundred and thirteen precepts, which were divided into two classes, affirmative and negative, two hundred and forty-eight in the former, and three hundred and sixty-five in the latter. It may serve to give the reader some idea of the low state of moral philosophy among the Jews in the middle age, to add that of the two hundred and forty-eight affirmative precepts, only three were considered as obligatory upon women, and that in order to obtain salvation, it was judged sufficient to fulfil any one single law in the hour of death; the observance of the rest being deemed necessary, only to increase the felicity of the future life. What a wretched depravity of sentiment and manners must have prevailed, before such corrupt maxims could have obtained credit! It is impossible to collect from these writings a consistent series of moral doc-

[1] Letter to John Adams.

trine."[2] Enfield, B. 4, chap. 3. It was the reformation of this "wretched depravity" of morals which Jesus undertook.

In extracting the pure principles which he taught, we should have to strip off the artificial vestments in which they have been muffled by priests, who have travestied them into various forms, as instruments of riches and power to themselves. We must dismiss the Platonists and Plotinists, the Stagyrites and Gamalielites, the Eclectics, the Gnostics and Scholastics, their essences and emanations, their Logos and Demiurgos, Æons and Daemons, male and female, with a long train of &c. &c. &c., or, shall I say at once, of nonsense. We must reduce our volume to the simple evangelists, select, even from them, the very words only of Jesus, paring off the amphiboligisms into which they have been led, by forgetting often, or not understanding, what had fallen from him, by giving their own misconceptions as his dicta, and expressing unintelligibly for others what they had not understood themselves. There will be found remaining the most sublime and benevolent code of morals which has ever been offered to man. I have performed this operation for my own use, by cutting verse by verse out of the printed book, and arranging the matter which is evidently his, and which is as easily distinguishable as diamonds in a dunghill. The result is an octavo of forty-six pages, of pure and unsophisticated doctrines, such as were professed and acted on by the *unlettered* Apostles, the Apostolic Fathers, and the Christians of the first century. [*See the line cut on the following page.*] Their Platonising successors, indeed, in after times, in order to legitimate the corruptions which they had incorporated into the doctrines of Jesus, found it necessary to disavow the primitive Christians, who had taken their principles from the mouth of Jesus himself, of his Apostles, and the Fathers contemporary with them. They excommunicated their followers as heretics, branding them with the opprobrious name of Ebionites or Beggars.

[2] In thus inferentially rejecting the ancient Hebrew writings as containing no moral doctrines, Jefferson repeated an eighteenth-century belief that was originally promulgated by Voltaire in his attack on the historic traditions of Christianity. Voltaire gave currency to the cynical remark that the "Jews have never had but one good institution, that of having a horror of virginity."

On this subject John Adams disagreed with his friend Jefferson. Adams wrote: "In spite of Bolingbroke and Voltaire, I will insist that the Hebrews have done more to civilize men than any other nation. If I were an atheist, and believed in blind eternal fate, I should still believe that fate had ordained the Jews to be the most essential instrument for civilizing the nations. If I were an atheist of the other sect, who believe or pretend to believe that all is ordered by chance, I should believe that chance had ordered the Jews to preserve and propagate to all mankind the doctrine of a supreme, intelligent, wise, almighty sovereign of the universe, which I believe to be the great essential principle of all morality, and consequently of all civilization."

# A Table

of the Texts ~~of this Extract~~ from the Evan-
-gelists, employed in this Narrative, and of the order of their arrangement.

page

1. Luke. 2. 1–7. Joseph & Mary go to Bethlehem, where Jesus is born.
21. 39. he is circumcised & named & they return to Nazareth.
40. 42–48. 51. 52. at 12. years of age he accompanies his
2. parents to Jerusalem and returns.
L. 3. 1. 2. Mk. 1. 4 Mt. 3. 4. 5. 6. John baptises in Jordan.
Mt. 3. 13. Jesus is baptised. L. 3. 23. at 30. years of age.
3. J. 2. 12–16. drives the traders out of the temple.
J. 3. 22. Mt. 4. 12. Mk. 6. 17–28. he ~~goes~~ baptises but retires into Galilee on the death of John
4. Mk. 1. 21. 22. he teaches in the Synagogue.
5. Mt. 12. 1–5. 9–12. Mk. 2. 27. Mt. 12. 14. 15. explains the Sabbath.
L. 6. 12–17. call of his disciples.
6. to 15. Mt. 5. 1–12. L. 6. 24. 25. 26. Mt. 5. 13–47. L. 6. 34. 35. 36. Mt. 6. 1.–34. 7. 1.
L. 6. 38. Mt. 7. 3–20. 12. 35. 36. 37. 7. 24–29. the Sermon in the Mount.
Mt. 8. 1. Mk. 6. 6. Mt. 11. 28. 29. 30. exhorts.
16. L. 7. 36–46. a woman anointeth him.
17. Mk. 3. 31–35. L. 12. 1–7. 13–15 precepts
18. L. 12. 16.–21. parable of the rich man.
20 22–48. 54–59. L. 13. 1–5 precepts.
21. L. 13. 6–9. parable of the figtree.
22. L. 11. 37–46. 52. 53. 54. precepts.
23. Mt. 13. 1–9. Mk. 4. 10. Mt. 13. 18–23. parable of the Sower.
4.25 Mk. 4. 21. 22. 23. precepts. Mt. 13. 24–30. 36–52. parable of the Tares
.27 Mk. 4. 26–34. L. 9. 57–62. L. 5. 27–29. Mk. 2. 15–17. precepts
L. 5. 36–39. parable of new wine in old bottles.
28. Mt. 13. 53–57. a prophet hath no honor in his own country.
29. Mt. 9. 36. Mk. 6. 7. Mt. 10. 5. 6. 9–18. 23. 26–31. Mk. 6. 12. 30. mission, instrn, return of apostles
30. 31. J. 7. 1. Mk. 7. 1–5. 14–24. Mt. 18. 1–4. 7–9. 12–17. 21–25. precepts.
33. Mt. 18. 23.–35. parable of the wicked servant.

# NO POLITICS IN THE PULPIT[1]

## March 13, 1815

On one question only I differ from him, and it is that which constitutes the subject of his first discourse, the right of discussing public affairs *in the pulpit.* I add the last words, because I admit the right in *general conversation* and in *writing;* in which last form it has been exercised in the valuable book you have now favored me with.[2]

The mass of human concerns, moral and physical, is so vast, the field of knowledge requisite for man to conduct them to the best advantage is so extensive, that no human being can acquire the whole himself, and much less in that degree necessary for the instruction of others. It has of necessity, then, been distributed into different departments, each of which, singly, may give occupation enough to the whole time and attention of a single individual. Thus we have teachers of Languages, teachers of Mathematics, of Natural Philosophy, of Chemistry, of Medicine, of Law, of History, of Government, &c. Religion, too, is a separate department, and happens to be the only one deemed requisite for all men, however high or low. Collections of men associate together, under the name of congregations, and employ a religious teacher of the particular sect of opinions of which they happen to be, and contribute to make up a stipend as a compensation for the trouble of delivering them, at such periods as they agree on, lessons in the religion they profess. If they want instruction in other sciences or arts, they apply to other instructors; and this is generally the business of early life. But I suppose there is not an instance of a single congregation which has employed their preacher for the mixed purposes of lecturing them *from the pulpit* in Chemistry, in Medicine, in Law, in the science and principles of Government, or in anything but Religion exclusively. Whenever, therefore, preachers, instead of a lesson in religion, put them off with a discourse on the Copernican system, on chemical affinities, on the construction of government, or the characters or conduct of those administering it, it is a breach of contract, depriving their audience of the kind of service for which they are salaried, and giving them, instead of it, what they did not want, or, if wanted, would rather seek from better sources in that particular art or science. In choosing our pastor we look to his religious qualifications, without inquiring into his physical or political dogmas, with which we mean to have nothing to do. I am aware that arguments may be found, which may twist a thread of politics into the cord of religious duties. So may they for every other branch of human art or science. Thus, for example, it is a religious duty to

[1] Letter to Wendover. ("Not sent.")

[2] Alexander McLeod's *Scriptural View of the Character, Causes and Ends of the Present War* (1815). The Rev. McLeod defended Madison's war policy.

obey the laws of our country; the teacher of religion, therefore, must instruct us in those laws, that we may know how to obey them. It is a religious duty to assist our sick neighbors; the preacher must, therefore, teach us medicine, that we may do it understandingly. It is a religious duty to preserve our own health; our religious teacher, then, must tell us what dishes are wholesome, and give us recipes in cookery, that we may learn how to prepare them. And so, ingenuity, by generalizing more and more, may amalgamate all the branches of science into any one of them, and the physician who is paid to visit the sick, may give a sermon instead of medicine, and the merchant to whom money is sent for a hat, may send a handkerchief instead of it. But notwithstanding this possible confusion of all sciences into one, common sense draws lines between them sufficiently distinct for the general purposes of life, and no one is at a loss to understand that a recipe in medicine or cookery, or a demonstration in geometry, is not a lesson in religion. I do not deny that a congregation may, if they please, agree with their preacher that he shall instruct them in Medicine also, or Law, or Politics. Then, lectures in these, from the pulpit, become not only a matter of right, but of duty also. But this must be with the consent of every individual; because the association being voluntary, the mere majority has no right to apply the contributions of the minority to purposes unspecified in the agreement of the congregation. I agree, too, that on all other occasions, the preacher has the right, equally with every other citizen, to express his sentiments, in speaking or writing, on the subjects of Medicine, Law, Politics, &c., his leisure time being his own, and his congregation not obliged to listen to his conversation or to read his writings; and no one would have regretted more than myself, had any scruple as to this right withheld from us the valuable discourses which have led to the expression of an opinion as to the true limits of the right. I feel my portion of indebtment to the reverend author for the distinguished learning, the logic and the eloquence with which he has proved that religion, as well as reason, confirms the soundness of those principles on which our government has been founded and its rights asserted.

These are my views on this question. They are in opposition to those of the highly respected and able preacher, and are, therefore, the more doubtingly offered. Difference of opinion leads to inquiry, and inquiry to truth; and that, I am sure, is the ultimate and sincere object of us both. We both value too much the freedom of opinion sanctioned by our constitution, not to cherish its exercise even where in opposition to ourselves.

Unaccustomed to reserve or mystery in the expression of my opinions, I have opened myself frankly on a question suggested by your letter and present. And although I have not the honor of your acquaintance, this mark of attention, and still more the sentiments of esteem so kindly expressed in your letter, are entitled to a confidence that observations not intended for the public will not be ushered to their notice, as has happened to me sometimes. Tranquillity, at my age, is the balm of life. While I know I am safe in the honor and charity of a McLeod, I do not wish to be cast forth to the Marats, the Dantons, and the Robespierres of the priesthood; I mean the Parishes, the Ogdens, and the Gardiners of Massachusetts.

## PERSONAL CREED[1]

August 6, 1816

I recognize the same motives of goodness in the solicitude you express on the rumor supposed to proceed from a letter of mine to Charles Thomson, on the subject of the Christian religion. It is true that in writing to the translator of the Bible and Testament, that subject was mentioned: but equally so that no adherence to any particular mode of Christianity was there expressed; nor any change of opinions suggested. A change from what? The Priests, indeed, have heretofore thought proper to ascribe to me religious, or rather anti-religious sentiments of their own fabric, but such as soothed their resentments against the Act of Virginia for establishing religious freedom. They wish him to be thought atheist, deeist, or devil, who could advocate freedom from their religious dictations, but I have ever thought religion a concern purely between our God and our consciences for which we were accountable to him, and not to the priests. I never told my own religion nor scrutinized that of another. I never attempted to make a convert, nor wish to change another's creed. I have ever judged of the religion of others by their lives; and by this test, my dear Madam, I have been satisfied yours must be an excellent one, to have produced a life of such exemplary virtue and correctness, for it is in our lives and not from our words, that our religion must be read. By the same test the world must judge me.

But this does not satisfy the priesthood, they must have a positive, a declared assent to all their interested absurdities. My opinion is that there would never have been an infidel, if there had never been a priest. The artificial structure they have built on the purest of all moral systems for the purpose of deriving from it pence and power revolts those who think for themselves and who read in that system only what is really there. These, therefore, they brand with such nicknames as their enmity chooses gratuitously to impute. I have left the world in silence, to judge of causes from their effects: and I am consoled in this course, my dear friend, when I perceive the candor with which I am judged by your justice and discern-

[1] Letter to Mrs. Samuel Harrison Smith.

ment; and that, notwithstanding the slander of the Saints, my fellow citizens have thought me worthy of trust. The imputations of irreligion having spent their force, they think an imputation of change might now be turned to account as a bolster for their duperies. I shall leave them as heretofore to grope on in the dark.

## THE DOCTRINES OF JESUS[1]

June 26, 1822

The doctrines of Jesus are simple, and tend all to the happiness of man.

1. That there is one only God, and he all perfect.
2. That there is a future state of rewards and punishments.
3. That to love God with all thy heart and thy neighbor as thyself, is the sum of religion. These are the great points on which he endeavored to reform the religion of the Jews. But compare with these the demoralizing dogmas of Calvin.

1. That there are three Gods.
2. That good works, or the love of our neighbor, are nothing.
3. That faith is everything, and the more incomprehensible the proposition, the more merit in its faith.
4. That reason in religion is of unlawful use.
5. That God, from the beginning, elected certain individuals to be saved, and certain others to be damned; and that no crimes of the former can damn them; no virtues of the latter save.

Now, which of these is the true and charitable Christian? He who believes and acts on the simple doctrines of Jesus? Or the impious dogmatists, as Athanasius and Calvin? Verily I say these are the false shepherds foretold as to enter not by the door into the sheepfold, but to climb up some other way. They are mere usurpers of the Christian name, teaching a counter-religion made up of the *deliria* of crazy imaginations, as foreign from Christianity as is that of Mahomet. Their blasphemies have driven thinking men into infidelity, who have too hastily rejected the supposed author himself, with the horrors so falsely imputed to him. Had the doctrines of Jesus been preached always as pure as they came from his lips, the whole civilized world would now have been Christian. I rejoice that in this blessed country of free inquiry and belief, which has surrendered its creed and conscience to neither kings nor priests, the genuine doctrine of one only God is reviving, and I trust that there is not a *young man* now living in the United States who will not die an Unitarian.

But much I fear, that when this great truth shall be re-established, its

[1] Letter to Dr. Benjamin Waterhouse.

votaries will fall into the fatal error of fabricating formulas of creed and confessions of faith, the engines which so soon destroyed the religion of Jesus, and made of Christendom a mere Aceldama; that they will give up morals for mysteries, and Jesus for Plato. How much wiser are the Quakers, who, agreeing in the fundamental doctrines of the gospel, schismatize about no mysteries, and, keeping within the pale of common sense, suffer no speculative differences of opinion, any more than of feature, to impair the love of their brethren. Be this the wisdom of Unitarians, this the holy mantle which shall cover within its charitable circumference all who believe in one God, and who love their neighbor!

## FREEDOM OF RELIGION AT THE UNIVERSITY OF VIRGINIA

October 7, 1822

In the same report of the commissioners of 1818 it was stated by them that "in conformity with the principles of constitution, which place all sects of religion on an equal footing, with the jealousies of the different sects in guarding that equality from encroachment or surprise, and with the sentiments of the legislature in freedom of religion, manifested on former occasions, they had not proposed that any professorship of divinity should be established in the University; that provision, however, was made for giving instruction in the Hebrew, Greek and Latin languages, the depositories of the originals, and of the earliest and most respected authorities of the faith of every sect, and for courses of ethical lectures, developing those moral obligations in which all sects agree. That, proceeding thus far, without offence to the constitution, they had left, at this point, to every sect to take into their own hands the office of further instruction in the peculiar tenet of each."

It was not, however, to be understood that instruction in religious opinion and duties was meant to be precluded by the public authorities, as indifferent to the interests of society. On the contrary, the relations which exist between man and his Maker, and the duties resulting from those relations, are the most interesting and important to every human being, and the most incumbent on his study and investigation. The want of instruction in the various creeds of religious faith existing among our citizens presents, therefore, a chasm in a general institution of the useful sciences. But it was thought that this want, and the entrustment to each society of instruction in its own doctrine, were evils of less danger than a permission to the public authorities to dictate modes or principles of religious instruction, or than opportunities furnished them by giving countenance or ascendancy to any one sect over another. A remedy, however, has been suggested of promising aspect, which, while it excludes the public authorities from the domain of religious freedom, will give to the sectarian schools of divinity the full benefit the public provisions made for instruction in the other branches of science. These branches are equally necessary to the divine as to the other professional or civil characters, to enable them to fulfill the duties of their calling with understanding and usefulness. It has, therefore, been in contemplation, and suggested by some pious individuals, who perceive the advantages of associating other studies with those of religion, to establish their religious schools on the confines of the University, so as to give to their students ready and convenient access and attendance on the scientific lectures of the University; and to maintain, by that means, those destined for the religious professions on as high a standing of science, and of personal weight and respectability, as may be obtained by others from the benefits of the University. Such establishments would offer the further and greater advantage of enabling the students of the University to attend religious exercises with the professor of their particular sect, either in the rooms of the building still to be erected, and destined to that purpose under impartial regulations, as proposed in the same report of the commissioners, or in the lecturing room of such professor. To such propositions the Visitors are disposed to lend a willing ear, and would think it their duty to give every encouragement, by assuring to those who might choose such a location for their schools, that the regulations of the University should be so modified and accommodated as to give every facility of access and attendance to their students, with such regulated use also as may be permitted to the other students, of the library which may hereafter be acquired, either by public or private munificence. But always understanding that these schools shall be independent of the University and of each other. Such an arrangement would complete the circle of the useful sciences embraced by this institution, and would fill the chasm now existing, on principles which would leave inviolate the constitutional freedom of religion, the most inalienable and sacred of all human rights, over which the people and authorities of this state, individually and publicly, have ever manifested the most watchful jealousy: and could this jealousy be now alarmed, in the opinion of the legislature, by what is here suggested, the idea will be relinquished on any surmise of disapprobation which they might think proper to express.

*Chapter XX*

# SCIENCE AND INVENTION

## NOTES ON THE ESTABLISHMENT OF A MONEY UNIT, AND OF A COINAGE FOR THE UNITED STATES[1]

April, 1784

In fixing the Unit of Money, these circumstances are of principal importance.

I. That it be of *convenient size* to be applied as a measure to the common money transactions of life.

II. That its parts and multiples be in an *easy proportion* to each other, so as to facilitate the money arithmetic.

III. That the Unit and its parts, or divisions, *be so nearly of the value of some of the known coins,* as that they may be of easy adoption for the people.

The Spanish Dollar seems to fulfil all these conditions.

I. Taking into our view all money transactions, great and small, I question if a common measure of more *convenient size* than the Dollar could be proposed. The value of 100, 1000, 10,000 dollars is well estimated by the mind; so is that of the tenth or the hundredth of a dollar. Few transactions are above or below these limits. The expediency of attending to the size of the money Unit will be evident, to anyone who will consider how inconvenient it would be to a manufacturer or merchant, if, instead of the yard for measuring cloth, either the inch or the mile had been made the Unit of Measure.

II. The most *easy ratio* of multiplication and division, is that by ten. Everyone knows the facility of Decimal Arithmetic. Everyone remembers, that, when learning Money-Arithmetic, he used to be puzzled with adding the farthings, taking out the fours and carrying them on; adding the pence,

[1] This is the famous paper that led to the establishment of the dollar-unit system in the United States. The reader is referred to Jefferson's Autobiography, p. 000, for an explanation of how he came to write it.

taking out the twelves and carrying them on; adding the shillings, taking out the twenties and carrying them on; but when he came to the pounds, where he had only tens to carry forward, it was easy and free from error. The bulk of mankind are school-boys through life. These little perplexities are always great to them. And even mathematical heads feel the relief of an easier, substituted for a more difficult process. Foreigners, too, who trade and travel among us, will find a great facility in understanding our coins and accounts from this ratio of subdivision. Those who have had occasion to convert the livres, sols, and deniers of the French; the gilders, stivers, and frenings of the Dutch; the pounds, shillings, pence, and farthings of these several States, into each other, can judge how much they would have been aided, had their several subdivisions been in a decimal ratio. Certainly, in all cases, where we are free to choose between easy and difficult modes of operation, it is most rational to choose the easy. The Financier, therefore, in his report, well proposes that our Coins should be in decimal proportions to one another. If we adopt the Dollar for our Unit, we should strike four coins, one of gold, two of silver, and one of copper, *viz.:*

1. A golden piece, equal in value to ten dollars:
2. The Unit or Dollar itself, of silver:
3. The tenth of a Dollar, of silver also:
4. The hundredth of a Dollar, of copper.

Compare the arithmetical operations, on the same sum of money expressed in this form, and expressed in the pound sterling and its division.

| Addition. | £ | S. | D. | QRS. | | DOLLARS |
|---|---|---|---|---|---|---|
| | 8 | 13 | 11 | 1-2 | = | 38.65 |
| | 4 | 12 | 8 | 3-4 | = | 20.61 |
| | 13 | 6 | 8 | 1-4 | = | 59.26 |

| Subtraction. | £ | S. | D. | QRS. | | DOLLARS |
|---|---|---|---|---|---|---|
| | 8 | 13 | 11 | 1-2 | = | 38.65 |
| | 4 | 12 | 8 | 3-4 | = | 20.61 |
| | 4 | 1 | 2 | 3-4 | = | 18.04 |

Multiplication by 8.

| £ | S. | D. | QRS. | | DOLLARS |
|---|---|---|---|---|---|
| 8 | 13 | 11 | 1-2 | = | 38.65 |
| 20 | | | | | 8 |
| 173 | | | | | $309.20 |
| 12 | | | | | |
| 2087 | | | | | |
| 4 | | | | | |
| 8350 | | | | | |
| 8 | | | | | |
| 4)66.800 | | | | | |
| 12)16.700 | | | | | |
| 20)1391 | 8 | | | | |
| £69 | 11 | 8 | | | |

Division by 8.

| £ | S. | D. | QRS. | | DOLLARS |
|---|---|---|---|---|---|
| 8 | 13 | 11 | 1-2 | = | 8)38.65 |
| 20 | | | | | 4.83 |
| 173 | | | | | |
| 12 | | | | | |
| 2087 | | | | | |
| 4 | | | | | |
| 8)8350 | | | | | |
| 4)1043 | | | | | |
| 12)260 | 3-4 | | | | |
| 20)21 | 8 | 3-4 | | | |
| £1 | 1 | 8 | 3-4 | | |

A bare inspection of the above operations will evince the labor which is occasioned by subdividing the Unit into 20ths, 240ths, and 960ths, as the English do, and as we have done; and the ease of subdivision in a decimal ratio. The same difference arises in making payment. An Englishman, to pay £8, 13*s*. 11*d*. 1-2 qrs., must find, by calculation, what combination of the coins of his country will pay this sum; but an American, having the same sum to pay, thus expressed $38.65, will know, by inspection only, that three golden pieces, eight units or dollars, six tenths, and five coppers, pay it precisely.

III. The third condition required is, that the Unit, its multiples, and subdivisions, coincide in value with some of the known coins so nearly, that the people may, by a quick reference in the mind, estimate their value. If this be not attended to, they will be very long in adopting the innovation, if ever they adopt it. Let us examine, in this point of view, each of the four coins proposed.

1. The golden piece will be 1-5 more than a half joe, and 1-15 more than a double guinea. It will be readily estimated, then, by reference to either of them; but more readily and accurately as equal to ten dollars.

2. The Unit, or Dollar, is a known coin, and the most familiar of all, to the minds of the people. It is already adopted from South to North; has identified our currency, and therefore happily offers itself as a Unit already introduced. Our public debt, our requisitions, and their appointments, have given it actual and long possession of the place of Unit. The course of our commerce, too, will bring us more of this than of any other foreign coin, and therefore renders it more worthy of attention. I know of no Unit which can be proposed in competition with the Dollar, but the Pound. But what is the Pound? 1547 grains of fine silver in Georgia; 1289 grains in Virginia, Connecticut, Rhode Island, Massachusetts, and New Hampshire; 1031 1-4 grains in Maryland, Delaware, Pennsylvania, and New Jersey; 966 3-4 grains in North Carolina and New York. Which of these shall we adopt? To which State give that pre-eminence of which all are so jealous? And on which impose the difficulties of a new estimate of their corn, their cattle, and other commodities? Or shall we hang the pound sterling, as a common badge, about all their necks? This contains 1718 3-4 grains of pure silver. It is difficult to familiarize a new coin to the people; it is more difficult to familiarize them to a new coin with an old name. Happily, the dollar is familiar to them all, and is already as much referred to for a measure of value, as their respective provincial pounds.

3. The tenth will be precisely the Spanish bit, or half pistereen. This is a coin perfectly familiar to us all. When we shall make a new coin, then, equal in value to this, it will be of ready estimate with the people.

4. The hundredth, or copper, will differ little from the copper of the four

Eastern States, which is 1-108 of a dollar; still less from the penny of New York and North Carolina, which is 1-96 of a dollar; and somewhat more from the penny or copper of Jersey, Pennsylvania, Delaware, and Maryland, which is 1-90 of a dollar. It will be about the medium between the old and the new coppers of these States, and will therefore soon be substituted for them both. In Virginia, coppers have never been in use. It will be as easy, therefore, to introduce them there of one value as of another. The copper coin proposed will be nearly equal to three-fourths of their penny, which is the same with the penny lawful of the Eastern States.

A great deal of small change is useful in a State, and tends to reduce the price of small articles. Perhaps it would not be amiss to coin three more pieces of silver, one of the value of five-tenths, or half a dollar, one of the value of two-tenths, which would be equal to the Spanish pistereen, and one of the value of five coppers, which would be equal to the Spanish half-bit. We should then have five silver coins, *viz.*:

1. The Unit or Dollar:
2. The half dollar or five-tenths:
3. The double tenth, equal to 2, or one-fifth of a dollar, or to the pistereen:
4. The tenth, equal to a Spanish bit:
5. The five copper piece, equal to .5, or one-twentieth of a dollar, or the half-bit.

The plan reported by the Financier is worthy of his sound judgment. It admits, however, of objection, in the size of the Unit. He proposes that this shall be the 1440th part of a dollar: so that it will require 1440 of his units to make the one before proposed. He was led to adopt this by a mathematical attention to our old currencies, all of which this Unit will measure without leaving a fraction. But as our object is to get rid of those currencies, the advantage derived from this coincidence will soon be past, whereas the inconveniences of this Unit will forever remain, if they do not altogether prevent its introduction. It is defective in two of the three requisites of a Money Unit. 1. It is inconvenient in its application to the ordinary money transactions. 10.000 dollars will require eight figures to express them, to wit 14,400,000 units. A horse or bullock of eighty dollars value, will require a notation of six figures, to wit, 115,200 units. As a money of account, this will be laborious, even when facilitated by the aid of decimal arithmetic: as a common measure of the value of property, it will be too minute to be comprehended by the people. The French are subjected to very laborious calculations, the Livre being their ordinary money of account, and this but between 1-5th and 1-6th of a dollar; but what will be our labors, should our money of account be 1-1440th of a dollar? 2. It is neither equal, nor near to any of the known coins in value.

If we determine that a Dollar shall be our Unit, we must then say with precision what a Dollar is. This coin, struck at different times, of different weights and fineness, is of different values. Sir Isaac Newton's assay and representation to the Lords of the Treasury, in 1717, of those which he examined, make their values as follows:

| | DWTS. GRS. | | |
|---|---|---|---|
| The Seville piece of eight | 17—12 | containing | 387 grains of pure silver |
| The Mexico piece of eight | 17—10 5-9 | " | 385 1-2 |
| The Pillar piece of eight | 17—9 | " | 385 3-4 |
| The new Seville piece of eight | 14— | " | 308 7-10 |

The Financier states the old Dollar as containing 376 grains of fine silver, and the new 365 grains. If the Dollars circulating among us be of every date equally, we should examine the quantity of pure metal in each, and from them form an average for our Unit. This is a work proper to be committed to mathematicians as well as merchants, and which should be decided on actual and accurate experiment.

The quantum of alloy is also to be decided. Some is necessary, to prevent the coin from wearing too fast; too much, fills our pockets with copper, instead of silver. The silver coin assayed by Sir Isaac Newton, varied from 1 1-2 to 76 pennyweights alloy, in the pound troy of mixed metal. The British standard has 18 dwt.; the Spanish coins assayed by Sir Isaac Newton, have from 18 to 19 1-2 dwt.; the new French crown has in fact 19 1-2, though by edict, it should have 20 dwt., that is 1-12.

The taste of our countrymen will require, that their furniture plate should be as good as the British standard. Taste cannot be controlled by law. Let it then give the law, in a point which is indifferent to a certain degree. Let the Legislature fix the alloy of furniture plate at 18 dwt., the British standard, and Congress that of their coin at one ounce in the pound, the French standard. This proportion has been found convenient for the alloy of gold coin, and it will simplify the system of our mint to alloy both metals in the same degree. The coin, too, being the least pure, will be the less easily melted into plate. These reasons are light, indeed, and, of course, will only weigh, if no heavier ones can be opposed to them.

The proportion between the values of gold and silver is a mercantile problem altogether. It would be inaccurate to fix it by the popular exchanges of a half Joe for eight dollars, a Louis for four French crowns, or five Louis for twenty-three dollars. The first of these, would be to adopt the Spanish proportion between gold and silver; the second, the French; the third, a mere popular barter, wherein convenience is consulted more than accuracy. The legal proportion in Spain is 16 for 1; in England, 15 1-2 for 1; in France, 15 for 1. The Spaniards and English are found, in experience, to retain an over-proportion of gold coins, and to lose their silver. The French have a greater proportion of silver. The difference at market has been on the decrease. The Financier states it at present, as at 14 1-2 for one. Just principles will lead us to disregard legal proportions altogether; to enquire into the market price of gold, in the several countries with which we shall principally be connected in commerce, and to take an average from them. Perhaps we might, with safety, lean to a proportion somewhat above par for gold, considering our neighborhood, and commerce with the sources of the coins, and the tendency which the high price of gold in Spain has, to draw thither all that of their mines, leaving silver principally for our and other markets. It is not impossible that 15 for 1, may be found an eligible proportion. I state it, however, as a conjecture only.

As to the alloy for gold coin, the British is an ounce in the pound; the French, Spanish, and Portuguese differ from that, only from a quarter of a grain, to a grain and a half. I should, therefore, prefer the British, merely because its fraction stands in a more simple form, and facilitates the calculations into which it enters.

Should the Unit be fixed at 365 grains of pure silver, gold at 15 for 1, and the alloy of both be one-twelfth, the weight of the coins will be as follows:

| | GRAINS | | GRAINS | | DWT. GRAINS |
|---|---|---|---|---|---|
| The Golden piece containing | 242⅓ | of pure metal, | 22.12 | of alloy, will weigh | 11—1.45 |
| The Unit or Dollar | 365 | " | 33.18 | " | 16—14.18 |
| The half dollar, or five tenths | 182½ | " | 16.59 | " | 8— 7.09 |
| The fifth, or Pistereen | 73 | " | 6.63 | " | 3— 7.63 |
| The tenth, or Bit | 36½ | " | 3.318 | " | 1—15.818 |
| The twentieth, or half Bit | 18¼ | " | 1.659 | " | 19.9 |

The quantity of fine silver which shall constitute the Unit, being settled, and the proportion of the value of gold to that of silver; a table should be formed from the assay before suggested, classing the several foreign coins according to their fineness, declaring the worth of a pennyweight or grain in each class, and that they shall be lawful tenders at those rates, if not clipped or otherwise diminished; and, where diminished, offering their value for them at the mint, deducting the expense of re-coinage. Here the Legislatures should co-operate with Congress, in providing that no money be received or paid at their treasuries, or by any of their officers, or any bank, but on actual weight; in making it criminal, in a high degree, to diminish their own coins, and, in some smaller degree, to offer them in payment when diminished.

That this subject may be properly prepared, and in readiness for Congress to take up at their meeting in November, something must now be done. The present session drawing to a close, they probably would not choose to enter far into this undertaking themselves. The Committee of the States, however, during the recess, will have time to digest it thoroughly, if Congress will fix some general principles for their government. Suppose they be instructed,

To appoint proper persons to assay and examine, with the utmost accuracy practicable, the Spanish milled dollars of different dates, in circulation with us.

To assay and examine, in like manner, the fineness of all the other coins which may be found in circulation within these States.

To report to the Committee the result of these assays, by them to be laid before Congress.

To appoint, also, proper persons to enquire what are the proportions between the values of fine gold, and fine silver, at the markets of the several countries with which we are, or probably may be, connected in commerce; and what would be a proper proportion here, having regard to the average of their values at those markets, and to other circumstances, and to report the same to the Committee, by them to be laid before Congress.

To prepare an Ordinance for establishing the Unit of Money within these States; for subdividing it; and for striking coins of gold, silver, and copper, on the following principles:

That the Money Unit of these States shall be equal in value to a Spanish milled dollar containing so much fine silver as the assay, before directed, shall show to be contained, on an average, in dollars of the several dates in circulation with us.

That this Unit shall be divided into tenths and hundredths; that there shall be a coin of silver of the value of a Unit; one other of the same metal, of the value of one-tenth of a Unit; one other of copper, of the value of the hundredth of a Unit.

That there shall be a coin of gold of the value of ten Units, according to the report before directed, and the judgment of the Committee thereon.

That the alloy of the said coins of gold and silver, shall be equal in weight to one-eleventh part of the fine metal.

That there be proper devices for these coins.

That measures be proposed for preventing their diminution, and also their currency, and that of any others, when diminished.

That the several foreign coins be described and classed in the said Ordinance, the fineness of each class stated, and its value by weight estimated in Units and decimal parts of Units.

And that the said draught of an Ordinance be reported to Congress at their next meeting, for their consideration and determination.

The preceding notes having been submitted to the consideration of the Financier, he favored me with his opinion and observations on them, which render necessary the following supplementary explanations.

I observed, in the preceding notes, that the true proportion of value between gold and silver was a mercantile problem altogether, and that, perhaps, fifteen for one, might be found an eligible proportion. The Financier is so good as to inform me, that this would be higher than the market would justify. Confident of his better information on this subject, I recede from that idea.[2]

He also informs me, that the several coins, in circulation among us, have been already assayed with accuracy, and the result published in a work on that subject. The assay of Sir Isaac Newton had superseded, in my mind, the necessity of this operation as to the older coins, which were the subject of his examination. This later work, with equal reason, may be considered as saving the same trouble as to the latter coins.

So far, then, I accede to the opinions of the Financier. On the other hand, he seems to concur with me, in thinking his smallest fractional division too minute for a Unit, and, therefore, proposes to transfer that denomination to his largest silver coin, containing 1000 of the units first proposed, and worth about 4s. 2d. lawful, or 25-36 of a Dollar. The only question then remaining between us is, whether the Dollar, or this coin, be best for the Unit. We both agree that *the ease of adoption with the people,* is the thing to be aimed at.

1. As to the Dollar, events have overtaken and superseded the question. It is no longer a doubt whether the people can adopt it with ease; they have adopted it, and will have to be turned out of that, into another tract of calculation, if another Unit be assumed. They have now two Units, which they use with equal facility, *viz.,* the Pound of their respective State, and the Dollar. The first of these is peculiar to each State: the second, happily, common to all. In each State, the people have an easy rule of converting the pound of their State into dollars, or dollars into pounds; and this is enough for them, without knowing how this may be done in every State of the Union. Such of them as live near enough the borders of their State to have dealings with their neighbors, learn also the rule of their neighbors: thus, in Virginia and the Eastern States, where the dollar is 6s. or 3-10 of a

[2] In a newspaper, which frequently gives good details in political economy, I find, under the Hamburgh head, that the present market price of Gold and Silver is, in England, 15.5 for 1: in Russia, 15: in Holland, 14.75: in Savoy, 14.6: in France, 14.42: in Spain, 14.3: in Germany, 14.155: the average of which is 14.675 or 14 5-8. I would still incline to give a little more than the market price for gold, because of its superior convenience in transportation.—T. J.

pound, to turn pounds into dollars, they multiply by 10 and divide by 3. To turn dollars into pounds, they multiply by 3, and divide by 10. Those in Virginia who live near to Carolina, where the dollar is 8s. or 4-10 of a pound, learn the operation of that State, which is a multiplication by 4, and division by 10, *et e converso*. Those who live near Maryland, where the dollar is 7s. 6d. or 3-8 of a pound, multiply by 3, and divide by 8, *et e converso*. All these operations are easy, and have been found, by experience, not too much for the arithmetic of the people, when they have occasion to convert their old Unit into dollars, or the reverse.

2. As to the Unit of the Financier; in the States where the dollars is 3-10 of a pound, this Unit will be 5-24. Its conversion into the pound then, will be by a multiplication of 5, and a division by 24. In the States where the dollar is 3-8 of a pound, this Unit will be 25-96 of a pound, and the operation must be to multiply by 25, and divide by 96, *et e converso*. Where the dollar is 4-10 of a pound, this Unit will be 5-18. The simplicity of the fraction, and of course the facility of conversion and reconversion, is therefore against this Unit, and in favor of the dollar, in every instance. The only advantage it has over the dollar, is, that it will in every case express our farthing without a remainder; whereas, though the dollar and its decimals will do this in many cases, it will not in all. But, even in these, by extending your notation one figure further, to wit, to thousands, you approximate to perfect accuracy within less than the two-thousandth part of a dollar; an atom in money which everyone would neglect. Against this single inconvenience, the other advantages of the dollar are more than sufficient to preponderate. This Unit will present to the people a new coin, and whether they endeavor to estimate its value by comparing it with a Pound, or with a Dollar, the Units they now possess, they will find the fraction very compound, and of course less accommodated to their comprehension and habits than the dollar. Indeed the probability is, that they could never be led to compute in it generally.

The Financier supposes that the 1-100 part of a dollar is not sufficiently small, where the poor are purchasers or vendors. If it is not, make a smaller coin. But I suspect that it is small enough. Let us examine facts, in countries where we are acquainted with them. In Virginia, where our towns are few, small, and of course their demand for necessaries very limited, we have never yet been able to introduce a copper coin at all. The smallest coin which anybody will receive there, is the half-bit, or 1-20 of a dollar. In those States where the towns are larger and more populous, a more habitual barter of small wants, has called for a copper coin of 1-90, 1-96, or 1-108 of a dollar. In England, where the towns are many and populous, and where ages of experience have matured the conveniences of intercourse, they have found that some wants may be supplied for a farthing, or 1-208 of a dollar, and they have accommodated a coin to this want. This business is evidently progressive. In Virginia, we are far behind. In some other States, they are further advanced, to wit, to the appreciation of 1-90, 1-96, 1-108 of a dollar. To this most advanced state, then, I accommodated my smallest coin in the decimal arrangement, as *a money of payment,* corresponding with the *money of account.* I have no doubt the time will come when a smaller coin will be called for. When that comes, let it be made. It will probably be the half of the copper I suppose, that is to say, 5-1000 or .005 of a dollar, this being very nearly the farthing of England. But it will be time enough to make it, when the people shall be ready to receive it.

My proposition then, is, that our notation of money shall be decimal, descending *ad libitum* of the person noting; that the Unit of this notation shall be a Dollar; that coins shall be accommodated to it from ten dollars to the hundreth of a dollar; and that, to set this on foot, the resolutions be adopted which were proposed in the notes, only substituting *an enquiry into the fineness of the coins* in lieu of *an assay of them.*

## MUSICAL VIBRATION[1]

January 3, 1786

Turning to your Encyclopedie, Arts et Metiers, tome 3, part 1, page 393, you will find mentioned an instrument, invented by a Monsieur Renaudin, for determining the true time of the musical movements, largo, adagoio, &c. I went to see it. He showed me his first invention; the price of the machine was twenty-five guineas; then his second, which he had been able to make for about half that sum. Both of these had a mainspring and a balance wheel, for their mover and regulator. The strokes were made by a small hammer. He then showed me his last, which is moved by a weight and regulated by a pendulum, and which cost only two guineas and a half. It presents, in front, a dial-plate like that of a clock, on which are arranged, in a circle, the words largo, adagio, andante, allegro, presto. The circle is moreover divided into fifty-two equal degrees. Largo is at 1, adagio at 11, andante at 22, allegro at 36, and presto at 46. Turning the index to any one of these, the pendulum (which is a string, with a ball hanging to it) shortens or lengthens, so that one of its vibrations gives you a crotchet for that movement. This instrument has been examined by the academy of music here, who are so well satisfied of its utility, that they have ordered all music which shall be printed here, in future, to have the movements numbered in correspondence with this plexi-chronometer. I need not tell you that the numbers between two movements, as between 22 and 36, give

[1] Letter to Francis Hopkinson, Paris.

the quicker or slower degrees of the movements, such as the quick andante, or moderate allegro. The instrument is useful, but still it may be greatly simplified. I got him to make me one, and having fixed a pendulum vibrating seconds, I tried by that the vibrations of his pendulum, according to the several movements.

I find the pendulum regulated to

| | | | |
|---|---|---|---|
| Largo | vibrates | 52 | times in a minute. |
| Adagio | | 60 | |
| Andante | | 70 | |
| Allegro | | 95 | |
| Presto | | 135 | |

Everyone, therefore, may make a chronometer adapted to his instrument.

For a harpsichord, the following occurs to me.

In the wall of your chamber, over the instrument, drive five little brads, as 1, 2, 3, 4, 5, in the following manner. Take a string with a bob to it, of such length, as that hung on No. 1, it shall vibrate fifty-two times in a minute. Then proceed by trial to drive No. 2, at such a distance, that drawing the loop of the string to that, the part remaining between 1 and the bob, shall vibrate sixty times in a minute. Fix the third for seventy vibrations, &c.; the cord always hanging over No. 1, as the centre of vibration. A person, playing on the violin, may fix this on his music stand. A pendulum thrown into vibration, will continue in motion long enough to give you the time of your piece. I have been thus particular, on the supposition that you would fix one of these simple things for yourself.

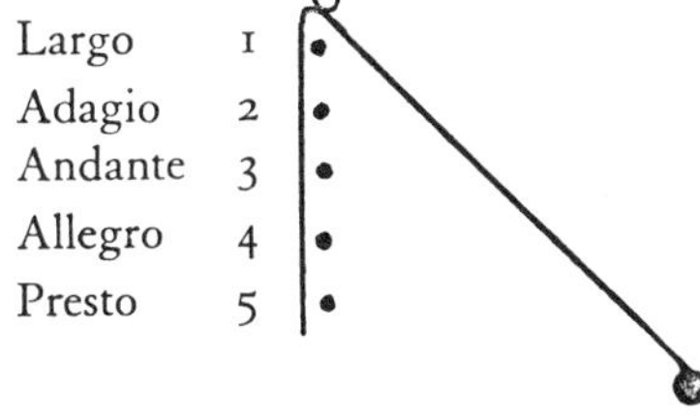


## PEDOMETER[1]

May 3, 1788

I send your pedometer. To the loop at the bottom of it, you must sew a tape, and at the other end of the tape, a small hook (such as we use under the name of hooks and eyes) cut a little hole in the bottom of your left watch pocket, pass the hook and tape through it, and down between the breeches and drawers, and fix the hook on the edge of your knee band, an inch from the knee buckle; then hook the instrument itself by its swivel hook, on the upper edge of the watch pocket. Your tape being well adjusted in length, your double steps will be exactly counted by the instrument, the

[1] Letter to James Madison.

shortest hand pointing out the thousands, the flat hand the hundreds, and the long hand the tens and units. Never turn the hands backward; indeed, it is best not to set them to any given place, but to note the number they stand at when you begin to walk. The adjusting the tape to its exact length is a critical business, and will cost you many trials. But once done, it is done for ever. The best way is, to have a small buckle fixed on the middle of the tape, by which you can take it up, and let it out at pleasure. When you choose it should cease to count, unhook it from the top of the watch pocket, and let it fall down on the bottom of the pocket.

## REPORT ON THE METHODS FOR OBTAINING FRESH WATER FROM SALT

*c.* 1790

The Secretary of State, to whom was referred by the House of Representatives of the United States, the petition of Jacob Isaacs of Newport in Rhode Island, has examined into the truth and importance of the allegations therein set forth, and makes thereon the following report:

The petitioner sets forth, that by various experiments, with considerable labor and expense, he has discovered a method of converting salt-water into fresh, in the proportion of 8 parts out of 10, by a process so simple that it may be performed on board of vessels at sea by the common iron caboose, with small alterations, by the same fire, and in the same time, which is used for cooking the ship's provisions, and offers to convey to the government of the United States a faithful account of his art or secret, to be used by, or within the United States, on their giving to him a reward suitable to the importance of the discovery, and in the opinion of government, adequate to his expenses and the time he has devoted to the bringing it into effect.

In order to ascertain the merit of the petitioner's discovery, it becomes necessary to examine the advances already made in the art of converting salt-water into fresh.

Lord Bacon, to whom the world is indebted for the first germs of so many branches of science, had observed, that with a heat sufficient for distillation, salt will not rise in vapor, and that salt-water distilled is fresh; and it would seem, that all mankind might have observed that the earth is supplied with fresh water chiefly by exhalation from the sea, which is, in fact, an insensible distillation effected by the heat of the sun; yet this, although the most obvious, was not the first idea in the essays for converting salt-water into fresh; filtration was tried in vain, and congelation could be resorted to only in the coldest regions and seasons. In all the earlier trials by distillation, some mixture was thought necessary to aid the operation by a partial precipitation of the salt, and other foreign matters contained in sea-water. Of this kind, were the methods of Sir Richard Hawkins in the sixteenth century, of Glauber, Hauton, and Lister, in the seventeenth, and of Hales, Appleby, Butler, Chapman, Hoffman, and Dore, in the eighteenth; nor was there anything in these methods worthy noting on the present occasion, except the very simple still contrived extempore by Captain Chapman, and made from such materials as are to be found on board every ship, great or small; this was a common pot, with a wooded lid of the usual form; in the centre of which a hole was bored to receive perpendicularly, a short wooden tube made with an inch-and-a-half auger, which perpendicular tube received at its top, and at an acute angle, another tube of wood also, which descended until it joined a third of pewter made by rolling up a dish and passing it obliquely through a cask of cold water; with this simple machine he obtained two quarts of fresh water an hour, and observed that the expense of fuel would be very trifling, if the still was contrived to stand on the fire along with the ship's boiler.

In 1762, Doctor Lind, proposing to make experiment of several different mixtures, first distilled rain-water, which he supposed would be the purest, and then sea-water, without any mixture, which he expected would be the least pure, in order to arrange between these two supposed extremes, the degree of merit of the several ingredients he meant to try; "to his great surprise," as he confesses, the sea-water distilled without any mixture, was as pure as the rain-water; he pursued the discovery and established the fact, that a pure and potable fresh water may be obtained from salt-water by simple distillation, without the aid of any mixture for fining or precipitating its foreign contents. In 1767, he proposed an extempore still, which, in fact, was Chapman's, only substituting a gun-barrel instead of Chapman's pewter tube, and the hand-pump of the ship to be cut in two obliquely and joined again at an acute angle, instead of Chapman's wooden tubes bored expressly; or instead of the wooden lid and upright tube, he proposed a tea-kettle (without its lid or handle) to be turned bottom upwards over the mouth of the pot by way of still-head, and a wooden tube leading from the spout to a gun-barrel passing through a cask of water, the whole luted with equal parts of chalk and meal moistened with salt-water. With this apparatus of a pot, tea-kettle, and gun-barrel, the Dolphin, a twenty-gun ship, in her voyage around the world in 1768, from 56 gallons of sea-water and with 9 lbs. of wood and 69 lbs. of pit-coal made 42 gallons of good fresh water, at the rate of 8 gallons an hour. The Dorsetshire, in her passage from Gibraltar to Mahon in 1769, made 19 quarts of pure water in four hours with 10 lbs. of wood, and the Slambal in 1773, between

Bombay and Bengal, with the hand-pump, gun-barrel, and a pot of 6 gallons of sea-water, made ten quarts of fresh water in three hours.

In 1771, Dr. Irvin putting together Lind's idea of distilling without a mixture, Chapman's still, and Dr. Franklin's method of cooling by evaporation, obtained a premium of five thousand pounds from the British parliament. He wet his tube constantly with a mop instead of passing it through a cask of water; he enlarged its bore also, in order to give a free passage to the vapor, and thereby increase its quantity by lessening the resistance or pressure on the evaporating surface. This last improvement was his own; it doubtless contributed to the success of his process; and we may suppose the enlargement of the tube to be useful to that point at which the central parts of the vapor passing through it would begin to escape condensation. Lord Mulgrave used his method in his voyage towards the north pole in 1773, making from 34 to 40 gallons of fresh water a day, without any great addition of fuel, as he says.

M. de Bougainville, in his voyage round the world, used very successfully a still which had been contrived in 1763 by Poyssonier to guard against the water being thrown over from the boiler into the pipe, by the agitation of the ship. In this, one singularity was, that the furnace or fire-box was in the middle of the boiler, so that the water surrounded it in contact. This still, however, was expensive, and occupied much room.

Such was the advances already made in the art of obtaining fresh from salt-water, when Mr. Isaacs, the petitioner, suggested his discovery. As the merit of this could be ascertained by experiment only, the Secretary of State asked the favor of Mr. Rittenhouse, President of the American Philosophical Society, of Dr. Wistar, professor of chemistry in the college at Philadelphia, and Dr. Hutchinson, professor of chemistry in the University of Pennsylvania, to be present at the experiments. Mr. Isaacs fixed the pot, a small caboose, with a tin cap and straight tube of tin passing obliquely through a cask of cold water; he made use of a mixture, the composition of which he did not explain, and from 24 pints of sea-water, taken up about three miles out of the Capes of Delaware, at flood-tide, he distilled 22 pints of fresh water in four hours with 20 lbs. of seasoned pine, which was a little wetted by having lain in the rain.

In a second experiment of the 21st of March, performed in a furnace, and five-gallon still at the college, from 32 pints of sea-water he drew 31 pints of fresh water in 7 hours and 24 minutes, with 51 lbs. of hickory, which had been cut about six months. In order to decide whether Mr. Isaacs' mixture contributed in any and what degree to the success of the operation, it was thought proper to repeat his experiment under the same circumstances exactly, except the omission of the mixture. Accordingly, on the next day, the same quantity of sea-water was put into the same still, the same furnace was used, and fuel from the same parcel; it yielded, as his had done, 31 pints fresh water in 11 minutes more of time, and with 10 lbs. less of wood.

On the 24th of March, Mr. Isaacs performed a third experiment. For this, a common iron pot of three and a half gallons was fixed in brick work, and the flue from the hearth wound once around this pot spirally, and then passed off up a chimney.

The cap was of tin, and a straight tin tube of about two inches diameter passing obliquely through a barrel of water, served instead of a worm. From sixteen pints of sea-water he drew off fifteen pints of fresh water, in two hours fifty-five minutes, with 3 lbs. of dry hickory and 8 lbs. of seasoned pine. This experiment was also repeated the next day, with the same apparatus, and fuel from the same parcel; but without the mixture, sixteen pints of sea-water yielded in like manner fifteen pints of fresh in one minute more of time, and with ½ lb. less of wood. On the whole, it was evident that Mr. Isaacs' mixture produced no advantage either in the process or result of the distillation.

The distilled water in all these instances, was found on experiment to be as pure as the best pump water of the city; its taste, indeed, was not as agreeable, but it was not such as to produce any disgust. In fact, we drink, in common life, in many places, and under many circumstances, and almost always at sea, a worse tasted and probably a less wholesome water.

The obtaining fresh from salt-water was for ages considered as an important desideratum for the use of navigators. The process for doing this by simple distillation is so efficacious, the erecting an extempore still with such utensils as are found on board of every ship, is so practicable, as to authorize the assertion that this desideratum is satisfied to a very useful degree. But though this has been done for upwards of thirty years, though its reality has been established by the actual experience of several vessels which have had recourse to it, yet neither the fact nor the process is known to the mass of seamen, to whom it would be the most useful, and for whom it was principally wanted. The Secretary of State is therefore of opinion that since the subject has now been brought under observation, it should be made the occasion of disseminating its knowledge generally and effectually among the seafaring citizens of the United States. The following is one of the many methods which might be proposed for doing this: Let the clearance for every vessel sailing from the ports of the United States be printed on a paper, in the back whereof shall be a printed account of the essays which have been made for obtaining fresh from salt-water, mentioning shortly those which have been unsuccessful, and more fully those which have succeeded, describing the methods which have been found to answer for constructing extempore stills of such implements as are generally on board of every vessel, with a recommendation in all cases where they shall have occasion to resort to this expedient for obtaining water, to publish the result of their trial in some gazette on their return to the United States, or to communicate it for publication to the office of the Secretary of State, in order that others may, by their success, be encouraged to make similar trials, and be benefited by any improvements or new ideas which may occur to them in practice.

## NOTES ON WEIGHTS AND MEASURES[1]

June 14, 1790

I enclosed you the day before yesterday a rough draught of the report I had prepared on the subject of weights and measures. I have this morning received from Mr. Short a proposition made by the Bishop of Autun to the National Assembly of France, on the same subject, which I enclose you, and will beg the favor of you to return it by post after you shall have perused it. He mentions that the latitude of 45°, as being a middle term between the equator and pole, had been proposed as the general standard for measures, and he makes the proposition anew, and desires it may be made to England. As this degree of latitude is our northern boundary, as it may form a link between us and Europe, and as the degree which shall otherwise give the standard is not otherwise very material, I have thought of proposing it in my report instead of the 38th degree. I have in consequence gone over my calculations again upon the ground of a pendulum of 36.–8.428. (Sir Isaac Newton's calculation for 45°) 39.14912 inches giving a rod of 58.72368 inches, and reformed the tables (last page of the report), of which reformation I send you a copy. The alterations in the body of the work may be easily made from this. The Bishop says the pendulum has been calculated for 45° to be 36.–8.52 this 1-10 of a line less than Sir Isaac Newton's, and the Bishop accordingly adds, that there may be in this calculation an error of 1-10 of a line.

I had taken no notice of the precaution of making the experiment of the pendulum on the sea shore, because the highest mountain in the United States would not add 1-5000 part to the length of the earth's radius, nor 1-128 of an inch to the length of the pendulum; the highest part of the Andes indeed might add about 1-1000 to the earth's radius, and 1-25 of an inch to the pendulum; as it has been thought worth mention, I will insert it also.

Your letter of April 20th, was duly attended to by me, but I fancy the successor had been decided on before it was known to the public that there would be a vacancy.

[1] Letter to David Rittenhouse.

I am, with great esteem, my dear Sir, your sincere friend and humble servant.

DEAR SIR:[2] I enclosed you on the 17th the alterations I had made in my report in consequence of the Bishop of Autun's proposition, which had come to my hands two days before. On the 18th, I received from Mr. Cutter in London a packet of newspapers, among which were the two enclosed, containing the speech in Parliament of Sir John Riggs Miller, on the subject of weights and measures. I observe, he states the estimate of 39.2 I. for the length of the pendulum as confessedly erroneous. I had adopted it from memory only, and before I had been able to get a single book of any kind, in the first part of the report, wherein I endeavor to ascertain and fix invariably the system of measures and weights now in use with us. But before I proceeded to the second part, proposing a thorough reform, and reducing the whole to the decimal ratio, I had been able to procure here a copy of the Principia, and so to recur to the fountain head for Sir I. Newton's calculations, and then added the note, which you will find page 3 of the report, doubting what could have been the foundation of the common imputation of the estimate of 39.2 to Sir I. Newton, and stating the grounds of that of 39.1682 for the latitude of 51° 31′ of 39.1285 for 38°, which I had at first adopted, and 39.14912 for 45°, which I took on receiving the Bishop of Autun's proposition. I have now thought I might venture to take for granted, that the estimate of 39.2 is as erroneous as I had supposed it, and therefore to expunge it from the first branch of the report, and substitute in its stead 39.1682; and to change a passage under the head of "Measures of length" into the following form:

"They furnish no means to persons at a distance of knowing what this standard is. This, however, is supplied by the evidence of the second pendulum, which, according to the authority before quoted, being 39.1682 I. for the latitude of London, and consequently the second rod for the same latitude being 58.7523, we are first to find by actual trial the rod for 45°, and to add to that 287/10,000 of an inch, or rather 3/10 of a line (which in practice will endanger less error than an attempt at so minute a fraction as 10,000th parts of an inch), this will give us the true measure of 58¾ English inches. Or, to shorten the operation, and yet obtain the result we seek, let the standard rod of 45° be divided into 587⅕ equal parts, and let each of these parts be declared a line, and ten lines an inch," &c.

I propose also to strike out the note (page 3) before mentioned, and to substitute the following in its place:

"The length of the pendulum has been differently estimated by different

[2] Letter to David Rittenhouse, June 20, 1790.

persons. Knowing no reason to respect any of them more than Sir Isaac Newton for skill, care, or candor, I had adopted his estimate of 39.149 I. for our northern limit of 45°, before I saw the different propositions of the Bishop of Autun, and Sir John Riggs Miller. The first of these gentlemen quotes Mairan's calculation for 48° 50′, the latitude of Paris, to wit, 504 : 257 : : 72 : to a 4th proportional, which will be 36.71428 = 39.1923 inches. The difference between the pendulum for 48° 50′ and 45°, as calculated by Sir I. Newton, is .0112 I : so that the pendulum for 45° would be estimated, according to the Bishop of Autun, at 39.1923 — .0112 = 39.1811. Sir John Riggs Miller proposes 39.126, being Graham's determination for 51° 31′, the latitude of London. The difference between the pendulum for 51° 31′, and 45° by Sir I. Newton, is .019 I., so that the pendulum for 45° should be estimated according to Sir J. R. Miller, at 39.126 — .019 = 39.107 I. Now, dividing our respect between these two results, by taking their mean, to wit, $\frac{39.181 + 39.107}{2} = 39.144$, we find ourselves almost exactly with Sir I. Newton, whose estimate of 39.149 we had already adopted."

I propose also to reform a passage under the head of Weights, in the first branch of the report, to stand thus:

"Let it then be established, that an ounce is the weight of a cube of rain water of one-tenth of a foot, *or rather, that it is the thousandth part of the weight of a cubic foot of rain water* weighed in the standard temperature," &c.

All which I submit to your judgment, and I will ask you particularly to examine the numbers .0112 and .019, as I have no help here to find them otherwise than by approximation. I have wished much, but in vain, Emerson's and Ferguson's books here. In short, I never was cut off from the resources of my own books and papers at so unlucky a moment. There is a Count Andriani, of Milan, here, who says there is a work on the subject of weights and measures published by Trisi of Milan. Perhaps you may have it at Philadelphia, and be able to send it to me. Were it not for my confidence in your assistance, I should not have ventured to take up this business till I received my books.

I am, my dear Sir, with great and sincere esteem, your friend and servant.

# PLAN FOR ESTABLISHING UNIFORMITY IN THE COINAGE, WEIGHTS, AND MEASURES OF THE UNITED STATES

COMMUNICATED TO THE HOUSE OF REPRESENTATIVES, JULY 13, 1790

July 4, 1790 [1]

SIR: In obedience to the order of the House of Representatives of January 15th, I have now the honor to enclose you a report on the subject of measures, weights, and coins. The length of time which intervened between the date of the order and my arrival in this city, prevented my receiving it till the 15th of April; and an illness which followed soon after added, unavoidably, some weeks to the delay; so that it was not till about the 20th May that I was able to finish the report. A desire to lessen the number of its imperfections induced me still to withhold it awhile, till, on the 15th of June, came to my hands, from Paris, a printed copy of a proposition made by the Bishop of Autun, to the National Assembly of France, on the subject of weights and measures; and three days afterwards I received, through the channel of the public papers, the speech of Sir John Riggs Miller, of April 13th, in the British House of Commons, on the same subject. In the report which I had prepared, and was then about to give in, I had proposed the latitude of 38°, as that which should fix our standard, because it was the medium latitude of the United States; but the proposition before the National Assembly of France, to take that of 45° as being a middle term between the equator and both poles, and a term which consequently might unite the nations of both hemispheres, appeared to me so well chosen, and so just, that I did not hesitate a moment to prefer it to that of 38°. It became necessary, of course, to conform all my calculations to that standard—an operation which has been retarded by my other occupations.

These circumstances will, I hope, apologize for the delay which has attended the execution of the order of the House; and, perhaps, a disposition on their part to have due regard for the proceedings of other nations, engaged on the same subject, may induce them still to defer deciding ultimately on it till their next session. Should this be the case, and should any new matter occur in the meantime, I shall think it my duty to communicate it to the House, as supplemental to the present report.

I have the honor to be, with sentiments of the most profound respect,

Sir, your most obedient and most humble servant.

The Secretary of State, to whom was referred, by the House of Representatives, to prepare and report a proper plan or plans for establishing uni-

[1] December 18, 1792: Th. Jefferson has the honor to send the President 2 cents made on Voigt's plan, by putting a silver plug worth ¾ of a cent into a copper worth ¼ of a cent. Mr. Rittenhouse is about to make a few by mixing the same plug by fusion with the same quantity of copper. He will then make of copper alone of the same size, and lastly he will make the real cent, as ordered by Congress, four times as big. Specimens of these several ways of making the cent will be delivered to the Committee of Congress now having that subject before them. (MS., National Archives, Misc. Letters, Dept. of State.)

formity in the currency, weights, and measures of the United States, in obedience thereto, makes the following report:

To obtain uniformity in measures, weights, and coins, it is necessary to find some measure of invariable length, with which, as a standard, they may be compared.

There exists not in nature, as far as has been hitherto observed, a single subject or species of subject, accessible to man, which presents one constant and uniform dimension.

The globe of the earth itself, indeed, might be considered as invariable in all its dimensions, and that its circumference would furnish an invariable measure; but no one of its circles, great or small, is accessible to admeasurement through all its parts, and the various trials to measure definite portions of them, have been of such various result as to show there is no dependence on that operation for certainty.

Matter, then, by its mere extension, furnishing nothing invariable, its motion is the only remaining resource.

The motion of the earth round its axis, though not absolutely uniform and invariable, may be considered as such for every human purpose. It is measured obviously, but unequally, by the departure of a given meridian from the sun, and its return to it, constituting a solar day. Throwing together the inequalities of solar days, a mean interval, or day, has been found, and divided, by very general consent, into 86,400 equal parts.

A pendulum, vibrating freely, in small and equal arcs, may be so adjusted in its length, as, by its vibrations, to make this division of the earth's motion into 86,400 equal parts, called seconds of mean time.

Such a pendulum, then, becomes itself a measure of determinate length, to which all others may be referred to as to a standard.

But even a pendulum is not without its uncertainties.

1. The difficulty of ascertaining, in practice, its centre of oscillation, as depending on the form of the bob, and its distance from the point of suspension; the effect of the weight of the suspending wire towards displacing the centre of oscillation; that centre being seated within the body of the bob, and therefore inaccessible to the measure, are sources of considerable uncertainty.

2. Both theory and experience prove that, to preserve its isochronism, it must be shorter towards the equator, and longer towards the poles.

3. The height of the situation above the common level, as being an increment to the radius of the earth, diminishes the length of the pendulum.

4. The pendulum being made of metal, as is best, it varies its length with the variations in the temperature of the atmosphere.

5. To continue small and equal vibrations, through a sufficient length of time, and to count these vibrations, machinery and a power are necessary,

which may exert a small but constant effort to renew the waste of motion; and the difficulty is so to apply these, as that they shall neither retard or accelerate the vibrations.

1. In order to avoid the uncertainties which respect the centre of oscillation, it has been proposed by Mr. Leslie, an ingenious artist of Philadelphia, to substitute, for the pendulum, a uniform cylindrical rod, without a bob.

Could the diameter of such a rod be infinitely small, the centre of oscillation would be exactly at two-thirds of the whole length, measured from the point of suspension. Giving it a diameter which shall render it sufficiently inflexible, the centre will be displaced, indeed; but, in a second rod not the (1) six hundred thousandth part of its length, and not the hundredth part as much as in a second pendulum with a spherical bob of proper diameter. This displacement is so infinitely minute, then, that we may consider the centre of oscillation, for all practical purposes, as residing at two-thirds of the length from the centre of suspension. The distance between these two centres might be easily and accurately ascertained in practice. But the whole rod is better for a standard than any portion of it, because sensibly defined at both its extremities.

2. The uncertainty arising from the difference of length requisite for the second pendulum, or the second rod, in different latitudes, may be avoided by fixing on some one latitude, to which our standard shall refer. That of 38°, as being the middle latitude of the United States, might seem the most convenient, were we to consider ourselves alone; but connected with other nations by commerce and science, it is better to fix on that parallel which bids fairest to be adopted by them also. The 45th, as being the middle term between the equator and pole, has been heretofore proposed in Europe, and the proposition has been lately renewed there under circumstances which may very possibly give it some effect. This parallel is distinguished with us also as forming our principal northern boundary. Let the completion of the 45th degree, then, give the standard for our union, with the hope that it may become a line of union with the rest of the world.

The difference between the second rod for 45° of latitude, and that for 31°, our other extreme, is to be examined.

The second *pendulum* for 45° of latitude, according to Sir Isaac Newton's computation, must be of (2) 39.14912 inches English measure; and a *rod,* to vibrate in the same time, must be of the same length between the centres of suspension and oscillation; and, consequently, its whole length 58.7 (or, more exactly, 58.72368) inches. This is longer than the rod which shall vibrate seconds in the 31° of latitude, by about 1/679 part of its whole length; a difference so minute, that it might be neglected, as insensible, for the common purposes of life, but, in cases requiring perfect exactness, the second rod, found by trial of its vibrations in any part of the United States, may be corrected by computation for the (3) latitude of the place, and so brought exactly to the standard of 45°.

3. By making the experiment in the level of the ocean, the difference will be avoided, which a higher position might occasion.

4. The expansion and contraction of the rod with the change of temperature, is the fourth source of uncertainty before mentioned. According to the high authority so often quoted, an iron rod, of given length, may vary, between summer and winter, in temperate latitudes, and in the common exposure of house clocks, from $\frac{1}{1728}$ to $\frac{1}{2592}$ of its whole length, which, in a rod of 58.7 inches, will be from about two to three hundredths of an inch. This may be avoided by adjusting and preserving the standard in a cellar, or other place, the temperature of which never varies. Iron is named for this purpose, because the least expansible of the metals.

5. The practical difficulty resulting from the effect of the machinery and moving power is very inconsiderable in the present state of the arts; and, in their progress towards perfection, will become less and less. To estimate and obviate this, will be the artist's province. It is as nothing when compared with the sources of inaccuracy hitherto attending measures.

Before quitting the subject of the inconveniences, some of which attend the pendulum alone, others both the pendulum and rod, it must be added that the rod would have an accidental but very precious advantage over the pendulum in this country, in the event of our fixing the foot at the nearest aliquot part of either; for the difference between the common foot, and those so to be deduced, would be three times greater in the case of the pendulum than in that of the rod.

Let the standard of measure, then, be a uniform cylindrical rod of iron, of such length as, in latitude 45°, in the level of the ocean, and in a cellar, or other place, the temperature of which does not vary through the year, shall perform its vibrations in small and equal arcs, in one second of mean time.

A standard of invariable length being thus obtained, we may proceed to identify, by that, the measures, weights and coins of the United States; but here a doubt presents itself as to the extent of the reformation meditated by the House of Representatives. The experiment made by Congress in the year one thousand seven hundred and eighty-six, by declaring that there should be one money of account and payment through the United States, and that its parts and multiples should be in a decimal ratio, has obtained such general approbation, both at home and abroad, that nothing seems wanting but the actual coinage, to banish the discordant pounds, shillings, pence, and farthings of the different States, and to establish in their stead the new denominations. Is it in contemplation with the House of Representatives to extend a like improvement to our measures and weights, and to arrange them also in a decimal ratio? The facility which this would introduce into the vulgar arithmetic would, unquestionably, be soon and sensibly felt by the whole mass of the people, who would thereby be enabled to compute for themselves whatever they should have occasion to buy, to sell, or to measure, which the present complicated and difficult ratios place beyond their computation for the most part. Or, is it the opinion of the Representatives that the difficulty of changing the established habits of a whole nation opposes an insuperable bar to this improvement? Under this uncertainty, the Secretary of State thinks it his duty to submit alternative plans, that the House may, at their will, adopt either the one or the other, exclusively, or the one for the present and the other for a future time, when the public mind may be supposed to have become familiarized to it.

I. And first, on the supposition that the present measures and weights are to be retained but to be rendered uniform and invariable, by bringing them to the same invariable standard.

The first settlers of these States, having come chiefly from England, brought with them the measures and weights of that country. These alone are generally established among us, either by law or usage; and these, therefore, are alone to be retained and fixed. We must resort to that country for information of what they are, or ought to be.

This rests, principally, on the evidence of certain standard measures and weights, which have been preserved, of long time, in different deposits. But differences among these having been known to exist, the House of Commons, in the years 1757 and 1758, appointed committees to inquire into the original standards of their weights and measures. These committees, assisted by able mathematicians and artists, examined and compared with each other the several standard measures and weights, and made reports on them in the years 1758 and 1759. The circumstances under which these reports were made entitle them to be considered, as far as they go, as the best written testimony existing of the standard measures and weights of England; and as such, they will be relied on in the progress of this report.

### MEASURES OF LENGTH

The measures of length in use among us are:

The league of 3 miles
The mile of 8 furlongs
The furlong of 40 poles or perches
The pole or perch of 5½ yards
The fathom of 2 yards
The ell of a yard and quarter
The yard of 3 feet
The foot of 12 inches, and
The inch of 10 lines

On this branch of their subject, the committee of 1757-1758, says that the standard measures of length at the receipt of the exchequer, are a yard, supposed to be of the time of Henry VII, and a yard and ell supposed to have been made about the year 1601; that they are brass rods, very coarsely made, their divisions not exact, and the rods bent; and that in the year 1742, some members of the Royal Society had been at great pains in taking an exact measure of these standards, by very curious instruments, prepared by the ingenious Mr. Graham; that the Royal Society had had a brass rod made pursuant to their experiments, which was made so accurately, and by persons so skilful and exact, that it was thought not easy to obtain a more exact one; and the committee, in fact, found it to agree with the standards at the exchequer, as near as it was possible. They furnish no means, to persons at a distance, of knowing what this standard is. This, however, is supplied by the evidence of the second pendulum, which, according to the authority before quoted, is, at London, 39.1682 English inches, and, consequently, the second rod there is of 58.7523 of the same inches. When we shall have found, then, by actual trial, the second rod for 45° by adding the difference of their computed length, to wit: 287/10,000 of an inch, or rather 3/10 of a line (which in practice will endanger less error than an attempt at so minute a fraction as the ten thousandth parts of an inch) we shall have the second rod of London, or a true measure of 58¾ English inches. Or, to shorten the operation, without varying the result,

Let the standard rod of 45° be divided into 587⅕ equal parts, and let each of these parts be declared a line.

| | |
|---|---|
| 10 lines an inch | 5½ yards a perch or pole |
| 12 inches a foot | 40 poles or perches a furlong |
| 3 feet a yard | 8 furlongs a mile |
| 3 feet 9 inches an ell | 3 miles a league |
| 6 feet a fathom | |

### SUPERFICIAL MEASURES

Our measures of surface are, the acre of 4 roods and the rood of 40 square poles; so established by a statute of 33 Edw. 1. Let them remain the same.

### MEASURES OF CAPACITY

The measures of capacity in use among us are of the following names and proportions:

The gill, four of which make a pint.

Two pints make a quart.

Two quarts a pottle.

Two pottles a gallon.

Two gallons a peck, dry measure.

Eight gallons make a measure called a firkin, in liquid substances, and a bushel, dry.

Two firkins, or bushels, make a measure called a rundlet or kilderkin, liquid, and a strike, dry.

Two kilderkins, or strikes, make a measure called a barrel, liquid, and a coomb, dry; this last term being ancient and little used.

Two barrels, or coombs, make a measure called a hogshead, liquid, or a quarter, dry; each being the quarter of a ton.

A hogshead and a third make a tierce, or third of a ton.

Two hogsheads make a pipe, butt, or puncheon; and

Two pipes make a ton.

But no one of these measures is of a determinate capacity. The report of the committee of 1757-8, shows that the gallon is of very various content; and that being the unit, all the others must vary with it.

The gallon and bushel contain—

224 and 1792 cubic inches, according to the standard wine gallon preserved at Guildhall.

231 and 1848, according to the statute of 5th of Anne.

264.8 and 2118.4, according to the ancient Rumford quart, of 1228, examined by the committee.

265.5 and 2124, according to three standard bushels preserved in the Exchequer, to wit: one of Henry VII, without a rim; one dated 1091, supposed for 1591, or 1601, and one dated 1601.

266.25 and 2130, according to the ancient Rumford gallon of 1228, examined by the committee.

268.75 and 2150, according to the Winchester bushel, as declared by statute 13, 14, William III, which has been the model for some of the grain States.

271, less 2 spoonfuls, and 2168, less 16 spoonfuls, according to a standard gallon of Henry VII, and another dated 1601, marked E. E., both in the Exchequer.

271 and 2168, according to a standard gallon in the Exchequer, dated 1601, marked E., and called the corn gallon.

272 and 2176, according to the three standard corn gallons last mentioned, as measured in 1688, by an artist for the Commissioners of the Excise, generally used in the seaport towns, and by mercantile people, and thence introduced into some of the grain States.

277.18 and 2217.44, as established for the measure of coal by the statute 12 Anne.

278 and 2224, according to the standard bushel of Henry VII, with a copper rim, in the Exchequer.

278.4 and 2227.2, according to two standard pints of 1601 and 1602, in the Exchequer.

280 and 2240, according to the standard quart of 1601, in the Exchequer.

282 and 2256, according to the standard gallon for beer and ale in the Treasury.

There are, moreover, varieties on these varieties, from the barrel to the ton, inclusive; for, if the barrel be of herrings, it must contain 28 gallons by the statute 13 Eliz. c. 11. If of wine, it must contain 31½ gallons by the statute 2 Henry VI. c. 11, and I Rich. III. c. 15. If of beer or ale, it must contain 34 gallons by the statute 1 William and Mary, c. 24, and the higher measures in proportion.

In those of the United States which have not adopted the statutes of William and Mary, and of Anne before cited, nor their substance, the wine gallon of 231 cubic inches rests on the authority of very long usage, before the 5th of Anne, the origin and foundation of which are unknown; the bushel is the Winchester bushel, by the 11 Henry VII undefined; and the barrel of ale 32 gallons, and of beer 36 gallons, by the statute 23 Henry VIII c. 4.

The Secretary of State is not informed whether there have been any, and what, alterations of these measures by the laws of the particular States.

It is proposed to retain this series of measures, but to fix the gallon to one determinate capacity, as the unit of measure, both wet and dry; for convenience is in favor of abolishing the distinction between wet and dry measures.

The wine gallon, whether of 224 or 231 cubic inches, may be altogether disregarded, as concerning, principally, the mercantile and the wealthy, the least numerous part of the society, and the most capable of reducing one measure to another by calculation. This gallon is little used among the mass of farmers, whose chief habits and interests are in the size of the corn bushel.

Of the standard measures before stated, two are principally distinguished in authority and practice. The statute bushel of 2150 cubic inches, which gives a gallon of 268.75 cubic inches, and the standard gallon of 1601, called the corn gallon of 271 or 272 cubic inches, which has introduced the mercantile bushel of 2276 inches. The former of these is most used in some of the grain States, the latter in others. The middle term of 270 cubic inches may be taken as a mutual compromise of convenience, and as offering this general advantage: that the bushel being of 2160 cubic inches, is exactly a cubic foot and a quarter, and so facilitates the conversion of wet and dry measures into solid contents and tonnage, and simplifies the connection of measures and weights, as will be shown hereafter. It may be added, in favor of this, as a medium measure, that eight of the standard, or statute measures before enumerated, are below this term, and nine above it.

The measures to be made for use, being four sided, with rectangular sides and bottom.

The pint will be 3 inches square, and 3¾ inches deep;

The quart 3 inches square, and 7½ inches deep;

The pottle 3 inches square, and 15 inches deep, or 4½, 5, and 6 inches.

The gallon 6 inches square, and 7½ inches deep, or 5, 6, and 9 inches;

The peck 6, 9, and 10 inches;

The half bushel 12 inches square, and 7½ inches deep; and

The bushel 12 inches square, and 15 inches deep, or 9, 15, and 16 inches.

Cylindrical measures have the advantage of superior strength, but square ones have the greater advantage of enabling everyone who has a rule in his pocket, to verify their contents by measuring them. Moreover, till the circle can be squared, the cylinder cannot be cubed, nor its contents exactly expressed in figures.

Let the measures of capacity, then, for the United States be—

A gallon of 270 cubic inches;

The gallon to contain 2 pottles;

The pottle 2 quarts;

The quart 2 pints;

The pint 4 gills;

Two gallons to make a peck;

Eight gallons a bushel or firkin;

Two bushels, or firkin, a strike or kilderkin;

Two strikes, or kilderkins, a coomb or barrel;

Two coombs, or barrels, a quarter or hogshead;

A hogshead and a third one tierce;

Two hogsheads a pipe, butt, or puncheon; and

Two pipes a ton.

And let all measures of capacity of dry subjects be stricken with a straight strike.

## WEIGHTS

There are two series of weights in use among us; the one called avoirdupois, the other troy.

### *In the Avoirdupois series*

The pound is divided into 16 ounces;

The ounce into 16 drachms;

The drachm into 4 quarters.

The pound is divided into 12 ounces;

The ounce (according to the subdivision of the apothecaries) into 8 drachms;

The drachm into 3 scruples;

The scruple into 20 grains.

According to the subdivision for gold and silver, the ounce is divided into twenty pennyweights, and the pennyweight into twenty-four grains.

So that the pound troy contains 5760 grains, of which 7000 are requisite to make the pound avoirdupois; of course the weight of the pound troy is to that of the pound avoirdupois as 5760 to 7000, or as 144 to 175.

It is remarkable that this is exactly the proportion of the ancient liquid gallon of Guildhall of 224 cubic inches, to the corn gallon of 272; for 224 are to 272 as 144 to 175. (4.)

It is further remarkable still, that this is also the exact proportion between the specific weight of any measure of wheat, and of the same measure of water: for the statute bushel is of 64 pounds of wheat. Now as 144 to 175, so are 64 pounds to 77.7 pounds; but 77.7 pounds is known to be the weight of (5.) 2150.4 cubic inches of pure water, which is exactly the content of the Winchester bushel, as declared by the statute 13, 14, Will. 3. That statute determined the bushel to be a cylinder of 18½ inches diameter, and 8 inches depth. Such a cylinder, as nearly as it can be cubed, and expressed in figures, contains 2150.425 cubic inches; a result which reflects authority on the declaration of Parliament, and induces a favorable opinion of the care with which they investigated the contents of the ancient bushel, and also a belief that there might exist evidence of it at that day, unknown to the committees of 1758 and 1759.

We find, then, in a continued proportion 64 to 77.7 as 224 to 272, and as 144 to 175, that is to say, the specific weight of a measure of wheat, to that of the same measure of water, as the cubic contents of the wet gallon, to those of the dry; and as the weight of a pound troy to that of a pound avoirdupois.

This seems to have been so combined as to render it indifferent whether a thing were dealt out by weight or measure; for the dry gallon of wheat, and the liquid one of wine, were of the same weight; and the avoirdupois pound of wheat, and the troy pound of wine, were of the same measure. Water and the vinous liquors, which enter most into commerce, are so nearly of a weight, that the difference, in moderate quantities, would be neglected by both buyer and seller; some of the wines being a little heavier, and some a little lighter, than water.

Another remarkable correspondence is that between weights and measures.

For 1000 ounces avoirdupois of pure water fill a cubic foot, with mathematical exactness.

What circumstances of the times, or purposes of barter or commerce, called for this combination of weights and measures, with the subjects to be exchanged or purchased, are not now to be ascertained. But a triple set of exact proportionals representing weights, measures, and the things to be weighed and measured, and a relation so integral between weights and solid measures, must have been the result of design and scientific calculation, and not a mere coincidence of hazard. It proves that the dry and wet measures, the heavy and light weights, must have been original parts of the system they compose—contrary to the opinion of the committee of 1757, 1758, who thought that the avoirdupois weight was not an ancient weight of the kingdom, nor ever even a legal weight, but during a single year of the reign of Henry VIII; and, therefore, concluded, otherwise than will be here proposed, to suppress it altogether. Their opinion was founded chiefly on the silence of the laws as to this weight. But the harmony here developed in the system of weights and measures, of which the avoirdupois makes an essential member, corroborated by a general use, from very high antiquity, of that, or of a nearly similar weight under another (6.) name, seem stronger proofs that this is legal weight, than the mere silence of the written laws is of the contrary.

Be this as it may, it is in such general use with us, that, on the principle of popular convenience, its higher denominations, at least, must be preserved. It is by the avoirdupois pound and ounce that our citizens have been used to buy and sell. But the smaller subdivisions of drachms and quarters are not in use with them. On the other hand, they have been used to weigh their money and medicine with the pennyweights and grains troy weight, and are not in the habit of using the pounds and ounces of that series. It would be for their convenience, then, to suppress the pound and ounce troy, and the drachm and quarter avoirdupois; and to form into one series the avoirdupois pound and ounce, and the troy pennyweight and grain. The avoirdupois ounce contains 18 pennyweights 5½ grains troy weight. Divide it, then, into 18 pennyweights, and the pennyweight, as heretofore, into 24 grains, and the new pennyweight will contain between a third and a quarter of a grain more than the present troy pennyweight; or, more accurately, it will be to that as 875 to 864—a difference not to be noticed, either in money or medicine, below the denomination of an ounce.

But it will be necessary to refer these weights to a determinate mass of some substance, the specific gravity of which is invariable. Rain water is such a substance, and may be referred to everywhere, and through all time. It has been found by accurate experiments that a cubic foot of rain water weighs

1000 ounces avoirdupois, standard weights of the exchequer. It is true that among these standard weights the committee report small variations; but this experiment must decide in favor of those particular weights, between which, and an integral mass of water, so remarkable a coincidence has been found. To render this standard more exact, the water should be weighed always in the same temperature of air; as heat, by increasing its volume, lessens its specific gravity. The cellar of uniform temperature is best for this also.

Let it, then, be established that an ounce is of the weight of a cube of rain water, of one-tenth of a foot; or, rather, that it is the thousandth part of the weight of a cubic foot of rain water, weighed in the standard temperature; that the series of weights of the United States shall consist of pounds, ounces, pennyweights, and grains; whereof

24 grains shall be one pennyweight
18 pennyweights one ounce
16 ounces one pound

COINS

Congress, in 1786, established the money unit at 375.64 troy grains of pure silver. It is proposed to enlarge this by about the third of a grain in weight, or a mill in value; that is to say, to establish it at 376 (or, more exactly, 375.989343) instead of 375.64 grains; because it will be shown that this, as the unit of coin, will link in system with the units of length, surface, capacity, and weight, whenever it shall be thought proper to extend the decimal ratio through all these branches. It is to preserve the possibility of doing this, that this very minute alteration is proposed.

We have this proportion, then, 875 to 864, as 375.989343 grains troy to 371.2626277; the expression of the unit in the new grains.

Let it be declared, therefore, that the money unit, or dollar of the United States, shall contain 371.262 American grains of pure silver.

If nothing more, then, is proposed, than to render uniform and stable the system we already possess, this may be effected on the plan herein detailed; the sum of which is: 1st. That the present measures of length be retained, and fixed by an invariable standard. 2d. That the measures of surface remain as they are, and be invariable also as the measures of length to which they are to refer. 3d. That the unit of capacity, now so equivocal, be settled at a medium and convenient term, and defined by the same invariable measures of length. 4th. That the more known terms in the two kinds of weights be retained, and reduced to one series, and that they be referred to a definite mass of some substance, the specific gravity of which never changes. And

5th. That the quantity of pure silver in the money unit be expressed in parts of the weights so defined.

In the whole of this no change is proposed, except an insensible one in the troy grain and pennyweight, and the very minute one in the money unit.

II. But if it be thought that, either now, or at any future time, the citizens of the United States may be induced to undertake a thorough reformation of their whole system of measures, weights and coins, reducing every branch to the same decimal ratio already established in their coins, and thus bringing the calculation of the principal affairs of life within the arithmetic of every man who can multiply and divide plain numbers, greater changes will be necessary.

The unit of measure is still that which must give law through the whole system; and from whatever unit we set out, the coincidences between the old and new ratios will be rare. All that can be done, will be to choose such a unit as will produce the most of these. In this respect the second rod has been found, on trial, to be far preferable to the second pendulum.

### MEASURES OF LENGTH

Let the second rod, then, as before described, be the standard of measure; and let it be divided into five equal parts, each of which shall be called a foot; for, perhaps, it may be better generally to retain the name of the nearest present measure, where there is one tolerably near. It will be about one quarter of an inch shorter than the present foot.

Let the foot be divided into 10 inches
The inch into 10 lines
The line into 10 points

Let 10 feet make a decad
10 decads one rood
10 roods a furlong
10 furlongs a mile

### SUPERFICIAL MEASURES

Superficial measures have been estimated, and so may continue to be, in squares of the measures of length, except in the case of lands, which have been estimated by squares, called roods and acres. Let the rood be equal to a square, every side of which is 100 feet. This will be 6.483 English feet less than the English (7.) rood every way, and 1311 square feet less in its whole contents; that is to say, about one-eighth; in which proportion, also, 4 roods will be less than the present acre.

### MEASURES OF CAPACITY

Let the unit of capacity be the cubic foot, to be called a bushel. It will contain 1620.05506862 cubic inches, English; be about one-fourth less than that before proposed to be adopted as a medium; one-tenth less than the bushel made from 8 of the Guildhall gallons; and one-fourteenth less than the bushel made from 8 Irish gallons of 217.6 cubic inches.

Let the bushel be divided into 10 pottles
Each pottle into 10 demi-pints
Each demi-pint into 10 metres, which will be of a cubic inch each
Let 10 bushels be a quarter, and
10 quarters a last, or double ton

The measures for use being four-sided, and the sides and bottoms rectangular, the bushel will be a foot cube.

The pottle 5 inches square and four inches deep
The demi-pint 2 inches square, and 2½ inches deep
The metre, an inch cube

### WEIGHTS

Let the weight of a cubic inch of rain water, or the thousandth part of a cubic foot, be called an ounce; and let the ounce be divided into 10 double scruples:

The double scruple into 10 carats
The carat into 10 minims or demi-grains
The minim into 10 mites
Let 10 ounces make a pound
10 pounds a stone
16 stones a kental
10 kentals a hogshead

### COINS

Let the money unit, or dollar, contain eleventh-twelfths of an ounce of pure silver. This will be 376 troy grains, (or more exactly, 375.989343 troy grains,) which will be about a third of a grain, (or more exactly, .349343 of a grain, more than the present unit. This, with the twelfth of alloy already established, will make the dollar or unit, of the weight of an ounce, or of a cubic inch of rain water, exactly. The series of mills, cents, dimes, dollars, and eagles, to remain as already established (8.)

The second rod, or the second pendulum, expressed in the measures of other countries, will give the proportion between their measures and those of the United States.

Measures, weights and coins, thus referred to standards unchangeable in their nature, (as is the length of a rod vibrating seconds, and the weight of a definite mass of rain water,) will themselves be unchangeable. These standards, too, are such as to be accessible to all persons, in all times and places. The measures and weights derived from them fall in so nearly with some of those now in use, as to facilitate their introduction; and being arranged in decimal ratio, they are within the calculation of everyone who possesses the first elements of arithmetic, and of easy comparison, both for foreigners and citizens, with the measures, weights, and coins of other countries.

A gradual introduction would lessen the inconveniences which might attend too sudden a substitution, even of an easier for a more difficult system. After a given term, for instance, it might begin in the custom-houses, where the merchants would become familiarized to it. After a further term, it might be introduced into all legal proceedings, and merchants and traders in foreign commodities might be required to use it in their dealings with one another. After a still further term, all other descriptions of people might receive it into common use. Too long a postponement, on the other hand, would increase the difficulties of its reception with the increase of our population.

*Appendix, containing illustrations and developments of some passages of the preceding report*

(1) In the second pendulum with a spherical bob, call the distance between the centres of suspension and of the bob, $2 \times 19.575$, or 2d, and the radius of the bob $= r$; then $2d : r :: r : \frac{rr}{2d}$ and ⅖ of this last proportional expresses the displacement of the centre of oscillation, to wit: $\frac{2rr}{5 \times 2d} = \frac{rr}{5d}$. Two inches have been proposed as a proper diameter for such a bob. In that case $r$ will be $=$ 1. inch, and $\frac{rr}{5d} = \frac{1}{9787}$ inches.

In the cylindrical second rod, call the length of the rod, $3 \times 19.575$. or 3d, and its radius $= r$ and $\frac{rr}{2 \times 3d} = \frac{rr}{6d}$ will express the displacement of the centre of oscillation. It is thought the rod will be sufficiently inflexible if it be ⅕ of an inch in diameter. Then $r$ will be $=$ .1 inch, and $\frac{rr}{6d} = \frac{1}{11{,}745}$ inches, which is but the 120th part of the displacement in the case of the pendulum with a spherical bob, and but the 689,710th part of the whole length of the rod. If the rod be even of half an inch diameter, the displacement will be but $\frac{1}{1879}$ of an inch, or $\frac{1}{110{,}356}$ of the length of the rod.

(2) Sir Isaac Newton computes the pendulum for 45° to be 36 pouces 8.428 lignes. Picard made the English foot 11 pouces 2.6 lignes, and Dr. Maskelyne 11 pouces 3.11 lignes. D'Alembert states it at 11 pouces 3 lignes, which

has been used in these calculations as a middle term, and gives us 36 pouces 8.428 lignes = 39.1491 inches. This length for the pendulum of 45° had been adopted in this report before the Bishop of Autun's proposition was known here. He relies on Mairan's ratio for the length of the pendulum in the latitude of Paris, to wit: 504:257::72 pouces to a 4th proportional, which will be 36.71428 pouces = 39.1619 inches, the length of the pendulum for latitude 48° 50′. The difference between this and the pendulum for 45° is .0113 of an inch; so that the pendulum for 45° would be estimated, according to Mairan, at 39.1619 — .0113 = 39.1506 inches, almost precisely the same with Newton's computation herein adopted.

(3) Sir Isaac Newton's computations for the different degrees of latitude, from 30° to 45°, are as follows:

| | PIEDS | LIGNES | | PIEDS | LIGNES |
|---|---|---|---|---|---|
| 30° | 3 | 7.948 | 42° | 3 | 8.327 |
| 35 | 3 | 8.099 | 43 | 3 | 8.361 |
| 40 | 3 | 8.261 | 44 | 3 | 8.394 |
| 41 | 3 | 8.294 | 45 | 3 | 8.428 |

(4) Or, more exactly, 144 : 175::224 : 272.2.

(5) Or, more exactly, 62.5 : 1728::77.7 : 2150.39.

(6) The merchant's weight.

(7) The English rood contains 10,890 sq. feet = 104.355 feet sq.

(8) *The Measures, Weights, and Coins of the Decimal System, estimated in those of England, now used in the United States.*

I. MEASURES OF LENGTH

| | FEET | EQUIVALENT IN ENGLISH MEASURE |
|---|---|---|
| The point | .001 | .011 inch |
| The line | .01 | .117 |
| The inch | .1 | 1.174, about 1/7 more than the English inch |
| The foot | 1. | 11.744736 / .978728 feet, about 1/48 less than the English foot |
| The decad | 10. | 9.787, about 1/48 less than the 10 feet rod of the carpenters |
| The rood | 100. | 97.872, about 1/16 less than the side of an English square rood |
| The furlong | 1000. | 978.728, about 1/3 more than the English furlong |
| The mile | 10000. | 9787.28, about 1 6/7 English mile, nearly the Scotch and Irish mile, and 1/2 the German mile |

### 2. SUPERFICIAL MEASURE

| | ROODS | |
|---|---|---|
| The hundredth | .01 | 95.69 square feet English |
| The tenth | .1 | 957.9 |
| The rood | 1. | 9579.085 |
| The double acre | 10. | 2.199, or say 2.2 acres English |
| The square furlong | 100. | 22 |

### 3. MEASURE OF CAPACITY

| | BUSHELS | CUB. INCHES |
|---|---|---|
| The metre | .001 | 1.62 |
| The demi-pint | .01 | 16.2, about 1/24 less than the English half-pint |
| The pottle | .1 | 162.005, about 1/6 more than the English pottle |
| The bushel | 1. | 1620.05506862 / .937531868414884352 cubic feet, about 1/4 less than the middle sized English bushel |
| The quarter | 10. | 9.375, about 1/5 less than the English quarter |
| The last | 100. | 93.753, about 1/7 more than the English last |

### 4. WEIGHTS

| | POUNDS | AVOIRDUPOIS | TROY |
|---|---|---|---|
| Mite | .00001 | | .041 grains, about 1/5 less than the English mite |
| Minim, or demi-grain | .0001 | | .4101, about 1/5 less than half-grain troy |
| Carat | .001 | | .4101, about 1/40 more than the carat troy |
| Double scruple | .01 | | 41.017, about 1/40 more than 2 scruples troy |
| Ounce | .1 | 937531868414884352 oz. | 410.170192431 / .85452 oz. about 1/16 less than the ounce avoirdupois |
| Pound | 1. | 9.375 / .585957417759 lb. | .712101 lb., about 1/4 less than the pound troy |
| Stone | 10. | 93.753 oz. / 5.8595 lb. | 7.121 about 1/4 less than the English stone of 8 lbs. avoirdupois |
| Kental | 100. | 937.531 oz. / 58.5957 lb. | 71.21 about 4/10 less than the English kental of 100 lbs. avoirdupois |
| Hogshead | 1000. | 9375.318 oz. / 585.9574 lb. | 712.101 |

## 5. COINS

| | DOLLARS | | | TROY GRAINS |
|---|---|---|---|---|
| The mill | .001 | Dollar | 1. | 375.98934306 pure silver |
| The cent | .01 | | | 34.18084937 alloy |
| The dime | .1 | Eagle | 10. | 410.17019243 |

### *Postscript*

January 10, 1791

It is scarcely necessary to observe that the measures, weights, and coins, proposed in the preceding report, will be derived altogether from mechanical operations, *viz.:* A rod, vibrating seconds, divided into five equal parts, one of these subdivided, and multiplied decimally, for every measure of length, surface, and capacity, and these last filled with water, to determine the weights and coins. The arithmetical estimates in the report were intended only to give an idea of what the new measures, weights, and coins, would be nearly, when compared with the old. The length of the standard or second rod, therefore, was assumed from that of the pendulum; and as there has been small differences in the estimates of the pendulum by different persons, that of Sir Isaac Newton was taken, the highest authority the world has yet known. But, if even he has erred, the measures, weights, and coins proposed, will not be an atom the more or less. In cubing the new foot, which was estimated at .978728 of an English foot, or 11.744736 English inches, an arithmetical error of an unit happened in the fourth column of decimals, and was repeated in another line in the sixth column, so as to make the result one ten thousandth and one millionth of a foot too much. The thousandth part of this error (about one ten millionth of a foot) consequently fell on the metre of measure, the ounce weight, and the unit of money. In the last it made a difference of about the twenty-fifth part of a grain Troy, in weight, or the ninety-third of a cent in value. As it happened, this error was on the favorable side, so that the detection of it approximates our estimate of the new unit exactly that much nearer to the old, and reduces the difference between them to 34, instead of 38 hundredths of a grain Troy; that is to say, the money unit instead of 375.64 Troy grains of pure silver, as established heretofore, will now be 375.98934306 grains, as far as our knowledge of the length of the second pendulum enables us to judge; and the current of authorities since Sir Isaac Newton's time, gives reason to believe that his estimate is more probably above than below the truth, consequently future corrections of it will bring the estimate of the new unit still nearer to the old.

The numbers in which the arithmetical error before mentioned showed itself in the table, at the end of the report, have been rectified, and the table re-printed.

The head of superficial measures in the last part of the report, is thought to be not sufficiently developed. It is proposed that the rood of land, being 100 feet square (and nearly a quarter of the present acre), shall be the unit of land measure. This will naturally be divided into tenths and hundredths, the latter of which will be a square decad. Its multiples will also, of course, be tens, which may be called double acres, and hundreds, which will be equal to a square furlong each. The surveyor's chain should be composed of 100 links of one foot each.

## A BILL TO PROMOTE THE PROGRESS OF THE USEFUL ARTS [1]

February 7, 1791

Be it enacted by the Senate and Representatives of the United States of America in Congress assembled, that when any person shall have invented any new and useful art, machine, or composition of matter or any new and useful improvement on any art, machine, or composition of matter, and shall desire to have an exclusive property in the same, he shall pay into the Treasury of the United States the sum of —— dollars, whereof he shall take a receipt from the Treasury in the usual form, and shall produce the same to the Secretary of State, in whose office he shall then deposit a description of the said inventions in writing and of the manner of using or process for compounding the same in such full, clear, and exact terms, as to distinguish the same from other things before known and to enable any person skilled in the art or science of which it is a branch, or with which it is most nearly connected to make, compound and use the same; and he shall accompany it with drawings and written references and also with exact models made in strong and workmanlike manner where the nature of the case admits of drawings or models, and with specimens of the ingredients, and of the composition of matter, sufficient in quantity for the purpose of experiment, where the invention is of a composition of matter; and he shall be entitled to receive from the Secretary of State a certificate thereof under the seal of his office wherein shall be inserted a shorter and more general description of the thing invented to be furnished by the applicant himself, in terms sufficient to point out the general nature thereof, and to warn others against an interference therewith, a copy of which certificate as also of the warrant of the Secretary of the Treasury and Treasurer's receipt he shall file of record in the clerk's office of every District Court of the United States, and shall pub-

[1] This "patent" bill was introduced into the House of Representatives on February 7, 1791, but no action was taken until the next Congress, which adopted it with a number of changes.

lish three times in some one Gazette of each of the said Districts. After which it shall not be lawful for any person without the permission of the owner of the said invention or of his agents to make or sell the thing so invented and discovered, for the term of fourteen years from the date of the Treasurer's receipt.

And be it further Enacted that it shall be lawful for the said inventor to assign his title and interest in the said invention at any time before or after the date of the Treasurer's receipt, and the assignee, having recorded the said assignment in the offices of the Secretary of State of the Clerks of the District Courts, and published the same three times in some one Gazette of each District, shall thereafter stand in the place of the original inventor, both as to right and responsibility, and so the assignees of assignees to any degree. And any person making or selling the thing so invented without permission as aforesaid shall be liable to an action at law, and to such damages as a jury shall assess, unless he can show that the same thing was known to others before the date of the Treasurer's receipt, and can show such probable grounds as the nature of a negative proof will admit that that knowledge was not derived from any party from, through or in whom the right is claimed, or unless he can show on like grounds that he did not know that there existed an exclusive right to the said invention, or can prove that (the same is so unimportant and obvious that it ought not be the subject of an exclusive right, or that) the description, model, specimen or ingredients deposited in the office of the Secretary of State do not contain the whole matter necessary to possess the public of the full benefit thereof after the expiration of the exclusive right, or that they contain superfluous matters intended to mislead the public, or that the effect pretended to cannot be produced by the means described. Provided that where any State before its accession to the present form of Government, or the adoption of the said form by nine States, shall have granted an exclusive right to any invention, the party claiming that right shall not be capable of obtaining an exclusive right under this act, but on relinquishing his right in and under such particular State, so as that obtaining equal benefits he may be subject to equal restrictions with the other Citizens of the United States, and of such relinquishment his obtaining an exclusive right under this act shall be sufficient evidence.

Provided also that the person whose applications for Patents were on the 1st day of February in this present year depending before the Secretary of State, Secretary at War, and Attorney General, according to the Act of 1790 for promoting the progress of useful Arts, on complying with all the conditions of this Act except the payment to the Treasurer herein before required, and instead of that payment obtaining from the said Secretary of State, Secretary at War and Attorney General, or any two of them, a certificate of the date of his application, and recording and publishing the said certificate instead of the warrant and receipt of Treasury shall be within the purview of this Act as if he had made such payment and his term of fourteen years shall be counted from the said date of his application.

And be it further Enacted, that after the expiration of any exclusive right to an invention, the public shall have reasonable and sufficient access to the descriptions, drawings, models, and specimens, of the same, so as to be enabled to copy them; and moreover that the Secretary of State shall cause the said descriptions and drawings to be printed, engraved and published, on the best terms he can, to the expences of which the Monies paid as before directed in to the Treasury shall be appropriated in the first place, and the balance to the purchase of books to form a public library at the seat of Government, under the direction of such persons as the President of the United States for the time being shall appoint.

And be it Enacted that the act passed in the year 1790 intitled "an act to promote the progress of the useful arts," be and is hereby repealed.

## MOULD-BOARD[1]

December 29, 1794

I have imagined and executed a mould-board which may be mathematically demonstrated to be perfect, as far as perfection depends on mathematical principles, and one great circumstance in its favor is that it may be made by the most bungling carpenter, and cannot possibly vary a hair's breadth in its form, by but gross negligence. You have seen the musical instrument called a sticcado. Suppose all its sticks of equal length, hold the fore-end horizontally on the floor to receive the turf which presents itself horizontally, and with the right hand twist the hind-end to the perpendicular, or rather as much beyond the perpendicular as will be necessary to cast over the turf completely. This gives an idea (though not absolutely exact) of my mould-board. It is on the principle of two wedges combined at right angles, the first in the direct line of the furrow to raise the turf gradually, the other across the furrow to turn it over gradually. For both these purposes the wedge is the instrument of the least resistance. I will make a model of the mould-board and lodge it with Colonel Harvie in Richmond for you.[2]

[1] Letter to John Taylor.

[2] Letter to Sylvestre, Secretary of the Société d'Agriculture de Paris, May 29, 1807: I have received, through the care of General Armstrong, the medal of gold by which the society of agriculture at Paris have been pleased to mark their approbation of the form of a mould-board which I had proposed; also the four first volumes of their memoirs, and the information that they had honored me with the title of foreign associate to their society. I receive with great thankfulness these testimonies of their favor, and should be happy to merit them by greater services. Attached to agriculture by inclination, as well as by a conviction that it is the most

I have just received information that a plough addressed to me has arrived at New York, from England . . . I presume it is the one sent by the Society of the Seine . . . I shall with great pleasure attend to the construction and transmission to the Society of a plough with my mould-board. This is the only part of that useful instrument to which I have paid any particular attention. But knowing how much the perfection of the plough must depend, 1st, on the line of traction; 2d, on the direction of the share; 3d, on the angle of the wing; 4th, on the form of the mould-board; and persuaded that I shall find the three first advantages eminently exemplified in that which the Society sends me, I am anxious to see combined with these a mould-board of my form, in the hope it will still advance the perfection of that machine. But for this I must ask time till I am relieved from the cares which have now a right to all my time, that is to say, till the next Spring. Then giving, in the leisure of retirement, all the time and attention this construction merits and requires, I will certainly render to the Society the result in a plough of the best form I shall be able to have executed.[3]

## MEMORIAL SUGGESTING MORE MINUTE CENSUS RETURNS[4]

January 10, 1800

TO THE HONORABLE THE SENATE AND HOUSE OF REPRESENTATIVES OF THE UNITED STATES

*The Memorial of the American Philosophical Society, Respectfully Sheweth*

That this Society, instituted for the promotion of useful knowledge, understanding that the Legislature of the Union have under their consideration a bill for taking a new census of the inhabitants of the United States, consider it as offering an occasion of great value, and not otherwise to be obtained, of ascertaining sundry facts highly interesting and important to Society. Under this impression they beg leave respectfully to submit to the wisdom of the Legislature, the expediency of requiring from their Officers, in addition to the table in the former Act for the same purpose, others presenting a more detailed View of the inhabitants of the United States, under several different aspects.

They consider it as important to determine the effect of the soil and

useful of the occupations of man, my course of life has not permitted me to add to its theories the lessons of practice.

[3] Letter to the same, July 15, 1808.

[4] Written and signed by Jefferson, as president of the American Philosophical Society. MS. in the National Archives.

climate of the United States on the inhabitants thereof; and, for this purpose, dividing life into certain epochs, to ascertain the existing numbers within each epoch, from whence may be calculated the ordinary duration of life in these States, the chances of life for every epoch thereof, and the ratio of the increase of their population: firmly believing that the result will be sensibly different from what is presented by the tables of other countries, by which we are, from necessity, in the habit of estimating the probabilities of life here. And they humbly suggest, as proper for these purposes, the intervals between the following epochs, to wit:—birth, two, five, ten, sixteen, twenty one, and twenty five years of age, and every term of five years from thence to one hundred.

For the purpose also of more exactly distinguishing the increase of population by birth, and by immigration, they propose that another table shall present, in separate columns, the respective numbers of native citizens, citizens of foreign birth, and of Aliens.

In order to ascertain more compleatly the causes which influence life and health, and to furnish a curious and useful document of the distribution of society in these States, and of the conditions and vocations of our fellow citizens, they propose, that still another table shall be formed, specifying, in different columns, the number of free male inhabitants of all ages engaged in business, under the following or such other descriptions as the greater wisdom of the Legislature shall approve, to wit: 1. men of the learned professions, including clergymen, lawyers, physicians, those employed in the fine arts, teachers and scribes, in general. 2. Merchants and traders, including bankers, insurers, brokers and dealers of every kind. 3. Mariners. 4. handy craftsmen. 5. Labourers in agriculture. 6. Labourers of other descriptions. 7. domestic servants. 8. paupers. 9. persons of no particular calling living on their income: care being to be taken, that every person be noted but once in this table, and that under the description to which he principally belongs.

They flatter themselves, that from these data, truths will result very satisfactory to our citizens; that under the joint influence of soil, climate and occupation, the duration of human life in this portion of the earth, will be found at least equal to what it is in any other; and that its population increases with a rapidity unequalled in all others.

What other views may be advantageously taken, they submit with those above suggested, to the superior wisdom of Congress, in whose decision they will acquiesce with unqualified respect.

By order of the society.

TH. JEFFERSON, *President*

# THE VELOCITY OF RIVERS[1]

March 13, 1804

DEAR SIR: Your favor of January 28 has been duly received, and I have read with great satisfaction your ingenuous paper on the subject of the Mississippi, which I shall immediately forward to the Philosophical Society, where it will be duly prized. To prove the value I set on it, and my wish that it may go to the public without any imperfection about it, I will take the liberty of submitting to your consideration the only passage which I think may require it. You say, page 9, "The velocity of rivers is greatest at the surface, and gradually diminishes downwards." And this principle

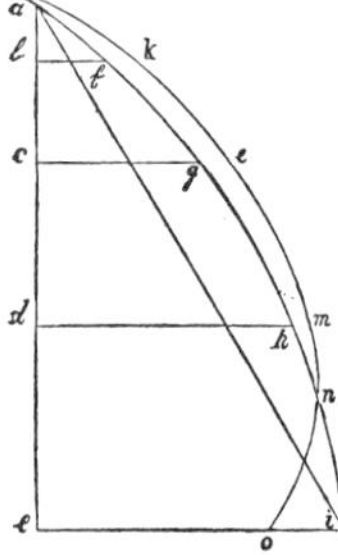


enters into some subsequent parts of the paper, and has too much effect on the phenomena of that river not to merit mature consideration. I can but suppose it at variance with the law of motion in rivers. In strict theory, the velocity of water at any given depth in a river is (in addition to its velocity at its surface) whatever a body would have acquired by falling through a space equal to that depth. If, in the middle of a river, we drop a vertical line, *a e,* from its surface to its bottom, and (using a perch, or rather a measure of 16.125 feet, for our unit of measure) we draw, at the depths, *b c d e,* (which suppose = 1.4 9.16 perch ordinates in the direction of the stream, equal to the odd numbers, 3, 5, 7, 9 perch, these ordinates will represent the additional velocities of the water per second of time, at the depth of their respective abscissæ, and will terminate in a curve, *a f g h i,*) which will represent the velocity of their current in every point, and the whole mass of water passing on in a second of time.[2] This would be the theory of the motion of rivers, were there no friction; but the bottom being rough, its friction with the lower sheet or lamina of water will retard that lamina; the friction or viscosity of the particles of which, again, with those of the one next above, will retard that somewhat less, the 2d retard the 3d, the 3d the 4th, and so on upwards, diminishing till the retardation becomes insensible; and the theoretic curve will be modified by that cause, as at *n o,* removing the maximum of motion from the bottom somewhere upwardly. Again, the same circumstances of friction and viscosity of the particles of water among themselves, will cause the lamina at the sur-

[1] Letter to William Dunbar.

[2] These ordinates are arithmetical progressionals, each of which is double the root of its abscissa, plus unit. The equation, therefore, expressing the law of the curve is $y = 2\sqrt{x} + 1$; that is, the velocity of the water of any depth will be double the root of that depth, plus unit. Were the line *a e* a wall, and *b f e g d h e i* troughs, along which water spouted from apertures at *b c d e,* their intersections with the curve at *f g h i* would mark the point in each trough to which the water would flow in a second of time, abating for friction.—T. J.

face to be accelerated by the quicker motion of the one next below it, the 2d still more by the 3d, the 3d by the 4th, and so on downwards, the acceleration always increasing till it reached the lamina of greatest motion. The exact point of the maximum of motion cannot be calculated, because it depends on friction; but it is probably much nearer the bottom than top, because the greater power of the current there sooner overcomes the effect of the friction. Ultimately, the curve will be sensibly varied by being swelled outwardly above, and retracted inwardly below, somewhat like *a k l m n o,* in the preceding diagram.

Indulging corollaries on this theory, let us suppose a plane surface, as a large sheet of cast-iron, let down by a cable from a boat, and made to present its surface to the current by a long vane fixed on its axis in the direction of the current. Would not the current below, laying hold of this plate, draw the boat down the stream with more rapidity than that with which it otherwise moves on the surface of the water? Again, at the cross current of the surface which flows into the Chafaleya, and endangers the drawing boats into that river, as you mention, page 18, would not the same plane surface, if let down into the under current, which moves in the direction of the bed of the main river, have the effect of drawing the vessel across the lateral current prevailing at its surface, and conduct the boat with safety along the channel of the river?

## TORPEDOES AND SUBMARINES [1]

August 16, 1807

I consider your torpedoes as very valuable means of the defence of harbors, and have no doubt that we should adopt them to a considerable degree. Not that I go the whole length (as I believe you do) of considering them as solely to be relied on. Neither a nation nor those entrusted with its affairs, could be justifiable, however sanguine its expectations, in trusting solely to an engine not yet sufficiently tried, under all the circumstances which may occur, and against which we know not as yet what means of parrying may be devised. If, indeed, the mode of attaching them to the cable of a ship be the only one proposed, modes of prevention cannot be difficult. But I have ever looked to the submarine boat as most to be depended on for attaching them, and though I see no mention of it in your letter, or your publications, I am in hopes it is not abandoned as impracticable. I should wish to see a corps of young men trained to this service. It would belong to the engi-

[1] Letter to Robert Fulton. On March 17, 1810, Jefferson wrote to Fulton: "Your torpedoes will be to cities what vaccination has been to mankind. It extinguishes their greatest danger. But there will still be navies."

neers if at hand, but being nautical, I suppose we must have a corps of naval engineers, to practise and use them. I do not know whether we have authority to put any part of our existing naval establishment in a course of training, but it shall be the subject of a consultation with the Secretary of the Navy. General Dearborn has informed you of the urgency of our want of you at New Orleans for the locks there.

## NATURAL HISTORY: COLLECTION [1]

July 14, 1808

SIR: If my recollection does not deceive me, the collection of the remains of the animal incognitum of the Ohio (sometimes called mammoth), possessed by the Cabinet of Natural History at Paris, is not very copious. Under this impression, and presuming that this Cabinet is allied to the National Institute, to which I am desirous of rendering some service, I have lately availed myself of an opportunity of collecting some of those remains.[2] General Clarke (the companion of Governor Lewis in his expedition to the Pacific Ocean) being, on a late journey, to pass by the Big-bone Lick of the Ohio, was kind enough to undertake to employ for me a number of laborers, and to direct their operations in digging for these bones at this important deposit of them. The result of these researches will appear in the enclosed catalogue of specimens which I am now able to place at the disposal of the National Institute. An aviso being to leave this place for some port of France on public service, I deliver the packages to Captain Haley, to be deposited with the Consul of the United States, at whatever port he may land. They are addressed to Mr. Warden of our legation at Paris, for the National Institute, and he will have the honor of delivering them. To these I have added the horns of an animal called by the natives the Mountain Ram, resembling the sheep by his head, but more nearly the deer in his other parts; as also the skin of another animal, resembling the sheep by his fleece but the goat in his other parts. This is called by the natives the Fleecy Goat, or in the style of the natural historian, the Pokotragos. I suspect it to be nearly related to the Pacos, and were we to group the fleecy animals together, it would stand perhaps with the Vigogne, Pacos, and Sheep. The Mountain Ram was found in abundance by Messrs. Lewis and Clarke on their western tour, and was frequently an article of food for their party, and esteemed more delicate than the deer. The Fleecy Goat they did not see, but procured two skins from the Indians, of which this is one. Their description will be given in the work of Governor Lewis, the

1 Letter to De La Capede.

2 On March 7, 1791, Jefferson wrote to Harry Innes: "Natural History . . . is my passion."

journal and geographical part of which may be soon expected from the press; but the parts relating to the plants and animals observed in his tour, will be delayed by the engravings. In the meantime, the plants of which he brought seeds, have been very successfully raised in the botanical garden of Mr. Hamilton of the Woodlands, and by Mr. McMahon, a gardener of Philadelphia; and on the whole, it is with pleasure I can assure you that the addition to our knowledge in every department, resulting from this tour of Messrs. Lewis and Clarke, has entirely fulfilled my expectations in setting it on foot, and that the world will find that those travellers have well earned its favor. I will take care that the Institute as well as yourself shall receive Governor Lewis's work as it appears.

It is with pleasure I embrace this occasion of returning you my thanks for the favor of your very valuable works, *sur les poissons et les cétacées,* which you were so kind as to send me through Mr. Livingston and General Turreau, and which I find entirely worthy of your high reputation in the literary world. That I have not sooner made this acknowledgment has not proceeded from any want of respect and attachment to yourself, or a just value of your estimable present, but from the strong and incessant calls of duty to other objects. The candor of your character gives me confidence of your indulgence on this head, and I assure you with truth that no circumstances are more welcome to me than those which give me the occasion of recalling myself to your recollection, and of renewing to you the assurances of sincere personal attachment, and of great respect and consideration.

*Contents of the large square Box*

A Fibia.

A Radius.

Two ribs belonging to the upper part of the thorax.

Two ribs from a lower part of the thorax.

One entire vertebra.

Two spinous processes of the vertebra broken from the bodies.

Dentes molares, which appear to have belonged to the full-grown animal.

A portion of the under-jaw of a young animal with two molar teeth in it.

These teeth appear to have belonged to a first set, as they are small, and the posterior has but three grinding ridges, instead of five, the common number in adult teeth of the lower jaw.

Another portion of the under-jaw, including the symphysis, or chin. In this portion the teeth of one side are every way complete; to wit, the posterior has five transverse ridges, and the anterior three.

A fragment of the upper-jaw with one molar tooth much worn.

Molar teeth which we suppose to be like those of the mammoth or elephant of Siberia. They are essentially different from those of the mammoth or elephant of this country, and although similar in some respects to the teeth of the Asiatic elephant, they agree more completely with the description of the teeth found in Siberia in the arrangement and size of the transverse lamina of enamel. This idea, however, is not derived from actual comparison of the different teeth with each other, for we have no specimens of Siberian teeth in this country; but from inferences deduced from the various accounts and drawings of these teeth to be found in books. A few of these teeth have been found in several places where the bones of the American animal have existed.

An Astragalus.

An Oscalcis.

Os naviculare.

In the large box in which the preceding bones are, is a small one containing a promiscuous mass of small bones, chiefly of the feet.

In the large irregular-shaped box, a tusk of large size. The spiral twist in all the specimens of these tusks which we have seen, was remarked so long ago as the time of Breyneus, in his description of the tusks of the Siberian mammoth in the Philosophical Transactions, if that paper is rightly recollected, for the book is not here to be turned to at present. Many fragments of tusks have been sent from the Ohio, generally resembling portions of such tusks as are brought to us in the course of commerce. But of these spiral tusks, in a tolerable complete state, we have had only four. One was found near the head of the north branch of the Susquehanna. A second possessed by Mr. Peale, was found with the skeleton, near the Hudson. A third is at Monticello, found with the bones of this collection at the Bigbone lick of Ohio, and the fourth is that now sent for the Institute, found at the same place and larger than that at Monticello.

The smallest box contains the horns of the mountain ram, and skin of the fleecy goat.

## STANDARDS OF MEASURES, WEIGHTS AND COINS[1]

November 10, 1811

DEAR SIR: Your favor of September 23d came to hand in due time, and I thank you for the nautical almanac it covered for the year 1813. I learn with pleasure that the Philosophical Society has concluded to take into consideration the subject of a fixed standard of meaures, weights and coins, and you ask my ideas on it; insulated as my situation is, I am sure I can offer nothing but what will occur to the committee engaged on it, with the advan-

[1] Letter to Dr. Robert Patterson.

tage on their part of correction by an interchange of sentiments and observations among themselves. I will, however, hazard some general ideas because you desire it, and if a single one be useful, the labor will not be lost.

The subject to be referred to as a standard, whether it be matter or motion, should be fixed by nature, invariable and accessible to all nations, independently of others, and with a convenience not disproportioned to its utility. What subject in nature fulfils best these conditions? What system shall we propose on this, embracing measures, weights and coins? and in what form shall we present it to the world? These are the questions before the committee.

Some other subjects have, at different times, been proposed as standards, but two only have divided the opinions of men: first, a direct admeasurement of a line on the earth's surface, or second, a measure derived from its motion on its axis. To measure directly such a portion of the earth as would furnish an element of measure, which might be found again with certainty in all future times, would be too far beyond the competence of our means to be taken into consideration. I am free, at the same time, to say that if these were within our power in the most ample degree, this element would not meet my preference. The admeasurement would of course be of a portion of some great circle of the earth. If of the equator, the countries over which that passes, their character and remoteness, render the undertaking arduous, and we may say impracticable for most nations. If of some meridian, the varying measures of its degrees from the equator to the pole, require a mean to be sought, of which some aliquot part may furnish what is desired. For this purpose the 45th degree has been recurred to, and such a length of line on both sides of it terminating at each end in the ocean, as may furnish a satisfactory law for a deduction of the unmeasured part of the quadrant. The portion resorted to by the French philosophers, (and there is no other on the globe under circumstances equally satisfactory), is the meridian passing through their country and a portion of Spain, from Dunkirk to Barcelona. The objections to such an admeasurement as an element of measure, are the labor, the time, the number of highly-qualified agents, and the great expense required. All this, too, is to be repeated whenever any accident shall have destroyed the standard derived from it, or impaired its dimensions. This portion of that particular meridian is accessible of right to no one nation on earth. France, indeed, availing herself of a moment of peculiar relation between Spain and herself, has executed such an admeasurement. But how would it be at this moment, as to either France or Spain? and how is it at all times as to other nations, in point either of right or of practice? Must these go through the same operation, or take their measures from the standard prepared by France?

Neither case bears that character of independence which the problem requires, and which neither the equality nor convenience of nations can dispense with. How would it now be, were England the deposit of a standard for the world? At war with all the world, the standard would be inaccessible to all other nations. Against this, too, are the inaccuracies of admeasurements over hills and valleys, mountains and waters, inaccuracies often unobserved by the agent himself, and always unknown to the world. The various results of the different measures heretofore attempted, sufficiently prove the inadequacy of human means to make such an admeasurement with the exactness requisite.

Let us now see under what circumstances the pendulum offers itself as an element of measure. The motion of the earth on its axis from noon to noon of a mean solar day, has been divided from time immemorial, and by very general consent, into 86,400 portions of time called seconds. The length of a pendulum vibrating in one of these portions, is determined by the laws of nature, is invariable under the same parallel, and accessible independently to all men. Like a degree of the meridian, indeed, it varies in its length from the equator to the pole, and like it, too, requires to be reduced to a mean. In seeking a mean in the first case, the 45th degree occurs with unrivalled preferences. It is the mid-way of the celestial ark from the equator to the pole. It is a mean between the two extreme degrees of the terrestrial ark, or between any two equi-distant from it, and it is also a mean value of all its degrees. In like manner, when seeking a mean for the pendulum, the same 45th degree offers itself on the same grounds, its increments being governed by the same laws which determine those of the different degrees of the meridian.

In a pendulum loaded with a Bob, some difficulty occurs in finding the centre of oscillation; and consequently the distance between that and the point of suspension. To lessen this, it has been proposed to substitute for the pendulum, a cylindrical rod of small diameter, in which the displacement of the centre of oscillation would be lessened. It has also been proposed to prolong the suspending wire of the pendulum below the Bob, until their centres of oscillation shall coincide. But these propositions not appearing to have received general approbation, we recur to the pendulum, suspended and charged as has been usual. And the rather as the laws which determine the centre of oscillation leave no room for error in finding it, other than that minimum in practice to which all operations are subject in their execution. The other sources of inaccuracy in the length of the pendulum need not be mentioned, because easily guarded against. But the great and decisive superiority of the pendulum, as a standard of measure, is in its accessibility to all men, at all times and in all places. To obtain the second pendulum for

45° it is not necessary to go actually to that latitude. Having ascertained its length in our own parallel, both theory and observation give us a law for ascertaining the difference between that and the pendulum of any other. To make a new measure therefore, or verify an old one, nothing is necessary in any place but a well-regulated time-piece, or a good meridian, and such a knowledge of the subject as is common in all civilized nations.

Those indeed who have preferred the other element, do justice to the certainty, as well as superior facilities of the pendulum, by proposing to recur to one of the length of their standard, and to ascertain its number of vibrations in a day. These being once known, if any accident impair their standard it is to be recovered by means of a pendulum which shall make the requisite number of vibrations in a day. And among the several commissions established by the Academy of Sciences for the execution of the several branches of their work on measures and weights, that respecting the pendulum was assigned to Messrs. Borda, Coulomb & Cassini, the result of whose labors, however, I have not learned.

Let our unit of measures then be a pendulum of such length as in the latitude of 45°, in the level of the ocean, and in a given temperature, shall perform its vibrations, in small and equal arcs, in one second of mean time.

What ratio shall we adopt for the parts and multiples of this unit? The decimal without a doubt. Our arithmetic being founded in a decimal numeration, the same numeration in a system of measures, weights and coins, tallies at once with that. On this question, I believe, there has been no difference of opinion.

In measures of length, then, the pendulum is our unit. It is a little more than our yard, and less than the ell. Its tenth or dime, will not be quite .4 inches. Its hundredth, or cent, not quite .4 of an inch; its thousandth, or mill, not quite .04 of an inch, and so on. The traveller will count his road by a longer measure. 1,000 units, or a kiliad, will not be quite two-thirds of our present mile, and more nearly a thousand paces than that.

For measures of surface, the square unit, equal to about ten square feet, or one-ninth more than a square yard, will be generally convenient. But for those of lands a larger measure will be wanted. A kiliad would be not quite a rood, or quarter of an acre; a myriad not quite 2½ acres.

For measures of capacity, wet and dry,

The cubic Unit = .1 would be about .35 cubic feet, .28 bushels dry, or ⅞ of a ton liquid
Dime = .1 would be about 3.5 cubic feet, 2.8 bushels, or about ⅞ of a barrel liquid
Cent = .01 about 50 cubic inches, or ⅞ of a quart
Mill = .001 = .5 of a cubic inch, or ⅔ of a gill

To incorporate into the same system our weights and coins, we must recur to some natural substance, to be found everywhere, and of a composition sufficiently uniform. Water has been considered as the most eligible substance, and rain-water more nearly uniform than any other kind found in nature. That circumstance renders it preferable to distilled water, and its variations in weight may be called insensible.

The cubic unit of this = .1 would weigh about 2,165 lbs. or a ton between the long and short.

| | |
|---|---|
| The Dime = | .1 a little more than 2. kentals |
| Cent = | .01 a little more than 20 lbs. |
| Mill = | .001 a little more than 2 lbs. |
| Decimmil = | .0001 about 3½ oz. avoirdupois |
| Centimmil = | .00001 a little more than 6 dwt. |
| Millionth = | .000001 about 15 grains |
| Decimmillionth = | .0000001 about 1½ grains |
| Centimmillionth = | .00000001 about .14 of a grain |
| Billionth = | .000000001 about .014 of a grain |

With respect to our coins, the pure silver in a dollar being fixed by law at 347¼ grains, and all debts and contracts being bottomed on that value, we can only state the pure silver in the dollar, which would be very nearly 23 millionths.

I have used loose and round numbers (the exact unit being yet undetermined) merely to give a general idea of the measures and weights proposed, when compared with those we now use. And in the names of the subdivisions I have followed the metrology of the ordinance of Congress of 1786, which for their series below unit adopted the Roman numerals. For that above unit the Grecian is convenient, and has been adopted in the new French system.

We come now to our last question, in what form shall we offer this metrical system to the world? In some one which shall be altogether unassuming; which shall not have the appearance of taking the lead among our sister institutions in making a general proposition. So jealous is the spirit of equality in the republic of letters, that the smallest excitement of that would mar our views, however salutary for all. We are in habits of correspondence with some of these institutions, and identity of character and of object, authorize our entering into correspondence with all. Let us then mature our system as far as can be done at present, by ascertaining the length of the second pendulum of 45° by forming two tables, one of which shall give the equivalent of every different denomination of measures, weights and coins in these States, in the unit of that pendulum, its decimals and multiples; and the other stating the equivalent of all the decimal parts and multiples of that pendulum, in the several denominations of measures, weights and coins of our existing system. This done, we might communicate to one or more of these institutions in every civilized country a copy of those tables, stating as our motive, the difficulty we had experienced, and often the impossibility of ascertaining the value of the measures, weights and coins of other countries, expressed in any standard which we possess; that desirous of being relieved from this, and of obtaining information which could be relied on for the purposes of science, as well as of business, we had concluded to ask it from the learned societies of other nations, who are especially qualified to give it with the requisite accuracy; that in making this request we had thought it our duty first to do ourselves, and to offer to others, what we meant to ask from them, by stating the value of our own measures, weights and coins, in some unit of measure already possessed, or easily obtainable, by all nations; that the pendulum vibrating seconds of mean time, presents itself as such an unit; its length being determined by the laws of nature, and easily ascertainable at all times and places; that we have thought that of 45° would be the most unexceptionable, as being a mean of all other parallels, and open to actual trial in both hemispheres. In this, therefore, as an unit, and in its parts and multiples in the decimal ratio, we have expressed, in the tables communicated, the value of all the measures, weights and coins used in the United States, and we ask in return from their body a table of the weights, measures and coins in use within their country, expressed in the parts and multiples of the same unit. Having requested the same favor from the learned societies of other nations, our object is, with their assistance, to place within the reach of our fellow citizens at large a perfect knowledge of the measures, weights and coins of the countries with which they have commercial or friendly intercourse; and should the societies of other countries interchange their respective tables, the learned will be in possession of an uniform language in measures, weights and coins, which may with time become useful to other descriptions of their citizens, and even to their governments. This, however, will rest with their pleasure, not presuming, in the present proposition, to extend our views beyond the limits of our own nation. I offer this sketch merely as the outline of the kind of communication which I should hope would excite no jealousy or repugnance.

Peculiar circumstances, however, would require letters of a more special character to the Institute of France, and the Royal Society of England. The magnificent work which France has executed in the admeasurement of so large a portion of the meridian, has a claim to great respect in our reference to it. We should only ask a communication of their metrical system, expressed in equivalent values of the second pendulum of 45° as ascertained by Messrs. Borda, Coulomb and Cassini, adding, perhaps, the request of an actual rod of the length of that pendulum.

With England, our explanations will be much more delicate. They are the older country, the mother country, more advanced in the arts and sciences, possessing more wealth and leisure for their improvement, and animated by a pride more than laudable.[2] It is their measures, too, which we undertake to ascertain and communicate to themselves. The subject should therefore be opened to them with infinite tenderness and respect, and in some way which might give them due place in its agency. The parallel of 45° being within our latitude and not within theirs, the actual experiments under that would be of course assignable to us. But as a corrective, I would propose that they should ascertain the length of the pendulum vibrating seconds in the city of London, or at the observatory of Greenwich, while we should do the same in an equi-distant parallel to the south of 45°, suppose in 38° 29′. We might ask of them, too, as they are in possession of the standards of Guildhall, of which we can have but an unauthentic account, to make the actual application of those standards to the pendulum when ascertained. The operation we should undertake under the 45th parallel (about Passamaquoddy), would give us a happy occasion, too, of engaging our sister society of Boston in our views, by referring to them the execution of that part of the work. For that of 38° 29′ we should be at a loss. It crosses the tide waters of the Potomac, about Dumfries, and I do not know what our resources there would be unless we borrow them from Washington, where there are competent persons.

Although I have not mentioned Philadelphia in these operations, I by no means propose to relinquish the benefit of observations to be made there. Her science and perfection in the arts would be a valuable corrective to the less perfect state of them in the other places of observation. Indeed, it is to be wished that Philadelphia could be made the point of observation south of 45°, and that the Royal Society would undertake the counterpoint on the north, which would be somewhere between the Lizard and Falmouth. The actual pendulums from both of our points of observation, and not merely the measures of them, should be delivered to the Philosophical Society, to be measured under their eye and direction.

As this is really a work of common and equal interest to England and the United States, perhaps it would be still more respectful to make our proposition to her Royal Society in the outset, and to agree with them on a partition of the work. In this case, any commencement of actual experiments on

[2] We are all occupied in industrious pursuits. They abound with persons living on the industry of their fathers, or on the earnings of their fellow citizens, given away by their rulers in sinecures and pensions. Some of these, desirous of laudable distinction, devote their time and means to the pursuits of science, and become profitable members of society by an industry of a higher order.—T. J.

our part should be provisional only, and preparatory to the ultimate results. We might, in the meantime, provisionally also, form a table adapted to the length of the pendulum of 45°, according to the most approved estimates, including those of the French commissioners. This would serve to introduce the subject to the foreign societies, in the way before proposed, reserving to ourselves the charge of communicating to them a more perfect one, when that shall have been completed.

We may even go a step further, and make a general table of the measures, weights and coins of all nations, taking their value hypothetically for the present, from the tables in the commercial dictionary of the encyclopédie méthodique, which are very extensive, and have the appearance of being made with great labor and exactness. To these I expect we must in the end recur, as a supplement for the measures which we may fail to obtain from other countries directly. Their reference is to the foot or inch of Paris, as a standard, which we may convert into parts of the second pendulum of 45°.

I have thus, my dear sir, committed to writing my general ideas on this subject, the more freely as they are intended merely as suggestions for consideration. It is not probable they offer anything which would not have occurred to the committee itself. My apology on offering them must be found in your request. My confidence in the committee, of which I take for granted you are one, is too entire to have intruded a single idea but on that ground.

Be assured of my affectionate and high esteem and respect.

## THE INVENTION OF ELEVATORS [1]

August 13, 1813

SIR: Your letter of August 3d asking information on the subject of Mr. Oliver Evans' exclusive right to the use of what he calls his Elevators, Conveyers, and Hopper-boys, has been duly received. My wish to see new inventions encouraged, and old ones brought again into useful notice, has made me regret the circumstances which have followed the expiration of his first patent. I did not expect the retrospection which has been given to the reviving law. For although the second proviso seemed not so clear as it ought to have been, yet it appeared susceptible of a just construction; and the retrospective one being contrary to natural right, it was understood to be a rule of law that where the words of a statute admit of two constructions, the one just and the other unjust, the former is to be given them. The first proviso takes care of those who had lawfully used Evans' improvements under the first patent; the second was meant for those who had lawfully

[1] Letter to Isaac McPherson.

erected and used them after that patent expired, declaring they "should not be liable to damages therefor." These words may indeed be restrained to uses already past, but as there is parity of reason for those to come, there should be parity of law. Every man should be protected in his lawful acts, and be certain that no *ex post facto* law shall punish or endamage him for them. But he is endamaged, if forbidden to use a machine lawfully erected, at considerable expense, unless he will pay a new and unexpected price for it. The proviso says that he who erected and used lawfully should not be liable to pay damages. But if the proviso had been omitted, would not the law, construed by natural equity, have said the same thing. In truth both provisos are useless. And shall useless provisos, inserted *pro majori cautela* only, authorize inferences against justice? The sentiment that *ex post facto* laws are against natural right, is so strong in the United States, that few, if any, of the State constitutions have failed to proscribe them. The federal constitution indeed interdicts them in criminal cases only; but they are equally unjust in civil as in criminal cases, and the omission of a caution which would have been right, does not justify the doing what is wrong. Nor ought it to be presumed that the legislature meant to use a phrase in an unjustifiable sense, if by rules of construction it can be ever strained to what is just. The law books abound with similar instances of the care the judges take of the public integrity. Laws, moreover, abridging the natural right of the citizen, should be restrained by rigorous constructions within their narrowest limits.

Your letter, however, points to a much broader question, whether what have received from Mr. Evans the new and proper name of Elevators, are of his invention. Because, if they are not, his patent gives him no right to obstruct others in the use of what they possessed before. I assume it is a Lemma, that it is the invention of the machine itself, which is to give a patent right, and not the application of it to any particular purpose, of which it is susceptible. If one person invents a knife convenient for pointing our pens, another cannot have a patent right for the same knife to point our pencils. A compass was invented for navigating the sea; another could not have a patent right for using it to survey land. A machine for threshing *wheat* has been invented in Scotland; a second person cannot get a patent right for the same machine to thresh *oats,* a third *rye,* a fourth *peas,* a fifth *clover,* &c. A string of buckets is invented and used for raising water, ore, &c., can a second have a patent right to the same machine for raising wheat, a third oats, a fourth rye, a fifth peas, &c? The question then whether such a string of buckets was invented first by Oliver Evans, is a mere question of fact in mathematical history. Now, turning to such books only as I happen to possess, I find abundant proof that this simple machinery has been in use from time immemorial. Doctor Shaw, who visited Egypt and the Barbary coast in the years 1727-8-9, in the margin of his map of Egypt, gives us the figure of what he calls a Persian wheel, which is a string of round cups or buckets hanging on a pulley, over which they revolved, bringing up water from a well and delivering it into a trough above. He found this used at Cairo, in a well 264 feet deep, which the inhabitants believe to have been the work of the patriarch Joseph. Shaw's travels, 341, Oxford edition of 1738 in folio, and the Universal History, I. 416, speaking of the manner of watering the higher lands in Egypt, says, "formerly they made use of Archimedes's screw, thence named the Egyptian pump, but they now generally use wheels (wallowers) which carry a rope or chain of earthen pots holding about seven or eight quarts apiece, and draw the water from the canals. There are besides a vast number of wells in Egypt, from which the water is drawn in the same manner to water the gardens and fruit trees; so that it is no exaggeration to say, that there are in Egypt above 200,000 oxen daily employed in this labor." Shaw's name of Persian wheel has been since given more particularly to a wheel with buckets, either fixed or suspended on pins, at its periphery. Mortimer's husbandry, I. 18, Duhamel III. II., Ferguson's Mechanic's plate, XIII; but his figure, and the verbal description of the Universal History, prove that the string of buckets is meant under that name. His figure differs from Evans' construction in the circumstances of the buckets being round, and strung through their bottom on a chain. But it is the principle, to wit, a string of buckets, which constitutes the invention, not the form of the buckets, round, square, or hexagon; nor the manner of attaching them, nor the material of the connecting band, whether chain, rope, or leather. Vitruvius, L. x. c. 9, describes this machinery as a windlass, on which is a chain descending to the water, with vessels of copper attached to it; the windless being turned, the chain moving on it will raise the vessel, which in passing over the windlass will empty the water they have brought up into a reservoir. And Perrault, in his edition of Vitruvius, Paris, 1684, fol. plates 61, 62, gives us three forms of these water elevators, in one of which the buckets are square, as Mr. Evans' are. Bossut, Histoire des Mathématiques, i. 86, says, "the drum wheel, the wheel with buckets and the *Chapelets,* are hydraulic machines which come to us from the ancients. But we are ignorant of the time when they began to be put into use." The *Chapelets* are the revolving bands of the buckets which Shaw calls the Persian wheel, the moderns a chain-pump, and Mr. Evans elevators. The next of my books in which I find these elevators is Wolf's Cours de Mathématiques, i. 370, and plate 1, Paris 1747, 8vo; here are two forms. In one of them the buckets are square, attached to two chains, passing over a cylinder or wallower at top, and under another at bottom, by which they are made to revolve. It is a nearly exact representation of Evans' Elevators. But a more exact one is to be seen in Desagulier's Experimental Philosophy,

ii. plate 34; in the Encyclopédie de Diderot et D'Alembert, 8vo edition of Lausanne, 1st volume of plates in the four subscribed Hydraulique. Norie, is one where round eastern pots are tied by their collars between two endless ropes suspended on a revolving lantern or wallower. This is said to have been used for raising ore out of a mine. In a book which I do not possess, L'Architecture Hydraulique de Belidor, the 2d volume of which is said [De la Lande's continuation of Montuclas' Histoire de Mathématiques, iii. 711] to contain a detail of all the pumps, ancient and modern, hydraulic machines, fountains, wells, &c, I have no doubt this Persian wheel, chain pump, chapelets, elevators, by whichever name you choose to call it, will be found in various forms. The last book I have to quote for it is Prony's Architecture Hydraulique i., Avertissement vii., and § 648, 649, 650. In the latter of which passages he observes that the first idea which occurs for raising water is to lift it in a bucket by hand. When the water lies too deep to be reached by hand, the bucket is suspended by a chain and let down over a pulley or windlass. If it be desired to raise a continued stream of water, the simplest means which offers itself to the mind is to attach to an endless chain or cord a number of pots or buckets, so disposed that, the chain being suspended on a lanthorn or wallower above, and plunged in water below, the buckets may descend and ascend alternately, filling themselves at bottom and emptying at a certain height above, so as to give a constant stream. Some years before the date of Mr. Evans' patent, a Mr. Martin of Caroline county in this State, constructed a drill-plough, in which he used the band of buckets for elevating the grain from the box into the funnel, which let them down into the furrow. He had bands with different sets of buckets adapted to the size of peas, of turnip seed, &c. I have used this machine for sowing Benni seed also, and propose to have a band of buckets for drilling Indian Corn, and another for wheat. Is it possible that in doing this I shall infringe Mr. Evans' patent? That I can be debarred of any use to which I might have applied my drill, when I bought it, by a patent issued after I bought it?

These verbal descriptions, applying so exactly to Mr. Evans' elevators, and the drawings exhibited to the eye, flash conviction both on reason and the senses that there is nothing new in these elevators but their being strung together on a strap of leather. If this strap of leather be an invention, entitling the inventor to a patent right, it can only extend to the strap, and the use of the string of buckets must remain free to be connected by chains, ropes, a strap of hempen girthing, or any other substance except leather. But, indeed, Mr. Martin had before used the strap of leather.

The screw of Archimedes is as ancient, at least, as the age of that mathematician, who died more than 2,000 years ago. Diodorus Siculus speaks of it, L. i., p. 21, and L. v., p. 217, of Stevens' edition of 1559, folio; and

Vitruvius, xii. The cutting of its spiral worm into sections for conveying flour or grain, seems to have been an invention of Mr. Evans, and to be a fair subject of a patent right. But it cannot take away from others the use of Archimedes' screw with its perpetual spiral, for any purposes of which it is susceptible.

The hopper-boy is an useful machine, and so far as I know, original.

It has been pretended by some (and in England especially), that inventors have a natural and exclusive right to their inventions, and not merely for their own lives, but inheritable to their heirs. But while it is a moot question whether the origin of any kind of property is derived from nature at all, it would be singular to admit a natural and even an hereditary right to inventors. It is agreed by those who have seriously considered the subject, that no individual has, of natural right, a separate property in an acre of land, for instance. By an universal law, indeed, whatever, whether fixed or movable, belongs to all men equally and in common, is the property for the moment of him who occupies it; but when he relinquishes the occupation, the property goes with it. Stable ownership is the gift of social law, and is given late in the progress of society. It would be curious then, if an idea, the fugitive fermentation of an individual brain, could, of natural right, be claimed in exclusive and stable property. If nature has made any one thing less susceptible than all others of exclusive property, it is the action of the thinking power called an idea, which an individual may exclusively possess as long as he keeps it to himself; but the moment it is divulged, it forces itself into the possession of everyone, and the receiver cannot dispossess himself of it. Its peculiar character, too, is that no one possesses the less, because every other possesses the whole of it. He who receives an idea from me, receives instruction himself without lessening mine; as he who lights his taper at mine, receives light without darkening me. That ideas should freely spread from one to another over the globe, for the moral and mutual instruction of man, and improvement of his condition, seems to have been peculiarly and benevolently designed by nature, when she made them, like fire, expansible over all space, without lessening their density in any point, and like the air in which we breathe, move, and have our physical being, incapable of confinement or exclusive appropriation. Inventions then cannot, in nature, be a subject of property. Society may give an exclusive right to the profits arising from them, as an encouragement to men to pursue ideas which may produce utility, but this may or may not be done, according to the will and convenience of the society, without claim or complaint from anybody. Accordingly, it is a fact, as far as I am informed, that England was, until we copied her, the only country on earth which ever, by a general law, gave a legal right to the exclusive use of an idea. In some other countries it is sometimes done, in a great case, and by a special and personal act, but, generally speaking, other nations have thought that these monopolies produce more embarrassment than advantage to society; and it may be observed that the nations which refuse monopolies of invention, are as fruitful as England in new and useful devices.

Considering the exclusive right to invention as given not of natural right, but for the benefit of society, I know well the difficulty of drawing a line between the things which are worth to the public the embarrassment of an exclusive patent, and those which are not. As a member of the patent board for several years, while the law authorized a board to grant or refuse patents, I saw with what slow progress a system of general rules could be matured. Some, however, were established by that board. One of these was, that a machine of which we were possessed, might be applied by every man to any use of which it is susceptible, and that this right ought not to be taken from him and given to a monopolist, because the first perhaps had occasion so to apply it. Thus a screw for crushing plaster might be employed for crushing corn-cobs. And a chain-pump for raising water might be used for raising wheat: this being merely a change of application. Another rule was that a change of material should not give title to a patent. As the making a ploughshare of cast rather than of wrought iron; a comb of iron instead of horn or of ivory, or the connecting buckets by a band of leather rather than of hemp or iron. A third was that a mere change of form should give no right to a patent, as a high-quartered shoe instead of a low one; a round hat instead of a three-square; or a square bucket instead of a round one. But for this rule, all the changes of fashion in dress would have been under the tax of patentees. These were among the rules which the uniform decisions of the board had already established, and under each of them Mr. Evans' patent would have been refused. First, because it was a mere change of application of the chain-pump, from raising water to raise wheat. Secondly, because the using a leathern instead of a hempen band, was a mere change of material; and thirdly, square buckets instead of round, are only a change of form, and the ancient forms, too, appear to have been indifferently square or round. But there were still abundance of cases which could not be brought under rule, until they should have presented themselves under all their aspects; and these investigations occupying more time of the members of the board than they could spare from higher duties, the whole was turned over to the judiciary, to be matured into a system, under which everyone might know when his actions were safe and lawful. Instead of refusing a patent in the first instance, as the board was authorized to do, the patent now issues of course, subject to be declared void on such principles as should be established by the courts of law. This business, however, is but little analogous to their course of reading, since we might in vain turn over all the lubberly volumes of the law to find a single ray which would lighten the path of the mechanic or the mathematician. It is more within the information of a board of academical professors, and a previous refusal of patent would better guard our citizens against harassment by law-suits. But England had given it to her judges, and the usual predominancy of her examples carried it to ours.

It happened that I had myself a mill built in the interval between Mr. Evans' first and second patents. I was living in Washington, and left the construction to the mill-wright. I did not even know he had erected elevators, conveyers and hopper-boys, until I learnt it by an application from Mr. Evans' agent for the patent price. Although I had no idea he had a right to it by law (for no judicial decision had then been given), yet I did not hesitate to remit to Mr. Evans the old and moderate patent price, which was what he then asked, from a wish to encourage even the useful revival of ancient inventions. But I then expressed my opinion of the law in a letter, either to Mr. Evans or to his agent.

I have thus, Sir, at your request, given you the facts and ideas which occur to me on this subject. I have done it without reserve, although I have not the pleasure of knowing you personally. In thus frankly committing myself to you, I trust you will feel it as a point of honor and candor, to make no use of my letter which might bring disquietude on myself. And particularly, I should be unwilling to be brought into any difference with Mr. Evans, whom, however, I believe too reasonable to take offence at an honest difference of opinion. I esteem him much, and sincerely wish him wealth and honor. I deem him a valuable citizen, of uncommon ingenuity and usefulness. And had I not esteemed still more the establishment of sound principles, I should now have been silent. If any of the matter I have offered can promote that object, I have no objection to its being so used; if it offers nothing new, it will of course not be used at all. I have gone with some minuteness into the mathematical history of the elevator, because it belongs to a branch of science in which, as I have before observed, it is not incumbent on lawyers to be learned; and it is possible, therefore, that some of the proofs I have quoted may have escaped on their former arguments. On the law of the subject I should not have touched, because more familiar to those who have already discussed it; but I wished to state my own view of it merely in justification of myself, my name and approbation being subscribed to the act. With these explanations, accept the assurance of my respect.

# NATURAL HISTORY: CLASSIFICATION[1]

February 22, 1814

SIR: The opinion which, in your letter of January 24, you are pleased to ask of me, on the comparative merits of the different methods of classification adopted by different writers on Natural History, is one which I could not have given satisfactorily, even at the earlier period at which the subject was more familiar; still less, after a life of continued occupation in civil concerns has so much withdrawn me from studies of that kind. I can, therefore, answer but in a very general way. And the text of this answer will be found in an observation in your letter, where, speaking of nosological systems, you say that disease has been found to be an unit. Nature has, in truth, produced units only through all her works. Classes, orders, genera, species, are not of her work. Her creation is of individuals. No two animals are exactly alike; no two plants, nor even two leaves or blades of grass; no two crystallizations. And if we may venture from what is within the cognizance of such organs as ours, to conclude on that beyond their powers, we must believe that no two particles of matter are of exact resemblance. This infinitude of units or individuals being far beyond the capacity of our memory, we are obliged, in aid of that, to distribute them into masses, throwing into each of these all the individuals which have a certain degree of resemblance; to subdivide these again into smaller groups, according to certain points of dissimilitude observable in them, and so on until we have formed what we call a system of classes, orders, genera and species. In doing this, we fix arbitrarily on such characteristic resemblances and differences as seem to us most prominent and invariable in the several subjects, and most likely to take a strong hold in our memories. Thus Ray formed one classification on such lines of division as struck him most favorably; Klein adopted another; Brisson a third, and other naturalists other designations, till Linnæus appeared. Fortunately for science, he conceived in the three kingdoms of nature, modes of classification which obtained the approbation of the learned of all nations. His system was accordingly adopted by all, and united all in a general language. It offered the three great desiderata: First, of aiding the memory to retain a knowledge of the productions of nature. Secondly, of rallying all to the same names for the same objects, so that they could communicate understandingly on them. And Thirdly, of enabling them, when a subject was first presented, to trace it by its character up to the conventional name by which it was agreed to be called. This classification was indeed liable to the imperfection of bringing into the same group individuals which, though resembling in the char-

[1] Letter to Dr. John Manners.

acteristics adopted by the author for his classification, yet have strong marks of dissimilitude in other respects. But to this objection every mode of classification must be liable, because the plan of creation is inscrutable to our limited faculties. Nature has not arranged her productions on a single and direct line. They branch at every step, and in every direction, and he who attempts to reduce them into departments, is left to do it by the lines of his own fancy. The objection of bringing together what are disparata in nature, lies against the classifications of Blumenbach and of Cuvier, as well as that of Linnæus, and must forever lie against all. Perhaps not in equal degree; on this I do not pronounce. But neither is this so important a consideration as that of uniting all nations under one language in Natural History. This had been happily effected by Linnæus, and can scarcely be hoped for a second time. Nothing indeed is so desperate as to make all mankind agree in giving up a language they possess, for one which they have to learn. The attempt leads directly to the confusion of the tongues of Babel. Disciples of Linnæus, of Blumenbach, and of Cuvier, exclusively possessing their own nomenclatures, can no longer communicate intelligbly with one another. However much, therefore, we are indebted to both these naturalists, and to Cuvier especially, for the valuable additions they have made to the sciences of nature, I cannot say they have rendered her a service in this attempt to innovate in the settled nomenclature of her productions; on the contrary, I think it will be a check on the progress of science, greater or less, in proportion as their schemes shall more or less prevail. They would have rendered greater service by holding fast to the system on which we had once all agreed, and by inserting into that such new genera, orders, or even classes, as new discoveries should call for. Their systems, too, and especially that of Blumenbach, are liable to the objection of giving too much into the province of anatomy. It may be said, indeed, that anatomy is a part of natural history. In the broad sense of the word, it certainly is. In that sense, however, it would comprehend all the natural sciences, every created thing being a subject of natural history in extenso. But in the subdivisions of general science, as has been observed in the particular one of natural history, it has been necessary to draw arbitrary lines, in order to accommodate our limited views. According to these, as soon as the structure of any natural production is destroyed by art, it ceases to be a subject of natural history, and enters into the domain ascribed to chemistry, to pharmacy, to anatomy, &c. Linnæus' method was liable to this objection so far as it required the aid of anatomical dissection, as of the heart, for instance, to ascertain the place of any animal, or of a chemical process for that of a mineral substance. It would certainly be better to adopt as much as possible such exterior and visible characteristics as every traveller is competent to observe, to ascertain and to relate. But with this objection, lying but in a small degree, Linnæus' method was received, understood, and conventionally settled among the learned, and was even getting into common use. To disturb it then was unfortunate. The new system attempted in botany, by Jussieu, in mineralogy, by Haüiy, are subjects of the same regret, and so also the no-system of Buffon, the great advocate of individualism in opposition to classification. He would carry us back to the days and to the confusion of Aristotle and Pliny, give up the improvements of twenty centuries, and co-operate with the neologists in rendering the science of one generation useless to the next by perpetual changes of its language. In botany, Wildenow and Persoon have incorporated into Linnæus the new discovered plants. I do not know whether anyone has rendered us the same service as to his natural history. It would be a very acceptable one. The materials furnished by Humboldt, and those from New Holland particularly, require to be digested into the catholic system. Among these, the Ornithorhyncus mentioned by you is an amusing example of the anomalies by which nature sports with our schemes of classification. Although without mammæ, naturalists are obliged to place it in the class of mammiferæ; and Blumenbach, particularly, arranges it in his order of Palmipeds and toothless genus, with the walrus and manatie. In Linnæus' system it might be inserted as a new genus between the anteater and manis, in the order of Bruta. It seems, in truth, to have stronger relations with that class than any other in the construction of the heart, its red and warm blood, hairy integuments, in being quadruped and viviparous, and may we not say, in its *tout ensemble,* which Buffon makes his sole principle of arrangement? The mandible, as you observe, would draw it towards the birds, were not this characteristic overbalanced by the weightier ones before mentioned. That of the Cloaca is equivocal, because although a character of birds, yet some mammalia, as the beaver and sloth, have the rectum and urinary passage terminating at a common opening. Its ribs also, by their number and structure, are nearer those of the bird than of the mammalia. It is possible that further opportunities of examination may discover the mammæ. Those of the Opossum are asserted, by the Chevalier d'Aboville, from his own observations on that animal, made while here with the French army, to be not discoverable until pregnancy, and to disappear as soon as the young are weaned. The Duckbill has many additional particularities which liken it to other genera, and some entirely peculiar. Its description and history needs yet further information.

In what I have said on the method of classing, I have not at all meant to insinuate that that of Linnæus is intrinsically preferable to those of Blumenbach and Cuvier. I adhere to the Linnæan because it is sufficient as a ground-work, admits of supplementary insertions as new productions are discovered, and mainly because it has got into so general use that it will not be easy to displace it, and still less to find another which shall have the same singular fortune of obtaining the general consent. During the attempt we shall become unintelligible to one another, and science will be really retarded by efforts to advance it made by its most favorite sons. I am not myself apt to be alarmed at innovations recommended by reason. That dread belongs to those whose interests or prejudices shrink from the advance of truth and science. My reluctance is to give up an universal language of which we are in possession, without an assurance of general consent to receive another. And the higher the character of the authors recommending it, and the more excellent what they offer, the greater the danger of producing schism.

I should seem to need apology for these long remarks to you who are so much more recent in these studies, but I find it in your particular request and my own respect for it, and with that be pleased to accept the assurance of my esteem and consideration.

## SURVEYING[1]

March 18, 1814

You likewise requested for the use of your school, an explanation of a method of platting the courses of a survey, which I mentioned to you as of my own practice. This is so obvious and simple, that as it occurred to myself, so I presume it has to others, although I have not seen it stated in any of the books. For drawing parallel lines, I use the triangular rule, the hypothenusal side of which being applied to the side of a common straight rule, the triangle slides on that, as thus, always parallel to itself. Instead of drawing meridians on his paper, let the pupil draw a parallel of latitude, or east and west line, and note in that a point for his first station, then applying to it his protractor, lay off the first course and distance in the usual way to ascertain his second station. For the second course, lay the triangular rule to the east and west line, or first parallel, holding the straight or guide rule firmly against its hypothenusal side. Then slide up the triangle (for a northerly course) to the point of his second station, and pressing it firmly there, lay the protractor to that, and mark off the second course, and distance as before, for the third station. Then lay the triangle to the first parallel again, and sliding it as before to the point of the third station, there apply to it the protractor for the third course and distance, which gives the fourth station; and so on. Where a course is southwardly, lay the protractor, as before, to the northern edge of the triangle, but prick its

[1] Letter to Louis Hue Girardin, Professor of Modern Languages, William and Mary College.

reversed course, which reversed again in drawing, gives the true course. When the station has got so far from the first parallel, as to be out of the reach of the parallel rule sliding on its hypothenuse, another parallel must be drawn by laying the edge, or longer leg of the triangle, to the first parallel as before, applying the guide-rule to the end, or short leg (instead of the hypothenuse), as in the margin, and sliding the triangle up to the point for the new parallel. I have found this, in practice, the quickest and most correct method of platting which I have ever tried, and the neatest also, because it disfigures the paper with the fewest unnecessary lines.

If these mathematical trifles can give any facilities to your pupils, they may in their hands become matters of use, as in mine they have been of amusement only.

## WHAT CONSTITUTES A MULATTO? [1]

March 4, 1815

You asked me in conversation, what constituted a mulatto by our law? And I believe I told you four crossings with the whites. I looked afterwards into our law, and found it to be in these words: "Every person, other than a Negro, of whose grandfathers or grandmothers anyone shall have been a Negro, shall be deemed a mulatto, and so every such person who shall have one-fourth part or more of Negro blood, shall in like manner be deemed a mulatto"; L. Virgà 1792, December 17: the case put in the first member of this paragraph of the law is *exempli gratiâ*. The latter contains the true canon, which is that one-fourth of Negro blood, mixed with any portion of white, constitutes the mulatto. As the issue has one-half of the blood of each parent, and the blood of each of these may be made up of a variety of fractional mixtures, the estimate of their compound in some cases may be intricate, it becomes a mathematical problem of the same class with those on the mixtures of different liquors or different metals; as in these, therefore, the algebraical notation is the most convenient and intelligible. Let us express the pure blood of the white in the capital letters of the printed alphabet, the pure blood of the Negro in the small letters of the printed alphabet, and any given mixture of either, by way of abridgement in MS. letters.

Let the first crossing be of *a*, pure Negro, with A, pure white. The unit of blood of the issue being composed of the half of that of each parent, will be $\frac{a}{2} + \frac{A}{2}$. Call it, for abbreviation, *h* (half blood).

[1] Letter to Francis C. Gray.

Let the second crossing be of $h$ and B, the blood of the issue will be $\frac{h}{2} + \frac{B}{2}$, or substituting for $\frac{h}{2}$ its equivalent, it will be $\frac{a}{4} + \frac{A}{4} + \frac{B}{2}$ call it $q$ (quarteroon) being $\frac{1}{4}$ Negro blood.

Let the third crossing be of $q$ and C, their offspring will be $\frac{q}{2} + \frac{C}{2} = \frac{a}{8} + \frac{A}{8} + \frac{B}{4} + \frac{C}{2}$, call this $e$ (eighth), who having less than $\frac{1}{4}$ of $a$, or of pure Negro blood, to wit $\frac{1}{8}$ only, is no longer a mulatto, so that a third cross clears the blood.

From these elements let us examine their compounds. For example, let $h$ and $q$ cohabit, their issue will be $\frac{h}{2} + \frac{q}{2} = \frac{a}{4} + \frac{A}{4} + \frac{a}{8} + \frac{A}{8} + \frac{B}{4} = \frac{3a}{8} + \frac{3A}{8} + \frac{B}{4}$ wherein we find $\frac{3}{8}$ of $a$, or Negro blood.

Let $h$ and $e$ cohabit, their issue will be $\frac{h}{2} + \frac{e}{2} = \frac{a}{4} + \frac{A}{4} + \frac{a}{16} + \frac{A}{16} + \frac{B}{8} + \frac{c}{4} = \frac{5a}{16} + \frac{5A}{16} + \frac{B}{8} + \frac{c}{4}$, wherein $\frac{5}{16}$ $a$ makes still a mulatto.

Let $q$ and $e$ cohabit, the half of the blood of each will be $\frac{q}{2} + \frac{e}{2} = \frac{a}{8} + \frac{A}{8} + \frac{B}{4} + \frac{a}{16} + \frac{A}{16} + \frac{B}{8} + \frac{C}{4} = \frac{3a}{16} + \frac{3A}{16} + \frac{3B}{8} + \frac{C}{4}$, wherein $\frac{3}{16}$ of $a$ is no longer a mulatto, and thus may every compound be noted and summed, the sum of the fractions composing the blood of the issue being always equal to unit. It is understood in natural history that a fourth cross of one race of animals with another gives an issue equivalent for all sensible purposes to the original blood. Thus a Merino ram being crossed, first with a country ewe, second with his daughter, third with his granddaughter, and fourth with the great-granddaughter, the last issue is deemed pure Merino, having in fact but $\frac{1}{16}$ of the country blood. Our canon considers two crosses with the pure white, and a third with any degree of mixture, however small, as clearing the issue of the Negro blood. But observe, that this does not re-establish freedom, which depends on the condition of the mother, the principle of the civil law, *partus sequitur ventrem*, being adopted here. But if $e$ be emancipated, he becomes a free *white* man, and a citizen of the United States to all intents and purposes. So much for this trifle by way of correction.

# THE STEAM ENGINE AND THE HEMP-BREAK[1]

December 29, 1815

At the date of your favor of October 30th, I had just left home on a journey to a distant possession of mine, from which I am but recently returned, and I wish that the matter of my answer could compensate for its delay. But, Sir, it happens that of all the machines which have been employed to aid human labor, I have made myself the least acquainted with (that which is certainly the most powerful of all) the steam engine. In its original and simple form indeed, as first constructed by Newcomen and Savary, it had been a subject of my early studies; but once possessed of the principle, I ceased to follow up the numerous modifications of the machinery for employing it, of which I do not know whether England or our own country has produced the greatest number. Hence, I am entirely incompetent to form a judgment of the comparative merit of yours with those preceding it; and the cession of my library to Congress has left me without any examples to turn to. I see, indeed, in yours, the valuable properties of simplicity, cheapness and accommodation to the small and more numerous calls of life, and the calculations of its power appear sound and correct. Yet experience and frequent disappointment have taught me not to be over-confident in theories or calculations, until actual trial of the whole combination has stamped it with approbation. Should this sanction be added, the importance of your construction will be enhanced by the consideration that a smaller agent, applicable to our daily concerns, is infinitely more valuable than the greatest which can be used only for great objects. For these interest the few alone, the former the many. I once had an idea that it might perhaps be possible to economize the steam of a common pot, kept boiling on the kitchen fire until its accumulation should be sufficient to give a stroke, and although the strokes might not be rapid, there would be enough of them in the day to raise from an adjacent well the water necessary for daily use; to wash the linen, knead the bread, beat the hominy, churn the butter, turn the spit, and do all other household offices which require only a regular mechanical motion. The unproductive hands now necessarily employed in these, might then increase the produce of our fields. I proposed it to Mr. Rumsey, one of our greatest mechanics, who believed in its possibility, and promised to turn his mind to it. But his death soon after disappointed this hope. Of how much more value would this be to ordinary life than Watts & Bolton's thirty pair of mill-stones to be turned by one engine, of which I saw seven pair in actual operation.

[1] Letter to George Fleming.

It is an interesting part of your question, how much fuel would be requisite for your machine?

Your letter being evidence of your attention to mechanical things, and to their application to matters of daily interest, I will mention a trifle in this way, which yet is not without value. I presume, like the rest of us in the country, you are in the habit of household manufacture, and that you will not, like too many, abandon it on the return of peace, to enrich our late enemy, and to nourish foreign agents in our bosom, whose baneful influence and intrigues cost us so much embarrassment and dissension. The shirting for our laborers has been an object of some difficulty. Flax is injurious to our lands, and of so scanty produce that I have never attempted it. Hemp, on the other hand, is abundantly productive, and will grow forever on the same spot. But the breaking and beating it, which has been always done by hand, is so slow, so laborious, and so much complained of by our laborers, that I had given it up and purchased and manufactured cotton for their shirting. The advanced price of this, however, now makes it a serious item of expense; and in the meantime, a method of removing the difficulty of preparing hemp occurred to me, so simple and so cheap, that I return to its culture and manufacture. To a person having a threshing machine, the addition of a hemp-break will not cost more than twelve or fifteen dollars. You know that the first mover in that machine is a horizontal horse-wheel with cogs on its upper face. On these are placed a wallower and shaft, which give motion to the threshing apparatus. On the opposite side of this same wheel I place another wallower and shaft, through which, and near its outer end, I pass a cross-arm of sufficient strength, projecting on each side fifteen inches in this form:

nearly under the cross-arm is placed a very strong hemp-break, much stronger and heavier than those for the hand. Its head block particularly is massive, and four feet high, and near its upper end in front is fixed a strong pin (which we may call its horn), by this the cross-arm lifts and lets fall the break twice in every revolution of the wallower. A man feeds the break with hemp stalks, and a little person holds under the head block a large twist of the hemp which has been broken, resembling a twist of tobacco but larger, where it is more perfectly beaten than I have ever seen done by hand. If the horse-wheel has one hundred and forty-four cogs, the wallower eleven rounds, and the horse goes three times round in a minute, it will give about eighty strokes in a minute. I had fixed a break to be moved by the gate of my saw-mill, which broke and beat at the rate of two hundred pounds a day. But the inconveniences of interrupting that, induced me to try the power of a horse, and I have found it to answer perfectly. The power being less, so also probably will be the effect, of which I cannot make a fair trial until I commence on my new crop. I expect that a single horse will do the breaking and beating of ten men. Something of this kind has been so long wanted by the cultivators of hemp, that as soon as I can speak of its effect with certainty, I shall probably describe it anonymously in the public papers, in order to forestall the prevention of its use by some interloping patentee. I shall be happy to learn that an actual experiment of your steam engine fulfils the expectations we form of it, and I pray you to accept the assurances of my esteem and respect.

## A METHOD OF FINDING THE LONGITUDE OF A PLACE AT LAND, WITHOUT A TIME-KEEPER

November 29, 1821

If two persons, at different points of the same hemisphere (as Greenwich and Washington, for example), observe the same celestial phenomenon, at the same instant of time, the difference of the times marked by their respective clocks is the difference of their longitudes, or the distance between their meridians. To catch with precision the same instant of time for these simultaneous observations, the moon's motion in her orbit is the best element; her change of place (about a half second of space in a second of time) is rapid enough to be ascertained by a good instrument with sufficient precision for the object. But suppose the observer at Washington, or in a desert, to be without a time-keeper; the equatorial is the instrument to be used in that case. Again, we have supposed a cotemporaneous observer at Greenwich. But his functions may be supplied by the nautical almanac, adapted to that place, and enabling us to calculate for any instant of time the meridian distances there of the heavenly bodies necessary to be observed for this purpose.

The observer at Washington, choosing the time when their position is suitable, is to adjust his equatorial to his meridian, to his latitude, and to the plane of his horizon; or if he is in a desert where neither meridian nor latitude is yet ascertained, the advantages of this noble instrument are, that it enables him to find both in the course of a few hours. Thus prepared, let him ascertain by observation the right ascension of the moon from that of a known star, or their horary distance; and, at the same instant, her horary distance from his meridian. Her right ascension at the instant thus ascertained, enter with that of the nautical almanac, and calculate, by its tables, what was her horary distance from the meridian of Greenwich at the instant she had attained that point of right ascension, or that horary distance from the same star. The addition of these meridian distances, if the moon was between the two meridians, or the subtraction of the lesser from the greater, if she was on the same side of both, is the differences of their longitudes.

This general theory admits different cases, of which the observer may avail himself, according to the particular position of the heavenly bodies at the moment of observation.

Case 1st. When the moon is on his meridian, or on that of Greenwich.

Second. When the star is on either meridian.

Third. When the moon and star are on the same side of his meridian.

Fourth. When they are on different sides.

For instantaneousness of observation, the equatorial has great advantage over the circle or sextant; for being truly placed in the meridian beforehand, the telescope may be directed sufficiently in advance of the moon's motion, for time to note its place on the equatorial circle, before she attains that point. Then observe, until her limb touches the cross-hairs; and in that instant direct the telescope to the star; that completes the observation, and the place of the star may be read at leisure. The apparatus for correcting the effects of refraction and parallax, which is fixed on the eye-tube of the telescope, saves time by rendering the notation of altitudes unnecessary, and dispenses with the use of either a time-keeper or portable pendulum.

I have observed that, if placed in a desert where neither meridian nor latitude is yet ascertained, the equatorial enables the observer to find both in a few hours. For the latitude, adjust by the cross-levels the azimuth plane of the instrument to the horizon of the place. Bring down the equatorial plane to an exact parallelism with it, its pole then becoming vertical. By the nut and pinion commanding it, and by that of the semi-circle of declination, direct the telescope to the sun. Follow its path with the telescope by the combined use of these two pinions, and when it has attained its greatest altitude, calculate the latitude as when taken by a sextant.

For finding the meridian, set the azimuth circle to the horizon, elevate the equatorial circle to the complement of the latitude, and fix it by the clamp and tightening screw of the two brass segments of arches below. By the declination semicircle set the telescope to the sun's declination of the moment. Turn the instrument towards the meridian by guess, and by the combined movement of the equatorial and azimuth circles direct the telescope to the sun, then by the pinion of the equatorial alone, follow the path of the sun with the telescope. If it swerves from that path, turn the azimuth circle until it shall follow the sun accurately. A distant stake or tree should mark the meridian, to guard against its loss by any accidental jostle of the instrument. The 12 o'clock line will then be in the true meridian, and the axis of the equatorial circle will be parallel with that of the earth. The instrument is then in its true position for the observations of the night. To the competence and the advantages of this method, I will only add that these instruments are high-priced. Mine cost thirty-five guineas in Ramsden's shop, a little before the Revolution. I will lengthen my letter, already too long, only by assurances of my great esteem and respect.

## A LOCK-DOCK FOR NAVY VESSELS[1]

November 27, 1825

SIR: Disqualified by age and ill health from undertaking minute investigations, I find it will be easier for me to state to you my proposition of a lock-dock, for laying up vessels, high and dry, than to investigate yours. You will then judge for yourself whether any part of mine has anticipated any part of yours.

While I was at Washington, in the administration of the government, Congress was much divided in opinion on the subject of a navy, a part of them wishing to go extensively into preparation of a fleet, another part opposed to it, on the objection that the repairs and preservation of a ship, even idle in harbor, in ten or twelve years, amount to her original cost. It has been estimated in England, that if they could be sure of peace a dozen years it would be cheaper for them to burn their fleet, and build a new one when wanting, than to keep the old one in repair during that term. I learnt that, in Venice, there were then ships, lying on their original stocks, ready for launching at any moment, which had been so for eighty years, and were still in a state of perfect preservation; and that this was effected by disposing of them in docks pumped dry, and kept so by constant pumping. It occurred to me that this expense of constant pumping might be saved by combining a lock with the common wet dock, wherever there was a running stream of water, the bed of which, within a reasonable distance, was of a sufficient height above the high-water level of the harbor. This was the case at the navy-yard, on the eastern branch at Washington, the high-water line of which was seventy-eight feet lower than the ground on which the Capitol stands, and to which it was found that the water of the Tyber creek could be brought for watering the city. My proposition then was as follows: Let *a b* be the high-water level of the harbor, and the vessel to be laid up draw eighteen feet of water. Make a chamber A twenty feet deep below high water and twenty feet high above it, as *c d e f*, and at the upper end make another chamber, B,

[1] Letter to Lewis M. Wiss.

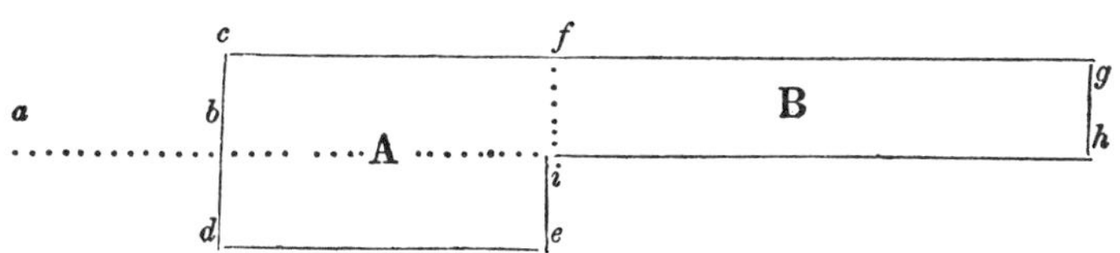


the bottom of which should be in the high-water level, and the tops twenty feet above that. *g h* is the water of the Tyber. When the vessel is to be introduced, open the gate at *c b a.* The tide water rises in the chamber A to the level *b i,* and floats the vessel in with it. Shut the gate *c b d* and open that of *f i.* The water of the Tyber fills both chambers to the level *c f g,* and the vessel floats into the chamber B; then opening both gates *c b d* and *f i,* the water flows out, and the vessel settles down on the stays previously prepared at the bottom *i h* to receive her. The gate at *g h* must of course be closed, and the water of the feeding stream be diverted elsewhere. The chamber B is to have a roof over it of the construction of that over the meal market at Paris, except that that is hemispherical, this semi-cylindrical. For this construction see Delenne's architecture, whose invention it was. The diameter of the dome of the meal market is considerably over one hundred feet.

It will be seen at once, that instead of making the chamber B of sufficient width and length for a single vessel only, it may be widened to whatever span the semi-circular framing of the roof can be trusted, and to whatever length you please, so as to admit two or more vessels in breadth, and as many in length as the localities render expedient.

I had a model of this lock-dock made and exhibited in the President's house, during the session of Congress at which it was proposed. But the advocates for a navy did not fancy it, and those opposed to the building of ships altogether were equally indisposed to provide protection for them. Ridicule was also resorted to, the ordinary substitute for reason, when that fails, and the proposition was passed over. I then thought and still think the measure wise, to have a proper number of vessels always ready to be launched, with nothing unfinished about them, except the planting their masts, which must of necessity be omitted, to be brought under a roof. Having no view in this proposition but to combine for the public a provision for defence, with economy in its preservation, I have thought no more of it since. And if any of my ideas anticipated yours, you are welcome to appropriate them to yourself, without objection on my part, and, with this assurance, I pray you to accept that of my best wishes and respects.

# *Chapter XXI*

# PHILOSOPHY AND CONDUCT

## PHILOSOPHERS IN FRANCE[1]

December, 1803

I find nothing surprising in the raining of stones in France—nor yet had they been Mill stones. There are in France more real Philosophers than in any country on Earth but there are also a greater proportion of pseudo Philosophers there. The reason is that the exuberant imagination of a French-man gives him a greater facility of writing and runs away with his judgment unless he has a good stock of it. It even creates facts for him which never happened and he tells them with good faith. Count Rumford after discovering that cold is a positive body will doubtless find out that darkness is so too. As many as two or three times during my seven years residence in France new discoveries were made which overset the whole Newtonian Philosophy.

## CONDUCT AND MANNERS[2]

November 24, 1808

I have mentioned good humor as one of the preservatives of our peace and tranquillity. It is among the most effectual, and its effect is so well imitated and aided, artificially, by politeness, that this also becomes an acquisition of first rate value. In truth, politeness is artificial good humor, it covers the natural want of it, and ends by rendering habitual a substitute nearly equivalent to the real virtue. It is the practice of sacrificing to those whom we meet in society, all the little conveniences and preferences which

[1] Letter to Major Andrew Ellicott, in reply to an account from France of a shower of stones. This letter is included here chiefly because of its rare whimsicality.

[2] Letter to his grandson, Thomas Jefferson Randolph.

will gratify them, and deprive us of nothing worth a moment's consideration; it is the giving a pleasing and flattering turn to our expressions, which will conciliate others, and make them pleased with us as well as ourselves. How cheap a price for the good will of another! When this is in return for a rude thing said by another, it brings him to his senses, it mortifies and corrects him the most salutary way, and places him at the feet of your good nature, in the eyes of the company.

But in stating prudential rules for our government in society, I must not omit the important one of never entering into dispute or argument with another. I never saw an instance of one of two disputants convincing the other by argument. I have seen many, on their getting warm, becoming rude, and shooting one another. Conviction is the effect of our own dispassionate reasoning, either in solitude, or weighing within ourselves, dispassionately, what we hear from others, standing uncommitted in argument ourselves. It was one of the rules which, above all others, made Doctor Franklin the most amiable of men in society, "never to contradict anybody." If he was urged to announce an opinion, he did it rather by asking questions, as if for information, or by suggesting doubts.

When I hear another express an opinion which is not mine, I say to myself, he has a right to his opinion, as I to mine; why should I question it? His error does me no injury, and shall I become a Don Quixote, to bring all men by force of argument to one opinion? If a fact be misstated, it is probable he is gratified by a belief of it, and I have no right to deprive him of the gratification. If he wants information, he will ask it, and then I will give it in measured terms; but if he still believes his own story, and shows a desire to dispute the fact with me, I hear him and say nothing. It is his affair, not mine, if he prefers error.

There are two classes of disputants most frequently to be met with among us. The first is of young students, just entered the threshold of science, with a first view of its outlines, not yet filled up with the details and modifications which a further progress would bring to their knowledge. The other consists of the ill-tempered and rude men in society, who have taken up a passion for politics. (Good humor and politeness never introduce into mixed society a question on which they foresee there will be a difference of opinion.) From both of those classes of disputants, my dear Jefferson, keep aloof, as you would from the infected subjects of yellow fever or pestilence. Consider yourself, when with them, as among the patients of Bedlam, needing medical more than moral counsel.

Be a listener only, keep within yourself, and endeavor to establish with yourself the habit of silence, especially on politics. In the fevered state of our country, no good can ever result from any attempt to set one of these fiery zealots to rights, either in fact or principle. They are determined as to the facts they will believe, and the opinions on which they will act. Get by them, therefore, as you would an angry bull; it is not for a man of sense to dispute the road with such an animal.

## THE MORAL INSTINCT[1]

June 13, 1814

Of all the theories on this question, the most whimsical seems to have been that of Wollaston, who considers *truth* as the foundation of morality. The thief who steals your guinea does wrong only inasmuch as he acts a lie in using your guinea as if it were his own. Truth is certainly a branch of morality, and a very important one to society. But presented as its foundation, it is as if a tree taken up by the roots, had its stem reversed in the air, and one of its branches planted in the ground. Some have made the *love of God* the foundation of morality. This, too, is but a branch of our moral duties, which are generally divided into duties to God and duties to man. If we did a good act merely from the love of God and a belief that it is pleasing to Him, whence arises the morality of the Atheist? It is idle to say, as some do, that no such being exists. We have the same evidence of the fact as of most of those we act on, to wit: their own affirmations, and their reasonings in support of them. I have observed, indeed, generally, that while in Protestant countries the defections from the Platonic Christianity of the priests is to Deism, in Catholic countries they are to Atheism. Diderot, d'Alembert, d'Holbach, Condorcet, are known to have been among the most virtuous of men. Their virtue, then, must have had some other foundation than the love of God.

The To καλον of others is founded in a different faculty, that of taste, which is not even a branch of morality. We have indeed an innate sense of what we call beautiful, but that is exercised chiefly on subjects addressed to the fancy, whether through the eye in visible forms, as landscape, animal figure, dress, drapery, architecture, the composition of colors, &c., or to the imagination directly, as imagery, style, or measure in prose or poetry, or whatever else constitutes the domain of criticism or taste, a faculty entirely distinct from the moral one. Self-interest, or rather self-love, or *egoism,* has been more plausibly substituted as the basis of morality. But I consider our relations with others as constituting the boundaries of morality. With ourselves we stand on the ground of identity, not of relation, which last, requiring two subjects, excludes self-love confined to a single one. To ourselves, in strict language, we can owe no duties, obligation requiring also two parties. Self-love, therefore, is no part of morality. Indeed it is exactly

[1] Letter to Thomas Law.

its counterpart. It is the sole antagonist of virtue, leading us constantly by our propensities to self-gratification in violation of our moral duties to others. Accordingly, it is against this enemy that are erected the batteries of moralists and religionists, as the only obstacle to the practice of morality. Take from man his selfish propensities, and he can have nothing to seduce him from the practice of virtue. Or subdue those propensities by education, instruction or restraint, and virtue remains without a competitor. Egoism, in a broader sense, has been thus presented as the source of moral action. It has been said that we feed the hungry, clothe the naked, bind up the wounds of the man beaten by thieves, pour oil and wine into them, set him on our own beast and bring him to the inn, because we receive ourselves pleasure from these acts. So Helvetius, one of the best men on earth, and the most ingenious advocate of this principle, after defining "interest" to mean not merely that which is pecuniary, but whatever may procure us pleasure or withdraw us from pain, [*de l'esprit* 2, 1,] says, [*ib.* 2, 2,] "the humane man is he to whom the sight of misfortune is insupportable, and who to rescue himself from this spectacle, is forced to succor the unfortunate object." This indeed is true. But it is one step short of the ultimate question. These good acts give us pleasure, but how happens it that they give us pleasure? Because nature hath implanted in our breasts a love of others, a sense of duty to them, a moral instinct, in short, which prompts us irresistibly to feel and to succor their distresses, and protests against the language of Helvetius, [*ib.* 2, 5,] "what other motive than self-interest could determine a man to generous actions? It is as impossible for him to love what is good for the sake of good, as to love evil for the sake of evil." The Creator would indeed have been a bungling artist, had he intended man for a social animal, without planting in him social dispositions. It is true they are not planted in every man, because there is no rule without exceptions; but it is false reasoning which converts exceptions into the general rule. Some men are born without the organs of sight, or of hearing, or without hands. Yet it would be wrong to say that man is born without these faculties, and sight, hearing, and hands may with truth enter into the general definition of man. The want or imperfection of the moral sense in some men, like the want or imperfection of the senses of sight and hearing in others, is no proof that it is a general characteristic of the species. When it is wanting, we endeavor to supply the defect by education, by appeals to reason and calculation, by presenting to the being so unhappily conformed, other motives to do good and to eschew evil, such as the love, or the hatred, or rejection of those among whom he lives, and whose society is necessary to his happiness and even existence; demonstrations by sound calculation that honesty promotes interest in the long run; the rewards and penalties established by the laws; and ultimately the prospects of a future state of retribution for the evil as well as the good done while here. These are the correctives which are supplied by education, and which exercise the functions of the moralist, the preacher, and legislator; and they lead into a course of correct action all those whose disparity is not too profound to be eradicated. Some have argued against the existence of a moral sense, by saying that if nature had given us such a sense, impelling us to virtuous actions, and warning us against those which are vicious, then nature would also have designated, by some particular ear-marks, the two sets of actions which are, in themselves, the one virtuous and the other vicious. Whereas, we find, in fact, that the same actions are deemed virtuous in one country and vicious in another. The answer is that nature has constituted *utility* to man the standard and test of virtue. Men living in different countries, under different circumstances, different habits and regimens, may have different utilities; the same act, therefore, may be useful, and consequently virtuous in one country which is injurious and vicious in another differently circumstanced. I sincerely, then, believe with you in the general existence of a moral instinct. I think it the brightest gem with which the human character is studded, and the want of it as more degrading than the most hideous of the bodily deformities. I am happy in reviewing the roll of associates in this principle which you present in your second letter, some of which I had not before met with. To these might be added Lord Kaims, one of the ablest of our advocates, who goes so far as to say, in his Principles of Natural Religion, that a man owes no duty to which he is not urged by some impulsive feeling. This is correct, if referred to the standard of general feeling in the given case, and not to the feeling of a single individual. Perhaps I may misquote him, it being fifty years since I read his book.

## THE NONSENSE OF PLATO[1]

July 5, 1814

I amused myself with reading seriously Plato's Republic. I am wrong, however, in calling it amusement, for it was the heaviest task-work I ever went through. I had occasionally before taken up some of his other works, but scarcely ever had patience to go through a whole dialogue. While wading through the whimsies, the puerilities, and unintelligible jargon of this work, I laid it down often to ask myself how it could have been, that the world should have so long consented to give reputation to such nonsense as this? How the *soi-disant* Christian world, indeed, should have done it,

[1] Letter to John Adams.

is a piece of historical curiosity. But how could the Roman good sense do it? And particularly, how could Cicero bestow such eulogies on Plato? Although Cicero did not wield the dense logic of Demosthenes, yet he was able, learned, laborious, practised in the business of the world, and honest. He could not be the dupe of mere style, of which he was himself the first master in the world. With the moderns, I think, it is rather a matter of fashion and authority. Education is chiefly in the hands of persons who, from their profession, have an interest in the reputation and the dreams of Plato. They give the tone while at school, and few in their after years have occasion to revise their college opinions. But fashion and authority apart, and bringing Plato to the test of reason, take from his sophisms, futilities and incomprehensibilities, and what remains? In truth, he is one of the race of genuine sophists, who has escaped the oblivion of his brethren, first, by the elegance of his diction, but chiefly by the adoption and incorporation of his whimsies into the body of artificial Christianity. His foggy mind is forever presenting the semblances of objects which, half seen through a mist, can be defined neither in form nor dimensions. Yet this, which should have consigned him to early oblivion, really procured him immortality of fame and reverence. The Christian priesthood, finding the doctrines of Christ levelled to every understanding, and too plain to need explanation, saw in the mysticism of Plato materials with which they might build up an artificial system, which might, from its indistinctness, admit everlasting controversy, give employment for their order, and introduce it to profit, power and pre-eminence. The doctrines which flowed from the lips of Jesus himself are within the comprehension of a child; but thousands of volumes have not yet explained the Platonisms engrafted on them; and for this obvious reason, that nonsense can never be explained. Their purposes, however, are answered. Plato is canonized; and it is now deemed as impious to question his merits as those of an Apostle of Jesus. He is peculiarly appealed to as an advocate of the immortality of the soul; and yet I will venture to say, that were there no better arguments than his in proof of it, not a man in the world would believe it. It is fortunate for us, that Platonic republicanism has not obtained the same favor as Platonic Christianity; or we should now have been all living, men, women and children, pell mell together, like beasts of the field or forest. Yet "Plato is a great philosopher," said La Fontaine. But, says Fontenelle, "do you find his ideas very clear?" "Oh, no! He is of an obscurity impenetrable." "Do you not find him full of contradictions?" "Certainly," replied La Fontaine, "he is but a sophist." Yet immediately after, he exclaims again, "Oh, Plato was a great philosopher." Socrates had reason, indeed, to complain of the misrepresentations of Plato; for in truth, his dialogues are libels on Socrates.

## THE DOCTRINES OF EPICURUS AND OTHER MORALISTS[1]

November 7, 1819

As you say of yourself, I too am an Epicurean. I consider the genuine (not the imputed) doctrines of Epicurus as containing everything rational in moral philosophy which Greece and Rome have left us. Epictetus, indeed, has given us what was good of the Stoics; all beyond, of their dogmas, being hypocrisy and grimace. Their great crime was in their calumnies of Epicurus and misrepresentations of his doctrines; in which we lament to see the candid character of Cicero engaging as an accomplice. Diffuse, vapid, rhetorical, but enchanting. His prototype Plato, eloquent as himself, dealing out mysticisms incomprehensible to the human mind, has been deified by certain sects usurping the name of Christians; because, in his foggy conceptions, they found a basis of impenetrable darkness whereon to rear fabrications as delirious, of their own invention. These they fathered blasphemously on him whom they claimed as their founder, but who would disclaim them with the indignation which their caricatures of his religion so justly excite. Of Socrates we have nothing genuine but in the Memorabilia of Xenophon; for Plato makes him one of his Collocutors merely to cover his own whimsies under the mantle of his name; a liberty of which we are told Socrates himself complained. Seneca is indeed a fine moralist, disfiguring his work at times with some Stoicisms, and affecting too much of antithesis and point, yet giving us on the whole a great deal of sound and practical morality. But the greatest of all the reformers of the depraved religion of his own country, was Jesus of Nazareth. Abstracting what is really his from the rubbish in which it is buried, easily distinguished by its lustre from the dross of his biographers, and as separable from that as the diamond from the dunghill, we have the outlines of a system of the most sublime morality which has ever fallen from the lips of man; outlines which it is lamentable he did not live to fill up. Epictetus and Epicurus give laws for governing ourselves, Jesus a supplement of the duties and charities we owe to others. The establishment of the innocent and genuine character of this benevolent moralist, and the rescuing it from the imputation of imposture, which has resulted from artificial systems,[2] invented by ultra-Christian sects, unauthorized by a single word ever uttered by him, is a most desirable object, and one to which Priestley has successfully devoted his labors and learning. It would in time, it is to be hoped, effect a

[1] Letter to John Adams.

[2] *E.g.,* The immaculate conception of Jesus, his deification, the creation of the world by him, his miraculous powers, his resurrection and visible ascension, his corporeal presence in the Eucharist, the Trinity, original sin, atonement, regeneration, election, orders of Hierarchy, &c. —T. J.

quiet euthanasia of the heresies of bigotry and fanaticism which have so long triumphed over human reason, and so generally and deeply afflicted mankind; but this work is to be begun by winnowing the grain from the chaff of the historians of his life. I have sometimes thought of translating Epictetus (for he has never been tolerably translated into English) by adding the genuine doctrines of Epicurus from the Syntagma of Gassendi, and an abstract from the Evangelists of whatever has the stamp of the eloquence and fine imagination of Jesus. The last I attempted too hastily some twelve or fifteen years ago. It was the work of two or three nights only, at Washington, after getting through the evening task of reading the letters and papers of the day. But with one foot in the grave, these are now idle projects for me. My business is to beguile the wearisomeness of declining life, as I endeavor to do, by the delights of classical reading and of mathematical truths, and by the consolations of a sound philosophy, equally indifferent to hope and fear.

I take the liberty of observing that you are not a true disciple of our master Epicurus, in indulging the indolence to which you say you are yielding. One of his canons, you know, was that "that indulgence which presents a greater pleasure, or produces a greater pain, is to be avoided." Your love of repose will lead, in its progress, to a suspension of healthy exercise, a relaxation of mind, an indifference to everything around you, and finally to a debility of body, and hebetude of mind, the farthest of all things from the happiness which the well-regulated indulgences of Epicurus ensure; fortitude, you know, is one of his four cardinal virtues. That teaches us to meet and surmount difficulties; not to fly from them, like cowards; and to fly, too, in vain, for they will meet and arrest us at every turn of our road. Weigh this matter well; brace yourself up; take a seat with Correa, and come and see the finest portion of your country, which, if you have not forgotten, you still do not know, because it is no longer the same as when you knew it. It will add much to the happiness of my recovery to be able to receive Correa and yourself, and prove the estimation in which I hold you both. Come, too, and see our incipient University, which has advanced with great activity this year. By the end of the next, we shall have elegant accommodations for seven professors, and the year following the professors themselves. No secondary character will be received among them. Either the ablest which America or Europe can furnish, or none at all. They will give us the selected society of a great city separated from the dissipations and levities of its ephemeral insects.

I am glad the bust of Condorcet has been saved and so well placed. His genius should be before us; while the lamentable, but singular act of ingratitude which tarnished his latter days, may be thrown behind us.

I will place under this a syllabus of the doctrines of Epicurus, somewhat in the lapidary style, which I wrote some twenty years ago; a like one of the philosophy of Jesus, of nearly the same age, is too long to be copied. *Vale, et tibi persuade carissimum te esse mihi.*

*Syllabus of the doctrines of Epicurus*

*Physical.*—The Universe eternal.

Its parts, great and small, interchangeable.

Matter and Void alone.

Motion inherent in matter which is weighty and declining.

Eternal circulation of the elements of bodies.

Gods, an order of beings next superior to man, enjoying in their sphere, their own felicities; but not meddling with the concerns of the scale of beings below them.

*Moral.*—Happiness the aim of life.

Virtue the foundation of happiness.

Utility the test of virtue.

Pleasure active and In-do-lent.

In-do-lence is the absence of pain, the true felicity.

Active, consists in agreeable motion; it is not happiness, but the means to produce it.

Thus the absence of hunger is an article of felicity; eating the means to obtain it.

The *summum bonum* is to be not pained in body, nor troubled in mind.

*I.e.,* In-do-lence of body, tranquillity of mind.

To procure tranquillity of mind we must avoid desire and fear, the two principal diseases of the mind.

Man is a free agent.

Virtue consists in 1. Prudence. 2. Temperance. 3. Fortitude. 4. Justice.

To which are opposed, 1. Folly. 2. Desire. 3. Fear. 4. Deceit.

## A DECALOGUE OF CANONS FOR OBSERVATION IN PRACTICAL LIFE [1]

February 21, 1825

1. Never put off till tomorrow what you can do today.
2. Never trouble another for what you can do yourself.
3. Never spend your money before you have it.

[1] This accompanied a letter to a young namesake, Thomas Jefferson Smith, whose father asked Jefferson to give the boy some rules to go by. In his letter to young Smith, Jefferson explained: "Few words will be necessary, with good dispositions on your part. Adore God. Reverence and cherish your parents. Love your neighbor as yourself, and your country more than yourself. Be just. Be true. Murmur not at the ways of Providence."

4. Never buy what you do not want, because it is cheap; it will be dear to you.

5. Pride costs us more than hunger, thirst, and cold.

6. We never repent of having eaten too little.

7. Nothing is troublesome that we do willingly.

8. How much pain have cost us the evils which have never happened.

9. Take things always by their smooth handle.

10. When angry, count ten before you speak; if very angry, an hundred.

# *Part V*

# EDUCATION

## *Chapter XXII*

# IDEAS AND PROJECTS

## EDUCATION FOR A LAWYER[1]

*c.*1767

Before you enter on the study of the law a sufficient groundwork must be laid. For this purpose an acquaintance with the Latin and French languages is absolutely necessary. The former you have; the latter must now be acquired. Mathematics and Natural Philosophy are so useful in the most familiar occurrences of life, and are so peculiarly engaging and delightful as would induce everyone to wish an acquaintance with them. Besides this, the faculties of the mind, like the members of the body, are strengthened and improved by exercise. Mathematical reasonings and deductions are therefore a fine preparation for investigating the abstruse speculations of the law. In these and the analogous branches of science the following books are recommended:

*Mathematics.*—Beyzout, Cours de Mathématiques—the best for a student ever published; Montucla or Bossut, Histoire des Mathématiques.

*Astronomy.*—Ferguson, and le Monnier or de Lalande.

*Geography.*—Pinkerton.

*Natural Philosophy.*—Joyce's Scientific Dialogues; Martin's Philosophia Britannica, Muschenbroek's Cours de Physique.

This foundation being laid, you may enter regularly on the study of the law, taking with it such of its kindred sciences as will contribute to eminence in its attainment. The principal of these are Physics, Ethics, Religion, Natural Law, Belles Lettres, Criticism, Rhetoric, and Oratory. The carrying

[1] This was written at the time when Jefferson began to practice law. Half a century later, 1814, he sent a revised copy to a friend, with the comment: "I have at length found the paper of which you requested a copy. It was written near fifty years ago, for the use of a young friend whose course of reading was confided to me; and it formed a basis for the studies of others subsequently placed under my direction." He apologized that the paper "betrays sufficiently its juvenile date."

on several studies at a time is attended with advantage. Variety relieves the mind as well as the eye, palled with too long attention to a single object, but, with both, transitions from one object to another may be so frequent and transitory as to leave no impression. The mean is therefore to be steered, and a competent space of time allotted to each branch of study. Again, a great inequality is observable in the vigor of the mind at different periods of the day. Its powers at these periods should therefore be attended to, in marshalling the business of the day. For these reasons I should recommend the following distribution of your time:

*Till Eight o'clock in the morning, employ yourself in Physical Studies*

Ethics, Religion, natural and sectarian, and Natural Law, reading the following books:

*Agriculture.*—Dickson's Husbandry of the Ancients; Tull's Horse-hoeing Husbandry; Lord Kames' Gentleman Farmer; Young's Rural Economy; Hale's Body of Husbandry; De Serres's Théâtre d'Agriculture.

*Chemistry.*—Lavoisier, Conversations in Chemistry.

*Anatomy.*—John and James Bell's Anatomy.

*Zoology.*—Abrégé du Système de la nature de Linné par Gilibert; Manuel d'Histoire Naturelle by Blumenbach, Buffon, including Montbeiliard and La Cepède; Wilson's American Ornithology.

*Botany.*—Barton's Elements of Botany; Turton's Linneus; Persoon's Synopsis Plantarum.

*Ethics and Natural Religion.*—Locke's Essay; Locke's Conduct of the Mind in the Search after Truth; Stewart's Philosophy of the Human Mind; Enfield's History of Philosophy; Condorcet, Progrès de l'Esprit Humain; Cicero de Officiis, Tusculanae, de Senectute, Somnia Scipionis; Senecae Philosophica; Hutchinson's Introduction to Moral Philosophy; Lord Kames' Natural Religion; Traité Elémentaire de Morale et Bonheur; La Sagesse de Charron.

*Religion, Sectarian.*—Bible: New Testament, Commentaries on them by Middleton in his Works, and by Priestley in his Corruptions of Christianity and Early Opinions of Christ; The Sermons of Sterne, Massillon and Bourdaloue.

*Natural Law.*—Vattel, Droit des Gens; Rayneval, Institutions du Droit de la Nature et des Gens.

*From Eight to Twelve read Law*

The general course of this reading may be formed on the following grounds. Lord Coke has given us the first views of the whole body of law worthy now of being studied; for so much of the admirable work of Bracton is now obsolete that the students should turn to it occasionally only, when tracing the history of particular portions of the law. Coke's Institutes are a perfect digest of the law in his day. After this, new laws were added by the Legislature, and new developments of the old law by the judges, until they had become so voluminous as to require a new digest. This was ably executed by Matthew Bacon, although unfortunately under an alphabetical instead of analytical arrangement of matter. The same process of new laws and new decisions on the old laws going on, called at length for the same operation again, and produced the inimitable Commentaries of Blackstone. In the department of the Chancery, a similar progress has taken place. Lord Kames has given us the first digest of the principles of that branch of our jurisprudence, more valuable for the arrangement of matter than for its exact conformity with the English decisions. The reporters from the early times of that branch to that of the same Matthew Bacon are well digested, but alphabetically also in the abridgment of the cases in equity, the second volume of which is said to be done by him. This was followed by a number of able reporters, of which Fonblanque has given us a summary digest by commentaries on the text of the earlier work, ascribed to Ballow, entitled "A Treatise on Equity." The course of reading recommended then in these two branches of law is the following:

*Common Law.*—Coke's Institutes; Select Cases from the Subsequent Reporters to the time of Matthew Bacon; Bacon's Abridgment; Select Cases from the Subsequent Reporters to the Present Day; Select Tracts on Law, among which those of Baron Gilbert are all of the first merit; the Virginia Laws; Reports on them.

*Chancery.*—Lord Kames' Principles of Equity, 3d edition; Select Cases from the Chancery Reporters to the time of Matthew Bacon; the Abridgment of Cases in Equity; Select Cases from the Subsequent Reporters to the Present Day; Fonblanque's Treatise of Equity.

Blackstone's Commentaries (Tucker's edition) as the best perfect digest of both branches of law.

In reading the Reporters, enter in a common-place book every case of value, condensed into the narrowest compass possible, which will admit of presenting distinctly the principles of the case. This operation is doubly useful, insomuch as it obliges the student to seek out the pith of the case, and habituates him to a condensation of thought, and to an acquisition of the most valuable of all talents, that of never using two words where one will do. It fixes the case, too, more indelibly in the mind.

*From Twelve to One read Politics*

*Politics, General.*—Locke on Government, Sidney on Government, Priestley's First Principles of Government, Review of Montesquieu's Spirit of Laws. De Lolme sur la constitution d'Angleterre; De Burgh's Political Disquisitions; Hatsell's Precedents of the House of Commons; Select Parliamentary Debates of England and Ireland; Chipman's Sketches of the Principles of Government; The Federalist.[2]

*Political Economy.*—Say's Economie Politique; Malthus on the Principles of Population; de Tracy's work on Political Economy, now about to be printed, 1814.

*In the Afternoon read History*

*History, Ancient.*—The Greek and Latin originals; select histories from the Universal History; Gibbon's Decline of the Roman Empire; Histoire ancienne de Millot.

*Modern.*—Histoire moderne de Millot; Russel's History of Modern Europe; Robertson's Charles V.

*English.*—The original historians, *to wit:* The History of Edward 2nd, by E. F.; Habington's Edward 4th; More's Richard 3rd; Lord Bacon's Henry 7th; Lord Herbert's Henry 8th; Goodwin's Henry 8th, Edward 7th, Mary; Camden's Elizabeth, James, Ludlow; Macaulay [Catharine]; Fox; Belsham; Baxter's History of England; Hume republicanized and abridged; Robertson's History of Scotland.

*American.*—Robertson's History of America; Gordon's History of the Independence of the U.S.; Ramsay's History of the American Revolution; Burk's History of Virginia; Continuation of d°., by Jones and Girardin, nearly ready for the press.

*From Dark to Bedtime*

Belles Lettres; Criticism; Rhetoric; Oratory, *to wit:*

*Belles Lettres.*—Read the best of the poets, epic, didactic, dramatic, pastoral, lyric, etc.; but among these, Shakespeare must be singled out by one who wishes to learn the full powers of the English language. Of him we must declare as Horace did of the Grecian models, "*Vos exemplaria Graeca nocturna versate manu, versate diurna.*"

*Criticism.*—Lord Kames' Elements of Criticism; Tooke's Diversions of Purley. Of Bibliographical criticism, the Edinburgh Review furnishes the finest models extant.

[2] This, together with a number of other works (for example, Robertson's *History of America,* which was not published until 1777), was inserted in 1814, when Jefferson made the copy for Bernard Moore.

*Rhetoric.*—Blair's Rhetoric; Sheridan on Elocution; Mason on Poetic and Prosaic Numbers.

*Oratory.*—This portion of time (borrowing some of the afternoon when the days are long and the nights short) is to be applied also to acquiring the art of writing and speaking correctly by the following exercises: Criticize the style of any book whatsoever, committing the criticism to writing. Translate into the different styles, *to wit,* the elevated, the middling, and the familiar. Orators and poets will furnish subjects of the first, historians of the second, and epistolary and comic writers of the third. Undertake, at first, short compositions as themes, letters, etc., paying great attention to the elegance and correctness of your language. Read the orations of Demosthenes and Cicero; analyze these orations, and examine the correctness of the disposition, language, figures, state of the cases, arguments, etc.; read good samples also of English eloquence. Some of these may be found in Small's American Speaker, and some in Carey's Criminal Recorder; in which last the defence of Eugene Aram is distinguished as a model of logic, condensation of matter and classical purity of style. Exercise yourself afterwards in preparing orations on feigned cases. In this, observe rigorously the disposition of Blair into introduction, narration, etc. Adapt your language to the several parts of the oration, and suit your arguments to the audience before which it is supposed to be delivered. This is your last and most important exercise. No trouble should therefore be spared. If you have any person in your neighborhood engaged in the same study, take each of you different sides of the same cause, and prepare pleadings according to the custom of the bar, where the plaintiff opens, the defendant answers, and the plaintiff replies. It will further be of great service to pronounce your oration (having before you only short notes to assist the memory) in the presence of some person who may be considered as your judge.

NOTE.—Under each of the preceding heads, the books are to be read in the order in which they are named. These by no means constitute the whole of what might be usefully read in each of these branches of science. The mass of excellent works going more into detail is great indeed. But those here noted will enable the student to select for himself such others of detail as may suit his particular views and dispositions. They will give him a respectable, an useful and satisfactory degree of knowledge in these branches, and will themselves form a valuable and sufficient library for a lawyer who is at the same time a lover of science.

# A BILL FOR THE MORE GENERAL DIFFUSION OF KNOWLEDGE[1]

1779

SECTION I. Whereas it appeareth that however certain forms of government are better calculated than others to protect individuals in the free exercise of their natural rights, and are at the same time themselves better guarded against degeneracy, yet experience hath shewn, that even under the best forms, those entrusted with power have, in time, and by slow operations, perverted it into tyranny; and it is believed that the most effectual means of preventing this would be, to illuminate, as far as practicable, the minds of the people at large, and more especially to give them knowledge of those facts, which history exhibiteth, that, possessed thereby of the experience of other ages and countries, they may be enabled to know ambition under all its shapes, and prompt to exert their natural powers to defeat its purposes; And whereas it is generally true that that people will be happiest whose laws are best, and are best administered, and that laws will be wisely formed, and honestly administered, in proportion as those who form and administer them are wise and honest; whence it becomes expedient for promoting the public happiness that those persons, whom nature hath endowed with genius and virtue, should be rendered by liberal education worthy to receive, and able to guard the sacred deposit of the rights and liberties of their fellow citizens, and that they should be called to that charge without regard to wealth, birth or other accidental condition or circumstance; but the indigence of the greater number disabling them from so educating, at their own expence, those of their children whom nature hath fitly formed and disposed to become useful instruments for the public, it is better that such should be sought for and educated at the common expence of all, than that the happiness of all should be confined to the weak or wicked:

SECTION II. Be it therefore enacted by the General Assembly, that in every county within this commonwealth, there shall be chosen annually, by the electors qualified to vote for Delegates, three of the most honest and able men of their county, to be called the Aldermen of the county; and that the election of the said Aldermen shall be held at the same time and place, before the same persons, and notified and conducted in the same manner as by law is directed, for the annual election of Delegates for the county.

SECTION III. The person before whom such election is holden shall certify to the court of the said county the names of the Aldermen chosen, in order that the same may be entered of record, and shall give notice of their election to the said Aldermen within a fortnight after such election.

[1] Ch. LXXIX of the *Report of the Revisors.*

SECTION IV. The said Aldermen on the first Monday in October, if it be fair, and if not, then on the next fair day, excluding Sunday, shall meet at the court-house of their county, and proceed to divide their said county into hundreds, bounding the same by water courses, mountains, or limits, to be run and marked, if they think necessary, by the county surveyor, and at the county expence, regulating the size of the said hundreds, according to the best of their discretion, so as that they may contain a convenient number of children to make up a school, and be of such convenient size that all the children within each hundred may daily attend the school to be established therein, and distinguishing each hundred by a particular name; which division, with the names of the several hundreds, shall be returned to the court of the county and be entered of record, and shall remain unaltered until the increase or decrease of inhabitants shall render an alteration necessary, in the opinion of any succeeding Alderman, and also in the opinion of the court of the county.

SECTION V. The electors aforesaid residing within every hundred shall meet on the third Monday in October after the first election of Aldermen, at such place, within their hundred, as the said Aldermen shall direct, notice thereof being previously given to them by such person residing within the hundred as the said Aldermen shall require who is hereby enjoined to obey such requisition, on pain of being punished by amercement and imprisonment. The electors being so assembled shall choose the most convenient place within their hundred for building a school-house. If two or more places, having a greater number of votes than any others, shall yet be equal between themselves, the Aldermen, or such of them as are not of the same hundred, on information thereof, shall decide between them. The said Aldermen shall forthwith proceed to have a school-house built at the said place, and shall see that the same shall be kept in repair, and, when necessary, that it be rebuilt; but whenever they shall think necessary that it be rebuilt, they shall give notice as before directed, to the electors of the hundred to meet at the said school-house, on such a day as they shall appoint, to determine by vote, in the manner before directed, whether it shall be rebuilt at the same, or what other place in the hundred.

SECTION VI. At every of those schools shall be taught reading, writing, and common arithmetick, and the books which shall be used therein for instructing the children to read shall be such as will at the same time make them acquainted with Graecian, Roman, English, and American history. At these schools all the free children, male and female, resident within the respective hundred, shall be intitled to receive tuition gratis, for the term of three years, and as much longer, at their private expence, as their parents, guardians, or friends shall think proper.

SECTION VII. Over every ten of these schools (or such other number nearest thereto, as the number of hundreds in the county will admit, without fractional divisions) an overseer shall be appointed annually by the Aldermen at their first meeting, eminent for his learning, integrity, and fidelity to the commonwealth, whose business and duty it shall be, from time to time, to appoint a teacher to each school, who shall give assurance of fidelity to the commonwealth, and to remove him as he shall see cause; to visit every school once in every half year at the least; to examine the scholars; see that any general plan of reading and instruction recommended by the visiters of William and Mary College shall be observed; and to superintend the conduct of the teacher in everything relative to his school.

SECTION VIII. Every teacher shall receive a salary of — by the year, which, with the expences of building and repairing the school-houses, shall be provided in such manner as other county expences are by law directed to be provided and shall also have his diet, lodging, and washing found him, to be levied in like manner, save only that such levy shall be on the inhabitants of each hundred for the board of their own teacher only.

SECTION IX. And in order that grammar schools may be rendered convenient to the youth in every part of the commonwealth, be it therefore enacted, that on the first Monday in November, after the first appointment of overseers for the hundred schools, if fair, and if not, then on the next fair day, excluding Sunday, after the hour of one in the afternoon, the said overseer appointed for the schools in the counties of Princess Ann, Norfolk, Nansemond and Isle-of-Wight, shall meet at Nansemond court-house; those for the counties of Southampton, Sussex, Surry and Prince George, shall meet at Sussex court-house; those for the counties of Brunswick, Mecklenburg and Lunenburg, shall meet at Lunenburg court-house; those for the counties of Dinwiddie, Amelia and Chesterfield, shall meet at Chesterfield court-house; those for the counties of Powhatan, Cumberland, Goochland, Henrico and Hanover, shall meet at Henrico court-house; those for the counties of Prince Edward, Charlotte and Halifax, shall meet at Charlotte court-house; those for the counties of Henry, Pittsylvania and Bedford, shall meet at Pittsylvania court-house; those for the counties of Buckingham, Amherst, Albemarle and Fluvanna, shall meet at Albemarle court-house; those for the counties of Botetourt, Rockbridge, Montgomery, Washington and Kentucky, shall meet at Botetourt court-house; those for the counties of Augusta, Rockingham and Greenbriar, shall meet at Augusta court-house; those for the counties of Accomack and Northampton, shall meet at Accomack court-house; those for the counties of Elizabeth City, Warwick, York, Gloucester, James City, Charles City and New-Kent, shall meet at James City court-house; those for the counties of Middlesex, Essex, King and Queen, King William and Caroline, shall meet at King and Queen court-house; those for the counties of Lancaster, Northumberland, Richmond and Westmoreland, shall meet at Richmond court-house; those for the counties of King George, Stafford, Spotsylvania, Prince William and Fairfax, shall meet at Spotsylvania court-house; those for the counties of Loudoun and Fauquier, shall meet at Loudoun court-house; those for the counties of Culpeper, Orange and Louisa, shall meet at Orange court-house; those for the county of Shenandoah and Frederick, shall meet at Frederick court-house; those for the counties of Hampshire and Berkeley, shall meet at Berkeley court-house; and those for the counties of Yohogania, Monongalia, and Ohio, shall meet at the Monongalia court-house; and shall fix on such place in some of the counties in their district as shall be most proper for situating a grammar school-house, endeavoring that the situation be as central as may be to the inhabitants of the said counties, that it be furnished with good water, convenient to plentiful supplies of provision and fuel, and more than all things that it be healthy. And if a majority of the overseers present should not concur in their choice of any one place proposed, the method of determining shall be as follows: If two places only were proposed, and the votes be divided, they shall decide between them by fair and equal lot; if more than two places were proposed, the question shall be put on those two which on the first division had the greater number of votes; or if no two places had a greater number of votes than the others, then it shall be decided by fair and equal lot (unless it can be agreed by a majority of votes) which of the places having equal numbers shall be thrown out of the competition, so that the question shall be put on the remaining two, and if on this ultimate question the votes shall be equally divided, it shall then be decided finally by lot.

SECTION X. The said overseers having determined the place at which the grammar school for their district shall be built, shall forthwith (unless they can otherwise agree with the proprietors of the circumjacent lands as to location and price) make application to the clerk of the county in which the said house is to be situated, who shall thereupon issue a writ, in the nature of a writ of ad quod damnum, directed to the sheriff of the said county commanding him to summon and impanel twelve fit persons to meet at the place, so destined for the grammer school-house, on a certain day, to be named in the said writ, not less than five, nor more than ten, days from the date thereof; and also to give notice of the same to the proprietors and tenants of the lands to be viewed if they be found within the county, and if not, then to their agents therein if any they have. Which freeholders shall be charged by the said sheriff impartially, and to the best of their skill and judgment to view the lands round about the said place, and to locate and circumscribe, by certain meets and bounds, one hundred acres thereof, having regard therein principally to the benefit and convenience of the said school, but respecting in some measure also the convenience of the said proprietors, and to value and appraise the same in so many several and distinct parcels as shall be owned or held by several and distinct owners or tenants, and according to their respective interests and estates therein. And after such location and appraisement so made, the said sheriff shall forthwith return the same under the hands and seals of the said jurors, together with the writ, to the clerk's office of the said county and the right and property of the said proprietors and tenants in the said lands so circumscribed shall be immediately devested and be transferred to the commonwealth for the use of the said grammar school, in full and absolute dominion, any want of consent or disability to consent in the said owners or tenants notwithstanding. But it shall not be lawful for the said overseers so to situate the grammer school-house, nor to the said jurors so to locate the said lands, as to include the mansion-house of the proprietor of the lands, nor the offices, curtilage, or garden, thereunto immediately belonging.

SECTION XI. The said overseers shall forthwith proceed to have a house of brick or stone, for the said grammar school, with necessary offices, built on the said lands, which grammar school-house shall contain a room for the school, a hall to dine in, four rooms for a master and usher, and ten or twelve lodging rooms for the scholars.

SECTION XII. To each of the said grammar schools shall be allowed out of the public treasury, the sum of — pounds, out of which shall be paid by the Treasurer, on warrant from the Auditors, to the proprietors or tenants of the lands located, the value of their several interests as fixed by the jury, and the balance thereof shall be delivered to the said overseers to defray the expense of the said buildings.

SECTION XIII. In either of these grammar schools shall be taught the Latin and Greek languages, English Grammar, geography, and the higher part of numerical arithmetick, to wit, vulgar and decimal fractions, and the extrication of the square and cube roots.

SECTION XIV. A visiter from each county constituting the district shall be appointed, by the overseers, for the county, in the month of October annually, either from their own body or from their county at large, which visiters, or the greater part of them, meeting together at the said grammar school on the first Monday in November, if fair, and if not, then on the next fair day, excluding Sunday, shall have power to choose their own Rector, who shall call and preside at future meetings, to employ from time to time a master, and if necessary, an usher, for the said school, to remove them at their will, and to settle the price of tuition to be paid by the scholars. They shall also visit the school twice in every year at the least, either together or separately at their discretion, examine the scholars, and see that any general plan of instruction recommended by the visiters, of William and Mary College shall be observed. The said masters and ushers, before they enter on the execution of their office, shall give assurance of fidelity to the commonwealth.

SECTION XV. A steward shall be employed, and removed at will by the master, on such wages as the visiters shall direct; which steward shall see to the procuring provisions, fuels, servants for cooking, waiting, house cleaning, washing, mending, and gardening on the most reasonable terms; the expence of which, together with the steward's wages, shall be divided equally among all the scholars boarding either on the public or private expence. And the part of those who are on private expence, and also the price of their tuitions due to the master or usher, shall be paid quarterly by the respective scholars, their parents, or guardians, and shall be recoverable, if withheld, together with costs, on motion in any Court of Record, ten days' notice thereof being previously given to the party, and a jury impanelled to try the issue joined, or enquire of the damages. The said steward shall also, under the direction of the visiters, see that the houses be kept in repair, and necessary enclosures be made and repaired, the accounts for which, shall, from time to time, be submitted to the Auditors, and on their warrant paid by the Treasurer.

SECTION XVI. Every overseer of the hundred schools shall, in the month of September annually, after the most diligent and impartial examination and inquiry, appoint from among the boys who shall have been two years at the least at some one of the schools under his superintendence, and whose parents are too poor to give them farther education, someone of the best and most promising genius and disposition, to proceed to the grammer school of his district; which appointment shall be made in the court-house of the county, and on the court day for that month if fair, and if not, then on the next fair day, excluding Sunday, in the presence of the Aldermen, or two of them at the least, assembled on the bench for that purpose, the said overseer being previously sworn by them to make such appointment, without favor or affection, according to the best of his skill and judgment, and being interrogated by the Aldermen, either on their own motion, or on suggestions from the parents, guardians, friends, or teachers of the children, competitors for such appointment; which teachers the parents shall attend for the information of the Aldermen. On which interrogatories the said Aldermen, if they be not satisfied with the appointment proposed, shall have right to negative it; whereupon the said visiter may proceed to make a new appointment, and the said Aldermen again to interrogate and negative, and so toties quoties until an appointment be approved.

SECTION XVII. Every boy so appointed shall be authorized to proceed to the grammer school of his district, there to be educated and boarded during such time as is hereafter limited; and his quota of the expences of the house together with a compensation to the master or usher for his tuition, at the rate of twenty dollars by the year, shall be paid by the Treasurer quarterly on warrant from the Auditors.

SECTION XVIII. A visitation shall be held, for the purpose of probation, annually at the said grammer school on the last Monday in September, if fair, and if not, then on the next fair day, excluding Sunday, at which one third of the boys sent thither by appointment of the said overseers, and who shall have been there one year only, shall be discontinued as public foundationers, being those who, on the most diligent examination and enquiry, shall be thought to be the least promising genius and disposition; and of those who shall have been there two years, all shall be discontinued save one only the best in genius and disposition, who shall be at liberty to continue there four years longer on the public foundation, and shall thence forward be deemed a senior.

SECTION XIX. The visiters for the districts which, or any part of which, be southward and westward of James river, as known by that name, or by the names of Fluvanna and Jackson's river, in every other year, to wit, at the probation meetings held in the years, distinguished in the Christian computation by odd numbers, and the visiters for all the other districts at their said meetings to be held in those years, distinguished by even numbers, after diligent examination and enquiry as before directed, shall chuse one among the said seniors, of the best learning and most hopeful genius and disposition, who shall be authorized by them to proceed to William and Mary College; there to be educated, boarded, and clothed, three years; the expence of which annually shall be paid by the Treasurer on warrant from the Auditors.

## A BILL FOR ESTABLISHING A PUBLIC LIBRARY[1]

1779

SECTION I. Be it enacted by the General Assembly, that on the first day of January, in every year, there shall be paid out of the treasury the sum of two thousand pounds, to be laid out in such books and maps as may be proper to be preserved in a public library, and in defraying the expences necessary for the care and preservation thereof; which library shall be established at the town of Richmond.[2]

SECTION II. The two houses of Assembly shall appoint three persons of learning and attention to literary matters, to be visiters of the said library, and shall remove them, and fill any vacancies from time to time, as they shall think fit; which visiters shall have power to receive the annual sums before mentioned, and therewith to procure such books and maps as afore-

[1] This is Chapter LXXXXI of the *Report of the Revisors.*
[2] Richmond became the capital of Virginia in 1779.

said, and shall superintend the preservation thereof. Whensoever a keeper shall be found necessary they shall appoint such keeper, from time to time, at their will, on such annual salary (not exceeding one hundred pounds) as they shall think reasonable.

SECTION III. If during the time of war the importation of books and maps shall be hazardous, or if the rate of exchange between this commonwealth and any state from which such articles are wanted, shall from any cause be such that they cannot be imported to such advantage as may be hoped at a future day, the visiters shall place the annual sums, as they become due, in the public loan office, if any there be, for the benefit of interest, or otherwise shall suffer them to remain in the treasury until fit occasions shall occur of employing them.

SECTION IV. It shall not be lawful for the said keeper, or the visiters themselves, or any other person to remove any book or map out of the said library, unless it be for the necessary repair thereof; but the same be made useful by indulging the researches of the learned and curious, within the said library, without fee or reward, and under such rules for preserving them safe and in good order and condition as the visiters shall constitute.

SECTION V. The visiters shall annually settle their accounts with the Auditors and leave with them the vouchers for the expenditure of the monies put into their hands.

## OBJECTIONS TO SENDING AMERICAN STUDENTS TO EUROPE [1]

October 15, 1785

But why send an American youth to Europe for education? What are the objects of an useful American education? Classical knowledge, modern languages, chiefly French, Spanish, and Italian; Mathematics, Natural philosophy, Natural history, Civil history, and Ethics. In Natural philosophy, I mean to include Chemistry and Agriculture, and in Natural history, to include Botany, as well as the other branches of those departments. It is true that the habit of speaking the modern languages cannot be so well acquired in America; but every other article can be as well acquired at William and Mary College, as at any place in Europe. When college education is done with, and a young man is to prepare himself for public life, he must cast his eyes (for America) either on Law or Physics. For the former, where can he apply so advantageously as to Mr. Wythe? For the latter, he must come to Europe: the medical class of students, therefore, is the only one which need come to Europe. To enumerate them all, would require a volume. I will

[1] Letter, from Paris, to J. Bannister.

select a few. If he goes to England, he learns drinking, horse racing, and boxing. These are the peculiarities of English education. The following circumstances are common to education in that and the other countries of Europe. He acquires a fondness for European luxury and dissipation, and a contempt for the simplicity of his own country; he is fascinated with the privileges of the European aristocrats, and sees, with abhorrence, the lovely equality which the poor enjoy with the rich, in his own country; he contracts a partiality for aristocracy or monarchy; he forms foreign friendships which will never be useful to him, and loses the seasons of life for forming, in his own country, those friendships which, of all others, are the most faithful and permanent; he is led, by the strongest of all the human passions, into a spirit for female intrigue, destructive of his own and others' happiness, or a passion for whores, destructive of his health, and, in both cases, learns to consider fidelity to the marriage bed as an ungentlemanly practice, and inconsistent with happiness; he recollects the voluptuary dress and arts of the European women, and pities and despises the chaste affections and simplicity of those of his own country; he retains, through life, a fond recollection, and a hankering after those places, which were the scenes of his first pleasures and of his first connections; he returns to his own country, a foreigner, unacquainted with the practices of domestic economy, necessary to preserve him from ruin, speaking and writing his native tongue as a foreigner, and therefore unqualified to obtain those distinctions, which eloquence of the pen and tongue ensures in a free country; for I would observe to you, that what is called style in writing or speaking is formed very early in life, while the imagination is warm, and impressions are permanent. I am of opinion, that there never was an instance of a man's writing or speaking his native tongue with elegance, who passed from fifteen to twenty years of age out of the country where it was spoken. Thus, no instance exists of a person's writing two languages perfectly. That will always appear to be his native language, which was most familiar to him in his youth. It appears to me, then, that an American, coming to Europe for education, loses in his knowledge, in his morals, in his health, in his habits, and in his happiness. I had entertained only doubts on this head before I came to Europe: what I see and hear, since I came here, proves more than I had even suspected. Cast your eye over America: who are the men of most learning, of most eloquence, most beloved by their countrymen and most trusted and promoted by them? They are those who have been educated among them, and whose manners, morals, and habits are perfectly homogeneous with those of the country.

Did you expect by so short a question, to draw such a sermon on yourself? I dare say you did not. But the consequences of foreign education are alarming to me, as an American. I sin, therefore, through zeal, whenever I enter on the subject.

## EDUCATION OF A YOUNG MAN[1]

August 10, 1787

DEAR PETER: I have received your two letters of December the 30th and April the 18th, and am very happy to find by them, as well as by letters from Mr. Wythe, that you have been so fortunate as to attract his notice and good will; I am sure you will find this to have been one of the most fortunate events of your life, as I have ever been sensible it was of mine. I enclose you a sketch of the sciences to which I would wish you to apply, in such order as Mr. Wythe shall advise; I mention, also, the books in them worth your reading, which submit to his correction. Many of these are among your father's books, which you should have brought to you. As I do not recollect those of them not in his library, you must write to me for them, making out a catalogue of such as you think you shall have occasion for, in eighteen months from the date of your letter, and consulting Mr. Wythe on the subject. To this sketch, I will add a few particular observations:

1. Italian. I fear the learning this language will confound your French and Spanish. Being all of them degenerated dialects of the Latin, they are apt to mix in conversation. I have never seen a person speaking the three languages, who did not mix them. It is a delightful language, but late events having rendered the Spanish more useful, lay it aside to prosecute that.

2. Spanish. Bestow great attention on this, and endeavor to acquire an accurate knowledge of it. Our future connections with Spain and Spanish America, will render that language a valuable acquisition. The ancient history of that part of America, too, is written in that language. I send you a dictionary.

3. Moral Philosophy. I think it lost time to attend lectures on this branch. He who made us would have been a pitiful bungler, if he had made the rules of our moral conduct a matter of science. For one man of science, there are thousands who are not. What would have become of them? Man was destined for society. His morality, therefore, was to be formed to this object. He was endowed with a sense of right and wrong, merely relative to this. This sense is as much a part of his nature, as the sense of hearing, seeing, feeling; it is the true foundation of morality, and not the το καλον, truth, &c., as fanciful writers have imagined. The moral sense, or conscience, is as much a part of man as his leg or arm. It is given to all human beings in a stronger or weaker degree, as force of members is given them in a greater

[1] Letter to Peter Carr, Jefferson's nephew.

or less degree. It may be strengthened by exercise, as may any particular limb of the body. This sense is submitted, indeed, in some degree, to the guidance of reason; but it is a small stock which is required for this: even a less one than what we call common sense. State a moral case to a ploughman and a professor. The former will decide it as well, and often better than the latter, because he has not been led astray by artificial rules. In this branch, therefore, read good books, because they will encourage, as well as direct your feelings. The writings of Sterne, particularly, form the best course of morality that ever was written. Besides these, read the books mentioned in the enclosed paper; and, above all things, lose no occasion of exercising your dispositions to be grateful, to be generous, to be charitable, to be humane, to be true, just, firm, orderly, courageous, &c. Consider every act of this kind, as an exercise which will strengthen your moral faculties and increase your worth.

4. Religion. Your reason is now mature enough to examine this object. In the first place, divest yourself of all bias in favor of novelty and singularity of opinion. Indulge them in any other subject rather than that of religion. It is too important, and the consequences of error may be too serious. On the other hand, shake off all the fears and servile prejudices, under which weak minds are servilely crouched. Fix reason firmly in her seat, and call to her tribunal every fact, every opinion. Question with boldness even the existence of a God; because, if there be one, he must more approve of the homage of reason, than that of blindfolded fear. You will naturally examine first, the religion of your own country. Read the Bible, then, as you would read Livy or Tacitus. The facts which are within the ordinary course of nature, you will believe on the authority of the writer, as you do those of the same kind in Livy and Tacitus. The testimony of the writer weighs in their favor, in one scale, and their not being against the laws of nature, does not weigh against them. But those facts in the Bible which contradict the laws of nature, must be examined with more care, and under a variety of faces. Here you must recur to the pretensions of the writer to inspiration from God. Examine upon what evidence his pretensions are founded, and whether that evidence is so strong, as that its falsehood would be more improbable than a change in the laws of nature, in the case he relates. For example, in the book of Joshua, we are told, the sun stood still several hours. Were we to read that fact in Livy or Tacitus, we should class it with their showers of blood, speaking of statues, beasts, &c. But it is said, that the writer of that book was inspired. Examine, therefore, candidly, what evidence there is of his having been inspired. The pretension is entitled to your inquiry, because millions believe it. On the other hand, you are astronomer enough to know how contrary it is to the law of nature that a body revolving on its axis, as the earth does, should have stopped, should not, by that sudden stoppage,

have prostrated animals, trees, buildings, and should after a certain time have resumed its revolution, and that without a second general prostration. Is this arrest of the earth's motion, or the evidence which affirms it, most within the law of probabilities? You will next read the New Testament. It is the history of a personage called Jesus. Keep in your eye the opposite pretensions: 1, of those who say he was begotten by God, born of a virgin, suspended and reversed the laws of nature at will, and ascended bodily into heaven; and 2, of those who say he was a man of illegitimate birth, of a benevolent heart, enthusiastic mind, who set out without pretensions to divinity, ended in believing them, and was punished capitally for sedition, by being gibbeted, according to the Roman law, which punished the first commission of that offence by whipping, and the second by exile, or death *in furea*. See this law in the Digest, Lib. 48. tit. 19. § 28. 3. and Lipsius Lib. 2. de cruce. cap. 2. These questions are examined in the books I have mentioned, under the head of Religion, and several others. They will assist you in your inquiries; but keep your reason firmly on the watch in reading them all. Do not be frightened from this inquiry by any fear of its consequences. If it ends in a belief that there is no God, you will find incitements to virtue in the comfort and pleasantness you feel in its exercise, and the love of others which it will procure you. If you find reason to believe there is a God, a consciousness that you are acting under his eye, and that he approves you, will be a vast additional incitement; if that there be a future state, the hope of a happy existence in that increases the appetite to deserve it; if that Jesus was also a God, you will be comforted by a belief of his aid and love. In fine, I repeat, you must lay aside all prejudice on both sides, and neither believe nor reject anything, because any other persons, or description of persons, have rejected or believed it. Your own reason is the only oracle given you by heaven, and you are answerable, not for the rightness, but uprightness of the decision. I forgot to observe, when speaking of the New Testament, that you should read all the histories of Christ, as well of those whom a council of ecclesiastics have decided for us to be Pseudo-evangelists, as those they named Evangelists. Because these Pseudo-evangelists pretended to inspiration, as much as the others, and you are to judge their pretensions by your own reason, and not by the reason of those ecclesiastics. Most of these are lost. There are some, however, still extant, collected by Fabricius, which I will endeavor to get and send you.

5. Travelling. This makes men wiser, but less happy. When men of sober age travel, they gather knowledge, which they may apply usefully for their country; but they are subject ever after to recollections mixed with regret; their affections are weakened by being extended over more objects; and they learn new habits which cannot be gratified when they return

home. Young men, who travel, are exposed to all these inconveniences in a higher degree, to others still more serious, and do not acquire that wisdom for which a previous foundation is requisite, by repeated and just observations at home. The glare of pomp and pleasure is analogous to the motion of the blood; it absorbs all their affection and attention, they are torn from it as from the only good in this world, and return to their home as to a place of exile and condemnation. Their eyes are forever turned back to the object they have lost, and its recollection poisons the residue of their lives. Their first and most delicate passions are hackneyed on unworthy objects here, and they carry home the dregs, insufficient to make themselves or anybody else happy. Add to this, that a habit of idleness, an inability to apply themselves to business is acquired, and renders them useless to themselves and their country. These observations are founded in experience. There is no place where your pursuit of knowledge will be so little obstructed by foreign objects, as in your own country, nor any, wherein the virtues of the heart will be less exposed to be weakened. Be good, be learned, and be industrious, and you will not want the aid of travelling, to render you precious to your country, dear to your friends, happy within yourself. I repeat my advice, to take a great deal of exercise, and on foot. Health is the first requisite after morality. Write to me often, and be assured of the interest I take in your success, as well as the warmth of those sentiments of attachment with which I am, dear Peter, your affectionate friend.

## ON THE SCIENCE OF MEDICINE[1]

June 21, 1807

I have a grandson, the son of Mr. Randolph, now about fifteen years of age, in whose education I take a lively interest. . . .

I am not a friend to placing young men in populous cities, because they acquire there habits and partialities which do not contribute to the happiness of their after life. But there are particular branches of science, which are not so advantageously taught anywhere else in the United States as in Philadelphia. The garden at the Woodlands for Botany, Mr. Peale's Museum for Natural History, your Medical school for Anatomy, and the able professors in all of them, give advantages not to be found elsewhere. We propose, therefore, to send him to Philadelphia to attend the schools of Botany, Natural History, Anatomy, and perhaps Surgery; but not of Medicine. And why not of Medicine, you will ask? Being led to the subject, I will avail myself of the occasion to express my opinions on that science, and the extent

[1] Letter to Dr. Caspar Wistar, Professor of Anatomy, University of Pennsylvania.

of my medical creed. But, to finish first with respect to my grandson, I will state the favor I ask of you, and which is the object of this letter.

✦

This subject dismissed, I may now take up that which it led to, and further tax your patience with unlearned views of medicine; which, as in most cases, are, perhaps, the more confident in proportion as they are less enlightened.

We know, from what we see and feel, that the animal body is in its organs and functions subject to derangement, inducing pain, and tending to its destruction. In this disordered state, we observe nature providing for the re-establishment of order, by exciting some salutary evacuation of the morbific matter, or by some other operation which escapes our imperfect senses and researches. She brings on a crisis, by stools, vomiting, sweat, urine, expectoration, bleeding, &c., which, for the most part, ends in the restoration of healthy action. Experience has taught us, also, that there are certain substances, by which, applied to the living body, internally or externally, we can at will produce these same evacuations, and thus do, in a short time, what nature would do but slowly, and do effectually, what perhaps she would not have strength to accomplish. Where, then, we have seen a disease, characterized by specific signs or phenomena, and relieved by a certain natural evacuation or process, whenever that disease recurs under the same appearances, we may reasonably count on producing a solution of it, by the use of such substances as we have found produce the same evacuation or movement. Thus, fulness of the stomach we can relieve by emetics; diseases of the bowels, by purgatives; inflammatory cases, by bleeding; intermittents, by the Peruvian bark; syphilis, by mercury; watchfulness, by opium; &c. So far, I bow to the utility of medicine. It goes to the well-defined forms of disease, and happily, to those the most frequent. But the disorders of the animal body, and the symptoms indicating them, are as various as the elements of which the body is composed. The combinations, too, of these symptoms are so infinitely diversified, that many associations of them appear too rarely to establish a definite disease; and to an unknown disease, there cannot be a known remedy. Here then, the judicious, the moral, the humane physician should stop. Having been so often a witness to the salutary efforts which nature makes to re-establish the disordered functions, he should rather trust to their action, then hazard the interruption of that, and a greater derangement of the system, by conjectural experiments on a machine so complicated and so unknown as the human body, and a subject so sacred as human life. Or, if the appearance of doing something be necessary to keep alive the hope and spirits of the patient, it should be of the most innocent character. One of the most successful physicians

I have ever known, has assured me, that he used more bread pills, drops of colored water, and powders of hickory ashes, than of all other medicines put together. It was certainly a pious fraud. But the adventurous physician goes on, and substitutes presumption for knowledge. From the scanty field of what is known, he launches into the boundless region of what is unknown. He establishes for his guide some fanciful theory of corpuscular attraction, of chemical agency, of mechanical powers, of stimuli, of irritability accumulated or exhausted, of depletion by the lancet and repletion by mercury, or some other ingenious dream, which lets him into all nature's secrets at short hand. On the principle which he thus assumes, he forms his table of nosology, arrays his diseases into families, and extends his curative treatment, by analogy, to all the cases he has thus arbitrarily marshalled together. I have lived myself to see the disciples of Hoffman, Boerhaave, Stahl, Cullen, Brown, succeed one another like the shifting figures of a magic lantern, and their fancies, like the dresses of the annual doll-babies from Paris, becoming, from their novelty, the vogue of the day, and yielding to the next novelty their ephemeral favor. The patient, treated on the fashionable theory, sometimes gets well in spite of the medicine. The medicine therefore restored him, and the young doctor receives new courage to proceed in his bold experiments on the lives of his fellow creatures. I believe we may safely affirm, that the inexperienced and presumptuous band of medical tyros let loose upon the world, destroys more of human life in one year, than all the Robin hoods, Cartouches, and Macheaths do in a century. It is in this part of medicine that I wish to see a reform, an abandonment of hypothesis for sober facts, the first degree of value set on clinical observation, and the lowest on visionary theories. I would wish the young practitioner, especially, to have deeply impressed on his mind, the real limits of his art, and that when the state of his patient gets beyond these, his office is to be a watchful, but quiet spectator of the operations of nature, giving them fair play by a well-regulated regimen, and by all the aid they can derive from the excitement of good spirits and hope in the patient. I have no doubt, that some diseases not yet understood may in time be transferred to the table of those known. But, were I a physician, I would rather leave the transfer to the slow hand of accident, than hasten it by guilty experiments on those who put their lives into my hands. The only sure foundations of medicine are, an intimate knowledge of the human body, and observation on the effects of medicinal substances on that. The anatomical and clinical schools, therefore, are those in which the young physician should be formed. If he enters with innocence that of the theory of medicine, it is scarcely possible he should come out untainted with error. His mind must be strong indeed, if, rising above juvenile credulity, it can maintain a wise infidelity against the authority of his instructors, and the bewitching delusions of their theories. You see that I estimate justly that portion of instruction which our medical students derive from your labors; and, associating with it one of the chairs which my old and able friend, Doctor Rush, so honorably fills, I consider them as the two fundamental pillars of the edifice. Indeed, I have such an opinion of the talents of the professors in the other branches which constitute the school of medicine with you, as to hope and believe, that it is from this side of the Atlantic, that Europe, which has taught us so many other things, will at length be led into sound principles in this branch of science, the most important of all others, being that to which we commit the care of health and life.

I dare say, that by this time, you are sufficiently sensible that old heads as well as young, may sometimes be charged with ignorance and presumption. The natural course of the human mind is certainly from credulity to scepticism; and this is perhaps the most favorable apology I can make for venturing so far out of my depth, and to one too, to whom the strong as well as the weak points of this science are so familiar. But having stumbled on the subject in my way, I wished to give a confession of my faith to a friend; and the rather, as I had perhaps, at times, to him as well as others, expressed my scepticism in medicine, without defining its extent or foundation. At any rate, it has permitted me, for a moment, to abstract myself from the dry and dreary waste of politics, into which I have been impressed by the times on which I happened, and to indulge in the rich fields of nature, where alone I should have served as a volunteer, if left to my natural inclinations and partialities.

I salute you at all times with affection and respect.

## AN ACADEMICAL VILLAGE[1]

May 6, 1810

I consider the common plan followed in this country, but not in others, of making one large and expensive building, as unfortunately erroneous. It is infinitely better to erect a small and separate lodge for each separate professorship, with only a hall below for his class, and two chambers above for himself; joining these lodges by barracks for a certain portion of the students, opening into a covered way to give a dry communication between all the schools. The whole of these arranged around an open square of grass and trees, would make it, what it should be in fact, an academical village, instead of a large and common den of noise, of filth and of fetid air. It would afford that quiet retirement so friendly to study, and lessen the dangers of fire, infection and tumult. Every professor would be the police of-

[1] Letter to the Trustees for the Lottery of East Tennessee College.

ficer of the students adjacent to his own lodge, which should include those of his own class of preference, and might be at the head of their table, if, as I suppose, it can be reconciled with the necessary economy to dine them in smaller and separate parties, rather than in a large and common mess. Those separate buildings, too, might be erected successively and occasionally, as the number of professorships and students should be increased, or the funds become competent.

I pray you to pardon me if I have stepped aside into the province of counsel; but much observation and reflection on these institutions have long convinced me that the large and crowded buildings in which youths are pent up, are equally unfriendly to health, to study, to manners, morals and order.

## PLAN FOR AN EDUCATIONAL SYSTEM[1]

September 7, 1814

DEAR SIR: On the subject of the academy or college proposed to be established in our neighborhood, I promised the trustees that I would prepare for them a plan, adapted, in the first instance, to our slender funds, but susceptible of being enlarged, either by their own growth or by accession from other quarters.

I have long entertained the hope that this, our native State, would take up the subject of education, and make an establishment, either with or without incorporation, into that of William and Mary, where every branch of science, deemed useful at this day, should be taught in its highest degree. With this view, I have lost no occasion of making myself acquainted with the organization of the best seminaries in other countries, and with the opinions of the most enlightened individuals, on the subject of the sciences worthy of a place in such an institution. In order to prepare what I have promised our trustees, I have lately revised these several plans with attention; and I am struck with the diversity of arrangement observable in them—no two alike. Yet, I have no doubt that these several arrangements have been the subject of mature reflection, by wise and learned men, who, contemplating local circumstances, have adapted them to the conditions of the section of society for which they have been framed. I am strengthened in this conclusion by an examination of each separately, and a conviction that no one of them, if adopted without change, would be suited to the circumstances and pursuit of our country. The example they set, then, is authority for us to select from their different institutions the materials which are good for us, and, with them, to erect a structure, whose arrangement

[1] Letter to Peter Carr.

shall correspond with our own social condition, and shall admit of enlargement in proportion to the encouragement it may merit and receive. As I may not be able to attend the meetings of the trustees, I will make you the depository of my ideas on the subject, which may be corrected, as you proceed, by the better view of others, and adapted, from time to time, to the prospects which open upon us, and which cannot be specifically seen and provided for.

In the first place, we must ascertain with precision the object of our institution, by taking a survey of the general field of science, and marking out the portion we mean to occupy at first, and the ultimate extension of our views beyond that, should we be enabled to render it, in the end, as comprehensive as we would wish.

### 1. ELEMENTARY SCHOOLS

It is highly interesting to our country, and it is the duty of its functionaries, to provide that every citizen in it should receive an education proportioned to the condition and pursuits of his life. The mass of our citizens may be divided into two classes—the laboring and the learned. The laboring will need the first grade of education to qualify them for their pursuits and duties; the learned will need it as a foundation for further acquirements. A plan was formerly proposed to the legislature of this State for laying off every county into hundreds or wards of five or six miles square, within each of which should be a school for the education of the children of the ward, wherein they should receive three years' instruction gratis, in reading, writing, arithmetic as far as fractions, the roots and ratios, and geography. The Legislature at one time tried an ineffectual expedient for introducing this plan, which having failed, it is hoped they will some day resume it in a more promising form.

### 2. GENERAL SCHOOLS

At the discharging of the pupils from the elementary schools, the two classes separate—those destined for labor will engage in the business of agriculture, or enter into apprenticeships to such handicraft art as may be their choice; their companions, destined to the pursuits of science, will proceed to the college, which will consist, 1st of general schools; and, 2d, of professional schools. The general schools will constitute the second grade of education.

The learned class may still be subdivided into two sections: 1, Those who are destined for learned professions, as means of livelihood; and, 2, The wealthy, who, possessing independent fortunes, may aspire to share in conducting the affairs of the nation, or to live with usefulness and respect in the private ranks of life. Both of these sections will require instruction in all the higher branches of science; the wealthy to qualify them for either public or private life; the professional section will need those branches, especially, which are the basis of their future profession, and a general knowledge of the others, as auxiliary to that, and necessary to their standing and association with the scientific class. All the branches, then, of useful science, ought to be taught in the general schools, to a competent degree, in the first instance. These sciences may be arranged into three departments, not rigorously scientific, indeed, but sufficiently so for our purposes. These are, I. Language; II. Mathematics; III. Philosophy.

I. Language. In the first department, I would arrange a distinct science. 1, Languages and History, ancient and modern; 2, Grammar; 3, Belles Lettres; 4, Rhetoric and Oratory; 5, A school for the deaf, dumb and blind. History is here associated with languages, not as a kindred subject, but on the principle of economy, because both may be attained by the same course of reading, if books are selected with that view.

II. Mathematics. In the department of Mathematics, I should give place distinctly: 1, Mathematics pure; 2, Physico-Mathematics; 3, Physics; 4, Chemistry; 5, Natural History, *to wit:* Mineralogy; 6, Botany; and 7, Zoology; 8, Anatomy; 9, the Theory of Medicine.

III. Philosophy. In the Philosophical department, I should distinguish: 1, Ideology; 2, Ethics; 3, the Law of Nature and Nations; 4, Government; 5, Political Economy.

But, some of these terms being used by different writers, in different degrees of extension, I shall define exactly what I mean to comprehend in each of them.

I. 3. Within the term of Belles Lettres I include poetry and composition generally, and criticism.

II. 1. I consider pure mathematics as the science of, 1, Numbers, and 2, Measure in the abstract; that of numbers comprehending Arithmetic, Algebra and Fluxions; that of Measure (under the general appellation of Geometry), comprehending Trigonometry, plane and spherical, conic sections, and transcendental curves.

II. 2. Physico-Mathematics treat of physical subjects by the aid of mathematical calculation. These are Mechanics, Statics, Hydrostatics, Hydrodynamics, Navigation, Astronomy, Geography, Optics, Pneumatics, Acoustics.

II. 3. Physics, or Natural Philosophy (not entering the limits of Chemistry), treat of natural substances, their properties, mutual relations and action. They particularly examine the subjects of motion, action, magnetism, electricity, galvanism, light, meteorology, with an etc. not easily enumerated. These definitions and specifications render immaterial the question whether I use the generic terms in the exact degree of comprehension in which others use them; to be understood is all that is necessary to the present object.

### 3. PROFESSIONAL SCHOOLS

At the close of this course the students separate; the wealthy retiring, with a sufficient stock of knowledge, to improve themselves to any degree to which their views may lead them, and the professional section to the professional schools, constituting the third grade of education, and teaching the particular sciences which the individuals of this section mean to pursue, with more minuteness and detail than was within the scope of the general schools for the second grade of instruction. In these professional schools each science is to be taught in the highest degree it has yet attained. They are to be the

1st *Department,* the fine arts, to wit: Civil Architecture, Gardening, Painting, Sculpture, and the Theory of Music; the

2d *Department,* Architecture, Military and Naval; Projectiles, Rural Economy (comprehending Agriculture, Horticulture and Veterinary), Technical Philosophy, the Practice of Medicine, Materia Medica, Pharmacy and Surgery. In the

3d *Department,* Theology and Ecclesiastical History; Law, Municipal and Foreign.

To these professional schools will come those who separated at the close of their first elementary course, to wit:

The lawyer to the school of law.

The ecclesiastic to that of theology and ecclesiastical history.

The physician to those of medicine, materia medica, pharmacy and surgery.

The military man to that of military and naval architecture and projectiles.

The agricultor to that of rural economy.

The gentleman, the architect, the pleasure gardener, painter and musician to the school of fine arts.

And to that of technical philosophy will come the mariner, carpenter, shipwright, pumpmaker, clockmaker, machinist, optician, metallurgist, founder, cutler, druggist, brewer, vintner, distiller, dyer, painter, bleacher, soapmaker, tanner, powdermaker, saltmaker, glassmaker, to learn as much as shall be necessary to pursue their art understandingly, of the sciences of geometry, mechanics, statics, hydrostatics, hydraulics, hydrodynamics, navigation, astronomy, geography, optics, pneumatics, physics, chemistry, natural history, botany, mineralogy and pharmacy.

The school of technical philosophy will differ essentially in its functions from the other professional schools. The others are instituted to ramify and dilate the particular sciences taught in the schools of the second grade on a general scale only. The technical school is to abridge those which were taught there too much *in extenso* for the limited wants of the artificer or practical man. These artificers must be grouped together, according to the particular branch of science in which they need elementary and practical instruction; and a special lecture or lectures should be prepared for each group. And these lectures should be given in the evening, so as not to interrupt the labors of the day. The school, particularly, should be maintained wholly at the public expense, on the same principles with that of the ward schools. Through the whole of the collegiate course, at the hours of recreation on certain days, all the students should be taught the manual exercise; military evolutions and manœuvers should be under a standing organization as a military corps, and with proper officers to train and command them.

A tabular statement of this distribution of the sciences will place the system of instruction more particularly in view:

*1st or Elementary Grade in the Ward Schools.*

Reading, Writing, Arithmetic, Geography.

*2d, or General Grade.*

1. Language and History, ancient and modern.

2. Mathematics, *viz.:* Mathematics pure, Physico-Mathematics, Physics, Chemistry, Anatomy, Theory of Medicine, Zoology, Botany and Mineralogy.

3. Philosophy, *viz.:* Ideology, and Ethics, Law of Nature and Nations, Government, Political Economy.

*3d, or Professional Grades.*

Theology and Ecclesiastical History; Law, Municipal and Foreign; Practice of Medicine; Materia Medica and Pharmacy; Surgery; Architecture, Military and Naval, and Projectiles; Technical Philosophy; Rural Economy; Fine Arts.

On this survey of the field of science, I recur to the question, what portion of it we mark out for the occupation of our institution? With the first grade of education we shall have nothing to do. The sciences of the second grade are our first object; and, to adapt them to our slender beginnings, we must separate them into groups, comprehending many sciences each, and greatly more, in the first instance, than ought to be imposed on, or can be competently conducted by a single professor permanently. They must be subdivided from time to time, as our means increase, until each professor shall have no more under his care than he can attend to with advantage to his pupils and ease to himself. For the present, we may group the sciences into professorships, as follows, subject, however, to be changed, according to the qualifications of the persons we may be able to engage.

I. *Professorship.*

Language and History, ancient and modern.
Belles Lettres, Rhetoric and Oratory.

II. *Professorship.*

Mathematics pure, Physico-Mathematics.
Physics, Anatomy, Medicine, Theory.

III. *Professorship.*

Chemistry, Zoology, Botany, Mineralogy.

IV. *Professorship.*

Philosophy.

The organization of the branch of the institution which respects its government, police and economy, depending on principles which have no affinity with those of its institution, may be the subject of separate and subsequent consideration.

## OBSERVATIONS ON THE TRANSPORTATION OF THE MONTICELLO LIBRARY[1]

February 27, 1815

The books stand at present in pine cases with backs and shelves without fronts. The cases are generally of three tier, one upon another, about 9 feet high in the whole. The lowest case is generally 13 inches deep, the second 6¾ inches and the uppermost 5¾, averaging 8½ inches, to that add ¾ inch for the front of boards to be nailed on, and it makes 9¼ inches depth. I have measured the surface of wall which these cases cover and find it to be 855.39 feet, which divided into the depth of 9½ inches equals 676 cubic feet; of this 232 cubic feet would be the wood of the cases and 444 cubic feet the books. I find a cubical foot of books to weigh 40 pounds, and as this is the weight of dry pine also, we need not distinguish between the weight of the wood and the books, but say the whole 676 cubic feet at 40 pounds makes 27,046 pounds, or eleven waggon loads of 2,458 each.

It is said that waggon hire at Washington is eight dollars a day, finding themselves here it is exactly half that price, or a half dozen waggons can be

[1] This accompanied a letter to Samuel Harrison Smith, Jefferson's agent. Congress had authorized the purchase of Jefferson's library, consisting of nearly 6,500 volumes, on January 30, 1815. Altogether it took 10 wagons to transport the books, the last wagon leaving Monticello on May 8. The trip from Monticello to Washington took six days. Of his library, Jefferson wrote to Smith, May 8, 1815: "It is the choicest collection of books in the United States, and I hope it will not be without some general effect on the literature of our country." The library became the foundation of the great Library of Congress. Jefferson received $23,950 for his superb collection.

got here at four dollars, who will undertake to carry 2,500 pounds. I think it would be better, therefore, to employ the waggons of this neighborhood, and let them make two trips, but as the interstices between the books and shelves (which, however, are very small), will require a certain quantity of book binder's paper-parings; a great many elegant bindings will require to be wrapped in waste paper, and all should have slips of paper between them, which cannot be had here. Would it not be necessary to send on a waggon load from Washington to be deposited here before the books are packed? It might take a return load of the books. And the books should go in their cases, every one its station, so that the cases on their arrival need only be set up on end, and they will be arranged exactly as they stand in the catalogue. I will have the fronts closed with boards for the journey, which, being taken off on their arrival at Washington, sash doors may be made there at little expense. But the books will require careful and skilful packing, to prevent their being rubbed in so long and rough a journey, by the jolting of the waggons.[2]

The best road, by far, for waggons at this season, is from Monticello by Orange Court House, Culpeper Court House, Fauquier Court House, Emil's mill, Sorgater Lanes, and George T. ferry, because it is along cross roads nearly the whole way, which are very little travelled by waggons. The road by Fredericksburg is considerably further, and deeply cut through the whole. That by Stephensburg is the shortest and levellest of all, but being generally a deep living clay is absolutely unpassable from November to May. The worst circumstance of the road by the Court Houses is that two branches of the Rappahannock and three of the Occoquam are to be forded, and they are liable to sudden swells. I presume a waggon will go loaded in seven days, and return empty in six, and allowing one for loading and accidents, the trip will be of a fortnight and come to $56.[3] I will have the waggons engaged if it is desired, to attend on any day which may be named.

## LIBRARY CLASSIFICATION[4]

May 7, 1815

I have duly received your favor of April 26th,[5] in which you are pleased to ask my opinion on the subject of the arrangement of libraries. I shall

[2] Jefferson packed the books so well that not one was damaged during the transportation.

[3] Joseph Dougherty, the master wagoner, wrote to Samuel Harrison Smith, on March 20: "I will now state what my travelling expenses will amount to per day—so that you may see what my compensation would amount to per day. Horse-hire, $1.25 per day; breakfast, $0.50; dinner, $0.75; supper and lodging, $0.75, for gallons oats and hay, $0.87. Expence per day, $4.12." Dougherty asked $6.00 per day, but was finally paid $5.00.

[4] Letter to George Watterston, Librarian of Congress.

[5] On that date Librarian Watterston wrote to Jefferson: "I am solicitous to obtain your opinion as a gentleman of literary taste on the subject of arrangement. Your long acquaintance

communicate with pleasure what occurs to me on it. Two methods offer themselves, the one alphabetical, the other according to the subject of the book. The former is very unsatisfactory, because of the medley it presents to the mind, the difficulty sometimes of recalling an author's name, and the greater difficulty, where the name is not given, of selecting the word in the title, which shall determine its alphabetical place. The arrangement according to subject is far preferable, although sometimes presenting difficulty also, for it is often doubtful to what particular subject a book should be ascribed. This is remarkably the case with books of travels, which often blend together the geography, natural history, civil history, agriculture, manufactures, commerce, arts, occupations, manners, &c., of a country, so as to render it difficult to say to which they chiefly relate. Others again, are polygraphical in their nature, as Encyclopedias, magazines, etc. Yet on the whole I have preferred arrangement according to subject, because of the peculiar satisfaction, when we wish to consider a particular one, of seeing at a glance the books which have been written on it, and selecting those from which we effect most readily the information we seek. On this principle the arrangement of my library was formed, and I took the basis of its distribution from Lord Bacon's table of science, modifying it to the changes in scientific pursuits which have taken place since his time, and to the greater or less extent of reading in the science which I proposed to myself. Thus the law having been my profession, and politics the occupation to which the circumstances of the times in which I have lived called my particular attention, my provision of books in these lines, and in those most nearly connected with them was more copious, and required in particular instances subdivisions into sections and paragraphs, while other subjects of which general views only were contemplated are thrown into masses. A physician or theologist would have modified differently, the chapters, sections, and paragraphs of a library adapted to their particular pursuits.

You will receive my library arranged very perfectly in the order observed in the catalogue, which I have sent with it. In placing the books on their shelves, I have generally, but not always, collocated distinctly the folios, quarto, octavo, and duodecimo, placing with the last all smaller sizes. On every book is a label, indicating the chapter of the catalogue to which it belongs, and the other it holds among those of the same format. So that, although the numbers seem confused on the catalogue, they are consecutive on the volumes as they stand on their shelves, and indicate at once the place

with books and your literary habits have, doubtless, led you to the adoption of some plan of arrangement with respect to libraries, which I should be happy if you would communicate." Jefferson sent him a scientifically classified catalogue. "I am happy to inform you," Watterston wrote to Jefferson, October 13, 1815, "that the catalogue is now in press . . . I have preserved your arrangement." The Librarian made but a few minor changes.

they occupy there. Mr. Milligan in packing them has preserved their arrangement so exactly, in their respective presses, that on setting the presses up on end, he will be able readily to replace them in the order corresponding with the catalogue, and thus save you the immense labor which their rearrangement would otherwise require.

To give to my catalogue the convenience of the alphabetical arrangement I have made at the end an alphabet of authors' names and have noted the chapter or chapters, in which the name will be found; where it occurs several times in the same chapter, it is indicated, by one or more perpendicular scores, thus ||||, according to the number of times it will be found in the chapter. Where a book bears no author's name, I have selected in its title some leading word for denoting it alphabetically. This member of the catalogue would be more perfect if, instead of the score, the number on the book were particularly noted. This could not be done when I made the catalogue, because no label of numbers had then been put on the books. That alteration can now be readily made, and would add greatly to the convenient use of the catalogue.

## AN ACT FOR ESTABLISHING ELEMENTARY SCHOOLS [1]

September 9, 1817

1. Be it enacted by the General Assembly of Virginia, that at the first session of the Superior Court in every county within this commonwealth, next ensuing the passage of this act, the judge thereof shall appoint three discreet and well-informed persons, residents of the county, and not being ministers of the gospel [2] of any denomination, to serve as visitors of the Elementary Schools in the said county; of which appointment the sheriff shall, within fifteen days thereafter, deliver a certificate, under the hand of the clerk of the said court, to each of the persons so appointed.

2. The said visitors shall meet at the court-house of their county on the first county court day after they shall have received notice of their appointment, and afterwards at such times and places as they, or any two of them,

[1] In sending this Act to Joseph C. Cabell, Jefferson wrote: "I should apologize, perhaps, for the style of this bill. I dislike the verbose and intricate style of the English statutes. . . . You, however, can easily correct this bill to the taste of my brother lawyers, by making every other word a 'said' or 'aforesaid,' and saying everything over two or three times, so that nobody but we of the craft can untwist the diction, and find out what it means; and that, too, not so plainly but that we may conscientiously divide one half on each side."

The text of this Bill is taken from H. A. Washington's edition of Jefferson's *Writings*. The version in N. F. Cabell's *Early History of the University of Virginia* (1856), p. 413-17, contains some variations and omissions.

[2] Ministers of the Gospel are excluded to avoid jealousy from the other sects, were the public education committed to the ministers of a particular one; and with more reason than in the case of their exclusion from the legislative and executive functions.—T. J.

with reasonable notice to the third, shall have agreed; and shall proceed to divide their county into wards,[3] by metes and bounds so designated as to comprehend each, about the number of militia sufficient for a company, and so also as not to divide, and throw into different wards[4] the lands of any one person held in one body; which division into wards shall, within six months from the date of their appointment, be completely designated, published, and reported, by their metes and bounds, to the office of the clerk of the Superior Court, there to be recorded, subject, however, to such alterations, from time to time afterwards, as changes of circumstances shall, in the opinion of the said visitors or their successors, with the approbation of the said court, render expedient.

3. The original division into wards being made, the visitors shall appoint days for the first meeting of every ward, at such place as they shall name within the same, of which appointment notice shall be given at least two weeks before the day of meeting, by advertisement at some public place within the ward, requiring every free, white male citizen, of full age, resident within the ward, to meet at the place, and by the hour of twelve of the day so appointed, at which meeting some one of the visitors shall also attend, and a majority of the said warders being in attendance, the visitor present shall propose to them to decide by a majority of their votes,—1. The location of a school-house for the ward, and a dwelling-house for the teacher (the owner of the ground consenting thereto). 2. The size and structure of the said houses; and 3. Whether the same shall be built by the joint labor of the warders, or by their pecuniary contributions; and also 4. To elect by a plurality of their votes a warden, resident, who shall direct and superintend the said buildings, and be charged with their future care.

4. And if they decide that the said buildings[5] shall be erected by the joint labor of the warders, then all persons within the said ward liable to work

[3] § 2. This designation of the size of a ward is founded on these considerations: 1st. That the population which furnishes a company of militia will generally about furnish children enough for a school. 2d. That in most instances, at present, the militia captaincies being laid off compactly by known and convenient metes and bounds, many will be adopted without change, and others will furnish a canvas to work on and to reform. 3d. That these wards once established, will be found convenient and salutary aids in the administration of government, of which they will constitute the organic elements, and the first integral members in the composition of the military.—T. J.

[4] § 3. The prohibition to place among different wards the lands of a single individual, held in a body is, 1st. To save the proprietor from the perplexity of multiplied responsibilities; and 2. To prevent arbitrary and inconsistent apportionments, by different wardens, of the comparative values of the different portions of his lands in their respective wards.—T. J.

[5] § 4. It is presumed that the wards will generally build such log-houses for the school and teacher as they now do, and will join force and build them themselves, experience proving them to be as comfortable as they are cheap. Nor would it be advisable to build expensive houses in the country wards, which, from changes in their population, will be liable to changes of their boundaries and consequent displacements of their centre, drawing with it a removal of their school-house. In towns, better houses may be more safely built, or rented for both purposes.—T. J.

in the highways, shall attend at the order of the warden, and, under his direction, shall labor thereon until completed, under the same penalties as provided by law to enforce labor on the highways. And if they decide on erection by pecuniary contributions, the residents and owners of property within the ward shall contribute toward the cost, each in proportion to the taxes they last paid to the State for their persons and for the same property: of which the sheriff or commissioners shall furnish a statement to the warden, who, according to the ratio of that statement, shall apportion and assess the quota of contribution for each, and be authorized to demand, receive, and apply the same to the purposes of the contribution, and to render account thereof, as in all other his pecuniary transactions for the school, to the visitors; and on failure of payment by any contributor, the sheriff, on the order of the warden, shall collect and render the same under like powers and regulations as provided for the collection of the public taxes. And in every case it shall be the duty of the warden to have the buildings completed within six months from the date of his election.

5. It shall be the duty of the said visitors to seek and to employ for every ward,[6] whenever the number and ages of its children require it, a person

[6] § 5. Estimating eight hundred militia to a county, there will be twelve captaincies or wards in a county on an average. Suppose each of these, three years in every six, to have children enough for a school, who have not yet had three years' schooling; such a county will employ six teachers, each serving two wards by alternate terms. These teachers will be taken from the laboring classes, as they are now, to wit: from that which furnishes mechanics, overseers and tillers of the earth; and they will chiefly be the cripples, the weakly and the old, of that class, who will have been qualified for these functions by the ward schools themselves. If put on a footing then, for wages and subsistence, with the young and the able of their class, they will be liberally compensated: say with one hundred and fifty dollars wages and the usual allowance of meat and bread. The subsistence will probaby be contributed in kind by the warders, out of their family stock. The wages alone will be a pecuniary tax of about nine hundred dollars. To a county, this addition would be of about one-fifth of the taxes we now pay to the State, or about one-fifth of one per cent on every man's taxable property; if tax can be called that which we give to our children in the most valuable of all forms, that of instruction. Were those schools to be established on the public funds, and to be managed by the Governor and council, or the commissioners of the Literary fund, brick houses to be built for the schools and teachers, high wages and subsistence given them, they would be badly managed, depraved by abuses, and would exhaust the whole Literary fund. While under the eye and animadversion of the wards, and the control of the wardens and visitors, economy, diligence, and correctness of conduct, will be enforced, the whole Literary fund will be spared to complete the general system of education, by colleges in every district for instruction in the languages, and an university for the whole of the higher sciences; and this, by an addition to our contributions almost insensible, and which, in fact, will not be felt as a burthen, because applied immediately and visibly to the good of our children.

A question of some doubt might be raised on the latter part of this section, as to the rights and duties of society towards its members, infant and adult. Is it a right or a duty in society to take care of their infant members in opposition to the will of the parent? How far does this right and duty extend?—to guard the life of the infant, his property, his instruction, his morals? The Roman father was supreme in all these: we draw a line, but where?—public sentiment does not seem to have traced it precisely. Nor is it necessary in the present case. It is better to tolerate the rare instance of a parent refusing to let his child be educated, than to shock the common feelings and ideas by the forcible asportation and education of the infant against the will of the father. What is proposed here is to remove the objection of expense, by offering education gratis, and to strengthen parental excitement by the disfranchisement of his child while uneducated. Society has certainly a right to disavow him whom they offer,

of good moral character, qualified to teach reading, writing, numeral arithmetic and geography, whose subsistence shall be furnished by the residents and proprietors of the ward, either in money or in kind, at the choice of each contributor, and in the ratio of their public taxes, to be apportioned and levied as on the failures before provided for. The teacher shall also have the use of the house and accommodations provided for him, and shall moreover receive annually such standing wages as the visitors shall have determined to be proportioned on the residents and proprietors of the ward, and to be paid, levied and applied as before provided in other cases of pecuniary contribution.

6. At this school shall be received and instructed gratis, every infant of competent age who has not already had three years' schooling. And it is declared and enacted, that no person unborn or under the age of twelve years at the passing of this act, and who is *compos mentis,* shall, after the age of fifteen years, be a citizen of this commonwealth until he or she can read readily in some tongue, native or acquired.

7. To keep up a constant succession of visitors, the judge of the Superior Court of every county shall at his first session in every bissextile year, appoint visitors as before characterized, either the same or others, at his discretion. And in case of the death or resignation of any visitor during the term of his appointment, or of his removal by the said judge for good cause, moral or physical, he shall appoint another to serve until the next bissextile appointment. Which visitors shall have their first meeting at their court house on the county court day next ensuing their appointment, and afterwards at such times and places as themselves or any two of them with reasonable notice to the third shall agree. But the election of wardens shall be annually, at the first meeting of the ward after the month of March, until which election the warden last elected shall continue in office.

8. All ward meetings shall be at their school house, and on a failure of the meeting of a majority of the wardens on the call of a visitor, or of their warden, such visitor or warden may call another meeting.

9. At all times when repairs or alterations of the buildings before provided for shall be wanting, it shall be the duty of the warden or of a visitor, to call a ward meeting and to take the same measures towards such repairs or alterations as are herein before authorized for the original buildings.

10. When, on the application of any warden, authorized thereto by the vote of his ward, the judge of the Superior Court shall be of opinion that the contributors of any particular ward are disproportionably and oppressively overburthened with an unusual number of children of non-contributors of their ward, he may direct an order to the county court to assess in

and are not permitted to qualify for the duties of a citizen. If we do not force instruction, let us at least strengthen the motives to receive it when offered.—T. J.

their next county levy the whole or such part of the extra burthen as he shall think excessive and unreasonable, to be paid to the warden for its proper use, to which order the said county court is required to conform.

11. The said teachers shall, in all things relating to the education and government of their pupils, be under the direction and control of the visitors; but no religious reading, instruction or exercise, shall be prescribed or practiced inconsistent with the tenets of any religious sect or denomination.

12. Some one of the visitors, once in every year at least, shall visit the several schools: shall inquire into the proceedings and practices thereat: shall examine the progress of the pupils, and give to those who excel in reading, in writing, in arithmetic, or in geography, such honorary marks and testimonies of approbation, as may encourage and excite to industry and emulation.

13. All decisions and proceedings of the visitors relative to the original designation of wards at any time before the buildings are begun, or changes of wards at any time after, to the quantum of subsistence, or wages allowed to the teacher, and to the rules prescribed to him for the education and government of his pupils, shall be subject to be controlled and corrected by the judge of the Superior Court of the county, on the complaint of any individual aggrieved or interested.

## A BILL FOR THE ESTABLISHMENT OF DISTRICT COLLEGES AND UNIVERSITY[1]

October 24, 1817

And for the establishment of colleges whereat the youth of the Commonwealth may, within convenient distances from their homes, receive a higher grade of education,

14.[2] *Be it further enacted as follows:* The several counties of this Commonwealth shall be distributed into nine collegiate districts, whereof one shall be composed of the counties of Accomac, Northampton, Northumberland, Lancaster, Richmond, Westmoreland, Middlesex, Essex, Matthews, Gloucester, King & Queen, King William, Elizabeth City, Warwick, York, James City, New Kent, and Charles City; one other of the counties of Princess Anne, Norfolk, Norfolk borough, Nansemond, Isle of Wight, Southampton, Surry, Prince George, Sussex, and Greensville; one other of the counties of Fairfax, Loudoun, King George, Stafford, Prince William,

[1] This is, in effect, a continuation of the preceding Bill which Jefferson prepared soon after he sent the former to J. C. Cabell. Combining the two into a "A Bill for Establishing a System of Public Education," Jefferson submitted the new draft to Cabell on October 24.

The text above is from N. F. Cabell's *Early History of the University of Virginia,* pp. 417-27.

[2] This number follows number 13 in the preceding Bill.

Fauquier, Culpeper, Madison, Caroline, and Spotsylvania; one other of the counties of Hanover, City of Richmond, Goochland, Louisa, Fluvanna, Powhatan, Cumberland, Buckingham, Orange, Albemarle, Nelson, Amherst, Augusta, and Rockbridge; one other of the counties of Chesterfield, town of Petersburg, Dinwiddie, Brunswick, Amelia, Nottoway, Lunenburg, Mecklenburg, Prince Edward, Charlotte, and Halifax; one other of the counties of Campbell, Pittsylvania, Bedford, Franklin, Henry, Patrick, Botetourt, and Montgomery; one other of the counties of Frederick, Jefferson, Berkeley, Hampshire, Shenandoah, Hardy, Rockingham, and Pendleton; one other of the counties of Monongalia, Brooke, Ohio, Randolph, Harrison, Wood, and Mason; and one other of the counties of Bath, Greenbrier, Kanawha, Cabell, Giles, Monroe, Tazewell, Wythe, Grayson, Washington, Russell, and Lee.

15. Within three months after the passing of this act, the President and Directors of the Literary Fund, who shall henceforward be called the Board of Public Instruction, shall appoint one fit person in every county, in each of the districts, who, with those appointed in the other counties of the same district, shall compose the Board of Visitors for the College of that district; and shall, within four months after passing this act, cause notice to be given to each individual so appointed, prescribing to them a day, within one month thereafter, and a place within their district, for their first meeting, with supplementary instructions for procuring a meeting subsequently, in the event of failure at the time first appointed.

16. The said Visitors, or so many of them as, being a majority, shall attend, shall appoint a rector, of their own body, who shall preside at their meetings, and a secretary to record and preserve their proceedings; and shall proceed to consider of the site for a college most convenient for their district, having regard to the extent, population and other circumstances, and within the term of six months from the passing of this act shall report the same to the Board of Public Instruction, with the reasons on which each site is preferred; and if any minority of two or more members prefer any other place, the same shall be reported, with the reasons for and against the same.

17. Within seven months after the passing of this act the said Board of Public Instruction shall determine on such of the sites reported as they shall think most eligible for the college of each district, shall notify the same to the said Visitors, and shall charge them with the office of obtaining from the proprietor, with his consent, the proper grounds for the building, and its appurtenances, either by donation or purchase; or if his consent, on reasonable terms, cannot be obtained, the clerk of the county, wherein the site is, shall, on their request, issue and direct to the sheriff of the same county a writ of *ad quod damnum,* to ascertain by a jury the value of the grounds selected, and to fix their extent by metes and bounds, so, however, as not

to include the dwelling house, or buildings appurtenant, the curtilage, gardens or orchards of the owner; which writ shall be executed according to the ordinary forms prescribed by the laws in such cases; and shall be returned to the same clerk to be recorded: *Provided,* that in no case, either of purchase or valuation by a jury, shall more grounds be located than of the value of $500; which grounds, if by donation or purchase, shall, by the deed of the owner, or if by valuation of a jury, shall, by their inquest, become vested in the said Board of Public Instruction, as trustees for the Commonwealth, and for the uses and purposes of a college of instruction.

18. On each of the sites so located shall be erected one or more substantial buildings—the walls of which shall be of brick or stone, with two school rooms, and four rooms for the accommodation of the professors, and with sixteen dormitories in or adjacent to the same, each sufficient for two pupils, and in which no more than two shall be permitted to lodge, with a fireplace in each, and the whole in a comfortable and decent style, suitable to their purpose.

19. The plan of the said buildings, and their appurtenances, shall be furnished or approved by the said Board of Public Instruction, and that of the dormitories shall be such as may conveniently receive additions from time to time. The Visitors shall have all the powers which are necessary and proper for carrying them into execution, and shall proceed in their execution accordingly. Provided, that in no case shall the whole cost of the said buildings and appurtenances of any one college exceed the sum of $7,500.

20. The college of the district first in this act described, to wit: of Accomac, &c. shall be called the Wythe College, or the College of the District of Wythe; that of the second description, to wit: Princess Anne, &c. shall be called the ——; that of the third description, to wit: Fairfax, &c. shall be called the ——; that of the fourth description, to wit: Hanover, &c. shall be called the ——; that of the fifth description, to wit: Chesterfield, &c. shall be called the ——; that of the sixth description, to wit: Campbell, &c. shall be called the ——; that of the seventh description, to wit: Frederick, &c. shall be called the ——; that of the eighth description, to wit: Monongalia, &c. shall be called the ——; and that of the ninth description, to wit: Bath, &c. shall be called the ——.

21. In the said colleges shall be taught the Greek, Latin, French, Spanish, Italian and German languages, English grammar, geography, ancient and modern, the higher branches of numerical arithmetic, the mensuration of land, the use of the globes, and the ordinary elements of navigation.

22. To each of the said colleges shall be appointed two professors, the one for teaching Greek, Latin, and such other branches of learning before described, as he may be qualified to teach, and the other for the remaining branches thereof, who shall each be allowed the use of the apartments pro-

vided for him, and a standing salary of $500 yearly, to be drawn from the literary fund, with such tuition fee from each pupil as the Visitors shall establish.

23. The said Visitors shall be charged with the preservation and repair of the buildings, the care of the ground and appurtenances for which, and other necessary purposes, they may employ a steward and competent laborers; they shall have power to appoint and remove the professors, to prescribe their duties, and the course of education to be pursued; they shall establish rules for the government and discipline of the pupils, for their subsistence and board, if boarded in the college, and for their accommodation, and the charges to which they shall be subject for the same, as well as the rent for the dormitories they occupy. They may draw from the literary fund such moneys as are hereby charged on it for their institution. And, in general, they shall direct and do all matters and things which, not being inconsistent with the laws of the land, to them shall seem most expedient for promoting the purposes of the said institution; which several functions may be exercised by them in the form of by-laws, resolutions, orders, instructions, or otherwise, as they shall deem proper.

24. The rents of the dormitories, the profits of boarding the pupils, donations and other occasional resources shall constitute the fund, and shall be at their disposal for the necessary purposes of the said institution, and not otherwise provided for; and they shall have authority to draw on the said Board of Public Instruction for the purchase or valuation money of the site of their college, for the cost of the buildings and improvements authorized by law, and for the standing salaries of the professors herein allowed—for the administration of all which they may appoint a bursar.

25. They shall have two stated meetings in the year, at their colleges, on the first Mondays of April and October, and occasional meetings at the same place, and at such other times, as they shall appoint; giving due notice thereof to every individual of their board.

26. A majority of them shall constitute a quorum for business, and on the death or resignation of a member, or on his removal by the Board of Public Instruction, or out of the county from which he was appointed, the said Board shall appoint a successor, resident in the same county.

27. The Visitors of every collegiate district shall be a body politic and corporate, to be called the Visitors of the College, by name, for which they are appointed, with capacity to plead, or be impleaded, in all courts of justice, and in all cases interesting to their college, which may be the subject of legal cognizance and jurisdiction, which pleas shall not abate by the determination of the office of all or any of them, but shall stand revived in the name of their successors; and they shall be capable in law, and in trust for their college, of

receiving subscriptions and donations, real and personal, as well from bodies corporate, or persons associated, as from private individuals.

28. Some member, or members, of the Board of Visitors, to be nominated by the said Board, or such other persons as they shall nominate, shall, once in every year, at least, visit the college of their district, enquire into the proceedings and practices thereat, examine the progress of the pupils, and give to those who excel in any branch of learning prescribed for the said college, such honorary marks and testimonies of approbation as may encourage or excite to industry and emulation.

29. The decisions and proceedings of the said Visitors shall be subject to control and correction by the Board of Public Instruction, either on the complaint of any individual, aggrieved or interested, or on the proper motion of the said board.

30. On every 29th day of February, or, if that be Sunday, then on the next or earliest day thereafter, on which a meeting can be effected, the Board of Public Instruction shall be in session, and shall appoint, in every county of each district, a Visitor, resident therein, either the same before appointed, or another, at their discretion, to serve until the ensuing 29th day of February, duly and timely notifying to them their appointment, and prescribing a day for their first meeting at the college of their district, after which, their stated meetings shall be at their college, on the first Mondays of April and October, annually; and their occasional meetings at the same place, and at such times as themselves shall appoint, due notice thereof being given to every member of their board.

*Utrum horum?*

And for establishing in a central and healthy part of the State an University wherein all the branches of useful science may be taught, Be it enacted as follows:

31. Within the limits of the county of —— there shall be established an University, to be called the University of Virginia; and so soon as may be after the passage of this act the Board of Public Instruction shall appoint eight fit persons to constitute the Board of Visitors for the said University; and shall forthwith give notice to each individual so ap-

And for establishing in a central and healthy part of the State and University wherein all the branches of useful science may be taught, Be it further enacted as follows:

31. Whensoever the Visitors of the Central College in Albemarle, authorized thereto by the consent in writing of the subscribers of the major part of the amount subscribed to that institution, shall convey or cause to be conveyed to the Board of Public Instruction, for the use of this Commonwealth, all the lands, buildings, property and rights of the said

pointed, prescribing to them a day for their first meeting at the Court-house of the said county, with supplementary instruction for procuring a meeting subsequently in the event of failure at the time first appointed.

32. The said Visitors, or so many of them as, being a majority, shall attend, shall appoint a Rector of their own body, who shall preside at their meetings, and a Secretary to record and preserve their proceedings, and shall proceed to enquire into and select the most eligible site for the University, and to obtain from the proprietor, with his consent, the proper grounds for the buildings and appurtenances, either by donation or purchase, or, if his consent on reasonable terms cannot be obtained, the clerk of the county shall, on their request, issue and direct to the sheriff of the county a writ of *ad quod damnum* to ascertain by a jury the value of the grounds selected, and to fix their extent by metes and bounds, so however as

College, in possession, in interest or in action (save only so much as may discharge their engagements then existing), the same shall be thereupon vested in this Commonwealth, and shall be appropriated to the institution of an University to be called the University of Virginia, which shall be established on the said lands. The said Board of Public Instruction shall thereupon forthwith appoint eight fit persons who shall compose the Board of Visitors for the government of the said University, notifying thereof the persons so appointed, and prescribing to them a day for their first meeting at Charlottesville, with supplementary instructions for procuring a meeting subsequently, in the event of failure at the time first appointed.

32. The said Visitors, or so many of them as, being a majority, shall attend, shall appoint a Rector of their own body to preside at their meetings, and a Secretary to record and preserve their proceedings, and shall proceed to examine into the state of the property conveyed as aforesaid, shall make an inventory of the same, specifying the items whereof it consists, shall notice the buildings and other improvements already made, and those which are in progress, shall take measures for their completion, shall consider what others may be necessary in addition, and of the best plan for effecting the same, with estimates of the probable cost, and shall make report of the whole to the said Board of Public Instruction, which is authorized to

not to include the dwelling house or buildings appurtenant, the curtilage, gardens or orchards of the owner; which writ shall be executed according to the ordinary forms prescribed by the laws in such cases, and shall be returned to the same clerk to be recorded: *Provided,* That in no case, either of purchase or valuation by a jury, shall more grounds be located than of the value of $2,000; which grounds, if by donation or purchase, shall, by the deed of the owner, or if by valuation of a jury, shall, by their inquest, become vested in the Board of Public Instruction aforesaid, as trustees for the commonwealth, for the uses and purposes of an University.

33. A plan of the buildings and appurtenances necessary and proper for an University being furnished or approved by the Board of Public Instruction, in which that of the dormitories shall be such as may conveniently admit additions from time to time, the Visitors shall have all the powers which shall be necessary and proper for carrying them into execution, and shall proceed in their execution accordingly.

approve, negative or modify any of the measures so proposed by the said Visitors.

33. The said measures being approved or modified, the Visitors shall have all the powers relative thereto which shall be necessary or proper for carrying them into execution, and shall proceed in their execution accordingly.

34. In the said University shall be taught history and geography, ancient and modern; natural philosophy, agriculture, chemistry and the theories of medicine; anatomy, zoology, botany, mineralogy and geology; mathematics, pure and mixed; military and naval science; ideology, ethics, the law of nature and of nations; law, municipal and foreign; the science of civil government and political economy; languages, rhetoric, belles lettres, and the fine arts generally; which branches of science shall be so distributed and under so many professorships, not exceeding ten, as the Visitors shall think most proper.

35. Each professor shall be allowed the use of the apartments and accommodations provided for him, and such standing salary, not exceeding $1,000

yearly, as the Visitors shall think proper, to be drawn from the literary fund, with such tuition fees from the students as the Visitors shall establish.

36. The said Visitors shall be charged with the erection, preservation and repair of the buildings, the care of the grounds and appurtenances, and of the interests of the University generally; they shall have power to appoint a bursar, employ a steward and all other necessary agents; to appoint and remove professors; to prescribe their duties, and the course of education to be pursued; to establish rules for .the government and discipline of the students, for their subsistence, board and accommodation, if boarded by the University, and the charges to which they shall be subject for the same, as well as for the dormitories they occupy; to provide and control the duties and proceedings of all officers, servants and others, with respect to the buildings, lands, appurtenances, and other property and interests of the University; to draw from the literary fund such moneys as are hereby charged on it for this institution; and in general to direct and do all matters and things which, not being inconsistent with the laws of the land, to them shall seem most expedient for promoting the purposes of the said institution; which several functions may be exercised by them in the form of by-laws, rules, resolutions, orders, instructions, or otherwise, as they shall deem proper.

37. They shall have two stated meetings in the year, to wit: on the first Mondays of April and October, and occasional meetings at such other times as they shall appoint, due notice thereof being given to every individual of their Board, which meetings shall be at the said University; a majority of them shall constitute a quorum for business; and on the death or resignation of a member, or on his removal by the Board of Public Instruction, or change of habitation to a greater than his former distance from the University, the said Board shall appoint a successor.

38. The Visitors of the said University shall be a body politic and corporate under the style and title of the Visitors of the University of Virginia, with capacity to plead or be impleaded in all courts of justice, and in all cases interesting to their College, which may be the subjects of legal cognizance and jurisdiction, which pleas shall not abate by the determination of their office, but shall stand revived in the name of their successors; and they shall be capable in law, and in trust for their College, of receiving subscriptions and donations, real and personal, as well from bodies corporate or persons associated, as from private individuals.

39. Some member or members of the Board of Visitors, to be nominated by the said Board, or such other person as they shall nominate, shall, once in every year at least, visit the said University, enquire into the proceeding and practices thereat, examine the progress of the students, and give to those who excel in any branch of science there taught such honorary marks and

testimonies of approbation as may encourage and excite to industry and emulation.

40. All decisions and proceedings of the Visitors shall be subject to control and direction by the Board of Public Instruction, either on the complaint of any individual aggrieved or interested, or on the proper motion of the said Board.

41. On every 29th day of February, or, if that be Sunday, then on the next or earliest day thereafter on which a meeting can be effected, the said Board of Public Instruction shall be in session, and shall appoint Visitors for the said University, either the same or others, at their discretion, to serve until the 29th day of February next ensuing, duly and timely notifying to them their appointment, and prescribing a day for their first meeting at the University, after which their stated meetings shall be on the first Mondays of April and October annually, and their occasional meetings at the same place, and at such times as themselves shall appoint, due notice thereof being given to every member of their Board.

[NOTE.—If the Central College be adopted for the University, the following section may be added: "Provided, that nothing in this act contained shall suspend the proceedings of the Visitors of the said Central College of Albemarle; but, for the purpose of expediting the objects of the said institution, they shall be authorized, under the control of the Board of Public Instruction, to continue the exercise of their functions until the first meeting of the Visitors of the University."]

And to avail the Commonwealth of those talents and virtues which nature has sown as liberally among the poor as rich, and which are lost to their country by the want of means for their cultivation, Be it further enacted as follows:

42. On every 29th day of February, or, if that be Sunday, then on the next day, the Visitors of the Ward-schools in every county shall meet at the Court-House of their county, and after the most diligent and impartial observation and enquiry of the boys who have been three years at the Ward-schools, and whose parents are too poor to give them a collegiate education, shall select from among them some one of the most promising and sound understanding, who shall be sent to the first meeting of the Visitors of their collegiate district, with such proofs as the case requires and admits, for the examination and information of that Board; who, from among the candidates so offered from the several counties of their district, shall select two of the most sound and promising understanding, who shall be admitted to their College, and there be maintained and educated five years at the public expense, under such rules and limitations as the Board of Public Instruction shall prescribe; and at the end of the said five years the said Collegiate Visitors shall select that one of the two who shall, on their most diligent

and impartial enquiry and best information, be adjudged by them to be of the most sound and promising understanding and character, and most improved by their course of education, who shall be sent on immediately thereafter to the University, there to be maintained and educated in such branches of the sciences taught there as are most proper to qualify him for the calling to which his parents or guardians may destine him; and to continue at the said University three years at the public expense, under such rules and limitations as the Board of Public Instruction shall prescribe. And the expenses of the persons so to be publicly maintained and educated at the Colleges and University shall be drawn by their respective Visitors from the literary fund.

## FEMALE EDUCATION[1]

March 14, 1818

A plan of female education has never been a subject of systematic contemplation with me. It has occupied my attention so far only as the education of my own daughters occasionally required. Considering that they would be placed in a country situation where little aid could be obtained from abroad, I thought it essential to give them a solid education, which might enable them, when become mothers, to educate their own daughters, and even to direct the course for sons, should their fathers be lost, or incapable, or inattentive. My surviving daughter accordingly, the mother of many daughters as well as sons, has made their education the object of her life, and being a better judge of the practical part than myself, it is with her aid and that of one of her *élèves,* that I shall subjoin a catalogue of the books for such a course of reading as we have practised.[2]

A great obstacle to good education is the inordinate passion prevalent for novels, and the time lost in that reading which should be instructively employed. When this poison infects the mind, it destroys its tone and revolts it against wholesome reading. Reason and fact, plain and unadorned, are rejected. Nothing can engage attention unless dressed in all the figments of fancy, and nothing so bedecked comes amiss. The result is a bloated imagination, sickly judgment, and disgust towards all the real businesses of life. This mass of trash, however, is not without some distinction; some few modeling their narratives, although fictitious, on the incidents of real life, have been able to make them interesting and useful vehicles of a sound morality. Such, I think, are Marmontel's new moral tales, but not his old ones, which are really immoral. Such are the writings of Miss Edgeworth, and some of those of Madame Genlis. For a like reason, too, much poetry should not be indulged. Some is useful for forming style and taste. Pope,

[1] Letter to N. Burwell.

[2] The catalogue is not available.

Dryden, Thomson, Shakespeare, and of the French, Molière, Racine, the Corneilles, may be read with pleasure and improvement.

The French language, become that of the general intercourse of nations, and from their extraordinary advances, now the depository of all science, is an indispensable part of education for both sexes. In the subjoined catalogue, therefore, I have placed the books of both languages indifferently, according as the one or the other offers what is best.

The ornaments, too, and the amusements of life, are entitled to their portion of attention. These, for a female, are dancing, drawing, and music. The first is a healthy exercise, elegant, and very attractive for young people. Every affectionate parent would be pleased to see his daughter qualified to participate with her companions and without awkwardness at least, in the circles of festivity, of which she occasionally becomes a part. It is a necessary accomplishment, therefore, although of short use; for the French rule is wise, that no lady dances after marriage. This is founded in solid physical reasons, gestation and nursing leaving little time to a married lady when this exercise can be either safe or innocent. Drawing is thought less of in this country than in Europe. It is an innocent and engaging amusement, often useful, and a qualification not to be neglected in one who is to become a mother and an instructor. Music is invaluable where a person has an ear. Where they have not, it should not be attempted. It furnishes a delightful recreation for the hours of respite from the cares of the day, and lasts us through life. The taste of this country, too, calls for this accomplishment more strongly than for either of the others.

I need say nothing of household economy, in which the mothers of our country are generally skilled, and generally careful to instruct their daughters. We all know its value, and that diligence and dexterity in all its processes are inestimable treasures. The order and economy of a house are as honorable to the mistress as those of the farm to the master, and if either be neglected, ruin follows, and children destitute of the means of living.

This, sir, is offered as a summary sketch on a subject on which I have not thought much. It probably contains nothing but what has already occurred to yourself, and claims your acceptance on no other ground than as a testimony of my respect for your wishes, and of my great esteem and respect.

## THE STUDY OF GREEK AND LATIN [1]

August 24, 1819

You ask my opinion on the extent to which classical learning should be carried in our country. A sickly condition permits me to think, and a

[1] Letter to John Brazier.

rheumatic hand to write too briefly on this litigated question. The utilities we derive from the remains of the Greek and Latin languages are, first, as models of pure taste in writing. To these we are certainly indebted for the national and chaste style of modern composition which so much distinguishes the nations to whom these languages are familiar. Without these models we should probably have continued the inflated style of our northern ancestors, or the hyperbolical and vague one of the east. Second. Among the values of classical learning, I estimate the luxury of reading the Greek and Roman authors in all the beauties of their originals. And why should not this innocent and elegant luxury take its preëminent stand ahead of all those addressed merely to the senses? I think myself more indebted to my father for this than for all the other luxuries his cares and affections have placed within my reach; and more now than when younger, and more susceptible of delights from other sources. When the decays of age have enfeebled the useful energies of the mind, the classic pages fill up the vacuum of *ennui,* and become sweet composers to that rest of the grave into which we are all sooner or later to descend. Third. A third value is in the stores of real science deposited and transmitted us in these languages, to-wit: in history, ethics, arithmetic, geometry, astronomy, natural history, &c.

But to whom are these things useful? Certainly not to all men. There are conditions of life to which they must be forever estranged, and there are epochs of life too, after which the endeavor to attain them would be a great misemployment of time. Their acquisition should be the occupation of our early years only, when the memory is susceptible of deep and lasting impressions, and reason and judgment not yet strong enough for abstract speculations. To the moralist they are valuable, because they furnish ethical writings highly and justly esteemed: although in my own opinion, the moderns are far advanced beyond them in this line of science, the divine finds in the Greek language a translation of his primary code, of more importance to him than the original because better understood; and, in the same language, the newer code, with the doctrines of the earliest fathers, who lived and wrote before the simple precepts of the founder of this most benign and pure of all systems of morality became frittered into subtleties and mysteries, and hidden under jargons incomprehensible to the human mind. To these original sources he must now, therefore, return, to recover the virgin purity of his religion. The lawyer finds in the Latin language the system of civil law most conformable with the principles of justice of any which has ever yet been established among men, and from which much has been incorporated into our own. The physician as good a code of his art as has been given us to this day. Theories and systems of medicine, indeed, have been in perpetual change from the days of the good Hippocrates to the days of the good Rush, but which of them is the true one? the present, to be sure, as long as it is the present, but to yield its place in turn to the next novelty, which is then to become the true system, and is to mark the vast advance of medicine since the days of Hippocrates. Our situation is certainly benefited by the discovery of some new and very valuable medicines; and substituting those for some of his with the treasure of facts, and of sound observations recorded by him (mixed to be sure with anilities of his day) and we shall have nearly the present sum of the healing art. The statesman will find in these languages history, politics, mathematics, ethics, eloquence, love of country, to which he must add the sciences of his own day, for which of them should be unknown to him? And all the sciences must recur to the classical languages for the etymon, and sound understanding of their fundamental terms. For the merchant I should not say that the languages are a necessary. Ethics, mathematics, geography, political economy, history, seem to constitute the immediate foundations of his calling. The agriculturist needs ethics, mathematics, chemistry and natural philosophy. The mechanic the same. To them the languages are but ornament and comfort. I know it is often said there have been shining examples of men of great abilities in all the businesses of life, without any other science than what they had gathered from conversations and intercourse with the world. But who can say what these men would not have been had they started in the science on the shoulders of a Demosthenes or Cicero, of a Locke or Bacon, or a Newton? To sum the whole, therefore, it may truly be said that the classical languages are a solid basis for most, and an ornament to all the sciences.

## A COURSE OF LAW READING[1]

February 26, 1821

While you were in this neighborhood, you mentioned to me your intention of studying the law, and asked my opinion as to the sufficient course of reading. I gave it to you, *ore tenus,* and with so little consideration that I do not remember what it was; but I have since recollected that I once wrote a letter to Dr. Cooper,[2] on good consideration of the subject. He was then law-lecturer, I believe, at Carlisle. My stiffening wrist makes writing now a slow and painful operation, but my granddaughter Ellen undertakes to copy the letter, which I shall enclose herein.

I notice in that letter four distinct epochs at which the English laws have been reviewed, and their whole body, as existing at each epoch, well digested into a code. These digests were by Bracton, Coke, Matthew Bacon and Blackstone. Bracton having written about the commencement of the

[1] Letter to Dabney Terrell.

[2] January 16, 1814.—T. J.

extant statutes, may be considered as having given a digest of the laws then in being, written and unwritten, and forming, therefore, the textual code of what is called the common law, just at the period too when it begins to be altered by statutes to which we can appeal. But so much of his matter is become obsolete by change of circumstances or altered by statute, that the student may omit him for the present, and

1st. Begin with [3] Coke's four Institutes. These give a complete body of the law as it stood in the reign of the first James, an epoch the more interesting to us, as we separated at that point from English legislation, and acknowledge no subsequent statutary alterations.

2. Then passing over (for occasional reading as hereafter proposed) all the reports and treatises to the time of Matthew Bacon, read his abridgment, compiled about one hundred years after Coke's, in which they are all embodied. This gives numerous applications of the old principles to new cases, and gives the general state of the English law at that period.

Here, too, the student should take up the chancery branch of the law, by reading the first and second abridgments of the cases in Equity. The second is by the same Matthew Bacon, the first having been published some time before. The alphabetical order adopted by Bacon, is certainly not as satisfactory as the systematic. But the arrangement is under very general and leading heads, and these, indeed, with very little difficulty, might be systematically instead of alphabetically arranged and read.

3. Passing now in like manner over all intervening reports and tracts, the student may take up Blackstone's Commentaries, published about twenty-five years later than Bacon's abridgment, and giving the substance of these new reports and tracts. This review is not so full as that of Bacon, by any means, but better digested. Here, too, Woodeson should be read as supplementary to Blackstone, under heads too shortly treated by him. Foublanque's edition of Francis' Maxims of Equity, and Bridgman's digested Index, into which the latter cases are incorporated, are also supplementary in the chancery branch, in which Blackstone is very short.

This course comprehends about twenty-six 8vo volumes, and reading four or five hours a day would employ about two years.

[3] Since the date of this letter, a most important and valuable edition has been published of Coke's First Institute. The editor, Thomas, has analyzed the whole work, and re-composed its matter in the order of Blackstone's Commentaries, not omitting a sentence of Lord Coke's text, nor inserting one not his. In notes, under the text, he has given the modern decisions relating to the same subjects, rendering it thus as methodical, lucid, easy and agreeable to the reader as Blackstone, and more precise and profound. It can now be no longer doubted that this is the very best elementary work for a beginner in the study of the law. It is not, I suppose, to be had in this State, and questionable if in the North, as yet, and it is dear, costing in England four guineas or nineteen dollars, to which add the duty here on imported books, which, on the three volumes 8vo, is something more than three dollars, or one dollar the 8vo volume. This is a tax on learned readers to support printers for the readers of "The Delicate Distress," and "The Wild Irish Boy."—T. J.

After these, the best of the reporters since Blackstone should be read for the new cases which have occurred since his time. Which they are I know not, as all of them are since my time.

By way of change and relief for another hour or two in the day, should be read the law-tracts of merit which are many, and among them all those of Baron Gilbert are of the first order. In these hours, too, may be read Bracton (now translated), and Justinian's Institute. The method of these two last works is very much the same, and their language often quite so. Justinian is very illustrative of the doctrines of equity, and is often appealed to, and Cooper's edition is the best on account of the analogies and contrasts he has given of the Roman and English law. After Bracton, Reeves' History of the English Law may be read to advantage. During this same hour or two of lighter law reading, select and leading cases of the reporters may be successively read, which the several digests will have pointed out and referred to.

✦

I have here sketched the reading in common law and chancery which I suppose necessary for a reputable practitioner in those courts. But there are other branches of law in which, although it is not expected he should be an adept, yet when it occurs to speak of them, it should be understandingly to a decent degree. There are the Admiralty law, Ecclesiastical law, and the Law of Nations. I would name as elementary books in these branches, Molloy de Jure Maritimo. Brown's Compend of the Civil and Admiralty Law, 2 vols. 8vo. The Jura Ecclesiastica, 2 vols. 8vo. And Les Institutions du droit de la Nature et des Gens de Reyneval, 1 vol. 8vo.

Besides these six hours of law reading, light and heavy, and those necessary for the repasts of the day, for exercise and sleep, which suppose to be ten or twelve, there will still be six or eight hours for reading history, politics, ethics, physics, oratory, poetry, criticism, &c., as necessary as law to form an accomplished lawyer.

The letter to Dr. Cooper, with this as a supplement, will give you those ideas on a sufficient course of law reading which I ought to have done with more consideration at the moment of your first request. Accept them now as a testimony of my esteem, and of sincere wishes for your success; and the family, *unâ voce,* desires me to convey theirs with my own affectionate salutations.

## LIBRARY CLASSIFICATION[1]

Between 1820 and 1825

*An Explanation of the Views on which this Catalogue has been Prepared*

1. Great standard works of established reputation, too voluminous and too expensive for private libraries, should have a place in every public library, for the free resort of individuals.

2. Not merely the best books in their respective branches of science should be selected, but such also as were deemed good in their day, and which consequently furnish a history of the advance of the science.

3. The *opera omnia* of writers on various subjects are sometimes placed in that chapter of this Catalogue to which their principal work belongs, and sometimes referred to the Polygraphical chapter.

4. In some cases, besides the *opera omnia,* a detached tract has been also placed in its proper chapter, on account of editorial or other merit.

5. Books in very rare languages are considered here as specimens of language only, and are placed in the chapter of Philology, without regard to their subject.

6. Of the classical authors, several editions are often set down on account of some peculiar merit in each.

7. Translations are occasionally noted, on account of their peculiar merit or of difficulties of their originals.

8. Indifferent books are sometimes inserted, because none good are known on the same subject.

9. Nothing of mere amusement should lumber a public library.

10. The 8vo. form is generally preferred, for the convenience with which it is handled, and the compactness and symmetry of arrangement on the shelves of the library.

11. Some chapters are defective for the want of a more familiar knowledge of their subject in the compiler, others from schisms in the science they relate to. In Medicine, *e.g.,* the changes of theory which have successively prevailed, from the age of Hippocrates to the present day, have produced distinct schools, acting on different hypotheses, and headed by respected names, such as Stahl, Boerhaave, Sydenham, Hoffman, Cullen, and our own good Dr. Rush, whose depletive and mercurial systems have formed a school, or perhaps revived that which arose on Harvey's discovery of the circulation of the blood. In Religion, divided as it is into multifarious creeds, differing in their bases, and more or less in their superstructure, such moral

[1] This is from the preface of "A Catalogue of Books Forming the Body of a Library for the University of Virginia," which Jefferson wrote sometime between 1820 and 1825. The catalogue is in the University of Virginia and was printed for the first time in that University's *Alumni Bulletin,* November, 1895, pp. 79-80.

works have been chiefly selected as may be approved by all, omitting what is controversial and merely sectarian. Metaphysics have been incorporated with Ethics, and little extension given to them. For, while some attention may be usefully bestowed on the operations of thought, prolonged investigations of a faculty unamenable to the test of our senses, is an expense of time too unprofitable to be worthy of indulgence. Geology, too, has been merged in Mineralogy, which may properly embrace what is useful in this science, that is to say, a knowledge of the general stratification, collocation and sequence of the different species of rocks and other mineral substances, while it takes no cognisance of theories for the self-generation of the universe, or the particular revolutions of our own globe by the agency of water, fire, or other agent, subordinate to the fiat of the Creator.

Books are addressed to the three faculties of

MEMORY REASON IMAGINATION

To these belong respectively

| HISTORY | | PHILOSOPHY | | FINE ARTS |
|---|---|---|---|---|
| *Civil* | *Physical* | *Mathematical* | *Moral* | |
| 1. Ancient | 6. Physics, pure and mixed | 17. Arithmetic | 19. Ethics | 29. Architecture |
| 2. Modern, Foreign | 7. Agriculture | 18. Geometry | 20. Religion | Gardening |
| 3. " British | 8. Chemistry | | 21. Law—Nature and Nations | 30. Painting |
| 4. " American | 9. Anatomy | | 22. Law of Equity | Sculpture |
| 5. " Ecclesiastical | Surgery | | 23. " Common | Music |
| | 10. Medicine | | 24. " Merchant | 31. Poetry, Epic |
| | 11. Zoology | | 25. " Maritime | 32. " Romance |
| | 12. Botany | | 26. " Ecclesiastical | 33. " Pastoral |
| | 13. Mineralogy | | 27. " Foreign | 34. " Didactic |
| | 14. Technics | | 28. Politics | 35. " Tragedy |
| | 15. Astronomy | | | 36. " Comedy |
| | 16. Geography | | | 37. " Dialogue and Epistolary |
| | | | | 38. Rhetoric |
| | | | | 39. Criticism, Theory |
| | | | | 40. " Bibliography |
| | | | | 41. " Philology |
| | | 42. Polygraphical | | |

# THE STUDY OF HISTORY[1]

October 25, 1825

DEAR SIR: I do not know whether the professors to whom ancient and modern history are assigned in the University, have yet decided on the course of historical reading which they will recommend to their schools. If they have, I wish this letter to be considered as not written, as their course, the result of mature consideration, will be preferable to anything I could recommend. Under this uncertainty, and the rather as you are of neither of these schools, I may hazard some general ideas, to be corrected by what they may recommend hereafter.

In all cases I prefer original authors to compilers. For a course of ancient history, therefore, of Greece and Rome especially, I should advise the usual suite of Herodotus, Thucydides, Xenophon, Diodorus, Livy, Cæsar, Suetonius, Tacitus, and Dion, in their originals if understood, and in translations if not. For its continuation to the final destruction of the empire we must then be content with Gibbons, a compiler, and with Segur, for a judicious recapitulation of the whole. After this general course, there are a number of particular histories filling up the chasms, which may be read at leisure in the progress of life. Such is Arrian, Q. Curtius, Polybius, Sallust, Plutarch, Dionysius, Halicarnassus, Micasi, &c. The ancient universal history should be on our shelves as a book of general reference, the most learned and most faithful perhaps that ever was written. Its style is very plain but perspicuous.

In modern history, there are but two nations with whose course it is interesting to us to be intimately acquainted, to wit: France and England. For the former, Millot's General History of France may be sufficient to the period when I Davila commences. He should be followed by Perefixe, Sully, Voltaire's Louis XIV and XV, la Cretelle's XVIII$^{me}$ siècle, Marmontel's Regence, Foulongion's French Revolution, and Madame de Staël's, making up by a succession of particular history, the general one which they want.

Of England there is as yet no general history so faithful as Rapin's. He may be followed by Ludlow, Fox, Belsham, Hume and Brodie. Hume's, were it faithful, would be the finest piece of history which has ever been written by man. Its unfortunate bias may be partly ascribed to the accident of his having written backwards. His maiden work was the History of the Stuarts. It was a first essay to try his strength before the public. And whether as a Scotchman he had really a partiality for that family, or thought that the lower their degradation, the more fame he should acquire by raising

[1] Letter to an unnamed member of the University faculty.

them up to some favor, the object of his work was an apology for them. He spared nothing, therefore, to wash them white, and to palliate their misgovernment. For this purpose he suppressed truths, advanced falsehoods, forged authorities, and falsified records. All this is proved on him unanswerably by Brodie. But so bewitching was his style and manner, that his readers were unwilling to doubt anything, swallowed everything, and all England became Tories by the magic of his art. His pen revolutionized the public sentiment of that country more completely than the standing armies could ever have done, which were so much dreaded and deprecated by the patriots of that day.

Having succeeded so eminently in the acquisition of fortune and fame by this work, he undertook the history of the two preceding dynasties, the Plantagenets and Tudors. It was all-important in this second work, to maintain the thesis of the first, that "it was the people who encroached on the sovereign, not the sovereign who usurped on the rights of the people." And, again, chapter 53d, "the grievances under which the English labored [to wit: whipping, pillorying, cropping, imprisoning, fining, &c.,] when considered in themselves, without regard to the Constitution, scarcely deserve the name, nor were they either burthensome on the people's properties, or anywise shocking to the natural humanity of mankind." During the constant wars, civil and foreign, which prevailed while these two families occupied the throne, it was not difficult to find abundant instances of practices the most despotic, as are wont to occur in times of violence. To make this second epoch support the third, therefore, required but a little garbling of authorities. And it then remained, by a third work, to make of the whole a complete history of England, on the principles on which he had advocated that of the Stuarts. This would comprehend the Saxon and Norman conquests, the former exhibiting the genuine form and political principles of the people constituting the nation, and founded in the rights of man; the latter built on conquest and physical force, not at all affecting moral rights, nor even assented to by the free will of the vanquished. The battle of Hastings, indeed, was lost, but the natural rights of the nation were not staked on the event of a single battle. Their will to recover the Saxon constitution continued unabated, and was at the bottom of all the unsuccessful insurrections which succeeded in subsequent times. The victors and vanquished continued in a state of living hostility, and the nation may still say, after losing the battle of Hastings,

What though the field is lost?
All is not lost; the unconquerable will
And study of revenge, immortal hate
And courage never to submit or yield.

The government of a nation may be usurped by the forcible intrusion of an individual into the throne. But to conquer its will, so as to rest the right on that, the only legitimate basis, requires long acquiescence and cessation of all opposition. The Whig historians of England, therefore, have always gone back to the Saxon period for the true principles of their constitution, while the Tories and Hume, their Coryphæus, date it from the Norman conquest, and hence conclude that the continual claim by the nation of the good old Saxon laws, and the struggles to recover them, were "encroachments of the people on the crown, and not usurpations of the crown on the people." Hume, with Brodie, should be the last histories of England to be read. If first read, Hume makes an English Tory, from whence it is an easy step to American Toryism. But there is a history, by Baxter, in which, abridging somewhat by leaving out some entire incidents as less interesting now than when Hume wrote, he has given the rest in the identical words of Hume, except that when he comes to a fact falsified, he states it truly, and when to a suppression of truth, he supplies it, never otherwise changing a word. It is, in fact, an editic expurgation of Hume. Those who shrink from the volume of Rapin, may read this first, and from this lay a first foundation in a basis of truth.

For modern continental history, a very general idea may be first aimed at, leaving for future and occasional reading the particular histories of such countries as may excite curiosity at the time. This may be obtained from Mollet's Northern Antiquities, Vol. Esprit et Mœurs des Nations, Millot's Modern History, Russel's Modern Europe, Hallam's Middle Ages, and Robertson's Charles V.

You ask what book I would recommend to be first read in law. I am very glad to find from a conversation with Mr. Gilmer, that he considers Coke Littleton, as methodized by Thomas, as unquestionably the best elementary work, and the one which will be the text book of his school. It is now as agreeable reading as Blackstone, and much more profound. I pray you to consider this hasty and imperfect sketch as intended merely to prove my wish to be useful to you, and that with it you will accept the assurance of my esteem and respect.

# *Chapter XXIII*

# THE UNIVERSITY OF VIRGINIA

## AIM AND CURRICULUM[1]

August 1-4, 1818

In proceeding to the third and fourth duties prescribed by the Legislature, of reporting "the branches of learning, which should be taught in the University, and the number and description of the professorships they will require," the Commissioners were first to consider at what point it was understood that university education should commence. Certainly not with the alphabet, for reasons of expediency and impracticability, as well from the obvious sense of the Legislature, who, in the same act, make other provision for the primary instruction of the poor children, expecting, doubtless, that in other cases it would be provided by the parent, or become, perhaps, subject of future and further attention of the Legislature. The objects of this primary education determine its character and limits. These objects would be,

To give to every citizen the information he needs for the transaction of his own business;

To enable him to calculate for himself, and to express and preserve his ideas, his contracts and accounts, in writing;

To improve, by reading, his morals and faculties;

To understand his duties to his neighbors and country, and to discharge with competence the functions confided to him by either;

To know his rights; to exercise with order and justice those he retains; to choose with discretion the fiduciary of those he delegates; and to notice their conduct with diligence, with candor, and judgment;

And, in general, to observe with intelligence and faithfulness all the social relations under which he shall be placed.

To instruct the mass of our citizens in these, their rights, interests and

[1] From the report of the Commissioners for the University of Virginia, meeting in Rockfish Gap, on the Blue Ridge, to the Legislature of the State. Jefferson wrote the report.

duties, as men and citizens, being then the objects of education in the primary schools, whether private or public, in them should be taught reading, writing and numerical arithmetic, the elements of mensuration (useful in so many callings), and the outlines of geography and history. And this brings us to the point at which are to commence the higher branches of education, of which the Legislature require the development; those, for example, which are,

To form the statesmen, legislators and judges, on whom public prosperity and individual happiness are so much to depend;

To expound the principles and structure of government, the laws which regulate the intercourse of nations, those formed municipally for our own government, and a sound spirit of legislation, which, banishing all arbitrary and unnecessary restraint on individual action, shall leave us free to do whatever does not violate the equal rights of another;

To harmonize and promote the interests of agriculture, manufactures and commerce, and by well informed views of political economy to give a free scope to the public industry;

To develop the reasoning faculties of our youth, enlarge their minds, cultivate their morals, and instill into them the precepts of virtue and order;

To enlighten them with mathematical and physical sciences, which advance the arts, and administer to the health, the subsistence, and comforts of human life;

And, generally, to form them to habits of reflection and correct action, rendering them examples of virtue to others, and of happiness within themselves.

These are the objects of that higher grade of education, the benefits and blessings of which the Legislature now propose to provide for the good and ornament of their country, the gratification and happiness of their fellow-citizens, of the parent especially, and his progeny, on which all his affections are concentrated.

In entering on this field, the Commissioners are aware that they have to encounter much difference of opinion as to the extent which it is expedient that this institution should occupy. Some good men, and even of respectable information, consider the learned sciences as useless acquirements; some think they do not better the condition of man; and others that education, like private and individual concerns, should be left to private individual effort; not reflecting that an establishment embracing all the sciences which may be useful and even necessary in the various vocations of life, with the buildings and apparatus belonging to each, are far beyond the reach of individual means, and must either derive existence from public patronage, or not exist at all. This would leave us, then, without those callings which depend on education, or send us to other countries to seek the instruction they require. But the Commissioners are happy in considering the statute under which they are assembled as proof that the Legislature is far from the abandonment of objects so interesting. They are sensible that the advantages of well-directed education, moral, political and economical, are truly above all estimate. Education generates habits of application, of order, and the love of virtue; and controls, by the force of habit, any innate obliquities in our moral organization. We should be far, too, from the discouraging persuasion that man is fixed, by the law of his nature, at a given point; that his improvement is a chimera, and the hope delusive of rendering ourselves wiser, happier or better than our forefathers were. As well might it be urged that the wild and uncultivated tree, hitherto yielding sour and bitter fruit only, can never be made to yield better; yet we know that the grafting art

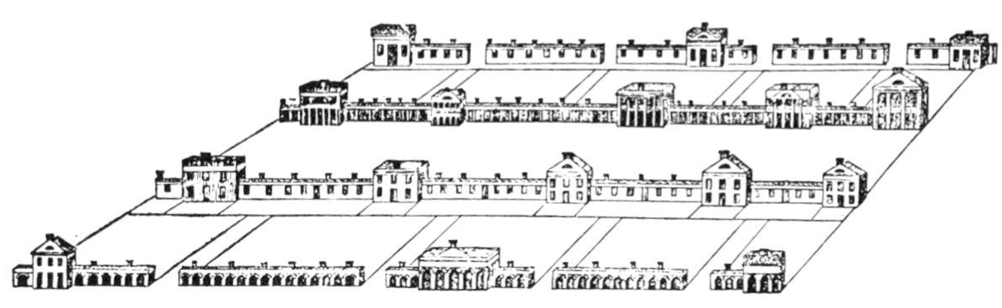

JEFFERSON'S DRAWINGS OF THE BUILDINGS OF THE UNIVERSITY OF VIRGINIA

implants a new tree on the savage stock, producing what is most estimable both in kind and degree. Education, in like manner, engrafts a new man on the native stock, and improves what in his nature was vicious and perverse into qualities of virtue and social worth. And it cannot be but that each generation succeeding to the knowledge acquired by all those who preceded it, adding to it their own acquisitions and discoveries, and handing the mass down for successive and constant accumulation, must advance the knowledge and well-being of mankind, not *infinitely,* as some have said, but *indefinitely,* and to a term which no one can fix and foresee. Indeed, we need look back half a century, to times which many now living remember well, and see the wonderful advances in the sciences and arts which have been made within that period. Some of these have rendered the elements themselves subservient to the purposes of man, have harnessed them to the yoke of his labors, and effected the great blessings of moderating his own, of accomplishing what was beyond his feeble force, and extending the comforts of life to a much enlarged circle, to those who had before known its necessaries only. That these are not the vain dreams of sanguine hope, we have before our eyes real and living examples. What, but education, has advanced us beyond the condition of our indigenous neighbors? And what chains them to their present state of barbarism and wretchedness, but a bigoted veneration for the supposed superlative wisdom of their fathers, and the preposterous idea that they are to look backward for better things, and not forward, longing, as it should seem, to return to the days of eating acorns and roots, rather than indulge in the degeneracies of civilization? And how much more encouraging to the achievements of science and improvement is this, than the desponding view that the condition of man cannot be ameliorated, that what has been must ever be, and that to secure ourselves where we are, we must tread with awful reverence in the footsteps of our fathers. This doctrine is the genuine fruit of the alliance between Church and State; the tenants of which, finding themselves but too well in their present condition, oppose all advances which might unmask their usurpations, and monopolies of honors, wealth, and power, and fear every change, as endangering the comforts they now hold. Nor must we omit to mention, among the benefits of education, the incalculable advantage of training up able counsellors to administer the affairs of our country in all its departments, legislative, executive and judiciary, and to bear their proper share in the councils of our national government; nothing more than education advancing the prosperity, the power, and the happiness of a nation.

Encouraged, therefore, by the sentiments of the Legislature, manifested in this statute, we present the following tabular statement of the branches of learning which we think should be taught in the University, forming them into groups, each of which are within the powers of a single professor:

I. Languages, ancient:
- Latin
- Greek
- Hebrew

II. Languages, modern:
- French
- Spanish
- Italian
- German
- Anglo-Saxon

III. Mathematics, pure:
- Algebra
- Fluxions
- Geometry, Elementary
  - Transcendental
- Architecture, Military
  - Naval

IV. Physico-Mathematics:
- Mechanics
- Statics
- Dynamics
- Pneumatics
- Acoustics
- Optics
- Astronomy
- Geography

V. Physics, or Natural Philosophy:
- Chemistry
- Mineralogy

VI. Botany
- Zoology

VII. Anatomy
- Medicine

VIII. Government
- Political Economy
- Law of Nature and Nations
- History, being interwoven with Politics and Law

IX. Law, municipal

X. Ideology
- General Grammar
- Ethics
- Rhetoric
- Belles Lettres and the fine arts.

Some of the terms used in this table being subject to a difference of acceptation, it is proper to define the meaning and comprehension intended to be given them here:

Geometry, Elementary, is that of straight lines and of the circle.
Transcendental, is that of all other curves; it includes, of course, *Projectiles,* a leading branch of military art.
Military Architecture includes Fortification, another branch of that art.
Statics respect matter generally, in a state of rest, and include Hydrostatics, or the laws of fluids particularly, at rest or in equilibrio.
Dynamics, used as a general term, include
Dynamics proper, or the laws of *solids* in motion; and
Hydrodynamics, or Hydraulics, those of *fluids* in motion.
Pneumatics teach the theory of air, its weight, motion, condensation, rarefaction, &c.
Acoustics, or Phonics, the theory of sound.
Optics, the laws of light and vision.
Physics, or Physiology, in a general sense, mean the doctrine of the physical objects of our senses.
Chemistry is meant, with its other usual branches, to comprehend the theory of agriculture.
Mineralogy, in addition to its peculiar subjects, is here understood to embrace what is real in geology.
Ideology is the doctrine of thought.
General Grammar explains the construction of language.

Some articles in this distribution of sciences will need observation. A professor is proposed for ancient languages, the Latin, Greek, and Hebrew, particularly; but these languages being the foundation common to all the sciences, it is difficult to foresee what may be the extent of this school. At the same time, no greater obstruction to industrious study could be proposed than the presence, the intrusions and the noisy turbulence of a multitude of small boys; and if they are to be placed here for the rudiments of the languages, they may be so numerous that its character and value as an University will be merged in those of a Grammar school. It is, therefore, greatly to be wished, that preliminary schools, either on private or public establishment, could be distributed in districts through the State, as preparatory to the entrance of students into the University. The tender age at which this part of education commences, generally about the tenth year, would weigh heavily with parents in sending their sons to a school so distant as the central establishment would be from most of them. Districts of such extent as that every parent should be within a day's journey of his son at school, would be desirable in cases of sickness, and convenient for supplying their ordinary wants, and might be made to lessen sensibly the expense of this part of their education. And where a sparse population would not, within such a compass, furnish subjects sufficient to maintain a school, a competent enlargement of district must, of necessity, there be submitted to. At these district schools or colleges, boys should be rendered able to read the easier authors, Latin and Greek. This would be useful and sufficient for many not intended for an University education. At these, too, might be taught English grammar, the higher branches of numerical arithmetic, the geometry of straight lines and of the circle, the elements of navigation, and geography to a sufficient degree, and thus afford to greater numbers the means of being qualified for the various vocations of life, needing more instruction than merely menial or praedial labor, and the same advantages to youths whose education may have been neglected until too late to lay a foundation in the learned languages. These institutions, intermediate between the primary schools and University, might then be the passage of entrance for youths into the University, where their classical learning might be critically completed, by a study of the authors of highest degree; and it is at this stage only that they should be received at the University. Giving then a portion of their time to a finished knowledge of the Latin and Greek, the rest might be appropriated to the modern languages, or to the commencement of the course of science for which they should be destined. This would generally be about the fifteenth year of their age, when they might go with more safety and contentment to that distance from their parents. Until this preparatory provision shall be made, either the University will be overwhelmed with the grammar school, or a separate establishment, under one or more ushers, for its lower classes, will be advisable, at a mile or two distant from the general one; where, too, may be exercised the stricter government necessary for young boys, but unsuitable for youths arrived at years of discretion.

The considerations which have governed the specification of languages to be taught by the professor of modern languages were, that the French is the language of general intercourse among nations, and as a depository of human science, is unsurpassed by any other language, living or dead; that the Spanish is highly interesting to us, as the language spoken by so great a portion of the inhabitants of our continents, with whom we shall probably have great intercourse ere long, and is that also in which is written the greater part of the earlier history of America. The Italian abounds with works of very superior order, valuable for their matter, and still more distinguished as models of the finest taste in style and composition. And the German now stands in a line with that of the most learned nations in richness and erudition and advance in the sciences. It is too of common descent with the language of our own country, a branch of the same original Gothic stock, and furnishes valuable illustrations for us. But in this point of view, the Anglo-Saxon is of peculiar value. We have placed it among the modern languages, because it is in fact that which we speak, in the earliest form in which we have knowledge of it. It has been undergoing, with time, those gradual changes which all languages, ancient and modern, have experienced; and even now needs only to be printed in the modern character and orthography to be intelligible, in a considerable degree, to an English reader. It has this value, too, above the Greek and Latin, that while it gives the radix of the mass of our language, they explain its innovations only. Obvious proofs of this have been presented to the modern reader in the disquisitions of Horn Tooke; [2] and Fortescue Aland has well explained the great instruction which may be derived from it to a full understanding of our ancient common law, on which, as a stock, our whole system of law is engrafted. It will form the first link in the chain of an historical review of our language through all its successive changes to the present day, will constitute the foundation of that critical instruction in it which ought to be found in a seminary of general learning, and thus reward amply the few weeks of attention which would alone be requisite for its attainment; a language already fraught with all the eminent science of our parent country, the future vehicle of whatever we may ourselves achieve, and destined to occupy so much space on the globe, claims distinguished attention in American education.

Medicine, where fully taught, is usually subdivided into several professorships, but this cannot well be without the accessory of an hospital, where the student can have the benefit of attending clinical lectures, and of assisting at operations of surgery. With this accessory, the seat of our University is not yet prepared, either by its population or by the numbers of poor who would leave their own houses, and accept of the charities of an hospital. For the present, therefore, we propose but a single professor for both medicine and anatomy. By him the medical science may be taught, with a history and explanations of all its successive theories from Hippocrates to the present day; and anatomy may be fully treated. Vegetable pharmacy will make a part of the botanical course, and mineral and chemical pharmacy of those of mineralogy and chemistry. This degree of medical information is such as the mass of scientific students would wish to possess, as enabling them in their course through life, to estimate with satisfaction the extent and limits of the aid to human life and health, which they may understandingly expect from that art; and it constitutes such a foundation for those intended for the profession, that the finishing course of practice at the bedsides of the sick, and at the operations of surgery in a hospital, can neither

[2] John Horne Tooke (1736-1812), English philologist and author of *The Diversions of Purley*.

be long nor expensive. To seek this finishing elsewhere, must therefore be submitted to for a while.

In conformity with the principles of our Constitution, which places all sects of religion on an equal footing, with the jealousies of the different sects in guarding that equality from encroachment and surprise, and with the sentiments of the Legislature in favor of freedom of religion, manifested on former occasions, we have proposed no professor of divinity; and the rather as the proofs of the being of a God, the creator, preserver, and supreme ruler of the universe, the author of all the relations of morality, and of the laws and obligations these infer, will be within the province of the professor of ethics; to which adding the developments of these moral obligations, of those in which all sects agree, with a knowledge of the languages, Hebrew, Greek, and Latin, a basis will be formed common to all sects. Proceeding thus far without offence to the Constitution, we have thought it proper at this point to leave every sect to provide, as they think fittest, the means of further instruction in their own peculiar tenets.

We are further of opinion, that after declaring by law that certain sciences shall be taught in the University, fixing the number of professors they require, which we think should, at present, be ten, limiting (except as to the professors who shall be first engaged in each branch) a maximum for their salaries (which should be a certain but moderate subsistence, to be made up by liberal tuition fees, as an excitement to assiduity), it will be best to leave to the discretion of the visitors, the grouping of these sciences together, according to the accidental qualifications of the professors; and the introduction also of other branches of science, when enabled by private donations, or by public provision, and called for by the increase of population, or other change of circumstances; to establish beginnings, in short, to be developed by time, as those who come after us shall find expedient. They will be more advanced than we are in science and in useful arts, and will know best what will suit the circumstances of their day.

We have proposed no formal provision for the gymnastics of the school, although a proper object of attention for every institution of youth. These exercises with ancient nations, constituted the principal part of the education of their youth. Their arms and mode of warfare rendered them severe in the extreme; ours, on the same correct principle, should be adapted to our arms and warfare; and the manual exercise, military manoeuvres, and tactics generally, should be the frequent exercises of the students, in their hours of recreation. It is at that age of aptness, docility, and emulation of the practices of manhood, that such things are soonest learnt and longest remembered. The use of tools too in the manual arts is worthy of encouragement, by facilitating to such as choose it, an admission into the neighboring workshops. To these should be added the arts which embellish life, dancing, music, and drawing; the last more especially, as an important part of military education. These innocent arts furnish amusement and happiness to those who, having time on their hands, might less inoffensively employ it. Needing, at the same time, no regular incorporation with the institution, they may be left to accessory teachers, who will be paid by the individuals employing them, the University only providing proper apartments for their exercise.

The fifth duty prescribed to the Commissioners, is to propose such general provisions as may be properly enacted by the Legislature, for the better organizing and governing the University.

In the education of youth, provision is to be made for, 1, tuition; 2, diet; 3, lodging; 4, government; and 5, honorary excitements. The first of these constitutes the proper functions of the professors; 2, the dieting of the students should be left to private boarding houses of their own choice, and at their own expense; to be regulated by the Visitors from time to time, the house only being provided by the University within its own precincts, and thereby of course subjected to the general regimen, moral or sumptuary, which they shall prescribe. 3. They should be lodged in dormitories, making a part of the general system of buildings. 4. The best mode of government for youth, in large collections, is certainly a desideratum not yet attained with us. It may be well questioned whether *fear* after a certain age, is a motive to which we should have ordinary recourse. The human character is susceptible of other incitements to correct conduct, more worthy of employ, and of better effect. Pride of character, laudable ambition, and moral dispositions are innate correctives of the indiscretions of that lively age; and when strengthened by habitual appeal and exercise, have a happier effect on future character than the degrading motive of fear. Hardening them to disgrace, to corporal punishments, and servile humiliations cannot be the best process for producing erect character. The affectionate deportment between father and son, offers in truth the best example for that of tutor and pupil; and the experience and practice of other[3] countries, in this respect, may be worthy of enquiry and consideration with us. It will then be for the wisdom and discretion of the Visitors to devise and perfect a proper system of government, which, if it be founded in reason and comity, will be more likely to nourish in the minds of our youth the combined spirit of order and self-respect, so congenial with our political institutions, and so important to be woven into the American character.

[3] A police exercised by the students themselves, under proper discretion, has been tried with success in some countries, and the rather as forming them for initiation into the duties and practices of civil life.—T. J.

## REGULATIONS

October 4, 1824

The Board then proceeded to consider of the regulations necessary for constituting, governing and conducting the institution in addition to those passed at their last session, agreed to the following supplementary enactments:

Each of the schools of the University shall be held two hours of every other day of the week; and that every student may be enabled to attend those of his choice, let their sessions be so arranged, as to days and hours, that no two of them shall be holden at the same time. Therefore,

The school of ancient languages shall occupy from 7.30 to 9.30 A.M., on Mondays, Wednesdays and Fridays.

That of modern languages shall occupy the same hours on Tuesdays, Thursdays and Saturdays.

That of mathematics shall occupy from 9.30 to 11.30 A.M. on Mondays, Wednesdays and Fridays.

That of natural philosophy the same hours on Tuesdays, Thursdays and Saturdays.

That of natural history shall occupy from 11.30 A.M. to 1.30 P.M. on Mondays, Wednesdays and Fridays.

That of anatomy and medicine the same hours on Tuesdays, Thursdays and Saturdays.

That of moral philosophy shall occupy from 1.30 to 3.30 P.M. on Mondays, Wednesdays and Fridays.

That of law the same hours on Tuesdays, Thursdays and Saturdays.

The Visitors of the University shall be free, severally or together, to attend occasionally any school, during its session, as inspectors and judges of the mode in which it is conducted.

Wherein the instruction is by lessons, and the class too numerous for a single instructor, assistant tutors may be employed, to be chosen by the professor, to have the use of two adjacent dormitories each, rent free, and to divide with the professor the tuition fees, as shall be agreed between them.

The professors, tutors and all officers of the University shall reside constantly in the apartments of the University, or of its precincts, assigned to them.

At a meeting of the faculty of professors, on matters within their functions, one of them shall preside, by rotation, for the term of one year each. A majority of the members shall make a quorum for business. They may appoint a secretary of their own body, or otherwise, who shall keep a journal of their proceedings, and lay the same before the Board of Visitors at their first ensuing meeting, and whenever else required. The compensation for such secretary shall be fifty dollars yearly, payable from the funds of the University.

Meetings of the faculty may be called by the presiding member of the year, or by any three of the professors, to be held in an apartment of the rotunda, and the object of the call shall be expressed in the written notification to be served by the janitor. But when assembled, other business also may be transacted.

The faculty may appoint a janitor, who shall attend its meetings, and the meetings of the Visitors, and shall perform necessary menial offices for them, for which he shall receive 150 dollars yearly from the funds of the University, and be furnished with a lodging room.

No student is to be received under sixteen years of age, rigorously proved. None to be admitted into the mathematical school, or that of natural philosophy, who is not an adept in all the branches of numerical arithmetic; and none into the school of ancient languages, unless qualified, in the judgment of the professor, to commence reading the higher Latin classics; nor to receive instruction in Greek, unless qualified in the same degree in that language.

No one shall enter as a student of the University, either at the beginning or during the progress of the session, but as for the whole session, ending on the 15th day of December, and paying as for the whole.

The dormitories shall be occupied by two students each, and no more, at fifteen dollars yearly rent, to be paid to the proctor at or before the end of the session, one-half by each occupant, or the whole by one, if there be only one. And every student, within the same term, shall pay to the proctor, also, for the University, fifteen dollars annually for his participation in the use of the public apartments during the session.

The students shall be free to diet themselves in any of the hotels of the University, at their choice, or elsewhere, other than in taverns, as shall suit themselves, but not more than fifty shall be allowed to diet at the same hotel.

No keeper of any of the hotels of the University shall require or receive more than 100 dollars for dieting any student and for performing the necessary offices of his dormitory, during the session of ten months and a half, nor shall suffer ardent spirits or wine, mixed or unmixed, to be drank within his tenement, on pain of an immediate determination of his lease, and removal by the Faculty; nor shall any person boarding elsewhere than with their parents, in any house, and using wine or ardent spirits, mixed or unmixed, within such house, or its tenement, or paying more than 120 dollars for diet, lodging, and other offices and accommodations of the house and tenement, during a like term, be admitted to any school of the University.

Every student shall be free to attend the schools of his choice, and no other than he chooses.

There will be one vacation only in the year, and that shall be from the 15th day of December to the last day of January.

Examination of the candidates for honorary distinctions shall be held in the presence of all the professors and students, in the week preceding the commencement of the vacation. At these examinations shall be given, to the highly meritorious only, and by the vote of a majority of the professors, diplomas, or premiums of medals or books, to be provided by the University, to wit: Diplomas to those of the highest qualifications, medals of more or less value to those of the second grade of acquisition, and books of more or less value to those of a third. These diplomas shall be of two degrees; the highest of doctor, the second of graduate. And the diploma of each shall express the particular school or schools in which the candidate shall have been declared eminent, and shall be subscribed by the particular professors approving it. But no diploma shall be given to anyone who has not passed such an examination in the Latin language as shall have proved him able to read the highest classics in that language with ease, thorough understanding and just quantity; and if he be also a proficient in the Greek, let that, too, be stated in his diploma. The intention being that the reputation of the University shall not be committed but to those who, to an eminence in some one or more of the sciences taught in it, add a proficiency in these languages which constitute the basis of good education, and are indispensable to fill up the character of a "well-educated man."

Punishment for major offences shall be expulsion, temporary suspension, or interdiction of residence or appearance within the precincts of the University. The minor punishment shall be restraint within those precincts, within their own chamber, or in diet, reproof by a professor, privately or in presence of the school of the offender, or of all the schools, a seat of degradation in his school-room of longer or shorter duration, removal to a lower class, dismission from the school-room for the day, imposition of a task; and insubordination to these sentences shall be deemed and punished as contumacy.

Contumacy shall be liable to any of the minor punishments.

The precincts of the University are to be understood as co-extensive with the lot or parcel of its own grounds on which it is situated.

The major punishments of expulsion from the University, temporary suspension of attendance and presence there, or interdiction of residence or appearance within its precincts, shall be decreed by the professors themselves. Minor cases may be referred to a board of six censors, to be named by the faculty, from the most discreet of the students, whose duty it shall be, sitting as a board, to inquire into the facts, propose the minor punishment which they think proportioned to the offence, and to make report thereof to the professors for their approbation, or their commutation of the penalty, if it be beyond the grade of the offence. The censors shall hold their offices until the end of the session of their appointment, if not sooner revoked by the faculty.

Inattendance on school, inattention to the exercises prescribed, and misbehavior or indecorum in school shall be subject to any of the minor punishments; and the professor of the school may singly reprove, impose a task, or dismiss from the room for the day.

Habits of expense, of dissoluteness, dissipation, or of playing at games of chance, being obstructive to the acquisition of science by the student himself and injurious by example to others, shall be subject in the first instance to admonition and reproof to the offender, and to communication and warning to the parent or guardian, and, if not satisfactorily corrected, to a refusal of further continuance at the University.

No student shall make any festive entertainment within the precincts of the University, nor contribute or be present at them, there or elsewhere, but with the consent of each of the professors whose school he attends, on pain of a minor punishment.

No student shall admit any disturbing noises in his room, or make them anywhere within the precincts of the University, or fire a gun or pistol within the same, on pain of such minor sentence as the faculty shall decree or approve. But the proper use of musical instruments shall be freely allowed in their rooms, and in that appropriated for instruction in music.

Riotous, disorderly, intemperate or indecent conduct of any student within the precincts shall be punished by interdiction of a residence within the precincts; and repetitions of such offences, by expulsion from the University.

Fighting with weapons which may inflict death, or a challenge to such fight, given or accepted, shall be punished by instant expulsion from the University, not remissible by the Faculty; and it shall be the duty of the proctor to give information thereof to the civil magistrate, that the parties may be dealt with according to law.

Offences cognisable by the laws of the land shall be left to the cognisance of the civil magistrate, if claimed by him, or otherwise to the judgment of the faculty; all others to that of the faculty. And such of these as are not specially designated in enactments of the Visitors may be subjected by the faculty to any of the minor punishments permitted by these enactments.

Sentences of expulsion from the University (except in the case of challenge or combat with arms) shall not be final until approved by the Board of Visitors or, when they are not in session, by a majority of them, separately consulted. But residence within the precincts, and attendance on the schools may be suspended in the meantime.

No student shall, within the precincts of the University, introduce, keep or use any spiritous or vinous liquors, keep or use weapons or arms of any kind, or gunpowder, keep a servant, horse or dog, appear in school with a stick, or any weapon, nor while in school, be covered without permission of the professor, nor use tobacco by smoking or chewing, on pain of any of the minor punishments at the discretion of the faculty, or of the board of censors, approved by the faculty.

All damages done to instruments, books, buildings or other property of the University by any student, shall be made good at his expense; and wilful injury to any tree, shrub or other plant within the precincts, shall be punished by fine, not exceeding ten dollars, at the discretion of the faculty.

When a professors knocks at the door of a student's room, any person being within, and announces himself, it shall be opened, on pain of minor punishment; and the professor may, if refused, have the door broken open; and the expenses of repair shall be levied on the student or students within.

At the hour appointed for the meeting of every school, the roll of the school shall be called over, the absentees and those appearing tardily, shall be noted, and if no sufficient cause be offered, at the rising of the school, to the satisfaction of the professor, the notation shall stand confirmed, and shall be given in to the faculty, the presiding member of which for the time being shall, on the 15th days of May, August and December, or as soon after each of these days as may be, transmit by mail a list of these notations to the parent or guardian of each delinquent.

When testimony is required from a student, it shall be voluntary, and not on oath. And the obligation to give it shall—(if unwilling to give it, let the moral obligation be explained and urged, under which everyone is bound to bear witness, where wrong has been done, but finally let it)—be left to his own sense of right.

Should the religious sects of this State, or any of them, according to the invitation held out to them, establish within, or adjacent to, the precincts of the University, schools for instruction in the religion of their sect, the students of the University will be free, and expected to attend religious worship at the establishment of their respective sects, in the morning, and in time to meet their school in the University at its stated hour.

The students of such religious school, if they attend any school of the University, shall be considered as students of the University, subject to the same regulations, and entitled to the same rights and privileges.

The room provided for a school-room in every pavilion shall be used for the school of its occupant professor, and shall be furnished by the University with necessary benches and tables.

The upper circular room of the rotunda shall be reserved for a library.

One of its larger elliptical rooms on its middle floor shall be used for annual examinations, for lectures to such schools as are too numerous for their ordinary school-room, and for religious worship, under the regulations allowed to be prescribed by law. The other rooms on the same floor may be used by schools of instruction in drawing, music, or any other of the innocent and ornamental accomplishments of life; but under such instructors only as shall be approved and licensed by the faculty.

The rooms in the basement story of the rotunda shall be, one of them for a chemical laboratory, and the others for any necessary purpose to which they may be adapted.

The two open apartments, adjacent to the same story of the rotunda, shall be appropriated to the gymnastic exercises and games of the students, among which shall be reckoned military exercises.

A military instructor shall be provided at the expense of the University, to be appointed by the faculty, who shall attend on every Saturday from half after one o'clock to half after three P.M., and shall instruct the students in the manual exercise, in field evolutions, manœuvres and encampments. The students shall attend these exercises, and shall be obedient to the military orders of their instructor. The roll shall be regularly called over by him at the hour of meeting, absences and insubordinations shall be noted, and the list of the delinquents shall be delivered to the presiding member of the faculty for the time being to be animadverted on by the faculty, and such minor punishment imposed as each case shall, in their discretion, require. The school of modern languages shall be pretermitted on the days of actual military exercise.

Substitutes in the form of arms shall be provided by the proctor, at the expense of the University; they shall be distinguished by numbers, delivered out, received in and deposited under the care and responsibility of the instructor, in a proper depository to be furnished him; and all injuries to them by a student shall be repaired at the expense of such student.

Work-shops shall be provided, whenever convenient, at the expense of the University, wherein the students who choose, may exercise themselves in the use of tools, and such mechanical practices as it is convenient and useful for every person to understand, and occasionally to practice. These shops may be let, rent free, to such skillful and orderly mechanics as shall be approved by the faculty, on the condition that they will permit the use of their tools, instruments and implements, within the shop, to such students as shall desire and use the permission discreetly, and under a liability for any injury they may do them; and on the further condition, if necessary, of such mechanics receiving instruction gratis in the mechanical and philosophical principles of his art, so far as taught in any of the schools.

## POLITICAL SCIENCE

March 4, 1825

Whereas, it is the duty of this Board [of Visitors of the University of Virginia] to the government under which it lives, and especially to that of which this University is the immediate creation, to pay especial attention to the principles of government which shall be inculcated therein, and to provide that none shall be inculcated which are incompatible with those on which the Constitutions of this State, and of the United States were genuinely based, in the common opinion; and for this purpose it may be necessary to point out specially where these principles are to be found legitimately developed:

Resolved, that it is the opinion of this Board that as to the general principles of liberty and the rights of man, in nature and in society, the doctrines of Locke, in his "Essay concerning the true original extent and end of civil government," and of Sidney in his "Discourses on government," may be considered as those generally approved by our fellow citizens of this, and the United States, and that on the distinctive principles of the government of our State, and of that of the United States, the best guides are to be found in, 1. The Declaration of Independence, as the fundamental act of union of these States. 2. The book known by the title of "The Federalist," being an authority to which appeal is habitually made by all, and rarely declined or denied by any as evidence of the general opinion of those who framed, and of those who accepted the Constitution of the United States, on questions as to its genuine meaning. 3. The Resolutions of the General Assembly of Virginia in 1799 on the subject of the alien and sedition laws, which appeared to accord with the predominant sense of the people of the United States. 4. The valedictory address of President Washington, as conveying political lessons of peculiar value. And that in the branch of the school of law, which is to treat on the subject of civil polity, these shall be used as the text and documents of the school.

## LIBRARY REGULATIONS

March 5, 1825

Books may be lent to the students of the University, by the librarian, and by no other person, on a written permit from a professor whom such student attends, specifying the day beyond which they will not be retained. But it is meant that the books lent are for reading only, and not for the ordinary purpose of getting lessons in them as school books.

No student shall carry any book borrowed from the library, out of the precincts of the University; nor shall any student be permitted to have more than three volumes in his possession at any time.

If a student shall not return a borrowed book on or before the day limited in his permit, he shall receive no other until it be returned; and he shall pay, moreover, for every week's detention beyond the limitation, ten cents for a 12mo. or book of smaller size, twenty cents for an 8mo., thirty cents for a 4mo. and forty cents for a folio.

Not every book in the library shall be free to be lent to students, but such only as shall not be expressly prohibited by the faculty on account of their rarity, value or liableness to injury.

No student shall ever be in the library but in presence of the librarian, or of some professor whom he attends, nor shall be allowed to take any book from the shelves, nor remain in the room to read or consult any book, but during such presence.

If any student deface, injure, or lose any book of the library, he shall pay the value of the book if defaced, double value if injured, and three-fold, if lost; and shall be suspended from the privilege of borrowing during such term as the faculty shall adjudge.

On some one day of every week during term, and during one hour of that day (such day and hour to be fixed on by the faculty) the librarian shall attend in the library, to receive books returned, and to lend such others as shall be applied for according to rule. And at some one hour of every day (to be fixed by the faculty) the librarian shall attend, if requested by any such professor, such book or books as he may require, and to receive any he may have to return.

The librarian shall make an entry of every book lent, and cancel the same when returned, so that it may always be known in what hands every book is.

Strangers whom the librarian may be willing to attend, may visit the library; but, to prevent derangement of the books, they are to take no book from the shelf, but in his presence. They may also be permitted to consult any book, to read in it, make notes or quotations from it, at the table, under such accommodations and arrangements as the librarian shall prescribe, on his own responsibility.

Resolved, that the salary of the librarian be raised to the sum of 150 dollars.

## PROBLEMS OF DISCIPLINE

### October 3, 1825

Resolved, that it be communicated to the Faculty of the professors of the University, as the earnest request and recommendation of the rector and

Visitors, that so far as can be effected by their exertions, they cause the statutes and rules enacted for the government of the University, to be exactly and strictly observed; that the roll of each school particularly be punctually called at the hour at which its students should attend; that the absent and the tardy, without reasonable cause, be noted, and a copy of these notations be communicated by mail or otherwise to the parent or guardian of each student respectively, on the first days of every month during the term (instead of the days prescribed in a former statute for such communications).

That it is requested of them to make known to the students that it is with great regret that some breaches of order, committed by the unworthy few who lurk among them unknown, render necessary the extension to all of processes afflicting to the feelings of those who are conscious of their own correctness, and who are above all participation in these vicious irregularities. While the offenders continue unknown the tarnish of their faults spreads itself over the worthy also, and confounds all in a common censure. But that it is in their power to relieve themselves from the imputations and painful proceedings to which they are thereby subjected, by lending their aid to the faculty, on all occasions towards detecting the real guilty. The Visitors are aware that a prejudice prevails too extensively among the young that it is dishonorable to bear witness one against another. While this prevails, and under the form of a matter of conscience, they have been unwilling to authorize constraint, and have therefore, in their regulations on this subject, indulged the error, however unfounded in reason or morality. But this loose principle in the ethics of school-boy combinations, is unworthy of mature and regulated minds, and is accordingly condemned by the laws of their country, which, in offences within their cognisance, compel those who have knowledge of a fact, to declare it for the purposes of justice, and of the general good and safety of society. And certainly, where wrong has been done, he who knows and conceals the doer of it, makes himself an accomplice, and justly censurable as such. It becomes then but an act of justice to themselves, that the innocent and the worthy should throw off with disdain all communion of character with such offenders, should determine no longer to screen the irregular and the vicious under the respect of their cloak, and to notify them, even by a solemn association for the purpose, that they will co-operate with the faculty in future, for preservation of order, the vindication of their own character, and the reputation and usefulness of an institution which their country has so liberally established for their improvement, and to place within their reach those acquirements in knowledge on which their future happiness and fortunes depend. Let the good and the virtuous of the alumni of the University do this, and the disorderly will then be singled out for observation, and deterred by punishment, or disabled by expulsion, from infecting with their inconsideration the institution itself, and the sound mass of those which it is preparing for virtue and usefulness.

Although nocturnal absences from their chambers occasionally happening are not entirely forbidden, yet if frequent, habitual, or without excusable cause, they should be also noted and reported, with other special delinquencies, to the parent or guardian.

October 5, 1825

Resolved that the 47th enactment be amended, by inserting after the word "chewing" the words "or smoking."

No student shall appear out of his dormitory masked or disguised in any manner whatever, which may render the recognition of his person more difficult, on pain of suspension or expulsion by the faculty of professors.

Intoxication shall, for the first offence, be liable to any of the minor punishments, and any repetition of the offence to any of the major punishments.

Resolved, that the 40th enactment be amended, by inserting after the word "dissipation," the words "of profane swearing."

No person who has been a student at any other incorporated seminary of learning shall be received at this University, but on producing a certificate from such seminary or other satisfactory evidence to the faculty with respect to his general good conduct.

The professors being charged with the execution of the laws of the University, it becomes their duty to pursue proper means to discover and prevent offences. Respect from the student to the professor being at all times due, it is more especially so when the professor is engaged in his duty. Such respect, therefore, is solemnly enjoined on every student, and it is declared and enacted, that if any student refuse his name to a professor, or being required by him to stop, shall fail to do so, or shall be guilty of any other disrespect to a professor, he shall be liable to any of the punishments, minor or major.

*Part VI*

# PERSONAL PAPERS

## *Chapter XXIV*

# AUTOBIOGRAPHY

January 6–July 21,* 1821

January 6, 1821. At the age of 77, I begin to make some memoranda, and state some recollections of dates and facts concerning myself, for my own more ready reference, and for the information of my family.

The tradition in my father's family was, that their ancestor came to this country from Wales, and from near the mountain of Snowdon, the highest in Great Britain. I noted once a case from Wales, in the law reports, where a person of our name was either plaintiff or defendant; and one of the same name was secretary to the Virginia Company. These are the only instances in which I have met with the name in that country. I have found it in our early records; but the first particular information I have of any ancestor was of my grandfather, who lived at the place in Chesterfield called Ozborne's, and owned the lands afterwards the glebe of the parish. He had three sons; Thomas who died young, Field who settled on the waters of Roanoke and left numerous descendants, and Peter, my father, who settled on the lands I still own, called Shadwell, adjoining my present residence. He was born February 29, 1707–8, and intermarried 1739, with Jane Randolph, of the age of 19, daughter of Isham Randolph, one of the seven sons of that name and family, settled at Dungeness in Goochland. They trace their pedigree far back in England and Scotland, to which let everyone ascribe the faith and merit he chooses.

My father's education had been quite neglected; but being of a strong mind, sound judgment, and eager after information, he read much and improved himself, insomuch that he was chosen, with Joshua Fry, Professor of Mathematics in William and Mary college, to continue the boundary line between Virginia and North Carolina, which had been begun by Colonel Byrd; and was afterwards employed with the same Mr. Fry, to make the first map of Virginia which had ever been made, that of Captain Smith being merely a conjectural sketch. They possessed excellent materials for so much of the country as is below the blue ridge; little being then known beyond that ridge. He was the third or fourth settler, about the year 1737, of the part of the country in which I live. He died, August 17th, 1757, leaving my mother a widow, who lived till 1776, with six daughters and two sons, myself the elder. To my younger brother he left his estate on James River, called Snowden, after the supposed birth-place of the family: to myself, the lands on which I was born and live.

He placed me at the English school at five years of age; and at the Latin at nine, where I continued until his death. My teacher, Mr. Douglas, a clergyman from Scotland, with the rudiments of the Latin and Greek languages, taught me the French; and on the death of my father, I went to the Reverend Mr. Maury, a correct classical scholar, with whom I continued two years; and then, to wit, in the spring of 1760, went to William and Mary college, where I continued two years. It was my great good fortune, and what probably fixed the destinies of my life, that Dr. William Small of Scotland, was then professor of Mathematics, a man profound in most of the useful branches of science, with a happy talent of communication, correct and gentlemanly manners, and an enlarged and liberal mind. He, most happily for me, became soon attached to me, and made me his daily companion when not engaged in the school; and from his conversation I got my first views of the expansion of science, and of the system of things in which we are placed. Fortunately, the philosophical chair became vacant soon after my arrival at college, and he was appointed to fill it *per interim:* and he was the first who ever gave, in that college, regular lectures in Ethics, Rhetoric and Belles lettres. He returned to Europe in 1762, having previously filled up the measure of his goodness to me, by procuring for me, from his most intimate friend, George Wythe, a reception as a student of law, under his direction, and introduced me to the acquaintance and familiar table of Governor Fauquier, the ablest man who had ever filled that office. With him, and at his table, Dr. Small and Mr. Wythe, his *amici omnium horarum,* and myself, formed a *partie quarree,* and to the habitual conversations on these occasions I owed much instruction. Mr. Wythe continued to be my faithful and beloved mentor in youth, and my most affectionate friend through life. In 1767, he led me into the practice of the law at the bar of the General court, at which I continued until the Revolution shut up the courts of justice.[1]

In 1769, I became a member of the legislature by the choice of the county in which I live, and so continued until it was closed by the Revolution. I made one effort in that body for the permission of the emancipation of

[1] For Jefferson sketch of Wythe, see pp. 927-28.

slaves, which was rejected: and indeed, during the regal government, nothing liberal could expect success. Our minds were circumscribed within narrow limits, by an habitual belief that it was our duty to be subordinate to the mother country in all matters of government, to direct all our labors in subservience to her interests, and even to observe a bigoted intolerance for all religions but hers. The difficulties with our representatives were of habit and despair, not of reflection and conviction. Experience soon proved that they could bring their minds to rights, on the first summons of their attention. But the King's Council, which acted as another house of legislature, held their places at will, and were in most humble obedience to that will: the Governor too, who had a negative on our laws, held by the same tenure, and with still greater devotedness to it: and, last of all, the Royal negative closed the last door to every hope of amelioration.

On the 1st of January, 1772, I was married to Martha Skelton, widow of Bathurst Skelton, and daughter of John Wayles, then twenty-three years old. Mr. Wayles was a lawyer of much practice, to which he was introduced more by his great industry, punctuality, and practical readiness, than by eminence in the science of his profession. He was a most agreeable companion, full of pleasantry and good humor, and welcomed in every society. He acquired a handsome fortune, and died in May, 1773, leaving three daughters: the portion which came on that event to Mrs. Jefferson, after the debts should be paid, which were very considerable, was about equal to my own patrimony, and consequently doubled the ease of our circumstances.

When the famous Resolutions of 1765, against the Stamp-act, were proposed, I was yet a student of law in Williamsburgh. I attended the debate, however, at the door of the lobby of the House of Burgesses, and heard the splendid display of Mr. Henry's talents as a popular orator. They were great indeed; such as I have never heard from any other man. He appeared to me to speak as Homer wrote. Mr. Johnson, a lawyer, and member from the Northern Neck, seconded the resolutions, and by him the learning and the logic of the case were chiefly maintained. My recollections of these transactions may be seen page 60 of the life of Patrick Henry, by Wirt, to whom I furnished them.

In May, 1769, a meeting of the General Assembly was called by the Governor, Lord Botetourt. I had then become a member; and to that meeting became known the joint resolutions and address of the Lords and Commons, of 1768–9, on the proceedings in Massachusetts. Counter-resolutions, and an address to the King by the House of Burgesses, were agreed to with little opposition, and a spirit manifestly displayed itself of considering the cause of Massachusetts as a common one. The Governor dissolved us: but we met the next day in the Apollo of the Raleigh tavern, formed ourselves into a voluntary convention, drew up articles of association against the use of any merchandise imported from Great Britain, signed and recommended them to the people, repaired to our several counties, and were re-elected without any other exception than of the very few who had declined assent to our proceedings.

Nothing of particular excitement occurring for a considerable time, our countrymen seemed to fall into a state of insensibility to our situation; the duty on tea, not yet repealed, and the declaratory act of a right in the British Parliament to bind us by their laws in all cases whatsoever, still suspended over us. But a court of inquiry held in Rhode Island in 1762, with a power to send persons to England to be tried for offences committed here, was considered, at our session of the spring of 1773, as demanding attention. Not thinking our old and leading members up to the point of forwardness and zeal which the times required, Mr. Henry, Richard Henry Lee, Francis L. Lee, Mr. Carr and myself agreed to meet in the evening, in a private room of the Raleigh, to consult on the state of things. There may have been a member or two more whom I do not recollect. We were all sensible that the most urgent of all measures was that of coming to an understanding with all the other colonies, to consider the British claims as a common cause to all, and to produce a unity of action: and, for this purpose, that a committee of correspondence in each colony would be the best instrument for intercommunication: and that their first measure would probably be, to propose a meeting of deputies from every colony, at some central place, who should be charged with the direction of the measures which should be taken by all. We, therefore, drew up the resolutions which may be seen in Wirt, page 87. The consulting members proposed to me to move them, but I urged that it should be done by Mr. Carr, my friend and brother-in-law, then a new member, to whom I wished an opportunity should be given of making known to the house his great worth and talents. It was so agreed; he moved them, they were agreed to *nem. con.*, and a committee of correspondence appointed, of whom Peyton Randolph, the speaker, was chairman. The Governor (then Lord Dunmore) dissolved us, but the committee met the next day, prepared a circular letter to the speakers of the other colonies, inclosing to each a copy of the resolutions, and left it in charge with their chairman to forward them by expresses.

The origination of these committees of correspondence between the colonies has been since claimed for Massachusetts, and Marshall [2] has given into this error, although the very note of his appendix to which he refers, shows that their establishment was confined to their own towns. This matter will be seen clearly stated in a letter of Samuel Adams Wells to me of April 2nd, 1819, and my answer of May 12th. I was corrected by the letter of Mr. Wells

[2] Life of Washington, ii, p. 151.

in the information I had given Mr. Wirt, as stated in his note, page 87, that the messengers of Massachusetts and Virginia crossed each other on the way, bearing similar propositions; for Mr. Wells shows that Massachusetts did not adopt the measure, but on the receipt of our proposition, delivered at their next session. Their message, therefore, which passed ours, must have related to something else, for I well remember Peyton Randolph's informing me of the crossing of our messengers.

The next event which excited our sympathies for Massachusetts, was the Boston port bill, by which that port was to be shut up on the 1st of June, 1774. This arrived while we were in session in the spring of that year. The lead in the House, on these subjects, being no longer left to the old members, Mr. Henry, R. H. Lee, Fr. L. Lee, three or four other members, whom I do not recollect, and myself, agreeing that we must boldly take an unequivocal stand in the line with Massachusetts, determined to meet and consult on the proper measures, in the council-chamber, for the benefit of the library in that room. We were under conviction of the necessity of arousing our people from the lethargy into which they had fallen, as to passing events; and thought that the appointment of a day of general fasting and prayer would be most likely to call up and alarm their attention. No example of such a solemnity had existed since the days of our distresses in the war of '55, since which a new generation had grown up. With the help, therefore, of Rushworth, whom we rummaged over for the revolutionary precedents and forms of the Puritans of that day, preserved by him, we cooked up a resolution, somewhat modernizing their phrases, for appointing the 1st day of June, on which the port bill was to commence, for a day of fasting, humiliation, and prayer, to implore Heaven to avert from us the evils of civil war, to inspire us with firmness in support of our rights, and to turn the hearts of the King and Parliament to moderation and justice. To give greater emphasis to our proposition, we agreed to wait the next morning on Mr. Nicholas, whose grave and religious character was more in unison with the tone of our resolution, and to solicit him to move it. We accordingly went to him in the morning. He moved it the same day; the 1st of June was proposed; and it passed without opposition. The Governor dissolved us, as usual. We retired to the Apollo, as before, agreed to an association, and instructed the committee of correspondence to propose to the corresponding committees of the other colonies, to appoint deputies to meet in Congress at such place, *annually,* as should be convenient, to direct, from time to time, the measures required by the general interest: and we declared that an attack on any one colony, should be considered as an attack on the whole. This was in May. We further recommended to the several counties to elect deputies to meet at Williamsburgh, the 1st of August ensuing, to consider the state of the colony, and particularly to appoint delegates to a general Congress, should that measure be acceded to by the committees of correspondence generally. It was acceded to; Philadelphia was appointed for the place, and the 5th of September for the time of meeting. We returned home, and in our several counties invited the clergy to meet assemblies of the people on the 1st of June, to perform the ceremonies of the day, and to address to them discourses suited to the occasion. The people met generally, with anxiety and alarm in their countenances, and the effect of the day, through the whole colony, was like a shock of electricity, arousing every man, and placing him erect and solidly on his centre. They chose, universally, delegates for the convention. Being elected one for my own county, I prepared a draught of instructions to be given to the delegates whom we should send to the Congress, which I meant to propose at our meeting. In this I took the ground that, from the beginning, I had thought the only one orthodox or tenable, which was, that the relation between Great Britain and these colonies was exactly the same as that of England and Scotland, after the accession of James, and until the union, and the same as her present relations with Hanover, having the same executive chief, but no other necessary political connection; and that our emigration from England to this country gave her no more rights over us, than the emigrations of the Danes and Saxons gave to the present authorities of the mother country, over England. In this doctrine, however, I had never been able to get anyone to agree with me but Mr. Wythe. He concurred in it from the first dawn of the question, What was the political relation between us and England? Our other patriots, Randolph, the Lees, Nicholas, Pendleton, stopped at the half-way house of John Dickinson, who admitted that England had a right to regulate our commerce, and to lay duties on it for the purposes of regulation, but not of raising revenue. But for this ground there was no foundation in compact, in any acknowledged principles of colonization, nor in reason: expatriation being a natural right, and acted on as such, by all nations, in all ages. I set out for Williamsburgh some days before that appointed for our meeting, but was taken ill of a dysentery on the road, and was unable to proceed. I sent on, therefore, to Williamsburgh, two copies of my draught, the one under cover to Peyton Randolph, who I knew would be in the chair of the convention, the other to Patrick Henry. Whether Mr. Henry disapproved the ground taken, or was too lazy to read it (for he was the laziest man in reading I ever knew) I never learned: but he communicated it to nobody. Peyton Randolph informed the convention he had received such a paper from a member, prevented by sickness from offering it in his place, and he laid it on the table for perusal. It was read generally by the members, approved by many, though thought too bold for the present state of things; but they printed it in pamphlet form, under the title of "A Summary View of the Rights of British America." It found its way to England, was taken up by the opposition, interpolated a little by Mr. Burke so as to make it answer opposition purposes, and in that form ran rapidly through several editions. This information I had from Parson Hurt, who happened at the time to be in London, whither he had gone to receive clerical orders; and I was informed afterwards by Peyton Randolph, that it had procured me the honor of having my name inserted in a long list of proscriptions, enrolled in a bill of attainder commenced in one of the Houses of Parliament, but suppressed in embryo by the hasty step of events, which warned them to be a little cautious. Montague, agent of the House of Burgesses in England, made extracts from the bill, copied the names, and sent them to Peyton Randolph. The names, I think, were about twenty, which he repeated to me, but I recollect those only of Hancock, the two Adamses, Peyton Randolph himself, Patrick Henry, and myself. The convention met on the 1st of August, renewed their association, appointed delegates to the Congress, gave them instructions very temperately and properly expressed, both as to style and matter; and they repaired to Philadelphia at the time appointed. The splendid proceedings of that Congress, at their first session, belong to general history, are known to everyone, and need not therefore be noted here. They terminated their session on the 26th of October, to meet again on the 10th of May ensuing. The convention, at their ensuing session of March, '75, approved of the proceedings of Congress, thanked their delegates, and reappointed the same persons to represent the colony at the meeting to be held in May: and foreseeing the probability that Peyton Randolph, their president, and speaker also of the House of Burgesses, might be called off, they added me, in that event, to the delegation.

Mr. Randolph was, according to expectation, obliged to leave the chair of Congress, to attend the General Assembly summoned by Lord Dunmore, to meet on the 1st day of June, 1775. Lord North's conciliatory propositions, as they were called, had been received by the Governor, and furnished the subject for which this assembly was convened. Mr. Randolph accordingly attended, and the tenor of these propositions being generally known, as having been addressed to all the governors, he was anxious that the answer of our Assembly, likely to be the first, should harmonize with what he knew to be the sentiments and wishes of the body he had recently left. He feared that Mr. Nicholas, whose mind was not yet up to the mark of the times, would undertake the answer, and therefore pressed me to prepare it. I did so, and, with his aid, carried it through the House, with long and doubtful scruples from Mr. Nicholas and James Mercer, and a dash of cold water on it here and there, enfeebling it somewhat, but finally with unanimity, or a vote approaching it. This being passed, I repaired immediately to Philadelphia, and conveyed to Congress the first notice they had of it. It was entirely approved there. I took my seat with them on the 21st of June. On the 24th, a committee which had been appointed to prepare a declaration of the causes of taking up arms, brought in their report (drawn I believe by J. Rutledge) which, not being liked, the House recommitted it, on the 26th, and added Mr. Dickinson and myself to the committee. On the rising of the House, the committee having not yet met, I happened to find myself near Governor W. Livingston, and proposed to him to draw the paper. He excused himself and proposed that I should draw it. On my pressing him with urgency, "we are as yet but new acquaintances, sir," said he, "why are you so earnest for my doing it?" "Because," said I, "I have been informed that you drew the Address to the people of Great Britain, a production, certainly, of the finest pen in America." "On that," says he, "perhaps, sir, you may not have been correctly informed." I had received the information in Virginia from Colonel Harrison on his return from that Congress. Lee, Livingston, and Jay had been the committee for that draught. The first, prepared by Lee, had been disapproved and recommitted. The second was drawn by Jay, but being presented by Governor Livingston, had led Colonel Harrison into the error. The next morning, walking in the hall of Congress, many members being assembled, but the House not yet formed, I observed Mr. Jay speaking to R. H. Lee, and leading him by the button of his coat to me. "I understand, sir," said he to me, "that this gentleman informed you, that Governor Livingston drew the Address to the people of Great Britain." I assured him, at once, that I had not received that information from Mr. Lee, and that not a word had ever passed on the subject between Mr. Lee and myself; and after some explanations the subject was dropped. These gentlemen had had some sparrings in debate before, and continued ever very hostile to each other.

I prepared a draught of the declaration committed to us. It was too strong for Mr. Dickinson. He still retained the hope of reconciliation with the mother country, and was unwilling it should be lessened by offensive statements. He was so honest a man, and so able a one, that he was greatly indulged even by those who could not feel his scruples. We therefore requested him to take the paper, and put it into a form he could approve. He did so, preparing an entire new statement, and preserving of the former only the last four paragraphs and half of the preceding one. We approved and reported it to Congress, who accepted it. Congress gave a signal proof of their indulgence to Mr. Dickinson, and of their great desire not to go too fast for any respectable part of our body, in permitting him to draw their second petition to the King according to his own ideas, and passing it with scarcely any amendment. The disgust against this humility was general; and Mr. Dickinson's delight at its passage was the only circumstance which reconciled them to it. The vote being passed, although further observation on it was out of order, he could not refrain from rising and expressing his satisfaction, and concluded by saying, "there is but one word, Mr. President, in the paper which I disapprove, and that is the word *Congress*"; on which Ben Harrison rose and said, "There is but one word in the paper, Mr. President, of which I approve, and that is the word *Congress*."

On the 22d of July, Dr. Franklin, Mr. Adams, R. H. Lee, and myself, were appointed a committee to consider and report on Lord North's conciliatory resolution. The answer of the Virginia Assembly on that subject having been approved, I was requested by the committee to prepare this report, which will account for the similarity of feature in the two instruments.

On the 15th of May, 1776, the convention of Virginia instructed their delegates in Congress, to propose to that body to declare the colonies independent of Great Britain, and appointed a committee to prepare a declaration of rights and plan of government.

In Congress, Friday, June 7, 1776. The delegates from Virginia moved, in obedience to instructions from their constituents, that the Congress should declare that these United colonies are, and of right ought to be, free and independent states, that they are absolved from all allegiance to the British crown, and that all political connection between them and the state of Great Britain is, and ought to be, totally dissolved; that measures should be immediately taken for procuring the assistance of foreign powers, and a Confederation be formed to bind the colonies more closely together.

The House being obliged to attend at that time to some other business, the proposition was referred to the next day, when the members were ordered to attend punctually at ten o'clock.

Saturday, June 8. They proceeded to take it into consideration, and referred it to a committee of the whole, into which they immediately resolved themselves, and passed that day and Monday, the 10th, in debating on the subject.

It was argued by Wilson, Robert R. Livingston, E. Rutledge, Dickinson, and others—

That, though they were friends to the measures themselves, and saw the impossibility that we should ever again be united with Great Britain, yet they were against adopting them at this time:

That the conduct we had formerly observed was wise and proper now, of deferring to take any capital step till the voice of the people drove us into it:

That they were our power, and without them our declarations could not be carried into effect:

That the people of the middle colonies (Maryland, Delaware, Pennsylvania, the Jerseys and New York) were not yet ripe for bidding adieu to British connection, but that they were fast ripening, and, in a short time, would join in the general voice of America:

That the resolution, entered into by this House on the 15th of May, for suppressing the exercise of all powers derived from the crown, had shown, by the ferment into which it had thrown these middle colonies, that they had not yet accommodated their minds to a separation from the mother country:

That some of them had expressly forbidden their delegates to consent to such a declaration, and others had given no instructions, and consequently no powers to give such consent:

That if the delegates of any particular colony had no power to declare such colony independent, certain they were, the others could not declare it for them; the colonies being as yet perfectly independent of each other:

That the assembly of Pennsylvania was now sitting above stairs, their convention would sit within a few days, the convention of New York was now sitting, and those of the Jerseys and Delaware counties would meet on the Monday following, and it was probable these bodies would take up the question of Independence, and would declare to their delegates the voice of their state:

That if such a declaration should now be agreed to, these delegates must retire, and possibly their colonies might secede from the Union:

That such a secession would weaken us more than could be compensated by any foreign alliance:

That in the event of such a division, foreign powers would either refuse to join themselves to our fortunes, or, having us so much in their power as that desperate declaration would place us, they would insist on terms proportionably more hard and prejudicial:

That we had little reason to expect an alliance with those to whom alone, as yet, we had cast our eyes:

That France and Spain had reason to be jealous of that rising power, which would one day certainly strip them of all their American possessions:

That it was more likely they should form a connection with the British court, who, if they should find themselves unable otherwise to extricate themselves from their difficulties, would agree to a partition of our territories, restoring Canada to France, and the Floridas to Spain, to accomplish for themselves a recovery of these colonies:

That it would not be long before we should receive certain information of the disposition of the French court, from the agent whom we had sent to Paris for that purpose:

That if this disposition should be favorable, by waiting the event of the present campaign, which we all hoped would be successful, we should have reason to expect an alliance on better terms:

That this would in fact work no delay of any effectual aid from such ally, as, from the advance of the season and distance of our situation, it was impossible we could receive any assistance during this campaign:

That it was prudent to fix among ourselves the terms on which we should form alliance, before we declared we would form one at all events:

And that if these were agreed on, and our Declaration of Independence ready by the time our Ambassador should be prepared to sail, it would be as well as to go into that Declaration at this day.

On the other side, it was urged by J. Adams, Lee, Wythe, and others, that no gentleman had argued against the policy or the right of separation from Britain, nor had supposed it possible we should ever renew our connection; that they had only opposed its being now declared:

That the question was not whether, by a Declaration of Independence, we should make ourselves what we are not; but whether we should declare a fact which already exists:

That, as to the people or parliament of England, we had always been independent of them, their restraints on our trade deriving efficacy from our acquiescence only, and not from any rights they possessed of imposing them, and that so far, our connection had been federal only, and was now dissolved by the commencement of hostilities:

That, as to the King, we had been bound to him by allegiance, but that this bond was now dissolved by his assent to the last act of Parliament, by which he declares us out of his protection, and by his levying war on us, a fact which had long ago proved us out of his protection; it being a certain position in law, that allegiance and protection are reciprocal, the one ceasing when the other is withdrawn:

That James the II never declared the people of England out of his protection, yet his actions proved it, and the Parliament declared it:

No delegates then can be denied, or ever want, a power of declaring an existing truth:

That the delegates from the Delaware counties having declared their constituents ready to join, there are only two colonies, Pennsylvania and Maryland, whose delegates are absolutely tied up, and that these had, by their instructions, only reserved a right of confirming or rejecting the measure:

That the instructions from Pennsylvania might be accounted for from the times in which they were drawn, near a twelvemonth ago, since which the face of affairs has totally changed:

That within that time, it had become apparent that Britain was determined to accept nothing less than a *carte-blanche,* and that the King's answer to the Lord Mayor, Aldermen and Common Council of London, which had come to hand four days ago, must have satisfied everyone of this point:

That the people wait for us to lead the way:

That *they* are in favor of the measure, though the instructions given by some of their *representatives* are not:

That the voice of the representatives is not always consonant with the voice of the people, and that this is remarkably the case in these middle colonies:

That the effect of the resolution of the 15th of May has proved this, which, raising the murmurs of some in the colonies of Pennsylvania and Maryland, called forth the opposing voice of the freer part of the people, and proved them to be the majority even in these colonies:

That the backwardness of these two colonies might be ascribed, partly to the influence of proprietary power and connections, and partly, to their having not yet been attacked by the enemy:

That these causes were not likely to be soon removed, as there seemed no probability that the enemy would make either of these the seat of this summer's war:

That it would be vain to wait either weeks or months for perfect unanimity, since it was impossible that all men should ever become of one sentiment on any question:

That the conduct of some colonies, from the beginning of this contest, had given reason to suspect it was their settled policy to keep in the rear of the confederacy, that their particular prospect might be better, even in the worst event:

That, therefore, it was necessary for those colonies who had thrown themselves forward and hazarded all from the beginning, to come forward now also, and put all again to their own hazard:

That the history of the Dutch Revolution, of whom three states only confederated at first, proved that a secession of some colonies would not be so dangerous as some apprehended:

That a declaration of Independence alone could render it consistent with European delicacy, for European powers to treat with us, or even to receive an Ambassador from us:

That till this, they would not receive our vessels into their ports, nor acknowledge the adjudications of our courts of admiralty to be legitimate, in cases of capture of British vessels:

That though France and Spain may be jealous of our rising power, they must think it will be much more formidable with the addition of Great Britain; and will therefore see it their interest to prevent a coalition; but should they refuse, we shall be but where we are; whereas without trying, we shall never know whether they will aid us or not:

That the present campaign may be unsuccessful, and therefore we had better propose an alliance while our affairs wear a hopeful aspect:

That to wait the event of this campaign will certainly work delay, because, during the summer, France may assist us effectually, by cutting off those supplies of provisions from England and Ireland, on which the enemy's armies here are to depend; or by setting in motion the great power they have collected in the West Indies, and calling our enemy to the defence of the possessions they have there:

That it would be idle to lose time in settling the terms of alliance, till we had first determined we would enter into alliance:

That it is necessary to lose no time in opening a trade for our people, who will want clothes, and will want money too, for the payment of taxes:

And that the only misfortune is, that we did not enter into alliance with France six months sooner, as, besides opening her ports for the vent of our last year's produce, she might have marched an army into Germany, and prevented the petty princes there, from selling their unhappy subjects to subdue us.

It appearing in the course of these debates, that the colonies of New York, New Jersey, Pennsylvania, Delaware, Maryland, and South Carolina were not yet matured for falling from the parent stem, but that they were fast advancing to that state, it was thought most prudent to wait a while for them, and to postpone the final decision to July 1st; but, that this might occasion as little delay as possible, a committee was appointed to prepare a Declaration of Independence. The committee were John Adams, Dr. Franklin, Roger Sherman, Robert R. Livingston, and myself. Committees were also appointed, at the same time, to prepare a plan of confederation for the colonies, and to state the terms proper to be proposed for foreign alliance. The committee for drawing the Declaration of Independence, desired me to do it. It was accordingly done, and being approved by them, I reported it to the House on Friday, the 28th of June, when it was read, and ordered to lie on the table. On Monday, the 1st of July, the House resolved itself into a committee of the whole, and resumed the consideration of the original motion made by the delegates of Virginia, which, being again debated through the day, was carried in the affirmative by the votes of New Hampshire, Connecticut, Massachusetts, Rhode Island, New Jersey, Maryland, Virginia, North Carolina and Georgia. South Carolina and Pennsylvania voted against it. Delaware had but two members present, and they were divided. The delegates from New York declared they were for it themselves, and were assured their constituents were for it; but that their instructions having been drawn near a twelvemonth before, when reconciliation was still the general object, they were enjoined by them to do nothing which should impede that object. They, therefore, thought themselves not justifiable in voting on either side, and asked leave to withdraw from the question; which was given them. The committee rose and reported their resolution to the House. Mr. Edward Rutledge, of South Carolina, then requested the determination might be put off to the next day, as he believed his colleagues, though they disapproved of the resolution, would then join in it for the sake of unanimity. The ultimate question, whether the House would agree to the resolution of the committee, was accordingly postponed to the next day, when it was again moved, and South Carolina concurred in voting for it. In the meantime, a third member had come post from the Delaware counties, and turned the vote of that colony in favor of the resolution. Members of a different sentiment attending that morning from Pennsylvania also, her vote was changed, so that the whole twelve colonies who were authorized to vote at all, gave their voices for it; and, within a few days, the convention of New York approved of it, and thus supplied the void occasioned by the withdrawing of her delegates from the vote.

Congress proceeded the same day to consider the Declaration of Independence, which had been reported and lain on the table the Friday preceding, and on Monday referred to a committee of the whole. The pusillanimous idea that we had friends in England worth keeping terms with, still haunted the minds of many. For this reason, those passages which conveyed censures on the people of England were struck out, lest they should give them offence. The clause too, reprobating the enslaving the inhabitants of Africa, was struck out in complaisance to South Carolina and Georgia, who had never attempted to restrain the importation of slaves, and who, on the contrary, still wished to continue it. Our northern brethren also, I believe, felt a little tender under those censures; for though their people had very few slaves themselves, yet they had been pretty considerable carriers of them to others. The debates, having taken up the greater parts of the 2d, 3d, and 4th days of July, were, on the evening of the last, closed; the Declaration was reported by the committee, agreed to by the House, and signed by every member present, except Mr. Dickinson. As the sentiments of men are known not only by what they receive, but what they reject also, I will state the form of the Declaration as originally reported. The parts struck out by Congress shall be distinguished by a black line drawn under them; [3] and those inserted by them shall be placed in the margin, or in a concurrent column.

The Declaration thus signed on the 4th, on paper, was engrossed on parchment, and signed again on the 2d of August.

[Some erroneous statements of the proceedings on the Declaration of Independence having got before the public in latter times, Mr. Samuel A. Wells asked explanations of me, which are given in my letter to him of May 12, '19, before and now again referred to.[4] I took notes in my place while these things were going on, and at their close wrote them out in form

[3] The Declaration is omitted here; it is printed in ch. 1, pp. 28-34.
[4] See pp. 81-86.

and with correctness, and from 1 to 7 of the two preceding sheets, are the originals then written; as the two following are of the earlier debates on the Confederation, which I took in like manner.]

On Friday, July 12, the committee appointed to draw the articles of Confederation reported them, and, on the 22d, the House resolved themselves into a committee to take them into consideration. On the 30th and 31st of that month, and 1st of the ensuing, those articles were debated which determined the proportion, or quota, of money which each state should furnish to the common treasury, and the manner of voting in Congress. The first of these articles was expressed in the original draught in these words: "Art. XI. All charges of war and all other expenses that shall be incurred for the common defence, or general welfare, and allowed by the United States assembled, shall be defrayed out of a common treasury, which shall be supplied by the several colonies in proportion to the number of inhabitants of every age, sex, and quality, except Indians not paying taxes, in each colony, a true account of which, distinguishing the white inhabitants, shall be triennially taken and transmitted to the Assembly of the United States."

Mr. Chase moved that the quotas should be fixed, not by the number of inhabitants of every condition, but by that of the "white inhabitants." He admitted that taxation should be always in proportion to property, that this was, in theory, the true rule; but that, from a variety of difficulties, it was a rule which could never be adopted in practice. The value of the property in every State, could never be estimated justly and equally. Some other measure for the wealth of the State must therefore be devised, some standard referred to, which would be more simple. He considered the number of inhabitants as a tolerably good criterion of property, and that this might always be obtained. He therefore thought it the best mode which we could adopt, with one exception only: he observed that negroes are property, and as such, cannot be distinguished from the lands or personalities held in those States where there are few slaves; that the surplus of profit which a Northern farmer is able to lay by, he invests in cattle, horses, &c., whereas a Southern farmer lays out the same surplus in slaves. There is no more reason, therefore, for taxing the Southern States on the farmer's head, and on his slave's head, than the Northern ones on their farmer's heads and the heads of their cattle; that the method proposed would, therefore, tax the Southern States according to their numbers and their wealth conjunctly, while the Northern would be taxed on numbers only: that negroes, in fact, should not be considered as members of the State, more than cattle, and that they have no more interest in it.

Mr. John Adams observed, that the numbers of people were taken by this article, as an index of the wealth of the State, and not as subjects of taxation; that, as to this matter, it was of no consequence by what name you called your people, whether by that of freemen or of slaves; that in some countries the laboring poor were called freemen, in others they were called slaves; but that the difference as to the state was imaginary only. What matters it whether a landlord, employing ten laborers on his farm, gives them annually as much money as will buy them the necessaries of life, or gives them those necessaries at short hand? The ten laborers add as much wealth annually to the State, increase its exports as much in the one case as the other. Certainly five hundred freemen produce no more profits, no greater surplus for the payment of taxes, than five hundred slaves. Therefore, the State in which are the laborers called freemen, should be taxed no more than that in which are those called slaves. Suppose, by an extraordinary operation of nature or of law, one half the laborers of a State could in the course of one night be transformed into slaves; would the State be made the poorer or the less able to pay taxes? That the condition of the laboring poor in most countries, that of the fishermen particularly of the Northern States, is as abject as that of slaves. It is the number of laborers which produces the surplus for taxation, and numbers, therefore, indiscriminately, are the fair index of wealth; that it is the use of the word "property" here, and its application to some of the people of the State, which produces the fallacy. How does the Southern farmer procure slaves? Either by importation or by purchase from his neighbor. If he imports a slave, he adds one to the number of laborers in his country, and proportionably to its profits and abilities to pay taxes; if he buys from his neighbor, it is only a transfer of a laborer from one farm to another, which does not change the annual produce of the State, and therefore, should not change its tax: that if a Northern farmer works ten laborers on his farm, he can, it is true, invest the surplus of ten men's labor in cattle; but so may the Southern farmer, working ten slaves; that a State of one hundred thousand freemen can maintain no more cattle, than one of one hundred thousand slaves. Therefore, they have no more of that kind of property; that a slave may indeed, from the custom of speech, be more properly called the wealth of his master, than the free laborer might be called the wealth of his employer; but as to the State, both were equally its wealth, and should, therefore, equally add to the quota of its tax.

Mr. Harrison proposed, as a compromise, that two slaves should be counted as one freeman. He affirmed that slaves did not do as much work as freemen, and doubted if two effected more than one; that this was proved by the price of labor; the hire of a laborer in the Southern colonies being from 8 to £12, while in the Northern it was generally £24.

Mr. Wilson said, that if this amendment should take place, the Southern colonies would have all the benefit of slaves, whilst the Northern ones would bear the burthen: that slaves increase the profits of a State, which the Southern States mean to take to themselves; that they also increase the burthen of defence, which would of course fall so much the heavier on the Northern: that slaves occupy the places of freemen, and eat their food. Dismiss your slaves, and freemen will take their places. It is our duty to lay every discouragement on the importation of slaves; but this amendment would give the *jus trium liberorum* to him who would import slaves: that other kinds of property were pretty equally distributed through all the colonies: there were as many cattle, horses and sheep, in the North as the South, and South as the North; but not so as to slaves: that experience has shown that those colonies have been always able to pay most, which have the most inhabitants, whether they be black or white; and the practice of the Southern colonies has always been to make every farmer pay poll taxes upon all his laborers, whether they be black or white. He acknowledges, indeed, that freemen work the most; but they consume the most also. They do not produce a greater surplus for taxation. The slave is neither fed nor clothed so expensively as a freeman. Again, white women are exempted from labor generally, but negro women are not. In this, then, the Southern States have an advantage as the article now stands. It has sometimes been said, that slavery is necessary, because the commodities they raise would be too dear for market if cultivated by freemen; but now it is said that the labor of the slave is the dearest.

Mr. Payne urged the original resolution of Congress, to proportion the quotas of the States to the number of souls.

Dr. Witherspoon was of opinion, that the value of lands and houses was the best estimate of the wealth of a nation, and that it was practicable to obtain such a valuation. This is the true barometer of wealth. The one now proposed is imperfect in itself, and unequal between the States. It has been objected that negroes eat the food of freemen, and, therefore, should be taxed; horses also eat the food of freemen; therefore they also should be taxed. It has been said too, that in carrying slaves into the estimate of the taxes the State is to pay, we do no more than those States themselves do, who always take slaves into the estimate of the taxes the individual is to pay. But the cases are not parallel. In the Southern colonies slaves pervade the whole colony; but they do not pervade the whole continent. That as to the original resolution of Congress, to proportion the quotas according to the souls, it was temporary only, and related to the moneys heretofore emitted: whereas we are now entering into a new compact, and therefore stand on original ground.

August 1. The question being put, the amendment proposed was rejected by the votes of New Hampshire, Massachusetts, Rhode Island, Connecticut, New York, New Jersey, and Pennsylvania, against those of Delaware, Maryland, Virginia, North and South Carolina. Georgia was divided.

The other article was in these words: "Art. XVII. In determining questions, each colony shall have one vote."

JULY 30, 31, AUGUST 1. Present forty-one members. Mr. Chase observed this article was the most likely to divide us, of any one proposed in the draught then under consideration: that the larger colonies had threatened they would not confederate at all, if their weight in Congress should not be equal to the numbers of people they added to the confederacy; while the smaller ones declared against a union, if they did not retain an equal vote for the protection of their rights. That it was of the utmost consequence to bring the parties together, as, should we sever from each other, either no foreign power will ally with us at all, or the different States will form different alliances, and thus increase the horrors of those scenes of civil war and bloodshed, which in such a state of separation and independence, would render us a miserable people. That our importance, our interests, our peace required that we should confederate, and that mutual sacrifices should be made to effect a compromise of this difficult question. He was of opinion, the smaller colonies would lose their rights, if they were not in some instances allowed an equal vote; and, therefore, that a discrimination should take place among the questions which would come before Congress. That the smaller States should be secured in all questions concerning life or liberty, and the greater ones, in all respecting property. He, therefore, proposed, that in votes relating to money, the voice of each colony should be proportioned to the number of its inhabitants.

Dr. Franklin thought, that the votes should be so proportioned in all cases. He took notice that the Delaware counties had bound up their delegates to disagree to this article. He thought it a very extraordinary language to be held by any State, that they would not confederate with us, unless we would let them dispose of our money. Certainly, if we vote equally, we ought to pay equally; but the smaller States will hardly purchase the privilege at this price. That had he lived in a State where the representation, originally equal, had become unequal by time and accident, he might have submitted rather than disturb government; but that we should be very wrong to set out in this practice, when it is in our power to establish what is right. That at the time of the Union between England and Scotland, the latter had made the objection which the smaller States now do; but experience had proved that no unfairness had ever been shown them: that their advocates had prognosticated that it would again happen, as in times of old, that the whale would swallow Jonas, but he thought the prediction reversed in event, and that Jonas had swallowed the whale; for the Scotch had in fact got possession of the government, and gave laws to the English. He reprobated the original agreement of Congress to vote by colonies, and, therefore, was for their voting, in all cases, according to the number of taxables.

Dr. Witherspoon opposed every alteration of the article. All men admit that a confederacy is necessary. Should the idea get abroad that there is likely to be no union among us, it will damp the minds of the people, diminish the glory of our struggle, and lessen its importance; because it will open to our view future prospects of war and dissension among ourselves. If an equal vote be refused, the smaller States will become vassals to the larger; and all experience has shown that the vassals and subjects of free States are the most enslaved. He instanced the Helots of Sparta, and the provinces of Rome. He observed that foreign powers, discovering this blemish, would make it a handle for disengaging the smaller States from so unequal a confederacy. That the colonies should in fact be considered as individuals; and that, as such, in all disputes, they should have an equal vote; that they are now collected as individuals making a bargain with each other, and, of course, had a right to vote as individuals. That in the East India Company they voted by persons, and not by their proportion of stock. That the Belgic confederacy voted by provinces. That in questions of war the smaller States were as much interested as the larger, and therefore, should vote equally; and indeed, that the larger States were more likely to bring war on the confederacy, in proportion as their frontier was more extensive. He admitted that equality of representation was an excellent principle, but then it must be of things which are co-ordinate; that is, of things similar, and of the same nature: that nothing relating to individuals could ever come before Congress; nothing but what would respect colonies. He distinguished between an incorporating and a federal union. The union of England was an incorporating one; yet Scotland had suffered by that union; for that its inhabitants were drawn from it by the hopes of places and employments: nor was it an instance of equality of representation; because, while Scotland was allowed nearly a thirteenth of representation, they were to pay only one fortieth of the land tax. He expressed his hopes, that in the present enlightened state of men's minds, we might expect a lasting confederacy, if it was founded on fair principles.

John Adams advocated the voting in proportion to numbers. He said that we stand here as the representatives of the people: that in some States the people are many, in others they are few; that therefore, their vote here should be proportioned to the numbers from whom it comes. Reason, justice and equity never had weight enough on the face of the earth, to govern the councils of men. It is interest alone which does it, and it is interest alone which can be trusted: that therefore the interests within doors, should be the mathematical representatives of the interests without doors: that the individuality of the colonies is a mere sound. Does the individuality of a colony increase its wealth or numbers? If it does, pay equally. If it does not add weight in the scale of the confederacy, it cannot add to their rights, nor weigh in argument. A. has £50, B. £500, C. £1000 in partnership. Is it just they should equally dispose of the moneys of the partnership? It has been said, we are independent individuals making a bargain together. The question is not what we are now, but what we ought to be when our bargain shall be made. The confederacy is to make us one individual only; it is to form us like separate parcels of metal, into one common mass. We shall no longer retain our separate individuality, but become a single individual as to all questions submitted to the confederacy. Therefore, all those reasons, which prove the justice and expediency of equal representation in other assemblies, hold good here. It has been objected that a proportional vote will endanger the smaller States. We answer that an equal vote will endanger the larger. Virginia, Pennsylvania, and Massachusetts, are the three greater colonies. Consider their distance, their difference of produce, of interests, and of manners, and it is apparent they can never have an interest or inclination to combine for the oppression of the smaller: that the smaller will naturally divide on all questions with the larger. Rhode Island, from its relation, similarity and intercourse, will generally pursue the same objects with Massachusetts; Jersey, Delaware, and Maryland, with Pennsylvania.

Dr. Rush took notice, that the decay of the liberties of the Dutch republic proceeded from three causes. 1. The perfect unanimity requisite on all occasions. 2. Their obligation to consult their constituents. 3. Their voting by provinces. This last destroyed the equality of representation, and the liberties of Great Britain also are sinking from the same defect. That a part of our rights is deposited in the hands of our legislatures. There, it was admitted, there should be an equality of representation. Another part of our rights is deposited in the hands of Congress: why is it not equally necessary there should be an equal representation there? Were it possible to collect the whole body of the people together, they would determine the questions submitted to them by their majority. Why should not the same majority decide when voting here, by their representatives? The larger colonies are so providentially divided in situation, as to render every fear of their combining visionary. Their interests are different, and their circumstances dissimilar. It is more probable they will become rivals, and leave it in the power of the smaller States to give preponderance to any scale they please. The voting by the number of free inhabitants, will have one excellent effect, that of inducing the colonies to discourage slavery, and to encourage the increase of their free inhabitants.

Mr. Hopkins observed, there were four larger, four smaller, and four middle-sized colonies. That the four largest would contain more than half the inhabitants of the confederated States, and therefore, would govern the others as they should please. That history affords no instance of such a thing as equal representation. The Germanic body votes by States. The Helvetic body does the same; and so does the Belgic confederacy. That too little is known of the ancient confederations, to say what was their practice.

Mr. Wilson thought, that taxation should be in proportion to wealth, but that representation should accord with the number of freemen. That government is a collection or result of the wills of all: that if any government could speak the will of all, it would be perfect; and that, so far as it departs from this, it becomes imperfect. It has been said that Congress is a representation of States, not of individuals. I say, that the objects of its care are all the individuals of the States. It is strange that annexing the name of "State" to ten thousand men, should give them an equal right with forty thousand. This must be the effect of magic, not of reason. As to those matters which are referred to Congress, we are not so many States; we are one large State. We lay aside our individuality, whenever we come here. The Germanic body is a burlesque on government; and their practice, on any point, is a sufficient authority and proof that it is wrong. The greatest imperfection in the constitution of the Belgic confederacy is their voting by provinces. The interest of the whole is constantly sacrificed to that of the small States. The history of the war in the reign of Queen Anne sufficiently proves this. It is asked, shall nine colonies put it into the power of four to govern them as they please? I invert the question, and ask, shall two millions of people put it in the power of one million to govern them as they please? It is pretended, too, that the smaller colonies will be in danger from the greater. Speak in honest language and say, the minority will be in danger from the majority. And is there an assembly on earth, where this danger may not be equally pretended? The truth is, that our proceedings will then be consentaneous with the interests of the majority, and so they ought to be. The probability is much greater, that the larger States will disagree, than that they will combine. I defy the wit of man to invent a possible case, or to suggest any one thing on earth, which shall be for the interests of Virginia, Pennsylvania and Massachusetts, and which will not also be for the interest of the other States.

These articles, reported July 12, '76, were debated from day to day, and time to time, for two years, were ratified July 9, '78, by ten States, by New Jersey on the 26th of November of the same year, and by Delaware on the 23d of February following. Maryland alone held off two years more, acceding to them March 1, '81, and thus closing the obligation.

Our delegation had been renewed for the ensuing year, commencing August 11; but the new government was now organized, a meeting of the legislature was to be held in October, and I had been elected a member by my county. I knew that our legislation, under the regal government, had many very vicious points which urgently required reformation, and I thought I could be of more use in forwarding that work. I therefore retired from my seat in Congress on the 2d of September, resigned it, and took my place in the legislature of my State, on the 7th of October.

On the 11th, I moved for leave to bring in a bill for the establishment of courts of justice, the organization of which was of importance. I drew the bill; it was approved by the committee, reported and passed, after going through its due course.

On the 12th, I obtained leave to bring in a bill declaring tenants in tail to hold their lands in fee simple. In the earlier times of the colony, when lands were to be obtained for little or nothing, some provident individuals procured large grants; and, desirous of founding great families for themselves, settled them on their descendants in fee tail. The transmission of this property from generation to generation, in the same name, raised up a distinct set of families, who, being privileged by law in the perpetuation of their wealth, were thus formed into a Patrician order, distinguished by the splendor and luxury of their establishments. From this order, too, the king habitually selected his counsellors of State; the hope of which distinction devoted the whole corps to the interests and will of the crown. To annul this privilege, and instead of an aristocracy of wealth, of more harm and danger, than benefit, to society, to make an opening for the aristocracy of virtue and talent, which nature has wisely provided for the direction of the interests of society, and scattered with equal hand through all its conditions, was deemed essential to a well-ordered republic. To effect it, no violence was necessary, no deprivation of natural right, but rather an enlargement of it by a repeal of the law. For this would authorize the present holder to divide the property among his children equally, as his affections were divided; and would place them, by natural generation, on the level of their fellow citizens. But this repeal was strongly opposed by Mr. Pendleton, who was zealously attached to ancient establishments; and who, taken all in all, was the ablest man in debate I have ever met with. He had not indeed the poetical fancy of Mr. Henry, his sublime imagination, his lofty and overwhelming diction; but he was cool, smooth and persuasive; his language flowing, chaste and embellished; his conceptions quick, acute and full of resource; never vanquished: for if he lost the main battle, he returned upon you, and regained so much of it as to make it a drawn one, by dexterous manœuvres, skirmishes in detail, and the recovery of small advantages which, little singly, were important all together. You never knew when you were clear of him, but were harassed by his perseverance, until the patience was worn down of all who had less of it than himself. Add to this, that he was one of the most virtuous and benevolent of men, the kindest friend, the most amiable and pleasant of companions, which ensured a favorable reception to whatever came from him. Finding that the general principle of entails could not be maintained, he took his stand on an amendment which he proposed, instead of an absolute abolition, to permit the tenant in tail to convey in fee simple, if he chose it; and he was within a few votes of saving so much of the old law. But the bill passed finally for entire abolition.

In that one of the bills for organizing our judiciary system, which proposed a court of Chancery, I had provided for a trial by jury of all matters of fact, in that as well as in the courts of law. He defeated it by the introduction of four words only, *"if either party choose."* The consequence has been, that as no suitor will say to his judge, "Sir, I distrust you, give me a jury," juries are rarely, I might say, perhaps, never, seen in that court, but when called for by the Chancellor of his own accord.

The first establishment in Virginia which became permanent, was made in 1607. I have found no mention of negroes in the colony until about 1650. The first brought here as slaves were by a Dutch ship; after which the English commenced the trade, and continued it until the revolutionary war. That suspended, *ipso facto,* their further importation for the present, and the business of the war pressing constantly on the legislature, this subject was not acted on finally until the year '78, when I brought in a bill to prevent their further importation. This passed without opposition, and stopped the increase of the evil by importation, leaving to future efforts its final eradication.

The first settlers of this colony were Englishmen, loyal subjects to their king and church, and the grant to Sir Walter Raleigh contained an express proviso that their laws "should not be against the true Christian faith, now professed in the church of England." As soon as the state of the colony admitted, it was divided into parishes, in each of which was established a minister of the Anglican church, endowed with a fixed salary, in tobacco, a glebe house and land with the other necessary appendages. To meet these expenses, all the inhabitants of the parishes were assessed, whether they were or not members of the established church. Towards Quakers who came here, they were most cruelly intolerant, driving them from the colony by the severest penalties. In process of time, however, other sectarisms were introduced, chiefly of the Presbyterian family; and the established clergy, secure for life in their glebes and salaries, adding to these, generally, the emoluments of a classical school, found employment enough, in their farms and school-rooms, for the rest of the week, and devoted Sunday only to the edification of their flock, by service, and a sermon at their parish church. Their other pastoral functions were little attended to. Against this inactivity, the zeal and industry of sectarian preachers had an open and undisputed field; and by the time of the revolution, a majority of the inhabitants had become dissenters from the established church, but were still obliged to pay contributions to support the pastors of the minority.

This unrighteous compulsion, to maintain teachers of what they deemed religious errors, was grievously felt during the regal government, and without a hope of relief. But the first republican legislature, which met in '76, was crowded with petitions to abolish this spiritual tyranny. These brought on the severest contests in which I have ever been engaged. Our great opponents were Mr. Pendleton and Robert Carter Nicholas; honest men, but zealous churchmen. The petitions were referred to the committee of the whole house on the state of the country and, after desperate contests in that committee, almost daily from the 11th of October to the 5th of December, we prevailed so far only, as to repeal the laws which rendered criminal the maintenance of any religious opinions, the forbearance of repairing to church, or the exercise of any mode of worship; and further, to exempt dissenters from contributions to the support of the established church; and to suspend, only until the next session, levies on the members of that church for the salaries of their own incumbents. For although the majority of our citizens were dissenters, as has been observed, a majority of the legislature were churchmen. Among these, however, were some reasonable and liberal men, who enabled us, on some points, to obtain feeble majorities. But our opponents carried, in the general resolutions of the committee of November 19, a declaration that religious assemblies ought to be regulated, and that provision ought to be made for continuing the succession of the clergy, and superintending their conduct. And, in the bill now passed, was inserted an express reservation of the question, Whether a general assessment should not be established by law, on everyone, to the support of the pastor of his choice; or whether all should be left to voluntary contributions; and on this question, debated at every session, from '76 to '79 (some of our dissenting allies, having now secured their particular object, going over to the advocates of a general assessment), we could only obtain a suspension from session to session until '79, when the question against a general assessment was finally carried, and the establishment of the Anglican church entirely put down. In justice to the two honest but zealous opponents who have been named, I must add, that although, from their natural temperaments, they were more disposed generally to acquiesce in things as they are, than to risk innovations, yet whenever the public will had once decided, none were more faithful or exact in their obedience to it.

The seat of our government had originally been fixed in the peninsula of Jamestown, the first settlement of the colonists; and had been afterwards removed a few miles inland to Williamsburg. But this was at a time when our settlements had not extended beyond the tide waters. Now they had crossed the Alleghany; and the centre of population was very far removed from what it had been. Yet Williamsburg was still the depository of our archives, the habitual residence of the Governor and many other of the public functionaries, the established place for the sessions of the legislature, and the magazine of our military stores; and its situation was so exposed that it might be taken at any time in war, and, at this time particularly, an enemy might in the night run up either of the rivers, between which it lies, land a force above, and take possession of the place, without the possibility of saving either persons or things. I had proposed its removal so early as October, '76; but it did not prevail until the session of May, '79.

Early in the session of May, '79, I prepared, and obtained leave to bring in a bill, declaring who should be deemed citizens, asserting the natural right of expatriation, and prescribing the mode of exercising it. This, when I withdrew from the house, on the 1st of June following, I left in the hands of George Mason, and it was passed on the 26th of that month.

In giving this account of the laws of which I was myself the mover and draughtsman, I, by no means, mean to claim to myself the merit of obtaining their passage. I had many occasional and strenuous coadjutors in debate, and one, most steadfast, able and zealous; who was himself a host. This was George Mason, a man of the first order of wisdom among those who acted on the theatre of the revolution, of expansive mind, profound judgment, cogent in argument, learned in the lore of our former constitution, and earnest for the republican change on democratic principles. His elocution was neither flowing nor smooth; but his language was strong, his manner most impressive, and strengthened by a dash of biting cynicism, when provocation made it seasonable.

Mr. Wythe, while speaker in the two sessions of 1777, between his return from Congress and his appointment to the Chancery, was an able and constant associate in whatever was before a committee of the whole. His pure integrity, judgment and reasoning powers, gave him great weight. Of him, see more in some notes inclosed in my letter of August 31, 1821, to Mr. John Saunderson.[5]

[5] Letter to John Saunderson, Esq., Monticello, August 31, 1820.

SIR: Your letter of the 19th was received in due time, and I wish it were in my power to furnish you more fully, than in the enclosed paper, with materials for the biography of George Wythe; but I possess none in writing, am very distant from the place of his birth and early life, and know not a single person in that quarter from whom inquiry could be made, with the expectation of collecting anything material. Add to this, that feeble health disables me, almost, from writing; and entirely from the labor of going into difficult research. I became acquainted with Mr. Wythe when he was about thirty-five years of age. He directed my studies in the law, led me into business, and continued, until death, my most affectionate friend. A close intimacy with him, during that period of forty odd years, the most important of his life, enables me to state its leading facts, which, being of my own knowledge, I vouch their truth. Of what precedes that period, I speak from hearsay only, in which there may be error, but of little account, as the character of the facts will themselves manifest. In the epoch of his birth, I may err a little, stating that from the recollection of a particular incident, the date of which, within a year or two, I do not distinctly remember. These scanty outlines you will be able, I hope, to fill up from other information, and they may serve you, sometimes, as landmarks to distinguish truth from error, in what you hear from others. The

Mr. Madison came into the House in 1776, a new member and young; which circumstances, concurring with his extreme modesty, prevented his venturing himself in debate before his removal to the Council of State, in November, '77. From thence he went to Congress, then consisting of few members. Trained in these successive schools, he acquired a habit of self-possession, which placed at ready command the rich resources of his luminous and discriminating mind, and of his extensive information, and rendered him the first of every assembly afterwards, of which he became a member. Never wandering from his subject into vain declamation, but pursuing it closely, in language pure, classical and copious, soothing always the feelings of his adversaries by civilities and softness of expression, he rose to the eminent station which he held in the great National Convention of 1787; and in that of Virginia which followed, he sustained the new constitution in all its parts, bearing off the palm against the logic of George Mason, and the fervid declamation of Mr. Henry. With these consummate powers, were united a pure and spotless virtue which no calumny has ever attempted to sully. Of the powers and polish of his pen, and of the wisdom of his administration in the highest office of the nation, I need say nothing. They have spoken, and will forever speak for themselves.

So far we were proceeding in the details of reformation only; selecting points of legislation, prominent in character and principle, urgent, and indicative of the strength of the general pulse of reformation. When I left Congress, in '76, it was in the persuasion that our whole code must be reviewed, adapted to our republican form of government; and, now that we had no negatives of Councils, Governors, and Kings to restrain us from doing right, that it should be corrected, in all its parts, with a single eye to reason, and the good of those for whose government it was framed. Early, therefore, in the session of '76, to which I returned, I moved and presented a bill for the revision of the laws, which was passed on the 24th of October; and on the 5th of November, Mr. Pendleton, Mr. Wythe, George Mason, Thomas L. Lee, and myself, were appointed a committee to execute the work. We agreed to meet at Fredericksburg to settle the plan of operation, and to distribute the work. We met there accordingly, on the 13th of January, 1777. The first question was, whether we should

exalted virtue of the man will also be a polar star to guide you in all matters which may touch that element of his character. But on that you will receive imputation from no man: for, as far as I know, he never had an enemy. Little as I am able to contribute to the just reputation of this excellent man, it is the act of my life most gratifying to my heart; and leaves me only to regret that a waning memory can do no more.

Of Mr. Hancock I can say nothing, having known him only in the chair of Congress. Having myself been the youngest man but one in that body, the disparity of age prevented any particular intimacy. But of him there can be no difficulty in obtaining full information in the North.

I salute you, Sir, with sentiments of great respect,

Th. Jefferson

propose to abolish the whole existing system of laws, and prepare a new and complete Institute, or preserve the general system, and only modify it to the present state of things. Mr. Pendleton, contrary to his usual disposition in favor of ancient things, was for the former proposition, in which he was joined by Mr. Lee. To this it was objected, that to abrogate our whole system would be a bold measure, and probably far beyond the views of the legislature; that they had been in the practice of revising, from time to time, the laws of the colony, omitting the expired, the repealed, and the obsolete, amending only those retained, and probably meant we should now do the same, only including the British statutes as well as our own: that to compose a new Institute, like those of Justinian and Bracton, or that of Blackstone, which was the model proposed by Mr. Pendleton, would be an arduous undertaking, of vast research, of great consideration and judgment; and when reduced to a text, every word of that text, from the imperfection of human language, and its incompetence to express distinctly every shade of idea, would become a subject of question and chicanery, until settled by repeated adjudications; and this would involve us for ages in litigation and render property uncertain, until, like the statutes of old, every word had been tried and settled by numerous decisions, and by new volumes of reports and commentaries; and that no one of us, probably, would undertake such a work, which to be systematical, must be the work of one hand. This last was the opinion of Mr. Wythe, Mr. Mason, and myself. When we proceeded to the distribution of the work, Mr. Mason excused himself, as, being no lawyer, he felt himself unqualified for the work, and he resigned soon after. Mr. Lee excused himself on the same ground, and died, indeed, in a short time. The other two gentlemen, therefore, and myself divided the work among us. The common law and statutes to the 4 James I. (when our separate legislature was established) were assigned to me; the British statutes, from that period to the present day, to Mr. Wythe; and the Virginia laws to Mr. Pendleton. As the law of Descents, and the criminal law fell of course within my portion, I wished the committee to settle the leading principles of these, as a guide for me in framing them; and, with respect to the first, I proposed to abolish the law of primogeniture, and to make real estate descendible in parcenary to the next of kin, as personal property is, by the statute of distribution. Mr. Pendleton wished to preserve the right of primogeniture, but seeing at once that that could not prevail, he proposed we should adopt the Hebrew principle, and give a double portion to the elder son. I observed, that if the eldest son could eat twice as much, or do double work, it might be a natural evidence of his right to a double portion; but being on a par in his powers and wants, with his brothers and sisters, he should be on a par also in the partition of the patrimony; and such was the decision of the other members.

On the subject of the Criminal law, all were agreed, that the punishment of death should be abolished, except for treason and murder; and that, for other felonies, should be substituted hard labor in the public works, and in some cases, the *Lex talionis.* How this last revolting principle came to obtain our approbation I do not remember. There remained, indeed, in our laws, a vestige of it in a single case of a slave; it was the English law, in the time of the Anglo-Saxons, copied probably from the Hebrew law of "an eye for an eye, a tooth for a tooth," and it was the law of several ancient people; but the modern mind had left it far in the rear of its advances. These points, however, being settled, we repaired to our respective homes for the preparation of the work.

In the execution of my part, I thought it material not to vary the diction of the ancient statutes by modernizing it, nor to give rise to new questions by new expressions. The text of these statutes had been so fully explained and defined, by numerous adjudications, as scarcely ever now to produce a question in our courts. I thought it would be useful, also, in all new draughts, to reform the style of the later British statutes, and of our own acts of Assembly; which, from their verbosity, their endless tautologies, their involutions of case within case, and parenthesis within parenthesis, and their multiplied efforts at certainty, by *saids* and *aforesaids,* by *ors* and by *ands,* to make them more plain, are really rendered more perplexed and incomprehensible, not only to common readers, but to the lawyers themselves. We were employed in this work from that time to February, 1779, when we met at Williamsburg, that is to say, Mr. Pendleton, Mr. Wythe and myself; and meeting day by day, we examined critically our several parts, sentence by sentence, scrutinizing and amending, until we had agreed on the whole. We then returned home, had fair copies made of our several parts, which were reported to the General Assembly, June 18, 1779, by Mr. Wythe and myself, Mr. Pendleton's residence being distant, and he having authorized us by letter to declare his approbation. We had, in this work, brought so much of the Common law as it was thought necessary to alter, all the British statutes from *Magna Charta* to the present day, and all the laws of Virginia, from the establishment of our legislature, in the 4th Jac. 1. to the present time, which we thought should be retained, within the compass of one hundred and twenty-six bills, making a printed folio of ninety pages only. Some bills were taken out, occasionally, from time to time, and passed; but the main body of the work was not entered on by the legislature until after the general peace, in 1785, when, by the unwearied exertions of Mr. Madison, in opposition to the endless quibbles, chicaneries, perversions, vexations and delays of lawyers and demi-lawyers, most of the bills were passed by the legislature, with little alteration.

The bill for establishing religious freedom, the principles of which had, to a certain degree, been enacted before, I had drawn in all the latitude of reason and right. It still met with opposition; but, with some mutilations in the preamble, it was finally passed; and a singular proposition proved that its protection of opinion was meant to be universal. Where the preamble declares, that coercion is a departure from the plan of the holy author of our religion, an amendment was proposed, by inserting the word "Jesus Christ," so that it should read, "a departure from the plan of Jesus Christ, the holy author of our religion"; the insertion was rejected by a great majority, in proof that they meant to comprehend, within the mantle of its protection, the Jew and the Gentile, the Christian and Mahometan, the Hindoo, and Infidel of every denomination.

Beccaria, and other writers on crimes and punishments, had satisfied the reasonable world of the unrightfulness and inefficacy of the punishment of crimes by death; and hard labor on roads, canals and other public works, had been suggested as a proper substitute. The Revisors had adopted these opinions; but the general idea of our country had not yet advanced to that point. The bill, therefore, for proportioning crimes and punishments, was lost in the House of Delegates by a majority of a single vote. I learned afterwards, that the substitute of hard labor in public, was tried (I believe it was in Pennsylvania) without success. Exhibited as a public spectacle, with shaved heads and mean clothing, working on the high roads, produced in the criminals such a prostration of character, such an abandonment of self-respect, as, instead of reforming, plunged them into the most desperate and hardened depravity of morals and character. To pursue the subject of this law.—I was written to in 1785 (being then in Paris) by directors appointed to superintend the building of a Capitol in Richmond, to advise them as to a plan, and to add to it one of a Prison. Thinking it a favorable opportunity of introducing into the State an example of architecture, in the classic style of antiquity, and the Maison quarrée of Nismes, an ancient Roman temple, being considered as the most perfect model existing of what may be called Cubic architecture, I applied to M. Clerissault, who had published drawings of the Antiquities of Nismes, to have me a model of the building made in stucco, only changing the order from Corinthian to Ionic, on account of the difficulty of the Corinthian capitals. I yielded, with reluctance, to the taste of Clerissault, in his preference of the modern capital of Scamozzi to the more noble capital of antiquity. This was executed by the artist whom Choiseul Gouffier had carried with him to Constantinople, and employed, while Ambassador there, in making those beautiful models of the remains of Grecian architecture which are to be seen at Paris. To adapt the exterior to our use, I drew a plan for the interior, with the apartments necessary for legislative, executive, and judiciary purposes; and accommodated in their size and distribution to the form and dimensions of the building. These were forwarded to the Directors, in 1786, and were carried into execution, with some variations, not for the better, the most important of which, however, admit of future correction. With respect to the plan of a Prison, requested at the same time, I had heard of a benevolent society, in England, which had been indulged by the government, in an experiment of the effect of labor, in *solitary confinement,* on some of their criminals; which experiment had succeeded beyond expectation. The same idea had been suggested in France, and an Architect of Lyons had proposed a plan of a well-contrived edifice, on the principle of solitary confinement. I procured a copy, and as it was too large for our purposes, I drew one on a scale less extensive, but susceptible of additions as they should be wanting. This I sent to the Directors, instead of a plan of a common prison, in the hope that it would suggest the idea of labor in solitary confinement, instead of that on the public works, which we had adopted in our Revised Code. Its principle, accordingly, but not its exact form, was adopted by Latrobe in carrying the plan into execution, by the erection of what is now called the Penitentiary, built under his direction. In the meanwhile, the public opinion was ripening, by time, by reflection, and by the example of Pennsylvania, where labor on the highways had been tried, without approbation, from 1786 to '89, and had been followed by their Penitentiary system on the principle of confinement and labor, which was proceeding auspiciously. In 1796, our legislature resumed the subject, and passed the law for amending the Penal laws of the commonwealth. They adopted solitary, instead of public, labor, established a gradation in the duration of the confinement, approximated the style of the law more to the modern usage, and, instead of the settled distinctions of murder and manslaughter, preserved in my bill, they introduced the new terms of murder in the first and second degree. Whether these have produced more or fewer questions of definition, I am not sufficiently informed of our judiciary transactions to say. I will here, however, insert the text of my bill, with the notes I made in the course of my researches into the subject.[6]

The acts of Assembly concerning the College of William and Mary, were properly within Mr. Pendleton's portion of our work; but these related chiefly to its revenue, while its constitution, organization and scope of science, were derived from its charter. We thought that on this subject, a systematical plan of general education should be proposed, and I was re-

[6] See Ch. III, pp. 90-102.

quested to undertake it. I accordingly prepared three bills for the Revisal, proposing three distinct grades of education, reaching all classes. 1st. Elementary schools, for all children generally, rich and poor. 2d. Colleges, for a middle degree of instruction, calculated for the common purposes of life, and such as would be desirable for all who were in easy circumstances. And, 3d, an ultimate grade for teaching the sciences generally, and in their highest degree. The first bill proposed to lay off every county into Hundreds, or Wards, of a proper size and population for a school, in which reading, writing, and common arithmetic should be taught; and that the whole State should be divided into twenty-four districts, in each of which should be a school for classical learning, grammar, geography, and the higher branches of numerical arithmetic. The second bill proposed to amend the constitution of William and Mary College, to enlarge its sphere of science, and to make it in fact a University. The third was for the establishment of a library. These bills were not acted on until the same year, '96, and then only so much of the first as provided for elementary schools. The College of William and Mary was an establishment purely of the Church of England; the Visitors were required to be all of that Church; the Professors to subscribe its thirty-nine Articles; its Students to learn its Catechism; and one of its fundamental objects was declared to be, to raise up Ministers for that church. The religious jealousies, therefore, of all the dissenters, took alarm lest this might give an ascendancy to the Anglican sect, and refused acting on that bill. Its local eccentricity, too, and unhealthy autumnal climate, lessened the general inclination towards it. And in the Elementary bill, they inserted a provision which completely defeated it; for they left it to the court of each county to determine for itself, when this act should be carried into execution, within their county. One provision of the bill was, that the expenses of these schools should be borne by the inhabitants of the county, every one in proportion to his general tax rate. This would throw on wealth the education of the poor; and the justices, being generally of the more wealthy class, were unwilling to incur that burden, and I believe it was not suffered to commence in a single county. I shall recur again to this subject, towards the close of my story, if I should have life and resolution enough to reach that term; for I am already tired of talking about myself.

The bill on the subject of slaves, was a mere digest of the existing laws respecting them, without any intimation of a plan for a future and general emancipation. It was thought better that this should be kept back, and attempted only by way of amendment, whenever the bill should be brought on. The principles of the amendment, however, were agreed on, that is to say, the freedom of all born after a certain day, and deportation at a proper age. But it was found that the public mind would not yet bear the proposition, nor will it bear it even at this day. Yet the day is not distant when it must bear and adopt it, or worse will follow. Nothing is more certainly written in the book of fate, than that these people are to be free; nor is it less certain that the two races, equally free, cannot live in the same government. Nature, habit, opinion have drawn indelible lines of distinction between them. It is still in our power to direct the process of emancipation and deportation, peaceably, and in such slow degree, as that the evil will wear off insensibly, and their place be, *pari passu,* filled up by free white laborers. If, on the contrary, it is left to force itself on, human nature must shudder at the prospect held up. We should in vain look for an example in the Spanish deportation or deletion of the Moors. This precedent would fall far short of our case.

I considered four of these bills, passed or reported, as forming a system by which every fibre would be eradicated of ancient or future aristocracy; and a foundation laid for a government truly republican. The repeal of the laws of entail would prevent the accumulation and perpetuation of wealth, in select families, and preserve the soil of the country from being daily more and more absorbed in mortmain. The abolition of primogeniture, and equal partition of inheritances, removed the feudal and unnatural distinctions which made one member of every family rich, and all the rest poor, substituting equal partition, the best of all Agrarian laws. The restoration of the rights of conscience relieved the people from taxation for the support of a religion not theirs; for the establishment was truly of the religion of the rich, the dissenting sects being entirely composed of the less wealthy people; and these, by the bill for a general education, would be qualified to understand their rights, to maintain them, and to exercise with intelligence their parts in self-government; and all this would be effected, without the violation of a single natural right of any one individual citizen. To these, too, might be added, as a further security, the introduction of the trial by jury, into the Chancery courts, which have already ingulfed, and continue to ingulf, so great a proportion of the jurisdiction over our property.

On the 1st of June, 1779, I was appointed Governor of the Commonwealth, and retired from the legislature. Being elected, also, one of the Visitors of William and Mary college, a self-electing body, I effected, during my residence in Williamsburg that year, a change in the organization of that institution, by abolishing the Grammar school, and the two professorships of Divinity and Oriental languages, and substituting a professorship of Law and Police, one of Anatomy, Medicine and Chemistry, and one of Modern languages; and the charter confining us to six professorships, we added the Law of Nature and Nations, and the Fine Arts to the duties of the Moral professor, and Natural History to those of the professor of Mathematics and Natural Philosophy.

Being now, as it were, identified with the Commonwealth itself, to write my own history, during the two years of my administration, would be to write the public history of that portion of the revolution within this State. This has been done by others, and particularly by Mr. Girardin, who wrote his Continuation of Burke's History of Virginia, while at Milton, in this neighborhood, had free access to all my papers while composing it, and has given as faithful an account as I could myself. For this portion, therefore, of my own life, I refer altogether to his history. From a belief that, under the pressure of the invasion under which we were then laboring, the public would have more confidence in a Military chief, and that the Military commander, being invested with the Civil power also, both might be wielded with more energy, promptitude and effect for the defence of the State, I resigned the administration at the end of my second year, and General Nelson was appointed to succeed me.

Soon after my leaving Congress, in September, '76, to wit, on the last day of that month, I had been appointed, with Dr. Franklin, to go to France, as a Commissioner, to negotiate treaties of alliance and commerce with that government. Silas Deane, then in France, acting as agent for procuring military stores, was joined with us in commission. But such was the state of my family that I could not leave it, nor could I expose it to the dangers of the sea, and of capture by the British ships, then covering the ocean. I saw, too, that the laboring oar was really at home, where much was to be done, of the most permanent interest, in new modelling our governments, and much to defend our fanes and fire-sides from the desolations of an invading enemy, pressing on our country in every point. I declined, therefore, and Dr. Lee was appointed in my place. On the 15th of June, 1781, I had been appointed, with Mr. Adams, Dr. Franklin, Mr. Jay, and Mr. Laurens, a Minister Plenipotentiary for negotiating peace, then expected to be effected through the mediation of the Empress of Russia. The same reasons obliged me still to decline; and the negotiation was in fact never entered on. But, in the autumn of the next year, 1782, Congress receiving assurances that a general peace would be concluded in the winter and spring, they renewed my appointment on the 13th of November of that year. I had, two months before that, lost the cherished companion of my life, in whose affections, unabated on both sides, I had lived the last ten years in unchequered happiness. With the public interests, the state of my mind concurred in recommending the change of scene proposed; and I accepted the appointment, and left Monticello on the 19th of December, 1782, for Philadelphia, where I arrived on the 27th. The Minister of France, Luzerne, offered me a passage in the Romulus frigate, which I accepted; but she was then lying a few miles below Baltimore, blocked up in the ice. I remained, therefore, a month in Philadelphia, looking over the papers in the office of State, in order to possess myself of the general state of our foreign relations, and then went to Baltimore, to await the liberation of the frigate from the ice. After waiting there nearly a month, we received information that a Provisional treaty of peace had been signed by our Commissioners on the 3d of September, 1782, to become absolute, on the conclusion of peace between France and Great Britain. Considering my proceeding to Europe as now of no utility to the public, I returned immediately to Philadelphia, to take the orders of Congress, and was excused by them from further proceeding. I, therefore, returned home, where I arrived on the 15th of May, 1783.

On the 6th of the following month, I was appointed by the legislature a delegate to Congress, the appointment to take place on the 1st of November ensuing, when that of the existing delegation would expire. I, accordingly, left home on the 16th of October, arrived at Trenton, where Congress was sitting, on the 3d of November, and took my seat on the 4th, on which day Congress adjourned, to meet at Annapolis on the 26th.

Congress had now become a very small body, and the members very remiss in their attendance on its duties, insomuch, that a majority of the States, necessary by the Confederation to constitute a House even for minor business, did not assemble until the 13th of December.

They, as early as January 7, 1782, had turned their attention to the moneys current in the several States, and had directed the Financier, Robert Morris, to report to them a table of rates, at which the foreign coins should be received at the treasury. That officer, or rather his assistant, Gouverneur Morris, answered them on the 15th, in an able and elaborate statement of the denominations of money current in the several States, and of the comparative value of the foreign coins chiefly in circulation with us. He went into the consideration of the necessity of establishing a standard of value with us, and of the adoption of a money Unit. He proposed for that Unit, such a fraction of pure silver as would be a common measure of the penny of every State, without leaving a fraction. This common divisor he found to be 1-1440 of a dollar, or 1-1600 of the crown sterling. The value of a dollar was, therefore, to be expressed by 1,440 units, and of a crown by 1,600; each Unit containing a quarter of a grain of fine silver. Congress turning again their attention to this subject the following year, the Financier, by a letter of April 30, 1783, further explained and urged the Unit he had proposed; but nothing more was done on it until the ensuing year, when it was again taken up, and referred to a committee, of which I was a member. The general views of the Financier were sound, and the principle was ingenious on which he proposed to found his Unit; but it was too minute for ordinary use, too laborious for computation, either by the head or in figures. The price of a loaf of bread, 1/20 of a dollar, would be 72 units.

A pound of butter, 1/5 of a dollar, 288 units.

A horse or bullock, of eighty dollars value, would require a notation of six figures, to wit, 115,200, and the public debt, suppose of eighty millions, would require twelve figures, to wit, 115,200,000,000 units. Such a system of money-arithmetic would be entirely unmanageable for the common purposes of society. I proposed, therefore, instead of this, to adopt the Dollar as our Unit of account and payment, and that its divisions and sub-divisions should be in the decimal ratio. I wrote some Notes on the subject, which I submitted to the consideration of the Financier. I received his answer and adherence to his general system, only agreeing to take for his Unit one hundred of those he first proposed, so that a Dollar should be 14 40/100, and a crown 16 units. I replied to this, and printed my notes and reply on a flying sheet, which I put into the hands of the members of Congress for consideration, and the Committee agreed to report on my principle. This was adopted the ensuing year, and is the system which now prevails. I insert, here, the Notes and Reply, as showing the different views on which the adoption of our money system hung.[7] The divisions into dimes, cents, and mills is now so well understood, that it would be easy of introduction into the kindred branches of weights and measures. I use, when I travel, an Odometer of Clarke's invention, which divides the mile into cents, and I find every one comprehends a distance readily, when stated to him in miles and cents; so he would in feet and cents, pounds and cents, &c.

The remissness of Congress, and their permanent session, began to be a subject of uneasiness; and even some of the legislatures had recommended to them intermissions, and periodical sessions. As the Confederation had made no provision for a visible head of the government, during vacations of Congress, and such a one was necessary to superintend the executive business, to receive and communicate with foreign ministers and nations, and to assemble Congress on sudden and extraordinary emergencies, I proposed, early in April, the appointment of a committee, to be called the "Committee of the States," to consist of a member from each State, who should remain in session during the recess of Congress: that the functions of Congress should be divided into executive and legislative, the latter to be reserved, and the former, by a general resolution, to be delegated to that Committee. This proposition was afterwards agreed to; a Committee appointed, who entered on duty on the subsequent adjournment of Congress, quarrelled very soon, split into two parties, abandoned their post, and left the government without any visible head, until the next meeting in Con-

[7] See Ch. XX, pp. 959-68.

gress. We have since seen the same thing take place in the Directory of France; and I believe it will forever take place in any Executive consisting of a plurality. Our plan, best, I believe, combines wisdom and practicability, by providing a plurality of Counsellors, but a single Arbiter for ultimate decision. I was in France when we heard of this schism, and separation of our Committee, and, speaking with Dr. Franklin of this singular disposition of men to quarrel, and divide into parties, he gave his sentiments, as usual, by way of Apologue. He mentioned the Eddystone lighthouse, in the British channel, as being built on a rock, in the mid-channel, totally inaccessible in winter, from the boisterous character of that sea, in that season; that, therefore, for the two keepers employed to keep up the lights, all provisions for the winter were necessarily carried to them in autumn, as they could never be visited again till the return of the milder season; that, on the first practicable day in the spring, a boat put off to them with fresh supplies. The boatmen met at the door one of the keepers, and accosted him with a "How goes it, friend? Very well. How is your companion? I do not know. Don't know? Is not he here? I can't tell. Have not you seen him today? No. When did you see him? Not since last fall. You have killed him? Not I, indeed." They were about to lay hold of him, as having certainly murdered his companion; but he desired them to go up stairs and examine for themselves. They went up, and there found the other keeper. They had quarrelled, it seems, soon after being left there, had divided into two parties, assigned the cares below to one, and those above to the other, and had never spoken to, or seen, one another since.

But to return to our Congress at Annapolis. The definitive treaty of peace which had been signed at Paris on the 3d of September, 1783, and received here, could not be ratified without a House of nine States. On the 23d of December, therefore, we addressed letters to the several Governors, stating the receipt of the definitive treaty; that seven States only were in attendance, while nine were necessary to its ratification; and urging them to press on their delegates the necessity of their immediate attendance. And on the 26th, to save time, I moved that the Agent of Marine (Robert Morris) should be instructed to have ready a vessel at this place, at New York, and at some Eastern port, to carry over the ratification of the treaty when agreed to. It met the general sense of the House, but was opposed by Dr. Lee, on the ground of expense, which it would authorize the Agent to incur for us; and, he said, it would be better to ratify at once, and send on the ratification. Some members had before suggested, that seven States were competent to the ratification. My motion was therefore postponed, and another brought forward by Mr. Read, of South Carolina, for an immediate ratification. This was debated the 26th and 27th. Reed, Lee, Williamson and Jeremiah Chase, urged that ratification was a mere matter of form, that the treaty was conclusive from the moment it was signed by the ministers; that, although the Confederation requires the assent of *nine States* to *enter into* a treaty, yet, that its conclusion could not be called *entrance into it;* that supposing nine States requisite, it would be in the power of five States to keep us always at war; that nine States had virtually authorized the ratification, having ratified the provisional treaty, and instructed their ministers to agree to a definitive one in the same terms, and the present one was, in fact, substantially, and almost verbatim, the same; that there now remain but sixty-seven days for the ratification, for its passage across the Atlantic, and its exchange; that there was no hope of our soon having nine States present; in fact, that this was the ultimate point of time to which we could venture to wait; that if the ratification was not in Paris by the time stipulated, the treaty would become void; that if ratified by seven States, it would go under our seal, without its being known to Great Britain that only seven had concurred; that it was a question of which they had no right to take cognizance, and we were only answerable for it to our constituents; that it was like the ratification which Great Britain had received from the Dutch, by the negotiations of Sir William Temple.

On the contrary, it was argued by Monroe, Gerry, Howel, Ellery and myself, that by the modern usage of Europe, the ratification was considered as the act which gave validity to a treaty, until which, it was not obligatory.[8] That the commission to the ministers reserved the ratification to Congress; that the treaty itself stipulated that it should be ratified; that it became a second question, who were competent to the ratification? That the Confederation expressly required nine States to enter into any treaty; that, by this, that instrument must have intended, that the assent of nine States should be necessary, as well to the *completion* as to the *commencement* of the treaty, its object having been to guard the rights of the Union in all those important cases where nine States are called for; that by the contrary construction, seven States, containing less than one-third of our whole citizens, might rivet on us a treaty, commenced indeed under commission and instructions from nine States, but formed by the minister in express contradiction to such instructions, and in direct sacrifice of the interests of so great a majority; that the definitive treaty was admitted not to be a verbal copy of the provisional one, and whether the departures from it were of substance, or not, was a question on which nine States alone were competent to decide; that the circumstances of the ratification of the provisional articles by nine States, the instructions to our ministers to form a definitive one by them, and their actual agreement in substance,

[8] Vattel L. 2, § 156. L. 4, § 77. 1. Mably Droit D'Europe, 86.—T. J.

do not render us competent to ratify in the present instance; if these circumstances are in themselves a ratification, nothing further is requisite than to give attested copies of them, in exchange for the British ratification; if they are not, we remain where we were, without a ratification by nine States, and incompetent ourselves to ratify; that it was but four days since the seven States, now present, unanimously concurred in a resolution, to be forwarded to the Governors of the absent States, in which they stated, as a cause for urging on their delegates, that nine States were necessary to ratify the treaty; that in the case of the Dutch ratification, Great Britain had courted it, and therefore was glad to accept it as it was; that they knew our Constitution, and would object to a ratification by seven; that, if that circumstance was kept back, it would be known hereafter, and would give them ground to deny the validity of a ratification, into which they should have been surprised and cheated, and it would be a dishonorable prostitution of our seal; that there is a hope of nine States; that if the treaty would become null, if not ratified in time, it would not be saved by an imperfect ratification; but that, in fact, it would not be null, and would be placed on better ground, going in unexceptionable form, though a few days too late, and rested on the small importance of this circumstance, and the physical impossibilities which had prevented a punctual compliance in point of time; that this would be approved by all nations, and by Great Britain herself, if not determined to renew the war, and if so determined, she would never want excuses, were this out of the way. Mr. Read gave notice, he should call for the yeas and nays; whereon those in opposition, prepared a resolution, expressing pointedly the reasons of their dissent from his motion. It appearing, however, that his proposition could not be carried, it was thought better to make no entry at all. Massachusetts alone would have been for it; Rhode Island, Pennsylvania and Virginia against it, Delaware, Maryland and North Carolina, would have been divided.

Our body was little numerous, but very contentious. Day after day was wasted on the most unimportant questions. A member, one of those afflicted with the morbid rage of debate, of an ardent mind, prompt imagination, and copious flow of words, who heard with impatience any logic which was not his own, sitting near me on some occasion of a trifling but wordy debate, asked me how I could sit in silence, hearing so much false reasoning, which a word should refute? I observed to him, that to refute indeed was easy, but to silence was impossible; that in measures brought forward by myself, I took the laboring oar, as was incumbent on me; but that in general, I was willing to listen; that if every sound argument or objection was used by some one or other of the numerous debaters, it was enough; if not, I thought it sufficient to suggest the omission, without going into a repetition of what had been already said by others: that this was a waste and abuse of the time and patience of the House, which could not be justified. And I believe, that if the members of deliberate bodies were to observe this course generally, they would do in a day, what takes them a week; and it is really more questionable, than may at first be thought, whether Bonaparte's dumb legislature, which said nothing, and did much, may not be preferable to one which talks much, and does nothing. I served with General Washington in the legislature of Virginia, before the revolution, and, during it, with Dr. Franklin in Congress. I never heard either of them speak ten minutes at a time, nor to any but the main point, which was to decide the question. They laid their shoulders to the great points, knowing that the little ones would follow of themselves. If the present Congress errs in too much talking, how can it be otherwise, in a body to which the people send one hundred and fifty lawyers, whose trade it is to question everything, yield nothing, and talk by the hour? That one hundred and fifty lawyers should do business together, ought not to be expected. But to return again to our subject.

Those who thought seven States competent to the ratification, being very restless under the loss of their motion, I proposed, on the third of January, to meet them on middle ground, and therefore moved a resolution, which premised, that there were but seven States present, who were unanimous for the ratification, but that they differed in opinion on the question of competency; that those however in the negative were unwilling that any powers which it might be supposed they possessed, should remain unexercised for the restoration of peace, provided it could be done, saving their good faith, and without importing any opinion of Congress, that seven States were competent, and resolving that the treaty be ratified so far as they had power; that it should be transmitted to our ministers, with instructions to keep it uncommunicated; to endeavor to obtain three months longer for exchange of ratifications; that they should be informed, that so soon as nine States shall be present, a ratification by nine shall be sent them: if this should get to them before the ultimate point of time for exchange, they were to use it, and not the other; if not, they were to offer the act of the seven States in exchange, informing them the treaty had come to hand while Congress was not in session; that but seven States were as yet assembled, and these had unanimously concurred in the ratification. This was debated on the third and fourth; and on the fifth, a vessel being to sail for England, from this port (Annapolis), the House directed the President to write to our ministers accordingly.

January 14. Delegates from Connecticut having attended yesterday, and another from South Carolina coming in this day, the treaty was ratified without a dissenting voice; and three instruments of ratification were ordered to be made out, one of which was sent by Colonel Harmer, another by Colonel Franks, and the third transmitted to the Agent of Marine, to be forwarded by any good opportunity.

Congress soon took up the consideration of their foreign relations. They deemed it necessary to get their commerce placed with every nation, on a footing as favorable as that of other nations; and for this purpose, to propose to each a distinct treaty of commerce. This act too would amount to an acknowledgment, by each, of our independence, and of our reception into the fraternity of nations; which, although as possessing our station of right, and in fact we would not condescend to ask, we were not unwilling to furnish opportunities for receiving their friendly salutations and welcome. With France, the United Netherlands, and Sweden, we had already treaties of commerce; but commissions were given for those countries also, should any amendments be thought necessary. The other States to which treaties were to be proposed, were England, Hamburg, Saxony, Prussia, Denmark, Russia, Austria, Venice, Rome, Naples, Tuscany, Sardinia, Genoa, Spain, Portugal, the Porte, Algiers, Tripoli, Tunis, and Morocco.

On the 7th of May Congress resolved that a Minister Plenipotentiary should be appointed, in addition to Mr. Adams and Dr. Franklin, for negotiating treaties of commerce with foreign nations, and I was elected to that duty. I accordingly left Annapolis on the 11th, took with me my eldest daughter, then at Philadelphia (the two others being too young for the voyage), and proceeded to Boston, in quest of a passage. While passing through the different States, I made a point of informing myself of the state of the commerce of each; went on to New Hampshire with the same view, and returned to Boston. Thence I sailed on the 5th of July, in the Ceres, a merchant ship of Mr. Nathaniel Tracey, bound to Cowes. He was himself a passenger, and, after a pleasant voyage of nineteen days, from land to land, we arrived at Cowes on the 26th. I was detained there a few days by the indisposition of my daughter. On the 30th, we embarked for Havre, arrived there on the 31st, left it on the 3d of August, and arrived at Paris on the 6th. I called immediately on Dr. Franklin, at Passy, communicated to him our charge, and we wrote to Mr. Adams, then at the Hague, to join us at Paris.

Before I had left America, that is to say, in the year 1781, I had received a letter from M. de Marbois, of the French legation in Philadelphia, informing me, he had been instructed by his government to obtain such statistical accounts of the different States of our Union, as might be useful for their information; and addressing to me a number of queries relative to the State of Virginia. I had always made it a practice, whenever an opportunity occurred, of obtaining any information of our country, which might be of use to me in any station, public or private, to commit it to writing. These memoranda were on loose papers, bundled up without order, and difficult of recurrence, when I had occasion for a particular one. I thought this a good occasion to embody their substance, which I did in the order of Mr. Marbois' queries, so as to answer his wish, and to arrange them for my own use. Some friends, to whom they were occasionally communicated, wished for copies; but their volume rendering this too laborious by hand, I proposed to get a few printed, for their gratification. I was asked such a price, however, as exceeded the importance of the object. On my arrival at Paris, I found it could be done for a fourth of what I had been asked here. I therefore corrected and enlarged them, and had two hundred copies printed, under the title of "Notes on Virginia." I gave a very few copies to some particular friends in Europe, and sent the rest to my friends in America. An European copy, by the death of the owner, got into the hands of a bookseller, who engaged its translation, and when ready for the press, communicated his intentions and manuscript to me, suggesting that I should correct it, without asking any other permission for the publication. I never had seen so wretched an attempt at translation. Interverted, abridged, mutilated, and often reversing the sense of the original, I found it a blotch of errors, from beginning to end. I corrected some of the most material, and, in that form, it was printed in French. A London bookseller, on seeing the translation, requested me to permit him to print the English original. I thought it best to do so, to let the world see that it was not really so bad as the French translation had made it appear. And this is the true history of that publication.

Mr. Adams soon joined us at Paris, and our first employment was to prepare a general form, to be proposed to such nations as were disposed to treat with us. During the negotiations for peace with the British Commissioner, David Hartley, our Commissioners had proposed, on the suggestion of Dr. Franklin, to insert an article, exempting from capture by the public or private armed ships, of either belligerent, when at war, all merchant vessels and their cargoes, employed merely in carrying on the commerce between nations. It was refused by England, and unwisely, in my opinion. For, in the case of a war with us, their superior commerce places infinitely more at hazard on the ocean, than ours; and, as hawks abound in proportion to game, so our privateers would swarm, in proportion to the wealth exposed to their prize, while theirs would be few, for want of subjects of capture. We inserted this article in our form, with a provision against the molestation of fishermen, husbandmen, citizens unarmed, and following their occupations in unfortified places, for the humane treatment of prisoners of war, the abolition of contraband of war, which exposes merchant vessels to such vexatious and ruinous detentions and abuses; and for the principle of free bottoms, free goods.

In a conference with the Count de Vergennes, it was thought better to leave to legislative regulation, on both sides, such modifications of our commercial intercourse, as would voluntarily flow from amicable dispositions. Without urging, we sounded the ministers of the several European nations, at the court of Versailles, on their dispositions towards mutual commerce, and the expediency of encouraging it by the protection of a treaty. Old Frederic, of Prussia, met us cordially, and without hesitation, and appointing the Baron de Thulemeyer, his minister at the Hague, to negotiate with us, we communicated to him our Projét, which, with little alteration by the King, was soon concluded. Denmark and Tuscany entered also into negotiations with us. Other powers appearing indifferent, we did not think it proper to press them. They seemed, in fact, to know little about us, but as rebels, who had been successful in throwing off the yoke of the mother country. They were ignorant of our commerce, which had been always monopolized by England, and of the exchange of articles it might offer advantageously to both parties. They were inclined, therefore, to stand aloof, until they could see better what relations might be usefully instituted with us. The negotiations, therefore, begun with Denmark and Tuscany, we protracted designedly, until our powers had expired; and abstained from making new propositions to others having no colonies; because our commerce being an exchange of raw for wrought materials, is a competent price for admission into the colonies of those possessing them; but were we to give it, without price, to others, all would claim it, without price, on the ordinary ground of *gentis amicissimæ*.

Mr. Adams being appointed Minister Plenipotentiary of the United States, to London, left us in June, and in July, 1785, Dr. Franklin returned to America, and I was appointed his successor at Paris. In February, 1786, Mr. Adams wrote to me, pressingly, to join him in London immediately, as he thought he discovered there some symptoms of better disposition towards us. Colonel Smith, his secretary of legation, was the bearer of his urgencies for my immediate attendance. I, accordingly, left Paris on the 1st of March, and, on my arrival in London, we agreed on a very summary form of treaty, proposing an exchange of citizenship for our citizens, our ships, and our productions generally, except as to office. On my presentation, as usual, to the King and Queen, at their levées, it was impossible for anything to be more ungracious, than their notice of Mr. Adams and myself. I saw, at once, that the ulcerations of mind in that quarter, left nothing to be expected on the subject of my attendance; and, on the first conference with the Marquis of Caermarthen, the Minister for foreign affairs, the distance and disinclination which he betrayed in his conversation, the vagueness and evasions of his answers to us, confirmed me in the belief of their aversion to have anything to do with us. We delivered him, however, our Projét, Mr. Adams not despairing as much as I did, of its effect. We afterwards, by one or more notes, requested his appointment of an interview and conference, which, without directly declining, he evaded, by pretences of other pressing occupations for the moment. After staying there seven weeks, till within a few days of the expiration of our commission, I informed the minister, by note, that my duties at Paris required my return to that place, and that I should, with pleasure, be the bearer of any commands to his Ambassador there. He answered, that he had none, and, wishing me a pleasant journey, I left London the 26th, and arrived at Paris the 30th of April.

While in London, we entered into negotiations with the Chevalier Pinto, Ambassador of Portugal, at that place. The only article of difficulty between us was, a stipulation that our bread stuff should be received in Portugal, in the form of flour as well as of grain. He approved of it himself, but observed that several Nobles, of great influence at their court, were the owners of wind-mills in the neighborhood of Lisbon, which depended much for their profits on manufacturing our wheat, and that this stipulation would endanger the whole treaty. He signed it, however, and its fate was what he had candidly portended.

My duties, at Paris, were confined to a few objects; the receipt of our whale-oils, salted fish, and salted meats, on favorable terms; the admission of our rice on equal terms with that of Piedmont, Egypt and the Levant; a mitigation of the monopolies of our tobacco by the Farmers-general, and a free admission of our productions into their islands, were the principal commercial objects which required attention; and, on these occasions, I was powerfully aided by all the influence and the energies of the Marquis de La Fayette, who proved himself equally zealous for the friendship and welfare of both nations; and, in justice, I must also say, that I found the government entirely disposed to befriend us on all occasions, and to yield us every indulgence, not absolutely injurious to themselves. The Count de Vergennes had the reputation, with the diplomatic corps, of being wary and slippery in his diplomatic intercourse; and so he might be with those whom he knew to be slippery, and double-faced themselves. As he saw that I had no indirect views, practised no subtleties, meddled in no intrigues, pursued no concealed object, I found him as frank, as honorable, as easy of access to reason, as any man with whom I had ever done business; and I must say the same for his successor, Montmorin, one of the most honest and worthy of human beings.

Our commerce, in the Mediterranean, was placed under early alarm, by the capture of two of our vessels and crews by the Barbary cruisers. I was very unwilling that we should acquiesce in the European humiliation, of paying a tribute to those lawless pirates, and endeavored to form an association of the powers subject to habitual depredations from them. I accordingly prepared, and proposed to their Ministers at Paris, for consultation with their governments, articles of a special confederation, in the following form:

"Proposals for concerted operation among the powers at war with the piratical States of Barbary.

1. "It is proposed, that the several powers at war with the piratical States of Barbary, or any two or more of them who shall be willing, shall enter into a convention to carry on their operations against those States, in concert, beginning with the Algerines.

2. "This convention shall remain open to any other powers, who shall, at any future time, wish to accede to it; the parties reserving the right to prescribe the conditions of such accession, according to the circumstances existing at the time it shall be proposed.

3. "The object of the convention shall be, to compel the piratical States to perpetual peace, without price, and to guarantee that peace to each other.

4. "The operations for obtaining this peace shall be constant cruises on their coast, with a naval force now to be agreed on. It is not proposed that this force shall be so considerable as to be inconvenient to any party. It is believed that half a dozen frigates, with as many Tenders or Xebecs, one half of which shall be in cruise, while the other half is at rest, will suffice.

5. "The force agreed to be necessary, shall be furnished by the parties, in certain quotas, now to be fixed; it being expected, that each will be willing to contribute, in such proportion as circumstances may render reasonable.

6. "As miscarriages often proceed from the want of harmony among officers of different nations, the parties shall now consider and decide, whether it will not be better to contribute their quotas in money, to be employed in fitting out and keeping on duty, a single fleet of the force agreed on.

7. "The difficulties and delays, too, which will attend the management of these operations, if conducted by the parties themselves separately, distant as their courts may be from one another, and incapable of meeting in consultation, suggest a question, whether it will not be better for them to give full powers, for that purpose, to their Ambassadors, or other Ministers resident at some one court of Europe, who shall form a Committee, or Council, for carrying this convention into effect; wherein, the vote of each member shall be computed in proportion to the quota of his sovereign, and the majority so computed, shall prevail in all questions within the view of this convention. The court of Versailles is proposed, on account of its neighborhood to the Mediterranean, and because all those powers are represented there, who are likely to become parties to this convention.

8. "To save to that Council the embarrassment of personal solicitations for office, and to assure the parties that their contributions will be applied solely to the object for which they are destined, there shall be no establish-

ment of officers for the said Council, such as Commissioners, Secretaries, or any other kind, with either salaries or perquisites, nor any other lucrative appointments but such whose functions are to be exercised on board the said vessels.

9. "Should war arise between any two of the parties to this convention, it shall not extend to this enterprise, nor interrupt it; but as to this they shall be reputed at peace.

10. "When Algiers shall be reduced to peace, the other piratical States, if they refuse to discontinue their piracies, shall become the objects of this convention, either successively or together, as shall seem best.

11. "Where this convention would interfere with treaties actually existing between any of the parties and the States of Barbary, the treaty shall prevail, and such party shall be allowed to withdraw from the operations against that State."

Spain had just concluded a treaty with Algiers, at the expense of three millions of dollars, and did not like to relinquish the benefit of that, until the other party should fail in their observance of it. Portugal, Naples, the two Sicilies, Venice, Malta, Denmark and Sweden, were favorably disposed to such an association; but their representatives at Paris expressed apprehensions that France would interfere, and, either openly or secretly, support the Barbary powers; and they required, that I should ascertain the dispositions of the Count de Vergennes on the subject. I had before taken occasion to inform him of what we were proposing, and, therefore, did not think it proper to insinuate any doubt of the fair conduct of his government; but, stating our propositions, I mentioned the apprehensions entertained by us, that England would interfere in behalf of those piratical governments. "She dares not do it," said he. I pressed it no further. The other Agents were satisfied with this indication of his sentiments, and nothing was now wanting to bring it into direct and formal consideration, but the assent of our government, and their authority to make the formal proposition. I communicated to them the favorable prospect of protecting our commerce from the Barbary depredations, and for such a continuance of time, as, by an exclusion of them from the sea, to change their habits and characters, from a predatory to an agricultural people: towards which, however, it was expected they would contribute a frigate, and its expenses, to be in constant cruise. But they were in no condition to make any such engagement. Their recommendatory powers for obtaining contributions were so openly neglected by the several States, that they declined an engagement which they were conscious they could not fulfil with punctuality; and so it fell through.

In 1786, while at Paris, I became acquainted with John Ledyard, of Connecticut, a man of genius, of some science, and of fearless courage and enterprise. He had accompanied Captain Cook in his voyage to the Pacific, had distinguished himself on several occasions by an unrivalled intrepidity, and published an account of that voyage, with details unfavorable to Cook's deportment towards the savages, and lessening our regrets at his fate. Ledyard had come to Paris, in the hope of forming a company to engage in the fur trade of the Western coast of America. He was disappointed in this, and, being out of business, and of a roaming, restless character, I suggested to him the enterprise of exploring the Western part of our continent, by passing through St. Petersburg to Kamschatka, and procuring a passage thence in some of the Russian vessels to Nootka Sound, whence he might make his way across the continent to the United States; and I undertook to have the permission of the Empress of Russia solicited. He eagerly embraced the proposition, and M. de Sémoulin, the Russian Ambassador, and more particularly Baron Grimm, the special correspondent of the Empress, solicited her permission for him to pass through her dominions, to the Western coast of America. And here I must correct a material error, which I have committed in another place, to the prejudice of the Empress. In writing some notes of the life of Captain Lewis, prefixed to his "Expedition to the Pacific," I stated that the Empress gave the permission asked, and afterwards retracted it. This idea, after a lapse of twenty-six years, had so insinuated itself into my mind, that I committed it to paper, without the least suspicion of error. Yet I find, on recurring to my letters of that date, that the Empress refused permission at once, considering the enterprise as entirely chimerical. But Ledyard would not relinquish it, persuading himself that, by proceeding to St. Petersburg, he could satisfy the Empress of its practicability, and obtain her permission. He went accordingly, but she was absent on a visit to some distant part of her dominions, and he pursued his course to within two hundred miles of Kamschatka, where he was overtaken by an arrest from the Empress, brought back to Poland, and there dismissed. I must therefore, in justice, acquit the Empress of ever having for a moment countenanced, even by the indulgence of an innocent passage through her territories, this interesting enterprise.

The pecuniary distresses of France produced this year a measure of which there had been no example for near two centuries, and the consequences of which, good and evil, are not yet calculable. For its remote causes, we must go a little back.

Celebrated writers of France and England had already sketched good principles on the subject of government; yet the American Revolution seems first to have awakened the thinking part of the French nation in general, from the sleep of despotism in which they were sunk. The officers too, who had been to America, were mostly young men, less shackled by habit and prejudice, and more ready to assent to the suggestions of common sense, and feeling of common rights, than others. They came back with new ideas and impressions. The press, notwithstanding its shackles, began to disseminate them; conversation assumed new freedoms; Politics became the theme of all societies, male and female, and a very extensive and zealous party was formed, which acquired the appellation of the Patriotic party, who, sensible of the abusive government under which they lived, sighed for occasions of reforming it. This party comprehended all the honesty of the kingdom, sufficiently at leisure to think, the men of letters, the easy Bourgeois, the young nobility, partly from reflection, partly from mode; for these sentiments became matter of mode, and as such, united most of the young women to the party. Happily for the nation, it happened, at the same moment, that the dissipations of the Queen and court, the abuses of the pension-list, and dilapidations in the administration of every branch of the finances, had exhausted the treasures and credit of the nation, insomuch that its most necessary functions were paralyzed. To reform these abuses would have overset the Minister; to impose new taxes by the authority of the King, was known to be impossible, from the determined opposition of the Parliament to their enregistry. No resource remained then, but to appeal to the nation. He advised, therefore, the call of an Assembly of the most distinguished characters of the nation, in the hope that, by promises of various and valuable improvements in the organization and regimen of the government, they would be induced to authorize new taxes, to control the opposition of the Parliament, and to raise the annual revenue to the level of expenditures. An Assembly of Notables therefore, about one hundred and fifty in number, named by the King, convened on the 22d of February. The Minister (Calonne) stated to them, that the annual excess of expenses beyond the revenue, when Louis XVI came to the throne, was thirty-seven millions of livres; that four hundred and forty millions had been borrowed to re-establish the navy; that the American war had cost them fourteen hundred and forty millions (two hundred and fifty-six millions of dollars), and that the interest of these sums, with other increased expenses, had added forty millions more to the annual deficit. (But a subsequent and more candid estimate made it fifty-six millions). He proffered them an universal redress of grievances, laid open those grievances fully, pointed out sound remedies, and, covering his canvas with objects of this magnitude, the deficit dwindled to a little accessory, scarcely attracting attention. The persons chosen were the most able and independent characters in the kingdom, and their support, if it could be obtained, would be enough for him. They improved the occasion for redressing their grievances, and agreed that the public wants should be relieved; but went into an examination of the causes of them. It was supposed that Colonne was conscious that his accounts could not bear examination; and it was said, and believed, that he asked of the King, to send four members to the Bastille, of whom the Marquis de La Fayette was one, to banish twenty others, and two of his Ministers. The King found it shorter to banish him. His successor went on in full concert with the Assembly. The result was an augmentation of the revenue, a promise of economies in its expenditure, of an annual settlement of the public accounts before a council, which the Comptroller, having been heretofore obliged to settle only with the King in person, of course never settled at all; an acknowledgment that the King could not lay a new tax, a reformation of the Criminal laws, abolition of torture, suppression of corvees, reformation of the gabelles, removal of the interior Custom Houses, free commerce of grain, internal and external, and the establishment of Provincial Assemblies; which, altogether, constituted a great mass of improvement in the condition of the nation. The establishment of the Provincial Assemblies was, in itself, a fundamental improvement. They would be of the choice of the people, one-third renewed every year, in those provinces where there are no States, that is to say, over about three-fourths of the kingdom. They would be partly an Executive themselves, and partly an Executive Council to the Intendant, to whom the Executive power, in his province, had been heretofore entirely delegated. Chosen by the people, they would soften the execution of hard laws, and, having a right of representation to the King, they would censure bad laws, suggest good ones, expose abuses, and their representations, when united, would command respect. To the other advantages, might be added the precedent itself of calling the Assemblée des Notables, which would perhaps grow into habit. The hope was, that the improvements thus promised would be carried into effect; that they would be maintained during the present reign, and that that would be long enough for them to take some root in the constitution, so that they might come to be considered as a part of that, and be protected by time, and the attachment of the nation.

The Count de Vergennes had died a few days before the meeting of the Assembly, and the Count de Montmorin had been named Minister of Foreign Affairs, in his place. Villedeuil succeeded Calonne, as Comptroller General, and Loménie de Brienne, Archbishop of Toulouse, afterwards of Sens, and ultimately Cardinal Loménie, was named Minister principal, with whom the other Ministers were to transact the business of their departments, heretofore done with the King in person; and the Duke de Nivernois, and M. de Malesherbes, were called to the Council. On the nomination of the Minister principal, the Marshals de Ségur and de Castries retired from the departments of War and Marine, unwilling to act subordinately, or to share the blame of proceedings taken out of their direction. They were succeeded by the Count de Brienne, brother of the Prime Minister, and the Marquis de La Luzerne, brother to him who had been Minister in the United States.

A dislocated wrist, unsuccessfully set, occasioned advice from my surgeon, to try the mineral waters of Aix, in Provence, as a corroborant. I left Paris for that place therefore, on the 28th of February, and proceeded up the Seine, through Champagne and Burgundy, and down the Rhone through the Beaujolais by Lyons, Avignon, Nismes to Aix; where, finding on trial no benefit from the waters, I concluded to visit the rice country of Piedmont, to see if anything might be learned there, to benefit the rivalship of our Carolina rice with that, and thence to make a tour of the seaport towns of France, along its Southern and Western coast, to inform myself, if anything could be done to favor our commerce with them. From Aix, therefore, I took my route by Marseilles, Toulon, Hieres, Nice, across the Col de Tende, by Coni, Turin, Vercelli, Novara, Milan, Pavia, Novi, Genoa. Thence, returning along the coast of Savona, Noli, Albenga, Oneglia, Monaco, Nice, Antibes, Frejus, Aix, Marseilles, Avignon, Nismes, Montpellier, Frontignan, Cette, Agde, and along the canal of Languedoc, by Bezieres, Narbonne, Carcassonne, Castelnaudari, through the Souterrain of St. Feriol, and back by Castelnaudari, to Toulouse; thence to Montauban, and down the Garonne by Langon to Bordeaux. Thence to Rochefort, la Rochelle, Nantes, L'Orient; then back by Rennes to Nantes, and up the Loire by Angers, Tours, Amboise, Blois to Orleans, thence direct to Paris, where I arrived on the 10th of June. Soon after my return from this journey, to wit, about the latter part of July, I received my younger daughter, Maria, from Virginia, by the way of London, the youngest having died some time before.

The treasonable perfidy of the Prince of Orange, Stadtholder and Captain General of the United Netherlands, in the war which England waged against them, for entering into a treaty of commerce with the United States, is known to all. As their Executive officer, charged with the conduct of the war, he contrived to baffle all the measures of the States General, to dislocate all their military plans, and played false into the hands of England against his own country, on every possible occasion, confident in her protection, and in that of the King of Prussia, brother to his Princess. The States General, indignant at this patricidal conduct, applied to France for aid, according to the stipulations of the treaty concluded with her in '85. It was assured to them readily, and in cordial terms, in a letter from the Count de Vergennes, to the Marquis de Verac, Ambassador of France at the Hague, of which the following is an extract:

*"Extrait de la depéche de Monsieur le Comte de Vergennes à Monsieur le Marquis de Verac, Ambassadeur de France à la Haye, du 1er Mars, 1786.*

*"Le Roi concourrera, autant, qu' il sera en son pouvoir, au succès de la chose, et vous inviterez, de sa part, les patriotes de lui communiquer leurs vues, leurs plans, et leurs envieux. Vous les assurerez, que le roi prend un interet véritable à leurs personnes comme à leur cause, et qu' ils peuvent compter sur sa protection. Ils doivent y compter d' autant plus, Monsieur, que nous ne dissimulons pas, que si Monsieur le Stadhoulder reprend son ancienne influence, le système Anglois ne tardera pas de prévaloir, et que notre alliance deviendroit un être de raison. Les Patriotes sentiront facilement, que cette position seroit incompatible avec la dignité, comme avec la considération de sa majesté. Mais dans le cas, Monsieur, ou les chefs des Patriotes auroient à craindre une scission, ils auroient le temps suffisant pour ramener ceux de leurs amis, que les Anglomanes ont égarés, et préparer les choses de manière que la question de nouveau mise en déliberation, soit decidée selon leurs désirs. Dans cette hypothèse, le roi vous autorise à agir de concert avec eux, de suivre la direction qu' ils jugeront devoir vous donner, et d' employer tous les moyens pour augmenter le nombre des partisans de la bonne cause. Il me reste, Monsieur, de vous parler de la sureté personnelle des Patriotes. Vous les assurerez, que dans tout état de cause, le roi les prend sous sa protection immédiate, et vous ferez connoitre, partout ou vous le jugerez nécessaire, que sa Majesté regarderoit comme une offense personnelle, tout ce qu' on entreprenderoit contre leur liberté. Il est à presumer que ce langage, tenu avec énergie, en imposéra a l'audace des Anglomanes, et que Monsieur le Prince de Nassau croira courir quelque risque en provoquant le ressentiment de sa Majesté."*

This letter was communicated by the Patriots to me, when at Amsterdam, in 1788, and a copy sent by me to Mr. Jay, in my letter to him of March 16, 1788.

The object of the Patriots was, to establish a representative and republican government. The majority of the States General were with them, but the majority of the populace of the towns was with the Prince of Orange; and that populace was played off with great effect, by the triumvirate of * * * Harris, the English Ambassador, afterwards Lord Malmesbury, the Prince of Orange, a stupid man, and the Princess as much a man as either of her colleagues, in audaciousness, in enterprise, and in the thirst of domination. By these, the mobs of the Hague were excited against the members of the States General; their persons were insulted and endangered in the streets; the sanctuary of their houses was violated; and the Prince, whose function and duty it was to repress and punish these violations of order, took no steps for that purpose. The States General, for their own protection, were therefore obliged to place their militia under the command of a Committee. The Prince filled the courts of London and Berlin with complaints at this usurpation of his prerogatives, and, forgetting that he was but the first servant of a Republic, marched his regular troops against the city of Utrecht, where the States were in session. They were repulsed by the militia. His interests now became marshalled with those of the public enemy, and against his own country. The States, therefore, exercising their rights of sovereignty, deprived him of all his powers. The great Frederic had died in August, '86. He had never intended to break with France in support of the Prince of Orange. During the illness of which he died, he had, through the Duke of Brunswick, declared to the Marquis de La Fayette, who was then at Berlin, that he meant not to support the English interest in Holland: that he might assure the government of France, his only wish was, that some honorable place in the Constitution should be reserved for the Stadtholder and his children, and that he would take no part in the quarrel, unless an entire abolition of the Stadtholderate should be attempted. But his place was now occupied by Frederic William, his great-nephew, a man of little understanding, much caprice, and very inconsiderate; and the Princess, his sister, although her husband was in arms against the legitimate authorities of the country, attempting to go to Amsterdam, for the purpose of exciting the mobs of that place, and being refused permission to pass a military post on the way, he put the Duke of Brunswick at the head of twenty thousand men, and made demonstrations of marching on Holland. The King of France hereupon declared, by his Chargé des Affaires in Holland, that if the Prussian troops continued to menace Holland with an invasion, his Majesty, in quality of Ally, was determined to succor that province. In answer to this, Eden gave official information to Count Montmorin, that England must consider as at an end its convention with France relative to giving notice of its naval armaments, and that she was arming generally. War being now imminent, Eden, since Lord Aukland, questioned me on the effect of our treaty with France, in the case of a war, and what might be our dispositions. I told him frankly, and without hesitation, that our dispositions would be neutral, and that I thought it would be the interest of both these powers that we should be so; because, it would relieve both from all anxiety as to feeding their West India islands; that England, too, by suffering us to remain so, would avoid a heavy land war on our Continent, which might very much cripple her proceedings elsewhere; that our treaty, indeed, obliged us to receive into our ports the armed vessels of France, with their prizes, and to refuse admission to the prizes made on her by her enemies: that there was a clause, also, by which we guaranteed to France her American possessions, which might perhaps force us into the war, if these were attacked. "Then it will be war," said he, "for they will assuredly be attacked." Liston, at Madrid, about the same time, made the same inquiries of Carmichael. The Government of France then declared a determination to form a camp of observation at Givet, commenced arming her marine, and named the Bailli de Suffrein their Generalissimo on the Ocean. She secretly engaged, also, in negotiations with Russia, Austria, and Spain, to form a quadruple alliance. The Duke of Brunswick having advanced to the confines of Holland, sent some of his officers to Givet, to reconnoitre the state of things there, and report them to him. He said afterwards, that "if there had been only a few tents at that place, he should not have advanced further, for that the King would not, merely for the interest of his sister, engage in a war with France." But, finding that there was not a single company there, he boldly entered the country, took their towns as fast as he presented himself before them, and advanced on Utrecht. The States had appointed the Rhingrave of Salm their Commander-in-Chief; a Prince without talents, without courage, and without principle. He might have held out in Utrecht for a considerable time, but he surrendered the place without firing a gun, literally ran away and hid himself, so that for months it was not known what had become of him. Amsterdam was then attacked, and capitulated. In the meantime, the negotiations for the quadruple alliance were proceeding favorably; but the secrecy with which they were attempted to be conducted, was penetrated by Fraser, Chargé des Affaires of England at St. Petersburg, who instantly notified his court, and gave the alarm to Prussia. The King saw at once what would be his situation, between the jaws of France, Austria, and Russia. In great dismay, he besought the court of London not to abandon him, sent Alvensleben to Paris to explain and soothe; and England, through the Duke of Dorset and Eden, renewed her conferences for accommodation. The Archbishop, who shuddered at the idea of war, and preferred a peaceful surrender of right to an armed vindication of it, received them with open arms, entered into cordial conferences, and a declaration, and counter-declaration, were cooked up at Versailles, and sent to London for approbation. They were approved there, reached Paris at one o'clock of the 27th, and were signed that night at Versailles. It was said and believed at Paris, that M. de Montmorin, literally *"pleuroit comme un enfant,"* when obliged to sign this counter-declaration; so distressed was he by the dishonor of sacrificing the Patriots, after assurances so solemn of protection, and absolute encouragement to proceed. The Prince of Orange was reinstated in all his powers, now become regal. A great emigration of the Patriots took place; all were deprived of office, many exiled, and their property confiscated. They were received in France, and subsisted, for some time, on her bounty. Thus fell Holland, by the treachery of her Chief, from her honorable independence, to become a province of England; and so, also, her Stadtholder, from the high station of the first citizen of a free Republic, to be the servile Viceroy of a foreign Sovereign. And this was effected by a mere scene of bullying and demonstration; not one of the parties, France, England, or Prussia, having ever really meant to encounter actual war for the interest of the Prince of Orange. But it had all the effect of a real and decisive war.

Our first essay, in America, to establish a federative government had fallen, on trial, very short of its object. During the war of Independence, while the pressure of an external enemy hooped us together, and their enterprises kept us necessarily on the alert, the spirit of the people, excited by danger, was a supplement to the Confederation, and urged them to zealous exertions, whether claimed by that instrument or not; but, when peace and safety were restored, and every man became engaged in useful and profitable occupation, less attention was paid to the calls of Congress. The fundamental defect of the Confederation was, that Congress was not authorized to act immediately on the people, and by its own officers. Their power was only requisitory, and these requisitions were addressed to the several Legislatures, to be by them carried into execution, without other coercion than the moral principle of duty. This allowed, in fact, a negative to every Legislature, on every measure proposed by Congress; a negative so frequently exercised in practice, as to benumb the action of the Federal government, and to render it inefficient in its general objects, and more especially in pecuniary and foreign concerns. The want, too, of a separation of the Legislative, Executive, and Judiciary functions, worked disadvantageously in practice. Yet this state of things afforded a happy augury of the future march of our Confederacy, when it was seen that the good sense and good dispositions of the people, as soon as they perceived the incompetence of their first compact, instead of leaving its correction to insurrection and civil war, agreed, with one voice, to elect deputies to a general Convention, who should peaceably meet and agree on such a Constitution as "would ensure peace, justice, liberty, the common defence and general welfare."

This Convention met at Philadelphia on the 25th of May, '87. It sat with closed doors, and kept all its proceedings secret, until its dissolution on the 17th of September, when the results of its labors were published all together. I received a copy, early in November, and read and contemplated its provisions with great satisfaction. As not a member of the Convention, however, nor probably a single citizen of the Union, had approved it in all its parts, so I, too, found articles which I thought objectionable. The absence of express declarations ensuring freedom of religion, freedom of the press, freedom of the person under the uninterrupted protection of the Habeas corpus, and trial by jury in Civil as well as in Criminal cases, excited my jealousy; and the re-eligibility of the President for life, I quite disapproved. I expressed freely, in letters to my friends, and most particularly to Mr. Madison and General Washington, my approbations and objections. How the good should be secured and the ill brought to rights, was the difficulty. To refer it back to a new Convention might endanger the loss of the whole. My first idea was, that the nine States first acting, should accept it unconditionally, and thus secure what in it was good, and that the four last should accept on the previous condition, that certain amendments should be agreed to; but a better course was devised, of accepting the whole, and trusting that the good sense and honest intentions of our citizens would make the alterations which should be deemed necessary. Accordingly, all accepted, six without objection, and seven with recommendations of specified amendments. Those respecting the press, religion, and juries, with several others, of great value, were accordingly made; but the Habeas corpus was left to the discretion of Congress, and the amendment against the re-eligibility of the President was not proposed. My fears of that feature were founded on the importance of the office, on the fierce contentions it might excite among ourselves, if continuable for life, and the dangers of interference, either with money or arms, by foreign nations, to whom the choice of an American President might become interesting. Examples of this abounded in history; in the case of the Roman Emperors, for instance; of the Popes, while of any significance; of the German Emperors; the Kings of Poland, and the Deys of Barbary. I had observed, too, in the feudal history, and in the recent instance, particularly, of the Stadtholder of Holland, how easily offices, or tenures for life, slide into inheritances. My wish, therefore, was, that the President should be elected for seven years, and be ineligible afterwards. This term I thought sufficient to enable him, with the concurrence of the Legislature, to carry through and establish any system of improvement he should propose for the general good. But the practice adopted, I think, is better, allowing his continuance for eight years, with a liability to be dropped at half way of the term, making that a period of probation. That his continuance should be restrained to seven years, was the opinion of the Convention at an earlier stage of its session, when it voted that term, by a majority of eight against two, and by a simple majority that he should be ineligible a second time. This opinion was confirmed by the House so late as July 26, referred to the Committee of detail, reported favorably by them, and changed to the present form by final vote, on the last day but one only of their session. Of this change, three States expressed their disapprobation; New York, by recommending an amendment, that the President should not be eligible a third time, and Virginia and North Carolina that he should not be capable of serving more than eight, in any term of sixteen years; and though this amendment has not been made in form, yet practice seems to have established it. The example of four Presidents voluntarily retiring at the end of their eighth year, and the progress of public opinion, that the principle is salutary, have given it in practice the force of precedent and usage; insomuch, that, should a President consent to be a candidate for a third election, I trust he would be rejected, on this demonstration of ambitious views.

But there was another amendment, of which none of us thought at the time, and in the omission of which, lurks the germ that is to destroy this happy combination of National powers in the General government, for matters of National concern, and independent powers in the States, for what concerns the States severally. In England, it was a great point gained at the Revolution, that the commissions of the Judges, which had hitherto been during pleasure, should thenceforth be made during good behavior. A Judiciary, dependent on the will of the King, had proved itself the most oppressive of all tools, in the hands of that Magistrate. Nothing, then, could be more salutary, than a change there, to the tenure of good behavior; and the question of good behavior, left to the vote of a simple majority in the two Houses of Parliament. Before the Revolution, we were all good English Whigs, cordial in their free principles, and in their jealousies of their Executive Magistrate. These jealousies are very apparent, in all our state Constitutions; and, in the General government in this instance, we have gone even beyond the English caution, by requiring a vote of two-thirds, in one of the Houses, for removing a Judge; a vote so impossible, where any defence is made, before men of ordinary prejudices and passions, that our Judges are effectually independent of the nation. But this ought not to be. I would not, indeed, make them dependent on the Executive authority, as they formerly were in England; but I deem it indispensable to the continuance of this government, that they should be submitted to some practical and impartial control; and that this, to be imparted, must be compounded of a mixture of State and Federal authorities. It is not enough that honest men are appointed Judges. All know the influence of interest on the mind of man, and how unconsciously his judgment is warped by that influence. To this bias add that of the *esprit de corps,* of their peculiar maxim and creed, that "it is the office of a good Judge to enlarge his jurisdiction," and the absence of responsibility; and how can we expect impartial decision between the General government, of which they are themselves so eminent a part, and an individual State, from which they have nothing to hope or fear? We have seen, too, that contrary to all correct example, they are in the habit of going out of the question before them, to throw an anchor ahead, and grapple further hold for future advances of power. They are then, in fact, the corps of sappers and miners, steadily working to undermine the independent rights of the States, and to consolidate all power in the hands of that government in which they have so important a freehold estate. But it is not by the consolidation, or concentration of powers, but by their distribution, that good government is effected. Were not this great country already divided into States, that division must be made, that each might do for itself what concerns itself directly, and what it can so much better do than a distant authority. Every State again is divided into counties, each to take care of what lies within its local bounds; each county again into townships or wards, to manage minuter details; and every ward into farms, to be governed each by its individual proprietor. Were we directed from Washington when to sow, and when to reap, we should soon want bread. It is by this partition of cares, descending in gradation from general to particular, that the mass of human affairs may be best managed, for the good and prosperity of all. I repeat, that I do not charge the Judges with wilful and ill-intentioned error; but honest error must be arrested, where its toleration leads to public ruin. As, for the safety of society, we commit honest maniacs to Bedlam, so judges should be withdrawn from their bench, whose erroneous biases are leading us to dissolution. It may, indeed, injure them in fame or in fortune; but it saves the Republic, which is the first and supreme law.

Among the debilities of the government of the Confederation, no one was more distinguished or more distressing, than the utter impossibility of obtaining, from the States, the moneys necessary for the payment of debts, or even for the ordinary expenses of the government. Some contributed a little, some less, and some nothing; and the last furnished at length an excuse for the first to do nothing also. Mr. Adams, while residing at the Hague, had a general authority to borrow what sums might be requisite, for ordinary and necessary expenses. Interest on the public debt, and the maintenance of the diplomatic establishment in Europe, had been habitually provided in this way. He was now elected Vice-President of the United States, was soon to return to America, and had referred our bankers to me for future counsel, on our affairs in their hands. But I had no powers, no instructions, no means, and no familiarity with the subject. It had always been exclusively under his management, except as to occasional and partial deposits in the hands of Mr. Grand, banker in Paris, for special and local purposes. These last had been exhausted for some time, and I had fervently pressed the Treasury board to replenish this particular deposit, as Mr. Grand now refused to make further advances. They answered candidly, that no funds could be obtained until the new government should get into action, and have time to make its arrangements. Mr. Adams had received his appointment to the court of London, while engaged at Paris, with Dr. Franklin and myself, in the negotiations under our joint commissions. He had repaired thence to London, without returning to the Hague, to take leave of that government. He thought it necessary, however, to do so now, before he should leave Europe, and accordingly went there. I learned his departure from London, by a letter from Mrs. Adams, received on the very day on which he would arrive at the Hague. A consultation with him, and some provision for the future, was indispensable, while we could yet avail ourselves of his powers; for when they would be gone, we should be without resource. I was daily dunned by a Company who had formerly made a small loan to the United States, the principal of which was now become due; and our bankers in Amsterdam, had notified me that the interest on our general debt would be expected in June; that if we failed to pay it, it would be deemed an act of bankruptcy, and would effectually destroy the credit of the United States, and all future prospect of obtaining money there; that the loan they had been authorized to open, of which a third only was filled, had now ceased to get forward, and rendered desperate that hope of resource. I saw that there was not a moment to lose, and set out for the Hague on the second morning after receiving the information of Mr. Adams's journey. I went the direct road by Louvres, Senlis, Roye, Pont St. Maxence, Bois le duc, Gournay, Peronne, Cambray, Bouchain, Valenciennes, Mons, Bruxelles, Malines, Antwerp, Mordick, and Rotterdam, to the Hague, where I happily found Mr. Adams. He concurred with me at once in opinion, that something must be done, and that we ought to risk ourselves on doing it without instructions, to save the credit of the United States. We foresaw, that before the new government could be adopted, assembled, establish its financial system, get the money into the Treasury, and place it in Europe, considerable time would elapse; that, therefore, we had better provide at once, for the years '88, '89, and '90, in order to place our government at its ease, and our credit in security, during that trying interval. We set out, therefore, by the way of Leyden, for Amsterdam, where we arrived on the 10th. I had prepared an estimate, showing that

| | | FLORINS |
|---|---|---|
| There would be necessary for the year | '88— | 531,937–10 |
| | '89— | 538,540 |
| | '90— | 473,540 |
| Total, | | 1,544,017–10 |

| | FLORINS | |
|---|---|---|
| To meet this, the bankers had in hand, | 79,268–2–8 | |
| and the unsold bonds would yield, | 542,800 | 622,068–2–8 |
| Leaving a deficit of | | 921,949–7–4 |
| We proposed then to borrow a million, yielding | | 920,000 |
| Which would leave a small deficiency of | | 1,949–7–4 |

Mr. Adams accordingly executed 1000 bonds, for 1000 florins each, and deposited them in the hands of our bankers, with instructions, however, not to issue them until Congress should ratify the measure. This done, he returned to London, and I set out for Paris; and, as nothing urgent forbade it, I determined to return along the banks of the Rhine, to Strasburg, and thence strike off to Paris. I accordingly left Amsterdam on the 30th of March, and proceeded by Utrecht, Nimeguen, Cleves, Duysberg, Dusseldorf, Cologne, Bonn, Coblentz, Nassau, Hocheim, Frankfort, and made an excursion to Hanau, thence to Mayence, and another excursion to Rudesheim, and Johansberg; then by Oppenheim, Worms, and Mannheim, making an excursion to Heidelberg, then by Spire, Carlsruh, Rastadt and Kehl, to Strasbourg, where I arrived April the 16th, and proceeded again on the 18th, by Phalsbourg, Fenestrange, Dieuze, Moyenvie, Nancy, Toul, Ligny, Barleduc, St. Diziers, Vitry, Châlons sur Marne, Epernay, Chateau Thierry, Meaux, to Paris, where I arrived on the 23d of April; and I had the satisfaction to reflect, that by this journey our credit was secured, the new government was placed at ease for two years to come, and that, as well as myself, relieved from the torment of incessant duns, whose just complaints could not be silenced by any means within our power.

A Consular Convention had been agreed on in '84, between Dr. Franklin and the French government, containing several articles, so entirely inconsistent with the laws of the several States, and the general spirit of our citizens, that Congress withheld their ratification, and sent it back to me, with instructions to get those articles expunged, or modified so as to render them compatible with our laws. The Minister unwillingly released us from these concessions, which, indeed, authorized the exercise of powers very offensive in a free State. After much discussion, the Convention was reformed in a considerable degree, and was signed by the Count Montmorin and myself, on the 14th of November, '88; not, indeed, such as I would have wished, but such as could be obtained with good humor and friendship.

On my return from Holland, I found Paris as I had left it, still in high fermentation. Had the Archbishop, on the close of the Assembly of Notables, immediately carried into operation the measures contemplated, it was believed they would all have been registered by the Parliament; but he was slow, presented his edicts, one after another, and at considerable intervals, which gave time for the feelings excited by the proceedings of the Notables to cool off, new claims to be advanced, and a pressure to arise for a fixed constitution, not subject to changes at the will of the King. Nor should we wonder at this pressure, when we consider the monstrous abuses of power under which this people were ground to powder; when we pass in review the weight of their taxes, and the inequality of their distribution; the oppressions of the tithes, the tailles, the corvees, the gabelles, the farms and the barriers; the shackles on commerce by monopolies; on industry by guilds and corporations; on the freedom of conscience, of thought, and of speech; on the freedom of the press by the Censure; and of the person by Lettres de

Cachet; the cruelty of the Criminal code generally; the atrocities of the Rack; the venality of the Judges, and their partialities to the rich; the monopoly of Military honors by the Noblesse; the enormous expenses of the Queen, the Princes and the Court; the prodigalities of pensions; and the riches, luxury, indolence and immorality of the Clergy. Surely under such a mass of misrule and oppression, a people might justly press for a thorough reformation, and might even dismount their rough-shod riders, and leave them to walk on their own legs. The edicts, relative to the corvees and free circulation of grain, were first presented to the Parliament and registered; but those for the impôt territorial, and stamp tax, offered some time after, were refused by the Parliament, which proposed a call of the States General, as alone competent to their authorization. Their refusal produced a Bed of justice, and their exile to Troyes. The Advocates, however, refusing to attend them, a suspension in the administration of justice took place. The Parliament held out for awhile, but the ennui of their exile and absence from Paris, began at length to be felt, and some dispositions for compromise to appear. On their consent, therefore, to prolong some of the former taxes, they were recalled from exile; the King met them in session, November 19, '87, promised to call the States General in the year '92, and a majority expressed their assent to register an edict for successive and annual loans from 1788 to '92; but a protest being entered by the Duke of Orleans, and this encouraging others in a disposition to retract, the King ordered peremptorily the registry of the edict, and left the assembly abruptly. The Parliament immediately protested, that the votes for the enregistry had not been legally taken, and that they gave no sanction to the loans proposed. This was enough to discredit and defeat them. Hereupon issued another edict, for the establishment of a cour plenière, and the suspension of all the Parliaments in the kingdom. This being opposed, as might be expected, by reclamations from all the Parliaments and Provinces, the King gave way, and by an edict of July 5th, '88, renounced his cour plenière, and promised the States General for the 1st of May, of the ensuing year; and the Archbishop, finding the times beyond his faculties, accepted the promise of a Cardinal's hat, was removed [September '88] from the Ministry, and M. Necker was called to the department of finance. The innocent rejoicings of the people of Paris on this change provoked the interference of an officer of the city guards, whose order for their dispersion not being obeyed, he charged them with fixed bayonets, killed two or three, and wounded many. This dispersed them for the moment, but they collected the next day in great numbers, burnt ten or twelve guardhouses, killed two or three of the guards, and lost six or eight more of their own number. The city was hereupon put under Martial law, and after awhile the tumult subsided. The effect of this change of ministers, and the promise of the States General at an early day, tranquillized the nation. But two great questions now occurred. 1st. What proportion shall the number of deputies of the Tiers état bear to those of the Nobles and Clergy? And 2d, shall they sit in the same or in distinct apartments? M. Necker, desirous of avoiding himself these knotty questions, proposed a second call of the same Notables, and that their advice should be asked on the subject. They met, November 9, '88; and, by five bureaux against one, they recommended the forms of the States General of 1614; wherein the Houses were separate, and voted by orders, not by persons. But the whole nation declaring at once against this, and that the Tiers état should be, in numbers, equal to both the other orders, and the Parliament deciding for the same proportion, it was determined so to be, by a declaration of December 27th, '88. A Report of M. Necker, to the King, of about the same date, contained other very important concessions. 1. That the King could neither lay a new tax, nor prolong an old one. 2. It expressed a readiness to agree on the periodical meeting of the States. 3. To consult on the necessary restriction on Lettres de Cachet; and 4. How far the press might be made free. 5. It admits that the States are to appropriate the public money; and 6. That Ministers shall be responsible for public expenditures. And these concessions came from the very heart of the King. He had not a wish but for the good of the nation; and for that object, no personal sacrifice would ever have cost him a moment's regret; but his mind was weakness itself, his constitution timid, his judgment null, and without sufficient firmness even to stand by the faith of his word. His Queen, too, haughty and bearing no contradiction, had an absolute ascendency over him; and around her were rallied the King's brother d'Artois, the court generally, and the aristocratic part of his Ministers, particularly Breteuil, Broglie, Vauguyon, Foulon. Luzerne. men whose principles of government were those of the age of Louis XIV. Against this host, the good counsels of Necker, Montmorin, St. Priest, although in unison with the wishes of the King himself, were of little avail. The resolutions of the morning, formed under their advice, would be reversed in the evening, by the influence of the Queen and court. But the hand of heaven weighed heavily indeed on the machinations of this junto; producing collateral incidents, not arising out of the case, yet powerfully co-exciting the nation to force a regeneration of its government, and overwhelming with accumulated difficulties, this liberticide resistance. For, while laboring under the want of money for even ordinary purposes, in a government which required a million of livres a day, and driven to the last ditch by the universal call for liberty, there came on a winter of such severe cold, as was without example in the memory of man, or in the written records of history. The Mercury was at times 50° below the freezing point of Fahrenheit, and 22° below that of Reaumur. All out-door labor was suspended, and the poor, without the wages of labor, were, of course, without either bread or fuel. The government found its necessities aggravated by that of procuring immense quantities of fire-wood, and of keeping great fires at all the cross streets, around which the people gathered in crowds, to avoid perishing with cold. Bread, too, was to be bought, and distributed daily, gratis, until a relaxation of the season should enable the people to work; and the slender stock of bread stuff had for some time threatened famine, and had raised that article to an enormous price. So great, indeed, was the scarcity of bread, that, from the highest to the lowest citizen, the bakers were permitted to deal but a scanty allowance per head, even to those who paid for it; and, in cards of invitation to dine in the richest houses, the guest was notified to bring his own bread. To eke out the existence of the people, every person who had the means, was called on for a weekly subscription, which the Curés collected, and employed in providing messes for the nourishment of the poor, and vied with each other in devising such economical compositions of food, as would subsist the greatest number with the smallest means. This want of bread had been foreseen for some time past, and M. de Montmorin had desired me to notify it in America, and that, in addition to the market price, a premium should be given on what should be brought from the United States. Notice was accordingly given, and produced considerable supplies. Subsequent information made the importations from America, during the months of March, April and May, into the Atlantic ports of France, amount to about twenty-one thousand barrels of flour, besides what went to other ports, and in other months; while our supplies to their West Indian islands relieved them also from that drain. This distress for bread continued till July.

Hitherto no acts of popular violence had been produced by the struggle for political reformation. Little riots, on ordinary incidents, had taken place as at other times, in different parts of the kingdom, in which some lives, perhaps a dozen or twenty, had been lost; but in the month of April, a more serious one occurred in Paris, unconnected, indeed, with the Revolutionary principle, but making part of the history of the day. The Fauxbourg St. Antoine is a quarter of the city inhabited entirely by the class of day laborers and journeymen in every line. A rumor was spread among them, that a great paper manufacturer, of the name of Reveillon, had proposed, on some occasion, that their wages should be lowered to fifteen sous a day. Inflamed at once into rage, and without inquiring into its truth, they flew to his house in vast numbers, destroyed everything in it, and in his magazines and work-shops, without secreting, however, a pin's worth to themselves, and were continuing this work of devastation, when the regular troops were called in. Admonitions being disregarded, they were of necessity fired on, and a regular action ensued, in which about one hundred of them were killed, before the rest would disperse. There had rarely passed a year without such a riot, in some part or other of the Kingdom; and this is distinguished only as cotemporary with the Revolution, although not produced by it.

The States General were opened on the 5th of May, '89, by speeches from the King, the Garde des Sceaux, Lamoignon, and M. Necker. The last was thought to trip too lightly over the constitutional reformations which were expected. His notices of them in this speech, were not as full as in his previous "Rapport au Roi." This was observed, to his disadvantage; but much allowance should have been made for the situation in which he was placed, between his own counsels, and those of the ministers and party of the court. Overruled in his own opinions, compelled to deliver, and to gloss over those of his opponents, and even to keep their secrets, he could not come forward in his own attitude.

The composition of the Assembly, although equivalent, on the whole, to what had been expected, was something different in its elements. It had been supposed, that a superior education would carry into the scale of the Commons a respectable portion of the Noblesse. It did so as to those of Paris, of its vicinity, and of the other considerable cities, whose greater intercourse with enlightened society had liberalized their minds, and prepared them to advance up to the measure of the times. But the Noblesse of the country, which constituted two-thirds of that body, were far in their rear. Residing constantly on their patrimonial feuds, and familiarized, by daily habit, with Seigneurial powers and practices, they had not yet learned to suspect their inconsistence with reason and right. They were willing to submit to equality of taxation, but not to descend from their rank and prerogatives to be incorporated in session with the Tiers état. Among the Clergy, on the other hand, it had been apprehended that the higher orders of the Hierarchy, by their wealth and connections, would have carried the elections generally; but it turned out, that in most cases, the lower clergy had obtained the popular majorities. These consisted of the Curés, sons of the peasantry, who had been employed to do all the drudgery of parochial services for ten, twenty, or thirty Louis a year; while their superiors were consuming their princely revenues in palaces of luxury and indolence.

The objects for which this body was convened, being of the first order of importance, I felt it very interesting to understand the views of the parties of which it was composed, and especially the ideas prevalent as to the organization contemplated for their government. I went, therefore, daily from Paris to Versailles, and attended their debates, generally till the hour of adjournment. Those of the Noblesse were impassioned and tempestuous. They had some able men on both sides, actuated by equal zeal. The debates of the Commons were temperate, rational, and inflexibly firm. As preliminary to all other business, the awful questions came on, shall the States sit in one, or in distinct apartments? And shall they vote by heads or houses? The opposition was soon found to consist of the Episcopal order among the clergy, and two-thirds of the Noblesse; while the Tiers état were, to a man, united and determined. After various propositions of compromise had failed, the Commons undertook to cut the Gordian knot. The Abbé Siéyès, the most logical head of the nation (author of the pamphlet "Qu'est ce que le Tiers état?" which had electrified that country, as Paine's Common Sense did us), after an impressive speech on the 10th of June, moved that a last invitation should be sent to the Noblesse and Clergy, to attend in the hall of the States, collectively or individually, for the verification of powers, to which the Commons would proceed immediately, either in their presence or absence. This verification being finished, a motion was made, on the 15th, that they should constitute themselves a National Assembly; which was decided on the 17th, by a majority of four-fifths. During the debates on this question, about twenty of the Curés had joined them, and a proposition was made, in the chamber of the Clergy, that their whole body should join. This was rejected, at first, by a small majority only; but, being afterwards somewhat modified, it was decided affirmatively, by a majority of eleven. While this was under debate, and unknown to the court, to wit, on the 19th, a council was held in the afternoon, at Marly, wherein it was proposed that the King should interpose, by a declaration of his sentiments, in a *séance royale*. A form of declaration was proposed by Necker, which, while it censured, in general, the proceedings, both of the Nobles and Commons, announced the King's views, such as substantially to coincide with the Commons. It was agreed to in Council, the *séance* was fixed for the 22d, the meetings of the States were till then to be suspended, and everything, in the meantime, kept secret. The members, the next morning (the 20th) repairing to their house, as usual, found the doors shut and guarded, a proclamation posted up for a *séance royale* on the 22d, and a suspension of their meetings in the meantime. Concluding that their dissolution was now to take place, they repaired to a building called the "Jeu de paume" (or Tennis court) and there bound themselves by oath to each other, never to separate, of their own accord, till they had settled a constitution for the nation, on a solid basis, and, if separated by force, that they would reassemble in some other place. The next day they met in the church of St. Louis, and were joined by a majority of the clergy. The heads of the Aristocracy saw that all was lost without some bold exertion. The King was still at Marly. Nobody was permitted to approach him but their friends. He was assailed by falsehoods in all shapes. He was made to believe that the Commons were about to absolve the army from their oath of fidelity to him, and to raise their pay. The court party were now all rage and desperation. They procured a committee to be held, consisting of the King and his Ministers, to which Monsieur and the Count d'Artois should be admitted. At this committee, the latter attacked M. Necker personally, arraigned his declaration, and proposed one which some of his prompters had put into his hands. M. Necker was brow-beaten and intimidated, and the King shaken. He determined that the two plans should be deliberated on the next day, and the *séance royale* put off a day longer. This encouraged a fiercer attack on M. Necker the next day. His draught of a declaration was entirely broken up, and that of the Count d'Artois inserted into it. Himself and Montmorin offered their resignation, which was refused; the Count d'Artois saying to M. Necker, "No sir, you must be kept as the hostage; we hold you responsible for all the ill which shall happen." This change of plan was immediately whispered without doors. The Noblesse were in triumph; the people in consternation. I was quite alarmed at this state of things. The soldiery had not yet indicated which side they should take, and that which they should support would be sure to prevail. I considered a successful reformation of government in France, as insuring a general reformation through Europe, and the resurrection, to a new life, of their people, now ground to dust by the abuses of the governing powers. I was much acquainted with the leading patriots of the Assembly. Being from a country which had successfully passed through a similar reformation, they were disposed to my acquaintance, and had some confidence in me. I urged, most strenuously, an immediate compromise; to secure what the government was now ready to yield, and trust to future occasions for what might still be wanting. It was well understood that the King would grant, at this time, 1. Freedom of the person by Habeas corpus: 2. Freedom of conscience: 3. Freedom of the press: 4. Trial by jury: 5. A representative Legislature: 6. Annual meetings: 7. The origination of laws: 8. The exclusive right of taxation and appropriation: and 9. The responsibility of Ministers; and with the exercise of these powers they could obtain, in future, whatever might be further necessary to improve and preserve their constitution. They thought otherwise, however, and events have proved their lamentable error. For, after thirty years of war, foreign and domestic, the loss of millions of lives, the prostration of private happiness, and the foreign subjugation of their own country for a time, they have obtained no more, nor even that securely. They were unconscious of (for who could foresee?) the melancholy sequel of their well-meant perseverance; that their physical force would be usurped by a first tyrant to trample on the independence, and even the existence, of other nations: that this would afford a fatal example for the atrocious conspiracy of Kings against their people; would generate their unholy and homicide alliance to make common cause among themselves, and to crush, by the power of the whole, the efforts of any part to moderate their abuses and oppressions.

When the King passed, the next day, through the lane formed from the Château to the "Hotel des états," there was a dead silence. He was about an hour in the House, delivering his speech and declaration. On his coming out, a feeble cry of "vive le Roi" was raised by some children, but the people remained silent and sullen. In the close of his speech, he had ordered that the members should follow him, and resume their deliberations the next day. The Noblesse followed him, and so did the Clergy, except about thirty, who, with the Tiers, remained in the room, and entered into deliberation. They protested against what the King had done, adhered to all their former proceedings, and resolved the inviolability of their own persons. An officer came, to order them out of the room in the King's name. "Tell those who sent you," said Mirabeau, "that we shall not move hence but at our own will, or the point of the bayonet." In the afternoon, the people, uneasy, began to assemble in great numbers in the courts, and vicinities of the palace. This produced alarm. The Queen sent for M. Necker. He was conducted, amidst the shouts and acclamations of the multitude, who filled all the apartments of the palace. He was a few minutes only with the Queen, and what passed between them did not transpire. The King went out to ride. He passed through the crowd to his carriage, and into it, without being in the least noticed. As M. Necker followed him, universal acclamations were raised of "vive Monsieur Necker, vive le sauveur de la France opprimée." He was conducted back to his house with the same demonstrations of affection and anxiety. About two hundred deputies of the Tiers, catching the enthusiasm of the moment, went to his house, and extorted from him a promise that he would not resign. On the 25th, forty-eight of the Nobles joined the Tiers, and among them the Duke of Orleans. There were then with them one hundred and sixty-four members of the Clergy, although the minority of that body still sat apart, and called themselves the Chamber of the Clergy. On the 26th, the Archbishop of Paris joined the Tiers, as did some others of the Clergy and of the Noblesse.

These proceedings had thrown the people into violent ferment. It gained the soldiery, first of the French guards, extended to those of every other denomination, except the Swiss, and even to the body guards of the King. They began to quit their barracks, to assemble in squads, to declare they would defend the life of the King, but would not be the murderers of their fellow-citizens. They called themselves the soldiers *of the nation,* and left now no doubt on which side they would be, in case of rupture. Similar accounts came in from the troops in other parts of the kingdom, giving good reason to believe they would side with their fathers and brothers, rather than with their officers. The operation of this medicine at Versailles was as sudden as it was powerful. The alarm there was so complete, that in the afternoon of the 27th, the King wrote, with his own hand, letters to the Presidents of the

Clergy and Nobles, engaging them immediately to join the Tiers. These two bodies were debating, and hesitating, when notes from the Count d'Artois decided their compliance. They went in a body, and took their seats with the Tiers, and thus rendered the union of the orders in one chamber complete.

The Assembly now entered on the business of their mission, and first proceeded to arrange the order in which they would take up the heads of their constitution, as follows:

First, and as Preliminary to the whole, a general Declaration of the Rights of Man. Then, specifically, the Principles of the Monarchy; Rights of the Nation; rights of the King; rights of the Citizens; organization and rights of the National Assembly; forms necessary for the enactment of Laws; organization and functions of the Provincial and Municipal Assemblies; duties and limits of the Judiciary power; functions and duties of the Military power.

A Declaration of the Rights of Man, as the preliminary of their work, was accordingly prepared and proposed by the Marquis de La Fayette.

But the quiet of their march was soon disturbed by information that troops, and particularly the foreign troops, were advancing on Paris from various quarters. The King had probably been advised to this, on the pretext of preserving peace in Paris. But his advisers were believed to have other things in contemplation. The Marshal de Broglie was appointed to their command, a high-flying aristocrat, cool and capable of everything. Some of the French guards were soon arrested, under other pretexts, but really, on account of their dispositions, in favor of the National cause. The people of Paris forced their prison, liberated them, and sent a deputation to the Assembly to solicit a pardon. The Assembly recommended peace and order to the people of Paris, the prisoners to the King, and asked from him the removal of the troops. His answer was negative and dry, saying they might remove themselves, if they pleased, to Noyons or Soissons. In the meantime, these troops, to the number of twenty or thirty thousand, had arrived, and were posted in, and between Paris and Versailles. The bridges and passes were guarded. At three o'clock in the afternoon of the 11th of July, the Count de La Luzerne was sent to notify M. Necker of his dismission, and to enjoin him to retire instantly, without saying a word of it to anybody. He went home, dined, and proposed to his wife a visit to a friend, but went in fact to his country house at St. Ouen, and at midnight set out for Brussels. This was not known till the next day (the 12th), when the whole Ministry was changed, except Villedeuil, of the domestic department, and Barenton, Garde des sceaux. The changes were as follows:

The Baron de Breteuil, President of the Council of Finance; de la Galaisière, Comptroller General, in the room of M. Necker; the Marshal de

Broglie, Minister of War, and Foulon under him, in the room of Puy-Ségur; the Duke de la Vauguyon, Minister of Foreign Affairs, instead of the Count de Montmorin; de La Porte, Minister of Marine, in place of the Count de La Luzerne; St. Priest was also removed from the Council. Luzerne and Puy-Ségur had been strongly of the Aristocratic party in the Council, but they were not considered equal to the work now to be done. The King was now completely in the hands of men, the principal among whom had been noted, through their lives, for the Turkish despotism of their characters, and who were associated around the King, as proper instruments for what was to be executed. The news of this change began to be known at Paris, about one or two o'clock. In the afternoon, a body of about one hundred German cavalry were advanced, and drawn up in the Place Louis XV, and about two hundred Swiss posted at a little distance in their rear. This drew people to the spot, who thus accidentally found themselves in front of the troops, merely at first as spectators; but, as their numbers increased, their indignation rose. They retired a few steps, and posted themselves on and behind large piles of stones, large and small, collected in that place for a bridge, which was to be built adjacent to it. In this position, happening to be in my carriage on a visit, I passed through the lane they had formed, without interruption. But the moment after I had passed, the people attacked the cavalry with stones. They charged, but the advantageous position of the people, and the showers of stones, obliged the horse to retire, and quit the field altogether, leaving one of their number on the ground, and the Swiss in the rear not moving to their aid. This was the signal for universal insurrection, and this body of cavalry, to avoid being massacred, retired towards Versailles. The people now armed themselves with such weapons as they could find in armorers, shops, and private houses, and with bludgeons; and were roaming all night, through all parts of the city, without any decided object. The next day (the 13th), the Assembly pressed on the King to send away the troops, to permit the Bourgeoisie of Paris to arm for the preservation of order in the city, and offered to send a deputation from their body to tranquillize them; but their propositions were refused. A committee of magistrates and electors of the city were appointed by those bodies, to take upon them its government. The people, now openly joined by the French guards, forced the prison of St. Lazare, released all the prisoners, and took a great store of corn, which they carried to the corn-market. Here they got some arms, and the French guards began to form and train them. The city-committee determined to raise forty-eight thousand Bourgeois, or rather to restrain their numbers to forty-eight thousand. On the 14th, they sent one of their members (Monsieur de Corny) to the Hotel des Invalides, to ask arms for their Garde Bourgeoise. He was followed by, and he found there, a great collection of people. The Governor of the Invalids came out, and represented the impossibility of his delivering arms, without the orders of those from whom he received them. De Corny advised the people then to retire, and retired himself; but the people took possession of the arms. It was remarkable, that not only the Invalids themselves made no opposition, but that a body of five thousand foreign troops, within four hundred yards, never stirred. M. de Corny, and five others, were then sent to ask arms of M. de Launay, Governor of the Bastille. They found a great collection of people already before the place, and they immediately planted a flag of truce, which was answered by a like flag hoisted on the parapet. The deputation prevailed on the people to fall back a little, advanced themselves to make their demand of the Governor, and in that instant, a discharge from the Bastille killed four persons of those nearest to the deputies. The deputies retired. I happened to be at the house of M. de Corny, when he returned to it, and received from him a narrative of these transactions. On the retirement of the deputies, the people rushed forward, and almost in an instant, were in possession of a fortification of infinite strength, defended by one hundred men, which in other times had stood several regular sieges, and had never been taken. How they forced their entrance has never been explained. They took all the arms, discharged the prisoners, and such of the garrison as were not killed in the first moment of fury; carried the Governor and Lieutenant Governor to the Place de Grève (the place of public execution), cut off their heads, and sent them through the city, in triumph, to the Palais royal. About the same instant, a treacherous correspondence having been discovered in M. de Flesselles, Prevôt des Marchands, they seized him in the Hotel de Ville, where he was in the execution of his office, and cut off his head. These events, carried imperfectly to Versailles, were the subject of two successive deputations from the Assembly to the King, to both of which he gave dry and hard answers; for nobody had as yet been permitted to inform him, truly and fully, of what had passed at Paris. But at night, the Duke de Liancourt forced his way into the King's bed chamber, and obliged him to hear a full and animated detail of the disasters of the day in Paris. He went to bed fearfully impressed. The decapitation of de Launay worked powerfully through the night on the whole Aristocratic party; insomuch, that in the morning, those of the greatest influence on the Count d'Artois, represented to him the absolute necessity that the King should give up everything to the Assembly. This according with the dispositions of the King, he went about eleven o'clock, accompanied only by his brothers, to the Assembly, and there read to them a speech, in which he asked their interposition to re-establish order. Although couched in terms of some caution, yet the manner in which it was delivered, made it evident that it was meant as a surrender at discretion. He returned to the Château a foot, accompanied by the Assembly. They sent off a deputation to quiet Paris, at the head of which was the Marquis de La Fayette, who had, the same morning, been named Commandant en chef of the Milice Bourgeoise; and Monsieur Bailly, former President of the States General, was called for as Prevôt des Marchands. The demolition of the Bastille was now ordered and begun. A body of the Swiss guards, of the regiment of Ventimille, and the city horse guards joined the people. The alarm at Versailles increased. The foreign troops were ordered off instantly. Every Minister resigned. The King confirmed Bailly as Prevôt des Marchands, wrote to M. Necker, to recall him, sent his letter open to the Assembly, to be forwarded by them, and invited them to go with him to Paris the next day, to satisfy the city of his dispositions; and that night, and the next morning, the Count d'Artois, and M. de Montesson, a deputy connected with him, Madame de Polignac, Madame de Guiche, and the Count de Vaudreuil, favorites of the Queen, the Abbé de Vermont her confessor, the Prince of Conde, and Duke of Bourbon fled. The King came to Paris, leaving the Queen in consternation for his return. Omitting the less important figures of the procession, the King's carriage was in the centre; on each side of it, the Assembly, in two ranks a foot; at their head the Marquis de La Fayette, as Commander-in-chief, on horseback, and Bourgeois guards before and behind. About sixty thousand citizens, of all forms and conditions, armed with the conquests of the Bastille and Invalids, as far as they would go, the rest with pistols, swords, pikes, pruning-hooks, scythes, &c., lined all the streets through which the procession passed, and with the crowds of people in the streets, doors, and windows, saluted them everywhere with the cries of "vive la nation," but not a single "vive le Roi" was heard. The King stopped at the Hotel de Ville. There M. Bailly presented and put into his hat, the popular cockade, and addressed him. The King being unprepared, and unable to answer, Bailly went to him, gathered from him some scraps of sentences, and made out an answer, which he delivered to the audience, as from the King. On their return, the popular cries were "vive le Roi et la nation." He was conducted by a Garde Bourgeoise to his palace at Versailles, and thus concluded an "amende honorable," as no sovereign ever made, and no people ever received.

And here, again, was lost another precious occasion of sparing to France the crimes and cruelties through which she has since passed, and to Europe, and finally America, the evils which flowed on them also from this mortal source. The King was now become a passive machine in the hands of the National Assembly, and had he been left to himself, he would have willingly acquiesced in whatever they should devise as best for the nation. A wise constitution would have been formed, hereditary in his line, himself placed at its head, with powers so large as to enable him to do all the good of his station, and so limited, as to restrain him from its abuse. This he would have faithfully administered, and more than this, I do not believe, he ever wished. But he had a Queen of absolute sway over his weak mind and timid virtue, and of a character the reverse of his in all points. This angel, as gaudily painted in the rhapsodies of Burke, with some smartness of fancy, but no sound sense, was proud, disdainful of restraint, indignant at all obstacles to her will, eager in the pursuit of pleasure, and firm enough to hold to her desires, or perish in their wreck. Her inordinate gambling and dissipations, with those of the Count d'Artois, and others of her *clique,* had been a sensible item in the exhaustion of the treasury, which called into action the reforming hand of the nation; and her opposition to it, her inflexible perverseness, and dauntless spirit, led herself to the Guillotine, drew the King on with her, and plunged the world into crimes and calamities which will forever stain the pages of modern history. I have ever believed, that had there been no Queen, there would have been no revolution. No force would have been provoked, nor exercised. The King would have gone hand in hand with the wisdom of his sounder counsellors, who, guided by the increased lights of the age, wished only, with the same pace, to advance the principles of their social constitution. The deed which closed the mortal course of these sovereigns, I shall neither approve nor condemn. I am not prepared to say, that the first magistrate of a nation cannot commit treason against his country, or is unamenable to its punishment; nor yet, that where there is no written law, no regulated tribunal, there is not a law in our hearts, and a power in our hands, given for righteous employment in maintaining right, and redressing wrong. Of those who judged the King many thought him wilfully criminal; many, that his existence would keep the nation in perpetual conflict with the horde of Kings who would war against a generation which might come home to themselves, and that it were better that one should die than all. I should not have voted with this portion of the legislature. I should have shut up the Queen in a convent, putting harm out of her power, and placed the King in his station, investing him with limited powers, which, I verily believe, he would have honestly exercised, according to the measure of his understanding. In this way, no void would have been created, courting the usurpation of a military adventurer, nor occasion given for those enormities which demoralized the nations of the world, and destroyed, and is yet to destroy, millions and millions of its inhabitants. There are three epochs in history, signalized by the total extinction of national morality. The first was of the successors of Alexander, not omitting himself: The next, the successors of the first Cæsar: The third, our own age. This was begun by the partition of Poland, followed by that of the treaty of Pillnitz; next the conflagration of Copenhagen; then the enormities of Bonaparte, partitioning the earth at his will, and devastating it with fire and sword; now the conspiracy of Kings, the successors of Bonaparte, blasphemously calling themselves the Holy Alliance, and treading in the footsteps of their incarcerated leader; not yet, indeed, usurping the government of other nations, avowedly and in detail, but controlling by their armies the forms in which they will permit them to be governed; and reserving, *in petto,* the order and extent of the usurpations further meditated. But I will return from a digression, anticipated, too, in time, into which I have been led by reflection on the criminal passions which refused to the world a favorable occasion of saving it from the afflictions it has since suffered.

M. Necker had reached Basle before he was overtaken by the letter of the King, inviting him back to resume the office he had recently left. He returned immediately, and all the other Ministers having resigned, a new administration was named, to wit: St. Priest and Montmorin were restored; the Archbishop of Bordeaux was appointed Garde des sceaux, La Tour du Pin, Minister of War; La Luzerne, Minister of Marine. This last was believed to have been effected by the friendship of Montmorin; for although differing in politics, they continued firm in friendship, and Luzerne, although not an able man, was thought an honest one. And the Prince of Bauvau was taken into the Council.

Seven Princes of the blood Royal, six ex-Ministers, and many of the high Noblesse, having fled, and the present Ministers, except Luzerne, being all of the popular party, all the functionaries of government moved, for the present, in perfect harmony.

In the evening of August the 4th, and on the motion of the Viscount de Noailles, brother in law of La Fayette, the Assembly abolished all titles of rank, all the abusive privileges of feudalism, the tithes and casuals of the Clergy, all Provincial privileges, and, in fine, the Feudal regimen generally. To the suppression of tithes, the Abbé Siéyès was vehemently opposed; but his learned and logical arguments were unheeded, and his estimation lessened by a contrast of his egoism (for he was beneficed on them), with the generous abandonment of rights by the other members of the Assembly. Many days were employed in putting into the form of laws, the numerous demolitions of ancient abuses; which done, they proceeded to the preliminary work of a Declaration of rights. There being much concord of sentiment on the elements of this instrument, it was liberally framed, and passed with a very general approbation. They then appointed a Committee for the "reduction of a projet" of a constitution, at the head of which was the Archbishop of Bordeaux. I received from him, as chairman of the Committee, a letter of July 20th, requesting me to attend and assist at their deliberations; but I excused myself, on the obvious considerations, that my mission was to the King as Chief Magistrate of the nation, that my duties were limited to the concerns of my own country, and forbade me to intermeddle with the internal transactions of that, in which I had been received under a specific character only. Their plan of a constitution was discussed in sections, and so reported from time to time, as agreed to by the Committee. The first respected the general frame of the government; and that this should be formed into three departments, Executive, Legislative and Judiciary, was generally agreed. But when they proceeded to subordinate developments, many and various shades of opinion came into conflict, and schism, strongly marked, broke the Patriots into fragments of very discordant principles. The first question, Whether there should be a King? met with no open opposition; and it was readily agreed, that the government of France should be monarchical and hereditary. Shall the King have a negative on the laws? shall that negative be absolute, or suspensive only? Shall there be two Chambers of Legislation? or one only? If two, shall one of them be hereditary? or for life? or for a fixed term? and named by the King? or elected by the people? These questions found strong differences of opinion, and produced repulsive combinations among the Patriots. The Aristocracy was cemented by a common principle, of preserving the ancient regime, or whatever should be nearest to it. Making this their polar star, they moved in phalanx, gave preponderance on every question to the minorities of the Patriots, and always to those who advocated the least change. The features of the new constitution were thus assuming a fearful aspect, and great alarm was produced among the honest Patriots by these dissensions in their ranks. In this uneasy state of things, I received one day a note from the Marquis de La Fayette, informing me that he should bring a party of six or eight friends to ask a dinner of me the next day. I assured him of their welcome. When they arrived, they were La Fayette himself, Duport, Barnave, Alexander la Meth, Blacon, Mounier, Maubourg, and Dagout. These were leading Patriots, of honest but differing opinions, sensible of the necessity of effecting a coalition by mutual sacrifices, knowing each other, and not afraid, therefore, to unbosom themselves mutually. This last was a material principle in the selection. With this view, the Marquis had invited the conference, and had fixed the time and place inadvertently, as to the embarrassment under which it might place me. The cloth being removed, and wine set on the table, after the American manner, the Marquis introduced the objects of the conference, by summarily reminding them of the state of things in the Assembly, the course which the principles of the Constitution were taking, and the inevitable result, unless checked by more concord among the Patriots themselves. He observed, that although he also had his opinion, he was ready to sacrifice it to that of his brethren of the same cause; but that a common opinion must now be formed, or the Aristocracy would carry everything, and that, whatever they should now agree on, he, at the head of the National force, would maintain. The discussions began at the hour of four, and were continued till ten o'clock in the evening; during which time, I was a silent witness to a coolness and candor of argument, unusual in the conflicts of political opinion; to a logical reasoning, and chaste eloquence, disfigured by no gaudy tinsel of rhetoric or declamation, and truly worthy of being placed in parallel with the finest dialogues of antiquity, as handed to us by Xenophon, by Plato and Cicero. The result was, that the King should have a suspensive veto on the laws, that the legislature should be composed of a single body only, and that to be chosen by the people. This Concordate decided the fate of the constitution. The Patriots all rallied to the principles thus settled, carried every question agreeably to them, and reduced the Aristocracy to insignificance and impotence. But duties of exculpation were now incumbent on me. I waited on Count Montmorin the next morning, and explained to him, with truth and candor, how it had happened that my house had been made the scene of conferences of such a character. He told me, he already knew everything which had passed, that so far from taking umbrage at the use made of my house on that occasion, he earnestly wished I would habitually assist at such conferences, being sure I should be useful in moderating the warmer spirits, and promoting a wholesome and practicable reformation only. I told him, I knew too well the duties I owed to the King, to the nation, and to my own country, to take any part in councils concerning their internal government, and that I should persevere, with care, in the character of a neutral and passive spectator, with wishes only, and very sincere ones, that those measures might prevail which would be for the greatest good of the nation. I have no doubts, indeed, that this conference was previously known and approved by this honest Minister, who was in confidence and communication with the Patriots, and wished for a reasonable reform of the Constitution.

Here I discontinue my relation of the French Revolution. The minuteness with which I have so far given its details, is disproportioned to the general scale of my narrative. But I have thought it justified by the interest which the whole world must take in this Revolution. As yet, we are but in the first chapter of its history. The appeal to the rights of man, which had been made in the United States, was taken up by France, first of the European nations. From her, the spirit has spread over those of the South. The tyrants of the North have allied indeed against it; but it is irresistible. Their opposition will only multiply its millions of human victims; their own satellites will catch it, and the condition of man through the civilized world will be finally and greatly ameliorated. This is a wonderful instance of great events from small causes. So inscrutable is the arrangement of causes and consequences in this world, that a two-penny duty on tea, unjustly imposed in a sequestered part of it, changes the condition of all its inhabitants. I have been more minute in relating the early transactions of this regeneration, because I was in circumstances peculiarly favorable for a knowledge of the truth. Possessing the confidence and intimacy of the leading Patriots, and more than all, of the Marquis Fayette, their head and Atlas, who had no secrets from me, I learned with correctness the views and proceedings of that party; while my intercourse with the diplomatic missionaries of Europe at Paris, all of them with the court, and eager in prying into its councils and proceedings, gave me a knowledge of these also. My information was always, and immediately committed to writing, in letters to Mr. Jay, and often to my friends, and a recurrence to these letters now insures me against errors of memory.

These opportunities of information ceased at this period, with my retirement from this interesting scene of action. I had been more than a year soliciting leave to go home, with a view to place my daughters in the society and care of their friends, and to return for a short time to my station at Paris. But the metamorphosis through which our government was then passing from its Chrysalid to its Organic form suspended its action in a great degree; and it was not till the last of August, that I received the permission I had asked. And here, I cannot leave this great and good country, without expressing my sense of its pre-eminence of character among the nations of the earth. A more benevolent people I have never known, nor greater warmth and devotedness in their select friendships. Their kindness and accommodation to strangers is unparalleled, and the hospitality of Paris is beyond anything I had conceived to be practicable in a large city. Their eminence, too, in science, the communicative dispositions of their scientific men, the politeness of the general manners, the ease and vivacity of their conversation, give a charm to their society, to be found nowhere else. In a comparison of this, with other countries, we have the proof of primacy, which was given to Themistocles, after the battle of Salamis. Every general voted to himself the first reward of valor, and the second to Themistocles. So, asked the travelled inhabitant of any nation, in what country on earth would you rather live?—Certainly, in my own, where are all my friends, my relations, and the earliest and sweetest affections and recollections of my life. Which would be your second choice? France.

On the 26th of September I left Paris for Havre, where I was detained by contrary winds until the 8th of October. On that day, and the 9th, I crossed over to Cowes, where I had engaged the Clermont, Capt. Colley, to touch for me. She did so; but here again we were detained by contrary winds, until the 22d, when we embarked, and landed at Norfolk on the 23d of November. On my way home, I passed some days at Eppington, in Chesterfield, the residence of my friend and connection, Mr. Eppes; and, while there, I received a letter from the President, General Washington, by express, covering an appointment to be Secretary of State. I received it with real regret. My wish had been to return to Paris, where I had left my household establishment, as if there myself, and to see the end of the Revolution, which I then thought would be certainly and happily closed in less than a year. I then meant to return home, to withdraw from political life, into which I had been impressed by the circumstances of the times, to sink into the bosom of my family and friends, and devote myself to studies more congenial to my mind. In my answer of December 15th, I expressed these dispositions candidly to the President, and my preference of a return to Paris; but assured him, that if it was believed I could be more useful in the administration of the government, I would sacrifice my own inclinations without hesitation, and repair to that destination; this I left to his decision. I arrived at Monticello on the 23d of December, where I received a second letter from the President, expressing his continued wish that I should take my station there, but leaving me still at liberty to continue in my former office, if I could not reconcile myself to that now proposed. This silenced my reluctance, and I accepted the new appointment.

In the interval of my stay at home, my eldest daughter had been happily married to the eldest son of the Tuckahoe branch of Randolphs, a young gentleman of genius, science, and honorable mind, who afterwards filled a dignified station in the General Government, and the most dignified in his own State. I left Monticello on the first of March, 1790, for New York. At Philadelphia I called on the venerable and beloved Franklin. He was then on the bed of sickness from which he never rose. My recent return from a country in which he had left so many friends, and the perilous convulsions to which they had been exposed, revived all his anxieties to know what part they had taken, what had been their course, and what their fate. He went over all in succession, with a rapidity and animation almost too much for his strength. When all his inquiries were satisfied, and a pause took place, I told him I had learned with much pleasure that, since his return to America, he had been occupied in preparing for the world the history of his own life. I cannot say much of that, said he; but I will give you a sample of what I shall leave; and he directed his little grandson (William Bache) who was standing by the bedside, to hand him a paper from the table, to which he pointed. He did so; and the Doctor putting it into my hands, desired me to take it and read it at my leisure. It was about a quire of folio paper, written in a large and running hand, very like his own. I looked into it slightly, then shut it, and said I would accept his permission to read it, and would carefully return it. He said, "No, keep it." Not certain of his meaning, I again looked into it, folded it for my pocket, and said again, I would certainly return it. "No," said he, "keep it." I put it into my pocket, and shortly after took leave of him. He died on the 17th of the ensuing month of April; and as I understood that he had bequeathed all his papers to his grandson, William Temple Franklin, I immediately wrote to Mr. Franklin, to inform him I possessed this paper, which I should consider as his property, and would deliver to his order. He came on immediately to New York, called on me for it, and I delivered it to him. As he put it into his pocket, he said carelessly, he had either the original, or another copy of it, I do not recollect which. This last expression struck my attention forcibly, and for the first time suggested to me the thought that Dr. Franklin had meant it as a confidential deposit in my hands, and that I had done wrong in parting from it. I have not yet seen the collection he published of Dr. Franklin's works, and, therefore, know not if this is among them. I have been told it is not. It contained a narrative of the negotiations between Dr. Franklin and the British Ministry, when he was endeavoring to prevent the contest of arms which followed. The negotiation was brought about by the intervention of Lord Howe and his sister, who, I believe, was called Lady Howe, but I may misremember her title. Lord Howe seems to have been friendly to America, and exceedingly anxious to prevent a rupture. His intimacy with Dr. Franklin, and his position with the Ministry, induced him to undertake a mediation between them; in which his sister seemed to have been associated. They carried from one to the other, backwards and forwards, the several propositions and answers which passed, and seconded with their own intercessions, the importance of mutual sacrifices, to preserve the peace and connection of the two countries. I remember that Lord North's answers were dry, unyielding, in the spirit of unconditional submission, and betrayed an absolute indifference to the occurrence of a rupture; and he said to the mediators distinctly, at last, that "a rebellion was not to be deprecated on the part of Great Britain; that the confiscations it would produce would provide for many of their friends." This expression was reported by the mediators to Dr. Franklin, and indicated so cool and calculated a purpose in the Ministry, as to render compromise hopeless, and the negotiation was discontinued. If this is not among the papers published, we ask, what has become of it? I delivered it with my own hands, into those of Temple Franklin. It certainly established views so atrocious in the British government, that its suppression would, to them, be worth a great price. But could the grandson of Dr. Franklin be, in such degree, an accomplice in the parricide of the memory of his immortal grandfather? The suspension for more than twenty years of the general publication, bequeathed and confided to him, produced, for awhile, hard suspicions against him; and if, at last, all are not published, a part of these suspicions may remain with some.

I arrived at New York on the 21st of March, where Congress was in session.

So far July 29, 1821.

# *Chapter XXV*

# DIARIES AND NOTES

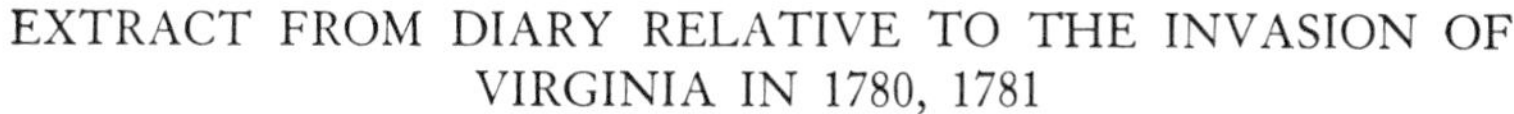

## EXTRACT FROM DIARY RELATIVE TO THE INVASION OF VIRGINIA IN 1780, 1781

Saturday, December the 31st, 1780, eight o'clock, A.M. Received first intelligence that twenty-seven sail were, on the morning of December the 29th, just below Willoughby's Point. Sent off General Nelson, with full powers.

1781. January the 1st. No intelligence.

January the 2d, ten o'clock, A.M. Information from N. Burwell, that their advance was at Warrasqueak Bay. Gave orders for militia, a quarter from some, and half from other counties. Assembly rose.

Wednesday, January the 3d, eight o'clock, P.M. Received a letter from E. Archer, Swan's Point, that at twelve o'clock that day they were at anchor a little below Jamestown. At five o'clock, P.M., of the same day, I had received a letter from R. Andrews for General Nelson, that they were at Jamestown the evening of the 2d.

Thursday, January the 4th, five o'clock, A.M. Mr. Eppes and family, &c., came and informed me from the Speaker, that they had passed Kennon's and Hood's the evening before; the tide having made for them at one o'clock, P.M., of the 3d, and the wind shifted to the east strong. They had not, however, passed Hood's, but anchored at Kennon's. Called whole militia from adjacent counties. I was then anxious to know whether they would pass Westover, or not, as that would show the side they would land.

Five o'clock, P.M. Learned by Captain De Ponthiere, that at two o'clock, P.M., they were drawn up at Westover. Then ordered arms, and stores, &c. (which till then had been carrying to Westham), to be thrown across the river at Richmond; and at half-past seven o'clock, P.M., set out to the foundry and Westham, and set Captain Brush, Captain Irish, and Mr. Hylton, to see everything wagoned from the magazine and laboratory to Westham, and there thrown over; to work all night. The enemy encamped at Four-Mile Creek. I went to Tuckahoe and lodged.

January the 5th. Went early over the river with my family; sent them up to Fine Creek; went myself to Westham; gave orders for withdrawing ammunition and arms (which lay exposed on the bank to the effect of artillery from opposite shore), behind a point. Then went to Manchester; had a view of the enemy. My horse sunk under me with fatigue; borrowed one, went to Chetwood's, appointed by Baron Steuben as a rendezvous and head-quarters; but finding him not there, and understanding he would go to Colonel Henry's, I proceeded there for quarters. The enemy arrived in Richmond at one o'clock, P.M. One regiment of infantry and thirty horse proceeded, without stopping, to the foundry; burned that and the magazine and Ballendine's house, and went as far as Westham. They returned that evening to Richmond. Sent me a proposition to compound for property. Refused.

January the 6th. In the morning they burned certain houses and stores, and at twelve o'clock of that day left Richmond, and encamped at Four-Mile Creek. I went to Westham, ordered books and papers particularly from magazine. In the evening I went up to Fine Creek.

January the 7th. I returned to Westham, and then came down to Manchester, where I lodged. The enemy encamped at Westover and Berkley. It had rained excessively the preceding night, and continued to do so till about noon. Gibson has one thousand; Steuben, eight hundred; Davis, two hundred; Nelson, two hundred and fifty.

January the 8th, at half-past seven o'clock, A.M. I returned to Richmond. The wind gets, about this time, to north-west; a good gale; in the afternoon becomes easterly. The enemy remain in their last encampment. General Nelson at Charles City C. H. Colonel Nicholas with three hundred men at the Forest.

January the 9th, eleven o'clock. The wind is south-east, but almost nothing. The enemy remain in their last encampment, except embarking their horse.

January the 10th, at one o'clock, P.M. They embark infantry, and fall down the river, the wind having shifted a little north of west, and pretty fresh. Baron Steuben gets to Bland's Mills tonight, nine miles short of Hood's.

January the 11th, eight o'clock, A.M. The wind due west, and strong.

*Loss sustained by the public*

The papers and books of the Council since the revolution. The papers of the auditors, but not their books. Five brass field-pieces, four pounders, which had been sunk in the river, but were weighed by the enemy. About one hundred and fifty arms in the Capitol loft. About one hundred and fifty in a wagon on the Brook road. About five tons of powder, and some made ammunition at magazine. Some small proportion of the linens, cloths, &c., in the public store. Some quartermasters' stores; the principal articles was one hundred and twenty sides of leather. Some of the tools in the artificers' shops. Foundry, magazine, four artificers' shops, public store, quartermasters' store, one artificers' shop, three wagons.

The legislature was sitting when the entrance of the enemy into James river was made known. They were informed, without reserve, of the measures adopted. Every suggestion from the members was welcomed and weighed, and their adjournment on the 2d of January furnished the most immediate and confidential means of calling for the militia of their several counties. They accordingly became the bearers of those calls, and they were witnesses themselves, that every preparation was making which the exhausted and harassed state of the country admitted.

They met again at Richmond in May, and adjourned to Charlottesville, where they made a house on the 28th. My office of Governor expired on the 2d of June, being the fifth day of the session; and no successor had been appointed, when an enterprise on the 4th by Tarleton's cavalry drove them thence, and they met again at Staunton on the 7th. Some members attended there who had not been at Richmond at the time of Arnold's enterprise. One of these, George Nicholas, a very honest and able man, then, however, young and ardent, supposing there had been some remissness in the measures of the Executive on that occasion, moved for an inquiry into them, to be made at the succeeding session. The members who had been present and privy to the transactions, courted the inquiry on behalf of the executive. Mr. Nicholas, as a candid and honorable man, sent me, through a friend, a copy of the topics of inquiry he proposed to go into; and I communicated to him, with the same frankness, the justifications I should offer, that he might be prepared to refute them if not founded in fact. The following is a copy of both:

*1st Objection.*—That General Washington's information was, that an embarkation was taking place, destined for this State.

*Answer.*—His information was, that it was destined for the Southward, as was *given out* at New York. Had similar informations from General Washington, and Congress, been considered as sufficient ground at all times for calling the militia into the field, there would have been a standing army of militia kept up; because there has never been a time, since the invasion expected in December, 1779, but what we have had those intimations hanging over our heads. The truth is, that General Washington always considered as his duty to convey every rumor of an embarkation; but we (for some time past, at least) never thought anything but actual invasion should induce us to the expense and harassment of calling the militia into the field; except in the case of December, 1779, when it was thought proper to do this in order to convince the French of our disposition to protect their ships. Inattention to this necessary economy, in the beginning, went far towards that ruin of our finances which followed.

*2d Objection.*—Where were the post-riders, established last summer?

*Answer.*—They were established at Continental expense, to convey speedy information to Congress of the arrival of the French fleet, then expected here. When that arrived at Rhode Island, these expenses were discontinued. They were again established on the invasion in October, and discontinued when that ceased. And again on the first intimation of the invasion of December. But it will be asked, why were they not established on General Washington's letters? Because those letters were no more than we had received upon many former occasions, and would have led to a perpetual establishment of post-riders.

*3d Objection.*—If a proper number of men had been put into motion on Monday, for the relief of the lower country, and ordered to march to Williamsburg, that they would at least have been in the neighborhood of Richmond on Thursday.

*Answer.*—The order could not be till Tuesday, because we then received our first certain information. Half the militia of the counties round about Richmond were then ordered out, and the whole of them on the 4th, and ordered not to wait to come in a body, but in detachments as they could assemble. Yet were there not on Friday more than two hundred collected, and they were principally of the town of Richmond.

*4th Objection.*—That we had not the signals.

*Answer.*—This, though a favorite plan of some gentlemen, and perhaps a practicable one, has hitherto been thought too difficult.

*5th Objection.*—That we had not look-outs.

*Answer.*—There had been no cause to order look-outs more than has been ever existing. This is only in fact asking why we do not always keep look-outs.

*6th Objection.*—That we had not heavy artillery on travelling carriages.

*Answer.*—The gentlemen who acted as members of the Board of War a twelvemonth can answer this question, by giving the character of the artificers whom, during that time, they could never get to mount the heavy artillery. The same reason prevented their being mounted from May, 1780, to December. We have even been unable to get those heavy cannon moved from Cumberland by the whole energy of government. A like difficulty which occurred in the removal of those at South Quay, in their day, will convince them of the possibility of this.

*7th Objection.*—That there was not a body of militia thrown into Portsmouth, the great bridge, Suffolk.

*Answer.*—In the summer of 1780, we asked the favor of General Nelson, to call together the County Lieutenants of the lower counties, and concert the general measures which should be taken for instant opposition, on any invasion, until aid could be ordered by the Executive; and the County Lieutenants were ordered to obey his call; he did so the first moment, to wit, on Saturday, December the 31st, at 8 o'clock A.M., of our receiving information of the appearance of a fleet in the bay. We asked the favor of General Nelson to go down, which he did, with full powers to call together the militia of any counties he thought proper, to call on the keepers of any public arms or stores, and to adopt for the instant such measures as exigencies required, till we could be better informed.

*Query.*—Why were not General Nelson, and the brave officers with him, particularly mentioned?

*Answer.*—What should have been said of them? The enemy did not land, nor give them an opportunity of doing what nobody doubts they would have done; that is, something worthy of being minutely recited.

*Query.*—Why publish Arnold's letter without General Nelson's answer?

*Answer.*—Ask the printer. He got neither from the Executive.

*Objection.*—As to the calling out a few militia, and that late.

*Answer.*—It is denied that they were few or late. Four thousand and seven hundred men (the number required by Baron Steuben) were called out the moment an invasion was known to have taken place, that is on Tuesday, January 2d.

*Objection.*—The abandonment of York and Portsmouth fortifications.

*Answer.*—How can they be kept without regulars, on the large scale on which they were formed? Would it be approved of to harass the militia with garrisoning them?

To place me on equal ground for meeting the inquiry, one of the representatives of my county resigned his seat, and I was unanimously elected in his place. Mr. Nicholas, however, before the day, became better satisfied as to what had been done, and did not appear to bring forward the inquiry; and in a publication, several years after, he made honorable acknowledgment of the erroneous views he had entertained on those transactions. I therefore read in my place the inquiries he had proposed to make, and stated the justifications of the Executive. And nearly every member present having been a witness to their truth, and conscious all was done which could have been done, concurred at once in the following resolution:

"The following resolution was *unanimously* agreed to by both houses of the General Assembly of Virginia, December the 19th, 1781.

*"Resolved,* That the sincere thanks of the General Assembly be given to our former Governor, Thomas Jefferson, Esquire, for his impartial, upright, and attentive administration whilst in office. The Assembly wish in the strongest manner to declare the high opinion they entertain of Mr. Jefferson's ability, rectitude, and integrity as Chief Magistrate of this Commonwealth, and mean, by thus publicly avowing their opinion, to obviate and to remove all unmerited censure."

And here it is but proper to notice the parody of these transactions which General Lee has given as their history. He was in a distant State at the time, and seems to have made up a random account from the rumors which were afloat where he then was. It is a tissue of errors from beginning to end.

The nonsense which has been uttered on the *coup de main* of Tarleton on Charlottesville is really so ridiculous, that it is almost ridiculous seriously to notice it. I will briefly, however, notice facts and dates. It has been said before, that the legislature was driven from Charlottesville by an incursion of the enemy's cavalry. Since the adjournment from Richmond, their force in this country had been greatly augmented by reinforcements under Lord Cornwallis and General Phillips; and they had advanced up into the country as far as Elk Island, and the Fork of James river. Learning that the legislature was in session at Charlottesville, they detached Colonel Tarleton with his legion of horse to surprise them. As he was passing through Louisa on the evening of the 3d of June, he was observed by a Mr. Jouett, who, suspecting the object, set out immediately for Charlottesville, and knowing the byways of the neighborhood, passed the enemy's encampment, rode all night, and before sunrise of the 4th, called at Monticello with notice of what he had seen, and passed on to Charlottesville to notify the members of the legislature. The Speakers of the two houses, and some other members were lodging with us. I ordered a carriage to be ready to carry off my family; we breakfasted at leisure with our guests, and after breakfast they had gone to Charlottesville; when a neighbor rode up full speed to inform me that a troop of horse was then ascending the hill to the house. I instantly sent off my family, and after a short delay for some pressing arrangements, I mounted my horse; and knowing that in the public road I should be liable to fall in with the enemy, I went through the woods, and joined my family at the house of a friend, where we dined. Would it be believed, were it not known, that this flight from a troop of horse, whose whole legion, too, was within supporting distance, has been the subject, with party writers, of volumes of reproach on me, serious or sarcastic? That it has been sung in verse, and said in humble prose, that forgetting the noble example of the hero of La Mancha, and his wind-mills, I declined a combat singly against a troop, in which victory would have been so glorious? Forgetting, themselves, at the same time, that I was not provided with the enchanted arms of the Knight, nor even with his helmet of Mambrino. These closet heroes, forsooth, would have disdained the shelter of a wood, even singly and unarmed, against a legion of armed enemies.

Here, too, I must note another instance of the want of that correctness in writing history, without which it becomes romance. General Lee says that Tarleton, in another enterprise some time after, penetrated up the south side of James river to New London, in Bedford county. To that neighborhood precisely, where I had a possession, I had carried my family, and was confined there several weeks by the effects of a fall from my horse; and I can assure the readers of General Lee's history, that no enemy ever came within forty miles of New London.

## MEMORANDUM RELATIVE TO INVASION OF VIRGINIA IN 1780, 1781

*c.* 1805

Among Jefferson's manuscripts is the following paper in relation to the invasion of Virginia in 1780-1781. It is in Jefferson's own handwriting, although it refers to him in the third person.

Richmond, 1780. Dec. 31st, at 8 A.M. The Governor received the first intelligence that twenty-seven sail of ships had entered Chesapeake Bay, and were in the morning of the 29th just below Willoughby's point [the southern cape of James river], their destination unknown.

1781. January 2, at 10 A.M. Information received that they had entered James river, their advance being at Warrasqueak Bay. Orders were immediately given for calling in the militia, one-fourth from some, and half from other counties. The members of the legislature, which rises this day, are the bearers of the orders to their respective counties. The Governor directs the removal of the records into the country, and the transportation of the military stores from Richmond to Westham [on the river seven miles above], there to be carried across the river.

January 3d, 8 P.M. The enemy are said to be a little below Jamestown; convenient for landing, if Williamsburg is their object.

January 4th, at 5 A.M. Information is received that they had passed Kennon's and Hoods the evening before with a strong easterly wind, which determines their object to be either Petersburg or Richmond. The Governor now calls in the whole militia from the adjacent counties.

At 5 P.M. Information that at 2 P.M. they were landed and drawn up at Westover [on the north side of the river, and twenty-five miles below Richmond], and consequently Richmond was their destination. Orders are now given to discontinue wagoning the military stores from Richmond to Westham, and to throw them across directly at Richmond.

The Governor having attended to this till an hour and a half in the night, then rode up to the foundry [one mile below Westham], ordered Captains Brush and Irish, and Mr. Hylton to continue all night wagoning to Westham the arms and stores still at the foundry, to be thrown across the river at Westham, then proceeded to Westham to urge the pressing the transportation there across the river, and thence went to Tuckahoe [eight miles above, and on the same side of the river] to see after his family, which he had sent that far in the course of the day. He arrived there at 1 o'clock in the night.

Early in the morning he carried his family across the river there, and sending them to Teine creek [eight miles higher up], went himself to Breton's on the south side of the river [opposite to Westham], finding the arms, &c., in a heap near the shore, and exposed to be destroyed by cannon from the north bank. He had them removed under cover of a point of land near by. He proceeded to Manchester [opposite to Richmond]. The enemy had arrived at Richmond at 1 P.M. Having found that nearly the whole arms had been got there from Richmond, he set out for Chetwood's to meet with Baron Steuben, who had appointed that place as a rendezvous and head-quarters; but not finding him there, and understanding that he would be at Colonel Fleming's [six miles above Breton's], he proceeded thither. The enemy had now a detachment at Westham, and sent a deputation from the city of Richmond to the Governor at Colonel Fleming's to propose terms for ransoming the safety of the city, which terms he rejected. The Governor returned to Breton's, had measures taken more effectually to secure the books and papers there. The enemy having burnt some houses and stores, left Richmond, after twenty-four hours stay there, and encamped at Four-Mile Creek [eight or ten miles below], and the Governor went to look to his family at Fine Creek.

He returned to Breton's to see further to the arms there, exposed on the ground to heavy rains which had fallen the night before, and then proceeded to Manchester, and lodged there. The enemy encamped at Westover.

At half-past 7 A.M. he crossed over to Richmond, and resumed his residence there. The enemy are still retained in their encampment at Westover by an easterly wind. Col. John Nicholas has now three hundred militia at the Forest [six miles off from Westover], General Nelson two hundred at Charles City Court House [eight miles below Westover], Gibson one thousand, and Baron Steuben eight hundred on the south side the river.

January 9th. The enemy are still encamped at Westover.

January 10th. At 1 P.M. they embark; and the wind having shifted a little to the north of the west, and pretty fresh, they fall down the river. Baron Steuben marches for Hood's, where their passage may be checked. He reaches Bland's Mills in the evening, within nine miles of Hood's.

January 11th. At 8 A.M. the wind due west and strong, they may make good their retreat. During this period time and place have been minutely cited, in order that those who think there was any remissness in the movements of the Governor, may lay their finger on the point, and say when and where it was. Hereafter less detail will suffice.

Soon after this General Phillips having joined Arnold with a reinforcement of two thousand men, they advanced again up to Petersburg, and about the last of April to Manchester. The Governor had remained constantly in and about Richmond, exerting all his powers collecting militia, and providing such means for the defence of the State as its exhausted resources admitted. Never assuming a guard, and with only the river between him and the enemy, his lodgings were frequently within four, five, or six miles of them.

M. de la Fayette, about this time, arrived at Richmond with some Continental troops, with which, and the militia collected, he continued to occupy that place, and the north bank of the river, while Phillips and Arnold held Manchester and the south bank. But Lord Cornwallis, about the middle of May, joining the main southern armies, M. de la Fayette was obliged to retire. The enemy crossed the river, and advanced up into the country about fifty miles, and within thirty miles of Charlottesville, at which place the legislature being to meet in June, the Governor proceeded to his seat at Monticello, two or three miles from it. His office was now near expiring, the country under invasion by a powerful army, no services but military of any avail, unprepared by his line of life and education for the command of armies, he believed it right not to stand in the way of talents better fitted than his own to the circumstances under which the country was placed. He therefore himself proposed to his friends in the legislature that General Nelson, who commanded the militia of the State, should be appointed Governor, as he was sensible that the union of the civil and military power in the same hands at this time, would greatly facilitate military measures. This appointment accordingly took place on the 12th of June, 1781.

This was the state of things when, his office having actually expired, and no successor as yet in place, Colonel Tarleton, with his regiment of horse, was detached by Lord Cornwallis to surprise Mr. Jefferson (whom they thought still in office) and the legislature now sitting in Charlottesville. The Speakers of the two houses, and some other members of the legislature, were lodging with Mr.

Jefferson at Monticello. Tarleton, early in the morning, when within ten miles of that place, detached a company of horse to secure him and his guests, and proceeded himself rapidly with his main body to Charlottesville, where he hoped to find the legislature unapprized of his movement. Notice of it, however, had been brought, both to Monticello and Charlottesville, about sun-rise. The Speakers, with their colleagues, returned to Charlottesville, and with the other members of the legislature, had barely time to get out of his way. Mr. Jefferson sent off his family to secure them from danger, and was himself still at Monticello making arrangements for his own departure, when a Lieutenant Hudson arrived there at half speed, and informed him that the enemy were then ascending the hill of Monticello. He departed immediately, and knowing that he would be pursued if he took the high road, he plunged into the woods of the adjoining mountain, where being at once safe, he proceeded to overtake his family. This is the famous adventure of Carter's mountain, which has been so often resounded through the slanderous chronicles of federalism. But they have taken care never to detail the facts, lest these should show that this favorite charge amounted to nothing more than that he did not remain in his house, and there singly fight a whole troop of horse, or suffer himself to be taken prisoner. Having accompanied his family one day's journey, he returned to Monticello. Tarleton had retired after eighteen hours' stay in Charlottesville. Mr. Jefferson then rejoined his family, and proceeded with them to an estate he had in Bedford, about eighty miles south-west, where, riding on his farm some time after, he was thrown from his horse, and disabled from riding on horseback for a considerable time. But Mr. Turner finds it more convenient to give him this fall in his retreat before Tarleton, which had happened some weeks before, as a proof that he withdrew from a troop of horse with a precipitancy which Don Quixote would not have practiced.

The facts here stated most particularly, with date of time and place, are taken from the notes made by the writer hereof for his own satisfaction at the time. The others are from memory, but so well recollected that he is satisfied there is no material fact mis-stated. Should any person undertake to contradict any particular on evidence which may at all merit the public respect, the writer will take the trouble (though not at all in the best situation for it) to produce the proof in support of it. He finds, indeed, that of the persons whom he recollects to have been present on these occasions, few have survived the intermediate lapse of four and twenty years. Yet he trusts that some, as well as himself, are yet among the living; and he is positively certain that no man can falsify any material fact here stated. He well remembers, indeed, that there were then, as there are at all times, some who blamed everything done contrary to their own opinion, although their opinions were formed on a very partial knowledge of facts. The censures which have been heralded by such men as Wm. Turner, are nothing but revivals of these half-informed opinions. Mr. George Nicholas, then a very young man, but always a very honest one, was prompted by these persons to bring specific charges against Mr. Jefferson; the heads of these in writing were communicated through a mutual friend to Mr. Jefferson, who committed to writing also the heads of justification on each of them. I well remember this paper, and believe the original of it still exists; and though framed when every real fact was fresh in the knowledge of everyone, this fabricated flight from Richmond was not among the charges stated in this paper, nor any charge against Mr. Jefferson for not fighting singly the troop of horse. Mr. Nicholas candidly relinquished further proceeding. The House of Representatives of Virginia pronounced an honorable sentence of entire approbation of Mr. Jefferson's conduct, and so much the more honorable as themselves had been witness to it. And Mr. George Nicholas took a conspicuous occasion afterwards, of his own free will, and when the matter was entirely at rest, to retract publicly the erroneous opinions he had been led into on that occasion, and to make just reparation by a candid acknowledgment of them.

## THE ANAS[1]

### 1791-1806

*Explanations of the 3 volumes bound in marbled paper*

February 4, 1818

In these 3 volumes will be found copies of the official opinions given in writing by me to General Washington, while I was Secretary of State, with sometimes the documents belonging to the case. Some of these are the rough draughts, some press-copies, some fair ones. In the earlier part of my acting in that office, I took no other note of the passing transactions: but after awhile, I saw the importance of doing it, in aid of my memory. Very often therefore I made memorandums on loose scraps of paper, taken out of my pocket in the moment, and laid by to be copied fair at leisure, which however they hardly ever were. These scraps therefore, ragged, rubbed, and scribbled as they were, I had bound with the others by a binder who came into my cabinet, did it under my own eye, and without the opportunity of reading a single paper.

At this day, after the lapse of 25 years, or more, from their dates, I have given the whole a calm revisal, when the passions of the time are passed away, and the reasons of the transactions act alone on the judgment. Some of the informations I had recorded are now cut out from the rest, because I have seen that they were incorrect, or doubtful, or merely personal or private, with which we have nothing to do. I should perhaps have thought the rest not worth preserving, but for their testimony against the only history of that period which pretends to have been compiled from authentic and unpublished documents. Could these documents, all, be laid open to the public eye, they might be compared, contrasted, weighed, and the truth fairly sifted out of them, for we are not to suppose that every thing found among General Washington's papers is to be taken as gospel truth. Facts indeed of his own writing and inditing, must be believed

[1] The Anas, which Jefferson called "loose scraps," is a kind of diary, particularly important for the years of his service as Secretary of State. Its history is explained in the first two paragraphs.

by all who knew him; and opinions, which were his own, merit veneration and respect; for few men have lived whose opinions were more unbiassed and correct. Not that it is pretended he never felt bias. His passions were naturally strong; but his reason, generally, stronger. But the materials from his own pen make probably an almost insensible part of the mass of papers which fill his presses. He possessed the love, the veneration, and confidence of all. With him were deposited suspicions and certainties, rumors and realities, facts and falsehoods, by all those who were, or who wished to be thought, in correspondence with him, and by the many Anonymi who were ashamed to put their names to their slanders. From such a Congeries history may be made to wear any hue, with which the passions of the compiler, royalist or republican, may chuse to tinge it. Had General Washington himself written from these materials a history of the period they embrace, it would have been a conspicuous monument of the integrity of his mind, the soundness of his judgment, and its powers of discernment between truth and falsehood; principles and pretensions.

But the party feelings of his biographer, to whom after his death the collection was confided, has culled from it a composition as different from what General Washington would have offered, as was the candor of the two characters during the period of the war. The partiality of this pen is displayed in lavishments of praise on certain military characters, who had done nothing military, but who afterwards, and before he wrote, had become heroes in party, although not in war; and in his reserve on the merits of others, who rendered signal services indeed, but did not earn his praise by apostatising in peace from the republican principles for which they had fought in war. It shews itself too in the cold indifference with which a struggle for the most animating of human objects is narrated. No act of heroism ever kindles in the mind of this writer a single aspiration in favor of the holy cause which inspired the bosom, and nerved the arm of the patriot warrior. No gloom of events, no lowering of prospects ever excites a fear for the issue of a contest which was to change the condition of man over the civilized globe. The sufferings inflicted on endeavors to vindicate the rights of humanity are related with all the frigid insensibility with which a monk would have contemplated the victims of an auto da fé. Let no man believe that General Washington ever intended that his papers should be used for the suicide of the cause, for which he had lived, and for which there never was a moment in which he would not have died. The abuse of these materials is chiefly however manifested in the history of the period immediately following the establishment of the present constitution; and nearly with that my memorandums begin. Were a reader of this period to form his idea of it from this history alone, he would suppose the republican party (who were in truth endeavoring to keep the government within the line of the Constitution, and prevent its being monarchised in practice) were a mere set of grumblers, and disorganisers, satisfied with no government, without fixed principles of any, and, like a British parliamentary opposition, gaping after loaves and fishes, and ready to change principles, as well as position, at any time, with their adversaries.

But a short review of facts omitted, or uncandidly stated in this history will shew that the contests of that day were contests of principle, between the advocates of republican, and those of kingly government, and that, had not the former made the efforts they did, our government would have been, even at this early day, a very different thing from what the successful issue of those efforts have made it.

The alliance between the States under the old Articles of Confederation, for the purpose of joint defence against the aggression of Great Britain, was found insufficient, as treaties of alliance generally are, to enforce compliance with their mutual stipulations; and these, once fulfilled, that bond was to expire of itself, and each State to become sovereign and independent in all things. Yet it could not but occur to everyone, that these separate independencies, like the petty States of Greece, would be eternally at war with each other, and would become at length the mere partisans and satellites of the leading powers of Europe. All then must have looked forward to some further bond of union, which would insure eternal peace, and a political system of our own, independent of that of Europe. Whether all should be consolidated into a single government, or each remain independent as to internal matters, and the whole form a single nation as to what was foreign only, and whether that national government should be a monarchy or republic, would of course divide opinions, according to the constitutions, the habits, and the circumstances of each individual. Some officers of the army, as it has always been said and believed (and Steuben and Knox have ever been named as the leading agents), trained to monarchy by military habits, are understood to have proposed to General Washington to decide this great question by the army before its disbandment, and to assume himself the crown on the assurance of their support. The indignation with which he is said to have scouted this parricide proposition was equally worthy of his virtue and wisdom. The next effort was (on suggestion of the same individuals, in the moment of their separation), the establishment of an hereditary order under the name of the Cincinnati, ready prepared by that distinction to be ingrafted into the future frame of government, and placing General Washington still at their head. The General wrote to me on this subject, while I was in Congress at Annapolis, and an extract from my letter is inserted in 5th Marshall's history, page 28. He afterwards called on me at that place on his way to a meeting of the society, and after a whole evening of consultation, he left that place fully determined to use all his endeavors for its total suppression. But he found it so firmly riveted in the affections of the members, that, strengthened as they happened to be by an adventitious occurrence of the moment, he could effect no more than the abolition of its hereditary principle. He called again on his return, and explained to me fully the opposition which had been made, the effect of the occurrence from France, and the difficulty with which its duration had been limited to the lives of the present members. Further details will be found among my papers, in his and my letters, and some in the *Encyclopédie Méthodique et Dictionnaire d'Économie Politique,* communicated by myself to

M. Meusnier, its author, who had made the establishment of this society the ground, in that work, of a libel on our country.

The want of some authority which should procure justice to the public creditors, and an observance of treaties with foreign nations, produced, some time after, the call of a convention of the States at Annapolis. Although, at this meeting, a difference of opinion was evident on the question of a republican or kingly government, yet, so general through the States was the sentiment in favor of the former, that the friends of the latter confined themselves to a course of obstruction only, and delay, to everything proposed; they hoped, that nothing being done, and all things going from bad to worse, a kingly government might be usurped, and submitted to by the people, as better than anarchy and wars internal and external, the certain consequences of the present want of a general government. The effect of their manœuvres, with the defective attendance of Deputies from the States, resulted in the measure of calling a more general convention, to be held at Philadelphia. At this, the same party exhibited the same practices, and with the same views of preventing a government of concord, which they foresaw would be republican, and of forcing through anarchy their way to monarchy. But the mass of that convention was too honest, too wise, and too steady, to be baffled and misled by their manœuvres. One of these was a form of government proposed by Colonel Hamilton, which would have been in fact a compromise between the two parties of royalism and republicanism. According to this, the executive and one branch of the legislature were to be during good behavior, *i.e.,* for life, and the governors of the States were to be named by these two permanent organs. This, however, was rejected; on which Hamilton left the convention, as desperate, and never returned again until near its final conclusion. These opinions and efforts, secret or avowed, of the advocates for monarchy, had begotten great jealousy through the States generally; and this jealousy it was which excited the strong opposition to the conventional constitution; a jealousy which yielded at last only to a general determination to establish certain amendments as barriers against a government either monarchical or consolidated. In what passed through the whole period of these conventions, I have gone on the information of those who were members of them, being absent myself on my mission to France.

I returned from that mission in the first year of the new government, having landed in Virginia in December, 1789, and proceeded to New York in March, 1790, to enter on the office of Secretary of State. Here, certainly, I found a state of things which, of all I had ever contemplated, I the least expected. I had left France in the first year of her revolution, in the fervor of natural rights, and zeal for reformation. My conscientious devotion to these rights could not be heightened, but it had been aroused and excited by daily exercise. The President received me cordially, and my colleagues and the circle of principal citizens apparently with welcome. The courtesies of dinner parties given me, as a stranger newly arrived among them, placed me at once in their familiar society. But I cannot describe the wonder and mortification with which the table conversations filled me. Politics were the chief topic, and a preference of kingly over republican government was evidently the favorite sentiment. An apostate I could not be, nor yet a hypocrite; and I found myself, for the most part, the only advocate on the republican side of the question, unless among the guests there chanced to be some member of that party from the legislative Houses. Hamilton's financial system had then passed. It had two objects; 1st, as a puzzle, to exclude popular understanding and inquiry; 2d, as a machine for the corruption of the legislature; for he avowed the opinion, that man could be governed by one of two motives only, force or interest; force, he observed, in this country was out of the question, and the interests, therefore, of the members must be laid hold of, to keep the legislative in unison with the executive. And with grief and shame it must be acknowledged that his machine was not without effect; that even in this, the birth of our government, some members were found sordid enough to bend their duty to their interests, and to look after personal rather than public good.

It is well known that during the war the greatest difficulty we encountered was the want of money or means to pay our soldiers who fought, or our farmers, manufacturers and merchants, who furnished the necessary supplies of food and clothing for them. After the expedient of paper money had exhausted itself, certificates of debt were given to the individual creditors, with assurance of payment so soon as the United States should be able. But the distresses of these people often obliged them to part with these for the half, the fifth, and even a tenth of their value; and speculators had made a trade of cozening them from the holders by the most fraudulent practices, and persuasions that they would never be paid. In the bill for funding and paying these, Hamilton made no difference between the original holders and the fraudulent purchasers of this paper. Great and just repugnance arose at putting these two classes of creditors on the same footing, and great exertions were used to pay the former the full value, and to the latter, the price only which they had paid, with interest. But this would have prevented the game which was to be played, and for which the minds of greedy members were already tutored and prepared. When the trial of strength on these several efforts had indicated the form in which the bill would finally pass, this being known within doors sooner than without, and especially, than to those who were in distant parts of the Union, the base scramble began. Couriers and relay horses by land, and swift sailing pilot boats by sea, were flying in all directions. Active partners and agents were associated and employed in every State, town, and country neighborhood, and this paper was bought up at five shillings, and even as low as two shillings in the pound, before the holder knew that Congress had already provided for its redemption at par. Immense sums were thus filched from the poor and ignorant, and fortunes accumulated by those who had themselves been poor enough before. Men thus enriched by the dexterity of a leader, would follow of course the chief who was leading them to fortune, and become the zealous instruments of all his enterprises.

This game was over, and another was on the carpet at the moment of my arrival; and to this I was most ignorantly and innocently made to hold the candle. This fiscal maneuvre is well known by the name of the Assumption. Independently of the debts of Congress, the States had during the war contracted separate and heavy debts; and Massachusetts particularly, in an absurd attempt, absurdly conducted, on the British post of Penobscott: and the more debt Hamilton could rake up, the more plunder for his mercenaries. This money, whether wisely or foolishly spent, was pretended to have been spent for general purposes, and ought, therefore, to be paid from the general purse. But it was objected, that nobody knew what these debts were, what their amount, or what their proofs. No matter; we will guess them to be twenty millions. But of these twenty millions, we do not know how much should be reimbursed to one State, or how much to another. No matter; we will guess. And so another scramble was set on foot among the several States, and some got much, some little, some nothing. But the main object was obtained, the phalanx of the Treasury was reinforced by additional recruits. This measure produced the most bitter and angry contest ever known in Congress, before or since the Union of the States. I arrived in the midst of it. But a stranger to the ground, a stranger to the actors on it, so long absent as to have lost all familiarity with the subject, and as yet unaware of its object, I took no concern in it. The great and trying question, however, was lost in the House of Representatives. So high were the feuds excited by this subject, that on its rejection business was suspended. Congress met and adjourned from day to day without doing any thing, the parties being too much out of temper to do business together. The eastern members particularly, who, with Smith from South Carolina, were the principal gamblers in these scenes, threatened a secession and dissolution. Hamilton was in despair. As I was going to the President's one day, I met him in the street. He walked me backwards and forwards before the President's door for half an hour. He painted pathetically the temper into which the legislature had been wrought; the disgust of those who were called the creditor States; the danger of the *secession* of their members, and the separation of the States. He observed that the members of the administration ought to act in concert; that though this question was not of my department, yet a common duty should make it a common concern; that the President was the centre on which all administrative questions ultimately rested, and that all of us should rally around him, and support, with joint efforts, measures approved by him; and that the question having been lost by a small majority only, it was probable that an appeal from me to the judgment and discretion of some of my friends, might effect a change in the vote, and the machine of government, now suspended, might be again set into motion. I told him that I was really a stranger to the whole subject; that not having yet informed myself of the system of finances adopted, I knew not how far this was a necessary sequence; that undoubtedly, if its rejection endangered a dissolution of our Union at this incipient stage, I should deem that the most unfortunate of all consequences, to avert which all partial and temporary evils should be yielded. I proposed to him, however, to dine with me the next day, and I would invite another friend or two, bring them into conference together, and I thought it impossible that reasonable men, consulting together coolly, could fail, by some mutual sacrifices of opinion, to form a compromise which was to save the Union. The discussion took place. I could take no part in it but an exhortatory one, because I was a stranger to the circumstances which should govern it. But it was finally agreed, that whatever importance had been attached to the rejection of this proposition, the preservation of the Union and of concord among the States was more important, and that therefore it would be better that the vote of rejection should be rescinded, to effect which, some members should change their votes. But it was observed that this pill would be peculiarly bitter to the southern States, and that some concomitant measure should be adopted, to sweeten it a little to them. There had before been propositions to fix the seat of government either at Philadelphia, or at Georgetown on the Potomac; and it was thought that by giving it to Philadelphia for ten years, and to Georgetown permanently afterwards, this might, as an anodyne, calm in some degree the ferment which might be excited by the other measure alone. So two of the Potomac members (White and Lee, but White with a revulsion of stomach almost convulsive), agreed to change their votes, and Hamilton undertook to carry the other point. In doing this, the influence he had established over the eastern members, with the agency of Robert Morris with those of the middle States, effected his side of the engagement; and so the Assumption was passed, and twenty millions of stock divided among favored States, and thrown in as a pabulum to the stock-jobbing herd. This added to the number of votaries to the Treasury, and made its chief the master of every vote in the legislature, which might give to the government the direction suited to his political views.

I know well, and so must be understood, that nothing like a majority in Congress had yielded to this corruption. Far from it. But a division, not very unequal, had already taken place in the honest part of that body, between the parties styled republican and federal. The latter being monarchists in principle, adhered to Hamilton of course, as their leader in that principle, and this mercenary phalanx added to them, insured him always a majority in both Houses: so that the whole action of legislature was now under the direction of the Treasury. Still the machine was not complete. The effect of the funding system, and of the Assumption, would be temporary; it would be lost with the loss of the individual members whom it has enriched, and some engine of influence more permanent must be contrived, while these myrmidons were yet in place to carry it through all opposition. This engine was the Bank of the United States. All that history is known, so I shall say nothing about it. While the government remained at Philadelphia, a selection of members of both Houses were constantly kept as directors who, on every question interesting to that institution, or to the views of the federal head, voted at the will of that head; and, together with the stockholding members, could always make the federal vote that of the majority. By this combination, legislative expositions were given to the constitution, and all the administrative laws were shaped on the model of England, and so passed. And from this influence we were not relieved, until the removal from the precincts of the bank, to Washington.

Here then was the real ground of the opposition which was made to the course of administration. Its object was to preserve the legislature pure and independent of the executive, to restrain the administration to republican forms and principles, and not permit the constitution to be construed into a monarchy, and to be warped, in practice, into all the principles and pollutions of their favorite English model. Nor was this an opposition to General Washington. He was true to the republican charge confided to him; and has solemnly and repeatedly protested to me, in our conversations, that he would lose the last drop of his blood in support of it; and he did this the oftener and with the more earnestness, because he knew my suspicions of Hamilton's designs against it, and wished to quiet them. For he was not aware of the drift, or of the effect of Hamilton's schemes. Unversed in financial projects and calculations and budgets, his approbation of them was bottomed on his confidence in the man.

But Hamilton was not only a monarchist, but for a monarchy bottomed on corruption. In proof of this, I will relate an anecdote, for the truth of which I attest the God who made me. Before the President set out on his southern tour in April, 1791, he addressed a letter of the fourth of that month, from Mount Vernon, to the Secretaries of State, Treasury and War, desiring that if any serious and important cases should arise during his absence, they would consult and act on them. And he requested that the Vice President should also be consulted. This was the only occasion on which that officer was ever requested to take part in a cabinet question. Some occasion for consultation arising, I invited those gentlemen (and the Attorney General, as well as I remember), to dine with me, in order to confer on the subject. After the cloth was removed, and our question agreed and dismissed, conversation began on other matters, and by some circumstance, was led to the British constitution, on which Mr. Adams observed, "Purge that constitution of its corruption, and give to its popular branch equality of representation, and it would be the most perfect constitution ever devised by the wit of man." Hamilton paused and said, "Purge it of its corruption, and give to its popular branch equality of representation, and it would become an *impracticable* government: as it stands at present, with all its supposed defects, it is the most perfect government which ever existed." And this was assuredly the exact line which separated the political creeds of these two gentlemen. The one was for two hereditary branches and an honest elective one: the other, for an hereditary King, with a House of Lords and Commons corrupted to his will, and standing between him and the people. Hamilton was, indeed, a singular character. Of acute understanding, disinterested, honest, and honorable in all private transactions, amiable in society, and duly valuing virtue in private life, yet so bewitched and perverted by the British example, as to be under thorough conviction that corruption was essential to the government of a nation. Mr. Adams had originally been a republican. The glare of royalty and nobility, during his mission to England, had made him believe their fascination a necessary ingredient in government; and Shays's rebellion, not sufficiently understood where he then was, seemed to prove that the absence of want and oppression was not a sufficient guarantee of order. His book on the American constitutions having made known his political bias, he was taken up by the monarchical federalists in his absence, and on his return to the United States, he was by them made to believe that the general disposition of our citizens was favorable to monarchy. He here wrote his Davila, as a supplement to a former work, and his election to the Presidency confirmed him in his errors. Innumerable addresses, too, artfully and industriously poured in upon him, deceived him into a confidence that he was on the pinnacle of popularity, when the gulf was yawning at his feet, which was to swallow up him and his deceivers. For when General Washington was withdrawn, these *energumeni* of royalism, kept in check hitherto by the dread of his honesty, his firmness, his patriotism, and the authority of his name, now mounted on the car of State and free from control, like Phaeton on that of the sun, drove headlong and wild, looking neither to right nor left, nor regarding anything but the objects they were driving at; until, displaying these fully, the eyes of the nation were opened, and a general disbandment of them from the public councils took place.

Mr. Adams, I am sure, has been long since convinced of the treacheries with which he was surrounded during his administration. He has since thoroughly seen, that his constituents were devoted to republican government, and whether his judgment is re-settled on its ancient basis, or not, he is conformed as a good citizen to the will of the majority, and would now, I am persuaded, maintain its republican structure with the zeal and fidelity belonging to his character. For even an enemy has said, "He is always an honest man, and often a great one." But in the fervor of the fury and follies of those who made him their stalking horse, no man who did not witness it can form an idea of their unbridled madness, and the terrorism with which they surrounded themselves. The horrors of the French revolution, then raging, aided them mainly, and using that as a raw head and bloody bones, they were enabled by their stratagems of X. Y. Z. in which . . . was a leading mountebank, their tales of tub-plots, ocean massacres, bloody buoys, and pulpit lyings and slanderings, and maniacal ravings of their Gardeners, their Osgoods and parishes, to spread alarm into all but the firmest breasts. Their Attorney General had the impudence to say to a republican member, that deportation must be resorted to, of which, said he, "you republicans have set the example;" thus daring to identify us with the murderous Jacobins of France. These transactions, now recollected but as dreams of the night, were then sad realities; and nothing rescued us from their liberticide effect, but the unyielding opposition of those firm spirits who sternly maintained their post in defiance of terror, until their fellow citizens could be aroused to their own danger, and rally and rescue the standard of the constitution. This has been happily done. Federalism and monarchism have languished from that moment, until their treasonable combinations with the enemies of their country during the late war, their plots of dismembering the Union, and their Hartford convention, have consigned them to the tomb of the dead; and I fondly hope, "we may now truly say, we are all republicans, all federalists," and that the motto of the standard to which our country will forever rally, will be, "federal union, and republican government;" and sure I am we may say, that we are indebted for the preservation of this point of ralliance, to that opposition of which so injurious an idea is so artfully insinuated and excited in this history.

Much of this relation is notorious to the world; and many intimate proofs of it will be found in these notes. From the moment where they end, of my retiring from the administration, the federalists [2] got unchecked hold of General Washington. His memory was already sensibly impaired by age, the firm tone of mind for which he had been remarkable, was beginning to relax, its energy was abated, a listlessness of labor, a desire for tranquillity had crept on him, and a willingness to let others act, and even think for him. Like the rest of mankind, he was disgusted with atrocities of the French revolution, and was not sufficiently aware of the difference between the rabble who were used as instruments of their perpetration, and the steady and rational character of the American people, in which he had not sufficient confidence. The opposition too of the republicans to the British treaty, and the zealous support of the federalists in that unpopular but favorite measure of theirs, had made him all their own. Understanding, moreover, that I disapproved of that treaty, and copiously nourished with falsehoods by a malignant neighbor of mine, who ambitioned to be his correspondent, he had become alienated from myself personally, as from the republican body generally of his fellow-citizens; and he wrote the letters to Mr. Adams and Mr. Carroll, over which, in devotion to his imperishable fame, we must forever weep as monuments of mortal decay.

*February 4th,* 1818.

## *The Anas*

August the 13th, 1791. Notes of a conversation between Alexander Hamilton and Thomas Jefferson. Th: Jefferson mentioned to him a letter received from John Adams, disavowing Publicola, and denying that he ever entertained a wish to bring this country under an hereditary executive, or introduce an hereditary branch of Legislature, &c. See his letter. Alexander Hamilton condemning Mr. Adams' writings, and most particularly Davila, as having a tendency to weaken the present government, declared in substance as follows: "I own it is my own opinion, though I do not publish it in Dan or Bersheba, that the present government is not that which will answer the ends of society, by giving stability and protection to its rights, and that it will probably be found expedient to go into the British form. However, since we have undertaken the experiment, I am for giving it a fair course, whatever my expectations may be. The success, indeed, so far, is greater than I had expected, and therefore, at present, success seems more possible than it had done heretofore, and there are still other and other stages of improvement which, if the present does not succeed, may be tried, and ought to be tried, before we give up the republican

[2] See conversation with General Washington, October 1, 1792, pp. 1227-29.

form altogether; for that mind must be really depraved, which would not prefer the equality of political rights, which is the foundation of pure republicanism, if it can be obtained consistently with order. Therefore, whoever by his writings disturbs the present order of things, is really blameable, however pure his intentions may be, and he was sure Mr. Adams' were pure." This is the substance of a declaration made in much more lengthy terms, and which seemed to be more formal than usual for a private conversation between two, and as if intended to qualify some less guarded expressions which had been dropped on former occasions. Th: Jefferson has committed it to writing in the moment of A. Hamilton's leaving the room.

December the 25th, 1791. Colonel Gunn (of Georgia) dining the other day with Colonel Hamilton, said to him, with that plain freedom he is known to use, "I wish, Sir, you would advise your friend King, to observe some kind of consistency in his votes. There has been scarcely a question before the Senate on which he has not voted both ways. On the representation bill, for instance, he first voted for the proposition of the Rrepesentatives, and ultimately voted against it." "Why," says Colonel Hamilton, "I'll tell you as to that, Colonel Gunn, that it never was intended that bill should pass." Gunn told this to Butler, who told it to Th: Jefferson.

### CONVERSATIONS WITH THE PRESIDENT

February the 28th, 1792. I was to have been with him long enough before three o'clock (which was the hour and day he received visits), to have opened to him a proposition for doubling the velocity of the post riders, who now travel about fifty miles a day, and might, without difficulty, go one hundred, and for taking measures (by way bills) to know where the delay is, when there is any. I was delayed by business, so as to have scarcely time to give him the outlines. I run over them rapidly, and observed afterwards, that I had hitherto never spoken to him on the subject of the post office, not knowing whether it was considered as a revenue law, or a law for the general accommodation of the citizens: that the law just passed seemed to have removed the doubt, by declaring that the whole profits of the office should be applied to extending the posts, and that even the past profits should be refunded by the treasury for the same purpose: that I therefore conceive it was now in the department of the Secretary of State: that I thought it would be advantageous so to declare it for another reason, to wit: that the department of the Treasury possessed already such an influence as to swallow up the whole executive powers, and that even the future Presidents (not supported by the weight of character which himself possessed), would not be able to make head against this department. That in urging this measure I had certainly no personal interest, since, if I was supposed to have any appetite for power, yet as my career would certainly be exactly as short as his own, the intervening time was too short to be an object. My real wish was to avail the public of every occasion, during the residue of the President's period, to place things on a safe footing. He was now called on to attend his company, and he desired me to come and breakfast with him the next morning.

February the 29th. I did so; and after breakfast we retired to his room, and I unfolded my plan for the post office, and after such an approbation of it as he usually permitted himself on the first presentment of any idea, and desiring me to commit it to writing, he, during that pause of conversation which follows a business closed, said in an affectionate tone, that he had felt much concern at an expression which dropped from me yesterday, and which marked my intention of retiring when he should. That as to himself, many motives obliged him to it. He had, through the whole course of the war, and most particularly at the close of it, uniformly declared his resolution to retire from public affairs, and never to act in any public office; that he had retired under that firm resolution: that the government, however, which had been formed, being found evidently too inefficacious, and it being supposed that his aid was of some consequence towards bringing the people to consent to one of sufficient efficacy for their own good, he consented to come into the convention, and on the same motive, after much pressing, to take a part in the new government, and get it under way. That were he to continue longer, it might give room to say, that having tasted the sweets of office, he could not do without them: that he really felt himself growing old, his bodily health less firm, his memory, always bad, becoming worse, and perhaps the other faculties of his mind showing a decay to others of which he was insensible himself; that this apprehension particularly oppressed him: that he found, moreover, his activity lessened, business therefore more irksome, and tranquility and retirement become an irresistible passion. That however he felt himself obliged, for these reasons, to retire from the government, yet he should consider it as unfortunate, if that should bring on the retirement of the great officers of the government, and that this might produce a shock on the public mind of dangerous consequence.

I told him that no man had ever had less desire of entering into public offices than myself; that the circumstance of a perilous war, which brought every thing into danger, and called for all the services which every citizen could render, had induced me to undertake the administration of the government of Virginia; that I had both before and after refused repeated appointments of Congress to go abroad in that sort of office, which, if I had consulted my own gratification, would almost have been the most agreeable to me; that at the end of two years, I resigned the government of Virginia, and retired with a firm resolution never more to appear in public life; that a domestic loss, however, happened, and made me fancy that absence and a change of scene for a time might be expedient for me; that I therefore accepted a foreign appointment, limited to two years; that at the close of that, Doctor Franklin having left France, I was appointed to supply his place, which I had accepted, and though I continued in it three or four years, it was under the constant idea of remaining only a year or two longer; that the revolution in France coming on, I had so interested myself in the event of that, that when obliged to bring my family home, I had still an idea of returning and awaiting the close of that, to fix the era of my final retirement; that on my arrival here I found he had appointed me to my present office; that he knew I had not come into it without some reluctance; that it was, on my part, a sacrifice of inclination to the opinion that I might be more serviceable here than in France, and with a firm resolution in my mind, to indulge my constant wish for retirement at no very distant day; that when, therefore, I had received his letter, written from Mount Vernon, on his way to Carolina and Georgia (April the 1st, 1791), and discovered, from an expression in that, that he meant to retire from the government ere long, and as to the precise epoch there could be no doubt, my mind was immediately made up, to make that the epoch of my own retirement from those labors of which I was heartily tired. That, however, I did not believe there was any idea in any of my brethren in the administration of retiring; that on the contrary, I had perceived at a late meeting of the trustees of the sinking fund, that the Secretary of the Treasury had developed the plan he intended to pursue, and that it embraced years in its view.

He said, that he considered the Treasury department as a much more limited one, going only to the single object of revenue, while that of the Secretary of State, embracing nearly all the objects of administration, was much more important, and the retirement of the officer therefore, would be more noticed: that though the government had set out with a pretty general good will of the public, yet that symptoms of dissatisfaction had lately shown themselves far beyond what he could have expected, and to what height these might arise, in case of too great a change in the administration, could not be foreseen.

I told him, that in my opinion, there was only a single source of these discontents. Though they had indeed appeared to spread themselves over the War department also, yet I considered that as an overflowing only from their real channel, which would never have taken place, if they had not first been generated in another department, to wit, that of the Treasury. That a system had there been contrived, for deluging the States with paper money instead of gold and silver, for withdrawing our citizens from the pursuits of commerce, manufactures, buildings, and other branches of useful industry, to occupy themselves and their capitals in a species of gambling, destructive of morality, and which had introduced its poison into the government itself. That it was a fact, as certainly known as that he and I were then conversing, that particular members of the legislature, while those laws were on the carpet, had feathered their nests with paper, had then voted for the laws, and constantly since lent all the energy of their talents, and instrumentality of their offices, to the establishment and enlargement of this system; that they had chained it about our necks for a great length of time, and in order to keep the game in their hands had, from time to time, aided in making such legislative constructions of the constitution, as made it a very different thing from what the people thought they had submitted to; that they had now brought forward a proposition far beyond any one ever yet advanced, and to which the eyes of many were turned, as the decision which was to let us know, whether we live under a limited or an unlimited government. He asked me to what proposition I alluded? I answered, to that in the report on manufactures, which, under color of giving *bounties* for the encouragement of particular manufactures, meant to establish the doctrine, that the power given by the constitution to collect taxes to provide for the *general welfare* of the United States, permitted Congress to take everything under their management which *they* should deem for the *public welfare,* and which is susceptible of the application of money; consequently, that the subsequent enumeration of their powers was not the description to which resort must be had, and did not at all constitute the limits of their authority; that this was a very different question from that of the bank, which was thought an incident to an enumerated power; that, therefore, this decision was expected with great anxiety; that, indeed, I hoped the proposition would be rejected, believing there was a majority in both Houses against it, and that if it should be, it would be considered as a proof that things were returning into their true channel; and that, at any rate, I looked forward to the broad representation which would shortly take place, for keeping the general constitution on its true ground; and that this would remove a great deal of the discontent which had shown itself. The conversation ended with this last topic. It is here stated nearly as much at length as it really was; the expressions preserved where I could recollect them, and their substance always faithfully stated.

March 1, 1792.

On the 2d of January, 1792, Messrs. Fitzsimmons and Gerry (among others) dined with me. These two staid, with a Mr. Larned of Connecticut, after the company was gone. We got on the subject of references by the legislature to the Heads of departments, considering their mischief in every direction. Gerry and Fitzsimmons clearly opposed to them.

Two days afterwards (January the 4th), Mr. Bourne from Rhode Island presented a memorial from his State, complaining of inequality in the Assumption, and moved to refer it to the Secretary of the Treasury. Fitzsimmons, Gerry and others opposed it; but it was carried.

January the 19th. Fitzsimmons moved, that the *President of the United States* be requested to direct the Secretary of the Treasury, to lay before the House information to enable the legislature to judge of the additional revenue necessary on the increase of the military establishment. The House, on debate, struck out the words, "President of the United States."

March the 7th. The subject resumed. An animated debate took place on the tendency of references to the Heads of departments; and it seemed that a great majority would be against it; the House adjourned. Treasury greatly alarmed, and much industry supposed to be used before next morning, when it was brought on again, and debated through the day, and on the question, the Treasury carried it by thirty-one to twenty-seven; but deeply wounded, since it was seen that all Pennsylvania, except Jacobs, voted against the reference; that Tucker of South Carolina voted for it, and Sumpter absented himself, debauched for the moment only, because of the connection of the question with a further Assumption which South Carolina favored; but showing that they never were to be counted on among the Treasury votes. Some others absented themselves. Gerry changed sides. On the whole, it showed that Treasury influence was tottering.

Committed to writing this 10th of March, 1792.

March the 11th, 1792. Consulted verbally by the President, on whom a committee of the Senate (Izard, Morris, and King) are to wait tomorrow morning, to know whether he will think it proper to redeem our Algerine captives, and make a treaty with the Algerines, on the single vote of the Senate, without taking that of the Representatives.

My opinions run on the following heads:

We must go to Algiers with cash in our hands. Where shall we get it? By loan? By converting money now in the treasury?

Probably a loan might be obtained on the President's authority; but as this could not be repaid without a subsequent act of legislature, the Representatives might refuse it. So if money in the treasury be converted, they may refuse to sanction it.

The subsequent approbation of the Senate being necessary to validate a treaty, they expect to be consulted beforehand, if the case admits.

So the subsequent act of the Representatives being necessary where money is given, why should not they expect to be consulted in like manner, when the case admits. A treaty is a law of the land. But prudence will point out this difference to be attended to in making them; *viz.,* where a treaty contains such articles only as will go into execution of themselves, or be carried into execution by the judges, they may be safely made; but where there are articles which require a law to be passed afterwards by the legislature, great caution is requisite.

For example; the consular convention with France required a very small legislative regulation. This convention was unanimously ratified by the Senate. Yet the same identical men threw by the law to enforce it at the last session, and the Representatives at this session have placed it among the laws which they may take up or not, at their own convenience, as if that was a higher motive than the public faith.

Therefore, against hazarding this transaction without the sanction of both Houses.

The President concurred. The Senate express the motive for this proposition, to be a fear that the Representatives would not keep the secret. He has no opinion of the secrecy of the Senate. In this very case, Mr. Izard made the communication to him, sitting next to him at table, on one hand, while a lady (Mrs. McLane) was on his other hand, and the French minister next to her; and as Mr. Izard got on with his communication, his voice kept rising, and his stutter bolting the words out loudly at intervals, so that the minister might hear if he would. He said he had a great mind at one time to have got up, in order to put a stop to Mr. Izard.

March the 11th, 1792. Mr. Sterret tells me, that sitting round a fire the other day with four or five others [Mr. Smith of South Carolina was one], somebody mentioned that the murderers of Hogeboom, sheriff of Columbia county, New York, were acquitted. "Aye," says Smith, "this is what comes of your damned *trial by jury.*"

1791. Towards the latter end of November, Hamilton had drawn Ternant into a conversation on the subject of the treaty of commerce recommended by the National Assembly of France to be negotiated with us, and, as he had no ready instructions on the subject, he led him into a proposal that Ternant should take the thing up as a volunteer with me, that we should arrange conditions, and let them go for confirmation or refusal. Hamilton communicated this to the President, who came into it, and proposed it to me. I disapproved of it, observing, that such a volunteer project would be binding on us, and not them; that it would enable them to find out how far we would go, and avail themselves of it. However, the President thought it worth trying, and I acquiesced. I prepared a plan of treaty for exchanging the privileges of native subjects, and fixing all duties forever as they now stood. Hamilton did not like this way of fixing the duties, because, he said, many articles here would bear to be raised, and therefore, he would prepare a tariff. He did so, raising duties for the French, from twenty-five to fifty per cent. So they were to give us the privileges of native subjects, and we, as a compensation, were to make them pay higher duties. Hamilton, having made his arrangements with Hammond to pretend that though he had no powers to conclude a treaty of commerce, yet his general commission authorized him to enter into the discussion of one, then proposed to the President at one of our meetings, that the business should be taken up with Hammond in the same informal way. I now discovered the trap which he had laid, by first getting the President into that step with Ternant. I opposed the thing warmly. Hamilton observed, if we did it with Ternant we should also with Hammond. The President thought this reasonable. I desired him to recollect, I had been against it with Ternant, and only acquiesced under his opinion. So the matter went off as to both. His scheme evidently was, to get us engaged first with Ternant, merely that he might have a pretext to engage us on the same ground with Hammond, taking care, at the same time, by an extravagant tariff, to render it impossible we should come to any conclusion with Ternant: probably meaning, at the same time, to propose terms so favorable to Great Britain, as would attach us to that country by treaty. On one of those occasions he asserted, that our commerce with Great Britain and her colonies was put on a much more favorable footing than with France and her colonies. I therefore prepared the tabular comparative view of the footing of our commerce with those nations, which see among my papers. See also my project of a treaty and Hamilton's tariff.

Committed to writing March the 11th, 1792.

It was observable, that whenever, at any of our consultations, anything was proposed as to Great Britain, Hamilton had constantly ready something which Mr. Hammond had communicated to him, which suited the subject and proved the intimacy of their communications; insomuch, that I believe he communicated to Hammond all our views, and knew from him, in return, the views of the British court. Many evidences of this occurred; I will state some. I delivered to the President my report of instructions for Carmichael and Short, on the subject of navigation, boundary and commerce, and desired him to submit it to Hamilton. Hamilton made several just criticisms on different parts of it. But where I asserted that the United States had no right to alienate an inch of the territory of any State, he attacked and denied the doctrine. See my report, his note, and my answer. A few days after came to hand Kirkland's letter, informing us that the British, at Niagara, expected to run a new line between themselves and us; and the reports of Pond and Stedman, informing us it was understood at Niagara, that Captain Stevenson had been sent here by Simcoe to settle that plan with Hammond. Hence Hamilton's attack of the principle I had laid down, in order to prepare the way for this new line. See minute of March the 9th. Another proof. At one of our consultations, about the last of December, I mentioned that I wished to give in my report on commerce, in which I could not avoid recommending a commercial retaliation against Great Britain. Hamilton opposed it violently; and among other arguments, observed, that it was of more importance to us to have the posts than to commence a commercial war; that this, and this alone, would free us from the expense of the Indian wars; that it would therefore be the height of imprudence in us, while treating for the surrender of the posts, to engage in anything which would irritate them; that if we did so, they would naturally say, "These people mean war, let us therefore hold what we have in our hands." This argument struck me forcibly, and I said, "If there is a hope of obtaining the posts, I agree it would be imprudent to risk that hope by a commercial retaliation. I will, therefore, wait till Mr. Hammond gives me in his assignment of breaches, and if that gives a glimmering of hope that they mean to surrender the posts, I will not give in my report till the next session." Now, Hammond had received my assignment of breaches on the 15th of December, and about the 22d or 23d had made me an apology for not having been able to send me his counter-assignment of breaches; but in terms which showed I might expect it in a few days. From the moment it escaped my lips in the presence of Hamilton, that I would not give in my report till I should see Hammond's counter-complaint, and judge if there was a hope of the posts, Hammond never said a word to me on any occasion, as to the time he should be ready. At length the President got out of patience, and insisted I should jog him. This I did on the 21st of February, at the President's assembly: he immediately promised I should have it in a few days, and accordingly, on the 5th of March I received it.

Written March the 11th, 1792.

March the 12th, 1792. Sent for by the President, and desired to bring the letter he had signed to the King of France. Went. He said the House of Representatives had, on Saturday, taken up the communication he had made of the King's letter to him, and come to a vote in their own name; that he did not expect this when he sent this message and the letter, otherwise he would have sent the message without the letter, as I had proposed. That he apprehended the legislature would be endeavoring to invade the executive. I told him, I had understood the House had resolved to request him to join their congratulations to his on the completion and acceptance of the constitution; on which part of the vote, there were only two dissentients (Barnwell and Benson); that the vote was thirty-five to sixteen on that part which expressed an approbation of the wisdom of the constitution; that in the letter he had signed, I had avoided saying a word in approbation of the constitution, not knowing whether the King, in his heart, approved it. Why, indeed, says he, I begin to doubt very much of the affairs of France; there are papers from London as late as the 10th of January, which represent them as going into confusion. He read over the letter he had signed, found there was not a word which could commit his judgment about the constitution, and gave it to me back again. This is one of many proofs I have had, of his want of confidence in the event of the French revolution. The fact is, that Gouverneur Morris, a high-flying monarchy man, shutting his eyes and his faith to every fact against his wishes, and believing everything he desires to be true, has kept the President's mind constantly poisoned with his forebodings. That the President wishes the revolution may be established, I believe from several indications. I remember, when I received the news of the King's flight and capture, I first told him of it at his assembly. I never saw him so much dejected by any event in my life. He expressed clearly, on this occasion, his disapprobation of the legislature referring things to the Heads of departments.

Written March the 12th.

*Eodem die.* Ten o'clock, A.M. The preceding was about nine o'clock. The President now sends Lear to me, to ask what answer he shall give to the committee, and particularly, whether he shall add to it, that, "in making the communication, it was not his expectation that the House should give any answer." I told Mr. Lear that I thought the House had a right, independently of legislation, to express sentiments on other subjects. That when these subjects did not belong to any other branch particularly, they would publish them by their own authority; that in the present case, which respected a foreign nation, the President being the organ of our nation with other nations, the House would satisfy their duty, if, instead of a direct communication, they should pass their sentiments through the President; that if expressing a sentiment were really an invasion of the executive power, it was so faint a one, that it would be difficult to demonstrate it to the public, and to a public partial to the French revolution, and not disposed to consider the approbation of it from any quarter as improper. That the Senate, indeed, had given many indications of their wish to invade the executive power: the Representatives had done it in one case, which was indeed mischievous and alarming; that of giving orders to the Heads of the executive departments, without consulting the President; but that the late vote for directing the Secretary of the Treasury to report ways and means, though carried, was carried by so small a majority, and with the aid of members so notoriously under a local influence on that question, as to give a hope that the practice would be arrested, and the constitutional course be taken up, of asking the President to have information laid before them. But that in the present instance, it was so far from being clearly an invasion of the executive, and would be so little approved by the general voice, that I could not advise the President to express any dissatisfaction at the vote of the House; and I gave Lear, in writing, what I thought should be his answers. See it.

March the 31st. A meeting at the President's; present, Thomas Jefferson, Alexander Hamilton, Henry Knox and Edmund Randolph. The subject was the resolution of the House of Representatives, of March the 27th, to appoint a committee to inquire into the causes of the failure of the late expedition under Major General St. Clair, with the power to call for such persons, papers and records, as may be necessary to assist their inquiries. The committee had written to Knox for the original letters, instructions, &c. The President had called us to consult, merely because it was the first example, and he wished that so far as it should become a precedent, it should be rightly conducted. He neither acknowledged nor denied, nor even doubted the propriety of what the House were doing, for he had not thought upon it, nor was acquainted with subjects of this kind: he could readily conceive there might be papers of so secret a nature, as that they ought not to be given up. We were not prepared, and wished time to think and inquire.

April the 2d. Met again at the President's, on the same subject. We had all considered, and were of one mind, first, that the House was an inquest, and therefore might institute inquiries. Second, that it might call for papers generally. Third, that the executive ought to communicate such papers as the public good would permit, and ought to refuse those, the disclosure of which would injure the public: consequently were to exercise a discretion. Fourth, that neither the committee nor House had a right to call on the Head of a department, who and whose papers were under the President alone; but that the committee should instruct their chairman to move the House to address the President. We had principally consulted the proceedings of the Commons in the case of Sir Robert Walpole, 13 Chandler's Debates. For the first point, see pages 161, 170, 172, 183, 187, 207; for the second, pages 153, 173, 207; for the third, 81, 173, appendix page 44; fourth, page 246. Note; Hamilton agreed with us in all these points, except as to the power of the House to call on Heads of departments. He observed, that as to his department, the act constituting it had made it subject to Congress in some points, but he thought himself not so far subject, as to be obliged to produce all the papers they might call for. They might demand secrets of a very mischievous nature. [Here I thought he began to fear they would go on to examining how far their own members and other persons in the government had been dabbling in stocks, banks, &c., and that he probably would choose in this case to deny their power; and, in short, he endeavored to place himself subject to the House, when the executive should propose what he did not like, and subject to the executive, when the House should propose anything disagreeable]. I observed here a difference between the British parliament and our Congress; that the former was a legislature, an inquest, and a council (S. C. page 91), for the King. The latter was, by the constitution, a legislature and an inquest, but not a council. Finally agreed, to speak separately to the members of the committee, and bring them by persuasion into the right channel. It was agreed in this case, that there was not a paper which might not be properly produced; that copies only should be sent, with an assurance, that if they should desire it, a clerk should attend with the originals to be verified by themselves. The committee were Fitzsimmons, Steele, Mercer, Clarke, Sedgwick, Giles and Vining.

April the 9th, 1792. The President had wished to redeem our captives at Algiers, and to make peace with them on paying an annual tribute. The Senate were willing to approve this, but unwilling to have the lower House applied to previously to furnish the money; they wished the President to take the money from the treasury, or open a loan for it. They thought that to consult the Representatives on one occasion, would give them a handle always to claim it, and would let them into a participation of the power of making treaties, which the constitution had given exclusively to the President and Senate. They said too, that if the particular sum was voted by the Representatives, it would not be a secret. The President had no confidence in the secrecy of the Senate, and did not choose to take money from the treasury or to borrow. But he agreed he would enter into provisional treaties with the Algerines, not to be binding on us till ratified here. I prepared questions for consultation with the Senate, and added, that the Senate were to be apprized, that on the return of the provisional treaty, and after they should advise the ratification, he would not have the seal put to it till the two Houses should vote the money. He asked me, if the treaty stipulating a sum and ratified by him, with the advice of the Senate, would not be good under the constitution, and obligatory on the Representatives to furnish the money? I answered it certainly would, and that it would be the duty of the Representatives to raise the money; but that they might decline to do what was their duty, and I thought it might be incautious to commit himself by a ratification with a foreign nation, where he might be left in the lurch in the execution: it was possible too, to conceive a treaty, which it would not be their duty to provide for. He said that he did not like throwing too much into democratic hands, that if they would not do what the constitution called on them to do, the government would be at an end, and must *then assume another form*. He stopped here; and I kept silence to see whether he would say anything more in the same line, or add any qualifying expression to soften what he had said; but he did neither.

I had observed, that wherever the agency of either, or both Houses would be requisite subsequent to a treaty, to carry it into effect, it would be prudent to consult them previously, if the occasion admitted. That thus it was, we were in the habit of consulting the Senate previously, when the occasion permitted, because their subsequent ratification would be necessary. That there was the same reason for consulting the lower House previously, where they were to be called on afterwards, and especially in the case of money, as they held the purse strings, and would be jealous of them. However, he desired me to strike out the intimation that the seal would not be put till both Houses should have voted the money.

April the 6th. The President called on me before breakfast, and first introduced some other matter, then fell on the representation bill, which he had now in his possession for the tenth day. I had before given him my opinion in writing, that the method of apportionment was contrary to the constitution. He agreed that it was contrary to the common understanding of that instrument, and to what was understood at the time by the makers of it; that yet it would bear the construction which the bill put, and he observed that the vote for and against the bill was perfectly geographical, a northern against a southern vote, and he feared he should be thought to be taking side with a southern party. I admitted the motive of delicacy, but that it should not induce him to do wrong; urged the dangers to which the scramble for the fractionary members would always lead. He here expressed his fear that there would, ere long, be a separation of the Union; that the public mind seemed dissatisfied and tending to this. He went home, sent for Randolph, the Attorney General, desired him to get Mr. Madison immediately and come to me, and if we three concurred in opinion that he should negative the bill, he desired to hear nothing more about it, but that we would draw the instrument for him to sign. They came. Our minds had been before made up. We drew the instrument. Randolph carried it to him, and told him we all concurred in it. He walked with him to the door, and as if he still wished to get off, he said, "And you say you approve of this yourself." "Yes, Sir," says Randolph, "I do upon my honor." He sent it to the House of Representatives instantly. A few of the hottest friends of the bill expressed passion, but the majority were satisfied, and both in and out of doors it gave pleasure to have, at length, an instance of the negative being exercised.

Written this the 9th of April.

July the 10th, 1792. My letter of —— to the President, directed to him at Mount Vernon, had not found him there, but came to him here. He told me of this, and that he would take an occasion of speaking with me on the subject. He did so this day. He began by observing that he had put it off from day to day because the subject was painful, to wit, his remaining in office, which that letter solicited. He said that the declaration he had made when he quitted his military command, of never again entering into public life, was sincere. That, however, when he was called on to come forward to set the present government in motion, it appeared to him that circumstances were so changed as to justify a change in his resolution: he was made to believe that in two years all would be well in motion, and he might retire. At the end of two years he found some things still to be done. At the end of the third year, he thought it was not worth while to disturb the course of things, as in one year more his office would expire, and he was decided then to retire. Now he was told there would still be danger in it. Certainly, if he thought so, he would conquer his longing for retirement. But he feared it would be said his former professions of retirement had been mere affectation, and that he was like other men, when once in office he could not quit it. He was sensible, too, of a decay of his hearing, perhaps his other faculties might fall off and he not be sensible of it. That with respect to the existing causes of uneasiness, he thought there were suspicions against a particular party, which had been carried a great deal too far; there might be *desires,* but he did not believe there were *designs* to change the form of government into a monarchy; that there might be a few who wished it in the higher walks of life, particularly in the great cities, but that the main body of the people in the eastern States were as steadily for republicanism as in the southern. That the pieces lately published, and particularly in Freneau's paper, seemed to have in view the exciting opposition to the government. That this had taken place in Pennsylvania as to the excise law, according to information he had received from General Hand. That they tended to produce a separation of the Union, the most dreadful of all calamities, and that whatever tended to produce anarchy, tended, of course, to produce a resort to monarchical government. He considered those papers as attacking him directly, for he must be a fool indeed to swallow the little sugar plums here and there thrown out to him. That in condemning the administration of the government, they condemned him, for if they thought there were measures pursued contrary to his sentiments, they must conceive him too careless to attend to them, or too stupid to understand them. That though, indeed, he had signed many acts which he did not approve in all their parts, yet he had never put his name to one which he did not think, on the whole, was eligible. That as to the bank, which had been an act of so much complaint, until there was some infallible criterion of reason, a difference of opinion must be tolerated. He did not believe the discontents extended far from the seat of government. He had seen and spoken with many people in Maryland and Virginia in his late journey. He found the people contented and happy. He wished, however, to be better informed on this head. If the discontents were more extensive than he supposed, it might be that the desire that he should remain in the government was not general.

My observations to him tended principally to enforce the topics of my letter. I will not, therefore, repeat them, except where they produced observations from him. I said that the two great complaints were, that the national debt was unnecessarily increased, and that it had furnished the means of corrupting both branches of the legislature; that he must know, and everybody knew, there was a considerable squadron in both, whose votes were devoted to the paper and stock-jobbing interest, that the names of a weighty number were known, and several others suspected on good grounds. That on examining the votes of these men, they would be found uniformly for every Treasury measure, and that as most of these measures had been carried by small majorities, they were carried by these very votes. That, therefore, it was a cause of just uneasiness, when we saw a legislature legislating for their own interests, in opposition to those of the people. He said not a word on the corruption of the legislature, but took up the other point, defended the Assumption, and argued that it had not increased the debt, for that all of it was honest debt. He justified the excise law, as one of the best laws which could be passed, as nobody would pay the tax who did not choose to do it. With respect to the increase of the debt by the Assumption, I observed to him that what was meant and objected to was, that it increased the debt of the General Government, and carried it beyond the possibility of payment. That if the balances had been settled, and the debtor States directed to pay their deficiencies to the creditor States, they would have done it easily, and by resources of taxation in their power, and acceptable to the people; by a direct tax in the south, and an excise in the north. Still, he said, it would be paid by the people. Finding him decided, I avoided entering into argument with him on those points.

Sept. the 30th, 1792. The constitution as agreed to till a fortnight before the Convention rose, was such a one as he would have set his hand and heart to. 1st. The President was to be elected for seven years. Then ineligible for seven years more. 2d. Rotation in the Senate. 3d. A vote of two-thirds in the legislature on particular subjects, and expressly on that of navigation. The three New England States were constantly with us in all questions (Rhode Island not there, and New York seldom), so that it was these three States, with the five southern ones, against Pennsylvania, New Jersey, and Delaware.

With respect to the importation of slaves, it was left to Congress. This disturbed the two southernmost States, who knew that Congress would immediately suppress the importation of slaves. These two States, therefore, struck up a bargain with the three New England States. If they would join to admit slaves for some years, the southernmost States would join in changing the clause which required two-thirds of the legislature in any vote. It was done. These articles were changed accordingly, and from that moment the two southernmost States, and the three northern ones, joined Pennsylvania, New Jersey and Delaware, and made the majority eight to three against us, instead of eight to three for us, as it had been through the whole Convention. Under this coalition, the great principles of the constitution were changed in the last days of the Convention.

Anecdote. Yates, Lawsing and Hamilton represented New York. Yates and Lawsing never voted in one single instance with Hamilton, who was so much mortified at it that he went home. When the season for courts came on, Yates, a judge, and Lawsing, a lawyer, went to attend their courts. Then Hamilton returned.

Anecdote. The constitution as agreed at first was, that amendments might be proposed either by Congress or the legislatures. A committee was appointed to digest and redraw. Gouverneur Morris and King were of the committee. One morning Gouverneur Morris moved an instrument for certain alterations (not one-half the members yet come in). In a hurry and without understanding, it was agreed to. The committee reported so that Congress should have the exclusive power of proposing amendments. George Mason observed it on the report, and opposed it. King denied the construction. Mason demonstrated it, and asked the committee by what authority they had varied what had been agreed. Gouverneur Morris then impudently got up, and said, by authority of the Convention, and produced the blind instruction before mentioned, which was unknown by one-half of the House, and not till then understood by the other. They then restored it, as it originally stood.

He said he considered Hamilton as having done us more injury than Great Britain and all her fleets and armies. That his (Mason's) plan of settling our debts would have been something in this way. He would have laid as much tax as could be paid without oppressing the people;—particularly he would have laid an impost of about the amount of the first, laid by Congress, but somewhat different in several of its articles. He would have suspended all application of it one year, during which an office should have been open to register unalienated certificates. At the end of the year he would have appropriated his revenue. 1st. To pay the civil list. 2d. The interest of these certificates. 3d. Instalments of the principal. 4th. A surplus to buy up the alienated certificates, still avoiding to make any other provision for these last. By the time the unalienated certificates should have been all paid, he supposed half the alienated ones would have been bought up at market. He would then have proceeded to redeem the residue of them.

Bladensburg, October the 1st, 1792. This morning, at Mount Vernon, I had the following conversation with the President. He opened it by expressing his regret at the resolution in which I appeared so fixed, in the letter I had written him, of retiring from public affairs. He said, that he should be extremely sorry that I should do it, as long as he was in office, and that he could not see where he should find another character to fill my office. That, as yet, he was quite undecided whether to retire in March or not. His inclinations led him strongly to do it. Nobody disliked more the ceremonies of his office, and he had not the least taste or gratification in the execution of its functions. That he was happy at home alone, and that his presence there was now peculiarly called for by the situation of Major Washington, whom he thought irrecoverable, and should he get well, he would remove into another part of the country, which might better agree with him. That he did not believe his presence necessary; that there were other characters who would do the business as well or better. Still, however, if his aid was thought necessary to save the cause to which he had devoted his life principally, he would make the sacrifice of a longer continuance. That he therefore reserved himself for future decision, as his declaration would be in time if made a month before the day of election. He had desired Mr. Lear to find out from conversation, without appearing to make the inquiry, whether any other person would be desired by any body.

He had informed him, he judged from conversations that it was the universal desire he should continue, and he believed that those who expressed a doubt of his continuance, did it in the language of apprehension, and not of desire. But this, says he, is only from the north; it may be very different in the south. I thought this meant as an opening to me to say what was the sentiment in the south, from which quarter I came. I told him, that as far as I knew, there was but one voice there, which was for his continuance. That as to myself, I had ever preferred the pursuits of private life to those of public, which had nothing in them agreeable to me. I explained to him the circumstances of the war which had first called me into public life, and those following the war, which had called me from a retirement on which I had determined. That I had constantly kept my eye on my own home, and could no longer refrain from returning to it. As to himself, his presence was important; that he was the only man in the United States who possessed the confidence of the whole; that government was founded in opinion and confidence, and that the longer he remained, the stronger would become the habits of the people in submitting to the government, and in thinking it a thing to be maintained; that there was no other person who would be thought anything more than the head of a party. He then expressed his concern at the difference which he found to subsist between the Secretary of the Treasury and myself, of which he said he had not been aware. He knew, indeed, that there was a marked difference in our political sentiments, but he had never suspected it had gone so far in producing a personal difference, and he wished he could be the mediator to put an end to it. That he thought it important to preserve the check of my opinions in the administration, in order to keep things in their proper channel, and prevent them from going too far. That as to the idea of transforming this government into a monarchy, he did not believe there were ten men in the United States whose opinions were worth attention, who entertained such a thought. I told him there were many more than he imagined. I recalled to his memory a dispute at his own table, a little before we left Philadelphia, between General Schuyler on one side and Pinckney and myself on the other, wherein the former maintained the position, that hereditary descent was as likely to produce good magistrates as election. I told him, that though the people were sound, there were a numerous sect who had monarchy in contemplation; that the Secretary of the Treasury was one of these. That I had heard him say that this constitution was a shilly shally thing, of mere milk and water, which could not last, and was only good as a step to something better. That when we reflected, that he had endeavored in the convention, to make an English constitution of it, and when failing in that, we saw all his measures tending to bring it to the same thing, it was natural for us to be jealous; and particularly, when we saw that these measures had established corruption in the legislature, where there was a squadron devoted to the nod of the Treasury, doing whatever he had directed, and ready to do what he should direct. That if the equilibrium of the three great bodies, legislative, executive and judiciary, could be preserved, if the legislature could be kept independent, I should never fear the result of such a government; but that I could not but be uneasy, when I saw that the executive had swallowed up the legislative branch. He said, that as to that interested spirit in the legislature, it was what could not be avoided in any government, unless we were to exclude particular descriptions of men, such as the holders of the funds, from all office. I told him, there was great difference between the little accidental schemes of self-interest, which would take place in every body of men, and influence their votes, and a regular system for forming a corps of interested persons, who should be steadily at the orders of the Treasury. He touched on the merits of the funding system, observed there was a difference of opinion about it, some thinking it very bad, others very good; that experience was the only criterion of right which he knew, and this alone would decide which opinion was right. That for himself, he had seen our affairs desperate and our credit lost, and that this was in a sudden and extraordinary degree raised to the highest pitch. I told him, all that was ever necessary to establish our credit, was an efficient government and an honest one, declaring it would sacredly pay our debts, laying taxes for this purpose, and applying them to it. I avoided going further into the subject. He finished by another exhortation to me not to decide too positively on retirement, and here we were called to breakfast.

October the 31st, 1792. I had sent to the President, Viar and Jaudenes's letter of the 29th instant, whereupon he desired a consultation of Hamilton, Knox, E. Randolph, and myself, on these points: 1. What notice was to be taken hereof to Spain? 2. Whether it should make part of the communication to the legislature? I delivered my opinion, that it ought to be communicated to both Houses, because the communications intended to be made, being to bring on the question, whether they would declare war against any, and which of the nations or parts of the nations of Indians to the south, it would be proper this information should be before them, that they might know how far such a declaration would lead them. There might be some who would be for war against the Indians, if it were to stop there, but who would not be for it, if it were to lead to a war against Spain. I thought it should be laid before both Houses, because it concerned the question of declaring war, which was the function equally of both Houses. I thought a simple acknowledgment of the receipt of the letter should be made by me to the Spanish Chargés, expressing that it contained some things very unexpected to us, but that we should refer the whole, as they had proposed, to the negotiators at Madrid. This would secure to us a continuation of the suspension of Indian hostilities, which the Governor of New Orleans said he had brought about till the result of the negotiation at Madrid should be known; would not commit us as to running or not running the line, or imply any admission of doubt about our territorial right; and would avoid a rupture with Spain, which was much to be desired, while we had similar points to discuss with Great Britain.

Hamilton declared himself the advocate for peace. War would derange our affairs greatly; throw us back many years in the march towards prosperity; be difficult for us to pursue, our countrymen not being disposed to become soldiers; a part of the Union feeling no interest in the war, would with difficulty be brought to exert itself; and we had no navy. He was for everything which would procrastinate the event. A year, even, was a great gain to a nation strengthening as we were. It laid open to us, too, the chapter of accidents, which, in the present state of Europe, was a very pregnant one. That while, however, he was for delaying the event of war, he had no doubt it was to take place between us for the object in question; that jealousy and perseverance were remarkable features in the character of the Spanish government, with respect to their American possessions; that so far from receding as to their claims against us, they had been strengthening themselves in them. He had no doubt the present communication was by authority from the court. Under this impression, he thought we should be looking forward to the day of rupture, and preparing for it. That if we were unequal to the contest ourselves, it behoved us to provide allies for our aid. That in this view, but two nations could be named, France and England. France was too intimately connected with Spain in other points, and of too great mutual value, ever to separate for us. Her affairs, too, were such, that whatever issue they had, she could not be in a situation to make a respectable mediation for us. England alone, then, remained. It would not be easy to affect it with her; however, he was for trying it, and for sounding them on the proposition of a defensive treaty of alliance. The inducements to such a treaty, on their part, might be, 1. The desire of breaking up our former connections, which we knew they had long wished. 2. A continuance of the *status quo* in commerce for ten years, which he believed would be desirable to them. 3. An admission to some navigable part of the Mississippi, by some line drawn from the Lake of the Woods to such navigable part. He had not, he said, examined the map to see how such a line might be run, so as not to make too great a sacrifice. The navigation of the Mississippi being a joint possession, we might then take measures in concert for the joint security of it. He was, therefore, for immediately sounding them on this subject through our ministers at London; yet so as to keep ourselves unengaged as long as possible, in hopes a favorable issue with Spain might be otherwise effected. But he was for sounding immediately, and for not letting slip an opportunity of securing our object.

E. Randolph concurred, in general, with me. He objected that such an alliance could not be effected without pecuniary consideration probably, which we could not give. And what was to be their aid? If men, our citizens would see their armies get foothold in the United States, with great jealousy; it would be difficult to protect them. Even the French, during the distress of the late war, excited some jealous sentiments.

Hamilton said, money was often, but not always demanded, and the aid he should propose to stipulate would be in ships. Knox *non dissentiente*.

The President said the remedy would be worse than the disease, and stated some of the disagreeable circumstances which would attend our making such overtures.

November, 1792. Hamilton called on me to speak about our furnishing supplies to the French colony of St. Domingo. He expressed his opinion, that we ought to be cautious, and not go too far in our application of money to their use, lest it should not be recognized by the mother country. He did not even think that some kinds of government they might establish could give a sufficient sanction.[3] I observed, that the National Convention was now met, and would certainly establish a form of government; that as we had recognized the former government because established by authority of the *nation,* so we must recognize any other which should be established by the authority of the nation. He said we had recognized the former, because it contained an important member of the ancient, to wit: the King, and wore the appearance of his consent; but if, in any future form, they should omit the King, he did not know that we could with safety recognize it, or pay money to its order.

November the 19th, 1792. Beckley brings me the pamphlet written by Hamilton, before the war, in answer to Common Sense. It is entitled "Plain Truth." Melancthon Smith sends it to Beckley, and in his letter says, it was not printed in New York by Loudon, because prevented by a mob, and was printed in Philadelphia, and that he has these facts from Loudon.

November the 21st, 1792. Mr. Butler tells me, that he dined last winter with Mr. Campbell from Denmark, in company with Hamilton, Lawrence, Dr. Shippen, T. Shippen, and one other person whom he cannot recollect. That after dinner political principles became the subject of conversation; that Hamilton declared openly, that "there was no stability, no security in any kind of government but a monarchy." That Lawrence took him up, and entered the lists of argument against him; that the dispute continued long, and grew warm, remarkably so as between them; that T. Shippen, at length, joined Lawrence in it; and in fine, that it broke up the company. Butler recommended to the company, that the dispute having probably gone farther than was intended, it ought to be considered as confined to the company.

December the 10th, 1792. Present: Alexander Hamilton, General Knox, Edmund Randolph, and Th: Jefferson, at the President's.

It was agreed to reject meeting the Indians at the proposed treaty, rather

[3] There had been a previous consultation at the President's (about the first week in November) on the expediency of suspending payments to France, under her present situation. I had admitted that the late constitution was dissolved by the dethronement of the King; and the management of affairs surviving to the National Assembly only, this was not an integral Legislature, and therefore not competent to give a legitimate discharge for our payments: that I thought, consequently, that none should be made till some legitimate body came into place; and that I should consider the National Convention called, but not met as we had yet heard, to be a legitimate body. Hamilton doubted whether it would be a legitimate body, and whether, if the King should be re-established, he might not disallow such payments on good grounds. Knox, for once, dared to differ from Hamilton, and to express, very submissively, an opinion, that a convention named by the whole body of the nation, would be competent to do anything. It ended by agreeing, that I should write to Gouverneur Morris to suspend payment generally, till further orders.—T. J.

than to admit a *mediation* by Great Britain; but to admit the presence of Governor Simcoe, not as a *party* (if that was insisted on); and that I should make a verbal communication to Mr. Hammond, in substance, as on the back hereof, which I previously read to the President.

December the 12th. I made the communication to Mr. Hammond. He said the attendance of Governor Simcoe was a circumstance only mentioned by him, but not desired; that he would decline it without difficulty; declared it to be their most ardent wish that peace should take place, for their fur-trade was entirely interrupted; and he urged as decisive proof of the sincerity of their wish,—1st. That they had kept the late Indian council together six weeks at a very great expense, waiting for the Six Nations. 2d. That the Indians at that council were so perfectly satisfied of their desire that they should make peace, that they had not so much as mentioned in council the applying to the British for any supplies. I immediately communicated this to the President.

December the 13th, 1792. The President called on me to see the model and drawings of some mills for sawing stone. After showing them, he in the course of a subsequent conversation asked me if there were not some good manufactories of porcelain in Germany; that he was in want of table china, and had been speaking to Mr. Shaw, who was going to the East Indies to bring him a set, but he found that it would not come till *he should no longer be in a situation to want it.* He took occasion a second time to observe that Shaw said it would be two years, at least, before he could have the china here, before which time he said he should be where he should not need it. I think he asked the question about the manufactories in Germany merely to have an indirect opportunity of telling me he meant to retire, and within the limits of two years.

December the 17th. Hammond says the person is here to whom the Six Nations delivered the invitation for Simcoe to attend, who says they insisted on it, and would consider his non-attendance as an evidence that he does not wish for peace; but he says that Simcoe has not the least idea of attending; that this gentleman says we may procure in Upper Canada any quantity of provisions, which the people will salt up express during winter; and that he will return and carry our request whenever we are ready.

Thursday, December the 27th, 1792. I waited on the President on some current business. After this was over, he observed to me, that he thought it was time to endeavor to effect a stricter connection with France, and that Gouverneur Morris should be written to on this subject. He went into the circumstances of dissatisfaction between Spain and Great Britain, and us, and observed, there was no nation on whom we could rely, at all times, but France; and that, if we did not prepare in time some support, in the event of rupture with Spain and England, we might be charged with a criminal negligence. [I was much pleased with the tone of these observations. It was the very doctrine which had been my polar star, and I did not need the successes of the republican arms in France, lately announced to us, to bring me to these sentiments. For it is to be noted, that on Saturday last (the 22d) I received Mr. Short's letters of October the 9th and 12th, with the Leyden gazettes to October the 13th, giving us the first news of the retreat of the Duke of Brunswick, and the capture of Spires and Worms by Custine, and that of Nice by Anselme]. I therefore expressed to the President my cordial approbation of these ideas; told him I had meant on that day (as an opportunity of writing by the British packet would occur immediately) to take his orders for removing the suspension of payments to France, which had been imposed by my last letter to Gouverneur Morris, but was meant, as I supposed, only for the interval between the abolition of the late constitution by the dethronement of the King, and the meeting of some other body, invested by the will of the nation with powers to transact their affairs; that I considered the National Convention, then assembled, as such a body; and that, therefore, we ought to go on with the payments to them, or to any government they should establish; that, however, I had learned last night, that some clause in the bill for providing reimbursement of the loan made by the bank to the United States, had given rise to a question before the House of Representatives yesterday, which might affect these payments; a clause in that bill proposing, that the money formerly borrowed in Amsterdam, to pay the French debt, and appropriated by law (1690, August 4th, c. 34, s. 2) to that purpose, lying dead as was suggested, should be taken to pay the bank, and the President be authorized to borrow two millions of dollars more, out of which it should be replaced; and if this should be done, the removal of our suspension of payments, as I had been about to propose, would be premature. He expressed his disapprobation of the clause above mentioned; thought it highly improper in the Legislature to change an appropriation once made, and added, that no one could tell in what that would end. I concurred, but observed, that on a division of the House, the ayes for striking out the clause were twenty-seven, the noes twenty-six; whereon the Speaker gave his vote against striking out, which divides the House: the clause for the disappropriation remained of course. I mentioned suspicions, that the whole of this was a trick to serve the bank under a great existing embarrassment; that the debt to the bank was to be repaid by instalments; that the first instalment was of two hundred thousand dollars only, or rather one hundred and sixty thousand dollars (because forty thousand of the two hundred thousand dollars would be the United States' own dividend of the instalment). Yet here were two millions to be paid them at once, and to be taken from a purpose of gratitude and honor, to which it had been appropriated.

December the 30th, 1792. I took the occasion furnished by Pinckney's letter of September the 19th, asking instructions how to conduct himself as to the French revolution, to lay down the catholic principal of republicanism, to wit, that every people may establish what form of government they please, and change it as they please; the will of the nation being the only thing essential.

I was induced to do this, in order to extract the President's opinion on the question which divided Hamilton and myself in the conversation of November, 1792, and the previous one of the first week of November, on the suspension of payments to France; and if favorable to mine, to place the principles of record in the letter books of my office. I therefore wrote the letter of December the 30th, to Pinckney, and sent it to the President, and he returned me his approbation in writing, in his note of the same date, which see.

February the 7th, 1793. I waited on the President with letters and papers from Lisbon. After going through these, I told him that I had for some time suspended speaking with him on the subject of my going out of office, because I had understood that the bill for intercourse with foreign nations was likely to be rejected by the Senate, in which case, the remaining business of the department would be too inconsiderable to make it worth while to keep it up. But that the bill being now passed, I was freed from the considerations of propriety which had embarrassed me. That &c. [nearly in the words of a letter to Mr. T. M. Randolph, of a few days ago], and that I should be willing, if he had taken no arrangements to the contrary, to continue somewhat longer, how long I could not say, perhaps till summer, perhaps autumn. He said, so far from taking arrangements on the subject, he had never mentioned to any mortal the design of retiring which I had expressed to him, till yesterday, when having heard that I had given up my house, and that it was rented by another, he thereupon mentioned it to Mr. E. Randolph, and asked him, as he knew my retirement had been talked of, whether he had heard any persons suggested in conversation to succeed me. He expressed his satisfaction at my change of purpose, and his apprehensions that my retirement would be a new source of uneasiness to the public. He said Governor Lee had that day informed him of the general discontent prevailing in Virginia, of which he never had had any conception, much less sound information. That it appeared to him very alarming. He proceeded to express his earnest wish that Hamilton and myself could coalesce in the measures of the government, and urged here the general reasons for it which he had done to me in two former conversations. He said he had proposed the same thing to Hamilton, who expressed his readiness, and he thought our coalition would secure the general acquiescence of the public. I told him my concurrence was of much less importance than he seemed to imagine; that I kept myself aloof from all cabal and correspondence on the subject of the government, and saw and spoke with as few as I could. That as to a coalition with Mr. Hamilton, if by that was meant that either was to sacrifice his general system to the other, it was impossible. We had both, no doubt, formed our conclusions after the most mature consideration; and principles conscientiously adopted, could not be given up on either side. My wish was, to see both Houses of Congress cleansed of all persons interested in the bank or public stocks; and that a pure legislature being given us, I should always be ready to acquiesce under their determinations, even if contrary to my own opinions; for that I subscribe to the principle, that the will of the majority, honestly expressed, should give law. I confirmed him in the fact of the great discontents to the south; that they were grounded on seeing that their judgments and interests were sacrificed to those of the eastern States on every occasion, and their belief that it was the effect of a corrupt squadron of voters in Congress, at the command of the Treasury; and they see that if the votes of those members who had any interest distinct from, and contrary to the general interest of their constituents, had been withdrawn, as in decency and honesty they should have been, the laws would have been the reverse of what they are on all the great questions. I instanced the new Assumption carried in the House of Representatives by the Speaker's vote. On this subject he made no reply. He explained his remaining in office to have been the effect of strong solicitations after he returned here; declaring that he had never mentioned his purpose of going out but to the Heads of departments and Mr. Madison; he expressed the extreme wretchedness of his existence while in office, and went lengthily into the late attacks on him for levees, &c., and explained to me how he had been led into them by the persons he consulted at New York; and that if he could but know what the sense of the public was, he would most cheerfully conform to it.

February the 16th, 1793. E. Randolph tells J. Madison and myself, a curious fact which he had from Lear. When the President went to New York, he resisted for three weeks the efforts to introduce levees. At length he yielded, and left it to Humphreys and some others to settle the forms. Accordingly, an antichamber and presence room were provided, and when those who were to pay their court were assembled, the President set out, preceded by Humphreys. After passing through the ante-chamber, the door of the inner room was thrown open, and Humphreys entered first, calling out with a loud voice, "The President of the United States." The President was so much disconcerted with it, that he did not recover from it the whole time of the levee, and when the company was gone, he said to Humphreys, "Well, you have taken me in once, but by God you shall never take me in a second time."

There is reason to believe that the rejection of the late additional Assumption by the Senate, was effected by the President through Lear, operating on Langdon. Beckley knows this.

February the 20th, 1793. Colonel W. S. Smith called on me to communicate intelligence from France. He had left Paris November the 9th. He says the French ministers are entirely broken with Gouverneur Morris; shut their doors to him, and will never receive another communication from him. They wished Smith to be the bearer of a message from the President, to this effect, but he declined; and they said in that case they would press it through their own minister here. He says they are sending Genet here with full powers to give us all the privileges we can desire in their countries, and particularly in the West Indies; that they even contemplate to set them free the next summer; that they propose to emancipate South America, and will send forty-five ships of the line there next spring, and Miranda at the head of the expedition; that they desire our debt to be paid them in provisions, and have authorized him to negotiate this. In confirmation of this, he delivers a letter to the President from Le Brun, minister for foreign affairs, in which Le Brun says that Colonel Smith will communicate plans worthy of his (the President's) great mind, and he shall be happy to receive his opinion as to the means the most suitable to effect it.

I had, five or six days ago, received from Ternant, extracts from the lives of his ministers, complaining of both Gouverneur Morris and Mr. Short. I sent them this day to the President with an extract from a private letter of Mr. Short, justifying himself, and I called this evening on the President. He said he considered the extracts from Ternant very serious—in short, as decisive; that he saw that Gouverneur Morris could be no longer continued there consistent with the public good; that the moment was critical in our favor, and ought not to be lost; that he was extremely at a loss what arrangement to make. I asked him whether Gouverneur Morris and Pinckney might not change places. He said that would be a sort of remedy, but not a radical one. That if the French ministry conceived Gouverneur Morris to be hostile to them; if they would be jealous merely on his proposing to visit London, they would never be satisfied with us at placing him at London permanently. He then observed, that though I had unfixed the day on which I had intended to resign, yet I appeared fixed in doing it at no great distance of time; that in this case, he could not but wish that I would go to Paris; that the moment was important: I possessed the confidence of both sides, and might do great good; that he wished I could do it, were it only to stay there a year or two. I told him that my mind was so bent on retirement that I could not think of launching forth again in a new business; that I could never again cross the Atlantic; and that as to the opportunity of doing good, this was likely to be the scene of action, as Genet was bringing powers to do the business here; but that I could not think of going abroad. He replied that I had pressed him to continue in the public service, and refused to do the same myself. I said the case was very different; he united the confidence of all America, and was the only person who did so: his services therefore were of the last importance; but for myself, my going out would not be noted or known. A thousand others could supply my place to equal advantage, therefore I felt myself free; and that as to the mission to France, I thought perfectly proper. He desired me then to consider maturely what arrangement should be made.

Smith, in speaking of Morris, said, that at his own table, in presence of his company and servants, he cursed the French ministers, as a set of damned rascals; said the king would still be replaced upon his throne. He said he knew they had written to have him recalled, and expected to be recalled. He consulted Smith to know whether he would bring his furniture here duty free. Smith has mentioned the situation of Gouverneur Morris freely to others here. Smith said also that the ministers told him they meant to begin their attack at the mouth of the Mississippi, and to sweep along the Bay of Mexico southwardly, and that they would have no objection to our incorporating into our government the two Floridas.

February the 25th, 1793. The President desires the opinions of the heads of the three departments, and of the Attorney-General, on the following question, to wit.: Mr. Ternant having applied for money equivalent to three millions of livres, to be furnished on account of our debt to France at the request of the executive of that country, which sum is to be laid out in provisions within the United States, to be sent to France. Shall the money be furnished?

The Secretary of the Treasury stated it as his opinion, that making a liberal allowance for the depreciation of assignats (no rule of liquidation having been yet fixed), a sum of about three hundred and eighteen thousand dollars may not exceed the arrearages equitably due to France to the end of 1792, and that the whole sum asked for may be furnished within periods capable of answering the purpose of Mr. Ternant's application, without a derangement of the Treasury.

Whereupon the Secretaries of State and War, and the Attorney General, are of opinion that the whole sum asked for by Mr. Ternant ought to be furnished: the Secretary of the Treasury is of opinion that the supply ought not exceed the above-mentioned sum of three hundred and eighteen thousand dollars.

The President having required the attendance of the heads of the three departments, and of the Attorney General, at his house, on Monday the 25th of February, 1793, the following questions were proposed, and answers given:

1. The Governor of Canada having refused to let us obtain provisions from that province, or to pass them along the water communication to the place of treaty with the Indians; and the Indians having refused to let them pass peaceably along what they call the bloody path, the Governor of Canada at the same time proposing to furnish the whole provisions necessary, ought the treaty to proceed? Answer unanimously, it ought to proceed.

2. Have the Executive, or the Executive and Senate together, authority to relinquish to the Indians the right of soil of any part of the land north of the Ohio, which has been validly obtained by former treaties?

The Secretary of the Treasury, the Secretary at War, and Attorney General, are of opinion that the Executive and Senate have such authority, provided that no grants to individuals, nor reservations to States, be thereby infringed. The Secretary of State is of opinion they have no such authority to relinquish.

3. Will it be expedient to make any such relinquishments to the Indians, if essential to peace?

The Secretaries of the Treasury and War, and the Attorney General, are of opinion it will be expedient to make such relinquishments if essential to peace, provided it do not include any lands sold or received for special purposes (the reservations for trading places excepted). The Secretary of State is of opinion that the Executive and Senate have authority to stipulate with the Indians, and that if essential to peace, it will be expedient to stipulate that we will not settle any lands between those already sold, or reserved for special purposes, and the lines heretofore validly established with the Indians.

Whether the Senate shall be previously consulted on this point. The opinion unanimously is, that it will be better not to consult them previously.

February the 26th, 1793. Notes on the proceedings of yesterday. [See the formal opinions given to the President in writing, and signed].

First question. We are all of opinion that the treaty should proceed merely to gratify the public opinion, and not from an expectation of success. I expressed myself strongly, that the event was so unpromising, that I thought the preparations for a campaign should go on without the least relaxation, and that a day should be fixed with the commissioners for the treaty, beyond which they should not permit the treaty to be protracted, by which day orders should be given for our forces to enter into action. The President took up the thing instantly, after I had said this, and declared that he was so much in the opinion that the treaty would end in nothing, that he then, in the presence of us all, gave orders to General Knox, not to slacken the preparations for the campaign in the least, but to exert every nerve in preparing for it. Knox said something about the ultimate day for continuing the negotiations. I acknowledged myself not a judge on what day the campaign should begin, but that whatever it was, that day should terminate the treaty. Knox said he thought a winter campaign was always the most efficacious against the Indians. I was of opinion, since Great Britain insisted on furnishing provisions, that we should offer to repay. Hamilton thought we should not.

Second question. I considered our right of pre-emption of the Indian lands, not as amounting to any dominion, or jurisdiction, or paramountship whatever, but merely in the nature of a remainder after the extinguishment of a present right, which gave us no present right whatever, but of preventing other nations from taking possession, and so defeating our expectancy; that the Indians had the full, undivided and independent sovereignty as long as they choose to keep it, and that this might be forever; that as fast as we extend our rights by purchase from them, so fast we extend the limits of our society, and as soon as a new portion became encircled within our line, it became a fixed limit of our society; that the executive, with either or both branches of the legislature, could not alien any part of our territory; that by the law of nations it was settled, that the unity and indivisibility of the society was so fundamental, that it could not be dismembered by the constituted authorities, except, 1, where *all power* was delegated to them (as in the case of despotic governments), or, 2, where it was expressly delegated; that neither of these delegations had been made to our General Government, and therefore, that it had no right to dismember or alienate any portion of territory once ultimately consolidated with us; and that we could no more cede to the Indians than to the English or Spaniards, as it might, according to acknowledged principles, remain as irrevocably and eternally with the one as the other. But I thought, that as we had a right to sell and settle lands once comprehended within our lines, so we might forbear to exercise that right, retaining the property till circumstances should be more favorable to the settlement, and this I agreed to do in the present instance, if necessary for peace.

Hamilton agreed to the doctrine of the law of nations, as laid down in Europe, but that it was founded on the universality of settlement there; consequently, that no lopping off of territory could be made without a lopping off of citizens, which required their consent; but that the law of nations for us must be adapted to the circumstance of our unsettled country, which he conceived the President and Senate may cede; that the power of treaty was given to them by the Constitution, without restraining it to particular objects; consequently, that it was given in as plenipotentiary a form as held by any sovereign in any other society. Randolph was of opinion there was a difference between a cession to Indians and to any others, because it only restored the ceded part to the condition in which it was before we bought it, and consequently, that we might buy it again hereafter; therefore, he thought the executive and Senate could cede it. Knox joined in the main opinion. The President discovered no opinion, but he made some efforts to get us to join in some terms which could unite us all, and he seemed to direct those efforts more towards me; but the thing could not be done.

Third question. We agreed in idea as to the line to be drawn, to wit, so as to retain all lands appropriated, or granted, or reserved.

Fourth question. We all thought if the Senate should be consulted, and consequently apprized of our line, it would become known to Hammond, and we should lose all chance of saving anything more at the treaty than our ultimatum.

The President, at this meeting, mentioned the declaration of some person, in a paper of Fenno, that he would commence an attack on the character of Dr. Franklin. He said the theme was to him excessively disagreeable on other considerations, but most particularly so, as the party seemed to do it as a means of defending him (the President) against the late attacks on him; that such a mode of defence would be peculiarly painful to him, and he wished it could be stopped. Hamilton and Randolph undertook to speak to Fenno to suppress it, without mentioning it as the President's wish. Both observed that they had heard this declaration mentioned in many companies, and that it had excited universal horror and detestation.

The paper in Fenno must lie between two persons, *viz.,* Adams and Izard, because they are the only persons who could know such facts as are there promised to be unfolded. Adams is an enemy to both characters, and might choose this ground as an effectual position to injure both. Izard hated Franklin with unparalleled bitterness, but humbly adores the President, because he is in *loco regis.* If the paper proceeds, we shall easily discover which of these two gentlemen is the champion. In the meantime, the first paper leads our suspicions more towards Izard than Adams, from the circumstance of style, and because he is quite booby enough not to see the injury he would do to the President by such a mode of defence.

February the 28th. Knox, E. Randolph and myself met at Knox's, where Hamilton was also to have met, to consider the time, manner and place of the President's swearing in. Hamilton had been there before, and had left his opinion with Knox, to wit, that the President should ask a judge to attend him in his own house to administer the oath, in the presence of the Heads of departments, which oath should be deposited in the Secretary of State's office. I concurred in this opinion. Randolph was for the President's going to the Senate's chamber to take the oath, attended by the marshal of the United States, who should then make proclamation, &c. Knox was for this, and for adding the House of Representatives to the presence, as they would not yet be departed. Our individual opinions were written, to be communicated to the President, out of which he might form one. In the course of our conversation, Knox, stickling for parade, got into great warmth, and swore that our government must either be entirely new modeled, or it would be knocked to pieces in less than ten years; and that as it is at present, he would not give a copper for it; that it is the President's character, and not the written constitution, which keeps it together.

Same day. Conversation with Lear. He expressed the strongest confidence that republicanism was the universal creed of America, except of a very few; that a republican administration must of necessity immediately overbear the contrary faction; said that he had seen with extreme regret that a number of gentlemen had for a long time been endeavoring to instil into the President, that the noise against the administration of the government was that of a little faction, which would soon be silent, and which was detested by the people, who were contented and prosperous; that this very party, however, began to see their error, and that the sense of America was bursting forth to their conviction.

March the 2d, 1793. See in the papers of this date, Mr. Giles's resolutions. He and one or two others were sanguine enough to believe that the palpableness of these resolutions rendered it impossible the House could reject them. Those who knew the composition of the House, 1, of bank directors; 2, holders of bank stock; 3, stock jobbers; 4, blind devotees; 5, ignorant persons, who did not comprehend them; 6, lazy and good-humored persons, who comprehended and acknowledged them, yet were too lazy to examine, or unwilling to pronounce censure; the persons who knew these characters, foresaw that the three first descriptions making one-third of the House, the three latter would make one-half of the residue; and, of course, that they would be rejected by a majority of two to one. But they thought that even this rejection would do good, by showing the public the desperate and abandoned dispositions with which their affairs were conducted. The resolutions were proposed, and nothing spared to present them in the fulness of demonstration. There were not more than three or four who voted otherwise than had been expected.

March the 30th, 1793. At our meeting at the President's, February the 25th, in discussing the question, whether we should furnish to France the three millions of livres desired, Hamilton, in speaking on the subject, used this expression, "When Mr. Genet arrives, whether we shall receive him or not, will then be a question for discussion," which expression I did not recollect till E. Randolph reminded me of it a few days after. Therefore, on the 20th instant, as the President was shortly to set out for Mount Vernon, I observed to him, that as Genet might arrive in his absence, I wished to know beforehand how I should treat him, whether as a person who would or would not be received? He said he could see no ground of doubt but that he ought to be received. On the 24th he asked E. Randolph's opinion on the subject, saying he had consulted Colonel Hamilton thereon, who went into lengthy considerations of doubt and difficulty, and viewing it as a very unfortunate thing that the President should have the decision of so critical a point forced on him; but, in conclusion, said, since he was brought into that situation, he did not see but that he must receive Mr. Genet. Randolph told the President he was clear he should be received, and the President said he had never had any doubt on the subject in his mind. Afterwards, on the same day, he spoke to me again on it, and said Mr. Genet should unquestionably be received; but he thought not with too much warmth or cordiality, so only as to be satisfactory to him. I wondered at first at this restriction; but when Randolph afterwards communicated to me his conversation of the 24th, I became satisfied it was a small sacrifice to the opinion of Hamilton.

March the 31st. Mr. Beckley tells me, that the merchants' bonds for duties on six months' credit became due the 1st instant to a very great amount, that Hamilton went to the bank on that day, and directed the bank to discount for those merchants all their bonds at thirty days, and that he would have the collectors credited for the money at the treasury. Hence, the treasury lumping its receipts by the month in its printed accounts, these sums will be considered by the public as only received on the last day; consequently, the bank makes the month's interest out of it. Beckley had this from a merchant who had a bond discounted, and supposes a million of dollars were discounted at the bank here. Mr. Brown got the same information from another merchant, who supposed only six hundred thousand dollars discounted here. But they suppose the same orders went to all the branch banks to a great amount.

*Eodem die*. Mr. Brown tells me he has it from a merchant, that during the last winter the directors of the bank ordered the freest discounts. Every man could obtain it. Money being so flush, the six per cents run up to twenty-one and twenty-two shillings. Then the directors sold out their private stocks. When the discounted notes were becoming due, they stopped discounts, and not a dollar was to be had. This reduced six per cents to eighteen shillings and three pence; then the same directors bought in again.

April the 7th, 1793. Mr. Lear called on me, and introduced of himself a conversation on the affairs of the United States. He laughed at the cry of prosperity, and the deriving it from the establishment of the treasury: he said, that so far from giving into this opinion, and that we were paying off our national debt, he was clear the debt was growing on us; that he had lately expressed this opinion to the President, who appeared much astonished at it. I told him I had given the same hint to the President last summer, and lately again had suggested, that we were even depending for the daily subsistence of government on borrowed money. He said, that was certain, and was the only way of accounting for what was become of the money drawn over from Holland to this country. He regretted that the President was not in the way of hearing full information, declared he communicated to him everything he could learn himself; that the men who vaunted the present government so much on some occasions, were the very men who at other times declared it was a poor thing, and such a one as could not stand, and he was sensible they only esteemed it as a stepping stone to something else, and had availed themselves of the first moments of the enthusiasm in favor of it, to pervert its principles and make of it what they wanted; and that though they raised the cry of anti-federalism against those who censured the mode of administration, yet he was satisfied, whenever it should come to be tried, that the very men whom they called anti-federalists, were the men who would save the government, and he looked to the next Congress for much rectification.

April the 18th. The President sends a set of questions to be considered, and calls a meeting. Though those sent me were in his own hand writing, yet it was palpable from the style, their ingenious tissue and suite, that they were not the President's, that they were raised upon a prepared chain of argument, in short, that the language was Hamilton's, and the doubts his alone. They led to a declaration of the executive, that our treaty with France is void. E. Randolph, the next day, told me that the day before the date of these questions, Hamilton went with him through the whole chain of reasoning of which these questions are the skeleton, and that he recognized them the moment he saw them.

We met. The first question, whether we should receive the French minister, Genet, was proposed, and we agreed unanimously that he should be received; Hamilton, at the same time, expressing his great regret that any incident had happened, which should oblige us to recognize the government. The next question was, whether he should be received absolutely, or with qualifications. Here Hamilton took up the whole subject, and went through it in the order in which the questions sketch it. See the chain of his reasoning in my opinions of April the 28th. Knox subscribed at once to Hamilton's opinion that we ought to declare the treaty void, acknowledging, at the same time, like a fool as he is, that he knew nothing about it. I was clear it remained valid. Randolph declared himself of the same opinion, but on Hamilton's undertaking to present to him the authority in Vattel (which we had not present) and to prove to him, that if the authority was admitted, the treaty might be declared void, Randolph agreed to take further time to consider. It was adjourned. We determined, unanimously, the last question, that Congress should not be called. There having been an intimation by Randolph, that in so great a question he should choose to give a written opinion, and this being approved by the President, I gave in mine April the 28th. Hamilton gave in his. I believe Knox's was never thought worth offering or asking for. Randolph gave his May the 6th, concurring with mine. The President told me, the same day, he had never had a doubt about the validity of the treaty; but that since a question had been suggested, he thought it ought to be considered; that this being done, I might now issue passports to sea vessels in the form prescribed by the French treaty. I had for a week past only issued the Dutch form; to have issued the French, would have been presupposing the treaty to be in existence. The President suggested, that he thought it would be as well that nothing should be said of such a question having been under consideration.

Written May the 6th.

May the 6th, 1793. When the question was, whether the proclamation of April the 22d should be issued, Randolph observed, that there should be a letter written by me to the ministers of the belligerent powers, to declare that it should not be taken as conclusive evidence against our citizens in foreign courts of admiralty, for contraband goods. Knox suddenly adopted the opinion, before Hamilton delivered his. Hamilton opposed it pretty strongly. I thought it an indifferent thing, but rather approved Randolph's opinion. The President was against it; but observed that *as there were three for it, it should go.* This was the first instance I had seen of an opportunity to decide by a mere majority, including his own vote.

May the 12th. Lear called on me today. Speaking of the lowness of stocks, (sixteen shillings), I observed it was a pity we had not money to buy on public account. He said, yes, and that it was the more provoking, as two millions had been borrowed for that purpose, and drawn over here, and yet were not here. That he had no doubt those would take notice of the circumstance whose duty it was to do so. I suppose he must mean the President.

May the 23d. I had sent to the President yesterday, draughts of a letter from him to the Provisory Executive Council of France, and of one from myself to Mr. Ternant, both on the occasion of his recall. I called on him today. He said there was an expression in one of them, which he had never before seen in any of our public communications, to wit, "our republic." The letter prepared for him to the Council, began thus: "The Citizen Ternant has delivered to me the letter wherein you inform me, that yielding, &c., you had determined to recall him from his mission, as your Minister Plenipotentiary to *our republic.*" He had underscored the words, *our republic.* He said that certainly ours was a republican government, but yet we had not used that style in this way; that if any body wanted to change its form into a monarchy, he was sure it was only a few individuals, and that no man in the United States would set his face against it more than himself; but that this was not what he was afraid of; his fears were from another quarter; that there was more danger of anarchy being introduced. He averted to a piece in Freneau's paper of yesterday; he said he despised all their attacks on him personally, but that there never had been an act of the government, not meaning in the executive line only, but in any line, which that paper had not abused. He had also marked the word republic thus √, where it was applied to the French republic. (See the original paper). He was evidently sore and warm, and I took his intention to be, that I should interpose in some way with Freneau, perhaps withdraw his appointment of translating clerk to my office. But I will not do it. His paper has saved our constitution, which was galloping fast into monarchy, and has been checked by no one means so powerfully as by that paper. It is well and universally known, that it has been that paper which has checked the career of the monocrats; and the President, not sensible of the designs of the party, has not with his usual good sense and *sang froid,* looked on the efforts and effects of this free press, and seen that, though some bad things have passed through it to the public, yet the good have preponderated immensely.

June the 7th, 1793. Mr. Beckley, who has returned from New York within a few days, tells me that while he was there, Sir John Temple, Consul General of the northern States for Great Britain, showed him a letter from Sir Gregory Page Turner, a member of Parliament for a borough in Yorkshire, who, he said, had been a member for twenty-five years, and always confidential for the ministers, in which he permitted him to read particular passages of the following purport: "that the government was well apprized of the predominancy of the British interest in the United States; that they considered Colonel Hamilton, Mr. King, and Mr. W. Smith of South Carolina, as the main supports of that interest; that particularly, they considered Colonel Hamilton, and not Mr. Hammond, as their effective minister here; that if the anti-federal interest (that was his term), at the head of which they considered Mr. Jefferson to be, should prevail, these gentlemen *had secured* an asylum to themselves in England." Beckley could not understand whether they had secured it *themselves,*[4] or whether they were only notified that it was secured to them. So that they understand that they may go on boldly in their machinations to change the government, and if they should be overset and choose to withdraw, they will be secure of a pension in England, as Arnold, Deane, &c., had. Sir John read passages of a letter (which he did not put into Beckley's hand, as he did the other) from Lord Grenville, saying nearly the same things. This letter mentions to Sir John, that though they had divided the Consul Generalship, and given the southern department to Bond, yet he, Sir John, was to retain his whole salary. [By this it would seem, as if, wanting to use Bond, they had covered his employment with this cloak]. Mr. Beckley says that Sir John Temple is a strong republican. I had a proof of his intimacy with Sir John in this circumstance. Sir John received his new commission of Consul for the northern department, and instead of sending it through Mr. Hammond, got Beckley to enclose it to me for his exequatur. I wrote to Sir John that it must come through

[4] Jefferson wrote in the margin: "Impossible as to Hamilton; he was far above that."

Mr. Hammond, enclosing it back to him. He accordingly then sent it to Mr. Hammond.

In conversation with the President today, and speaking about General Greene, he said that he and General Greene had always differed in opinion about the manner of using militia. Greene always placed them in his front: himself was of opinion, they should always be used as a reserve to improve any advantage, for which purpose they were the *finest fellows* in the world. He said he was on the ground of the battle of Guilford, with a person who was in the action, and who explained the whole of it to him. That General Greene's front was behind a fence at the edge of a large field, through which the enemy were obliged to pass to get at them; and that in their passage through this, they must have been torn all to pieces, if troops had been posted there who would have stood their ground; and that the retreat from that position was through a thicket, perfectly secure. Instead of this, he posted the North Carolina militia there, who only gave one fire and fell back, so that the whole benefit of their position was lost. He thinks that the regulars, with their field pieces, would have hardly let a single man get through that field.

*Eodem die* (June the 7th). Beckley tells me that he has the following fact from Governor Clinton. That before the proposition for the present General Government, *i.e.*, a little before Hamilton conceived a plan for establishing a monarchial government in the United States, he wrote a draught of a circular letter, which was to be sent to about —— persons, to bring it about. One of these letters, in Hamilton's handwriting, is now in possession of an old militia General up the North River, who, at that time, was thought *orthodox* enough to be entrusted in the execution. This General has given notice to Governor Clinton that he has this paper, and that he will deliver it into his hands, and no one's else. Clinton intends, the first interval of leisure, to go for it, and he will bring it to Philadelphia. Beckley is a man of perfect truth as to what he affirms of his own knowledge, but too credulous as to what he hears from others.

June the 10th, 1793. Mr. Brown gives me the following specimen of the phrenzy which prevailed at New York on the opening of the new government. The first public ball which took place after the President's arrival there, Colonel Humphreys, Colonel W. S. Smith and Mrs. Knox were to arrange the ceremonials. These arrangements were as follows: a sofa at the head of the room, raised on several steps, whereon the President and Mrs. Washington were to be seated. The gentlemen were to dance in swords. Each one, when going to dance, was to lead his partner to the foot of the sofa, make a low obeisance to the President and his lady, then go and dance, and when done, bring his partner again to the foot of the sofa for new obeisances, and then to retire to their chairs. It was to be understood, too, that gentlemen should be dressed in bags. Mrs. Knox contrived to come with the President, and to follow him and Mrs. Washington to their destination, and she had the design of forcing an invitation from the President to a seat on the sofa. She mounted up the steps after them unbidden, but unfortunately the wicked sofa was so short, that when the President and Mrs. Washington were seated, there was not room for a third person; she was obliged, therefore, to descend in the face of the company, and to sit where she could. In other respects the ceremony was conducted rigorously according to the arrangements, and the President made to pass an evening which his good sense rendered a very miserable one to him.

June the 12th. Beckley tells me that Klingham has been with him today, and relates to him the following fact: A certificate of the old Congress had been offered at the treasury and refused payment, and so indorsed in red ink as usual. This certificate came to the hands of Francis (the quondam clerk of the treasury, who, on account of his being dipped in the infamous case of the Baron Glaubec, Hamilton had been obliged to dismiss, to save appearances, but with an assurance of all future service, and he accordingly got him established in New York). Francis wrote to Hamilton that such a ticket was offered him, but he could not buy it unless he would inform him and give him his certificate that it was good. Hamilton wrote him a most friendly letter, and sent him the certificate. He bought the paper, and came on here and got it recognized, whereby he made twenty-five hundred dollars. Klingham saw both the letter and certificate.

Irving, a clerk in the treasury, an Irishman, is the author of the pieces now coming out under the signature of Veritas, and attacking the President. I have long suspected this detestable game was playing by the fiscal party, to place the President on their side.

June the 17th, 1793. At a meeting of the Heads of department at the President's this day, on summons from him, a letter from Mr. Genet of the 15th inst. (addressed to the Secretary of State on the subject of the seizure of a vessel by the Governor of New York, as having been armed, equipped and manned in that port, with a design to cruize on the enemies of France), was read, as also the draught of an answer prepared by the Secretary of State, which was approved.

Read, also, a letter of June 14th from Mr. Hammond to the Secretary of State, desiring to know whether the French privateers, the Citizen Genet, and Sans Culottes, are to be allowed to return or send their prizes into the ports of the United States. It is the opinion that he be informed that they were required to depart to the dominions of their own sovereign, and nothing expressed as to their ulterior proceedings; and that in answer to that part which states that the Sans Culottes had increased its force in the port of Baltimore, and remained there in the avowed intention of watching the motions of a valuable ship now lying there, it be answered that we expect the speedy departure of those privateers will obviate the inconveniences apprehended, and that it will be considered whether any practical arrangements can be adopted to prevent the augmentations of the force of armed vessels.

THOMAS JEFFERSON
ALEXANDER HAMILTON
HENRY KNOX

June the 20th, 1793. At a meeting this day of the Heads of department at the President's, on summons from him, a letter from Messrs. Viar and Jaudines, dated June 18th, and addressed to the Secretary of State, was read; whereupon it is the opinion that a full detail of the proceedings of the United States with respect to the southern Indians and the Spaniards be prepared, and a justification as to the particular matters charged in the said letter; that this be sent, with all the necessary documents, to our commissioners at the court of Madrid, leaving to them a discretion to change expressions in it which to them may appear likely to give offence in the circumstances under which they may be at the time of receiving it; and that a copy be sent to Mr. Pinckney for his information, and to make such use of the matter it contains as to him should seem expedient; that an answer be written to Messrs. Viar and Jaudines informing them that we shall convey our sentiments on the subject to their court through our commissioners at Madrid, and letting them see that we are not insensible to the style and manner of their communications.

A draught of a letter from the Secretary of State to Mr. Hammond, asking when an answer to his letter of May 29th, 1792, might be expected, was read and approved.

THOMAS JEFFERSON
ALEXANDER HAMILTON
HENRY KNOX

July the 5th, 1793. A meeting desired by Alexander Hamilton at my office. Himself, Knox, and myself met accordingly. He said that according to what had been agreed on in presence of the President, in consequence of Mr. Genet's declining to pay the $45,000 at his command in the treasury, to the holders of the St. Domingo bills, we had agreed to pay the holders out of other moneys to that amount; that he found, however, that these bills would amount to $90,000, and the question was whether he should assume $90,000 to be paid out of the September instalment. This, he said, would enable holders to get discounts at the banks, would therefore be equal to ready money, and save them from bankruptcy. Unanimously agreed to. We also agreed to a letter written by General Knox to Governor Mifflin, to have a particular inquiry made whether the Little Sarah is arming, &c., or not. I read also Governor Lee's letter about the Governor of South Carolina's proclamation respecting pestilential disease in West Indies. We are all of opinion the evidence is too slight for interference, and doubt the power to interfere. Therefore let it lie.

Mr. Genet called on me, and read to me very rapidly instructions he had prepared for Michaud, who is going to Kentucky; an address to the inhabitants of Louisiana, and another to those of Canada. In these papers it appears that, besides encouraging those inhabitants to insurrection, he speaks of two generals in Kentucky who have proposed to him to go and take New Orleans, if he will furnish the expense, about £3,000 sterling. He declines advancing it, but promises that sum ultimately for their expenses; proposes that officers shall be commissioned by himself in Kentucky and Louisiana; that they shall rendezvous *out of the territories of the United States*,—suppose in Louisiana, and there making up a battalion to be called the —— of inhabitants of Louisiana and Kentucky, and getting what Indians they could, to undertake the expedition against New Orleans, and then Louisiana to be established into an independent State, connected in commerce with France and the United States; that two frigates shall go into the river Mississippi, and co-operate against New Orleans. The address to Canada was to encourage them to shake off English yoke, to call Indians to their assistance, and to assure them of the friendly dispositions of their neighbors of the United States.

He said he communicated these things to me, not as Secretary of State, but as Mr. Jefferson. I told him that his enticing officers and soldiers from Kentucky to go against Spain, was really putting a halter about their necks; for that they would assuredly be hung if they commenced hostilities against a nation at peace with the United States. That leaving out that article I did not care what insurrections should be excited in Louisiana. He had about a fortnight ago sent me a communication for Michaud as consul of France at Kentucky, and desired an Exequatur. I told him this could not be given, that it was only in the *ports* of the United States they were entitled to consuls, and that if France should have a consul at Kentucky, England and Spain would soon demand the same, and we should have all our interior country filled with foreign agents. He acquiesced, and asked me to return the commission and his note, which I did; but he desired I would give Michaud a letter of introduction for Governor Shelby. I sent him one a day or two after. He now observes to me that in that letter I speak of him only as a person of botanical and natural pursuits, but that he wished the Governor to view him as something more; as a French citizen possessing his confidence. I took back the letter and wrote another.

## *Memorandum of a Meeting at the State House, Philadelphia, relative to the case of the Little Sarah*

July the 8th, 1793. At a meeting at the State House of the City of Philadelphia,

Present: the Secretary of State, the Secretary of the Treasury, the Secretary of War.

It appears that a brigantine, called the Little Sarah, has been fitted out at the port of Philadelphia, with fourteen cannon and all other equipment, indicating that she is intended to cruise under the authority of France, and that she is now lying in the river Delaware, at some place between this city and Mud Island; that a conversation has been had between the Secretary of State and the Minister Plenipotentiary of France, in which conversation the Minister refused to give any explicit assurance that the brigantine would continue until the arrival of the President, and his decision in the case, but made declarations respecting her not being ready to sail within the time of the expected return of the President, from which the Secretary of State infers with confidence, that she will not sail till the President will have an opportunity of considering and determining the case; that in the course of the conversation, the Minister declared that the additional guns which had been taken in by the Little Sarah were French property, but the Governor of Pennsylvania declared that he has good ground to believe that two of her cannon were purchased here of citizens of Philadelphia.

The Governor of Pennsylvania asks advice what steps, under the circumstances, he shall pursue?

The Secretary of the Treasury and the Secretary of War are of opinion, that it is expedient that immediate measures should be taken provisionally for establishing a battery on Mud Island, under cover of a party of militia, with direction that if the brig Sarah should attempt to depart before the pleasure of the President shall be known concerning her, military coercion be employed to arrest and prevent her progress.

The Secretary of State dissents from this opinion.

### *Reasons for his Dissent*

I am against the preceding opinion of the Secretaries of the Treasury and War, for ordering a battery to be erected on Mud Island, and firing on the Little Sarah, an armed vessel of the Republic of France:

Because I am satisfied, from what passed between Mr. Genet and myself at our personal interview yesterday, that the vessel will not be ordered to sail till the return of the President, which, by a letter of this day's post, we may certainly expect within eight and forty hours from this time.

Because the erecting a battery and mounting guns to prevent her passage might cause a departure not now intended, and produce the fact it is meant to prevent.

Because were such battery and guns now in readiness and to fire on her, in the present ardent state of her crew just in the moment of leaving port, it is morally certain that bloody consequences would follow. No one could say how many lives would be lost on both sides, and all experience has shown, that blood once seriously spilled between nation and nation, the contest is continued by subordinate agents, and the door of peace is shut. At this moment, too, we expect in the river twenty of their ships of war, with a fleet of from one hundred to one hundred and fifty of their private vessels, which will arrive at the scene of blood in time to continue it, if not to partake in it.

Because the actual commencement of hostilities against a nation, for such this act may be, is an act of too serious consequence to our countrymen to be brought on their heads by subordinate officers, not chosen by them nor clothed with their confidence; and too presumptuous on the part of those officers, when the chief magistrate, into whose hands the citizens have committed their safety, is within eight and forty hours of his arrival here, and may have an opportunity of judging for himself and them, whether the buying and carrying away two cannon (for according to information, the rest are the nation's own property), is sufficient cause of war between Americans and Frenchmen.

Because, should the vessel, contrary to expectation, depart before the President's arrival, the adverse powers may be told the truth of the case: that she went off contrary to what we had a right to expect; that we shall be justifiable in future cases to measure our confidence accordingly; that for the present we shall demand satisfaction from France, which, with the proof of good faith we have already given, ought to satisfy them. Above all, Great Britain ought not to complain: for, since the date of the order forbidding that any of the belligerent powers should equip themselves in our ports with our arms, these two cannon are all that have escaped the vigilance of our officers on the part of their enemies, while their vessels have carried off more than ten times the number, without any impediment; and if the suggestion be true (and as yet it is but suggestion) that there are fifteen or twenty Americans on board the Little Sarah, who have gone with their own consent, it is equally true that more than ten times that number of Americans are at this moment on board English ships of war, who have been taken forcibly from our merchant vessels at sea or in port, wherever met with, and compelled to bear arms against the friends of their country. And is it less a breach of our neutrality towards France to suffer England to strengthen herself with our force, than towards England to suffer France to do so? And are we equally ready and disposed to sink the British vessels in our ports by way of reprisal for this notorious and avowed practice?

Because it is inconsistent for a nation which has been patiently bearing for ten years the grossest insults and injuries from their late enemies, to rise at a feather against their friends and benefactors; and that, too, in a moment when circumstances have kindled the most ardent affections of the two people towards each other; when the little subjects of displeasure which have arisen are the acts of a particular individual, not yet important enough to have been carried to his government as causes of complaint; are such as nations of moderation and justice settle by negociation, not making war their first step; are such as that government would correct at a word, if we may judge from the late unequivocal demonstrations of their friendship towards us; and are very slight shades of the acts committed against us by England, which we have been endeavoring to rectify by negociation, and on which they have never condescended to give any answer to our minister.

Because I would not gratify the combination of kings with the spectacle of the two only republics on earth destroying each other for two cannon; nor would I, for infinitely greater cause, add this country to that combination, turn the scale of contest, and let it be from our hands that the hopes of man received their last stab.

It has been observed that a general order has been already given to stop by force vessels arming contrary to rule in our ports, in which I concurred. I did so because it was highly presumeable that the destination of such a vessel would be discovered in some early stage, when there would be few persons on board, these not yet disposed nor prepared to resist, and a small party of militia put aboard would stop the procedure without a marked infraction of the peace. But it is a much more serious thing when a vessel has her full complement of men (here said to be one hundred and twenty), with every preparation and probably with disposition to go through with their enterprise. A serious engagement is then a certain consequence. Besides, an act of force, committed by an officer in a distant port, under general orders, given long ago, to take effect on all cases, and with less latitude of discretion in him, would be a much more negociable case than a recent order, given by the general government itself (for that is the character we are to assume) on the spot, in the very moment, pointed at this special case, professing full discretion and not using it. This would be a stubborn transaction, not admitting those justifications and explanations which might avert a war, or admitting such only as would be entirely humiliating to the officers giving the order, and to the government itself.

On the whole, respect to the chief magistrate, respect to our countrymen, their lives, interests, and affection, respect to a most friendly nation, who, if we give them the opportunity, will answer our wrongs by correcting and not by repeating them; respect to the most sacred cause that ever man was engaged in, poising maturely the evils which may flow from the commitment of an act which it would be in the power and probably in the temper of subordinate agents to make an act of continued war, and those which may flow from an eight and forty hours suspension of the act, are motives with me for suspending it eight and forty hours, even should we thereby lose the opportunity of committing it altogether.

### *Copy of a minute given to the President*

July the 12th, 1793. At a meeting of the Heads of the departments at the President's, on summons from him, and on consideration of various representations from the Minister Plenipotentiary of France and Great Britain, on the subject of vessels arming and arriving in our ports, and of prizes;—it is their opinion that letters be written to the said ministers, informing them that the executive of the United States is desirous of having done what shall be strictly conformable to the treaties of the United States and the laws respecting the said cases; has determined to refer the questions arising therein to persons learned in the laws; that as this reference will occasion some delay, it is expected that, in the meantime, the Little Sarah, or Little Democrat, the ship Jane, and the ship William, in the Delaware, the Citoyen Genet and her prizes, the brigs Lovely-Lass and Prince William Henry, and the brig in the Chesapeake, do not depart till the further order of the President.

That letters be addressed to the judges of the Supreme Court of the United States, requesting their attendance at this place on Thursday the 18th instant, to give their advice on certain matters of public concern, which will be referred to them by the President.

That the Governor be desired to have the ship Jane attended to with vigilance, and if she be found augmenting her force and about to depart, that he cause her to be stopped.

THOMAS JEFFERSON
ALEXANDER HAMILTON
HENRY KNOX

Does the treaty with France leave us free to prohibit her from arming vessels in our ports? Thomas Jefferson, Hamilton, Knox, and Randolph—unanimous—it does. As the treaty obliges us to prohibit the enemies of France from arming in our ports, and leaves us free to prohibit France, do not the laws of neutrality oblige us to prohibit her? Same persons answer they do.

How far may a prohibition now declared be retrospective to the vessels armed in Charleston before the prohibition, to wit, the Citoyen Genet and Sans Culottes, and what is to be done with these prizes? Thomas Jefferson,—It cannot be retrospective at all; they may sell their prizes, and continue to act freely as other armed vessels of France. Hamilton and Knox,—The prizes ought to be given up to the English, and the privateers suppressed. Randolph,—They are free to sell their prizes, and the privateers should be ordered away, not to return here till they shall have been to the dominions of their own sovereign, and thereby purged the illegality of their origin. This last opinion was adopted by the President.

Our citizens who have joined in these hostilities against nations at peace with the United States, are they punishable? E. Randolph gave an official opinion—they were. Thomas Jefferson, Hamilton and Knox joined in the opinion. All thought it our duty to have prosecutions instituted against them, that the laws might pronounce on their case. In the first instance, two only were prosecuted merely to try the question, and to satisfy the complaint of the British men; and because it was thought they might have offended unwittingly. But a subsequent armament of a vessel at New York taking place with full knowledge of this prosecution, all the persons engaged in it, citizens and foreigners, were ordered to be prosecuted.

May the prohibition extend to the means of the party arming, or are they only prohibited from using our means for the annoyance of their enemies? Thomas Jefferson of opinion they are free to use their own means, *i.e.*, to mount their own guns, &c. Hamilton and Knox of opinion they are not to put even their own implements or means into a posture of annoyance. The President has as yet not decided this.

May an armed vessel arriving here be prohibited to employ their own citizens found here as seamen or mariners? Thomas Jefferson,—They cannot be prohibited to recruit their own citizens. Hamilton and Knox,—They may and ought to be prohibited. No decision yet by the President.

It appears to me the President wished the Little Sarah had been stopped by military coercion, that is, by firing on her; yet I do not believe he would have ordered it himself had he been here, though he would be glad if we had ordered it. The United States being a ship-building nation, may they sell ships, prepared for war, to both parties? Thomas Jefferson,—They may sell such ships in their ports to both parties, or carry them for sale to the dominions of both parties. E. Randolph of opinion they could not sell them here; and that if they attempted to carry them to the dominions of the parties for sale, they might be seized by the way as *contraband*. Hamilton of same opinion, except that he did not consider them as seizable for contraband, but as the property of a power, making itself a party in the *war* by an aid of such a nature, and consequently that it would be a breach of neutrality.

Hamilton moves that the government of France be desired to recall Mr. Genet. Knox adds that he be in the meantime suspended from his functions. Thomas Jefferson proposes that his correspondence be communicated to his government, with friendly observations. President silent.

July the 15th. Thomas Jefferson, Hamilton and Knox met at the President's. Governor Mifflin had applied to Knox for the loan of four cannon to mount at Mud Island. He informed him he should station a guard of thirty-five militia there, and asked what arrangement for rations the general government had taken. Knox told him nothing could be done as to rations, and he would ask the President for the cannon. In the meantime, he promised him to put the cannon on board a boat, ready to send off as soon as permission was obtained. The President declared his own opinion *first* and fully, that when the orders were given to the government to stop vessels arming, &c., in our ports, even by military force, he took for granted the government would use such diligence as to stop those projects in embryo, and stop them when no force was requisite, or a very small party of militia would suffice; that here was a demand from the government of Pennsylvania to land four cannon under pretext of executing orders of the general government; that if this was granted, we should be immediately applied to by every other governor, and that not for one place only, but for several, and our cannon would be dispersed all over the United States; that for this reason we would refuse the same request to the governors of South Carolina, Virginia, and Rhode Island; that if they erected batteries, they must establish men for them, and would come on us for this too. He did not think the executive had a power to establish permanent guards: he had never looked to anything permanent when the orders were given to the governors, but only an occasional call on small parties of militia in the moments requiring it. These sentiments were so entirely my own, that I did little more than combat on the same grounds the opinions of Hamilton and Knox. The latter said he would be ready to lend an equal number to every government to carry into effect orders of such importance; and Hamilton, that he would be willing to lend them in cases where they happened to be as near the place where they were to be mounted.

Hamilton submitted the purchase of a large quantity of saltpetre, which would outrun the funds destined to objects of that class by Congress. We were unanimous we ought to venture on it, and to the procuring supplies of military stores in the present circumstances, and take on us the responsibility to Congress, before whom it should be laid.

The President was fully of the same opinion.

In the above case of the cannon, the President gave no final order while I remained; but I saw that he was so impressed with the disagreeableness of taking them out of the boat again, that he would yield. He spoke sharply to Knox for having put them in that position without consulting him, and declared that, but for that circumstance, he would not have hesitated one moment to refuse them.

July the 18th, 1793. Lear calls on me. I told him that Irving, an Irishman, and a writer in the treasury, who, on a former occasion, had given the most decisive proofs of his devotion to his principal, was the author of the pieces signed Veritas; and I wished he could get at some of Irving's acquaintances and inform himself of the fact, as the person who told me of it would not permit the name of his informer to be mentioned; [*Note.*—Beckley told me of it, and he had it from Swaine, the printer to whom the pieces were delivered]; that I had long before suspected this excessive foul play in that party, of writing themselves in the character of the most exaggerated democrats, and incorporating with it a great deal of abuse on the President, to make him believe it was that party who were his enemies, and so throw him entirely into the scale of the monocrats. Lear said he no longer ago than yesterday expressed to the President his suspicions of the artifices of that party to work on him. He mentioned the following fact as a proof of their writing in the character of their adversaries; to wit, the day after the little incident of Richet's toasting "the man of the people" (see the gazettes), Mrs. Washington was at Mrs. Powel's, who mentioned to her that when the toast was given, there was a good deal of disapprobation appeared in the audience, and that many put on their hats and went out; on inquiry, he had not found the fact true, and yet it was put into ——'s paper, and written under the character of a republican, though he is satisfied it is altogether a slander of the monocrats. He mentioned this to the President, but he did not mention to him the following fact, which he knows; that in New York, the last summer, when the parties of Jay and Clinton were running so high, it was an agreed point with the former, that if any circumstances should ever bring it to a question, whether to drop Hamilton or the President, they had decided to drop the President. He said that lately one of the loudest pretended friends to the government, damned it, and said it was good for nothing, that it could not support itself, and it was time to put it down and set up a better; and yet the same person, in speaking to the President, puffed off that party as the only friends to the government. He said he really feared, that by their artifices and industry, they would aggravate the President so much against the republicans, as to separate him from the body of the people. I told him what the same cabals had decided to do, if the President had refused his assent to the bank bill; also what Brockhurst Livingston said to ——, that Hamilton's life was much more precious to the community than the President's.

July the 29th, 1793. At a meeting at the President's on account of the British letter-of-marque, ship Jane, said to have put up waste boards, to have pierced two port holes, and mounted two cannon (which she brought in) on new carriages which she did not bring in, and consequently having sixteen, instead of fourteen, guns mounted, it was agreed that a letter-of-marque, or vessel armé en guerre, and en marchandise, is not a privateer, and therefore not to be ordered out of our ports. It was agreed by Hamilton, Knox, and myself, that the case of such a vessel does not depend on the treaties, but on the law of nations. Edmund Randolph thought, as she had a mixed character of merchant vessel and privateer, she might be considered under the treaty; but this being overruled, the following paper was written:

Rules proposed by Attorney General:

1st. That all equipments purely for the accommodation of vessels, as merchantmen, be admitted. [Agreed.]

2d. That all equipments, doubtful in their nature, and applicable equally to commerce or war, be admitted, as producing too many minutia. [Agreed.]

3d. That all equipments, solely adapted to military objects, be prohibited. [Agreed.]

Rules proposed by the Secretary of the Treasury:

1st. That the original arming and equipping of vessels for military service, offensive or defensive, in the ports of the United States, be considered as prohibited to all. [Agreed.]

2d. That vessels which were armed before their coming into our ports, shall not be permitted to augment these equipments in the ports of the United States, but may repair or replace any military equipments which they had when they began their voyage for the United States; that this, however, shall be with the exception of privateers of the parties opposed to France, who shall not refit or repair. [Negatived—the Secretary of the Treasury only holding the opinion.]

3d. That for convenience, vessels armed and commissioned before they come into our ports, may engage their own citizens, not being inhabitants of the United States. [Agreed.]

I subjoined the following:

I concur in the rules proposed by the Attorney General, as far as respects materials or means of annoyance furnished by us; and I should be for an additional rule, that as to means or materials brought into this country, and belonging to themselves, they are free to use them.

August the 1st. Met at the President's, to consider what was to be done with Mr. Genet. All his correspondence with me was read over. The following propositions were made: 1. That a full statement of Mr. Genet's conduct be made in a letter to G. Morris, and be sent with his correspondence, to be communicated to the Executive Council of France; the letter to be so prepared, as to serve for the form of communication to the Council. Agreed unanimously. 2. That in that letter his recall be required. Agreed by all, though I expressed a preference of expressing that desire with great delicacy; the others were for peremptory terms. 3. To send him off. This was proposed by Knox; but rejected by every other. 4. To write a letter to Mr. Genet, the same in substance with that written to G. Morris, and let him know we had applied for his recall. I was against this, because I thought it would render him extremely active in his plans, and endanger confusion. But I was overruled by the other three gentlemen and the President. 5. That a publication of the whole correspondence, and statement of the proceedings, should be made by way of appeal to the people. Hamilton made a jury speech of three-quarters of an hour, as inflammatory and declamatory as if he had been speaking to a jury. E. Randolph opposed it. I chose to leave the contest between them. Adjourned to next day.

August the 2d. Met again. Hamilton spoke again three-quarters of an hour. I answered on these topics. *Object* of the appeal.—The democratic society; this the great circumstance of alarm; afraid it would extend its connections over the continent; chiefly meant for the local object of the ensuing election of Governor. If left alone, would die away after that is over. If opposed, if proscribed, would give it importance and vigor; would give it a new object, and multitudes would join it merely to assert the right of voluntary associations. That the measure was calculated to make the President assume the station of the head of a party, instead of the head of the nation. *Plan* of the appeal.—To consist of *facts* and the *decisions* of the President. As to facts we are agreed; but as to the decisions, there have been great differences of opinion among us. Sometimes as many opinions as persons. This proves there will be ground to attack the decisions. Genet will appeal also; it will become a contest between the President and Genet—anonymous writers—will be same difference of opinion in *public,* as in our cabinet—will be same difference in *Congress,* for it must be laid before them—would, therefore, work very unpleasantly *at home.* How would it work *abroad?* France—unkind—after such proofs of her friendship, should rely on that friendship, and her justice. Why appeal to the world? Friendly nations always negotiate little differences in private. Never appeal to the world, but when they appeal to the sword. Confederacy of Pillnitz was to overthrow the government of France. The interference of France to disturb other governments and excite insurrections, was a measure of reprisal. Yet these Princes have been able to make it believed to be the system of France. Colonel Hamilton supposes Mr. Genet's proceedings here are in pursuance of that system; and we are so to declare it to the world, and to add our testimony to this base calumny of the Princes. What a triumph to them to be backed by our testimony. What a fatal stroke at the cause of liberty; *et tu Brute.* We indispose the French government, and they will retract their offer of the treaty of commerce. The President manifestly inclined to the appeal to the people.[5] Knox, in a foolish incoherent sort of a speech, introduced the pasquinade lately printed, called the funeral of George W—n, and James W—n, King and Judge, &c., where the President was placed on a guillotine. The President was much inflamed; got into one of those passions when he cannot command himself; ran on much on

[5] He said that Mr. Morris, taking a family dinner with him the other day, went largely, and of his own accord, into this subject; advised this appeal, and promised, if the President adopted it, that he would support it himself, and engage for all his connections. The President repeated this twice, and with an air of importance. Now, Mr. Morris has no family connections: he engaged them for his political friends. This shows that the President has not confidence enough in the virtue and good sense of mankind, to confide in a government bottomed on them, and thinks other props necessary.—T. J.

the personal abuse which had been bestowed on him; defied any man on earth to produce one single act of his since he had been in the government, which was not done on the purest motives; that he had never repented but once the having slipped the moment of resigning his office, and that was every moment since; that *by God* he had rather be in his grave than in his present situation; that he had rather be on his farm than to be made *Emperor of the world;* and yet that they were charging him with wanting to be a King. That that *rascal Freneau* sent him three of his papers every day, as if he thought he would become the distributor of his papers; that he could see in this, nothing but an impudent design to insult him: he ended in this high tone. There was a pause. Some difficulty in resuming our question; it was, however, after a little while, presented again, and he said there seemed to be no necessity for deciding it now; the propositions before agreed on might be put into a train of execution, and perhaps events would show whether the appeal would be necessary or not. He desired we would meet at my office the next day, to consider what should be done with the vessels armed in our ports by Mr. Genet, and their prizes.

August the 3d. We met. The President wrote to take our opinions, whether Congress should be called. Knox pronounced at once against it. Randolph was against it. Hamilton said his judgment was against it, but that if any two were for it, or against it, he would join them to make a majority. I was for it. We agreed to give separate opinions to the President. Knox said we should have had fine work, if Congress had been sitting these two last months. The fool thus let out the secret. Hamilton endeavored to patch up the indiscretion of this blabber, by saying "he did not know; he rather thought they would have strengthened the executive arm." It is evident they do not wish to lengthen the session of the *next Congress,* and probably they particularly wish it should not meet till Genet is gone. At this meeting I received a letter from Mr. Remson at New York, informing me of the event of the combat between the Ambuscade and the Boston. Knox broke out into the most unqualified abuse of Captain Courtany. Hamilton, with less fury, but with the deepest vexation, loaded him with censures. Both showed the most unequivocal mortification at the event.

August the 6th, 1793. The President calls on me at my house in the country, and introduces my letter of July the 31st, announcing that I should resign at the close of the next month. He again expressed his repentance at not having resigned himself, and how much it was increased by seeing that he was to be deserted by those on whose aid he had counted; that he did not know where he should look to find characters to fill up the offices; that mere talents did not suffice for the department of State, but it required a person conversant in foreign affairs, perhaps acquainted with foreign courts; that without this, the best talents would be awkward and at a loss. He told me that Colonel Hamilton had three or four weeks ago written to him, informing him that private as well as public reasons had brought him to the determination to retire, and that he should do it towards the close of the next session. He said he had often before intimated dispositions to resign, but never as decisively before; that he supposed he had fixed on the latter part of next session, to give an opportunity to Congress to examine into his conduct; that our going out at times so different, increased his difficulty; for if he had both places to fill at once, he might consult both the particular talents and geographical situation of our successors. He expressed great apprehensions at the fermentation which seemed to be working in the mind of the public; that many descriptions of persons, actuated by different causes, appeared to be uniting; what it would end in he knew not; a new Congress was to assemble, more numerous, perhaps of a different spirit; the first expressions of their sentiments would be important; if I would only stay to the end of that, it would relieve him considerably.

I expressed to him my excessive repugnance to public life, the particular uneasiness of my situation in this place, where the laws of society oblige me always to move exactly in the circle which I know to bear me peculiar hatred; that is to say, the wealthy aristocrats, the merchants connected closely with England, the new created paper fortunes; that thus surrounded, my words were caught, multiplied, misconstrued, and even fabricated and spread abroad to my injury; that he saw also, that there was such an opposition of views between myself and another part of the administration, as to render it peculiarly unpleasing, and to destroy the necessary harmony. Without knowing the views of what is called the republican party here, or having any communication with them, I could undertake to assure him, from my intimacy with that party in the late Congress, that there was not a view in the republican party as spread over the United States, which went to the frame of the government; that I believed the next Congress would attempt nothing material, but to render their own body independent; that that party were firm in their dispositions to support the government; that the manœuvres of Mr. Genet might produce some little embarrassment, but that he would be abandoned by the republicans the moment they knew the nature of his conduct; and on the whole, no crisis existed which threatened anything.

He said he believed the views of the republican party were perfectly pure, but when men put a machine into motion, it is impossible for them to stop it exactly where they would choose, or to say where it will stop. That the constitution we have is an excellent one, if we can keep it where it is; that it was, indeed, supposed there was a party disposed to change it into a monarchical form, but that he could conscientiously declare there was not a man in the United States who would set his face more decidedly against it than himself. Here I interrupted him, by saying, "No rational man in the United States suspects you of any other disposition; but there does not pass a week, in which we cannot prove declarations dropping from the monarchical party that our government is good for nothing, is a milk and water thing which cannot support itself, we must knock it down, and set up something of more energy." He said if that was the case, he thought it a proof of their insanity, for that the republican spirit of the Union was so manifest and so solid, that it was astonishing how anyone could expect to move it.

He returned to the difficulty of naming my successor; he said Mr. Madison would be his first choice, but that he had always expressed to him such a decision against public office, that he could not expect he would undertake it. Mr. Jay would prefer his present office. He said that Mr. Jay had a great opinion of the talents of Mr. King; that there was also Mr. Smith of South Carolina, and E. Rutledge; but he observed, that name whom he would, some objections would be made, some would be called speculators, some one thing, some another; and he asked me to mention any characters occurring to me. I asked him if Governor Johnson of Maryland had occurred to him? He said he had; that he was a man of great good sense, an honest man, and he believed, clear of speculations; but this, says he, is an instance of what I was observing; with all these qualifications, Governor Johnson, from a want of familiarity with foreign affairs, would be in them like a fish out of water; everything would be new to him, and he awkward in everything. I confessed to him that I had considered Johnson rather as fit for the Treasury Department. Yes, says he, for that he would be the fittest appointment that could be made; he is a man acquainted with figures, and having as good a knowledge of the resources of this country as any man. I asked him if Chancellor Livingston had occurred to him? He said yes; but he was from New York, and to appoint him while Hamilton was in, and before it should be known he was going out, would excite a newspaper conflagration, as the ultimate arrangement would not be known. He said McLurg had occurred to him as a man of first-rate abilities, but it is said that he is a speculator. He asked me what sort of a man Wolcott was. I told him I knew nothing of him myself; I had heard him characterized as a cunning man. I asked him whether some person could not take my office *par interim,* till he should make an appointment, as Mr. Randolph, for instance. Yes, says he, but there you would raise the expectation of keeping it, and I do not know that he is fit for it, nor what is thought of Mr. Randolph. I avoided noticing the last observation, and he put the question to me directly. I then told him, I went into society so little as to be unable to answer it: I knew that the embarrassments in his private affairs had obliged him to use expedients, which had injured him with the merchants and shop-keepers, and affected his character of independence; that these embarrassments were serious, and not likely to cease soon. He said if I would only stay in till the end of another quarter (the last of December) it would get us through the difficulties of this year, and he was satisfied that the affairs of Europe would be settled with this campaign; for that either France would be overwhelmed by it, or the confederacy would give up the contest. By that time, too, Congress will have manifested its character and view. I told him that I had set my private affairs in motion in a line which had powerfully called for my presence the last spring, and that they had suffered immensely from my not going home; that I had now calculated them to my return in the fall, and to fail in going then, would be the loss of another year, and prejudicial beyond measure. I asked him whether he could not name Governor Johnson to my office, under an express arrangement that at the close of the session he should take that of the Treasury. He said that men never chose to descend; that being once in a higher department, he would not like to go into a lower one. He asked me whether I could not arrange my affairs by going home. I told him I did not think the public business would admit of it; that there never was a day now in which the absence of the Secretary of State would not be inconvenient to the public. And he concluded by desiring that I would take two or three days to consider whether I could not stay in till the end of another quarter, for that like a man going to the gallows, he was willing to put it off as long as he could; but if I persisted, he must then look about him and make up his mind to do the best he could; and so he took leave.

August the 20th. We met at the President's to examine by paragraphs the draught of a letter I had prepared to Gouverneur Morris on the conduct of Mr. Genet. There was no difference of opinion on any part of it, except on this expression, "An attempt to embroil both, to add still another nation to the enemies of his country, and to draw on both a reproach which it is hoped will never stain the history of either, that of *liberty warring on herself.*" Hamilton moved to strike out these words, "that of liberty warring on herself." He urged generally that it would give offence to the combined powers; that it amounted to a declaration that they were warring on liberty; that we were not called on to declare that the cause of France was that of liberty; that he had at first been with them with all his heart, but that he had long since left them, and was not for encouraging the idea here, that the cause of France was the cause of liberty in general, or could have either connection or influence in our affairs. Knox, according to custom, jumped plump into all his opinions. The President, with a good deal of positiveness, declared in favor of the expression; that he considered the pursuit of France to be that of liberty, however they might sometimes fail of the best means of obtaining it; that he had never at any time entertained a doubt of their ultimate success, if they hung well together; and that as to their dissensions, there were such contradictory accounts given, that no one could tell what to believe. I observed that it had been supposed among us all along that the present letter might become public; that we had therefore three parties to attend to,—1st, France; 2d, her enemies; 3d, the people of the United States; that as to the enemies of France, it ought not to offend them because the passage objected to, only spoke of an attempt to make the United States, a *free nation,* war on France, a *free nation,* which would be liberty warring against liberty; that as to France, we were taking so harsh a measure (desiring her to recall her minister) that a precedent for it could scarcely be found; that we knew that minister would represent to his government that our executive was hostile to liberty, leaning to monarchy, and would endeavor to parry the charges on himself, by rendering suspicions the source from which they flowed; that, therefore, it was essential to satisfy France, not only of our friendship to her, but our attachment to the general cause of liberty, and to hers in particular; that as to the people of the United States, we knew there were suspicions abroad that the executive, in some of its parts, was tainted with a hankering after monarchy, an indisposition towards liberty, and towards the French cause; and that it was important, by an explicit declaration, to remove these suspicions, and restore the confidence of the people in their government. Randolph opposed the passage on nearly the same ground with Hamilton. He added, that he thought it had been agreed that this correspondence should contain no expressions which could give offence to either party. I replied that it had been my opinion in the beginning of the correspondence, that while we were censuring the conduct of the French minister, we should make the most cordial declarations of friendship to them; that in the first letter or two of the correspondence, I had inserted expressions of that kind, but that himself and the other two gentlemen had struck them out; that I thereupon conformed to their opinions in my subsequent letters, and had carefully avoided the insertion of a single term of friendship to the French nation, and the letters were as dry and husky as if written between the generals of two enemy nations; that on the present occasion, however, it had been agreed that such expressions ought to be inserted in the letter now under consideration, and I had accordingly charged it pretty well with them; that I had further thought it essential to satisfy the French and our own citizens of the light in which we viewed their cause, and of our fellow feeling for the general cause of liberty, and had ventured only four words on the subject; that there was not from beginning to end of the letter one other expression or word in favor of liberty, and I should think it singular, at least, if the single passage of that character should be struck out.

The President again spoke. He came into the idea that attention was due to the two parties who had been mentioned, France and the United States; that as to the former, thinking it certain their affairs would issue in a government of some sort—of considerable freedom—it was the only nation with whom our relations could be counted on; that as to the United States, there could be no doubt of their universal attachment to the cause of France, and of the solidity of their republicanism. He declared his strong attachment to the expression, but finally left it to us to accommodate. It was struck out, of course, and the expressions of affection in the context were a good deal taken down.

August the 23d, 1793. In consequence of my note of yesterday to the President, a meeting was called this day at his house to determine what should be done with the proposition of France to treat. The importance of the matter was admitted; and being of so old a date as May 22d, we might be accused of neglecting the interests of the United States, to have left it so long unanswered, and it could not be doubted Mr. Genet would avail himself of this inattention. The President declared it had not been inattention, that it had been the subject of conversation often at our meetings, and the delay had proceeded from the difficulty of the thing.

If the struggles of France should end in the old despotism, the formation of such a treaty with the present government would be a matter of offence; if it should end in any kind of free government, he should be very unwilling, by inattention to their advances, to give offence, and lose the opportunity of procuring terms so advantageous to our country. He was, therefore, for writing to

Mr. Morris to get the powers of Mr. Genet renewed to his successor. [As he had expressed this opinion to me the afternoon before, I had prepared the draught of a letter accordingly.] But how to explain the delay? The Secretary of the Treasury observed on the letter of the National Convention, that as it did not seem to require an answer, and the matters it contained would occasion embarrassment if answered, he should be against answering it; that he should be for writing to Mr. Morris, mentioning our readiness to treat with them, and suggesting a renewal of Mr. Genet's powers to his successor, but not in as strong terms as I had done in my draught of the letter—not as a thing anxiously wished for by us, lest it should suggest to them the asking a price; and he was for my writing to Mr. Genet *now,* an answer to his letter of May 22d, referring to the meeting of the Senate the entering on the treaty. Knox concurred with him, the Attorney General also,—except that he was against suggesting the renewal of Mr. Genet's powers, because that would amount to a declaration that we would treat with that government, would commit us to lay the subject before the Senate, and his principle had ever been to do no act, not unavoidably necessary, which, in the event of a counter revolution, might offend the future governing powers of that country. I stated to them that having observed from our conversations that the propositions to treat might not be acceded to immediately, I had endeavored to prepare Mr. Genet for it, by taking occasion in conversations to apprize him of the control over treaties which our constitution had given to the Senate; that though this was indirectly done (because not having been authorized to say anything official on the subject, I did not venture to commit myself directly), yet, on some subsequent conversation, I found it had struck him exactly as I had wished; for, speaking on some other matter, he mentioned incidentally his propositions to treat, and said, however, as I know now that you cannot take up that subject till the meeting of the Senate, I shall say no more about it now, and so proceeded with his other subject, which I do not now recollect. I said I thought it possible by recalling the substance of these conversations to Mr. Genet, in a letter to be written now, I might add that the Executive had at length come to a conclusion, that on account of the importance of the matter, they would await the meeting of the Senate; but I pressed strongly the urging Mr. Morris to procure a renewal of Genet's powers, that we might not lose the chance of obtaining so advantageous a treaty. Edmund Randolph had argued against our acceding to it, because it was too advantageous; so much so that they would certainly break it, and it might become the cause of war. I answered that it would be easy, in the course of the negociation, to cure it of its inequality by giving some compensation; but I had no fear of their revoking it, that the islanders themselves were too much interested in the concessions ever to suffer them to be revoked; that the best thinkers in France had long been of opinion that it would be for the interest of the mother country to let the colonies obtain subsistence wherever they could cheapest; that I was confident the present struggles in France would end in a free government of some sort, and that such a government would consider itself as growing out of the present one, and respect its treaties. The President recurred to the awkwardness of writing a letter now to Mr. Genet, in answer to his of May 22d; that it would certainly be construed as merely done with a design of exculpation of ourselves, and he would thence inculpate us. The more we reflected on this, the more the justice of the observation struck us. Hamilton and myself came into it—Knox still for the letter—Randolph half for it, half against it, according to custom.

It was at length agreed I should state the substance of my verbal observations to Mr. Genet, in a letter to Mr. Morris, and let them be considered as the answer intended; for being from the Secretary of State, they might be considered as official, though not in writing.

It is evident that taking this ground for their future justification to France and to the United States, they were sensible they had censurably neglected these overtures of treaty; for not only what I had said to Mr. Genet was without authority from them, but was never communicated to them till this day. To rest the justification of delay on answers given, it is true in time; but of which they had no knowledge till now, is an ostensible justification only.

September the 4th, 1793. At a meeting held some days ago, some letters from the Governor of Georgia were read, in which a consultation of officers, and a considerable expedition against the Creeks was proposed. We were all of opinion no such expedition should be undertaken. My reasons were that such a war might bring on a Spanish, and even an English war; that for this reason the aggressions of the Creeks had been laid before the last Congress, and they had not chosen to declare war, therefore the Executive should not take on itself to do it; and that according to the opinions of Pickens and Blount, it was too late in the season.

I thought, however, that a temperate and conciliatory letter should be written to the Governor, in order that we might retain the disposition of the people of the State to assist in an expedition when undertaken. The other gentlemen thought a strong letter of disapprobation should be written. Such a one was this day produced, strong and reprehendatory enough, in which I thought were visible the personal enmities of Knox and Hamilton, against Telfair, Gun, and Jackson—the two last having been of the council of officers. The letter passed without objection, being of the complexion before determined.

Wayne's letter was read, proposing that six hundred militia should set out from Fort Pitt to attack certain Miami towns, while he marched against the principal towns. The President disapproved it, because of the difficulty of concerted movements at six hundred miles distance; because these six hundred men might, and probably would have the whole force of the Indians to contend with; and because the object was not worth the risking such a number of men. We all concurred. It appeared to me, further, that to begin an expedition from Fort Pitt, the very first order for which is to be given now, when we have reason to believe Wayne advanced as far as Fort Jefferson, would be either too late for his movements, or would retard them very injuriously. [*Note.*—The letters from the Commissioners were now read, announcing the refusal of the

Indians to treat, unless the Ohio were made the boundary; and that they were on their return.]

A letter from Governor Clinton read, informing of his issuing a warrant to arrest Governor Galbaud, at the request of the French Consul, and that he was led to interfere because the judge of the district lived at Albany. It was proposed to write to the judge of the district, that the place of his residence was not adapted to his duties; and to Clinton, that Galbaud was not liable to arrest. Hamilton said, that by the laws of New York, the Governor has the powers of a justice of peace, and had issued the warrant as such.

I was against writing letters to judiciary officers. I thought them independent of the Executive, not subject to its coercion, and, therefore, not obliged to attend to its admonitions.

The other three were for writing the letters. They thought it the duty of the President to see that the laws were executed; and if he found a failure in so important an officer, to communicate it to the legislature for impeachment.

Edmund Randolph undertook to write the letters, and I am to sign them as if mine. The President brought forward the subject of the ports, and thought a new demand of answers should be made to Mr. Hammond. As we had not Mr. Hammond's last answer (of June 20th) on that subject, agreed to let it lie over to Monday.

Hammond proposed, that on Monday we should take into consideration the fortification of the rivers and ports of the United States, and that though the Executive could not undertake to do it, preparatory surveys should be made to be laid before Congress, to be considered on Monday.

The letters to Genet covering a copy of mine to Gouv. Morris—of —— to the French consuls, threatening the revocation of their Exequaturs—to Mr. Pinckney on the additional instructions of Great Britain to their navy for shipping our corn, flour, &c., and to Gouv. Morris on the similar order of the French National Assembly, are to be ready on Monday.

My letter to Mr. Hammond, in answer to his of August 30th, was read and approved. Hamilton wished not to narrow the ground of compensation so much as to cases after August 7th. Knox joined him, and by several observations showed he did not know what the question was. He could not comprehend that the letter of August 7th, which promised compensation (because we had not used all the means in our power for restricting), would not be contradicted by a refusal to compensate in cases after August 7th, where we should naturally use all the means in our power for restriction, and these means should be insufficient. The letter was agreed to on Mr. Randolph's opinion and mine; Hamilton acquiescing, Knox opposing.

At sundry meetings of the Heads of departments and Attorney General, from the 1st to the 28th of November, 1793, at the President's, several matters were agreed upon, as stated in the following letters from the Secretary of State, to wit:—

November the 8th. Circular letter to the representatives of France, Great

Britain, Spain, and the United Netherlands, fixing provisionally the extent of our jurisdiction into the sea at a sea league.

10th. Circular letter to the district attorneys, notifying the same, and committing to them the taking depositions in those cases.

10th. Circular to the foreign representatives, notifying how depositions are to be taken in those cases.

The substance of the preceding letters was agreed to by all; the rough draughts were submitted to them and approved.

November the 14th. To Mr. Hammond, that the United States are not bound to restore the Rochampton. This was agreed by all. The rough draught was submitted to and approved by Colonel Hamilton and Mr. Randolph. General Knox was on a visit to Trenton.

10th. Letters to Mr. Genet and Hammond, and the 14th to Mr. Hollingsworth, for taking depositions in the cases of the Conningham and Pilgrim.

13th. Ditto, to Mr. Genet, Hammond, and Bowle, for depositions in the case of the William.

14th. Ditto, to Hollingsworth, to ascertain whether Mr. Moissonier had passed sentence on the Rochampton and Pilgrim.

These last-mentioned letters of the 10th, 13th, and 14th were, as to their substance, agreed to by all, the draughts were only communicated to Mr. Randolph, and approved by him.

November the 13th. To Mr. Hammond, inquiring when we shall have an answer on the inexecution of the treaty. The substance agreed by all. The letter was sent off without communication, none of the gentlemen being at Germantown.

22d. To Mr. Genet, returning the commissions of Pennevert and Chervi, because not addressed to the President.

22d. To Mr. Genet, inquiring whether the Lovely-Lass, Prince William Henry, and Jane, of Dublin, have been given up; and if not, requiring that they be restored to owners. These were agreed to by all, as to their matter, and the letters themselves were submitted before they were sent to the President, the Secretary of War, and the Attorney-General.

22d. To Mr. Gore, for authentic evidence of Dannery's protest on the President's revocation of Duplaine's Exequatur. The substance agreed by all. The letter sent off before communication.

THOMAS JEFFERSON
HENRY KNOX
EDMUND RANDOLPH
ALEXANDER HAMILTON

November 23d, 1793.

November the 5th, 1793. E. Randolph tells me, that Hamilton, in conversation with him yesterday, said, "Sir, if all the people in America were now assembled, and to call on me to say whether I am a friend to the French revolution, I would declare that *I have it in abhorrence*."

November the 8th, 1793. At a conference at the President's, where I read several letters of Mr. Genet; on finishing one of them, I asked what should be the answer? The President thereupon took occasion to observe, that Mr. Genet's conduct continued to be of so extraordinary a nature, that he meant to propose to our serious consideration, whether he should not have his functions discontinued, and be ordered away? He went lengthily into observations on his conduct, to raise against the executive, 1, the people; 2, the State governments; 3, the Congress. He showed he felt the venom of Genet's pen, but declared he would not choose his insolence should be regarded any further, than as might be thought to affect the honor of the country. Hamilton and Knox readily and zealously argued for dismissing Mr. Genet. Randolph opposed it with firmness, and pretty lengthily. The President replied to him lengthily, and concluded by saying he did not wish to have the thing hastily decided, but that we should consider of it, and give our opinions on his return from Reading and Lancaster.

Accordingly, November the 18th, we met at his house; read new volumes of Genet's letters, received since the President's departure; then took up the discussion of the subjects of communication to Congress. 1. The Proclamation. E. Randolph read the statement he had prepared; Hamilton did not like it; said much about his own views; that the President had a right to declare his opinion to our citizens and foreign nations; that it was not the interest of this country to join in the war, and that we were under no obligation to join in it; that though the declaration would not legally bind Congress, yet the President had a right to give his opinion of it, and he was against any explanation in the speech, which should yield that he did not intend that foreign nations should consider it as a declaration of neutrality, future as well as present; that he understood it as meant to give them that sort of assurance and satisfaction, and to say otherwise now, would be a deception on them. He was for the President's using such expressions, as should neither affirm his right to make such a declaration to foreign nations, nor yield it. Randolph and myself opposed the right of the President to declare anything future on the question, shall there or shall there not be war, and that no such thing was intended; that Hamilton's construction of the effect of the proclamation, would have been a determination of the question of the *guarantee,* which we both denied to have intended, and I had at the time declared the executive incompetent to. Randolph said he meant that foreign nations should understand it as an intimation of the President's opinion, that neutrality would be our interest. I declared my meaning to have been, that foreign nations should understand no such thing; that on the contrary, I would have chosen them to be doubtful, and to come and bid for our neutrality. I admitted the President, having received the nation at the close of Congress in a state of peace, was bound to preserve them in that state till Congress should meet again, and might proclaim anything which went no farther. The President declared he never had an idea that he could bind Congress against declaring war, or that anything contained in his proclamation could look beyond the first day of their meeting. His main view was to keep our people in peace; he apologized for the use of the term neutrality in his answers, and justified it, by having submitted the first of them (that to the merchants, wherein it was used) to our consideration, and we had not objected to the term. He concluded in the end, that Colonel Hamilton should prepare a paragraph on this subject for the speech, and it should then be considered. We were here called to dinner.

After dinner, the *renvoi* of Genet was proposed by himself. I opposed it on these topics. France, the only nation on earth sincerely our friend. The measure so harsh a one, that no precedent is produced where it has not been followed by war. Our messenger has now been gone eighty-four days; consequently, we may hourly expect the return, and to be relieved by their revocation of him. Were it now resolved on, it would be eight or ten days before the matter on which the order should be founded, could be selected, arranged, discussed, and forwarded. This would bring us within four or five days of the meeting of Congress. Would it not be better to wait and see how the pulse of that body, new as it is, would beat. They are with us now, probably, but such a step as this may carry many over to Genet's side. Genet will not obey the order, &c., &c. The President asked me what I would do if Genet sent the accusation to us to be communicated to Congress, as he threatened in the letter to Moultrie? I said I would not send it to Congress; but either put it in the newspapers, or send it back to him to be published if he pleased. Other questions and answers were put and returned in a quicker altercation than I ever before saw the President use. Hamilton was for the *renvoi;* spoke much of the dignity of the nations; that they were now to form their character; that our conduct now would tempt or deter other foreign ministers from treating us in the same manner; touched on the President's personal feelings; did not believe France would make it a cause of war; if she did, we ought to do what was right, and meet the consequences, &c. Knox on the same side, and said he thought it very possible Mr. Genet would either declare us a department of France, or levy troops here and endeavor to reduce us to obedience. Randolph of my opinion, and argued chiefly on the resurrection of popularity to Genet, which might be produced by this measure. That at present he was dead in the public opinion, if we would but leave him so. The president lamented there was not unanimity among us; that as it was, we had left him exactly where we found him; and so it ended.

November the 21st. We met at the President's. The manner of explaining to Congress the intentions of the proclamation, was the matter of debate. Randolph produced his way of stating it. This expressed its views to have been, 1, to keep our citizens quiet; 2, to intimate to foreign nations that it was the President's opinion, that the interests and dispositions of this country were for peace. Hamilton produced his statement, in which he declared his intention to be, to say nothing which could be laid hold of for any purpose; to leave the proclamation to explain itself. He entered pretty fully into all the argumentation of Pacificus; he justified the right of the President to declare his opinion for a *future neutrality,* and that there existed no circumstances to oblige the

United States to enter into the war on account of the guarantee; and that in agreeing to the proclamation, he meant it to be understood as conveying both those declarations; *viz.,* neutrality, and that the *casus fœderis* on the guarantee did not exist. He admitted the Congress might declare war, notwithstanding these declarations of the President. In like manner, they might declare war in the face of a treaty, and in direct infraction of it. Among other positions laid down by him, this was with great positiveness; that the constitution having given power to the President and Senate to make treaties, they might make a treaty of neutrality which should take from Congress the right to declare war in that particular case, and that under the form of a treaty they might exercise any powers whatever, even those exclusively given by the constitution to the House of Representatives. Randolph opposed this position, and seemed to think that where they undertook to do acts by treaty (as to settle a tariff of duties), which were exclusively given to the Legislature, that an act of the Legislature would be necessary to confirm them, as happens in England, when a treaty interferes with duties established by law. I insisted that in giving to the President and Senate a power to make treaties, the constitution meant only to authorize them to carry into effect, by way of treaty, any powers they might constitutionally exercise. I was sensible of the weak points in this position, but there were still weaker in the other hypothesis; and if it be impossible to discover a rational measure of authority to have been given by this clause, I would rather suppose that the cases which my hypothesis would leave unprovided, were not thought of by the convention, or if thought of, could not be agreed on, or were thought of and deemed unnecessary to be invested in the government. Of this last description, were treaties of neutrality, treaties offensive and defensive, &c. In every event, I would rather construe so narrowly as to oblige the nation to amend, and thus declare what powers they would agree to yield, than too broadly, and indeed, so broadly as to enable the executive and Senate to do things which the constitution forbids. On the question, which form of explaining the principles of the proclamation should be adopted, I declared for Randolph's, though it gave to that instrument more objects than I had contemplated. Knox declared for Hamilton's. The President said he had had but one object, the keeping our people quiet till Congress should meet; that nevertheless, to declare he did not mean a declaration of neutrality, in the technical sense of the phrase, might perhaps be crying *peccavi* before he was charged. However, he did not decide between the two draughts.

November the 23d. At the President's. Present, Knox, Randolph, and Th: Jefferson. Subject, the heads of the speech. One was, a proposition to Congress to fortify the principal harbors. I opposed the expediency of the General Government's undertaking it, and the expediency of the President's proposing it. It was amended, by substituting a proposition to adopt means for enforcing respect to the jurisdiction of the United States within its waters. It was proposed to recommend the establishment of a military academy. I objected that none of the specified powers given by the constitution to Congress, would authorize this. It was, therefore, referred for further consideration and inquiry. Knox was for both propositions. Randolph against the former, but said nothing as to the latter. The President acknowledged he had doubted of the expediency of undertaking the former; and as to the latter, though it would be a good thing, he did not wish to bring on anything which might generate heat and ill humor. It was agreed that Randolph should draw the speech and the messages.

November the 28th. Met at the President's. I read over a list of the papers copying, to be communicated to Congress on the subject of Mr. Genet. It was agreed that Genet's letter of August the 13th to the President, mine of August the 16th, and Genet's of November to myself and the Attorney General, desiring a prosecution of Jay and King should not be sent to the legislature: on a general opinion, that the discussion of the fact certified by Jay and King had better be left to the channel of the newspapers, and in the private hands in which it now is, than for the President to meddle in it, or give room to a discussion of it in Congress.

Randolph had prepared a draught of the speech. The clause recommending fortifications was left out; but that for a military academy was inserted. I opposed it, as unauthorized by the constitution. Hamilton and Knox approved it without discussion. Randolph was for it, saying that the words of the constitution authorizing Congress to lay taxes, &c., *for the common defence,* might comprehend it. The President said he would not choose to recommend anything against the constitution, but if it was *doubtful,* he was so impressed with the necessity of this measure, that he would refer it to Congress, and let them decide for themselves whether the constitution authorized it or not. It was, therefore, left in. I was happy to see that Randolph had, by accident, used the expression "our republic," in the speech. The President, however, made no objection to it, and so, as much as it had disconcerted him on a former occasion with me, it was now put into his own mouth to be pronounced to the two Houses of legislature.

No material alterations were proposed or made in any part of the draught.

After dinner, I produced the draught of messages on the subject of France and England, proposing that that relative to Spain should be subsequent and secret.

Hamilton objected to the draught *in toto*; said that the contrast drawn between the conduct of France and England amounted to a declaration of war; he denied that France had ever done us favors; that it was mean for a nation to acknowledge favors; that the dispositions of the people of this country towards France, he considered as a serious calamity; that the executive ought not, by an echo of this language, to nourish that disposition in the people; that the offers in commerce made us by France, were the offspring of the moment, of circumstances which would not last, and it was wrong to receive as permanent, things merely temporary; that he could demonstrate that Great Britain showed us more favors than France. In complaisance to him I whittled down the expressions without opposition; struck out that of "favors ancient and recent" from France; softened some terms, and omitted some sentiments respecting Great Britain. He still was against the whole, but insisted that, at any rate, it should be a secret communication, because the matters it stated were still depending. These were, 1, the inexecution of the treaty; 2, the restraining our commerce to their own ports and those of their friends. Knox joined Hamilton in everything. Randolph was for the communications; that the documents respecting the first should be given in as public; but that those respecting the second should not be given to the legislature at all, but kept secret. I began to tremble now for the whole, lest all should be kept secret. I urged, especially, the duty now incumbent on the President, to lay before the legislature and the public what had passed on the inexecution of the treaty, since Mr. Hammond's answer of this month might be considered as the last we should ever have; that, therefore, it could no longer be considered as a negotiation pending. I urged that the documents respecting the stopping our corn ought also to go, but insisted that if it should be thought better to withhold them, the restrictions should not go to those respecting the treaty; that neither of these subjects was more in a state of *pendency* than the recall of Mr. Genet, on which, nevertheless, no scruples had been expressed. The President took up the subject with more vehemence than I have seen him show, and decided without reserve, that not only what had passed on the inexecution of the treaty should go in as public (in which Hamilton and Knox had divided in opinion from Randolph and myself), but also that those respecting the stopping our corn should go in as public (wherein, Hamilton, Knox, and Randolph had been against me). This was the first instance I had seen of his deciding on the opinion of one against that of three others, which proved his own to have been very strong.

December the 1st, 1793. Beckley tells me he had the following fact from Lear. Langdon, Cabot, and some others of the Senate, standing in a knot before the fire after the Senate had adjourned, and growling together about some measure which they had just lost; "Ah!" said Cabot, "things will never go right till you have a President for life, and an hereditary Senate." Langdon told this to Lear, who mentioned it to the President. The President seemed struck with it, and declared he had not supposed there was a man in the United States who could have entertained such an idea.

March the 2d, 1797. I arrived at Philadelphia to qualify as Vice-President, and called instantly on Mr. Adams, who lodged at Francis's, in Fourth street. The next morning he returned my visit at Mr. Madison's, where I lodged. He found me alone in my room, and shutting the door himself, he said he was glad to find me alone, for that he wished a free conversation with me. He entered immediately on an explanation of the situation of our affairs with France, and the danger of rupture with that nation, a rupture which would convulse the attachments of this country; that he was impressed with the necessity of an immediate mission to the Directory; that it would have been the first wish of his heart to have got me to go there, but that he supposed it was out of the question, as it did not seem justifiable for him to send away the person destined to take his place in case of accident to himself, nor decent to remove from competition one who was a rival in the public favor. That he had, therefore, concluded to send a mission, which, by its dignity, should satisfy France, and by its selection from the three great divisions of the continent, should satisfy all parts of the United States; in short, that he had determined to join Gerry and Madison to Pinckney, and he wished me to consult Mr. Madison for him. I told him that as to myself, I concurred in the opinion of the impropriety of my leaving the post assigned me, and that my inclinations, moreover, would never permit me to cross the Atlantic again; that I would, as he desired, consult Mr. Madison, but I feared it was desperate, as he had refused that mission on my leaving it, in General Washington's time, though it was kept open a twelvemonth for him. He said that if Mr. Madison should refuse, he would still appoint him, and leave the responsibility on him. I consulted Mr. Madison, who declined as I expected. I think it was on Monday the 6th of March, Mr. Adams and myself met at dinner at General Washington's, and we happened, in the evening, to rise from table and come away together. As soon as we got into the street, I told him the event of my negotiation with Mr. Madison. He immediately said, that, on consultation, some objections to that nomination had been raised which he had not contemplated; and was going on with excuses which evidently embarrassed him, when we came to Fifth street, where our road separated, his being down Market street, mine off along Fifth, and we took leave; and he never after that said one word to me on the subject, or ever consulted me as to any measures of the government. The opinion I formed at the time on this transaction, was, that Mr. Adams, in the first moments of the enthusiasm of the occasion (his inauguration), forgot party sentiments, and as he never acted on any system, but was always governed by the feeling of the moment, he thought, for a moment, to steer impartially between the parties; that Monday, the 6th of March, being the first time he had met his cabinet, on expressing ideas of this kind, he had been at once diverted from them, and returned to his former party views.

July, 1797. Murray is rewarded for his services by an appointment to Amsterdam; W. Smith of Charleston, to Lisbon.

August the 24th. About the time of the British treaty, Hamilton and Talleyrand, bishop of Autun, dined together, and Hamilton drank freely. Conversing on the treaty, Talleyrand says, "*mais vraiment, Monsieur Hamilton, ce n'est pas bien honnête,* after making the Senate ratify the treaty, to advise the President to reject it." "The treaty," says Hamilton, "is an execrable one, and Jay was an old woman for making it; but the whole credit of saving us from it must be given to the President." After circumstances had led to a conclusion that the President also must ratify it, he said to the same Talleyrand, "though the treaty is a most execrable one, yet when once we have come to a determination on it, we must carry it through thick and thin, right or wrong." Talleyrand told this to Volney, who told it to me.

There is a letter now appearing in the papers, from Pickering to Monroe, dated July the 24th, 1797, which I am satisfied is written by Hamilton. He was in Philadelphia at that date.

December the 26th, 1797. Langdon tells me, that at the second election of President and Vice-President of the United States, when there was a considerable vote given to Clinton in opposition to Mr. Adams, he took occasion to remark it in conversation in the Senate chamber with Mr. Adams, who, gritting his teeth, said, "damn 'em, damn 'em, damn 'em, you see that an elective government will not do." He also tells me that Mr. Adams, in a late conversation, said, "republicanism must be disgraced, Sir." The Chevalier Yruho called on him at Braintree, and conversing on French affairs, and Yruho expressing his belief of their stability, in opposition to Mr. Adams, the latter lifting up and shaking his finger at him, said, "I'll tell you what, the French republic will not last three months." This I had from Yruho.

Harper, lately in a large company, was saying that the best thing the friends of the French could do, was to pray for the restoration of their monarch. "Then," says a bystander, "the best thing we could do, I suppose, would be to pray for the establishment of a monarch in the United States." "Our people," says Harper, "are not yet ripe for it, but it is the best thing we can come to, and we shall come to it." Something like this was said in presence of Findlay. He now denies it in the public papers, though it can be proved by several members.

December the 27th. Tenche Coxe tells me, that a little before Hamilton went out of office, or just as he was going out, taking with him his last conversation, and among other things, on the subject of their differences, "for my part," says he, "I avow myself a monarchist; I have no objection to a trial being made of this thing of a republic, but," &c.

January the 5th, 1798. I receive a very remarkable fact indeed in our history, from Baldwin and Skinner. Before the establishment of our present government, a very extensive combination had taken place in New York and the eastern States, among that description of people who were partly monarchical in principle, or frightened with Shays's rebellion and the impotence of the old Congress. Delegates in different places had actually had consultations on the subject of seizing on the powers of a government, and establishing them by force; had corresponded with one another, and had sent a deputy to General Washington to solicit his co-operation. He refused to join them. The new convention was in the meantime proposed by Virginia and appointed. These people believed it impossible the States should ever agree on a government, as this must include the impost and all the other powers which the States had, a thousand times, refused to the general authority. They therefore let the proposed convention go on, not doubting its failure, and confiding that on its failure would be a still more favorable moment for their enterprise. They therefore wished it to fail, and especially, when Hamilton, their leader, brought forward his plan of government, failed entirely in carrying it, and retired in disgust from the convention. His associates then took every method to prevent any form of government being agreed to. But the well-intentioned never ceased trying, first one thing, then another, till they could get something agreed to. The final passage and adoption of the constitution completely defeated the views of the combination, and saved us from an attempt to establish a government over us by force. This fact throws a blaze of light on the conduct of several members from New York and the eastern States in the convention of Annapolis, and the grand convention. At that of Annapolis, several eastern members most vehemently opposed Madison's proposition for a more general convention, with more general powers. They wished things to get more and more into confusion, to justify the violent measure they proposed. The idea of establishing a government by reasoning and agreement, they publicly ridiculed as an Utopian project, visionary and unexampled.

February the 6th, 1798. Mr. Baldwin tells me that in a conversation yesterday with Goodhue, on the state of our affairs, Goodhue said, "I'll tell you what, I have made up my mind on this subject; I would rather the old ship should go down than not"; (meaning the Union of the States). Mr. Hillhouse coming up, "well," says Mr. Baldwin, "I'll tell my old friend Hillhouse what you say"; and he told him. "Well," says Goodhue, "I repeat that I would rather the old ship should go down, if we are to be always kept pumping so." "Mr. Hillhouse," says Baldwin, "you remember when we were learning logic together at school, there was the case *categorical* and the case *hypothetical*. Mr. Goodhue stated it to me first as the case categorical. I am glad to see that he now changes it to the case hypothetical, by adding, 'if we are always to be kept pumping so.'" Baldwin went on then to remind Goodhue what an advocate he had been for our tonnage duty, wanting to make it one dollar instead of fifty cents; and how impatiently he bore the delays of Congress in proceeding to retaliate on Great Britain before Mr. Madison's propositions came on. Goodhue acknowledged that his opinions had changed since that.

February the 15th, 1798. I dined this day with Mr. Adams (the President). The company was large. After dinner I was sitting next to him, and our conversation was first on the enormous price of labor,[6] house rent, and other things. We both concurred in ascribing it chiefly to the floods of bank paper now afloat, and in condemning those institutions. We then got on the constitution; and in the course of our conversation he said, that no republic could ever last which had not a Senate, and a Senate deeply and strongly rooted, strong enough to bear up against all popular storms and passions; that he thought our Senate as well constituted as it could have been, being chosen by the legislatures; for

[6] He observed, that eight or ten years ago, he gave only fifty dollars to a common laborer for his farm, finding him food and lodging. Now he gives one hundred and fifty dollars, and even two hundred dollars to one.—T. J.

if these could not support them, he did not know what could do it; that perhaps it might have been as well for them to be chosen by the State at large, as that would insure a choice of distinguished men, since none but such could be known to a whole people; that the only fault in our Senate was, that it was not durable enough; that hitherto, it had behaved very well; however, he was afraid they would give way in the end. That as to trusting to a popular assembly for the preservation of our liberties, it was the merest chimera imaginable; they never had any rule of decision but their own will; that he would as lieve be again in the hands of our old committees of safety, who made the law and executed it at the same time; that it had been observed by some writer (I forget whom he named), that anarchy did more mischief in one night, than tyranny in an age; and that in modern times we might say with truth, that in France, anarchy had done more harm in one night, than all the despotism of their Kings had ever done in twenty or thirty years. The point in which he views our Senate, as the colossus of the constitution, serves as a key to the politics of the Senate, who are two-thirds of them in his sentiments, and accounts for the bold line of conduct they pursue.

March the 1st. Mr. Tazewell tells me, that when the appropriations for the British treaty were on the carpet, and very uncertain in the lower House, there being at that time a number of bills in the hands of committees of the Senate, none reported, and the Senate idle for want of them, he, in his place, called on the committees to report, and particularly on Mr. King, who was of most of them. King said that it was true the committees kept back their reports, waiting the event of the question about appropriation; that if that was not carried, they considered legislation as at an end; that they might as well break up and consider the Union as dissolved. Tazewell expressed his astonishment at these ideas, and called on King to know if he had misapprehended him. King rose again and repeated the same words. The next day, Cabot took an occasion in debate, and so awkward a one as to show it was a thing agreed to be done, to repeat the same sentiments in stronger terms, and carried further, by declaring a determination on their side to break up and dissolve the government.

March the 11th. In conversation with Baldwin, and Brown of Kentucky, Brown says that in a private company once, consisting of Hamilton, King, Madison, himself, and someone else making a fifth, speaking of the *"federal government"*; "Oh!" says Hamilton, "say the *federal monarchy,* let us call things by their right names, for a monarchy it is."

Baldwin mentions at table the following fact: When the bank bill was under discussion in the House of Representatives, Judge Wilson came in, and was standing by Baldwin. Baldwin reminded him of the following fact which passed in the grand convention: Among the enumerated powers given to Congress, was one to erect corporations. It was, on debate, struck out. Several particular powers were then proposed. Among others, Robert Morris proposed to give Congress a power to establish a national bank. Gouverneur Morris opposed it, observing that it was extremely doubtful whether the constitution they were framing could ever be passed at all by the people of America; that to give it its best chance, however, they should make it as palatable as possible, and put nothing into it not very essential, which might raise up enemies; that his colleague (Robert Morris) well knew that "a bank" was, in their State, (Pennsylvania), the very watch-word of party; that *a bank* had been the great bone of contention between the two parties of the State from the establishment of their constitution, having been erected, put down, and erected again, as either party preponderated; that therefore, to insert this power, would instantly enlist against the whole instrument, the whole of the anti-bank party in Pennsylvania. Whereupon it was rejected, as was every other special power, except that of giving copyrights to authors, and patents to inventors; the general power of incorporating being whittled down to this shred. Wilson agreed to the fact.

Mr. Hunter, of South Carolina, who lodges with Rutledge, tells me that Rutledge was explaining to him the plan they proposed to pursue as to war measures when Otis came in. Rutledge addressed Otis. Now, sir, says he, you must come forward with something liberal for the southern States, fortify their harbors, and build gallies, in order to obtain their concurrence. Otis said, we insist on convoys for our European trade, and *guarda costas,* on which conditions alone we will give them gallies and fortifications. Rutledge observed, that in the event of war, McHenry and Pickering must go out; Wolcott, he thought, might remain, but the others were incapable of conducting a war. Otis said the eastern people would never abandon Pickering, he must be retained; McHenry might go. They considered together whether General Pinckney would accept the office of Secretary of War. They apprehended he would not. It was agreed in this conversation that Sewall had more the ear of the President than any other person.

March the 12th. When the bill for appropriations was before the Senate, Anderson moved to strike out a clause recognizing (by way of appropriation) the appointment of a committee by the House of Representatives to sit during their recess to collect evidence on Blount's case, denying they had power, but by a law, to authorize a committee to sit during recess. Tracy advocated the motion, and said, "We may as well speak out. The committee was appointed by the House of Representatives to take care of the British minister, to take care of the Spanish minister, to take care of the Secretary of State, in short, to take care of the President of the United States. They were afraid the President and Secretary of State would not perform the office of collecting evidence faithfully; that there would be collusion, &c. Therefore, the House appointed a committee of their own. We shall have them next sending a committee to Europe to make a treaty, &c. Suppose that the House of Representatives should resolve, that after the adjournment of Congress, they should continue to sit as a committee of the whole House during the whole recess." This shows how the appointment of that committee has been viewed by the President's friends.

April the 5th. Doctor Rush tells me he had it from Mrs. Adams, that not a scrip of a pen has passed between the late and present President since he came into office.

April the 13th. New instructions of the British government to their armed ships now appear, which clearly infringe their treaty with us, by authorizing them to take our vessels carrying produce of the French colonies from those colonies to Europe, and to take vessels bound to a blockaded port. See them in Brown's paper, of April the 18th, in due form.

The President has sent a government brig to France, probably to carry despatches. He has chosen as the bearer of these one Humphreys, the son of a ship carpenter, ignorant, under age, not speaking a word of French, most abusive of that nation, whose only merit is, the having mobbed and beaten Bache on board the frigate built here, for which he was indicted and punished by fine.

April the 25th. At a dinner given by the bar to the federal judges, Chase and Peters, present about twenty-four lawyers, and William Tilghman in the chair, this toast was given, "Our *King* in old England." Observe the double *entendre* on the word King. Du Ponceau, who was one of the bar present, told this to Tenche Coxe, who told me in presence of H. Tazewell. Dallas was at the dinner; so was Colonel Charles Sims, of Alexandria, who is here on a lawsuit *vs.* General Irving.

May the 3d. The President some time ago appointed Steele, of Virginia, a commissioner to the Indians, and recently Secretary of the Mississippi Territory. Steele was a Counsellor of Virginia, and was voted out by the Assembly because he turned tory. He then offered for Congress, and was rejected by the people. Then offered for the Senate of Virginia, and was rejected. The President has also appointed Joseph Hopkinson commissioner to make a treaty with the Oneida Indians. He is a youth of about twenty-two or twenty-three, and has no other claims to such an appointment than extreme toryism, and the having made a poor song to the tune of the President's March.

October the 13th, 1798. Littlepage, who has been on one or two missions from Poland to Spain, said that when Gardoqui returned from America, he settled with his court an account of secret service money of six hundred thousand dollars. *Ex-relatione* Colonel Monroe.

January, 1799. In a conversation between Dr. Ewen and the President, the former said one of his sons was an aristocrat, the other a democrat. The President asked if it was not the youngest who was the democrat. "Yes," said Ewen. "Well," said the President, "a boy of fifteen who is not a democrat is good for nothing, and he is no better who is a democrat at twenty." Ewen told Hurt, and Hurt told me.

January the 14th. Logan tells me that in his conversation with Pickering on his arrival, the latter abused Gerry very much; said he was a traitor to his country, and had deserted the post to which he was appointed; that the French temporized at first with Pinckney, but found him too much of a man for their purpose. Logan observing, that notwithstanding the pacific declarations of France, it might still be well to keep up the military ardor of our citizens, and to have the militia in good order; "the militia," said Pickering, "the militia never did any good to this country, except in the single affair of Bunker Hill; that we must have a standing army of fifty thousand men, which being stationed in different parts of the continent, might serve as rallying points for the militia, and so render them of some service." In his conversation with Mr. Adams, Logan mentioned the willingness of the French to treat with Gerry. "And do you know why," said Mr. Adams. "Why, sir?" said Logan. "Because," said Mr. Adams, "they know him to have been an anti-federalist, against the constitution."

January the 2d, 1800. Information from Tenche Coxe. Mr. Liston had sent two letters to the Governor of Canada by one Sweezy. He had sent copies of them, together with a third (original) by one Cribs. Sweezy was arrested (being an old horse thief), and his papers examined. T. Coxe had a sight of them. As soon as a rumor got out that there were letters of Mr. Liston disclosed, but no particulars yet mentioned, Mr. Liston suspecting that *Cribs* had betrayed him, thought it best to bring all his *three* letters, and lay them before Pickering, Secretary of State. Pickering thought them all very innocent. In his office they were seen by a Mr. Hodgen of New Jersey, commissary of military stores, and the intimate friend of Pickering. It happens that there is some land partnership between Pickering, Hodgen and Coxe, so that the latter is freely and intimately visited by Hodgen, who, moreover, speaks freely with him on political subjects. They were talking the news of the day, when Mr. Coxe observed that these intercepted letters of Liston were serious things; (nothing being yet out but a general rumor). Hodgen asked which he thought the most serious. Coxe said the second; (for he knew yet of no other). Hodgen said he thought little of any of them, but that the third was the most exceptionable. This struck Coxe, who, not betraying his ignorance of a third letter, asked generally what part of that he alluded to. Hodgen said to that wherein he *assured the Governor of Canada, that if the French invaded Canada, an army would be marched from these States to his assistance.* After this it became known that it was Sweezy who was arrested, and not Cribs; so that Mr. Liston had made an unnecessary disclosure of his third letter to Mr. Pickering, who, however, keeps his secret for him. In the beginning of the conversation between Hodgen and Coxe, Coxe happened to name Sweezy as the bearer of the letters. "That's not his name," says Hodgen (for he did not know that two of the letters had been sent by Sweezy also), "his name is Cribs." This put Coxe on his guard, and sent him fishing for the new matter.

January the 10th. Doctor Rush tells me that he had it from Samuel Lyman, that during the X Y Z Congress, the federal members held the largest caucus they have ever had, at which he was present, and the question was proposed and debated, whether they should declare war against France, and determined in the negative. Lyman was against it.

He tells me, that Mr. Adams told him, that when he came on in the fall to Trenton, he was there surrounded constantly by the opponents of the late mission to France. That Hamilton pressing him to delay it, said, "Why, sir, by Christmas, Louis the XVIII will be seated on his throne." Mr. A. "By whom?" H. "By the coalition." Mr. A. "Ah! then farewell to the independence of Europe. If a coalition moved by the finger of England, is to give a government to France, there is an end to the independence of every country."

January the 12th. General Samuel Smith says that Pickering, Wolcott, and McHenry, wrote a joint letter from Trenton to the President, then at Braintree, dissuading him from the mission to France. Stoddard refused to join in it. Stoddard says the instructions are such, that if the Directory have any disposition to reconciliation, a treaty will be made. He observed to him, also, that Ellsworth looks beyond this mission to the Presidential chair. That with this view, he will endeavor to make a treaty, and a good one. That Davie has the same vanity and views. All this communicated by Stoddard to S. Smith.

January the 13th. Baer and Harrison G. Otis told J. Nicholas, that in the caucus mentioned ante 10th, there wanted but five votes to produce a declaration of war. Baer was against it.

January the 19th. W. C. Nicholas tells me, that in a conversation with Dexter three or four days ago, he asked Dexter whether it would not be practicable for the States to agree on some uniform mode of choosing electors of President. Dexter said, "I suppose you would prefer an election by districts." "Yes," said Nicholas, "I think it would be best; but would nevertheless agree to any other consistent with the constitution." Dexter said he did not know what might be the opinion of his State, but his own was, that no mode of *election* would answer any good purpose; that he should prefer one *for life*. "On that reasoning," said Nicholas, "you should prefer an hereditary one." "No," he said, "we are not ripe for that yet. I suppose," added he, "this doctrine is not very popular with you." "No," said Nicholas, "it would effectually damn any man in my State." "So it would in mine," said Dexter; "but I am under no inducement to belie my sentiment, I have nothing to ask from anybody; I had rather be at home than here, therefore I speak my sentiments freely." Mr. Nicholas, a little before or after this, made the same proposition of a uniform election to Ross, who replied that he saw no good in any kind of election. "Perhaps," said he, "the present one may last awhile." On the whole, Mr. Nicholas thinks he perceives in that party, a willingness and a wish to let everything go from bad to worse, to amend nothing, in hopes it may bring on confusion, and open a door to the kind of government they wish. In a conversation with Gunn, who goes with them, but thinks in some degree with us, Gunn told him that the very game which the minority of Pennsylvania is now playing with McKean (see substitute of minority in lower House, and address of Senate in upper), was meditated by the same party in the federal government, in case of the election of a republican President; and that the eastern States would in that case throw things into confusion, and break the Union. That they have in a great degree got rid of their paper, so as no longer to be creditors, and the moment they cease to enjoy the plunder of the immense appropriations now exclusively theirs, they would aim at some other order of things.

January the 24th. Mr. Smith, a merchant of Hamburg, gives me the following information: The St. Andrew's Club of New York (all of Scotch tories), gave a public dinner lately. Among other guests, Alexander Hamilton was one. After dinner, the first toast was, "The President of the United States." It was drank without any particular approbation. The next was, "George the Third." Hamilton started up on his feet, and insisted on a bumper and three cheers. The whole company accordingly rose and gave the cheers. One of them, though a federalist, was so disgusted at the partiality shown by Hamilton to a foreign sovereign over his own President, that he mentioned it to a Mr. Schwarthouse, an American merchant of New York, who mentioned it to Smith.

Mr. Smith also tells me, that calling one evening on Mr. Evans, then Speaker of the House of Representatives of Pennsylvania, and asking the news, Evans said, Harper had been just there, and speaking of the President's setting out to Braintree, said, "he prayed to God that his horses might run away with him, or some other accident happen to break his neck before he reached Braintree." This was indignation at his having named Murray, &c., to negotiate with France. Evans approved of the wish.

February the 1st. Doctor Rush tells me that he had it from Asa Green, that when the clergy addressed General Washington on his departure from the government, it was observed in their consultation, that he had never, on any occasion, said a word to the public which showed a belief in the Christian religion, and they thought they should so pen their address, as to force him at length to declare publicly whether he was a Christian or not. They did so. However, he observed, the old fox was too cunning for them. He answered every article of their address particularly except that, which he passed over without notice. Rush observes, he never did say a word on the subject in any of his public papers, except in his valedictory letter to the Governors of the States, when he resigned his commission in the army, wherein he speaks of "the benign influence of the Christian religion."

I know that Gouverneur Morris, who pretended to be in his secrets and believed himself to be so, has often told me that General Washington believed no more of that system than he himself did.

March, 1800. Heretical doctrines maintained in Senate, on the motion against the Aurora. That there is in every legal body of men a right of self-preservation, authorizing them to do whatever is necessary for that purpose: by Tracy, Read, and Lawrence. That the common law authorizes the proceeding proposed against the Aurora, and is in force here: by Read. That the privileges of Congress are and ought to be indefinite: by Read.

Tracy says, he would not say exactly that the common law of England in all its extent is in force here; but common sense, reason and morality, which are the foundations of the common law, are in force here, and establish a common law. He held himself so nearly half way between the common law of England and what everybody else has called natural law, and not common law, that he could hold to either the one or the other, as he should find expedient.

Dexter maintained that the common law, as to crimes, is in force in the United States.

Chipman says, that the principles of common right are common law.

March the 11th. Conversing with Mrs. Adams on the subject of the writers in the newspapers, I took occasion to mention that I never in my life had, directly or indirectly, written one sentence for a newspaper; which is an absolute truth. She said that Mr. Adams, she believed, had pretty well ceased to meddle in the newspapers, since he closed the pieces on Davila. This is the first direct avowal of that work to be his, though long and universally understood to be so.

March the 14th. Freneau, in Charleston, had the printing of the laws in his paper. He printed a pamphlet of Pinckney's letters on Robbins' case. Pickering has given the printing of the laws to the tory paper of that place, though not of half the circulation. The printing amounted to about one hundred dollars a year.

March the 24th. Mr. Perez Morton of Massachusetts tells me that Thatcher, on his return from the war Congress, declared to him he had been for a declaration of war against France, and many others also; but that on counting noses they found they could not carry it, and therefore did not attempt it.

March the 27th. Judge Breckenridge gives me the following information: He and Mr. Ross were originally very intimate; indeed, he says, he found him keeping a little Latin school, and advised and aided him in the study of law, and brought him forward. After Ross became a Senator, and particularly at the time of the western insurrection, they still were in concert. After the British treaty, Ross, on his return, informed him there was a party in the United States who wanted to overturn the government, who were in league with France; that France, by a secret article of treaty with Spain, was to have Louisiana; and that Great Britain was likely to be our best friend and dependence. On this information, he, Breckenridge, was induced to become an advocate for the British treaty. During this intimacy with Ross, he says, that General Collot, in his journey to the western country, called on him, and he frequently led Breckenridge into conversations on their grievances under the government, and particularly the western expedition; that he spoke to him of the advantages that country would have in joining France when she should hold Louisiana; showed him a map he had drawn of that part of the country; pointed out the passes in the mountain, and the facility with which they might hold them against the United States, and with which France could support them from New Orleans. He says, that in these conversations, Collot let himself out with common prudence. He says, Michaud (to whom I, at the request of Genet, had given a letter of introduction to the Governor of Kentucky as a botanist, which was his real profession), called on him; that Michaud had a commissary's commission for the expedition, which Genet had planned from that quarter against the Spaniards; that ——, the late Spanish commandant of St. Genevieve, with one Powers, an Englishman, called on him. That from all these circumstances, together with Ross' stories, he did believe that there was a conspiracy to deliver our country, or some part of it at least, to the French; that he made notes of what passed between himself and Collot and the others, and lent them to Mr. Ross, who gave them to the President, by whom they were deposited in the office of the Board of War; that when he complained to Ross of this breach of confidence, he endeavored to get off by compliments on the utility and importance of his notes.. They now cooled towards each other; and his opposition to Ross's election as Governor has separated them in truth, though not entirely to appearance.

Doctor Rush tells me, that within a few days he has heard a member of Congress lament our separation from Great Britain, and express his sincere wishes that we were again dependent on her.

December the 25th, 1800. Colonel Hitchburn tells me what Col. Monroe had before told me of, as coming from Hitchburn. He was giving me the characters of persons in Massachusetts. Speaking of Lowell, he said he was, in the beginning of the Revolution, a timid whig, but as soon as he found we were likely to prevail, he became a great office hunter. And in the very breath of speaking of Lowell, he stopped: says he, I will give you a piece of information which I do not venture to speak of to others. There was a Mr. Hale in Massachusetts, a reputable, worthy man, who becoming a little embarrassed in his affairs, I aided him, which made him very friendly to me. He went to Canada on some business. The Governor there took great notice of him. On his return, he took occasion to mention to me that he was authorized by the Governor of Canada to give from three to five thousand guineas each to himself and some others, to induce them, not to do anything to the injury of their country, but to befriend a good connection between England and it. Hitchburn said he would think of it, and asked Hale to come and dine with him tomorrow. After dinner he drew Hale fully out. He told him he had his doubts, but particularly, that he should not like to be alone in such a business. On that, Hale named to him four others who were to be engaged, two of whom, said Hitchburn, are now dead, and two living. Hitchburn, when he had got all he wanted out of

Hale, declined in a friendly way. But he observed those four men, from that moment, to espouse the interests of England in every point and on every occasion. Though he did not name the men to me, yet as the speaking of Lowell was what brought into his head to tell me this anecdote, I concluded he was one. From other circumstances respecting Stephen Higginson, of whom he spoke, I conjectured him to be the other living one.

December the 26th. In another conversation, I mentioned to Colonel Hitchburn, that though he had not named names, I had strongly suspected Higginson to be one of Hale's men. He smiled and said, if I had strongly suspected any man wrongfully from his information, he would undeceive me; that there were no persons he thought more strongly to be suspected himself, than Higginson and Lowell. I considered this as saying they were the men. Higginson is employed in an important business about our navy.

February the 12th, 1801. Edward Livingston tells me, that Bayard applied today or last night to General Samuel Smith, and represented to him the expediency of his coming over to the States who vote for Burr, that there was nothing in the way of appointment which he might not command, and particularly mentioned the Secretaryship of the Navy. Smith asked him if he was authorized to make the offer. He said he was authorized. Smith told this to Livingston, and to W. C. Nicholas who confirms it to me. Bayard in like manner tempted Livingston, not by offering any particular office, but by representing to him his, Livingston's, intimacy and connection with Burr; that from him he had everything to expect, if he would come over to him. To Doctor Linn of New Jersey, they have offered the government of New Jersey. See a paragraph in Martin's Baltimore paper of February the 10th, signed, "A LOOKER ON," stating an intimacy of views between Harper and Burr.

February the 14th. General Armstrong tells me, that Gouverneur Morris, in conversation with him today on the scene which is passing, expressed himself thus. "How comes it," says he, "that Burr who is four hundred miles off (at Albany), has agents here at work with great activity, while Mr. Jefferson, who is on the spot, does nothing?" This explains the ambiguous conduct of himself and his nephew, Lewis Morris, and that they were holding themselves free for a prize; *i.e.,* some office, either to the uncle or nephew.

February the 16th. See in the Wilmington Mirror of February the 14th, Mr. Bayard's elaborate argument to prove that the common law, as modified by the laws of the respective States at the epoch of the ratification of the constitution, attached to the courts of the United States.

June the 23d, 1801. Andrew Ellicot tells me, that in a conversation last summer with Major William Jackson of Philadelphia, on the subject of our intercourse with Spain, Jackson said we had managed our affairs badly; that he himself was the author of the papers against the Spanish ministers signed Americanus; that his object was irritation; that he was anxious, if it could have been brought about, to have plunged us in a war with Spain, that the people might have been occupied with that, and not with the conduct of the administration, and other things they had no business to meddle with.

December the 13th, 1803. The Reverend Mr. Coffin of New England, who is now here soliciting donations for a college in Greene county, in Tennessee, tells me that when he first determined to engage in this enterprise, he wrote a paper recommendatory of the enterprise, which he meant to get signed by clergymen, and a similar one for persons in a civil character, at the head of which he wished Mr. Adams to put his name, he being then President, and the application going only for his name, and not for a donation. Mr. Adams, after reading the paper and considering, said, "he saw no possibility of continuing the union of the States; that their dissolution must necessarily take place; that he therefore saw no propriety in recommending to New England men to promote a literary institution in the south; that it was in fact giving strength to those who were to be their enemies; and, therefore, he would have nothing to do with it."

December the 31st. After dinner today, the pamphlet on the conduct of Colonel Burr being the subject of conversation, Matthew Lyon noticed the insinuations against the republicans at Washington, pending the Presidential election, and expressed his wish that everything was spoken out which was known; that it would then appear on which side there was a bidding for votes, and he declared that John Brown of Rhode Island, urging him to vote for Colonel Burr, used these words: "What is it you want, Colonel Lyon? Is it office, is it money? Only say what you want, and you shall have it."

January the 2d, 1804. Colonel Hitchburn of Massachusetts, reminding me of a letter he had written me from Philadelphia, pending the Presidential election, says he did not therein give the details. That he was in company at Philadelphia with Colonel Burr and . . . that in the course of the conversation on the election, Colonel Burr said, "we must have a President, and a constitutional one, in some way." "How is it to be done," says Hitchburn; "Mr. Jefferson's friends will not quit him, and his enemies are not strong enough to carry another." "Why," says Burr, "our friends must join the federalists, and give the President." The next morning at breakfast, Colonel Burr repeated nearly the same, saying, "we cannot be without a President, our friends must join the federal vote." "But," says Hitchburn, "we shall then be without a Vice-President; who is to be our Vice-President?" Colonel Burr answered, "Mr. Jefferson."

January the 26th. Colonel Burr, the Vice-President, calls on me in the evening, having previously asked an opportunity of conversing with me. He began by recapitulating summarily, that he had come to New York a stranger, some years ago; that he found the country in possession of two rich families (the Livingstons and Clintons); that his pursuits were not political, and he meddled not. When the crisis, however, of 1800 came on, they found their influence worn out, and solicited his aid with the people. He lent it without any views of promotion. That his being named as a candidate for Vice-President was unexpected by him. He acceded to it with a view to promote my fame and advancement, and from a desire to be with me, whose company and conversation had always been fascinating to him. That since, those great families had become hostile to him, and had excited the calumnies which I had seen published. That in this Hamilton had joined, and had even written some of the pieces against him. That his attachment to me had been sincere, and was still unchanged, although many little stories had been carried to him, and he supposed to me also, which he despised; but that attachments must be reciprocal or cease to exist, and therefore he asked if any change had taken place in mine towards him; that he had chosen to have this conversation with myself directly, and not through any intermediate agent. He reminded me of a letter written to him about the time of counting the votes (say February, 1801), mentioning that his election had left a chasm in my arrangements; that I had lost him from my list in the administration, &c. He observed, he believed it would be for the interest of the republican cause for him to retire; that a disadvantageous schism would otherwise take place; but that were he to retire, it would be said he shrunk from the public sentence, which he never would do; that his enemies were using my name to destroy him, and something was necessary from me to prevent and deprive them of that weapon, some mark of favor from me which would declare to the world that he retired with my confidence.

I answered by recapitulating to him what had been my conduct previous to the election of 1800. That I had never interfered directly or indirectly with my friends or any others, to influence the election either for him or myself; that I considered it as my duty to be merely passive, except that in Virginia, I had taken some measures to procure for him the unanimous vote of that State, because I thought any failure there might be imputed to me. That in the election now coming on, I was observing the same conduct, held no councils with anybody respecting it, nor suffered anyone to speak to me on the subject, believing it my duty to leave myself to the free discussion of the public; that I do not at this moment know, nor have ever heard, who were to be proposed as candidates for the public choice, except so far as could be gathered from the newspapers. That as to the attack excited against him in the newspapers, I had noticed it but as the passing wind; that I had seen complaints that Cheetham, employed in publishing the laws, should be permitted to eat the public bread and abuse its second officer; that as to this, the publishers of the laws were appointed by the Secretary of the State, without any reference to me; that to make the notice general, it was often given to one republican and one federal printer of the same place; that these federal printers did not in the least intermit their abuse of me, though receiving emoluments from the governments and that I have never thought it proper to interfere for myself, and consequently not in the case of the Vice-President. That as to the letter he referred to, I remembered it, and believed he had only mistaken the date at which it was written; that I thought it must have been on the first notice of the event of the election of South Carolina; and that I had taken that occasion to mention to him, that I had intended to have proposed to him one of the great offices, if he had not been elected; but that his election in giving him a higher station had deprived me of his aid in the administration. The letter alluded to was, in fact, mine to him of December the 15th, 1800. I now went on to explain to him verbally, what I meant by saying I had lost him from my list. That in General Washington's time, it had been signified to him that Mr. Adams, the Vice-President, would be glad of a foreign embassy; that General Washington mentioned it to me, expressed his doubts whether Mr. Adams was a fit character for such an office, and his still greater doubts, indeed his conviction, that it would not be justifiable to send away the person who, in case of his death, was provided by the constitution to take his place; that it would moreover appear indecent for him to be disposing of the public trusts, in apparently buying off a competitor for the public favor. I concurred with him in the opinion, and, if I recollect rightly, Hamilton, Knox, and Randolph were consulted and gave the same opinions. That when Mr. Adams came to the administration, in his first interview with me, he mentioned the necessity of a mission to France, and how desirable it would have been to him if he could have got me to undertake it; but that he conceived it would be wrong in him to send me away, and assigned the same reasons General Washington had done; and therefore, he should appoint Mr. Madison, &c. That I had myself contemplated his (Colonel Burr's) appointment to one of the great offices, in case he was not elected Vice-President; but that as soon as that election was known, I saw it could not be done, for the good reasons which had led General Washington and Mr. Adams to the same conclusion; and therefore, in my first letter to Colonel Burr, after the issue was known, I had mentioned to him that a chasm in my arrangements had been produced by this event. I was thus particular in rectifying the date of this letter, because it gave me an opportunity of explaining the grounds on which it was written, which were, indirectly, an answer to his present hints. He left the matter with me for consideration, and the conversation was turned to indifferent subjects. I should here notice, that Colonel Burr must have thought that I could swallow strong things in my own favor, when he founded his acquiescence in the nomination as Vice-President, to his desire of promoting my honor, the being with me, whose company and conversation had always been fascinating with him, &c. I had never seen Colonel Burr till he came as a member of Senate. His conduct very soon inspired me with distrust. I habitually cautioned Mr. Madison against trusting him too much. I saw afterwards, that under General Washington's and Mr. Adams' administrations, whenever a great military appointment or a diplomatic one was to be made, he came post to Philadelphia to show himself, and in fact that he was always at market, if they had wanted him. He was indeed told by Dayton in 1800, he might be Secretary at War; but this bid was too late. His election as Vice-President was then foreseen. With these impressions of Colonel Burr, there never had been an intimacy between us, and but little association. When I destined him for a high appointment, it was out of respect for the favor he had obtained with the republican party, by his extraordinary exertions and successes in the New York election in 1800.

April the 15th, 1806. About a month ago, Colonel Burr called on me, and entered into a conversation, in which he mentioned, that a little before my coming into office, I had written to him a letter intimating that I had destined him for a high employ, had he not been placed by the people in a different one; that he had signified his willingness to resign as Vice-President, to give aid to the administration in any other place, that he had never asked an office, however; he asked aid of nobody, but could walk on his own legs and take care of himself; that I had always used him with politeness, but nothing more; that he aided in bringing on the present order of things; that he had supported the administration; and that he could do me much harm; he wished, however, to be on different ground; he was now disengaged from all particular business—willing to engage in something—should be in town some days, if I should have anything to propose to him. I observed to him, that I had always been sensible that he possessed talents which might be employed greatly to the advantage of the public, and that as to myself, I had a confidence that if he were employed, he would use his talents for the public good; but that he must be sensible the public had withdrawn their confidence from him, and that in a government like ours it was necessary to embrace in its administration as great a mass of public confidence as possible, by employing those who had a character with the public, of their own, and not merely a secondary one through the executive. He observed, that if we believed a few newspapers, it might be supposed he had lost the public confidence, but that I knew how easy it was to engage newspapers in anything. I observed, that I did not refer to that kind of evidence of his having lost the public confidence, but to the late Presidential election, when, though in possession of the office of Vice-President, there was not a single voice heard for his retaining it. That as to any harm he could do me, I knew no cause why he should desire it, but, at the same time, I feared no injury which any man could do me; that I never had done a single act, or been concerned in any transaction, which I feared to have fully laid open, or which could do me any hurt, if truly stated; that I had never done a single thing with a view to my personal interest, or that of any friend, or with any other view than that of the greatest public good; that, therefore, no threat or fear on that head would ever be a motive of action with me. He has continued in town to this time; dined with me this day week, and called on me to take leave two or three days ago.

I did not commit these things to writing at the time, but I do it now, because in a suit between him and Cheetham, he has had a deposition of Mr. Bayard taken, which seems to have no relation to the suit, nor to any other object than to calumniate me. Bayard pretends to have addressed to me, during the pending of the Presidential election in February, 1801, through General Samuel Smith, certain conditions on which my election might be obtained, and that General Smith, after conversing with me, gave answers from me. This is absolutely false. No proposition of any kind was ever made to me on that occasion by General Smith, nor any answer authorized by me. And this fact General Smith affirms at this moment.

For some matters connected with this, see my notes of February the 12th and 14th, 1801, made at the moment. But the following transactions took place about the same time, that is to say, while the Presidential election was in suspense in Congress, which, though I did not enter at the time, they made such an impression on my mind, that they are now as fresh, as to their principal circumstances, as if they had happened yesterday. Coming out of the Senate chamber one day, I found Gouverneur Morris on the steps. He stopped me, and began a conversation on the strange and portentous state of things then existing, and went on to observe, that the reasons why the minority of States was so opposed to my being elected, were, that they apprehended that, 1, I would turn all federalists out of office; 2, put down the navy; 3, wipe off the public debt. That I need only to declare, or authorize my friends to declare, that I would not take these steps, and instantly the event of the election would be fixed. I told him, that I should leave the world to judge of the course I meant to pursue by that which I had pursued hitherto, believing it to be my duty to be passive and silent during the present scene; that I should certainly make no terms; should never go into the office of President by capitulation, nor with my hands tied by any conditions which should hinder me from pursuing the measures which I should deem for the public good. It was understood that Gouverneur Morris had entirely the direction of the vote of Lewis Morris of Vermont, who, by coming over to Matthew Lyon, would have added another vote, and decided the election. About the same time, I called on Mr. Adams. We conversed on the state of things. I observed to him, that a very dangerous experiment was then in contemplation, to defeat the Presidential election by an act of Congress declaring the right of the Senate to name a President of the Senate, to devolve on him the government during any interregnum; that such a measure would probably produce resistance by force, and incalculable consequences, which it would be in his power to prevent by negativing such an act. He seemed to think such an act justifiable, and observed, it was in my power to fix the election by a word in an instant, by declaring I would not turn out the federal officers, nor put down the navy, nor spunge the national debt. Finding his mind made up as to the usurpation of the government by the President of the Senate, I urged it no further, observed the world must judge as to myself of the future by the past, and turned the conversation to something else. About the same time, Dwight Foster of Massachusetts called on me in my room one night, and went into a very long conversation on the state of affairs, the drift of which was to let me understand, that the fears above mentioned were the only obstacle to my election, to all of which I avoided giving any answer the one way or the other. From this moment he became most bitterly and personally opposed to me, and so has ever continued. I do not recollect that I ever had any particular conversation with General Samuel Smith on this subject. Very possibly I had, however, as the general subject and all its parts were the constant themes of conversation in the private *tête à têtes* with our friends. But certain I am that neither he, nor any other republican ever uttered the most distant hint to me about submitting to any conditions or giving any assurances to anybody; and still more certainly was neither he nor any other person ever authorized by me to say what I would or would not do. See a very exact statement of Bayard's conduct on that occasion in a piece among my notes of 1801, which was published by G. Granger with some alterations in the papers of the day under the signature of —— [blank].

## JEFFERSON'S SERVICES TO HIS COUNTRY

1800(?)

I have sometimes asked myself, whether my country is the better for my having lived at all? I do not know that it is. I have been the instrument of doing the following things; but they would have been done by others; some of them, perhaps, a little better.

The Rivanna had never been used for navigation; scarcely an empty canoe had ever passed down it. Soon after I came of age, I examined its obstructions, set on foot a subscription for removing them, got an Act of Assembly passed, and the thing effected, so as to be used completely and fully for carrying down all our produce.

The Declaration of Independence.

I proposed the demolition of the church establishment, and the freedom of religion. It could only be done by degrees; to wit, the Act of 1776, c. 2, exempted dissenters from contributions to the Church, and left the Church clergy to be supported by voluntary contributions of their own sect; was continued from year to year, and made perpetual 1779, c. 36. I prepared the act for religious freedom in 1777, as part of the revisal, which was not reported to the Assembly till 1779, and that particular law not passed till 1785, and then by the efforts of Mr. Madison.

The act putting an end to entails.

The act prohibiting the importation of slaves.

The act concerning citizens, and establishing the natural right of man to expatriate himself, at will.

The act changing the course of descents, and giving the inheritance to all the children, &c., equally, I drew as part of the revisal.

The act for apportioning crimes and punishments, part of the same work, I drew. When proposed to the legislature, by Mr. Madison, in 1785, it failed by a single vote. G. K. Taylor afterwards, in 1796, proposed the same subject; avoiding the adoption of any part of the diction of mine, the text of which had been studiously drawn in the technical terms of the law, so as to give no occasion for new questions by new expressions. When I drew mine, public labor was thought the best punishment to be substituted for death. But, while I was in France, I heard of a society in England, who had successfully introduced solitary confinement, and saw the drawing of a prison at Lyons, in France, formed on the idea of solitary confinement. And, being applied to by the Governor of Virginia for the plan of a Capitol and Prison, I sent him the Lyons plan, accompanying it with a drawing on a smaller scale, better adapted to our use. This was in June, 1786. Mr. Taylor very judiciously adopted this idea (which had now been acted on in Philadelphia, probably from the English model), and substituted labor in confinement, to the public labor proposed by the Committee of revisal; which themselves would have done, had they been to act on the subject again. The public mind was ripe for this in 1796, when Mr. Taylor proposed it, and ripened chiefly by the experiment in Philadelphia; whereas, in 1785, when it had been proposed to our Assembly, they were not quite ripe for it.

In 1789 and 1790, I had a great number of olive plants, of the best kind, sent from Marseilles to Charleston, for South Carolina and Georgia. They were planted, and are flourishing; and, though not yet multiplied, they will be the germ of that cultivation in those States.

In 1790, I got a cask of heavy upland rice, from the river Denbigh, in Africa, about lat. 9° 30′ North, which I sent to Charleston, in hopes it might supersede the culture of the wet rice, which renders South Carolina and Georgia so pestilential through the summer. It was divided, and a part sent to Georgia. I know not whether it has been attended to in South Carolina; but it has spread in the upper parts of Georgia, so as to have become almost general, and is highly prized. Perhaps it may answer in Tennessee and Kentucky. The greatest service which can be rendered any country is, to add an useful plant to its culture; especially, a bread grain; next in value to bread is oil.

Whether the act for the more general diffusion of knowledge will ever be carried into complete effect, I know not. It was received by the legislature with great enthusiasm at first; and a small effort was made in 1796, by the act to establish public schools, to carry a part of it into effect, *viz.*, that for the establishment of free English schools; but the option given to the courts has defeated the intention of the act.

## THOUGHTS ON LOTTERIES[1]

February, 1826

It is a common idea that games of chance are immoral. But what is chance? Nothing happens in this world without a cause. If we know the cause, we do not call it chance; but if we do not know it, we say it was produced by chance. If we see a loaded die turn its lightest side up, we know the cause, and that it is not an effect of chance; but whatever side an unloaded die turns up, not knowing the cause, we say it is the effect of chance. Yet the morality of a thing cannot depend on our knowledge or ignorance of its cause. Not know-

[1] Burdened with debt, and threatened with the loss of his home, Jefferson hoped to pay his debts by selling his lands through a lottery, which required the approval of the State Legislature. While the bill was pending in the Legislature, Jefferson wrote the above paper as a justification of this unusual way of selling land.

ing why a particular side of an unloaded die turns up, cannot make the act of throwing it, or of betting on it, immoral. If we consider games of chance immoral, then every pursuit of human industry is immoral; for there is not a single one that is not subject to chance, not one wherein you do not risk a loss for the chance of some gain. The navigator, for example, risks his ship in the hope (if she is not lost in the voyage) of gaining an advantageous freight. The merchant risks his cargo to gain a better price for it. A landholder builds a house on the risk of indemnifying himself by a rent. The hunter hazards his time and trouble in the hope of killing game. In all these pursuits, you stake some one thing against another which you hope to win. But the greatest of all gamblers is the farmer. He risks the seed he puts into the ground, the rent he pays for the ground itself, the year's labor on it, and the wear and tear of his cattle and gear, to win a crop, which the chances of too much or too little rain, and general uncertainties of weather, insects, waste, &c., often make a total or partial loss. These, then, are games of chance. Yet so far from being immoral, they are indispensable to the existence of man, and everyone has a natural right to choose for his pursuit such one of them as he thinks most likely to furnish him subsistence. Almost all these pursuits of chance produce something useful to society. But there are some which produce nothing, and endanger the well-being of the individuals engaged in them, or of others depending on them. Such are games with cards, dice, billiards, &c. And although the pursuit of them is a matter of natural right, yet society, perceiving the irresistible bent of some of its members to pursue them, and the ruin produced by them to the families depending on these individuals, consider it as a case of insanity, *quoad hoc,* step in to protect the family and the party himself, as in other cases of insanity, infancy, imbecility, &c., and suppress the pursuit altogether, and the natural right of following it. There are some other games of chance, useful on certain occasions, and injurious only when carried beyond their useful bounds. Such are insurances, lotteries, raffles, &c. These they do not suppress, but take their regulation under their own discretion. The insurance of ships on voyages is a vocation of chance, yet useful, and the right to exercise it therefore is left free. So of houses against fire, doubtful debts, the continuance of a particular life, and similar cases. Money is wanting for a useful undertaking, as a school, &c., for which a direct tax would be disapproved. It is raised therefore by a lottery, wherein the tax is laid on the willing only, that is to say, on those who can risk the price of a ticket without sensible injury for the possibility of a higher prize. An article of property, insusceptible of division at all, or not without great diminution of its worth, is sometimes of so large value as that no purchaser can be found while the owner owes debts, has no other means of payment, and his creditors no other chance of obtaining it but by its sale at a full and fair price. The lottery is here a salutary instrument for disposing of it, where many run small risks for the chance of obtaining a high prize. In this way the great estate of the late Colonel Byrd (in 1756) was made competent to pay his debts, which, had the whole been brought into the market at once, would have overdone the demand, would have sold at half or quarter the value, and sacrificed the creditors, half or three-fourths of whom would have lost their debts. This method of selling was formerly very much resorted to, until it was thought to nourish too much a spirit of hazard. The legislature were therefore induced not to suppress it altogether, but to take it under their own special regulation. This they did for the first time by their act of 1769, c. 17, before which time every person exercised the right freely; and since which time, it is made unlawful but when approved and authorized by a special act of the legislature.

Since then this right of sale, by way of lottery, has been exercised only under the jurisdiction of the legislature. Let us examine the purposes for which they have allowed it in practice, not looking beyond the date of our independence.

1. It was for a long time an item of the standing revenue of the State.

1813. c. 1, § 3. An act imposing taxes for the support of government, and c. 2, § 10.
1814. Dec. c. 1, § 3. 1814. Feb. c. 1, § 3. 1818. c. 1, § 1.
1819. c. 1. 1820. c. 1.

This, then, is a declaration by the nation, that an act was not immoral, of which they were in the habitual use themselves as a part of the regular means of supporting the government; the tax on the vender of tickets was their share of the profits, and if their share was innocent, his could not be criminal.

2. It has been abundantly permitted to raise money by lottery for the purposes of schools; and in this, as in many other cases, the lottery has been permitted to retain a part of the money (generally from ten to fifteen per cent) for the use to which the lottery has been applied. So that while the adventurers paid one hundred dollars for tickets, they received back eighty-five or ninety dollars only in the form of prizes, the remaining ten or fifteen being the tax levied on them, with their own consent. Examples are,

1784. c. 34. Authorizing the city of Williamsburg to raise £2,000 for a grammar school.
1789. c. 68. For Randolph Academy, £1,000.
1789. c. 73. For Fauquier Academy, £500.
c. 74. For the Fredericksburg Academy, £4,000.
1790. c. 46. For the Transylvanian Seminary, £500.
For the Southampton Academy, £300.
1796. c. 82. For the New London Academy.
1803. c. 49. For the Fredericksburg Charity School.
c. 50. For finishing the Strasburg Seminary.
c. 58. For William and Mary College.
c. 62. For the Bannister Academy.
c. 79. For the Belfield Academy.
c. 82. For the Petersburg Academy.
1804. c. 40. For the Hotsprings Seminary.
c. 76. For the Stevensburg Academy.
c. 100. For William and Mary College.
1805. c. 24. For the Rumford Academy.
1812. c. 10. For the Literary Fund. To sell the privilege for $30,000 annually, for seven years.

1816. c. 80. For Norfolk Academy, $12,000.
Norfolk Female Society, $2,000.
Lancastrian School, $6,000.

3. The next object of lotteries has been rivers.

1790. c. 46. For a bridge between Gosport and Portsmouth, £400.
1796. c. 83. For clearing Roanoke River.
1804. c. 62. For clearing Quantico Creek.
1805. c. 42. For a toll bridge over Cheat River.
1816. c. 49. For the Dismal Swamp, $50,000.

4. For roads.

1790. c. 46. For a road to Warminster, £200.
For cutting a road from Rockfish gap to Scott's and Nicholas's landing, £400.
1796. c. 85. To repair certain roads.
1803. c. 60. For improving roads to Snigger's and Ashby's gaps.
c. 61. For opening a road to Brock's gap.
c. 65. For opening a road from the town of Monroe to Sweet Springs and Lewisburg.
c. 71. For improving the road to Brock's gap.
1805. c. 5. For improving the road to Clarksburg.
c. 26. For opening a road from Monongalia Glades to Fishing Creek.
1813. c. 44. For opening a road from Thornton's gap.

5. Lotteries for the benefit of counties.

1796. c. 78. To authorize a lottery in the county of Shenandoah.
c. 84. To authorize a lottery in the county of Gloucester.

6. Lotteries for the benefit of towns.

1782. c. 31. Richmond, for a bridge over Shockoe, amount not limited.
1789. c. 75. Alexandria, to pave its streets, £1,500.
1790. c. 46. do. do. £5,000.
1796. c. 79. Norfolk, one or more lotteries authorized.
c. 81. Petersburg, a lottery authorized.
1803. c. 12. Woodstock, do.
c. 48. Fredericksburg, for improving its main street.
c. 73. Harrisonburg, for improving its streets.

7. Lotteries for religious congregations.

1785. c. 111. Completing a church in Winchester.
For rebuilding a church in the parish of Elizabeth River.
1790. c. 46. For building a church in Warminster, £200.
in Halifax, £200.
in Alexandria, £500.
in Petersburg, £750.
in Shepherdstown, £250.
1791. c. 69. For the benefit of the Episcopal society.

8. Lotteries for private societies.

1790. c. 46. For the Amicable Society in Richmond, £1,000.
1791. c. 70. For building a Freemason's Hall in Charlotte, £750.

9. Lotteries for the benefit of private individuals. [To raise money for them].

1781. c. 6. For completing titles under Byrd's lottery.
1790. c. 46. To erect a paper mill in Staunton, £300.
To raise £2,000 for Nathaniel Twining.
1791. c. 73. To raise £4,000 for William Tatham, to enable him to complete his geographical work.
To enable —— to complete a literary work.[2]
1796. c. 80. For the sufferers by fire in the town of Lexington.

We have seen, then, that every vocation in life is subject to the influence of chance; that so far from being rendered immoral by the admixture of that ingredient, were they abandoned on that account, man could no longer subsist; that, among them, everyone has a natural right to choose that which he thinks most likely to give him comfortable subsistence; but that while the greater number of these pursuits are productive of something which adds to the necessaries and comforts of life, others again, such as cards, dice, &c., are entirely unproductive, doing good to none, injury to many, yet so easy, and so seducing in practice to men of a certain constitution of mind, that they cannot resist the temptation, be the consequences what they may; that in this case, as in those of insanity, idiocy, infancy, &c., it is the duty of society to take them under its protection, even against their own acts, and to restrain their right of choice of these pursuits, by suppressing them entirely; that there are others, as lotteries particularly, which, although liable to chance also, are useful for many purposes, and are therefore retained and placed under the discretion of the Legislature, to be permitted or refused according to the circumstances of every special case, of which they are to judge; that between the years 1782 and 1820, a space of thirty-eight years only, we have observed seventy cases, where the permission of them has been found useful by the Legislature, some of which are in progress at this time. These cases relate to the emolument of the whole State, to local benefits of education, of navigation, of roads, of counties, towns, religious assemblies, private societies, and of individuals under particular circumstances which may claim indulgence or favor. The latter is the case now submitted to the Legislature, and the question is, whether the individual soliciting their attention, or his situation, may merit that degree of consideration which will justify the Legislature in permitting him to avail himself of the mode of selling by lottery, for the purpose of paying his debts.

That a fair price cannot be obtained by sale in the ordinary way, and in the present depressed state of agricultural industry, is well known. Lands in this State will now sell for more than a third or fourth of what they would have brought a few years ago, perhaps at the very time of the contraction of the

[2] I found such an act, but not noting it at the time, I have not been able to find it again. But there is such an one.—T. J.

debts for which they are now to be sold. The low price in foreign markets, for a series of years past, of agricultural produce, of wheat generally, of tobacco most commonly, and the accumulation of duties on the articles of consumption not produced within our State, not only disable the farmer or planter from adding to his farm by purchase, but reduces him to sell his own, and remove to the western country, glutting the market he leaves, while he lessens the number of bidders. To be protected against this sacrifice is the object of the present application, and whether the applicant has any particular claim to this protection, is the present question.

Here the answer must be left to others. It is not for me to give it. I may, however, more readily than others, suggest the offices in which I have served. I came of age in 1764, and was soon put into the nomination of justice of the county in which I live, and at the first election following I became one of its representatives in the Legislature.

I was thence sent to the old Congress.

Then employed two years with Mr. Pendleton and Mr. Wythe, on the revisal and reduction to a single code of the whole body of the British statutes, the acts of our Assembly, and certain parts of the common law.

Then elected Governor.

Next to the Legislature, and to Congress again.

Sent to Europe as Minister Plenipotentiary.

Appointed Secretary of State to the new government.

Elected Vice-President, and

President. And lastly, a Visitor and Rector of the University. In these different offices, with scarcely any interval between them, I have been in the public service now sixty-one years; and during the far greater part of the time, in foreign countries or in other States. Everyone knows how inevitably a Virginia estate goes to ruin, when the owner is so far distant as to be unable to pay attention to it himself; and the more especially, when the line of his employment is of a character to abstract and alienate his mind entirely from the knowledge necessary to good, and even to saving management.

If it were thought worth while to specify any particular services rendered, I would refer to the specification of them made by the Legislature itself in their Farewell Address, on my retiring from the Presidency, February, 1809. [This will be found in 2 Pleasant's Collection, page 144.] There is one, however, not therein specified, the most important in its consequences, of any transaction in any portion of my life; to wit, the head I personally made against the federal principles and proceedings, during the administration of Mr. Adams. Their usurpations and violations of the constitution at that period, and their majority in both Houses of Congress, were so great, so decided, and so daring, that after combating their aggressions, inch by inch, without being able in the least to check their career, the republican leaders thought it would be best for them to give up their useless efforts there, go home, get into their respective Legislatures, embody whatever of resistance they could be formed into, and if ineffectual, to perish there as in the last ditch. All, therefore, retired, leaving Mr. Gallatin alone in the House of Representatives, and myself in the Senate, where I then presided as Vice-President. Remaining at our posts, and bidding defiance to the brow beatings and insults by which they endeavored to drive us off also, we kept the mass of republicans in phalanx together, until the Legislature could be brought up to the charge; and nothing on earth is more certain, than that if myself particularly, placed by my office of Vice-President at the head of the republicans, had given way and withdrawn from my post, the republicans throughout the Union would have given up in despair, and the cause would have been lost forever. By holding on, we obtained time for the Legislature to come up with their weight; and those of Virginia and Kentucky particularly, but more especially the former, by their celebrated resolutions, saved the constitution at its last gasp. No person who was not a witness of the scenes of that gloomy period, can form any idea of the afflicting persecutions and personal indignities we had to brook. They saved our country however. The spirits of the people were so much subdued and reduced to despair by the X Y Z imposture, and other stratagems and machinations, that they would have sunk into apathy and monarchy, as the only form of government which could maintain itself.

If Legislative services are worth mentioning, and the stamp of liberality and equality, which was necessary to be imposed on our laws in the first crisis of our birth as a nation, was of any value, they will find that the leading and most important laws of that day were prepared by myself, and carried chiefly by my efforts; supported, indeed, by able and faithful coadjutors from the ranks of the House, very effective as seconds, but who would not have taken the field as leaders.

The prohibition of the further importation of slaves was the first of these measures in time.

This was followed by the abolition of entails, which broke up the hereditary and high-handed aristocracy, which, by accumulating immense masses of property in single lines of families, had divided our country into two distinct orders, of nobles and plebeians.

But further to complete the equality among our citizens so essential to the maintenance of republican government, it was necessary to abolish the principle of primogeniture. I drew the law of descents, giving equal inheritance to sons and daughters, which made a part of the revised code.

The attack on the establishment of a dominant religion, was first made by myself. It could be carried at first only by a suspension of salaries for one year, by battling it again at the next session for another year, and so from year to year, until the public mind was ripened for the bill for establishing religious freedom, which I had prepared for the revised code also. This was at length established permanently, and by the efforts chiefly of Mr. Madison, being myself in Europe at the time that work was brought forward.

To these particular services, I think I might add the establishment of our University, as principally my work, acknowledging at the same time, as I do, the great assistance received from my able colleagues of the Visitation. But my residence in the vicinity threw, of course, on me the chief burthen of the enterprise, as well of the buildings as of the general organization and care of the whole. The effect of this institution on the future fame, fortune and prosperity of our country, can as yet be seen but at a distance. But an hundred well-educated youths, which it will turn out annually, and ere long, will fill all its offices with men of superior qualifications, and raise it from its humble state to an eminence among its associates which it has never yet known; no, not in its brightest days. That institution is now qualified to raise its youth to an order of science unequalled in any other State; and this superiority will be the greater from the free range of mind encouraged there, and the restraint imposed at other seminaries by the shackles of a domineering hierarchy, and a bigoted adhesion to ancient habits. Those now on the theatre of affairs will enjoy the ineffable happiness of seeing themselves succeeded by sons of a grade of science beyond their own ken. Our sister States will also be repairing to the same fountains of instruction, will bring hither their genius to be kindled at our fire, and will carry back the fraternal affections which, nourished by the same *alma mater,* will knit us to them by the indissoluble bonds of early personal friendships. The good Old Dominion, the blessed· mother of us all, will then raise her head with pride among the nations, will present to them that splendor of genius which she has ever possessed, but has too long suffered to rest uncultivated and unknown, and will become a centre of ralliance to the States whose youth she has instructed, and, as it were, adopted.

I claim some share in the merits of this great work of regeneration. My whole labors, now for many years, have been devoted to it, and I stand pledged to follow it up through the remnant of life remaining to me. And what remuneration do I ask? Money from the treasury? Not a cent. I ask nothing from the earnings or labors of my fellow citizens. I wish no man's comforts to be abridged for the enlargement of mine. For the services rendered on all occasions, I have been always paid to my full satisfaction. I never wished a dollar more than what the law had fixed on. My request is, only to be permitted to sell my own property freely to pay my own debts. To *sell* it, I say, and not to *sacrifice* it, not to have it gobbled up by speculators to make fortunes for themselves, leaving unpaid those who have trusted to my good faith, and myself without resource in the last and most helpless stage of life. If permitted to sell it in a way which will bring me a fair price, all will be honestly and honorably paid, and a competence left for myself, and for those who look to me for subsistence. To sell it in a way which will offend no moral principle, and expose none to risk but the willing, and those wishing to be permitted to take the chance of gain. To give me, in short, that permission which you often allow to others for purposes not more moral.

Will it be objected, that although not evil in itself, it may, as a precedent, lead to evil? But let those who shall quote the precedent bring their case within the same measure. Have they, as in this case, devoted three-score years and one of their lives, uninterruptedly, to the service of their country? Have the times of those services been as trying as those which have embraced our Revolution, our transition from a colonial to a free structure of government? Have the stations of their trial been of equal importance? Has the share they have borne in holding their new government to its genuine principles, been equally marked? And has the cause of the distress, against which they seek a remedy, proceeded, not merely from themselves, but from errors of the public authorities, disordering the circulating medium, over which they had no control, and which have, in fact, doubled and trebled debts, by reducing, in that proportion, the value of the property which was to pay them? If all these circumstances, which characterize the present case, have taken place in theirs also, then follow the precedent. Be assured, the cases will be so rare as to produce no embarrassment, as never to settle into an injurious habit. The single feature of a sixty years' service, as no other instance of it has yet occurred in our country, so it probably never may again. And should it occur, even once and again, it will not impoverish your treasury, as it takes nothing from that, and asks but a simple permission, by an act of natural right, to do one of moral justice.

## TESTAMENT

March 16 and 17, 1826

I, Thomas Jefferson, of Monticello, in Albemarle, being of sound mind and in my ordinary state of health, make my last will and testament in manner and form as follows:

I give to my grandson Francis Eppes, son of my dear deceased daughter Mary Eppes, in fee simple, all that part of my lands at Poplar Forest lying west of the following lines, to wit: beginning at Radford's upper corner, near the double branches of Bear Creek and the public road, and running thence in a straight line to the fork of my private road, near the barn; thence along that private road (as it was changed in 1817), to its crossing of the main branch of North Tomahawk Creek; and from that crossing, in a direct line over the main ridge which divides the North and South Tomahawk, to the South Tomahawk, at the confluence of two branches where the old road to the Waterlick crossed it, and from that confluence up the northernmost branch (which separate M'Daniels' and Perry's fields), to its source; and thence by the shortest line to my western boundary. And having, in a former correspondence with my deceased son-in-law John W. Eppes, contemplated laying off for him, with remainder to my grandson Francis, a certain portion in the southern part of my lands in Bedford and Campbell, which I afterwards found to be generally more indifferent than I had supposed, and therefore determined to change its location for the better; now to remove all doubt, if any could arise on a purpose merely voluntary and unexecuted, I hereby declare that what I have herein given to my said grandson Francis, is instead of, and not additional to, what I had formerly contemplated. I subject all my other property to the payment of my debts in the first place. Considering the insolvent state of the affairs of my friend and son-in-law Thomas Mann Randolph, and that what will remain of my property will be the only resource against the want in which his family would otherwise be left, it must be his wish, as it is my duty, to guard that resource against all liability for his debts, engagements or purposes whatsoever, and to preclude the rights, powers, and authorities over it, which might result to him by operation of law, and which might, independently of his will, bring it within the power of his creditors, I do hereby devise and bequeath all the residue of my property, real and personal, in possession or in action, whether held in my own right, or in that of my dear deceased wife, according to the powers vested in me by deed of settlement for that purpose, to my grandson Thomas J. Randolph, and my friends Nicholas P. Trist and Alexander Garrett, and their heirs, during the life of my said son-in-law Thomas M. Randolph, to be held and administered by them, in trust, for the sole and separate use and behoof of my dear daughter Martha Randolph, and her heirs; and aware of the nice and difficult distinction of the law in these cases, I will further explain by saying, that I understand and intend the effect of these limitations to be, that the legal estate and actual occupation shall be vested in my said trustees, and held by them in base fee, determinable on the death of my said son-in-law, and the remainder during the same time be vested in my said daughter and her heirs, and of course disposable by her last will, and that at the death of my said son-in-law, the particular estate of the trustees shall be determined, and the remainder, in legal estate, possession, and use, become vested in my said daughter and her heirs, in absolute property forever. In consequence of the variety and indescribableness of the articles of property within the house at Monticello, and the difficulty of inventorying and appraising them separately and specifically, and its inutility, I dispense with having them inventoried and appraised; and it is my will that my executors be not held to give any security for the administration of my estate. I appoint my grandson Thomas Jefferson Randolph, my sole executor during his life, and after his death, I constitute executors my friends Nicholas P. Trist and Alexander Garrett, joining to them my daughter Martha Randolph, after the death of my said son-in-law Thomas M. Randolph. Lastly, I revoke all former wills by me heretofore made; and in witness that this is my will, I have written the whole with my own hand on two pages, and have subscribed my name to each of them this sixteenth day of March, one thousand eight hundred and twenty-six.

I, Thomas Jefferson, of Monticello, in Albemarle, make and add the following codicil to my will, controlling the same so far as its provisions go:

I recommend to my daughter Martha Randolph, the maintenance and care of my well beloved sister Anne Scott, and trust confidently that from affection to her, as well as for my sake, she will never let her want a comfort. I have made no specific provision for the comfortable maintenance of my son-in-law Thomas M. Randolph, because of the difficulty and uncertainty of devising terms which shall vest any beneficial interest in him, which the law will not transfer to the benefit of his creditors, to the destitution of my daughter and her family, and disablement of her to supply him: whereas, property placed under the exclusive control of my daughter and her independent will, as if she were a feme sole, considering the relation in which she stands both to him and his children, will be a certain resource against want for all.

I give to my friend James Madison, of Montpellier, my gold-mounted walking staff of animal horn, as a token of the cordial and affectionate friendship which for nearly now an half century, has united us in the same principles and pursuits of what we have deemed for the greatest good of our country.

I give to the University of Virginia my library, except such particular books only, and of the same edition, as it may already possess, when this legacy shall take effect; the rest of my said library, remaining after those given to the University shall have been taken out, I give to my two grandsons-in-law Nicholas P. Trist and Joseph Coolidge. To my grandson Thomas Jefferson Randolph, I give my silver watch in preference of the golden one, because of its superior excellence. My papers of business going of course to him, as my executor, all others of a literary or other character I give to him as of his own property.

I give a gold watch to each of my grandchildren, who shall not have already received one from me, to be purchased and delivered by my executor to my grandsons, at the age of twenty-one, and grandaughters at that of sixteen.

I give to my good, affectionate, and faithful servant Burwell, his freedom, and the sum of three hundred dollars, to buy necessaries to commence his trade of glazier, or to use otherwise, as he pleases.

I give also to my good servants John Hemings and Joe Fosset, their freedom at the end of one year after my death; and to each of them respectively, all the tools of their respective shops or callings; and it is my will that a comfortable log-house be built for each of the three servants so emancipated, on some part of my lands convenient to them with respect to the residence of their wives, and to Charlottesville and the University, where they will be mostly employed, and reasonably convenient also to the interests of the proprietor of the lands, of which houses I give the use of one, with a curtilage of an acre to each, during his life or personal occupation thereof.

I give also to John Hemings the service of his two apprentices Madison and Eston Hemings, until their respective ages of twenty-one years, at which period respectively, I give them their freedom; and I humbly and earnestly request of the legislature of Virginia a confirmation of the bequest of freedom to these servants, with permission to remain in this State, where their families and connections are, as an additional instance of the favor, of which I have received so many other manifestations in the course of my life, and for which I now give them my last, solemn, and dutiful thanks.

In testimony that this is a codicil to my will of yesterday's date, and that it is to modify so far the provisions of that will, I have written it all with my own hand in two pages, to each of which I subscribe my name, this seventeenth day of March, one thousand eight hundred and twenty-six.

✦

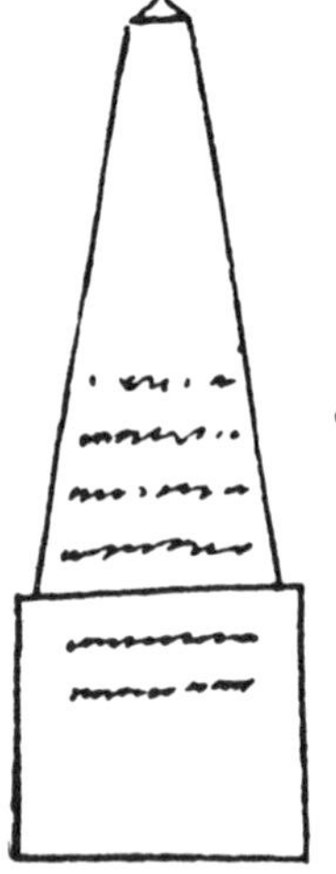

could the dead feel any interest in Monu-
-ments or other remembrances of them, when, as
Anacreon says Ολιγη δε κεισομεσθα
Κονις, οστεων λυθεντων
the following would be to my Manes the most
gratifying.
On the grave
a plain die or cube of 3.f without any
mouldings, surmounted by an Obelisk
of 6.f. height, each of a single stone:
on the faces of the Obelisk the following
inscription, & not a word more
'Here was buried
Thomas Jefferson
Author of the Declaration of American Independance
of the Statute of Virginia for religious freedom
& Father of the University of Virginia.'
because by these, as testimonials that I have lived, I wish most to
be remembered. ~~[struck out]~~ to be of the coarse stone of which
my columns are made, that no one might be tempted
hereafter to destroy it for the value of the materials.
my bust by Ciracchi, with the pedistal and truncated
column on which it stands, might be given to the University
if they would place it in the Dome room of the Rotunda.
on the Die of the Obelisk might be engraved
Born Apr. 2. 1743. O.S.
Died ——

JEFFERSON'S SKETCH AND INSCRIPTION FOR HIS TOMBSTONE

# SELECTED BIBLIOGRAPHY

Jefferson's writings, including his letters, have been published in three major collections:

H. A. Washington's *The Writings of Thomas Jefferson* (9 vols., 1853-54).

P. L. Ford's *The Writings of Thomas Jefferson* (10 vols., 1892-99).

A. A. Lipscomb and A. E. Bergh's *The Writings of Thomas Jefferson* (2 vols., 1903).

Other important collections, containing mostly letters, are the following:

N. F. Cabell, *Early History of the University of Virginia, As Contained in the Letters of Thomas Jefferson and Joseph C. Cabell, Hitherto Unpublished* (1856).

G. Chinard, *The Commonplace Book of Thomas Jefferson: A Repertory of His Ideas on Government* (1926).

*Ibid., The Correspondence of Jefferson and du Pont de Nemours* (1931).

*Ibid., Houdon in America: A Collection of Documents in the Jefferson Papers in the Library of Congress* (1930).

*Ibid., The Letters of Lafayette and Jefferson* (1929).

*Ibid., Trois amitiés françaises de Jefferson d'après sa correspondance inédite avec Madame de Bréhan, Madame de Tessé et Madame de Corny* (1927).

W. D. Johnston, *History of the Library of Congress* (vol. I, 1904).

R. J. Honeywell, *The Educational Work of Thomas Jefferson* (1931).

C. F. Jenkins and W. J. Campbell, *Jefferson's Germantown Letters* (1906).

D. Malone, *Correspondence between Thomas Jefferson and Pierre Samuel du Pont de Nemours, 1798-1817* (1930).

T. J. Randolph, *Memoir, Correspondence and Miscellanies, from the Papers of Thomas Jefferson* (4 vols., 1829).

*Magazine of History,* "Letters of Thomas Jefferson" (1915).

Massachusetts Historical Society, Collections, *The Jefferson Papers* (ser. 7, vol. I, 1900).

Missouri Historical Society, "Correspondence of Thomas Jefferson, 1788-1826," (vol. III, 1936).

New York Historical Society, Collections, *The Papers of Charles Thomson, Secretary of the Continental Congress, 1765-1816* (vol. I, 1878)—about 100 letters exchanged between Jefferson and Thomson.

*Washington, Jefferson, Lincoln, and Agriculture* (U. S. Department of Agriculture, 1937), pp. 41-71.

Jefferson's official messages are to be found in:

J. D. Richardson's *A Compilation of the Messages and Papers of the Presidents* (vol. I, 1897), 306-446.

Other writings, primarily letters, are scattered in various historical publications. The reader is referred to the Bibliography by R. H. Johnson in the Lipscomb and Bergh edition of Jefferson's *Writings,* vol. XX, and to Saul K. Padover's *Jefferson* (1942), pp. 435-47.

# INDEX